Hawai'i Reader in Traditional Chinese Culture

Hawai'i Reader in

Traditional Chinese Culture

Edited by

Victor H. Mair

Nancy S. Steinhardt and Paul R. Goldin

University of Hawai'i Press

Honolulu

© 2005 University of Hawai'i Press
All rights reserved
Printed in the United States of America
10 09 08 07 06 05   6 5 4 3 2 1

Library of Congress Cataloging-in-Publication Data

Hawai'i reader in traditional Chinese culture / edited by
Victor H. Mair, Nancy S. Steinhardt, and Paul R. Goldin.
    p. cm.
  Includes bibliographical references and index.
  ISBN 0-8248-2785-6 (hardcover : alk. paper)
    1. China—Civilization—Sources—Textbooks. I. Mair,
Victor H. II. Steinhardt, Nancy Shatzman. III. Goldin,
Paul Rakita.
DS721.H338 2005
951—dc22

2004012418

Selections 12, 13, 32, 69, 84, and 92 first appeared in the following
copyrighted works and are used with permission: *Tao Te Ching:
The Classic Book of Integrity and the Way,* trans. Victor H. Mair
(Bantam Press, 1990) (selection 12); *Wandering on the Way: Early
Taoist Tales and Parables of Chuang Tzu,* trans. Victor H. Mair
(University of Hawai'i Press, 1998) (selection 13); Xiao Tong,
comp., *Wen xuan,* under the title *Selections of Refined Literature,*
vol. 1: *Rhapsodies on Metropolises and Capitals,* trans. David R.
Knechtges (Princeton University Press, 1982) (selection 32);
"Ni Tsan and His 'Cloud Forest Hall Collection of Rules for
Drinking and Eating,'" trans. Teresa Wang and E. N. Anderson,
Petits Propos Culinaires, 60: 24–41 (London: Prospect Books, 1998)
(selection 69); with permission of the Harvard University Asia
Center from Emma Teng, *From "Savage Island" to "Chinese Province":
Taiwan in the Imagined Geography of the Qing Empire* (©The President
and Fellows of Harvard College, 2004) (selection 84); Britta
Erickson, ed., *The Art of Xu Bing: Words without Meaning, Meaning
without Words* (University of Washington Press and Smithsonian
Institution/Arthur M. Sackler Gallery, 2001) (selection 92).

University of Hawai'i Press books are printed on acid-free paper
and meet the guidelines for permanence and durability of the
Council on Library Resources.

Designed by April Leidig-Higgins

Printed by The Maple-Vail Book Manufacturing Group

For Derk Bodde,
Schuyler Van Rensselaer Cammann,
and W. Allyn Rickett

三人行，必有我師焉。

"When three people are walking along,
there will certainly be a teacher for me
among them."—*Analects* 7.22

Present-day China, showing archaeological and historical sites

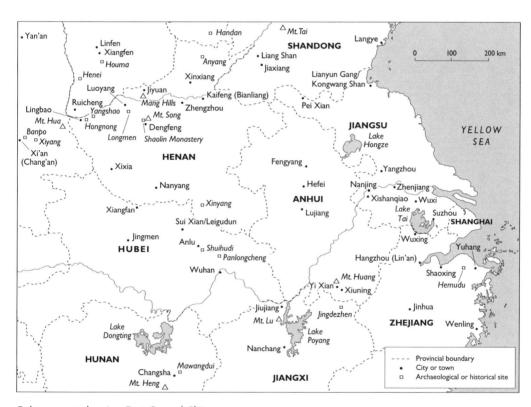

Enlargement showing East Central China

CONTENTS

Color illustrations follow pages 150, 294, 422, and 566.

AB   Alan Berkowitz (Swarthmore College)

ALH   Ann L. Huss (Wellesley College)

AS   Angela Sheng (Ottawa, Canada)

BH   Barbara Hendrischke (Australian National University)

CF   Charlotte Furth (University of Southern California)

DAG   David A. Graff (Kansas State University)

DB   Daniel Boucher (Cornell University)

DM   Denis Mair (poet, independent scholar)

DRK   David R. Knechtges (University of Washington)

DSS   Donald S. Sutton (Carnegie Mellon University)

DWP   David Pankenier (Lehigh University)

ENA   Eugene N. Anderson (University of California, Riverside)

ET   Emma Teng (Massachusetts Institute of Technology)

GLM   Gilbert L. Mattos (Seton Hall University, deceased)

GS   Gary Seaman (University of Southern California)

HC   Hugh Clark (Ursinus College)

HYS   Hsio-yen Shih (University of Hong Kong, deceased)

JH   John Hay (University of California, Santa Cruz)

JLH   Jan L. Hagman (Lexington, Massachusetts)

KC   Katherine Carlitz (University of Pittsburgh)

KK   Keith Knapp (The Citadel)

KL   Kathryn Lowry (University of California, Santa Barbara)

LDS   Lowell Skar (University of Colorado at Boulder)

LH   Laura Hostetler (University of Illinois, Chicago)

LLM   Lindy Li Mark (California State University, Hayward)

LMJ   Lionel M. Jensen (University of Notre Dame)

LS   Lynn Struve (Indiana University)

MRD   Michael R. Drompp (Rhodes College)

MS   Meir Shahar (Tel Aviv University)

NCS   Narayan Chandra Sen (Asiatic Society, Calcutta)

NSS   Nancy S. Steinhardt (University of Pennsylvania)

PRG   Paul R. Goldin (University of Pennsylvania)

PYW   Pei-yi Wu (Columbia University)

RF   Robert Foster (Berea College)

RK   Robin Kornman (University of Wisconsin, Milwaukee)

RM   Richard Mather (University of Minnesota)

RT   Romeyn Taylor (University of Minnesota)

SB   Susan Bush (Cambridge, Massachusetts)

SHW   Stephen H. West (University of California, Berkeley)

SLM   Susan L. Mann (University of California, Davis)

SM   Sucheta Mazumdar (Duke University)

TB   Thomas Bartlett (La Trobe University)

TL   Tina Lu (University of Pennsylvania)

TS   Tansen Sen (Baruch College)

TW   Teresa Wang (University of California, Riverside)

VCX   Victor Cunrui Xiong (Western Michigan University)

VHM   Victor H. Mair (University of Pennsylvania)

WS   Wayne Schlepp (University of Toronto)

XFT   Xiaofei Tian (Harvard University)

XRL   Xinru Liu (College of New Jersey)

ZQC   Zong-qi Cai (University of Illinois, Urbana-Champaign)

ca. 1600–ca. 1045 B.C.E.	SHANG DYNASTY
ca. 1045–221 B.C.E.	ZHOU DYNASTY

Western Zhou ca. 1045–771 B.C.E.
Eastern Zhou 770–256 B.C.E.
    Spring and Autumn Period 722–481 B.C.E.
    Warring States Period 475–221 B.C.E.

221–206 B.C.E.   QIN DYNASTY

206 B.C.E.–220 C.E.   HAN DYNASTY

Western Han 206 B.C.E.–8 C.E.
Xin (Wang Mang Interregnum) 8–23 C.E.
Eastern Han 25–220

220–280   THREE KINGDOMS

Wei 220–265
Shu 221–263
Wu 222–280

281–420   JIN DYNASTY

Western Jin 281–317
Eastern Jin 317–420

304–439   SIXTEEN STATES

During this period, there were actually at least eighteen different
states that controlled various parts of North China and Sichuan.
Of these eighteen states, fourteen were ruled over by five
different non-Han groups.

386–589   NORTHERN DYNASTIES

Northern Wei 386–534
Eastern Wei 534–550
Western Wei 535–556
Northern Qi 550–577
Northern Zhou 557–581

420–589   SOUTHERN DYNASTIES

Liu Song 420–479
Southern Qi 479–502

Liang 502–557
Chen 557–589

The period from the fall of the Han dynasty to the reunification by the Sui dynasty is called the Six Dynasties.

581–618	SUI DYNASTY
618–907	TANG DYNASTY
907–960	FIVE DYNASTIES (in the north)

Later Liang 907–923
Later Tang 923–936
Later Jin 936–946
Later Han 947–950
Later Zhou 951–960

902–979	TEN KINGDOMS (in the south)

Shu 907–925
Later Shu 934–965
Chu 907–951
Nanping or Jingnan 924–963
Wu 902–937
Southern Tang 937–975
Wu-Yue 907–978
Min 909–945
Southern Han 917–971
Northern Han 951–979

907–1125	LIAO DYNASTY
960–1279	SONG DYNASTY

Northern Song 960–1127
Southern Song 1127–1279

1038–1227	XI XIA (WESTERN XIA) DYNASTY
1115–1234	JIN DYNASTY
1271–1368	YUAN DYNASTY
1368–1644	MING DYNASTY
1636–1912	QING DYNASTY
1912–	REPUBLIC OF CHINA
1949–	PEOPLE'S REPUBLIC OF CHINA

THIS *READER* IS DESIGNED to serve as a fund of primary texts for introductory college courses on the history, culture, and society of China, both modern and premodern. Unique in the breadth of its coverage, the *Reader* can be used either as the main textbook for studying about Chinese civilization or to accompany, for example, one of the many excellent histories of China that are available.

Since literature is an important component of culture, we have naturally included a number of literary texts. However, this volume is not intended to serve as an anthology of Chinese literature, since there are already several excellent literary anthologies available and, furthermore, they tend to be used in classes dealing exclusively with literature.

An unusual characteristic of this volume is its exceptionally strong coverage of visual and material culture. The illustrations have been carefully chosen not merely to showcase Chinese art and architecture, but to provide direct exposure to archaeological artifacts, objects from daily life, and the Chinese landscape. In other words, a close examination of the illustrations in this volume will greatly enhance the reading of the texts by helping to establish their substance and settings. Thus, we consider the abundant illustrations to be an integral part of our presentation. The ample captions are full of valuable information and are intended to serve as a bridge between the verbal and the visual components of the book. We believe that the illustrations and their captions should be assigned to students by number in the same way as the texts they are designed to complement.

Another feature of this *Reader* that sets it apart from other comparable collections of translated texts is its incorporation of recently excavated materials (see selections 10, 12, 22, 23, 25, and 49). Such newly discovered texts from places like Yinqueshan, Mawangdui, Shuihudi, Guodian, and Dunhuang have revolutionized the study of Chinese thought, society, and literature. Not only does this make the *Reader* as up to date as possible; it also presents Chinese civilization in a more accurate light than permitted by reliance on canonical texts alone.

Chinese culture consists of numerous facets. In order to give a nuanced picture of the complex whole, we try to touch upon as many of them as possible. The ninety-two selections are arranged in chronological order, but they need not be read that way. It would also be possible for a teacher to assign individual texts, or groups of texts, according to specific themes. Among these might be the following:

art and aesthetics 57, 86, 92
biography and legend 24, 29, 35, 37, 41, 66, 89
Buddhism 42, 43, 46, 47, 49, 52, 56, 66, 86, 87, 88
classics 6, 7, 10, 67
Confucianism 7, 9, 16, 18, 35, 52, 53, 58, 63, 64, 67, 71, 82, 88, 90
courtly and daily life 32, 62
culinary arts 69
divination 4
education 49, 75
ethics, mores, and social values 16, 44, 60, 67, 78, 70, 80
ethnography 84, 85

The above list may be thought of as a sort of user's guide to the texts in this volume, but with the caveat that it by no means exhausts the selections that may be relevant to a given category. And, of course, the illustrations cover many of the same topics, but also touch upon themes not mentioned here.

We have endeavored to supply a judicious mix of short, medium, and long texts. Our purpose here is to maximize the number of different types of materials included while at the same time affording students the experience of engaging with readings of greater amplitude. Each selection is preceded by a brief introduction that (where pertinent) identifies its author, establishes the context, and raises important issues and questions.

With only a few exceptions, all of the translations in this volume are new and have been undertaken expressly for it. The translators are identified by their initials at the end of each text (see the list of contributors for their full names and affiliations).

Unless otherwise indicated, all of the illustration captions are by Nancy S. Steinhardt.

—Victor H. Mair

EXCEPT WHERE OTHERWISE specified, the pronunciations of all Chinese words in this volume are given according to Modern Standard Mandarin (MSM) in pinyin romanization. While this is historically inaccurate for texts deriving from earlier periods and phonologically imprecise for non-Mandarin topolects (q.v. below), it is a nearly universal convention in contemporary Chinese studies.

C. Chinese transcription in Mandarin.

East Asian Heartland (EAH) essentially consisting of the Yellow River Valley and immediately adjoining areas.

J. Japanese

jing customarily rendered as "classic" in Confucian contexts, "scripture" in Taoist contexts, and "sutra" in Buddhist contexts, there has recently been a shift toward the use of the rendering "canon," particularly among specialists on the intellectual history of the Han and earlier periods. In this volume, we generally use simply "book" in the titles of Confucian classics.

jinshi ("Advanced Scholar" or "Presented Scholar")—the most coveted degree in the civil service examination system. The date of passage of this degree was often the single most salient biographical fact known about a scholar-official.

juan (scroll) Chinese texts were originally divided into a number of scrolls. Out of habit, this usage was retained even after the development of books with pages sewn together along a spine. Consequently, this word is often left untranslated or rendered as "chapter."

khaghan medieval ruler of a Turkic, Tartar, or Mongol tribe or country; sometimes spelled *qaghan;* also appears in the contracted form "khan."

morpheme the smallest unit of meaning in a language.

MSM Modern Standard Mandarin, as determined by the State Language Commission of the People's Republic of China.

pinyin (literally, "spelling") the official MSM romanization of the People's Republic of China.

qaghan see *khaghan*

qi (also transcribed as *ch'i* and pronounced as *ki* in Japanese; "material energy")—the stuff and spirit that informs everything in the universe. Cf. Sanskrit *prāṇa,* Greek *pneuma,* and Hebrew *ruaḥ.*

semantosyllabic a twofold characteristic of written symbols that are a syllable in length and convey meaning.

Sino-, Sinitic Arabo-Graeco-Latinate terms meaning "Chinese" that, like it, ultimately derive from the name (viz., Qin or Ch'in) of the first nonfeudal, bureaucratically organized state to unify all the territory of the East Asian Heartland.

Skt. Sanskrit

supratopolectal a characteristic of written symbols that transcend local and regional pronunciations of the morphemes they are used to write.

sūtra Buddhist scripture.

tael refers to various units of weight for silver, but usually the *liang* (ounce).

Tao(ism) Although this word is now occasionally written as Dao(ism), it is so deeply ensconced in English in the earlier form that we bow to tradition except in cases where a contributor has expressed a strong preference in favor of the newer romanization.

Tib. Tibetan

topolect a literal translation of the highly problematic term *fangyan,* which is usually misleadingly rendered as "dialect." See the discussion in the Introduction and the entry for this word in the 4th edition of *The American Heritage Dictionary of the English Language.*

tricent signifying three hundred (in later periods sometimes 360) paces or approximately one-third of a mile (a thousand paces), this was the most common unit of distance (i.e., the *li*) employed in premodern China.

xing consistently rendered as "[human] nature" until very recently. Lately, however, some scholars have opted to leave it untranslated.

Zeng Shen the traditional pronunciation of the name of one of Confucius's disciples who was known for his extreme filial piety. An alternative, philologically grounded reading is Zeng Can (which may be phonetically rendered as *ts'ahn*).

A NOTE ON THE TRANSCRIPTION AND TRANSLATION OF THE TITLES OF CHINESE TEXTS

THERE ARE NO established standards for how to handle Chinese titles in English and in romanization. For example, the title of the famous historical work by Sima Qian (145?–86? B.C.E.) may be romanized in pinyin as *Shiji, Shi ji,* or *Shi Ji,* and it has been translated into English as *Historical Records, Records of the Historian, Records of the Grand Historian, Records of the Scribe, The Grand Scribe's Records,* and so forth. In neither case is it possible to say with absolute certitude which version is correct. For example, although it is more in accord with the grammar of Literary Sinitic to separate the syllables of the Chinese title, orthographic rules emerging in China (see the references at the end of this note) stipulate that they be combined on the grounds that they constitute a single unit when pronounced by modern Chinese speakers. Although none of the widely varying English translations can be declared to be definitely wrong or the sole correct version, we have generally standardized the titles here for ease of reading and indexing.

Calendrical Terminology

Chinese days and years are traditionally designated by binomial terms in a recurring cycle of sixty. Hence, 1943 was a *guiwei* year, and so was 2003. This accounts for such expressions as *"guisi* day" and *"renxu* day" that occur in the texts translated in this book. Chinese years are also often designated by the reign titles of various emperors. Thus, the third year of the Tianbao (Heavenly Treasure) reign period, which began in 742 C.E., would be 744.

A Note on the Use of Brackets and Parentheses

Brackets [ ] indicate elements absent in the Chinese text but necessary for grammaticality or intelligibility in English.

Parentheses ( ) indicate explanatory or amplificatory material added by the translator (i.e., in-text notes).

References

DeFrancis, John, ed. *ABC Chinese-English Comprehensive Dictionary.* See Appendix I (pp. 1341–1349): "Basic Rules for Hanyu Pinyin Orthography." Honolulu: University of Hawai'i Press, 2003.

Xinhua pinxie cidian (Xinhua spelling dictionary). Beijing: Shangwu yinshuguan, 2002.

Yin Binyong with Mary Felley. *Chinese Romanization: Pronunciation and Orthography.* Beijing: Sinolingua, 1990.

ACKNOWLEDGMENTS

THE IDEA OF compiling a reader on traditional Chinese culture was first proposed to me in 1998 by Patricia Crosby, Executive Editor at the University of Hawai'i Press. Considering it to be an eminently worthwhile project, I happily accepted the challenge and immediately began to contact possible contributors. One of the first individuals to respond positively was my colleague, Paul R. Goldin. Much to my delight, and far beyond my expectations, Goldin offered to provide translations and introductions for more than two dozen texts dating to the Warring States period through the Eastern Han (and even a bit beyond in one case). With tremendous proficiency and expert philological skills, Goldin finished all of his contributions within half a year of promising to do them.

Since Goldin's response was so enthusiastic and gratifying, and since Pat Crosby had from the very beginning wanted the *Reader* to include a rich assortment of illustrations, I then approached my art historian colleague, Nancy S. Steinhardt, and asked whether she would be willing to take on the responsibility for assembling the requisite visual materials and writing the captions for them. The results, as are evident to anyone who leafs through the *Reader,* have been nothing short of wonderful. I am deeply indebted to Steinhardt, not only for her splendid selection of illustrations, but also for the extraordinarily informative explanations that accompany them.

I am also profoundly grateful to all of the other scholars who have contributed to this volume, both for the quality of their learning and for their generosity in sharing it with students and fellow teachers. In some cases I have asked them to go through two or even three drafts of their translations, but no one grumbled and everyone was prompt in getting things back to me. I also appreciate the conscientiousness of the contributors in keeping me informed of their whereabouts and the patience they kindly displayed when other commitments prevented me from pushing the project forward more rapidly.

Others who deserve recognition are Carrie Reed for her timely help with the Cinderella story (selection 54); W. Allyn Rickett and Kenneth W. Holloway for insights on the "Five Forms of Conduct" (selection 10); David Knechtges, W. South Coblin, and David Prager Branner for authoritative explanations of the title of Yang Xiong's *Fang yan* (selection 91); Joseph Farrell, Ralph Rosen, A[ngus] John Graham, and Georg Knauer for their assistance with the Latin of selection 67; Paul D. Buell, Philip F. C. Williams, Yenna Wu, James Bosson, and Françoise Sabban for help and advice concerning selection 69 (especially Ms. Sabban for her interpretation of the first sentence in the sixth recipe and for many other good suggestions); and Sangye Khandro and Khenpo Chöying Namgyal for their assistance with the translation of selection 87.

Thanks to Cheri Dunn, Managing Editor at the University of Hawai'i Press, for conscientiously and skillfully seeing this volume through the final stages of production.

I wish to express special gratitude to one of the reviewers for the press who provided numerous, detailed suggestions for improvement, many of which we have adopted.

I would also like to take this opportunity to thank my wife, Li-ching, for listening to me rattle on about this *Reader* for hours over meals and on walks, and for proffering wise counsel when it was needed.

Above all, I wish once again to thank Pat Crosby for suggesting this project in the first place; for meeting with us in Montreal, Philadelphia, Honolulu, and elsewhere to discuss its contents and progress; and just generally for guiding us along every step of the path to its completion.

—VHM
July 1, 2004
Swarthmore

Introduction | A Constantly Shifting Mosaic of Peoples and Cultures

FOR MANY STUDENTS, this book will be part of their first systematic exposure to learning about China. As such, we wanted to make it as comprehensive as possible within the limits naturally imposed by the amount of material that can reasonably be absorbed within a single semester. One of our main goals has been to help the student realize that China is not a monolithic state with a monotonous culture and a static past. The myth of a thoroughly homogeneous, ultrastable empire, although widespread and persistent, is far from true. China never existed as the "nation of uniformity" that it is often alleged to be. Quite the contrary, we are faced with a multifaceted country that possesses an extremely complicated history and a richly varied mix of regional and ethnic traditions.

Take language, for example. When one thinks of what defines "China," perhaps the first thing that comes to mind is that it is a place where the people all speak "Chinese." But what is this "Chinese" that everyone is supposedly speaking to each other? Unfortunately, China does not today possess, nor has it ever in the past possessed, such a universally understood tongue. For starters, we have to take into account the tens of millions of speakers of non-Sinitic languages who make up a significant proportion of the population of the Chinese nation as it is currently configured. Among the bewildering panoply of languages in question—in no particular order—are Tibetan, Mongolian, Uyghur, Yugur, Kazakh, Kirghiz, Zhuang, Korean, Dai, Sibe (akin to Manchu), Tajik, Tatar, Shui, Bai, Yi (also called Lolo, Ne, Nosu, and Nasu), Lisu, Lahu, Miao (Hmong), Mulam, Naxi (also known as Naxhi, Nashee, Lukhi, Luhsi, Luxi, Moso, Nachri, Nahsi, Nashi, Na-khi, Nakhi, Nari, Nasi, Nazo, and Hlikhin), Gelao (Klo or Klau), Blang, Pumi, Wa, Achang, De'ang, Akadaw, Russian (!), and countless others (the list could effortlessly be extended manyfold). These languages belong to such disparate groups and families as Tibeto-Burman, Austroasiatic, Austronesian, Turkic, Tungusic, Iranian, and Slavic. These are the "minorities" of the People's Republic of China, all of whom have roots that lie deep in the past of East Asia, West Asia, Central Asia, Southeast Asia, and Northeast Asia.

And then there is the so-called majority group who, it is claimed, speak a language called "Hanyu" or "Chinese." While the current government and its predecessor (the Republic of China, now restricted to Taiwan) have energetically promoted what is variously called Mandarin (Language of the Officials [a name that accurately betrays its origins]), Putonghua (Common Speech), Guoyu (National Language), or Huayu (Language of the [Culturally] Florescent [People]) as a lingua franca, there is as much mutual unintelligibility within Hanyu/Chinese as there is outside of it. The designation "Hanyu" (literally, "language of the Han [people]") as *the* language of China is problematic in many respects, not the least of which is arriving at an accurate and acceptable definition of Han ethnicity. That, of course, is far too big and nettlesome an issue to tackle here, so we shall merely focus on the question of the homogeneity of Hanyu itself.

However we ultimately choose to define it, Hanyu is related in some fashion (not yet well understood by scholars) to Tibeto-Burman. Since the combined family is customarily styled Sino-Tibetan, we may—for the sake of linguistic precision—refer to Hanyu as "Sinitic" in English. Sinitic is often said to have eight (or more) major *fangyan* (topolects—see the discussion of terms at the conclusion of the Preface). Among these *fangyan* are "Northern" (i.e., Mandarin in the broadest of terms; it actually stretches to the far southwest), Wu (typified by Suzhou and Shanghai), Xiang (Hunanese), Gan (spoken in Jiangxi), Hakka (the language of those displaced "guests" from the north who have played a particularly important role in modern Chinese history), Northern Min, Southern Min (including Amoy and Taiwanese), and Cantonese. If analyzed by the standards applied to languages in Europe or South Asia, these *fangyan* would be classified as branches of the Sinitic group.

Speakers from any one of the major *fangyan* are incapable of conversing with speakers from those of any of the other major *fangyan*. Even within the major *fangyan* or branches of Sinitic, there are numerous more or less unintelligible varieties of speech. What is more, it is essential to note that, throughout history, the *fangyan* have never been written down in their unalloyed form, except latterly by missionaries using alphabets. Traditionally, there have been only two acceptable forms of writing in China: Literary Sinitic (*wenyan* or Classical Chinese), strictly a book language about which we will have more to say at the conclusion of this essay, and Vernacular Sinitic *(baihua[wen]),* a written manifestation of Mandarin that developed—largely under the influence of Buddhism[1]—out of a presumed Tang-period koine. Despite their lack of a written form, the *fangyan* are still vibrant. As clear indications of the continuing vitality of *fangyan,* Taiwanese is now the preferred mode of expression on Formosa, and the Chinese government on the mainland is constantly threatening to cashier officials and teachers who fail to learn Mandarin.

Sinitic evolved through a complex process of interaction with the non-Sinitic languages mentioned above, borrowing (and lending) not only words, but also structures and phonemes. The internal development of Sinitic is equally intricate, such that historical linguists are still seriously puzzled over the relationships among the various *fangyan,* the phonology of their earlier stages, and the identification of the fundamental etyma for the group en masse.

Linguistic multifariousness is only one of the more obvious features of "the Chinese mosaic."[2] The same may be said of almost any other aspect of Chinese culture and society. Perhaps the most obvious symbol of Chineseness in the larger world is cuisine. Yet it is impossible to point to any particular type of fare that stands for Chinese cooking in general. Hot pots have a Mongolic ancestry, pasta products are derived from Central and Southwest Asia, tea is ultimately from the hills of the Assam-Burma-Yunnan "Golden Triangle," and so forth. Milk products are anathema to most lactose-intolerant denizens of the Central Kingdom, yet they are a staple of the people living along its northern reaches. The more sophisticated American aficionado of Chinese cooking knows very well the difference between Szechwanese and Cantonese cooking, staying clear of the former if he or she does not like spicy hot food and avoiding the latter if his or her palate is not attracted to gelatinous, gooey comestibles.

When we watch a Chinese film and see the heroine encased in a tight sheath slit to the thigh, she is basically sporting an item of Manchu dress. Some Chinese (those who wanted to ride horses) began to wear trousers in the latter part of the fourth century B.C.E., but only because they wanted to ward off the steppe peoples who introduced the domesticated horse (*and* the trousers) to their land, with devastating consequences. In premodern times, it would not have been difficult to recognize the ethnicity of a citizen of the Chinese empire by his or his costume.

As for Chinese empires, there was not one of them, but a long series of dynasties, more often than not erected on the ashes of their predecessors. Also more often than not, those who established new dynasties were—a supreme incongruity—groups from the north and northwest who either were themselves "barbarians" dreaded for their awesome military prowess or who had exceptionally close affinities with them. Numerous recent archaeological discoveries have led to a salutary reconsideration of the nature of the millennial interactions between the inhabitants of the East Asian Heartland (EAH) and their septentrional neighbors.[3] As a result, it is no longer possible to think of the latter only as "traders or raiders." Instead, what we are finding is that—already at least from the late Neolithic period and continuing right through to the twentieth century—the northern peoples were involved not only in state formation, but also in the importation of vital cultural elements such as bronze metallurgy and the chariot. Consequently, in this *Reader* we place greater emphasis than usual upon the northern peoples, for we believe that, unless one takes them duly into account, one's comprehension of Chinese history and appreciation of Chinese culture are bound to be flawed.

The intricacy of Chinese involvement with wide-ranging steppe peoples can be demonstrated by the derivation of Gesar (see selection 87) from Caesar. How, why, and when this originally Etruscan title of the Roman emperors came to be applied by the bards of a Central Asia nomadic confederation to their greatest hero is an intriguing story. What is not in doubt is that the Tibetans contested with the Chinese for hegemony during the Tang period (618–907).[4] Indeed, the Tibetans not only occupied the strategically crucial Gansu Corridor for a century, but even invested the capital, Chang'an, for a while during the year 763 and were dislodged only when the Tang authorities pleaded with the Uyghurs (see selection 55) to drive them off. Thus, a dynasty that was initially founded by individuals in whose veins ran nomadic blood and who maintained intimate ties with their northern ancestors found temporary salvation from destruction at the hands of northwestern nomads by a confederation of Turkic tribes (whom the Tang actually detested)—a typical series of events that recurred over and over again during the more than three thousand years of known Chinese history. We should remember, moreover, that the Tang dynasty represents the acme of cultural cosmopolitanism in East Asia. It should further be noted that the location of the Tibetans was by no means restricted solely to that of their current nation, which is occupied by Chinese troops. During the medieval period, they were also identified with the border areas to the northwest of the East Asian Heartland, and still today there are large concentrations of Tibetans in the provinces of Gansu and Qinghai.

Just as due consideration of the non-Sinitic peoples of the north and northwest is essential for any adequate study of the development of Chinese civilization, the same may be said for the non-Sinitic inhabitants of the south. Chinese culture (including Sinitic languages) marched southward slowly during the latter part of the first millennium B.C.E., gained momentum during the first millennium C.E., and was far from reaching its culmination even by the end of the twentieth century. The large and small pockets of non-Sinitic speakers that pepper all of the provinces south of the Yangtze River attest to the ongoing presence of peoples from radically different traditions within the territory of the modern Chinese state. The fusion of Chinese culture with the indigenous populations has led to a distinctive mix of regional cultures and ethnicities that is conspicuous in customs, languages, surnames, and physical types.[5]

The ramifications of the sharp distinction between north and south—played out in art, poetry, theories of enlightenment, social values, business practices, burial customs, and endless other respects—may be examined in the person of Gu Yanwu (1613–1682; see selection 83), arguably the foremost exponent of Qing-period philological scholarship. Gu was born into a distinguished family of Kunshan (Suzhou Prefecture), itself renowned as the birthplace of southern drama. A staunch Ming loyalist who witnessed the fall of the last Chinese dynasty to the despised Manchus, Gu spent the last quarter-century of his life as a sojourner in north China. There he experienced an agonizing psychological alienation between north and south China, arising from and reinforced by the fault line between northern and southern topolect groups. Sensing that China could not possibly hold together as a strong nation if this dramatic rift were not somehow surmounted, he threw himself into research on the geographical and phonological sources of division. Strange as it may seem, statecraft was the primary motivation for Gu's phonological studies.

Although Gu made many valuable contributions to the study of ancient Chinese, his basic premises were flawed by the same misconceptions that had limited language studies ever since the Han period. Namely, Gu was unable to realize that fixation on the supratopolectal, semanto-syllabic characters masked the tremendous contrasts in morphology, phonology, and grammar among Sinitic languages. Merely devoting attention to rationalizing the pronunciation of the characters against a hypothetical ancient standard was useless for effecting a reconciliation between north and south. Nonetheless, we must admit that Gu was well intentioned and that he clarified much about the nature of pre-Tang initials and finals. Given the constraints of the scholarly apparatus with which he was endowed, Gu Yanwu must be judged an outstanding exemplar of the best Chinese scholarship, a worthy successor to the long line of thinkers passionately committed to the preservation of "this culture [of ours]" (*si wen;* see selection 7 [9.5]).[6]

Standing at the beginning of the line and counted among the glories of Chinese civilization are the scintillating intellectual debates that went on during the Warring States period (475–221 B.C.E.). Well represented in this volume, the contending schools of thought—with their starkly discrepant proposals for solutions to the problem of how to organize a successful state—demonstrate that Chinese thinkers were far from being boring epigones of some mythical (in every sense of the word) founder figure.

As for philosophy, so for religion—but with even more exuberant dissimilarity. Among spiritual traditions that have flourished in China during the last three millennia and more are Magianism, shamanism, Taoism, Buddhism, Zoroastrianism (Mazdaism), Nestorian Christianity, Hinduism (among Indian emigrants), Judaism, Islam, Catholicism, Protestantism, and—above all—ancestor worship. It is immediately apparent that most of these traditions entered China from abroad. Although adherents of some of them were persecuted (and even extirpated) from time to time, several of the traditions took root in Chinese soil, found sustenance there, and—in turn—enriched the lives of the people.

We could go on in this vein—citing evidence from science, medicine, architecture, music, dance, the performing arts, folklore, social structures, and other areas—but the picture should be clear by now. Chinese civilization is richly varied and, as eloquently explained by Valerie Hansen,[7] very much open to influence from outside and change from within. To reiterate a point made at the outset of this essay, China's society was not static, and its culture was far from unvariegated. Coupled with the cyclical collapse of dynasties, this sociocultural volatility might well have led to the utter disintegration of Chinese civilization. What, then, held it together? What was the quintessential glue that prevented the dissolution of "this culture [of ours]"? We have no hesitation whatsoever in declaring that it was none other than dedication to the hallowed culture itself, bearing in mind that *wen* means both "culture" *and* "writing." That is to say, it was the traditional culture *(wenhua)* and all its attendant values, as embodied in the sacred script *(wenzi),* that bound Chinese civilization in a cohesive and enduring whole.

But to whom exactly did "this culture/script [of ours]" belong? In other words, who were the implicit "we" that lay claim to the role of proprietors of the culture/script that both symbolized and sustained traditional Chinese civilization? The answer is simple: the literati. And who were the literati? How did one become a literatus and thereby gain access to the ranks of those who were the powerful custodians of the culture/script? The answer is likewise straightforward: master fine writing *(wenzhang)* and belles lettres *(wenxue).*[8] By dint of diligence and through the good fortune of privilege, approximately two percent of the populace in premodern China attained full literacy and all the perquisites that pertained to it, which were not inconsiderable.

Given that full literacy normally brought with it both prestige and pecuniary benefit, it is small wonder that many men devoted their lives to the acquisition and exercise of the ability to write well. (With a few very rare exceptions, women were excluded from the enterprise of fine writing.) Those accustomed to universal literacy using an alphabetic script and a living, vernacular language may find it hard to imagine the exceptional effort required to gain an advanced degree of competency in a highly allusive, dead (i.e., not used for speech) language written with an elaborate logographic script.[9] For those who did put forward the required exertion, their command of the script, plus the satisfaction of knowing that they were contributing to the preservation of Chinese culture, made it all worthwhile.

With the twentieth century, however, the combination of culture and script began to unravel. With the overthrow of the Qing (Manchu) dynasty in 1911 by revolutionaries led by Sun Yat-sen (1866–1925),[10] the institutional support for the examination system that upheld "this culture [of ours]" evaporated. By 1919, progressive intellectuals were promoting writing in the vernacular, and radical activists were proposing the adoption of an alphabetic script. A direct assault on the script itself came with the promulgation of thousands of simplified characters by the Communist government during the 1950s and 1960s. An outrageous affront to those who cherish the script and all that it embraces, the simplified characters were seen by reformers as essential for expanding literacy to workers and farmers and necessary for the sake of efficiency in diverse types of communication.

By the end of the twentieth century and the beginning of the twenty-first century, a new threat to the traditional script was emerging: the computer. IT (Information Technology) specialists are acutely aware of the tremendous stumbling blocks in the way of free and easy access to electronic data processing by users of Chinese characters. The input, storage, and management of a script consisting of tens of thousands of discrete elements pose mind-boggling problems in comparison with the couple hundred letters and typographic characters of the ASCII (American Standard Code for Information Interchange). The economic costs in terms of vastly larger memories, slower manipulations, more frequent crashes and bugs due to overly intricate programming, and so forth are staggering.

One of the most poignant ironies of the saga of characters in computers is that the alphabet has come to their (partial) rescue. Of the hundreds and hundreds of schemes that have been devised for inputting Chinese characters in computers, by far the most popular are those relying on the alphabet. And, of the alphabetic schemes, those that rely on whole words rather than single syllables are much more user-friendly and computer-friendly. For example, both computers and human beings find it easier to analyze the following eight syllables of a journal title as *Zhongguo lishi dili luncong (Collected Papers on Chinese Historical Geography)* than as *zhong guo li shi di li lun cong (central kingdom successive scribe/history ground principle discussion cluster)*. Herein lurks a danger. Once computers and human beings get used to parsing strings of syllables into words rather than resolutely keeping them separate, alphabetic inputting is on its way to becoming an independent script.

The defenders of the characters, who also view themselves as defenders of the last bastion of Chinese culture, have not been slow to recognize this threat, and they have been adamantly opposed to any hint of a move toward legitimation of the formal establishment of what is called *fenci lianxie* (word division). Throughout history, Chinese scholars have always resisted the insertion of spaces between words. In fact, until the twentieth century, there was no concept of *ci* (word), only that of *zi* ([syllabic] graph/character). Despite the vociferous opposition of the defenders of characters, the Chinese government has officially established a set of Basic Rules for Hanyu Pinyin Orthography,[11] and private software companies and individuals are producing their own refinements apace.[12]

Willy-nilly, pinyin orthography is becoming a reality. This leads to a host of thorny questions. What will happen when the character system is weakened still further (after the twin enactment of vernacularization and simplification)? As we have argued above, the writing system that perpetuated "this culture [of ours]" was the matrix that held the mosaic in place. If the matrix dissolves or is irretrivably weakened, what is to prevent the multitudinous pieces of glittering color in the Chinese mosaic from flying off in a thousand different directions?

The battle lines have been drawn between the defenders of the Old Order and the proponents of the New Vision. Lu Xun, the greatest Chinese writer of the twentieth century, was an ardent advocate of romanization (see selection 91). Xu Bing, perhaps the best-known artist at the dawn of the twenty-first century, has boldly tampered with the characters, simultaneously recognizing that their acquisition by generations of Chinese youths constitutes the most fundamental kind of cultural conditioning (see selection 92).

Should the character system falter or fail, is there something else that might serve as a substitute matrix for the Chinese mosaic? That depends upon the ingenuity of China's citizens and their collective will to stay together as one nation. In the end, however, the determining factor for Chinese civilization may prove to be ecology, not culture.[13] The precarious environment, distinctively shaped through the centuries by the Chinese masses of diverse ethnicities, is extraordinarily sensitive to natural disasters. Now, even more gigantic transformations of the landscape are being wrought than ever before in China's past. A good example is the damming of the Three Gorges on the Yangtze and the diversion of its waters to the north. Not only is this environmental engineering of unprecedented proportions, it is also a geopolitical act of more far-reaching consequences than the construction of the Grand Canal in 605–606, which the Sui Emperor Yang Di (r. 604–617) had built to transport southern grain to the relatively impoverished (but militarily mighty) north.[14] Also operative in Yang Di's mobilization of tens of thousands of workers to build the Grand Canal was the same sort of psychological anxiety about the lack of a linkage between the Yellow River Valley and the Yangtze River Valley that plagued Gu Yanwu.

While adherence to historical veracity demands that we emphasize the complexity of Chinese culture, we by no means wish to deny its commonalities. Hence, we have adopted an integral and, we hope, balanced approach which bears testimony to the unity in diversity in Chinese civilization. We have seen how China is a congeries of varied constituents. Traditionally, they have been kept together by "this culture/script [of ours]" whose ever-alert guardians were the impressively accomplished literati. For a succession of twenty-five[15] dynasties, they did their job surprisingly well.

—VHM

Notes

1. Victor H. Mair, "Buddhism and the Rise of the Written Vernacular: The Making of National Languages," *Journal of Asian Studies* 53.3 (August 1994), 707–751.

2. Here we borrow an apt expression from *The Chinese Mosaic*, an extraordinarily perceptive, but regrettably poorly known, volume by Leo J. Moser (see under Ethnography and Folklore in the list of Suggestions for Further Reading).

3. Nicola Di Cosmo's new book, *Ancient China and Its Enemies*, marks a watershed in thinking about the historiography of Sino-"Barbarian" relations (see under Neighboring Peoples).

4. Christopher Beckwith, *The Tibetan Empire in Central Asia* (see under Neighboring Peoples).

5. See "China's Vernacular Cultures," the brilliant inaugural lecture of Glen Dudbridge, which was delivered at the University of Oxford on June 1, 1995 (Oxford: Clarendon Press, 1996), and the statistically documented study of Ruofu Du, Yida Yuan, Juliana Hwang, Joanna Mountain, and L. Luca Cavalli-Sforza, *Chi-

nese Surnames and the Genetic Differences between North and South China, Journal of Chinese Linguistics Monograph Series, 5 (Berkeley: University of California, 1992).

6. I am obviously indebted to Peter Bol for this felicitous rendering of the phrase, although he is not responsible for our clumsy brackets. For a nuanced discussion of *wen,* see Haun Saussy's "The Prestige of Writing: *wén,* Letter, Picture, Image, Ideography," in his *Great Walls of Discourse and Other Adventures in Cultural China* (Cambridge: Harvard University Asia Center, 2001), chap. 3, pp. 35–74.

7. See Hansen, *The Open Empire: A History of China to 1600* (New York and London: W. W. Norton, 2000).

8. I am grateful to Jidong Yang for the first insight and to Zong-qi Cai for the second.

9. Strictly speaking, the Chinese characters are not logographs, because not every character is equal to a word. Much less are the characters ideographs, a term that is often irresponsibly applied to them. Technically speaking, the Chinese script may be designated as morphosyllabic or semantosyllabic. The grounds for such a designation are outlined in John DeFrancis, *The Chinese Language* (see under Languages and Scripts).

10. It is an intriguing fact of history that a disproportionately large number of the core leaders of the 1911 revolution, including perhaps Sun Yat-sen himself, were Hakkas. The same is true of many of the main generals and chief supporters of Mao Zedong (1893–1976).

11. Conveniently published as Appendix I (pp. 835–845) in John DeFrancis, ed., *ABC Chinese-English Dictionary* (Honolulu: University of Hawai'i Press, 1996).

12. No scholar has done more to perfect and promote pinyin as a fully functioning orthography than the late Yin Binyong (1930–2003). See his *Chinese Romanization: Pronunciation and Orthography,* written with Mary Felley (Beijing: Sinolingua, 1990), and the landmark *Xinhua Spelling Dictionary (Xinhua pinxie cidian)* (Beijing: Shangwu, 2002).

13. Two thought-provoking works on this subject are Leon E. Stover, *The Cultural Ecology of Chinese Civilization: Peasants and Elites in the Last of the Agrarian States* (New York: Pica, 1974), and *Sediments of Time: Environment and Society in Chinese History,* ed. Mark Elvin and Liu Ts'ui-jung (Cambridge: Cambridge University Press, 1998).

14. The actual designer of the canal was Yuwen Kai (555–612), who was of Xianbei (Särbi) ethnicity. Yuwen also supervised the construction of the capital cities that served as the foundations of the Tang metropolises of Chang'an and Luoyang, and oversaw many other large and important public works projects.

15. The exact number is difficult to pin down, since there were numerous small dynasties, and two or more dynasties often ruled concurrently in different parts of what is now referred to as China. The number twenty-five is taken from the official dynastic histories.

1 | Shang Dynasty Oracle-Bone Inscriptions

DATING AS FAR back as the early twelfth century B.C.E., the Shang oracle-bone inscriptions are the earliest paleographical records remaining from China's ancient past. Yet as records they are unique—and certainly very specialized—in that they consist for the most part of the terse notes of diviners about particular divinations that had been performed by using the bones on which these inscriptions appear. This method of seeking divine guidance was performed by using specially prepared bones, such as turtle plastrons and bovine scapulae. After the bones were properly treated, small hollows were bored on one side of a bone, so that when heat was applied to them with a hot poker, cracking would occur on the other side. The resulting ╡-shaped cracks would then be interpreted by the diviner (as well as the Shang king). In many cases, particularly in the early periods, the matters of concern put to the oracle were phrased as positive-negative propositions. Thus the bones had to be cracked twice and heat applied to opposing hollows that had been scraped out of the surface (see fig. 1.2). In many instances, the same proposition would be put to the oracle several times, perhaps for the sake of clarification or verification. By inspecting the shapes of the cracks, the diviner could then determine whether or not the matters divined would materialize in the future. Afterward, the diviner would have the details of the divination recorded (i.e., engraved) on the bone used. These records usually include the date on which the divination took place (i.e., based on the sixty-day cycle used at that time), the name of the diviner who performed it, and a brief statement about the specific matter that had been put to the oracle. If the same proposition was divined more than once, the inscribed text was then often subsequently abbreviated to avoid redundancy. In addition, the diviner would also have notations engraved near the cracks, registering their nature and significance, as well as other relevant comments pertaining to the outcome of the events that followed. Quite often a number of different divinations performed at different times would be made using the same bone, so that the texts inscribed on them have no connection with one another. These are normally distinguishable by the different dates on which the divinations were performed and also by the different names of the diviners who performed them. We also find other extraneous notations engraved on these bones, such as the delivery of a "shipment" of fresh bones.

Archaeological excavations near Anyang, Henan Province—the last site of the Shang capital—have shown that the royal house of Shang relied heavily on this method of divination in its day-to-day operations and decision making from the time it established its capital there about 1200 B.C.E. until the fall of the dynasty about 1045 B.C.E. Many thousands of these inscribed bones have been discovered at Anyang, though most of them are nothing more than fragments now. Nevertheless, enough nearly complete inscribed shells and bones have been excavated and painstakingly reassembled to allow us to learn a good deal about the political, religious, and cultural practices of that era. In this sense, the contents of these divinatory texts are quite rich, as they provide detailed—if not always transparent—insights into the concerns that mattered most to the members of the ruling class, everything from harvests to warfare to childbirth to sacrificial offerings to fortuitous and evil omens to health matters and so forth. As a rule, the propositions put to the oracle were phrased with great precision and care, often involving finely tuned levels of modality, rather than simple positive-negative propositions, and therefore no doubt were equally open to carefully crafted interpretations. The gravity of these divinations is attested by the use of professional diviners, in addition to the fact that the Shang kings themselves almost always got involved in them and proffered their own interpretations of the cracks, which are also recorded on the oracle bones.—GLM

Inscription 1

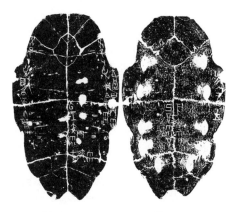

Figure 1.1 **Figure 1.2**

Front side:

Divining (i.e., cracking the bone) on *guisi* (day 30), Zheng tested [the proposition]: It will rain during the current month. The king, prognosticating, said, "It will rain on a *bing* day."[1]

Divining on *guisi* (day 30), Zheng tested [the proposition]: It may not rain during the current month. [Comment:] It rained on *renyin* (day 39) during the next ten-day period. On *jiachen* (day 41) it also rained. (*Bingbian* 368)

Back side:

[Comment:] On *jiyou* (day 46) it rained. On *xinhai* (day 48) it also rained. [Notation:] The Que [people] brought in 250 [turtle shells]. (*Bingbian* 369)

Inscription 2

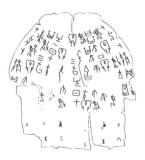

Figure 1.3

Divining on *jiashen* (day 21), Nan tested [the proposition]: When Lady Hao gives birth, it will be felicitous (i.e., she will give birth to a son).[2] The king, prognosticating, said, "Perhaps if it is on a *ding* day that she gives birth, there will be extended auspiciousness." [Comment:] After 31 days, on *jiayin* (51), she gave birth and it was not felicitous; it was a girl.

Divining on *jiashen* (day 21), Nan tested [the proposition]: When Lady Hao gives birth, it may not be felicitous. [Comment:] After 31 days, on *jiayin* (51), she gave birth and it really was not felicitous; it was a girl. (*Yibian* 7731)

Inscription 3

Divining on *jichou* (day 26), Nan tested [the proposition]: That the king had a dream was [due to] Ancestor Yi. Tested [the proposition]: That the king had a dream was not due to Ancestor Yi.

Divining on *jichou* (day 26), Nan tested [the proposition]: That the king had a dream was [due to] Ancestor Yi. Tested [the proposition]: That the king had a dream was not [due to] Ancestor Yi.

Divining on *jichou* (day 26), Nan tested [the proposition]: Perform the x-sacrifice at Qiushang. Tested [the proposition]: Do not specifically perform the x-sacrifice at Qiushang. On the next *xinmao* (day 28) make a sacrificial offering to Ancestor Xin. Tested [the proposition]: Offer Ancestor Xin three specially reared sheep. On the next *xin* day offer one ox to Ancestor Xin. One ox to Ancestor Xin. Offer a specially reared sheep to Ancestor Xin. Tested [the proposition]: To Ancestor Xin make a sacrificial offering. Make a sacrificial offering to Ancestor Yi.

Divining on *renchen* (day 29), Nan [tested the proposition]: Offer a specially reared sheep to Shi Ren. Offer two oxen to Shi Ren.

Divining on *jiawu* (day 31), Zheng [tested the proposition]: [Make a sacrifice] to the River God.

Divining on *jiawu* (day 31), Zheng [tested the proposition]: Do not [make a sacrifice] to the River God.

[Divining] on [*jia*]*wu* (day 31), Nan [tested the proposition]: [Make it] a captive and three dancers.

[Divining] on [*jia*]*wu* (day 31), Nan [tested the proposition]: Do not [make it a captive and three dancers].

Divining on *renyin* (day 39), Nan [tested the proposition]: The River God will harm the king.

Divining on *renyin* (day 39), Nan tested [the proposition]: The River God will not harm the king.

Divining on *renyin* (day 39), Nan tested [the proposition]: That it does not rain means that this [house of] Shang is being afflicted with misfortune. Tested [the proposition]: That it does not rain does not mean that this [house of] Shang is being afflicted with misfortune.

Divining on *guimao* (day 40), Nan [tested the proposition]: On the next *jiachen* (day 41) make an offering of ten oxen to Shangjia.

Inscription 4

Divining on *jiawu* (day 31), Zheng tested [the proposition]: On the next *yiwei* (day 32) use Qiang [tribesmen in sacrifice].[3] [Comment:] [They were] used. That day was overcast.

Divining on *jiawu* (day 31), Zheng tested [the proposition]: On the next *yiwei* (day 32) do not specifically use Qiang [tribesmen in sacrifice]. Tested [the proposition]: On the next *yiwei* (day 32) use Qiang [tribesmen in sacrifice].

Divining on *yiwei* (day 32), Bin tested [the proposition]: Bring in sacrificial victims from Wu. [Do not] bring in sacrificial victims from Wu. Tested [the proposition]: Sacrificial victims may not be brought in from Wu. Make an offering to Tang Zi and perform the decapitation sacrifice. Tested [the proposition]: Call for the taking of a Zi [clansman?] and perform the decapitation sacrifice. Tested [the proposition]: Make a burnt offering to the divinity of the soil. Make an offering to Father Yi. Tested [the proposition]: That the king had a dream spells [impending] disaster. It does not spell [impending] disaster. Tested [the proposition]: The king may have an eye ailment. Tested [the proposition]: The king does not have an eye ailment.

Inscription 5

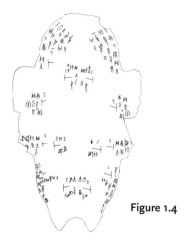

Figure 1.4

Divining on *yimao* (day 52), Nan tested [the proposition]: The king ought to follow Wang Cheng in attacking the Xiagui, [and by doing so he] will receive much [divine?] assistance.

Divining on *yimao* (day 52), Nan tested [the proposition]: The king ought not follow Wang Cheng in attacking the Xiagui, [and by doing so he] may not receive much assistance. Tested [the proposition]: The king ought to follow Wang Cheng. Tested [the proposition]: The king ought not follow Wang Cheng.

Divining on *dingsi* (day 54), Nan tested [the proposition]: The king ought to train the multitude of people at Maofang, [and by doing so he] will receive much assistance.

Divining on *dingsi* (day 54), Nan tested [the proposition]: The king ought not train the multitude of people at Maofang, [and by doing so he] may not receive much assistance. Going out to inspect is what the king should do. Going out to inspect is not what the king should do.

Divining on *gengshen* (day 57), Nan tested [the proposition]: [He] ought to be made a guest.

Divining on *gengshen* (day 57), Nan tested [the proposition]: [He] ought not be made a guest. Tested [the proposition]: It ought to be Zhi Jia whom the king follows in attacking the [Bafang]. Tested [the proposition]: The king ought not follow Zhi Jia in attacking the Ba[fang]. It ought to be Jia whom [he] follows. It ought not be the case that [he] follows Jia. (*Bingbian* 22)

—GLM

Notes

1. Note that the king was apparently wrong in this instance. Yet in other instances an inscription may note in relation to the king's prognostication: "It really rained on such and such a day."

2. Lady Hao was the consort of King Wu Ding (r. early 12th c. B.C.E.). Her tomb was excavated in 1996 and yielded a total of approximately sixteen hundred finely crafted bronze artifacts, jades, cowries, and so forth. See plate 9.

3. The Qiang, a non-Shang nomadic people, were frequently used as sacrificial victims along with a variety of animals. Exactly who the Qiang were and whether or not their descendants survive today has been a subject of much scholarly debate, although it is widely believed that they were Proto-Tibetans.

THE INSCRIBING OF bronzes used in the performance of ritual sacrifices to one's ancestors began during the second half of the second millennium B.C.E. Initially, the inscriptions were usually short, consisting of little more than a clan emblem, indicating ownership; sometimes the posthumous title of the ancestor to whom the bronze was being dedicated was also included. But as time passed, the inscriptions grew in length and complexity and were increasingly used to record significant events in the lives of their composers. Usually these events focus on the receipt of awards from the Shang and Western Zhou kings in recognition of one's service to the state. While the exact reasons for these awards are rarely stated, the fact that one had been singled out for an award in recognition of one's meritorious service was sufficient evidence of one's great accomplishments. No additional elaboration in the inscription was needed. Desire for humility might also have been a factor. Emphasis in these inscriptions is usually placed more on what the king did or said than on what the person being awarded had done to warrant an award. Thus ritual bronzes in turn came to serve as a personal yet permanent medium for announcing through their inscriptions one's deeds and accomplishments to one's ancestors and descendants alike. The fact that these inscriptions normally were placed inconspicuously on the interior surfaces of vessels suggests that they were not intended for others' casual perusal and were meant more for spiritual than human consumption.

All this changed when the house of Zhou was forced by invaders to move its capital eastward from Zongzhou (near present-day Xi'an) to Luoyi (present-day Luoyang) in 770 B.C.E. after the earlier capital became all but a nonentity politically. Clear evidence of this is seen in the Eastern Zhou period (770–221 B.C.E.) bronze inscriptions, for from this point on the Zhou kings are seldom even mentioned in bronze texts. The days of the investiture ritual, enfeoffments, and award ceremonies as recorded on bronzes in which the Western Zhou kings had figured so prominently had clearly passed, and with them went the ritual bronze texts glorifying and extolling the virtues of the Sons of Heaven for their generous rewards in recognition of meritorious service. The feudal lords, who had been among the primary recipients of these awards, now simply took what they wanted by brute force when they had the wherewithal to do so. The once all-powerful Sons of Heaven were now at their mercy.

Yet after the royal award ceremonies had faded into history and the nobility began manufacturing bronzes on their own at will, the composers of inscriptions eventually found it necessary to adopt a new rhetorical style to announce their own deeds and accomplishments directly to their ancestors and descendants. The style that finally evolved may be termed "self-panegyrical," in that the composer literally enumerates his finest virtues. So the focus was now placed on the character and accomplishments of the person responsible for the production of the bronze, along with his request of the spirits for endless longevity and well-being. What is more, the dedication of bronzes to a particular ancestor also fell out of vogue, and in many cases references to one's ancestors are only vague at best. While this does not necessarily indicate a sudden decline in the veneration of ancestors during the Eastern Zhou, it does reveal that one's ancestors no longer were as integral a consideration in the production of bronzes as they had been during the Shang and Western Zhou. On the contrary, the stated reasons for casting bronzes during the Eastern Zhou became considerably more vague. This may well have been an outcome of the eventual commonality of the manufacture of bronzes, which had earlier been regarded as a significant event because the metals used in their production were relatively rare. Ironically, by the end of the Eastern Zhou, bronze inscriptions became shorter once again and often record little more than the names of the persons who had them produced, or at most etched names indicating ownership.—GLM

Petty Officer Yu's Ritual *Zun*-vessel Inscription (Xiaochen Yu *zun*) (fig. 2.1; see plate 8) Late Shang (ca. 11th c. B.C.E.)

Figure 2.1

On *dingsi* (day 54) the king made an inspection tour of Kuizu. The king presented Petty Officer Yu (i.e., me) Kui cowry shells.[1] It was when the king came on a campaign against Renfang. It was the king's tenth sacrificial cycle and fifth (i.e., the fifteenth year of his reign), second-day sacrifice.[2]

Petty Officer Yi's Ritual *Jia*-vessel Inscription (Yi *jia*)
Late Shang (ca. 11th c. B.C.E.)

On *guisi* (day 30), the king presented Petty Officer Yi cowry shells, amounting to ten strings. On this occasion [I] make for Mother Gui (a posthumous title) [this] sacrificial vessel. It was the king's sixth sacrificial cycle (i.e., sixth year), second-day sacrifice. It was in the fourth month. Clan emblem.

Yu's Ritual *Ding*-tripod Inscription (Da Yu *ding*)
Early Western Zhou (ca. early 10th c. B.C.E.)

It was the ninth month when the king was in Zongzhou and laid charge on Yu (i.e., me). The king spoke thus: "Yu, the greatly illustrious King Wen received Heaven's great mandate. When King Wu succeeded King Wen, he built a state, ridded it of evils (i.e., the defeated Yin rulers), extensively possessed the four quarters [of the realm], and grandly governed its people. In tending to affairs [of state], alas, in the case of spirits, none dared overindulge(?),[3] and in making burnt offerings and performing the winter sacrifices, none dared get intoxicated(?).[4] Thus Heaven safeguarded and watched over [its] children and greatly protected the former kings, and so they x-ly[5] possessed the four quarters [of the realm]. We have heard that Yin lost its Mandate. It was [because the officials in] Yin's outlying *hou* and *dian* administrative zones and Yin's officials and administrators all overindulged in alcoholic spirits that it lost its multitudes. Oh! In the dawn [of your life] you had great responsibilities but it was I that instructed you a little. Do not form cliques against me, your ruler, the One Man. Now let us attain to the model inherent in King Wen's correct virtue. Just as King Wen commanded two or three government officials, now I command you, Yu, to assist in regulating [the state]. Respectfully harmonize the norms of virtue. From morning till night diligently submit admonitions; in performing the sacrifices, (make haste:) bestir [yourself] and stand in awe of Heaven's awesome majesty." The king said, "Oh! [I] command you, Yu, emulate your grandfather whom you succeed, the Duke of Nan." The king said, "Yu, now assist until death in taking charge of the weaponry. Diligently press for punishments and litigations. From early morning till night assist me, the One Man, in (upholding:) taking care of the four quarters [of the realm]. For me [you] will go on an inspection tour of the peoples and territories received by the former kings. [I] confer on you one jar of aromatic sacrificial spirits, an unlined slipover robe, a knee cover and slippers,[6] and a chariot and horses. [I] confer on you the banner of your grandfather, the Duke of Nan; use it in hunting. [I] confer on you state officers, numbering four, and people and serfs(?) from charioteers down to commoners, numbering 659. [I] confer on you barbarian officers and royal servants, numbering 13, and people and serfs(?) numbering 1,050. Reaching as far as X (a place name?) remove(?) [them] from their lands." The king said, "Yu, compliantly respect your official duties and do not neglect my charge." On this occasion, Yu extols the king's patronage and herewith makes for [his] grandfather, the Duke of Nan, [this] precious *ding*-cauldron. It is the king's twenty-third year.

Food Steward Ke's Ritual *Ding*-tripod Inscription (Da Ke *ding*)
(fig. 2.2; see plate 12) Mid Western Zhou (ca. mid-9th c. B.C.E.)

Figure 2.2

Ke said, "August was my accomplished ancestor, Shi Huafu. Discriminating and yielding was his heart. Vigilant and at ease was he in the affairs [of state]. Kind and wise was his moral character.

bells→music

So was he able to reverently protect his sovereign, King Gong, and regulate and supervise the king's household. Being kind to the myriad people and gentle to those distant and (capable in) handling competently those near, so was he able to be x-ed by August Heaven. He exhibited probity to those above and below, attained greatness without distress, and was presented gifts without limit. He is everlastingly remembered by his grandson's sovereign, the Son of Heaven. The Son of Heaven is intelligent and discerning; and he is profoundly filial to the spirits. Thinking of his (i.e., Ke's) sagacious, protective ancestor, Shi Huafu, he (the king) selected [me], Ke, for the king's service, to issue and bring in [reports on] the king's decrees; and he copiously presented [me] precious favors. May the Son of Heaven live for ten thousand years without end. May he protect and regulate the Zhou state and eminently rule the four quarters [of the realm]."

The king was in Zongzhou.[7] At dawn, the king proceeded to the Mu Temple and assumed position.[8] Zhong Ji assisted Food Steward Ke to enter the gate and stand in the central hall, facing north. The king called on the Yinshi (an official title) to issue the charge to Food Steward Ke. The king spoke thus: "Ke, formerly I commanded you to issue and bring in [reports on] my decrees. Now I am reaffirming your charge. [I] confer on you x-knee cover and unlined slipover robe.[9] [I] confer on you fields at Ye. [I] confer on you fields at Pi. [I] confer on you the fields of the Suo people in Jun that are inhabited by the Jing people, along with their male and female slaves. [I] confer on you fields at Kang. [I] confer on you fields at Yan. [I] confer on you fields at Boyuan. [I] confer on you fields at Hanshan. [I] confer on you scribes, retainers, flutists, and a drum and bell [master]. [I] confer on you the Suo people conscripted by the Jing people to x (meaning uncertain). I confer on you the Jing people hurrying about (i.e., toiling) at Liang. Day and night, reverently employ [all of these] in serving [me]; do not neglect my charge." Ke saluted with hands cupped and touched his head to the floor, and dared in response to extol the Son of Heaven's greatly illustrious patronage. On this occasion [I] make for my accomplished ancestor, Shi Huafu, a precious vessel for carrying out sacrificial offerings. May [I] Ke live for ten thousand years without end and [his] son's sons and grandsons forever treasure and use [this vessel].

Duke Wu of Qin's Bell Inscription (Qin Wugong *zhong*)
Mid Spring and Autumn Period (early 7th c. B.C.E.)

The Duke of Qin said, "Our ancestors received Heaven's decree. [They] were rewarded a place to dwell and received a state. Majestically eminent were Duke Wen, Duke Jing, and Duke Xian. [They] grandly advanced (i.e., ascended) on high, and eminently acted in accord with August Heaven and thereby vigilantly attended to [the tribes of] the Man regions."[10] The Duke said to Lady Ji of the royal house (i.e., his wife), "As for me, the little child (i.e., a term of humility), morning and evening I make reverent and respectful my sacrifices in order to receive many blessings, to enlighten [my] mind, to stabilize and harmonize the administrators and knights, and to unite and foster [those] on the left and the right (i.e., my ministers). Being truly righteous in great measure, having respectfully received radiant virtue, and having harmonized my state by means of peace and stability, [I] will bring about the submission of all the many Man tribes. [I] make his (i.e., my) harmonizing bells, [whose] felicitous tone is pure and harmonious, so as to please the august dukes (during the performance of sacrificial rituals) and thereby receive great blessings, abundant generosity and many gifts, and a grand longevity of ten thousand years. May the Duke of Qin (i.e., I) be everlastingly perfect on the throne and receive the great mandate, and enjoy longevous old age without end and extensively possess the four quarters. May [these bells] be treasured in tranquility.

Yizhe's Bell Inscription (Wangsun Yizhe *zhong*)
Late Spring and Autumn Period (late 6th c. B.C.E.)

+ bells. please spirits

It was the first month, *chuji* (beginning auspiciousness: first quarter), *dinghai* (day 24) that the king's grandson, Yizhe, selected his fine metal and on his own initiative made [this] harmonizing bell. [Its tone] is both sonorous and resounding, and [its] fine sound is ever so grand. [I] will use [it] to make sacrificial offerings and thereby show filial devotion to my august ancestors and refined deceased father, and will use [it] to pray for longevous old age. I am mild and respectful and am at ease and composed; cautiously standing in awe, [I] am reverent, wise, sagacious, and valiant. Being kind in [my] administrative demeanor and being proper in [my] sense of decorum, [my] strategies and plans are greatly prudent. Loud and strong is this harmonizing bell. [I] will use [it] in feasting to rejoice and use [it] to please honored guests, elders, and elder brothers, together with our associates and friends. I make responsible my heart and make far-reaching and constant my deportment, and [I] harmonize and settle the people. I am omnipresent in the state. Brilliantly and extensively, for ten thousand years without end, with generations numbering ten thousand, [may] grandsons and sons eternally safeguard and strike it (i.e., this bell).

—GLM

Notes

1. Cowry shells were used as currency in early China.
2. This was a supplementary sacrifice performed the day after a primary one.
3. It should be stated that these laconic texts, written in very archaic script, are still in the process of being deciphered by epigraphers. While we are able to read substantial portions of them, the meanings and pronunciations of some words and phrases in them still present riddles to be solved and are indicated here by question marks.
4. King Wen's stern prohibition against intemperance by state officials is covered at length in the "Announcement about Spirits" section of the *Book of Documents,* where insobriety is treated as a crime worthy of the death penalty.
5. Occasionally we know from its position the grammatical part of speech of a character but not its exact meaning. In such cases we write "x-ly," "x-ed," and so forth.
6. These were evidently ceremonial garments worn at court.
7. None of the place-names in this inscription can be identified with confidence.
8. The ceremony depicted here is typical of the investiture ceremonies recorded in numerous Western Zhou bronze inscriptions.
9. The exact nature of the garments mentioned here is uncertain.
10. The Man were apparently a persistent thorn in the side of the more agriculturally oriented Zhou people. The Zhou people themselves, however, had a background in the pastoral northwest, yet developed over the course of their dynasty into one of the greatest settled civilizations on earth.

REFERENCES TO CELESTIAL bodies and astronomical phenomena in Chinese texts first make their appearance in the late Shang dynasty oracle-bone (divinatory) inscriptions dating from the thirteenth to mid-eleventh centuries B.C.E., most of which pertain to various aspects of Shang cultic ritual. Identifiable stars and asterisms and the like named in the inscriptions include the Northern (Big) Dipper, the "Fire Star" Antares (α Scorpii), Orion the "Triaster" asterism (δ Orionis), the Dragon constellation (corresponding to the portion of the zodiac we know as Virgo through Scorpio), the planet Jupiter, and, of course Sun and Moon. A small number of inscriptions also record important transitory phenomena such as sunspots, solar and lunar eclipses, solstices, comets, and possibly supernovas. Here are some representative examples.

[Preface:] Crack-making on day *bingyin* (3),[1] Que divined: [Charge:] We should perhaps perform a *you*-ritual to the Fire [star].

[Preface:] [Divined] on day *xinsi* (18): [Charge:] The Sun has a blemish (i.e., a sunspot) [on the] west. . . . ["There will be a] calamity." [Verification:] Indeed there was a blemish.

[Preface:] Crack-making on day [*gui*]*chou* (50), Bin divined: [Charge:] On the coming *yi*[*mao*] (52) we should offer steamed millet to [ancestor] Zu Yi. [Prognostication:] The king read the cracks and said, "There will be disasters. . . . It may not rain." [Verification:] [After] 6 days, on the night of day [*wu*]*wu* (55), the Moon was eclipsed. . . .

IT IS NOTEWORTHY that both Antares and Orion's belt figure importantly from this early date, for, as we shall see, the volume of astral lore connected with these two crucial seasonal indicators attests to their great significance to the early Chinese. Knowledge of the stars was, of course, vital in ancient times, before the advent of reliable calendars. As the celebrated Qing-dynasty scholar Gu Yanwu (1613–1682; see selection 83) once said, "Before the Three Dynasties (Xia, Shang, Zhou), everyone knew astronomy."

Also worth noting in the Shang inscriptions is the implication that astronomical phenomena may serve as omens of good or ill fortune, so that both aspects of "applied" astronomy—calendar science and astrology—are represented in the literature from the earliest times. Before turning to a more general consideration of cosmology in the early imperial period, we reproduce examples from the formative period of Chinese civilization that reflect a concern first with calendrical astronomy and then with astrology.

Calendrical Astronomy in the "Canon of Yao" (Yao dian)

One early canonical text that describes the systematic seasonal observation of stellar phenomena is the "astronomical foundation charter" in the "Yao dian" chapter of the *Book of Documents,* originally composed around the middle of the first millennium B.C.E. but modified in Han times. In this text, the legendary Emperor Yao charges his royal astrologers with the responsibility of scrupulously observing the evening transit *(zhong)*, the moment of culmination on the observer's meridian (i.e., the imaginary north-south line that passes directly overhead), of four cardinal asterisms in order to inform the people of the passage of the seasons. This canonical text clearly illustrates the calendrical significance of the four season-defining asterisms, makes plain how vital their observation was to the interests of the state, and describes the observational technique of "centering"—*zhong* (i.e., observing meridian transit)—by means of which the sun's position among the stars, and hence the date, could be more or less accurately inferred.[2]

Then [yao] commanded Xi and He, in reverent accord with august Heaven, to calculate and delineate the Sun, Moon, stars, and constellations, so as to respectfully confer the seasons on the people.

He separately charged Xi Zhong to reside at Yuyi, [in the place] called Yanggu (Bright Valley), there respectfully to host the rising Sun and to arrange and regulate the works of the East. "When the day is of medium length, and the star is Niao (Bird; α Hydrae), you may thereby determine midspring. The people disperse and the birds and beasts breed and mate."

He further charged Xi Shu to reside at Nanjiao (South Crossing), there to arrange and regulate the works of the South, paying respectful attention to the summer solstice. "When the day is longest and the star is Fire (α Scorpii), you may thereby determine midsummer. The people avail themselves [of the season]; the feathers and coats of birds and beasts are thin and hide-like."

He separately charged He Zhong to reside in the West, [in the place] called Meigu (Dark Valley), there to respectfully send off the setting Sun and to arrange and regulate the achievements of the West. "When the night is of medium length and the star is Xu (Void; α, β Aquarii), you may thereby determine midautumn. The people are at their ease, and the feathers and coats of birds and beasts are glossy."

He further charged He Shu to reside in the North, [in the place] called Youdu (Somber Capital), there to arrange and examine the works of the North. "When the day is at its shortest and the star is Mao (Pleiades; η Tauri), you may thereby determine midwinter. The people keep to the warmth [of their houses], and the feathers and coats of birds and beasts are downy and thick."

The emperor said, "Ah! You, Xi, and He. A round year consists of three hundred sixty-six days. By means of an intercalary month you should fix the four seasons and complete the year. If you thus faithfully regulate the many functionaries, their accomplishments will all be resplendent."[3]

GIVEN, SAY, OBSERVATION of the meridian transit of the reference star α Hydrae of the Vermilion Bird constellation at evening twilight, "when the day is of medium length," it can be inferred that the sun must be some 90° behind at the vernal equinox in Mao (lunar lodge no. 18,[4] Pleiades; η Tauri). It follows also that three months hence, at the summer solstice, the sun should have moved along to the vicinity of α Hydrae in the Vermilion Bird, at which time the star transiting the meridian at dusk should now be the distinctly reddish "Fire Star." From such rudimentary beginnings stellar indications for the whole year were gradually worked out in a way that made it possible to mark the passage of each month and season with precision. One such early calendrical almanac from the fifth century B.C.E., the *Lesser Annuary of Xia* or *Xia xiao zheng*, does precisely that, by mentioning fifteen distinct stellar phenomena associated with eight of the twelve months. These include the first and last visibility of certain asterisms at night, the orientation of the handle of the Northern Dipper (Ursa Major) at dusk or dawn, and meridian transits of three stars at dawn or dusk. At the same time, much of this information, in a less specialized form, would have been familiar to "everyman" in early China, much as was Hesiod's poetic *Works and Days* in ancient Greece. For example, here is a representative passage from the late-fourth-century-B.C.E. historical narrative *Discourses of the States (Guoyu)*:

When [the asterism] Dragon's Horn (lunar lodge no. 1, α Virginis) appears, the rain stops. When [the asterism] Heaven's Taproot (Virgo/Libra) appears, the rivers dry up. When [the asterism] Root (Libra) appears, the plants shed their leaves. When [the asterism] Quadriga (π Scorpii) appears, frost falls. When [the asterism] Fire (α Scorpii) appears, the clear winds warn of cold. Thus the teachings of the former kings say, "When the rains stop, clear the paths. When the rivers dry up, complete the bridges. When the plants shed their leaves, store the harvest. When the frost falls, make ready the fur garments. When the clear wind comes, repair the inner and outer defense walls and the palaces and buildings." Therefore, the *Ordinances of Xia* says, "In the ninth month clear the paths, in the tenth month complete the bridges." Its *Seasonal Advisories* says, "Gather in your harvest floor's bounty; prepare your baskets and spades. When [the asterism] Plan the House (lunar lodge no. 13, α Pegasi) is centered, look to begin earth moving. The Fire [star's] first appearance is already anticipated by the village headmen." This is how the former kings broadly promulgated their virtuous sway throughout the realm, without resorting to monetary incentives.[5]

BY THE EARLY imperial period, seasonal observations such as these were systematized and spelled out in great detail, in accordance with the *yinyang* and Five Phases[6] correlative cosmology that increasingly came to dominate cosmo-political thinking in the third to first centuries B.C.E. The opening passage from the "Monthly Ordinances" (Yue ling) chapter of the *Book of Rites (Liji)* illustrates the inseparability of the cosmological, natural, ritual, and political spheres in the ideology of the early empire:[7]

In the first month of the year the sun is in Plan the House (α Pegasi). At dusk Triaster (lunar lodge no. 21, α Orionis) is centered and at dawn Tail (lunar lodge no. 6, λ Scorpii) is centered. This month's [propitious] heavenly stems are *jia* and *yi*, its ruler Tai Hao, and its tutelary spirit Gou Mang. Its insects are the scaly sort, its keynote is *Jue*, and among the [12 tones of the] pitch pipes it corresponds to Great Budding. Its number is eight, its taste sour, and its odor rank. Its sacrifice is the Household, and sacrificial offerings give preference to the spleen. The east wind dissipates the freezing cold, and the hibernating insects begin to stir. The fish swim upstream, the otter makes an offering of his fish, and the wild geese arrive. The Son of Heaven dwells in the left (i.e., east) or blue-green wing [of the palace]. He rides the *luan*-carriage, drives the azure dragon[-steeds], and flies blue-green pennants. He dons blue-green ceremonial robes, wears azure jade pendants, dines on wheat and mutton, and the [motifs] of his incised vessels are [seasonally] apt. As this is the month of the Beginning of Spring, three days beforehand the

Prefect Grand Astrologer reports to the Son of Heaven, "such-and-such day is the Beginning of Spring; the influence of Wood is in the ascendant." The Son of Heaven then fasts, and on the day of the Beginning of Spring he personally leads the Three Eminences, Nine Ministers, Lords, and Grandees in ceremoniously welcoming the Spring in the eastern suburbs. On their return [the Son of Heaven] rewards his Eminences, Ministers, Lords, and Grandees at court.

THIS IMPERATIVE TO harmonize human activity with the rhythms of the cosmos underlies the rhetorical question that begins Sima Qian's (fl. ca. 100 B.C.E.) summation of the astronomical knowledge of his day in the "Treatise on the Heavenly Offices" (Tian guan shu) in *Records of the Grand Historian (Shiji):* "Ever since the people have existed, when have successive rulers not systematically followed the movements of Sun, Moon, stars, and asterisms?" In what follows, however, Sima Qian emphasizes the application of this knowledge not to calendrical science, but to discerning the will of Heaven and prognosticating the future—that is, to astrology: "The twenty-eight lunar lodges govern the twelve provinces and the handle of the Dipper seconds them; the origin (of these conceptions) is ancient."

So now we turn to a consideration of the principles and practice of astrology in early China.

Field Allocation Astrology

From the observation in hoary antiquity that the cycles of sun and moon directly influence human activity it naturally came to be assumed that whatever transpired in the skies had consequences below. In an effort to render such phenomena intelligible, and hence manageable, there gradually developed a scheme of astral-terrestrial correspondences in which locations in the sky were coupled with locations on the ground. In this scheme, the Heavenly River arching across the night sky, which we know as the Milky Way, was thought to correspond to the archetypal terrestrial River (i.e., the Yellow River), and the stellar fields surrounding it were the heavenly correlates of the terrestrial polities. When something transpired in the stellar field allocated to a terrestrial region it was taken as an omen of things to come, and it was the responsibility of specialized officials to report the event and its interpretation to the ruler.

The early antecedents of this system of Field Allocation *(fenye)* astrology are to be found in certain conceptions already influential in the second millennium B.C.E. Several passages in pre-Qin works preserve the remnants of etiological myths and traditions that establish the existence of definite connections between celestial locations and terrestrial polities. One of the most famous is the legend of E Bo and Shi Chen, which is preserved in the *Zuo Commentary* (Duke Zhao, first year):

Formerly, Gao Xin had two sons, the eldest was named E Bo and the younger one Shi Chen. They lived in Kuanglin but could not get along, daily taking up shield and lance against one another. In the end, Gao Xin could no longer condone it and removed E Bo to Shangqiu to have charge of [the asterism] Chen (Great Fire in Scorpio). The Shang people emulated him in this; therefore Great Fire is the Shang asterism. [Gao Xin also] moved Shi Chen to Daxia to have charge of Shen (Orion), and the people of Tang emulated him, and served the houses of Xia and Shang there. The last of their line was Tang Shuyu. When [Zhou] King Wu's wife Yi

Jiang was pregnant with Tai Shu (i.e., Tang Shuyu), she dreamt that the Lord on High told her, "I have named your son Yu and will give Tang to him, make Tang belong to Shen (Orion), and cause his descendants to flourish." When the child was born he had the character Yu on his hand, and so his name was called Yu. When [Zhou] King Cheng extinguished the Tang [line] he enfoeffed Tai Shu there; hence, Orion is the star of Jin. From this we can see that Shi Chen is the spirit of Shen (Orion).

AGAIN, ON THE occasion of a disastrous fire in Song, the successor state of Shang (Duke Xiang, ninth year):

The Marquis of Jin asked Shi Ruo the reason for the assertion he had heard, that the fires in Song are a manifestation of the workings (i.e., Dao) of Heaven. Shi Ruo replied, "The ancient Regulator of Fire offered sacrificial nourishment to the asterisms Heart (α Scorpii) and Beak (α Hydrae) [at their spring and autumn culminations] when [the people] carry out and bring in the [hearth] fires. For this reason, Beak is [known as] Quail Fire and Heart as Great Fire. Tao Tang's (i.e., Emperor Yao's) Regulator of Fire, E Bo, dwelt at Shangqiu and sacrificed to Great Fire (α Scorpii), using Fire to mark the seasons there. Xiang Tu (grandson of Xie and father of the Shang people) continued in like manner, and so the Shang people principally focused on Great Fire (α Scorpii). They observed that the incipient signs of their calamities and defeats inevitably began with Fire, hence from the date one can deduce that the Way of Heaven is implicated." The Duke of Jin said, "Is it inevitably so?" to which [Shi Ruo] responded, "It depends on the Way. If a state is disordered but such manifest signs are lacking, [the workings of Heaven] cannot be known."

THE SAME LEGEND is alluded to in an equally famous passage in *Guoyu,* "Jinyu" (Discourses of Jin): "I have heard that when Jin was first enfeoffed, Jupiter was in Great Fire, which is the star of E Bo; in truth, it marked the periods of the Shang."

This famous nexus of astral lore involving E Bo and Shi Chen weaves together various elements of cultural significance in characteristic fashion. At bottom, it is a classic example of the kind of etiological myth dating from the preliterate period that served both to explain and to transmit vital astronomical and calendrical knowledge. In so doing it also laid the foundation for the subsequent elaboration of an astrological theory based on celestial and terrestrial correspondences. In this pithy story we have a tale about the human origins of the deities associated with the principal constellations of spring and autumn, Scorpio and Orion, which are diametrically opposed or "at odds" in the heavens and hence never appear in the sky simultaneously. Just as if unable to abide each other's presence, E Bo invariably ducks beneath the western horizon just before Shi Chen rises in the east. These personified asterisms are then linked to the cardinal directions (East and West), to seasonal activity for which they anciently served as harbingers (carrying out and in of the hearth fires marking the beginning and end of the agricultural season), as well as to the dominant political entities of the early Bronze Age (Shang and Xia), their descendants, and the hereditary lines of astrologers and calendar specialists who served them. In this and other examples of such astral lore it is possible to discern the ancient nucleus of the system of astral-terrestrial correlations that over time was to become amplified and ultimately standardized in the field allocation system.

The following is an example of a famous prognostication, which purports to date from the mid-seventh century B.C.E.[8] It concerns the restoration of Chong Er to power in the state of Jin[9] and his subsequent elevation to the status of hegemon. Like most examples of field allocation astrology from the preimperial period, the prognostication is based on well-established correlations between twelve states and their assigned stellar fields, here identified using the names of Jupiter stations. These stations, denoted "stages of Jupiter's march" *(Sui ci),* are regular 30° spaces containing two or three lunar lodges each. Each corresponds to Jupiter's annual movement during one of the approximately twelve years the planet takes to complete a circuit of the heavens. Fundamentally, Jupiter's presence in a state's astral space was thought to confer political and military advantage. As we have already seen, Jupiter station Shi Chen, which is named for one of the feuding brothers of legend, contains lunar lodge no. 21 Shen (Orion). Shen is the astral space of the state of Jin, having anciently been the astral correlate of Tang, the fiefdom Jin supplanted. As we also saw, when Jin was first founded Jupiter was in Great Fire, or Scorpio. Here, as Chong Er hesitates at the southern bank of the Yellow River on his return from nineteen years of forced exile, the future Duke Wen of Jin is persuaded by the historiographer/astrologer *(baozhang shi)* Dong Yin to cross into Jin and reclaim his rightful place as ruler:

[Historiographer] Dong Yin [of Jin] came out to meet Duke [Wen] at the Yellow River. The Duke asked, "Might I cross?" [Dong] replied, "Jupiter is in Great Bridge (lunar lodges nos. 17–19) and about to complete its heavenly travel. Thus, in your First Year you will start by gaining the star of Shi Chen. As for the space Shi Chen, [its terrestrial correlate] is the abode of the people of Jin and it is that whereby Jin arose. Now that My Lord's return coincides with Shi Chen [it means] you have but to cross! When My Lord departed, Jupiter was in Great Fire (lunar lodges nos. 3–5), which is the star of E Bo. [Great Fire] is called the Great Asterism. The Great Asterism is for bringing the goodness [of the harvest] to fruition; Hou Ji emulated it, and Tang Shu was enfeoffed during it. The historical records of the blind [historiographer] say, 'Successors will continue the ancestral line, like the increase of grain; there must needs be a Jin State.' Your servant divined by milfoil and obtained all eights for [hexagram] Tai [Peace], [whose judgment] says, 'Heaven and Earth unite in receiving sacrifice; the smaller departs and the greater approaches. [Good Fortune. Success].' The present [circumstances] correspond to this, so how could you not cross? What's more, you left under Chen (Great Fire = Scorpio) and you return under Shen (Shi Chen = Orion); these are both auspicious signs for Jin; they are Heaven's great seasonal markers. If you cross and complete your grasp [of power in Jin], you are sure to dominate the lords of the states as hegemon. Your descendants are depending on it; have no fear, My Lord." The prince crossed the river and summoned [local headmen]; [the localities of] Linghu, Jiushuai, and Sangquan all capitulated. The people of Jin were frightened, and [the usurper] Duke Huai [of Jin] fled to Gaoliang, leaving Lü Sheng and Ji Rui in command of the army. On day *jiawu* (31) [the Jin army] encamped at Luliu. The Earl of Qin sent Gongzi Zhi into the army; then the army withdrew and encamped at Xun. On day *xinchou* (38), Hu Yan together with grandees from Qin and Jin entered into a covenant at Xun. On day *renyin* (39), Duke (Wen) went among the Jin army. On day *jiachen* (41), the Earl of Qin returned [home]. On day *bingwu* (43), [Duke Wen] entered Quwo. On day *dingwei* (44), he entered [the Jin capital at] Jiang and ascended the throne in the temple of Duke Wu. On day *mushen* (45), [Duke Wen had] Duke Huai killed at Gaoliang.

Heavenly Cycles and Cosmo-political Consequences

THE JOB DESCRIPTION of those who, like Dong Yin, occupied the office of historiographer/ astrologer in ancient China is succinctly stated in the canonical *Rites of Zhou (Zhouli):*

[The *baozhang shi*] concerns himself with the stars in the heavens, keeping a record of the changes and movements of the stars and planets, sun and moon, in order to discern [corresponding] trends in the terrestrial world, with the object of distinguishing (i.e., prognosticating) good and bad fortune. He divides the territories of the nine regions of the empire in accordance with their dependence on particular celestial bodies; all the fiefs and territories are connected with distinct stars, based on which their prosperity or misfortune can be ascertained. He makes prognostications, according to the twelve years [of the Jupiter cycle], of good and evil in the terrestrial world." [10]

THE MORE UNUSUAL the changes and movements of the stars and planets, the more grave the implications, particularly since unanticipated events such as comets and eclipses were viewed with foreboding. In contrast, the most auspicious of all celestial events were dense gatherings of the five visible planets (Saturn, Jupiter, Mars, Venus, and Mercury), which occurred only at rare intervals. These planetary "minions" of the Lord Above were already a focus of attention in the Shang oracle-bone inscriptions, where they are referred to collectively as the Supreme Lord's Five Minister Regulators *(wu chen zheng).* In the late Warring States period, their gatherings were understood to have heralded the founding of each of the Three Dynasties, so that by the late third century B.C.E. a planetary massing had virtually become an ideological necessity if a new ruling dynasty were legitimately to claim to have received Heaven's Mandate. Moreover, given the obvious analogy between the operations of the Five Phases on earth and the changes foretold by the movements of the Five Planets up above, in the correlative cosmology of the times a massing of all five was an unmistakable sign that a phase-transition was in the offing. And so it is not surprising that a somewhat less than impressive gathering of planets in 205 B.C.E. was pressed into service and dutifully linked with the rise of the Han dynasty by the "Grand Historian," Sima Qian, in his "Treatise on the Heavenly Offices": "When Han arose, the Five Planets gathered in Eastern Well (lunar lodge no. 22; Gemini)."

At a time when rulership entailed comprehensive mastery of the cosmos, human affairs, and the phenomena of nature, observing and interpreting the motions of heavenly bodies was a matter of utmost concern to the state. Indeed, it was flawless performance of this role that enabled the ideal ruler to "promulgate his virtuous influence throughout the realm" as we saw above in the first passage from *Guoyu.* Here then is the rest of Sima Qian's concluding summary of the astrological knowledge of his day, displaying both ancient conceptual roots as well as the Han theoretical framework based on the prevailing *yinyang* and Five Phases correlative cosmology:

Ever since the people have existed, when have successive rulers not systematically followed the movements of sun, moon, stars, and asterisms? Coming to the Five Houses (Huang Di, Gao Yang, Gao Xin, Tang Yu, Yao-Shun) and the Three Dynasties, they continued by making this [knowledge] clear, they distinguished wearers of cap and sash from the barbarian peoples as inner is to outer, and they divided the Middle Kingdom into twelve regions. Looking up they observed the figures in the heavens, looking down they modeled themselves on the categories of earth. Therefore, in Heaven there are Sun and Moon; on Earth there are yin and yang; in Heaven there are the Five Planets; on Earth there are the Five Phases; in Heaven are arrayed the lunar lodges, and on Earth there are the terrestrial regions.

THEREFORE,

When the Five Planets gather, this is a change of phase: the possessor of [fitting] virtue is celebrated, a new Great Man is set up to possess the four quarters, and his descendants flourish and multiply. But the one lacking in virtue suffers calamities to the point of destruction.

THE ASTROLOGICAL AND calendrical functions of the office of Prefect Grand Astrologer could only be neglected at one's peril, for the risk was great that if one overlooked the incipient signs of a shift in the workings of Heaven, failure to align oneself properly with the new trend could lead to disaster. During the reign of Emperor Wu of Han (141–87 B.C.E.) when it became impossible to ignore the inaccuracy of the calendar inherited from the Qin, long overdue reform of the system of mathematical astronomy became a necessity. Thus it was that at the same time that other aspects of imperial ceremonial were being reinvented, supposedly based on ancient precedents, an imperial commission was appointed to reform the calendar. These experts confronted the daunting task of correcting and redesigning the calendar so that it both correctly predicted the timing of new moons and solstices and also conformed with esoteric texts that supposedly revealed how the Yellow Emperor had achieved immortality. The end result was the Grand Inception *(Tai chu)* calendrical regime whose commencement in 104 B.C.E. marked the inauguration of a new era and a belated official confirmation that the Han dynasty, in power for a hundred years, now ruled by virtue of the influence of Earth:

When it came to the accession of the Sovereign, he summoned the specialists in recondite arts, Tang Du, to reapportion the heavenly sectors (lunar lodges), and Luoxia Hong of Ba to convert the angular measurements into a calendrical system. After that the graduations of the chronograms conformed to the regulations of Xia. Thereupon, a new regnal era was begun, the titles of offices were changed, and [the emperor] performed the *Feng* sacrifice on Mount Tai (in the summer of 110 B.C.E.). Accordingly, [Emperor Wu] issued an edict to the Imperial Scribes, which said, "Recently, We were informed by the responsible officials that the astronomical system still has not been fixed. Having widely solicited advice about bringing order to the stellar graduations, they have been unable to resolve the matter.

"Now, We have heard that in antiquity the Yellow Emperor achieved perfection and did not die. He is renowned for having examined into the graduation [of the stellar regions] and verification [of their portents], determined the clear and turbid [notes of the musical scale], initiated the [sequence of the] Five Phases, and established the division and number of the [24 fortnightly] *qi*-nodes and their [associated] phenomena. Thus, [concern with such matters] goes back to high antiquity. We deeply regret that the ancient writings are lost and the music abandoned, so that We are unable to perpetuate the brilliance [of antiquity], [now that] the accumulation of days and temporal divisions properly conform to the subduing of the influence of Water [of the Qin].

"Now, in accordance with the regulations of Xia, Yellow Bell will make the note *Gong* (of the pentatonic scale), Forest Bell will make the note *Zheng,* Great Budding will make the note *Shang,* Southern Regulator will make the note *Yu,* and Maiden Purity will make the note *Jue.* Henceforth, the seasonal *qi*-nodes will be correct again, the sound of the note *Yu* will be clear again, names will once again change properly, so that a *zi* [eleventh month] day will coincide with the winter solstice; in this way the operations of separating and coming together of yin and yang will proceed [normally]. Inasmuch as winter solstice on new-moon day *jiazi* [1] in the eleventh month is already anticipated, let the seventh year [of the present Primal *Feng*-Sacrifice reign period] be changed to be the origination year of the Grand Inception reign period. The year will be called *yanfeng shetige,* and the month will be called *bizou;* new moon will occur at midnight on day *jiazi,* and winter solstice will occur at dawn."

Two years later, in the eleventh month, new moon on day *jiazi* (25 December 105 B.C.E.) and winter solstice at dawn were to coincide, so those responsible for computing the calendar took this day as the base epoch (for the new calendar). The Son of Heaven proceeded in person to Mount Tai and at dawn on the day *jiazi* in the eleventh month, the day of the new moon and winter solstice, he sacrificed to the Lord on High in the Hall of Light, but did not renew the *Feng* and *Shan* sacrifices. The laudatory sacrificial liturgy said,

"Heaven has further bestowed on me the Sovereign Emperor the numinous reckoning of the Supreme Origin: the cycles have come round and now begin again. The Sovereign Emperor makes reverent obeisance to the Supreme Ultimate." ... [That] summer, the Han [dynasty] changed the calendrical system, taking the Regulation (1st) Month as the beginning of the year. Among the colors, yellow (of Earth) was given precedence (over the former black), the offices of state were renamed, and the officials' seals of office now carried (inscriptions of) five characters (instead of six as prescribed by the Qin). With that, this became the origination year of the Grand Inception reign period.

—DWP

Notes

1. Numbers in brackets after bisyllabic italicized terms refer to the cycle of sixty days.

2. Various attempts to establish the epoch of observation based on the seasonal stellar phenomena mentioned in this text have failed to produce a consensus because of such factors as uncertainty about the exact time of observation, the precise identity of the reference stars or asterisms referred to, whether all four date from the same epoch, and the like. It is probably safe to assume that the seasonal stellar indications all date from sometime in the second millennium B.C.E.

3. Tr. B. Karlgren, *The Book of Documents* (Stockholm: Museum of Far Eastern Antiquities, 1950), p. 3 (modified).

4. For a list of the twenty-eight lunar lodges *(xiu),* see *Mathews' Chinese-English Dictionary* (Cambridge: Harvard University Press, 1975), Appendix A, Table V.

5. Note that this passage from the *Guoyu* begins by citing the first five lunar lodges in sequence by way of illustration. Analogous seasonal and behavioral correlations certainly existed for the remaining twenty-three lodges as well.

6. The Five Phases (formerly referred to as Five Elements) and related concepts are discussed in selection 26.

7. These detailed prescriptions for seasonally appropriate rituals and occupations for the twelve months of the year were originally included in the *Lost Documents of Zhou* or *Yi Zhou shu*. They also provided the organizational motif for an important section of the encyclopedic Qin treatise *Spring and Autumn Annals of Master Lü (Lü shi chun qiu),* compiled at the behest of Chancellor Lü Buwei in 239 B.C.E.

8. The text is translated from the *Guoyu, juan* 10.

9. Jin was one of the major states during the Spring and Autumn (841–476 B.C.E.) and the Warring States (475–221 B.C.E.) periods, coming to an end in the year 369 B.C.E.

10. Joseph Needham et al., *Science and Civilisation in China,* vol. 3: *Sciences of the Heavens and the Earth* (Cambridge: Cambridge University Press, 1959), p. 190 (modified).

SCAPULIMANCY (I.E., DIVINATION by means of bone or turtle-shell), discussed above in the section on oracle-bone inscriptions, was one of the two major forms of divination in ancient China. The other technique involved the use of stalks of a plant called "yarrow" or "milfoil." Traditions differ concerning the precise details of milfoil-divination, but in its essentials, the procedure was as follows: the stalks were cast in such a way as to produce a result that could be recorded either as a broken or an unbroken horizontal line; this step was then repeated five times, yielding a combination of six broken or unbroken lines drawn one above the other in the form of a column. This figure is known as a "hexagram," of which there are sixty-four (2^6) possible permutations. Each hexagram has a different name and meaning.

The *Changes of Zhou (Zhouyi)* or *Yijing* (frequently written *I ching* in English) is an ancient manual of milfoil-divination that has survived through the centuries. It lists each of sixty-four hexagrams in order, along with a comment (the so-called "line statement" or *yaoci*) on the significance of each of the six lines of which each hexagram is formed, after an introductory comment on the hexagram as a whole (the "hexagram statement" or *guaci*). These comments are clearly very old—perhaps as old as the Zhou dynasty itself. (In its present form, the *Yijing* [Book of changes] includes later commentaries and appendixes to the original text; these are discussed elsewhere in this reader.) One sure sign of the antiquity of the line statements is their diction, which is extremely archaic and reminiscent of the language of Shang and Zhou oracle-bone inscriptions. The famous opening line of the first hexagram (Qian), for example, reads *yuan heng li zhen,* which does not make much sense in standard Classical Chinese. Commentators have debated the meaning of the phrase for centuries, generally taking each word as the name of a particular virtue (thus, e.g., "originality, pervasiveness, benefit, correction"). Most scholars today understand the phrase as a divinatory formula ("Primary receipt: beneficial to divine"), but this possibility could not have been imagined before the discovery of the oracle-bone inscriptions.

Archaic syntax is not the only reason why the line statements are difficult to interpret: like oracles the world over, they appear to be deliberately inscrutable. Since it is not always clear how the phrases are to be parsed, the prognostications can be read in different ways—and even when the sense is relatively clear, the significance may not be, as is illustrated by the very first line statement in the book: "The submerged dragon ought not be used." The proliferation of commentaries on the *Yijing* over the centuries (a phenomenon that continues down to the present day) should come as no surprise: without a guide to the meaning of the text, one usually cannot tell whether one's results augur good or ill. But it would be a mistake to say that the line statements are random or unconnected to human experience. Even with our partial knowledge of the mysteries of milfoil-divination, we can still discern the general import of many of the hexagrams. Hexagram 49, for example, is named Ge ("Overturning"; see the translation below), the same term that is used in the *Exalted Documents* for the overturning of a licentious nation's Heavenly Mandate (such as the violent "overturning" of the Shang mandate by Zhou). This explains why the line statements for the hexagram refer repeatedly to "conquest." Each hexagram has been analyzed exhaustively along such lines by generations of commentators.—PRG

(Hexagram 1:) Qian ("Creativity"). Primary receipt: beneficial to divine.

First Nine:[1] The submerged dragon ought not to be used.

Nine in the Second: See the dragon in the field. It is beneficial to see a great man.

Nine in the Third: The noble man is creative to the end of the day. In the evening he is wary, as though in danger. There is no trouble.

Nine in the Fourth: Someone jumps into the pool. There is no trouble.

Nine in the Fifth: There is a flying dragon in Heaven. It is beneficial to see a great man.

Top Nine: The haughty dragon is regretful.

The Use of the Nine: See a flock of dragons without heads. Auspicious.

(Hexagram 4:) Meng ("Folly"). Folly is received. It is not that we seek youthful folly; youthful folly seeks us. The first milfoil-divination is reported; if it is muddled repeatedly, it is not reported. Beneficial to divine.

First Six: Initiating folly. Beneficial to use a convict and use [the opportunity] to remove his shackles and manacles. He has already gone through a calamity.

Nine in the Second: Wrapping folly. Auspicious. Taking in a wife. Auspicious. The son can marry.

Six in the Third: Do not use [this opportunity] to marry a girl. See the man of bronze; he does not have a torso. There is no place beneficial.

Six in the Fourth: Binding folly. Calamity.

Six in the Fifth: Youthful folly. Auspicious.

Top Nine: Smiting folly. It is not beneficial to be an aggressor. It is beneficial to defend against aggressors.

(Hexagram 10:) Lü ("Stepping"). Stepping on a tiger's tail. It does not bite one. Receipt.

First Nine: Stepping ahead plainly. There is no trouble.

Nine in the Second: Stepping along a road smoothly. The benighted one's divination is auspicious.

Six in the Third: The blind can see; the lame can move forward. Stepping on a tiger's tail: if it bites one, it is inauspicious. The martial man acts for the great lord.

Nine in the Fourth: Stepping on a tiger's tail in panic. In the end auspicious.

Nine in the Fifth: Resolutely stepping. The divination is dangerous.

Top Nine: Seeing the steps, investigate the omens. May they circle back to the origin. Auspicious.

(Hexagram 18:) Gu ("Plague"). Plague. Primary receipt. It is beneficial to ford a great river. Precede *jia*-day by three days; follow *jia*-day by three days.

First Six: Occupied by the father's plague. There is a son and a deceased father. There is no trouble. Dangerous. In the end auspicious.

Nine in the Second: Occupied by the mother's plague. Cannot be divined.

Nine in the Third: Occupied by the father's plague. There is slight regret; there is no great trouble.

Six in the Fourth: Dealing leniently with the father's plague. Going to see calamity.

Six in the Fifth: Occupied by the father's plague. Use it [as an opportunity for] praise.

Top Nine: One does not serve king or overlord, but one's service is highly esteemed.

(Hexagram 37:) Jiaren ("Members of the Family"). Members of the Family. Beneficial for the girl to divine.

First Nine: Greatly having family. Regret perishes.

Six in the Second: There is no place to follow in the middle of the food. The divination is auspicious.

Nine in the Third: The members of the family holler. Regret. Danger. Auspicious. The wife and child holler. In the end calamity.

Six in the Fourth: A wealthy family. Greatly auspicious.

Nine in the Fifth: The king has family in abundance. Do not pity him. Auspicious.

Top Nine: There is a conquest, as though awesome. In the end auspicious.

(Hexagram 49:) Ge ("Overturning"). Overturning. On *si*-day there will be conquest. Primary receipt: beneficial to divine. Regret perishes.

First Nine: For strengthening, use the hide of a brown ox.

Six in the Second: On *si*-day there will be a campaign of conquest. Auspicious. There is no trouble.

Nine in the Third: Campaign. Inauspicious. The divination is dangerous. Approach three times with words of overturning. There is a conquest.

Nine in the Fourth: Regret perishes. There is a conquest that changes the Mandate. Auspicious.

Nine in the Fifth: The great man changes into a tiger. Without a prognostication, there is conquest.

Top Six: The noble man changes into a leopard. The petty man overturns his face. On the campaign, inauspicious; at home, the divination is auspicious.

(Hexagram 50:) Ding ("Tripod"). The Tripod. Prime auspiciousness. Receipt.

First Six: The tripod's legs are upturned. Beneficial to expel what is negative. Obtaining a concubine with her children. There is no trouble.

Nine in the Second: The tripod is full. Our enemy is sick and is unable to draw near to us. Auspicious.

Nine in the Third: The tripod's ears are overturned. Its motion is blocked. The fat of the pheasant is inedible. Soon rain. Diminishing regret. In the end auspicious.

Nine in the Fourth: The tripod has a broken leg. Cover the duke's stew. Its form is glossy. Inauspicious.

Six in the Fifth: The tripod's yellow ears and brazen crossbar. Beneficial to divine.

Top Nine: The tripod's jade crossbar. Greatly auspicious. There is nothing that is not beneficial.

(Hexagram 53:) Jian ("Gradual-Advance"). Gradual-Advance. A girl is brought home. Auspicious. Beneficial to divine.

First Six: The wild-geese gradually advance to the riverbank. A child. Danger. There are words. There is no trouble.

Six in the Second: The wild-geese gradually advance to the rock. Food and drink, happy, happy. Auspicious.

Nine in the Third: The wild-geese gradually advance to the land. The husband is on campaign and does not return. The wife is pregnant and does not give birth. Inauspicious. Beneficial to defend against aggressors.

Six in the Fourth: The wild-geese gradually advance to the trees. Perhaps they will attain a perch. There is no trouble.

Nine in the Fifth: The wild-geese gradually advance to the mound. The wife has not been pregnant for three years. In the end nothing overcomes it. Auspicious.

Top Nine: The wild-geese gradually advance to the land. Their feathers can be used as a standard. Auspicious.

—PRG

Notes

1. The line statements are organized by line, which are counted (starting at the bottom) as First, Second, Third, Fourth, Fifth, and Top. Numerological convention dictates that an unbroken line is referred to as "Nine," a broken line as "Six." Thus, for example, "First Nine" signifies an unbroken bottom line; "Top Six" signifies a broken top line.

ONE OF THE GREATEST ideological accomplishments of the Zhou dynasty is the concept of Heaven's Mandate (Tianming). After having vanquished the powerful state of Shang in the mid-1040s B.C.E., the Zhou suzerains were faced with a significant problem of legitimation, which they solved by appealing to an innovative notion of "Heaven." The idea was that Heaven, an irresistible ethical force, would choose a virtuous individual on earth as its vicegerent and install him and his descendants to rule on earth as the so-called "Heaven's Son" (Tianzi). If, however, the Son of Heaven were to fail in his obligation to rule with virtue, Heaven would swiftly choose another champion to overthrow him. This was the reasoning that the lords of Zhou put forward when explaining their astonishing success (we must remember that the nation of Shang seemed to all observers far mightier than its conqueror): the last king of Shang was evil; he mistreated his subjects; and Heaven appointed the Zhou to punish him and take his place. The avowed intention of the Zhou, in other words, was not brute conquest, but beneficent and Heaven-ordained rule. (Incidentally, the term for "overturning the Mandate"—*geming*—is used in Modern Chinese to mean "revolution.")

This idea of Heaven's Mandate went on to become one of the dominant elements of Chinese political culture. Later emperors may not have believed earnestly that an august and terrifying Heaven would strike them down if they were to misgovern their domain—but it was still typical for rulers and political advisers to discuss exhaustively the consequences that any proposed legislation might have for even the lowliest members of the population. This genuine concern for the welfare of the people can be traced back directly to the ancient ideal of Heaven's Mandate.

The following text, known as "The Many Officers" (Duoshi), is taken from the canonical *Exalted Documents* (*Shangshu;* i.e., the *Book of Documents*) and is generally accepted as a document from very early Zhou times. It is a speech allegedly delivered by the Duke of Zhou (a brother of King Wu, the Conqueror) soon after quelling a Shang uprising. A new city, known as Luo, was built in the east, and the remnants of the Shang population were collected and moved there, so that they could be more efficiently governed and controlled. The Duke of Zhou arrived in Luo to rule over the Shang subjects, and addressed "the many officers" of Shang. The translation is complete, with the exception of the very last line of the original, which is garbled and hence deleted here.—PRG

The Many Officers

In the third month, the Duke of Zhou first came to the new city of Luo. He used [this opportunity] to address the officers of the Shang king.

The king says to this effect,[1] "You many remaining officers of Shang! It is a misfortune; autumnal Heaven has greatly sent down destruction on Yin.[2] We, possessors of Zhou, assisted in the mandate; led by Heaven's brilliant authority, we brought about the king's punishment, setting the mandate of Yin aright and [thereby] fulfilling [the will of] Di.[3] Thus, you many officers, it was not that our small nation dared to take aim at the mandate of Yin; it was that Heaven, not

Di
heaven

cooperating with those who are deceitful, prevaricatory, ignorant, and disorderly, supported us. Would we dare seek this status [ourselves]? It was that Di would not cooperate [with you]. What our lowly people uphold and act upon is the brilliant dreadfulness of Heaven.

"I have heard it said, 'Di Above leads one to tranquility.' The possessor of Xia[4] did not recognize the patterns of tranquility, so Di sent down visitations to provide guidance to the times. The Xia had no use for Di; they were greatly licentious and dissolute, for which [behavior] they invented pretexts. Thereupon Heaven no longer cared for them or heard them, but discontinued their primal mandate, sending down punishments. So your former ancestor Tang the Successful was commanded to overturn Xia; with your capable people he governed the four quarters. From Tang the Successful down to Emperor Yi, none [of your rulers] failed to make his virtue brilliant and attend to the sacrifices. Thus Heaven grandly established you, and protected and gave order to the possessors of Yin. The kings of Yin, for their part, did not dare to lose [the support of] Di, and did not fail to be adequate to Heaven and [receive] its emoluments. But more recently, their descendant and successor has been vastly unenlightened with respect to Heaven. How could it be said of him that he would comply with and care about the diligent heritage of the former kings? He was vastly licentious and dissolute; he did not look upon Heaven's manifest [presence] or the misery of the people. At this time, Di Above did not protect him, and sent down such great destruction as this. Heaven does not cooperate with those who do not make their virtue brilliant. Every territory that was destroyed within the four quarters, whether great or small—in no case is its punishment unjustified."

The king says to this effect, "You many officers of Yin! Recently, our kings of Zhou have been very god-fearing; they have been charged with the service of Di. There was a Mandate: 'Cut off Yin!' We announce to Di that we have corrected [the licentious ruler of Yin]. In our business, we have no duplicitous objectives: your royal house is our [only] enemy. Let me say that you have been unrestrained like a flood. We did not move you [to be impious]; it came from your own city. Moreover, I keep in mind that Heaven has brought [punishments] upon [the king of] Yin for his great crimes; therefore, I do not punish [you, who are not guilty]."

The king says, "Yea! I announce to you, the many officers: it is because of this that I move your residence and bring you to the west.[5] It is not that I, the One Man, bear a disquiet character; this [affair] is Heaven's Mandate. If you do not disobey me, I will not dare make any further [demands]. Do not resent me. You know that the former people of Yin possessed books and canons [telling how] Yin overturned the Mandate of Xia. So now you say, '[After we defeated them,] the Xia were promoted and chosen [as attendants] in the royal court; they served among the hundred officials.' I, the One Man, comply with and employ only the virtuous; thus I dared to seek you out in your great city of Shang. I am led to pardon and pity you. This is not a crime on my part; this is Heaven's Mandate."

The king says, "You many officers! In the past, when I came from Yan, I sent my illustrious Mandate down to your territories in all directions. Then I clearly executed the punishment [ordained by] Heaven. I have removed you to a distant place, bringing you near the ministers serving in our capital with much obedience."

The king says, "I announce to you, the many officers of Yin! Now, since I will not lay you low, I repeat this commandment [to you]. I have now built a great city here in Luo, since I had no other place in the four quarters where I might host you. It was also so that you, many officers, would have a place where you might serve, in haste and running, as ministers to us with much obedience. So you still have your [own] grounds, and you still rest in your [own] dwellings. If you can be respectful, Heaven will cooperate with you and have pity on you. If you cannot be respectful, then not only will you lose your grounds, but I will also render Heaven's punishment on you to the utmost. Now you may dwell here in your city; you may perpetuate your houses; you will have your affairs and [live out] your years in this Luo. Then your children will flourish. This is the consequence of your being moved."

—PRG

Notes

1. The text sometimes reads "The king says to this effect," because the speaker is really the Duke of Zhou acting as the king's representative. The reigning king at the time was probably King Wu's son (and thus the Duke of Zhou's nephew), King Cheng.

2. "Yin" is the name of the Shang capital and is used interchangeably with the dynastic name "Shang."

3. "Di" is the name of the chief divinity of the Shang, but the speaker here merely uses it as another appellation of Heaven—implying deftly that the Zhou notion of Heaven is greater than the old Shang religion, because it can incorporate the faith of the defeated.

4. The Duke of Zhou refers to the Xia dynasty, which was destroyed by the Shang centuries earlier, as another example of Heaven's Mandate at work: the Shang founder was a virtuous ruler, like the present king of Zhou; it was only the last king of Shang who deserved punishment.

5. The new city lay to the west of the old Shang capital and to the east of the Zhou capital.

ACCORDING TO LEGEND, the Zhou established a corps of officials called Music-Masters, who were given the task of roaming throughout the realm, noting down the songs that the people sang in various provinces. This institution reflected the belief that an insightful ruler could gauge the sentiment of the people by diligently studying their songs and dances. The songs collected in this manner are said to form the core of the extant *Book of Odes* or *Poetry Classic (Shijing)*, an anthology allegedly redacted and transmitted by Confucius. We cannot test the veracity of the attribution to Confucius, but it is true that philosophers of the Confucian school cherished the *Odes* and cited them frequently—suggesting that we may indeed owe the transmission of the text to the followers of Confucius, if not to the Master himself.

The collection is made up of 305 works of different length, which are divided into four categories: the "Airs of the States" (Guofeng), which comprise 160 poems; the "Lesser Elegantiae" (Xiaoya), with seventy-four poems; the "Greater Elegantiae" (Daya), with thirty-one poems; and the "Hymns" (Song), with forty poems. The poems range widely in style and content. The Airs of the States are typically written in a simple, lyrical form and take as their subject the daily experiences of regular people—often dealing straightforwardly with the subject of sexual love and its attendant emotions. The Elegantiae, especially the Greater Elegantiae, are composed in a more self-consciously grandiose manner and tend to deal with correspondingly loftier matters: virtuous government, sacrifice to the spirits, and Heaven's Mandate. The Hymns are paeans and liturgies, some of which are thought to have been used in religious ceremonies.

The *Odes* are famous for their pregnant, allusive style, which greatly influenced Chinese poetry through the centuries. The *Odes* may display an appearance of rustic innocence, but they yield layers of sophisticated meanings after careful and sympathetic reading. Traditional commentators to the *Odes* are often criticized for having wandered too far in their speculations—as, for example, when they read overly specific historical allusions into the poems—but their basic conviction was doubtless correct: the poems often contain more meaning than their literal significations. A good example of this Confucian conviction is found in *Analects* 3.8, where Confucius and a disciple interpret a poem that ostensibly discusses a woman's facial powder as a profound comment on the place of ritual in moral education. Similarly, the standard interpretation of "The Nine-Meshed Net" (Mao 159; translated below) held that the speaker entreating her beloved not to leave was to be understood as a representation of the people yearning for the beneficent rule of the Duke of Zhou. Regardless of whether the specific reference to the Duke of Zhou is acceptable, it is apparent that the *Odes,* with their pointed use of imagery, lent themselves to such interpretations.

The poems here are listed with their eponymous "Mao number," after the editors (Mao Heng and Mao Chang, both fl. 1st c. B.C.E.) who gave the collection its present arrangement. From its Mao number, one can tell easily the formal category of a given poem: numbers 1–160 comprise the Airs; numbers 161–234 the Lesser Elegantiae; numbers 235–265 the Greater Elegantiae; and numbers 266–305 the Hymns.—PRG

[Mao 1:] The *Guan*-ing Ospreys

"Guan, guan" [cry] the ospreys
on the isle in the river.
The reclusive, modest girl
is a good mate for the noble man.
Long and short is the duckweed
To the left and to the right we look for it.
The reclusive, modest girl—
waking and sleeping he seeks her.
He seeks her and does not obtain her.
Waking and sleeping he pines and yearns for her.
Oh, anxious! Oh, anxious!
He tosses and twists and turns onto his side.

Long and short is the duckweed.
To the left and to the right we gather it.
The reclusive, modest girl—
among citherns and lutes, he shows her his friendship.
Long and short is the duckweed.
To the left and to the right we pick it.
The reclusive, modest girl—
as a bell to a drum, he delights in her.

[Mao 23:] In the Field There Is a Dead Roe

In the field there is a dead roe.
With white grass we wrap it.
There is a girl who longs for spring.
A fine fellow seduces her.

In the forest there is the *pusu*-tree.
In the field there is a dead deer.
With white grass we bind it.
There is a girl like jade.

Oh, undress me slowly.
Oh, do not upset my kerchief.
Do not make the shaggy-dog bark.

[Mao 32:] The Gentle Wind

The gentle wind from the south
blows on the heart of that jujube tree.
The jujube tree is verdant.
The mother pains and toils.

The gentle wind from the south
blows on the wood of that jujube tree.

The mother is sage and good.
We do not have a compassionate man.

There is a cold spring
beneath [the city of] Jun
There are seven sons.
The mother toils in misery.

Dazzling are the yellow birds,
lovely their tones.
There are seven sons.
They do not soothe the mother's heart.

[Mao 34:] The Gourds Have Bitter Leaves

The gourds have bitter leaves.
The ford has a deep crossing.
Where it is deep, they cross with their clothes on.
Where it is shallow, they cross by lifting their clothes.

Overflowing, the ford is swollen!
Resoundingly, the female pheasant calls!
The ford, though swollen, will not wet my axle.
The female pheasant calls to seek her male.

Harmoniously, harmoniously cry the wild geese.
The morning sun begins to rise.
If a man brings home a wife,
it is while the ice has not yet melted.

He beckons, he beckons, the ferryman.
Others cross, but I do not.
I am waiting for my friend.

[Mao 86:] The Crafty Youth

Oh, that crafty youth!
Oh, he does not talk to me.
It is your fault.
Oh, you make me unable to eat.

Oh, that crafty youth!
Oh, he does not eat with me.
It is your fault.
Oh, you make me unable to rest.

[Mao 115:] On the Mountain There Are Thorn-Elms

On the mountain there are thorn-elms.
In the marshes there are elms.

You have a robe and gown.
You do not train them, do not trail them.
You have carriage and horse.
You do not gallop them, do not spur them.
It is as though you are dead!
Another will enjoy them.

On the mountain there are *kao*-trees.
In the marshes there are *niu*-trees.
You have courts and halls.
You do not sprinkle them, do not sweep them.
You have bells and drums.
You do not strike them, do not beat them.
It is as though you are dead!
Another will take care of them.

On the mountain there are lacquer trees.
In the marshes there are chestnut trees.
You have wine and food.
Why do you not play your cithern daily?
You should be happy and pleased.
You should make your days endless.
It is as though you are dead!
Another will enter your chamber.

[Mao 131:] The Yellow Birds

Back and forth [fly] the yellow birds.[1]
They settle on the jujube tree.
Who follows Duke Mu?
Ziju Yanxi.
This Yanxi
is the finest in a hundred.
He approaches the pit.
In fear, in fear he trembles.
That azure Heaven
annihilates our good man.
Oh, how can he be redeemed?
A hundred men for him alone.

Back and forth [fly] the yellow birds.
They settle on the mulberry tree.
Who follows Duke Mu?
Ziju Zhonghang.
This Zhonghang
can hold his own against a hundred.
He approaches the pit.
In fear, in fear he trembles.

That azure Heaven
annihilates our good man.
Oh, how can he be redeemed?
A hundred men for him alone.

Back and forth [fly] the yellow birds.
They settle on the thorn tree.
Who follows Duke Mu?
Ziju Qianhu.
This Qianhu
is as mighty as a hundred.
He approaches the pit.
In fear, in fear he trembles.
That azure Heaven
annihilates our good man.
Oh, how can he be redeemed?
A hundred men for him alone.

[Mao 138:] The Crossbeam of the Door

Under the crossbeam of the door
one can rest at leisure.
By the swelling flow of the spring,
one can delight one's appetite.

When you eat a fish,
must it be a bream from the river?
When you take a wife,
must she be a Jiang of Qi?[2]

When you eat a fish,
must it be a carp from the river?
When you take a wife,
must she be a Zi of Song?

[Mao 159:] The Nine-Meshed Net

The fish in the nine-meshed net
are rudd and bream.
I see this young man
in regal robes and embroidered skirt.

The wild geese fly along the sandbar.
When the Duke goes back, there will be no place [for us].
I will stay with you one more time.

The wild geese fly along the hill.
The Duke is going back and will not return.
I will lodge with you one more time.

Oh, here we had the regal robes.
Oh, do not go back with our Duke.
Oh, do not make my heart grieve.

[Mao 161:] The Deer Cries

"You, you," the deer cries.
It eats the artemisia in the wild.
I have a lucky guest.
Sound the cithern; blow the pipes.
Blow the pipes; sound the reeds.
This receiving basket—take it.
The man who likes me
will show me the practices of Zhou.

"You, you," the deer cries.
It eats the southernwood in the wild.
I have a lucky guest.
The renown of his virtue is very bright.
His regard for the people is not fickle.
The noble men take him as a model and imitate him.
I have good wine.
May the lucky guest feast and be happy.

"You, you," the deer cries.
It eats the *qin*-plant in the wild.
I have a lucky guest.
Sound the lute; sound the cithern.
Sound the lute; sound the cithern.
Harmonious is the music while we indulge.
I have good wine
to feast and delight the heart of the lucky guest.

[Mao 175:] The Red-Lacquered Bows

Oh, the red-lacquered bows are unbent.
We receive and store them.
I have a lucky guest.
The core of my heart I bestow on him.
The bells and drums are already set up.
All morning I feast him.

Oh, the red-lacquered bows are unbent.
We receive and carry them.
I have a lucky guest.
The core of my heart delights in him.
The bells and drums are already set up.
All morning I honor him.

Oh, the red-lacquered bows are unbent.
We receive and set them in their cases.
I have a lucky guest.
The core of my heart loves him.
The bells and drums are already set up.
All morning I toast him.

[Mao 187:] Yellow Birds

Yellow birds, yellow birds,
do not gather on the corn.
Do not peck at my grain.
The people in this country
are not willing to nourish me.
I will return; I will go back,
back to my country and kin.

Yellow birds, yellow birds,
do not gather on the mulberry.
Do not peck at my *liang*-millet.
The people in this country
I cannot ally with.
I will return; I will go back,
back to my several brothers.

Yellow birds, yellow birds,
do not gather in the oak.
Do not peck at my *li*-millet.
The people in this country
I cannot dwell with.
I will return; I will go back,
back to my several ancestors.

[Mao 247:] We Are Now Drunk

We are now drunk with wine.
We are now satiated by your virtue.
Myriad years to the noble man!
Increased be your resplendent fortune.

We are now drunk with wine.
Your sacrifices have been conducted.
Myriad years to the noble man!
Increased be your shining brilliance.

Your shining brilliance is extensive.
Your lofty brightness comes to an illustrious end.
The illustrious end has its beginning.
The impersonator[3] of the revered [deceased] has made an announcement of blessing.

What is his announcement?
"The *bian* and *dou*-vessels are pure and fine.
The friends who anxiously assist [in the sacrifice]
do so with awed demeanor.

"Your awed demeanor is quite appropriate to the occasion.
The noble man has filial sons,
no dearth of filial sons.
Forever will goods be granted to you.

"What are these goods?
The corridors of your house and home.
Myriad years to the noble man!
Forever will dignity and posterity be granted to you.

"What is this posterity?
Heaven covers you in emoluments.
Myriad years to the noble man!
The resplendent Mandate will be attached [to your lineage].

"What is this attachment?
You will be given female attendants.
You will be given female attendants.
From them will come sons and grandsons."

[Mao 256:] Dignified [Excerpt]

Does he not exert himself, he who is humane?
Are the four quarters not instructed by him?
Sensing his virtuous conduct,
the four regions obey him.
With grandiloquent counsel he confirms his Mandate.
With farsighted plans and timely announcements
he is reverently cautious about his awesome deportment.
He is a pattern for the people.

The one of today
is aroused and seduced by disorder in government.
He overturns his own power.
He abandons and dissipates himself in wine.
You devote yourself only to dissipated pleasures.
You do not ponder your lineage.
Why do you not apply yourself to seeking the [Way of the] former kings
so that you could hold fast to their enlightened law?

[Mao 264:] I See on High

I see great Heaven on high,
but it is not kind to us.
Very long has it been disquiet.

It sends down these great horrors.
In the state, there is nothing that is settled.
The grain-grubs gnaw as grubs do.
There is no peace, no end.
Those who instigate crimes are not apprehended.
There is no peace, no cure.

People had land and fields
but you possess them.
People had followers
but you seize them.
This one is properly without guilt
but you arrest him.
That one is properly with guilt
but you set him loose.

A clever man completes a city;
a clever woman overturns a city.
Alas, that clever woman!
She is a harpy; she is an owl.
Women have long tongues.
They are the foundation of cruelty.
Disorder does not descend from Heaven.
It is born of woman.
There is no one to instruct or admonish [the king]
because those who attend him are always women.

They exhaust others; they are jealous and fickle.
At first they slander; in the end they turn their backs [on authority].
Will you say it is not so extreme?
Oh, how they are wicked!
They are like merchants who make a threefold profit.
The noble man knows this.
There is no public service for women.
They stay with their silkworms and weaving.

[Mao 271:] Sublime Heaven Had a Definite Mandate

Sublime Heaven had a definite Mandate.
The two sovereigns[4] received it.
King Cheng did not dare take his ease.
Day and night, he laid the foundations for his Mandate, deep and still.
Oh, perpetually splendid,
he expanded his heart.
Thus he pacified [his realm].

—PRG

Notes

1. This poem alludes to an infamous historical event. Duke Mu of Qin (r. 659–621 B.C.E.) ordered three brothers of the Ziju clan (named Yanxi, Zhonghang, and Qianhu) to accompany him in death. "The Yellow Birds" is said to have been composed by the grieving populace in their memory. Keep in mind that the poems rhymed in Old Chinese (though they do not rhyme perfectly when read in Modern Mandarin), and in "The Yellow Birds," this feature is exploited chillingly: the name of the brother about to be executed always rhymes with the name of the tree where the yellow birds are said to alight in the previous line. In other words, the movements of the yellow birds take on the significance of prognostications.

2. The names "Jiang of Qi" and "Zi of Song" (in the next stanza) refer to the surnames of the ducal houses of Qi and Song. The point is that one need not marry a woman of elevated birth to find conjugal bliss.

3. The "impersonator" is a medium, that is, a supplicant who is chosen to receive the spirit of a deceased ancestor within his body. The subsequent "announcement" is thus understood as a message directly from the ancestral spirits.

4. The "two sovereigns" are conventionally understood as Kings Wen and Wu of Zhou; King Cheng, whom we have met before, was King Wu's son and successor.

KONG QIU (551–479 B.C.E.), known in the West as Confucius (see selection 35), stands as one of the most influential figures in Chinese history. An impoverished minor noble of murky ancestry, Confucius made a name for himself as China's first renowned teacher. Though Confucius considered himself to be a "transmitter" and not a "creator," his teachings laid the foundations for the dominant philosophical tradition in premodern China. While the oft-heard pronouncement that traditional China was a Confucian civilization may be an oversimplification, it is still true that no figure or intellectual movement contributed more to the experience and character of the Chinese nation.

Through the ages, many different statements and doctrines have been attributed to the historical Confucius, but the most authoritative repository of his teachings is generally considered to be the *Analects (Lunyu)*, or "Selected Sayings" of the Master, said to have been compiled by disciples after his death. Since Confucius left no original works of his own, our view of him is necessarily colored by the impressions and interests of the editors of the *Analects,* who naturally included only those statements that they considered representative and fitting. Moreover, the format of the *Analects,* which consist mostly of informal teachings and *obiter dicta,* forces the modern student of Confucius to reconstruct his philosophy piece by piece, in a way that is not necessary for writers who conveyed their philosophies in coherent essays and similar expository forms.

Still, the *Analects* reveal enough for us to tell that the core of Confucius's philosophy was moral practice centered on the virtue of *ren,* or "humanity." Though Confucius rarely defines *ren* (or any other concept) in unambiguous terms, he does inform us that the "method of humanity" lies in "taking what is near as an analogy" (6.30). The notion of "taking what is near as an analogy," furthermore, is designated as *shu,* or "reciprocity"—a principle that is also conveniently defined by the variant of the Golden Rule in 15.23: "What you yourself do not desire, do not do to others." In other words, Confucius presents us with an ethical scheme constructed around the idea of sympathy. Assuming that other people's feelings and desires are essentially similar to ours, we can say that moral action begins by treating other people as we would like ourselves to be treated.

Other crucial elements of Confucius's worldview include the role of ritual as a blueprint for social harmony, the obligation of self-cultivation, filial piety and respect for one's superiors, and the importance of moral education in government. But for the most part, we must discover Confucius's philosophy on our own. Confucius's intention is to make us think for ourselves, not to hand us ready-made formulas that inhibit intellectual growth. As the Master said, "I begin with one corner; if a student cannot return with the other three corners, I do not repeat myself."—PRG

[1.1.][1] The Master said, "To study and then practice [what you have learned] in a timely way— is this not a delight? To have friends come from distant places—is this not a joy? To be unknown by others, and yet not to be indignant—is this not a noble man?"

[1.4.] Master Zeng (i.e., Zeng Shen, 505–436 B.C.E.?—a disciple of Confucius) said, "Every day, I examine myself on three counts: in planning on behalf of others, whether I have been without integrity; in my intercourse with friends, whether I have been untrustworthy; and whether I do not practice what I transmit."

☆ [1.6.] The Master said, "Young men are to be filial at home, courteous when abroad. They are to be careful and trustworthy; they are to overflow with love of the multitude and be intimate with humanity. If they have energy left over from their actions, then they use it to study refinements."[2]

☆ [1.8.] The Master said, "If a noble man is not grave, then he will not be awe-inspiring, and his studies will not be solid. Make integrity and trustworthiness your chief [aims]. Do not have friends who are unequal to yourself. If you have faults, do not shirk from correcting them."

☆ [1.11.] The Master said, "When someone's father is alive, observe his or her ambitions. When the father is deceased, observe [the person's] actions. If, after three years, he or she has not changed from the way of the father, then he or she can be called filial."

[1.16.] The Master said, "I am not vexed at others' not knowing me; I am vexed at not knowing others."

[2.1.] The Master said, "One who effects government with virtue is like the Pole Star. It dwells in its place, while the many stars turn respectfully toward it."

[2.3.] The Master said, "If you guide them with legislation, and unify them with punishments, then the people will avoid [the punishments] but have no conscience. If you guide them with virtue, and unify them with ritual, then they will have a conscience; moreover, they will correct themselves."

[2.4.] The Master said, "At fifteen, my intention was to study. At thirty, I was established. At forty, I was not deluded. At fifty, I knew Heaven's Mandate. At sixty, my ear was compliant. At seventy, I could follow the desires of my heart without overstepping the bounds."

[2.7.] Ziyou (i.e., the disciple Yan Yan, b. 506 B.C.E.) asked about filial piety. The Master said, "What is 'filial' nowadays refers to the ability to feed [one's parents]. Even dogs and horses can be fed. If one is not reverent, wherein lies the difference?"

[2.11.] The Master said, "One who warms up the old in order to know the new can be a teacher."

[2.12.] The Master said, "The noble man does not act as a utensil."

[3.8.] Zixia (i.e., the disciple Bu Shang, b. 507 B.C.E.) asked, "'Oh, her artful smile is dimpled. Oh, her beautiful eye is black-and-white. Oh, a plain [background] on which to apply the highlights.'[3] What does this refer to?"

The Master said, "In painting, everything follows the plain [background]."

[Zixia] said, "Does ritual follow [in similar fashion]?"

The Master said, "Shang, it is you who have inspired me. Finally I have someone to discuss the *Odes* with."[4]

[3.15.] The Master entered the Great Temple and asked about everything. Someone said, "Who says that fellow from Zou knows ritual? He entered the Great Temple and asked about everything." Confucius heard of this, and said, "This is ritual."[5]

[3.17.] Zigong (i.e., the disciple Duanmu Ci, b. 520 B.C.E.) wished to do away with the sacrificing of a sheep when announcing the new moon. The Master said, "Ci, you love the sheep; I love the rite."

[3.18.] Lord Ding (of Lu, r. 509–496 B.C.E.) asked how a lord should employ his ministers and how a minister should serve his lord. Confucius answered, "A lord should serve a minister with ritual; a minister should serve his lord with integrity."

[4.8.] The Master said, "If one hears the Way in the morning, it is acceptable to die in the evening."

[4.10.] The Master said, "In his associations with the world, there is nothing that the noble man [invariably] affirms or denies. He is a participant in what is right."

[4.15.] The Master said, "Shen![6] In my Way, there is one thing with which to string [everything] together."[7]

Master Zeng said, "Yes."

The Master went out, and the disciples asked, "What was he referring to?"

Master Zeng said, "The Way of the Master is nothing other than integrity and reciprocity."

[4.18.] The Master said, "In serving your parents, remonstrate slightly. If you see that they do not intend to follow [your advice], remain respectful and do not disobey. Toil and do not complain."

[4.25.] The Master said, "The virtuous are not orphans. They will have neighbors."

[5.11.] Zigong said, "What I do not desire others to do to me, I do not desire to do to them." The Master said, "Ci, you have not attained to that."[8]

[6.20.] Fan Chi (b. 515 B.C.E.) asked about wisdom. The Master said, "To take what is due to the people as one's duty, and to revere the ghosts and spirits, but keep them at a distance, can be called wisdom." He asked about humanity. The Master said, "One who is humane reaps after facing the difficulties first. That can be called humanity."

[6.23.] The Master said, "A *gu*-goblet is not a *gu*-goblet. Oh, *gu*-goblet! Oh, *gu*-goblet!"[9]

[6.28.] Zigong said, "Suppose there is someone who extensively confers benefits on the people and was able to help the multitude. What about that—can one call this humanity?"

The Master said, "Why make an issue of humanity? Would this not have to be sagehood? Could even Yao or Shun (two Sage Kings) find infirmity in someone [like that]? Now as for humanity—what one wishes to establish in oneself one establishes in others; what one wishes to advance in oneself, one advances in others. The ability to take what is near as an analogy can be called the method of humanity."

[7.1.] The Master said, "Transmitting and not creating, trusting and loving what is ancient, I humbly compare myself to our Old Peng."[10]

[7.8.] The Master said, "I do not open up [knowledge] to those who are not desperate for it; I do not disclose anything to those who are not anxious to speak. I begin with one corner; if [a student] cannot return with the other three corners, I do not repeat myself."

[7.21.] The Master said, "When I walk with people in a threesome, there must be some respect in which they can be a teacher to me. I pick what is good in them and follow it. What is not good in them, I correct."

[7.34.] The Master was critically ill. Zilu (i.e., the disciple Zhong You, 542–480 B.C.E.) asked leave to pray. The Master said, "Is there such a thing?"

Zilu responded, "There is. The eulogy says, 'We pray for you above and below to the spirits of the upper and lower worlds.'"

The Master said, "My prayer is of long standing."

[9.3.] The Master said, "A cap of hemp [is prescribed by] the rites, but today [one uses] jet-black silk. This is frugal,[11] and I follow the majority. To bow at the bottom of the hall [is prescribed by] the rites, but today one bows at the top [of the hall]. This is self-aggrandizing, so although I oppose the majority, I follow [the tradition of] the bottom [of the hall]."

[9.5.] The Master was terrorized in Kuang. He said, "Since the death of King Wen, has Culture not still been here?[12] If Heaven were about to let This Culture die, then I, a later mortal, would not have been able to partake of This Culture. Since Heaven has not let This Culture die, what can the people of Kuang do to me?"

[9.12.] Zigong said, "There is a beautiful jade here. Should we enclose it in a case and store it, or should we seek a good price and sell it?"

The Master said, "Sell it! Sell it! I am waiting for the right price."

[9.13.] The Master wished to dwell among the several barbarians. Someone said, "They are rude; how will you get along?"

The Master said, "If a noble man dwelled there, what rudeness would there be?"

[9.17.] The Master said, "I have never seen anyone who loves virtue as much as sex."

[9.22.] The Master said, "The young can be held in awe. How do we know that the future will not measure up to the present? Someone who is forty or fifty and has not been heard from—such a one indeed is not worth holding in awe."

[9.27.] The Master said, "Only after the year has grown cold does one know that the pine and cypress are the last to wither."

[10.12.] The stables caught fire. The Master retired from court, and asked, "Was anyone injured?" He did not ask about the horses.

[11.11.] Zilu asked about the services for ghosts and spirits. The Master said, "You do not yet know how to serve people. How will you be able to serve ghosts?"

"May I be so bold as to ask about death?"

[Confucius] said, "You do not yet know life. How can you know death?"

[12.1.] Yan Yuan (b. 521 B.C.E.) asked about humanity. The Master said, "Overcome the self and return to ritual in order to practice humanity. If you can overcome the self and return to ritual for one day, the world will bring humanity home to you. Does the practice of humanity emerge from the self, or does it arise from others?"[13]

Yan Yuan said, "May I ask for an overview?"

The Master said, "Do not look in opposition to the rites. Do not listen in opposition to the rites. Do not speak in opposition to the rites. Do not move in opposition to the rites."

Yan Yuan said, "Although I am not clever, I ask leave to make this saying my business."[14]

[12.7.] Zigong asked about government. The Master said, "Sufficient food, sufficient arms, and popular trust [in the ruler]."

Zigong said, "If this were impossible, and we would have to dispense with one of these three, which should come first?"

[Confucius] said, "Dispense with arms."

Zigong said, "If this were impossible, and we would have to dispense with one of these two, which should come first?"

[Confucius] said, "Dispense with food. Since antiquity, there has always been death. But people without trust have no standing."

[12.11.] Lord Jing of Qi (r. 547–490 B.C.E.) asked Confucius about government. Confucius answered, "The lord acts as a lord, the minister as a minister, the father as a father, the son as a son."

The lord said, "Excellent! Surely, if the lord does not act as a lord, nor the minister as a minister, nor the father as a father, nor the son not as a son, then although I might have grain, would I be able to eat it?"

[12.13.] The Master said, "In hearing litigation, I am like other people. What is necessary is to cause there to be no litigation."

[12.17.] Ji Kangzi (i.e., Jisun Fei, d. 468 B.C.E.) asked Confucius about government. Confucius answered, "To govern is to correct.[15] If you lead with rectitude, who will dare not be correct?"

[12.18.] Ji Kangzi was vexed at the thieving [in his state] and asked Confucius about it. Confucius answered, "If you, sir, were not covetous, then even if you were to reward them for it, they would not steal."

[13.3.] Zilu said, "The Lord of Wei is waiting for you to effect government. What will you do first?"

The Master said, "What is necessary is to rectify names!"

Zilu said, "Is there such a thing? Master, you are wide of the mark. Why such rectification?"

The Master said, "You,[16] you are uncouth. A noble man should appear more reserved about what he does not know. If names are not rectified, then speech does not flow properly. If speech does not flow properly, then affairs are not completed. If affairs are not completed, then ritual and music do not flourish. If ritual and music do not flourish, then punishments and penalties do not hit the mark. If punishments and penalties do not hit the mark, the people have no way to move hand or foot. Thus, for the noble man, names must be able to be spoken, and what he speaks must be able to be carried out. With regard to his speech, the noble man's [concern] is simply that there be nothing that is careless."

[13.10.] The Master said, "If there were one [among the princes] who would make use of me, within no more than twelve months, [the government] would be acceptable. Within three years there would be success."

[13.18.] The Lord of Shě said to Confucius, "In our village there is one Upright Gong.[17] His father stole a sheep, so the son testified against him."

Confucius said, "The upright people of my village are different from this. The fathers are willing to conceal their sons; the sons are willing to conceal their fathers. Uprightness lies therein."

[14.25.] The Master said, "Those who studied in the past did it for themselves. Those who study today do it for others."

[14.36.] Someone said, "'To repay resentment with kindness'[18]—how about that?"

The Master said, "[Then] with what should one repay kindness? Repay resentment with uprightness. Repay kindness with kindness."

[14.41.] Zilu was lodging at the Stone Gate. The gatekeeper said, "Whence do you come?"

Zilu said, "From Confucius."

[The gatekeeper] said, "Is he not the one who knows that it is not possible, but still does it?"

[15.1.] Lord Ling of Wei (r. 534–493 B.C.E.) asked Confucius about battle. Confucius answered, "I have heard of matters pertaining to sacrificial vessels, but I have not studied matters pertaining to armies and brigades." Thereupon he left the next day.

In Chen, they ran out of rations. The followers became ill, and none could get up. Zilu's irritation showed, and he said, "Does the noble man also encounter hard times?"

The Master said, "The noble man is firm in hard times; when the lesser man falls on hard times, he becomes dissolute."

[15.2.] Confucius said, "Ci,[19] do you consider me one who knows things by having studied much?"

[Zigong] replied, "Yes. Is that not so?"

[Confucius] said, "It is not so. I have one thing with which to string everything together."[20]

[15.23.] Zigong asked, "Is there one word that one can practice throughout one's life?"

The Master said, "Is it not reciprocity? What you yourself do not desire, do not do to others."

[15.26.] The Master said, "Artful words bring disorder on virtue. Who is not forbearing in small matters brings disorder on great plans."

[15.28.] The Master said, "People can enlarge the Way. It is not that the Way can enlarge people."

[17.2.] The Master said, "By nature, people are close to each other. They grow distant from each other through practice."

[17.19.] The Master said, "I wish to be without speech."

Zigong said, "If you do not speak, then what will we, your children, have to transmit from you?"

The Master said, "What does Heaven say? The four seasons progress by it; the many creatures are born by it. What does Heaven say?"

[17.20.] Ru Bei wished to see Confucius. Confucius made a pretext of illness. When the messenger went out of the door, he took up his lute and sang, making sure that [Ru] heard him.

☆ [17.25.] The Master said, "Only women and petty men are difficult to nurture. If you are familiar with them, they become insubordinate; if you are distant from them, they become resentful."

[18.4.] The people of Qi sent some female musicians. Ji Huanzi [i.e., Jisun Si, d. 492 B.C.E.] received them, and for three days court was not held. Confucius left.

—PRG

Notes

1. There are various conventions by which the *Analects* are divided into chapter and verse; I follow here the numberings given by James Legge (1815–1897).

2. I.e., pursuits such as literature and archery that are not directly related to moral practice.

3. The first two lines (though not the third line) are found in Mao 57, a poem in the *Odes*.

4. As is typical of the *Analects,* the point of this passage is not transparent. Presumably Zixia means to say that the rituals, significant though they may be, are still nothing more than a set of embellishments that are effective only if practiced by those who have prepared themselves for the task.

5. In other words, ritual itself requires one to ask about everything in the Great Temple. The "fellow from Zou," of course, is Confucius (whose father was from that state).

6. Confucius is addressing Master Zeng by his personal name, Shen, alternatively read as Can (pronounced *ts'ahn*).

7. Compare 15.2 below.

8. Not doing to others what one does not wish others to do to oneself is understood as *shu* (reciprocity), one of the central Confucian virtues. Thus Zigong declares here his intention to pursue *shu,* and Confucius gently reminds him that it is not as easy as it sounds. Compare 15.23 below.

9. *Gu* is the name of a bronze goblet used in a ritual ceremony. This enigmatic saying is usually understood as a lament to the effect that people were willing to use the designation "*gu*-goblet" for vessels which failed to satisfy the scrupulous ritual requirements of a genuine *gu*. Confucius uses the example of the *gu*-goblet to point to the pervasive and philosophically dangerous misuse of language. Also, the *gu*-goblet may be intended as a concrete image of the entire system of rituals, which the people of Confucius's day evidently no longer understand well.

10. It is not clear precisely who "our old Peng" is supposed to be; he is evidently a beloved mythical figure.

11. In Confucius's day, the ritual cap of hemp was considered more extravagant than one of silk (which was a plentiful material).

12. Or perhaps "has Culture not been here [with me]?"

13. A rhetorical question intended to convey that the practice of humanity surely emerges from the self, and does not depend on others.

14. A formula of thanks for an instruction.

15. A keen paronomasia in Chinese: the word for "government" *(zhèng)* is a derivative of the word for "rectitude" *(zhèng).*

16. Zilu's personal name is romanized as You (pronounced Yō).

17. The name can also be taken to mean "Self-Righteous."

18. A maxim that is found in the extant *Lao Zi (Daode jing).*

19. He is addressing Zigong by his personal name, Ci.

20. Compare 4.15 above.

MO DI (D. CA. 390 B.C.E.) or Mo Zi (Master Mo) led the first great intellectual response to Confucianism. The fundamental idea of Mohism was that good and bad can be measured in concrete terms of profit and loss: whatever brings about profit is good; whatever brings about loss is bad; and the more profit, the better. Mohism is most famous for the doctrine of "Universal Love," which attributes all the harm and loss in the world to humanity's desire for wealth. If only people could be made to love each other as they love themselves, then they would not attack each other for their goods because they would regard an attack on someone else as an attack on themselves. Greed, competition, and strife would be eliminated. In less rarefied terms, Mo Zi means that a world of unbridled competition brings about a situation that is detrimental to everyone. While his proposal of Universal Love has been rejected as idealistic and impracticable, Mo Zi is surely not the only thinker to have observed that violence against others is fundamentally imprudent and that a more prosperous society would result if we could neutralize the human desire to steal our neighbors' wealth.

Mo Zi is usually categorized as a utilitarian and a consequentialist (that is, a philosopher who believes that ethical judgments should be made on the basis of the consequences of human action), but the issue is somewhat unclear. The crucial point is that Mo Zi justifies his utilitarianism explicitly on the grounds that it is Heaven's will. In other words, if Mo Zi happened to believe that Heaven's will were otherwise, would he still say that acts bringing about the greatest benefit are always good in themselves, even if they might at times run counter to the intentions of Heaven? There is no way to know how Mo Zi would have responded to this dilemma because he simply takes it as an axiom that Heaven desires maximal utility. In practice, therefore, Mo Zi's philosophy is thoroughly utilitarian, and we find that his ethical assessments are consistently based on material and calculable concerns. Something is good, as far as Mo Zi is concerned, only if it brings about palpable and discernible benefit to the world.

The most significant Chinese criticism of Mohism has been that with its uncompromising materialism, it overlooks the importance of spiritual self-cultivation. In an ethical system where all acts are judged forthwith by a raw calculus of material benefit, such Confucian virtues as honesty, integrity, humanity, and reciprocity are valuable only insofar as they contribute to the general utility; they have no intrinsic value in themselves. (Consequently the Mohist understanding of the term *yi,* or "righteousness," is completely different from its meaning in Confucian contexts.) According to Mohism, people need not strive to perfect themselves or cultivate their virtues; they need only act in such a way as to bring about the greatest "benefit." Since most philosophical camps discountenanced material benefit as little more than a temptation that may lead humanity away from moral excellence, the failure of Mohism to develop a concept of self-cultivation has typically been considered a grave defect.

We know very little about the historical Mo Di. Since *mo* means "tattoo" (tattooing was a common punishment in ancient China), it has been suggested that Mo Di may have been a convict— and that "Mo Zi" is not a name but an epithet: "the Tattooed Master." *Mo* can also mean "inkline," and because of the very mechanical and repetitive style of the Mohist writings, as well as their penchant for analogies taken from workmen's experience, other scholars suspect that Mo Zi and his followers may have originally been artisans or craftsmen. Be that as it may, Mohism burgeoned quickly into an influential philosophical school with a firm hierarchy and organization. Whatever their origins, most Mohists soon came to be professional thinkers.

The following selection from the *Mo Zi,* or the Mohist corpus, contains two discursive essays ("Universal Love" and "The Will of Heaven") and two passages from the so-called "Mohist Analects," which are accounts of Mo Zi's discussions with his disciples and other contemporaries. The *Mo Zi,* which is very large, also contains some of the earliest Chinese treatises on warfare, optics, and other technological subjects (not discussed here).—PRG

Universal Love, Part 1

In taking it as his duty to order the world, the Sage must know whence disorder arises. Then he can put it in order. If he does not know whence disorder arises, he cannot bring about order. Compare this to a physician who is attacking someone's disease. He must know whence the disease arises; then he can attack it. If he does not know whence the disease arises, he cannot attack it. Why should putting disorder into order be any different [in this respect]? One must know whence disorder arises; then one can put it in order. If one does not know whence disorder arises, one cannot put it in order.

In taking it as his duty to order the world, the Sage cannot fail to investigate whence disorder arises. If we investigate disorder—whence does it arise? It arises from a lack of mutual love. When subjects and sons are not filial to their rulers and fathers, this is what is called disorder. When a son loves himself and does not love his father, he causes his father loss and benefits himself. When a younger brother loves himself and does not love his elder brother, he causes his elder brother loss and benefits himself. When a subject loves himself and does not love his lord, he causes his lord loss and benefits himself. This is what is called disorder. If the father is not kind to his son, nor the elder brother kind to his younger brother, nor the lord kind to his subjects, this is also what is called disorder. When a father loves himself and does not love his son, he causes his son loss and benefits himself. When an elder brother loves himself and does not love his younger brother, he causes his younger brother loss and benefits himself. When a lord loves himself and does not love his subjects, he causes his subjects loss and benefits himself. Why is this? These [disorders] all arise from a lack of mutual love. This is so even among the thieves and robbers in the world. A thief loves his house and does not love others' houses; thus he steals from others' houses in order to benefit his own house. A robber loves himself and does not love other people; thus he robs other people in order to benefit himself. Why is this? These [disorders] all arise from a lack of mutual love. This is so even among the feuding ministerial families and landed lords who attack each other's domains. The ministers each love their own families and do not love other families; thus they feud with other families in order to benefit their own families. Landed lords each love their own domains and do not love others' domains; thus they attack others' domains to benefit their own domains. There is nothing more than this to all the disorderly affairs in the world.

If we investigate these [problems]—whence do they arise? They all arise from a lack of mutual love. If we were to make everyone in the world love each other, so that they loved other people as they love themselves, would there still be a lack of filial piety? If they regarded their father, elder brother, and lord as they do themselves, how would they do anything unfilial? And would there still be a lack of kindness? If people regarded their sons, younger brothers, and subjects as they do themselves, how would they do anything unkind? Thus unfilial and unkind [acts] would be eliminated. Would there still be thieves and robbers? If people regarded others' houses as they do their own house, who would steal? If they regarded other people as they do themselves, who would rob? Thus thieves and robbers would be eliminated. Would there still be feuding ministerial families and landed lords who attack each other's domains? If people regarded others' families as they do their own families, who would feud? If they regarded other people's domains as they do their own domains, who would attack? Thus the feuding ministerial families and landed lords who attack each other's domains would be eliminated. If we were to make [the people of] the world all love each other—then domain and domain would not attack each other; family and family would not feud with each other; thieves and robbers would not exist; lords and subjects and fathers and sons would all be able to be filial and kind. If things were like this, the world would be ordered.

Thus in taking it as his duty to order the world, the Sage cannot fail to prohibit hatred and encourage love. Thus if [the people of] the world all love each other, there will be order. If they hate each other in their interactions, then there will be disorder. This is what Master Mo Zi meant when he said that one cannot fail to encourage the love of others.

The Will of Heaven, Part 1 [Excerpt]

What does Heaven desire and what does it hate? Heaven desires righteousness and hates unrighteousness. In that case, if we were to lead the Hundred Clans[1] of the world to tend to their affairs with righteousness, we would be doing what Heaven desires. If we do what Heaven desires, Heaven will also do what we desire. This being the case—what do we desire and what do we hate? We desire wealth and emoluments and hate disaster and calamity. So if we were to lead the Hundred Clans of the world to tend to their affairs unrighteously, then we would be doing what Heaven does not desire. If we do what Heaven does not desire, Heaven will also do what we do not desire. Thus we would be leading the Hundred Clans of the world into the midst of disaster and calamity.

But how do we know that Heaven desires righteousness and hates unrighteousness? It is said, If there is righteousness in the world, there is life; if there is no righteousness, there is death. If there is righteousness, there is wealth; if there is no righteousness, there is poverty. If there is righteousness, there is order; if there is no righteousness, there is disorder. So Heaven desires life and hates death, desires wealth and hates poverty, desires order and hates disorder; this is how we know that Heaven desires righteousness and hates unrighteousness. . . .

How do we know that Heaven loves the Hundred Clans of the world? In that it shines on them all. How do we know that it shines on them all? In that it possesses them all. How do we know that it possesses them all? In that it is fed by them all. How do we know that it is fed by them all? It is said, Within the four seas, none of the peoples that eat grain[2] fail to feed grass to their oxen and sheep, grain to their dogs and pigs,[3] nor to clean their containers of millet and [vessels] for refined and unrefined wine in order to sacrifice to Di Above and to the ghosts and spirits. Heaven possesses civilized people, so what would be the use of not loving them? Moreover, as I have said, if one kills one innocent person, there must be one inauspicious [result]. Who is it who kills innocent people? It is mankind. Who is it who delivers inauspicious [results]? It is Heaven. Now if Heaven did not love the Hundred Clans of the world, for what reason would it deliver inauspicious [results] when people kill each other? This is how we know that Heaven loves the Hundred Clans of the world.

To comply with the intentions of Heaven is to govern with righteousness. To oppose the intentions of Heaven is to govern by force. What will they do who govern with righteousness? Master Mo Zi has said, "Those who are seated in a great state do not attack smaller states; those who are seated in a great family do not take over smaller families. The strong do not plunder the weak; the noble are not haughty to the base; the clever do not cheat the foolish." This must be beneficial to Heaven above, to the ghosts in the middle, and to the people below. [A ruler like this] is beneficial in these three respects; there is no respect in which he is not beneficial. Thus he acquires an attractive reputation in the world and adds to it; one calls him a "Sage King."

"Mohist Analects" [Excerpts]

Wuma Zi said to Mo Zi, "I am different from you. I cannot love universally. I love people from Zou more than people from Yue, people from Lu more than people from Zou, people from my district more than people from Lu, people in my family more than people from my district, my parents more than people in my family, and myself more than my parents. I go by what is closer to myself. If you strike me, it hurts; if you strike someone else, it does not hurt me. For what reason should I not resist what hurts me and indeed resist what does not hurt me? Because I exist, there are [cases] where I would kill someone else in order to benefit myself, but there are no [cases] where I would kill myself in order to benefit someone else."

Mo Zi said, "Will you conceal your morality? Will you tell people your opinion?"

Wuma Zi said, "Why would I conceal my morality? I would tell people."

Mo Zi said, "Then if one person is persuaded by you, one person will want to kill you in order to benefit himself. If ten people are persuaded by you, ten people will want to kill you in order to benefit themselves. If the whole world is persuaded by you, the whole world will want to kill you in order to benefit itself."

There was a rustic from the south of Lu named Wu Lü. In the winter he made pottery and in the summer he plowed; he compared himself to Shun.[4] Master Mo Zi heard of him and went to see him. Wu Lü addressed Master Mo Zi, saying, "Righteousness, righteousness—what's the use of talking about it?"[5]

. . . Master Mo Zi said, "I have calculated this. I considered plowing and feeding the people of the world. If I were successful, I would do the plowing of one farmer. Divide this among the world, and each person cannot get one cup of grain. Even if one could get one cup of grain, it is obvious that that is not enough to satisfy those who are starving in the world. I considered weaving and clothing the people of the world. If I were successful, I would do the weaving of one woman. Divide this among the world, and each person cannot get one foot of cloth. Even if one could get one foot of cloth, it is obvious that that is not enough to warm those who are cold in the world. . . . "

Wu Lü said, "Righteousness, righteousness—what's the use of talking about it?"

Master Mo Zi said, "Suppose the world does not know how to plow. Wherein is there a greater accomplishment: in teaching people to plow; or in not teaching them to plow, and plowing by oneself?"

Wu Lü said, "The greater accomplishment is in teaching people to plow."

Master Mo Zi said, "Suppose you were attacking an unrighteous state. Wherein is there a greater accomplishment: in beating the drums and causing the army to advance to battle; or in not beating the drums and causing the army to advance to battle and advancing to battle by oneself?"

Wu Lü said, "The greater accomplishment is in beating the drums and causing the army to advance."

Master Mo Zi said, "The ordinary men and foot soldiers in the world know little about righteousness, and the accomplishment of those who teach the world with righteousness is surely great. Why do you not say so? If I had a drum and made them advance to righteousness, then would my own righteousness not be increased and advanced thereby?"

—PRG

Notes

1. I.e., the common people.
2. I.e., agrarian cultures and, by extension, civilized cultures.
3. The point evidently is that they fatten their domesticated animals for sacrifice to Heaven.
4. An ancient Sage King famed for his virtuous simplicity.
5. Wu Lü is saying that Mo Zi talks too much, and should spend his time farming instead.

MENCIUS (371–289 B.C.E.) was the second great teacher in the Confucian tradition and one of the most revered philosophers in imperial China. Mencius's core teaching is that all human beings are naturally good, a tenet he attempts to demonstrate repeatedly in his discussions with disciples and intellectual opponents. As it emerges from these debates, Mencius's theory is as follows. Human beings are endowed by Heaven with what he calls the "Four Beginnings" *(siduan),* which represent the incipience of the four cardinal virtues, namely humanity, righteousness, ritual, and wisdom. Mencius is convinced that in situations where our natural instincts determine our actions—that is, where we have neither time nor opportunity for rational analysis—our inherent goodness will come through. His most famous illustration of this phenomenon is the example of the baby about to fall into a well (2A.6): Mencius argues that anyone who sees a baby in such peril would rush to intercede—immediately and without thinking. To Mencius, this scenario demonstrates the inborn goodness in human beings (compare also 1A.7).

However, while we are all born with the incipience of virtue, we must not fail to cultivate our Beginnings, lest they wither and die. There are surely evil people in the world, and to account for them, Mencius points out that the incipience of virtue is not virtue itself. We must cultivate our innate Beginnings so that they grow into full-fledged virtues, and this process demands constant energy and sincerity throughout our lives. The fact that there are many people who let their Beginnings decay does not convince Mencius that there are people in whom evil exists naturally. As he explains through the parable of Ox Mountain (6A.8), evil people have merely allowed their surroundings to thwart their potential for goodness, just as the trees on Ox Mountain have all been felled by axes and hatchets.

The example of Ox Mountain is typical for Mencius: he repeatedly uses naturalistic images to illustrate his points, and he is especially fond of analogies involving plant life. Our incipient goodness is like sprouts in a field, which need to be tended and cultivated actively if they are to flourish. To say that a plant does not thrive because it has been neglected or damaged does not refute the basic contention that a plant's natural tendency is to grow, and similarly, for Mencius, to say that such-and-such a person is evil does not refute the fundamental conviction that the natural destiny of all human beings is to be virtuous (see especially 7A.2). Therefore, Mencius's conception of *xing*—which is usually translated as "human nature"—is best understood as the natural course of development that an organism may be expected to undergo given nourishing conditions. When Mencius says that our *xing* is good, he means not that we are born good, but that we are born with the potential to become good. Recently excavated texts from ancient times make it increasingly clear that this understanding of *xing* was unique in Mencius's own time; as we shall see, it was opposed vigorously by Xunzi, a later Confucian thinker. Controversial as it was in antiquity, however, the Mencian view of human nature became orthodox in imperial times. (To emphasize the uniqueness of Mencius's conception of *xing,* the term is left untranslated below.)

Like Confucius, Mencius considered his own teaching to be of global importance for the transmission of the Way. Mencius continually sought out representatives of other schools of thought in order to engage them in debate—to the extent that some contemporaries branded him as "disputatious" *(haobian).* His opposition to Mohism is celebrated; his view, essentially, is that the Mohist dictates—which prohibit lavish funerals for one's parents and require us to love strangers as we love our own families—are unnatural. He is also critical of the Mohists' emphasis on "profit" and "benefit" as opposed to moral self-cultivation.

As with so many ancient Chinese philosophers, very little is known about Mencius's life and origins. It is often said that he studied with Zisi, Confucius's famous grandson, but this is not likely: Mencius was probably born after Zisi was already dead. Most of what we can say about Mencius the man is derived, therefore, from the surviving records of his teachings. In these accounts, he emerges as a thinker with abiding faith in the goodness of humanity and as a staunch defender of the Confucian tradition.—PRG

[1A.1.] Mencius had an audience with King Hui of Liang.[1] The king said, "Venerable man, you have not considered it [too] far to come here from a thousand tricents[2] away; surely you will have some means to profit my state?"

Mencius responded, "Your Majesty, why must you speak of 'profit'? Indeed, I possess nothing more than humanity and righteousness. If the king says, 'How can I profit my state?' then the Grand Masters will say, 'How can I profit my family?' and the men-of-service and commoners will say, 'How can I profit myself?' Superiors and inferiors will wage war on each other for profit, and the state will be imperiled. In a state with ten thousand chariots, the one who assassinates his lord will be from a family with a thousand chariots; in a state with a thousand chariots, the one who assassinates his lord will be from a family of a hundred chariots. To have one thousand in ten thousand, or one hundred in one thousand, is not an inconsiderable [share],[3] but if one were to put righteousness last and profit first, then they would not be satiated without snatching more. There has never been one with humanity who yet abandoned his family; there has never been one with righteousness who yet placed his lord last (sc. in his list of obligations). Surely Your Majesty [should] say 'Humanity and righteousness, and nothing more!' Why must you speak of profit?"

[1A.7. Excerpt.] Mencius said, "I have heard that Hu He said, 'The king[4] was sitting at the top of the hall. There was someone with a sacrificial ox passing by the bottom of the hall. The king saw him, and said, What ox is that? The man answered, We are going to use it for a blood-sacrifice with a bell. The king said, Leave it; I cannot bear its fearful expression. It is like that of an innocent person approaching the execution ground. The man answered, Then will you do away with the blood-sacrifice and bell? The king said, How can I do away with that? Change it for a sheep.' I am not aware whether that happened."

The king said, "It happened."

Mencius said, "This type of mind is sufficient for a [true] king. The Hundred Clans all thought that you begrudged [the expense of the animal], but I know surely that it was because you could not bear the sight."

The king said, "That is so. But there was indeed [an appearance] of what the Hundred Clans supposed. Although the state of Qi is narrow and small, how would I begrudge one ox? Since I could not bear its frightened appearance—like that of an innocent person approaching the execution ground—I exchanged it for a sheep."

"Your Majesty, do not think it strange that the Hundred Clans thought you begrudged [the expense]. When you exchanged a large [animal] for a small one, how would they know [the real reason]? If you felt compassion on account of its [appearance as] an innocent person approaching the execution ground, then what was there to choose between an ox and a sheep?"

The king laughed and said, "Indeed! What was in my mind? I did not begrudge the expense, but I exchanged it for a sheep. It was appropriate that the Hundred Clans called me stingy!"

"Do not be hurt by it. [Your conduct] was an instantiation of humanity. You saw the ox; you did not see the sheep. With regard to beasts, the noble man [acts] as follows. When he sees them alive, he cannot bear to see them die. When he hears their sounds, he cannot bear to eat their flesh. Therefore the noble man keeps a distance from the kitchen."

[2A.2. Excerpt.] [Gongsun Chou][5] asked, "I venture to ask: may I hear about your unmoved mind and Master Gao's[6] unmoved mind?"

[Mencius said,] "Master Gao says, 'What is not obtained in words, do not seek in the mind; what is not obtained in the mind, do not seek in the *qi*.'[7] 'What is not obtained in the mind, do not seek in the *qi*'—that is acceptable; but 'What is not obtained in words, do not seek in the mind'—that is not acceptable. The will is the director of the *qi*; the *qi* is what fills the body. The will is superior among them; the *qi* comes second among them. Thus it is said: 'Maintain the will and do not violate the *qi*.'" . . .

[Gongsun Chou said,] "I venture to ask: wherein lie your strengths, Master?"

[Mencius] said, "I know words. I am good at nourishing my flood-like *qi*."

"I venture to ask, what do you mean by 'flood-like *qi*'?"

"It is difficult to say. It is the kind of *qi* that is greatest and firmest. If it is nourished with uprightness and is not damaged, then it fills in the space between Heaven and Earth. It is the kind of *qi* that is the consort of righteousness and the Way. Without it, [the body] starves. It is engendered by the accumulation of righteousness and is not obtained through sporadic righteousness. If there is something in one's actions that does not satisfy the mind, then [the flood-like *qi*] starves. Thus I say, Master Gao never knew righteousness, because he considered it external.[8] You must take it as your duty and do not let it out of your mind.[9] Do not let it out of your mind and do not 'help it grow.' Do not be like the man of Song. There was a man of Song who was sorry that his sprouts were not growing and pulled them up. He came home appearing weary and said to his people, 'Today I am worn out; I have helped my sprouts grow.' His son rushed out and went to look; the sprouts were all withered. There are few people in the world who do not 'help their sprouts grow.' Those who abandon them, thinking that they cannot [do anything to] benefit them, do not weed their sprouts. Those who 'help them grow' pull up their sprouts; not only are they not [doing anything to] benefit them—they are also damaging them."

[2A.6.] Mencius said, "All people have a mind that cannot bear [the suffering] of others. The Former Kings had a mind that could not bear [the suffering] of others, and thus had a government that could not bear [the suffering] of others. By using a mind that cannot bear [the suffering] of others to put into practice a government that cannot bear [the suffering] of others, ruling the world is [as easy as] moving it around in one's palm.

"What is meant by 'All people have a mind that cannot bear [the suffering] of others' is as follows. Suppose a person suddenly saw a child about to fall into a well. Everyone [in such a situation] would have a frightened, compassionate mind, not in order to ingratiate himself with the child's parents, not because he wants praise from his neighbors and friends, and not because he would hate to have the reputation [of one who would not save an innocent child]. From this we see: Who does not have a commiserating heart is not human. Who does not have a heart of shame is not human. Who does not have a heart of deference is not human. Who does not have a heart of right and wrong is not human. The heart of commiseration is the beginning of humanity. The heart of shame is the beginning of righteousness. The heart of deference is the beginning of ritual. The heart of right and wrong is the beginning of wisdom.

"Humans have these Four Beginnings as we have our four limbs. To have these Four Beginnings and say that one is incapable (sc. of developing them) is to make oneself into a brigand; to say that one's lord is incapable (of developing them) is to make one's lord into a brigand. Since we all have these Four Beginnings within ourselves, if we know to broaden them all and make them full, then it is like a fire beginning to blaze or a spring beginning to rise up. If one can make them full, they will be sufficient to protect the Four Seas; if one cannot make them full, they will not be sufficient [even] to serve one's father and mother."

[3A.5.] The Mohist Yi Zhi sought an audience with Mencius through Xu Bi.[10] Mencius said, "I am certainly willing to have an audience with him, but now I am slightly ill. When my illness recedes, I will go to see him; Master Yi need not come here." On another day, he sought an audience with Mencius again. Mencius said, "Today I can see him. If I do not correct him, the Way will not be apparent. So let me correct him. I have heard that Master Yi is a Mohist. According to the Mohist precepts on funerals, sparseness is their way. If Master Yi thinks that he can change the world with [the Mohist precepts], then would he not consider them correct and would he not honor them? But Master Yi buried his own parents richly and thus served his parents in a way that he considers base."

Master Xu told Master Yi about this, and Master Yi said, "According to the Way of the Confucians, the ancients 'were as though protecting a baby.' What does this refer to? To me, it means to love without differences of degree, but the practice (sc. of love) begins with one's parents."

Master Xu told Mencius about this, and Mencius said, "Does that Master Yi really think that a person's closeness to his elder brother's child is equal to his closeness to his neighbor's baby? What we can take from his [teachings] is this. If a baby were crawling around and were about to fall into a well, this would not be the fault of the baby. Moreover, when Heaven engenders creatures, it gives them one base, but Master Yi has two bases.[11] This is the cause [of his errors].

"In earliest times, there were those who did not bury their parents. When their parents died, they carried them and cast them into a ditch. On another day, they passed by [and saw] that foxes and wildcats had eaten [their parents' corpses] and that flies and gnats were gnawing at them. Their foreheads became sweaty, and they glanced away so as not to see. Now as for their sweat—it was not that they were sweating for other people. The [emotions] of their innermost heart reached their faces and eyes; they went home forthwith, and [came back] to cover [the corpses] with overturned baskets and shovels. If covering them was indeed right, then the filial son and humane person must also be with the Way in covering their parents."

Master Xu told Master Yi about this, and Master Yi was pensive for a while. Then he said, "He has taught me."

[3B.9. Excerpt.] "The words of Yang Zhu and Mo Di swell across the world. [People's] words throughout the world find their home in Mo if they do not do so in Yang. Mr. Yang's [credo] is 'For Me!'—there is no ruler in that. Mr. Mo's [credo] is 'Universal Love!'—there is no father in that.[12] To be without ruler or father is to be a beast.... If the ways of Yang and Mo are not quelled and the Way of Confucius not made manifest, then these heterodox propositions will delude the people and will fully obstruct humanity and righteousness. When humanity and righteousness are completely obstructed, then they will lead beasts to eat people, and people will eat each other.

"I am alarmed by this, and defend the Way of the Former kings. I resist Yang and Mo and banish their licentious statements, so that their heterodox propositions have no opportunity to operate. If they operate on [people's] minds, then they will damage their affairs; if they operate on their affairs, then they will damage the government. When a Sage rises again, he will not alter my words."

[6A.1.] Master Gao said, "Human xing is like a willow; righteousness is like cups and bowls. Making human xing humane and righteous is like making cups and bowls out of a willow."

Mencius said, "Can you accord with the xing of the willow and still make it into cups and bowls? You must injure and plunder the willow before you can make it into cups and bowls. If you must injure and plunder the willow in order to make it into cups and bowls, then [by your account] you must also injure and plunder people in order to make them humane and righteous. Your words will necessarily lead the people of the world to think of humanity and righteousness as a calamity."

[6A.2.] Master Gao said, "Human *xing* is like a torrent of water. If you clear a passage for it to the east, it will flow to the east; if you clear a passage for it to the west, it will flow to the west. Human *xing* is not divided into good or not good, just as water is not divided into east and west."

Mencius said, "Water is indeed not divided into east and west, but is it not divided into higher and lower? The goodness of human *xing* is like water's tendency to go downward. There is no person without goodness; there is no water that does not go downward. Now as for water, if you strike it and make it leap up, you can cause it to pass over your forehead; if you dam it and make it move [in a certain direction], you can cause it to stay on a mountain. Is this the *xing* of the water? Or is it force that makes it so? When people are caused to become bad, their *xing* is also like this."[13]

[6A.4.] Master Gao said, "Human *xing* is food and sex. Humanity is internal and not external. Righteousness is external and not internal."

Mencius said, "Why do you say that humanity is internal and righteousness external?"

[Master Gao] said, "If that man is older, then I treat him as an elder.[14] It is not that the oldness is in me. Just as if that man is hoary, then I treat him as hoary, following [the principle] that his hoariness is external to me. That is why I call it external."

[Mencius] said, "[Righteousness] is different from hoariness. There is no respect in which the whiteness of a white horse is different from the hoariness of a hoary man. But I do not know about the oldness of an old horse. Is there no respect in which it is different from the oldness of an elderly man? Moreover, what is righteousness—that he is old, or that we treat him as an elder?"

"If it is my younger brother, I love him; if it is the younger brother of a man from Qin, I do not love him. I am the criterion; thus I say that [humanity] is internal.[15] I treat an old man from Chu as an elder, just as I treat an old man from among our people as an elder. The oldness is the criterion; thus I say that [righteousness] is external."

"There is no respect in which relishing the roast meat of a man from Qin differs from relishing our own roast meat. Even among [inanimate] objects, there is some respect in which [what you say] is so.[16] So is there something external even in the way that we relish roast meat?"

[6A.8.] Mencius said, "The trees of Ox Mountain were once beautiful. Because it was in the suburbs of a great city, with axes and hatchets chopping at it, could it remain beautiful? With the respite that [the mountain] was afforded by the nights,[17] and the moisture of the rain and dew, it was not without buds and sprouts that grew on it; but then the cattle and goats came to pasture there. That is why it is so bald. People see its baldness and suppose that it never had timber on it. Is this the *xing* of the mountain?

"Even what exists within human beings—are we without a mind of humanity and righteousness? The manner in which we let go of our good minds is like axes and hatchets with respect to trees. If [the trees] are chopped down every morning, can they remain beautiful? With the respite that we are afforded by the nights,[18] and the [restorative influence] of the morning airs, our likes and dislikes are close to those of other people. [But the power of this restorative process] is slight, and it is fettered and destroyed by what takes place during the day. When this fettering is repeated again and again, the [restorative] nocturnal airs are insufficient to preserve [our goodness]. If the nocturnal airs are insufficient to preserve [our goodness], then we are not far from being disobedient beasts. People see our bestiality, and suppose that there was never any ability[19] in us. Is this human *xing?*

"Thus, if it obtains its nourishment, no creature will fail to grow; if it loses its nourishment, no creature will fail to decay.

"Confucius said, 'It is to the mind alone that the following refers! If you grasp it, it will be preserved; if you discard it, it will be destroyed. There is no time to its comings and goings, and no one knows its province.'"

[6A.10.] Mencius said, "Fish is what I desire; bear's paw[20] is also what I desire. Of the two, if I cannot have both, I will set aside fish and take bear's paw. Life is what I desire; righteousness is also what I desire. Of the two, if I cannot have both, I will set aside life and take righteousness.

"Life is surely something I desire, but there are things I desire more than life, and thus I will not act improperly in order to retain [life]. Death is surely something I hate, but there are things I hate more than death, and thus there are troubles that I do not avoid.

"If one were to make people desire nothing more than life, then why would they not use every means by which they could retain their lives? If one were to make people hate nothing more than death, then why would they not do anything by which they could avoid trouble?

"There are cases where we do not use some means that would ensure our life, and there are cases where we do not do something that would ensure our avoidance of trouble.

"Therefore, there are things that we desire more than life, and there are things that we hate more than death—and it is not only a moral paragon who has such a mind. All people have it; the moral paragon is able to keep it from perishing."

[6A.15.] Master Gongdu[21] asked, "We are all equally human. Why is it that some of us become great people, and some become lesser people?"

Mencius said, "Those who follow their greater parts become great people; those who follow their lesser parts become lesser people."[22]

[Master Gongdu] said, "We are all equally human. Why is it that some people follow their greater parts, and some follow their lesser parts?"

[Mencius] said, "The organs of the ears and eyes do not think, and are blinded by objects. When an object interacts with another object, it simply leads it astray.[23] But the organ of the mind thinks. If it thinks, it obtains its [object] (i.e., morality); if it does not think, it does not obtain it. These are what Heaven has imparted to us; if we first establish ourselves in the greater [parts], then the lesser ones cannot snatch [our attention]. To be a great person is nothing more than this."

[7A.1.] Mencius said, "Those who exhaust their minds know their *xing*. If they know their *xing*, then they know Heaven. Preserving one's mind and nourishing one's *xing* is how one serves Heaven. Not being of two minds in the face of premature death or long life and cultivating oneself in order to await [one's fate] is how one establishes one's destiny."

[7A.2.] Mencius said, "There is nothing that is not destined. One should compliantly receive one's proper [destiny]. Therefore those who know destiny do not stand by a precipitous wall. To die having exhausted the Way is proper destiny. To die in manacles and fetters is not proper destiny."

—PRG

Notes

1. R. 370–319 B.C.E.
2. A tricent *(li)* is a unit of distance roughly equivalent to a third of a mile.
3. That is to say, the assassins already possess one-tenth of their state's total number of chariots.

4. King Xuan of Qi (r. 319–310 B.C.E.).

5. A disciple of Mencius.

6. Master Gao was probably an older contemporary of Mencius, one who represented another branch of Confucianism. He is Mencius's interlocutor in a famous debate in section 6A of the *Mencius* (translated below).

7. The *qi* is understood here as the amorphous material of the human body. As Mencius goes on to concede, the concept is difficult to grasp.

8. See 6A.4 below.

9. The original is confusing here and may be garbled. Presumably Mencius means that one must make it one's constant duty to nourish one's "flood-like *qi*."

10. Xu Bi was a disciple of Mencius, Yi Zhi a follower of Mohism.

11. Mencius's meaning is somewhat obscure here. The phrase "two bases" probably refers to the fact that Yi Zhi espoused one set of views regarding appropriate burial customs but then went ahead and buried his parents as his conscience guided him, though this was in direct violation of the Mohist way.

12. In other words, the Mohist concept of "universal love" does not allow for the fact that we properly love our parents more deeply than we do other people's parents. Yang Zhu was another ancient philosopher, about whom little is known beyond his famous credo, "For Me!" Mencius's criticism presupposes that Yang Zhu considers the most important thing in the world to be his own person, and consequently that he would not obey his ruler if it required any self-sacrifice. But it is not clear that this is really what Yang Zhu meant by "For Me!"

13. That is to say, although people are naturally good, they can be made bad, just as water naturally flows downward, but can be dammed and maneuvered into flowing in an unnatural direction.

14. Meaning to treat an elder with the appropriate deference and respect.

15. Master Gao is saying that his own relation to the object determines whether he loves or does not love; hence the virtue of "humanity" is internal to the self.

16. I.e., that there is some element of Master Gao's "externality" in our relationship to any object in the world.

17. Literally, "by the days' nights," but clearly the nighttime, when the lumberjacks are not attacking the mountain, is intended here.

18. Ibid.

19. The Chinese word is *cai,* which is related to the word that Mencius has used above to refer to the timber *(cai)* on Ox Mountain. This paronomasia is intentional.

20. A rare, succulent dish.

21. A disciple of Mencius.

22. As Mencius goes on to explain, the "greater part" is the mind, the "lesser parts" the sense organs.

23. That is to say, the objects of the senses' desires merely attract the senses and lead them astray.

10 | The *Great Learning, Doctrine of the Mean,* and *Five Forms of Conduct*

THESE THREE ANONYMOUS Confucian texts—the *Great Learning, Doctrine of the Mean,* and *Five Forms of Conduct*—share a similar philosophy and rhetoric and probably date to more or less the same period in the development of the Confucian tradition. All three discuss the importance and methods of moral self-cultivation and portray human nature in a manner reminiscent of Mencius: we are born with "shoots" of goodness imparted to us from Heaven, but it is our own obligation to develop this endowment through constant introspection and self-perfection. Along with the teachings of Mencius himself, these works represent one of the dominant worldviews in early Confucianism.

The *Great Learning (Daxue)* and *Doctrine of the Mean (Zhongyong;* sometimes called *Application of Equilibrium)* have been transmitted for centuries as chapters in a compendium known as the *Book of Rites (Liji).* The *Five Forms of Conduct (Wuxing),* however, was lost for centuries and was completely unknown before it was discovered in a tomb at Mawangdui (cf. selection 26). Another edition of the text was found twenty years later in a tomb at Guodian, and it is clear now that the *Five Forms of Conduct* was recognized as a foundational work in ancient times. It does not have the same literary merit as the *Doctrine of the Mean* (the text to which it comes closest in philosophical orientation and expository technique), and its relatively pedestrian style may at least partly explain why it was not preserved by the Confucian tradition, but it is especially revealing in that it highlights both the strengths and the weaknesses of this branch of early Confucianism. For example, the veneration accorded to the *Odes* is evident from the repeated references in both the *Doctrine of the Mean* and *Five Forms of Conduct,* and the hermeneutic by which the latter text continually finds moral meaning in these poems is ingenious. But this reliance on the canon and the audience's familiarity with it also particularizes the Confucian vision: the value of the *Five Forms of Conduct* is diminished for readers who do not consider the authority of such texts as the *Odes* to be axiomatic.

The *Great Learning* is included here primarily because it was singled out in the Neo-Confucian period—over a thousand years after the time of its original composition—as one of the four most important books in the Confucian corpus (the other three being the *Analects, Mencius,* and *Doctrine of the Mean*). Its influence on ancient philosophy, however, is hardly discernible. The *Doctrine of the Mean* is a more substantial work and includes the classic discussion of the concept of "perfection" *(cheng;* often misleadingly translated as "sincerity"). In line with the Mencian idea of cultivating our Beginnings, the *Doctrine of the Mean* teaches that we must "perfect" ourselves by fulfilling our potential as moral paragons. The effective meaning of *cheng* is to bring oneself in accord with the Way of Heaven; literally the term means "completion," which can be understood as the completion of one's destiny as a collaborator with Heaven and Earth in the universal plan.

The following selections include a complete translation of the *Great Learning,* excerpts from the *Doctrine of the Mean,* and a complete translation of the *Five Forms of Conduct.*—PRG

Great Learning

The Way of great learning lies in making brilliant one's brilliant virtue, in being intimate with the people, and in coming to rest in supreme goodness. After one knows one's resting place, one is settled; after one is settled, one can be tranquil; after one is tranquil, one can be at peace; after one is at peace, one can deliberate; after one deliberates, one can attain [the Way]. Things have their roots and branches; affairs have their beginnings and endings. If one knows what comes first and what comes last, one will be close to the Way.

Because the ancients desired to make their brilliant virtue shine throughout the world, they first ordered their states; desiring to order their states, they first regulated their families; desiring to regulate their families, they first cultivated themselves; desiring to cultivate themselves, they first rectified their minds; desiring to rectify their minds, they first made their intentions sincere; desiring to make their intentions sincere, they first brought about knowledge; desiring to bring about knowledge, they first investigated things.[1] After things are investigated, knowledge is brought about; after knowledge is brought about, one's intentions are sincere; after one's intentions are sincere, one's mind is rectified; after one's mind is rectified, one cultivates oneself; after one has cultivated oneself, one's family is regulated; after one's family is regulated, the state is ordered; after the state is ordered, the world is peaceful.

From the Son of Heaven down to the common people, [everyone] takes this as primary; all must take self-cultivation as their root. For the roots to be disordered and the branches ordered—this will not occur. There has never been a case where one neglects what should be emphasized and emphasizes what should be neglected.[2]

Doctrine of the Mean

[1.] What Heaven endows is called *xing*; what leads the *xing* is called "the Way"; cultivating the Way is called "teaching." The Way cannot be left even for an instant. If it can be left, it is not the Way. Therefore, the noble man is cautious about what he does not see and fearful of what he does not hear. There is nothing more apparent than what is hidden; there is nothing more manifest than what is subtle. Thus the noble man is cautious when alone. When happiness, anger, grief, and joy have not yet stirred, this is called "equilibrium." When they stir and all attain their appropriate measure, this is called "harmony." Equilibrium is the great foundation of the world. Harmony is the far-reaching Way of the world. If one brings about equilibrium and harmony, Heaven and Earth will have their respective positions and the Myriad Creatures will be nourished thereby.

[2.] Confucius said, "The noble man [exemplifies] the application of equilibrium; the petty man opposes the application of equilibrium. The noble man's application of equilibrium—being a noble man, he is in constant equilibrium. The petty man's [opposition to] the application of equilibrium—being a petty man, he lacks caution."

[3.] The Master[3] said, "How supreme is the application of equilibrium! The people are rarely able to do it for a long time."

[4.] The Master said, "I know why the Way is not practiced. Those who are knowledgeable go past it; those who are foolish do not reach it. I know why the Way is not illuminated. The worthy go past it; the ignoble do not reach it. There are no people who do not drink and eat, but few are able to know flavors."

[5.] The Master said, "Oh, how the Way is not practiced! Alas!"

[6.] The Master said, "Shun—was he not greatly knowledgeable? Shun loved to ask questions and loved to investigate other people's words. He concealed their evil and broadcast their goodness. He grasped the two endpoints and applied the equilibrium to the people. It was by this that he was Shun!"

[7.] The Master said, "People all say: 'I am knowledgeable.' They rush forward and are caught by a net, trap, or pitfall, and none know how to avoid it. People all say: 'I am knowledgeable.' But when they choose the application of equilibrium, none can maintain it for a period of one month."

[8.] The Master said, "As a person, Hui⁴ was as follows. He chose the application of equilibrium. When he obtained one thing at which he was adept, he would clench it in his fist, wear it on his breast, and never lose it."

[9.] The Master said, "The nations and families of the world can be ruled. Rank and emolument can be declined. Brazen blades can be trampled. The application of equilibrium cannot be 'abilitied.'"⁵

[11.] The Master said, "[There are] simple hermits who yet practice wonders, so that their [names] are transmitted to later generations—I do not do this. [There are] noble men who walk along the Way, but give it up after half the journey—I cannot do this. [There are] noble men who accord with the application of equilibrium, who retire from the world and are not seen or known, yet do not regret it. Only a Sage can do this.

[12.] The Way of the Noble Man requires expenditure [of energy] and is hidden. Foolish men and women can take part in knowledge of it, but in its utmost reaches, there are respects in which even a Sage does not know it. Ignoble men and women can practice it, but in its utmost reaches, there are respects in which even a Sage cannot [practice] it. As great as Heaven and Earth are, people are still dissatisfied with them in some respects. Thus if the noble man speaks of the greatness [of the Way], nothing in the world can contain it; if he speaks of its smallness, nothing in the world can break it. The *Odes* say, "The hawk flies up to heaven; the fish leaps into the deep."⁶ This speaks of how [the Way] is displayed above and below. The Way of the Noble Man originates among men and women, but in its utmost reaches, it is displayed throughout Heaven and Earth.

[13.] The Master said, "The Way is not remote from humanity. People who [attempt to] practice the Way but keep a distance from other people cannot practice the Way. The *Odes* say, "In cutting an ax-handle, in cutting an ax-handle, the pattern is not far away."⁷ We grasp an ax-handle to cut [another] ax-handle, but if we look at it from a distance, it may appear remote. Thus the noble man uses people to put people in order; when they have been improved, he stops. Integrity and reciprocity are not far from the Way. What you do not wish done to you, do not do to others.

"There are four [elements] of the Way of the Noble Man of which I have not been able to achieve one. I have not been able to serve my father as I demand from my son; I have not been able to serve my ruler as I demand from my servants; I have not been able to serve my elder brother as I demand from my younger brother; I have not been able to do unto my friends as I demand from them.

"In the practice of applying virtue, in the care with which he applies speech, if there is any insufficiency, [the noble man] dares not fail to exert himself; if there is any excess, he dares not go to the limit. His actions correspond to his words; his words correspond to his actions. Is the noble man not sincere?"

[14.] The noble man acts as befits his station and is unwilling to go beyond it. Facing wealth and nobility, his actions pertain to wealth and nobility; facing poverty and turpitude, his actions pertain to poverty and turpitude; facing barbarous tribes, his actions pertain to barbarous tribes; facing vexation and difficulty, his actions pertain to vexation and difficulty. The noble man does not enter into a situation in which he cannot find himself. In a superior position, he does not humiliate his inferiors; in an inferior position, he is not obsequious with his superiors. If he rectifies himself and seeks nothing from others, he will have no cause for resentment. Above, he does not resent Heaven; below, he does not blame humanity. Thus the noble man lives easily and attends to his destiny; the petty man walks on a precipice and prays for fortune. The Master said, "There is one respect in which the archer is like the noble man. If he misses the target, he turns inward and seeks the cause within himself."

[20. Excerpts.] Duke Ai asked about government. The Master said, "The government of [Kings] Wen and Wu is exhibited in the manuscripts of wood and bamboo. If such people exist, such government will arise; if such people do not exist, such government will cease. The Way of Humanity is for government to grow rapidly; the Way of Earth is for trees to grow rapidly. Government is like rushes and reeds. . . .[8]

"[The virtue of] humanity pertains to humans.[9] Its greatest form is in intimacy with one's parents. Righteousness [derives from] what is appropriate. Its greatest form is in honoring moral paragons. One's decreasing intimacy with relatives [of more remote relation] and the ranks with which one honors moral paragons are born of ritual. Thus the noble man cannot fail to cultivate himself. Thinking of cultivating himself, he cannot fail to serve his parents. Thinking of serving his parents, he cannot fail to know humanity. Thinking of knowing humanity, he cannot fail to know Heaven.

"There are five aspects to the far-reaching Way in the world, and three means by which it can be practiced. It is said: the intercourse between lord and subject, father and son, husband and wife, elder brother and younger brother, and between friends—these five relations [make up] the far-reaching Way in the world. Knowledge, humanity, and courage—these three are the far-reaching virtues in the world. They are all practiced by a single means. Some are born knowing it; some know it through study; some know it through hardship—but in attaining knowledge of it, these amount to one and the same thing. Some practice it easily; some practice it keenly; some practice it through strenuous effort—but in completing the achievement of it, these amount to one and the same thing."

The Master said, "To be fond of study is to be close to knowledge; to practice with energy is to be close to humanity; to know one's conscience is to be close to courage. If one knows these three things, one knows how to cultivate oneself; if one knows how to cultivate oneself, one knows how to put people in order; if one knows how to put people in order, one knows how to put in order the states and families in the world. . . .

"Perfection is the Way of Heaven; to become perfect is the Way of Humanity. One who is perfect hits the mark without effort, comprehends without thinking, and naturally attains equilibrium with the Way; he is a Sage. One who perfects himself chooses goodness and grasps it solidly. He studies it broadly; he investigates and inquires of it; he thinks carefully about it; he analyzes it clearly; he practices it genuinely."

[22.] Only the most perfect people in the world are able to fulfill their *xing*.[10] If they can fulfill their *xing,* they can fulfill the *xing* of others; if they can fulfill the *xing* of others, they can fulfill the *xing* of creatures; if they can fulfill the *xing* of creatures, they can assist in the transformation and nourishment of Heaven and Earth; if they can assist in the transformation and nourishment of Heaven and Earth, they can form a triad with Heaven and Earth.

[23.] Second to these are those who develop their shoots. With one's shoots, one can possess perfection; if one is perfected, one will be realized; if one is realized, one will be manifest; if one is manifest, one will be brilliant; if one is brilliant, one will move [others]; if one moves [others], one will change them; if one changes them, one will transform them. Only the most perfect people in the world can effect such transformation.

[24.] With the Way of Utmost Perfection, one can know things in advance. When states and families are about to prosper, there must be auspicious omens; when states and families are about to perish, there must be portents of catastrophe. They are visible in the milfoil and tortoise and affect the movements of the four limbs. When disaster and fortune are about to arrive—if it is good, one must know of it; if it is not good, one must know of it. Thus a person of utmost perfection is like a spirit.

[25.] "Perfection" is self-completion, and the Way is self-directing. Perfection is the beginning and end of things. Without perfection, there are no things. Thus the noble man considers it noble to become perfect. One who is perfect does not simply complete himself; he uses [his perfection] to complete other things. Completing the self is humanity; completing other things is knowledge. These are virtues of the *xing;* they are the way by which one unites inner and outer. Thus it is appropriate to employ [these virtues] at the right times.

Five Forms of Conduct

The five forms of conduct: When humanity is realized within [oneself], this is called virtuous conduct. When it is not realized within, this is called conduct. When righteousness is realized within, this is called virtuous conduct. When it is not realized within, this is called conduct. When ritual is realized within, this is called virtuous conduct. When it is not realized within, this is called conduct. When wisdom is realized within, this is called virtuous conduct. When it is not realized within, this is called conduct. When sagehood is realized within, this is called virtuous conduct. When it is not realized within, this is called conduct.

There are five forms of virtuous conduct. When they are harmonized, this is called virtue. When four of the forms of conduct are harmonized, this is called adeptness. Adeptness is the Way of Humanity; virtue is the Way of Heaven. If a noble man does not have concern in his inner mind, then he will not have wisdom in his inner mind. If he does not have wisdom in his inner mind, then he will not have happiness in his inner mind. If he does not have happiness in his inner mind, then he will not be at peace. If he is not at peace, he will not be joyous. If he is not joyous, he will lack virtue.

One who has realized the five forms of conduct within [himself] and practices them at the appropriate times is called a "noble man." A *shi*[11] who has his aspirations set on the Way of the Noble Man is called an "aspiring *shi.*" If one does not act with adeptness, one will fail to come closer (sc. to the Way, etc.); if one does not aspire for virtue, one will not complete (sc. one's process of self-cultivation, etc.); if one does not think with wisdom, one will not comprehend. One who thinks without clarity has no insight; one who thinks without extending [his thoughts] will not realize [the five forms of conduct]. If [the five forms of conduct] are not realized, one will not be at peace. If one is not at peace, one will not be joyous. If one is not joyous, one will lack virtue.

If one is not humane, one's thoughts cannot be clear. If one is not wise, one's thoughts cannot be extended. Without humanity and wisdom, one's "concerned heart cannot be agitated, not having seen one's lord."[12] One's "heart cannot be delighted, having seen one's lord." This is what is meant by "Indeed when I have seen him, indeed when I have met him, then my heart will be delighted."[13] If one is not humane, one's thoughts cannot be clear. If one is not sage, one's thoughts cannot be light. Without humanity and sagehood, one's "concerned heart cannot be sorrowful, not having seen one's lord." One's "heart cannot be calmed, having seen one's lord."[14]

Humane thoughts are clear. If one is clear, one will be insightful; if one is insightful, one will be at peace; if one is at peace, one will be gentle; if one is gentle, one will be happy; if one is happy, one will be kind; if one is kind, one will be intimate; if one is intimate, one will be loving; if one is loving, one will have a jade-like visage; if one has a jade-like visage, one will realize [virtue]; if one has realized [virtue], one will be humane.

Wise thoughts are extended. If one extends [one's thoughts], one will comprehend; if one comprehends, one will not be vacuous; if one is not vacuous, one will be keen of sight; if one is keen of sight, one will discern moral paragons;[15] if one discerns moral paragons, one will have a jade-like visage; if one has a jade-like visage, one will realize [virtue]; if one has realized [virtue], one will be wise.

Sage thoughts are light. If one is light, one will be formed; if one is formed, one will not be vacuous; if one is not vacuous, one will be keen of hearing; if one is keen of hearing, one will hear the Way of the Noble Man; if one hears the Way of the Noble Man, one will have a jade-like tone; if one has a jade-like tone, one will realize [virtue]; if one realizes [virtue], one will be sage.

"The good man, the noble man—his deportment is unified."[16] Only after one can act in a unified manner can one be a noble man, [who is] cautious when alone.

"I watched until I could no longer see her, and then I wept like rain."[17] Only after one "displays one's feathers unevenly"[18] is one capable of utmost grief. The noble man is cautious when alone. In his practice of adeptness, there is that with which the noble man begins and that with which he ends. In his practice of virtue, there is that with which the noble man begins, but there is nothing with which he ends. One who turns the sound of bronze into the vibrations of jade is one who possesses virtue.[19]

The sound of bronze [pertains to] adeptness; the jade-like tone [pertains to] sagehood. Adeptness is the Way of Humanity; virtue is the Way of Heaven. Only after one possesses virtue can one turn the sounds of bronze into the vibrations of jade. If one is not keen of hearing, one will not be keen of sight; if one is not keen of sight, one will not be wise;[20] if one is not wise, one will not be humane; if one is not humane, one will not be at peace; if one is not at peace, one will not be joyous; if one is not joyous, one will lack virtue.

If one is not changeable, one will not be happy; in one is not happy, one will not be kind; if one is not kind, one will not be intimate; if one is not intimate, one will not be loving; if one is not loving, one will not be humane.

If one is not upright, one will not be X;[21] if one is not X, one will not be resolute; if one is not resolute, one will not be decisive; if one is not decisive, one will not act; if one does not act, one will not be righteous.

If one is not distant, one will not be respectful; if one is not respectful, one will not be stern; if one is not stern, one will not honor [others]; if one does not honor [others], one will not be reverent; if one is not reverent, one will not possess ritual.

One who has never heard the Way of the Noble Man is called "not keen of hearing." One who has never seen a moral paragon is called "not keen of sight." One who has heard the Way of the Noble Man but does not know that it is the Way of the Noble Man is called "not sage." One who has seen a moral paragon but does not know that he possesses virtue is called "not wise."

To see and to know [what one sees] is wisdom. To hear and to know [what one hears] is sagehood. To make brilliant what is brilliant is wisdom;[22] to dread what is dreadful is sagehood. This is what is meant by "Brilliant, brilliant below; dreadful, dreadful above."[23]

To hear the Way of the Noble Man is to be keen of hearing. To hear and know [what one hears] is to be sage. A sage knows the Way of Heaven. To know something and practice it is righteousness. To practice something at the appropriate time is virtue. To see a moral paragon is to be keen of sight. To see and know [what one sees] is wisdom. To know something and to be at peace with it is humanity. To be at peace with something and to be reverent about it is to possess ritual. Sagehood, wisdom, ritual, and music are born when the five forms of conduct are harmonized. If one has harmonized [the five forms of conduct], one will be joyous; if one is joyous, one will possess virtue; if one possesses virtue, then the state and its families can prosper. Such was the appearance of King Wen. This is what is meant by "King Wen is on high; oh, he shines from Heaven."[24]

To see and know [what one sees] is wisdom. To know something and to be at peace with it is humanity. To be at peace with something and practice it is righteousness. To practice something and to be reverent about it is to possess ritual. Humanity and ritual are born when four of the [five] forms of conduct are harmonized. If they are harmonized, one will understand;[25] if one understands, one will be adept.

One's visage and countenance should be gentle and changeable. To use one's inner mind in one's intercourse with others is to be happy. To be happy and follow one's brothers is to be kind. To be kind and trustworthy is to be intimate. To be intimate and affectionate is to be loving. To love one's father and secondarily love others is humanity.

To discriminate with one's inner mind and act correctly is uprightness. To be upright and be followed (sc. in one's uprightness, etc.) is X. To be X and not fear the mighty and powerful is resoluteness. Not to thwart the Great Way with lesser ways is decisiveness. To execute greatly those who have [committed] great crimes is [correct] action. To treat the noble as noble and honor moral paragons according to their ranks is righteousness.

To use one's outer mind in one's intercourse with others is to be distant. To be distant and earnest is to be respectful. To be respectful but not [overly] self-regulating is to be stern. To be stern and awed is to honor [others]. To honor [others] and not be haughty is reverence. To be reverent and have broad intercourse is to possess ritual.

If one is not decisive, one will not act. If one is not merciful, one will not have insight into the Way. To execute greatly those who have [committed] great crimes is to be decisive. To pardon those who have [committed] lesser crimes is mercy. Not to execute greatly those who have [committed] great crimes is not to act. Not to pardon those who have [committed] lesser crimes is not to have insight into the Way.

As a manner of speaking, "decisiveness" is like "selecting":[26] it is for great and rare [cases]. As a manner of speaking, "mercy" is like "covering over a misdeed":[27] it is for lesser [cases] in which one should be compassionate. Decisiveness is an element of righteousness. Mercy is an element of humanity. Hardness is an element of righteousness. Softness is an element of humanity. This is what is meant by "neither restless nor lax, neither hard nor soft."[28]

A noble man accumulates great accomplishments. Those who can advance [their accomplishments] become noble men; those who cannot advance them stop at their respective dwelling places. In great and rare [cases], [the noble man] is able to adopt [decisiveness]; in lesser [cases] where one should be compassionate, he is able to adopt [mercy]. One who, searching like a hound,[29] reaches the Way of the Noble Man is called a "moral paragon." One who knows and recruits a noble man is called "one who honors moral paragons." One who follows and serves a noble man is called "one who honors moral paragons." The former is the manner in which kings and dukes honor moral paragons; the latter is the manner is which a *shi* honors a moral paragon.

The six [organs]—the ears, the eyes, the nose, the mouth, the hands and the feet—are the mind's servants. If the mind says "yes," none of them dare say "no"; if it says "affirmative," none of them dare not affirm; if it says "advance," none of them dare not advance; if it says "retreat," none of them dare not retreat; if it says "deep," none of them dare not go deep; if it says "shallow," none of them dare not go shallow. If they are harmonized, one will understand; if one understands, one will be adept.

To know by means of one's eyes is called "advancement." To know by means of an analogy is called "advancement." To know by means of an example is called "advancement." To know by means of an omen is heavenly. This is what is meant by "Di Above is near you; do not be of two minds."[30]

What bestows greatly on humanity is Heaven. What people bestow on each other is X.

One who hears of the Way and delights in it is one who loves humanity. One who hears of the Way and is awed by it is one who loves righteousness. One who hears of the Way and reveres it is one who loves ritual. One who hears of the Way and takes joy in it is one who loves virtue.

—PRG

Notes

1. This is one possible translation of the phrase *gewu,* which can also mean "to classify things" or "to categorize things." Since the stage of *gewu* is obviously pivotal in this text, commentators have been debating its precise meaning for centuries.

2. The last sentence is unclear and has been the subject of much commentarial dispute. The penultimate sentence is more comprehensible: the idea is that one cannot expect to have an orderly state and family if one does not first cultivate oneself.

3. I.e., Confucius.

4. Yan Hui, Confucius's favorite disciple.

5. This saying sounds as odd in Chinese as it does in English. The point is that one cannot speak of "applying equilibrium" as though it were just another action that one could accomplish by virtue of one's talents and abilities. It is difficult for anyone and requires constant effort.

6. Mao 239 ("The Foothills of Han").

7. Mao 158 ("Cutting an Ax-Handle").

8. Plants that grow rapidly—and erect.

9. A paronomasia in Chinese as well as English. The name of the virtue translated as "humanity" *(ren)* is phonologically indistinguishable from the word for "human being" *(ren).* There is a similar effect in the next clause: the word for "righteousness" *(yi)* is similar (though not identical) to the word for "appropriate" *(yi).*

10. That is, develop the *xing* fully, in a Mencian sense.

11. The word is not easy to translate; it means, roughly, a man of service, honor, and scholarship.

12. A subtle and intentional misquotation of the *Odes.* Mao 14 ("The Grass-Insects") reads, "I have not yet seen my lord; my concerned heart is agitated." The text here is saying that without humanity and wisdom, one cannot have this emotional response.

13. A correct quotation from "The Grass-Insects."

14. Another intentional misquotation from "The Grass-Insects," which reads, "I have not yet seen my lord; my concerned heart is sorrowful. Indeed when I have seen him, indeed when I have met him, then my heart will be calmed." Mao 168 ("The Chariots Go Out") also reads, "I have not yet seen my lord; my concerned heart is sorrowful. Now I have seen my lord, so my heart is calmed."

15. That is, apperceive them as the moral paragons that they are. As the text defines the term below, a "moral paragon" *(xian)* is someone who possesses virtue and who searches for the Way of the Noble Man.

16. A quote from Mao 152 ("The Turtledove").

17. A quote from Mao 28 ("The Swallows").

18. In "The Swallows," the birds' uneven feathers constitute an image prefiguring the speaker's grief at his lady's departure.

19. As the text immediately goes on to explain, the "sound of bronze" is an image of adeptness, the "vibration of jade" that of virtue.

20. The text is probably garbled here; the present translation represents my supposition as to how this passage should run.

21. The original character has not been deciphered.

22. Presumably "what is brilliant" refers to one's virtue, as in the opening line of the *Great Learning:* "The Way of great learning lies in making brilliant one's brilliant virtue."

23. A quote from Mao 236 ("Great Brilliance").

24. A quote from Mao 235 ("King Wen").

25. The text is difficult to construe here.

26. The words for "decisive" and "select" (*jian* and *lian,* respectively) are cognate in classical Chinese.

27. The characters for "mercy" (literally, "to cover") and "misdeed" (*ni* and *te,* respectively) happen to share the same grapheme. In other words, the text is explaining why the terms *jian* and *ni,* which are not common, should be used for "decisiveness" and "mercy."

28. A quote from Mao 304 ("They Extensively Issued Forth").

29. The text is unclear here and permits various possible interpretations.

30. A quotation from "Great Brilliance."

ONE OF THE Thirteen Canons (or Thirteen Classics) of the Confucian tradition is the *Spring and Autumn Annals (Chunqiu)*, a chronicle covering the years 722 to 483 B.C.E. compiled at the feudal court of Lu (the home state of Confucius). Though generally reliable from a historical point of view, the *Springs and Autumns* is highly elliptical; consequently, it has been transmitted along with three commentaries that elucidate the terse statements of the canon and provide background information that later readers could not be expected to know. Two of these commentaries (the so-called *Gongyang* and *Guliang* commentaries) are written as catechisms: it is asked why the text of the *Spring and Autumn Annals* uses such-and-such an expression to convey its meaning, whereupon the work provides an answer intended to shed light on the hidden meaning of the annals.

The third orthodox commentary is attributed to one "Mr. Zuo" and is known as the *Zuo Commentary (Zuozhuan)*. It is far longer than the other two and has been handed down as a collection of interrelated narratives elaborating on the various entries of the *Spring and Autumn Annals*. As the most extensive of the historical or quasi-historical works in the Confucian corpus, the *Zuozhuan* has had an enormous influence on the historical imagination and sensibility of the generations that read it as part of their basic education. For Chinese intellectuals before the twentieth century, the *Zuozhuan* was the preeminent source for their nation's ancient history.

Modern readers are apt to treat the *Zuozhuan* differently, because its earlier standing as an infallible record of fact has recently been questioned. Though it was certainly compiled with the help of primary sources, the *Zuozhuan* is now usually dated to the fourth century B.C.E.—or as many as four hundred years removed from the events and personages that it discusses. Moreover, the purpose of the work seems to be not so much to relate historical data as to derive moral lessons from the pattern of the past. If one were to imagine a didactic and romanticized history of the Americas from Columbus down to the Revolutionary War, based partly on genuine documents, but containing a generous assortment of legends and thrilling anecdotes, this would be a contemporary analogy of the *Zuozhuan*.

The following narrative exemplifies many of the features of the *Zuozhuan*. The central characters are two half-brothers, Shensheng and Yiwu, who are sons of Lord Xian of Jin (r. 676–652 B.C.E.). Shensheng is the legitimate Heir Apparent, but he is driven to suicide before attaining the throne, so Yiwu is eventually ordained Marquis of Jin. Yiwu is a rash and thoughtless ruler, however, and his demise is foretold by the ghost of Shensheng, whose body Yiwu has ordered exhumed and transferred to a different grave. Through a series of offensive acts, Yiwu provokes a war with his brother-in-law, Lord Mu of Qin (r. 659–621 B.C.E.), in which he is captured by the latter's forces. Then the story focuses on the negotiations between the states of Jin and Qin, culminating in Lord Mu's wise and forbearing decision to send his prisoner home, suitably chastened. The tale is supposed to show that the only justifiable motivation for war is to punish the moral and ritual transgressions of one's enemies. Furthermore, a victorious lord must, like Lord Mu, help the vanquished recognize their faults and lead them back to the path of right conduct, rather than exploit their discomfiture by enriching himself at their expense. This is the high-minded view of the *Zuozhuan*—but at the same time, the authors of the work use this weighty issue as a pretext to tell a rousing battle story.

The names Shensheng and Yiwu may be intended as epithets. "Shensheng" can mean "Repeated Birth"—a fitting name for an injured spirit who roams the earth as a revenant. "Yiwu" means "Destroy Me!"—PRG

(Lord Xi of Lu, 10th year; 650 B.C.E.) The Marquis of Jin moved the grave of Heir Apparent Gong.[1] In the autumn, Hu Tu was traveling to the city of Quwo when he happened upon the Heir Apparent.[2] The Heir Apparent made him climb into [his own chariot] and serve as his driver. He announced to him, "Yiwu has no ritual! Di has acceded to my request that the state of Jin be conferred upon Qin, and [the people] of Qin will sacrifice to me."

[Hu Tu] replied, "Your servant has heard, 'Spirits are not fed by those who are not of their kind, and people do not sacrifice to those who are not of their clan.'[3] [If Jin is conquered by Qin], will my Lord's sacrifices not be terminated? Moreover, what crime have the people [of Jin committed]? The penalties [that you propose] are incommensurate, and you will be wanting for sacrifices. Lord, will you not reconsider?"[4]

Lord [Shensheng] said, "Very well. I will go and make another request [of Di]. In seven days, there will be a spirit-medium at the western side of the New City; you can see me through him." [Hu Tu] agreed to this, whereupon [Shenseng] disappeared. When the appointed time came and [Hu Tu] went [to see the medium, Shensheng] announced to him, "Di has permitted me to punish the guilty. [Yiwu] will be defeated at Han." . . .

(Lord Xi, 15th year; 645 B.C.E.) When the Marquis of Jin returned to his state [to be enthroned as the new ruler], Lady Mu of Qin [who was his sister] entrusted Lady Jia to his care.[5] She also said, "Take in all the princes." The Marquis of Jin fornicated with Lady Jia and did not take in all of the princes; therefore Lady Mu was resentful of him. The Marquis of Jin had agreed to present gifts to some Central Grand Masters, but then he turned his back on all of [his promises]. He was to present the Earl of Qin [who was his sister's husband] with five cities beyond the Yellow River, extending to the east all the way to the frontier of the state of Guo, to the south to Mount Hua, and to the north to the city of Jieliang. But then he did not grant [the territory]. When Jin was starving, Qin transported grain to them, but when Qin was starving, Jin refused to let them buy grain. Thus the Earl of Qin attacked Jin.

Diviner Tufu cast yarrow stalks [on behalf of Qin]; the result was auspicious: "After crossing the river, the marquis's chariot will be smashed." [The Earl of Qin] asked for details, and [the diviner] replied, "This is greatly auspicious. After three defeats, you will surely capture the Lord of Jin. The hexagram happens to be Gu ("Pests"), which says, 'A thousand chariots are driven away three times. Among those that remain after being driven away three times, we will catch their male fox.'[6] Now the fox is a pest, and must be their lord. The lower part of the hexagram Gu is Feng ("Wind"); the upper part is Shan ("Mountain"). The season is now autumn. We will take down their fruit and seize their timber; that is how we will vanquish them. If one's fruit is taken down and one's timber destroyed, what can one expect but defeat?"

After three defeats, [the army of Jin retreated] to Han. The Marquis of Jin addressed Qing Zheng, saying, "They have invaded deeply. What shall we do?"

He replied, "It was in fact you, my Lord, who brought them in so deep. What can be done?"

The lord said, "Impudent!" He divined to see who should be his right-hand man, and [the suggestion of] Qing Zheng was found to be auspicious. But he did not employ him.[7] Bu Yang drove the war chariot and Jia Putu served as [the lord's] right-hand man. The chariot was drawn by a team of four small horses, which had been received [as a gift] from the state of Zheng.

Qing Zheng said, "In ancient times, one would always use [horses] produced by one's own country in great matters. They are native to the waters and lands and know their people's minds; they are easily instructed and are accustomed to the roads. Wherever one may lead them, they are never unconformable to one's will. Now you use [horses] produced by a different country to carry out warlike affairs; once they become frightened, they will be changeable and will defy their drivers. With this disorderly temper, they will be unruly and frustrated; their blood will circulate, inflating their veins so that they bulge with arousal. They will have a superficial [appearance] of strength but will be withered to the core. They will not be able to advance, retreat, or turn around. Lord, you will certainly regret this." [The ruler of Jin] did not heed him.

In the ninth month, the Marquis of Jin encountered the army of Qin; he sent Han Jian to observe the [enemy] army. He returned and said, "Their army is smaller than ours, but they have twice as many bellicose warriors."

The lord said, "Why is this?"

He replied, "When you left [your homeland], you relied on their aid; when you returned, you made use of their favors;[8] and when you were starving, you ate their grain. Thrice they succored you, but without requital. This is why they have come. Now that they are about to strike, our [forces] are listless, and those of Qin fervent. To say that they have twice as many [bellicose warriors] does not even [approach the truth]."

The lord said, "One cannot let even one man become an arrogant cur [by yielding to him]—let alone an entire country." Then he sent an embassy requesting battle, saying, "I am not eloquent; I am able to assemble my forces but cannot disperse them. My Lord, if you do not go back, there will be no way for me avoid your command [to battle.]"

The Earl of Qin sent Noble Grandson Zhi, who replied, "My Lord, before you had entered [your state to become ruler of Jin], I was fearful for you; when you had entered your state but had not consolidated your position, I was still worried. If your position is now consolidated, would I dare not accept your command?"[9]

Han Jian returned and said, "I will be fortunate to be captured."

On *renxu* day, they fought on the plain of Han. The warhorses of Jin were confounded by the mud and forced to halt. The Lord [of Jin] called for Qing Zheng. Qing Zheng said, "You rejected my remonstrance and disobeyed the divination.[10] You were resolutely seeking defeat—why flee from it now?" Then he abandoned [his lord].

Liang Youmi was driving for Han Jian; Guo She was the right-hand man. They came upon the carriage of the Earl of Qin and were about to stop him. [Qing] Zheng misled them by [calling for someone] to save the Lord [of Jin]; thus they lost the Earl of Qin. Qin caught the Marquis of Jin and returned with him. The Grand Masters of Jin followed him, letting their hair loose and camping in the wilderness. The Earl of Qin sent an embassy [asking them] to desist, saying, "Gentlemen, why are you so aggrieved? I am accompanying the Lord of Jin to the west only in order to comply with the ominous dream of Jin.[11] Would I dare do anything excessive?"

The Grand Masters of Jin paid their respects by kowtowing three times and said, "Lord, you tread on the Earth Deity and bear up August Heaven. August Heaven and the Earth Deity have surely heard your words, my Lord, so we, your flock of subjects, dare to be inspired by them beneath you."

When Lady Mu heard that the Marquis of Jin was about to arrive, she ascended a terrace with Heir Apparent Ying, [her other son] Hong, and her daughter Jianbi, and stood upon a pyre there. She sent an embassy clad in mourning cap and gown to meet [her husband], and then she said, "Heaven Above has sent down catastrophe, causing my two lords to meet each other without jade and silk,[12] and to be aroused to warfare. If the Lord of Jin enters [the capital] in the morning, I and my children will die in the evening; if he enters in the evening, we will die the next morning. Only my Lord can decide [the hour of my death]!" Thereupon [the Lord of Jin] was lodged in the Spirit Terrace.

The Grand Masters [of Qin] requested that he be brought into [the capital], but the Lord [of Qin] said, "When I caught the Marquis of Jin, I supposed that I should come home with riches, but now that I have come home to a funeral, where is the utility in [having captured my enemy]? What [good] is there in this for you, Grand Masters? Moreover, the grief and worry of the people of Jin move me. Heaven and Earth have made a covenant with me. If I do not consider the worries of Jin, I will redouble their anger. If I swallow my words,[13] I will be turning my back on Heaven and Earth. Redoubled anger is difficult to bear, and turning one's back on Heaven is inauspicious. I must send the Lord of Jin home."

Noble Son Zhi said, "It is better to kill him, lest he gather [resources] for misdeeds against us."

Zisang said, "If we send him home but take his heir apparent hostage, that would be the greatest accomplishment. Jin cannot be annihilated, and to kill their lord would only bring about their hatred. Moreover, Historian Yi once said, 'Do not initiate misfortune; do not await [others'] disorders; do not redouble anger.' Redoubled anger is difficult to bear, and to abuse others is inauspicious." Thereupon they granted peace with Jin.

The Marquis of Jin sent Xi Qi to inform Lü Yisheng of Xia [of the news] and summoned the latter. Zijin[14] instructed [the Lord of Jin] with these words: "Bring the denizens of the state to court and reward them by your command as Lord. Then tell them, 'Although I am coming home, I have disgraced the altars of soil and grain. Let us divine whether [my son] Yu should replace me.'" The multitudes all wept. This is how the state of Jin came to redistribute its fields.[15]

Lü Yisheng of Xia said, "Our Lord was not troubled at his loss, but worried about us, his flock of subjects; this is the epitome of grace.[16] How do you think of him as a ruler?"

The multitudes said, "What can we do [to repay him]?"

[Lü Yisheng] replied, "We will raise funds and monies to support his young son. When the feudal lords hear of it, [they will know that] we grieve for one lord but have another, that his flock of subjects is harmonious and friendly, that our armor and weapons are more numerous than ever. Those who like us will encourage us; those who hate us will fear us. This would be advantageous in many respects!" . . .

In the tenth month, Yisheng of Yin[17] met with the Earl of Qin; they concluded an alliance in the Royal City. The Earl of Qin said, "Is the state of Jin at peace?"

[Yisheng] replied, "It is not at peace. The lesser people are ashamed at having lost their lord and grieve painfully for their kinsmen [who died in battle]. They are not reluctant to raise funds and monies in order to establish [his son] Yu [as his successor], saying, 'We must take revenge on our enemies, rather than serve those barbarians.' The noble men love their lord and know their faults. They are not reluctant to raise funds and monies in order to attend the commands of Qin, saying, 'We must requite their kindness; even should we die, we will not be duplicitous.' In this manner [the state] is not at peace."

The Earl of Qin said, "What do they say about their lord in the state [of Jin]?"

He replied, "The lesser people are aggrieved, and say that he will not avoid [execution]. The noble men put themselves in Qin's place and consider that he must be sent home. The lesser people say, 'We have been venomous to Qin; will Qin return our lord?' The noble men say, 'We know our faults. Qin must return our lord. He was duplicitous and they took hold of him; now that he is submissive they will let him go. There is no richer form of virtue than this, no more dreadful form of punishment. The submissive will cherish your virtue; the duplicitous will fear your punishments. As a result of this one engagement, Qin can be a hegemon. If [the Lord of Qin] sends him back but does not consolidate [his position], or deposes him and does not establish [a successor], then his kindness will become [a cause for] resentment. Qin will not act like this.'"

The Earl of Qin said, "These are my thoughts [as well]." He improved the Marquis of Jin's residence and provided him with seven *lao*-sacrifices.[18]

[Meanwhile], E Xi addressed Qing Zheng, saying, "Why do you not go?"

He replied, "I caused my Lord to fall into defeat. I was defeated but did not die; if I were also not to let him punish me, I would not be a proper minister. A minister who is not a minister—wherever he may go, where will he be taken in?" In the eleventh month, the Marquis of Jin came home. On *dingchou* day, he killed Qing Zheng and then entered [the capital].

That year, there was another famine in Jin, and the Earl of Qin supplied them with grain, saying, "I am resentful of their lord, but I pity their people. Moreover, I have heard that when Tang-shu[19] was enfeoffed, Master Ji said, 'Your descendants will surely be great!' How can Jin be eradicated? For now, I will sow kindness with them, while waiting for a more competent [ruler in Jin]." This was how Qin first collected taxes on the lands of Jin east of the Yellow River; they instituted a bureaucracy to oversee [the territory].[20]

—PRG

Notes

1. Shensheng is still called "Heir Apparent" even though he is deceased.

2. Quwo was the ancestral burial site of the rulers of Jin, so it makes sense that Hu Tu (who had been Shensheng's chariot-driver) should "happen upon" the ghost of his lord near that city.

3. The point is that only direct descendants of a spirit are allowed to sacrifice to it. The people of Qin will be unable to support Shensheng's ghost because they are not related to him by blood.

4. It is odd that Hu Tu should be better versed in the principles of ritual sacrifice than the Crown Prince of Jin—not to mention the High God Di!

5. Ostensibly, "Lady Jia" refers to the childless first wife of Yiwu's father (who was from the state of Jia). But since we are immediately told that Yiwu fornicated with this Lady Jia, commentators doubt that the text can be speaking of his father's wife: she would have been twenty to thirty years his senior. So they often suggest that the lady in question must have been Shensheng's widow. What is clear, in any case, is that by ravishing his kinsman's widow, Yiwu confirmed his half-brother's damning assessment of him by proving that he was, indeed, "without ritual."

6. None of the sayings quoted by this diviner appear in the extant *Changes*. He is either following some other codex or inventing his own prognostications.

7. Evidently the spirits are trying to tell Yiwu that he should listen to Qing Zheng's difficult remonstrations, but Yiwu is not sensitive to the warning.

8. Han Jian is alluding to the support that Yiwu received from Lord Mu of Qin before attaining rulership of Jin.

9. This is a stylized declaration of war.

10. That is, the earlier divination recommending Qing Zheng as the Marquis's right-hand man.

11. The Lord of Qin is evidently referring to Shensheng's prediction that Yiwu would be punished at Han.

12. That is to say, without a pledge of alliance, which would be concluded with ceremonial objects of jade and silk.

13. I.e., go back on his solemn promise.

14. Lü Yisheng's courtesy name.

15. The original text is difficult to construe, but it seems to mean that the state's resources were redistributed more equitably.

16. The word "grace" *(hui)* was later used as Yiwu's posthumous name (Lord Hui).

17. Lü Yisheng possessed the fiefs of Xia and Yin, so he is named variously as "Yisheng of Xia" and "Yisheng of Yin." Sometimes it is said that Lü, interpreted here as his surname, was originally the name of yet a third fief.

18. One *lao*-sacrifice consists of an ox, sheep, and pig.

19. The first Lord of Jin, enfeoffed in the eleventh century B.C.E.

20. The purpose of the final comment is to indicate that Yiwu finally delivered to Qin the lands he had long promised.

PROBABLY THE MOST widely known Chinese book anywhere on earth is the *Lao Zi (Old Master* or *Master Lao),* also called the *Daode jing (Canon of the Way and Its Power* or *Classic Book of Integrity and the Way).* It has been translated into dozens of languages and has been recognized for centuries as a profound work of philosophy. Two exegetical treatises on the *Lao Zi* attributed to the writer Han Fei (d. 233 B.C.E.) attest to the early interest in the text in China.

Archaeological discoveries of the past three decades have led to considerable advances in our knowledge and understanding of the *Lao Zi.* In 1973, two ancient manuscripts of the text were discovered in a tomb at Mawangdui (where the *Five Forms of Conduct,* examined in selection 10, was also found for the first time), and twenty years later, at Guodian,[1] archaeologists excavated what are now taken to be the oldest extant redactions (ca. 300 B.C.E.). Comparison between the received versions of the *Lao Zi* and the manuscripts from Mawangdui and Guodian reveal that the text underwent significant changes over the centuries. We can no longer speak simply of the *Lao Zi* as a monolithic scripture; we must always specify which edition we are using and take into account the many variant readings that we now possess.

Furthermore, recently discovered works dealing with medicine and macrobiotics help us situate the *Lao Zi* in the intellectual milieu of the mid to late Warring States period. It is evident that the author or authors of the *Lao Zi* were aware of this newly recovered technical literature and frequently alluded to its practices. For example, the "bellows" in *Lao Zi* 5 (see below) must be interpreted in the context of manuals on breath control that liken the space between the mouth and the anus to a bellows through which one can pump air. Similarly, the recurring motif of "playing the part of the female" (e.g., sections 10 and 61) may be understood as a reference to sexual practices designed to promote health and longevity.

Finally, current research has demonstrated that the *Lao Zi* did not emerge ex nihilo, but represents the most celebrated example of a philosophical tradition stretching back to even earlier times. *The Internal Enterprise (Neiye,* translated below), a chapter of an ancient miscellany called *Master Guan (Guan Zi),* is a mystical text describing techniques of meditation and breath control that aim to provide the practitioner with a more intimate knowledge of the Way. It is demonstrably older than the *Lao Zi* and is clearly one of the sources of the conception of the Way in the latter text. *The Internal Enterprise* has been known for centuries as a manual of physical self-cultivation, but its relation to the *Lao Zi* has only recently been appreciated.

The philosophy of the *Lao Zi* is distinctive yet deliberately vague. As we are told at the very beginning, the eternal Way cannot be explained in words; moreover, it cannot be perceived by our corporeal sense organs, but if we know where and how to sense it, we realize that the Way is everywhere. This is part of the difficulty involved in interpreting the book: it attempts to convey an idea that it concedes one cannot convey in language. Another major idea of the work is that masculinity, firmness, and other commonly prized attributes are actually signs of failure and decrepitude. We must pattern ourselves after the Way, which is like water: formless, yielding, and therefore capable of filling any space and passing through any crevice. Consequently, we must try to make ourselves soft and supple like a baby, the embodiment of vitality. The *Lao Zi* also expresses its characteristic skepticism of Confucian virtues, which it sees as artificial constructs that oppose nature. The ideal society, as the *Lao Zi* depicts it, is one where the inhabitants live naturally and harmoniously, in spontaneous accord with the Way of the universe. The sage ruler "hollows their hearts, stuffs their stomachs, weakens their wills, builds up their bones" (section 3)—banishing from their minds all considerations of competition and profit seeking.

The following selections include excerpts from *The Internal Enterprise* and the *Lao Zi* (Mawang-dui recension).—PRG

The Internal Enterprise [Excerpts]

The vital essence of all creatures—
it is this that endows them with life.
Below, it gives birth to the five grains;
above, it creates the arrayed stars.
When it flows between Heaven and Earth,
it is called "ghostly" and "spirit-like."
Those who store it within their breasts
are called "Sages." . . .

As a rule, the form of the mind[2]
is naturally filled and pregnant [with *qi*];
it is naturally born [of *qi*] and naturally completed by it.
What causes [a sound mind] to be lost
must be worry, joy, happiness, anger, desire, and profit-seeking.
If one can eliminate worry, joy, happiness, anger, desire, and profit-seeking,
the mind will return to equanimity.
The condition of the mind
is such that it is benefited by peace and quiet.
Do not importune it; do not disturb it.
Then harmony will be naturally complete. . . .

The Way is what fills one's body,
but people cannot consolidate it [within themselves].
It goes and does not return;
it comes but does not stay.
It is silent! None can hear its tones.
It is urgent! Thus it is present in the mind.
It is obscure! One cannot see its form.
It is torrential! It lives together with us.
One does not see its form;
one does not hear its sound;
but there is an order to its fulfillment.
It is called "the Way."

The Way has no location;
in an adept mind—there it resides.
If the mind is tranquil and the *qi* patterned,

the Way can come to rest [within one].
The Way is not distant;
people are procreated when it is attained.
The Way does not separate itself [from us];
people rely on it for harmony.
Therefore:
It is urgent, as though one could be bound by it!
It is vast, as though inexhaustibly without location!
How could the condition of the Way
be such that it [possessed] tones and sounds?
If you cultivate your mind and still your tones,
the Way can be attained.[3]

The Way
is what the mouth cannot speak,
what the eyes cannot see,
what the ears cannot hear;
it is what one uses to cultivate one's mind and rectify one's body.
People die if they lose it,
and live if they attain it.
Undertakings fail if they lose it,
and succeed if they attain it.
Whatever is the Way has no root or stalk,
no leaves or flowers.
The Myriad Creatures are born by it;
The Myriad Creatures are completed by it.
It is named "the Way."

Only after one is able to be rectified and tranquil
is one able to be settled.
With a settled mind within,
the ears and eyes will be keen of hearing and keen of sight;
the four limbs will be firm and solid,
and [one's body] can be a lodging place for vital essence.
Vital essence is the refined essence of *qi*.
If the *qi* is guided, there is life;
if there is life, there are thoughts;
if there are thoughts, there is knowledge;
if there is knowledge, stop.
As a rule, the form of the mind
loses its life if it knows too much.

One who can transform to be at one with things is called "spirit-like."
One who can change to be at one with affairs is called "wise."
To transform without altering the *qi* and to change without altering wisdom—
only a Noble Man who grasps the One can do this!
By grasping the One and not losing it,
one can be a lord to the Myriad Things.

The Noble Man employs things
and is not employed by things.
This is the principle of attaining the One. . . .

When vital essence is preserved and naturally born [within people],
their exterior is peaceful and lustrous.
They store it within themselves as a spring, as a source.
Expansive, it is placid and calm;
they use it as a reservoir of *qi*.
If the reservoir is not drained,
the four limbs will be solid.
If the spring is not exhausted,
[vital essence] will pass freely through the nine apertures.[4]
Then one can go to the limit of Heaven and Earth
and cover the four seas.
Within, there will be no deluded ideas;
without, there will be no abnormalities or injuries.
Those whose minds are pristine within,
and whose bodies are pristine without,
who do not meet with natural disaster,
who do not encounter man-made destruction,
are called "Sages." . . .

Whatever is the Way
must be universal, must be mysterious,
must be broad, must be easy,
must be firm, must be solid.
Maintain goodness and do not let go of it.
Chase away overflowing and meagerness.
When you know the extremes,
you will return to the Way and its power.

—PRG

The Classic Book of Integrity and the Way [Excerpts]

1. The ways that can be walked are not the eternal Way;
The names that can be named are not the eternal name.
The nameless is the origin of the myriad creatures;
The named is the mother of the myriad creatures.

Therefore,
    Always be without desire
        in order to observe its wondrous subtleties;
    Always have desire
        so that you may observe its manifestations.
    Both of these derive from the same source;
    They have different names but the same designation.

Mystery of mysteries,
The gate of all wonders!

3. Not exalting men of worth
    prevents the people from competing;
Not putting high value on rare goods
    prevents the people from being bandits;
Not displaying objects of desire
    prevents the people from being disorderly.

For these reasons,
    The sage, in ruling,
            hollows their hearts,
            stuffs their stomachs,
            weakens their wills,
            builds up their bones,
    Always causing the people
            to be without knowledge and desire.
    He ensures that
            the knowledgeable dare not be hostile,
                    and that is all.

Thus,
    His rule is universal.

5. Heaven and earth are inhumane;
    they view the myriad creatures as straw dogs.
The sage is inhumane;
    he views the common people as straw dogs.

The space between heaven and earth,
    how like a bellows it is!
Empty but never exhausted,
The more it pumps, the more comes out.

Hearing too much leads to utter exhaustion;
Better to remain in the center.

6. The valley spirit never dies—
    it is called "the mysterious female";
The gate of the mysterious female
    is called "the root of heaven and earth."
Gossamer it is,
    seemingly insubstantial,
    yet never consumed through use.

10. While you
    Cultivate the soul and embrace unity,
            can you keep them from separating?
    Focus your vital breath until it is supremely soft,
            can you be like a baby?

Cleanse the mirror of mysteries,
    can you make it free of blemish?
Love the people and enliven the state,
    can you do so without cunning?
Open and close the gate of heaven,
    can you play the part of the female?
Reach out with clarity in all directions,
    can you refrain from action?

It gives birth to them and nurtures them,
It gives birth to them but does not possess them,
It rears them but does not control them.
    This is called "mysterious integrity."

11.   Thirty spokes converge on a single hub,
        but it is in the space where there is nothing
            that the usefulness of the cart lies.
    Clay is molded to make a pot,
        but it is in the space where there is nothing
            that the usefulness of the clay pot lies.
    Cut out doors and windows to make a room,
        but it is in the spaces where there is nothing
            that the usefulness of the room lies.
Therefore,
    Benefit may be derived from something,
        but it is in nothing that we find usefulness.

25. There was something featureless yet complete,
    born before heaven and earth;
Silent—amorphous—
    it stood alone and unchanging.

We may regard it as the mother of heaven and earth.
Not knowing its name,
    I style it the "Way."
If forced to give it a name,
    I would call it "great."
Being great implies flowing ever onward,
Flowing ever onward implies far-reaching,
Far-reaching implies reversal.

The Way is great,
Heaven is great,
Earth is great,
The king, too, is great.

Within the realm there are four greats,
    and the king is one among them.

Man
>   patterns himself on earth,

Earth
>   patterns itself on heaven,

Heaven
>   patterns itself on the Way,

The Way
>   patterns itself on nature.

28. Know masculinity,
Maintain femininity,
>   and be a ravine for all under heaven.

By being a ravine for all under heaven,
Eternal integrity will never desert you.
If eternal integrity never deserts you,
You will return to the state of infancy.

Know you are innocent,
Remain steadfast when insulted,
>   and be a valley for all under heaven.

By being a valley for all under heaven,
Eternal integrity will suffice.
If eternal integrity suffices,
You will return to the simplicity of the unhewn log.

Know whiteness,
Maintain blackness,
>   and be a model for all under heaven.

By being a model for all under heaven,
Eternal integrity will not err.
If eternal integrity does not err,
You will return to infinity.

When the unhewn log is sawn apart,
>   it is made into tools;

When the sage is put to use,
>   he becomes the chief of officials.

For
>   Great Carving does no cutting.

43. The softest thing under heaven
>   gallops triumphantly over

The hardest thing under heaven.

Nonbeing penetrates nonspace.
Hence,
>   I know the advantages of nonaction.

The doctrine without words,
The advantages of nonaction—
> few under heaven can realize these!

55. He who embodies the fullness of integrity
> is like a ruddy infant.

Wasps, spiders, scorpions, and snakes
> will not sting or bite him;
Rapacious birds and fierce beasts
> will not seize him.

His bones are weak and his sinews soft,
> yet his grip is tight.
He knows not the joining of male and female,
> yet his penis is aroused.
His essence has reached a peak.

He screams the whole day without being hoarse;
His harmony has reached perfection.

Harmony implies constancy;
Constancy requires insight.

Striving to increase one's life is ominous;
To control the vital breath with one's mind entails force.

Something that grows old while still in its prime
> is said to be not in accord with the Way;
Not being in accord with the Way
> leads to an early demise.

61. A large state is like a low-lying estuary,
> the female of all under heaven.
In the congress of all under heaven,
> the female always conquers the male through her stillness.
Because she is still,
> it is fitting for her to lie low.
By lying beneath a small state,
> a large state can take over a small state.
By lying beneath a large state,
> a small state can be taken over by a large state.

Therefore,
> One may either take over or be taken over by lying low.

Therefore,
> The large state wishes only to annex and nurture others;
> The small state wants only to join with and serve others.

Now,

> Since both get what they want,
> It is fitting for the large state to lie low.

80. Let there be a small state with few people,
> where military devices find no use;
Let the people look solemnly upon death,
> and banish the thought of moving elsewhere.

They may have carts and boats,
> but there is no reason to ride them;
They may have armor and weapons,
> but they have no reason to display them.

Let the people go back to tying knots
> to keep records.
Let their food be savory,
> their clothes beautiful,
> their customs pleasurable,
> their dwellings secure.

Though they may gaze across at a neighboring state,
> and hear the sounds of its dogs and chickens,
The people will never travel back and forth,
> till they die of old age.

—VHM

Notes

1. Like Mawangdui (near Changsha, Hunan Province), Guodian (Jingmen, Hubei Province) was part of the ancient Chu Culture sphere.

2. Commentators disagree as to the meaning of this phrase.

3. The text asserts that the Way is fundamentally silent and that we should imitate this condition.

4. The two eyes, the two ears, the two nostrils, the mouth, the anus, and the vagina or opening of the penis.

THE ANCIENT TEXT most often associated with the *Lao Zi* is the *Zhuang Zi (Master Zhuang)*, named after and attributed to Zhuang Zhou (d. ca. 320 B.C.E.). The two works are often called the foundations of Taoism (or "philosophical Taoism"), an intellectual category that is rarely defined and best avoided. It is true that the understanding of the Way in the *Zhuang Zi* is compatible with that of the *Lao Zi*—and the *Zhuang Zi* may even surpass the *Lao Zi* in the sheer glee with which it denigrates and ridicules the Confucian tradition. (In the famous anecdote in chapter 26, for example, the *Zhuang Zi* suggests that by quoting right and left from their canonical scriptures, the Confucians try to justify and gloss over all manner of unscrupulous activities, including grave-robbing.) The *Zhuang Zi* refers to the figure of Lao Zi repeatedly and admiringly, and its doctrines of nonduality and the relativity of experience and knowledge (as related especially in chapter 2) are probably inspired by the *Lao Zi* tradition.

However, the world view espoused by the *Zhuang Zi* is substantially different from that of the *Lao Zi*. Whereas the *Lao Zi,* as we have seen, tries to apply its cosmological speculations to the problem of government on earth, the *Zhuang Zi* is typically suspicious of *all* political philosophy and recommends that we simply distance ourselves from the tumultuous world of statecraft and administration. Moreover, the literary style of the *Zhuang Zi* is unique. While it includes some metaphysical musings reminiscent of the *Lao Zi,* most of the *Zhuang Zi* is made up of incisive anecdotes and discussions between fabulous characters, all composed in a skillful mixture of poetry and prose. Many of these stories are intentionally amusing, and all are decidedly fantastical; while some of the personages appearing in the text are known from history (such as Confucius and his disciples, Zhuang Zhou's friend Hui Shi, and Zhuang Zhou himself), the tales about them are hardly to be taken as factual.

We know virtually nothing about Zhuang Zhou, except what is told about him in the *Zhuang Zi.* His boon friend Hui Shi, or Master Hui, was the author of a famous set of ten paradoxes, which are translated and examined in the next selection. Although Zhuang Zhou does not seem to have subscribed to Hui Shi's philosophical outlook, he clearly enjoyed debating with him, and after Hui Shi's death is said to have mourned the loss of his only significant interlocutor (chapter 24).

Modern scholarship has demonstrated convincingly that the *Zhuang Zi* is the product of several hands. Although the precise details are disputed, most specialists today agree that the so-called "Inner Chapters" (chapters 1–7) are closer to Zhuang Zhou's original oeuvre and that the "Outer Chapters" (chapters 8–22) and "Mixed Chapters" (chapters 23–33) are works of disciples and later writers influenced by Zhuang Zi's mode of thought. Nevertheless, taken as a whole, the book still represents a coherent statement, and materials from the later sections can often be used to help elucidate the more authentic "Inner Chapters." The passages on death in chapter 18, for example, square well with the story of the four gentlemen in chapter 6 and elaborate on the idea of the basic unity of life and death expounded in the earlier chapter.

The following selections include excerpts from all three divisions of the text, with an emphasis on the "Inner Chapters."—PRG

Zhuang Zi

1. Carefree Wandering

In the darkness of the Northern Ocean, there is a fish named Kun. The Kun is so big that no one knows how many thousands of tricents its body extends. After it metamorphoses into a bird, its name becomes Peng. The Peng is so huge that no one knows how many thousands of tricents its back stretches. Rousing itself to flight, its wings are like clouds suspended in the sky. When the seas stir, the Peng prepares for its journey to the Southern Ocean, the Lake of Heaven.

In the words of *The Drolleries of Qi,* a record of marvels, "On its journey to the Southern Ocean, the Peng beats the water with its wings for three thousand tricents, then it rises up on a whirlwind to a height of ninety thousand tricents and travels on the jet streams of late summer."

There galloping gusts and motes of dust are blown about by the breath of living organisms. Is azure the true color of the sky? Or is the sky so distant that its farthest limits can never be reached? When the Peng looks down at the sky from above, it must appear just the same as when we look up. . . .

A cicada and a dovelet laughed at the Peng, saying, "Wings aflutter, we fly up until we land in an elm or a dalbergia tree. Sometimes, when we don't make it, we just fall back to the ground and that's that. What's the use of flying up ninety thousand tricents to go south?"

If you're going on an outing to the verdant suburbs you only need to take along three meals and you'll still come back with a full stomach. If you're traveling a hundred tricents, you need to husk enough grain for an overnight stay. But if you're journeying a thousand tricents, you've got to set aside three months' worth of grain. What do these two creatures know?

Small knowledge is no match for great knowledge, nor is a short life span a match for a long one. How do we know this is so? The mushroom that sprouts in the morning and dies by the evening doesn't know the difference between night and day. The locust doesn't know the difference between spring and autumn. These are examples of short life spans. In the southern part of the state of Chu, there is a tortoise called Dark Spirit for whom spring and autumn each last five hundred years. In high antiquity, there was a large cedrela tree for which spring and autumn each lasted eight thousand years. These are examples of long life spans. Nowadays Progenitor Peng[1] is famous for his more than seven hundred years of longevity. Isn't it pathetic that people try to emulate him?

A question put by Tang, the first emperor of the Shang dynasty, to his wise minister Ji is similar. Tang asked, "Do up, down, and the four directions have a limit?"

"Beyond their limitlessness there is another limitlessness," said Ji. "In the barren north there is a dark sea, the Lake of Heaven. In the sea there is a fish named Kun that is several thousand tricents in breadth, but no one knows its length. There is also a bird named Peng whose back is like Mount Tai and whose wings are like clouds suspended in the sky. It rises upon a twisting whirlwind to a height of ninety thousand tricents, pierces the clouds and then heads south on its journey to the distant Southern Ocean with the blue sky touching its back.

"A marsh sparrow laughs at the Peng, saying, 'Where does he think he's going? I spring up into the air and come back down after not much more than a few yards. Flitting about amidst the bushes and brambles, this is the ultimate in flying! So where does he think he's going?'

"This shows the difference between the great and the small."

Master Hui said to Master Zhuang, "The king of Wei presented me with the seeds of a large gourd. I planted them and they grew to bear a fruit that could hold five bushels. I filled the gourd with liquid, but its walls were not strong enough for me to pick it up. I split the gourd into ladles, but their curvature was so slight they wouldn't hold anything. Although the gourd was admittedly of huge capacity, I smashed it into bits because it was useless."

"Sir," said Master Zhuang, "it's you who were obtuse about utilizing its bigness. There was a man of Song who was good at making an ointment for chapped hands. For generations, the family occupation had been to wash silk floss. A stranger who heard about the ointment offered him a hundred pieces of gold for the formula. The man of Song gathered his clan together and said to them, 'We have been washing silk floss for generations and have earned no more than a few pieces of gold. Now we'll make a hundred pieces of gold in one morning if we sell the technique. Please let me give it to the stranger.' After the stranger obtained the formula, he persuaded the king of Ngwa of its usefulness. Viet embarked on hostilities against Ngwa, so the king of Ngwa appointed the stranger to the command of his fleet. That winter, he fought a naval battle with the forces of Viet and totally defeated them (because his sailors' hands didn't get chapped). The king set aside a portion of land and enfeoffed him there.

"The ability to prevent chapped hands was the same, but one person gained a fief with it while the other couldn't even free himself from washing floss. This is because the uses to which the ointment was put were different. Now you, sir, had a five-bushel gourd. Why didn't you think of tying it on your waist as a big buoy so that you could go floating on the lakes and rivers instead of worrying that it couldn't hold anything because of its shallow curvature? This shows, sir, that you still have brambles for brains!" . . .

2. On the Equality of Things

Speech is not merely blowing of air. Speech is intended to say something, but what is spoken may not necessarily be valid. If it is not valid, has anything actually been spoken? Or has speech never actually occurred? We may consider speech to be distinct from the chirps of hatchlings, but is there really any difference between them?

How has the Way become so obscured that there are true and false? How has speech become so obscured that there are right and wrong? Could it be that the Way has gone off and is no longer present? Could it be that speech is present but has lost its ability to validate? The Way is obscured by partial achievements; speech is obscured by eloquent verbiage. Thus there are controversies between Confucians and Mohists over what's right and what's wrong. They invariably affirm what their opponents deny and deny what their opponents affirm. If one wishes to affirm what others deny and deny what others affirm, nothing is better than lucidity.

Everything is "that" in relation to other things and "this" in relation to itself. We may not be able to see things from the standpoint of "that," but we can understand them from the standpoint of "this." Therefore, it may be said that "that" derives from "this" and that "this" is dependent upon "that." Such is the notion of the cogenesis of "this" and "that." Nonetheless, from the moment of birth death begins simultaneously, and from the moment of death birth begins simultaneously. Every affirmation is a denial of something else, and every denial is an affirmation of something else. "This" and "that" are mutually dependent; right and wrong are also mutually dependent. For this reason, the sage does not subscribe to [the view of absolute opposites] but sees things in the light of nature, accepting "this" for what it is.

"This" is also "that"; "that" is also "this." "This" implies a concept of right and wrong; "that" also implies a concept of right and wrong. But is there really a "this" and a "that"? Or is there really no "this" and no "that"? Where "this" and "that" cease to be opposites, there lies the pivot of the Way. Only when the pivot is located in the center of the circle of things can we respond to their infinite transformations. The transformations of "right" are infinite and so are the transformations of "wrong." Therefore, it is said that nothing is better for responding to them than lucidity. . . .

Gnaw Gap inquired of Princely Scion, "Do you know wherein all things agree?"

"How could I know that?"

"Do you know what you don't know?"

"How could I know that?"

"Well, then, is it possible to know anything at all?"

"How could I know that? Nonetheless, I'll try to say something about it. How can we know that what I call knowledge is not really ignorance? How can we know that what I call ignorance is not really knowledge? But let me try to ask you a few questions. If people sleep in damp places, they develop lumbago or even partial paralysis. But would the same thing happen if a loach did so? If people dwell in trees, they will tremble with vertigo. But would the same thing happen if a gibbon did so? Of these three, which knows the proper place to dwell? People eat meat, deer eat grass, giant centipedes savor snakes, hawks and crows relish mice. Of these four, which knows the proper food to eat? Gibbons go for gibbons, buck mates with doe, loaches cavort with fish. Mao Qiang and Xi Shi[2] were considered by men to be beautiful, but if fish took one look at them they would dive into the depths, if birds saw them they would fly high into the sky, if deer saw them they would run away pell-mell. Of these four, which knows the correct standard of beauty for all under heaven? As I see it, the principle of humaneness and righteousness, the paths of right and wrong, are inextricably confused. How could I be able to distinguish among them?"

"If you," asked Gnaw Gap, "do not know the difference between benefit and harm, does the ultimate man likewise not know the difference between them?"

"The ultimate man is spiritous," said Princely Scion. "If the great marshes were set on fire, he would not feel hot. If the rivers turned to ice, he would not feel cold. If violent thunder split the mountains, he would not be injured. If whirlwinds lashed the seas, he would not be frightened. Such being the case, he rides the clouds, mounts the sun and moon, and wanders beyond the four seas. Since not even life and death have any transforming effect upon him, how much less so do benefit and harm?" . . .

3. Essentials for Nurturing Life

A cook was cutting up an ox for Lord Wenhui.
    Wherever

His hand touched,
His shoulder leaned,
His foot stepped,
His knee nudged,

the flesh would fall away with a swishing sound. Each slice of the cleaver was right in tune, zip zap! He danced in rhythm to "The Mulberry Grove," moved in concert with the strains of "The Managing Chief."

"Ah, wonderful," said Lord Wenhui, "that skill can attain such heights!"

The cook put down his cleaver and responded, "What your servant loves is the Way, which goes beyond mere skill. When I first began to cut oxen, what I saw was nothing but whole oxen. After three years, I no longer saw whole oxen. Today, I meet the ox with my spirit rather than looking at it with my eyes. My sense organs stop functioning and my spirit moves as it pleases. In accord with the natural grain, I slice at the great crevices, lead the blade through the great cavities. Following its inherent structure, I never encounter the slightest obstacle even where the veins and arteries come together or where the ligaments and tendons join, much less from obvious big bones. A good cook changes his cleaver once a year because he chops. An ordinary cook changes his cleaver once a month because he hacks. Now I've been using my cleaver for nineteen years and have cut up thousands of oxen with it, but the blade is still as fresh as though it had just come from the grindstone. Between the joints there are spaces, but the edge of the blade has no thickness. Since I am inserting something without any thickness into an empty space, there will certainly be lots of room for the blade to play around in. That's why the blade is still as fresh as though it had just come from the grindstone. Nonetheless, whenever I come to a complicated spot and see that it will be difficult to handle, I cautiously restrain myself, focus my vision, and slow my motion. With an imperceptible movement of the cleaver, plop! and the flesh is already separated, like a clump of earth collapsing to the ground. I stand there holding the cleaver in my hand, look all around me with complacent satisfaction, then I wipe off the cleaver and store it away."

"Wonderful!" said Lord Wenhui. "From hearing the words of the cook, I have learned how to nourish life." . . .

Sir Motley of Southunc made an excursion to the Hillock of Shang. There he saw an unusual tree so big that a thousand four-horse chariots could be shaded by its leaves.

"Goodness! What tree is this?" asked Sir Motley. "It must have unusual timber." Looking upward at the smaller branches, however, he saw that they were all twisted and unfit to be beams. Looking downward at the massive trunk, he saw that it was so gnarled as to be unfit for making coffins. If you lick one of its leaves, your mouth will develop ulcerous sores. If you smell its foliage, you fall into a drunken delirium that lasts for three days.

"This tree is truly worthless," said Sir Motley, "and that is why it has grown so large. Ah! The spiritual man is also worthless like this." . . .

Scattered Apart's chin was buried in his belly button, his shoulders were higher than the crown of his head, his cervical vertebrae pointed toward the sky, the five dorsal inductories were all up on top, and his thighbones were positioned like a couple of extra ribs. By sewing and washing clothes, he earned enough to make ends meet. By sifting grain with a winnowing-fan, he could make enough to feed ten people. When the authorities came to conscript soldiers, Scattered would wander about among them flailing his arms. When the authorities organized a massive labor project, Scattered would be excused because of his congenital defects. When the authorities handed out grain to the sick, he would receive three bags plus ten bundles of firewood. Though his body was scattered, it was sufficient to enable him to support himself and to live out the years allotted to him by heaven. How much more could someone whose virtue is scattered! . . .

6. The Great Ancestral Teacher

Sir Sacrifice, Sir Chariot, Sir Plow, and Sir Come were all four talking together. "Whoever can take nonbeing as his head, life as his spine, and death as his buttocks, whoever knows the oneness of life and death, of existence and nonexistence, we shall be his friends." The four men looked at each other and smiled. Since there was no discord in their hearts, they became friends with each other.

Before long, Sir Chariot fell ill. When Sir Sacrifice went to call on him, Sir Chariot said, "Great is the Creator of Things! She's making me all crookedy like this!" His back was all hunched up. On top were his five dorsal inductories. His chin was buried in his bellybutton. His shoulders were higher than the crown of his head. His neck bones pointed toward the sky. His vital yin and yang breaths were all out of kilter. Yet his mind was at ease, as though nothing were amiss. He hobbled over to a well and looked at his reflection in the water. "Alas!" he said. "The Creator of Things is making me all crookedy like this!"

"Do you resent it?" asked Sir Sacrifice.

"No, why should I resent it? Suppose that my left arm were transformed into a chicken; I would consequently go looking for a rooster that could call out the hours of the night. Supposing that my right arm were transformed into a crossbow; I would consequently go looking for an owl to roast. Supposing that my buttocks were transformed into wheels and my spirit into a horse; I would consequently mount upon them. What need would I have for any other conveyance?

"Furthermore, what we attain is due to timeliness and what we lose is the result of compliance. If we repose in timeliness and dwell in compliance, sorrow and joy cannot affect us. This is what the ancients called 'emancipation.' Those who are unable to win release for themselves are bound by things. Furthermore, long has it been that things do not win out against heaven. So why should I regret it?"

Before long, Sir Come fell ill. Gasping and on the verge of death, he was surrounded by his wife and children who were weeping. Sir Plow, who went to call on him, said to his family, "Shush! Go away! Do not disturb his transformation!" Then, leaning against the door, he spoke to Sir Come: "Great is the Transforming Creator! What next will he make of you? Where will he send you? Will he turn you into a rat's liver? Will he turn you into a bug's leg?" . . .

7. Responses for Emperors and Kings

The emperor of the Southern Sea was Lickety, the emperor of the Northern Sea was Split, and the emperor of the Center was Wonton. Lickety and Split often met each other in the land of Wonton, and Wonton treated them very well. Wanting to repay Wonton's kindness, Lickety and Split said, "All people have seven holes for seeing, hearing, eating, and breathing. Wonton alone lacks them. Let's try boring some holes for him." So every day they bored one hole, and on the seventh day Wonton died. . . .

13. The Way of Heaven

Duke Huan was reading in the upper part of the hall and Wheelwright Flat was hewing a wheel in the lower part. Setting aside his hammer and chisel, the wheelwright went to the upper part of the hall and inquired of Duke Huan, saying, "I venture to ask what words Your Highness is reading?"

"The words of the sages," said the duke.

"Are the sages still alive?"

"They're already dead," said the duke.

"Then what my lord is reading is merely the dregs of the ancients."

"How can you, a wheelwright, comment upon what I am reading?" asked Duke Huan. "If you can explain yourself, all right. If you cannot explain yourself, you shall die."

"I look at it from my own occupation," said Wheelwright Flat. "If the spokes are too loose, they'll fit sweet as a whistle but the wheel won't be solid. If they're too tight, you won't be able to insert them no matter how hard you try. To make them neither too loose nor too tight is something you sense in your hand and feel in your heart. There's a knack to it that can't be put into words. I haven't been able to teach it to my son, and my son hasn't been able to learn it from me. That's why I'm still hewing wheels after seventy years. When they died, the ancients took with them what they couldn't transmit. So what you are reading are the dregs of the ancients.". . .

17. Autumn Floods

Master Zhuang was fishing in the Pu River. The king of Chu dispatched two high-ranking officials to go before him with this message: "I wish to encumber you with the administration of my realm."

Without turning around, Master Zhuang just kept holding on to his fishing rod and said, "I have heard that in Chu there is a sacred tortoise that has already been dead for three thousand years.[3] The king stores it in his ancestral temple inside of a hamper wrapped with cloth. Do you think this tortoise would rather be dead and have its bones preserved as objects of veneration, or be alive and dragging its tail through the mud?"

"It would rather be alive and dragging its tail through the mud," said the two officials.

"Begone!" said Master Zhuang. "I'd rather be dragging my tail in the mud.". . .

Master Zhuang and Master Hui were strolling across the bridge over the Hao River. "The minnows have come out and are swimming so leisurely," said Master Zhuang. "This is the joy of fishes."

"You're not a fish," said Master Hui. "How do you know what the joy of fishes is?"

"You're not me," said Master Zhuang, "so how do you know that I don't know what the joy of fishes is?"

"I'm not you," said Master Hui, "so I certainly do not know what you do. But you're certainly not a fish, so it is irrefutable that you do not know what the joy of fishes is."

"Let's go back to where we started," said Master Zhuang. "When you said, 'How do you know what the joy of fishes is?' you asked me because you already knew that I knew. I know it by strolling over the Hao.". . .

18. Ultimate Joy

Master Zhuang's wife died. When Master Hui went to offer his condolences, he found Master Zhuang lolling on the floor with his legs sprawled out, beating a basin and singing.

"She lived together with you," said Master Hui, "raised your children, grew old, and died. It's enough that you do not wail for her, but isn't it a bit much for you to be beating on a basin and singing?"

"Not so," said Master Zhuang. "When she first died, how could I of all people not be melancholy? But I reflected on her beginning and realized that originally she was unborn. Not only was she unborn, originally she had no form. Not only did she have no form, originally she had no vital breath. Intermingling with nebulousness and blurriness, a transformation occurred and there was vital breath; the vital breath was transformed and there was form; the form was transformed and there was birth; now there has been another transformation and she is dead. This is like the progression of the four seasons—from spring to autumn, from winter to summer. There she sleeps blissfully in an enormous chamber. If I were to have followed her weeping and wailing, I think it would have been out of keeping with destiny, so I stopped.". . .

When Master Zhuang went to Chu, he saw an empty skull. Though brittle, it still retained its shape. Master Zhuang tapped the skull with his riding crop and asked, "Did you end up like this because of greed for life and loss of reason? Or was it because you were involved in some treasonous affair and had your head chopped off by an ax? Or was it because you were involved in some unsavory conduct, shamefully disgracing your parents, wife, and children? Or was it because you starved or froze? Or was it simply because your time was up?"

When he had finished with his questions, Master Zhuang picked up the skull and used it as a pillow when he went to sleep. At midnight, the skull appeared to him in a dream and said, "Your manner of talking makes you sound like a sophist. I perceive that what you mentioned are all burdens of the living. When you're dead, there's none of that. Would you like to hear me tell you about death, sir?"

"Yes," said Master Zhuang.

"When you're dead," said the skull, "there's no ruler above you and no subjects below you. There are no affairs of the four seasons; instead, time passes leisurely as it does for heaven and earth. Not even the joys of being a south-facing king[4] can surpass those of death."

Not believing the skull, Master Zhuang said, "If I were to have the Arbiter of Destiny[5] restore life to your physical form, to give you back your flesh, bones, and skin, to return you parents, wife, children, and village acquaintances, would you like that?"

Frowning in deep consternation, the skull said, "How could I abandon 'the joys of a south-facing king' and return to the toils of mankind?". . .

21. Sir Square Field

Lord Yuan of Song wished to have some charts drawn. A crowd of clerks arrived and, after receiving their instructions and bowing, they stood in line licking their brushes and mixing their ink. There were so many that half of them remained outside. There was one clerk who arrived late, casually and without hurrying. He received his instructions and bowed, but did not stand in line, returning instead to his dormitory. When the duke sent someone to look in on him, he was found half-naked, with his shirt off, sitting with his legs splayed out. "He will do," said the lord. "This is a true draftsman.". . .

24. Ghostless Xu

Master Zhuang was accompanying a funeral when he passed by the grave of Master Hui. Turning around, he said to his attendants, "There was a man from Ying who sent for carpenter Shi to slice off a speck of plaster like a fly's wing that had splattered the tip of his nose. Carpenter Shi whirled his ax so fast that it produced a wind. Letting the ax fall instinctively, he sliced off every last bit of the plaster but left the nose unharmed, while the man from Ying stood there without flinching. When Lord Yuan of Song heard about this, he summoned carpenter Shi and said, 'Try to do the same thing for me.' 'Your servant used to be able to slice off plaster like that,' said carpenter Shi, 'but my "chopping block" died long ago.' Since your death, Master Hui, I have had no one who can be my 'chopping block.' I have had no one with whom to talk.". . .

26. External Things

Some literati[6] were breaking open a grave mound in accordance with the *Odes* and the *Ritual*. The chief literatus shouted down to the others,

"The sun is rising in the east!
How is the affair getting on?"[7]
The lesser literati said,
"We haven't taken off his shirt and jacket yet,
But there's a pearl in his mouth."[8]

"Indeed, it is said in the *Odes:*

'The green, green wheat
Grows on the slopes of the tumulus.
While alive, he made no donations,
In death, why let him hold a pearl in his mouth?'

Grab hold of the hair on his temples and pull down on his beard. By tapping on his chin with a metal mallet, you should be able to open his jaws slowly, but don't damage the pearl in his mouth."

—VHM

Notes

1. Peng Zu, the Chinese Methuselah who lived in prehistoric times.
2. Fabled beauties of old.
3. Ostensibly, this "sacred tortoise" is an inscribed oracle bone that has been kept in the royal archives for centuries.
4. The ruler traditionally sat facing south.
5. The god controlling life and death.
6. I.e., Confucians.
7. The text imitates comically the style of the *Odes*. The alleged quote below is likewise obviously invented.
8. Presumably the pearl was intended to prevent the vital essence of the deceased from escaping through his mouth.

HUI SHI, THE renowned friend of Zhuang Zhou, is said to have disseminated ten interrelated paradoxes of great philosophical import. As they have survived today, and insofar as they can be understood without Hui Shi to explain them to us, the paradoxes seem to involve the consequences of infinite time and space. His sixth paradox ("The South has no limit but has a limit") is a good example: the southern quadrant of a map contains an infinite number of discrete points, but it is still strictly bounded and does not include every point on the map. The tenth paradox ("Let there be flowing love for the Myriad Things; Heaven and Earth are one body") is reminiscent of the Mohist dictate of "Universal Love," and there is reason to believe that Hui Shi not only was aware of recent developments within the Mohist school, but also was inspired by them. The important difference between Hui Shi's view and that of classical Mohism is that Hui Shi justifies his tenth paradox on ontological grounds, whereas the Mohist treatises, as we have seen, had argued for "Universal Love" by appealing to their characteristic utilitarianism. Hui Shi contends that Heaven and Earth are one body, and that we must love everything around us because every object is an equal component of the universe—not that we must practice "flowing love" because it should bring about the greatest good.

It was evidently fashionable in Hui Shi's day to suggest profound truths in the form of cryptic paradoxes. We are fortunate to possess a collection of later Mohist exercises that are apparently intended to help analyze the nature of such paradoxes by focusing on ambiguities of meaning in ordinary language. For example, "The fruit of the peach is the peach, but the fruit of the bramble is not the bramble": we can use the word "peach" to denote either the tree or its fruit (in modern English as in ancient Chinese), but the word "bramble" cannot be applied to the fruit of the bramble. These lighthearted etudes have one serious purpose: they show that if a crafty dialectician is allowed to use the same word in more than one sense, he can "deduce" a paradox that contradicts all common sense. It is a small step from the above observation about peaches and brambles to a falsidical paradox such as "Peaches are not fruit" (or "Peaches are not trees").

And contemporaries who were less scrupulous about observing logical principles took precisely this small step, producing such wild paradoxes as "Eggs have hair," "Tortoises are longer than snakes," and so forth. The solutions always lie in finding which term the sophist has used in an unexpected sense. Snakes are obviously longer than tortoises, but tortoises are longer than snakes with respect to their life spans. The tricky word is "long," which is ambiguous. This kind of wordplay may be fun, but it drew the ire of more sober philosophers who complained that the dialecticians were trivializing weighty philosophical issues and harming the dao by misusing language.—PRG

The Ten Paradoxes of Hui Shi

[1.] The greatest has nothing outside it; call it "Great Unity." The smallest has nothing inside it; call it "Small Unity."

[2.] Something without thickness cannot be accumulated, yet its size is a thousand tricents.[1]

[3.] Heaven is as low as Earth; mountains are as flat as swamps.

[4.] The sun is in the center and at an angle at the same time; creatures live and die at the same time.[2]

[5.] Being largely similar to, but different from, something that is slightly similar is called "small similarity and difference"; when the Myriad Things are completely similar and completely different, we call this "great similarity and difference."[3]

[6.] The South has no limit but has a limit.

[7.] Today I went to Yue but got there yesterday.

[8.] Linked rings can be loosed.

[9.] I know the center of the world: it is north of Yan and south of Yue.[4]

[10.] Let there be effusive love for the Myriad Things; Heaven and Earth are one body.

Some Later Mohist Paradoxes

Her younger brother is a handsome man, but loving her younger brother is not loving a handsome man.

A carriage is wood, but riding a carriage is not riding wood.

A boat is wood, but entering a boat is not entering wood.

Robbers are people, but having many robbers is not having many people, and having no robbers is not having no people.

Reading books is not books, but being fond of reading books is being fond of books.

Cockfights are not cocks, but being fond of cockfights is being fond of cocks.

Being about to fall into a well is not falling into a well, but stopping [someone] from being about to fall into a well is stopping [someone] from falling into a well.

The fruit of the peach is the peach, but the fruit of the bramble is not the bramble.

Asking about someone's illness is asking about the person, but disliking someone's illness is not disliking the person.

If this horse's eyes are blind, we call this horse "blind," but if this horse's eyes are big, we do not call this horse "big."

If this bull's hairs are yellow, we call this bull "yellow," but if this bull's hairs are many, we do not call this bull "many."

Some Paradoxes of Other Dialecticians

A white horse is not a horse.[5]

Eggs have hair.[6]

Dogs may be called sheep.[7]

Horses have eggs.

Frogs have tails.[8]

Fire is not hot.[9]

Eyes do not see.[10]

Tortoises are longer than snakes.

T-squares are not square; compasses cannot make circles.

The shadow of a flying bird has never moved.[11]

White dogs are black.[12]

If you have a foot-long stick, and remove half of it each day, in ten thousand generations it will not be exhausted.[13]

—PRG

Notes

1. This probably means that a two-dimensional plane can be infinitely large without having any thickness.

2. At the moment of high noon, the day begins to move into the afternoon; at the moment of birth, an organism begins to die.

3. This is probably the most difficult paradox to construe.

4. Yan is the northernmost state and Yue the southernmost.

5. Any kind of horse satisfies the requirement "horse," but only a white horse satisfies the requirement "white horse." So "white horse" is not the same thing as "horse."

6. Inside of an egg, there is hair (or feathers): the unhatched chick inside.

7. Dogs may be called whatever we like; if we define "sheep" to mean "dog," then we can call dogs "sheep."

8. Probably the idea is that frogs were once tadpoles.

9. According to the usual explanation of this paradox, fire produces heat but is not the same thing as heat.

10. Human beings see—with the aid of eyes.

11. At a given instant, a shadow is in a given place—and hence "not moving." Similar paradoxes are known from ancient Greece.

12. A white dog's eyes are black, so it is "black" in at least one respect. This idea is also explored in the later Mohist paradoxes, above.

13. This is actually a veridical paradox: a paradox based on sound reasoning that yields an unexpected result.

THE TERM "SHAMAN" is taken from the Tungusic word *šaman*, meaning literally "one who is aroused." The shaman is a member of a social group with special powers that allow him or her to act as a link to the spirit world. One characteristic feature of shamanism is the so-called "spirit voyage," in which the shaman's spirit temporarily leaves his or her body and travels—often with the aid of an animal familiar—to the unseen realm of the gods to negotiate with them on behalf of his or her people back home. It is also typical of shamans to serve as mediums who can be possessed by spirits or divinities and as faith healers (like the "medicine men" and *curanderas* of the Americas) who cure disease by banishing the evil influences that cause it.

Elements of shamanism can be found in religions all across the globe. Although the extent to which shamanism pervaded ancient Chinese religion is a matter of scholarly dispute, there can be little doubt that many communities relied on the unique talents of shamans for their quotidian spiritual needs. Indeed, shamans can be found throughout East and Southeast Asia to this day.

Some of our best evidence for shamanism in early China is found in the collection of poems known as the *Lyrics of Chu (Chuci)*. Many of these pieces contain depictions of spirit possession that were probably modeled after actual shamanic practices. In *Lyrics of Chu,* spirit possession is commonly conceived as hierogamic, with the union of the deity and his chosen shamaness portrayed in unmistakably erotic terms. Other poems in the anthology portray the spirit voyage as an ecstatic flight through the upper reaches of the empyrean.

However, while many of the motifs in *Lyrics of Chu* square well with shamanic rites as described by ethnographers who have observed them, it is important to remember that the poems are works of literature *inspired by* shamanism, and should not be taken as direct accounts of shamanic practices themselves. For example, a functioning shaman must always come back from his or her spirit voyage and report the disposition of the spirits to the awaiting community. By contrast, in "Distant Wandering," a poem in *Lyrics of Chu,* the explicitly stated goal of astral travel is to leave the "oppression and distress of the world today," never to return. So although the author has made liberal use of shamanic themes and imagery, we must not lose sight of the fact that "Distant Wandering" is an escapist work fundamentally incompatible with the structure and purposes of shamanic religion.

The aesthetic of spirit flight expressed so memorably in *Lyrics of Chu* came to inform the macrobiotic ideal of the "Transcendent" *(xian)* in late–Warring States and Han China. A "Transcendent" is a person who has learned how to halt the natural aging process and consequently enjoys eternity as an immortal, aloof from mundane society. Many of the manuals of techniques for attaining "Transcendence"—such as alchemical recipes for drugs of immortality—frequently describe the successful result in language that is manifestly derived from the classical depictions of spirit ascension in *Lyrics of Chu.*

Most of the poems in *Lyrics of Chu* are traditionally attributed to Qu Yuan (340?–278 B.C.E.), a legendary minister from Chu who supposedly committed righteous suicide after being spurned by his ruler. More recent research has demonstrated that the anthology includes pieces from various eras and has cast doubt on the historicity of the figure of Qu Yuan. But although we must probably accept the fact that we will never know the identity of the real authors of *Lyrics of Chu,* their anonymity does not diminish the literary and historical value of their poetry as an unparalleled source for shamanist aesthetics in ancient China.—PRG

The Eastern August Magnificent One[1]

Auspicious is the day, the hour good.
Respectfully we will please the Supreme August One.
Fondle the long sword, the jade hilt-ring.
The girdle gems chime and call out, *linlang.*
The *yao*-gem mats are laden with jade.
Why not take and hold the fragrance of the *qiong*-branch?
The melilotus and meat are presented on an orchid mat.
We offer cassia wine and pepper spirits.
Raise the drumstick and beat the drum
In broad and easy measures, a peaceful song.
They arrange in order the reed organs and zithers, the ocean of musicians.
The enchantress dances, with gorgeous robes.
The fragrance wafts in the air and fills the hall.
The Five Tones are mixed; luxuriously they combine.
The lord is rejoicing, happy and content.

The Lesser Administrator of Fate[2]

The autumn orchid and the *miwu*
grow in a carpet at the bottom of the hall.
The green leaves and white branches
have a fragrance that wafts and invades me.
The autumn orchids are blue,
with green leaves and purple stems.
The hall is filled with beauties.
Unexpectedly, his eyes fall entirely on me.
He enters me without a word, and exits without a farewell.
He rides back on the wind, his banners supported by the clouds.
No sorrow is more sorrowful than that of parting for the living.
No joy is more joyous than having someone new to know.
With a lotus robe and a melilotus belt
Quickly he comes and suddenly he departs.
In the evening he will lodge in the precincts of Di.
"Lord, whom are you awaiting at the edge of the clouds?
I will wander with you to the Nine Rivers.
The rushing wind arrives and the water raises waves.
I will bathe with you in Xian's pool.[3]
I will dry your hair on the bank of the sun."
I gaze at the Beautiful One, but he has not come.
Near the wild wind, I pour out my song.
With a peacock's canopy and a kingfisher's pennant,

He ascends the Nine Heavens and strokes the Broom Star.
Drawing up his long sword, he brings together young and old.
"Only you, Iris, are fit to be the ruler of the people."

Distant Wandering

Lamenting the oppression and distress of the world today,
I wish to rise up lightly and wander far away.
But my constitution is feeble and I have no means [to do so].
What carriage shall I commission so that I might float upward?
I have met with engulfing mire and foul stench.
I am lonely, depressed, and tied in knots—who is there to talk to?
At night I am restless and do not sleep.
My soul tosses anxiously until daybreak.
I think of the inexhaustibility of Heaven and Earth,
and mourn the long toil of human life.
Those who have gone before me—I cannot reach them;
those who will come after me—I will never hear of them.
I pace back and forth, agitated with longing.
I am sorrowful and frustrated, and yearn sulkily.
My thoughts, reckless and desultory, flow with abandon.
My heart is melancholy, with increasing lamentations.
Suddenly my spirit starts off and does not return.
My withered body alone remains.
I look inside myself to steady my self-control,
and seek the origin of *qi*.[4]
In vast emptiness and tranquility I will find calm and contentment.
In placid nonaction, I will attain myself.
I have heard how [Master] Red Pine[5] cleansed [the world] of dust;
I wish to be inspired by the standard that he left behind.
I pay homage to the blessed inner power of the Perfected Ones;
I admire the apotheosized Transcendents of past generations.[6]
Engaged in transformation, they departed and have not been seen,
but their name and reputation are manifest and have endured to latter days.
I marvel at how Fu Yue[7] commissioned the stars and constellations;
I am envious of Han Zhong's attainment of the One.[8]
Majestically, their bodies dissolved into the distance;
leaving the flock of humanity, they escaped.
They complied with the alterations of *qi* and then rose up.
Absconding suddenly, like a spirit, wondrously, like a ghost.
At times it seems as though they appear distantly,
their vital essence glimmering as they pass across [the sky].
They rid themselves of filth and dust and purged themselves of evil,
never to return to their old cities.
They have avoided the vexations of the multitudes and are not fearful.
None in this generation know their abode.
I fear the cyclical progression of the seasons.
The Splendid Numen[9] is radiant but marches westward.

I regret that before the fine frosts descend,
the fragrant herbs fall.
Oh, but to ramble and wander carefree,
for in this eternal succession of years I have accomplished nothing.
With whom can I enjoy this remaining fragrance [within me]?
Long have I faced the winds, unfurling my emotions.
Gaoyang[10] is remote and distant.
What shall I take as a pattern for myself?
I say again,[11] Springs become autumns—will they not tarry?
How can I remain for long in my old dwelling?
I cannot climb to [the position] of Xuanyuan,[12]
so I will follow Royal Qiao[13] and sport with him.
I dine on the Six Vapors and drink midnight dew;
I gargle with absolute yang and hold the morning mist in my mouth.
I conserve the purity of my spirit illumination,[14]
taking in the refined *qi* and expelling the rough contaminants.
Wandering along with the gentle winds,
I arrive at Chao in the south in a single breath.[15]
I see the Royal Son and lodge with him,
inquiring about the harmonious inner power [that comes of] unifying one's *qi*.
He says, "The Way can be received; it cannot be transmitted.
In its smallness, there is nothing inside it;
in its largeness, it has no boundaries.
Do not confuse your soul, and it will [arrive] spontaneously.
Unify your *qi* and increase your spirit,
visualizing them at midnight.
Await it with emptiness;
do not act before it.
All categories are completed by it:
this is the Gateway of Power."
Having heard this supremely valuable [teaching], I go,
and swiftly I resume my voyage.
I meet the feathered people at Cinnabar Hill,[16]
sojourning in the old home of immortality.
In the morning I wash my hair in the Valley of the Sun;
in the evening I dry myself in the ninefold sun.
I suck in the subtle liquor of the Flying Spring
and hold to my breast the florid luxuriance of the *wanyan*-jewel.
My countenance is lustrous like sericeous jade.
My refined essence is unadulterated and begins to grow strong.
My body melts, becoming soft and supple;
my spirit becomes *yaomiao*,[17] flowing freely.
Excellent, the fiery power of the southern regions!
Beautiful, the cassia trees that bloom even in the winter!
The mountains are desolate, without fauna;
the wilderness is vacuous and unpopulated.
While governing my soul and ascending the mists,
I seize hold of a floating cloud and go upward.

I command the ostiary of Heaven to open the gates.
Let him clear the *changhe*-gates,[18] expecting me.
I summon Fenglong[19] and make him lead the way,
asking for the dwelling of Great Subtlety.[20]
Collecting redoubled yang, I enter the palace of Di.
I advance to the Week Star and observe the Pure City.[21]
The next morning, I undo the wheel stops, setting out from Di's court;
not till evening do I approach the Yuweilü.[22]
I assemble my myriad chariots,
the tumultuous ocean of vehicles charging together.
I yoke eight undulating dragons [to my car],
bearing a flapping cloud banner.
I set up a male rainbow-monster as a colorful tail-banner,
its five colors intermingling and glittering.
The yoke-horses boldly raise and lower [their heads];
the trace-horses curl their hooves proudly.
The animals start wildly in confused disorder
as we divide into lines and begin to go.
I take up my reins and adjust the whip.
I will pass by Goumang,[23]
turning right to traverse [the realm of] the Great Luminance.[24]
I send ahead Feilian[25] to clear the path.
The sun is glistening but not yet radiant
as we ferry directly along the horizon.
The Earl of Wind gallops ahead of us;
dust and filth are cleared away, making [us] clean and refreshed.
Phoenixes form our flank, raising aloft our standards.
We come upon Rushou[26] in the Western Empyrean.
I grasp the Broom Star to use as a pennant;
I raise up the Dipper's Handle to use as a signal flag.
Winding and gleaming, we go up and down,
wandering amid the flowing waves of the rushing fog.
As it becomes dark and tenebrous,
I summon the Dark Warrior[27] to fly in our party.
Then I order Wenchang[28] to manage the procession;
I select the bureaucracy of spirits to join our naves.[29]
The road extends, lengthy and distant.
We move slowly, now haltingly, on our lofty journey.
The Master of Rains I send to the left as an upright attendant;
the Duke of Thunder I send to the right as my bodyguard.
I desire to cross into the next world and forget about returning.
My thoughts are unrestrained and vehement.
Within, I am cheerful and self-satisfied.
I [want] only to amuse myself and be joyous.
Fording the azure clouds and wandering randomly,
suddenly I approach and glance at my old home.
The groom feels it in his bosom and my heart laments;
the trace-horses look back and do not move.

I think of my old residence, images of it in my mind.
With a long sigh, I conceal my tears.
I ramble effusively and rise up still further.
I curb my will and restrain myself.
I point to the Fiery Spirit and charge straight toward him.
I will go to Yi[30] in the south.
I gaze at the barrenness beyond the world.
Abundant are the massive waters as I float over them.
Zhurong warns me to turn my yokes back.[31]
Soaring, I tell my *luan*-phoenixes to invite Fufei.[32]
She arranged to play "The Lake of Unity" and struck the rhythm to "Supporting the Clouds."
The Two Girls present songs from the "Ninefold Shao."[33]
I have the nymphs of the Xiang River[34] play their drums and cithers.
I command Ruo of the Sea to dance with Fengyi.[35]
Black krakens and aquatic monsters come out and advance in unison,
their bodies twisting and wriggling.
Female rainbow-monsters bend lithely;
volant *luan*-phoenixes fly overhead.
The music spreads broadly, without end or limit,
whereupon we depart and [resume] our roaming.
Losing order in our ranks, we charge and speed ahead.
We travel to the Absolute Boundary by the Gate of Cold.[36]
We race neck-and-neck with the swift winds to the Clear Source.[37]
We follow Zhuanxu to the swelling ice,
passing athwart Mysterious Obscurity.[38]
Levitating to the frontiers of the universe, I turn to look back.
I summon Qianlei[39] for an audience,
making him go in front of me to flatten the road.
I pass through the Four Wildernesses.
I flow around in the Six Directions.[40]
Above, I arrive at the Crack of Lightning;
I gaze down at the Great Gully.
Below, it is majestic, and there is no Earth.
Above, it is vast, and there is no Heaven.
I look, but quickly there is nothing to be seen.
In the agitated flurry, there is nothing to be heard.
I transcend Nonaction and arrive at Clarity.
I am a neighbor of the Magnificent Beginning.

—PRG

Notes

1. "Magnificent One" (Taiyi) is a well attested name of an ancient deity.
2. As in "The Eastern August Magnificent One," "The Lesser Administrator of Fate" (also called "Iris" below) is the name of the divinity invoked in this poem. As we have seen, the Administrator of Fate was an ancient god of life and death.

3. "Xian" is the name of a major deity. "Xian's Pool" may refer to a star.

4. The speaker, in other words, wishes to find the origin of the material universe.

5. Commentators all agree that Master Red Pine was an ancient immortal, but the various traditions concerning this figure are somewhat contradictory. According to one account, he was "Master of Rains" under the reign of the god known as the Divine Farmer.

6. The "Perfected Ones" and "Transcendents" are beings like Red Pine who learned how to become immortal.

7. An ancient counselor who turned into a star.

8. "Attaining the One" is a concept that we have encountered in *The Internal Enterprise* and *Lao Zi*. Not much is known about Han Zhong.

9. I.e., the sun, which sets in the west.

10. Otherwise known as Zhuanxu, an ancestral divinity.

11. These characters might also be an instruction of some kind for the musical accompaniment.

12. "Xuanyuan" is another name for the Yellow Emperor, a mythic ruler.

13. Royal Qiao (or Royal Son Qiao) was an heir apparent of Zhou who is said to have become a Transcendent.

14. "Spirit illumination" *(shenming)* is a religious term, used here to denote the speaker's physical vitality.

15. Or possibly, "and once there, rest." Chao in the South is rumored to be the dwelling place of the Royal Son Qiao.

16. The "feathered people" are other airy immortals. "Cinnabar Hill" is a fantastic name for a place where one would find such beings: cinnabar was often taken as a drug of immortality.

17. There are various definitions of *yaomiao:* "the appearance of being subtle"; "the appearance of being distant"; "beautiful." The word is probably onomatopoetic and untranslatable.

18. The gates of Heaven.

19. The god of clouds and rain.

20. The "dwelling of Great Subtlety" is a constellation where the god known as the "Magnificent One" resides.

21. The "Week Star" may be Venus; the "Pure City" is the palace of Di.

22. The "Yuweilü" (or simply "Weilü") is a mythic place in the east—either a mountain or a vortex in the Eastern Sea.

23. The god of the east.

24. The "Great Luminance" is a mythic ruler of the east.

25. The god of wind.

26. The god of the west.

27. The guardian of the north.

28. The patron god of officials.

29. "Naves" is used as a synecdoche for the army of chariots.

30. The name of a mountain.

31. Zhurong is the god of the south. The term "yokes," like "naves" above, refers to the speaker's chariots.

32. A beautiful goddess.

33. The "Two Girls" are identified by commentators as the two daughters of Yao, the ancient Sage king with whom "The Lake of Unity" is associated. The "Ninefold Shao" is the music of Yao's successor, Shun.

34. An important river in Chu.

35. "Ruo of the Sea" is the god of the sea, "Fengyi" the god of the rivers.

36. The "Absolute Boundary" is the end of the world; the "Gate of Cold" is entryway to the north.

37. The northern sea.

38. "Mysterious Obscurity" is the name of another guardian spirit of the north.

39. A creator spirit about whom little is known.

40. The four directions, plus up and down.

THE *CANON OF FILIAL PIETY (Xiaojing)* is probably the most controversial of all the Chinese classics, because it was singled out by critics in the early twentieth century as the quintessential expression of retrograde Confucian values. "Filial piety" is the common English translation of the Chinese term *xiao,* which generally denotes the reverence that children must show for their parents. It is understandable that this concept came under attack during the first years of the Chinese Republic, when intoxicating notions of progress and reform took hold among the intelligentsia. The prominent thinker Wu Yu (1871–1949), for example, conceived of *xiao* as nothing more than an ideological tool designed to defuse rebellious inclinations on the part of the people: "The effect of the idea of filial piety has been to turn China into a big factory for the manufacturing of obedient subjects."

By the twentieth century, the Chinese empire surely was a backward-looking institution, and wholesale reforms were obviously necessary at all levels of society. But in choosing *xiao* as a convenient target, many antiestablishmentarian voices grossly misrepresented Confucian ideals. The *Xiaojing* does not demand that children abnegate themselves for the sake of their parents and social superiors; on the contrary, one innovative idea of this text is that the highest manifestation of filial piety is the attainment of one's own reputation, through which one brings glory to one's progenitors. While we are told that we must "serve our parents," this "service" can take many different forms, of which the most praiseworthy is to develop ourselves into worthy successors to our parents' legacy. Indeed, the text goes on to deny explicitly that "filial piety" means only carrying out our parents' wishes (see section 15, "Remonstrating and Expostulating"). When we believe that our parents are wrong, we must expostulate with them. Nothing less can count as genuine "service."

The work is framed as a discussion between Confucius and his disciple Master Zeng (Zeng Zi), but by and large the text reads as a sustained lecture. (Master Zeng's role is confined to raising fruitful questions for his teacher to answer.) Scholars disagree about the date of the text; it is rarely accepted as a genuine record of the words of Confucius, but it may have attained its present form as early as the third or fourth century B.C.E. It has been said that the work contains at least two distinct layers: some of the chapters at the end elaborate on keywords found in the beginning of Confucius's lecture, and these sections may represent later exegesis of an older canonical core.

The following translation is complete.—PRG

1. Opening the Illustrious Discussion

Confucius was at leisure and Zeng Zi was attending him. The Master said, "The Former Kings had an essential Way of utmost virtue with which they instructed the world. They used the people with harmony and friendship, so that there was no resentment above or below. Do you know this [Way]?"

Zeng Zi rose from his mat and said, "I am not clever; how could [my ability] be sufficient to know it?"

The Master said, "Filial piety is the root of virtue and the origin of teaching.[1] Sit back down and I will lecture to you. You received your self, your body, your hair, and your skin from your mother and father: not daring to destroy or injure [these gifts] is the beginning of filial piety. Establishing oneself, practicing the Way, and displaying one's name unto later generations in order to manifest one's mother and father is the end of filial piety. The beginning of filial piety is serving one's parents; the middle is serving one's ruler; the end is establishing oneself. It is said in the 'Greater Elegantiae,' 'Why do you not remember your ancestors and cultivate your virtue?'"[2]

2. The Son of Heaven

The Master said, "Those who love their parents dare not be hateful to others. Those who revere their parents dare not be contemptuous of others. Love and reverence are fulfilled in serving one's parents. And when [the Son of Heaven's] teaching of virtue accrues to the Hundred Clans, he is a model for [everyone within] the Four Seas. The above is the filial piety of the Son of Heaven. It is said in the 'Laws of Fu,' 'I, the One Man, am blessed; the millions of people rely on me.'"[3]

3. The Feudal Lords

"Though in a superior position, they are not haughty; they are lofty but not precipitous. Restraining and moderating themselves, and remaining diligent about [proper] measure, they are replete but not overflowing. Being lofty but not precipitous is how one maintains longstanding nobility. Being replete but not overflowing is how one maintains longstanding wealth. Only when wealth and nobility do not depart from one's person can one protect the altars of soil and grain and bring harmony to one's people. The above is the filial piety of the feudal lords. It is said in the *Odes*, 'Take heed! Beware!—as though approaching a deep pool, as though treading on thin ice.'"[4]

4. The Ministers and Grand Masters

"If it is not a garment that was made standard by the Former Kings, they dare not wear it. If it is not a saying that was made standard by the Former Kings, they dare not speak it. If it is not a virtuous action of the Former Kings, they dare not practice it. Therefore they do not say anything that is not standard or practice anything that is not [in line with] the Way. There are no [deliberately] chosen words in their mouths or [deliberately] chosen actions [undertaken by] their body.[5] Their words fill the world but there are no transgressions in their mouths; their actions fill the world but there is no resentment or hatred. Only after these three [preconditions][6] are met can one maintain the temple of one's lineage. The above is the filial piety of the ministers and grand masters. It is said in the *Odes*, 'Never slackening, day or night, in serving the One Man.'"[7]

5. The *Shi* [8]

"What he undertakes in order to serve his father, he does to serve his mother; his love for them is the same. What he undertakes in order to serve his father, he does to serve his lord; his reverence for them is the same. Thus one's mother obtains one's love; one's lord obtains one's reverence; [both obligations] are combined in one's father. Thus if one serves one's lord with filial piety, one will have integrity; if one serves one's elders with reverence, one will be compliant. Only when one does not neglect integrity and compliance in serving one's superiors can one protect one's rank and station and maintain the altars (sc. to one's ancestors). The above is the filial piety of the *shi*. It is said in the *Odes*, 'Rising in the morning and sleeping at night, do not disgrace your origins.'"[9]

6. The Common People

"Using the Way of Heaven, dividing the benefits of the Earth,[10] being self-disciplined and moderating expenditure in order to serve one's father and mother—this is the filial piety of the common people. Thus from the Son of Heaven down to the common people, unless filial piety is [pursued] from beginning to end, calamities will arrive."

7. The Three Powers

Zeng Zi said, "Very great is filial piety!"

The Master said, "Filial piety is the warp of Heaven, the appropriate [standard] of Earth, and the practice of the people. The people take the warp of Heaven as their pattern; the brilliance of patterning oneself after Heaven and the benefits of complying with Earth are used to instruct the world. Thus [a ruler's] act of teaching is completed without being strict, and his government is ordered without being stern. The Former Kings saw the utility of teaching in transforming the people, so they led them with broad love, and there were none among the people who abandoned their parents. [The kings] explained virtue and righteousness to them, and the people were aroused to practice it. They led them with [the principles of] reverence and deference, and the people did not contend [with each other]. They led them with ritual and music, and the people were harmonious and friendly. They showed them what to like and dislike, and the people knew what was forbidden. It is said in the *Odes*, 'Awesome Master Yin! The people all look to you.'"[11]

8. Creating Order with Filial Piety

The Master said, "In the past, when the enlightened kings used filial piety to put the world in order, they dared not abandon the subjects of minor states, much less dukes, marquises, earls, viscounts, and barons! Thus they obtained the happy consent of the myriad states in serving their former kings.[12] Those who put their states in order dared not insult widowers and widows, much less *shi* and [common] people! Thus they obtained the happy consent of the Hundred Clans in serving their former rulers. Those who put their families in order dared not neglect their manservants and maidservants, much less their wives! Thus they obtained the happy consent of their people in serving their parents. Since this was so, parents were secure while living and received sacrifices as ghosts [after their death]. Therefore the world was harmonious and pacified. Disasters and catastrophes did not arise; misfortune and disorder did not occur. Thus when enlightened kings used filial piety to put the world in order, it was like this. It is said in the *Odes*, 'Sensing his virtuous conduct, the four regions obey him.'"[13]

9. The Order of the Sages

Zeng Zi said, "I venture to ask whether there is more to the virtue of the Sages than filial piety."

The Master said, "Of all the creations of Heaven and Earth, human beings are the most noble.

There is no greater form of human conduct than filial piety; there is no greater form of filial piety than being solemn with one's father; there is no greater form of being solemn with one's father than [sacrificing to] Heaven as a helpmate.[14] The Duke of Zhou was the one person [who did all this]. In the past, the Duke of Zhou sacrificed to the Millet Deity at the suburban altar; by this means he was a helpmate to Heaven. He sacrificed to his ancestor, King Wen, in the Brilliant Hall; by this means he was a helpmate to Di Above. Therefore, within the Four Seas, each person came to sacrifice according to his office. What more is there in the virtue of a Sage than filial piety? Thus intimacy [toward one's parents] is born when one is beneath [one's parents'] knees; in nurturing one's father and mother, one becomes more solemn every day. The Sages accord with this solemnity in order to teach reverence; they accord with intimacy in order to teach love. (The Sages' [act of] teaching is completed without being strict; their government is ordered without being stern.)[15] They accord with the root. The Way of father and son is imparted from Heaven, [as is] the righteous [relationship] between lord and subject. One's father and mother give birth to one: there is no greater form of continuity than this. One's lord and parents draw near to one: there is no richer form of kindness than this. Thus those who do not love their parents but love other people are called "perverters of virtue." Those who do not revere their parents but revere other people are called "perverters of ritual." If one complies [sc. with this principle], the people have a pattern [to follow]; if one rebels against it, the people will not have a pattern. If one does not remain in goodness, but always remains in a savage character, then even if one obtains [riches or power], the noble man does not value [such acquisitions]. The noble man is not like this. Whatever he thinks of saying can be spoken; whatever he thinks of doing can bring joy [to others]. His charismatic righteousness is honorable; his actions and undertakings can be taken as a standard; his demeanor can be observed; his advancing and retreating can be taken as an [appropriate] measure. This is how he draws near to his people. Therefore his people are awed by him and love him, and so they imitate him. Thus they can complete his virtuous teaching and put into practice his governmental decrees. It is said in the *Odes*, 'The good, noble man—there is nothing aberrant in his deportment.'"[16]

10. Being Regulated by Filial Piety

The Master said, "A filial son serves his parents as follows. At home, he is fully reverent; in nurturing them, he is fully joyous; when they are ill, he is fully concerned; when they die, he is fully grieved; in sacrificing to them, he is fully solemn. Only when these five [preconditions] are met can he serve his parents. One who serves his parents will not be haughty when occupying a superior [position], nor disorderly when in an inferior [position], nor contentious when among his peers. If one is haughty when occupying a superior [position], one will perish; if one is disorderly when in an inferior [position], one will be punished; if one is contentious when among one's peers, one will be attacked. If these three [faults] are not eliminated, even if one uses a threefold sacrifice[17] every day to nurture [the spirits of one's parents], one will still be unfilial."

11. The Five Punishments

The Master said, "There are three thousand categories [of offenses] pertaining to the five punishments,[18] but there is no greater crime than to be unfilial. One who extorts from his lord is insubordinate. One who opposes the Sages is without standards. One who is not filial has no parents. This is the Way of Great Disorder."

12. Elaborating on "The Essential Way"

The Master said, "To teach the people intimacy and love, there is nothing more efficacious than filial piety. To teach the people ritual and compliance, there is nothing more efficacious than fraternal piety.[19] To change habits and customs, there is nothing more efficacious than music. To make superiors secure and put the people in order, there is nothing more efficacious than ritual. Ritual is nothing more than reverence. Thus if he reveres his father, a son will be contented; if he reveres his elder brother, a younger brother will be fraternal; if he reveres his lord, a subject will be contented; if they revere the One Man, the millions of people will be contented. Those who are revered are few and those who are contented are many. This is what is called the 'essential Way.'"

13. Elaborating on "Utmost Virtue"

The Master said, "In teaching [people] by means of filial piety, the noble man does not go daily to their houses and watch them. He teaches by means of filial piety, so that the fathers in the world are revered. He teaches by means of fraternal piety, so that the elder brothers in the world are revered. He teaches by means of ministerial piety,[20] so that the lords in the world are revered. It is said in the *Odes*, 'The kind and fraternal noble man is the father and mother of the people.'[21] If not with utmost virtue, how could they instruct the people so greatly?"

14. Elaborating on "Displaying One's Name"

The Master said, "The noble man serves his parents filially; thus, with integrity, he can have influence over his lord. He serves his elder brothers with fraternal piety; thus, compliantly, he can have influence over his elders. He lives with his family in an organized manner; thus, well ordered, he can have influence over officials. Therefore when one's conduct is perfected internally, one's name will be established for later generations."

15. Remonstrating and Expostulating

Zeng Zi said, "Regarding kindness and love, reverence and respect, securing one's parents, and displaying one's name, I have heard your command. I venture to ask: If a son follows his father's decrees, can that be called 'filial piety'?"

The Master said, "What kind of talk is this? What kind of talk is this? In the past, the Son of Heaven had seven ministers to expostulate with him so that he would not lose the world even if he [were about to act] without the Way. The feudal lords had five ministers to expostulate with them so that they would not lose their states even if they [were about to act] without the Way. The grand masters had three ministers to expostulate with them so that they would not lose their families even if they [intended to act] without the Way. If a *shi* has friends to expostulate with him, he will not depart from his illustrious virtue; if a father has a son to expostulate with him, he will not fall into unrighteousness. Thus whenever there is unrighteousness, a son cannot but expostulate with his father and a minister cannot but expostulate with his lord. Thus whenever there is unrighteousness, one expostulates about it. To follow one's father's decrees—how can that be filial piety?"

16. Responding to Stimulus

The Master said, "In the past, enlightened kings served their fathers filially; thus they served Heaven brilliantly. They served their mothers filially; thus they served Earth insightfully. Old and young complied [with each other]; thus superiors and inferiors were ordered. When Heaven and Earth [are served] brilliantly and insightfully, the brilliance of spirits will shine. Thus even the Son of Heaven must have [someone] whom he honors, namely, his father. He must have [someone] whom he places ahead of himself, namely, his elder brothers.[22] In his lineage's temple, he is fully reverent; he does not forget his parents. He cultivates himself and is cautious about his conduct; he is afraid of disgracing his predecessors. If he is fully reverent in his lineage's temple, the ghosts and spirits will appear. If his filial and fraternal piety are realized, he will have congress with the brilliance of spirits. He will scintillate throughout the Four Seas and there will be no place where [his virtue] does not pervade. It is said in the *Odes,* 'From the west to the east, from the south to the north, there were no thoughts but of submission to him.'"[23]

17. Serving One's Lord

The Master said, "The noble man serves his superior as follows. His 'advancing' thoughts [pertain to] fulfilling his integrity; his 'retreating' thoughts [pertain to] mending his faults.[24] He helps his [ruler's] strengths flourish and assists him in correcting his weaknesses. Thus superior and inferior can be intimate with each other. It is said in the *Odes,* 'My heart! It loves him. Why not announce it? In the core of my heart I store him. What day will I forget him?'"[25]

18. Mourning One's Parents

The Master said, "Mourning his parents, the filial son weeps without wailing, [performs] the rites without [attention to] his appearance, and speaks without embellishment. He is not at peace wearing beautiful clothes; he is not joyous hearing music; he does not think sweet the taste of food. These are the emotions of grief and sorrow. After three days, he eats; this teaches the people that one does not take the dead to injure the living and that loss does not destroy what is inborn.[26] This was how the Sages governed. One's mourning does not exceed three years; this shows the people that there is an end. He makes a coffin, sarcophagus, vestments, and shroud and initiates [the funereal ceremonies]. He arranges the *fu* and *gui* vessels, grieves [for his parents] and feels sorrow. He beats his breast and leaps about, weeping. He sends them off, grieving; he divines their burial place and lays them to rest. He makes a lineage temple for them so that their ghosts might receive [his sacrifices]. He sacrifices to them in spring and in autumn, so as to remember them through the seasons. In life, he served them with love and reverence; in death, he serves them with grief and sorrow. When the fundamental [duties] of living people are discharged, a righteous [relationship] between the living and the dead is achieved. This is the end of the filial son's service to his parents."

—PRG

Notes

1. A play on words: the character for "teaching" *(jiao)* contains the character for "filial piety" *(xiao)* as a component grapheme. A close relationship was presumed between the two concepts.

2. A quote from Mao 235 ("King Wen"; see selection 6 for the Mao system of numbers). The text could be taken to mean "your virtue" or "their virtue," and this ambiguity is fitting: by cultivating one's own virtue, one is also perpetuating that of one's ancestors.

3. A quote from the *Documents*.

4. A quote from Mao 195 ("Minor Compassion").

5. The idea is that the ministers and grand masters are naturally and spontaneously good so they do not need to deliberate over their words and actions.

6. Namely, wearing standard garments, uttering standard sayings, and acting with virtue.

7. A quote from Mao 260 ("The Multitude of People").

8. This is the same difficult term that we have encountered before; it refers to the social and moral class of literate advisers to which Confucius and his disciples belonged. The conventional translation of "scholar" would be misleading in this context.

9. A quote from Mao 196 ("Minor Litheness").

10. The first two clauses probably refer to agriculture. "Dividing the benefits of Earth" denotes the process of marking off cultivable fields, while "using the Way of Heaven," in ancient usage, suggests sowing and plowing at the appropriate times of year.

11. A quote from Mao 191 ("The Crested Southern Mountain"). Master Yin is usually taken to be one of the highest ministers of state.

12. Presumably the former kings so "served" (like the "former rulers" in the next example) were deceased ancestors.

13. A quote from Mao 256 ("Dignified").

14. Heaven is conceived as the greatest "father" of all.

15. This line is probably out of place here; a similar sentence appears in section 7, "The Three Powers."

16. A quote from Mao 152 ("The Turtledove").

17. I.e., ox, sheep, and pig.

18. These are tattooing, amputating the nose, amputating one or both feet, castrating, and putting to death.

19. Strictly speaking, this term *(ti)* refers to the appropriately deferential attitude of a younger brother toward his elder brothers.

20. On the model of "fraternal piety," this term *(chen)* designates the appropriately deferential attitude of a subject toward his lord.

21. A quote from Mao 251 ("Vast Ladling").

22. In practice, these two requirements were often irrelevant, because the Son of Heaven did not typically have a living father or elder brothers of any kind. He was the Son of Heaven precisely because he was the oldest living son of the previous Son of Heaven.

23. A quote from Mao 244 ("King Wen Has a Reputation").

24. Commentators explain the "advancing" and "retreating" thoughts as ideas presented at court and deliberations at home, respectively.

25. A quote from Mao 228 ("The Mulberries in the Marsh"), where the object of the speaker's affections is an unnamed "noble man" *(junzi)*. The tone of the poem is subtly but unmistakably erotic.

26. A complex sentence. "What is inborn" *(xing)* refers ostensibly to the human need to eat, as when Gao Zi says, for example, "Human *xing* is food and sex" *(Mencius* 6A.4). But the character *xing* also shares a manifest graphemic connection with the character for "life" *(sheng),* so the implication here is that one's parents' death does not signal the end of one's own life.

ALONG WITH THE *Daode jing* and the *Analects* of Confucius, the *Methods of War (Bingfa,* often known by the less precise title *Art of War)* of Sun Zi (Master Sun) is one of the few classical Chinese texts to enjoy a global readership. The text is ascribed to Sun Wu, the renowned strategist who is said to have helped King Helu of Wu (r. 514–496 B.C.E.) dominate his neighbors and eventually be recognized by his peers as "Hegemon" *(ba),* the title given to the lord entrusted with the task of preserving the delicate balance of power among the various feudal states. While many modern scholars still accept this attribution, there are several reasons why it probably dates from a significantly later period.

One of the most noticeable features of *Methods of War* is its characteristic use of vocabulary taken from mainstream philosophical discourse, words such as "Heaven," "Earth," "the Way," "emptiness," "method." While these terms would have been familiar to ancient readers in their philosophical senses, in *Methods of War* they are used consistently to denote concepts in military theory. For example, as the text defines it, "Heaven" refers to "yin and yang, cold and heat, and the regular [progression] of the seasons," or in other words, natural factors influencing a commander's assessment of the battlefield, contingencies over which he has no direct control. This studied use of commonplace phraseology suggests an attempt to place military thought within an existing philosophical culture by showing that the well-known philosophical categories of the day could be applied reasonably to the field of military theory. The language of the text, therefore, squares better with a later period, after the maturation of Chinese philosophy, rather than with the time of King Helu, when Confucius was still teaching his disciples and no organized philosophical school was yet in existence.

While *Methods of War* is obviously aimed not at military careerists, but at general readers of a philosophical bent—with whom such categories as "Heaven" and "Earth" would have resounded with their intended significance—there can be little doubt that the author of the treatise possessed real combat experience. Most of the work deals with concrete issues of military strategy, such as deployment of troops, maneuver, attacking, and defending—unlike the *Zuozhuan,* which, as we have seen, also attempts to apply general philosophical principles to the theater of war, but without describing in any detail how battles were actually fought. In *Methods of War* and the *Zuozhuan* we have two complementary views of warfare in ancient times: in the former, a realistic glimpse of how commanders used their troops in battle; and in the latter, the idealized universe imagined by writers nostalgic for the mythic order of an earlier epoch.

It is related in Sun Wu's biography in *Records of the Grand Historian (Shiji,* a historical work completed ca. 90 B.C.E.) that he had a famous descendant named Sun Bin who also produced a book entitled *Methods of War.* Early bibliographies attest to the existence of this work in ancient times, but it was lost centuries ago. In 1972, however, an archaeological excavation at Yinqueshan (Shandong Province) uncovered manuscripts of both Sun Bin's *Methods of War* and Sun Wu's *Methods of War.* Subsequent analysis of the two texts shows that Sun Bin's work is probably the later of the two; it quotes extensively from Sun Wu's *Methods of War* and frequently elaborates on the general concepts found in that other source. But we have no more reliable information about the historical Sun Bin than we do about his ancestor. Indeed, neither name seems entirely credible. "Bin" means "kneecap" or "legless"—an unmistakable reference to the story that Sun Bin had both his feet amputated. Similarly, "Wu" means "martial" or "warlike"; it is suspicious that the most famous military theoretician in ancient China should have borne such a fitting name.

The following translations include the complete biographies of Sun Wu and Sun Bin from *Records of the Grand Historian,* as well as two selections from each *Methods.*—PRG

Biography of Master Sun

Master Sun Wu was a man of Qi. He obtained an audience with King Helu of Wu by virtue of his *Methods of War.* Helu said, "Master, I have read all thirteen of your essays. Can you train some troops as a little test?"

[Master Sun] replied, "I can."

Helu said, "Can you do the test with women?"

He said, "I can." Thereupon [Helu] allowed him to take 180 beautiful women from within the palace. Master Sun divided them into two companies and appointed the king's two favorite concubines as company leaders. He ordered them all to bear halberds. He ordered them, saying, "Do you know your heart, your left and right hands, and your back?"

The women said, "We know them."

Master Sun said, "When I say 'Forward!' look in the direction of your heart;[1] when I say 'Left!' look toward your left hand; when I say 'Right!' look toward your right hand; when I say 'Back!' look toward your back."

The women said, "Yes."

Having proclaimed the regulations, he readied hatchets and axes, and went over the orders again and again. Then he drummed the command to turn right, and the women laughed out loud. Master Sun said, "When the regulations are not clear, nor [the troops] familiar with the orders, it is the fault of the commander." So he went over the orders for maybe the fifth time and drummed the command to turn left. The women laughed out loud again. Master Sun said, "When the regulations are not clear, nor [the troops] acquainted with the orders, it is the fault of the commander; but when they have already been made clear, yet [the troops] do not conform to the standards, it is the fault of the officers." Then he intended to behead the Left and Right Company Leaders.

The King of Wu was watching from a terrace, and when he saw that [Master Sun] was about to behead his beloved concubines, he was amazed. He rushed a messenger with the order, "I know now that you, General, are competent at using troops. Without these two concubines, food has no taste to me. I entreat you not to behead them."

Master Sun said, "I have received your order to be your commander, and when the commander is among his troops, there are orders from his lord that he does not accept."[2] Thereupon he beheaded the two company leaders as an example. He used the second-highest-ranking [concubines] as the [new] company leaders and then beat the drum again. The women moved to the left, to the right, forward, and backward; they knelt and stood up; they were like a circle made by a compass, a right angle made by a T-square, a line made by an ink-string, and no one dared utter a sound. Then Master Sun sent a messenger to report to the king, saying, "Your troops are now disciplined. Your Majesty, you may inspect them yourself. You may use them however you wish; they can go even through water and fire!"

The King of Wu said, "General, go to your lodgings and rest. I do not wish to inspect them."

Master Sun said, "Your Majesty, you are interested only in words and are unable to apply them to reality."

This was how Helu came to know that Master Sun was competent at using troops, and in the end, he made him his commander. To the west, [Helu] overpowered and smashed Chu, entering the capital, Ying; to the north, he overawed Qi and Jin, displaying his name to the feudal lords. Master Sun contributed his might [to these successes].

More than a hundred years after Sun Wu died, there was [a man named] Sun Bin. Bin was born between Wo and Juan, and was also a direct descendant of Sun Wu. Sun Bin once studied the methods of war together with Pang Juan. Pang Juan came to serve in Wei and became King Hui's commander, but he considered his own abilities unequal to Sun Bin's. So he secretly sent a messenger to summon Sun Bin; when Bin arrived, Pang Juan feared that he would prove more talented and thus was envious of him. He used the penal laws to cut off both of [Sun Bin's] feet and had him tattooed, hoping to conceal him so that he would not be seen.

An envoy of Qi came to Liang [the capital of Wei], and Sun Bin went to see him secretly, even though he was a convict. He spoke to the envoy of Qi, who considered him so marvelous that he smuggled him into Qi. Qi's commander, Tian Ji, was good to [Sun Bin] and took him in as a retainer.

Ji often bet heavily on horse races with the various princes of Qi. Master Sun saw that the horses were not so far apart with respect to their speed. (The horses were divided into teams of three grades.) So Master Sun addressed Tian Ji, saying, "Lord, be sure to bet heavily! I can make you win." Tian Ji believed him and bet a thousand gold pieces with the king and various princes. When it came time to place the wagers, Master Sun said, "Lord, now match your worst team with their best; take your best team and match it with their second-best; and take your second-best team and match it with their worst." When the three races were finished, Tian Ji lost once but won twice, so in the end he earned a thousand gold pieces. Thus Ji presented Master Sun to King Wei [of Qi]; King Wei had heard of his methods of war, so he made him an adjutant.

Sometime later, the state of Wei attacked Zhao, and Zhao, in a state of emergency, begged Qi for aid. King Wei of Qi wished to place the troops under Sun Bin's command, but Bin declined, saying, "As a remnant of the penal code, I am unfit." Thus he made Tian Ji his commander, but with Sun Bin as an adjutant. He would stay in a covered carriage, sitting there to make plans and schemes. Tian Ji wished to lead the troops to Zhao, but Master Sun said, "To untie a tangled knot, you do not tug at it or fray it; to aid those who are fighting, you do not punch or jab. If we avoid what is fierce but pound at what is empty, then [the enemy's] form will be resisted without weapons and their dominance eliminated.[3] They will lift [the siege] of their own accord. Since Wei and Zhao are attacking each other, their speedy and keen troops have all been drained [to fight] outside the borders, leaving the aged and weak within. Lord, nothing is better than to lead your troops swiftly to Great Liang [the capital of Wei] and occupy their streets and roads; they will certainly let go of Zhao and come to save themselves. This is to relieve the siege of Zhao and harvest distress in Wei all in one stroke." Tian Ji followed [his advice], and Wei indeed left Handan [the capital of Zhao]. They fought with Qi at Guiling and were smashed.

Thirteen years later, Wei and Zhao attacked Han together; Han reported their emergency to Qi. Qi sent Tian Ji there as commander of the troops; he raced directly to Great Liang. Pang Juan, the general of Wei, hearing of this, left Han and went home, but the forces of Qi had already passed further west. Master Sun addressed Tian Ji, saying, "The troops of the Three Jin[4] are generally fierce and courageous; they make light of Qi, calling us cowards. One who is adept at warfare should comply with their [perceived] dominance and lure them with [the prospect of] profit.

According to the *Methods of War*,[5] the vanguard commanders [of an army] rushing for a hundred tricents [in pursuit] of an advantage may stumble; an army rushing for fifty tricents [in pursuit] of an advantage [may find] that but half its troops arrive. Send the forces of Qi into the territory of Wei and have them set up a hundred thousand campfires. The next day, make it fifty thousand campfires—the day after that, thirty thousand."

Pang Juan, who had been traveling for three days, was overjoyed, saying, "I was certain that the army of Qi was cowardly! They have been in our territory for three days, and more than half of their soldiers have deserted." He left behind his infantry divisions and chased [the army of Qi] with his speediest and keenest [troops] marching double-time.

Master Sun measured [Pang Juan's] movements and [determined] that by nightfall he should reach Maling. The road at Maling is narrow, with many defiles on both sides where one can lie in ambush. He stripped a great tree bare [of its bark] and wrote on it, "Pang Juan will die beneath this tree." Then he had ten thousand sharpshooters of Qi lie in ambush along the narrow road with the order, "At nightfall, all of you shoot as soon as you see a flame." As expected, Pang Juan arrived beneath the stripped tree in the evening; when he saw the writing on the bare [trunk], he lit a flame to illuminate it. Before he was finished reading, the ten thousand crossbowmen of Qi had all shot at him. The forces of Wei were thrown into great disorder and lost [communication] with each other.

Pang Juan knew that he was outwitted and his troops defeated, so he slit his own throat, saying, "I have made a name for that whipping boy!" Taking advantage of their victory, Qi thoroughly smashed the forces [of Wei]; they captured Shen, the heir apparent of Wei, and returned with him. Sun Bin's name was displayed to the world on this account, and the generations have transmitted his *Methods of War*.

Methods of War of Sun Wu

1. Calculation

Master Sun said,

War is the greatest affair of state. It is the province of death and life, the Way of survival and perdition, and cannot be left uninvestigated.

Thus one takes the following five [criteria] as its warp; one compares [the opposing armies] using the following calculations and thereby gains exhaustive knowledge of the situation. The first [criterion] is called the Way. The second is called Heaven. The third is called Earth. The fourth is called the commander. The fifth is called method.

The Way causes the people to have the same intentions as their superiors. Thus they can die with [their ruler]; they can live with their ruler; and they will not fear danger. Heaven is yin and yang, cold and heat, and the regular [progression] of the seasons. Earth is distance and proximity, difficulty and ease, expansiveness and narrowness, and death and life. The commander possesses wisdom, trustworthiness, humanity, courage, and strictness. Method is the regulation of troops, justice in [dispensing] ranks, and management of matériel. There is no general who has not heard of these five things. One who knows them will be victorious; one who does not know them will not be victorious.

Thus one compares [the opposing armies] using the following calculations and thereby gains exhaustive knowledge of the situation. Which ruler possessed the Way? Which general is more competent? Who has obtained Heaven and Earth? Whose methods and commands are carried out? Whose weapons and forces are stronger? Whose soldiers are better trained? Who is more enlightened with respect to rewards and punishments? On the basis of these [calculations], I know who will win and lose.

If a commander heeds my calculations, he will certainly be victorious if you use him, so retain him; if a commander does not heed my calculations, he will certainly be defeated if you use him, so dismiss him.

Once you have heeded the calculations of advantage, make [your army] dominant in order to complement external efforts.[6] "Dominance" means relying on relative advantages to take control of the balance.[7]

War is the Way of Deceit. Thus one who is competent pretends to be incompetent; one who uses [his army] pretends not to use it; one who draws near pretends to be distant; one who is distant pretends to draw near. If [the enemy desires] some advantage, entice him [with it]. If he is in disorder, seize him. If he is substantial, be prepared for him. If he is strong, evade him. If he is enraged, irritate him [further]. If he is humble, make him haughty. If he is rested, make him toil. If he is intimate [with his ranks], separate them. Attack where he does not expect it and go where he has not imagined. This is how military experts are victorious; these [factors] cannot be interpreted before [assessing the situation]. . . .

6. "Emptiness" and "Fullness"[8]

Master Sun said,

Whoever occupies the battlefield first and awaits his enemy will be rested. Whoever occupies the battlefield last and rushes to battle will be exhausted. Thus one who is adept at battle brings others [to the battlefield] and is not brought there by others.

One who is able to make his enemy arrive of his own accord does so by offering him an advantage; one who is able to prevent his enemy from arriving does so by harming him. Thus if the enemy is rested, one is able to exhaust him; if he is well fed, one is able to starve him; if he is secure, one is able to make him move. Go to places where he must rush [to meet you]; rush to places that he has not imagined. One who travels a thousand tricents without becoming exhausted travels through territory where there is no enemy. One who is sure to capture what he attacks will attack places that [the enemy] does not defend. One who is sure to keep what he defends will defend places that [the enemy] does not attack. Thus the enemy of one who is adept at attacking does not know where to defend; the enemy of one who is adept at defending does not know where to attack. Subtle, subtle, utterly without form! Divine, divine, utterly without sound! Thus one can be the Director of Fate of one's enemy.[9]

One who advances and cannot be warded off charges against [the enemy's] "emptiness"; one who retreats and cannot be pursued is so swift that one cannot reach him. Thus if we wish to do battle, we attack places that the enemy must rescue, so that he cannot avoid doing battle with us, even if he has high fortifications and deep moats. If we do not wish to do battle, we divert the enemy from where he is going, so that he cannot do battle with us, even if we [merely] draw a line in the ground and defend it.

Thus if we impose a form on others but have no form ourselves, then we will be concentrated and the enemy divided. If we are concentrated into one [group], and the enemy divided into ten, then we will attack each of his [groups] with tenfold strength. We will be many and the enemy few. If we are able to use many [troops] to attack few, then those with whom we do battle will be in straitened circumstances. [The enemy] cannot know the field where we will do battle. If he cannot know this, he will make preparations at many [points]; if he makes preparations at many [points], then those with whom we do battle will be few. Thus one who is prepared in the front will have few [troops] in the rear; one who is prepared in the rear will have few in the front; one who is prepared to the left will have few to the right; one who is prepared to the right will have few to the left. One who is prepared everywhere has few troops everywhere. One who has few [troops] is one who prepares for others; one who has many [troops] is one who makes others prepare for him.

Thus if one knows the field of battle and the day of battle, one can [march] a thousand tricents and meet for battle. If one does not know the field of battle or the day of battle, then the [troops on] the left cannot rescue those on the right; those on the right cannot rescue those on the left; those in the front cannot rescue those in the rear; those in the rear cannot rescue those in the front. How much more is this so when the distant [troops] are several tens of tricents away and the near ones several tricents away? As I measure it, although the troops of Yue are numerous, of what benefit is it to them with respect to victory and defeat? Thus I say, Victory can be made. Even if the enemy is numerous, one can cause them not to fight.

Therefore, make the enemy formulate a strategy so as to calculate his strengths and weaknesses. Make him act so as to know the pattern of his movement and stillness. Make him assume a form so as to know whether his territory will [mean] life or death [for him]. Probe him so as to know the points where he has excess and deficiency.

Thus the supreme [object] in forming one's troops is to be without form. If one is without form, then even those under deep cover will not be able to spy you out, and those who are wise will not be able to plan for you. By adjusting to forms, one provides victories for the multitudes, but the multitudes are unable to know this. Everyone will know the form that we use for victory, but no one will know the form that we used to determine victory. Thus when we are victorious in battle, we do not repeat ourselves, but respond to forms inexhaustibly.

The form of an army is like water. By virtue of its form, water avoids high [places] and rushes to low ones. By virtue of its form, an army evades "full" [places] and strikes "empty" ones. Water adjusts to the earth to determine its own flow. An army adjusts to the enemy to determine victory. Thus an army has no constant position; water has no constant form. One who can seize victory by complying with the enemy's vicissitudes is called "divine." None of the Five Phases constantly prevails; none of the four seasons has constant standing. The days grow shorter and longer; the moon dies and is reborn.

Methods of War of Sun Bin

King Wei Asked

King Wei of Qi asked Master Sun[10] about using troops, saying, "When two forces are evenly matched, when the two commanders face each other, both in a firm and solid [position], neither one daring to initiate action—what does one do?"

Master Sun answered, "Test them with light troops. Have a lowly but courageous [officer] lead them. Expect to flee; do not expect success [with this diversion]. Deploy an ambush in order to gore their flank. This is called 'Great Success.'"

King Wei said, "Is there a Way of using many and using few?"

Master Sun said, "There is."

King Wei said, "If we are strong and the enemy weak, if we are many and the enemy few, how do we use [our troops]?"

Master Sun bowed twice and said, "This is the question of an enlightened king. If you are many and strong, and still ask how to use [one's troops]—this is the Way of securing the state. The name [of the tactic] is 'Drawing Out the Army.' Break your ranks and move in disorder, so as to flow with [the enemy's] ambition. Then he will be certain to do battle."

King Wei said, "If the enemy is strong and we weak, if the enemy is many and we few, how do we use [our troops]?"

Master Sun said, "The name is 'Deferring to Authority.' You must hide your tail, affording [your troops] the ability to go back. Long weapons in the front, short weapons in the rear—and create meandering crossbow units to assist where there are emergencies. Do not move your main force, thereby waiting [to see] the enemy's abilities." . . .

King Wei said, "How do we strike those of equal [strength]?"

Master Sun said, "Dazzle them so that they disperse. We unite our troops and strike them, but do not let the enemy know [our intentions]. However, if they do not disperse, secure [your position] and halt. Do not strike if you are in doubt."

King Wei said, "Is there a Way of striking ten with one?"[11]

Master Sun said, "There is. Attack where they do not expect it, and go where they have not imagined."[12]

King Wei said, "If the ground is flat and the troops disciplined, but they are put to flight when combining [with the enemy], why is this?"

Master Sun said, "They were deployed without a vanguard."[13]

King Wei said, "How do I make the people obey by habit?"

Master Sun said, "Be trustworthy by habit."

King Wei said, "Good! In speaking of military strategies, you are inexhaustible." . . .

Preparations for Positional Dominance

Master Sun said,

[Animals] with fangs in their mouths and bearing horns [on their heads], with claws on their front [limbs] and spurs on the rear [limbs]—they come together when happy and fight when enraged. This is the Way of Heaven and cannot be stopped. Thus those who are without natural weapons must make preparations for themselves; this was a matter for the Sages. The Yellow Emperor invented swords, on which we model [the concept] of deployment. [Archer] Yi invented bows and crossbows, on which we model [the concept of] positional dominance. Yu invented boats and chariots, on which we model [the concept of] adaptability. Tang and Wu invented long weapons, on which we model [the concept] of balance. These four [concepts] are all applications of the weapons themselves.[14] . . .

The Nature of the Military

Master Sun said,

If you wish to know the nature of the military, take the crossbow and its bolts as a model. The bolts are the troops. The crossbow is the general. The one who releases [the bow] is the ruler. A bolt has metal in the front and feathers in the rear; thus it is sharp and swift. If [the troops] are heavy in the front and light in the rear, they will be well aligned and will be obedient. But recently, those who command troops make the rear heavy and the front light, so that they are manageable when deployed but disobedient when urged toward the enemy. Those who command troops do not take the bolt as their model.

The crossbow is the general. When the crossbow is drawn, if the handle is not straight, or if it is not balanced because one side is strong and one side weak, then in delivering the bolt, the two arms [of the crossbow] will not be united. Even if the bolt is light and heavy at the proper [places], even if its front and rear are suitable, it still will not hit the target. . . .

—PRG

Notes

1. I.e., look ahead.

2. This principle also appears in the *Methods of War*.

3. Sun Bin is using technical terms that are discussed in *Methods of War*. The basic idea is that Tian Ji should strike Wei in their own capital city, forcing them to respond and lift the siege in Zhao.

4. I.e., Zhao, Han, and Wei.

5. Sun Bin is referring to the *Methods of War* of his ancestor Sun Wu, which asserts that an army traveling too fast may lose its troops and commanders.

6. That is, preparations for war not directly involving the army (such as diplomacy and spying).

7. "Dominance" is used here to translate the Chinese term *shi,* which refers to relative and momentary advantages in battle. By taking advantage of fortuitous *shi*—and doing so at the right time—a wise commander will seize victory. But as *shi* is constantly changing, each military situation calls for a fresh calculation. The elusive, but obviously very important, term *shi* has also been variously translated as "configuration," "propensity," and so forth.

8. "Emptiness" is used here to denote the enemy's weak points, "fullness" his strong points.

9. The "Director of Fate" is the divinity that determines life and death.

10. This "Master Sun," of course, is Sun Bin.

11. I.e., attacking a force ten times stronger than one's own.

12. Chapter 1 of Sun Wu's treatise contains the same injunction.

13. Sun Wu's treatise also insists that troops must be deployed with a vanguard.

14. As we have seen, the concepts of deployment, strategic advantage, adaptability, and balance are fundamental to the military thought of Sun Wu and Sun Bin. This passage is asserting that those principles are modeled after the shapes and functions of various weapons invented by the Sages.

WITH XUN ZI (Master Xun, or Xun Kuang, ca. 310–ca. 210 B.C.E.) we come to a thinker unlike any that we have encountered before. He was a self-conscious Confucian who subscribed to the basic program of moral self-cultivation that had by his time already become the hallmark of that philosophical outlook. Unlike Confucius or Mencius, however, Xun Zi derived his entire world-view from the seminal concept of the Way. As Xun Zi understood it and expounded on it, the Way is the constant ethic of the cosmos, the Heaven-ordained plan and pattern of nature, the infallible standard of right reason and proper conduct. Our duty as human beings is to seek to comprehend the Way and conform to its order through rigorous and unceasing study. Those people who perfect themselves in this manner are called "Sages" (*sheng* or *shengren*), and their thoughts and actions, always in compliance with the Way, are necessarily flawless. This process of accumulating merit is called "artifice" *(wei)* or "learning" *(xue)*.

The rest of his philosophy falls into place logically if we begin from the foundation of the Way. We are not born with a sage comprehension of the Way: that exalted state is the end of a lifelong devotion to learning. It follows that human beings are originally evil, for we know nothing of the Way and its inherent moral standards when we are born; we must learn them. So Xun Zi divides human nature into two component parts: *xing,* which he uses to denote the natural and imperfect state of a human being at birth; and what he calls "artifice," or the gradual accumulation of moral perfection obtained by studying the Way.

These observations lead Xun Zi to contradict Mencius, who, as we have seen, declared that *xing* is essentially good. In his attempted refutation, however, Xun Zi fundamentally misrepresents Mencius's position by using the term *xing* in a sense that the earlier thinker did not intend. We recall that for Mencius, *xing* is conceived as the ideal flourishing state that we can attain if we cultivate our "Beginnings" of virtue; it does not refer to the condition of a human being at birth. Mencius himself would have largely agreed with Xun Zi's contention that we must overcome our baser urges before we can attain morality.

Nevertheless, in grounding the elements of morality in the very fabric of the cosmos, Xun Zi's philosophy departs significantly from that of Mencius. Mencius declared that the incipiences of virtue and right conduct were inborn and endowed by Heaven; but he never explained the connections, if any, between the Heavenly principles of our inborn goodness and the systems of the living world, such as the progressions of the stars or the processes of history. Xun Zi, on the other hand, claims that right is right for precisely the same reason that the sun rises in the east or that spring follows winter: everything in the universe follows the Way. The consequences of Xun Zi's view are considerable. Since the entire cosmos lies open to anyone who understands the Way, anyone can become a Sage.

But how do we start? Xun Zi asserts further that the Sage kings of antiquity bequeathed a code of conduct embodying the principles of the Way for posterity. This code is known as "ritual" *(li)* and is found in the canonical texts that the Sages left behind. Even if we are not yet Sages and thus cannot know the Way ourselves, we can still pattern ourselves after the Way and bring ourselves closer to moral perfection by modifying our conduct so as to conform with the rituals. Therefore, while the logical foundation of morality is unquestionably the Way, in practice, most people should focus on the rituals, since these are also immaculate and are much more accessible. As Xun Zi emphasizes repeatedly, the path to self-perfection and world peace lies in following the rituals.

Xun Zi's work also reveals a new attitude toward writing and authorship. His collected essays were clearly intended as a coherent oeuvre—what we would call a "book"—but the same cannot be said of any other text that we have yet examined. The *Analects* and *Mencius* were both redacted by disciples; the *Zhuang Zi* was compiled from diverse sources by unknown editors; the *Daode jing* probably coalesced over time. This is not to say that Xun Zi was necessarily the first person in Chinese history to have the idea of a book; rather, the synthetic format and presentation of his ideas, like the ideas themselves, reflect the revolutionary intellectual developments of the third century B.C.E.—PRG

---

1. Exhortation to Learning

The noble man says: Learning cannot cease. Blue dye is gained from the indigo plant, but is bluer than the indigo. Ice is made of water, but is colder than water. Wood may be as straight as a plumb line, but if bent into a wheel, it can become as round as a compass. Even if it is dried or heated, it will not become straight again because the bending has made it so. Thus wood set to the plumb line is straight; metal put to the grindstone is keen. The noble man learns broadly and examines himself trebly every day,[1] so that his knowledge is brilliant and his conduct without transgression. . . .

If one accumulates enough earth to complete a mountain, the wind and rain will prosper on it. If one accumulates enough water to complete a lake, serpents and dragons will be born in it. If one accumulates enough goodness to complete virtue, then spirit illumination[2] will be naturally attained, and a sage mind will be prepared within one. Thus, without accumulating half-paces and paces, there is no way to reach a thousand tricents;[3] without accumulating waters and streams, there is no way to complete rivers and oceans. Qiji[4] cannot [advance] ten paces in one prance, but a nag [can do so] if yoked ten times. Achievement rests in not desisting. If one carves but desists, rotten wood will not be pruned. If one carves and does not desist, metal and stone can be engraved. The earthworm does not have the benefit of claws and teeth, the strength of muscles and bones. Above, it eats dust and earth; below, it drinks from the Yellow Springs.[5] It employs its mind to one [purpose]. . . .

2. Self-Cultivation

By following ritual, there is order and success; by not following ritual, there is rebelliousness and disorder, indolence and neglect. When food and drink, clothing, residence, movement and quietude follow ritual, there is harmony and measure; when they do not follow ritual, they are offensive and lowly and beget disease. When appearance, attitude, entrance and exit, and rapid walking[6] follow ritual, there will be elegance; when they do not follow ritual, there will be sloth, depravity and perversion, vulgarity and wildness. Thus people cannot live without ritual; affairs cannot be completed without ritual; the state and its families cannot be at peace without ritual. . . .

4. Glory and Shame

In endowment, *xing,* knowledge, and ability, the noble man and the small are man are one. They like glory and hate shame; they like profit and hate harm. This is what is alike in noble men and small men. Only when it comes to the Way with which they seek things are they different. . . . All people are alike in one respect: hungry, they desire food; cold, they desire warmth; working, they desire respite; they like profit and hate harm. This is what is in human beings from birth; this is what is immediately so.[7] This is what is alike in Yu and Jie.[8] The eye distinguishes white, black, beautiful, and ugly; the ear distinguishes the pitches of tones and sounds; the mouth distinguishes sour, salty, sweet, and bitter; the nose distinguishes fragrant and foul; the bones and skin distinguish cold, heat, pain, and itching. This is what is in human beings from birth; this is what is immediately so. One can become Yao or Yu; one can become Jie or Zhi;[9] one can become a mechanic or artisan; one can become a farmer or merchant. [The difference] lies in the accumulated [benefit] of noting faults and habitual practice. . . .Yao and Yu were not fully developed when they were born: they arose by transforming their former selves; they perfected themselves through self-cultivation. When they cultivated themselves exhaustively, their [sagehood] became complete. Human *xing* is originally a small person's *xing.* . . .

Now if one were made to live without having gazed upon [the meat of] grass- and grain-fed [animals], or rice and millet, having gazed upon only beans, pulse, dregs, and chaff—then one would find utmost sufficiency to be in [the latter]. But if suddenly a sumptuous platter were to arrive with [the meat of] grass- and grain-fed [animals] and rice and millet, then one would behold it staring, and say, "What strange thing is this?" That [delicacy]—when one smells it, it is not disturbing to the nose; when one tastes it, it is sweet to the mouth; when one eats it, it brings comfort to the body. Thus no one does not reject this [old food] and choose that [new food]. Now take the Way of the Former Kings, the principles of humanity and righteousness. Are they not that by which societies live together, by which we support and nourish each other, by which we shield and adorn each other, by which we are peaceful and secure with each other? Do they not contrast with the Way of Jie and Zhi just as [the meat of] grass- and grain-fed [animals], rice, and millet contrast with dregs and chaff? . . .

To be honored as the Son of Heaven and richly to possess the world—this is the common desire of humans [by virtue of their] essence. But if people follow their desires, then boundaries cannot contain them and objects cannot satisfy them. Thus the Former Kings restrained them and established for them ritual and morality in order to divide them [into classes]. . . .

5. Refutation of Physiognomy[10]

What is it that makes humans human? I say: Their making of distinctions. Desiring food when hungry, desiring warmth when cold, desiring respite when toiling, liking profit and disliking harm—these [characteristics] are all possessed by people from birth. They are what is immediately so. This is the similarity between Yu and Jie. This being the case, what makes humans human is not specifically that they have two feet and no pelt [or plumage].[11] It is their making of distinctions. Now the *xingxing*-ape[12] resembles [humans] and also has two feet and no pelt. But the noble man sips his soup and eats his food cooked. Thus what makes humans human is not specifically that they have two feet and no pelt. It is their making of distinctions. Birds and beasts have fathers and sons, but no intimacy between fathers and sons. They have males and females but no separation between man and woman. Thus the Way of Humanity is nothing other than to make distinctions. There are no greater distinctions than social distinctions. There are no greater social distinctions than the rituals. There are no greater rituals than those of the Sage Kings. . . .

12. The Way of the Noble Man

An enlightened ruler hastens to gain [the support of] his people, while a benighted ruler hastens to gain stature. If he hastens to gain his people, then his body may be at leisure, and the state governed; his accomplishments will be great and his name admired. At best, he can be a king; at worst, he can be a hegemon.[13] If he does not hasten to gain his people, but hastens to gain stature, then his body may toil, yet the state will be in disorder; his accomplishments will be frustration, his name one of shame. The altars of grain and soil will be imperiled. Thus the lord toils at choosing [his assistants] and reposes as he commands them. . . .

The lord is the sundial. If the sundial is straight, the shadow is straight. The lord is the bowl. If the bowl is round, the water is round. The lord is the basin. If the basin is square, the water is square. . . .

15. Discussion of Warfare

From what I have heard of the Way of the ancients, the basis of all use of arms to attack in war is the unification of the people. If the bow and arrow are not aligned, then Yi[14] cannot hit the bull's-eye. If the six horses are not in harmony, then Zaofu[15] cannot make them go far. If the knights and common people are not close like family, then Tang and Wu[16] cannot be sure of victory. Thus, to be good at bringing the people close is to be good at using arms. . . .

Ritual is the ridgepole of order and discrimination; it is the foundation of a strong state, the Way of awesome practice, the chief precondition for a successful name. When kings and dukes follow [the rituals], that is how they obtain the world; when they do not follow them, that is how they bring about the perdition of their altars of soil and grain. Thus firm armor and keen weapons are not enough to bring about victory; lofty fortifications and deep moats are not enough to bring about security; strict commands and manifold punishments are not enough to bring about awesome [authority]. If one follows the Way, then one will progress; if one does not follow the Way, then one will perish. . . . The weapons of the ancients were nothing more than halberd, spear, bow, and arrow, but enemy states recoiled without contest. Fortifications and battlements were not managed, pits and moats were not dug, strongholds and fortresses were not planted, machinery and surprise tactics not brought to bear; however, that the state, in peace, did not fear foreigners and was secure—there was no other reason for this, than that [the rulers] were enlightened with respect to the Way and divided the [responsibilities] of the people equitably. . . .

16. Strengthening the State

If the mold is regular, the metal auspicious, the workmanship and casting skillful, and the fire and alloying appropriate, then cut open the mold and there will be a Moye.[17] But if one does not pare and expose it [when it becomes rough], does not sharpen it with a whetstone, then it will not be able to cut a rope. If one pares and exposes it, sharpens it with a whetstone, then it can slice a pan or basin and slash an ox or horse instantly. As for the state—there is also a "cutting open of the mold" for a strong state. If one does not teach and instruct, does not attune and unify, then one cannot defend against invasions or wage war outside [i.e., on other states]. But if one teaches and instructs them, attunes and unifies them, then the soldiers will be firm and the fortifications secure; enemy states will dare not close in. As for the state—there is also a "sharpening with a whetstone." This is ritual and morality, and restrictions [enacted] in due measure. . . .

17. Discourse on Heaven

Whoever strengthens the base and spends in moderation, Heaven cannot impoverish. Whoever completes the nourishment [sc. of the people] and moves in accordance with the seasons, Heaven cannot cause to be ill. Whoever cultivates the Way and is not of two [minds], Heaven cannot ruin. Thus floods and drought cannot bring about famine and thirst; cold and heat cannot bring about disease; portents and wonders cannot bring about an inauspicious situation. . . . Therefore one who is enlightened with respect to the division between Heaven and humanity can be called a "supreme person." Not to act, but to complete; not to seek, but to gain—this is called the work of Heaven. This being the case, such a person, however profound, does not apply deliberation to [Heaven]; however great, he does not apply inquiry to it. This is called not competing with Heaven in its work. Heaven has its seasons; Earth has its resources; humans have their order. This is called the ability to form a triad. . . .

Are order and disorder in Heaven? I say: The revolutions of the sun, moon, and stars, and the cyclical calendar—these were the same under Yu and Jie. Since Yu brought about order and Jie disorder, order and disorder are not in Heaven. And the seasons? I say: Multiflorously, [vegetation] begins to bloom and grow in spring and summer; crops are harvested and stored in autumn and winter. This, too, was the same under Yu and Jie. Since Yu brought about order and Jie disorder, order and disorder are not in the seasons. . . .

Heaven does not stop winter because people dislike cold; Earth does not stop its expansiveness because people dislike great distances. . . . Heaven has a constant Way. . . .

When a star falls or a tree calls out, the people of the state are all terrified. They say, "What is this?" I say: This is nothing. This is an [innocuous] change of Heaven and Earth, the transformation of yin and yang, or the presence of a material anomaly. To wonder at it is acceptable, but to fear it is not. Eclipses of the sun and moon, untimely winds and rain, unforeseen appearances of marvelous stars—there is no era that has not frequently [experienced] these things. . . . The falling of stars, the crying of trees—these are changes of Heaven and Earth, transformations of yin and yang, or the presence of material anomalies. To wonder at them is acceptable, but to fear them is not. Among material [anomalies] that may occur, it is human portents that are to be feared: poor plowing that harms the harvest, hoeing and weeding out of season, governmental malice that causes the loss of the people. When agriculture is untimely and the harvest bad, the price of grain is high and the people starve. In the roads and streets there are dead people. These are called human portents. When governmental commands are unenlightened, corvée miscalculated or untimely, fundamental affairs chaotic—these are called human portents. When ritual and morality are not cultivated, when internal and external are not separated, when male and female are licentious and disorderly, when father and son are suspicious of each other, when superior and inferior are obstinate and estranged, when crime and hardship occur together—these are called human portents. Portents are born of disorder; when the three types [of human portents][18] obtain, there is no peace in the country. . . .

If the sacrifice for rain [is performed], and it rains, what of it? I say: It is nothing. Even if there had been no sacrifice, it would have rained. When the sun and moon are eclipsed, we rescue them [sc. by performing the proper rites]; when Heaven sends drought we [perform] the sacrifice for rain; we decide great matters only after divining with turtle and milfoil. This is not in order to obtain what we seek, but in order to embellish [such occasions]. Thus the noble man takes [these ceremonies] to be embellishment, but the populace takes them to be spiritual. To take them as embellishment is auspicious; to take them as spiritual is inauspicious. . . .

19. Discourse on Ritual

Whence did rituals arise? I say: One is born with desires; if one desires and does not obtain [the object of one's desires], then one cannot but seek it. If, in seeking, people have no measures or limits, then there cannot but be contention. Contention makes disorder, and disorder privation. The Former Kings hated such disorder, and established ritual and morality in order to divide [the people into classes], in order to nourish people's desires and grant what people seek. They brought it about that desires need not be deprived of objects, that objects need not be depleted by desires; the two support each other and grow. This is where rituals arise. . . . The noble man having attained his nourishment, he will also be fond of separation. What is separation? I say: Noble and base have their ranks; old and young have their disparate [status]; poor and rich, light and heavy—all have what is fitting to them. . . .

A person has the incipience of both kinds of emotions[19] from birth. If they are stopped and continued, broadened and made shallow, increased and diminished, categorized and exhausted, made to flourish and be beautiful, and caused to be—in trunk and branch, from end to beginning—in all respects appropriate and suitable, so that they can be a standard for myriad generations, this standard is ritual. Other than the noble man who cultivates himself and acts appropriately and with maturity, no one can know this. Thus I say: The *xing* is the basis and origin, the material and simple [state of humanity]. Artifice is refinement and pattern, the exalted and flourishing [state]. Without *xing*, artifice has nothing to add itself onto; without artifice, *xing* cannot make itself beautiful. When *xing* and artifice are united, then we are at one with the name of "Sage." . . .

21. Resolving Blindness

Master Mo was blinded by utility and did not know refinement. Master Song was blinded by desire and did not know attainment. Master Shēn was blinded by laws and did not know [the value of] moral paragons. Master Shèn was blinded by [administrative] efficiency and did not know knowledge. Master Hui was blinded by propositions and did not know reality. Master Zhuang was blinded by Heaven and did not know humanity.[20] Thus, if we follow utility and call it [the Way], the Way will be entirely [a matter of] profit. If we follow desire and call it the Way, the Way will be entirely pleasure. If we follow laws and call them the Way, the Way will be entirely statecraft. If we follow efficiency and call it the Way, the Way will be entirely convenience. If we follow propositions and call them the Way, the Way will be entirely theories. If we follow Heaven and call it the Way, the Way will be entirely reliance [sc. on the forces of nature]. All these several [ideas] are one corner of the Way. The Way is constant in body and inexhaustibly changing. One corner does not suffice to extrapolate [the rest]. People with parochial knowledge look upon one corner of the Way, but are never able to recognize it [as such]. Thus they think it adequate and adorn it. Inside, they bring disorder upon themselves with it; outside, they use it to delude others. Superiors becloud inferiors with it; inferiors becloud superiors with it. This is the catastrophe of blind blockage. Confucius was humane, knowledgeable, and not blinded. Thus he studied the various arts to the point that he was the equal of the Former Kings. One school obtained the universal Way. They deduced from it and applied it, and were not blinded by their accomplishments. . . .

How does one know the Way? I say, the mind. How does the mind know? I say: emptiness, unity, and tranquility. The mind never stops storing, but it has something called "emptiness." The mind never stops being filled, but it has something called "unity." The mind never stops moving, but it has something called "tranquility." From birth humans have awareness; with awareness come thoughts; thoughts are stored. But [the mind] has something called "emptiness": it does not take what is stored to harm what is to be received; this is called "emptiness." From birth the mind has awareness; with awareness comes differentiation; different things are known at the same time. Knowing different things at the same time is duality. But [the mind] has something called "unity": it does not take one thing to harm another; this is called "unity." The mind dreams when it sleeps; it moves spontaneously when it relaxes; it plans when it is employed. Thus the mind never stops moving, but it has something called "tranquility": it does not take dreams and fancies to bring disorder upon knowledge; this is called "tranquility." . . .

The mind is the lord of the body and the master of spirit illumination. It issues commands but does not receive commands. It prohibits on its own; it employs on its own; it considers on its own; it takes on its own; it acts on its own; it ceases on its own. Thus the mouth can be forced to be silent or to speak; the body can be forced to contract or expand; the mind cannot be forced to change its intention. If it accepts [something], it receives it; if it rejects, it forgoes it. . . .

22. Rectifying Names

What does one rely upon to [determine] same and different? I say: One relies upon the senses. The senses of all members of the same species with the same essence—their senses perceive things in the same manner. Thus we associate things that appear similar upon comparison; in this manner we provide designated names for them in order to define them with respect to each other. Shape, body, color, and pattern are distinguished by the eyes. Sound, tone, treble, bass, mode, harmony—odd sounds are distinguished by the ears. Sweet, bitter, salty, bland, pungent, sour—odd tastes are distinguished by the mouth. Fragrant, foul, sweet-smelling, odorous, rank, fetid, putrid, acrid—odd smells are distinguished by the nose. Painful, itchy, cold, hot, smooth, sharp, light, and heavy are differentiated by the body. . . .

23. The Evil of *Xing*

Human *xing* is evil; what is good is artifice. Now human *xing* is as follows. At birth there is fondness for profit in it. Following this, contention and robbery arise, and deference and courtesy are destroyed. At birth there is envy and hatred in it. Following this, violence and banditry arise, and loyalty and trust are destroyed. At birth there are the desires of the ear and eye: there is fondness for sound and color in them. Following this, perversion and disorder arise, and ritual, morality, refinement, and principles are destroyed. Thus obeying one's *xing* and following one's emotions must result in contention and robbery. This is in accordance with the violation of [social] division and disruption in the natural order, and return to turmoil. Thus there must be the transformation [brought about by] the methods of a teacher and the Way of ritual and morality; then the result will be deference and courtesy, in accordance with refinement and principles, and return to order. Using these [considerations] to see it, human *xing* is clearly evil; what is good is artifice....

In ancient times, the Sage Kings considered human *xing* to be evil and thought people partial, malicious, and not upright; rebellious, disorderly, and not governed. For this reason they established ritual and morality for [the people]. They instituted laws and norms in order to rectify people's emotions and *xing* by reforming and adorning them, in order to guide people's emotions and *xing* by taming and transforming them. Only then did order ensue, in accordance with what is the Way. People today who are transformed by the methods of a teacher, who accumulate refinement and learning, who take ritual and morality as their Way, become noble men; those who indulge their *xing* and emotions, who are at peace in lust and staring, and who remain far from ritual and morality, become small men. Using these [considerations] to see it, human *xing* is clearly evil; what is good is artifice.

Mencius said: Since one can learn, one's *xing* is good. This is not so. This [point of view] does not attain to knowledge of human *xing* and does not investigate into the distinction between *xing* and artifice. *Xing* is what is spontaneous from Heaven, what cannot be learned, what cannot be acquired. Ritual and morality arise from the Sages. People become capable of them through learning; they perfect themselves by acquiring them. What cannot be learned, what cannot be acquired, and is in human beings, is called *xing*. What is in human beings, which they can be capable of through learning, which they can acquire to perfect themselves, is called "artifice." This is the distinction between *xing* and artifice....

Mencius said, Human *xing* is good. I say: This is not so. From ancient times until the present, all that has been called "good" in the world is rectitude, principle, peace, and order. What is called "evil" is partiality, malice, rebelliousness, and disorder. This is the distinction between good and evil. Now, can one sincerely believe that human *xing* is originally upright, principled, peaceful, and orderly? Then what use for the Sage Kings, what use for ritual and morality? . . .

A Sage is a person who has attained [Sagehood] through accumulation [of learning]. It was asked, Sagehood can be achieved by accumulating [learning], but not all of us can do so—why is this? I answered: We can, but we cannot be forced. Thus a small man could become a noble man, but is not willing to. A noble man could become a small man, but is not willing to. Small man, noble man—it is never the case that one cannot become the other. The [reason that] the one does not become the other is not that he cannot, but that he cannot be forced. This is how a person in the street can become Yu.[21]

—PRG

Notes

1. A reference to Master Zeng's triple self-examination in *Analects* 1.4 (see selection 7).
2. As we have seen in *Lyrics of Chu*, "spirit illumination" can refer to the physical vitality of the body, but here Xun Zi uses the term to denote intellectual lucidity.

3. This is the origin of the popular saying that a journey of a thousand miles begins with one step.

4. A legendary thoroughbred.

5. The "Yellow Springs" is the name for the subterranean home of the dead. The point is that the humble earthworm can tunnel all the way to the center of the earth by employing its faculties to one end.

6. A minister or gentleman was expected to walk rapidly in the presence of his superiors, so as not to importune them.

7. That is to say, these are the characteristics of human beings before they undertake the task of self-cultivation.

8. Yu was the Sage King who harnessed the waters, Jie the prodigal last king of the mythical Xia dynasty.

9. Yao was another Sage King, Zhi a legendary robber.

10. "Physiognomy" is a form of divination that uses the shapes of people's faces to tell their fortunes. The first half of this chapter is devoted to a refutation of physiognomy, whereupon Xun Zi moves on to other philosophical issues. It is from this later part of the chapter that the present excerpt is taken.

11. I.e., that humans are featherless bipeds.

12. A legendary ape with no hair.

13. Xun Zi invokes the familiar distinction between a "king," who rules by virtue, and a "hegemon," who rules by might.

14. A legendary archer.

15. A legendary charioteer.

16. The warlike founders of the Shang and Zhou dynasties, respectively.

17. The name of a legendary sword.

18. I.e., (1) lack of separation between internal and external, male and female; (2) friction between father and son, superior and inferior; and (3) crime and hardship.

19. I.e., joy and sorrow.

20. Masters Mo, Hui, and Zhuang are familiar to us from previous readings. Masters Shèn and Shēn were both famous as political philosophers; not much is known about Master Song, and his writings have not survived. The point of this passage is that only Confucius and his disciples were able to comprehend the Way in all its manifestations; the thinkers of the other schools could not perceive more than one corner.

21. That is to say, even a vagabond can become a Sage.

A BASIC IDEA in early Chinese philosophy is the notion that music is an essential attribute of the cosmos. For example, the discussion of the "pipes of Heaven and Earth" in the *Zhuang Zi* (translated below), while deliberately enigmatic, explains that the primordial movements of qi in the universe brought about a cacophony of sounds that finally culminated in a "mighty chorus." The context of the passage indicates that not everyone may be able to hear this cosmic music, but it is there nonetheless, howling and whirling, waiting for anyone with an attuned ear to hear and appreciate.

Similarly, the *Spring and Autumn Annals of Mr. Lü,* an encyclopedic text from the third century B.C.E., states that at the time of creation, the movements of yin and yang and the rotations of Heaven and Earth were all accompanied by sounds that marked the harmony and accord of the world and the Way. The consequence is that when we make music today, we are actually recreating the patterns of the universe. The *Spring and Autumn Annals of Mr. Lü* goes on to devote substantial space to the task of distinguishing proper music from perverse music. Music is a representation of the universe, and an improper rendition can only have inauspicious consequences.

The most thorough discussion of the difference between suitable and unsuitable music appears in the writings of Xun Zi. In his "Discourse on Music," Xun Zi begins by affirming that the urge to convey emotion through music is a natural component of human nature—an assumption in accord with the above view of the inherent musical propensity of the very cosmos. But since music can affect us deeply, Xun Zi argues, it is of paramount importance that our musical utterances assume the appropriate form. To this end, the Sage Kings handed down correct "patterns" *(wen)* that accord with the Way; we must regulate our spontaneous expressions of emotion by "patterning" them after the models of the Sage Kings, lest we sing impure odes that violate the Way and thus disseminate perversion throughout the world. As we can see, Xun Zi understands "music" *(yue)* as a special kind of ritual *(li):* the ritual of artistic expression.

In his essay on music, Xun Zi laid the groundwork of Chinese literary criticism. The idea that music and literature may be proper or improper insofar as they conform to the infallible standards of the Sage Kings became commonplace in subsequent discussions of the problem. The "Great Preface" to the *Odes* (probably written in the first century C.E., long after the *Odes* had coalesced as a canonical text) builds on an understanding of music and its didactic purposes characteristic of Xun Zi to explain why the *Odes* represent what it calls "the zenith of poetry." The authors of the *Odes* "sang their emotions" in order to inspire their neighbors to virtue, and succeeded in producing literary works that "obeyed the patterns" while "warning their audience."

Scholars often point out two major shortcomings of this theory. First, the idea that music and literature must reflect the genuine emotional state of the author is no longer popular in contemporary literary theory—much less so the Chinese idea that one can ascertain the feelings of artists through their work. Second, the conception of music as a "ritual" of emotional expression à la Xun Zi countenances only those compositions that serve a discernible moral purpose. Any kind of music or literature that does not limit itself to the "patterns" is immediately condemned rather than explored. But few people today believe that art should be judged according to its fulfillment of preconceived moral and aesthetic standards.—PRG

On the Equality of Things [From *Zhuang Zi*. Excerpt]

Sir Motley of Southurb sat leaning against his low table. He looked up to heaven and exhaled slowly. Disembodied, he seemed bereft of soul. Sir Wanderer of Countenance Complete, who stood in attendance before him, asked, "How can we explain this? Can the body really be made to become like withered wood? Can the mind really be made to become like dead ashes? The one who is leaning against the table now is not the one who was formerly leaning against the table."

"Indeed," said Sir Motley, "your question is a good one, Yan. Just now, I lost myself. Can you understand this? You may have heard the pipes of man, but not the pipes of earth. You may have heard the pipes of earth, but not the pipes of heaven."

"I venture," said Sir Wanderer, "to ask their secret."

"The Great Clod,"[1] said Sir Motley, "emits a vital breath called the wind. If it doesn't blow, nothing happens. Once it starts to blow, however, myriad hollows begin to howl. Have you not heard its moaning? The clefts and crevasses of the towering mountains, the hollows and cavities of huge trees a hundred spans around—they are like nostrils, like mouths, like ears, like sockets, like cups, like mortars, or like the depressions that form puddles and pools. The wind blowing over them makes the sound of rushing water, whizzing arrows, shouting, breathing, calling, crying, laughing, gnashing. The wind in front sings *aiee* and the wind that follows sings *wouu*. A light breeze evokes a small response; a powerful gale brings forth a mighty chorus. When the blast dies down, then all the hollows are silent. Have you not seen the leaves that quiver with tingling reverberations?"

"The pipes of earth," said Sir Wanderer, "are none other than all of the hollows you have described. The pipes of man are bamboo tubes arrayed in series. I venture to ask what the pipes of heaven are."

"As for the pipes of heaven," said Sir Motley, "the myriad sounds produced by the blowing of wind are different, yet all it does is elicit the natural propensities of the hollows themselves. What need is there for something else to stimulate them?"—VHM

Great Music [From *Spring and Autumn Annals of Mr. Lü*. Excerpt]

The source of tones and music is distant. They are born in measures and based on the Great Unity. The Great Unity emits the two attitudes (i.e., Heaven and Earth); the two attitudes emit yin and yang. Yin and yang change and transform: one rises; one sinks. They unite and create transformations. In primordial chaos, they separate and then unite again; they unite and then separate again. This is called Heaven's Constancy. Heaven and Earth [turn like] the wheel of a chariot: the end is again the beginning; [having reached] the highest point, it returns again. Everything is as it should be. [Among] the sun, moon, stars, and constellations, some are fast and some are slow. The sun and moon are dissimilar in their orbital period. The four seasons arise one after the other. Some are hot and some are cold; some are short and some are long; some are soft and some are hard. The origin of the Myriad Things—they are created by the Great Unity and transformed by yin and yang. Once the germs are excited, they congeal into a form; the form is embodied in a place, and nothing is without sound. The sound comes from harmony; harmony comes from accord. When the Former Kings established music, it was born of this.

Discourse on Music [From *Xun Zi*. Excerpts]

Music is joy; it is what human emotions cannot avoid. Thus humans cannot be without music. If we are joyous, then we must express it in sounds and tones and give form to it in movement and quietude. And the Way of Humanity is fulfilled in sounds and tones, in movement and quietude, and in the changes in the techniques of the *xing*.[2] Thus humans cannot be without joy, and joy cannot be without form, but if that form is not [in line with] the Way, then there cannot but be disorder. The Former Kings hated this disorder; thus they instituted the sounds of the Odes and Hymns to make them accord with the Way. They brought it about that their sounds were sufficient [to give form] to joy but were not dissipated; they brought it about that their patterned [compositions] were sufficient to make distinctions but were not timorous [?];[3] they brought it about that the directness, complexity, richness, and rhythm were sufficient to move people's good minds; they brought it about that heterodox and impure *qi* would have no opportunity to attach itself. . . . Sounds and music enter people deeply; they transform people quickly. Thus the Former Kings were careful to make [music] patterned. When music is centered and balanced, the people are harmonious and not dissipated. When music is stern and grave, the people are uniform and not disorderly. When the people are harmonious and uniform, the army is firm and the citadels secure; enemy states dare not invade. When this is the case, then none among the Hundred Clans are not at peace in their dwellings; all are joyous in the neighborhoods and fully satisfied with their superiors. Only then will the name and repute [of the ruler of such a state] be shining and his glory great; within the Four Seas, none among the people will be unwilling to accept him as their teacher. This is the beginning of kingship. When music is overwrought and seduces us to malice, then the people are dissipated, indolent, crude, and base. Dissipation and indolence lead to disorder, crudity and baseness to contention. When there is disorder and contention, the army is soft and the citadels pillaged; enemies will threaten [such a state]. When this is the case, the Hundred Clans are not at peace in their dwellings; they are not joyous in their neighborhoods or satisfied with their superiors. Thus when rituals and music lapse, and heterodox tones arise, this is the root of territorial encroachment, insult, and disgrace. Thus the Former Kings took ritual and music to be noble and heterodox tones to be base. This [principle] appears in the "Procedures of the Officials":[4] "The affairs of the Grand Music-Master are to cultivate the edicts and commands, to investigate poetic stanzas; to proscribe licentious sounds—so that [the people] act in accord with the seasons, and barbarous customs and heterodox tones dare not bring disorder upon the 'Elegantiae.'"[5]

Great Preface [to the *Odes*]

Poetry is where our intentions go. What is in the mind becomes an intention; we send forth words to make a poem. The emotions move about within us and are formed in words. When words are inadequate [to convey our emotions], we sigh and exclaim them; when sighs and exclamations are inadequate, we sing and chant them; when songs and chants are inadequate, we unconsciously dance and stamp them with our hands and feet. We send forth our emotions in sounds; sounds that are perfected and patterned are called "tones." The tones of an ordered age are peaceful and joyous: the government is harmonious. The tones of a disorderly age are resentful and angry: the government is perverse. The tones of a doomed state are mournful and longing: the people are in difficulty. Thus to rectify success and failure, to move Heaven and Earth, to stimulate the ghosts and spirits, nothing is closer to hand than poetry. The Former Kings used it to regulate husband

and wife, to perfect filial reverence, to enrich human relationships, to beautify moral education, and to change customs.

Thus there are six principles to the *Odes*. The first is the "Airs," the second "recitation," the third "comparison," the fourth "arousal," the fifth "Elegantiae," the sixth "Hymns."[6] Superiors transform inferiors by means of the Airs; inferiors criticize their superiors by means of the Airs. When a remonstrance obeys the [proper] patterns, the speaker is blameless, and [the words] sufficient to warn the audience. Thus it is called an "Air."[7] When the time came that the Way of kings declined, ritual and morality lapsed, government and filial piety were lost. States changed their governments, families [adopted] different customs, and the Airs of Change and Elegantiae of Change were composed. The historiographers of states were enlightened with respect to the traces of success and failure. Pained by the changes in human relationships and grieved by the cruelty of punishments and government, they sang their emotions in order to inspire their superiors because they understood the changes [that had taken place] and cherished the old customs. Thus the Airs of Change emerge from emotions and come to rest in ritual and morality. That they should emerge from emotions is human nature; that they should come to rest in ritual and morality is the fecund [influence] of the Former Kings.

Therefore, the affairs of a particular state, when related to the root (i.e., frame of reference) of a particular person, are called "Airs." [Odes that] indicate the affairs of the world and are formed by the habits of [all people] within the Four Quarters are called *Ya* ["Elegantiae"]. *Ya* means "correct." They indicate the origin of the rise or fall of kingly government. There are lesser and greater governments; thus there are the "Lesser Elegantiae" and "Greater Elegantiae."

The "Hymns" are the formed manifestation of flourishing virtue; they are used to inform the ghosts and spirits of one's accomplishments. These are the "Four Beginnings";[8] they are the zenith of poetry.

—PRG

Notes

1. A metaphor for the earth, the universe, or—in most cases—the Way (Dao/Tao).

2. This statement is difficult to construe, and there is a conspicuous lack of commentary about it. Perhaps Xun Zi means to say that music ("sounds and tones, movement and quietude") is a technique for improving the *xing* and thus fulfilling the Way of Humanity. This would be in line with his general views.

3. The original is unclear here.

4. "Procedures of the Officials" sounds like the title of an authoritative text of some kind, but Xun Zi is actually quoting his own words from a different essay.

5. By "Elegantiae," Xun Zi may mean either the section of the canonical *Odes* by that name or the "elegant" music sanctioned by the Sages—or both, since these alternatives amount to essentially the same thing.

6. The "Airs," "Elegantiae," and "Hymns" are sections of the *Odes*. "Comparison" *(bi)* and "arousal" *(xing)* are poetic techniques whose precise meanings are disputed; both refer to the use of imagery to convey meaning. "Recitation" *(fu)* can refer either to composing an ode or to reciting an extant one.

7. The operative image is that the audience is inspired by an "Air" as though by a righteous wind.

8. I.e., the Airs, Greater and Lesser Elegantiae, and Hymns. This set of Four Beginnings is different from the one discussed by Mencius (see selection 9).

WHEN EARLY CHINESE philosophers speak of "the rites" *(li)*, it is difficult to say precisely what they mean. Confucius mentions various rites in the *Analects* (e.g., *Analects* 9.3, which discusses the appropriate cap to be worn in a temple), but these brief references do not yield much information as to the scope of the rites, their origins, or their underlying principles. Moreover, the three great ritual compendia in the Confucian canon—the *Rites of Zhou (Zhouli),* the *Ceremonies and Rites (Yili),* and the *Book of Rites (Liji)*—are notoriously unreliable. The *Rites of Zhou,* though purporting to be a table of organization of the Zhou bureaucracy, dates in fact to the late Warring States or early Han period; the *Record of Rites* was compiled even later, at the end of the Han dynasty. The *Ceremonies and Rites* may be the oldest of the three codices, but the paucity of ancient references to it makes it impossible to assign the text a definite date.

"Vestments of Mourning" (Sangfu) is a short ritual digest that may provide some idea of what early thinkers understood by *li.* It prescribes the duration of mourning, as well as the different kinds of attire that one must wear, after the death of relatives of various degrees of consanguinity. The text has come down to us as a section of the *Ceremonies and Rites,* but there is evidence that it was originally circulated as an independent text. For example, it is the only section of the *Ceremonies and Rites* that has been transmitted with an ancient commentary. More important, the recently discovered manuscripts from Guodian (ca. 300 B.C.E.) allude to sartorial regulations that square with "Vestments of Mourning," showing that, at the very least, this ritual code descends from a genuinely ancient tradition.

While "Vestments of Mourning" is very clear about who should wear what, it does not attempt to elucidate the reasoning behind its requirements. And unfortunately, the accompanying commentary obfuscates as often as it enlightens. Hence it is omitted here; where its opinion is helpful, it is summarized in the notes.—PRG

Vestments of Mourning [Excerpts]

Untrimmed sackcloth [worn for] three years.

An untrimmed sackcloth garment with a skirt; a headband and waistband of the female nettle hemp; a staff; a twisted girdle; a cap with a hatband of cord; and rush sandals are worn in mourning

> for one's father;
> by the feudal lords, for the Son of Heaven;
> for one's lord;
> by a father, for his eldest son;
> for one's adopted successor;
> by a wife, for her husband;
> by a concubine, for her lord;
> by a daughter who is still at home,[1] for her father;

([Original Note: Women use] a linen fillet; they dress their hair with a pin of small-stemmed bamboo; they wear sackcloth for three years.)

> by a married daughter who has returned to her father's home, for her father.

The multitude of ministers of all ranks wear a linen girdle and string sandals for their lord.

Trimmed sackcloth [worn for] three years.

A coarse sackcloth garment with a skirt, trimmed; a headband and waistband of the male hemp plant; a cap with linen tassels; a pared staff; a linen girdle; and coarse sandals are worn for three years

> for one's mother, if one's father is dead;
> for one's stepmother as though for one's mother;
> for one's foster mother as though for one's mother;[2]
> by a mother, for her eldest son.

Trimmed sackcloth, with staff, [worn for] one year.

A coarse sackcloth garment with skirt, trimmed; a headband and waistband of the male hemp plant; a cap with linen tassels; a pared staff; a linen girdle; and coarse sandals are worn for one year

> for one's mother, if one's father is still alive;
> for one's wife;
> by children of a divorced wife, for their mother;
> as requital,[3] by those [children] who have accompanied their stepmother [to her new home] if she remarried after the death of their father.[4]

Trimmed sackcloth, without a staff, [worn for] one year.

[A trimmed sackcloth garment, as above], without a staff, and with sandals of hemp, is worn

> for one's grandfather and grandmother;
> for one's elder and younger paternal uncles and their wives;
> by the son of a grand master by his wife,[5] for his [own] wife;
> for one's elder and younger brothers;
> for the sons of one's elder and younger brothers;
> by the son of a grand master by his concubine, for his elder and younger half-brothers by the grand master's wife;
> for one's grandson by one's legitimate son's wife;
> as requital, by one who has been adopted as another's successor, for his [own] father and mother;
> by a daughter who has gone to her husband's house, for her father and mother, and for whoever among her elder and younger brothers should succeed her father;[6]
> for one's stepfather, if one has been living with him;
> for one's husband's lord;
> for an elder or younger paternal aunt, or for a daughter who has gone to her husband's house, but has no [son of her own to be her] patron[7] (as requital, in the case of the aunts);
> for the father, mother, wife, eldest son, grandfather, and grandmother of one's lord;
> by a concubine, for her lord's wife;

by a woman, for her father-in-law and mother-in-law;

for the sons of the elder and younger brothers of one's husband;

by the concubine of a duke or grand master for her son;

by a girl, for her grandfather and grandmother;

by the son of a grand master, for his elder and younger paternal uncles and their wives, for their sons, for his elder and younger brothers and their sons, for his elder and younger paternal aunts, for a daughter who has gone to her husband's house but has no patron, and for the grand master's titled lady (only in the case of the children is this not requital);

by a grand master, for the legitimate grandsons of his grandmother and grandfather, if they are of the rank of *shi*;[8]

by all concubines, from those of dukes to those of *shi*, for their father and mother.

—PRG

Notes

1. I.e., an unmarried daughter.

2. In other words, one wears the trimmed sackcloth garment for three years for one's mother, step-mother, or foster mother if one's father is deceased.

3. "Requital" is an unexplained principle that is repeatedly invoked in this text to justify various mourning requirements. Traditional commentators do not agree on the precise meaning of "requital" in this context.

4. The commentary says that the purpose of this requirement is to show esteem for mothers who love their children to the end. Those children who did not accompany their stepmother to her new home are not required to wear sackcloth for her at all when she dies. If one's stepmother did not remarry after the death of one's father, then one is required to wear sackcloth for her for three years (as we have seen above).

5. Here and following, the text distinguishes between sons borne by a man's primary wife and those borne by a concubine.

6. The commentaries explain that one cannot owe the heaviest mourning obligations (untrimmed sackcloth worn for three years) to two people at the same time. Thus a married woman owes the heaviest mourning obligations to her husband, rather than to her father, as long as she lives in her husband's house.

7. That is, no one to perform the regular sacrifices to her spirit.

8. The lowest rank of nobility.

AMONG XUN ZI'S many distinguished students, the two most famous names are Li Si (d. 208 B.C.E.) and Han Fei Zi (d. 233 B.C.E.). Both men attained renown as advisers in the state of Qin. Li Si gained office there first—he went on to become Counselor-in-Chief of the empire—and, fearing Han Fei Zi more than any other rival, allegedly drove his colleague to suicide. Before Han Fei Zi's untimely death, however, he had completed a voluminous collection of writings that have warranted his standing as one of the most admired political thinkers in Chinese history.

According to Han Fei Zi, the keys to rulership are the "Two Handles," by which he means rewards and punishments. A ruler must not let his ministers grasp the "Handles"—that is, dispense rewards and punishments in their own name—lest they use this power to usurp his authority. Rewards and punishments, furthermore, are determined according to a calculus called "forms and names." The ruler must never undertake any concrete action himself, but should always delegate responsibilities and offices to his inferiors. The ruler charges his ministers with various tasks based on their particular abilities; these tasks are the "names" of the ministers. The ministers must then carry out their duties and report their results, which are called the "forms." The ruler finally compares the "forms" with the foreordained "names," and if these match—that is to say, if the ruler's orders have been carried out precisely—then the ministers are rewarded. If not, the ministers must be punished.

Han Fei Zi adds that a ruler ought to conceal his own abilities, desires, and emotions, because his vulpine ministers will try to unseat him if they discover his strengths and weaknesses. A successful ruler is a silent and empty mystery, unfathomable and unpredictable. Clearly inspired by the *Lao Zi,* Han Fei Zi describes the characteristics of the ruler in language familiar from that text as attributes of the Way: "dark," "vacuous," "immeasurable," "constant." Like his teacher, Xun Zi, Han Fei Zi asserts that a ruler must emulate the Way; the great difference is that Han Fei Zi conceives of the Way in far more sinister terms. Whereas the universal Way of Xun Zi is open even to beggars in the street, Han Fei Zi reduces the Way to a Way of Rulership, a set of cosmic principles which the ruler and the ruler alone may know and which he applies for the sole purpose of confirming his vise-like hold on the "Handles" of government.

Surviving works by earlier political thinkers reveal Han Fei Zi's indebtedness to his predecessors. The fragmentary writings of Shen Buhai (fl. 354–340 B.C.E.), for example, also take a bureaucratic approach to government based on a notion of "names" similar to that of Han Fei Zi. Moreover, a text attributed to Lord Shang (i.e., Gongsun Yang, d. 338 B.C.E.) highlights the awesome effectiveness of a rational system of rewards and punishments. If the people's expectations are molded properly by means of the "Handles," then they will devote themselves entirely to agriculture and war, which are taken by Lord Shang to be the essential elements of statecraft, but are acknowledged as the two least pleasant pursuits of mankind. These earlier traditions of political philosophy show that Han Fei Zi did not fashion his image of the ideal state ex nihilo, but synthesized various received administrative concepts into a distinctive and chilling program.

The following translations include (1) "The Great Body," the longest surviving fragment of Shen Buhai's works; (2) "Outer and Inner," an essay attributed to Lord Shang but perhaps composed by a later hand; and (3) "The Way of Rulership," which is Han Fei Zi's most concise manifesto. The reader will notice that Han Fei Zi's prose is by far the most fluid of this genre. Earlier political writers, characteristically suspicious of literary refinement as nothing more than a sign of ineffective government (see "Outer and Inner," for example), tended to produce wooden and unadorned position papers. Han Fei Zi, on the other hand, evidently believed that a successful essay needs to be more than reasoned: it must be artful.—PRG

The Great Body [by Shen Buhai]

When one woman usurps [the power of] her husband, the multitude of [his other] women are thrown into disorder. When one minister monopolizes his lord, the [other] thronging ministers are overshadowed. Thus a jealous wife breaks up a household without difficulty; a disorderly minister breaks up his state without difficulty. Therefore, an enlightened lord causes his ministers to advance together, like the spokes of a hub, so that none is able to monopolize his lord.

Now the reason why a lord of men places high value on erecting walls and fortifications and is assiduous about the closure of gates and entryways is [to prepare for] the arrival of invading warriors and robbing brigands. But one who assassinates his lord and takes over the state need not climb over the walls and fortifications nor burst through the close gates and entryways. By obscuring the lord's ability to see, blocking the lord's hearing, and snatching his government, he may monopolize [the lord's ability] to command, possess his people, and take his state.

Suppose we let Wu Huo and Peng Zu[1] bear the weight of a thousand *jun*[2] on their backs and hold beautiful scepters and tablets to their breasts.[3] Command Meng Ben and Cheng Jing[4] to guard them with Ganjiang swords. If they were to go along a dark road, robbers would still steal from them. Now the strength of the lord of men does not exceed that of Wu Huo and Peng Zu, nor his bravery that of Meng Ben and Cheng Jing, while what he defends is not limited to beautiful scepters and tablets or a thousand-weight in gold. He may wish not to lose it, but how can he succeed?

The enlightened lord is like the self;[5] the ministers are like the hands. The lord is like an outcry; the minister is like an echo. The lord sets up the roots; the ministers manage the branches. The lord puts the essentials in order; the ministers carry out the details. The lord controls the "Handles";[6] the ministers take care of routine affairs. One who is a minister is held by a contract and obliged to [live up to] his name. Names are the main cord of the net of Heaven and Earth, the talismans of the Sages. If one casts the net of Heaven and Earth using the talismans of the Sages, then the Myriad Things are not disposed to flee.[7]

Thus one who is adept at ruling relies on [an appearance of] stupidity, erects himself in insufficiency, displays himself in cowardice, and conceals himself in lack of undertaking. He hides his reasons and covers his tracks. He exhibits his inaction to the world; therefore those who are near are intimate with him and those who are distant cherish him. People snatch from those who exhibit their surpluses and cooperate with those who exhibit their shortfalls. Those who are hard are felled; those who are endangered are protected. Those who move sway [precariously]; those who are quiet are secure.

Names rectify themselves; affairs settle themselves. Therefore, one who possesses the Way rectifies [the world] by beginning with names and settles it by according with affairs.

The drum does not take part in the Five Tones but is the ruler of the Five Tones.[8] One who possesses the Way does not do the work of the Five Offices but is the ruler of the government. The lord knows the Way; the ministers know their affairs. To speak appropriately ten times out of ten or to act appropriately a hundred times out of a hundred is the affair of a minister; it is not the Way of the lord of men.

In the past, Yao⁹ put the world in order by means of names. If names are rectified, then the world is in order. Jie also [tried to] put the world in order by means of names. If names are askew, then the world is in disorder. Therefore, the Sages value the rectification of names. The ruler dwells in the greater [considerations]; the ministers dwell in the finer [points]. [The ruler] listens to them according to their names, watches them according to their names, and commands them according to their names.

A mirror displays the essence [of an object]; without action, beauty and ugliness present themselves. The scale displays equilibrium; without action, light and heavy discover themselves. Anyone with the Way of Compliance partakes of everything without any [premeditated] undertakings. There are no undertakings, and yet the world aligns itself like a ridgepole.

Outer and Inner [from the *Writings of Lord Shang*]

Among the outer affairs of the people, nothing is harder than fighting [enemies]. Thus light methods cannot make them do it. What is meant by "light methods"? It is when rewards are few and authority meager. It refers to [a situation in which] licentious ways are not stopped. What is meant by "licentious ways"? It is when those who are sophistic and wise are valued, and when migrant¹⁰ bureaucrats are delegated responsibilities. It refers to [a situation in which] literature and private reputations are prominent. If these three [tendencies] are not stopped, the people will not fight, and undertakings will fail. Thus if rewards are few, those who are obedient will not profit; if authority is meager, then those who disobey will not suffer. Initiating licentious ways and using light methods to make [the people] fight is like baiting a mouse with a wildcat. Indeed, [the mouse] will not approach!

Thus whoever wishes to make his people fight must use heavy methods. Rewards must be manifold and authority strict. Licentious ways must be stopped. Those who are sophistic and wise should not be valued; migrant bureaucrats should not be delegated responsibilities; literature and private reputations should not be made prominent. If, when rewards are manifold and authority strict, the people see the many rewards of fighting, they will be heedless of death; if they see the disgrace of not fighting, they will be [content with] a bitter life.¹¹ Rewards make them heedless of death, and authority makes them [content with] a bitter life. And licentious ways will also be stopped. If one encounters an enemy with these [preparations], it will be like shooting at a floating leaf with a hundred-picul crossbow.¹² How could it be that they do not surrender?

Among the inner affairs of the people, nothing is more bitter than farming. Thus light regulations will not make them do it. What is meant by "light regulations"? It is when farmers are poor and merchants rich. Thus [the value of] food is low and that of money high. If [the value of] food is low, farmers are poor; if that of money is high, merchants are rich. If "branch affairs"¹³ are not prohibited, clever people will profit, and there will be multitudes of migrants [in search of] food. Thus farmers expend energy most bitterly, but the profit that they earn is slight and cannot be compared to that of merchants and clever people. If one could bring it about that merchants and clever people not multiply, the state would become rich even if one did not wish it.

Thus I say: Those who wish to enrich their state through farming must raise the value of grain within the borders. And the levies on those who are not farmers must be manifold; the taxes on profits in the markets must be heavy. Then the people will not be able to do without land. Since they will not be able to do without land, they will not think lightly of their food. If [the value of] food is high, landowners will profit. When landowners profit, there will be multitudes working [in the fields]. If [the value of] food is high and dealing in food not profitable—and, moreover, if one adds heavy taxes—then the people cannot but abandon their mercantile activities and their cleverness. And those who work on the earth will profit. Thus the people's energies will be entirely occupied by the profits of the earth. Thus one who engages in statecraft should bring all the profits of the frontiers home to the soldiers and all the profits of the markets to the farmers. One who brings all the profits of the frontiers home to the soldiers is strong; one who brings all the profits of the markets home to the farmers is rich. One who goes out to fight in strength and rests internally in richness is a king.

The Way of Rulership [from the *Han Fei Zi*]

The Way is the origin of the Myriad Things, the skein of right and wrong. Therefore, the enlightened lord holds to the origin in order to know the source of the Myriad Things and masters the skein in order to know the end points of gain and loss. Thus, in emptiness and tranquility, he awaits the commandment—the commandment for names to name themselves and for affairs to settle themselves. Since he is empty, he knows the essence of objects; since he is tranquil, he knows what is correct for everything that moves.[14] One who speaks spontaneously makes a name; one who acts spontaneously makes a form. When forms and names match identically, then everything returns to its essence without any action on the part of the ruler.[15]

Thus it is said: The lord ought not make his desires apparent. If the lord's desires are apparent, the ministers will carve and polish themselves [to deceive him]. The lord ought not make his intentions apparent. If the lord's intentions are apparent, the ministers will display themselves falsely. Thus it is said: Eliminate likes; eliminate dislikes. Then the ministers will appear plainly.[16] Eliminate tradition; eliminate wisdom. Then the ministers will prepare themselves. Thus [the lord] possesses wisdom, but does not use it to deliberate; he causes the Myriad Things to know their place. He possesses [the knowledge of proper] conduct, but does not use it to perform worthy acts; he observes what his ministers and inferiors comply with. He possesses courage, but does not use it in anger; he causes the thronging ministers to maximize their prowess. For these reasons, if one eliminates wisdom, there will be insight; if one eliminates worthiness, there will be accomplishments; if one eliminates courage, there will be strength. The thronging ministers will hold to their offices; the hundred officers will have a constant [routine]. To employ [subordinates] according to their abilities is called "practicing constancy."

Thus it is said: Silent! He has his place without taking a stand. Vacuous! No one can comprehend his location. The enlightened lord practices nonaction above; the thronging ministers tremble below. The Way of the enlightened lord is to cause the wise to make the most of their deliberations; the lord relies on [their wisdom] to decide affairs, but he does not exhaust his own wisdom. [He causes] the worthy to marshal their talents; he relies on [their abilities] to delegate responsibilities but does not exhaust his own abilities. If they should have accomplishments, it is the lord who is reckoned worthy for it, while if they commit transgressions, it is the ministers who are charged with the guilt; thus the lord does not exhaust his reputation. For this reason, he is not worthy, but is the master of the worthy; he is not wise, but is the corrector of the wise. The ministers have the toil, the lord the successes. This is what is meant by the warp[17] of a worthy ruler.

The Way lies in what cannot be seen; its uses lie in what cannot be known. Be empty, tranquil, and without undertaking; see the flaws [of others] from a dark [vantage point]. See but do not be seen; hear but do not be heard; know but do not be known. If you know the direction of some-one's words, do not change or improve them, but investigate whether they conform to [the deeds]. Establish one man in each office; if you do not let them talk freely to each other, every-thing will be maximized. If you cover your tracks and hide your reasons, inferiors cannot trace your origins. If you eliminate your wisdom and break off your abilities, inferiors cannot gauge you. Maintain your direction and examine whether it is identical [to your intentions]. Vigilantly grasp the "handles" (sc. of reward and punishment) and hold them firmly. Break their hopes, smash their intentions, and do not cause others to desire [the "handles"]. If you do not secure your gates, "tigers" will come into being. If you are not careful about your affairs and do not cover your emotions, "brigands" will arise. They slay their ruler, taking his place, none of them failing to participate; thus they are called "tigers." They dwell by their ruler's side; they are treach-erous ministers, hearing of their ruler's errors; thus they are called "brigands." Disperse their cliques; gather the rest [onto your side]; shut their gates; and snatch away their support. Then there will be no tigers in the state. Make your greatness immeasurable, your depth unfathomable; make forms and names match; investigate and test standards; execute those who act on their own. Then there will be no brigands in the state.

Thus there are five kinds of "blockages" for the ruler of men. When ministers shut out their ruler, it is called a "blockage." When ministers control resources and profits, it is called a "block-age." When ministers usurp [the right] to effect commands, it is called a "blockage." When min-isters are able to practice righteousness (sc. for their own reputation), it is called a "blockage." When ministers are able to plant others [in the bureaucracy], it is called a "blockage." If minis-ters shut out their ruler, the ruler loses his position. If ministers control resources and profits, the ruler loses power. If ministers usurp [the right] to effect commands, the ruler loses control. If ministers are able to practice righteousness, the ruler loses his reputation. If ministers are able to plant others [in the bureaucracy], the ruler loses [control of] his party. These are all [undertak-ings] that the ruler alone should execute; ministers should not be allowed to manage them.

According to the Way of the ruler of men, tranquility and reserve are treasures. Without man-aging affairs himself, he knows clumsiness from skill. Without deliberating and planning himself, he knows auspiciousness from inauspiciousness. Therefore, he does not speak, but good [words] respond; he does not act, but good [actions] multiply. When words respond, he takes hold of the contract; when actions multiply, he takes the tally in hand.[18] The extent to which the two halves of the tally conform determines rewards and punishments. Thus the thronging ministers utter their words; the lord hands down their duties according to their words and assesses their accom-plishments according to their duties. If their accomplishments match their duties and their duties match their words, they are rewarded. If their accomplishments do not match their duties or their duties do not match their words, they are punished. According to the Way of the enlightened lord, ministers do not utter words that they cannot match.

Thus, in bestowing rewards, an enlightened lord is bountiful like a seasonable rain; the Hun-dred Clans benefit from his fecundity. In carrying out punishments, he is dreadful like a thunder-clap; even spirits and sages cannot absolve themselves. Thus the enlightened lord does not reward recklessly or remit punishments. If he rewards recklessly, meritorious ministers will let their enter-prises slide. If he remits punishments, treacherous ministers will find it easy to do wrong. For this reason, those whose accomplishments are real must be rewarded, even if they are lowly and base; those whose transgressions are real must be punished, even if they are close and beloved. Then the lowly and base will not become insolent nor the close and beloved haughty.

—PRG

Notes

1. Legendary figures of great strength and longevity, respectively.

2. A *jun* was ancient unit of measure equivalent to thirty catties (or about sixteen and a half pounds).

3. Literally, "hold the beauty of scepters and tablets to their breasts."

4. Two famous swordsmen. "Ganjiang" is the name of a mythic sword.

5. I.e., the consciousness that commands the hands and other parts of the body.

6. I.e., rewards and punishments.

7. The general idea of this confusing passage seems to be that the ruler must use the principles of names to ensnare the Myriad Creatures within his net.

8. That is to say, a drum does not produce a note on a scale, but music is impossible without the rhythm of a drum.

9. A legendary Sage King. Jie, below, was a legendary tyrant.

10. And hence untrustworthy.

11. This sentence is somewhat convoluted; the point is that people who do not fight ought to be punished as examples to others.

12. A picul is a large unit of mass commonly used to measure the power of a bow. One picul is 120 catties, or approximately 66 pounds.

13. I.e., unessential undertakings in general, or trade in particular. The implied contrast is with "root affairs," or agriculture.

14. There is a subtle dimension to this sentence: *xu* (emptiness) is the natural opposite of *shi* (fullness), which can also mean "object" or "reality"; and *jing* (tranquility; repose) is a conventional opposite of *dong* (movement). The idea here is that the enlightened lord knows the essence of all real and moving objects because he is himself empty and motionless.

15. See the introduction to this selection. The concept of "forms and names" is explained in detail later in the book.

16. That is, without dissimulation.

17. An image from weaving: the "warp" (as opposed to the "weft" or "woof") determines the pattern to be woven.

18. The relationship between the lord and his ministers is likened here to a tally, which was a form of contract between a debtor and a creditor. At the time of the original agreement, the tally would be broken in two—one piece for each party. Like a creditor whose claim is embodied in his matching half of the tally, a lord assesses how well his ministers have lived up to their end of the bargain by the extent to which their actions conform to their stated obligations.

THE WARRING STATES period takes its name from *Stratagems of the Warring States (Zhanguo ce)*, a collection of anecdotes about the late Eastern Zhou period compiled from various sources during the Han dynasty. Even in ancient times, readers observed that the text can hardly be taken as a record of events as they actually transpired, but that the ingenious use of rhetorical techniques in the many orations contained in the *Stratagems* more than compensates for their questionable historicity. So the *Stratagems of the Warring States* are often explained as forensic exercises by unknown writers who tried to imagine what certain famous personages might have said at crucial moments in history.

Nevertheless, while clever speeches of persuasion are indeed a hallmark of the *Stratagems*, not all of the stories hinge on skillful rhetoric. The basic theme of the text is employing devious stratagems to fulfill one's worldly desires. Dulcet words represent only one possible avenue to success, and where the situation warrants other means—such as trickery, machination, or espionage—there is little need for a rhetorical display. Moreover, one of the primary aims of the *Stratagems* is to entertain. The implied world-view of the text is unambiguous: the more devious the plot, the more enjoyable; one deserves whatever one gets, by hook or by crook; virtue and loyalty are eminently unprofitable. Gleefully rejecting conventional standards of ethics and fair dealing, the *Stratagems of the Warring States* make up one of the most irreverent books in the early Chinese corpus.

Not all ancient examples of the anecdotal genre were intended to glorify intrigue and mendacity, however. As a literary device, it was common to use an illustrative little story to convey a deeper point—as we have seen, for example, in Mencius's analogy of the man from Song (*Mencius* 2A.2). "Lord Mu of Lu Asked Zisi" (translated below) is a miniature text that was discovered at Guodian along with the *Lao Zi*, "Five Forms of Conduct," and other materials. In the context of a brief discussion between the title characters (Zisi was Confucius's grandson), we not only hear Zisi's opinion of how a loyal minister should act, but also see that Zisi embodied the very principles of loyalty through his willingness to risk punishment by expressing a point of view that he knew would be displeasing to his lord. Using the same topos of an anecdote about a famous counselor, "Lord Mu of Lu Asked Zisi" articulates an ideal of ministerial conduct fundamentally opposed to that of the *Stratagems of the Warring States*.

The translations below include (1) "Lord Mu of Lu Asked Zisi"; (2) a selection from "Mr. He," a famous tale in the *Han Fei Zi*; (3) a story about Mencius from the *Outer Commentary to the Hán Odes (Han-Shi waizhuan)*, an early Han collection of exemplary tales; and (4) five representative pieces from the *Stratagems of the Warring States*.—PRG

Lord Mu of Lu Asked Zisi

Lord Mu of Lu asked Zisi, "Of what sort is he who can be called a loyal minister?"

Zisi said, "One who constantly cites his lord's weaknesses can be called a loyal minister."

Displeased, the lord had [Zisi] bow and retire. In an audience with Chengsun Ge, the lord said, "Before, I asked Zisi about loyal ministers, and Zisi said, 'One who constantly cites his lord's weaknesses can be called a loyal minister.' I was confused by this and did not comprehend."

Chengsun Ge said, "Oh, well spoken [by Zisi]! There have been those who have killed themselves for the sake of their lord. But there has never been one who constantly cites his lord's weaknesses. One who would kill himself for the sake of his lord is one who is committed to rank and emolument; one who constantly cites his lord's weaknesses keeps rank and emolument at a distance.[1] Practicing righteousness while keeping rank and emolument at a distance—other than Zisi, I have never heard of anyone [who does this]."

Mr. He [From *Han Fei Zi*. Excerpt]

One Mr. He of Chu obtained a jade gem from within Mount Chu; he took it and presented it to King Li. King Li had a jeweler examine it; the jeweler said, "It is [a mere] stone." The king thought [Mr.] He was a cozener, so he cut off his left foot.

When King Li died, King Wu assumed the throne, and He took his gem once again to present it to King Wu. King Wu had a jeweler examine it; the jeweler said, "It is [a mere] stone." Once again, the king thought [Mr.] He was a cozener, so he cut off his right foot.

When King Wu died, King Wen assumed the throne. Then [Mr.] He wrapped his arms around his gem and wept beneath Mount Chu. After three days and three nights, his tears were exhausted, so he continued by weeping blood. The king heard of this, and sent someone to ask [He's] reason, saying, "There are many people who have had their feet cut off; why do you weep so tragically?"

He said, "I am not weeping for my feet. I am weeping because a precious jade is labeled a stone, and an honest man-of-service is dubbed a cozener. That is what I consider tragic." Then the king had his jeweler polish the gem, and this revealed how precious it was. Consequently it was named "Mr. He's jade-disk."

From *Outer Commentary to the Hán Odes*

Mencius's wife was sitting by herself in a squatting position. Mencius came in through the door and saw her. He announced to his mother, "My wife is without ritual. I entreat you to expel her."

His mother said, "Why?"

He said, "She was squatting."

His mother said, "How do you know that?"

Mencius said, "I saw her."

His mother said, "Then *you* are without ritual, not your wife. Do the *Rites* not say, 'When you are about to go through a gate, ask who is there; when you are about to ascend a hall, you must make a sound; when you are about to go through a door, you must look down, lest you surprise someone who is unprepared'? Now you went to her place of respite and privacy, going through her door without a sound. That she was seen squatting is [the result of] your lack of ritual. It is not your wife's lack of ritual."

Thereupon Mencius blamed himself and did not dare expel his wife.

Stratagems of the Warring States [Excerpts]

The state of Zhao seized the sacrificial grounds of Zhou. The King of Zhou was upset by this and told Zheng Chao. Zheng Chao said, "Lord, do not be upset. Let me take [the grounds] back with [merely] thirty pieces of gold."

The Lord of Zhou granted him [the gold]. Zheng Chao presented it to the Grand Diviner of Zhao and told him about the matter of the sacrificial grounds. When the King [of Zhao] became ill, he sent for a divination. The Grand Diviner upbraided him, saying, "The sacrificial grounds of Zhou constitute an evil influence." So Zhao returned [the grounds].

When Gan Mao was Prime Minister in Qin, the King of Qin favored Gongsun Yan. One time when they were standing together at leisure, [the king] addressed [Gongsun Yan], saying, "I am about to make you Prime Minister."

One of Gan Mao's functionaries heard this while he was passing by and told Gan Mao. Gan Mao then went in to have an audience with the king. He said, "Your Majesty, you have gained a worthy Prime Minister. I venture to pay my respects and congratulate you."

The king said, "I have entrusted the state to you; why do I need another worthy Prime Minister?"

He replied, "Your Majesty, you are about to make the *xishou*[2] your Prime Minister."

The king said, "How did you hear that?"

He replied, "The *xishou* told me."

The king was enraged that the *xishou* should have leaked [this information], so he banished him.

King Xuan of Jing asked his flock of ministers, saying, "I have heard that the north fears Zhao Xixu. Verily, how shall we [proceed]?"[3]

None of the ministers answered. Then Jiang Yi said, "A tiger was seeking out the Hundred Beasts and eating them when he caught a fox. The fox said, 'You dare not eat me. Di in Heaven has made me the leader of the Hundred Beasts. If you were to eat me, you would be opposing the command of Di. If you think I am being untrustworthy, I shall walk ahead of you, and you will follow behind me. Observe whether there are any of the Hundred Beasts that dare not flee when they see me!' The tiger doubted the fox, so he walked with him. When the beasts saw them, they fled. The tiger did not know that the beasts fled because they were afraid of him, but thought they were afraid of the fox.

"Now, your Majesty, your territory is five thousand tricents square and contains a million armed [soldiers]. But they have all been assigned to Zhao Xixu alone. Thus, when the north fears Zhao Xixu, in reality they fear your Majesty's armed troops, as the Hundred Beasts fear the tiger."

The King of Wei sent a beautiful woman to the King of Chu; the King of Chu was pleased by her. His wife, Zheng Xiu, knew that the king was pleased by the new woman, and that he was very kind to her. Whatever clothing or baubles [the new woman] liked, [Zheng Xiu] gave her; whatever rooms and bed-furnishings she liked, [Zheng Xiu] gave her. She was kinder to her than the king was.

The king said, "A wife serves her husband with sex, but jealousy is her essence. Now you, Zheng Xiu, know that I am pleased by the new woman, and you are kinder to her than I am. This is how a filial son would serve his parents, how a loyal minister would serve his lord."

Relying on her knowledge that the king did not consider her jealous, Zheng Xiu addressed the new woman, saying, "The king loves your beauty! Though this is so, he dislikes your nose. When you see the king, you must cover your nose." So the new woman would cover her nose whenever she went to see the king.

The king addressed Zheng Xiu, saying, "Why does the new woman cover her nose when she sees me?"

Zheng Xiu said, "I know why."

The king said, "You must say it even if it is horrible."

Zheng Xiu said, "It seems she hates to smell your odor."[4]

The king said, "Shrew!" He ordered [the new woman's] nose cut off, and would not allow anyone to disobey the command.

There was a man who presented an herb of immortality to the King of Jing. The visitor was holding it in his hand as he entered, and a Mid-Rank Servitor[5] asked, "Can it be eaten?"

[The visitor] said, "It can."

Thereupon [the servitor] snatched it and ate it. The king was enraged and sent men to kill the Mid-Rank Servitor. The Mid-Rank Servitor sent a messenger to persuade the king, saying, "Your servant asked the visitor, and the visitor said it could be eaten; thus your servant ate it. Because of this, your servant is without guilt; the guilt is with the visitor. Furthermore, the guest was presenting an herb of immortality. If your servant eats it and you, king, kill your servant, then it must be an 'herb of mortality.' King, you will be killing a guiltless servant as well as making it plain that people deceive you." Thus the king did not kill him.

The state of Zhao was about to attack Yan. Su Dai addressed King Hui [of Zhao] on behalf of Yan, saying, "As I was coming here today, I passed the Yi River. A mussel had just come out [of its shell] to bask when a heron began to peck at its flesh; the mussel thereupon snapped closed on [the bird's] beak. The heron said, 'If it does not rain today or tomorrow, there will be a dead mussel.' The mussel said to the heron, 'If I do not come out today or tomorrow, there will be a dead heron.' Neither was willing to let the other go, and a fisherman was able to catch both of them.

"Now Zhao is about to attack Yan. Yan and Zhao will withstand each other for a long time, thereby straining their large populations. I fear that mighty Qin will be the fisherman. I request that you cook this plan through."[6]

King Hui said, "Very well." Thereupon he desisted.

—PRG

Notes

1. Presumably the idea here is that a minister willing to kill himself for the sake of his lord must be looking forward to the rewards and dignities that would be bestowed posthumously on his clan. Zisi, on the other hand, by pointing out his lord's flaws, proves himself so loyal that he endeavors to help his lord improve himself even at the cost of the lord's good graces.

2. *Xishou* was Gongsun Yan's title.

3. As the text goes on to explain, Zhao Xixu was the Commander-in-Chief of the army. It seems the king is not sure how to handle his powerful general.

4. A commentator opines at this juncture that the king must have suffered from some illness that produced a foul odor.

5. This is an official title.

6. I.e., consider it carefully.

BY THE MIDDLE of the third century B.C.E., the western state of Qin had emerged as the mightiest of all the Warring States, conquering its neighbors one by one until it occupied more than half the area of the Chinese world. The various eastern states joined in a desperate alliance of self-preservation, but it soon became evident that a new order was inevitable. The future of Qin was the future of China.[1]

Qin had never been a feeble power, but it would hardly have been clear to observers even as late as the fourth century that this was the contender destined to reunite the several states of China. For most of its history, Qin was considered a rude backwater inhabited by an impure and disreputable stock of semibarbarians. We have seen from the *Zuozhuan* that Duke Mu of Qin was respected in his time, but after his demise, few Qin rulers achieved any renown, and the annals rarely record any momentous happenings in that state. Therefore, we possess few materials, either archival or archaeological, to help explain the astonishing development of what was widely considered a frontier territory into a fearsome world leader. The rise of Qin was traditionally explained as a consequence of its cruel administration; after all, Lord Shang was often credited with transforming Qin into a fighting machine by emphasizing agriculture and war and by reorganizing the populace into a system of subdivisions inspired by military command structure. Through its terrifying laws, Qin was supposedly able to make its people more productive and docile. But the details of these laws were never known.

Our understanding of preimperial Qin was utterly transformed in 1975 when a substantial collection of statutes and legal manuals was discovered in a tomb near the town of Shuihudi, Hubei Province. Dating from the mid-third century B.C.E., these were the oldest legal texts ever discovered in China. The newfound Qin laws are difficult to read because they use many unglossed technical terms and routinely allude to statutes whose content we can only guess at. Nevertheless, we understand the laws well enough to see that they explode our received image of the Qin state. Though they may appear harsh indeed to a modern reader, they were not extraordinarily severe for the times and were by no means arbitrary.

On the contrary, the laws from Shuihudi display a sophisticated awareness of such concepts as criminal intent, judicial procedure, defendants' rights, and the difference between common law and statutory law. Defendants were even allowed to appeal for a second investigation into their case if they or their families disagreed with the results of the first. From our point of view, the most alienating aspects of the Qin laws are probably the mutilating punishments that they countenance, the instruments of collective responsibility (see n. 4, below), and the right of a father to demand the death of an "unfilial" son.

But even from our perspective, conditioned by our more liberal juridical traditions, it is impossible to deny the basic fairness of the Qin laws. If a man or woman were to be punished, it could not be simply at the whim of an invidious magistrate. Every subject of the Qin state could expect to be treated according to unambiguous and predetermined protocols—and that is precisely the judicial environment which every viable law code must bring about.—PRG

The Laws of Qin [Excerpts]

If they hide healthy youths[2] or are negligent about declaring the disabled, the [village] chieftain and elders pay [the punishment] of having their beards shaved off.[3] For those who dare to deceive or defraud [the state] by [declaring themselves] old when it is not warranted, or, upon reaching old age, [by removing themselves from the tax rolls] without bothering to request [a release], the fine is two suits of armor. If the chieftain and elders do not indict them, they are each fined one suit; the members of their "group of five" are to be fined one shield per household; and all are to be exiled. Enrollment Statute.[4]

A husband steals 1,000 [units of] cash and hides 300 in his wife's quarters. How is the wife to be sentenced? If the wife hid [the booty] knowing that the husband had stolen it, the warranted [punishment] is for having stolen 300 [cash]. If she did not know, she [is sentenced] for receiving [stolen goods].[5]

[Someone] accuses another of stealing 110 [units of cash]. The inquiry [reveals] that he stole 100 [cash]; how is the accuser to be sentenced? [The error] warrants a fine of two suits of armor. Suppose the [the criminal] stole 100 [cash] and [the accuser] intentionally added 10 cash to the stolen amount, then the question is: How is the accuser to be sentenced? [This crime] warrants a fine of one shield; the fine of one shield satisfies the statute. However, the practice of the court is to sentence those who bring false charges; the fine is two suits of armor.[6]

"For killing a child on one's own authority,[7] [the punishment] is to be tattooed and made a penal laborer or grain-pounder.[8] If the child is newborn and has strange marks on its body or is deformed, it is not a crime to kill it." Suppose someone gives birth to a child, and the child's body is not deformed and does not have strange marks, but [the family] does not want the child merely because it has many children. They do not raise it, but kill it—what is the sentence? It is for killing a child.

Commoner A was in a fight. Drawing his sword, he hacked and lopped off another's hair-knot.[9] What is the sentence? [The crime] warrants penal labor, but he is left intact.

If one draws a sheathed lance, halberd, or spear in a fight, but without causing injury, the sentence is as though [the weapon] were a sword.

If [someone] uses a poker, a *shu*-poker, or an awl in a fight, and injures another with that poker, *shu*-poker, or awl, how is he to be sentenced in each case?[10] If [the crime] is [the consequence] of a fight, it warrants a fine of two suits of armor; if it is premeditated, it warrants tattooing and penal labor.

"If members of a 'group of five' indict each other to avoid guilt by bringing a false charge, they are to be found guilty of the crime which they were [trying to] avoid." [The statutes] also say, "If one cannot determine the guilty party, and indicts someone else, this is bringing a false charge." Suppose A says that B, a member of his "group of five," has committed premeditated murder.

After B has been arrested, [it is determined] as a result of questioning that he did not commit the murder. A brought a false charge—is the warranted sentence that for bringing a false charge, or that for [the crime] which he [was trying to] avoid?[11] The warranted sentence is for what he [was trying to] avoid.

Bandits entered A's house and wounded him. A cried "Burglars!" but his four neighbors, [village] chieftain, and elders had all gone out and were not present, so they did not hear him cry "Burglars!" Question: Does this warrant sentencing or not? If the investigation [shows that his four neighbors] were not present, a sentence is not warranted; but for the chieftain and elders, even though they were not present, a sentence is warranted. What is meant by "four neighbors"? The "four neighbors" are the other members of his "group of five."

When one appeals for an inquest,[12] either for oneself or for another person, is the [appeal] heard after the case has been adjudicated, or is it heard even before the case has been adjudicated? It is heard after the case has been adjudicated.

How many rat burrows in a granary warrant a sentence or reprimand?[13] The practice of the court is to fine one shield for three or more rat burrows and to reprimand for two or fewer. Three mouse burrows count as one rat burrow.

Trying cases. In trying cases, if it is possible to track down the words [of a witness] by means of documents, it is better to obtain facts from a person without flogging him. Flogging is inferior because where there is fear, [the case] fails.

Interrogating in a case. While interrogating in a case, one must always first hear [witnesses'] words completely and write them down as each one lays out his statement. Even when you know that [a witness] is lying, there is no need to cross-examine hastily. If he cannot explain himself once his statement has been written down completely, cross-examine those points that are [vulnerable to] cross-examination. In cross-examination, once again, listen to his explanatory statements and have them written down. Again review the unexplained points and perform another cross-examination. If the cross-examination comes to an end and [the witness] has repeatedly lied or changed his words without acknowledging [the inconsistencies], then, in cases where the statutes warrant flogging,[14] flog him. The flogging must be recorded as follows: "Deposition: Since So-and-so repeatedly changed his words without an explanatory statement, he has been interrogated with the bastinado."

Accusing a son. Deposition: Commoner A of such-and-such a village indicted [his son], saying, "My natural son (Commoner C of the same village) is unfilial. Calling on [the court] for his death, I dare to indict him." Prefectural Clerk E was ordered to go and arrest him. Prefectural Clerk E's deposition: "With Prison Bondservant So-and-so I arrested C, apprehending him in the house of So-and-so." When Deputy So-and-so interrogated C, his statement was, "I am A's natural son. I have truly been unfilial to A. I have not been convicted of any other crime."[15]

—PRG

Notes

1. The name "China," incidentally, probably derives from "Qin," which sounds roughly like the English word "chin."

2. Such as would be eligible for military service.

3. As opposed to having their entire heads shaved, which would have been considered a more severe humiliation.

4. The so-called "group of five," which reappears below, was an institution of collective responsibility: if one member of the group committed a crime, the other members might all be subject to reprisals. "Enrollment" refers to registration on the tax rolls.

5. The punishment for stealing was significantly more severe than that for receiving stolen goods.

6. The principle of this item is clear: a defendant may not be charged for a crime greater than what he or she committed, and an accuser or prosecutor who exaggerates the severity of a crime is liable to be punished. The details, however, are confusing. On the one hand, the text seems to draw a distinction between cases in which the accuser overestimates the value of the stolen goods through sheer carelessness and those in which the accuser does so deliberately. However, the statutory fine for negligence (two suits of armor) sounds far heavier than that for intentionally misrepresenting the magnitude of a crime (one shield), though one would naturally expect the latter error to be considered more serious. Finally, the text asserts here, exceptionally, that the court may enforce a fine different from that mandated by the statutes; perhaps it was recognized that a penalty of one shield was too lenient in this case.

7. As we shall see, an irate father could petition the court for authority to slay his unfilial son, but this right had to be granted beforehand, or else the father would be convicted "for killing a child on his own authority."

8. Women were sentenced to be convict "grain-pounders" whereas men were sent to penal labor camps.

9. In other words, without causing any serious wounds—in which case the criminal would be mutilated as well as sentenced to penal labor.

10. The sentence for using these kinds of weapons is lighter because they do not have a sheath. Removing a weapon from its sheath is understood as a sign of some degree of premeditation. (A *shu* is defined as "a long poker.")

11. In other words, assuming that there was a murder and that A shared some blame in the affair, should he be tried for bringing false charges against B or for having committed premeditated murder himself?

12. The accused or a relative of the accused was regularly allowed to demand a second inquest into the case if there was reason to doubt the justice or fairness of the first.

13. I.e., of the functionaries in charge of the granary.

14. In other words, even a perjurer cannot be flogged except in accordance with the predetermined statutes.

15. The text does not relate the resolution of this conflict. The "Prison Bondservant" was apparently required to assist the Prefectural Clerk as part of his sentence.

1. Remains of Neolithic site, Banpo Village, Shaanxi, ca. 3000 B.C.E. A half-century of excavation has pushed back the date of China's Bronze Age to the first half of the second millennium B.C.E. and the date of Neolithic settlements from Gansu to Liaoning, Shandong, and Jiangsu even earlier. Yet Yangshao culture, one of the earliest studied and now encompassing more than a thousand sites in the Yellow River Valley from 5000 to 3000 B.C.E., has remained one of the most important. The four-sided wattle-and-daub structures supported by pillars and undecorated ceramic pots from the 300-by-200-meter settlement at Banpo, just east of the modern city of Xi'an, are typical of North Central China in about 3000 B.C.E.

2. Clay jar with raised human face and human figure, excavated at Shizhao Village, Gansu; ca. 3800–2000 B.C.E.; Institute of Archaeology, Beijing. One of the most exciting discoveries in tombs of Neolithic China has been the decoration of clay objects with human figures. The jar excavated at Shizhao, Gansu, is one of several superb examples of faces and human forms molded into a clay jar by potters of the Majiayao culture in the third millennium B.C.E. and perhaps earlier. Majiayao sites are prevalent in Gansu, Qinghai, and Shaanxi and in some instances have been found above the remains of Yangshao settlements.

3. "Goddess" temple, Niuheliang, Liaoning; ca. 3500–2500 B.C.E. It has been known since the 1970s that the Yellow River Valley was but one of the cradles of Chinese civilization. In Northeastern Liaoning Province, more than four hundred settlements of the Hongshan Culture have been uncovered. The so-called "Goddess" temple received its name from life-size human faces and hands found there. The plan of the "temple," roughly resembling the Chinese character for earth (*tu* [a plus symbol above a straight line]), may indicate the existence of elaborate ritual among the Hongshan people of Liaoning and Eastern Inner Mongolia in the third millennium B.C.E. Hongshan Culture is also known for superior jade carving, including jade objects nicknamed "pig-dragons" from the snout-like feature that merges with a curved body.

4. Pottery dish with coiled serpent motif, excavated at Taosi, Shanxi; ca. 2500–2000 B.C.E.; Institute of Archaeology, Beijing. Artifacts of another Neolithic culture, Longshan, have been uncovered at Taosi, Xiangfen County, Shanxi, also since the 1980s. Taosi objects feature serpentine creatures with prominent noses such as the one on this earthenware dish painted with red and black. The boldly painted creature and branch or foliage held between his sharp, evenly spaced teeth are characteristic of the flair for design observed in pottery from what seems to have been a wealthy Neolithic settlement in the Fen River Valley in southern Shanxi.

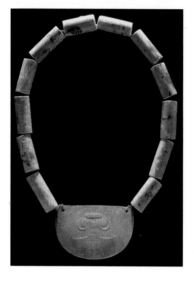

5. Jade necklace, excavated at Yaoshan, Yuhang County, Zhejiang; ca. 3200–2000 B.C.E.; Zhejiang Institute of Archaeology, Hangzhou. Jade carving was well under way in the late Neolithic cultures of both North and South China. Some of the most extraordinary jade objects have been excavated in the stretch from southern Jiangsu to northern Zhejiang that includes the modern cities of Shanghai and Hangzhou. Cylindrical ritual objects with anthropomorphic features, blades, and decorative objects, as well as jewelry, were buried in tombs of this third-millennium B.C.E. culture, sometimes known as Liangzhu Culture after the name of the site where jades displaying this extraordinary workmanship were first found in the 1930s.

6. Inscriptions on oracle bones excavated at Xiaotun, Anyang, Henan; *Zhongguo da baike quanshu, Yuyan wenzi* **juan, ca. 12th century B.C.E.** Inscriptions on the shoulder blades of bovines (especially oxen) and occasionally other animals and on shells of tortoises are the oldest known forms of Chinese writing. Discovered in great numbers by archaeologists in the village of Xiaotun, Anyang County, Henan, in the first decades of the twentieth century, and much earlier by local residents, the incised scapulae and plastrons (ventral portions) are commonly known as oracle bones. The name is a reference to their function: both scapulimancy and plastromancy were practiced by diviners of the Shang dynasty. The diviner would ask a question of the utmost human importance—for example, success in war, weather and its relation to the harvest, childbirth, or recovery from sickness—as he exposed the bone to the flame. The resulting cracks were then examined and interpreted to yield a positive or negative result. After the ceremony, a record of the divination would be inscribed on the bone for future reference.

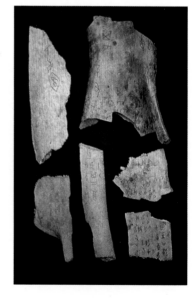

7. Royal tomb, Wuguan Village, Anyang, Henan; ca. 12th c. B.C.E. The cemetery of the Shang kings at their last capital, Yin (today Anyang), has aroused international attention since initial excavation in the 1930s. Oriented north-south with approach ramps from both sides and in some cases also from the east and west, the huge tombs measured nearly 20 by 16 meters at their upper sections, approximately 13 by 10 meters at the bottom, and were about 12 meters deep. Ramps could be twice the length of a tomb. Objects in bronze, jade, bone, shell, and rarer materials such as turquoise were stored in compartments of the tombs, together with necessities for the next life such as chariots and domestic animals. The decapitated corpses in the lower left are evidence of human sacrificial burial, a practice that seems to have been widespread among Shang kings.

8. Rhinoceros *zun* excavated at Mount Liang, Shouzhang County, Shandong; ca. 11th c. B.C.E.; Avery Brundage Collection, Asian Art Museum, San Francisco. Bronze vessels were common in many areas of what is now China by the middle of the second millennium B.C.E. Used for rituals and often buried with royalty, more than twenty different types are known. Each had a slightly different ceremonial function, but in general they can be divided into vessels for water, wine, and food, as well as weapons and musical instruments. Many shapes of Shang bronzes can be traced to pottery vessels of the Neolithic period, and each one evolved over centuries or even millennia. The smooth surface of this *zun* is unusual. More often patterns are cast into the surfaces of bronze vessels. In earlier examples, the design was often restricted to a band along the top of the vessel. Later, patterns covered every surface, and a single vessel could have incisions of more than one depth. Although the same shapes might be made in more than one place, many regional styles exist among Shang bronze objects. It is not known if the ceremonies in the various regions were the same, even where similarly shaped vessels have been found.

9. Jade human figurine with face and body on both sides, tomb of Lady Hao, Xiaotun, Anyang; ca. 14th–11th c. B.C.E.; Institute of Archaeology, Beijing. The broad, flat nose, wide lips, and large eyebrows are typical facial features of the late Shang period. Less typical are the carving on the front and back and the projections on either side of the top of the head. The extensions below the feet suggest that this small object, just less than 5 inches high, was inserted into something larger. More than 750 jade or stone objects and 527 hairpins were found among the nearly 2,000 items excavated in the simple pit tomb of Lady Hao. Included were numerous bronze vessels and oracle bones with her name and that of Wu Ding (d. 1189 B.C.E.), to whom she was consort, incised on them. The inscriptions have been invaluable in reconstructing the history of Shang China. In addition, the shapes of weapons, composition of jade, and turquoise inlay suggest interaction between the Anyang site and peoples of North or Central Asia.

10. Life-size bronze figure, pit 2, Sanxingdui, Guanghan County, Sichuan; ca. 1200–1000 B.C.E. The excavation of two pits containing bronze vessels, jade and gold objects, and elephant tusks at Sanxingdui in Sichuan Province revealed a heretofore unknown and still unidentified culture that flourished in southwestern China in the last centuries of the second millennium B.C.E. Human heads and masks, some with gold decoration, bird shapes and bird heads, blades, wheels, and diamond-shaped fittings are among the hoards found inside a 12 km² city wall made of layered mud-brick. Most spectacular, however, is this 172 cm figure standing on an 88 cm pedestal. The exaggerated facial features, oversized hands, and intricate patterns on his multilayer garment suggest that he may have been a participant in a ritual, and make his bare feet all the more noticeable. Priest, shaman, or cult leader —all are possible interpretations of his role in this intriguing society. There is more agreement that his hands originally held one of the 80 elephant tusks found in the Sanxingdui pits.

11. Chärchän Man, excavated at the village of Zaghunluq, Bayingholin County, Xinjiang, Uyghur Autonomous Region; ca. 1000 B.C.E.; Xinjiang Uyghur Autonomous Region Museum. This individual, popularly known as "Ur-David," is one of hundreds of mummies (more precisely, desiccated corpses) that have been unearthed at sites along the southern and eastern rim of the arid Tarim Basin in Eastern Central Asia. Those dating to the early period (first and second millennia B.C.E.) display primarily Caucasoid or Europoid anthropological and genetic affinities, while those from later periods show increasingly East Asian characteristics. Combined with evidence drawn from thousands of skeletons found in the same region, together with a wealth of extremely well-preserved textiles, pottery, wooden utensils, foodstuffs, bronze and iron implements, jewelry, and other associated artifacts, the recently discovered mummies of Eastern Central Asia have revolutionized our understanding of the movements of various peoples, as well as their languages and cultures, across Eurasia.

12. Da Ke Tripod, found in Ren Village, Fufeng County, Shaanxi; mid-9th c.; Shanghai Museum. The tripod for holding food known as ding is in many ways typical of bronze vessels of the early Zhou dynasty. Its form, like the four-legged variety known as *fangding,* is traceable to Shang and pottery prototypes. Its symmetrical pattern consists of fairly deep but neat and regular incisions, lacking the bold or inventive artistry that characterizes bronze vessels of the fifteenth–twelfth centuries B.C.E. In the place of creativity in pattern is a more overt purpose. Inscriptions on Zhou bronzes are long by comparison with their Shang counterparts, and often are extremely detailed. Through them the history and ideology of Zhou has been reconstructed. Part of the inscription on the inside of Food Steward Ke's *ding* can be seen in the photograph.

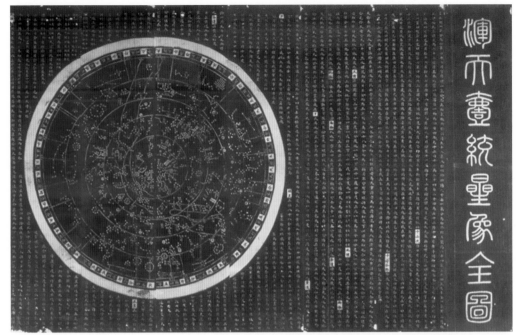

13. "Huntian yitong xingxiang quantu" (Complete chart of the standardized stars and constellations of the celestial sphere), a late-Qing dynasty planisphere attributed to Qian Yong (ca. 1826); Adler Planetarium. The star chart is centered on the north celestial pole and extends down to about −45°, with the regular asterisms arrayed in concentric rings set off by five declination circles. Graduations along the outermost ring give the names of the twelve Jupiter stations (suici) and allocated fields (fenye), reflecting the astrological correlations between regions of the sky and Chinese provinces. The accompanying notes explain these and other concepts, including the celestial equator (chidao), ecliptic (huangao), path of the moon (baidao), five planets (wu xing), and so forth. Although this chart dates from the early nineteenth century, the Chinese terms given in parentheses in the preceding two sentences would have been used already in the Han period, if not before.

14. Container for food, excavated at Liyu, Shanxi; late 6th–5th c. B.C.E.; Shanghai Museum. This vessel in the shape known as dou was one of numerous important bronze objects excavated in 1923 at Liyu in northern Shanxi Province. Two features of the dou are characteristic of the Eastern Zhou period (770–256 B.C.E.): the use of inlay and combat scenes. Copper is inlaid into this food vessel, but inlay of the period ranged from precious metals like silver and gold to mother-of-pearl. Combat scenes, both man vs. beast and animal vs. animal, as well as entwined animals, are popular motifs that were also present on portable objects in the shapes of animals or decorated in "animal style," buried in tombs of the so-called northern nomads of Siberia and the Russian steppe. Animal style art was known to Chinese craftsmen, and Chinese objects were known to the northern nomads. Also common at the time and found on bronze vessels excavated at Liyu were intricate patterns cast onto bronze vessels in multiple levels of depth.

15. Lacquer inner coffin of Marquis Yi of Zeng, Leigudun, Sui County, Hubei; ca. 433 B.C.E.; Suizhou Museum, Hubei. Marquis Yi of the small state of Zeng was buried in about the year 433 B.C.E. inside two nested lacquer coffins in the main chamber of a four-room wooden tomb sealed tight with charcoal. The corpses of twenty-one females, none older than about twenty-five, and a dog, all believed to have been sacrificed to accompany the marquis into his grave, also were buried in his funerary chamber or a second one. The inner coffin was decorated with hybrid creatures, paired figures, and four-sided motifs that perhaps represent doors or windows. Whether intended to permit light into the container for the corpse or to allow the deceased a view to the outside, the motifs at this time

are unique among sarcophagus patterns and surely were purposeful. Conceptually, the painted openings link Chinese burial practices of the Warring States period (481–256 B.C.E.) to those of ancient Egypt.

16. Set of 65 bronze bells from the tomb of Marquis Yi of Zeng, Leigudun, Hubei; ca. 433 B.C.E.; Hubei Provincial Museum. The set of bells excavated from the tomb of Marquis Yi of Zeng is the largest group found thus far in China. Among them are three types: 45 *yong*, 19 *niu*, and one *bo*, each used in ritual music of South China, including in the south-central state of Chu, where it is likely this set, weighing a total of more than 5,500 pounds, was produced. The individual bells, which have inscriptions that identify their pitches, could produce three steps in the standard scale, for a total range of more than five octaves. This was only one group of the 125 musical instruments found in the marquis's tomb, including other percussion instruments, winds, and strings, some of which were unknown prior to this excavation.

17. Wangcheng, or "Ruler's City," from 17th-c. version of "San-litu" (Three "ritual" classics illustrated). The fundamental principles of Chinese city planning can be observed in capitals of states from the first millennium B.C.E. Before the end of that millennium, principles of urban planning also were written down. The most famous literary passage that addresses the Chinese city plan is found in the "Kaogongji" (Record of the examination of craftsmen) section of the *Zhouli* (Rites of Zhou). It presents a formula for the ruler's city *(wangcheng)*: nine *li* (1 *li* = about ½ km) square with three gates on each side; three main north-south and three main east-west streets, the northern ones nine carriage-tracks in width; a temple dedicated to the ruler's ancestors east of the city center and twin altars for soil and grain to the west; a hall of audience in front of the residential palace quarters; and a marketplace. The majority of these stipulations persist in the latest Chinese imperial city, the Forbidden City of Beijing. The *Three Ritual Classics* are the *Rites of Zhou*, *Liji* (Record of rites), and *Yili* (Ceremonies and rites).

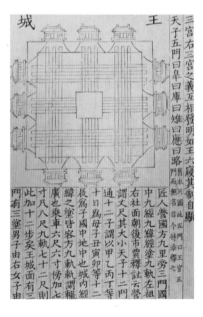

18. Detail of bronze *hu* (wine vessel); Eastern Zhou; Sichuan Provincial Museum. This extraordinary bronze vessel contains some of the earliest Chinese evidence of continuous narrative, or the telling of a story in which the same figures appear in different settings. Viewed from bottom to top, one sees first the world of the spirits, in which dwell exotic beasts and where occasionally man and beast combat each other. Separating them from the realm of man is a decorative border. In three bands of narration around the vessel, also separated by decorative borders, one sees first (lowest register), land and sea battles, individual scenes of which are shown simultaneously by the sophisticated use of parallel and diagonal lines; second (middle register), celebration of victory by the ringing of bells (shown here), beating of drums, dancing with spears, and hunting birds; and finally (top register), a return to normal life, illustrated by hunting and perhaps the picking of mulberry leaves. Like the base register, the lid again depicts the world of exotic creatures.

19. Bronze figurine of wrestlers; late Eastern Zhou; British Museum. Excavation continues to yield human figures modeled with sophistication in a variety of materials—especially bronze, jade, and clay—from the last two millennia B.C.E. Yet some of those known for more than half a century, such as these bronze wrestlers, remain extraordinary. Their purpose in a Warring States–period tomb was to entertain the occupant(s). Wrestlers continue to be found among figurines or subjects of wall paintings in Chinese tombs through the first several centuries C.E.

20. Zhaoyutu, from tomb of King Cuo, Zhongshan kingdom, Pingshan County, Hebei; 323–315 B.C.E.; Hebei Provincial Institute of Cultural Relics. *Zhaoyutu,* literally "map of the forbidden territory," is the earliest Chinese site plan. Both the diagram and this 96-by-48-cm, one-cm-thick bronze plate are inlaid in gold and silver. The obverse side, shown here, is a line drawing made to scale of three main structures and two smaller ones believed to depict the intended necropolis of King Cuo and his wives. The dimensions between each structure and the two enclosing walls are given in *chi* (approximately 23.1 cm; similar to a foot) and *bu* (paces). It is conjectured that the two tombs excavated at the Pingshan site may be two of those indicated on the plan. Most important is the inscription on the reverse. It states that this is one of two copies of the map, this one buried with the ruler and the second to be stored in the palace for the benefit of future generations. Thus is preserved startling proof of three fundamental ideas: the Chinese conceived of three-dimensional space in two dimensions in the fourth century B.C.E.; four-sided, enclosed building complexes existed at this time; and the Chinese believed that plans set forth in their classical age would serve as models for later times.

21. Lacquer horned creature with long tongue excavated at Xinyang, Henan; late 5th–4th c. B.C.E. Bizarre lacquer objects, often painted primarily in red and black with some yellow such as this one found in a tomb in Xinyang, Henan Province, are characteristic of the powerful and flamboyant state of Chu that spread from Hunan and Hubei into Henan and part of Anhui during the Eastern Zhou period. Masters in the production of lacquer ware, Chu artisans created monster-like figures believed by some to be tomb guardians, by others to be cult figures or totems, and by others graphic renderings of beings described in literature of the Chu state. Antlers, horns, long tongues, and combinations of ferocious beasts with benign winged creatures are prominent among the more than two hundred lacquer objects, some of which stand four feet or taller, that have been found at Chu sites.

22. Pit no. 1 from funerary complex of the First Emperor, Lishan, Lintong County, Shaanxi; ca. 210 B.C.E. Still one of the most dramatic images of Chinese archaeology, pit 1 contains more than seven thousand life-size terra-cotta soldiers and horses positioned erect as guards for the so-called First Emperor, Qin Shi Huangdi, the man who unified China in 221 B.C.E. The picture characterizes the man. The imperial aspirations of the First Emperor, called a megalomaniac by some, were, like the clay images he ordered made to guard his tomb, grandiose to the extreme. He unified weights and measures, standardized currency, ordered a common script, divided his empire into commanderies and districts, and established a central government. He also envisioned a defensive wall along China's northern border and worked a massive labor force under sometimes inhuman conditions to join disparate wall pieces to accomplish that goal; and he is said to have executed scholars and burned writings he deemed contrary to his grand plan.

23. (Above right) Gilt-bronze horses and charioteer, excavated near mausoleum of the First Emperor, Lishan, Shaanxi; ca. 210 B.C.E.; Qin Shi Huangdi Mausoleum Museum. The exquisite and costly horses and charioteer found in their own pit near the mausoleum of the First Emperor offer a glimpse at the splendors that are certain to be found in Qin Shi Huangdi's burial chambers when they are opened. The faces of the horses and face and hands of the driver are modeled with the kind of smooth detail accomplished in much softer clay for the faces of the emperor's soldiers (plate 22). About one-third life-size, the chariot has been identified as a "warm and cool carriage," a vehicle described in the *Shiji* (Records of the Grand Historian). According to the records, it was in this kind of carriage that Qin Shi Huangdi's corpse was transported to its final resting place while eunuch Zhao Gao and minister Li Si plotted to replace his legitimate heir with the weakling son who went on to become the Second Emperor.

THE DOCUMENTS THAT historians have long consulted for information about the Qin dynasty were all composed during the Han, for virtually no records have survived from the brief period between the unification of China in 221 B.C.E. and the collapse of the Qin empire fifteen years later. The significance of this limitation was not entirely appreciated until recent times, but today it is clear that the received view of the Qin empire is informed by the distortions and exaggerations of Han political thought. The Qin remains a poorly understood period in Chinese history.

The following selections include excerpts from the standard texts describing the rise and fall of the Qin empire: the biography of the influential merchant Lü Buwei; the biography of Li Si, the Counselor-in-Chief of the empire; and "The Transgressions of Qin" (Guo-Qin lun), an essay by the Han statesman Jia Yi (201–169 B.C.E.).[1] The first two items are taken from *Records of the Grand Historian (Shiji),* a monumental history of ancient China compiled by Sima Qian (145?–86? B.C.E.). These biographies recount the famous elements of the Qin myth: the illegitimate parentage of the First Emperor; his grandiose plans to unify the disparate customs of his new empire; Li Si's memorial calling for the destruction of all heterodox books; and the catastrophic plot of Zhao Gao, an ambitious eunuch, to eliminate the First Emperor's chosen successor and anoint instead his weakest son. While the recent discovery of the massive terracotta army near the First Emperor's burial tumulus attests to his megalomaniacal inclinations, few of the key events in Sima Qian's narrative can be verified by other sources. For example, not many modern scholars believe that the infamous biblioclasm transpired as Sima Qian says—if it took place at all; fewer still accept his scurrilous account of the First Emperor's birth. Though Sima Qian was a lively and engaging writer, we must, when assessing his great opus, bear in mind his tendency to embroider the truth and record history as he only wished it had occurred.

The last selection, "The Transgressions of Qin," is even more tendentious, because its author was a politician who consciously played into the hands of the new Han dynasts in their attempt to portray their own rule, in contrast to that of Qin, as one of pure humanity and righteousness. The theme of Jia Yi's essay is that the Qin emperors lost the support of the people through their cruelty and ignorance. Whether or not Jia Yi's arguments are justified, the significance of his essay, for our purposes, lies in its immense influence on later generations. As an exemplary discourse studied in every classroom, "The Transgressions of Qin" furthered the basic Chinese idea that a regime can survive only if it cares for the people. Since the history of the Qin was cast almost immediately to fit this fundamental dictate, reconstructing a more balanced model of the Qin state has proven to be a major challenge to modern historians.—PRG

Biography of Lü Buwei [Excerpts]

Lü Buwei was a great merchant from Yangdi. By traveling from one place to another, buying cheap and selling dear, he [amassed] a fortune of several thousand gold pieces.

In the fortieth year of King Zhao of Qin,[2] the Heir Apparent died. In his forty-second year, [King Zhao] made his second son, Lord Anguo, the [new] Heir Apparent. Lord Anguo had more than twenty sons. He had a concubine whom he loved dearly and whom he raised to the position of regular consort, calling her Consort Huayang. Consort Huayang had no sons. Lord Anguo had a son among [his many children] named Zichu; Zichu's mother was Lady Xia, and [Lord Anguo] did not love her. Zichu went as a hostage to Zhao,[3] and since Qin attacked Zhao numerous times, Zhao did not treat Zichu with much dignity.

As one of the many minor royal grandsons of Qin, and having been sent as a hostage to one of the feudal states, Zichu was not supplied abundantly with carriages and funds. His living conditions were hard, his ambitions unfulfilled. Lü Buwei, a merchant in Handan,[4] saw [Zichu] and felt compassion for him, saying, "This is marvelous merchandise for my warehouse!" So he went to see Zichu and said to him, "I can enlarge your gates."

Zichu laughed and said, "Sir, first enlarge your own gates, and then enlarge mine!"

Lü Buwei said, "What you do not know is that my gates depend on the size of yours." Zichu knew in his heart what Lü Buwei was referring to, so he invited him to sit with him and have a thorough conversation. Lü Buwei said, "The King of Qin is old, and Lord Anguo has become the Heir Apparent. I have heard secretly that Lord Anguo is in love with Consort Huayang. Consort Huayang has no sons, but she alone will be able to determine [Lord Anguo's] heir. Now you have more than twenty brothers; moreover, living in middling circumstances, you have not seen much fortune and have been the hostage of another feudal lord for a long time. Once the Great King dies, Lord Anguo will be raised as king, and you will have little chance to compete for the position of Heir Apparent with your elder brothers and the other sons who are present before [your father] day and night."

Zichu said, "It is so. What can be done about this?"

Lü Buwei said, "You are poor and are a guest in this [land]. You do not have anything to offer to your parents or to the clients that have crystallized around them. Although I am poor, I request leave to journey westward with a thousand gold pieces on your behalf. I will serve Lord Anguo and Consort Huayang, and establish you as the primary heir."

Zichu then bowed his head and said, "Certainly, if your stratagem [succeeds], you will allow me to divide the state of Qin and share it with you."

(There follows a lengthy description of how Lü Buwei persuaded Consort Huayang to request that Zichu be made Lord Anguo's heir.)

Lord Anguo consented and inscribed a jade tally with his consort, swearing that he would make [Zichu] his heir. Accordingly, Lord Anguo and his consort sent rich provisions to Zichu and requested that Lü Buwei be his tutor. Zichu's name thus became ever more eminent among the feudal lords.

Lü Buwei had taken from among the various ladies of Handan one who was surpassingly lovely and skilled at dancing. He lived with her and came to know that she was with child. Zichu visited Buwei to drink with him; he saw her and was pleased by her. Then he arose, made a toast to Lü's long life, and requested her. Lü Buwei was furious, but he remembered that in this enterprise, wishing to fish up something marvelous, he had already spent his fortune on behalf of Zichu. So he presented his lady to her. The lady concealed the fact that she was with child. When her term was up, she gave birth to the boy Zheng. Zichu then established the lady as his consort.

In the fiftieth year of his reign,[5] King Zhao of Qin sent Wang Yi to besiege Handan. In desperation, [the state of] Zhao wished to kill Zichu. Zichu and Lü Buwei conspired to take 600 catties of gold and present it to the officers who were guarding [Zichu]; thus attaining his freedom, he fled to the army of Qin and was able to return home. [The state of] Zhao wished to kill Zichu's wife and child, but since Zichu's consort was the daughter of a noble family of Zhao, she was able to hide out, and thus mother and child ultimately survived. In the fifty-sixth year of his reign,[6] King Zhao of Qin died, and the Heir Apparent, Lord Anguo, was raised to the throne. Consort Huayang became the Queen, and Zichu the Heir Apparent. [The state of] Zhao vouchsafed the return of Zichu's consort and child, Zheng.

In the first year of his reign, the [new] King of Qin died; he was known posthumously as King Xiaowen. The Heir Apparent, Zichu, succeeded him and is known as King Zhuangxiang. Queen Huayang, whom King Zhuangxiang treated as a mother, became Queen Dowager Huayang; his real mother, Lady Xia, was honored with the title Queen Dowager Xia. In the first year of his reign, King Zhuangxiang made Lü Buwei his Counselor-in-Chief and enfeoffed him as Marquis Wenxin with an appanage of a hundred thousand households in Luoyang, which is in Henan.

After having reigned for three years, King Zhuangxiang died. When the Heir Apparent, Zheng, was raised to the throne, he honored Lü Buwei with the title of Prime Minister, calling him "Uncle."[7] The King of Qin was still young, and the Queen Dowager[8] frequently had congress with Lü Buwei in secret. Buwei had a household of ten thousand servants. . . .

The First Emperor[9] was growing into manhood, but the Queen Dowager's licentiousness was ceaseless. Lü Buwei feared that if this became known, misfortune would reach him. So he privately found a man with a large penis named Lao Ai, and made him his retainer. At times he would indulge in song and music, making Lao Ai walk around with his penis stuck through a wheel of *tong*-wood. He had the Queen Dowager hear of this, in order to entice her. When the Queen Dowager heard, as expected, she wanted to have him in private. Lü Buwei then presented Lao Ai and conspired to have someone accuse him of a crime for which he should be castrated. Buwei then addressed the Queen Dowager secretly, saying, "If you permit this trumped-up castration, you can have him in your apartment." The Queen Dowager then secretly gave rich gifts to the official in charge of castrations, instructing him to pluck out [Lao Ai's] beard up to the eyebrows, making him a "eunuch" so that he could serve the Queen Dowager. The Queen Dowager had congress with him in private and loved him very much. She had a child by him, and, fearing that someone would come to know of it, she produced a sham divination saying that she should avoid [an inauspicious] period; she moved her palace and lived in Yong.[10] Lao Ai often visited her; she rewarded him with very rich gifts, and all the affairs [in the house] were decided by Lao Ai. Lao Ai had several thousand servants in his household, as well as more than a thousand henchmen who sought administrative office as his clients . . .

In the ninth year of the First Emperor,[11] someone reported that Lao Ai was not really a eunuch, that he often had secret illicit relations with the Queen Dowager, that she had given birth to two sons, and that they had concealed everything. He had conspired with the Queen Dowager, saying, "Once the king is dead, we will make one of these sons his successor." Therefore the King of Qin handed this [matter] down to his officials to investigate; they grasped the truth of the situation, and the affair was linked to the Prime Minister, Lü Buwei. In the ninth month, [the king] exterminated Lao Ai's clan to the third degree of relation, killed the two boys that the Queen Dowager had borne, and banished the Queen Dowager to Yong. All of Lao Ai's henchmen had their fortunes confiscated and were exiled to Shu.[12] The king wished to execute the Prime Minister, but because of the magnitude of his works on behalf of the former king[13] and the multitude of orators among [Lü Buwei's] clients who came to plea [for his life], the king could not bear to carry out the punishment.

In the tenth month of the tenth year of the King of Qin,[14] Lü Buwei was dismissed as Prime Minister. Subsequently, Mao Jiao, a man of Qi, persuaded the King of Qin to welcome the Queen Dowager back from Yong and allow her to return to Xianyang.[15] He also banished Marquis Wenxin [Lü Buwei] to his fief in Henan.

Within little more than a year, clients and emissaries of the feudal lords would encounter each other on the road, asking for Marquis Wenxin. The King of Qin feared that they would effect a coup, so he dispatched a letter to Marquis Wenxin, saying, "What have you achieved for Qin? Yet you have been enfeoffed as Lord of Henan with an appanage of a hundred thousand households. What is your relation to Qin? Yet you are called 'Uncle.' Move your family and retinue, and live in Shu." Lü Buwei reckoned himself slighted and abused, and, fearing execution, drank poison and died.[16] With Lü Buwei and Lao Ai—who had aroused the King of Qin's anger—both dead, [the king] allowed the return of all of Lao Ai's henchmen, whom he had exiled to Shu.

In the nineteenth year of the First Emperor,[17] the Queen Dowager died. She was given the posthumous title of Queen Dowager, and was buried with King Zhuangxiang at Zhiyang.

Biography of Li Si [Excerpts]

Li Si was from Shangcai in Chu. When he was young, he was a minor functionary in the local government. He saw that the rats in the privies and the functionaries' quarters ate refuse and would be terrified whenever people or dogs came close. When Si entered the granary, he observed that the rats in the granary ate mounds of grain and, living under a great portico, were not bothered by people or dogs. Therefore Si sighed and said, "People are worthy or ignoble just like rats: [one's fate] depends on where one is located!"

(The first part of the biography tells how Li Si left his teacher, Xun Zi, to seek his fortunes in Qin, where he impressed the king and eventually secured office.)

When [the First Emperor] finally united the world, being honored with the title Emperor, he made Li Si his Counselor-in-Chief. He demolished the fortifications of counties and commanderies[18] and melted down weapons, showing that there would be no more use for them. He decreed that Qin would not [part with] even a foot of land in fiefs; he did not establish his sons and younger brothers as princes nor his meritorious ministers as feudal lords, so that the turmoil of [territorial] warfare would never again come to pass.

In the thirty-fourth year of the First Emperor,[19] wine was laid out in the palace at Xianyang. Zhou Qingchen (Chief Administrator of the Erudites) and others lauded the First Emperor's awesome virtue. Chunyu Yue, a man of Qi, approached and remonstrated, saying: "I have heard that the kings of Yin[20] and Zhou [ruled] for more than a thousand years by enfeoffing their sons, younger brothers, and meritorious ministers, who then served as a support [for the king]. Now, Your Majesty, you possess everything within the seas, but your sons and younger brothers are but commoners. If there should be turmoil such as that of Tian Chang or the six ministers [of Jin],[21] you would not have anyone to support and assist you. How would you be saved? I have never heard of any cause that could endure without taking antiquity as its model. Now Qingchen and the others flatter you to your face, thereby compounding Your Majesty's errors; they are not loyal ministers."

The First Emperor sent this down to the Counselor-in-Chief for discussion; the Counselor-in-Chief considered the speech erroneous and its argument defective. So he submitted the following letter:

In ancient times, the world was dispersed and disordered; no one could unify it. Therefore, the feudal lords operated in concert; their words were always guided by the past and were harmful to the present. They embroidered empty talk to bring disorder to reality. Men esteemed their parochial learning and opposed the institutes of their superiors.

Now, Your Majesty, you possess the entire world; you distinguish white from black[22] and have confirmed [yourself] as the sole object of veneration. But private scholars now join with each other to oppose the regulations of your administration and your instructions; as soon as they hear that an order has been handed down, they each discuss it with reference to their parochial learning. When they enter [the court], they oppose it in their hearts; when they leave, they discuss it in the streets. They consider it reputable to oppose their ruler and lofty to have a dissenting inclination. They lead the flock of inferiors to fabricate defamation. If this is not prohibited, then the ruler's power will diminish among the higher [officials], and factions will form among the lower ones. Thus you ought to prohibit it.

I request that all those who possess literary works, the *Odes* and *Documents* and sayings of the Hundred Schools, [be forced to] abjure and discard these. Let it be commanded that anyone who does not discard them within thirty days be tattooed and sentenced to hard labor. Only writings on medicine, divination, and agriculture are not to be discarded. If someone wishes to study [these fields], he must have an official as his teacher.

The First Emperor approved of his opinion and confiscated the *Odes* and *Documents* and sayings of the Hundred Schools in order to keep the people ignorant and cause the world not to use the past to oppose the present. The rationalization of administrative measures and fixing of laws and edicts all began with the First Emperor. He standardized writing systems, erected palaces and buildings for sojourns abroad, and toured throughout the world. The next year, he campaigned again, driving out the Four Barbarians. [Li] Si was active in all these [undertakings]. . . .

In the tenth month of the thirty-seventh year of his reign,[23] the First Emperor traveled to Mount Guiji [in the south] and then reached Langya in the north by sea. Counselor-in-Chief [Li] Si and Zhao Gao, Eunuch Chief of the Carriage Bureau, traveled with him, [bearing] the official seals and administering affairs. The First Emperor had more than twenty sons; because the eldest, Fusu, had remonstrated forthrightly with the emperor on numerous occasions, he was sent to oversee the army at Shang Commandery,[24] where Meng Tian was stationed as General. His beloved younger son Huhai asked to go along [with the First Emperor on his trip], and the emperor acquiesced. None of the other sons went along.

In the seventh month of that year, the First Emperor arrived at Sand Hill and fell gravely ill. He ordered Zhao Gao to dispatch a letter to Prince Fusu, saying, "Entrust your troops to Meng Tian; join the funeral party at Xianyang and bury me." The letter had already been sealed, but the herald not yet sent, when the First Emperor died. The letter and the imperial seals were all in Zhao Gao's quarters; only [the First Emperor's] son Huhai, Counselor-in-Chief Li Si, Zhao Gao, and five or six favored eunuchs knew that the First Emperor had died. None of the other ministers were aware of it. Li Si considered that the emperor had died abroad without an undisputed heir, so he kept the matter confidential. He placed the First Emperor's [corpse] in a "warm and cool carriage";[25] the many officials sent up memorials and food as before, and the eunuchs would hastily approve of the memorials from within the "warm and cool carriage."

(Next the eunuch Zhao Gao convinces Huhai to suppress the First Emperor's letter to Fusu and claim the throne for himself. Li Si protests, but is finally persuaded by Zhao Gao to join the plot. Prince Fusu receives a forged letter with the imperial seal requesting his suicide, and he complies; General Meng Tian is imprisoned and executed. Thus Huhai is anointed as Second Emperor.)

When the Second Emperor was at leisure, he summoned Zhao Gao in order to plan affairs with him. He told him, "The duration of a man's life in this world is like [the time it takes] for a team of six thoroughbreds to gallop past a crack in a wall. Now that I govern the world, I wish to fulfill all the desires of my ears and eyes and enjoy to exhaustion everything that my heart and will delights in, while making the ancestral temples secure and bringing joy to the Hundred Clans. I wish to possess the world in perpetuity and live out my years. Is there a way to make this possible?"

[Zhao] Gao said, "It is a worthy ruler who is able to do this, and a benighted one who prohibits it. I ask leave to talk about this; not presuming to avoid execution by the ax,[26] I entreat Your Majesty to bear in mind for a little while [what I am about to say].

"The several princes and great ministers are all suspicious of the conspiracy at Sand Hill—and the princes are all elder brothers of the emperor, while the great ministers were established by the former emperor. Now Your Majesty has begun to take your stand, and this group is of a discontented mind and completely unsubmissive. I fear that they will carry out a coup. Moreover, now that Meng Tian is dead, [his younger brother] Meng Yi has taken up his troops and camps with them abroad. I shudder to think that you may not live out [your natural life]. Your Majesty, how can you attain in peace the pleasures [that you speak of]?"

The Second Emperor said, "What can be done about this?"

Zhao Gao said, "Make the administration harsher and punishments more severe. Order the guilty to denounce others for execution; arrest entire clans; annihilate the great ministers and estrange them from their flesh and blood. Enrich the poor and ennoble the base. When you have completely expelled the remaining ministers of the former emperor, set up those whom Your Majesty most trusts and draw them near to you. In this manner, those whom you favor personally will be grateful to you; harm will be expelled and treacherous conspiracies confounded. Among the thronging ministers, there will be none who are not smothered by your beneficent fecundity and enveloped by your munificent grace. Then, Your Majesty, you may repose loftily, indulge your whims, and enjoy your pleasures. No plan can exceed this."

The Second Emperor did as Zhao Gao had said and issued more administrative laws. Thus whenever a minister or prince committed a crime, he was sent down to [Zhao] Gao with orders [that the case be] examined and adjudicated. He killed Meng Yi and other great ministers. Twelve princes were massacred in the marketplace of Xianyang, and ten princesses were killed by quartering at Du. Their wealth and appurtenances were seized by the local courts. Those who were implicated in these affairs were too numerous to be counted. . . .

Thus administrative edicts and criminal punishments became more severe every day. Ministers all feared for their own [safety], and many were those who wished to rebel. On top of this, [the Second Emperor] constructed the Epang Palace[27] and organized grand highways. Tax collection became increasingly burdensome, and garrison and labor service was endless. Therefore Chen Shě, Wu Guang, and others, soldiers from a garrison in Chu, started a revolution in Shandong. Desperadoes took their stand everywhere, setting themselves up as marquises and princes and revolting against Qin. Troops reached Hongmen before being forced back.

(The rebellion of Chen Shě and Wu Guang was the beginning of the end. Zhao Gao's insatiable appetite for power led him to imprison and execute Li Si, thereby eliminating the last competent statesman in the cabinet. The text concludes by relating the bizarre sequence of events leading to the ignominious downfall of the Qin empire.)

After Li Si's death, the Second Emperor paid his respects to Zhao Gao by making him Eunuch Counselor-in-Chief. There were no affairs, great or small, that were not decided by Gao. Gao knew that his power was great, so he presented a deer [to the emperor], calling it a horse. The Second Emperor asked his attendants, "Is this not a deer?"

The attendants all said, "It is a horse."

The Second Emperor was alarmed and considered himself deluded. So he summoned the Grand Diviner and ordered him to cast milfoil. The Grand Diviner said, "Your Majesty, when you perform the *jiao*-sacrifice in the spring and autumn and make offerings to the ghosts and spirits in the ancestral temples, you are not clear about fasting and purifying yourself. Thus it has come to this. You can be clearer about fasting and purifying yourself, in accordance with your flourishing virtue." Therefore [the Second Emperor] entered Shanglin [Park] in order to fast and purify himself. But he would sport every day at archery and hunting, and when a wanderer entered Shanglin, the Second Emperor shot and killed him. Zhao Gao instructed his son-in-law, Yan Yue, magistrate of Xianyang, to impeach whoever it was who deliberately killed a man passing through Shanglin.

Then Gao remonstrated with the Second Emperor, saying, "Son of Heaven, you have deliberately killed an innocent man without reason; Di Above prohibits this. The ghosts and spirits will not receive [your sacrifices], and Heaven will soon send down misfortune. You ought to remove yourself far from the palace and expiate [your transgression]." So the Second Emperor left to go live in the Wangyi Palace. He had stayed there for three days when Zhao Gao forged an imperial mandate to the guards, ordering them to wear white vestments and aim their weapons toward the interior [of the palace]. He entered and addressed the Second Emperor, "The thronging bandits from Shandong have arrived in a mass!" When the Second Emperor arose to look, and saw [his guards], he was terrified. Zhao Gao then hectored him until he committed suicide. [Gao] removed the imperial seals [from the Second Emperor's cadaver] and hung them from his own belt, but the many officials in attendance would not follow him. When he ascended the main hall, it shook three times as though it were inclined to collapse. Gao knew that Heaven would not cooperate with him and that the ministers would not accept him, so he summoned the First Emperor's younger brother [Ziying][28] and bestowed the seals on him.

Ziying considered it a calamity to be raised to the throne, so he did not attend to affairs, citing illness. He plotted with the eunuch Han Tan and his son to kill Gao. When Gao came to visit, inquiring about [the emperor's] infirmity, [Ziying] called them in and commanded Han Tan to stab [Gao] to death. He destroyed [Zhao Gao's] clan to the third degree of relation.

In the third month of Ziying's reign, the troops of the Lord of Pei[29] entered [Qin] by way of the Wu Pass and reached Xianyang. The [imperial] ministers and officials were all disloyal and did not resist. Ziying and his wife and children tied ropes around their necks, surrendering by the side of the Zhi Road. The Lord of Pei remanded them to the custody of his functionaries; when King Xiang[30] arrived, he beheaded them. And so the world was lost.

The Transgressions of Qin [Excerpts]

The King of Qin[31] bore a covetous and boorish heart; he carried out his own ideas, did not trust his meritorious officials, and was not intimate with his men-of-service or with the people. He abrogated the Kingly Way and set up institutions according to his personal likes. He burned the books and made the penal law harsher, placing deception and power before humanity and righteousness; he was the leader of the world in violence and cruelty. One may esteem deception and power for the purpose of annexation, but to secure [one's gains], one must treasure compliance with justice. We can infer that there are different techniques for conquest and consolidation.

Although [the King of] Qin survived the Warring States and made himself king of the world, he did not change his ways or improve his government. This was because he thought there was no difference between conquest and consolidation. He possessed [the world] alone, like an orphan; thus his demise was simply a matter of time. If the King of Qin had been counseled by the affairs of earlier generations and the legacies of the Yin and Zhou dynasties in regulating his government, then, even though his descendant was a licentious and haughty ruler, there still would not have been any concern that [the government] could be overthrown or imperiled. Thus when the Three Kings[32] established [their government] over the world, their names and reputations were prominent and admired, their meritorious enterprises enduring.

Then the Second Emperor ascended the throne, and no one in the world failed to stretch his neck and observe the government. One who is freezing understands the benefit of coarse serge, as one who is starving reckons sweet the taste of dregs. The acclamation of the world might have been an aid to the new king: by this I mean that an exhausted populace is easy [to control] if treated with humanity. If the Second Emperor had acted like even an ordinary ruler and delegated authority to the loyal and worthy; if ruler and ministers had shown concern for the nation's problems with one mind; if he had regretfully corrected the former emperor's transgressions; if he had divided the land and people by enfeoffing the descendants of the meritorious ministers; if he had established principalities with lords who would [rule] the world with ritual; if he had emptied prisons and issued amnesties; if he had abolished penal slavery and other humiliating penalties, allowing all to return to their village; if he had opened granaries and storehouses, dispersing funds and monies to assist orphaned and straitened men-of-service; if he had lightened the burden of taxation and reduced corvée levies to relieve the desperation of the Hundred Clans; if he had made the administration conform to covenants and reexamined the penal code for the sake of posterity; if he had caused the people of the world to begin anew, so that each one would take care of himself through self-discipline and cultivated conduct; if he had fulfilled the hopes of the myriads of his people and engaged the world with flourishing virtue—then [the people of] the world would have gathered around him. Then, within the Four Seas, everyone would have considered himself fortunate in his station; the only fear would have been that there might be a coup.[33] Even if there had been crafty and mischievous people, no one else would have been of a mind to defy the emperor. Thus devious ministers would have had no means to dress up their schemes and treasonous uprisings would have been suppressed.

The Second Emperor did not practice such methods, but only compounded [the government's] failure to conform to the Way. In addition, he began construction on the Epang Palace. He multiplied punishments and executed harshly. The rule of his officers was even more severe; rewards and penalties were inappropriately matched; taxes and levies were immeasurable. There was so much corvée labor in the world that the officials could not manage it all. The Hundred Clans were in straitened circumstances, but their ruler did not take them in or pity them. Afterward, treachery and duplicity arose in concert, and superiors and inferiors deceived each other. So many were those entrapped by the law that convicts would gaze at each other on the roads. The world was bitter about this. From the several chamberlains down to the common rabble, everyone bore a heart of self-preservation. Everyone experienced personally the realities of misery and bitterness; everyone was insecure in his position, and thus easily moved [to insurgency]. Therefore Chen She did not have to be as worthy as Tang or Wu;[34] though he had no feudal dignities at his disposal, he rose up at Daze,[35] and the world responded like an echo, because the populace was imperiled. . . .

At the time, the world was not without men-of-service with profound designs and far-reaching deliberations who knew how to bring about change. But they did not dare manifest their loyalty by sweeping away the transgressions [of the emperor] because it was the habit of Qin frequently to prohibit [such rectitude] as though it were taboo. [Advisers] were doomed even before their loyal words had fully left their mouths. This caused the men-of-service in the world to incline their ears and listen, to stand firmly on their feet, to shut their mouths, and not to speak. Therefore, when the three rulers [of Qin] abandoned the Way, loyal ministers did not remonstrate with them and wise men-of-service did not plan on their behalf. The world was already in rebellion, but the treachery was not made known to the emperor—is this not tragic?

The Former Kings [of Zhou] knew that blocking [the flow of opinion] and remaining blind [to the people's concerns] would harm the state. Thus they established the various ranks of advisers to appoint the rest of the administration and set up laws so that the world would be ordered. When they were strong, they prohibited violence; they executed those who were disorderly, and the world submitted. When they became weak, the Five Hegemons carried out punitive expeditions and the feudal lords complied. When they were stripped [of territory], they preserved their interior [lands] while depending on foreign [powers], so that their altars of soil and grain endured.[36] However, when Qin was flourishing, it multiplied its laws and carried out punishments harshly, so that the world trembled; when it reached its decay, the Hundred Clans had become resentful, and [everyone] within the seas revolted. The protocols of the Zhou kings attained the Way, and they [survived] for more than a thousand years without interruption. Qin abandoned [the Way] at all levels, and thus could not endure. From this perspective, we see that the policies [which bring about] security are peril and far apart indeed.

A rustic proverb says: "Those who do not forget matters of the past are the teachers of posterity." Therefore, when a noble man manages the state, he observes [the practices] of ancient times, tests them in the current generation, and blends them with [the exigencies] of human affairs. He investigates the principles of flourishing and decay and is careful to wield power appropriately. He discards and rejects according to protocols; he institutes changes in compliance with the times; thus his days are many and his altars remain secure.

—PRG

Notes

1. The biography of the First Emperor himself is too long to be included here.
2. I.e., 267 B.C.E.
3. The kings of the various states commonly exchanged sons of low rank as hostages. Thus the presence of Zichu in Zhao was supposed to dissuade Qin from attacking Zhao; but as we are told here, the system did not always work.
4. The capital of Zhao.
5. I.e., 257 B.C.E. Note that the name of the king of Qin (Zhāo) and that of the state he was attacking (Zhào) are completely distinct in Chinese.
6. I.e., 251 B.C.E.
7. The great irony, of course, is that according to this story, Lü Buwei was really the king's father.
8. Zichu's consort, the girl whom Lü Buwei first found in Handan.
9. The text refers to Zheng by his future title; at this point he had not yet unified China and assumed the title of Emperor.
10. A city about a day's journey west of the capital.
11. I.e., 238 B.C.E.
12. An area in modern Sichuan, far to the southwest.
13. I.e., Zichu.
14. I.e., 237 B.C.E.
15. The capital of Qin, near modern Xi'an.
16. Execution would mean the death of his family as well.
17. I.e., 228 B.C.E.
18. To deter local insurrections.

19. I.e., 213 B.C.E.

20. I.e., Shang.

21. Tian Chang and the six ministers of Jin were ancient usurpers.

22. I.e., truth from falsehood.

23. I.e., 210 B.C.E. By a confusing convention, the "tenth month" here really means the first month.

24. In the extreme northwest of the empire.

25. A "warm and cool carriage" was a sleeping car with windows that could be opened or closed as the weather dictated.

26. In other words, he is prepared to die for his words.

27. A pleasure palace of obscene proportions.

28. According to another version, Ziying was the Second Emperor's eldest son, or the First Emperor's grandson.

29. I.e., Liu Bang, the eventual founder of the Han dynasty.

30. Another rebel leader.

31. I.e., the First Emperor.

32. The founders of the Xia, Shang, and Zhou dynasties.

33. That is to say, the people would have been so happy that they would have feared only a change in government.

34. The founders of the Shang and Zhou dynasties, respectively.

35. Two syllables.

36. Jia Yi is putting the best possible face on the history of the Zhou. The phrases "when they were weak" and "when they were stripped of territory" refer to the Spring and Autumn and Warring States periods, when the Zhou kings were no longer in a position to rule the world themselves.

VARIOUS ANCIENT SOURCES record that in the early years of the Han dynasty, the predominant political philosophy was that of "Huang-Lao." Scholars surmised that this school of thought must bear some relation to the political ideals expressed in the *Daode jing*, because "Huang-Lao" is apparently a portmanteau word composed of the first syllables of Huang Di (the Yellow Emperor) and Lao Zi. The Yellow Emperor is a mythic figure often associated with techniques of meditation and macrobiotics, so his juxtaposition to the *Lao Zi*—which, as we have seen, also alludes to such practices—makes some sense. But since no Huang-Lao works had been preserved down to modern times, the term long remained a mystery, and it was impossible to advance beyond the general supposition that Huang-Lao must denote some form of Daoism.

Then, in 1973, several previously unknown texts were discovered in a Western Han aristocrat's tomb in Mawangdui. Since these works frequently mention the Yellow Emperor, and since they were written on silk scrolls that also contained editions of the *Lao Zi*, it was evident that archaeologists had stumbled on the first known writings of the Huang-Lao persuasion. With great excitement, scholars set to work at analyzing and translating the new documents.

The central concept of Huang-Lao is the Way, which engenders the infallible standards of nature and which a wise ruler must learn to emulate. The patterns of Heaven, Earth, and the four seasons dictate the appropriate order of human activity. As the manuscripts declare, "If one obeys [the Way], one will live; if one [follows] its principles, one will be successful. If one opposes [the Way], one will die; if one fails to [conform, one will achieve no] name." Successful rulership is a matter of perceiving and complying with the chthonic and uranic rhythms on which all life depends.

These texts probably date to the early second century B.C.E., by which time such cosmological naturalism can no longer be considered original. Indeed, one is hard put to identify any idea in the so-called "Silk Manuscripts of Huang-Lao" that had not already been expressed in Warring States literature. Moreover, the texts are short on details; while they declare repeatedly that the ruler must "grasp the Way," they rarely explain, in concrete terms, what that entails. An ancient ruler might have found some high-flown principles in these works, but few tangible suggestions that could be readily applied to the practice of government. Finally, courtiers of a Confucian outlook criticized Huang-Lao on the grounds that it did not incorporate any notion of virtue and self-cultivation. The Confucian conviction is that good government is not the responsibility of the ruler alone, but the shared enterprise of all humanity.

Because of these shortcomings, the value of the Huang-Lao materials is primarily historical. We now have our first direct evidence concerning how early Han thinkers conceived of the state and its role in the universal plan. But Huang-Lao was too facile and derivative to endure as the prevailing paradigm of government.—PRG

Discourse on the Elements [of Government]

It is the Way of Heaven and Earth that one begin with patterns and end with war.[1] It is the principle of Heaven and Earth that the four seasons have their measure. It is the skein of Heaven and

Earth that the sun, moon, stars, and constellations have their orbital periods. It is the Way of Heaven and Earth that three seasons be [dedicated to] successful accomplishments and one to punishment and death.[2] The four seasons are timely and fixed; they do not miss or err. They constantly follow a standard model: [*lacuna*]; one arises when another declines; one is born when another dies. The four seasons govern successively, and with winter one returns to the beginning.

The principles of human affairs are a matter of maintaining opposition or obedience. If one's accomplishments overflow to Heaven, one will surely die and be punished. If one's accomplishments do not reach Heaven, one will retire without a name. If one's accomplishments are in accord with Heaven, one will achieve a great name. This is the principle of human affairs. If one obeys (sc. the Way), one will live; if one [follows] its principles, one will be successful. If one opposes [the Way], one will die; if one fails to [conform, one will achieve no] name.

If one rebels against the Way of Heaven, the state will have no ruler. In a state without a ruler, those who obey and those who oppose [the Way] will attack each other. They will assail the foundations and bring down its accomplishments. Disorder will be born and the state will be doomed. Acting [impiously] before Heaven, [the state] will lose its territory and have its ruler replaced. Not to follow Heaven's Constancy, not to regulate the energies of the people, to move around without accomplishment, to nourish death and assail life—this is called "opposing perfection." If [those who "oppose perfection"] are not executed by mankind, there will certainly be punishment from Heaven. When manifestations of opposition begin to arise, be sure not to correct them prematurely; those [who manifest opposition] will soon bring about their own punishment.

Thus one who grasps the Way must observe the world by examining the origin of affairs and their "forms and names." When forms and names are settled, opposition and obedience have their positions; death and life have their division; and survival and perdition, flourishing and decay have their place. Thereupon he gauges [forms and names] according to the eternal Way of Heaven and Earth; he determines the locations of calamity and fortune, death and life, survival and perdition, and flourishing and decay. In this manner, he does not depart from principles in myriad enterprises; he organizes the world without miscalculation. Thus he can raise the Son of Heaven and establish the Three Chief Ministers so that the world is transformed by their [moral instruction?]. This is called "Possessing the Way."

Guo Tong

The Yellow Emperor asked his four assistants, "I alone possess the entire world as one man. Now I wish to domesticate, rectify, balance, and pacify [the people]. How shall I do this?"

Guo Tong replied, "If you are not frugal, you cannot pacify them; if you are not sincere, you cannot rectify them. Observe Heaven above; regard Heaven below; and investigate men and women. Heaven has its trunk and Earth its constancy; [the trunk and][3] the constancy are combined, and thus there are darkness and light, yin and yang. Earth has mountains and valleys, blackness and whiteness, beauty and ugliness. Earth is tranquil with its abundant[4] power; Heaven is active by rectifying names. When tranquility and activity nourish each other, virtue and vice complete each other. If both [poles] have their names, they engage each other and are thus completed. When yin and yang are prepared, objects undergo the transformation of birth. 'There are those who, [when delegated one task], consider it heavy; there are others who are delegated a hundred but find it easy.'[5] People have their talents and objects have their forms; if one complies with them, one will be successful."

The Yellow Emperor said, "The people are born looking up to Heaven; they attend the Earth for food. They take Heaven as their father and Earth as their mother. Now that I wish to domesticate, rectify, balance, and pacify them, with whom is it fitting to start?"

[Guo Tong] replied, "If you are frugal, you will be able to pacify them; if you are sincere [you will be able to rectify them]. Noble and base must be contrasted so that rich and poor have their ranks. The older generation should be taken as a model for the younger generation to adhere[6] to. Start with me, Guo Tong."

Thereupon Guo Tong donned vestments of serge and, bearing a jug on his back, became hunchbacked. He walked alone and begged for food, meandering through the states in all four directions, in order to demonstrate the apex of poverty and abasement.

—PRG

Notes

1. The significance of this statement is unclear. "Patterns" and "war" are defined elsewhere in the Huang-Lao corpus as nourishing life and killing, respectively. So the idea here may be that the year begins with spring, the season of vitality, and ends with winter, the season of death.

2. The "three seasons" are spring, summer, and autumn; the "one" is winter.

3. There is a small lacuna here; "the trunk and" is a plausible supposition.

4. This is one possible meaning; the original character is hard to read.

5. This may be a quote or a well-known proverb: a similar saying appears in another ancient text. The point is that different people have different abilities, which the ruler must take into account when assigning them duties.

6. This graph is also difficult to construe. Guo Tong seems to be saying that as an elder counselor, he should set an example for the rest of the population.

THE COSMOLOGY OF the "Five Phases" is based on the materialist premise that the entire universe is made up of matter, called *qi*. Furthermore, *qi* is thought to pass eternally through a cyclical sequence of five aspects: Metal, Wood, Water, Fire, Earth—hence the term "Five Phases" *(wuxing)*. Since *qi* constantly transmutes from one phase to another, it is important to remember that the Five Phases are not conceived as elements. Whereas hydrogen, for example, cannot normally be converted into helium, Wood routinely transforms into Fire in the Five Phases scheme.

The Five Phases were associated with the seasons: Metal with autumn, Wood with spring, Water with winter, and Fire with summer. (Earth, remaining in the center, was not assigned a season.) Thus the progression of the year was understood as a single cycle of *qi*. At the beginning of the year, in the spring, Wood *qi* prevails. As the days move past the vernal equinox (the height of spring), gradually Wood *qi* wanes and Fire *qi* ascends, until the summer solstice, when Fire is at its zenith. Then Fire is gradually replaced by Metal, until the autumnal equinox, when Water takes its turn. At the winter solstice, Wood finally resumes its dominant position as the old year comes to a close and the new one is ushered in.

These correspondences could be amplified as each phase was correlated with a direction, a color, a theriomorphic guardian, and so on:

Metal	Wood	Water	Fire	Earth
autumn	spring	winter	summer	
west	east	north	south	center
white	green	black	red	yellow
tiger	dragon	warrior	bird	

The practical purpose of this cosmography becomes clear when we consider that *qi* was thought to obey a basic physical rule of "stimulus and response" *(ganying)*: if *qi* is stimulated in a certain way, it will respond sympathetically. (The most frequently adduced example of this rule was the phenomenon of sympathetic musical vibrations.) Since all human actions necessarily stimulate *qi* and elicit a physical response, everything we do must have a definite effect on the cosmic system. Consequently, a ruler needed to know which types of actions were appropriate to which times of year. If agriculture and hunting were untimely, for example, these activities were supposed to stimulate *qi* in such a way as to harm the Wood aspect. The inevitable repercussions would be madness, unremitting rainfall, and various portents and abominations involving creatures associated with Wood. Thinkers who embraced Five Phases philosophy therefore hastened to map out the correlations among the phases so as to provide a manual or almanac of appropriate action.

In stressing conformity with the sempiternal mechanics of nature, Five Phases philosophy resembles Huang-Lao, the other famous naturalistic world-view of the Han dynasty. Indeed, the two outlooks seem so compatible that some scholars identify the *Master of Huainan (Huainan Zi)*, one of the texts that laid the foundations of Five Phases thought, as a Huang-Lao work. But ancient texts that elucidate the Five Phases do not typically label themselves as Huang-Lao, and, conversely, the silk Huang-Lao manuscripts from Mawangdui do not ever refer to the Five Phases. Therefore, it is probably best to study Huang-Lao and Five Phases philosophy as separate schools of thought.

The following selections include (1) an excerpt from *Spring and Autumn Annals of Mr. Lü (Lüshi chunqiu)*, a compendium commissioned by Lü Buwei in the state of Qin; (2) an excerpt from "The Vast Plan" (Hongfan), a late chapter from the *Exalted Documents*, presented here with exegetical material from the so-called *Great Commentary to the Exalted Documents (Shangshu dazhuan)* attributed to Fu Sheng (d. early 2nd c. B.C.E.); and (3) excerpts from the *Huainan Zi*, a work modeled after the *Spring and Autumn Annals of Mr. Lü* and commissioned by Liu An (d. 122 B.C.E.), prince of Huainan.[1] The first and third items can be dated fairly precisely because we know when their patrons lived. The date of "The Vast Plan," on the other hand, is disputed. It can hardly have been written before the late Warring States period, but since it is already discussed in the *Great Commentary to the Exalted Documents*, "The Vast Plan" would appear to be a preimperial document. —PRG

Like Responds to Like [From *Spring and Autumn Annals of Mr. Lü*. Excerpt]

Whenever an emperor or king is about to flourish, Heaven must first cause an omen to appear to the people below.

At the time of the Yellow Emperor, Heaven first caused great earthworms and mole crickets to appear. The Yellow Emperor said, "Earth *qi* prevails." Since Earth *qi* prevailed, he exalted yellow as his color and modeled his activities after Earth.

When it came to the time of Yu,[2] Heaven first caused grasses and trees to appear throughout autumn and winter without dying. Yu said, "Wood *qi* prevails." Since Wood *qi* prevailed, he exalted green as his color and modeled his activities after Wood.

When it came to the time of Tang,[3] Heaven first caused metal blades to appear growing in the water. Tang said, "Metal *qi* prevails." Since Metal *qi* prevailed, he exalted white as his color and modeled his activities after Metal.

When it came to the time of King Wen,[4] Heaven first caused fire to appear, and red rooks with cinnabar writings in their beaks to gather at the altars of Zhou. King Wen said, "Fire *qi* prevails." Since Fire *qi* prevailed, he exalted red as his color and modeled his activities after Fire.

What will replace Fire is surely Water.[5] Heaven will first make it apparent that Water *qi* prevails; and since Water *qi* will prevail, [the new ruler] will exalt black as his color and model his activities after Water. Water *qi* will reach its limit, and then, without our knowing it, the sequence will come full circle and shift back to Earth.

The Vast Plan [From *Exalted Documents*. Excerpt. Commentary from *Great Commentary to the Exalted Documents*]

The Five Phases:

The first is called Water. The second is called Fire. The third is called Wood. The fourth is called Metal. The fifth is called Earth.

Water moistens and descends.

Commentary: If one diminishes one's ancestral temple, fails to pray to and worship one's forebears, lets sacrifices lapse, and opposes the Heavenly seasons, then Water will not moisten and descend.

Fire blazes and ascends.

Commentary: If one abrogates administrative laws, chases away meritorious ministers, kills the Heir Apparent, and makes one's concubine one's primary wife, then Fire will not blaze and ascend.

Wood is crooked and straight.

Commentary: If agriculture and hunting are out of season, if food and drink are offered as sacrifice without [the proper rituals], if exiting and entering are not moderated, if the people are snatched away during the farming seasons,[6] and if there are treacherous conspiracies, then Wood will not be crooked and straight.

Metal complies and changes.

Commentary: If one pursues warfare and battle, thinks lightly of the Hundred Clans, erects walls and fortifications like ornaments, and attacks neighboring territories, then Metal will not comply and change.

And Earth is [the phase of] sowing and harvesting.

Commentary: If one builds palatial dwellings and embellishes one's terraces and kiosks, if there is licentiousness and disorder in one's inner apartments,[7] if one violates one's relations and insults one's father and elder brother, then sowing and harvesting will not come to fruition.

Moistening and descending create saltiness; blazing and ascending create bitterness; crookedness and straightness create sourness; compliance and change create acridity; sowing and harvesting create sweetness.

The Five Actions:

The first is called Demeanor. The second is called Speech. The third is called Sight. The fourth is called Hearing. The fifth is called Thought.

Demeanor should be reverent. Speech should be compliant. Sight should be clear. Hearing should be keen. Thought should be astute.

Reverence creates decorousness.

Commentary: If one's demeanor is irreverent, this is called indecorousness. Its calamity is madness, its penalty constant rain; at its apex, it is evil. Sometimes there are portents involving clothing; sometimes there is retribution involving tortoises; sometimes there are catastrophes involving chickens; sometimes there are abominations such that the lower parts of the body grow on top;[8] sometimes there are internal and external omens involving green. This indicates that Metal is disrupting Wood.

Compliance creates orderliness.

Commentary: If one's speech is not compliant, this is called disorderliness. Its calamity is usurpation, its penalty constant yang; at its apex, it causes grief. Sometimes there are portents involving poetry; sometimes there is retribution involving little insects; sometimes there are catastrophes involving dogs; sometimes there are abominations involving the mouth and tongue; sometimes there are internal and external omens involving white. This indicates that Wood is disrupting Metal.

Clarity creates intelligence.

Commentary: If one's sight is not clear, this is called lack of intelligence. Its calamity is laxity, its penalty constant heat; at its apex, it causes disease. Sometimes there are portents involving grass; sometimes there is retribution involving armorless insects; sometimes there are catastrophes involving sheep; sometimes there are abominations involving the eyes; sometimes there are internal and external omens involving red. This indicates that Water is disrupting Fire.

Keenness creates deliberation.

Commentary: If hearing is not keen, this is called lack of deliberation. Its calamity is desperation, its penalty constant cold; at its apex it causes poverty. Sometimes there are portents involving drums; sometimes there is retribution involving fish; sometimes there are catastrophes involving pigs; sometimes there are abominations involving the ears; sometimes there are internal and external omens involving black. This indicates that Fire is disrupting Water.

Astuteness creates sagehood.

Commentary: If one's thinking mind is not astute, this is called lack of sagehood. Its calamity is fog, its penalty constant wind; at its apex it causes fierce deficiencies. Sometimes there are portents involving fat and the night;[9] sometimes there is retribution involving flowers; sometimes there are catastrophes involving oxen; sometimes there are abominations involving the heart and the fat; sometimes there are internal and external omens involving yellow. This indicates that Metal, Wood, Water, and Fire are disrupting Earth.

Treatise on the Patterns of Heaven [From *Huainan Zi*. Excerpt]

What are the five stars?

The eastern quadrant is Wood. Its god is Tai Hao. His assistant, Goumang, grasps the compass and governs spring. Its spirit is the Year Star, its beast the Blue-Green[10] Dragon, its tone *jue,* its days *jia* and *yi.*[11]

The southern quadrant is Fire. Its god is the Blazing Emperor. His assistant, Red Brightness, grasps the steelyard-beam and governs summer. Its spirit is Yinghuo, its beast the Vermilion Bird, its tone *zhi,* its days *bing* and *ding.*[12]

The center is Earth. Its god is the Yellow Emperor. His assistant, the Goddess of the Soil, grasps the marking-line and regulates the four quadrants. Its spirit is the Apotropaic Star, its beast the Yellow Dragon, its tone *gong,* its days *wu* and *ji.*[13]

The western quadrant is Metal. Its god is Shao Hao. His assistant, Rushou, grasps the T-square and governs autumn. Its spirit is the Grand Whiteness, its beast the White Tiger, its tone *shang,* its days *geng* and *xin.*[14]

The northern quadrant is Water. Its god is Zhuanxu. His assistant, Mysterious Obscurity, grasps the steelyard-weight and governs winter. Its spirit is the Morning Star, its beast the Mysterious Warrior, its tone *yu,* its days *ren* and *gui.*[15]

Treatise on the Shape of the Earth [Excerpt]

Wood vanquishes Earth; Earth vanquishes Water; Water vanquishes Fire; Fire vanquishes Metal; Metal vanquishes Wood. Thus grain is born in the spring and dies in the autumn. Pulse[16] is born in the summer and dies in the winter. Wheat is born in the autumn and dies in the summer. Shepherd's-purse is born in the winter and dies in midsummer.

When Wood is robust, Water is aging, Fire is born, Metal is imprisoned, and Earth is dead. When Fire is robust, Wood is aging, Earth is born, Water is imprisoned, and Metal is dead. When Earth is robust, Fire is aging, Metal is born, Wood is imprisoned, and Water is dead. When Metal is robust, Earth is aging, Water is born, Fire is imprisoned, and Wood is dead. When Water is robust, Metal is aging, Wood is born, Earth is imprisoned, and Fire is dead.

There are five tones; *gong* is their chief. There are five colors; yellow is their chief. There are five tastes; sweetness is their chief. There are five materials; earth is their chief.

Thus refined Earth engenders Wood; refined Wood engenders Fire; refined Fire engenders clouds [of Metal *qi*]; refined clouds engender Water; refined Water reverts to Earth. Refined sweetness engenders sourness; refined sourness engenders acridity; refined acridity engenders bitterness; refined bitterness engenders saltiness; refined saltiness reverts to sweetness. When *gong* is changed, it engenders *zhi*; when *zhi* is changed, it engenders *shang*; when *shang* is changed, it engenders *yu*; when *yu* is changed, it engenders *jue*; when *jue* is changed, it engenders *gong*.

Thus one uses Water to harmonize Earth, Earth to harmonize Fire, Fire to transform Metal, Metal to govern Wood; Wood reverts back to Earth. The Five Phases put each other in order, thereby constituting a useful instrument.

—PRG

Notes

1. The ancient text known as *Luxuriant Dew of the Springs and Autumns (Chunqiu fanlu)* is rich in Five Phases cosmology and is often used in sourcebooks; it is not included here because of modern doubts about its authenticity.
2. Founder of the Xia dynasty.
3. Founder of the Shang dynasty.
4. Founder of the Zhou dynasty.
5. Qin reckoned itself the dynasty pertaining to Water; since the *Spring and Autumn Annals of Mr. Lü* was compiled at the court of Qin, this paragraph claims cosmological justification for the dynastic rule of that state. Note, however, that it also predicts the ineluctable demise of Qin.
6. I.e., used for warfare and other enterprises.
7. The "inner apartments" housed the ruler's harem.
8. For example, when the legs of an ox emerge from its back (this example appears in an ancient subcommentary).
9. The significance of the connection between fat and night is not clear.
10. The color is *cang*, which can denote anything from the verdant color of vegetation to the pale blue of the sky.
11. The "Year Star" is Jupiter, *jue* the third note in the pentatonic scale. *Jia* and *yi* are the first two days of the ten-day week.
12. Yinghuo is Mars, *zhi* the fourth note in the scale, *bing* and *ding* the third and fourth days of the week.
13. The "Apotropaic Star" is Saturn, *gong* the first note in the scale, and *wu* and *ji* the fifth and sixth days.
14. "Grand Whiteness" is Venus, *shang* the second note in the scale, and *geng* and *xin* the seventh and eighth days.
15. The "Morning Star" is Mercury, *yu* the fifth note in the scale, and *ren* and *gui* the ninth and tenth days.
16. "Pulse" is a kind of plant, as is "shepherd's-purse," which appears below.

WHILE THE FIRST Emperor of Qin was cementing his empire in China, a mighty nomadic confederacy was forming on the northern steppes. This was the Xiongnu empire, an assemblage of various tribes and nations first united by a leader named Modu (d. 174 B.C.E.). As pastoral nomads, the Xiongnu had no fixed homes, but wandered across the steppe with their herds according to precise patterns, taking advantage of all the pasturelands at the most opportune times of the year. The Xiongnu tribesmen were also adept at mounted warfare—it is sometimes said that they learned to ride before they learned to walk—and exploited this advantage by attacking and plundering Chinese settlements along the northern frontier. We know that the First Emperor was concerned by their presence: General Meng Tian, whom we recall accompanying Prince Fusu in death, was stationed far in the north, contending with the Xiongnu menace.

But the Qin dynasty fell too quickly to gauge the success or failure of its Xiongnu policies. It was a consequence of the Han empire's very stability that its emperors were the first to have to face the steppe-nomadic threat as an endemic geopolitical problem. No single strategy provided a long-term solution. Attacking the Xiongnu was not only costly and risky—the first Han emperor was almost captured on such an expedition—but also futile because territorial gains could never be consolidated: the steppe was not easily incorporated into the Chinese empire and economy. The Han administration attempted to prepare for the Xiongnu raids by building garrisons along the frontier, but this approach was hardly less costly and was vitiated by the static nature of permanent fortifications. Sometimes the Han government would attempt to foment civil war among the Xiongnu by supporting a pretender to the steppe throne and encouraging him to wage war on his rivals, but too often the Han backed a weak contender without the resources to affect the balance of power on the steppe. So most Han emperors considered it expedient simply to buy off the Xiongnu with annual gifts and subsidies. But the high price of this modus vivendi strained the national treasury, and many Chinese patriots considered it shameful for the empire to prostrate itself before a horde of barbarians.

The financial burden of defending against the Xiongnu began to affect the domestic economy. Partly to help defray the cost of maintaining a fortified frontier, the Han administration established government monopolies in crucial industries over which it did not wish to lose control: salt, iron, liquor. Intellectuals protested that it was inappropriate for the government to engage in commerce. The basic mandate of government, in Confucian eyes, was the moral education of the populace; as soon as the government used its position to pursue profitable ventures, it was thought to be abusing its power. Thus a great conference was called in 81 B.C.E. between representatives of the imperial government and the Confucian intellectuals who opposed its economic policies. The Confucians scored a rhetorical victory, but the government monopolies, far from being abolished, were only confirmed as a standard element of imperial administration.

A transcript of the proceedings has come down to us in the form of a text called *Discourses on Salt and Iron (Yan tie lun)*. To modern readers, the proposals of the Confucians seem ethereal and impractical, their repeated quotes from scripture pedantic and unworldly. From the point of view of intellectual history, however, the text is valuable because it documents the rise of a kind of fundamentalist classicism: the belief that the correct blueprint for all human endeavors could be found in the Confucian canon. This outlook was to become mainstream in Later Han times.

The selections below include excerpts from the chapter on the Xiongnu in Sima Qian's *Records of the Grand Historian (Shiji)* and the opening pages of the *Discourses on Salt and Iron.*—PRG

The Xiongnu [From *Records of the Grand Historian*. Excerpts]

The progenitor of the Xiongnu was a descendant of the Xiahou clan named Chunwei. Since before the time of Tang and Yu,[1] there have been [tribes like the Xiongnu, named] Mountain Rong, Xianyun, and Xunyu. They live in the northern wastelands and wander about with their herds of pastoral animals. The majority of their animals consist of horses, oxen, and sheep, but they also have strange animals such as camels, asses, mules, *taotu,* and *dianxi.*[2] Though they move their abodes in pursuit of water and grasslands, and though they have no walls or fortifications, no permanent dwellings, and no agriculture, they do divide their lands into individual [territories].[3] They have no literature or writing and seal their covenants with oaths and speeches. As children, they can ride sheep and shoot birds and rodents with their bows; once they have grown a little, they shoot foxes and rabbits, which they use for food.

The men are all strong enough to bend a bow and serve as armed cavalry in cases of emergency. According to their custom, in times of peace they follow their herds and shoot wild animals for subsistence; in times of crisis the people wage war and attack. This is their Heaven-endowed nature. Their long-range weapon is the bow and arrow, their short-range weapons daggers and spears. In advantageous situations, they advance; in disadvantageous situations, they retreat. They are not ashamed to flee. Only profit attracts them; they know nothing of ritual and righteousness.

From the rulers on down, they all eat the meat of the herd-animals and use their skins and hides for clothing, covering themselves in felt and fur. Those who are most hardy eat the fattest and choicest [pieces]; the aged eat the remnants. They value hardiness and vigor and depreciate age and weakness. When a father dies, [the son] takes his stepmother as his own wife, and when their brothers die, they take their [brothers'] wives as their own. It is their custom to have personal names, but no taboo-names[4] or clan names.

(The text now recounts the ancient history of the steppe nomads, coming down at last to Touman, *chanyu*[5] or king of the Xiongnu, who lived at the time of the Qin dynasty.)

The *chanyu* had an heir named Modu. Later [the *chanyu*] obtained a *yanzhi,*[6] whom he loved and who bore him a younger son. Desiring to do away with Modu and establish his younger son [as his heir], the *chanyu* sent Modu as a hostage to the Yuezhi.[7] Once Modu had become a hostage of the Yuezhi, Touman quickly attacked them. The Yuezhi wanted to kill Modu, but Modu stole their best horse, mounted it, and charged home. Touman then considered him hardy and put him in charge of ten thousand cavalrymen.

Modu then made some whistling arrows and used them to train his cavalrymen. He commanded them: "I will behead anyone who does not shoot when I shoot my whistling arrows." When he was hunting game-birds, anyone who did not shoot in unison with his whistling arrows was summarily beheaded. Then Modu shot at his best horse with a whistling arrow, and some men in attendance did not dare shoot; Modu promptly beheaded those who did not shoot his best horse. A while later, he used his whistling arrows again to shoot his beloved wife, and some men in attendance were quite afraid and did not dare shoot; Modu beheaded them, too. Still later, Modu went out hunting and shot the *chanyu*'s best horse with a whistling arrow; all of his attendants shot it [as well]. Thus Modu knew that all of his attendants were reliable. He accompanied his father, the *chanyu* Touman, on a hunt, and shot Touman with a whistling arrow. His attendants all followed suit and shot the *chanyu* Touman to death. Then he executed all of his stepmothers and younger brothers, as well as those among the great advisers who did not obey him. Modu proclaimed himself *chanyu*.

At this time the Eastern Hu[8] were strong and prosperous. When they heard that Modu had killed his father and taken his place, they sent an embassy to Modu demanding Touman's thousand-tricent horse.[9] Modu consulted with his advisers, who all said, "The thousand-tricent horse is a treasured horse of the Xiongnu nation. Do not grant [their request]."

Modu said, "Why should I begrudge one horse to a neighboring nation?" So he granted them the thousand-tricent horse.

A while later, thinking Modu was scared of them, the Eastern Hu sent an embassy to Modu demanding a *yanzhi* from the *chanyu*. Modu again consulted with his advisers, who were all incensed and said, "The Eastern Hu have no decency, asking for your *yanzhi*. Attack them, we pray you."

Modu said, "Why should I begrudge one girl to a neighboring nation?" Then he selected his favorite *yanzhi* and bestowed her on the Eastern Hu.[10]

The king of the Eastern Hu, becoming more and more arrogant, attacked westward. Between [the Eastern Hu] and the Xiongnu, there was some unclaimed territory of over a thousand tricents that was uninhabited. Each [nation] placed frontier entrenchments on either side [of the buffer zone]. The Eastern Hu sent an embassy to Modu, saying, "Since you, the Xiongnu, are unable to occupy the unclaimed territory that lies between your frontier entrenchments and ours, we wish to possess it."

Modu consulted with his advisers, and some of them said, "This is unclaimed territory; granting their request and not granting it are both acceptable."

Thereupon Modu was greatly enraged and said, "Land is the basis of the nation. How could I grant their request?" He beheaded everyone who had said to do so. Modu ascended his horse, ordered that anyone in the nation who lagged behind would be beheaded; then he penetrated eastward and attacked the Eastern Hu. Since the Eastern Hu had earlier taken Modu lightly, they had not prepared for him. Thus when Modu arrived with his troops and attacked, he destroyed the Eastern Hu king, capturing his people and livestock. Once he had returned home, he attacked westward and routed the Yuezhi. To the south, he conquered the kings of Loufan and Boyang, which is south of the Yellow River.[11]

Discourses on Salt and Iron

Discussing "Roots"[12] [Excerpt]

In the sixth year of the Shiyuan era,[13] the Counselor-in-Chief and the Ombudsmen were sent by imperial decree to a conference with worthy literati who had been selected for that purpose. They asked about the afflictions of the people.

The literati responded, "We have humbly heard that the Way of ruling the people is to ward off the causes of licentiousness and indolence, broaden the incipiences of virtue,[14] rein in the profits of merchants, and cause humanity and righteousness to bloom. Only if one does not display profit [before the people] can the transformative effect of education flourish; only then can habits and customs be reformed. But now the territorial administrations have salt and iron [bureaus], the liquor monopoly, and 'equitable distribution';[15] they are contending with the people for profit. They dissipate the honest and kind simplicity [of the people], causing them to turn covetous and mean. Therefore, among the Hundred Clans, few people pursue the 'roots,' and many hanker after the 'branches.' When the blossoms are luxuriant, the fruits decay; when the branches flourish, the roots wilt. If the branches are cultivated, the people will be licentious; if the roots are cultivated, the people will be diligent. If the people are diligent, then resources and provisions will be adequate; if the people are perverse, then hunger and cold[16] will be born. We entreat you to abolish the salt and iron [bureaus], the liquor monopoly, and 'equitable distribution,' so as to advance the roots and abate the branches, and increase the profitability of agricultural enterprise. This would be expedient."

The Grand Masters[17] said, "The Xiongnu have turned their back on us, rebelling and refusing to be our subjects. They repeatedly plundered frontier settlements. If we prepare for them, we will be straining the soldiers of China; if we do not prepare for them, they will invade and rob incessantly. The former emperor,[18] grieved by the longstanding troubles of the frontiersmen and bitter at their capture by the 'caitiffs,'[19] built mote-and-bailey forts with a network of alarm towers and garrisons in order to prepare for them. The funds available to be spent on the frontier were inadequate, so he instituted the salt and iron [bureaus], organized the liquor monopoly, and established 'equitable distribution.' [These instruments] increased goods and wealth severalfold, thereby mitigating the frontier expenditures. Now the discussants wish to abolish them. At home, this would empty the reserves in the granaries and storehouses; abroad, this would diminish the funds available for defense and preparation. The soldiers who keep watch in the forts and mount the walls would be made to endure starvation and cold on the frontier. How do [the literati] expect to supply them? To abolish [the monopolies] is not expedient."

The literati said, "Confucius said: 'Heads of states or households worry not about poverty, but about inequality; they worry not about underpopulation, but about insecurity.'[20] Thus: 'The Son of Heaven does not speak of much or little; the feudal lords do not speak of advantage or detriment; the grand masters do not speak of gain or loss.'[21] If one influences [the people] by nurturing humanity and righteousness, and cherishes them by extending one's virtuous conduct, then those who are near will intimately attach themselves [to the ruler] and those who are distant will gladly submit. Thus: 'One who is adept at attacking does not wage war; one who is adept at waging war does not lead his soldiers; one who is adept at leading his soldiers does not deploy them in formation.'[22] Cultivate yourself in your ancestral hall; then incursions will be beaten back and you can return your troops.[23] One who is a king carries out humane government and has no enemies in the world. What need is there for [frontier] expenditures?"

—PRG

Notes

1. "Tang" and "Yu" are alternate names for the Sage Kings Yao and Shun, respectively. Therefore, this phrase means that steppe nomads had existed for as long as Chinese historians could remember.

2. A *taotu* is a wild horse, a *dianxi* perhaps a pony.

3. Modern research suggests that ancient steppe nomads did in fact engage in agriculture, though to a limited degree. The biography of Modu goes on to contradict the claim that the Xiongnu did not establish fortifications.

4. In China, a ruler's personal name was taboo and could not be uttered by his subjects.

5. This term is sometimes Romanized in Western works as *shanyu,* but *chanyu* is the preferred pronunciation in Chinese dictionaries.

6. This term is glossed by commentators as the Xiongnu word for "royal concubine."

7. The western neighbors of the Xiongnu.

8. The eastern neighbors of the Xiongnu.

9. I.e., a horse that could run a thousand tricents in one day (approximately three hundred miles).

10. The parallel between this tale and the preceding one is evident: Modu first sacrifices a valuable horse, then a favorite concubine.

11. The reference is to the area within the northern loop of the Yellow River, often called the Ordos region.

12. Here and in what follows, the "roots" are understood as agriculture, the "branches" as commerce.

13. I.e., 81 B.C.E.

14. An allusion to Mencius.

15. "Equitable distribution" *(junshu)* refers to the government practice of transporting goods across the state to equalize the supply and thereby stabilize prices.

16. By "cold" is meant homelessness.

17. I.e., the representatives of the imperial government.

18. I.e., Emperor Wu of Han (r. 140–87 B.C.E.).

19. The Chinese referred to the Xiongnu disdainfully as "caitiffs"; the (unintentional) irony here is that it is the "caitiffs" who are taking the prisoners.

20. A quote from *Analects* 16.1.

21. This saying was attributed to Xun Zi in ancient times, but it is not found in his extant writings today.

22. This was a kind of bromide in ancient times; a similar saying appears in the *Guliang Commentary* to the *Spring and Autumn Annals.*

23. A similar saying is attributed to Confucius in ancient times; it does not appear in the received *Analects.*

BIAN QUE, traditionally said to have lived sometime during the fifth–fourth centuries B.C.E., is the most celebrated of early Chinese practitioners of the medical arts and is considered the father of diagnosis by the pulse. His skills are legendary, as are the many stories about him in early Chinese writings. For example, one anecdote relates that he performed such a successful exchange of hearts between two men that upon recovery each took possession of the other's household. Somewhat less dramatic is Sima Qian's account of Bian Que's life included in his *Records of the Grand Historian (Shiji),* where it precedes the account of the historical physician Chunyu Yi (216–ca. 150 B.C.E.). Itself somewhat of a pastiche, Sima Qian's account translated below is the primary biography of Bian Que; but it too comes up short on historical verisimilitude. It begins by telling how secret arts and recipes were transmitted to Bian Que by a mysterious man known as Changsang Gong, Venerable Tall-Mulberry (a legendary transcendent who is mentioned in other literature as the transmitter of arcane arts); indeed, Bian Que acquires special abilities after ingesting a secret substance passed to him by Venerable Changsang. The rest of the account is overtly anecdotal and places Bian Que in historical contexts that range over several hundred years. There once may have been an actual man called Bian Que, or Qin Yueren, but the Bian Que esteemed for more than two millennia in traditional Chinese culture is the stuff of legend. A further problem with the Grand Historian's account of Bian Que is hermeneutical in nature. There are inconsistencies between the biography's recounting of medical concepts and terminology and those of early Chinese medical theory and practice, at least as far as either is presently envisioned and understood. The Grand Historian's recounting of events and dialogue could contain specific usages and vocabulary that had been preserved intact from earlier materials that now are nowhere else attested, perhaps conflated with contemporary understanding and jargon. But it may be more likely that the text reflects the editorial effects of years of literary iterations of anecdotes featuring Bian Que, with some specialized vocabulary perhaps used in places more for literary effect than for literal signification. While the text has been translated with primary attention to philological integrity, as well as to a suitable correspondence to the conceptual and practical systems of early Chinese medicine, the reader should bear in mind that numerous passages have had any number of contending interpretations over the centuries. The word *qi,* for instance, is variously translated as "vapor," "air," "breath," "vital energy," or "life force."—AB

Biography of Bian Que

Bian Que was a man of Zheng, of Bohai district (in northeastern China), whose family name was that of the Qin clan and his given name was Yueren (Surpassing Others). In his youth he acted as manager of a lodging house. Whenever the lodging guest Venerable Changsang passed by, Bian Que alone found him to be unique and would regularly meet him with respect. Venerable Changsang equally recognized that Bian Que was no common man. He came and went for more than ten years, and only then did he call Bian Que to sit with him privately. He leisurely conversed with Bian Que, then spoke with him thus, "I am in possession of taboo recipes; as I am old in years, I wish to pass them down to you. Do not divulge anything." Bian Que said, "I respectfully consent." Then, taking out some medicinal substance that had been concealed under his clothing, he gave it to Bian Que. "After drinking this mixed with waters of the pool on high (i.e., dew) for thirty days, you then will be able to comprehend material phenomena." Then he took out all of his books of taboo recipes and gave them all to Bian Que. Suddenly he disappeared: most probably he was not a mortal man.

Bian Que followed his instructions and drank the medicinal concoction for thirty days, and then upon looking he could see a person on the other side of a wall (i.e., he could see through a wall). Using this ability to examine ailments, he could completely see the obstructions and nodes in the five visceral "storage organs" (corresponding to heart, liver, spleen, lungs, and kidneys). But he especially achieved fame for examining the vessels (i.e., diagnosis by the pulse). Some of the areas where he practiced medicine were located in Qi, and some in Zhao. When in Zhao he was known as Bian Que.

Just at the time of Duke Zhao of Jin (ca. 531–526 B.C.E.), when the various grandees were becoming powerful and the ducal clan was weakening, in his position of grandee Jianzi of Zhao was monopolizing the state affairs. Jianzi became ill (in 501 B.C.E.) and was unconscious of others for five days. The grandees were all fearful, and so they summoned Bian Que. Bian Que entered and examined the ailment, then left. Dong Anyu (one of Jianzi's servants) questioned Bian Que, and Bian Que said, "The blood vessels are in order, so what is unusual? In the past, Duke Mu of Qin (r. 659–621 B.C.E.) once was like this for seven days and then he awoke. On the day he awoke he informed Gongsun Zhi and Ziyu (both of whom were in his service), 'I went to the residence of the (Celestial) Emperor, and it was extremely pleasing. The reason I stayed long is that there happened to be something to be learned. The emperor told me, "The state of Jin will soon be in great disorder. For five generations they will find no peace. Thereafter there will be a hegemony, but this man will die when not yet old. When the son of the hegemon is to command, in the state there will be no separating the men and the women."' Gongsun Zhi recorded it and stored it away. The Qin prophetic writings originate with this. The disorder of Duke Xian (r. 676–651 B.C.E.), the hegemony of Duke Wen (r. 636–628), and Duke Xiang (627–621) defeating the Qin army at Xiao and giving free reign to licentiousness upon returning home: these are things you have heard about. Now, the ailment of the ruling lord (Jianzi) is the same as that. Without going three days there is sure to be a break (in his condition). At the break, he surely will have something to say."

Remaining in that state for two and a half days, Jianzi then awoke. He recounted to the various grandees, saying, "I went to the residence of the (Celestial) Emperor, and it was extremely pleasing. With the hundred spirits I roamed in the Creator's Heaven. The Expansive Music, the Nine Arrangements, and the pantomime dances there cannot be classed with the music of the three (earthly) dynasties: their sounds moved the heart. There was a bear who wished to draw me away. The (Celestial) Emperor commanded me to shoot it; I hit the bear, and the bear died. There was (another) bear that approached. I again shot it; I hit the bear and the bear died. The (Celestial) Emperor was greatly pleased, and presented me with two baskets. Each (of the above) was a symbolic surrogate. (Similar to that of Duke Mu above, Jianzi's "ailment" actually was a prophetic dream trance. In Jianzi's trance, the two bears are surrogates for the totemic ancestors of two dignitaries Jianzi would vanquish in 490 B.C.E., and the two baskets represent two "barbarian" principalities.) I saw a child at the (Celestial) Emperor's side. The (Celestial) Emperor entrusted me with a dog of the (northern) Di tribe, and said: 'When it comes that your son has grown strong, bestow it upon him.' The (Celestial) Emperor told me that in the state of Jin the generations soon will weaken, and in the seventh generation it will be lost (indeed, the seventh ruler was deposed in 376 B.C.E.). The Ying clan (of the state of Zhao, i.e., Jianzi's clan) will greatly defeat the Zhou clan (of the state of Wei) to the west of Fankui, but they nevertheless will not be able to take possession." (In 372 B.C.E. Marquis Cheng of Zhao attacked Wei, taking seventy-three cities, but Wei did not give up its territories until 150 years later.) Dong Anyu received these words; he recorded them and stored them away. He told Jianzi the words of Bian Que, and Jianzi bestowed on Bian Que forty thousand *mu* of field lands (a bit less than five thousand acres).

After that, when Bian Que passed by (the state of) Guo, the heir designate (apparently) had died. Upon arriving at the Guo palace gates, Bian Que asked a palace cadet (an officer in the charge of the heir designate) who happened to appreciate arcane arts, "What was the heir designate's ailment? Throughout the state preparations for the exorcistic sacrifice (for burial) have taken precedence over all other affairs." The palace cadet said, "As for the heir designate's ailment, his blood and *qi* were not timely. Being intermixed and intermingled, they did not get to drain off. They were violently emitted on the exterior, and this as a consequence occasioned internal injury. The vital forces were unable to arrest the noxious *qi*; the noxious *qi* accumulated and built up, and did not get to drain off. On account of this, the yang was slackened and the yin excited. Therefore, with violent convulsions, he died." Bian Que asked, "How has his death been in terms of time?" "From cock's crow until the present." "Has he been removed yet (for burial)?" "Not yet. His death has not yet lasted half a day." "Say that I am Qin Yueren of Bohai district in Qi. As my home is located in Zheng, I have never yet gotten to gaze upon the pure brightness (of His Majesty's countenance), nor in service pay a visit before Him. I have heard that the heir designate most unfortunately has died. I, your subject, am able to make him live."

The palace cadet said, "Can it be that you, master, are not boasting of it? On what basis do you say that the heir designate can be made to live? I have heard that in the times of high antiquity, of physicians there was Yu Fu. In curing an ailment he did not use decoctions or fermented brews, sharp lancets or joint manipulation, pressure massages or medicated ironings. With one glance he would discern the bodily correspondences to the ailment. Following the incipiencies of the five storage organs, he then would cut open the skin and dissect the flesh, open up the vessels and knot the sinews, take hold of marrow and brain, pick out the fat and claw at the membranes, wash and bathe intestines and stomach, rinse the five storage organs, refine the vital force and transform the physical form. If, master, your arcane arts can match these, then the heir designate can be made to live; if, however, they cannot match these yet you would wish to make him live, then never could you convince even a cooing infant."

After some time, Bian Que looked up to the heavens and said with a sigh, "The way you practice healing arts is just like peeping at the sky through a tube, or looking at designs through a small crack (i.e., seeing only a small part of the whole). As to the way I, Yueren, practice healing arts, I need not wait to press on the vessels, observe the facial color, listen to the sound of the voice, or take note of the physical form to say where an ailment is located. Hearing about the yang of an ailment I can discuss its yin; hearing about the yin of an ailment I can discuss its yang. The bodily correspondences of an ailment are seen on the greater exterior. Without going a thousand tricents, the cases I've decided reach a multitude; it simply cannot be disputed. If you consider my words to be untrue, then for verification enter and examine the heir designate. You should perceive his ears resounding and his nostrils flaring. Follow his two thighs and reach his concealed parts: they should still be warm."

When the palace cadet heard Bian Que's words, his eyes revolved in their sockets and did not blink, and his tongue thrust upward and did not come down. Then he announced the words of

Bian Que to the Lord of Guo. When the Lord of Guo heard them he was greatly alarmed. He went out to see Bian Que at the central gate tower and said, "Long have I humbly heard of your high sense of duty, but I have never gotten to pay my respects before you. If you, master, in passing by this small state were to with great fortune raise up the heir designate, then the good fortune of this measly servant in this insignificant state would be extreme. With you, master, then he will live; without you, master, then he will be abandoned and discarded to the ditches and gullies, and for eternity he will be unable to return." Before his words were finished, he was moved to snivel and whimper, his soul and vital force dispersed in all directions, with flowing tears and long weeping streaming over his eyelashes; grieved and unable to stay himself, his countenance and appearance changed and transformed.

Bian Que said, "An ailment like that of the heir designate's is what is called a case of the 'cadaverous convulsions.' This is because the yang enters into the midst of the yin. Activating the stomach, binding up and winding around, it pierces the main vessels and ties up the auxiliary vessels. Separating, it goes below to the 'three heated spaces' and the urinary bladder. For this reason the yang pulse descends and falls off, and the yin pulse rises and contends. At the reunion points the *qi* is obstructed and does not circulate. The yin rises while the yang moves inward. Moving downward and inward, (the yang) drums and does not rise up; moving upward and outward, (the yin) is cut off and not sent out. Above, there are auxiliary vessels with interrupted yang; below, there are vascular nodes with disrupted yin. With disrupted yin and interrupted yang, the facial color is depleted and the pulse is disordered. Therefore, the physical form is still, with an appearance similar to death. The heir designate has not yet died. When it is a case of the yang entering the organs of the myriad yin conduits, one lives. In a case where the yin enters the organs of the myriad yang conduits, one dies. All these several events occur violently during the time when the five storage organs convulse. A good workman removes (the ailment); an unskilled one hesitates in confusion."

Bian Que then had his disciple Ziyang sharpen the needles and smooth the stones, and he selected the five reunion points on the three outer yang vessels. There was a break (in the condition), and the heir designate revived. Then Bian Que had Zibao (another disciple) perform a five-*fen* medicated ironing (i.e., the warming influences of "ironing on" the medicated application would reach to a depth of about one-half inch) and then blend and boil an eight-times-reduced compound and with this once more perform a medicated ironing on the (heir designate's) two flanks. The heir designate rose to a seated position. To once more harmonize his yin and yang, he but ingested a medicinal decoction for two ten-day periods, and then he was returned to his old state. Thus the whole world considered Bian Que to be able to bring to life a dead person. Bian Que said, "It is not that I, Yueren, am able to bring the dead to life. This was simply that I was able to cause someone to rise up who quite naturally was actually alive."

When Bian Que passed by (the state) of Qi, Marquis Huan of Qi retained him as a guest. Entering the court for an audience, (Bian Que) said, "You, lord, have an illness; it is located in the pores and fibers (of the skin). If not cured, it will go deeper." Marquis Huan said, "My humble self has no illness." Bian Que left, and Marquis Huan addressed his attendants, saying, "The way that physicians are fond of profiting is that they desire to achieve merit by way of ones who are not (really) ill." Five days later, Bian Que again had audience, and said, "You, lord, have an illness; it is located in the blood vessels. If not cured, I fear it will go deeper." Marquis Huan said, "My humble self has no illness." Bian Que left; Marquis Huan was not pleased. Five days later, Bian Que again had audience and said, "You, lord, have an illness; it is located amongst the intestines and the stomach. If not cured, it will go deeper." Marquis Huan did not respond. Bian Que left, and Marquis Huan was displeased. Five days later, Bian Que once again had audience.

Observing (from a distance), he looked at Marquis Huan, then withdrew and hurried away. Marquis Huan sent someone to ask the reason for it. Bian Que said, "When an illness is located in the pores and fibres of the skin, decoctions and medicated ironings are what can reach it. When located in the blood vessels, needles and stones are what can reach it. When it is located in the intestines and stomach, alcoholic brews are what can reach it. But when it is located in the bones and marrow, even the Controller of Destiny could not do anything about it. It is now located in the bones and marrow, and for this reason I have no requests (for the marquis in terms of a cure)." Five days later, Marquis Huan's body began to ail. He sent someone to summon Bian Que, but Bian Que already had fled and gone. Marquis Huan subsequently died.

If it is a given that the Sages can foresee subtleties, then if one could enable good physicians to proceed with their work early on, illness could be arrested and bodies could be kept alive. As for what ails people, they ail over (the fact that) illnesses are many; but what ails physicians is that the ways (of treatment) are few. Thus, of ailments there are six "incurables." Being arrogant and unrestrained, and not discussing with reason—this is the first incurable. Considering the body as unimportant and placing importance on wealth—this is the second incurable. Being unable to make clothing and food suitable—this is the third incurable. Having yin and yang mingled and the *qi* of the storage organs unstable—this is the fourth incurable. Having an emaciated physical form and being unable to ingest medicines—this is the fifth incurable. Trusting shamans and not trusting physicians—this is the sixth incurable. Having even one of these conditions makes it doubly difficult to cure.

Bian Que's renown was heard throughout the world. Passing by (the city of) Handan and hearing that they prized women, he accordingly practiced as a physician for matters below the sash. Passing by (the city of) Luoyang and hearing that the people of Zhou held their elderly folk dear, he accordingly practiced as a physician for the ear, the eye, and rheumatism. When he came to enter (the city of) Xianyang, hearing that the people of Qin doted on children, he accordingly practiced as a pediatrician. Conforming to the (local) customs, he effected changes (in his practice). Li Xi, grand officer of medicine in (the state of) Qin, being himself aware that in terms of skill he did not compare with Bian Que, sent someone to stab him to death. Up until the present, all under heaven that is spoken concerning the pulse derives from Bian Que.

—AB

A TERRIBLE THING happened to the historian Sima Qian (145?–86? B.C.E.) in 99 B.C.E. His contemporary Li Ling (d. 74 B.C.E.) was a general who had had great success in fighting the Xiongnu (see selection 27). After having penetrated deep into Central Asia, Li Ling was unexpectedly defeated by the enemy, whereupon he surrendered to the "barbarian" nomads—the supreme disgrace for a Chinese general. When Sima Qian saw that Emperor Wu (r. 140–87 B.C.E.) was displeased by the news, he praised Li Ling by pointing out that the defeated general had been outnumbered by the enemy and had fought bravely, adding that Li Ling was not entirely to blame, because his "relief troops never arrived." This comment was incautious, because the emperor understood Sima's lecture as a veiled attack on the so-called Nisaea General, Li Guangli (d. 90 B.C.E.), who was supposed to lead the relief column, and also happened to be the brother of one of the emperor's consorts. (He earned the sobriquet "Nisaea General" after his crafty successes in that Central Asian city.) The historian was promptly thrown into prison, convicted of "libel against the emperor," and sentenced to be castrated.

This penalty was intended to be humiliating, and Sima Qian was evidently expected to commit suicide rather than undergo it. But he chose to live on as a eunuch and eventually completed his magisterial history of ancient China, known as *Records of the Grand Historian (Shiji)*. Sometime later, he explained his decision in an epistle to Ren An (d. 91 B.C.E.?), an acquaintance who also found himself entangled in legal problems. This letter has been preserved as a testament to Sima Qian's courage and resolve, and as a shining example of his literary skills. In it he declares that he could not bear to leave his opus unfinished, and so he dedicated the rest of his life, scorned and contemned as he was because of his shameful punishment, to the work that would secure his fame for eternity.

Sima Qian's style is lively and relatively ornate, with frequent use of elegant locutions (e.g., "within the stations of the Secret Guard" for "the palace"; "the land of warlike steeds" for "the steppe"). Moreover, his tone in this piece is unmistakably bitter, with many sarcastic and incongruous combinations of words: "I was encumbered by talent that would not be bridled"; "our enlightened emperor did not understand deeply"; "our defilement would only be more copious." (The translation below attempts to convey the idiosyncratic, and at times bizarre, diction of the original.) He takes solace in the observation that most of the great works of Chinese literature were composed by authors who endured some grave tragedy and who, in his words, "issued their frustrations" in their writing. If pain and misery are prerequisites to literary renown, then surely he has paid his dues.

Thus Sima Qian places himself in an august line of national heroes extending back to King Wen himself, the Sage King who completed the *Changes* while in captivity. Though Sima repeatedly deprecates his own abilities, it is clear that he has no lack of esteem for his work. Toward the end of his letter to Ren An, he announces that when he is finished, he will deposit his book in a famous mountain. In ancient China, a text discovered in such a place was thought to be a divine revelation.—PRG

Letter to Ren An [Excerpts]

When I was young, I was encumbered by talent that would not be bridled, and grew up without the praise of my town. Fortunately, on account of my father, the emperor allowed me to present my meager skills, so I passed freely within the stations of the Secret Guard. Considering that there is no way to gaze up at Heaven while wearing a bowl on one's head, I renounced visits [to and from friends] and forgot my domestic affairs. Day and night I yearned to exert my inglorious talents; I sought the emperor's favor by discharging the duties of my office single-mindedly. But then I made a great mistake in my service, and nothing would be the same.

Li Ling and I both lived in the palace, but we had not become friendly with each other. Our likes and dislikes put us on different paths, so we never quaffed a cup of wine together or were linked in an earnest relationship. But I observed that his personality was that of an outstanding gentleman. He served his parents with filial piety, was trustworthy with other men, scrupulous where money was involved, and fair in his dealings. He would defer in matters of hierarchy, and was respectful, temperate, and humble with others. He always yearned to attend to national emergencies, fervently and without concern for his person. Such are the [virtues] that he nurtured and accumulated; I considered him an inspiration to men of state. A subject who would go out to face myriad deaths without concern for his life, who rushes to meet challenges to the commonwealth, is outstanding indeed. In handling his affairs, he acted inappropriately but once, and those ministers who look to their own safety and protect their wives and children immediately plotted retribution for his shortcoming. I was sincerely pained by this in my private heart.

Moreover, Li Ling was provided with fewer than five thousand foot soldiers. They marched deep into the land of warlike steeds; they reached [the Xiongnu] king's court on foot and dangled bait before the tiger's mouth, outrageously provoking the mighty barbarians. Facing an army of millions, they engaged the *chanyu* in battle for more than ten days, killing more than their own number. The caitiffs were unable to retrieve their dead or rescue their wounded. Their lords and chieftains, clad in felt and fur, all quaked with terror, so they summoned the Wise Princes of the Left and Right,[1] conscripted those among the people who could draw a bow, and attacked and surrounded [Li Ling] as one nation. [Li Ling's troops] fought on the move for a thousand *li* until their arrows were exhausted and the escape routes sealed off. The relief troops did not arrive; dead and wounded soldiers lay in heaps. But Li Ling stirred his battalion with a single shout, and none of the soldiers failed to rise up. He himself had tears and blood streaming down [his face] in rivulets. He swallowed his tears, drew his empty crossbow, braved their naked blades, and faced north to fight the enemy to the death.

Before Ling succumbed, a herald had brought a [favorable] report [to the imperial court], and the ministers and feudal lords of Han had all raised a goblet to his long life. Several days later, news of Ling's defeat was heard, and the emperor found no savor in his food and no pleasure in holding court. The great ministers were worried and afraid, not knowing what course to take. When I saw the emperor despondent and distressed, I sincerely wished to offer my candid opinion, without taking my lowly status into account.

Li Ling always shared his short rations with other gentlemen, renouncing what was most savory, so that he was able to get men to die for him. Even famous generals of ancient times did not surpass him in this. Though he fell in defeat, if one considered his intentions, his desire to succeed should have redeemed him and requited Han. Nothing could be done anymore about what had happened, but in the losses that he inflicted [on the Xiongnu], his merit was indeed sufficient to be renowned throughout the world.

In my breast, I wished to disclose [these views], but I had no avenue to do so. Then, coincidentally, [the emperor] summoned me for an interview. I extolled Ling's merit in this manner, wishing to broaden the emperor's point of view and put a stop to the supercilious comments [of Li Ling's enemies].

I was unable to make myself completely clear. Our enlightened emperor did not understand deeply: he thought I was maligning the Nisaea General and lobbying on behalf of Li Ling. So he remanded me to the judges. I was never able to display my solemn loyalty, and in the end, I was convicted of libeling the emperor. My family being poor, my resources were insufficient to buy my freedom. None of my acquaintances would save me, and my colleagues would not utter a single word. A body is not wood or stone. Alone with my jailers, in the deep, dark dungeon—to whom could I appeal? You, Shaoqing,[2] have experienced this yourself; should I have conducted myself any differently? Once Li Ling surrendered alive, he sullied his family's reputation. I, in my turn, was led to the Silkworm Chamber,[3] to become the laughingstock of the world. How tragic! How tragic!

It is not easy to tell this matter in one or two words to vulgar people. My father's accomplishments were not of the order of the tally and seal [of nobility]. As an annalist and astrologer, I am placed among diviners and theurgists and the like—surely a plaything of the emperor. He keeps me like a singer or actor, misprized by the fickle mob. Suppose I had prostrated myself before the law and accepted execution—how different would it have been from the loss of a single hair from nine oxen, or the [death] of an ant or cricket? And the world would never have granted that I had died for my integrity; rather, they would have thought that because of the limitations of my wisdom and the egregiousness of my crime, I was unable to avoid the death penalty. Why? Because of the office in which I had planted myself.

(Sima Qian goes on to explain why he did not commit suicide after his degrading punishment.)

There is no one who is not, by nature, greedy for life and averse to death. We remember our parents and relatives and care for our wives and children. But it is otherwise with those who are roused by righteousness and justice; indeed, they cannot help themselves. I was unlucky to lose both my parents early; I was without brothers, a lonely orphan. And Shaoqing, you see how I thought of my wife and children! But the brave do not necessarily die for their integrity, and even a timid man, if he reveres what is right, will struggle for it wherever he dwells. Although I am timid and weakly, and desire to live, however indecorously, I certainly recognize the difference between what one may and may not do. Then why did I let myself sink to the disgrace of being fettered and bound? Any Zang or Huo,[4] slave or slave-girl, is able to commit suicide; should I not have been able to? I forbore in silence and lived on indecorously, enveloping myself in night soil without apology, because I sensed with remorse that there was something unfinished within my breast. I was loath to depart from the world without exhibiting to posterity my literary brilliance.

In ancient times, there were innumerable wealthy and noble men whose names have been obliterated. Only the uncanny and extraordinary are mentioned [today]. When the Earl of the West[5] was in captivity, he elaborated on the *Rites of Zhou;* when Confucius was in straits, he produced the *Spring and Autumn Annals.* It was after Qu Yuan was exiled that he composed "Encountering Sorrow";[6] Zuoqiu lost his sight, and so we have the *Discourses of the States;* Master Sun had his legs amputated, and *Methods of War* was compiled; [Lü] Buwei was banished to Shu, and the world has transmitted his *Panoramas;*[7] Han Fei was imprisoned in Qin, and [wrote] "Difficulties of Persuasion" and "Solitary Frustration."[8] Most of the three hundred pieces in the *Odes* were produced by worthy sages who conveyed their frustrations. All these men had anxious and suppressed thoughts; they were unable to propagate their principles, so they bore posterity in mind by giving an account of past events. Those like Zuoqiu Ming, who did not have [the use of] his eyes, or Master Sun, whose feet were cut off, could never be employed; they retired to write books in which they expressed their frustrations, yearning to reveal themselves in the legacy of their insubstantial literature.

I have been impertinent enough to depute myself recently to my incompetent writing,[9] reticulating the world's neglected bits of ancient lore. I have examined [the record of] human action, investigating the principles of success and failure, flourishing and decline. In all there are 130 chapters. I wished also to understand the relation between Heaven and humanity and to be conversant with the vicissitudes of history, so as to complete a dissertation of a unified philosophy.[10] Before the first draft was done, this calamity happened to befall me. I was distraught that it might not be completed; therefore I submitted to this extreme punishment without an indignant countenance. Surely, when I have finished this book, I will store it in a famous mountain, where it will be left for someone to have it circulated throughout the cities and great metropolises. Thus I will repay the debt of my earlier disgrace; and though I might suffer myriad dismemberments, how should I regret it? But this can be said only to those who are wise; it is difficult to discuss it with the vulgar.

It is not easy to live with the burden of contempt; the lowly rabble mostly slanders and defames. I met with this calamity by speaking with my mouth; were I to compound the abuse and ridicule [that I endure] in my native district, thereby besmirching and disgracing my ancestors, how could I face the grave tumuli of my father and mother? Even after a succession of a hundred generations, our defilement would only be more copious. Therefore my guts ache several times a day. At home, I am disengaged, as though forgetting something; abroad, I do not know where I am going. Whenever I remember my shame, I sweat so that the clothes on my back are always soaked. By rights I should be a eunuch in the women's apartments, though I would rather withdraw to conceal myself deeply in the cliffs and caves. Thus I carry on for now, bobbing among the vulgar, undulating with the times, associating with fools and madmen.

—PRG

Notes

1. Two Xiongnu nobles.
2. Ren An's courtesy-name.
3. Where castrations were performed.
4. Stock names for a man and woman (like our "Jack and Jill").
5. The title of King Wen of Zhou before he received the Mandate of Heaven.
6. "Li sao," the longest poem in *Lyrics of Chu*.
7. *Spring and Autumn Annals of Mr. Lü* was also known as *Lü's Panoramas (Lülan)* in antiquity.
8. Two chapters in the *Han Fei Zi* (see selection 21).
9. Formal language of humility.
10. A biting pun: "a dissertation of a unified philosophy" (*yijia zhi yan*) can also mean "the words of one family." Denied a corporeal family as a result of his mutilation, Sima Qian intends his history as a surrogate.

WANG CHONG (27–ca. 100 C.E.) is one of the most original thinkers in Chinese history. He had a disappointing official career, and most of his works, being largely unappreciated in his own day, were lost. However, a collection of his essays, titled *The Scale of Discourses (Lunheng)*, was rediscovered in the century after his death and treasured as a repository of extraordinary wisdom. It has been in constant circulation ever since.

In his writings, Wang Chong adopts a tone of plain talking and common sense. He criticizes many of the elaborate metaphysical theories in vogue at the time, reducing them to absurdity by pointing out their inability to explain even the most basic elements of our everyday experience. He dismisses the conventional notion of an anthropomorphic Heaven as an irrational human invention: Heaven has no consciousness, no will, no intentions, no perceptions. People are born of nothing more than haphazard conjunctions of *qi*, not of a conative Heaven who created them for some lofty purpose. Similarly, Wang Chong ridicules as vulgar superstition the belief in ghosts and the idea that one might be able to increase one's allotted life span through occult techniques. Our life is like a candle: when the flame dies, the light goes out forever.

At times Wang Chong contradicts himself, and his arguments do not always hold water. But posterity is fortunate to have a book by an uninhibited ancient thinker who freely challenged all of the standard belief systems of his time, considering himself an adherent of none of them. Moreover, Wang Chong reveals a wide array of popular beliefs in his attempt to refute so many of them.

The following is an essay in which Wang Chong dismantles Five Phases cosmology. He does not deny the existence of *qi*, but he refuses to accept the complex set of correlations examined in selection 26.—PRG

The Conditions of Things [Excerpts]

The Confucians have a doctrine: "Heaven and Earth engender humanity intentionally." This statement is absurd. Humanity is born by chance when Heaven and Earth combine their *qi*, just as a child is born when a husband and wife combine their *qi*. A husband and wife combine their *qi* not because they desire to engender a child at that moment: they copulate because their emotions and desires have been moved, and, in copulating, they engender a child. Moreover, from the fact that a husband and wife do not engender a child intentionally, one knows that Heaven and Earth do not engender humanity intentionally. This being the case, people are born of Heaven and Earth as fish are born in a pond and as lice are born on people. They are born as a consequence of *qi*, each species reproducing according to its kind. The Myriad Things born amid Heaven and Earth are all one reality. . . .

If it cannot be that Heaven engenders humanity intentionally, then it also cannot be that it engenders the Myriad Things intentionally. Creatures are born by chance when Heaven and Earth combine their *qi*. Plowing, weeding, and sowing seeds are intentional acts, but whether [the seeds] ripen or not is a matter of chance. How do we prove this? If Heaven engendered the Myriad

Things intentionally, then it should have commanded them to love and be intimate with each other, and should not have commanded them to ravish and harm each other.

Some say, "Heaven engenders the Myriad Things with the Five Phases of *qi* and imbues the Myriad Things with the Five Phases of *qi*. And the Five Phases of *qi* ravish and harm each other."[1]

I say, "Heaven should have engendered the Myriad Things with One Phase of *qi* and commanded them to love and be intimate with each other; it should not have engendered the Myriad Things with Five Phases of *qi,* commanding them to ravish and harm each other."

Some say, "[Heaven] wishes them to be useful, so it commands them to ravish and harm each other; in pillaging and harming each other, things are perfected. Thus Heaven uses the Five Phases of *qi* to engender the Myriad Things, and people use the Myriad Things for the myriad actions. If things cannot regulate each other, they cannot employ each other; if they do not ravish and harm each other, they will not become useful. If Metal does not ravish Wood, Wood will not become useful;[2] if Fire does not melt Metal, Metal will not become a tool. Thus various objects ravish each other and benefit each other. When creatures imbued with blood vanquish each other and submit to each other, bite each other and are devoured by each other, it is because the Five Phases of *qi* make it so."

I say, "If Heaven engenders the Myriad Things, commanding them to make use of each other, and if they cannot but ravish and harm each other, then does Heaven engender such creatures as tigers, wolves, venomous snakes, and stinging wasps, which all ravish and harm people, because it wants people to be used by them?

"Furthermore, the body of a single person is imbued with Five Phases of *qi*; thus actions of a single person have the principles of the Five Constancies.[3] The Five Constancies are the ethical manifestation of the Five Phases. And the Five Storehouses within [the body] are associated with the Five Phases of *qi*. By the current argument, which is that creatures imbued with blood unceremoniously ravish and harm each other because they have the Five Phases of *qi* in their breasts, the Five Storehouses in the breast of a single person's body should ravish each other! And the heart of a person who carries out the principles of humanity and righteousness should be harmed.[4] Moreover, what reliable proof is there that creatures imbued with blood vanquish and submit to each other because the Five Phases of *qi* ravish and harm each other?"

They say, "The sign *yin*[5] is Wood; its beast is the tiger. *Xu* is Earth; its beast is the dog. *Chou* and *wei* are also Earth; *chou*'s beast is the ox, *wei*'s the goat. Wood vanquishes Earth; thus dogs, oxen, and goats submit to tigers. *Hai* is Water; its beast is the pig. *Si* is Fire; its beast is the snake. *Zi* is also Water; its beast is the rat. *Wu* is also Fire; its beast is the horse. Water vanquishes Fire; thus pigs eat snakes. Fire is harmed by Water; thus horses have distended bellies when they eat rat excrement."

I say, "If we investigate the current argument, we also find evidence that creatures imbued with blood do not vanquish each other. *Wu* is the horse, *zi* the rat, *you* the rooster, *mao* the rabbit.[6] Water vanquishes Fire—so why do rats not hunt horses? Metal vanquishes Wood—so why do roosters not peck at rabbits? *Hai* is the pig, *wei* the goat, *chou* the ox. Earth vanquishes Water— so why do oxen and goats not kill pigs? *Si* is the snake, *shen* the monkey.[7] Fire vanquishes Metal— so why do snakes not eat *mi*-monkeys?[8] *Mi*-monkeys are afraid of rats, and dogs bite *mi*-monkeys. The rat is Water, the *mi*-monkey Metal. Water does not vanquish Metal—so why are *mi*-monkeys afraid of rats? *Xu* is Earth, and *shen* the monkey. Earth does not vanquish Metal—so why are *mi*-monkeys afraid of dogs?"

—PRG

Notes

1. As we have seen, the Five Phases were thought to arise sequentially, each phase overcoming the previous one in the cycle.

2. That is to say, usable lumber is gained by chopping down trees with metal axes.

3. The "Five Constancies" (humanity, righteousness, ritual, wisdom, and trustworthiness) are correlated with the Five Phases, as are the "Five Storehouses" (heart, lungs, liver, kidneys, stomach), below.

4. This sentence may be garbled, but the import is clear. Humanity is associated with the liver, righteousness with the lungs, so part of the point may also be that neither of these virtues is associated with the heart.

5. *Yin* and the following terms enumerated by Wang Chong's imaginary interlocutor are elements of a duodecimal sequence; each sign is associated with an animal and a year in a twelve-year cycle (hence such Chinese expressions as "the Year of the Horse").

6. *You* is associated with Metal, *mao* with Wood.

7. *Shen* is associated with Metal.

8. *Mi* normally denotes a female monkey (especially with offspring), but commentators suggest here that "*mi*-monkey" refers to a large primate with a long tail.

IN *DISCOURSES ON SALT AND IRON,* we examined our first example of what might be called Han Confucian classicism: the idea that the Confucian classics constitute the supreme guide to human action. The scholars represented in that text, we remember, objected to state monopolies because they did not accord with the purpose of government as laid down by the august canon. This classicist view quickly gained favor among the intellectual class. The usurper Wang Mang (r. 9–23 C.E.) owed much of his support to the popularity of his overtly Confucian program.[1] And the eventual downfall of Wang Mang's regime did not prevent his philosophical orientation from flourishing in the succeeding Later Han dynasty; indeed, imperial historians must have sympathized with many of his ideals and condemned him in the sources only because he was not a legitimate heir to the throne.

This kind of classical traditionalism succeeded in uniting the literati by providing a universal scriptural foundation for all moral and political philosophy. But it had several major shortcomings. First, the Confucian canon proved inexpedient as a blueprint for national administration because it had congealed in an era that was ignorant of the exigencies of imperial government. It is no coincidence that many of Wang Mang's greatest failures—such as his disastrous restructuring of the bureaucracy—were reforms intended to reshape the country in the mold of the classics. Furthermore, by concentrating on a small body of sacred texts, much of Han thought became scholastic and insular. The range of philosophical positions espoused in this period was much narrower than in preimperial times.

The most serious weakness of the traditionalist outlook, however, was that it limited human behavior in ways that the classics themselves had not. This phenomenon is well illustrated in the infamous *Admonitions for Women (Nüjie),* by Ban Zhao (48–116? C.E.), the foremost female writer of her time. The avowed purpose of the work is to teach girls how to be good wives. Ban Zhao bemoans the fact that most families do not instruct their daughters, and her conviction that both males and females must be educated is surely appealing today. But the content of her lessons is far less liberal. As far as women are concerned, she tells us, the fundamental virtue of "humanity" *(ren)* consists of nothing more than safeguarding one's chastity, bathing regularly, and weaving with single-minded devotion (see chapter 4, "Womanly Conduct," translated below).

The catalog of "admonitions" continues in this vein, with the tacit premise that Ban Zhao is merely relating the age-old rituals for women in an easily understandable form. But the traditional standing of her prescriptions is questionable. We have seen that the Confucian classics demand genuine self-cultivation, an ethical engagement more complex than anything Ban Zhao discusses. (Confucius would never have equated *ren* with mindless obedience to a predetermined code of conduct.) The view that women should know their place, serve wine in silence, and never contradict their husbands and in-laws may not have been taken straight from the classics—since the classics present a view of humanity that is far richer and more problematic—yet scholars continue to debate the degree to which misogyny is inherent in Confucianism, with some pointing to statements such as that in the *Analects* (17.5) that women and underlings (literally, "small people") are "hard to handle" and others emphasizing the esteem in which wise women such as Mencius's mother were held.

The views that Ban Zhao articulated about the role of women in society are at odds with the pattern of her own life. She was by far the most educated woman of her day, and perhaps the most educated woman in Chinese history. She trained many important male scholars, including Ma Rong (79–166 C.E.), one of the titans of the Confucian lineage. And her greatest achievement may well have been one that posterity has insufficiently noted, namely, her contribution to the extant *History of the Han* (or *Documents of the Han; Hanshu*). This comprehensive history of the Former Han dynasty was originally the enterprise of her father, Ban Biao (3–54 C.E.), and her brother, Ban Gu (32–92). Both Biao and Gu died before completing the project, however, so the task of finishing it devolved on Ban Zhao. It was she who gave the work its present shape.—PRG

Admonitions for Women [Excerpts]

1. Baseness and Softness

In ancient times, on the third day after the birth of a girl, one would have her sleep beneath the bed, have her play with tiles,[2] and report [the birth to the ancestors] by fasting. Having her sleep beneath the bed makes clear her baseness and softness; it is a cardinal duty for her to be subordinate to others. Having her play with tiles makes clear her industry and toil; it is a cardinal duty for her to manage [household affairs] diligently. Fasting and reporting [her birth] to the former lords make clear that she should take it as a cardinal duty to continue the sacrifices and offerings.

These three [obligations are dictated] by the Constant Way for Women and the precepts and teachings of the ritual code. She should be modest, deferent, reverent, respectful. She should place others first and herself last. If she does something good, she should not refer to it; if she does something bad, she should not deny it. She should endure disgrace; she should taste filth in her mouth. She should be constantly as though in dread. This is what is meant by "baseness, softness, and subordination to others."

She should retire late and rise early; she should not shirk [her chores] whether by day or by night. She should not decline to handle domestic affairs, whether they are troublesome or easy. Whatever she does must be done completely. Her hands should show signs that she has been tidying and organizing [the house]. This is what is meant by "managing diligently."

Her bearing should be correct and her character decent, so that she may serve her husband, her master. She should maintain herself in purity and quietude, and not be fond of games and laughter. She should arrange and keep sanitary the food and wine presented in the ancestral temple. This is what is meant by "continuing the sacrifices and offerings."

[A woman who] fulfilled these three [obligations] and yet had to worry that her reputation would not be known, or who was personally disgraced—such has never been seen. But if she fails in these three respects, how can her reputation be known? How can she avoid disgrace?

2. Husband and Wife

The Way of Husband and Wife is associated with yin and yang and reaches to godliness; surely it is an expansive principle of Heaven and Earth and the greatest form of conjugation among human relationships. Therefore the *Rites* esteem the boundary between male and female; the *Odes* exhibit the principle of "The *Guan*-ing Ospreys."[3] From this point of view, one must not fail to emphasize [the relationship between husband and wife].

If a husband is unworthy, he will be unable to control the wife. If a wife is unworthy, she will be unable to serve her husband. If a husband does not control his wife, authority and ceremony will lapse and become deficient; if a wife does not serve her husband, righteousness and order will decline and be lacking. Effectively, these two matters[4] are the same.

If we examine the gentlemen of today, they know only that wives must be controlled and authority and ceremony maintained. Thus they instruct their males, educating them with documents and commentaries. They are quite unaware that husbands must be served and ritual and morality preserved. Are they not indeed blind to the respective obligations [of the sexes], teaching only their males and not teaching females? According to the *Rites,* one begins to teach [children] at eight years of age, and by fifteen they should advance to the point of [serious] study. Can we not take this as a rule? . . .

4. Womanly Conduct

The are four forms of conduct for females: womanly virtue, womanly speech, womanly appearance, and womanly merit. What is called "womanly virtue" need not be brilliant talent or extraordinary [ability]; "womanly speech" need not be eloquent and keen words; "womanly appearance" need not be a beautiful face; "womanly merit" need not be skill in one's work exceeding that of others.

She should safeguard her purity and chastity, keeping decorum and maintaining herself with probity. She should conduct herself with a sense of shame; her actions should follow the appropriate models. This is what is meant by "womanly virtue."

She should choose her phrases when she speaks, not uttering obscene words. She should speak only at the right time, so as not to oppress others [sc. with garrulousness]. This is what is meant by "womanly speech."

She should scrub away dust and dirt. Her clothing and jewelry should be fresh and clean. She should bathe regularly, so that her body is not disgraced by filth. This is what is meant by "womanly appearance."

She should sew and weave single-mindedly and not be fond of games and laughter. She should arrange and keep sanitary the food and wine to be presented to guests. This is what is meant by "womanly merit."

These four things are the great virtues of women; they are indispensable. However, practicing them is very easy: it is only a matter of bearing them in mind. This is what is meant by the saying of the ancients: "Is humanity distant? I desire humanity, and humanity is here!"[5]

5. Single-mindedness

According to the *Rites,* husbands have the right to remarry, but there is no clause [allowing] women to be mated twice.[6] Thus it is said that one's husband is one's Heaven.[7] One certainly cannot flee from Heaven, and one certainly cannot leave one's husband. If one disobeys the spirits of Heaven and Earth in one's actions, Heaven punishes one, and if [a wife] errs with respect to ritual and morality, her husband despises her. Thus it is said in *Women's Regulations:*[8] "To attain the favor of one man is called 'the eternal consummation.' To lose the favor of one man is called 'the eternal termination.'" From this point of view, one cannot fail to seek one's husband's heart. However, one should hardly seek it by means of deceitfulness, flattery, or indecorous insinuation. Certainly, [for this purpose], nothing can match single-mindedness and correct bearing.

She should live cleanly, in accordance with ritual and morality. Her ears should hear no turpitude; her eyes should see no perversion. When she goes out, she should not have a seductive appearance; at home she should not neglect her dress. She should not gather in groups with her peers. She should not watch at the gates. This is what is meant by "single-mindedness and correct bearing."

If her actions are frivolous and untrammeled; if she sees and hears wantonly; if she has disheveled hair and an unkempt body when at home; if she is sluttish and puts on airs when abroad; if she speaks of what ought not be said; if she watches what ought not be seen—then she cannot be single-minded or correct in her bearing.

—PRG

Notes

1. We should bear in mind, however, that Wang Mang also embraced state monopolies and other institutions that would have been decried by the dogmatists in *Discourses on Salt and Iron*.

2. Ban Zhao is alluding to the prescriptions in the *Ode* "These Banks" (Mao 189). The "tile" is sometimes explained as a loom-whorl and thus as an emblem of domesticity rather than humility.

3. "The *Guan*-ing Ospreys" (after the sound of the birds' call) is the title of the first poem in the *Odes*. Traditional commentators have consistently taken the ospreys in that piece as an image of chaste separation between the sexes.

4. I.e., the husband's control and the wife's service.

5. A quote from *Analects* 7.30.

6. In fact, the *Rites* are not unequivocal on this issue; as we have seen, "Vestments of Mourning" (see selection 20) discusses without stigma the case of stepmothers who remarry.

7. A reference to the canonical commentary to "Vestments of Mourning."

8. Evidently the title of a lost book.

ZHANG HENG (style Pingzi; 78–139) was a brilliant scientist, scholar, and poet of the Later Han dynasty. He was born in the area of Nanyang, the Southern Capital, which was located in Henan Province, where he lived much of his life. About the age of sixteen, he traveled north, first to Chang'an, the former Han capital, then to Luoyang, the later Han capital. He spent five years in Luoyang (from 95 to 99) seeking instruction in the classics, probably at the imperial academy. His first position was in his home commandery of Nanyang, where he served as Master of Documents under Bao De (d. ca. 110), governor of Nanyang. Zhang was employed mainly for his skill as a writer, and between 100 and 108 he wrote numerous official documents, dirges, and inscriptions on behalf of his patron.

While serving in Nanyang, Zhang found the leisure to complete his long, two-part poem on Chang'an and Luoyang, the "Two Metropolises Rhapsody," which he had begun ten years earlier. The "Western Metropolis Rhapsody" portrays Chang'an as a center of luxury and prodigality, promoted by emperors who were more interested in building lavish palaces, engaging in expensive hunts and excursions, and catering to the whims of petty concubines and court favorites than they were in attending to court affairs. The "Eastern Metropolis Rhapsody" describes Luoyang as a city of moderation and restraint, where all activity, including the imperial hunt, accords with classical ritual precepts.

In 108, Bao De was transferred to the capital, and Zhang Heng returned to his home in Xi'e prefecture north of Nanyang, where he resumed his scholarly studies. Around 111, Emperor Hu (r. 107–125), who had learned of Zhang's expertise in mathematics, summoned him to court, where he served in a variety of positions that mainly involved work with astronomy, the calendar, cartography, and mathematics. Zhang constructed an armillary sphere and a seismograph, which was remarkably accurate in predicting earthquakes.

Zhang rose through a series of high court positions to an appointment as Chancellor of Hejian (roughly modern central Hebei), in which capacity he served ably from 136 to 138. In the latter year, he was appointed Master of Writing, the position he held until his death the following year.

The "Western Metropolis Rhapsody," translated in full here, is both a brilliant example of the *fu* (rhapsody or rhyme-prose) genre and a rich source of information about courtly life during the Han dynasty. [Note: The line-numbering system employed here is based on the Chinese text and does not coincide exactly with the lines of the English translation, especially in the prose sections. For a map of Chang'an, see Plate 24.]—DRK, VHM

Western Metropolis Rhapsody

I

There was one Sir Based-on-nothing. His mind was bent on extravagance and his bearing was arrogant. Inveterately devoted to learning and ancient history, he studied in the old historians. Thus, he was quite conversant with the events of former ages. Speaking to Master Where-live, he said: "If a person is in a yang season,[1] he feels at ease. If he is in a yin season,[2] he is miserable.

This is something bound up with Heaven. If one dwells in fertile territory, he enjoys comfort. If one dwells in lean territory, he must toil hard. This is something tied to Earth. If one is miserable, he seldom is happy. If one must toil hard, he is not much inclined toward compassion. Few are those who are able to controvert this principle. The lesser man is certainly subject to these factors, and the prominent equally feels their effect. Therefore, emperors rely on Heaven and Earth to extend their moral influence, and the common people receive teachings from above to develop their customs. The basis of moral influence and customs shifts and changes from region to region. How does one verify this? Qin relied on the territory of Yong[3] and was strong. The Zhou proceeded to Yu[4] and became weak. Gaozu[5] established his capital in the west and was ostentatious. Guangwu[6] dwelled in the east and was frugal. The rise and fall of a government have always depended on these factors. But you, sir, have you alone not perceived the facts about the Western Metropolis? I request to lay them out for you."

      The first capital of the Han house
30   Lay on the banks of the Wei River.
      The Qin had dwelled to the north,
      And this place was called Xianyang.[7]
      To the left, there are
         The double defiles of Yao[8] and Han,[9]
         The barrier of Taolin,[10]
35   Connected by the Two Hua peaks.[11]
         Here the Giant Spirit,[12] exerting great force,
         Reaching high with his hands, kicked far with his legs,
         Thereby allowing the winding Yellow River to flow through.
         His prints still survive today.
      To the right, there is
40   The gap of Longdi,[13]
         Which partitions China from the barbarian lands.
         Mounts Qi, Liang, Qian, and Yong,[14]
         The Chen treasure,[15] with its crowing cocks, are here.
      At its southern front, there are
         Zhongnan and Taiyi,[16]
45   Twisting upward tall and stately,
         Jagged and rough, steeply scarped,
         Their ridges forming a chain with Bozhong.[17]
         They enfold Du, swallow Hu,
         Inhale the Feng, disgorge the Hao.[18]
50   Then, there is Lantian,[19]
         That source of precious jade.
      At its northern rear, there are
         High hills and level plains,
         Leaning on the Wei, nestled against the Jing.[20]
         Broad and flat, sloping and slanting,
55   They form a buttress for the capital environs.
      In the distance, there are
         Nine Peaks and Sweet Springs,[21]
         Frozen and dark, cloistered and cold.

Even when the sun reaches north[22] they are enveloped in a freezing chill,
And thus here one can be cool in summer's heat.[23]
    And then
60   The broad plateaus, fertile plains,
        Their fields are upper first class.
        This truly is the most mysterious region and most sacred frontier on earth![24]

Anciently, the Great Lord of Heaven was pleased with Duke Mu of Qin, invited him to court, and feted him with the "Grand Music of Harmonious Heaven." The Lord, in ecstasy, made a golden tablet, and bestowed him this land, which was situated under the Quail's Head.[25] At this time, those powerful states who had combined together numbered six.[26] But soon the entire empire came to live in unison under the Western Qin. Is that not amazing?

II

When our Exalted Ancestor first entered the Pass, the Five Wefts were in mutual accord and thereby lined up with the Eastern Well.[27] When Lou Jing cast off his cart yoke, he offered a corrective criticism of the emperor's opinion.[28] Heaven opened the founder's mind, and Man taught him the plan. When it came time for the emperor to make his plans, his mind also gave consideration to the spirits of Heaven and Earth, thus making certain it was right for him to establish Chang'an as the Celestial City.

        Did he not pay respectful attention to the Celestial Thoroughfare?[29]
        Did he not long for a return to Fenyu?[30]
        Heaven's decree is unvarying;
85   Who would dare change it?
    Thereupon:
        He measured the diameter and circumference,
        Reckoned the length and breadth.
        They built the city walls and moat,
        Constructed the outer enclosures.
90   He adopted various patterns from the capitals of the eight directions,
        And never considered following the measures of the ancient past.
    Then:
        He scanned the Qin regulations,[31]
        Exceeded the Zhou scale.
        He considered one hundred *du*[32] too narrow and crude,
95   Expanded the nine-mats[33] measure, which was too confining.
        They replicated the Purple Palace in the Everlasting Palace,[34]
        Placed lofty watchtowers to mark the Changhe gateway,[35]
        Leveled the Longshou Hills[36] to raise a hall,
        Whose form, imposing and tall, jutted precariously upward.
100   They ran crosswise long beams of the masculine arc,[37]
        Tied purlins and rafters[38] to link them together,
        Rooted inverted lotus stalks on the figured ceiling,[39]
        Which bloomed with red flowers joined one to another.
        They embellished the ornate rafters and jade finials,

105　　From which streamed sunlight's blazing radiance.
　　　　There were carved columns on jade pedestals,
　　　　Ornamented brackets with cloud-patterned rafters,
　　　　A triple staircase, a double platform,
　　　　Studded railings with figured edging.
110　　On the right was a ramp, on the left was a staircase;[40]
　　　　Blue was the door-engraving,[41] red was the floor.
　　　　They sheered off layered hills, leveled the humps,
　　　　Fixed the threshold at the margin.
　　　　The steps, clifflike, rose in stages,[42]
115　　Steep and serrated, tall and rugged,
　　　　With high banks, level roads,
　　　　Long avenues, climbing sheer and precipitously.
　　　　Double gates, reinforced and secure,
　　　　Against bandits and rebels were the defense.
120　　They gazed upon it as a counterpart to the Supreme Lord's abode,
　　　　Which glittered by day and disappeared at night.
　　　　It had a giant bell of ten thousand *jun,*[43]
　　　　Whose fierce frameposts stood mighty and strong.
　　　　Though supporting heavy crosspieces, they had fury to spare;
125　　Then, flapping their wings, they were poised ready for flight.[44]

III

　　　　The audience hall faced to the east;
　　　　The Warmth Modulator[45] stretched to the north,
　　　　On the west was the Jade Terrace,
　　　　Where it was joined by the Kunde Hall.[46]
130　All were tall and stately, jagged and peaked,
　　　　And there was no way to perceive their pattern.
　　　　As for:
　　　　　　Long Life, Divine Immortals,
　　　　　　Proclamation Chamber, Jade Hall,[47]
　　　　　　Unicorn, Vermilion Bird,
135　　　　Dragon Rising, Enfolding Splendor,[48]
　　　　They were like a mass of stars encircling the Pole Star,[49]
　　　　Blazing with fiery billiance, dazzling and resplendent.
　　　　The Main Hall—that Grand Chamber—[50]
　　　　Was used to receive the various lords.[51]
140　　In the great edifice, deep and cavernous,
　　　　Nine doors[52] stood opened wide.
　　　　Precious trees were planted in the courtyard;
　　　　Fragrant plants seemed as if heaped in piles.
　　　　Where the outer gate towered upward,
145　　Sat bronze barbarians[53] all in a row.
　　　　Inside the palace, there were

The regular attendants and internuncios,[54]
Who received commands and acted as servants.
At the Magnolia Terrace[55] and Bronze Horse Gate,[56]
They alternately lodged and dwelled.
  Next there were
150   The Tianlu and Stone Canal Pavilions,[57]
The places for collating texts.
Add to them Tiger Might and Splendid Moat,[58]
For the office of the strict watches.[59]
Patrol roads circled the exterior,[60]
155   A thousand guard huts[61] were attached to the interior.
The Commandant of the Guard's eight detachments
Kept watch at night, made the rounds during the day.
Planting their halberds, slinging their shields,
They took precautions against the unforeseen.

IV

  The Rear Palace contained
160   Bright Sunshine, Soaring Chamber,
Tiered Structure, Concordant Joy,
Thoroughwort Grove, Wafting Fragrance,
Phoenix, and Drake-Simurgh halls.[62]
Here assembled blossoming beauties, all modest and retiring.
165   Oh! Gazing inside one saw a spectacular sight!
Thus, their lodges and chambers, duty houses and dormitories[63]
Were colorfully adorned, finely decorated.
The beams were laced with intricate embroidery,
Embellished with vermeil and green.
170   Kingfisher plumes, fire-regulating pearls,[64]
Were strung with beautiful jade.
Light streamed from the night-glower of Xuanli,[65]
And they tied Sui pearls together as candles.[66]
Gold pavement, jade stairways,
175   And red courtyards shone with a fiery glow.
Coral, black jade, prase,
Red quartz, agate, and dark jade brightly sparkled.[67]
Precious objects grew in rows,
All glittering like the Kunlun peaks.
180   Though their construction was not grand,
Their extravagant beauty surpassed that of the most exalted residence.[68]
  And then, outside the Angular Array:[69]
Raised galleries, long and arching,
Connected Enduring Joy and Shining Brightness,[70]
185   Communicated directly north with Cinnamon Palace.[71]
They commanded skilled carpenters like Ban and Er[72]
To exhaust their versatile powers upon them.

The rear-palace ladies never left their chambers;
Musicians never moved their instrument frames.[73]

190 Everywhere were gate guards and equipment,
And officials to manage supplies item by item.
Wherever it pleased the emperor to go,
He dismounted from his cart and a feast was prepared.
Even if he spent his entire life, forgetting to return,

195 He still could not make the rounds of them all.
Though new marvels and wonders were presented daily,
There was an inexhaustible supply of things never seen before.
Such was the divine elegance of the emperor,
But he feared noble and mean were not properly distinguished.

200 Even though these buildings were spacious enough,
His heart was full of unreleased ambition.
He thought of comparing them to Ziwei,[74]
And regretted that Ebang[75] was uninhabitable.
He looked at the surviving lodges of the past,

205 And found Forest Light[76] among the Qin remains.
He occupied Sweet Springs' bright heights,
For it was tall and lofty, broad and spacious.
Having newly built Welcoming the Wind,
He added Dewy Chill and Storage.[77]

210 Tall foundations rested on mountain peaks,
Rising upright and tall.
The Sky-Piercing Tower rose straight up, far into the heavens;
Surpassing one hundred *chang*, alone and conspicuous it stood.[78]
The top was bathed in iridescent splendor, intricately blended;

215 The base was cut steep as if sheared with a blade.
The hovering great fowl,[79] neck craned upward, was unable to reach the spire;
How much less successful were the oriole and sparrow!
Leaning on the railing, peering downward and listening,
One could hear thunderclaps clashing one after another.

V

220 When the Cypress Beams Terrace burned down,
A Yue shaman presented his remedy.
The Jianzhang Palace was built
To suppress the fire's portent.[80]
The scale of construction

225 In every way was double that of Weiyang.[81]
The round watchtowers[82] thrust themselves upward, reaching the sky,
Like twin boulders[83] facing each other.
Phoenixes flapped their pinions at the top of the roof,[84]
Facing the wind as if about to soar away.

230 Within the Changhe Gate,[85]
The Watchtower for Distinguishing the Winds[86] stood rugged and tall.

How marvelous the craftsmanship!
Figured silk tied together formed latticed windows.[87]
Invading the clouds and mist, touching the firmament above,
235 Its form spired upward, far into the distance.
The Terrace of Divine Luminaries[88] stood tall and alone;
The Well-Curb Tower[89] rose hundreds of stories high.
They placed wandering rafters on floating columns,
Tied double brackets to support them.
240 Built in multiple stages, upward they climbed,
Edging toward the Pole Star, they ascended steadily higher.
Having dispelled the dust and filth of the central junction,[90]
They collected the purity of the multiple yang.[91]
One could perceive the spine of the long arching rainbow,
245 And inspect the place where the Cloud Master[92] dwelled.
Above the "flying doors" one could peer upward,
And directly sight Jasper Light and Jade Rope.[93]
As one was about to go forth, not yet halfway,
He became fearful, apprehensive, and quaked with terror.
250 Except for a nimble climber from Dulu,[94]
Who could vault it or climb all the way to the top?
Rapid Gallop and Relaxation[95]
Towered proudly upward, straight and tall.
Linden Hall[96] and Received Light[97]
255 Stood broad and open, hollow and gaping.
Multiple ridgepoles, double purlins,
Hung precipitously, ranged on high.
Their upturned roofs[98] were majestic and stately;
Their flying eaves soared on high.
260 Streaming light shone within the halls,
Which drew lumination from the sun and moon.
At the Palace of Celestial Beams,[99]
Here the gates were flung wide open.
Banners did not have their frame-locks removed,[100]
265 And fours-in-hand, joined together, marched harness to harness.
To the tapping on the spokes, they rapidly galloped,[101]
And easily passed through a single door-leaf.[102]
Long corridors, broad verandahs,
And interlocking galleries stretched like clouds.
270 Walled courtyards, most strange and unusual,
A thousand gates, ten thousand doors,
Double portals, secluded entryways,
Continuously crossed and intersected.
Seeing it so dark and deep, endlessly twining,
275 One was confused and did not know how to return.
And then:
    Precious terraces spiraled upward, supremely grand;
    An inclined passageway, snaking and twisting, led directly east.

        Just like the remote slopes of Langfeng,[103]
        It traversed the western moat, crossed the "metal" wall.[104]
280   The Guard of the City Gates never discarded his wooden clapper,
        Yet within and without one could secretly pass.[105]
    In front they opened a place for Middle Path Pond;[106]
    As far as one could see it was a vast expanse.
    Turning around, one could look down on the Grand Fluid,[107]
285   That azure lake broad and boundless.
    The Tower of Soaking Waters[108] stood in the center,
    Shining with a vermeil glitter, wide and spacious.
    In the Clear Pool,[109] surging and swelling,
    Sacred mountains stood tall and stately.
290   There were Yingzhou and Fangzhang ranged together,
    Joined with Penglai wedged between them.[110]
    Their summits were steep and sharp, rugged and scarped;
    Their bases were jagged and sloping, serrated and rough.
    A wind from the distance struck the separate islets,
295   Raising huge breakers, lifting waves
    That drenched the stone mushrooms on the high bank,
    And soaked the magic fungus on vermeil boughs.[111]
    Hairuo[112] played among the dark holms;
    A whale[113] washed ashore, writhing desperately.
    Thereupon:
300   Emperor Wu accepted the "absolute truth" of Shaojun,[114]
    Placed great hope in Luan Da's[115] "firm reliability."[116]
    He erected immortals' palms on tall stalks[117]
    To receive pure dew from beyond the clouds.
    He pulverized carnelian[118] stamens for his morning repast,
305   Certain that life could be prolonged.
    He praised Chisong[119] and Wang Qiao[120] of the past,
    Sought Xianmen[121] on the celestial highway.
    He longed to mount a dragon on Tripod Lake;[122]
    How was the profane world worth admiring?
310   But, if it were possible to live from generation to generation,
    Why such urgent building of mausoleums?[123]

VI

    Just look at the layout of the city walls—
    On every side there opened three gates,
    Each with a three-lane roadway level and straight.
315   Running parallel were chariot tracks, twelve in number;
    Streets and thoroughfares crossed back and forth.[124]
    The residential plots and wards followed regular lines;[125]
    The tiled roofs were even and smooth.
    The high-class residences[126] of the Northern Watchtower
320   Opened directly to the road.

They selected the most adept craftsmen to apply their skills,
And expected their dwellings never to crumble or collapse.
The timbers were garbed in pongee and brocade;
The ground was painted vermeil and purple.
325   The imperial arms of the Arsenal
Were placed in racks and crossbow frames.
Except for Shi,[127] except for Dong,[128]
Who could dwell there?
  And then:
They greatly expanded the Nine Markets,[129]
330   Joined by encircling walls, girdled by gates.
From the flag pavilions,[130] five stories high,
Officials looked down to inspect the countless shop rows.
The Zhou institution was the Chief of Assistants;[131]
Now it was the Commandant.[132]
335   Precious wares arriving from all quarters,
Gathered like birds, amassed like fish scales.
Sellers earned double profit,
But buyers were never lacking.
  And then:
The pedlars, shopkeepers, and common people,
340   Male and female vendors, selling cheap,[133]
Sold good quality mixed with the shoddy,
Dazzling the eyes of the country bumpkins.
Why exert oneself in performing labor,
When devious earnings were so plentiful?
345   The sons and daughters of these merchants
Were more beautifully garbed than the Xu and Shi.[134]
  As for:
Weng Bo, the Zhuo, the Zhi,
Or the families of Zhang Ward,[135]
With bells sounding, they ate from cauldrons,[136]
350   And line after line of riders passed their way.
The dukes and marquises of the Eastern Capital,
Their grandeur could never surpass them.
The knights-errant of the capital,
Men like Zhang and Zhao,[137]
355   Their ambition equalled that of Wuji,
And they wished to follow in the traces of Tian Wen.[138]
They took death lightly, valued spirit,
Organized cliques, formed gangs.
"Truly numerous were their disciples";[139]
360   "Their followers were as thick as clouds."[140]
Yuan of Mouling,[141]
Zhu of Yangling,[142]
Were fierce and brave,
Like tigers, like wildcats.

365   An angry look,[143] a paltry splinter,
        And a corpse fell at the side of the road.
        The Chancellor wished to ransom his son's crime;
        The princess of Yangshi was vilified and the Gongsuns were punished.[144]
    As for:
        The itinerant persuaders of the five prefectures,[145]
370   The masters of argument and disputation,
        They discoursed in the streets, debated in the lanes.
        Taking shots at the good and bad,
        Dissecting millimeters and centimeters,[146]
        Ripping the muscle, splitting the fiber.[147]
375   Whatever they liked grew down and feathers;[148]
        Whatever they detested grew wounds and ulcers.
    Within the suburbs and the royal domain[149]
           The district towns[150] were rich and wealthy.
           Merchandise from the Five Capitals[151]
380   Was traded and collected here.
           Carts of traveling merchants, yoke joined to yoke,
           Rumbled and rattled by.
           The "caps-and-sashes"[152] were seen here and there,
           Their chariot shafts side by side, their crossbars touching.
385   The imperial domain of a thousand tricents[153]
           Was controlled by the Governor of the Capital.[154]

VII

        The palaces and lodges of the commanderies and kingdoms[155]
        Were one hundred forty-five in number.[156]
        Their western limits extended to Zhouzhi,[157]
390 And encompassed the land of Feng and Hu.[158]
        The eastern bounds stretched to He and Hua,[159]
        And reached as far as the territory of Guo.[160]
        The forbidden Shanglin Park,
        Straddling valleys, covering hills,
395 Ranging eastward to Tripod Lake,[161]
        Diagonally intersecting Delicate Willows,[162]
        Enclosed Tall Poplars,[163] joined with Five Oaks,[164]
        Enfolded the Yellow Mountain,[165] reached Ox Head.[166]
        The encircling walls stretched continuously
400 Four hundred tricents and more.
        Plants here did grow;
        Animals here did rest.
        Flocks of birds fluttered about;
        Herds of beasts galloped and raced.
405 They scattered like startled waves,
        Gathered like tall islands in the sea.
        Bo Yi[167] would have been unable to name them;

Li Shou[168] would have been unable to count them.
The riches of the groves and forests—
410 In what were they lacking?
As for trees, there were:
Fir, juniper, windmill palm, *nanmu,*
Catalpa, spiny oak, elm, and sweet gum.[169]
Beautiful vegetation grew in thick clumps
As lush as Deng Grove.[170]
415 Luxuriant and dense, verdant and bosky,
They rose straight and tall, towering upward,
Spewing blossoms, sending forth blooms,
Spreading leaves, casting shadows.
As for plants, there were:
Oxalus, nutgrass, cogon grass, wool grass,[171]
420 Vetch, brake, iris,[172]
Arthraxon, frittilary, carex,[173]
Hollyhock, and *huaiyang.*[174]
They grew in clusters, overgrown and rank,
Covering the swamp margins, blanketing the ridges.
425 Arrow bamboo and giant bamboo thickly spread,
Forming fields and groves.
Mountains and valleys, plains and bogs,
Were boundless, without limit.
Then, there was
The divine pool of Kunming,
430 With its Black Water and Dark Foot shrine.[175]
It was surrounded by a "metal" dike,[176]
Planted with weeping willow and purple osier.[177]
The precious Camphor Lodge[178]
Thrusting itself upward, rose from the middle of the pond.
435 The Oxherd stood on the left;
The Weaving Maid occupied the right.[179]
The sun and moon exited and entered here,
Just like Fusang[180] and the Murky Shore.[181]
Within it there were:
Giant soft-shelled turtles, alligators, and the large trionyx,[182]
440 Sturgeon, carp, whitefish, ide,[183]
Paddlefish, giant salamanders, golden catfish, gobies.[184]
With their long foreheads, short necks,
Large mouths, cleft snouts,
They were most amazing creatures, most unusual species.
As for birds, there were:
445 Turquoise kingfishers, white-necked cranes, bustards,[185]
Wild geese and the great fowl.[186]
At the first of spring they came to visit;
In late autumn they headed for warmer climes.
South they flew to Hengyang;[187]

450   North they nested at Yanmen.[188]
       The swift peregrines, the homing mallards,
       Flapped their wings with an uproarious din.
       Their various forms and diverse sounds
       Cannot be completely described.

VIII

    And then:
455   In the first winter month the yin begins to rise
       And the chill winds turn stern and murderous.[189]
       Snow falls, whirling in the air;
       Ice and frost are freezing cold.
       All the plants wither and die;
460   The firm creatures[190] strike and seize their prey.
    Then:
       Preparing Heaven's headrope,
       Spreading Earth's net,[191]
       They churn up rivers and waterways,
       Shake forests and copses.
465   Birds are everywhere panicked;
       Beasts all spring to their feet.
       They cower in the grass, roost in the trees,
       Take refuge in temporary burrows.
       Flushed from one place, they gather in another,
470   Whirring and whizzing fast and furious.
       In the midst of that Divine Park,[192]
       Front and rear they form an endless line.
       The Forester is in charge,
       And lays out the boundaries.
475   They burn off the weeds, level the hunting ground,
       Remove standing trees, cut down thorny stickers.
       They string nets for a hundred tricents,
       And thus roads are obstructed, paths are blocked.
       "Does and bucks throng in great numbers,"[193]
480   Ranged in lines, crowded and pressed together.
    The Son of Heaven then
       Mounts his carved chariot,
       Drawn by six piebald chargers.
       There is a halcyon-plume sunshade over his head,
       And a golden sidebar for him to lean on.
485   The horse-bonnets and jade-studded bridles,
       Their trailing luster glitters and sparkles.
       They raise the Dark Lance,[194]
       Hoist the Twinkling Indicator,[195]
       Attach the Screeching Kite[196]
490   And unfurl Cloud Streamers[197] behind them.

There are Bow Flags[198] with warped arrows,
Rainbow pennants and iris banners.
The Flowery Baldaquin[199] covers the Chronogram;[200]
The Celestial Net[201] serves as the vanguard.
495 A thousand chariots roll like thunder;
Ten thousand riders speed like dragons.
The auxiliary chariot[202] of the cortege
Carries long-snouted and short-snouted hounds.
But it is not only for play and amusement;
500 For there are occult writings,
Stories, nine hundred in number,
Which originate from Yu Chu.[203]
In seeking leisure and relaxation,
These are ready and waiting.
    And then:
505 Chiyou[204] grasps a battle-ax,
And tossing his long hair, he dons a tiger skin.
He fends off the malevolent spirits,
And informs the people of demonic treachery,[205]
So that neither the *Chimei*[206] nor the *Wangliang*[207]
510 Is able to fall upon them.
They line up the Tiger and Troop Runners at Feilian,[208]
Replicate the Ramparts[209] in the Shanglan Belvedere.[210]
They organize the regiments and companies,
Straighten the columns and files.[211]
515 Upon igniting heaps of firewood,
And beating the thundering drums,
They release the hunters,
Who advance into the tall grass.
The imperial guards clear and watch the road;
520 The warriors blaze with fury.
Garbed in brown silk, dressed in red knee-covers,
Eyes glaring, they step forth menacingly.
Bright flames light the courtyard sky;
A noisy din shakes the strands of the sea.
525 Because of it, the He and Wei[212] rock with waves;
Because of it, the Wu and Yue peaks[213] crumble and collapse.
All the animals, quaking and quivering,
Running frantically, collide.
Bereft of spirit, devoid of soul,
530 They lose their way, forget direction.
Thrown against the wheels, caught in the spokes,
They are not intercepted, but fall into them on their own.
Flying nets tightly entangle them;
Streaming arrowheads pelt them.
535 Arrows are not discharged in vain;
Spears are not hurled for nothing.

Brushing against a foot, they are trampled;
Dashing into a wheel, they are crushed.
The fallen birds and slain beasts
540   Glisten like a pile of pebbles.
All one can see are
Things strangled and caught in nets and mesh,
Struck down by bamboo staves,
Impaled and stabbed by prongs and barbs,
Knocked and beaten by barehanded attack.
545   The bright sun has yet to shift its shadow,
And already they have killed seventy or eighty percent.
As for
The soaring pheasant winging on high,
Cutting across valleys, traversing marshes,
Or the wily hare, hopping and skipping about,
550   Climbing hills, overleaping gullies,
Just like Dongguo,[214]
Whom no one could catch,
There are the fleet-winged and light-footed,
Who could chase the sunlight, pursue the arrow nock.
555   Birds have no time to fly away;
Beasts have no chance to flee.
Blue-necked goshawks snatch birds beneath the gauntlets;[215]
Hanlu[216] hounds snap at hares from the end of their tethers.
As soon as the fierce beasts toss their shaggy manes,
560   Cast angry glances from piercing eyes,
They have overawed and daunted even the gaur and tiger,
And none dares to withstand them.
Then:
They send out warriors from Zhonghuang,[217]
The peer of Xia Yu[218] and Wu Huo.[219]
565   Wearing vermilion headbands and topknots,[220]
Their hair standing as straight as poles,
Bare-chested, brandishing their fists as halberds,
With long strides, they circle the quarry.
They seize the red elephant by his trunk,
570   Corral the giant *yan*,[221]
Catch langurs and hedgehogs,[222]
Strike the *yayu*[223] and lion.
They scour the hedges of hardy orange,[224]
Break through the pale of brambles.
575   The thorny groves are thus pulverized,
And the thick copses are smashed to pieces.
The light-footed and dauntless, nimble and quick,
Head for the caverns,
And drag out the giant foxes.
580   They scramble up the double-boiler slopes,[225]

And hunt the *kuntu*.[226]
They plunder the treetops,
Seize the macaques.[227]
Overleaping the tall hazel trees,[228]
585 They snatch the flying squirrels.

IX

At this time
The Rear-Palace favorites,
Women like the Brilliant Companion,[229]
Follow at the rear of the cortege.
They emulate Madame Jia, who traveled to Gao Preserve,[230]
590 Rejoice to the "North Wind" air with its "sharing the chariot."[231]
They amuse themselves in excursions and hunts;[232]
"Oh, how joyful it is!"[233]
And then:
With all the birds and beasts destroyed,
And having seen an exhaustive display,
595 They slowly withdraw, casting sidelong glances,
And gather at Tall Poplars Palace.[234]
Here they allow the couriers to rest,[235]
"Line up the chariots and horses,"[236]
Gather the game, lift the carcasses,
600 Count and tabulate the number.
They set up the meat racks, arrange the victims,
And distribute the catch.
They cut fresh meat for a feast in the field;
They remunerate effort, reward achievement.
605 To the five regiments and six divisions,[237]
With a thousand men to a file, one hundred rows deep,
From wine carts they pour fine spirits,
And from coupled chariots, they serve cooked meat.
They raise their goblets as the beacons are lit;
610 Upon draining their cups, they sound the bells.
The royal steward[238] gallops about on horseback,
Checking for surfeit, examining for deficiency.
Broiled and roasted meats are plentiful;
Clear wine is abundant.
615 Imperial grace is broadly bestowed;
Great bounty is generously given.
The footmen and drivers are pleased;
The warriors forget their fatigue.
The Carriage Intendant orders the chariots harnessed;
620 Reversing their banners, they turn off to the right.
They pause briefly at Five Oaks Lodge,
And rest at Kunming Pond.

They climb Camphor Belvedere,
Where selecting the red-cord arrow,
625   Puju[239] fires his bow.
He darts a high-flying goose,
Catches a white swan,
Impales a soaring duck.
The stone tip not only strikes a single bird,
630   But flies forth sure to fell a pair.
  And then:
They command the captain of boats
To begin the water games.
They set sail on the heron-prow.[240]
Shaded by a cloud-mushroom canopy,[241]
635   Festooned with pheasant-plume tassels,
Flying feathered banners.
They ready the oarswomen,
Who burst into a barcarole.
One sings the lead, the others chorus in;
640   To a lively tempo the reed pipe plays.
They perform the Huainan melodies,[242]
Sing to the "Yangle" tune.[243]
The music moves Pingyi,[244]
Affects the Xiang Beauty,[245]
645   Startles the *Wangliang,*
Terrifies crocodiles and snakes.
  Next:
They angle for bream and snakehead,
Net culter and hemiculter,[246]
Pick purple cowries,
650   Seize aged tortoises,
Catch water leopards,[247]
Fetter the diving ox.[248]
When the Forester of Preserves[249] wets the nets,[250]
How is there any regard for the season?
655   They search the creeks and brooks,
Explore the rivers and waterways,
Spread the nine-purse seine,[251]
Set the nets,
Strip the spawn and roe,
660   And exterminate the aquatic tribe.
Lotus roots are picked clean,
Giant clams and mussels are split open.
To their heart's content they hunt and fish,
Presenting fawns and baby elaphures as their catch.
665   Searching and seeking, rummaging and ransacking,
They drain the ponds, scour the marshes.
Above there is nothing left flying;

Below there is nothing left running.
They seize embryos, snatch eggs;
670 The ant larvae are all taken away.
They seize pleasure for today;
"How is there leisure for worry about the future?"[252]
Since the empire is settled and at peace,
How could one know it might totter and crumble?

X

675 When the Grand Equipage visited the Lodge of Peaceful Joy,[253]
They pitched A-rank and B-rank tents, and the emperor donned a halcyon-plume coat.[254]
He gathered precious treasures for play and amusement,
Mixed the rare and beautiful with the wasteful and extravagant.
He went down to the broad arena with a far-ranging view,
680 And judged the wondrous feats of competitive games.[255]
Wu Huo[256] hoisted cauldrons;
A Dulu climber[257] shinnied up a pole.
They "rushed the narrows" and performed a swallow dip,
Their chests thrusting at the sharp spear tips.[258]
685 They juggled balls and swords[259] whirling and twirling,
Walked a tightrope, meeting halfway across.[260]
Hua Peak[261] rose tall and stately,
With ridges and knolls of irregular heights,
And divine trees, magic plants,
690 Vermilion fruits hanging thickly.
They assembled a troupe of sylphine performers,
Made panthers frolic, brown bears dance.
The white tiger[262] plucked the zither;[263]
The azure dragon[264] played a flute.[265]
695 The Maiden and Beauty,[266] seated in place, sang loud and long;
Their voices, pure and clear, softly echoed.
Hongya[267] stood up and conducted the performance;
He was garbed in light, trailing plumes.
Before their song was ended,
700 Clouds rose, snow flew.
At first it seemed to flurry lightly;
Then it began to fall thick and fast.
From the covered roadways and storied galleries,
With rolling stones they created thunder.
705 Thunderbolts crashed and echoed repeatedly,
Their booming din similar to Heaven's rage.[268]
There was a giant beast one hundred *xun*[269] long;
This was the *manyan*.[270]
A sacred mountain, tall and rugged,

710   Suddenly appeared from its back.
      Bears and tigers climbed on, grappling one another;
      Gibbons and monkeys leaped up and clung to a high perch.
      Strange beasts wildly capered about,[271]
      And the great bird[272] proudly strutted in.

715   A white elephant marching along enacted [Buddha's] conception,[273]
      Its trunk drooping and undulating.
      A great sea-fish transformed itself into a dragon,[274]
      Its form writhing and wriggling, twisting and twining.
      The *hanli*,[275] mouth gaping,

720   Changed into a sylph's chariot,
      Drawn by a four-deer team.
      It carried a nine-petal mushroom canopy.[276]
      The toad and tortoise were there,
      And water denizens played with snakes.[277]

725   Amazing magicians, quicker than the eye,
      Changed forms, sundered bodies,
      Swallowed knives, exhaled fire,
      Darkened the arena with clouds and mist.[278]
      They drew on the ground and created rivers,

730   Making the Wei flow into the Jing.
      Master Huang from the Eastern Sea,[279]
      With red knife and Yue[280] incantations,
      Hoped to subdue the white tiger,
      But he could not save himself in the end.

735   Those with evil hearts, makers of black magic
      Thereafter could not sell their wares.[281]
      And then:
          They assembled the show wagon,[282]
          From which they hoisted a tall banner on a pole.
          Young lads displayed their skill,

740   Up and down doing glides and flips.
          Suddenly, they threw themselves upside down, catching themselves with their heels;
          Seemingly they were cut asunder and connected again.
          One hundred horses under the same bridle
          Raced side by side as fast as their feet could go.[283]

745   As for the tricks performed at the top of the pole—
          There was no end to their numerous postures.
          Drawing their bows, archers shot at a Western Qiang;[284]
          Looking back, they fired at a Xianbei.[285]

XI

      And then:
      When the diverse forms of entertainment came to an end,

750   The emperor's mind was fully intoxicated.

Just as the merriment reached its peak,
A feeling of discontent gathered inside him.
With a secret warning to the Rendezvous Gate,[286]
He went out incognito, bent and hunched like a commoner.
755 From his exalted place he descended to the lower plane;
He tucked away his seals and concealed his ribbons.
He strolled through the ward gates,
Toured the suburbs and outskirts.
Just like the transformation of a divine dragon—
760 This shows how noble was our sovereign![287]
He threaded his way through the lateral courtyards,[288]
And proceeded to the pleasure lodges.
He discarded faded beauties,
Consorted with the pretty and graceful.
765 They snuggled together on a narrow mat in the center of the hall,
And feathered goblets[289] made the rounds countless times.
Rarely seen dances were performed in succession;
Marvelous talents showed off their skills.
Their bewitching magic was more seductive than that of Xia Ji;[290]
770 Their beautiful voices were sweeter than that of Master Yu.[291]
At first they advanced slowly, with figures so thin,
They seemed unable to support their gossamer silks.
Singing the "Pure Shang,"[292] they suddenly whirled;
Ever more charming and graceful, they arched their backs.
775 All together, bodies relaxed, they quickened the tempo,
And returned just like a flock of startled cranes.[293]
Their vermilion slippers danced between plates and goblets,[294]
And they waved their long, dangling sleeves.
With a curvaceous, cultivated bearing,
780 Their lovely dresses fluttered like flowers in the wind.
Their eyes cast darting glances;
One look could overthrow a city.[295]
Even Zhan Ji[296] or a śramaṇa—[297]
No one—could not but be deluded.
785 Fourteen ranks in the harem,
Each one plied her charms in search of favor.
"Prosperity and decline" followed no constant rule;
They merely depended on personal whim.
Empress Wei[298] rose to prominence by virtue of her ebon hair;
790 Flying Swallow[299] was favored for her light body.
And then:
Indulging his desires, pursuing his wishes,
With his whole being he enjoyed himself to the full.
He took warning from the Tang ode:
"Others will enjoy them."[300]
795 When the ruler creates a precedent,

Why be restrained by the Rites?
They added "Brilliant Companion" to "Favored Beauty";[301]
Dong Xian was both duke and marquis.[302]
Emperor Cheng promised Lady Zhao none would stand higher than she;[303]
800   Emperor Ai considered elevating Dong Xian to the status of a Shun.
Wang Hong protested at the sovereign's elbow:
"The Han is stable and need not change."[304]

XII

Gaozu founded the heritage,
And his descendants continued his lineage, inherited his foundation.
805   There was temporary toil, then perpetual ease.
They governed by nonaction.
Addicted to pleasure—this they pursued.
Why be worried or concerned?[305]
A great amount of time passed—[306]
810   Over two hundred years.[307]
But, because the soil was rich and the plains were fertile,
Various products were in abundant supply.
The steep defiles, tight and secure,
These collars and belts were easy to defend.
815   Those who won this territory were strong;
Those who depended on it endured.
When a stream is long, its water is not easily exhausted.
When roots are deep, they do not rot easily.
Therefore, as extravagance and ostentation were given free rein,
820   The odor became pungent and increasingly fulsome.
A rustic scholar such as myself was born over three hundred years after the
        Han founding,
But I have been told things never heard of before.
All was a blur, as if I were dreaming,
And I have scarcely been able to glimpse into one corner.
825   How can one compare this transfer to Luoyang with the Yin who were always
        moving their capital?
In the former period there were eight and in the later period five.
They dwelled at Xiang, were flooded out at Geng.
They never permanently occupied the same land.
Pangeng made a declaration:
830   He led the people by making them suffer.[308]
Just now our sage sovereign
Being equal to Heaven, he is called Lord Radiance,[309]
He enfolds the Four Seas as his family.
Of all rich heritages none is greater than ours.
I only regret that lavish beauty may not serve as the glory of the state.
835   But mere frugality to the point of niggling and piffling

Ignores what the "Cricket" song [310] says.
Do we want it but are unable?
Or are we able but do not want it?
Beclouded in ignorance I am confused.
I should like to hear a discourse on how to explain it.

—DRK

Notes

1. Spring and summer.

2. Autumn and winter.

3. Yongzhou is the name of one of the nine provinces into which China was purportedly divided in remote antiquity. It was located in the extreme northwest and corresponded roughly to modern Shaanxi, Gansu, and Qinghai.

4. Yu is the ancient name for the territory that roughly corresponds to modern Henan Province. The eastern capital of Luoyang was located there.

5. First emperor (r. 206–195 B.C.E.,) of the Western Han.

6. First emperor (r. 25–57 C.E.) of the Eastern Han.

7. In 350 B.C.E., the Qin established its capital at Xianyang. The name literally means "Totally Yang" because the city was situated north of the Wei River (near its conjunction with the Yellow River in the modern province of Shaanxi) and south of the Nine Peaks (*yang* means "north of a river, south of a mountain," the sunny side in both cases).

8. Located sixty tricents north of modern Yongning, Henan.

9. One of the major strategic passes that protected the Western Capital. It was located south of modern Lingbao, Henan.

10. The Taolin (Peach Forest) "barrier," four hundred tricents east of Chang'an, is the ancient name of Tong Pass (Tong Guan), which stretched from Lingbao Prefecture west to Tongguan Prefecture (eastern Henan to western Shaanxi).

11. Great Mt. Hua (Taihua), south of Huayin, and Little Mt. Hua (Shaohua or Xiaohua), located southeast of Hua district town, Shaanxi. The two mountains were eighty tricents apart.

12. An ancient story tells how the two Hua mountains were formed. Originally, Mt. Hua was a single mountain. It blocked the Yellow River (He), which had to bend its course around it. The god of the Yellow River, also called Great Spirit, split open the top of the peak with his hands and kicked the base apart with his feet. The mountain divided into two sections, thus permitting the Yellow River to flow through in a straight course. The Great Spirit's handprints were visible on top of Mt. Hua, and his footprints could be seen at the base of Mt. Shouyang.

13. Slopes of Long (Long [pronounced Loong] is another name for the Shaanxi area) refers to a mountain range northwest of Chang'an.

14. Mt. Qi was located northwest of Meiyang Prefecture (northwest of modern Wugong, Shaanxi). Mt. Liang was north of Mt. Qi, near Haozhi Prefecture (east of modern Qian, Shaanxi). Mt. Qian was located in Qian Prefecture (south of modern Long, Shaanxi). It was the source of the Qian River, which flowed into the Wei River. Mt. Yong, located in Yong Prefecture (south of modern Fengxiang, Shaanxi), was the source of the Yong River.

15. Chenbao, also known as the Heavenly Treasure (Tianbao), was a supernatural creature that resembled a stone and had the head of a cock pheasant. There were frequent appearances of this creature in later periods. With each appearance, it emitted light like a shooting star. It always came from the east and landed on an altar. The loud noise it made caused "wild fowl" to crow at night. It is thought that the object may have been a meteorite, and the Chenbao sacrifices were part of a "meteorite cult."

16. Mt. Taiyi, the highest peak in the Zhongnan range, is located in modern Wugong district, Shaanxi.

17. Mt. Bozhong is located in modern Tianshui district, Gansu.

18. Du Mound is southeast of Chang'an district. Hu was the name of a Han prefecture that was southwest of Chang'an. The Feng River flowed through the imperial hunting park known as Shanglin (Supreme Forest). Its source was in the Qinling Mountains, which were also called the Zhongnan Mountains (see n. 16) after one of their prominent peaks, and it entered the Wei River west of Chang'an. The Hao River also had its source in the Zhongnan Mountains. It flowed into the Jue River, which in turn flowed into the Hao Pond, located north of the Kunming Pond.

19. The mountains around Lantian, south of Chang'an, were an important jade-producing area in Han times.

20. The Jing River flowed from central Gansu and joined the Wei River just east of Chang'an (at modern Gaoling, Shaanxi). The Wei River, the source of which was near modern Weiyuan, Gansu, flowed eastward into Shaanxi, where it passed through Chang'an. It joined the Yellow River to the east at Tongguan.

21. Jiuzong (Nine Peaks) was approximately 4,500 feet (1,400 meters) high and was an impressive promontory in the area near modern Liquan, Shaanxi. Ganquan (Sweet Springs) is the name of a mountain eighty tricents northwest of the Han prefecture of of Yunyang (northwest of modern Chunhua, Shaanxi). In 220 B.C.E. the First Qin Emperor built here the large Sweet Springs Palace. The mountain was three hundred tricents from Chang'an, but reportedly the walls of Chang'an could be seen from it.

22. Referring to the summer solstice.

23. The Sweet Springs Palace was used as a summer retreat by the Former Han emperors. It was located northwest of modern Chunhua in Shaanxi.

24. Because of its high elevation, Yongzhou (see n. 3) was considered a "refuge of spirits." In the Qin and Han, altars for sacrifices to various deities were built in the area.

25. These lines refer to the story of Duke Mu of Qin (r. 659–621 B.C.E.), who was unconscious for seven days. He dreamed that, during this time, he happily enjoyed himself at the palace of the Supreme Lord. He reported that he played with the hundred deities and heard the "Grand Music of Harmonious Heaven." The "Harmonious Heaven" occupies the center of the so-called "Nine Heavens" and is the location of the Great Lord's palace. The Quail's Head (Chun shou) is the name of the Jupiter Station associated with the lunar mansions Well (seven stars in Gemini) and Ghost (four stars in Cancer). Its "astral field" (fenye) corresponds to the territory of Qin (roughly Shaanxi, plus portions of Gansu and Sichuan). For an explanation of fenye, see selection 3.

26. These states included the six states of Han, Wei, Yan, Zhao, Qi, and Chu, who joined against Qin. This era (403–221 B.C.E.) was known as the Warring States period.

27. The "Five Wefts" (Wu Wei) are the five planets: the Year Star (Sui xing), which is Jupiter; Grand White (Taibo), which is Venus; the Chronographic Star (Chen xing), which is Mercury; the Sparkling Deluder (Ying huo), which is Mars; and the Quelling Star (Zhen xing), which is Saturn. The Well or Eastern Well (Dong jing) is the Chinese name for Gemini. Several Han dynasty accounts claim that when Liu Bang (founding emperor of the Former Han dynasty; 247–195 B.C.E., r. 202–195 B.C.E.) entered the Qin capital after having defeated the Qin army, the five planets "were in conjunction with the Eastern Well"). This celestial phenomenon was understood as Heaven's concurrence to the legitimacy of Liu Bang's rule.

28. Lou Jing (Liu Jing) was serving as a garrison soldier at the time he went to Liu Bang with the suggestion that he establish his capital at Chang'an. He "cast off his cart yoke, dressed in sheepskin," and went to see the emperor.

29. The "Celestial Thoroughfare" (Tian qu) refers to Luoyang.

30. Fenyu is the name of a village fifteen tricents northeast from Feng (modern Jiangsu Province), where Liu Bang was born. Liu Bang prayed at the altar of the soil god located there when he first began his rebellion against the Qin.

31. "Regulations" here is probably in the sense of rules pertaining to dimensions.

32. The du specifies both the height and length of a wall. It was roughly equivalent to 8 feet (2.4 meters).

33. "Nine mats" (jiu yan) is the east-west length of the classical Luminous Hall (Ming tang) as stipulated in the Rites of Zhou (Zhouli). One yan was approximately equivalent to 7 feet (2.1 meters).

34. Ziwei (or Ziwei yuan) is the name of the barrier of fifteen stars the Chinese pictured as encircling the celestial pole. Ziwei (yuan) has been variously translated into English as "Purple Forbidden Enclosure," "Purple Tenuity," and so forth. It was made up of stars from the following constellations: Draco, Cepheus,

Cassiopeia, and Ursa Major. Known as the palace of the Celestial Emperor, theoretically the Han emperor's palace was a replica of it. Some say that Purple Palace is another name for the Everlasting Palace. The main point, however, is that the latter was imagined as a replica of the celestial Purple Palace constellation.

35. Changhe, the exact meaning of which is uncertain, is the name of the main portal of the Purple Palace. The watchtowers are probably the Dark Warrior (Xuan wu) and Azure Dragon (Cang long) Watchtowers on the north and east sides of the Everlasting Palace.

36. The Longshou (Dragon Head) Hills extended over sixty tricents from the Wei River through the city of Chang'an to the Fan River, south of Chang'an. The highest point (near the Wei River) was just over 150 feet (46 meters) high. They gradually leveled off to about 39 feet (12 meters) near the Fan River. The early Han minister Xiao He (d. 193 B.C.E.) reputedly constructed the Everlasting Palace out of a leveled portion of these hills.

37. Rainbows were classed as male *(hong)* and female *(ni)*.

38. The term used for "purlin" is *fen*, glossed in old dictionaries as "the ridgepole of a double roof." The double roof was a two-story loft building that had two roofs, one for each story. The purlins (or ridgepoles) of this structure were called *fen*, and the rafters were called *liao*. This type of building is known as the "double-eave" *(chong yan)* style.

39. "Figured Well" (Zao jing) is another name for the ceiling called "Sky Well" (Tian jing). This was apparently intended to be a replica of the Eastern Well constellation, and water chestnuts *(sic)* were carved on it as talismans against fire. Such "wells" were constructed right in the middle of the ridgepoles by intersecting timbers to form a square like a Chinese well curb, which looks like a tick-tack-toe frame or a pound sign (#). A roundel was sunk or painted in each coffer of this flat, coffered ceiling. By staggering successively smaller layers of such "well"-frames at different angles on top of each other, a dome effect could be achieved.

40. The steps on the left (meaning the east) were restricted to foot traffic. Parallel to it on the right (west) was an inclined plane constructed of decorative brick. It was used as a ramp for chariots going in and out of the palace.

41. The engraving on the edge of the door was painted blue. The design resembled an "interlocking ring."

42. The steps were cut into the slope of the Longshou Hills. Thus, Zhang describes them in terms usually reserved for mountains.

43. A *jun* equaled 16 lb. (7.32 kg).

44. These lines describe the frame from which musical instruments such as stone chimes and bells were hung. Various types of animals were carved on the frame to symbolize fierceness and strength. In particular, the crosspiece at the top was supported by two flying beasts on either side.

45. The Warmth Modulator (Wen tiao) is another name for the Chamber of Warmth (Wen shi). It was the winter counterpart of the Hall of Coolness (Qingliang), a summer residence kept cool by ice stored underground during the winter. In contrast, the Chamber of Warmth was carpeted with thick Kashmir rugs and painted with a pepper-mud lacquer that provided a certain amount of heat.

46. Located west of the main hall of the Everlasting Palace.

47. These halls were all part of the Everlasting Palace.

48. These were all lodges south of the main hall.

49. The North Star (Beiji) constellation was the axis around which ancient Chinese astronomers believed all stars rotated.

50. According to the *Book of Rites (Liji),* the court would assemble in the palace at the crack of dawn. After the ruler daily reviewed the court, he would retire to the Grand Chamber to listen to government deliberations. After the grandees departed, he went to the Lesser Chamber and removed his robes.

51. The kings (princes), marquises, dukes, ministers, grandees, and scholars who visit the court.

52. The "nine doors" most likely refers to the nine chambers of the Main Hall.

53. In 221 B.C.E., the First Emperor of the Qin collected all the weapons in the empire and melted them down to make bell-stands and twelve metal statues. In Han times, these statues were located in front of the Palace of Enduring Joy.

54. The regular palace attendant *(zhong changshi)* in the Former Han was a personal servant to the emperor

in the Forbidden Palace. In the Later Han, it became a powerful position held exclusively by eunuchs. The internuncio *(yezhe)* was charged with the ceremonial concerned with receiving visitors to the palace.

55. Where documents and books were stored.

56. This was a large portal in the Everlasting Palace where scholar-officials visited to be summoned by the emperor. The name comes from a large Ferghana horse statue that stood in front of the gate. The famous "blood-sweating horses" of Ferghana (in Western Central Asia) were prized by the Chinese as the finest steeds on earth and were said to have descended from the fabled "Heavenly Horses" (Tian ma). In 101 B.C.E., the general Li Guangli defeated Ferghana after a four-year campaign. Upon his return to China, he presented Emperor Wu with a few of these splendid horses.

57. The Stone Canal Pavilion was the name of a library built by the early Han minister Xiao He (d. 193 B.C.E.). It was located north of the Main Hall of the Everlasting Palace. The Tianlu Pavilion was also built by Xiao He to store the imperial book collection and provide space for scholars to work on texts. Tianlu is the name of a one-horned animal with the features of a deer. Since its name literally means "Heavenly Recompense," it is obviously a felicitous symbol like the Qilin, another deer-like "unicorn."

58. These were the names of office buildings.

59. A kind of night watchman post responsible for patrolling the palace grounds. The watchman sounded a drum for each of the five night watches, which occurred every two hours from 7 P.M. to 5 A.M.

60. The capital was patrolled by police officials under the supervision of the Commandant at the Capital *(Zhong wei)*.

61. These served as quarters for the nightwatch.

62. The term "rear palace" *(hou gong)* is a general expression for the women's residences. All together there were a total of fourteen such residences, seven of which are mentioned here (Phoenix Hall, located east of the main hall, was constructed after a phoenix landed in the Shanglin Park). The most sumptuous of the women's quarters was the Bright Sunshine Lodge, in which the emperor's favorite stayed.

63. Duty houses were the quarters in which officials stayed while they were on duty, and the dormitories were where they lived when not on duty.

64. Such lustrous "pearls" were actually made of mica.

65. A precious gem owned by the state of Liang during the Warring States period.

66. The Marquis of Sui (Sui hou) was a noble who was descended from the Zhou clan. He encountered a snake that had been injured. He cared the snake's wounds with medicine. Later, the snake appeared to him with a large pearl, which it presented to him as repayment for his kindness. The pearl glowed in the dark and was famous as a luminous moon.

67. All six of these gems were extremely rare and precious.

68. I.e., the emperor's dwelling-place.

69. This is a group of six stars located within the Purple Palace. In addition to its function as the celestial counterpart of the Pear Palace, it had charge of the military guard. Here it refers to the empress's palace.

70. The Hall of Shining Brightness (Mingguang dian) was across from the Everlasting Palace on the large avenue reading to the main north portal of the city wall. It was constructed in 101 B.C.E. In the southeast part of Chang'an was the Palace of Enduring Joy (Changle gong), which Liu Bang (see nn. 5 and 30) erected out of an old Qin palace in 200 B.C.E. Connecting all these buildings was a network of raised galleries and carriage passageways.

71. This was the Gui gong, which was located north of the Everlasting Palace. Built in 101 B.C.E. by Emperor Wu, it had a circumference of more than ten tricents (approximately three miles [five kilometers]).

72. Master craftsmen of antiquity.

73. The emperor had so many ladies in his harem that he had access to them wherever he went. Similarly, there was such a large supply of musical instruments that they were available everywhere.

74. See n. 34.

75. The Ebang Palace was built by the First Qin Emperor south of the Wei River in Shanglin Park. It was connected to Xianyang, the Qin capital, by a series of elevated passageways. The palace was so large it reputedly could seat 10,000 people and accommodate banners five *zhang* (37 feet [11.55 meters]) high.

76. This palace was constructed by Hu Hai (d. 207 B.C.E.), the Second Qin Emperor.

77. Lines 208–209 contain the names of three lodges built by Emperor Wu in 109 B.C.E. as additions to the Sweet Springs Palace.

78. The Sky-Piercing Tower was also built by Emperor Wu in 109 B.C.E. for the purpose of attracting immortals to the Sweet Springs Palace. It was an exceptionally high structure, said by a third century C.E. commentator quoting an earlier source to have been 30 *zhang* (420 feet [129.3 meters]) high. Zhang Heng's figure of 100 *chang* (one *chang* = one *zhang*) is obviously hyperbole.

79. The semimythical *yun* bird, which seems to have been some sort of crane or stork.

80. The Cypress Beans Terrace was built by Emperor Wu in the spring of 115 B.C.E. It was located inside the Northern Watchtower of the Chang'an wall. The terrace burned down on January 15, 104 B.C.E. Emperor Wu consulted his advisers about what kind of omen this fire portended. Yongzhi, a shaman from the southern kingdom of Yue, told him that according to Yue custom, when one reconstructs a building after a fire, one must build the new structure even larger than the original to word off malevolent influences. Emperor Wu then ordered the construction of the Jianzhang Palace outside the Zhangcheng Gate of the western wall of the city. This was the largest of the Western Han palaces at Chang'an.

81. The main hall of the Jiangzhang Palace was higher than that of the Everlasting Palace (Weiyang Gong).

82. Probably a description of the twin watchtower gateways located at the Eastern Portal.

83. The paired watchtowers are portrayed as huge boulder mountains jutting up to the heavens.

84. It was not uncommon during Han times to place a bronze phoenix about three to six feet high on an acroterion (pedestal) atop the roof of a watchtower. There is evidence that beneath such phoenixes were rotating axles enabling them to turn with the wind. Hence, they seemed to have functioned as weather vanes. Compare the next line ("facing the wind"). Such phoenix acroteria were not restricted to the capital area.

85. The main south gate of the Jianzhang Palace.

86. Located at the eastern gate of the Jianzhang Palace.

87. This line describes the openwork windows made of figured silk woven in a crisscross pattern.

88. Located on the west side of the Jianzhang Palace. It reputedly was fifty *zhang* (375 feet [115.5 meters]) high. The name "Divine Luminaries" is derived from the belief that deities *(shenming)* lived at the top. The terrace had nine chambers, each occupied by a hundred Taoist priests.

89. This tower faced the Terrace of the Divine Luminaries and was also fifty *zhang* high. It was constructed of a series of trusses in the shape of well curbs (see n. 39).

90. This refers to the junction of Heaven and Earth.

91. "Multiple yang" *(chong yang)* is a way of referring to Heaven, which was considered to be yang and thought to consist of nine layers or stages.

92. Sometimes equated with the deity known as Fenglong (The Full and Lofty). The latter, however, is also identified as the god of thunder.

93. Jasper Light, also known as Wavering Light, and Jade Rope, also known as Jade Balance, are stars in Ursa Major.

94. Dulu is an abbreviated form of Fugan dulu (Old Sinitic *piwo- kam to- lo*), the name of a country located south of the Han commandery of Hepu (in modern Guangdong). This might credibly be a transcription for Pugandhara, the old Burmese city of Pagan (near Tagaung). Regardless of the correct identification, it seems clear that the Dulu were Burmese acrobats who specialized in pole-climbing.

95. The Relaxation Hall, known for its profusion of plants in the spring, lay to the front of the Hall of the Rapid Gallop, so named because it allegedly required an entire day to ride a horse from one end of the hall to the other.

96. Named for the wood out of which the timbers for the hall were constructed.

97. It is not certain whether this is the name of a terrace or of a hall.

98. The extended eaves of the roof that curved upward. This passage is one piece of evidence demonstrating the existence of the curved roof in ancient China.

99. Located behind the Linden Hall, this hall was so named because its beams seemed to raise to the highest region of the sky.

100. The doors were so high that the chariots could enter the palace without removing the banners, which were secured to the top of the chariot with a lock.

101. The driver tapped on the wheel spokes to signal the horses to increase speed.

102. The doors were so wide that a four-in-hand could pass through a single door-leaf.

103. The highest peak in the Kunlun Mountains.

104. The "metal" wall refers to the west wall of Chang'an. In Chinese correlative thought, the metal "element" symbolizes the west.

105. The wooden clapper was used to sound the alarm. There were so many labyrinthine passages that, in spite of the vigilance of the guards, it was possible to sneak in and out of the palace unnoticed.

106. A lake within the Jianzhang Palace complex, it had a circumference of twenty tricents (about six and a quarter miles [ten kilometers]).

107. This lake lay to the north of Jianzhang Palace. It was built to represent the Northern Sea. One would have to turn around to the north to see the Grand Fluid Pond.

108. The huge Tower of Soaking Waters rose over twenty *zhang* high from the middle of the Grand Fluid Pond. It was built at the same time as the Jianzhang Palace.

109. A lake north of the Jianzhang Palace.

110. Lines 290–291 contain the names of three magic islands in the Eastern Sea inhabited by immortals.

111. The "stone mushrooms" and the "magic fungus" were eaten as drugs of immortality.

112. A sea-god.

113. Perhaps a reference to the three-*zhang* statue of a whale that lay north of the Clear Pool.

114. Li Shaojun was an alchemist who gained Emperor Wu's favor in the 130s B.C.E. He had once been a retainer of the Marquis of Shenze and was a master of various magical techniques. He persuaded Emperor Wu to initiate sacrifices to the hearth, with the aim of learning from the hearth spirits the secret for transforming cinnabar into gold. Also at his suggestion, Emperor Wu sent an expedition into the Eastern Sea in search of the Penglai immortals.

115. Luan Da is the name of another alchemist-magician who achieved great influence with Emperor Wu in 113 B.C.E. He was named General of the Five Profits (Wuli jiangjun) but was executed the following year.

116. Zhang Heng, in these two lines, is clearly satirizing Emperor Wu's obsession with alchemy and his vain attempt to seek immortality.

117. These are the columns on which were erected bronze statues of immortals holding dew-collecting pans. The dew was drunk as a potion for prolonging life. The statues were reportedly twenty *zhang* (150 feet [46.2 meters]) high.

118. Or perhaps agate.

119. Chisong Zi is Master Red Pine. He reputedly lived at the time of the legendary ruler Shennong (the Divine Husbandman). He had the ability to ingest crystal. Much of his life was spent in the Kunlun Mountains where he resided in the Stone Chamber of the Queen Mother of the West. He is also known as the Rain Master.

120. Wangzi Qiao, also known as Wang Jin, was the heir apparent to King Ling of Zhou (r. 571–545 B.C.E.). He played the mouth organ *(sheng)* and could imitate the call of the phoenix. He learned the techniques of immortality from a Taoist.

121. Xianmen (or Xianmen Gao [the last syllable possibly a surname], as it appears in other Han texts) is customarily interpreted as the name of an immortal. Some scholars believe that Xianmen was actually an old Chinese transcription of the word "shaman," but this theory has not found wide acceptance.

122. The name of a palace located in Lantian, about twenty miles southeast of Chang'an. It was named for the Tripod Lake (situated below Mt. Jing just south of modern Wen xiang, Henan), associated in legend with the Yellow Emperor (Huang Di). An alchemist told Emperor Wu that, after the Yellow Emperor had cast a bronze tripod at the base of Mt. Jing, a dragon then appeared and carried him off into the sky. Emperor Wu was so impressed by this tale that he remarked, "Alas! If I truly could succeed in being like the Yellow Emperor, I would view leaving my wives and children the same as removing a sandal."

123. Emperor Wu in 139 B.C.E. had his tomb constructed in Mouling. Zhang points out the obvious contradiction between Emperor Wu's attempts to avoid death and his simultaneous elaborate preparations for death.

124. Each of Chang'an's four walls had three large gates. This gate arrangement was the same as that specified in the "Artificer's Record" (Kaogong ji) of the *Rites of Zhou (Zhouli),* a text that emerged around the middle of the second century B.C.E. Running from each gate was a three-lane avenue twelve chariot

gauges (about 71 feet [22 meters]) wide. The middle lane, called the "speedway" *(chi dao)* was reserved for the emperor, while the left lane was used for traffic entering the city and the right lane for traffic leaving the city.

125. Zhang Heng borrows two terms from the *Rites of Zhou* to designate the residential areas of Chang'an: *chan* (residential plot) and *li* (ward). The residential areas of Han Chang'an were called *li,* of which there were said to be 160.

126. These were mansions awarded to nobles and imperial favorites. Those near the North Watchtower were especially prestigious.

127. Shi refers to Shi Xian (fl. 74–79 B.C.E.), a eunuch who rose to a position of great influence under Emperor Yuan (r. 48–33 B.C.E.). Because Emperor Yuan was constantly ill, Shi Xian was entrusted with managing most of the court business.

128. Dong is Dong Xian (fl. 5–1 B.C.E.). He was the favorite of Emperor Ai. The handsome young man served as the emperor's catamite and eventually assumed the high position of Grand Minister of War. On one occasion, the emperor even proposed ceding the throne to Dong. Only after being admonished by the court official Wang Hong did the emperor desist.

129. Chang'an had nine markets, each of which was 266 *bu* (paces) square (33.57 acres [13.59 hectares]). There were six markets on the west side and three on the east.

130. The "flag pavilion" was a name for the market loft-buildings from which officials inspected the selling and trading in the marketplace. These five-story buildings received their names from the banners that hung from them.

131. The "Zhou" office mentioned here is that of the Director of the Market (Si shi), which, according to the *Rites of Zhou,* administered various offices concerned with market activities. For every twenty shops there was one supervising officer called the *xushi,* who was charged with policing transactions in the market.

132. During the Han, the overall supervision of the markets fell to officials with the title of Commandant *(wei).*

133. The terms Zhang uses here for sellers and buyers in the marketplace are all mentioned in the *Rites of Zhou.* The *shang* (peddlers) were the merchants who traveled to the market with their wares; the *gu* (shop-keepers) were the resident merchants. The *baizu* (literally, "hundred clans") were the common people who come to the afternoon market. The *fànfù* and *fànfù* were the male and female sellers who plied their wares at the evening market.

134. These were two of the most prominent clans of the Former Han. Both Emperor Xuan (r. 74–49 B.C.E.) and Emperor Cheng (r. 33–7 B.C.E.) had wives from the Xu family. The Good Lady Shi was the grandmother of Emperor Xuan.

135. Wang Bo earned a fortune selling land. The Zhuo clan sold fried tripe. The Zhi family cleaned and restored swords. The Zhang ward was known for its horse-doctors.

136. There is an old anecdote about Boyou of Zheng, who enjoyed drinking so much that he had an underground room built in which he drank and sounded bells throughout the night. "Sounding bells" implies music played during banquets. "Eating from cauldrons" implies the use of fancy dishes.

137. Zhang refers to Zhang Hui, the arrow maker, also known as Zhang Jin. Zhao is Zhao Fang, the wine-dealer. Both were knights-errant in Chang'an and were killed by Wang Zun, Governor of the Capital. While at the peak of their power, they kept many assassins as retainers.

138. Lord Xinling (Wei Wuji) of Wei and Lord Mengchang (Tian Wen) of Qi were wealthy princes of the third century B.C.E. who supported large numbers of retainers, some of whom were scholars and knights-errant.

139. This is a quotation from scroll 4 of the *Book of Documents (Shujing* or *Shangshu).*

140. This is a direct quotation from poem number 104 in the *Book of Odes (Shijing).*

141. Yuan is Yuan Shě, a knight-errant who lived toward the end of the Former Han.

142. Zhu is Zhu Anshi, a knight-errant who came from the mausoleum town of Yangling. In 92 B.C.E., Gongsun Jingsheng, the son of the Imperial Chancellor, Gongsun He, was arrested and imprisoned for lawless conduct. To ransom his son, Gongsun He promised to arrest the knight-errant Zhu Anshi. When Zhu was captured, he obtained revenge by charging Gongsun Jingsheng with various improprieties, including having intercourse with the princess of Yangshi. Gongsun He and his son were arrested. They both died in prison.

143. Scroll 92 of the *History of the Han (Hanshu)* says of Yuan Shě, "Outwardly he was gentle, kind, and humble, but inwardly he concealed his lust of killing. An angry look on the dusty road—those who died of the offense were quite numerous."

144. See n. 142.

145. The five prefectures are the five mausoleum towns north of Chang'an: Changling (Emperor Gaozu; forty tricents north of Chang'an), Anling (Emperor Hui; thirty-five tricents north of Chang'an), Mouling (Emperor Wu; eighty tricents northwest of Chang'an), Yangling (Emperor Jing; forty-five tricents northeast of Chang'an), Pingling (Emperor Zhao; seventy tricents northwest of Chang'an).

146. Zhang uses two metrological terms, *hao* and *li,* which are here loosely translated as millimeter and centimeter. The *li* in one system consisted of ten *hao.* Ten *li* equalled a *fen,* and ten *fen* equalled a *cun* (the Chinese "inch" = 0.9 in. [23.10 mm]). The compound *haoli* came to mean "a very small thing or matter."

147. The word *li* (fiber) could also be "vein" (as on a piece of jade). The metaphor of flesh and muscle works better with the following lines.

148. This implies the ability "to fly aloft," meaning that those praised by the scholars became famous.

149. The terms *jiao* (suburbs) and *dian* (royal domain) designate two zones that radiated out from the capital. The near suburb, *jiao,* extended fifty tricents (in all directions) from the capital, and the imperial domain was a hundred tricents from the capital.

150. The district town *(xiang yi)* was the administrative center of the district, which was the administrative unit below the prefecture *(xian).* The district consisted of ten cantons *(ting),* and the canton was divided into ten hamlets *(li).*

151. The major commandery capitals were Luoyang (Henan), Yuan (Nanyang), Linzi (Qi), Chengdu (Shu), and Handan, the capital of the Zhao kingdom.

152. A metonymy for "official."

153. The expression used here for "imperial domain" *(fengji),* which was a thousand tricents square, seems to indicate the totality of the land under the tax system, which was supposedly based on the "well-field" system. Once again, the geometrical pattern of the well curb (#; see n. 39) is drawn on, the land being laid out in eight peripheral squares of 100 *mu* (a sixth of an acre) arranged around a ninth square of the same size in the center. Eight families each worked one of the peripheral squares and jointly cultivated the common, central square, the produce from which was due to their lord as a tax.

154. *Jingzhao yin,* the title given by Emperor Wu in 104 B.C.E. to the office charged with administering the capital area.

155. The "commandery" *(jun)* was the most important subdivision of the Han administrative system. By the end of the Former Han there were eighty-three commanderies. The governor of a commandery, called a Grand Administrator *(taishou),* was directly responsible to the central government. The "kingdom" *(guo)* was an area given to a member of the imperial family to administer. At the end of the Former Han there were twenty kingdoms.

156. Presumably there would have been one such building in the capital for each of the empire's commanderies and kingdoms. There is some confusion among the early sources and commentators about the precise signification of the number 145 in relation to the palaces and lodges of the capital. The best modern authorities believe that the text is here referring to the area around the capital, for these are the royal buildings of Chang'an and its environs, not the entire realm. In the following lines, Zhang Heng speaks of the area south of the capital, where most of the touring palaces were located. Why he says 145 is a bit of a mystery. However, the *Old Events of the Three Capital Districts (Sanfu jiushi),* an account of the capital area, gives the same number, albeit for the Qin period. This is probably what Zhang Heng is referring to. More precisely, the *Sanfu jiushi* states, "The First Qin Emperor marked off the Yellow River as the eastern gate of the Qin, and marked off the Qian River as the western gate of the Qin. Outside (N.B.) the capital, there were 145 palaces and lodges." One might well argue that this refers to the entire realm. It should be noted, however, that the metropolitan area of the capital amounted to several hundred square miles. In sum, lines 387–388 most likely refer to the entire capital district and its environs, especially south into the Shanglin Park.

157. This imperial park was a Han prefecture that lay west of Chang'an (east of modern Zhouzhi). It was the location of Tall Poplars Palace.

158. See note 18.

159. He is the Yellow River. Hua is Taihua, a peak of the Qinling mountain range (south of modern Huayin, Shaanxi); it is the famous sacred mountain known as the Western Peak (Xiyue).

160. Guo was named for an old Zhou state. It was part of Youfufeng commandery (east of modern Baoji).

161. The exact location of the Tripod Lake (Dinghu) mentioned here is uncertain. One early commentator says that it was located east of Huayin, but there was also a Tripod Lake near Lantian (see n. 122), which was the location of a palace. The Lantian location would seem to be closer to the Shanglin Park (see n. 18).

162. A lodge located south of the Kunming Pond. The word "diagonal" is probably meant to indicate that it lay southwest of Chang'an.

163. This was a palace (Chanyang gong) in the Shanglin Park, one of its largest. From the terrace hall (xie) located here, the Han emperors viewed the hunt.

164. The Five Oaks Lodge (also referred to as a "detached palace") was located near Zhouzhi and was named for five large oak trees planted there.

165. The name of a palace located in the Han prefecture of Kuaili (southeast of modern Xingping, Shaanxi).

166. The name of a pond in the western end of the Shanglin Park. It is also identified as a mountain twenty-three tricents southwest of Hu Prefecture.

167. A minister to the legendary Emperor Shun. He accompanied the Great Yu (Shun's successor) to the Northern Sea and helped him identify the animals they encountered on the trip.

168. This dignitary was said to have made mathematical computations for the Yellow Emperor (Huang Di).

169. The scientific names of the eight trees in these two lines are (in order) *Abies firma* (Japanese fir or Momi fir), *Juniperus chinensis* (Chinese juniper), *Trachycarpus fortunei* (windmill palm), *Phoebe nanmu* (the nanmu tree), *Catalpa ovata* (or *bungei*), *Quercus spinosa*, *Ulmus macrocarpa* (big fruit), and *Liquidambar formosana* (sweet gum).

170. Deng Grove was formed from the staff of the great Kuafu (Father Kua), who tried to race the sun. He became thirsty and drank the Yellow and Wei rivers dry without quenching his thirst. He went north to drink the Great Marsh but died of thirst before he arrived. His discarded staff turned into the thick forest known as the Deng Grove.

171. The plants listed in this line are respectively *Oxalis cornuculata*, *Cyperus rotundus* (nut grass; *suo*, a sedge that was used to make mats and raincoats), *Themeda gigantea*, and *Scirpus eriophorum*.

172. *Vicia angustifalia* Benth./*sativa/pseudoorbus* Fisch. et Mey (a leguminous food plant), *Pteridium aquilinum* (common bracken), and *Iris ensata* (Chinese iris).

173. *Arthraxon hispidus* (joint head arthraxon; used for making yellow dye), *Fritillaria roylei* or *thunbergi* (a liliaceous plant whose corms are used in medicine), and *Carex dispalata*.

174. *Althaea rosea* (the common hollyhock) and a fragrant grass whose precise identification eludes the commentators.

175. The "Heavenly Questions" (Tian wen) of the *Lyrics of Chu (Chuci)* alludes to two mythical places called Black Water and Dark Foot. The latter was said to be the name of a mountain in the west, while the former was held to be a river that flows out of the Kunlun Mountains (also in the distant west; see line 179). The Kunming Pond near Chang'an had replicas of the Black Water and Dark Foot. The Kunming Pond in south China (Yunnan), of which the imperial pond outside Chang'an was a replica, had a Black Water Shrine. It is possible that the north China counterpart reproduced this shrine in some fashion.

176. This "metal" dike was actually made of stone. The term "metal" is metaphorical and indicates only that the dike was strong.

177. *Salix babylonica* and *Salix cheilophilia* or *purpurea*.

178. Camphor is the name of a lodge located at the Kunming Pond. It was also known as Kunming Lodge.

179. On the east and west shores of the Kunming Pond were stone replicas of the mythical lovers, Oxherd (Qian niu) and Weaving Girl (Zhi nü). They were depicted as constellations (our Altair and Vega) that occupied opposite sides of the Han River in the Clouds (Yun Han), the bright "Sky River" known in

the West as the Milky Way. They were allowed to meet only once a year, on the seventh day of the seventh moon, when a flock of magpies form a bridge for them to cross the river.

180. Fusang is the name of a "solar tree" located above the Dawn Valley at the extreme eastern limits of the world. According to accounts preserved in the *Classic of Mountains and Seas (Shanhai jing),* the ten suns bathed on the Fusang tree. Nine suns remained on the lower branches, while one rested on top. As soon as one sun arrived on a branch, another left. Each sun carried a three-legged crow.

181. Also known as the Murky Valley, this is the depression into which the sun sinks at the end of the day.

182. *Pelocheylys bibroni, Alligator sinensis,* and *Trionyx sinensis* (the lesser soft-shelled turtle).

183. *Acipenser sinensis, Cyprinus carpio, Hypophthalmichthys molitrix, Ctenopharyngdon idellus.*

184. *Psephurus gladius, Megalobatrachus* or *Andrias davidianas, Pseudo-bagrus aurantiacus,* and *Acanthogobius flavianus* (a small fish known to the ancient Chinese as the "sand-blower").

185. *Halcyon smyrnensis, Grus vipio,* and *Otis dybowskii.*

186. *Anser fabalis serrirotris* and *hong,* which refer to the larger species of wild goose.

187. "Hengyang" literally means "south of Mt. Heng" (in modern Nanyue district, Hunan). It was the site of the famous Returning Goose Peak (Hui yan feng), which was the southern ridge of Mt. Heng.

188. This is Wild Goose Portal, the name of a mountain located northwest of modern Dai, Shaanxi. The *Classic of Mountains and Seas* mentions it as a place from which geese took flight.

189. Present tense is used in this section to show the kinetic quality of Zhang Heng's narration of the Western Han hunt.

190. Hunting animals such as goshawks and hounds.

191. Zhang is using hyperbole here, comparing the size of the nets to "Heaven" and "Earth."

192. The park, which originally belonged to King Wen of Zhou, was seventy tricents square.

193. This line is a direct quotation from poem number 180 in the *Book of Odes.*

194. The name of a star that is sometimes portrayed as an addition to the handle of the (northern) Big Dipper. It was also known as the Shield and the Celestial Point.

195. Another star also imagined as part of the Northern Dipper, it had the alternative name Spear. Figures of these "martial stars" were drawn on the banners with the intention of fortifying the soldiers' courage.

196. A banner on which a black-eared kite *(Milvus migrans lineatus)* was painted. According to the *Book of Rites,* it was used when there was dust in front of the procession.

197. Banners made in the shape of clouds.

198. The Bow is the name of a constellation paired with the Arrow and located below the Celestial Wolf (or Sirius). This line is an exact quotation from the *Rites of Zhou.* An early commentator to the latter text says that the "warped arrows" are the "demonic stars," or comets, that are painted around the bow.

199. A constellation of seven stars in our Cassiopeia. It was imagined as shading the throne of the Celestial Lord.

200. Referring here to the Northern Chronogram, another name for the northern polestar. It corresponds to the imperial throne.

201. Hyades. It is also another name for the Rain Master.

202. The last chariot in the procession. It was decorated with a leopard's tail, symbolizing its position in the cortege.

203. This collection of stories is no longer extant. It is listed in the "Monograph on Literature" of the *Han History* under the title *Yu Chu's Tales of Zhou (Yu Chu Zhou shuo)* in 943 sections. Yu Chu was a native of Luoyang and was one of the many magicians who served at Emperor Wu's court.

204. Originally known as a warrior who rebelled against the Yellow Emperor, he was eventually slain by the latter in the dramatic battle of Zhuolu. Later, he became known as the inventor of weapons and plays a key role in the myth of the introduction of metallurgy to China. Zhang Heng perhaps is here referring to a person in the procession who impersonates Chiyou.

205. These lines are a paraphrase of the *Zuo Commentary (Zuozhuan),* Duke Xuan, year 3: "In the past . . . Xia cast tripods representing creatures . . . so that people would recognize demonic treachery. Therefore, when a person entered rivers and marshes, mountains and forests, he could not fall upon malevolent spirits (literally, 'the discordant')."

206. A spirit of mountains, forests, and marshes usually thought of as having bizarre animal form.

207. A spectral creature of mountains, rivers, grassy marshes, trees, and stones. One early-second-century C.E. text states that it is like "a three-year-old child, with red-black hair, red eyes, long ears, and beautiful hair."

208. Located in the Shanglin Park, this lodge was built by Emperor Wu in 109 B.C.E. The Feilian was a supernatural bird that had the power to attract wind and vapors. Emperor Wu had a bronze statue of a Feilian placed on top of the Feilian Lodge. This line uses the names of two offices mentioned in the *Rites of Zhou,* the Chiefs of the Tiger Runners and the Chiefs of the Troop Runners. The former were the emperor's bodyguard. The latter carried lances and shields, and ran in front of and behind the imperial chariot.

209. The name of a constellation of twelve stars that presided over the army and military encampments. The "ramparts" of the park were considered to be a replica of this constellation.

210. The name (Upper Thoroughwort?) of a belvedere in the Shanglin Park.

211. A column consisted of twenty-five men and a file of five men.

212. The Yellow River and the Wei River, which flows into it near Chang'an.

213. These two mountains lay in the Former Han prefecture of Qian (southwest of Long [34°54'N, 106°51'E] in western Shaanxi).

214. The *Stratagems of the Warring States (Zhanguo ce),* a collection compiled at the end of the first century B.C.E., twice refers to the wily hare, Dongguo Jun, who ran so fast nothing could catch him.

215. The hawks were so fast they captured the birds almost as soon as they left the gauntlet.

216. This especially fleet-footed dog is also twice mentioned in the *Stratagems of the Warring States.*

217. The name of a country whose location is unknown. Its ruler, the Earl of Zhonghuang, had a formidable reputation as a warrior who fought monsters and tigers.

218. A strongman who could lift incredibly heavy weights.

219. Another famous strongman who is mentioned numerous times in early texts.

220. Also called "exposed topknot" because no cap or kerchief was worn on the head; in this style the hair was tied up in small tufts and mixed with pieces of hemp.

221. Probably the same beast as the *manyan* (see n. 269).

222. *Rhinopithecus roxellanae* (moupin langur), *Erinaceus dealbatus.*

223. A mythical monster that is described in widely varying terms in early texts.

224. *Poncirus trifoliata,* a spiny, thorny shrub of central China often used for hedges.

225. The image is that of a mountain configuration piled up like an old double boiler, large above and small below.

226. China's oldest lexicon, the *Erya,* states that this is an animal with "cleft hooves that are flat. It is good at scrambling up double-boiler slopes." This entry, which seems to be describing some sort of mountain goat, must have been the source of Zhang Heng's lines 580–581.

227. *Macacus Sancti-Johannis.*

228. *Corylus heterophylla* (hazelnut or filbert).

229. During the Former (Western) Han, there were fourteen ranks of concubines. The highest of these was the "Brilliant Companion" *(Zhaoyi),* considered equal to the position of chancellor and the rank of noble and king. Each concubine rank was equated with a corresponding position and rank in the bureaucracy.

230. This line alludes to a story in the *Zuo Commentary,* Duke Zhao, year 28: "Grandee Jia was ugly, but he married a wife, and she was beautiful. For three years she did not speak or laugh. He drove her with him to Gao [Preserve]. He shot at a pheasant and hit it. His wife for the first time laughed and talked."

231. This line is an allusion to poem number 41 from the *Book of Odes,* in which a lady says to her lover, "Be kind and love me, / Take my hand and let me share your chariot."

232. This is a clever reversal of a phrase from the *Book of Documents (Shujing):* "King Wen [of the Zhou dynasty] dared not amuse himself in excursions and hunts." By removing the negative, Zhang Heng subtly casts aspersions on the excesses of the Han monarchs.

233. This line is a direct quotation from poem number 67 of the *Book of Odes.*

234. See note 163.

235. The couriers *(xingfu)* were in charge of carrying messages, especially those delivered without any ceremony. "Restoring the couriers" simply means they rested the soldiers.

236. This line is a direct quotation from the *Zuo Commentary,* Duke Cheng, year 16.

237. The "five regiments" *(wu jun)* is equivalent to the Han military term "five encampments" *(wu ying)*. The Chinese emperor's army was always thought of as consisting of six divisions.

238. A *Rites of Zhou* office that supervised preparation of all food and drink for the king.

239. The *Lie Zi* (late 1st c. B.C.E.–3rd c. C.E.) mentions Puju Zi, who was especially skilled in shooting the corded arrow.

240. A boat with the figure of a heron on the front. The ostensible purpose of the figure was to ward off demons.

241. A sunshade on which clouds and mushrooms were painted.

242. Part of the Music Repository at the end of the Former Han. There were four drum officers in charge of performing this music repertoire, which conformed to ancient military practice and was used for court congratulations and banquets.

243. Named for a famous entertainer of antiquity. Written with different (but similar) characters, it was the name of a southern Chu song used as dance music.

244. Pingyi, also called He Ping, is said to be the Earl of the Yellow River (He bo). He became a river sylph after eating eight stones. He is pictured as having a human face and riding two dragons.

245. The goddess of the Xiang River. Originally a single deity, by Han times some sources related that there were two Xiang goddesses, Ehuang and Nüying, daughters of the legendary sage-ruler who married his successor Shun. Two shamanistic hymns in the southern *Lyrics of Chu* are devoted to one or both of them.

246. These are small fish, *Culter brevicauda* and *Hemiculter leusiculus*.

247. Perhaps the reference is to seals of some sort.

248. A type of water buffalo, or possibly the extinct sea cow.

249. In charge of enforcing the regulations governing the "state preserves." This office did not exist in Han times, and Zhang is merely using the *Rites of Zhou* term to designate the person in charge of the hunting park.

250. An allusion to *Discourses of the States (Guoyu)*: "He wet the fishnets in the pools of the Si in order to catch fish."

251. Referring to the nine compartments in the net that the fish enter.

252. An exact quotation from poem number 35 of the *Book of Odes*.

253. Located in the Shanglin Park. In 105 B.C.E. Emperor Wu staged competitive games here that included various types of entertainment (see below, line 680).

254. This line quotes from Ban Gu's "Appraisal" at the end of the *Han History* chapter on the Western Regions: "They made A-rank and B-rank tents. . . . The Son of Heaven . . . donned a halcyon-plumed coat."

255. These competitions *(juedi)* included archery, chariot-driving, and possibly a ritual bullfight.

256. See note 219.

257. See note 94.

258. It is not known exactly what the acts described in lines 683–684 consisted of, but a fairly good idea can be had from this description by Xue Zong, a mid-third-century commentator: "They roll up bamboo-splint mats and stick spears into them. The performer throws himself into them and passes through (unharmed). . . . They place a plate of water in front of him. He sits behind it. Leaping up, with arms extended, he jumps forward. Using his feet to mark the rhythm, he clears the water. He then sits down like a swallow taking a bath."

259. This feat seems to have entered China from the Roman Orient (Da Qin). The *Wei Summary (Wei lüe)* by Yu Huan (3rd c. C.E.) specifically refers to the amazing performances of this area: "The customs of the country of Da Qin include many strange, magical tricks: producing fire from the mouth, tying oneself up and untying oneself, juggling twelve balls." Jugglers came to China as tribute from foreign countries such as Parthia and Shan on the Burmese border. Han mural paintings and reliefs prominently portray this activity.

260. A Han description of tightrope-walking is contained in the *Administrative Observances of Han Officialdom Selected for Use (Han guan dianzhi yishi xuanyong)* by Cai Zhi (d. 178): "They tie two large ropes between two columns separated by several *zhang* (tens of 'feet'). Two female entertainers dancing face to face move along the rope. When they meet, their shoulders rub but they do not fall off. Further, they walk with their bodies crouched and hide among the brackets *(dou,* in the upper parts of the building to which the rope is attached)."

261. Huayue, the sacred Western Peak near Huayin in Shaanxi. As part of the performance, a replica of Mt. Hua was made and paraded around on a cart. There were trees and plants on the miniature mountain.

262. The guardian spirit of the west.

263. This instrument had as many as fifty strings in the early period.

264. The guardian spirit of the east.

265. This is the *chi,* a short (ca. 11.7 in. [30 cm]) transverse flute with five fingerholes.

266. These are singers dressed as the Xiang goddesses Ehuang and Nüying (see n. 245).

267. A musician from the period of the semimythical Three August Ones (Yao, Shun, Yu—paradigmatically meritorious rulers of the remote past).

268. In lines 700–706, Zhang describes the creation of artificial clouds, snow, and thunder that concluded the musical performance.

269. One *xun* = eight *chi* (feet). Since a *chi* equaled 23.1 centimeters in Han times, this beast would have been 184.8 meters long (over 600 feet).

270. This performance would appear to have been a precursor of the modern Chinese lion and dragon dances in which numerous performers support the head, body, and tail of a beast above them. If the Han *manyan* really were six hundred feet (185 meters) long, it would have required at least one hundred to two hundred dancers. In any event, this beast gets its name from its prodigious length, since *manyan* (which is written in many different sinographic forms) literally means "elongated" or "stretched out," "extended."

271. These beasts were all men dressed in animal costumes.

272. The Chinese term is *daque,* which is the Han name for the ostrich, but it is possible that the peacock is intended here, since one of the Han murals depicting entertainments shows a man dressed as a peacock. The word for peacock *(kongque)* also means "big bird," and there may have been confusion between *daque,* the Parthian ostrich, and the peacock, which also came from the west.

273. This may be a ceremonial re-enactment of the birth of the Buddha. The night before Buddha was born, his pregnant mother dreamed that a white elephant entered her womb. Brahmans told her that the dream signified that she would give birth to a son who would become a universal ruler or a buddha.

274. These lines describe the procession known as the "fish-dragon." This is the beast known as the *sheli,* although this word is sometimes distorted as *hanli* because the graph for *han* is visually very similar to that for *she.* Since neither the characters for *sheli* (literally, "shed-sharpness") nor *hanli* (literally, "hold sharpness in the mouth") make much sense, it is assumed that the syllables must be the transcription of some foreign word. As a matter of fact, *sheli* is the usual transcription of Sanskrit *śarīra* (relic), but that meaning is clearly inappropriate here and, furthermore, Buddhism had exerted only a negligible impact on China at the time this rhapsody was written. More likely, as suggested by the Japanese scholar Fujita Toyohachi, *sheli* represented the same word as the name of the country later called Xili (viz., Sillah, a kingdom on the Irawaddy). Regardless of the name that is hiding behind *sheli,* the text cited in note 260 describes the performance in detail: "The *sheli* comes from the west, cavorts at the edge of the water, and finally enters in front of the hall (i.e., the Hall of Virtuous Light). It splashes water and changes into a pair-eyed fish. Jumping and leaping, it spurts water and makes a mist that screens the sun. When it has finished this, it changes into a yellow dragon eight *zhang* [about sixty feet (18.5 meters) long]. It comes out of the water and cavorts about the courtyard, gleaming and glistering like the rays of the sun."

275. See note 274.

276. The "nine petals" are the various ornaments on the canopy frame.

277. These "water denizens," who were excellent handlers of snakes, were from the southeastern tribe known as the Lier.

278. The musicians were able to make clouds and mist rise.

279. This is Donghai Huang gong, who is mentioned in the *Miscellanies of the Western Capital (Xi jing za ji),* a work that dates to about 500 C.E. but draws on Han materials:

> He was able to control dragons and direct tigers. He wore at his waist a red metal knife. He used a crimson silk to tie his hair. Standing up, he made clouds and mist rise. Seated, he created mountains and rivers. When he became old and decrepit, his vital force was sapped and weakened. He drank excessively and was no longer able to work his magic. At the end of the Qin a white tiger appeared before Master Huang from the Eastern Sea. He then went forth with his red knife to subdue him. His magic did not work, and he was killed by the tiger.

280. Yue is the name applied to the non-Chinese tribes of southern China. They included tribes located as far south as Vietnam (in Mandarin this name would be pronounced Yuenan, meaning "Yue-south") and Guangdong (Canton), and as far north as Zhejiang and Jiangxi (i.e., the region south of the mid- to lower reaches of the Yangtze River).

281. These lines pertain to Master Huang. They are intended as a satirical jab at the quacks and mountebanks who held sway in the Former Han period.

282. An elaborate conveyance that is depicted on one of the Han mural paintings. It shows a huge chariot pulled by three dragons. The chariot is large enough to carry a driver, four musicians, and a long vertical pole. Halfway up the pole is a large drum. There are also numerous streamers, plume tassels, and other decorations. On the top of the pole is a small platform on which a young boy or dwarf is performing a headstand.

283. Their pole-climbing antics seemed to create the illusion of a hundred horses marching together under the control of a single bridle.

284. A Tibetan people who occupied the western border areas of China (mostly Gansu, but they occasionally extended into Sichuan and Yunnan).

285. The Xianbei (i.e., Särbi), an Altaic people, occupied what is now southern Manchuria. The Han periodically undertook military action in an attempt to control these and other tribes. Effigies of the Qiang and Xianbei were attached to a pole, and archers shot at them.

286. A name first coined in 138 B.C.E. during Emperor Wu's incognito outing to the Shanglin Park.

287. One suspects that Zhang is being sarcastic here.

288. The lateral courtyards were occupied by second rank and lower concubines.

289. The feathers (kingfisher plumes) were attached to the goblets in order to "accelerate" the drinking (i.e., to symbolize flight).

290. One of the notorious depraved women of early Chinese history. She was the mother of the grandee of Chen, Xia Zhengshu (d. 598 B.C.E.). She was married seven times, and even in old age she attracted men.

291. One of the best singers at the beginning of the Han, he hailed from Lu (the home state of Confucius). The sound of his singing shook the dust in the rafters.

292. *Shang* is the second note of the pentatonic scale. The "Pure Shang" is a musical mode to which Music Master Juan played an especially mournful zither tune.

293. Cranes were trained to dance. Bao Zhao (ca. 414–466) wrote a rhapsody on the subject of dancing cranes.

294. There was a dance called "Cup and Plate Dance" in which the performers placed seven plates and an unspecified number of cups on the ground and danced around them. The Han murals have a painting that portrays this dance.

295. This line alludes to a famous song composed by the musician Li Yannian (ca. 140–ca. 87 B.C.E.):

In the north there is a beauty,
Matchless she stands alone;
One look will overturn a city,
A second look will overturn a state.

296. Also called Zhan Huo, and more often referred to as Liuxia Hui. He lived at the end of the seventh century B.C.E. and was particularly well known for his integrity and high moral character. One story about Liuxia Hui has him allowing a homeless woman to sit on his lap all night without any aspersions being cast on his reputation.

297. This is the Sanskrit word for "monastic," "ascetic." It is said by the Dutch scholar Erich Zürcher to be "the first mention of Buddhism in Chinese belles lettres."

298. Also known as Wei Zifu, she was a singer who was named empress by Emperor Wu in 128 B.C.E. The emperor was first attracted to her because of her beautiful hair.

299. Zhao Feiyan, a dancer whom Emperor Cheng selected as a consort. She eventually was named empress. Her younger sister was given the rank of Brilliant Companion (see n. 229).

300. This and the previous line refer to poem number 115 in the "Tang" section of the *Book of Odes*. Various early commentaries on the poem consider it to be a criticism of one or another of the dukes of the state of Jin. The poem contains the following lines:

You have coat and skirt,
You neither trail nor drag them;
You have carts and horses,
You neither galley nor spur them on.
Emaciated you will die.
"Others will enjoy them."

301. Emperor Yuan created the title of Brilliant Companion as the highest rank for his concubines (see n. 229). This rank was superior to the former highest rank, Favored Beauty.

302. See note 128.

303. Emperor Cheng had promised Brilliant Companion Zhao that "the empire will have no one standing higher than Lady Zhao."

304. Emperor Ai one day after drinking to excess casually suggested that he would abdicate to Dong Xian just as the legendary sage-ruler Yao had ceded the throne to Shun. Wang Hong sternly admonished him: "The empire is Emperor Gao's (i.e., the Han founder's) empire. It is not Your Majesty's possession. Your Majesty has received the ancestral temple, and you should propagate limitless numbers of descendants. The matter of succession is supremely important. The Son of Heaven should not jest about it." From the *Han History,* scroll 93.

305. Lines 807–808 are based in part on passages from the *Book of Documents,* the *Book of Odes,* and the *Book of Changes.*

306. This line is a verbatim quotation from the *Book of Documents:* "Therefore, in the Yin (i.e., Shang dynasty) rites [when a king] died, he became assessor to Heaven, and they passed through many years (i.e., a great amount of time passed)."

307. This figure refers to the period from Gaozu (founding emperor of the Western Han) to Wang Mang (usurper who brought a conclusion to the Western Han)—a total of 214 years for the dynasty.

308. Lines 825–830 allude to the numerous (as many as thirteen!) transfers of the capital undertaken by the Yin-dynasty rulers. Before Emperor Pangeng transferred his capital to West Bo, he made a long speech to his people in which he declared the reasons why a move was necessary. The "Pangeng" chapter in the *Book of Documents* purports to be a record of this speech. The line "they never permanently occupied the same land" here is derived from a similar line in the "Pangeng" chapter. The people were unwilling to leave their homes, and Pangeng had to cajole them into following him. Hence, the reference to "leading by making them suffer."

309. This line alludes to the celestial nature of the Han emperor, whose title "radiant lord" (*huangdi*) is derived from the notion that his virtue *(de)*—in the Latin sense—was compable to that of radiant Heaven *(huangtian)*.

310. A reference to poem number 114 from the *Book of Odes,* which has the following lines:

The cricket is at the hall,
The year is coming to its eve;
If we do not enjoy ourselves now,
The days and months will disappear.

—DRK (revised by VHM)

THE *SCRIPTURE ON GREAT PEACE (Taiping jing)* has been preserved in an edition prepared by sixth-century adherents of Upper Clarity (Shangqing) Daoism. Neither its authors nor date of writing is known. However, some circumstantial evidence points to eastern Shandong as the place of its origin, and judging by contents as well as language it seems to belong to the outgoing second century C.E. This period of political turmoil and economic decline saw the formation of several millenarian movements that addressed the worries of a large drifting population in search of food and social stability.

Most of the *Taiping jing* consists of original notes taken at meetings between a Celestial Master who claimed to be Heaven's spokesman and his disciples, a group of "Perfected." Since these notes did not undergo much editing, the text of the *Taiping jing* contains not only a number of unique ideas and concepts but also incoherent points and nonstandard language. The aim of these meetings was nothing less than to equip the Perfected with all the knowledge they needed to save mankind from immanent disaster. In preparation and before being permitted into the presence of the Celestial Master they would have studied a set of materials revealed by Heaven. Their questions target certain points in this material. The Perfected are expected to distribute and propagate this material as well as the notes (the *Taiping jing*) among political leaders. If those in charge could be persuaded to implement a program of social reforms, the world's evil might be quelled and the period of Great Peace draw nearer.

These reforms involve the flow of *qi* (literally, "vapor"), the material as well as spiritual substance of which the whole world consists. Human conduct can either hinder or promote this flow. Benevolent, generous, harmony-promoting conduct will allow *qi* to flow freely and life to go on, as do meditation and other ways of nourishing the "vital principle." Restrictive, aggressive, conflict- and resentment-producing conduct will have the opposite result. Celibacy and female infanticide, imprisonment, and the hoarding of goods are all seen as actions that hinder the flow of *qi*. Wrongful accusations, which the following chapter deals with, come under the same heading.—BH

Scripture on Great Peace, Chapter 37

Subchapter 47: A Model for Testing the Trustworthiness of Texts

This ignorant pupil's blindness is getting worse from day to day. I bow twice before you. Now there is another question that I would like to ask the Celestial Master, the divine man of superior majesty.

What would you like to ask?

I would like to ask about this text. In general terms, why has it been created, why has it been published?

Good! We may say that by the way you ask you show some understanding for what Majestic Heaven thinks. The text's message is to give an explanation.[1] Since the origin of Heaven and Earth both rulers and their people have received and transmitted [evil]. For this reason the text has been published.

But if it has been published for this reason, why does it first of all teach how to nourish the vital principle (yang xing)?

Yes, you have always been truly foolish and dumb, your vision blurred and your understanding hampered. Otherwise a listener might take what you have just said for modesty. But are you really and truly blind and dumb?

Yes, I am.

Perfected, you must open your ears and listen carefully. Now the common people are to blame because they are not good at nourishing their own person. Because they have all lost direction they are punished by the reception and transmission [of evil]. Compare this to the case of a father and mother, who in neglect of moral obligations have trespassed against their neighbors and their sons and grandsons, who later on will be injured by the same neighbors. This documents the punishment involved in receiving and transmitting [evil]. If the former kings in their government did not match the thoughts *(xin)* and intentions *(yi)* of heaven and earth, this did not happen because a single individual would have upset Heaven. Because Heaven was annoyed and angry, plagues and diseases and natural calamities occurred in ten thousand different forms. Those who later came to the throne continued to receive and transmit [evil]. Should this not be put to a halt? So the book has been published exactly for this purpose. Thus it says, "The great worthies of antiquity originally all knew the way of nourishing their own person." So they understood the purpose of government and suffered hardly any loss from the reception and transmission [of evil]. In the generations that followed masters who instructed others would often hide texts on the true and essential teachings. Instead they would teach how to indulge in luxuries. Thus men trespassed against the essential aim of the Dao of Heaven, which caused later generations to become more superficial and daily grow more shallow until they became unable to nourish and cherish their own person. Since this had lasted for a long period they moved away from the Dao. This is to say that the world lost the art by which men retain their person safe and complete. This gave rise to a neglect of affairs, a fight for income and position and thus the calamity of receiving and transmitting [evil]. How can you be [un]aware of what it means "to give an explanation"?

Excellent! To hear the Celestial Master speak is like the appearance of the sun when the clouds open up—in no way different.

Fine, let us assume that you now have grasped the intention of the Dao.

This foolish pupil is grateful for your kindness, and has already learned a lot. If my questions do not suffice, would the Celestial Master please continue to reprimand and to warn me?

Yes. A man can only nourish others when he can thoroughly nourish his own person. A man can only cherish others when he can truly cherish himself.[2] If someone who has a body[3] were to neglect it, how should he, unable to nourish his own person, be capable of nourishing someone else well? If he were not able to keep his own body intact by truly cherishing it in order to carefully safeguard the ancestral line, how should he be able to take care of others and keep them intact?

How foolish I am.

Don't you think that you should comprehend it more fully?

Yes, very well.

Fine. You propose that my book cannot be trusted. Imagine that you checked from beginning to end all the texts, which in early antiquity were seen to match the thoughts of Heaven and prolong happiness; and also the texts written on bamboo slips which in middle antiquity were judged to match the thoughts of Heaven; and furthermore the texts, which in late antiquity have been considered important for complying with the will of Heaven and prolonging self-preservation. You would find them all adhering to the same universal standards. As your blindness will dissolve, you will have great trust in the words of my book. Now that Heaven is upset with men, these later generations become every day more careless and easygoing. They risk their lives to test their talents. Some very foolish people say that Heaven is without knowledge and claim that it does not retaliate. But the earth does not deceive men. If you sow millet you will harvest millet, and if you sow wheat you will harvest wheat. If you work hard your harvest will be good. How much more so for Heaven! These very foolish people do not know that Heaven is filled with strong resentment. They go on teaching each other to take things easy and act foolishly. In later generations this has grown more serious from day to day. It brings about large numbers of natural disasters and monstrosities. These are in fact the profound favors that Heaven bestows on a ruler, just as it is a sign of kindness between father and son that they instruct each other. When a foolish person observes such disasters he will not in good time announce them to the ruler but instead keep them hidden. Thus he will cut off a path to Heaven, which will increase Heaven's rage. After this any increase in the reception and transmission [of evil] can no longer be influenced. Even a ruler who had the moral goodness of ten thousand men would still for no particular reason continue to suffer from it. Thus one might be led to presume that to do good is unreasonable, as it does not bring any benefit. This enables the very foolish to say that Heaven is without knowledge. Truly, how could there be any grounds for such a claim!

When I hear the words of the Celestial Master my heart is enlightened as if I had been born again. Excellent, indeed! Although this has often caused the Celestial Master trouble, I have asked questions at all costs. If I was mistaken to start with, I have now, after all the questioning, understood the meaning of "explanation." I feel happy and without regret. Not to ask about what one does not to know means that one has no way of comprehending clearly.

What you have said is right. You may go; the book is in all respects ready, from head to foot; from belly to back and from outside to inside it is complete, and will on its own inform all worthy people. There is no need for further questions.

Yes.

Subchapter 48: A Model to Explain the Reception and Transmission [of Evil] in Five Situations

This slow-witted pupil twice bows before the Celestial Master and says: If a person of great worth hears how a teacher discusses one aspect, he will know all four aspects. If a person of lesser worth hears how a teacher discusses one antithesis he will know all four antitheses. Thus it becomes easy to discuss matters. But I am so foolish and slow-witted that I cannot make use of the discussions that I have heard. I still continue to be in doubt. So I dare to ask you about everything: You have explained how majestic Heaven hates the reception and transmission [of evil], how august Earth puts forward natural disasters in response to it, how rulers suffer from it, what wrongdoings it evokes among the hundred families,[4] and how it afflicts all twelve thousand plants and creatures with punishments.

He said moreover: *This very foolish pupil is asking questions because Heaven wants me to do so. So I would not dare to risk leaving something unmentioned but want to hear the meaning of everything.*

Speak freely.

Now, ruler as well as the people receive [evil] and pass it on. Do all situations contain their own element of such reception and transmission?

Good! The question you have raised, on behalf of Heaven, is sincere, detailed, and circumspect.

Now whenever I meet the Celestial Master it is always understood that I raise questions concerning doubtful matters only because Heaven demands it. So how could I dare not to be detailed?

Good, your intentions are excellent, so let us proceed according to certain situations. Or would you prefer to have me explain it all in full? I would not mind the exertion, but I am afraid a text that is too long might be difficult to put to use. If I were to interpret all the world's reception and transmission [of evil], this would be difficult to manage in that ten million characters would still be too few. I will present you with an outline, and we will then let everyone who is worthy join the project so that our aim will be reached, as if by contract.

If only the Celestial Master would speak!

You must keep both your ears open, sit still, and listen with a calm heart.

Yes, I will.

Although Heaven and Earth have given birth to all creatures and plants, they also cause injuries when virtue is lacking. Thus the world is in disorder as if it were clouded. Families are poor and needy, the old and weak are hungry and cold, county offices derive no income, the granaries have been emptied. Although such evil stems from the earth when it inflicts harm on plants, men receive and transmit it. Now for one case the consequences have been explained. You must continue to listen carefully.

If one teacher addressing ten students should misrepresent the facts and the ten students would in turn each address ten students, this would amount to one hundred men speaking falsely. If these hundred men were to address ten men each this would amount to one thousand men giving wrong accounts. If a thousand men were to address ten men each there would be ten thousand men who speak falsely. If all these ten thousand men were to raise their voice into all four directions, the world as a whole would speak falsely. Moreover, should a large number of words from various traditions support each other, they would become irrefutable and be considered standard language. This goes back to one single person who missed the truth in what he said. But in turn this made all these men miss the truth, which upset the validity of the correct texts revealed by Heaven. For this reason customs would be altered and habits changed. Although the world might see all this as a great ill, they would not be able to bring it to a halt. It would get worse as time went by because peril would be received and transmitted from one generation to the next. Clearly, this would not just be a mistake committed by later generations. [However,] these later generations would not know that the point where it came from lay in the distance. Instead they would hold their contemporaries responsible, thereby intensifying the resentment felt by one against the other. This, in turn, would prevent the dissolution of embolized vital energy *(qi)* but would make it daily more persistent. Now two cases have been explained, but you must continue to listen carefully.

Imagine in the center of town, where roads from all directions cross, someone were to put on a great show in order to trick people. He would proclaim that the earth was flooded and about to turn into a lake. He might even shed tears while speaking. The people on their return home from the market would tell each other, all the thousand households would learn about it, the aged as well as the infirm, grown-ups as well as children would discuss it at the crossroads until the whole world would know. But once the world had been deceived, this deception would increase as if distance made it grow. It stemmed from the words of one man, so responsibility for it all rests with the receiving and transmitting of empty and false words. Where lies the mistake of later generations? In that they blame their contemporaries. Now three situations have been explained. You must however continue to listen carefully.

There is a large tree in the southern mountains which is so wide and long that it forms a ceiling over several hundred paces of ground, while its trunk is just one. Above the ground it has innumerable branches, leaves, and fruits, which may all suffer injury from storm or rain should the root below the ground not cling tightly to the soil. If this were the case, all the many millions of branches, leaves, and fruits would die from such injury. This is the big evil that is received and transmitted by all ten thousand plants and trees. This evil lies with the root and not with the branches. If the branches were accused instead, wouldn't they become even more resentful?

But if the branches are without fault, there is no reason why they should suffer death from such disasters.

This is exactly what the punishment of receiving and transmitting [evil] is all about. How can one accuse those who are born later? Four situations have been explained. You must, however, continue to listen carefully.

The southern mountains harbor poisonous vapors that they don't lock up very well. Thus in spring winds from the south bring disease along and will even hide sun and moon. Large numbers of people become infected and die. At the root is nothing else but the vapor released by the southern mountains. What reason should there be to let all the world receive and transmit a deadly disease? People of our times will, however, discuss this matter as if there were some moral transgression, and Heaven would kill because it found fault with a certain person. How should this not bring about resentment? If someone has received and transmitted this disaster without having done any wrong, his spirit will become resentful [after death]. Thus the living will heap even more accusations on him. His vital energy *(qi),* embolized by resentment, will affect Heaven above. All this distress is rooted in the mountains' bad vapors that are brought along by the wind. It is the same with the punishment of receiving and transmitting [evil].

Five situations have been explained, but you must continue to sit straight and listen to the particulars I shall speak about. All that was taught was originally reliable and correct. It would never falsely deceive men. But by confronting what former rulers, teachers, and fathers had taught, men lost a little of this correctness; that is, they lost the correct way of expression as well as the correct way of nourishing their own person. Since men learned from imitating each other it became worse from day to day for those born later. For this reason, over a long period nothing of what they taught each other has been true. They don't have the means to stop the world from being false. Thus natural calamities and monstrosities occur ten-thousand-fold, impossible to record. Their causes have been added one to the other over a long time, again and again. Yet foolish men know no better than to find fault with their own leaders and to make accusations against their contemporaries. So how should they avoid becoming entangled in even further resentment? The world is unable to become self-aware of all these perversities. Even if a single ruler had the virtue of ten thousand men, what could he do about this by himself? Concerning the conduct of men nowadays, how can they find a solution? Or supposing that there is food, and people wish to get all of it for themselves, so that only the sick man cannot eat and ends up dying. How can there be any solution? When in intercourse you reach the climax, you will look forward to having sons and grandsons. You might bring offerings to the deities and beg for good fortune, but still be unable to have children. How can there be any solution? When they have children men want them to be good and strong, but they might in fact be unworthy of their parents and turn out bad. How could there be any solution? All this is proof of the reception and transmission [of evil]. But to turn around and accuse one's contemporaries would lead to the destabilization of government. The men of our times have for so long suffered from deception. How should they all of a sudden be capable of reform? It has led to an ongoing resentment that has now lasted for so long that Heaven takes pity. Thus you must not be surprised should the highest majestic Dao in concert with the primordial vapor descend upon us.

Where should we begin?

By guarding the One in your thoughts.

How?

The One is the beginning of all numbers; the One is the way of life; the One is that which gives rise to the primordial vapor; the One is the hawser of Heaven. Therefore, if you keep thinking of the One, you move from high above to effect changes down below. But all ten thousand creatures make the mistake of stressing what equals the boughs and branches of an activity instead of referring back to its root. As long as these errors remain unresolved, a return to the root is even more appropriate.

Thus, when the wise men of antiquity where about to take action, they examined the patterns of the sky and investigated the structures of the earth. This clearly proves that they went back to the root of things. Do you understand?

Yes, I do.

Now, out of consideration for your distress, I have spelled out the gist of the doctrine of receiving and transmitting [evil]. Do you comprehend that all situations in this way involve this reception and transmission?

Yes. Now that you have given me the gist of it the knot in this foolish pupil's mind has become untied.

Fine. The essential message is the following: In early antiquity, men able to stabilize government through their grasp of the Way were merely engaged in nourishing their own person and preserving their root. In middle antiquity, when their grasp slackened, they became a little careless in regard to nourishing their own person and lost their root. In late antiquity, plans were not well drafted, and men held their body in light esteem, arguing that they could get another one. Thus, by greatly erring, they brought disorder upon their government. Nevertheless, this is not a mistake committed by the people of late antiquity, but the peril that results from receiving and transmitting [evil]. Since this has been repeatedly stressed in the text, I will speak no further. There is nothing to be gained from saying the same thing a hundred times. Now that Heaven's words have reached you there is no need for further additions to this text.

Yes.

You may go and return home to think about the essentials of [this message]. If given to a virtuous ruler, this book should dissolve (explain) the reception and transmission [of evil].

Yes, indeed!

—BH

Notes

1. *Jie:* this character means "to explain" and "to dissolve," an ambiguity that is of relevance to the wording of this chapter.

2. See *Daode jing* (i.e., *Tao te ching*), chap. 72.

3. See *Daode jing,* chap. 13.

4. The hundred families or hundred surnames refer to the populace as a whole.

CAO PI (187–226) was the second son of the formidable military dictator Cao Cao (155–220), whose story is told in *Romance of the Three Kingdoms (Sanguo yanyi),* and the elder brother of the poet Cao Zhi (192–232). He ended the puppet rule of the last Eastern Han emperor and founded the Wei dynasty in 220; thus he is also known as Emperor Wen of the Wei. Like his father and brother, Cao Pi was an accomplished writer and poet. His "Discourse on Literature" (Lun wen) survives from a critical work entitled *A Treatise on the Classics (Dianlun),* of which only some fragments are extant. One of the most notable things about this essay is Cao Pi's use of the notion of *qi,* breath or vital force, as a concept of literary criticism that has had an immense influence on classical Chinese literary thought.

"A Discourse on Literature" is itself a beautiful literary composition. It is particularly touching because we see in it a writer who was secretly anxious and insecure about the value of his work and the uncertain possibility of immortal fame. A great deal of the first part of the essay is devoted to the reasoning that one's literary talent is an inherent quality that cannot be learned or obtained by hard efforts *(li qiang);* in the second part of the essay, he claims that a person may achieve literary immortality by exerting himself *(qiang li).* The unconscious inconsistency in the argument is both human and poignant.—XFT

A Discourse on Literature

Literary men disparage one another; this has been so since antiquity. Fu Yi and Ban Gu were equal in their literary merit, and yet when Ban Gu wrote to his brother Ban Chao, he belittled Fu Yi by saying, "Wuzhong has been appointed the clerk of the Magnolia Terrace because he is skillful in composition, but his problem is that once he starts writing, he cannot stop himself."[1]

People are all eager to flaunt their special talent. However, there are many different literary genres, and few can excel at all of them. Thereupon each person takes pride in his particular strength and uses it to deprecate another's weakness. As a common saying has it, "A tattered broom is worth a thousand pieces of gold as long as it is mine." This is an evil caused by one's inability to know oneself.

Kong Rong of Lu, Chen Lin of Guangling, Wang Can of Shanyang, Xu Gan of Beihai, Ruan Yu of Chenliu, Ying Yang of Runan, Liu Zhen of Dongping—these seven masters are the literary men of the contemporary age.[2] There is nothing wanting in their learning, and there is nothing borrowed in their writings. Considering themselves as swift steeds that could effortlessly race a thousand leagues, they have galloped abreast at the same speed. No wonder they have found it difficult to concede to one another! But a true gentleman should always scrutinize himself first and then pass judgment on others, for only in this way may he be exempt from self-deception and discuss literature.

Wang Can is artful at writing poetic expositions and rhapsodies. Xu Gan sometimes falls into a rambling mode, but he is still Wang Can's match. Wang Can's rhapsodies such as "The First

Expedition," "Climbing a Tower," "Rhapsody on the Locust Tree," or "Thoughts of a Campaign" and Xu Gan's rhapsodies such as "The Black Gibbon," "The Clepsydra," "The Round Fan," or "The Tangerine" are what Zhang Heng and Cai Yong would not have been able to surpass.[3] However, it cannot be claimed that Wang and Xu are as accomplished in the other genres.

Chen Lin and Ruan Yu's memorials, letters, and memorandums are all of superior quality. Ying Yang's style is harmonious but not forceful. Liu Zhen's style is forceful but not thorough. Kong Rong's sentiments are lofty and subtle, and there is something extraordinary about him; but he cannot sustain an argument, and his propositions are often harmed by his rhetorical urge. Occasionally he mixes in bantering and jesting, and the best of these satiric pieces put him on a par with Yang Xiong and Ban Gu.[4]

Common people prize the faraway but scorn the nearby. They look up to reputation but turn their back against reality. What is more, they are afflicted by lack of self-knowledge and so tend to regard themselves as men of great worth. As far as literary writings are concerned, their root is the same but the branches are very unlike. Therefore elegance befits memorials and memorandums; lucidity well suits letters and treatises; in epigraphs and eulogies one values plain factualness; in poetry and rhapsodies one desires ornate embellishment. These genres are very different from one another, which is why a good writer is usually adept at just one of them. Only a comprehensive talent can master them all.

The essential element in literature is *qi* (vital force). One's vital force is either inherently clear or inherently turbid: one cannot change it by hard efforts. It is just like lute music: even though the score remains identical and the same rules of rhythms are followed, performances of a musical piece differ because the musicians' vital forces and individual abilities are unequal. Deftness and clumsiness are inborn qualities, which even a father cannot pass on to his son and an elder brother cannot hand down to his younger brother.

Alas! Literary works represent a great act of accomplishment that helps lead a country, a glorious enterprise that lasts throughout eternity. Sooner or later one's life will come to an end; both worldly fame and carnal pleasures are limited to a person's physical body. These things are all ephemeral and have their boundaries; none of them is as capable of permanence as great works of literature. That is why the ancient authors devoted themselves to brushes and ink, revealing their innermost thoughts in writings. Neither depending upon the records of a good historian nor the power of eminent patrons, their names have thus been transmitted to posterity.

Thus the Earl of the West[5] was imprisoned and he then completed the *Book of Changes;* the Duke of Zhou[6] became famous, and he then produced the *Rites:* the former did not abandon his endeavors because of disgrace and humiliation; the latter did not alter his resolve because of ease and comfort. Their examples show us how the ancients disdained a foot-long jade disk in favor of a moment, afraid that time would pass them by. However, people nowadays often do not exert themselves. When they are poor and lowly, they are fearful of hunger and cold; when they are rich and powerful, they indulge themselves in luxury and gaiety. In this way they only take care of the business of the present, neglecting the vocation that endures a thousand years. Days and months depart overhead; here below a person's face and body fade away. In an instant one is transformed together with a myriad of things. Herein lies the great sadness of all men with aspirations.

Kong Rong and the others have already perished; only Xu Gan, through his philosophical treatise, established a discourse of his own.

—XFT

Notes

1. Fu Yi (ca. 35–ca. 90), style Wuzhong, was a noted writer and scholar of the early Eastern Han. Ban Gu (32–92), a distinguished writer and historian, was the author of the *History of the Former Han (Hanshu)*. Ban Chao (32–102) was a famous explorer. Magnolia Terrace is where the Han emperors kept books and official archives for scholars and compilers to work on. Both Fu Yi and Ban Gu had once served in the capacity of the foreman clerk of Magnolia Terrace.

2. Kong Rong (153–208), a native of Lu (modern Shandong), was probably the eldest of the "Seven Masters of Jian'an," a designation for the seven eminent writers of the Jian'an period (196–220) that originated from this essay. Chen Lin (d. 217), a native of Guangling (in modern Jiangsu), is now primarily remembered for his poem "I Watered My Horse at a Spring by the Wall," but he had also left behind, among other things, a caustic proclamation against Cao Cao written when he was still serving the warlord Yuan Shao. Wang Can (177–217), a native of Shanyang (in modern Shandong), is acclaimed as the most distinguished of the seven in terms of his poetry and rhapsodies. Of Xu Gan's (171–217) rhapsodies, highly praised by Cao Pi, only fragments survive; but his "Treatise on the Middle Way" (Zhonglun), a philosophical work mentioned at the end of Cao Pi's essay, is still intact. Beihai is in modern Shandong. Ruan Yu (d. 212), a native of Chenliu (in modern Henan), was noted for drafting official letters and documents for Cao Cao. Ying Yang (d. 217), a native of Runan (in modern Henan), and Liu Zhen (d. 217), a native of Dongping (in modern Shandong), both served in the entourage of Cao Cao like the rest of the seven. Except for Kong Rong and Ruan Yu, all died of the great plague of 217.

3. Zhang Heng (78–139) and Cai Yong (133–192) were both famous writers and scholars of the Eastern Han.

4. Yang Xiong (53 B.C.E.–18 C.E.) was a leading scholar, poet, and philosopher of the late Western Han.

5. The Earl of the West later became King Wen of the Zhou dynasty.

6. Son of King Wen and brother of King Wu, for whom he served as counselor, of the Zhou dynasty. These three men were most important for the establishment of the second historically attested dynasty in the East Asian Heartland.

THE HISTORICITY OF Kong Zi (Master Kong), the figure known to Western audiences as Confucius, has long been a matter of speculation, particularly because there is no reliable evidence of a date of birth or death. What cannot be debated is the historical stature of a figure that by the fourth century B.C.E. appeared widely in Warring States literature. The first efforts to assign a date or occasion of birth to Kong Zi are in evidence late in the first century B.C.E. in two commentaries on the *Spring and Autumn Annals (Chunqiu),* a sketchy annalistic court chronicle of "events" in the reigns of twelve dukes of Kong Zi's home state of Lu beginning in 722 B.C.E. and ending in 481 B.C.E.

The provenance of this text, like so many of the *weishu* (apocrypha) genre, is obscure. However, according to the Tang scholar Li Xian's (651–684 C.E.) commentary on the *History of the Later Han,* the *Springs and Autumns Explanatory Kong Chart (Chunqiu wei Yan Kong tu)* is first cited in 178 C.E., although some scholars contend that it was written in the first century B.C.E. This textual tradition has not enjoyed the scholarly attention of the canonical texts; yet many of the latter contain in fragment what is complete in the former, and this is exquisitely the case with the birth stories of Kong Zi. The translated passage is taken from a late-Qing literary anthology, edited by Ma Guohan (1794–1857). It is believed that the short text (approximately seven hundred graphs) of this apocryphal excursus was assembled by the Six Dynasties–scholar Song Zhong sometime between the second and third centuries and, as is common to the *weishu,* establishes its authority through mere association with Kong Zi. In a fabulous postface to the birth account, it is stated that the *Yan Kong tu* emerged from a "blood book" which, when examined by Kong Zi's disciple Zixia, became a red bird that transformed into a white book. The themes of the birth story are those commonly found in many hero myths: fatherlessness, hierogamy, magical birth, curious physiognomy revealing the secondary mythologizing of Kong Zi characteristic of the hero cult literature of the latter Han.

Birth Story of Kong Zi from Latter Han Dynasty Apocrypha

Kong Zi's mother, Zhengzai,[1] wandered onto the slope of a large mound[2] and fell asleep. She dreamed of the Black Lord[3] whose envoy invited her to a marsh[4] on the *yisi*[5] day to copulate.[6] He said to her, "You will brood in the center of a hollow mulberry."[7] Afterward she awoke and felt pregnant[8] and gave birth to the mound[9] *(qiu)* in the center of a hollow mulberry. Thus, he was called "dark sage" *(yuansheng)*[10] when he was born. The top of his head resembled a dirt mound[11] *(niqiu);* thus [he acquired] the name.

HERE WE ARE given an explanation of the two names by which he has been known—Kong Qiu and Zhongni—and are shown that his was a miraculous birth, just like that of other culture heroes. The mound, a product of hierophany, is fatherless, something that is also explicit in the canonical account of Kong Zi's birth in Sima Qian's *Shiji*.

The narrative of the following text begins in the standard manner of the biographies in the *Records of the Grand Historian (Shiji)* with a citation of a figure's birthplace and principal ancestors. But unlike the more conventional accounts of other Warring States figures, say, Lao Zi or Zhuang Zi, Kong Zi's biography includes a terse, tantalizing account of his conception that threatens to exceed the narrative frame. Sima's official biography gives Kong Zi an interval in the era of one of Lu's rulers and explains much of what is mysterious about his birth and his name: copulation in the wild, sacrificial intercession, and the signal head deformity. The Grand Historian is unable to cast out the larger mythic themes that adhere to the story: miraculous conception and birth, orphanhood, and the overcoming of fatal adversity, all of which are found in the charter myths of the Shang and Zhou and in the *weishu* text. Moreover, Kong Zi, like so many redemptive heroes of western myth—Cyrus, *Romulus*, Hercules, Moses, and Oedipus—was orphaned and exposed, only to prevail and become the founder of a teaching later prominently patronized by the Chinese imperium.

Sima Qian, Kong Zi Birth Story from the *Records of the Grand Historian*

Chapter 47: "Hereditary Noble House of Kong Zi"

Kong Zi was born in Changping village, Zou district, Lu kingdom. His ancestor was a man of Song known as Kong Fangshu. Fangshu begot Boxia and Boxia begot Shu Liang He.[12] [Shu Liang] He and a woman of the Yan clan were joined in the wilds[13] and gave birth to Kong Zi; [it was] through sacrifice at the dirt hillock[14] [that she] got pregnant with Kong Zi. In the twenty-second year of Duke Xiang [551 B.C.E.] of Lu,[15] Kong Zi was born. He was born with a protuberance on the top of his head[16] and so he was given the name "mound." His style was Zhongni and his surname, Kong.[17] When Qiu was born, Shu Liang He died[18] and was buried at Fang Shan. Fang Shan is in eastern Lu, and so it was that Kong Zi had doubt about the place of his father's tomb;[19] his mother concealed it [from him]. Kong Zi, in playing games as a child, frequently set out and arranged ritual vessels.[20] When Kong Zi's mother died he buried her in the Road of the Five Fathers.

THE *FAMILY SAYINGS OF KONG ZI (Kong zi jiayu)* contains a far more comprehensive account of Kong Zi's antecedents in its thirty-ninth chapter, "Explication of the Original Surname," which describes the Kong clan's emergence from more than ten generations of apocryphal ancestors beginning with Weizi Qi, the first son of the legendary late-Shang king, Di Yi. The explicit attempt to join Kong Zi to the Shang signals the mythologizing temper of this narrative, a tale that begins with each male ancestor, quite fantastically, begetting his own heir. In this version, it turns out that Shu Liang He's principal wife, a woman of the Shi clan of Lu, bore him nine children, all daughters. Because he was without an heir, Shu sought an able male descendant through a concubine. This unnamed concubine gave Shu Liang He a son, Meng Pi or Boni, whose feeble foot represented a deformity sufficient to disqualify his inheritance, thus presenting a narrative stage for the arrival of Kong Zi.

Wang Su, *Family Sayings of Kong Zi*

Chapter 39: Explication of the Original Surname

Meng Pi, called Boni, had a foot disease. Thus [Shu] sought marriage in the Yan clan. The Yan clan[21] had three daughters, the youngest being called Zhengzai. Father Yan inquired of his three daughters saying, "[This is] the minister of Zou, whose father and grandfather were only scholars, but whose ancestors were the descendants of sages and kings of the Shang.[22] Today he has a height of ten feet[23] and [because of] his unparalleled martial prowess, I eagerly seek [to establish a bond with] him. While he is advanced in age and curmudgeonly, [however] I doubt you would be unsatisfied. Of the three of you, who is able to be his wife?" Two of the daughters did not respond. Zhengzai approached, saying, "Since it is from you, Father, that it is arranged, how will there be any question about it?" The father said, "Very well then, you can." It followed that [Shu He] took her (Zhengzai) as his wife. Zhengzai traveled to a temple to worship,[24] fearing that due to her husband's advanced age there would be no opportunity to bear a son.[25] She herself beseeched Mount Niqiu and offered sacrifice there.[26] She gave birth to Kong Zi, and thus called him "Mound," giving him the style Zhongni. When Kong Zi was three years old, Shu Liang He died[27] and was buried at Fang.

ADDITIONAL LAYERS OF the birth story are added in this account. The *Jiayu* elects to ignore the remarkable matter of outdoor intercourse (*yehe*) while directly addressing the fertility sacrifice of the *Shiji* fable, volunteering that Zhengzai's worship was conditioned by a reasonable fear of Shu Liang He's impotence. The received explanation for Sima Qian's use of *ye* to describe the relations of Shu Liang He and Zhengzai comes from the *Kong Zi jiayu* and insists that Zhengzai was a young girl, young enough to be Shu's granddaughter, and, therefore, their union was inappropriate. But was the marriage truly illicit? Lesser, or second, wives had already achieved a customary status among Zhou elite, not to mention with the grandees of Wang Su's day. Consequently, it is the explanation, rather than the union, that seems inappropriate, as it reaches beyond what the text tells us. On this matter the texts are in conscious dialogue, the *Kong Zi jiayu* story appearing as a justificatory explication of the ambiguities in the *Shiji* biography. And yet as they argue against each other, these normative accounts are both constituted against the grain of other ritual and mythic lore as revealed through juxtaposition with the *weishu* account. What emerges from this less obvious dialogue is the "narrative strain" of accommodating or even explaining mythic elements within the structure of a plot of biography and lineage citation.

—LMJ

Notes

1. Literally the name means "Summon Now" or "Fulfillment Has Arrived"; however, just as important is that the graph for Zheng also may be read as *zhi*, the last note of the Chinese pentatonic scale. In other magical accounts of the birth such as that found in the Song collection of Tang and earlier stories called *Taiping guangji*, the musicality of the union of Zhengzai and another god, Tiandi, is more prominent. In another *weishu* text from the Six Dynasties period, Kong Zi, ignorant of his name, blows on the pitchpipes to recover his identity in the sound of the fifth note, *zhi*, which astrologically linked him to the Black Lord (Hei di). See note 3.

2. *Dameng,* large mound. The mound and the marsh mark peculiar features in the physiognomy of the landscape signaling that the territory that the reader enters here is an unusual, even magical one.

3. This critical prologue to the birth story occurs in a dream, thus at a metanarrative level. Kong Zi's father is not a man but a god, Hei di (Black Lord), a mythical figure with distinct astrological associations. Hei di might refer to Hei hou (Black Ruler), one of the Five Celestial Rulers whose nature is described as the Black Warrior, the grand northern constellation, the fourth asterism of which is *qiu* of Kong Qiu. The Black Ruler is linked with the north, winter, and the fifth musical note, *zhi.* Furthermore, black is also the emblematic color of the Shang from whom, it is claimed, Kong Zi was descended. The symbolism suggests the winter solstice.

4. Marsh in this instance is *meng* and is graphically indistinguishable from *meng* "to dream," thus recalling Zhengzai's dream of the Black Lord.

5. *Yisi* is the darkest date of the Chinese cyclical calendar and represents the depth of the cosmic, female force of yin.

6. Through an ambiguous succession of dream and command, she is inseminated by the Black Lord.

7. *Kongsang zhi zhong* (center of a hollow mulberry) is a common image in legendary stories from the Warring States and Han periods. The mulberry also plays a central role in the charter myth of the Shang people. *Kongsang* (hollow mulberry) has been identified as an *axis mundi,* a magical juncture through which heaven and earth are connected. In a varied literature from the late Warring States era on, *kongsang* or *qiong* (exhausted; impoverished; empty) *sang* has been identified as a geographic site, a mountain, and a tree and located in the east, west, north, and south. Aside from the mythological symbolism, there is a distinct sexual symbolism at work in references to the mulberry *(Morus alba).* The mulberry, as is characteristic of plants of the nettle order, has small, clustered unisexual flowers, but it differs in possessing a milky sap. It is wind pollinated, and each female flower produces a single seed. A dicotyledon, the mulberry embryo sprouts two cotyledons with the seed leaves of one providing food for the other, which is enclosed in an ovary that later becomes a fruit. Its vascular tissue is arrayed in a ring and so is conducive to womb-like hollowing. The sexual sympathy explicit in the plant explains its usefulness as analogy for conception and birth, and the manner of its pollination and reproductive mechanism reiterates the male superfluity theme of the story. A similar theme is present in the birth stories of Jesus, the Buddha, and other founder figures.

8. The term *gan* is doubly significant. It is used here to refer to an incipience in the womb, and is also commonly employed to convey the harmony of sentiment binding the dead ancestor and the living worshiper in the cult of the dead. Thus, it reinforces the fertile associations of the burial mound site of Zhengzai's dream.

9. Though the story is identified as that of Kong Zi's birth, the celebrated figure is known only as "mound" in the narrative, unlike the stories from the normative texts such as the *Shiji* and the *Kong Zi jiayu* which refer to him as Kong Zi. The links between earthen mounds and successful birth are confirmed in recently excavated Warring States medical literature from the tombs at Mawangdui in Hunan. In the *Manual of Childbirth (Taichan shu),* readers are informed that, just before birth is to occur, a small mound of moist, clean earth is to be made. Following birth, the child is to be placed on the mound and covered with dirt. This practice ensures the strength of the child through its absorption of the yin nature of the earth. However, the earliest gloss of *qiu (Shuowen jiezi,* ca. 120 C.E.) asserts it is "elevated earth that is not man-made," explicitly distinguishing it from the dirt mound made by parents for the initiation of the child.

10. Here *yuan* is construed as standing for *xuan* (dark, black, abstruse), a term with which it is often exchanged in old texts. (Phonologically, their ancient pronunciations [respectively, **ngiwǎn* and **g'iwen*] are similar.) *Yuansheng* recalls the darkness of his male parent, affirming his descent from the Black Lord. *Yuan,* however, is more commonly glossed as "originary" or "primordial," suggesting an exclusiveness appropriate to a founder. The dark sage epithet has been explained as a metaphor for the dirt *(ni)* that rested in the concavity of his deformed head; yet it is more likely that it was an astrological designation, particularly considering the coincidence of the birth with the winter solstice.

11. Here the explanation of his name *qiu* is purely metaphorical, based, as it is, upon resemblance. Other accounts will elaborate upon the cranial metaphor to establish a "Mount Ni" at which petitional sacrifice was performed.

12. The original surname having been abandoned upon relocation to Zou, his father's surname is not Kong but Shu. The three graphs of the name—*shu* (a father's younger brother; to gather or harvest), *liang* (fishtrap; spiked millet), and *he* (fringe)—are wonderfully suggestive. Kong Zi's father never appears in the

Analects (Lunyu), and references to him are scant in the pre-Han literature, with only two vague mentions in the *Zuo Commentary (Zuozhuan),* neither of which asserts a definitive familial link between the two figures.

13. *Yehe* (wilderness union). The marsh of the *weishu* account and site of the magical insemination of Zhengzai is reduced to outdoor intercourse in the wild with a male figure. Later commentators on the *Shiji* such as Sima Zhen (8th c. C.E.) attempted to explain away the rude sexual conjunction by stating that the *ye* was a comment on the inappropriateness of the union between the youngest daughter of the Yan clan and a septuagenarian.

14. *Niqiu* (Mount Ni) is a mound in the wild either where Kong Zi was conceived or where Zhengzai performed a petitional sacrifice that ensured her bearing an heir. According to this reading, the magical site is memorialized in his names.

15. This is the date of birth as cited in the *Gongliang* (150 B.C.E.) and *Guliang* (100 B.C.E.) commentaries on the *Spring and Autumn Annals* and repeated here by Sima Qian. Though these earlier accounts note that the birth occurred after a sequence of total eclipses, Sima Qian neglects to mention the astronomy in favor of the year of the reign of Prince Xiang in the chronicle of the state of Lu.

16. This is the first instance of exposition of his given name. The descriptions of the top of his head vary from concave to convex, but what is consistent in all accounts is that this misshapenness was the reason for his unusual name.

17. The surname Kong itself is highly suggestive, because it literally means "hole, opening," recalling the hollow mulberry of the *weishu* account.

18. The fatherlessness of the mythic hero is asserted here in the simultaneity of Kong Zi's birth and his father's death. The intercourse and conception occurred between two parents rather than between Zhengzai and a god, but the implication is the same.

19. Indeed, Kong Zi knows nothing of his father, not even the location of his tomb. He is barred from conducting sacrifice to his progenitor and in this way is without a meaningful familial identity, and so he plays with ritual objects, the instrumental form of the rite whose details Kong Zi does not know.

20. The evident impropriety of the hero in the previous sentence is overcome here in the statement of his congenital inclination toward ritual objects, followed by the burial of his mother. Kong Zi's play with ritual artifacts may be used here to suggest his instinctual understanding of his ritual obligations to his father.

21. *Yan* (color), especially of the face or for painting, suggests the performing culture of the actor or the shaman. The surname itself recalls the claim of some scholars that the Yan were a clan of shamans.

22. Rather than astrological suggestions of descent from the Shang, Wang Su's account asserts the popular Han presumption of Kong Zi's descent from Shang royalty.

23. Even though the Chinese foot, *chi* is less than twelve inches, the height of ten feet is intended to convey the fantastic—a giant. Less fantastic than the *weishu* account, Wang's narrative still depends on making Kong Zi's father a narrative link joining Kong Zi with gods and the Shang. Later *weishu* accounts recuperate this fabulist physiognomy by putting Kong Zi's adult height in Chinese measurement at nine feet six inches.

24. *Miao* (temple), not an outdoor altar or funeral mound, marks the site of Zhengzai's prayer.

25. Here the suggestion that the union of Shu Liang He and Zhengzai was inappropriate is touched on in another way, that is, through the assertion of the latter's concern over her husband's infertility. In this instance, the account of the birth is expanded as a preface to the actual event.

26. Mount Ni has given way to Mount Niqiu on which there is a temple, and it is here that Zhengzai performs the *si* sacrifice. The *si* sacrifice, however, was not performed outdoors but inside the clan compound of the Zhou. It was the *yin* sacrifice, not mentioned here by Wang, that was performed outdoors on an earthen mound *(yin).*

27. Unlike the *Shiji* account, in which the father's death coincides with Kong Zi's birth, the *Kong Zi jiayu* displays the allusive remnants of the filial custom by giving Kong Zi three years of life before his father dies, thus solidifying his natal right to conduct cultic remembrances to his father.

PHARMACY AS AN integral facet of the healing arts in China has its roots in antiquity. Traditionally, the beginning of experiential botanical knowledge is credited to the legendary Divine Husbandman, Shennong, the so-called father of agriculture who is said to have lived almost five millennia ago. There has been a vast amount of information recorded over the centuries concerning the medicinal qualities of plants, minerals, and other substances, compiled into a very large number of compendia over the centuries. The two most renowned systematizers of materia medica are Tao Hongjing (456–536) and Li Shizhen (1518–1593), and their works are the standards of the genre known as *bencao,* literally "roots and grasses" (or, according to some traditions, "basic herbs"). *Bencao* actually signifies all types of organic and inorganic materials that were understood as having some kind of utility within the healing arts and within other esoteric traditions concerning the perfection of body and spirit. The genre itself commonly is traced back to a work known as *The Bencao of Shennong,* or *The Divine Husbandman's Canon of Materia Medica,* parts of which may date to the late Warring States and the Former Han, with accretions from as late as the Later Han. The early textual history of this work is highly problematic. The earliest known version was edited by Tao Hongjing together with commentaries, and the work mostly has existed over the centuries as excerpts in larger compendia; it has been reconstructed a number of times in various recensions, but since early in the twentieth century it has been widely available in the "standardized" edition from which the excerpts below are translated. People of the Han were interested in materia medica not only for curative purposes; equally important were the qualities of the substances that might be of alchemical or macrobiotic value. At the time much thought and practice was devoted to toning the mind and body of the adept toward prolonged life and the hope of becoming a *xian,* or transcendent. It probably is not coincidental that the first substance mentioned in the work attributed to Shennong is *dansha,* cinnabar, a naturally occurring form of mercuric sulfide that was seen as the elixir ingredient par excellence. The book is said to originally have described 365 substances (corresponding to the number of days in the year and implying completeness), divided into three categories according to their medicinal utility. While these categories also correspond to Han ideas of the two threefold groupings of heaven, earth, and man, and ruler, minister, and subject, a quotation from another source that is attributed to *Shennong's Canon of Materia Medica* describes the threefold division as follows: "Of all the medicinal substances, those of the highest order nourish one's life span, those of the middle order nourish one's nature, and those of the lowest order nourish the ailing." Materia medica on the whole are described according to their properties in terms of the categorical identifiers of "taste," "temperature," and modes of efficacy. The entries are terse and most often do not furnish much empirical information, such as description of the substance for the purposes of identification, or mention of curative value and how it should be ingested or otherwise used. The brief introductory notice to each of the three sections of the canon is translated below, followed by an example from each of the sections.—AB

Of the highest order of medicaments there are 120 varieties. They act in the role of "ruler." They have a controlling influence on the nourishing of one's life span and thereby correspond with Heaven. There are none that are toxic. Ingesting them often and over a long period of time will not harm a person. Those who desire to make their bodies light, increase their *qi,* not age, and extend their years take as their basis the first division of the canon.

Of the median order of medicaments there are 120 varieties. They act in the role of "minister." They have a controlling influence on the nourishing of one's nature and thereby correspond with man. Some are toxic and some are nontoxic. One should carefully consider their suitability (i.e., use them with discretion). Those who desire to curtail illness and replenish depletion take as their basis the middle division of the canon.

Of the inferior order of medicaments there are 125 varieties. They act in the role of "attendants and functionaries." They have a controlling influence on the curing of ailments and thereby correspond with earth. Most are toxic and cannot be ingested for long periods. Those who desire to expel "cold," "hot," and noxious *qi,* break down accumulations, and heal illness take as their basis the final division of the canon.

[From the first division:]

Ginseng *(renshen; Panax ginseng).* The taste is of the category of "sweet." It is classed as "slightly cold." It has a controlling influence on replenishing the five visceral "storage organs" (corresponding to heart, liver, spleen, lungs, and kidneys), calming the vital forces, stabilizing the souls, stopping alarm and fear, expelling noxious *qi,* clarifying vision, developing the heart, and increasing wisdom. Prolonged ingestion will make the body light and extend one's years. It also is called *renxian* or *guigai.* It grows in mountain valleys.

NOTE: GINSENG WAS, and still is, the medicinal substance par excellence, being prescribed for innumerable ailments and credited with great tonic and restorative properties. Its name likely derives from the resemblance of its root to a person [*ren*], and the influences it imparts from the Orion constellation [*shen*], but it has no fewer than ten other appellations. Although the part of the plant to receive the most attention has been the root, the leaves were also occasionally used. As with nearly all plants mentioned in *The Divine Husbandman's Canon of Materia Medica,* ginseng is still a part of traditional Chinese pharmacology; it also has had a place in Western European and North American healing traditions.

[From the middle division:]

Angelica *(baizhi; Angelica anomala).* The taste is of the category of "pungent." It is classed as "warm." It has a controlling influence on women's menstrual flow and reddens pale blood. It impedes yin-induced swelling, cold and hot "winds," oppression of the head, and tears from the eyes. It produces enduring sinews and flesh, and as it is moist and enriching, it can be used as a facial cosmetic. It also is called *fangxiang* and grows in river valleys.

NOTE: ANGELICA HAD no fewer than nine different names; both its root and leaves were used. Angelica also is part of the modern Chinese herbal tradition, as well as that of the West.

[From the final division:]

Skimmia *(yinyu; Skimmia japonica,* sometimes called *anquetilia).* The flavor is of the category of "bitter." It is classed as "warm." It has a controlling influence on noxious *qi* of the five visceral "storage organs"; on "cold" and "hot" of the heart and stomach; on consumption; on conditions similar to ague (or malaria) where the symptoms flare up at regular intervals; and on the pain of arthritis and rheumatism of the various joints. It grows in river valleys.

NOTE: THIS POISONOUS evergreen shrub was considered to have tonic and restorative properties. Pills and tinctures made from the leaves and stalks were considered particularly effective in relieving discomforts of the joints and extremities.

—AB

IN CHINA, THE customary path for the educated man was to become a scholar-official, one who could apply his knowledge and talent to the benefit of the state and the people through an official position in the state administration. While this path might lead to worldly success and an enduring legacy, it also could lead to frustration and compromise in terms of realizing one's personal aspirations, or perhaps to censure and punishment, or even execution, because of complicity in the doings of a faction that lost power or influence. Some men, however, forewent or withdrew from office, choosing instead to remain "in reclusion": disengaged from worldly affairs, freed from compromise, and resolved to the fulfillment of their lofty, individualistic pursuits. These High-minded Men achieved recognition by centuries and centuries of scholar-officials for having forged an alternative to the conventional life of service to the state, and as a rule they were appreciated as exponents of the sort of freedom that those bound to official position could never attain. Often portrayed as uncompromising in ethical conduct, unconventional in lifestyle, or unencumbered in mindset and doings, these High-minded Men were portrayed as the antithesis of the government official. They commonly were associated with mountains and the wilderness, their place of residence often being portrayed as a private spot far away from the centers of political and worldly activities, so they sometimes have been termed "recluses" or "hermits" in English; in Chinese they commonly are known as "Hidden Men," "Disengaged Persons," or "High-minded Men."

Copious references to High-minded Men are found throughout Chinese writings from the earliest times through the present, and at least since the beginning of the Common Era biographical accounts of these men were compiled in a very large number of books, for reference, for edification, or for appreciation. The earliest extant compilation of these accounts is Huangfu Mi's (215–282) *Accounts of High-minded Men (Gaoshi zhuan)*. Huangfu Mi himself practiced reclusion as a way of life, and later compilations of the lives of men in reclusion invariably would include an account of him, too. Like Huangfu Mi, all of the people whose accounts Huangfu Mi chose to include in his *Accounts of High-minded Men* practiced reclusion; in their own way they shunned political involvement and eschewed appointments in the central administration. Huangfu Mi's preface to his *Accounts* is brief, but it provides explicit information concerning the author's intentions and his understanding of the parameters of substantive reclusion; furthermore, Huangfu Mi's compilation by and large set the pattern for how reclusion came to be seen in traditional Chinese culture. Huangfu Mi's initial remarks establish the validity of reclusion since great antiquity and include a number of classical justifications. He then goes on to critique earlier compilations of accounts of reclusion and ends by expressing his own intentions. He is explicit that principled suicide was not to be considered within the compass of his vision of high-minded conduct. The individuals whose biographies are included below from Huangfu Mi's *Accounts* all have been celebrated in Chinese writings throughout the ages as High-minded Men par excellence.—AB

Preface

Confucius stated that "[King Wu of Zhou] called to office those who had retired into obscurity, so that throughout the kingdom the hearts of the people turned toward him." Master Hongya established the Way of High-mindedness during the age of the earliest emperors, and Xu You and Shanjuan would not let down their resolve during the reigns of Tang and Yu (i.e., the legendary Emperors Yao and Shun). [Through the Three Ages of Antiquity, the Qin and the Han, and down to the Wei arising and receiving the mandate, in all these times the rulers of worthy men in each and every case extended invitation to those who were secluded in the cliffside crannies, and sought after those who had withdrawn from the age. (Note from *Taiping yulan*)]

On account of this, in [the *Book of*] *Changes* there are the implications of (gifts to worthy men of) "bundled silk," and in [the *Book of*] *Rites* there is the institution of (ritually bestowed) "dark-colored pecuniary silks." The poets issued forth the song "White Colt" (about the flight of the worthy man from an unworthy court); the *Spring and Autumn* [*Annals*] extolled the integrity of Zizang (who declined the throne on principle); and according to the "Monthly Ordinances of the Hall of Clarity," during the final month of spring, one should "extend invitations to renowned gentlemen and pay ceremony to worthy ones." This being the case, then, gentlemen who loftily made renunciations were the ones promoted by the regal government, serving the function of curbing corruption and quelling avarice.

Many are those [men-in-reclusion] who were omitted or passed over by the [Grand] Historian [Sima Qian] and Ban [Gu] (in their comprehensive histories of the times). Liang Hong (before 24–after 80 B.C.E.) eulogized Disengaged Persons, and Su Shun (late 1st–early 2nd c. C.E.) classified High-minded Gentlemen. Some, in recording also cases of letting down one's resolve, were indiscriminate and adulterated. Others selected from the Qin and Han of recent times, and did not reach back to the distant past. Now, when we contemplate these men, we especially adore what they have established; how much more so should we acclaim their virtue and extoll their deeds!

I, Mi, have selected from past and present the men of eight ages who themselves were not humbled by a king or a lord and whose reputations were not dissipated by the passage of time, from [the time of] Yao down to the Wei, more than ninety men in all. All those who may [simply] have held fast to their resolve in the manner of [Bo] Yi and [Shu] Qi (who starved to death in the mountains rather than associate with a ruler they thought to be unworthy), whose chosen acts mayhaps were like those of the two Gong (Gong Sheng, who starved himself to death rather than visit the court of the "usurper" Wang Mang, and Gong She, who often was paired with Gong Sheng as a literary reference), I do not record. Authored by Huangfu Mi.

Biographies from Huangfu Mi's *Accounts of High-minded Men*

The Nest-dwelling Elder

The so-called Nest-dwelling Elder was a Hidden Man (i.e., a man in reclusion) of the time of (the legendary emperor) Yao. He lived in the mountains, and did not pursue worldly gain. As he was old in years and slept in a nest he had made in the trees, people of the time called him the Nest-dwelling Elder. When Yao wished to cede his rule to Xu You, Xu You told the Nest-dwelling Elder, who said, "Why do you not hide yourself and keep your brilliance inside? It's as if you're no friend of mine." He then pushed him down with a blow to the chest. Xu You felt mortified and could not contain himself. He then went over to a clear and cold waterflow to rinse out his ears and wipe his eyes, and said, "In making him listen to those covetous words, I have betrayed my friend." Thereupon he departed, and they did not see each other for the rest of their lives.

Xu You

Xu You, whose courtesy-name was Wuzhong, was a man from Huaili in Yangcheng. As a person he held fast to dutiful conduct and followed the path of uprightness. He would not sit at an inappropriate placement, would not eat inappropriate victuals. He later went into reclusion amid the marshes and fertile lands. When Yao wished to cede his rule to Xu You, he told Xu You, "When sun and moon have come out, yet one does not extinguish the candle's flames, then in terms of providing illumination, are they not disadvantaged? When timely rain has fallen, yet one still irrigates and waters, then in terms of providing moisture, is that not just making work? Now you, sir, are quite established and so all under heaven is ordered; yet still I act as your surrogate. I regard myself as inadequate, and request to convey the rule of the empire to you." Xu You replied, "You brought order to the empire. As the empire already is in good order, were I to go ahead and replace you, would I be doing it for a name? A name is the guest of reality; would I be doing it to be a guest? When the wren nests in the deep woods, it takes no more than a branch. When the mole rat drinks from the river, it does no more than fill its belly. Go home and desist, m'lord! I have no use at all for the empire. Even when the man in the kitchen has not put order to the kitchen, the surrogate of the ancestors who is leading the sacrificial ceremonies certainly will not leap over the goblets and platters to replace him."[1] He did not accept and escaped away.

Nieque (Xu You's teacher) met up with Xu You and asked, "Where are you off to?" Xu You replied, "I'm escaping Yao." Nieque asked, "What are you referring to?" Xu You answered, "Now Yao understands how worthy men profit the empire, yet he does not understand how they cheat the empire. It is only people other than the worthies who understand this." Xu You thenceforth hid out plowing in the area of Song shan, the central of the five sacred peaks, at the base of Ji Mountain on the northern bank of the Ying River. For the rest of his life he showed no fancy for governing the empire.

Yao once again summoned Xu You, to be leader of nine states. Xu You did not even wish to hear about it, and rinsed out his ears on the bank of the Ying. Just then his friend, the Nest-dwelling Elder, was leading his oxen over to water them. He saw Xu You rinsing his ears and asked the reason. Xu You replied, "Yao wished to summon me to be the leader of the nine states. I loathed hearing his words, and for this reason rinsed my ears." The Nest-dwelling Elder said, "If you were to place yourself on a high cliff or in a deep vale, the roads used by men would not reach you, and who would be able to see you? You purposely flit about wishing to be heard of, seeking your fame and renown. You have fouled my oxen's mouths." He led his oxen upstream to water them.

When Xu You died, he was buried at the top of Ji Mountain. Also called Xu You's Mountain, it is located a bit more than ten tricents south of Yangcheng. Yao subsequently visited his grave and gave him the posthumous title of Lord of Ji Mountain, and thus his spirit could receive sacrifices accessory to those provided to the Five Sacred Peaks. From generation to generation he has been presented sacrificial offerings, and this practice continues up until today.

Lao Zi

Lao Zi, Li Er, with the courtesy-name Boyang, was a man from Chen. He was born during the time of the Yin (Shang) dynasty and served as principal historian for the Zhou. He was devoted to nourishing his vital essence and *qi*. He placed value on receiving from others and did not make a show of himself. He transferred to the position of historian and conservator of the archives, where he remained for more than eighty years. The *Records of the Grand Historian (Shiji)* says that it was for more than two hundred years. At the time he was known as a hidden princely man. He was given the posthumous appellation "Dan." When Confucius went to Zhou he visited Lao Zi. Recognizing him as a sage, Confucius took him as his teacher. Later, when the virtue of the Zhou declined, Lao Zi mounted a cart pulled by a black ox and entered into the area of the Greater Qin (i.e., the far western, non-Sinitic civilizations). When he was passing through the western pass, the guardian of the pass, Yin Xi, observed the ethereal emanations and knew of his arrival in advance. So he posted a description, blocked the way, and waited for him. Finally, Lao Zi did arrive as expected. Yin Xi compelled him to compose writings, so he wrote down the *Classic of the Way and Virtue (Daode jing)* in more than five thousand words. Lao Zi is considered the patriarch of the lineage of Daoist teachings. Because he was old in years, his writing was known as the *Lao Zi (Master Lao)*.

Laolai Zi

The one known as Laolai Zi was a man from (the state of) Chu. Having met with a time when the world was in disorder, he fled from the world and farmed on the sunny side of Meng Mountain. Aster and reed served for his walls, tumbleweed and artemisia were used for his room. Branches and timber served for his bed, yarrow and mugwort were used for his mat. He drank from the waters and ate wild pulse; cultivating the mountains, he sowed and planted. Someone spoke of him to the King of Chu, and the King of Chu thereupon arrived by carriage at Lai Zi's gate. Lai Zi just then was weaving a basket. The king said, "I would humbly wish to trouble you, master, with looking after the government." Laolai Zi said, "I assent." The king departed. Laolai Zi's wife returned from wood-gathering and said, "Did you agree to it?" Laolai said, "It is so." His wife then said, "Your wife has heard that one who can feed you with wine and meat can follow up with whip and cane. One who can make designs with office and salary can follow up with the executioner's axe. Your wife is one who is unable to submit to the control of another." His wife then threw down her basket and departed. Laolai Zi also followed after his wife; they stopped when they had reached Jiangnan (the territory south of the Yangtze). They said, "The hairs and feathers of birds and beasts can be plaited into clothing, and their leftover kernels are sufficient for food." Confucius once heard of their rationale, and furrowing his brows he took on a renewed countenance over it. Laolai Zi composed writings amounting to fifteen rolls (of bamboo or wooden strips), which spoke of the utility of the lineage of Daoist teachings. No one knows how he came to his end.

Yan Hui

Yan Hui, with the courtesy-name of Ziyuan, was a man from the state of Lu. He was a disciple of Confucius. He was poor, but he found joy in the Way. He withdrew to reside in the humble alleyways, sleeping with crooked elbow (for his pillow). Confucius said, "Hui, you've come from a family that is poor, and you live in the most modest circumstances. Why do you not take an official position?" Hui replied, "I do not wish to serve in office. I possess fifty *mu* (a bit less than six acres) of land outside the city wall, sufficient enough to provide porridge and gruel, and ten *mu* of gardens inside the wall, sufficient enough to produce silk and hemp (for cloth). Drumming out the musical tones *gong* and *shang* is sufficient enough for my amusement. I repeat what I have heard from you, my Master, and this is sufficient for my happiness. What would I wish to take up official service for?" Confucius was moved and took on a renewed countenance, and said, "Excellent!, Hui's convictions."

Zhuang Zhou

Zhuang Zhou (also commonly referred to as Zhuang Zi, i.e., Master Zhuang) was a man from Meng in the state of Song. When young he studied the *Lao Zi* and worked as a deputy officer in the Lacquer Garden. He subsequently left the world behind, freed himself from constraint, and no longer served in office. Of kings, lords, and men of consequence, not one could obtain his services in any particular capacity.

King Wei of Chu sent his grandees to engage Zhuang Zhou's services with hundreds in gold. Zhou just then was fishing on the banks of the Pu; grasping his fishing pole he did not pay them heed. He said, "I have heard that in Chu there is a sacred tortoise that has been dead for two thousand years. Wrapped in cloth and kept in a basket, it is stored in the temple hall. Would this tortoise prefer being regarded as precious, having his bones preserved without anything for it to do, or would it prefer living and dragging its tail in the mud?" The grandees said, "It simply would rather drag its tail in the mud." Zhuang Zi said, "Be off. I am just now dragging my tail in the mud."

Someone further invited Zhou with coins worth thousands in gold to serve as prime minister. Zhou replied, "Do you not see the sacrificial ox used in the suburban sacrificial rites? It is clothed in patterned embroidery, and fed with grasses and pulse. At the moment it is led into the great temple, it wishes it were an orphan piglet, but can it get its wish?" To the end of his life he did not serve in office.

Heshang Zhangren

As for the one known as Heshang Zhangren (the Adept by the River), it is not known from which state he hailed. He had keen understanding of the arts of Lao Zi, and hid his family and personal names, residing by the banks of the (Yellow) River. He wrote a *Commentary to the Lao Zi by Line and Section,* and for this reason he was known to the world as the Adept by the River. At the end of the Warring States period, when the feudal lords were vying with one another, all the men who expounded ideologies overcame one another with power and position. Only the Adept hid himself in reclusion, practicing the Way. He had not declined even when aged. He passed on his vocation to Anqisheng, and through it has come to be considered as a patriarch of a lineage of Daoist teachings.

Anqisheng

The one known as Anqisheng (literally, "Born in What Period?") was a man from Langya. He received his teachings from the Adept by the River and sold medicinal substances by the shores of the sea. Even when old he did not serve in office. People of his time called him the Thousand-Year-Old Elder. When Qin Shihuang, the First August Emperor of Qin, traveled to the east, he requested to speak with Anqisheng, and for three days and three nights presented gold and ceremonial jades, which straightaway were counted in the hundreds of thousands. Anqisheng moved it out to the Fuxiang Pavilion, then departed. He left behind a vermilion-colored jade pillar-foot-ing in reciprocation and left a piece of writing to be given to the First August Emperor, which read, "After several tens of years, look for me at the foot of Penglai Mountain (where Transcendents lived on an island amid the ocean)." When the Qin was vanquished, Anqisheng and his friend Kuai Tong had some associations with Xiang Yu (a contender for the empire), who wished to grant him an entitlement, but he would not accept in the end.

The Four Hoaryheads (Si hao)

The ones known as the Four Hoaryheads (Si hao) were all from Zhi in Henei (north of Luoyang, near modern Jiyuan *xian,* Henan), or, according to one source, from Ji (northeast of modern Xinxiang City, Henan, west of modern Ji *xian*). The first was called Dongyuan gong (Elder of the Eastern Garden); the second, Luli xiansheng (Master from Lu Hamlet); the third, Qili ji (Younger One from Qi Hamlet); and the fourth, Xia Huang gong (Venerable Huang from Xia). They all (were dedicated to) cultivating the Way and refining themselves; if not for a higher purpose they would be unmoved. During the time of the First Emperor of Qin, when they perceived the tyrannical way of the Qin government, they withdrew into the mountains of Lantian (some twenty-five miles southeast of the capital) and composed a song, which goes:

Hazy so hazy, the high mountains;
The deep valley twists and twines.
Fulgent, refulgent, the purple polypore:
With it we remedy hunger.
The ages of Yao and Shun are distant,
Where might we find a home?
Horses in fours, baldachins tall—
The troubles they bring too great.
Wealth and nobility may awe people, but—
 that can't compare to the way
Being poor and humble frees the will.

They then together set off into the Shangluo region (near Lantian), going into reclusion at Mount Difei to await the settling of the world. When the Qin was overthrown, the Han Emperor Gao heard of them and summoned them (for office), but they did not go. They hid themselves deeply in the Southern Mountains (i.e., Zhongnan shan); he was unable to bend them.

Xiang Zhang

Xiang Zhang, with the courtesy-name of Ziping (also known as Shang Ziping), was a man from Chaoge in Henei (northeast of western Xinxiang City, Henan). He lived in reclusion and did not serve in office. By nature he esteemed equanimity, and he was fond of and proficient in the *Lao Zi* and the *Book of Changes.* Being impoverished, he lacked the wherewithal to feed himself, but charitable people repeatedly provided food on his behalf. He accepted this, and taking for himself only what was sufficient, returned the remainder. Wang Yi, Grand Minister of Works under Wang Mang, selected him for office year after year before he came (to the capital). Yi wished to recommend him to Mang and desisted only after steadfast refusal. Xiang Zhang then secluded himself in reclusion at home. Reading the *Book of Changes,* when he came to the hexagrams "Sun" and "Yi" ("Diminution" and "Increase," i.e., loss and gain), he sighed deeply and exclaimed, "I long have known that wealth is not comparable to poverty, and that prominent status is not as good as humble circumstances. Yet I never understood how superior life was when compared with death. During the Jianwu period (25–56 C.E.), the marriages of my sons and daughters were all completed; I now declare that I am severing all familial responsibilities and will not have any further interest in them. It is to be as if I were dead." With this he then set free his will and along with Qin Qing of Beihai, a man who shared his predilections, together roamed the five sacred peaks and the great mountains. In the end it is not known what became of him.

Yan Guang

Yan Guang (also known as Zhuang Guang), with the courtesy-name of Ziling, was a man from Yuyao in Guiji (near modern Shaoxing in Zhejiang Province). When young he made a name for being high-minded, and studied at the imperial academy with the future Guangwu emperor. When that emperor took the throne, Guang then changed his family and given names, and went off hidden in reclusion. The emperor remembered how worthy he was and issued a description of him in order to seek him out. Later, the state of Qi sent in a memorial stating that there was a lone man dressed in sheepskin who fished in the wetlands. The emperor suspected that this was Guang, and sent a comfortable carriage (with padded wheels) and bolts of rich dark silk to invite him in for an official post. Three times he turned it back, but he finally arrived.

The minister of affairs (Hou) Ba and Guang went way back as friends, and Ba wished to convince Guang to relent and come to Ba's residence to speak with him. He sent Hou Zidao, the subsidiary clerk in the western administrative bureau, to present a letter to Guang, but Guang would not get up from the bed, where he sat casually with his arms around his knees. When the letter was opened and read, he asked Zidao, "Junfang (i.e., Hou Ba) has always been foolish, and now that he is in one of the three highest posts, does he not rather seem an errand boy?" Zidao replied, "In rank he has reached to the highest office, and he is not foolish." Guang said, "What did he say to you when he sent you to come?" Zidao passed on what Ba had said, and Guang said, "You say he is not foolish; were those words foolish or not? The Son of Heaven summoned me three times before I came. Having yet to appear before the ruler of men, ought I to appear before the servant of men?" When Zidao sought a reply (for Hou Ba), Guang said, "My hand is unable to write." He then gave his reply verbally (for the messenger to record). The messenger objected that it was too skimpy a reply, and could it be made more ample? Guang replied, "Is this selling vegetables, this seeking for more?" Ba memorialized Guang's reply, and the emperor laughed, saying, "That's the old attitude of that crazy churl."

The imperial chariots and quadrigae arrived at Guang's lodging that very day, but Guang stayed abed and would not rise. The emperor approached his bedside and patted Guang's belly, saying, "Now, now, Ziling, would it not be reasonable to help out one another?" Guang remained asleep and did not respond for quite some time. Then he opened his eyes and said, "Of old, Yao of Tang displayed great virtue, but the Nest-dwelling Elder rinsed out his ears. Men for this reason may set their will. Why have you come to press me?" The emperor said, "Ziling, in the end will I be unable to make you give in?" He then climbed into the imperial carriage, breathed a sigh, and departed.

He later again led Guang into the (private quarters of the) palace. Discussion led to their friendship of former days. They conversed with each other for days on end, and accordingly slept in each other's company. Guang was selected for the post of grand master of remonstrance, but he did not let down his resolve. He then went to farm in the Fuchun Hills (in modern Zhejiang), where later people called his fishing spot Yan Ling Rapids. In the seventeenth year of the Jianwu period (41 C.E.) he was once again given a special summons, but he did not go. He died at home at the age of eighty.

Han Kang

Han Kang, with the courtesy-name of Boxiu, was a man from Baling in Jingzhao (outside the Han capital of Chang'an). He often roamed the famous mountains in search of medicinal plants, which he sold in the Chang'an market. For thirty years he would not haggle over prices. Once a girl was buying some simples from Kang, and she became angry when Kang held to his price. She said, "Be you, sir, Han Boxiu, and so no second price?" Kang said with a sigh, "I had desired to avoid a reputation, but now even little girls all know of me. Of what use could even medicines be?" So he ran off into the Baling mountains. He was repeatedly summoned for postings as an erudite and in the imperial conveyance bureau, but he never went. During the time of Emperor Huan (147–167), he was offered appointment with full ceremonial offerings of bolts of dark silk and a comfortable carriage. An envoy with the imperial proclamation in hand met up with Kang, and Kang had no recourse but to feign acceptance. He excused himself from the comfortable carriage and rode alone in a brushwood cart. He went forth one dawn before the others and arrived at a way station, where the station head was just then sending out men and oxen to repair the roads and bridges because Master Han, Recipient of Imperial Summons, was due to pass by. Seeing Kang's brushwood cart and his cloth headscarf, he took Kang for an old peasant, and requisitioned his ox. Kang straightaway released it from its yoke and gave it to him. After a while the envoy arrived, and as the oldster whose ox had been requisitioned was in fact the Recipient of Imperial Summons, the envoy wished to petition to have the station head executed. Kang said, "This is the result of an old man giving it up; what is the crime of the station head?" The envoy then desisted. Subsequently, along the way Kang ran away into hiding. He died in his longevity.

Pang gong

The one known as Venerable Pang (Pang gong) was a man from Xiangyang (modern Xiangfan City, Hubei) in the Southern Commandery. He lived to the south of the Xian hills and never once entered into the city compound. He and his wife treated each other with the respect accorded a guest. The Inspector of Jingzhou, Liu Biao (142–208; post held 190–195), repeatedly had extended invitations to him but could not get him to comply, so he personally went to inquire after him. He said, "How could preserving intact a single person compare with preserving intact all under Heaven?" Venerable Pang laughed, and said, "The wild goose and the grey crane nest atop the tall forests, and in the evening have their place to perch; the turtle and the alligator make their dens at the bottom of the deepest abyss, and at night have their place of lodging. Now, the choice of what to adopt or reject, when to act and when to refrain from action, likewise are the nest and den of a man. Moreover, each but finds his place to perch or lodge; it is not all under heaven that he would hold for his own." With this he excused himself to till upon the knoll, while his wife and children weeded ahead. Liu Biao pointed to them and asked, "If you, sir, would dwell in hardship amid the furrowed fields, and not consent to office and emolument, then what will your descendants have to bequeath to their posterity?" Venerable Pang replied, "People of the world all bequeath them peril; today I alone bequeath them peace. What I bequeath might be different, but it is not that I pass nothing down." Biao heaved a sigh and departed. Later, leading his wife and children, Venerable Pang climbed Deer Gate Mountain (Lumen shan), where he gathered simples, never to turn back.

—AB

Notes

1. This sentence, as indeed the whole paragraph, is based on the second section of the first chapter of the *Zhuang Zi*.

THE LAST CENTURY of Han rule saw a dismal succession of immature and ineffectual emperors. The national bureaucracy was paralyzed by factionalism and resentful of what it perceived as the inappropriate rise in the power of palace eunuchs. This bleak period witnessed protracted struggles among the three predominant and mutually antagonistic political groups: the scholar-officials; the eunuchs; and the great clans, who pretended to support the imperial structure by providing the emperors with their consorts but whose real interest was complete autonomy.

The general sense that the world was coming apart induced many writers to suggest what was wrong, who was at fault, and what might be done about it. Students at the Imperial Academy, for example, demonstrated repeatedly against the undue influence of the eunuchs—provoking the arrest of more than a thousand of them in a crackdown in 176 c.e.[1] Other observers, such as Wang Fu (ca. 82–167 c.e.), denounced the spendthrift elite, who devoted their resources and energies to luxury and extravagance rather than to the traditional literati aspirations of education and government service.

By the third century, however, many serious thinkers who were not simply hedonists began to question the merit of these same aspirations rather than criticize the world for failing to pursue them. They held that it was not necessarily reprehensible for men and women to challenge the received norms of behavior. It was fashionable to ask, with Ruan Ji (210–263), "Were the rituals established for people of our kind?" (see below). Never before, and certainly not during the heyday of the Han dynasty, could such a question have been posed. The view that the ancient rituals need not apply to people's everyday lives was revolutionary, and this deconstruction of traditional morality gradually became acceptable and even commonplace. How this momentous change in outlook came about is worth some reflection.

The new custodians of mainstream values were scions of the manorial gentry, the great families that came to dominate local administration during the period of imperial weakness in the third and fourth centuries. The last thing these aristocrats wanted to see was a resurgence of imperial power, and they devoted their energies to consolidating their own autonomy and undermining, as much as possible, the effectiveness of the national government. The gentry were consequently faced with two competing and irreconcilable commitments in their role as members of the bureaucratic elite: service to the empire as government officials and resistance to it as territorial aristocrats. In the intellectual sphere, the gentry's struggle for local hegemony manifested itself as a revolt against the tired and rigid doctrines of the Han. Just as the Han ideologues propounded their uniform behavioral standards in an effort to forge a unified empire centered on a single leader, so the new aristocratic elite of the post-Han era, in resisting imperialist demands on their loyalty, sought to undo the very idea of prescribed behavior.

The empty formalism of the rituals was a favorite target of the so-called "Seven Worthies of the Bamboo Grove": Ruan Ji, Ji Kang (223–262), Shan Tao (205–283), Liu Ling (d. after 265), Ruan Xian (234–305), Xiang Xiu (ca. 221–ca. 300), and Wang Rong (234–305). Ruan Ji, in particular, was a deliberate nonconformist who made serious moral statements with studied idiosyncrasies. For example, by attending parties while mourning his mother, he scandalized his more conservative contemporaries, who wrongly inferred from his outrageous violations of the rites that he was unmoved by her death. In private, we are told, he cried out, expectorated several quarts of blood, and lay ill for a long time. He considered the open disregard of propriety as the surest sign of sincere devotion.

The following selections include several representative stories about the "Seven Worthies" from a work called *Stories of the World Newly Told (Shishuo xinyu),* compiled under the direction of Liu Yiqing (403–444). *Stories of the World Newly Told* is a useful source revealing the general tenor of the intellectual world at the time.

The last selection below is an excerpt from "Refutation of 'The Natural Love of Learning,'" by Ji Kang.[2] Zhang Miao (d. 291), an obscure scholar-official, had written a fairly conventional essay entitled "The Natural Love of Learning," which Ji Kang used as a foil.—PRG

From *Stories of the World Newly Told*

Ruan Ji of Chenliu (Henan), Ji Kang of Jiao Principality (*guo;* Anhui), and Shan Tao of Henei (Henan) were all comparable in age, with Kang being the youngest. Liu Ling of Pei Principality (Jiangsu), Ruan Xian of Chenliu, Xiang Xiu of Henei, and Wang Rong of Langye (Shandong) were their sworn friends. The seven men would often gather in a bamboo grove, expressing their feelings with inebriated gusto. Thus the world called them "The Seven Worthies of the Bamboo Grove."

Liu Ling was sick from wine and, being extremely thirsty, asked his wife to find more wine. His wife cast away the wine and broke the vessels; she upbraided him in tears, saying, "You drink too much. This is no way to preserve your life. You must stop it."

Ling said, "Very well. Since I cannot prevent myself [from drinking], the only thing to do is pray to the ghosts and spirits and vow to stop. You may prepare the wine and meat."

His wife said, "Respectfully, I hear your command." She placed the wine and meat before the sprits, entreating Ling to pray and make his vow.

Ling knelt and prayed:

> Heaven gave birth to Liu Ling,
> who is famous on account of wine.[3]
> One *hu*[4] in one gulp—
> five *dou* dissolve the hangover.
> He is careful not to listen
> to his wife's speeches.

Then he took the wine and "presented" the meat, and soon he was roaring drunk.

[The post of] Infantry Commandant was vacant. In the commissary there was a hoard of several hundred *hu* of wine. So Ruan Ji asked to be made Infantry Commandant.

Liu Ling always indulged in wine and let himself be uninhibited. Sometimes he would take his clothes off and stay in his house stark naked. When visitors saw this, they criticized him. Ling said, "I take Heaven and Earth as my pillars and roof, and the rooms of my house as my trousers. Gentlemen, what are you doing in my trousers?"

Once, when Ruan Ji's sister-in-law was about to return to her [parents'] home, Ji saw her and said good-bye. Someone censured him for this;[5] Ji said, "Were the rites established for people of our kind?"

When Ruan Ji buried his mother, he steamed a fat suckling pig and drank two *dou* of wine. Only then did he attend the last rites. He kept saying, "It's over"; that was all he would cry. Then he coughed up blood and languished in depression for a good long time.

When Ruan of the "Infantry"[6] was mourning his mother, Pei Linggong went to offer his condolences. Ruan had just gotten drunk and was sitting on the couch with tousled hair; his legs were spread apart like the Sieve constellation,[7] and he did not weep. When Pei arrived, he put a mat [for himself] on the floor [and wept]. Once Pei was finished with his weeping and condolences, he left.

Someone asked Pei, "Whenever one offers one's condolences, the host may weep, but the guest acts in accordance with the rites. However, Ruan did not weep, so why did you?"[8]

Pei said, "Ruan is a man who is out of the common; thus he does not venerate the ritual institutes. Our kind are people of convention; thus we live along the tracks [laid down by] the ceremonies."

At the time, people marveled at how both men had attained balance.

Pei Chenggong's wife was Wang Rong's daughter. Wang Rong went to Pei's house early one morning and, without being announced, walked right inside. Pei got down from the south side of the bed and [Wang's] daughter got down from the north side. Facing each other, [Wang and the couple] acted as guest and host without blushing in the least.[9]

Ruan Zhongrong took pleasure in a Xianbei[10] slave girl in the household of his paternal aunt. While he was mourning his mother, his aunt thought it appropriate to move far away; she told him beforehand that she would leave the slave girl behind. But once she had set out, it turned out that she had taken her along. Zhongrong borrowed his guest's donkey and chased after them in his heavy [mourning] vestments. He returned [with the slave girl], seated with her on the same saddle. [Zhongrong] said, "One cannot lose one's seed!" She was the mother [of his son], Yaoji.

The wife of Wang Anfeng[11] would always call Anfeng "you."[12] Anfeng said, "According to the rites, it is disrespectful for a wife to call her husband 'you.' Do not do it again."

His wife said, "I am intimate with you and I love you; therefore I call you 'you.' If I do not call you 'you,' who should call you 'you'?"

Refutation of "The Natural Love of Learning" [by Ji Kang. Excerpt]

By nature, people love security and hate danger; they love idleness and hate toil. If they are not disturbed, they attain their wishes; if they are not oppressed, they follow their inclinations.

In the past, in the era of primeval chaos, Great Simplicity had not yet waned. Lords were not contriving above, the people not quarrelsome below. Things were whole and the Plan[13] flowed smoothly; no one failed to attain his [nature]. If people were full, they slept peacefully; if they were hungry, they went in search of food. They drummed on their bellies cheerfully. Unbeknownst to them, this was the era of ultimate virtue. How could they know the principles of humanity and righteousness or the contrivances of ritual and law?

When such "ultimate men"[14] no longer existed, the Great Way deteriorated and became decrepit; it was then that people first produced writing and ink in order to transmit their ideas. They differentiated among the teeming things, causing there to be species and clans. They invented humanity and righteousness and thereby hampered their minds. They instituted titles and duties to regulate [the world] around them. They "encouraged learning"[15] and lectured on writings to make their teachings seem spiritual. Thus the farrago of the Six Classics[16] and the multifarious Hundred Schools opened the road to glory and profit, and people raced along, astonished and unaware.

Just as birds, greedy for life, will eat grain or vegetables in parks and ponds, scholars in search of security betray their will and follow the vulgar. They hold their pens and grasp their tablets, well rested from head to toe. They accumulate learning and elucidate the canons instead of sowing and harvesting.[17] Therefore they [decide to] learn only when times are hard; they learn in order to achieve glory. They study only after calculating; they are fond of it, because they attain success by means of their studies.

[This love of learning] seems natural in some respect; thus it has brought you to say that it is natural. But let us investigate this from the beginning. The chief purpose of the Six Classics is to repress and guide, but human nature is such that we are happy when we are free. If we are repressed and guided, our wishes are thwarted; if we are free, we attain our natural state. Therefore, the attainment of our natural state does not derive from the repression and guidance of the Six Classics. The basis by which we keep our nature intact does not require rituals and laws, which oppose our emotions. Thus we know that humanity and righteousness are obligations of an artificial[18] order; they are not essential techniques for nourishing our genuine [nature]. Complaisance and deference are born of contention and depredation; they do not arise naturally. From this perspective, we might say that birds do not gather in flocks in order to be tamed; beasts do not form herds in order to be domesticated. Thus the genuine nature of humanity is "nonaction";[19] we are not naturally addicted to ritual and learning.

—PRG

Notes

1. One may arguably trace the origin of Chinese student movements, which have once again made headlines in recent years, to these demonstrations more than eighteen hundred years ago. Protesting, when circumstances call for it, is regarded as a basic element of students' identity and self-consciousness.

2. His surname is also sometimes read as Xi.

3. Or "whose destiny is wine."

4. About five and a half gallons (20.8 liters). One *hu* is ten *dou*.

5. According to the rites, sister-in-law and brother-in-law were not allowed to speak to each other directly.

6. An ironic epithet for Ruan Ji, whom we have seen assume the post of Commandant because of the army's well-stocked wine cellar.

7. Sagittarius. Ruan Ji's demeanor recalls Zhuang Zi's celebrated response to his wife's death (translated above in selection 13, chapter 18).

8. In other words, the guest is not expected to weep even if the host does, and since Ruan himself had not wept, Pei was under no obligation to do so.

9. Their lack of embarrassment can be contrasted with the behavior of Mencius when he found his wife in a compromising position in her bedroom (in the *Outer Commentary on the Hán Odes,* translated above in selection 22).

10. An Inner Asian tribe.

11. Wang Rong is cited here by his courtesy-name, "Anfeng."

12. As opposed to some honorific phrase.

13. *Li,* the fundamental pattern of the cosmos.

14. Ji Kang borrows this term from the *Zhuang Zi;* it denotes people who are in perfect harmony with the cosmos and are unencumbered by mundane concerns.

15. A reference to the first chapter of the *Xun Zi,* "Exhortation to Learning."

16. *Changes, Rites, Music, Odes, Documents,* and *Spring and Autumn Annals.* The *Music* was lost in ancient times.

17. The point of this sentence (and the preceding one) seems to be that scholars pursue a career of learning because it excuses them from the tiresome chores of a peasant life.

18. The term is *wei,* "artifice" or "forgery," which Xun Zi had used in a positive sense to refer to the process of self-cultivation by which people transform their evil natures. Ji Kang intends to disparage Xun Zi's view with this allusion.

19. *Wuwei,* a crucial concept in the *Lao Zi* and *Zhuang Zi.* "Nonaction" means not acting in a manner contrary to the Way.

39 | Lu Bao, "On the Money God"

LU BAO (fl. late 3rd c.–early 4th c.) was a recluse who lived during the Western Jin dynasty (265–316). Known for his erudition and simple lifestyle, he wrote this satirical essay to poke fun at the growing trend of money-worship around the Yuankang (291–299) period. Showing contempt for "filthy lucre," Lu lashed out at the corrupting effects of money through the mouth of a fictitious character, Sikong (an actual surname derived from an old Zhou-dynasty official title, Minister of Works). However, Lu went to such great lengths in depicting the omnipotence of money that his essay confirms the power of money rather than tarnishing its reputation as he intended. What is more significant, it also gives eloquent testimony to the existence of a lively money economy in early medieval China.—VCX

There was a gentleman by the name of Sikong who made light of wealth and nobility. Elaborately dressed, he came to the capital [Luoyang] for a visit and stayed in Pingshi Ward.[1] Seeing Mr. Qimu, gray-haired and walking, the gentleman said, "Hi, you are getting on in years. Walking like this empty-handed, where are you going?"

The man answered, "I want to go and see a nobleman."

The gentleman said, "Have you studied the *Book of Odes*?"

"Yes, I have."

"Have you studied the *Book of Rites*?"

"Yes, I have."

"Have you studied the *Book of Changes*?"[2]

"Yes, I have."

The gentleman said, "Doesn't the *Book of Odes* say, '[Fill up] the bamboo container with money and silk to express one's sincerity so that loyal ministers and honored guests can enjoy themselves.'[3] Doesn't the *Book of Rites* say, 'Men present jade, silk, wild geese, or pheasants. Women present hazelnuts, chestnuts, dates, or dried meat.'[4] Doesn't the *Book of Changes* say, 'Great indeed is the significance of following the times.'[5] I watch what you carry, and observe what you rely upon. [Judging by this] are you really following the [spirit of the] age? Although you claim to have studied [the Confucian classics], I daresay that you have not."

The man answered, "I will use pure conversation[6] as my bamboo container and penetrating insight[7] as my money and silk. Isn't the meaning of 'the *Rites* says, the *Rites* says' nothing more than 'jade and silk say'?"

Splitting his sides with laughter, the gentleman said, "What you just said is really stupid![8] You know neither the past nor the present. The exigencies of today don't need pure conversation at all. The world has been transformed with the change of the times. Past and present differ in customs. The rich are glorious and noble, while the poor are lowly and shameful. However, you still practice simplicity and stick to honesty. This is just like 'marking your boat in a river after you have lost your sword'[9] or 'tuning the *se*-zither with the pegs glued.'[10] Poverty never leaves you, and fame and glory never come out of your home. So you are patently stupid.

"Of old, after the death of Shennong, the Yellow Emperor (Huang Di), Yao, and Shun[11] taught the people farming and sericulture, with money and silk as capital. The wise and prophetic introduced more changes, digging up copper mountains. Looking up and down, they cast [the copper] into coins. Consequently, the square hole of the coin symbolizes Earth, and the circular shape Heaven. The essence of the coin is Qian and Kun.[12] The inner part is square, and the outer part round. It accumulates like mountains and flows like rivers. It follows its own tempo to move and stop. It appears and disappears according to its own rhythm. It facilitates the marketplace and never worries about wear and tear. Decaying slowly, it resembles longevity. Never-ending, it resembles the Way. So it can stay durable, becoming the divine treasure of the world.

"Endearing like an older brother, it has as its courtesy-name Square Hole (Kongfang). Lose it, you will become poor and weak; acquire it, you will become rich and strong, capable of flying with no wings and running with no feet, lighting up stern-looking faces and making the close-mouthed talk. Those with much money come to the front, and those with little money fall behind. Those in front become sovereigns and chieftains, and those behind become subjects and servants. Sovereigns and chieftains are wealthy and prosperous, and always have more to spare. Subjects and servants are poverty-stricken and exhausted, and never have enough. This is why the *Book of Odes* says,

> The rich may get through,
> But alas for the helpless and solitary.[13]

Isn't this (the importance of money) what is being referred to?

"Money *(qian)* may be defined (punningly) as fountain *(quan)*. The commoners use it every day, and its source never goes dry. No place is too far for it, and no depth is beyond its reach. In the capital city, those in formal dresses and caps are weary of oratory. They are so sick of listening to pure conversation that they fall asleep. When they see my older brother (money), they cannot help staring at him with wonder.

"The protection offered by money is auspicious without disadvantage. Why must one take the trouble to study to become rich and noble? Of old, Lü Gong was pleased with an empty calling tablet.[14] Gaozu of Han (Liu Bang) made it with two extra coins.[15] Zhuo Wenjun doffed her cloth garments and donned her embroidered dress, while Sima Xiangru untied the halter on the calf nose and rode in a canopied carriage.[16] High official rank and great fame are both the work of money. The empty tablet indeed looked blank, but it actually contained substance. Two extra coins was little, but it led to [Liu Bang's] close acquaintance [with Lü Gong]. In view of this, [money] can be called magic. It allows one to win respect without official status and become popular without power; to push open the Vermilion Gate and enter the Purple Gate.[17] With money, one can revive the dead and turn danger into safety. Without money, the noble can become lowly, and the living can get killed. In angry disputes and contentious lawsuits, one cannot win without money. The orphaned, the weak, the secluded, and the restricted can only pull out of their troubles with money. Grievances, feuds, dislike, and hatred cannot be addressed except with money. Interrogations[18] and cheerful conversations will not elicit a response without money. The officers in red[19] of Luoyang (the capital) and the powers that be all love my older brother unlimitedly. [My older brother says,] 'They hold me by the hand and carry me from beginning to end. They don't care about my quality, nor do they mind my age. Guests flock to my gate in carriage after carriage, and the constant hustle and bustle at my entrance recalls the marketplace.'

"A proverb says, 'Money does not have ears, and one can spend it blindly.' These are not just empty words! Another one says, 'If you have money, you can even make the devil work for you.'[20] How much more so with people! Zixia says, 'Life and death are a matter of destiny; wealth and honor depend on Heaven.'[21] I think, 'Life and death are no matter of destiny; wealth and honor depend on money.' How do I know? Money can turn misfortune into fortune, failure into success. The endangered will become safe, and the dead will come alive. The length of a life, physique, emolument, nobility and lowliness are all determined by money. What does it have to do with Heaven?

"Heaven has its shortcomings where money has its strength. Money is not as good as Heaven when it comes to continuing the four seasons and creating all creatures and things. But in reaching out to the poor and rescuing the stranded, energizing the destitute and assisting the needy, Heaven is not as good as money. If one has the wisdom of a Zang Wuzhong, the bravery of a Bian Zhuangzi, the arts of a Ran Qiu, then refine him with ritual and music, he would surely become an accomplished man.[22] Nowadays, an accomplished man does not have to proceed in this fashion. All he needs is Mr. Kongfang (square hole; i.e., money). Money can enlighten the destitute, warm the rich, and embolden the poor. Thus the saying goes, 'If you don't have wealth, no warriors will come. If you don't have rewards, no warriors will follow [your orders].' The proverb says, 'If an official doesn't have the support of insiders, he might as well go back to the country.' However, if one has the support of insiders but not my older brother, isn't that the same as 'trying to walk without feet and fly without wings'? Even if one is as talented as Yan Zi and as good-looking as Zizhang,[23] but only swings his arms empty-handed, what hope does he have? He will be much better off if he retires early to engage extensively in farming and trade, making Kongfang work for him on or off his boats and carts."

> Those one hundred gentlemen[24]
> Merge their dust and blend their light.[25]
> They connect with above and link with below,[26]
> Their fame and honor augment.

—VCX

Notes

1. Pingshi li was one of the residential wards in Jin period Luoyang. A number of Jin Luoyang ward names have survived in the *Gazetteer of Luoyang (Henan zhi)*, but Pingshi is not among them. Western Jin Luoyang, which was essentially the same city as Later Han Luoyang, had three marketplaces. One of them was named Pingle Market *(shi)*. It is possible that Pingshi Ward was named after that market and was located in its vicinity.

2. The *Book of Odes (Shijing), Book of Rites (Liji)*, and *Book of Changes (Yijing)* are all among the thirteen Confucian classics.

3. This sentence may be found in the Mao preface to the first poem (number 161) in the "Lesser Elegantiae" (Xiaoya) section of the *Book of Odes* titled "The Deer Calls" (Lu ming).

4. This passage is actually quoted from the *Zuo Commentary (Zuozhuan)*. It is a prescription for offerings that men of different ranks and women should carry out as befitting their status. The concept is also embodied in the *Book of Rites,* but not verbatim.

5. Quoted from the classical commentary *(zhuan)* of the *Yijing.*

6. This is *qingtan,* the rarefied Neo-Taoist repartee of the Wei-Jin period (early part of the Six Dynasties).

7. *Jishen* means "delicately precise and insightful." It is another term that was popular with the Neo-Taoists of the times.

8. *Gu* (solid; blockish) is here used in the sense of *gulou* (inferior, vulgar).

9. The earliest surviving record of the story is found in the *Spring and Autumn Annals of Mr. Lü (Lüshi chunqiu),* scroll 15.

10. The earliest surviving record of this story is found in the *Records of the Grand Historian (Shiji)*, scroll 81. Both this and the story cited in note 9 became set phrases *(chengyu)* that were commonly used until quite recently.

11. Shennong was the mythical first farmer; the Yellow Emperor was a legendary ruler and founder of civilization; Yao and Shun are semimythical figures who supposedly ruled during the third millennium B.C.E.

12. Qian and Kun are the two hexagrams with opposite attributes, with Qian symbolic of yang, male and Heaven, and Kun of yin, female and Earth.

13. From poem number 192 of the *Book of Odes* (translation by James Legge).

14. Lü Gong was a Qin period figure. *Ban* (calling tablet), also known as *ye*, refers to the bamboo tablet one presented when meeting with someone. In this case, on the tablet was written the amount of money the visitor would give as a present. The allusion is to Lü Gong's encounter with Liu Bang, founder of the Han dynasty. When Lü was the house guest of the magistrate of Pei County, local men of import all went to pay homage with money. Liu Bang brought no money at all, but wrote down on his calling tablet "10,000 cash as present." Lü, who was a master in physiognomy, noticed Liu's imperial looks and married his daughter (the future Empress Lü) to him in spite of his hoax.

15. *Ying'er* literally means "two coins extra." Here the sentence indicates that Liu Bang won the trust of Lü Gong by paying an extra amount of money. However, it seems that either the author, Lu Bao, was confused about the information or he had access to an account no longer extant which is different from that in the Standard Histories. In fact, the story has nothing to do with Lü Gong. It is Xiao He, Liu's superior in his predynastic days, who made the extra two (or two hundred) -coin payment to Liu each time after Liu worked for him as a corvée laborer. In gratitude, Liu Bang, as emperor of Han China, conferred an additional two thousand enfeoffment households upon Xiao.

16. The allusion is to the much-storied love affair between the Former Han literary giant Sima Xiangru and Zhuo Wenjun. While Sima was resident in Linqiong County (present-day Qionglai, Sichuan), he reluctantly made his appearance at a lavish party thrown by the local rich man Zhuo Wangsun, whose daughter Wenjun fell in love with Sima after listening to him playing the zither and eloped with him to Chengdu. Disowned by her rich father, Wenjun, together with her new husband, had to make a living selling wine. Wearing calf-nose pants (underpants that were shaped like a calf's nose), Sima Xiangru rubbed shoulders with slaves and menials in the marketplace, washing dishes. Hence the remark about "the calf nose." Zhuo Wangsun eventually reconciled with his daughter and son-in-law. With the assets they received from Wangsun, Sima Xiangru and Zhuo Wenjun became wealthy.

17. The Vermilion Gate (Zhumen) is a simile for the mansions of the rich and powerful. The Purple Gate (Zita) is a simile for the imperial residence. A variant reads Jinmen (Golden Gate) for Zhumen. Jinmen is short for Jinmamen (the Golden Horse Gate), which was located in the Weiyang Palace in Han Chang'an.

18. *Lingwen* is often used in the sense of "good reputation." But here it more likely means "to question officially."

19. *Zhuyi* generally refers to ritual officers.

20. Since these two proverbs were undoubtedly popular among the people, one would not expect them to be quoted from literary texts.

21. Zixia was the courtesy name of Bu Shang, a disciple of Confucius. These two lines are quoted from the *Analects (Lunyu)*, 12.5 (translation by D. C. Lau).

22. Zang Wuzhong was a grand master *(dafu)* in the Spring and Autumn state of Lu in present-day Shandong. Bian Zhuangzi was an ancient brave warrior. Ran Qiu, also known as Ran You, was a disciple of Confucius. Here Lu Bao takes his cue from the *History of the Han (Hanshu)*, which lumps these personages together as exemplary figures in their individual areas of achievement. In the *Hanshu* account, Ran is mentioned without his given name. The Tang exegete Yan Shigu identifies him with Ran Geng (Ran Boniu), another disciple of Confucius.

23. Yan Zi refers to Yan Yuan, one of Confucius's most gifted students. Zizhang was the courtesy-name of Zhuansun Shi. He was also a disciple of Confucius.

24. Among extant sources, the earliest use of the phrase *fan bai junzi* is found in the *Book of Odes*, number 194. It originally meant "all the ministers at court." Here it is used in a generic sense.

25. The phrase *tongchen heguang* can be traced to chapter 56 of the *Classic of Integrity and the Way (Daode jing)*.

26. The concept expressed here is embodied in the commentary on the judgment to hexagram 11 of the *Book of Changes*.

THE PROMINENT EARLY-FIFTH-CENTURY poet Xie Lingyun (385–433) has been acclaimed for his long, descriptive literary masterpiece "Rhapsody on Dwelling in the Mountains." He also earned an eternal niche in mountaineer lore for his use of footwear specially designed with removable platforms (literally, "teeth") front and rear to facilitate either ascent or descent of mountains. For Xie Lingyun, the mountains represented pleasurable relief from officialdom, and he took to making outings following his appointment in 422 as Governor of Yongjia (modern Wenzhou, Zhejiang). Perhaps based on these outings, Xie Lingyun chronicled local landscape in a work titled *Record of Excursions to Famous Mountains.* While only a few fragments remain of this work, much or all of its brief, yet revealing, preface has been preserved.

In early-medieval China, mountains were associated with the salutary release from worldly encumbrances and perturbations, even though such wilderness was the perennial home of ordinary woodcutters. Men of the scholar-official class who chose to withdraw from a positon in the administration were known by convention as "men of the mountain forests." In the Preface, Xie Lingyun implies that one ordinarily fulfills one's physical needs in places and situations which are not necessarily beneficent; he is certainly referring to government postings. Yet one's natural leanings are toward intimate communion with the natural world, the world of mountains and waters beyond the constraints of the world of men. Irrespective of Xie Lingyun's own personal vicissitudes (he was executed publicly for having supported an uprising against the ruling faction), the concepts expressed in his short preface evince a benign image of the natural world, a sentiment common to Xie's time that still is a commonplace in traditional Chinese cultural attitudes.—AB

Preface

Clothing and food are what human life requires, while mountains and waters are what one's natural disposition gravitates toward. Those of today, mired in the entanglements which accompany their needs, simply inhibit their natural inclinations.

The common view is that the root of joy fulfilled is found in a glorious (official) residence. Those, then, who bed in the cliffs and drink from the torrents are lacking in great aspirations, and thus always are found withered and haggard. I declare that it is not so. The Superior Man is solicitous about things by temperament, and by ability succors them. Damage due to things gone out of control can only be put in order by men of talent; thus at times there are cases of compromising oneself (i.e., compromising one's natural inclinations) so as to assist others. How could they consider the arena of fame and gain to be more worthy than the realm of purity and expansiveness?

Speaking in terms of emperors, then there was the one who released his sovereignty at Dinghu (the Yellow Emperor gave up temporal rule and ascended to the heavens at Dinghu). And in terms of heritors to the throne, then there was the one who severed all restraints at Mount Song (Xu You renounced Yao's offer of the throne and lived unfettered at Mount Song). Further, Tao Zhu (i.e., Fan Li) loftily forsook the stewardship of Yue, and the Lord of Liu (Zhang Liang) voluntarily retired from being Tutor of the Han. If we extrapolate from these examples, then it becomes clear.

—AB

FAN YE (398–446) included a separate biographical section in his *History of the Later Han (Hou Hanshu)* for "disengaged persons," that is, practitioners of reclusion, virtuous men of integrity who decline offers of service in local or state administration, men who exalt their private pursuits over a life as a scholar-official. Fan's section on reclusion is justifiably the most celebrated of early-medieval writings on reclusion, not only because of the richness of its accounts, but because of Fan Ye's own comments. Fan's discussion was the fullest to date concerning the nature of reclusion, the conduct of practitioners of reclusion, and criteria for delimiting entries in a compilation of notices of men-in-reclusion; thus, in great measure, Fan's discussion went far in defining the parameters of substantive reclusion. Further, his pronouncements, and in particular his Preface, have retained a certain authority through the ages: most subsequent discussions, especially those found within the sections on reclusion in later dynastic histories, in great measure derived from Fan Ye their approach and reasoning, and to a certain extent even their imagery and manner of expression. Fan Ye's prefatorial discussion, a model of poignant expression crafted in elegant language, was chosen for inclusion in the influential *Selections of Refined Writing (Wen xuan),* and as a result received particular attention since sometime during the late 520s, when compilation of *Wen xuan* was completed.

Fan Ye begins his preface to the section with a series of classical references to reclusion, then goes on to categorize the practice of reclusion as he saw it. In his view, "disengaged persons" from the Later Han (and earlier) did not willingly practice reclusion and accept resultant material duress because they eschewed human contact or rejoiced in the joys of the natural world. Reclusion was simply "where their innate nature led them." Fan next says that men-in-reclusion were obstinate, and as such were not unlike Confucius, who would ply his talent only under the proper circumstances. And he expresses approval of all of these individuals who can cast off their worldly fetters in favor of life beyond the confinement of conventional conduct. He remarks emphatically that they differed from seekers after personal advancement. Fan Ye goes on to relate that Wang Mang's usurpation (9–23 C.E., at the close of the Western Han dynasty) resulted in the withdrawal from public service of innumerable persons, while the first several Later Han emperors were deferential to the great hidden worthies of the day. Later, however, as the virtue of the emperors declined and the power of the eunuchs increased, a number of people considered it shameful to serve. Some were so indignant that they no longer felt constrained to a course of moderated conduct. Fan Ye ends his discussion by saying that the men whose accounts he has compiled were the match of preeminent men-in-reclusion from the distant past. His direct reference is to Confucius's cryptic declaration, "Ones who took action were seven in number" (*Analects* 14.40).

Fan Ye's section on reclusion contains the accounts of fourteen renowned "disengaged persons," with appended mentions of several of their confederates and three anecdotes concerning anonymous Wise Rustic types. This section, however, contains notices of only a fraction of known Later Han practitioners of reclusion. In the *Hou Han shu* alone there are notices or mentions of at least a hundred other men who might fit Fan Ye's own categorizations. Following the biographical accounts, Fan Ye closes the chapter with a rhymed "Encomium."—AB

The [Book of] Changes proclaims "Great indeed is the significance of the timeliness of (the hexagram) Dun (Withdrawal)." It also says (in the hexagram Gu [Bane]), "He does not serve a king or lord; he elevates in priority his [own] affairs." For this reason, although Yao was praised as "modeling Heaven," he could not humble the lofty integrity of [Xu You from] north of the Ying (who lived unencumbered in the mountains). And while King Wu was "utterly praiseworthy," still the purity of the [Lords of] Guzhu forever remains intact (referring to Bo Yi and Shu Qi, who starved to death in the mountains rather than compromise their principles).

From these examples on down, the influential current became increasingly prevalent. The path of prolonged departure has never varied, yet the tactics of those inspired to action are not single in kind. Some lived in seclusion, seeking to maintain their resolve. Some turned and fled to keep their inner principles intact. Some sought personal tranquility, thereby repressing their impatience. Some removed themselves from danger in pursuit of security. Some defiled themselves in the profane world and thereby stirred their mettle. Some condemned worldly things, thereby arousing their purity.

Nevertheless, in observing the way they gladly dwelt among the crosshatched cultivated fieldlands, or went worn and haggard out by the rivers and seas, must it necessarily be that they sought intimacy with fish and birds, and found pleasure in forests and plants? It might also be said that it simply was where their innate nature led them. Thus, a court appointee who had suffered disgrace, though repeatedly degraded would not depart from his state (referring to Liuxia Hui, a staunchly ethical man praised by Confucius), whereas one whose moral integrity would bring him to tread out on the sea could not be swayed by a ruler of a thousand-chariot state (referring to Lu Zhonglian, another paragon of morality lauded by Confucius). Even were one to try to convert or change their chosen course, one simply would be unable to affect them.

Although so obstinate they might be classed along with the one who would sell his name (only for the right price, referring to Confucius, in Analects 9.12), nevertheless, cicada-like they could cast off their slough amid the clamor and dust, and go off alone beyond the confines of the world. How different are they from those who would bedizen themselves with knowledge and craft in order to chase after fleeting gain! Xun Qing (i.e., Xun Zi) had a saying: "With will and purpose refined, one can be haughty before wealth and nobility; with the [proper] Way and justice exalted, one can slight kings and dukes."

When the Han ruling house weakened in the middle of its rule and Wang Mang usurped the throne, the pent-up righteous indignation of the scholar-officials was brought to the extreme. At that time, those who rent their official caps and destroyed their ceremonial headgear, who went hand in hand bolstering each other, and who abandoned him, seem incalculable in number. Yang Xiong (53 B.C.E.–8 C.E.) said, "When the wild goose flies in the distant heights, how could the archer catch it there?" This bespeaks their distant removal from harm.

Emperor Guangwu treated with respect "Remote Ones," seeking them out as if in fear of losing them. Plumed banners, bundled silk, and carriages with reed-padded wheels—the accoutrements of official summons—passed one another among the cliffs. Those such as Xue Fang and Pang Meng were invited to court yet declined to go, while Yan Guang, Zhou Dang, and Wang Ba went but were not to be humbled. Everyone in all directions acquiesced [to Guangwu's rule], and men of conviction cherished his humaneness. He most certainly was one who befit the dictum "he called to office those who had retired into obscurity, so that throughout the kingdom the hearts of the people turned toward him" (referring to King Wu of Zhou, from *Analects* 20.1).

Emperor Suzong likewise was deferential to Zheng Jun and summoned to audience Gao Feng, whereby they fulfilled their resolve. But after that time the virtue of the emperors gradually declined, and the perverse and wicked [eunuchs] dominated the court. The gentlemen who remained at home [and did not serve] stolidly upheld their integrity, ashamed to be ranked and associated with the ministers and highest officials. When it reached the point where their indignation was so roused that they paid no regard to consequence, many became extremists (literally "lost their moderate course of action"). Herein by and large I have recorded (accounts of) those who severed ties with the dusty world never to return, equals of the "Ones Who Took Action" *(zuo zhe),* arranging them in this section.

[The "Encomium" goes:]

> By rivers and seas they went obscured, forgotten;
> In mountains and forests they went off forever.
> They ranged their spirit afar on distant winds;
> They freed their feelings beyond the clouds.
> Their Way drew near to Vacuity and Wholeness;
> Their deeds turned away from taint and perversion.

—AB

WHEN BUDDHISM WAS first transmitted to China in the late Han dynasty (1st–2nd c. C.E.), it made itself most strongly felt in literati circles. By the early-medieval period hundreds of scriptures had become available to interested converts in translation. In addition to offering new doctrines and religious practices, Buddhist missionaries brought with them new languages and scripts, which forced the Chinese to confront a significant linguistic other for the first time.

Below is a short essay by the celebrated Buddhist scholar Sengyou (445–518), a monk from the southern capital of Jianye (modern Nanjing). Sengyou collected as many biographies, prefaces, colophons, and other notices as he could find to compose an authoritative catalog of all known Buddhist scriptures in China. His purpose was both to eliminate spurious scriptures (i.e., texts produced in China that purported to be translated from an Indian language) as well as to establish a textual foundation for orthodoxy. His catalog, *A Collection of Notes on the Translation of the Tripiṭaka,* is the earliest Buddhist bibliography available to us.

Sengyou's essay is an attempt to describe the differences between the Indic and Chinese languages. What is perhaps most telling about his description is his seeming equation of script and language. Sanskrit and related Indian languages in which Buddhist texts were composed use an alphasyllabic script of forty-eight letters, combining them to form words, much like other Indo-European languages. The most prevalent of the scripts in ancient times were *brāhmī* and *kharoṣṭhī,* both originally descended from Semitic sources. Chinese, by contrast, uses sinographs, each of which conveys both phonological and semantic significance. Sengyou's problem is to understand how Indian languages use nonmorphemic characters (i.e., written letters that are not in themselves words). His attempt to find parallels for this within the native Chinese tradition, though valiant, fails in a number of ways. Nevertheless, the very wrestling with these alien scripts and languages by Chinese Buddhist exegetes created entirely new means by which literati could think about their own literary and linguistic heritage. In many ways, China would never be the same again.—DB

A Record of Similarities and Differences in Pronunciation and Meaning When Translating Scriptures from Western Languages to Chinese[1]

Numinal concepts are without sound; we rely upon words and expressions in order to transcribe meaning. Words and expressions are without vestiges; we depend upon graphs and characters in order to depict pronunciation. Therefore, characters are "rabbit snares" for words; words are "fish traps" for concepts.[2] When pronunciation and meaning coincide, there cannot be any bias or loss. This is why writing should be used to comprehensively order the world. Although the vestiges are tied to brush and ink (i.e., the literary arts), concepts are suited to the numinous. In ancient times there were three progenitors of writing. The eldest was called Fan *(= Brāhmī);* his script went toward the right. Next was Qulou *(= Kharoṣṭhī);* his script went toward the left.[3] The youngest was Cang Jie; his script went downward.[4] *Brāhmī* and *Kharoṣṭhī* lived in India; Cang Jie, scribe to the Yellow Emperor, lived in China. *Brāhmī* and *Kharoṣṭhī* took their exemplars from the heaven of the Pure Abode (Skt. *Śuddhāvāsa*); Cang Jie relied upon impressions from bird tracks. The strokes of the scripts are certainly different, but in the end they convey concepts equally.

When we reverently inquire into what was taught by the formerly enlightened one (i.e., the Buddha), we find that there are sixty-four scripts.[5] The scribal techniques "deer wheel" and "rolling eye" are distinguished among them. The forms of the characters such as *nāga* (serpent), *yakṣa* (demon), and the eight classes (of supernatural beings) differ in style. Only *Brāhmī* and *Kharoṣṭhī* are the predominant scripts for our times. Therefore the various kingdoms in India call them the divine scripts. Despite the fact that, for copying sutras from the West, the common ancestor of the various scripts is *Brāhmī,* still the thirty-six countries (of the Western regions) frequently have variations in writing styles. If we compare this to the situation in China, is this not like the changing styles of the small seal script (of the Qin dynasty) and the great seal script (of the Western Zhou dynasty)? When we examine the changes in the ancient script of Cang Jie handed down over successive historical periods, we find that the ancient style changed into the great seal script, the great seal script changed into the small seal script, and the small seal script became the clerical script (of the Han). These transformations are many indeed. When we come to the eight styles tangentially derived, these include the "transcendent dragon," the "numinous fungus," (and so forth). Among the twenty-four styles of writing, there are the standard script, the grass script, the needle script, and the halberd script. Although such names and their referents are numerous, their application is on the whole limited. Nevertheless, when one is searching for the root meaning, style is fully realized in the six (analytical principles of) writing. If one is perspicacious according to the circumstances, then nothing is more essential than the clerical method (of writing). With it, the source of the Eastern and Western scripts can be grasped and for the most part mastered.

When we come to Western[6] pronunciation, [these languages] form words, simple and compounded, without consistency. Sometimes one graph is used to represent many concepts; sometimes several words generate but one meaning. Examining the *Mahāyāna-mahāparinirvāṇa-sūtra,* we find that it has enumerated in order the fifty letters (of the Sanskrit alphabet), completely explaining their various meanings.[7] The fourteen vowels it calls the root of the letter. We observe that in their uttering of phrases and discriminating of sounds, the permutations of pronunciation aid one another. Some are "tongue-root" sounds (i.e., velars) or "end of the lip" sounds (i.e., labials); some make distinctions with long or short (vowels). Moreover, a Western letter is a single phoneme but does not constitute a word. Additional words are necessary to complete the phrase; only then is a meaning is realized. When translators convey meaning, how could there not be difficulties!

Furthermore, compositions in Indic script have half-characters (i.e., letters) and full-characters (i.e., words). The reason some are called half-characters is that their meaning is not yet complete (i.e., they are only letters). Therefore, the form of the character is halved, as if the character "moon" (*yue* 月) in Chinese script were missing its side. The reason some are called full-characters is that with them concepts are fully expressed. Therefore, the form of the character is complete, as when the character "sun" (*ri* 日) in Chinese script fills out its shape. Therefore, half-characters poorly express meaning; one can liken them to the moral defilements. Full-characters are good at expressing meaning; one can liken them to constancy.[8] Furthermore, to take a half-character as the principal constituent is like the character "to say" (*yan* 言) in Chinese script; to take a full-character as the principal constituent is like the character "all" (*zhu* 諸) in Chinese script. To pair *yan* 言 with *zhe* 者 (nominalizing particle) constitutes forthwith the character *zhu* 諸. The character *zhu* unites both [elements, *yan* and *zhe*] and is thus an example of a full-character. The character *yan* standing by itself would be in the category of a half-character. Although half-characters (letters) are simple, they form the foundation of [morphemic] characters (words). We depend upon half-characters to form full-characters. It is like an ordinary man, at first being stuck in ignorance, afterward attaining constancy. Therefore, we rely on characters to create meaning; one can liken this to nirvana.

The Indic scripts are abstruse in conveying meaning; they are all like this. This is why the promulgation and understanding of the Indic scripts depends upon clear translation. To translate is to interpret. If, in the mutual interpretation between the two countries (India and China), the words are erroneous, then the concepts will be fallacious. From the end of the Former Han dynasty when the Dharma was first transmitted to China, the translations and transcriptions were all unreliable, so people could not yet become well versed [in the Buddha's teaching]. Therefore, words such as *futu* ("Buddha") and *sangmen* (Skt. *śramaṇa;* ascetic) are erroneous in the Han histories.[9] If transcriptions are [faulty] like this, how much more the meaning!

When we consider the Chinese model of reciting poetry and observing rites, we see that teachers instruct one another, but here, too, there are errors and confusions. The *Book of Odes (Shijing)* says, "There is a rabbit with a white head." *Si* 斯 (white) here should be written *xian* 鮮 (bright). In the language of (the ancient state of) Qi (in northeast China), the pronunciation was corrupt; consequently, it caused an alteration in the text of the *Book of Odes.*[10] This is an example of a *sangmen* [kind of mistake]. The *Book of Rites* says, "Master Kong awoke early." *Zao* 蚤 should be written *zao* 早; this character is the same as *zao* 蚤.... This is an example of the *futu* [kind of mistake]. In the archaic Chinese Buddhist translations, there are just such variants as the *si* and *zao* types. With Chinese and barbarian languages so far apart in translation, how can we find fault with [transcriptions like] *futu* and *sangmen?*

If one weighs the characters for conveying meaning, then diction depends upon the scribe. This is why among the various new and old translations, the similarities are great and the differences small. [For example, if we take] the Indian word Weimojie (Vimalakīrti; name of a lay bodhisattva): the archaic translations gloss it as *wugou cheng* (stainless praise); the translations from the Guanzhong region (modern Shaanxi province) call it *jingming* (pure fame). "Pure" *(jing)* means "stainless" *(wugou);* "fame" *(ming)* means "praise" *(cheng).* These words are different but their meaning is equivalent. The archaic translations say *zhongyou* (possessed of many blessings); the new translations have *shizun* (world-honored one; Skt. *bhagavat,* an epithet of the Buddha). This is the reason for the differences in establishing meaning. The archaic translations have *gantahe* (Skt. *gandharva;* class of celestial beings); the new translations have *gantapo.* These reflect differences of pronunciation among the different countries.[11] I have briefly presented three examples; others can be deduced by analogy.

This is why success or failure [in conveying] meaning depends upon the translator and the substance and form of expression is connected to those who hold the brush (i.e., the scribal assistants on translation committees). Some are skillful in [understanding and rendering] the Western meaning but are not versed in the Chinese sense; some have a clear understanding of the Chinese script but are not knowledgeable of the Western purport. Although they have partial understanding, in the end such limitations obstruct complete mastery of the text. If both the Western and Chinese languages are clearly understood, then the meaning will radiate unobstructedly in the four directions. Afterwards one can expound the abstruse points of the sutras, thereupon achieving precision. Among the old translators, there were none whose ability was thoroughly proficient. This is why the text and meaning of the old translations are transmitted with impediments. How could there be impediments in a sutra! It is only the shortcomings of the translation [that lead to such problems].[12]

In the old days [the translator] An Shigao of Parthia (ca. mid-2nd c. C.E.) was sagacious and without peer. The many sutras he translated were faithful and correct in substance and form. An Xuan and Yan Fotiao (ca. late 2nd c. C.E.) endeavored diligently in well ordering their translations; Zhi Yue and Zhu Shulan (early and late 3rd c. respectively) also balanced [style and simplicity] in making their translations elegant and fluent.[13] In general, these several virtuosos together appeared felicitous to former generations. When we come to Dharmarakṣa (late 3rd century), he was perspicacious, having mastered both the Chinese and barbarian languages. In translating texts and transmitting sutras, he was not misled by the archaic translations. We come next to the dharma-master Kumārajīva (early 5th century), whose genius was like the brilliance of gold, and (his disciples) Seng Rong and Seng Zhao of the [Latter] Qin dynasty (394–417), whose wisdom and natural talent were like a reflecting pool. Therefore, they were able to issue works that illumined the abstruse points of the sutras. The subtle words of the Mahayana shine brightly in them.

Coming next to Dharmakṣema's transmission of the *Mahāyāna-mahāparinirvāṇa-sūtra* and Buddhabhadra's translation of the *Avataṃsaka-sūtra* (both in the early 5th century), [we find that] their expressions and concepts were well expressed, with an illumination that surpasses the sun and moon. When we look into how they made [their translations] felicitous, we see that they followed the precedent of Kumārajīva. Coming next to the miscellaneous minor sutras, they derive for the most part from the *āgama*s (divisions of Mainstream Buddhist canons). Some come from the [Eastern] Han period (25–220 C.E.); others were translated during the Jin (265–420). Their translators are anonymous; nothing can be known about them in any detail.

So when embellishment is excessive, it damages beauty of expression; when simplicity is too much, the expression will be beset with coarseness. Crudeness and adornment are both undesirable; they equally lead to failure in the stylistic expression of the sutras. Therefore, genuinely wise masters are difficult to encounter in this world.

I, Sengyou, have modestly investigated the words of the sutras, the various treatises, the language and script of the magical formulae (*dhāraṇī*s)—they are all the teachings of the Buddha. Thus, the words [of the different translations] are fundamentally the same. Although the Western and Chinese [words] are distinguished in pronunciation, their meanings are fundamentally not different. Simplicity and adornment are but different styles. Although success and failure are incurred in the transmission and translation [of the sutras], their circulation depends on the circumstances. The revered sutras and their wondrous concepts profoundly and eternally illuminate [the world]. I have already reverentially gathered [information] about the early circumstances (of Buddhism); therefore I will next relate [details on] the subsequent [process of] translation. The early circumstances were initiated in the West; the subsequent translations circulated in the eastern kingdoms (i.e., China). Therefore, to inquire about the beginning we must pursue the end. I consign that (i.e., details about translation in China) to the end of the records which follow.

—DB

Notes

1. *Hu han yijing yin yi tongyi ji* in *Chu sanzang ji ji* (A collection of notes on the translation of the *Tripiṭaka*), *Taishō shinshū daizōkyō*, vol. 55:4b–5a. This essay was previously translated in Arthur Link, "The Earliest Chinese Accounts of the Compilation of the *Tripiṭaka* (II)," *Journal of the American Oriental Society* 81.2 (1961): 281–299.

2. The locus classicus for this allusion is the *Zhuang Zi*, chap. 26. The passage, in Victor Mair's felicitous

translation, goes as follows: "A fish-trap is for catching fish; once you've caught the fish, you can forget about the trap. A rabbit-snare is for catching rabbits; once you've caught the rabbit, you can forget about the snare. Words are for catching ideas; once you've caught the idea, you can forget about the words. Where can I find a person who knows how to forget about words so I can have a few words with him?" (*Wandering on the Way* [New York: Bantam Books, 1994; rpt. Honolulu: University of Hawai'i Press, 1998], 276–277).

3. *Brāhmī* and *kharoṣṭhī* are the two principal scripts used in ancient India. As Sengyou's description indicates, *brāhmī* was written left to right while *kharoṣṭhī,* which was modeled on Aramaic, was written right to left. Obviously both of these horizontally oriented scripts contrasted with Chinese, which is traditionally written top down and right to left.

4. Cang Jie was the minister of the legendary Yellow Emperor of hoary antiquity. He is traditionally accredited with inventing Chinese writing, modeling his script on the footprints of birds and animals.

5. This is a reference to the sixty-four scripts that the Buddha had mastered as a youth according to one of his early biographies. The following names are among the types of script listed.

6. *Hu* here is very difficult to translate. In ancient times *hu* typically referred to tribes on China's northern border with whom the Chinese frequently skirmished. By the Six Dynasties and Tang period, *hu* generally came to mean foreigners from the west, especially Iranians, but also Indians, Tokharians, Arabs, Uyghurs, and even Romans involved in the lucrative Silk Road trade.

7. The practice of assigning a meaning to each of the letters in the Sanskrit alphabet is well known in Buddhist texts.

8. Here Sengyou is drawing from the *Mahāyāna-mahāparinirvāṇa-sūtra:* "Moreover, the meanings of the half-characters [enumerated earlier in the text] are the source of the teachings on the moral defilements. Therefore they are called half-characters. The full-characters then are the basis for the teachings on all good things. It is like people engaged in bad actions being called 'half people' while those who cultivate good actions are called 'complete people.' Thus, all sutra texts and treatises depend on half-characters as their basis." (T 375, 12:655a.20–24)

9. *Futu* and *sangmen* are archaic transcriptions for "buddha" and "śramaṇa" respectively. For a brief account of the pre-Buddhist transcription system employed in the Han histories *(Hanshu* and *Hou Hanshu),* see Erik Zürcher, *The Buddhist Conquest of China* (Leiden: E. J. Brill, 1959), 39–40. As Zürcher notes, the attempt to transcribe foreign names in Chinese script may date to the first few centuries before the Common Era with the work of interpreters at the Office of Foreign Relations (Honglu si).

10. This example is taken from the *Shijing* (poem no. 231). Sengyou is here clearly following the great Han commentator Zheng Xuan (127–200), who glossed this passage as follows: "'*Si*' (this, this one) is equivalent to '*bai*' (white). People today say that the graphs '*si*' and '*bai*' are to be taken as '*xian*' (bright, fresh). During the time of the [ancient states of] Qi and Lu, its pronunciation was close to '*si*'." This exegesis is not entirely clear, and there are good reasons for rejecting Zheng Xuan's hypothesis despite the fact that Sengyou found it convincing.

11. What Sengyou is saying here is that these Chinese characters were chosen for their sound value to represent the same Indic word; they differ because of the different pronunciation habits of the respective translators. It is also possible, however, that the Indian originals of these translations were in fact written in different languages or topolects (Sanskrit, Gāndhārī, and various other Prakrits), a possibility Sengyou seems not to have been aware of.

12. Sengyou is almost certainly correct in claiming that most early translators did not thoroughly command both the Chinese and Indian languages. This is nonetheless a rather stark if not surprising admission by a very prominent Buddhist scholar.

13. With regard to balancing simplicity or plainness of style *(zhi)* and form or embellishment *(wen),* the locus classicus is the *Analects* 6.18: "The Master said: 'Simplicity over embellishment is coarseness; embellishment over simplicity is mere flourish. When embellishment and simplicity are balanced, then we have a true nobleman.'"

IN THE COURSE of the spread of the Buddhist religion from India to China, which had begun quietly during the first century of the Common Era, there came a point at which it began to arouse the opposition of certain members of the gentry who saw it as a threat to China's traditional values. By the end of the fifth century, resistance was especially strong among representatives of China's indigenous religion of Taoism in the Southern Dynasties of Qi (479–502) and Liang (502–557), whose rulers actively supported the foreign faith. Their resistance is the more interesting in view of the traditional Chinese belief, shared by both Confucianists and Taoists, that a Central Harmony, or Unitary Force, called "the Way" (Tao) pervades the entire universe, and that following the Tao is not only natural, but is the only principle by which the universe can run smoothly. Because of this Unitary Force, all apparent differences are treated as "outward manifestations" *(ji* 跡*),* which, if traced to the Center, will be found to be in harmony with the Tao. This basic characteristic of the Chinese world-view has made it possible for most Chinese to reconcile any variance from their own traditions as merely a superficial aberration. Even the harshest critics of the foreign religion insisted that they had no quarrel with Buddhism's ultimate goal of Enlightenment. What offended them most was the introduction of barbarous customs *(su),* such as monks and nuns deserting their families, and shaving off the hair bestowed on them by their parents, and, yes, squatting on their heels or in chairs instead of sitting respectfully on the ground.

The resulting crossfire of polemic attacks by members of the Taoist and Confucian gentry and defenses by Buddhist apologists, including occasional rejoinders by the original attackers, has filled large sections of two anthologies: the *Collection of [Documents] on the Propagation and Illumination [of the Dharma] (Hongming ji),* compiled by the monk Sengyou (see selection 42) around 510, and its sequel, the *Expanded Collection [of Documents] etc. (Guang hongming ji),* by Dao Xuan, a century later (both may be found in vol. 52 of the *Taishō Tripiṭaka).*

To give some sense at first hand of the issues involved, and the emotional intensity of the disputants, we have selected the greater portion of the "Treatise on Barbarians and Chinese" (Yixia lun) by the Taoist priest *(daoshi)* Gu Huan (d. after 483), included in his official biography in the *History of the Southern Qi (Nan Qi shu,* 54), followed by a rebuttal by the Liu-Song Director of Instruction, Yuan Can (420–477), through his friend, the monk Shi Huitong, and, finally, Gu Huan's rejoinder, all from the aforementioned biography.—RM

Gu Huan's "Treatise on Barbarians and Chinese"

In distinguishing between truth and falsehood it is appropriate to base one's opinion on sacred scriptures *(shengdian).* If one researches the sources of the two traditions (Buddhism and Taoism), indeed one finds that both point to scriptural passages. A Taoist scripture states, "Lao Zi entered the Pass (i.e., the Hindu Kush) and proceeded to the kingdom of Kapilavastu ([Jia-] wei-[luo]-wei). The wife of the king was named Māya (Jingmiao). Lao Zi, taking advantage of her daytime nap, entered into Māya's mouth riding on the essence of the sun *(rijing).* Later, on the eighth day of the fourth month, at midnight, he (Lao Zi/the Buddha) was born by opening up her left armpit. The moment he dropped to the ground, he walked seven paces. It was at this point that Buddhism came into being." This passage comes from the *Inner Chapters of the Mysterious Wonder (Xuanmiao neipian)*.[1]

A Buddhist scripture says, "Śākyamuni became the Buddha as many times as there are numberless *kalpas*." [This passage] comes from the section "The Infinite Life Span" of the *Lotus Sutra (Fahua, Wuliangshou)*.[2] [Another passage states,] "He became a National Preceptor, a Master of the Tao, the Ancestor of the Literati." "[This passage] comes from the *Sutra on the Auspicious Fulfillment of the Crown Prince ([Taizi] ruiying benqi jing)*."[3]

My thoughts on this are as follows: During the reigns of the Five Thearchs and Three August Ones,[4] none of these rulers was without an adviser. Among National Preceptors and Masters of the Tao, none ever surpassed Lao Zi and Zhuang Zi. As for the Ancestor of the Literati, who would have surpassed the Duke of Zhou and Confucius? If Confucius and Lao Zi were not the Buddha, then who were they? Thus, what the two traditions say are like the two halves of a tally. Tao is the Buddha; the Buddha is Tao. In their ideal of sageliness *(sheng)* they are identical; only in their outward manifestation *(ji)* are they at odds. One is the "Tempered Light" *(heguang* [of the Tao]), which illuminates what is near; the other is the "Radiant Spirit" *(yaoling)* [of the sun], which reveals what is distant.[5] The Tao sustains all under heaven; there is no quarter where it does not penetrate. [Buddha]-wisdom pervades all creation; no being is unaffected. But since their entrances have not been the same, their effects are also bound to differ. In each tradition [the adherents] fulfill their own natures *(xing),* and thus do not alter the things they do *(shi)*. Ceremonial caps and robes, with tablets of office tucked in their sashes, are the fashion of Chinese [officials]; shaved heads and loose garments are the habit of Barbarian [monks]. Kneeling reverently and bowing from the waist are expressions of respect within the [Chinese] royal domain; crouching like foxes and squatting like dogs are deemed to be dignified postures in the wilds. To be buried in a double coffin is the rule in China; to be incinerated on a funeral pyre or submerged under water is the custom among the western Barbarians. To preserve one's body whole and observe the proper rituals is the teaching that aims at perpetuating goodness; to disfigure one's appearance and alter one's nature is the study that seeks to terminate evil. Since [the latter] link up with strange beings, are they the same as humans? [Thus,] the kings of birds and the lords of beasts are often buddhas.

Through endless generations sages have arisen one after another. Some have expounded the *Five Canons (Wudian);* others have propagated the Three Vehicles (Sansheng).[6] Among birds [the sages] have chirped like birds, and among beasts they have roared like beasts. When instructing the Chinese they have spoken Chinese, when converting Barbarians they have spoken Barbarian, that's all. Although boats and carriages are equal when it comes to traveling distances, still there are limitations imposed by whether one is traveling by rivers or overland. Buddhism and Taoism are on a level when it comes to "achieving transformation" *(dahua)*. However, there are distinctions between Barbarians and Chinese. If one thinks that since the ends are the same, therefore the means are interchangeable, does that mean that carriages may cross rivers or boats may travel overland?

At present [some misguided people] are trying to make the nature of the Chinese conform to the doctrines of the western Barbarians. These two peoples are, on the one hand, not entirely the same, nor, on the other, are they entirely different. [The Barbarians] abandon their wives and children, and have done away with ancestral sacrifices. On the other hand, things to which they are attached and which they desire are promoted by their rituals; it is only the canons of filial piety and reverence that are suppressed by their doctrines. They have rebelled against the rites and violated compliance with them without ever being aware of it. Weak and lost, they have forgotten to return home. Who among them recognize their past? Furthermore, that which is most honorable in the noumenal world *(li* 理*)* is the Tao; that which is most contemptible in the phenomenal world *(shi* 事*)* is custom *(su)*. To reject the Chinese (Hua) and imitate the Barbarians (Yi)—where can morality be found in that? Should we follow the Tao? The Tao is definitely in accord with [our tradition]. Should we follow [Barbarian] custom? [Barbarian] custom is greatly at odds [with it].[7]

I have frequently observed "gunwale-notching" *(kexian)* Buddhist monks and "tree-trunk-guarding" *(shouzhu)* Taoist priests[8] arguing back and forth over which is greater or smaller, taking potshots at each other. Some delineate the Tao, considering it [and vulgar custom] to be two [different things]. Others obfuscate vulgar custom, considering it to be one and the same [with the Tao]. This is dragging together things that are different and considering them the same, and destroying things that are [really] the same and considering them different, with the result that they become the source of conflict and the basis of confusion. Even though [these two traditions] are the same in seeking sagehood *(xunsheng)*, their methods [in doing so] are as far apart as left and right. Their beginnings have no starting-point and their final goal no ending-point. Attaining nirvana *(nihuan)* and becoming a transcendent being *(xianhua)* are each distinct techniques. Buddhists call theirs "Correct Truth" *(zhengzhen)*; Taoists call theirs "Correct Unity" *(zhengyi)*. "Unity" results in "No Death" *(wusi)*. "Truth" coincides with "No Rebirth" *(wusheng)*. In name they are in opposition; in reality they are in agreement. But the doctrine of "No Rebirth" refers to a postponed future *(she)*, while the transformation of "No Death" deals with the immediate present *(qie)*. A doctrine of immediacy may be used to encourage humility and gentleness *(qianruo)*, whereas a doctrine of a postponed future may be used to discourage bragging and violence *(kuaqiang)*.[9] Buddhism is elaborate and diffuse; Taoism is plain and refined. The refined is not something crude people believe in, nor is diffuseness something refined people are capable of. Buddhist words are flowery and attractive; Taoist words are truthful and forbidding. If it is forbidding, then only the intelligent make progress; if it is attractive, then the unintelligent compete to move forward. Buddhist scriptures are prolix and obvious; Taoist scriptures are terse and obscure.[10] If it is obscure, then the "Subtle Gate" is hard to see; if it is obvious, then the "Correct Path" is easy to follow. These are the distinctions between the two doctrines.

The sage craftsman has no [prejudicial] thoughts *(wuxin)*, but square and round each has its [own distinctive] shape. So, just as each tool (whether a square or a compass) has its own special function, doctrines also have different applications. Buddhism is a formula for destroying evil; Taoism is a technique for encouraging goodness. To encourage goodness, naturalness *(ziran)* is paramount; to destroy evil, courage and ferocity *(yongmeng)* are valorized. The outward traces of Buddhism are brilliant and massive, suitable for converting living beings. The outward traces of Taoism, on the other hand, are secret and subtle, beneficial for use in self-development. The superiority or inferiority of one in relation to the other lies, for the most part, in these distinctions.

As for the posture of squatting on their heels *(dunyi)* and talking gibberish *(louluo)*, each of these comes out of their customs, which they understand among themselves. It's like the chirping of insects and twittering of birds. Why would it be worth transmitting or imitating?

Yuan Can's (420–477) Response to Gu Huan through the Monk Shi Huitong

When the sun halted its beams and the constant stars hid their light—the fulfillment of [the Buddha's] descent and birth—this event took place before [the time of] Lao Zi, so it would appear that [Lao Zi] did not first enter the Pass before this portent was manifested.[11] Furthermore [in the teachings of] Lao Zi, Zhuang Zi, [the Duke of] Zhou, and Confucius, if there is the possibility of survival [after death], it is like the fading rays of the sun. According to Śākyamuni's bequeathed teachings, an ox-thief who falsely claims to be good will, on the contrary, become a worm [in his next incarnation]. If you examine the original sources [of Taoism and Confucianism], in the end they simply differ from the way our [Buddhist] community practices the Tao, that's all.

[According to] records from the Western Regions *(xiyu)* and statements in the Buddhist sutras, it is customary *(su)* to consider crawling on hands and knees *(xixing)* to be a ceremonious act *(li)*. [Buddhists] do not favor squatting on their heels *(dunzuo)* as a respectful posture. And in their religious worship they consider a threefold circumambulation *(sanrao)* to be a sign of respectful humility. They do not esteem squatting haughtily *(ju'ao)* to be dignified. Why would it be only in the land of the Rong Barbarians [that this is done]? Indeed, it also happens here. When Xiang Tong (identity uncertain) paid a visit to the emperor, he approached him crawling on his knees. When the King of Zhao had an audience with the King of Zhou, he circumambulated [the throne] three times before stopping. At present, ever since Buddhism has been in China, those who have accepted it are always peaceful and law-abiding. Their rules of conduct are good in regard both to personal behavior and in relations with others, and those who walk in them are always in compliance. When King Wen founded the Zhou (ca. 1045 B.C.E.), and Taibo (King Wen's father) established Wu (in the Yangtze Delta), they totally transformed the Rong and the Yi, so that they no longer followed their old customs. How can Chinese and Barbarians be [compared to] boats and carriages, whose principles are not mutually interchangeable? As Buddhist doctrines have come down and evolved, some have been followed and some changed. Followers of "pure faith" *(qingxin,* a literal translation of *upāsaka,* or lay believer), have not changed their appearance or clothing. In the case of those "of tranquil mind" *(xixin,* a literal translation of *śramaṇa,* or monk), their clothing and appearance are changed by necessity. The change basically follows the Tao, and does not conform to local custom. The mores *(feng)* of the two religions are naturally divergent; there is no need to complain about any confusion.

Confucius, Lao Zi, and Śākyamuni, as persons, were in some respects the same. In their viewpoints, and in establishing their doctrines, [what each deemed to be] the "Tao" was necessarily different. For Confucius and Lao Zi, governing the world *(zhishi)* was their starting point. For Śākyamuni transcending the world *(chushi)* was his ideal. Since their starting points were divergent, their destinations were also different. The notion of their "matching like two halves of a tally" *(fuhe)* naturally proceeds from [unsupported] opinion.

Furthermore, "transformation into a transcendent being" *(xianhua)* puts "changing the body" *(bianshen)* in the ascendancy, whereas nirvana *(nihuan)* puts "molding the spirit" *(taoshen)* first. For those who change the body, their white hair may change to black, but they will never be able to become immortal. Those who mold the spirit, causing its dust and delusion daily to diminish, in a profound way will survive forever. When the Taos of Nirvana and of the Lands of Immortality are as diametrically opposed as this, how can you say they are the same?

Gu Huan's Rejoinder

In regard to the creation on the Taoist scriptures, they were written during the Western Zhou (ca. 1045–771 B.C.E.), whereas the coming [to China] of Buddhist scriptures began only during the Eastern Han (25–220 C.E.). The number of years that the Taoist scriptures preceded the Buddhist is thus more than eight hundred, and the reigns during that interval numbered several tens. If you think that, even though the Yellow Emperor and Lao Zi are ancient, it is still excessive [to claim they came] before Śākyamuni, this is [like saying] Lü Shang (who aided in overthrowing the Shang ruler, Zhou Xin) stole Chen Heng's state of Qi,[12] or that Liu Xiu usurped Wang Mang's state of Han.[13] The classic[14] states, "The Rong Barbarian temper is violent. They capture people and commandeer carts. Furthermore, the Yi Barbarian custom of kneeling upright is different from that of the Chinese. Their left knee sticks up and their right knee splays out, just as though they were 'squatting on their heels.'"

Also, in regard to the Yi Barbarian custom of constantly squatting, the way they do it is different from that of the Chinese, who raise the left [knee] and kneel on the right. The Barbarians always squat on their heels *(dunju)*. It was because of this that the Duke of Zhou first outlawed the practice,[15] and Confucius denounced it after him.[16] Furthermore, boats are for crossing streams and carriages for traveling on land. Buddhism (a religion that claims to rescue the deluded) originated among the Rong Barbarians. Doesn't this mean that the customs of the Rong Barbarians are habitually bad? Taoism (a religion that encourages self-development) originated in China. Doesn't this mean that Chinese customs are basically good? Today, now that Chinese customs have changed and become just as bad as those of the Rong and Di Barbarians, the fact that Buddhism has come here to destroy [these evil customs] is only natural. The Tao of the Buddha is indeed valuable, and therefore its commandments and practices are to be honored. But the customs of the Rong Barbarians are truly despicable; therefore their speech and their appearance should be rejected. Today all the Chinese gentlemen and ladies, as well as the common people, have not changed [their natures], but they insist on squatting with exposed heads, wantonly using the manners of the Yi Barbarians. They talk to the shorn-headed crowd, all of them Hu Barbarians. The state has its own long-standing mores; its laws are not to be altered.

Again, if we observe the Fashionable Teaching *(fengliu jiao),*[17] its Tao is bound to be different. Buddhism is not the Tao of the eastern Chinese, nor is Taoism the religion of the western Rong. Fish and birds from different bodies of water never have contact with each other. How is it that we get the two religions, Taoism and Buddhism, dealing with each other in all directions? Today, ever since Buddhism has spread eastward, Taoism has also moved westward. Thus we know that in the world there are the refined *(jing)* and the crude *(cu),* and among all religions there are the elaborate *(wen)* and the plain *(zhi).* Since this is so, then [we may say] Taoism grasps the root *(ben)* in order to control the branches *(mo),* while Buddhism rescues the branches in order to preserve the root.[18] I would like to ask: wherein do the differences lie? Of what do the [respective] goals *(gui)* consist? If we take shearing the head to be the difference, then chain-gang convicts *(xumi)* also have have their heads sheared. If we take setting up images to be the difference, then ordinary shamans *(suwu)* also set up images. These are not the [ultimate] goals. The [ultimate] goal [for both] consists in eternal life *(changzhu).* The symbol of eternal life—wherein does it differ from the Eternal Tao (Changdao)?

[To say that] Gods and Transcendent Beings *(shenxian)* are mortal is a statement of expedience *(quanbian zhi shuo).* "Gods" and "Transcendent Beings" are general terms for the Great Transformation *(dahua;* i.e., stages along the way to union with the Tao). They are not the Ultimate Name *(zhiming)* of the Totally Mysterious *(qiongmiao;* i.e., the Tao itself). The Ultimate Name is nameless *(wuming).* The ones that have names are the Twenty-seven Stages *(ershiqi pin);* Transcendent Beings *(xian)* become Realized Beings *(zhen);* Realized Beings become Gods *(shen)* or Sages *(sheng).* Each of these [three stages] has nine further gradations of its own (low-low, mid-low, high-low; low-mid, mid-mid, high-mid; low-high, mid-high, high-high). At the pinnacle of these gradations one enters Empty Silence *(kongji),* which is actionless and nameless. If one ingests [macrobiotic] herbs and polypores *(ruzhi),* one will prolong one's life span ten-thousand-fold or a million-fold. But when the life span is ended, one dies. When the herbs are exhausted, one withers away. These are merely gentlemen who cultivate longevity; they do not belong in the company of Gods and Transcendent Beings.[19]

—RM

Notes

1. Although the title of this scripture definitely has a Taoistic ring to it (the term *xuanmiao* was used in the *Daode jing,* and *Neipian* is a section of the *Zhuang Zi*), no such work can be found in the Taoist Canon. Gu Huan seems rather to be loosely misreading a passage from Zhi Qian's (320 C.E.) translation of the life of the historical Buddha, *Taizi ruiying benqi jing:*

> [The Bodhisattva] was reborn in the Kingdom of Kapilavastu in Sindh. The name of his father, the king, was Śuddhodana (Baijing), a wise and worthy man. The name of his mother, the queen, was Māya (Miao). . . . When the Bodhisattva first descended [to Earth] he transformed himself into a white elephant, crowned with the essence of the sun. While his mother was taking a daytime nap, he revealed himself to her in a dream, whereupon he entered [her body] through her right side. When she awoke from her dream she realized she was pregnant. . . . On the night of the eighth day of the fourth month, when the bright stars had come out, he transformed himself again and was born through her right side. The moment he dropped to the ground he walked seven paces.

2. Words to this effect may be found in section 16, "The Lifespan of the Tathāgata" *(Rulai shou),* of the *Lotus Sutra (Miaofa lianhua jing):* "Since I actually achieved Buddhahood there have been numberless, infinite, hundreds, thousands, myriads, millions of *ayutas* of *kalpas.*"

3. This passage does, indeed, come from the *Taizi ruiying benqi jing:* "As for [the Buddha's] transformations, he appears according to the times: sometimes as a Sage Thearch *(shengdi),* sometimes as the Ancestor of the Literati *(rulin zhi zong),* or as a National Preceptor *(guoshi).* Places where he has appeared or been transformed are more than can be recorded."

4. There is no unanimity regarding the identity or dates of the Five Thearchs *(wudi)* and Three August Ones *(sanhuang),* except that they go back to dim antiquity and include such luminaries as Fu Xi, Shen Nong, the Yellow Emperor (Huang Di, trad. r. 2698–2599 B.C.E.), and the Sage Kings, Yao (trad. r. 2357–2258 B.C.E.), Shun (trad. r. 2255–2208 B.C.E.), and Yu (trad. r. 2208–ca. 2195 B.C.E.).

5. See *Daode jing,* 4: "[The Tao] . . . blunts its sharpness, unties its tangles, tempers its light, identifies itself with the [world's] dust." See also the section entitled "Questions to Heaven" (Tianwen) in the *Lyrics of Chu (Chuci):* "When dawn has not yet broken in the lunar mansion, Horn (Jue), where has the Radiant Spirit (i.e., the sun) been hiding?"

6. See the *Zuo Commentary (Zuozhuan,* twelfth year of Duke Zhao): "Here is a good historiographer; . . . he can read the *Three Mounds (Sanfen),* the *Five Canons (Wudian),* the *Eight Rules (Basuo),* and the *Nine Hills (Jiuqiu)* (ancient lost works on government and morals attributed to the above-mentioned Five Thearchs and Three August Ones)." The Three Vehicles (Sansheng) are the Great Vehicle (Mahāyāna), so called because it carries all living beings to Enlightenment; the Disciple's Vehicle (Śrāvakayāna), which carries only monks and nuns, and is therefore called the "Lesser Vehicle" by Mahāyānists; and an intermediate category, the Pratyekabuddha-yāna, for those few who attain Buddhahood on their own without assistance from compassionate bodhisattvas. Though the correspondence with the "Five Canons" is not perfect, "Three Vehicles" is a convenient Buddhist numerical category to match one taken from Chinese tradition.

7. The somewhat tortured argument seems to be as follows: The Tao is the True Principle governing the universe. Chinese culture is built on the idea of following the Tao. For Barbarians, at least, human "affairs" *(shi)* are based on mere "custom" *(su),* which, for them, since they do not consciously follow the Tao, tends

to be "vulgar." Not having enjoyed the civilizing influence of Chinese culture, the Barbarians are therefore the victims of their own vulgar customs. Thus, when Gu Huan uses the term *su* (vulgar custom), it is for him a synonym for "Barbarian," while the term "Tao" is synonymous with "Chinese," not Taoism alone.

8. "Gunwale-notching" and "tree-trunk-guarding" are metaphors for simplemindedness. The first is based on a tale told in the *Lüshi chunqiu* 15, sec. 8, "Investigating the Present" (Chajin): "A man from Chu was crossing the Jiang (the Yangtze River) when his sword fell from inside the boat into the water. He instantly notched a mark on the gunwale of the boat, saying, 'This is the point from which my sword fell.' Whereupon [he ordered] the boat stopped while he jumped into the water from the point he had marked on the gunwale to look for it. Meanwhile, the boat had already drifted [downstream] while the sword had not. Was he not somewhat simpleminded to look for his sword in that way?" The second expression comes from *Han Fei Zi*, "The Five Vermin" (Wudu): "There was once a plowman from Song (modern Henan) in whose field there grew a large tree. One day a rabbit, racing [across the field], collided with the tree-trunk, breaking its neck and dying. The plowman forthwith forsook his plow and stood guard by the tree-trunk, hoping he would get another rabbit. But another rabbit never came and he became the laughingstock of the Song state."

9. It is unclear which Buddhist term Gu Huan had in mind when he characterized the final goal of Buddhism as "Correct Truth" *(zhengzhen)*. He may have been thinking of the "Four Noble Truths" (Skt. *catvāri āryasatyāni;* C. *sizhendi*): (1) that all existence is Suffering *(duḥkha)*, (2) that Suffering is caused by the Accumulation *(samudaya)* of desire and attachment, (3) that there is a way toward its Cessation *(nirodha)*, and (4) that the Way *(mārga)* is comprised of: Correct Views *(zhengjian)*, Correct Thought *(zhengsi)*, Correct Speech *(zhengyu)*, Correct Action *(zhengye)*, Correct Occupation *(zhengming)*, Correct Progress *(zheng jingjin)*, Correct Memory *(zhengnian)*, and Correct Meditation *(zhengding)*. On the Taoist side, "Correct Unity" *(zhengyi)* clearly refers to mystical unity with the Tao through meditation. See *The Master Who Embraces Simplicity (Baopuzi, Neipian)* 18, "Earthly Truth" (Dizhen): "[True] Unity is found in the middle of the vast depths of the Northern Culmen (Beiji = the North Star). In front [are the stars of] the Hall of Light (Mingtang = the head); behind, [the stars of] the Crimson Palace (Jianggong = the heart); high, high above is [the constellation] Floriate Canopy (Huagai = the lungs); [the constellation] Golden Loft (Jinlou = the kidneys) arches overhead; to the left are [the stars of] Gang (the bowl of the Big Dipper [pronounced Gahng, with the "a" sounding as it does in "father"]); to the right is Kuei (the handle of the Dipper). . . . This is the general scheme of True Unity."

Physical immortality ("No Death"), through both alchemical and meditative techniques, is basic to Taoist praxis. Cessation of the cycle of rebirths in nirvana or in the Western Paradise of Amitābha ("No Rebirth") is the ultimate goal of Buddhism. Gu Huan looked on the former as "immediate" *(qie)*, which for him meant "relevant to this life," whereas the promise of ultimate surcease, or threats of future punishment in Hell, as he saw it, tended to have no visible effect on present behavior.

10. To characterize the Buddhist *Tripiṭaka* as "elaborate and diffuse" *(wen er buo)*, in contrast to the "plain and refined" *(zhi er jing)* quality of the Taoist Canon, or to match Buddhist "prolixity and obviousness" *(fan er xian)* against Taoist "terseness and obscurity" *(jian er you)* may have been justifiable in the fifth century, before the Taoist scriptures themselves had expanded to the fifteen hundred or so titles of the Ming *Taoist Canon (Zhengtong Daozang)*, published during the fifteenth century, which includes many items strongly influenced by, or even directly imitating, titles in the *Tripiṭaka*. But, of course, Gu Huan is indulging here in a neat series of antithetical parallel couplets.

11. The fourteenth of the Thirty-two Portents marking the Buddha's birth, according to *Taizi ruiying benqi jing*, was: "The sun, moon, stars, and constellations all stood still and did not move."

12. The chronology here is admittedly confusing. Lü Shang (a.k.a. Taigong Wang) aided King Wu of Zhou in overthrowing the last Shang king. Chen Heng, during a coup in 481 B.C.E., overthrew his ruler, Duke Jian of Qi (see *Zuozhuan*, fourteenth year of Duke Ai). Gu seems to base his argument on the putative date of the oldest Taoist texts, such as the *Lao Zi* and works attributed to the mythical Yellow Emperor, rather than the uncertain dates of the earliest Chinese translations of Pāli and Sanskrit originals. He appears to be ignoring the Taoist texts of obviously later provenance.

13. Liu Ji is Emperor Guangwu, who overthrew the real usurper, Wang Mang, and founded the Later Han in 25 C.E. Gu Huan appears to be indulging in sarcasm.

14. The "classic" referred to here has not been identified.

15. This refers to the *Book of Documents (Shangshu)*, v.1.6: "[King Wu (trad. r. 1122–1115 B.C.E.) said], 'I, Fa, the Little Child, . . . observing the government of Shang, [find that its ruler], Shou (= Zhou Xin), does not have a contrite heart, but squats on his heels *(yiju)*, serving neither the Supreme God (Shang Di), nor the spirits of Heaven and Earth, and neglecting the temple of his ancestors by failing to sacrifice.'"

16. *Analects* 14. 46: "Yuan Rang was squatting on his heels waiting *(yisi)*. The Master said to him, 'Those who are disrespectful when they are young will achieve nothing to hand down when they are grown up. Merely to die of old age is to be nothing more than a robber!' With that he struck him across the shins with his staff." Obviously, in every educated Chinese gentleman's mind in those days squatting was symptomatic of disrespect and savagery. It is no coincidence that the name Yi, applied to the Eastern Barbarians, means "Squatters."

17. The "Fashionable Teaching" probably signifies the Buddho-Taoist blend of Confucianism, also known as "Dark Learning" or "Study of Mystery" *(xuanxue)*, popular in the Six Dynasties.

18. The idea seems to be that Taoism simply encourages natural growth, from root to branch, while Buddhism starts by trimming the sickly or distorted branches—the result of previous misdeeds—in the vain effort to recover a lost perfection.

19. Gu Huan's rejoinder basically reaffirms three points against which Yuan Can had raised objections: (1) that Buddhism did not originate before Lao Zi's reputed visit to India; (2) that the barbarous customs introduced into China by Buddhist missionaries, such as the disrespectful posture of squatting, are, despite Yuan's disclaimer, still practiced by Chinese Buddhists [the irony of this accusation is that it was the Buddhists who introduced the chair to China and the earliest folding chairs were called "Barbarian beds" *(huchuang)* because of their origin], and (3) that Yuan's insistence that the "Taos," or "Ultimate Goals" of the two religions are not the same is mistaken. According to Gu, Yuan has failed to note the difference between the proximate goal of longevity pursued by some Taoists through various macrobiotic techniques and the Ultimate Goal of transcendence of the world, which is the same for both religions.

THE FOLLOWING NARRATIVES are a modest sample of the hundreds, if not thousands, of tales of filial piety that circulated throughout early-medieval China (100–589 C.E.). In terms of popularity and number, the early-medieval period witnessed the golden age of this type of story. High officials and even emperors compiled them into collections called "Lives of Filial Offspring" (Xiaozi zhuan), and the best poets of the age lauded their exemplars in verse. "The Twenty-four Filial Exemplars" genre of popular literature incorporated many of these tales, which thereby became known to nearly every adult and child in late-imperial China. By showing historical personages whose conduct embodied the value of filial piety, these accounts made this abstract virtue comprehensible and provided models of correct behavior that the reader could either imitate or from which gain inspiration. Consequently, for nearly two millennia, filial piety stories shaped expectations of how children should serve their parents.

Rather than the later "Twenty-four Filial Exemplars" tales, this selection focuses on early-medieval stories because they are longer, more sophisticated, and more varied in content. This is probably due to the fact that adults were their primary audience. "Ji Mai," one of the longer filial piety tales, contains a virtual treasure trove of filial motifs, such as becoming a day laborer to support one's parents, mourning according to the exact regulations of the Confucian rites, avenging one's parents and then turning oneself in to the authorities, receiving heavenly rewards for one's piety, and, at one's parents' death, nearly dying from excessive grief. "Li Shan" illustrates another facet of the tales: his story indicates that filial piety was not merely a virtue confined to sons and daughters. In an era when one was supposed to also treat his or her lord and teacher as a parent, this was an important message. "Qiu Jie" reveals the narratives' lighter side, reminding us that although the tales' main purpose was didactic, they were entertaining as well. As for "Guo Ju," one of the most famous stories, I have included it because it disturbs both modern Chinese intellectuals and Western readers. Yet it was one of the most emotionally powerful narratives for premodern readers because Guo Ju has to choose between the two things that Chinese held to be most dear—their parents and their children. It also suggests that the poverty of many filial sons was voluntary. Note that all four stories emphasize the supernatural efficacy of filial piety— something we do not usually associate with supposedly rationalistic Confucians.—KK

Ji Mai[1]

Ji Mai was a man from Lujiang. He originally was surnamed Shu. Due to his birth on the fifth day of the fifth month, his mother abandoned him.[2] Woman Zhao, the wife of a fellow villager named Ji Shun, raised him. Upon reaching six years of age, his original mother and father came to see him, saying, "You are our child." Weeping, Mai told Zhao, who then told him everything from start to finish. Upon reaching ten years of age, Mai hired out his labor. He would divide his earnings: each mother would receive half [of his wages]. When [Ji] Shun died, he was without sons. In accordance with the most severe degree of mourning, Mai mourned him for three years. His original parents then died one after another. He then wore second-degree mourning clothes [for a year], but in his heart, he mourned them for three.[3]

Woman Zhao desired to obtain a wife for Mai. Wishing to present [gifts of] wine and rice, she went to the bride's home. Along the way, she encountered drunkards who beat her senseless. Suddenly a dog came straight to Mai and grabbed hold of his robe three times. Mai's heart was moved by this. While hurriedly running toward the bride's home, he happened upon the drunkards who were [sitting] in the grass toasting each other and drinking [the wine]. Mai used a pole to kill both of them. Woman Zhao was thus able to safely return home. Mai went to the prefectural yamen to confess, but the prefect forgave him [for his crime]. Mai thereupon swore he would never take a wife. Later when he was sleeping, there was suddenly a woman who said, "My surname is Wei. Yesterday I suddenly died violently. The Heavenly Deity pities you for having no wife. He has sent me to reward you." Mai reported everything to his mother. When mother and son reached the outside gate of the yamen, as expected, everything was as the dead woman said. Meanwhile her body was just about to be put on the hearse, but the oxen would not budge. Woman Zhao then explained everything to the chief mourner. He opened the coffin. His daughter was breathing. By dawn, she could talk. She told them everything from start to finish. It was just as Woman Zhao had said. Mai and the woman became man and wife. When Woman Zhao died, Mai expired but came back to life. This recurred for several days. When Mai was fifty, he became sick and almost died. He dreamed that a deity said, "You have perfect filial conduct. We will extend your life span so that you will almost reach one hundred." As expected, he died only after reaching ninety-seven years of age.

Li Shan[4]

Li Shan was a man from Nanyang. Originally, he was the family slave of Father Li. [One day] the whole [Li] family was completely wiped out [by disease]. The sole survivor was [Li's] son, who was only several months old. Li Shan cradled him in his arms and would not abandon him. Night and day, he would go around among his neighbors begging for milk so that he could satisfy [his young master's appetite] during the morning and evening audiences.[5] After this went on for a long time, his neighbors became fed up with this situation and were no longer willing to give him any milk. The child thereupon became emaciated; he was near death. Melancholy overcame Li Shan, and he could not curb his grief. He uncontrollably wailed and pitifully beseeched Heaven. He sought its help to save [the infant]. Heaven was moved by his determination. [Thereupon] liquid flowed out of his two breasts. Once the infant was able to obtain milk, he regained his health.

When he was already advanced in years of age, Li Shan accepted the office of Section Head (caozhu). During the morning and evening audiences, when he was paying respect to his superiors, he never was late. When commandery and prefectural officials submitted memorials, he would forward [all of them] to the emperor for his perusal. The emperor was moved by his righteousness (yi), and consequently bestowed upon him the surname Li. He then issued an edict throughout the realm that promoted Li to the position of Prefect of Yiling. His perfect filial conduct was famous throughout the Four Seas. Hence, this is what Confucius was referring to when he said, "He can be entrusted with an orphan six span tall."[6] This story comes from the *Lives of Filial Offspring*.

Qiu Jie[7]

Qiu Jie's style name was Weizhi. He was a man from Wucheng in Wuxing. Upon suffering his mother's death, he would not eat any cooked vegetables because they were tasty.[8] After being ill for more than a year, he suddenly dreamed that he met his mother who said, "To die only means to be apart. What in the world would made you endure this kind of hardship? When you ate raw vegetables, you met with frog poison. In front of my spirit bier there is a bowl that has three balls of medicine. Retrieve it and eat the balls." Jie awoke with a start. As expected he found a bowl that had three balls of medicine. He ate them. He thereupon excreted several pints of tadpoles.[9] For generations the Qiu family treasured that bowl, but in the seventh year of the Great Illumination reign of the [Liu-]Song dynasty (464), it was lost in a fire.

Guo Ju[10]

Guo Ju was a man from Wen in Henei. His family was exceedingly rich. When his father died, he divided the patrimony of twenty million cash into two portions. He gave one each to his two younger brothers. He alone took his mother to reverently support,[11] but they had to stay in temporary lodging. In their neighborhood, there was a haunted house. No one lived there. Everyone recommended that it be given to Guo Ju. When Guo lived there no calamities befell him. His wife gave birth to a son. However, Guo Ju thought that if he raised him, it would hinder his ability to reverently support his mother. He then ordered his wife to hold the child while he dug a hole in the ground to bury it. However, while digging, he obtained a pot of gold. An iron plate on it read, "This is to be bestowed upon the filial offspring Guo Ju." Guo Ju gave the pot of gold to the owner of the house, but the latter did not dare to take it. Guo thereupon reported the matter to the local official. In accordance with the statement on the plate, the official gave it back to Guo, who was thereby also able to support his child.

—KK

Notes

1. From Song Gong's *Lives of Filial Offspring (Xiaozi zhuan)* as quoted in the *Taiping yulan* (Imperially reviewed encyclopedia of the Taiping era), 411.7b–8a.
2. It was traditionally believed that a child born on the fifth day of the fifth month would eventually harm his or her parents.
3. According to the Confucian mourning system, there are five degrees of mourning. The longest lasted three years (in fact twenty-five months), and the shortest five months. Although second-degree mourning could vary in length, usually it lasted a year. Since his birth parents had abandoned Mai, according to the Confucian rites he could no longer perform the normal mourning rites for parents. Hence, to stay within the rules, he could mourn them for three years only by doing it mentally.
4. From *A Collection of Carved Jade (Diaoyu ji)*, pp. 46–47.
5. The morning and evening audiences were daily rituals in which inferiors would pay respect to their superiors. Li's feeding the infant during the morning and evening audiences underlines that he still treated the child as his master.
6. *Analects (Lunyu)* 8.6. The speaker is actually Zeng Zi (Master Zeng), one of Confucius's disciples, not Confucius himself. A span was equal to about nine inches, hence a six-span orphan would be fifty-four inches—below adult size and in need of guardianship.
7. From Song Gong's *Lives of Filial Offspring (Xiaozi zhuan)* as quoted in the *Taiping yulan* 411.6b.
8. While mourning, the grief of a filial son or daughter should be so intense that he or she should find no pleasure in eating, hence one should consume only the blandest of foods, such as unseasoned porridge.
9. A naturalistic explanation of what happened is that Qiu contracted intestinal parasites from eating uncooked vegetables that were probably fertilized with night soil. The medicine would have caused them

to leave his body during a bowel movement. Another interpretation, one that is more in harmony with the author's intention of illustrating the wonderful power of filial piety, is that, in eating raw vegetables, Qiu apparently swallowed frog eggs. The frog eggs somehow hatched, and the resulting tadpoles lived in his stomach.

10. From Liu Xiang's *Images of Filial Sons (Xiaozi tu)* as quoted in *Taiping yulan* 411.8b–9a.

11. "Reverently support" *(gongyang)* means that one does not merely feed his parents, but feeds them in a way that manifests their superior position, which is most commonly done by providing them with delicacies.

ALTHOUGH LITERATURE WAS produced in the earliest eras of Chinese civilization, it remained for a very long time as part of historical, philosophical, or different forms of practical discourses. It was not until after the Han that the Chinese began to discuss the intrinsic aesthetic value of literature, to advocate and institutionalize literary pursuits for their own sake, and to confer a respectable social status upon literary writers. Particularly remembered for such endeavors to elevate belles lettres are three brothers of the ruling family of the Liang dynasty: Xiao Tong (501–531), Xiao Gang (503–551), and Xiao Yi (508–554).

Xiao Tong, the crown prince who did not live long enough to succeed his father, is best known for his compilation of *Selections of Refined Writing (Wen xuan)*. In excluding all nonbelletristic writings from this anthology, he shows that refined writings can stand alone, proud and unashamed before the great Confucian classics. In the Preface to this anthology, this aim to legitimize and glorify literature comes to the fore. There, he traces the origin of literature to the creation of the Eight Trigrams, the purported source of civilization, and depicts the development of literature as a full flowering of civilization. To demonstrate its intrinsic aesthetic value, he characterizes it as being "born of deep contemplation" and "lying in the domain of refined phrases," and brings our attention to the artistic pleasures it affords.

Xiao Gang, who ascended the throne in 550 and ruled for only two years (as Jianwen Di), takes an even more radical line in promoting belles lettres. In his letter to a friend, he launches a blistering attack on those have belittled literary pursuits and considers their denigration of literature a crime worthy of severe punishment. In his letter to his son, he sets off literary pursuits from moral, social, and political endeavors by emphasizing their complete freedom from any restraints.

Xiao Yi, who succeeded Xiao Gang in 552 and ruled for about four years (part of the time as Yuan Di), is no less fervent an advocate of literary pursuits than his two brothers. What his eldest brother Xiao Tong has said about literature, he says about its practitioners. He identifies literary writers as a unique type of learned persons, who excel in the expression of emotions and the use of refined phrases. Judging by his comparison of literary writers with three other types of learned persons—the Confucians, the pedants, and the writers of practical prose—he undoubtedly holds literary writers in great esteem. According to him, their social standing is not only higher than those of pedants and writers of practical prose, but actually rivals that of Confucians.

The following excerpts afford a glimpse of the then revolutionary views of literature put forward by the three Xiao brothers.—ZQC

Xiao Tong (501–531), Preface to *Selections of Refined Writing*

Let us trace back to primordial times and carefully examine the customs of remote antiquity. In the time when people lived in caves in winter and built nests in summer and when people ate hairy animals raw and drank their blood, the world was pristine, people were naive, and writings were not yet produced. Coming to the time when Fu Xi ruled the world, the Eight Trigrams were drawn and writing was invented to replace the way of managing human affairs by tying knots.

Thereupon written documents *(wenji)* came into existence. The *Book of Changes* says, "Contemplate the pattern *(wen)* of heaven in order to observe the changes of seasons; contemplate the pattern of man in order to transform the world." The epochal significance of writing *(wen)* can be traced far back indeed!

Although spokeless wheels herald the making of a grand imperial carriage, does a grand imperial carriage still have the nature of spokeless wheels? Although layers of ice are formed of accumulated water, accumulated water lacks the coldness of ice. Why? This is because, as they develop and become elaborate, things outgrow their original nature and change radically. If physical things change this way, so do writings *(wen)*. As writings change with time, it is hard to discuss them in great detail.

Nonetheless, let me try to describe them. The Preface to the *Book of Odes* says, "There are six principles in the *Odes*. The first is called *feng* (airs); the second, *fu* (narrative mode); the third, *bi* (analogical mode); the fourth, *xing* (associational mode); the fifth, *ya* (odes); and the sixth, *song* (hymns)." The writers of our time differ from those of ancient times. Though *fu* is originally a poetic type in the *Odes,* they now use it solely to denote the rhapsody or rhyme-prose [of Han and later times]. This genre of *fu* begins with Xun (Xun Kuang, fl. 298–238 B.C.E.) and Song (Song Yu, fl. Warring States), followed by Jia (Jia Yi, 200–168 B.C.E.) and Ma (Sima Xiangru, 179–117 B.C.E.). From that time onward, the lineage of this genre becomes truly complex. Among the *fu* works that depict cities and houses, there are the "Sir Based-on-Nothing" and "Sir No-Such-Person."[1] Among those that admonish against imperial hunting excursions are "Tall Poplars" and "Plume Hunt." There are also those that document an event or sing about an object, those inspired by winds and clouds, grass and woods, and those written about fish and insects, fowl and beasts. If we extend and broaden this list of subjects, we can hardly record them all.

Then there is Qu Yuan (ca. 340–278 B.C.E.), a man of the Chu state, who upheld his loyalty and followed the path of purity. As his lord did not follow the right way, Qu submitted admonitions unpleasant to his ears. Qu's thoughts and concerns were deep and profound, but he ended up being exiled to the south of the Xiang. His intent of steadfastness was thwarted, and his feeling of anguish could not be expressed. When facing a deep pool, he would have the thought (of suicide) as hinted in his poem "Remembering the Sands."[2] When chanting a song by a swamp, he would display a worried and harrowed look. Thereupon the writings of disenchanted literati began.

Poetry is where the heart's intent goes. Emotion stirs within and finds expression in words. Thanks to "Crying Ospreys" and "Unicorn's Hoofs," the beginning of the correct way became luminous.[3] From the Sangjian area on the Pu River[4] came the music of a state in decline. Thus, the way of the Airs *(feng)* and the Odes *(ya)* can be eminently observed.

After the middle of the fiery Han, the path of poetic development gradually changed. The retired tutor composed "In Zou,"[5] and the surrendered general wrote the poem "The River Bridge."[6] Thus, the distinction between four-character-line and five-character-line poetry arose. With a character taken away, there appeared three-character-line poetry. With characters added, there appeared nine-character-line poetry. All these poetic forms flourished together, galloping ahead side by side but following their own paths. Hymns *(song)* are a form used to praise virtuous enterprises and extol accomplishments. [Regarding hymns], there are the phrase "dignified as [the pure wind]" uttered by Ji Fu[7] and the exclamatory remark "Perfect!" made by Master Ji.[8] When words are brought forth as a poem, they will be like those [written by the retired tutor and by the surrendered general]. All the works called Hymns will be like those [written by Ji Fu and praised by Master Ji].

Next, the exhortation *(zhen)* arises from the need to make up for deficiencies, and the admonition *(jie)* from the need to correct mistakes. The treatise *(lun)* is precise and subtle in its analysis of principles. The inscription *(ming)* is lucid and full in its account of events. When the life of a good man ends, a eulogy *(lei)* emerges. When a portrait is painted, an encomium *(zan)* comes forth. Then, there are the genres of imperial rescript *(zhao)*, imperial proclamation *(gao)*, imperial instruction *(jiao)*, and imperial command *(ling)*; and the genres of memorial *(biao)*, presentation *(zhou)*, letter to a superior expressing one's feelings *(jian)*, and letter to a superior expressing one's ideas *(ji)*. There are the genres of epistolary writing *(shu)*, oath *(shi)*, official tally *(fu)*, and official censure *(xi)*; works expressing condolence *(diao)*, sacrificial tribute *(ji)*, regret *(bei)*, and lament *(ai)*; compositions of reply to a guest *(dake)* and exempla *(zhishi)*; the Three-Character and Eight-Character [riddles]; texts that carry the title designators of "composed piece" *(pian)*, "Chu-style poems" *(ci)*, "introduction" *(yin)*, and "preface" *(xu)*; and finally, the grave inscription *(bei, jie)*, epitaph *(zhi)*, and obituary notice *(zhuang)*.

All of these genres emerged and developed from divergent sources. If we compare them to different instruments made of pottery and gourds, they are all for the entertainment of the ear. If we compare them to the varicolored patterns on a ritual robe, they are all objects of pleasure for the eye. Whatever sentiments writers wish to express, all these genres are indeed complete and ready to be used.

After supervising court affairs and addressing the people's needs, I have spent plenty of leisure time surveying the garden of literature thoroughly and browsing through the forest of refined phrases. It is not infrequently that I would let my mind roam afar and contemplate what I saw in the mind's eye. Even when the shadow of the sun lengthened, I would still be oblivious of the fatigue of reading. The span of time since the Zhou and the Han indeed stretches far and distant. Seven dynasties have been replaced, and more than a thousand years have elapsed. Men of letters and talented scholars let their fame issue forth from their blue-and-white book-bags. Dipping writing brushes in ink and dashing off line after line, they filled the yellow book-boxes with their manuscripts. Unless one weeds out the inferior and collects [only] the finest of their writings, it would be difficult for one to get through the better half of it, even with redoubled effort.

As for the writings of the Duke of Zhou and the works of Confucius, they hang alongside the sun and the moon, and their miraculous power rivals that of spirits and ghosts. They are the norms for practicing filial piety and reverence, and are the guide and companion for enhancing ethical human relationships. So, how can they be edited, cut, and excerpted? The writings of Lao [Zi] and Zhuang [Zi], along with those of Guan [Zi], and Mencius, have the primary goal of establishing their philosophical ideas, and literary competence is not essential to them. Therefore, from the present anthology they are also omitted.

Then there are the refined expressions of worthy people, upright words of loyal ministers, remarks of strategists, and speeches off the tongues of debaters—flowing eloquently like ice melting and water bubbling up from a spring and sending forth sounds as melodious as those produced by metal and jade. Among examples of these are the debate held on Ju Hill, the discussions held at Jixia,[9] the rebuke by Zhonglian[10] that sent the Qin army in retreat, the advice by Yiji[11] that brought about the submission of the Qi state, the eight objections raised by the Marquis of Liu,[12] and the six marvelous strategies devised by Quni.[13] Their deeds were the laudatory talk of their time, and their discourses have passed down a thousand years. Their deeds and discourses can all be found in written records and appear as well in philosophical and historical texts. Discourses like theirs are heterogeneous and wide-ranging. Though recorded on bamboo strips and tablets, they are different from refined writing. Hence the present anthology does not include them. As for the event-centered histories and chronicles, they are intended to praise what is right and criticize what is wrong, and to distinguish similarities and differences. They, too, are different from refined writing. Within them, however, there are commentaries *(zanlun)* strewn with elegant expressions and prefaces *(xu)* adorned with literary brilliance. [In these subgenres], the depiction of events is born of deep contemplation, and the locus of principles lies in the domain of refined phrases. Therefore, these subgenres are mixed and collected with poetical works in this anthology.

This anthology traces far back to the Zhou house and ends with this sacred dynasty, and contains a total of thirty volumes. It is entitled *Selections of Refined Writing*. It is organized in the order of genres, under which all works are grouped. Since the forms of the *shi* poetry and the *fu* poetry are different, I have further divided them by category. Within each generic category, I have arranged the works in a chronological sequence.

Xiao Gang (503–551), "A Letter Admonishing the Sun-Facing[14] Prince and Urging Him to Have a Great Aspiration" (Jie Pangyang Gong da xin shu)

You are still young in age, and what you lack is learning. Learning alone is what makes one great and everlasting, isn't it? For this reason, Confucius says, "Once I did not take any food the whole day and did not sleep the whole night in order to think, but that was of no avail. It is better to learn (than to think without learning)." To stand facing the wall [and not learn], or to act like a monkey [feigning a man by] donning a hat—this is what I would not do. The way of establishing oneself [in life] is different from [composing a piece of] refined writing. In establishing oneself [in life], one must first of all be cautious and prudent. [In composing a piece of] refined writing, one must allow oneself the greatest abandon.

Xiao Gang, "A Letter Thanking Zhang Zan after I Have Shown Him the Collection of My Works" (Da Zhang Zan xie shi ji shu)

It has been twenty-five years now since I, Gang, grew fond of refined writing. I have discussed it in these terms: the sun, the moon, and stars as well as to the multicolored patterns of fire and dragons [on an emperor's robe]. What is more, it makes manifest the metaphysical images and illuminates human affairs. So, how can it be possible that refined expressions be put to an end and the chanting of songs be forsaken? [In saying that] a man of great enterprise does not pursue [refined writing], Yang Xiong (53 B.C.E.–18 C.E.) is in fact destroying the Dao (Way) with his petty talk. [In saying that composing *ci* and *fu* poetry] cannot be regarded as [a worthy pursuit of] a gentleman, Cao Zhi (192–232) is similarly annulling words [as a means of achieving immortality] with his petty polemic. Speaking in terms of the punishments of the law, their crimes deserve no pardon.

As for [poetic description, there are] the scene of a springtime courtyard at sunset, the orchids waving in the wind, the morning sunshine after an autumn rain, the *wutong* trees by a house starting to shed their foliage, the floating clouds emerging from the wilderness, and the bright sunshine entering a tower. [There are also] the opportune gathering of guests and family members, the setting off of the imperial entourage, the frequent filling of the *chequ* wine-cups, and the instant emptying of the *yingwu* wine-cups.[15] Then there are the three ancient frontiers where the troops stayed a long time to fight off enemies from the four quarters. The fog in the land of the Huns hung over the skies, and the banners of the expedition troops brushed the sun. Hearing the notes of flutes from a settlement or listening to the distant sounds of reed-leaf pipes in the frontiers, one would succumb to the woe of homesickness or would be bursting with heroic ambitions. Therefore, [when confronting all these scenes], one will chant to oneself, pick up one's humble writing brush, and patch together one's mediocre music. Whether depicting what meets the eye or expressing what lies inside one's heart, one is always inspired by events in life to write.

Xiao Yi (508–554), from "Establishing Oneself by Means of Words" (Li yan), in *The Man of the Golden Tower (Jinlou Zi)*

Of learned persons, there are two types among ancients and four types among the people of our time. Confucius's disciples and other ancients through whom Confucius's teaching was transmitted had a thorough understanding of the classics of the sages, and they are therefore called Confucians (i.e., literati, *ru*). People like Qu Yuan, Song Yu, Mei Sheng (d. 141 B.C.E.), and Changqing (Sima Xiangru) were good only at *ci* and *fu* poetry, and therefore are called men of letters *(wen)*.

Today's *ru* are those who have made an exhaustive study of philosophical and historical texts but, despite their factual knowledge, cannot grasp the principles of things. They are called pedants *(xue)*. As for those [prose stylists] who were not skillful at writing poetry like Yan Zuan (fl. 300 C.E.) and those who were good at writing memorials like Bo Song (Zhang Song, fl. 6 C.E.), they are all called writers of practical prose *(bi)*. Those who chant and sing airs and give themselves to sorrowful brooding are called men of letters.

Most pedants are not conversant with refined expressions and cling to textual meanings of sentences and paragraphs. They are slow in grasping and adapting [the principles of the classics] to changing circumstances and are obtuse in the use of their minds. They cannot distinguish right from wrong in rituals and music or discern the essential purpose in the teaching of the classics. They can merely sum up what has already been said by others and delight in holding their hands and displaying their extensive knowledge. However, insofar as [philosophical and historical texts are] derived from the classics, their knowledge of these texts can be considered valuable.

If moved down [to be compared with men of letters], writers of practical prose cannot be seen as capable of producing refined works. If moved up [to be compared with the pedants], they cannot be seen as capable of finding the principles of things. They display their cleverness and intelligence in nothing other than their writing skill.

As for men of letters, they interweave expressions into brilliant embroidery, bring out the melodious music of words, capture the essence of speech, and send forth feelings like waves.

The *wen* and *bi* of ancient times and the *wen* and *bi* of our time also differ with respect to their sources. (Speaking of the ancient *wen* and *bi*), the "Commentary on the Judgments" the "Commentary on the Appended Phrases" (of the *Book of Changes*), the Airs, the Odes, and [the works of] the School of Names, the Mohist School, the Agriculturalist School, and the Legalist School all display beautiful patterns like those of tigers and leopards. They all display such a perfect balance of substance and style as seen in a gentleman. When Pu Shang (Zixia, 507 B.C.E.–?) talked about the Four Beginnings[16] and when a Mr. Li discussed the *Seven Summaries*,[17] the genealogies [of ancient writings] were delineated in great detail. Therefore, I merely list the examples above but do not discuss them. (Speaking of the *wen* and *bi* of the present time), Pan Anren's (Pan Yue, 247–300) works, pure and lucid as they are, are considered by the commentators as merely sincere in the expression of feelings. So, we can see how difficult it is to attain to the ideal of refined writing *(wen)*. Cao Zijian (Cao Zhi, 192–232) and Lu Shiheng (Lu Ji, 261–303) were both men of letters. Upon scrutiny, we find their diction dense and elegant, their narration clear and compact, their thinking orderly, and their choice of words never amiss. Even though they were not known as Confucians, they had a thorough understanding of the principles [of Confucian thought].

—ZQC

Notes

1. "Sir Based-on-Nothing" and "Sir No-Such-Person" are the interlocutors in Zhang Heng's (78–139) "*Fu* on the Western Metropolis" (see selection 32) and Xima Xiangru's "*Fu* on the Shanglin Park."

2. The title of one of Qu Yuan's "Nine Stanzas"; it refers to his intention to commit suicide in the Miluo River in Hunan by sinking himself while holding on to stones.

3. "Crying Ospreys" and "Unicorn's Hoofs" are the first and the last poems in the Airs section of the *Book of Odes.*

4. In Henan.

5. In Shandong.

6. Wei Meng is the retired tutor who oversaw the education of three generations of Chu kings. Li Ling (d. 74 B.C.E.) is the general who surrendered to Xiongnu, often identified as the Huns, after he failed to break their siege at the end of his doomed military campaign in 99 B.C.E.

7. Yin Ji Fu, a man of the Zhou state.

8. Master Ji was the Duke of Wu who made the remark ("Perfect") when he heard the hymns of the state of Lu (where Confucius was born).

9. Ju Hill and Jixia were both in the state of Qi. The former was where the sophist Tian Ba defeated a thousand opponents and the latter the site of a famous academy.

10. Lu Zhonglian, who persuaded the state of Zhao not to recognize the ruler of Qin as emperor.

11. Li Yiji, who persuaded the state of Qi to support the founder of the Han dynasty, Liu Bang.

12. Zhang Liang, who dissuaded the Han emperor from reestablishing the Six Feudal States.

13. Chen Ping, who was Chief Minister under the Han Emperor Gao Zu.

14. "Sun-facing" *(dangyang)* is an appellation reserved for a sovereign as a Chinese sovereign always sits facing south (hence the sun) in court. Here Xiao applies the appellation to his son the crown prince.

15. *Chequ* is one kind of jade produced in the western frontier regions. *Yingwu* signifies the parrot. Here the two words appear as the proper names of two particular kinds of wine-cups.

16. The phrase "Four Beginnings" *(sishi)* is used in the "Preface to the Mao Text of the *Book of Odes*" (Mao *Shi* xu) to denote the four sections of the *Book of Odes:* the Airs (Feng), the Lesser Elegantiae (Xiaoya), the Greater Elegantiae (Daya), and the Hymns (Song). Some scholars argue that "Four Beginnings" refers to only the first poems of these four sections.

17. *Seven Summaries* is a bibliographical catalog begun by Liu Xiang (ca. 79–ca. 6 B.C.E.) and completed by his son Liu Xin (ca. 50 B.C.E.–23 C.E.).

THE FOUR LEGENDS about the Buddhist savior of dead souls Dizang Pusa (Skt. Kṣitigarbha Bodhisattva) are embedded in the Buddhist scripture *The Original Vow of the Bodhisattva of the Earth Sanctuary (Dizang pusa benyuan jing)*, a sutra extant only in Chinese. This particular sutra has been somewhat neglected by scholars of Buddhism, a neglect due in part to scholarly preferences for more sophisticated philosophical works. Therefore, this work is seldom mentioned except in studies about spurious or apocryphal texts. Whether apocryphal or not, such works are particularly worthy of attention because they represent the process of innovation and adaptation of Buddhism in East Asia.

The Original Vow is in fact one of the best known Buddhist texts in Chinese lay society due mainly to its use in funeral rites, especially those for forebears. Among Chinese in China and in diaspora, filial piety is still an enduring value despite the cultural and political upheavals of the last century. Elaborate funeral rituals for parents remain an important expression of filial piety and constitute a rite of passage inside the People's Republic of China as well as abroad. Even the Communist Party has to close one eye to the resurgence of religious ceremonies (except for Christian sects presumably having foreign political ties), refurbishment of monasteries, home shrines, and grave sites. Funeral rites, especially for forebears, are also increasingly elaborate even as apostate priests are again pressed into service, a rather lucrative one at that.

In Buddhist rituals, funeral or otherwise, the act of chanting sutras in a sincere and pious frame of mind is more than an expression of religious faith; it is a magical act. Recitation energizes the sutra with supernatural power. For even the most skeptical, the experience of being surrounded by a mass of bowed heads, a chorus of voices slowly rising and falling in contrapuntal waves, has a transporting, hypnotic effect. Moreover, it matters not a whit that the lay chanter and acolyte, or even seasoned priest, do not understand a syllable of the text. Indeed, some parts of the text are syllabic transcriptions of the original Sanskrit or Pali words and meaningless in Chinese anyway. Fortunately, *The Original Vow* contains a minimum of incomprehensible magical syllables.

It is in the manner above that *The Original Vow* is chanted at funerals, with the chanting led by hired monks. In a full-scale funeral for deceased elders, the sutra is read several times on each day of the forty-nine-day rite. The sutra contains description and explanation of every act and meaning of the forty-nine-day rite as well as a hagiography of Dizang. The ritual as practiced today, or even in times past, has deviated considerably from the prescription herein. However, the essential efficacy of reciting the text has the same redemptive effect for the departed soul. In this introduction, discussion of the ritual is omitted, but the hagiography of Dizang in the four legends translated here contains the central ideology of filial piety so crucial to Chinese social philosophy. This is not to say that Chinese ancestor veneration originated in Buddhism, but that the ideological congruence herein has been vital to the spread of Buddhism in Confucian China and Confucian East Asia.

That filial piety is the central theme of this sutra is implied at the very outset in the narrative frame of the sutra. *The Original Vow* begins in the usual formulaic fashion where Buddha is said to be preaching at a certain place attended by myriad mortal and immortal beings. In this case,

Buddha is in the Trāyastriṃśa Heavenly Palace (Daoli tiangong) to preach the doctrine to his mother Queen Māyā (who died giving birth to him). In his discourse are two pairs of legends about the origins of Dizang's divine ability to rescue dead souls from purgatory. The first pair is in the beginning of Book 1, Section 1, in which he tells of Dizang's previous existence as Son of the Great Elder (Da Zhangzhezi, 135 characters in length), immediately followed by his existence as the Brahman woman (Poluomen nü, 1,005 characters). Then, toward the end of Section 4, he tells about Dizang's previous existence as one of two rulers of small kingdoms (Xiao wangguo, 125 characters), followed by his existence as Lady Bright Eyes (Guangmu nü, 633 characters).

What is unusual about these legends is that the female incarnate versions are much longer, more detailed, and more vivid than the male versions. As this translation will show, in both female versions Dizang's great power is derived from filial piety. There are several shorter sutras in the Japanese compendium of Chinese sutras, *Taishō shinshū daizōkyō* (1924–1934), dealing with the redemptive power of Dizang, but this is the only one in which the origin of his power is recounted.

It is even more unusual that the gender of the filial redeemer contradicts the strong male bias in Confucian ideology and ancestor worship. For this reason, it would seem that whatever the origin of this sutra, genuine or spurious, it is unlikely to have been Chinese. The sutra is traditionally accepted as having been translated into Chinese during the Tang dynasty by the Khotanese monk Śikṣānanda, but it is not known from what language, Sanskrit, Pali, or Tibetan. If there were a Sanskrit original, the title may be restored as *Kṣitigarbha-praṇidhāna-sūtra*.

That the Chinese did indeed feel uncomfortable about such powerful female figures is indicated by the fact that a male redeemer came into being, or was invented, in the persona of the priest Mulian, a.k.a. Da Muqianlian (Skt. *Mahāmaudgalyāyana*). The origin of this male filial priest, who was born Fu Luobu (Turnip Fu), is buried in mystery, but passion plays about his descent into hell to seek the soul of his gluttonous mother flourished during the Ming dynasty and were performed widely until the twentieth century. To aid his entry into the land of the dead, the Bodhisattva of Compassion, Guanyin, bestowed upon Fu Luobu a pewter staff (Skt. *khakkara*) with nine rings attached to its top *(jiuhuan xizhang)*. With this staff he breaks open the gates of hell, rescues his mother, and frees all the other dead souls. How Mulian/Fu Luobu became identified with Dizang is another mystery; presumably this is but another one of his incarnations. Mulian the male redeemer has completely eclipsed the female Dizang of *The Original Vow*. In East Asian iconography Dizang is always depicted as a tonsured handsome young man in monk's robe, holding a staff with nine rings attached (six rings in Japanese Jizō portraiture). However, there is no explicit account about the identification of Mulian with Dizang. Why the original female gender in the text was not tampered with can only be left to speculation. Perhaps the alteration of a sacred text will corrupt its divine power.

The oral-formulaic nature of the original is evident in the many repetitive phrases and expressions. Readers familiar with Homer's *Odessey* and *Iliad* will have no difficulty recognizing these. The lack of tense markers in Chinese also gives the narrative a timeless quality that is difficult to convey in English. Therefore, the present tense is intentionally used in some places where proper grammar would call for the past tense.

The most difficult and problematic aspect of the translation is the names of titles of the innumerable buddhas of the past worlds. *Fo* has been consistently translated as "buddha" and *rulai* as *tathāgata* (thus-come/gone), and both are capitalized if they appear as part of the name of a divinity or where they refer to the historic Buddha. The proper names of the *tathāgata/fo* are most difficult because there are so many of them in this text. With the exception of the most commonly known ones, there is no concordance between the Chinese and Sanskrit/Pali names. Names for which an established concordance cannot be found in available sources are translated according to common Chinese understanding of the words. This is perhaps justifiable on the grounds that the ordinary layperson would have understood the meaning this way.—LLM

Son of Great Elder

(Mañjuśrī asks Buddha to recount the great vow of Dizang for the benefit of future generations. Thereupon Buddha gives the following accounts.)

"Mañjuśrī, long ago before countless, countless eons of apocalyptic millennia, Dizang Bodhisattva Mahāsattva was the Son of the Great Elder. There was in the universe then a Tathāgata titled the Swift-Aroused Lion Fully Possessed of the Ten Thousand Modes of Salvation (Shizi fenxing juzu wanxing rulai). The Son of the Great Elder gazed upon him and saw a thousand blessings reflected upon his regal visage. Son of the Great Elder asked the Tathāgata what vow he had accomplished to attain such a presence. Then the Swift-Aroused Lion Tathāgata told the Son of the Great Elder, 'To attain such a presence one must strive to save all suffering beings.'

"Mañjuśrī, then the Son of the Great Elder made a vow, saying, 'From this moment onward until eons of apocalyptic millennia beyond calculation, I shall broadly provide for the release (Skt. *mukti*) from rebirth of all suffering beings in the six realms.[1] Only then shall I myself enter the path of Buddhahood.'

"Thus he made this great vow before the Buddha eons of incalculable apocalyptic millennia ago. Therefore, he remains now a bodhisattva still."

The Brahman Woman

"Again in the long past of time, infinite beyond thought, there was in the world a Tathāgata titled Sovereign Lord of the Flower of Enlightenment (Juehua ding zizai wang rulai). The lifetime of that Tathāgata was four hundred eons of millennia. Among his followers was a Brahman woman who was abundantly blessed. She was respected by everyone and, wherever she went, stayed, sat, or reclined, the heavenly hosts protected her.

"Her mother believed in evil and often blasphemed the Three Treasures (of Buddhism). At that time the holy woman distributed charity widely and remonstrated with her mother to return to the proper path. But the woman's mother did not keep the faith and soon her life ended. Her soul sank down into the Avīci earth dungeon (of ceaseless torment).

"The Brahman woman knew that her mother did not believe in retribution while she was alive and surmised that she must be in torment in accordance with her karma. Consequently, she sold her house and sought high and wide for precious incense, flowers, and offertorial furnishings, and dedicated a great ceremony at the shrine of said Tathāgata. When she saw the majestic image of the Sovereign Lord of the Flower of Enlightenment in the temple, her devotion became ever more fervent as she made obeisance. She thought to herself, this Tathāgata is named the Great Enlightenment so he must possess great wisdom. If he is in this world and I ask him where my mother went after her death, he surely will know. The Brahman woman stood reverently before the image and wept for a long time. Suddenly she heard a voice from high above saying, 'Weeping holy woman, grieve no longer! I will show you where your mother went.'

"The Brahman woman raised high her clasped palms and called out saying, 'Who is the divinity consoling me in my pain? Since I lost my mother I have grieved day and night. There is nowhere that I can ask to find out in which realm she has been reborn.'

"Then the voice from space again answered the woman: 'I am the one whom you venerate, Sovereign Lord of the Flower of Enlightenment from the past. I see that your grief for your mother is many times that of ordinary people. Therefore I have come to tell you.'

"When the Brahman woman heard these words, she pummeled herself all over injuring each of her limbs and joints. Those attending her supported her until she came to. She called out toward space, saying, 'May the Buddha be merciful toward me. Quickly tell me where my mother has been reborn. My heart and body are about to die soon too.'

"Lord of the Flower told her, saying, 'When you finish the offertorial ceremony, return home early. Sit quietly and meditate upon my name, and you will know where your mother is to be found.'

"When the Brahman woman finished her round of ceremonies, she went home immediately. Because she missed her mother so much, she sat straight up and recited the name of the Flower of Enlightenment Tathāgata.

"After one day and one night she suddenly found herself on the shore of a raging ocean. The waters swirled and swelled, and fearsome iron beasts swooped and galloped back and forth above the waters. She saw hundreds and thousands of men and women rising and sinking in the waves, chased and pecked by the beasts. Again she saw demons of strange appearance, with many hands, many eyes, many limbs, or many heads, with teeth sharp as swords protruding outside their mouth. The demons herded the sinners toward the iron beasts and fought among themselves head to head and foot to foot. There were ten thousand such apparitions, too frightful to look upon. But the Brahman woman, protected by the power of Buddha, was not afraid.

"Then came a demon king named Poisonless (Guiwang Wudu), who bowed and greeted the holy woman, saying, 'Good Bodhisattva,² why have you come here?'

"The Brahman woman asked the demon king, 'What is this place?'

"Poisonless replied, 'This is the first ocean to the west of the Great Iron Enclosure Mountain (Da tiewei shan).'

"The Brahman woman asked, 'I heard that inside the Great Iron Enclosure Mountain there is an earth dungeon *(diyu)*; is that true?'

"Poisonless replied, 'There is indeed.'

"The holy woman asked, 'How do I get to that dungeon?'

"Poisonless answered, 'Only by the power of the divinity and the power of karma. Without these two, no one can get there.'

"Again the holy woman asked, 'What is the source of this water, these waves, these sinners, and fearsome beasts?'

"Poisonless answered, 'These are the recently dead sinners of the sentient world. Forty-nine days after their recent deaths, they had no descendants to perform meritorious deeds to redeem their sins. When they were alive they had no good deeds; therefore they are condemned by their own karma to the earth dungeon. But first they must cross this ocean. Ten thousand miles east of this ocean there is another ocean twice as horrible. East of that ocean there is another, three times as horrible. These are retribution for the three sins and are called the Seas of Retribution. This is the place where she was.'

"The holy woman asked the demon King Poisonless again, 'Where is the earth dungeon?'

"Poisonless replied, 'In the middle of the three oceans are the great dungeons, hundreds and thousands of them, each of them different. The greatest of them number eighteen; the second greatest are five hundred in number, in which there is limitless suffering; then there are hundreds and thousands, all of boundless agony.'

"The holy woman asked the great demon king, 'My mother is not long dead; I wonder what punishment her soul is suffering.'

"The demon king asked the holy woman, 'How did the Bodhisattva's mother conduct herself in life?'

"The holy woman replied, 'My mother believed in evil and blasphemed the sacred triad.[3] Sometimes she held on to the faith, but soon she would lose her respect. Although she has not been dead long, I wonder where she will be reborn.'

"Poisonless asked, 'What is the Bodhisattva's mother's name?'

"The holy woman replied, 'My father and mother are both of the Brahman caste. My father's name is Shiluo Shanxian (Śīla Sudharśana); my mother is called Yuedili.'

"Poisonless joined his palms together and said to the holy woman, 'Holy one, return to your home and do not grieve or worry. The sinful woman Yuedili has already ascended to heaven three days ago. It is said that this is because her filial child set out offerings and performed meritorious deeds at the shrine of the Flower-of-Enlightenment Tathāgata. Not only was the Bodhisattva's mother released from the earth dungeon, but infinite numbers of other sinners received blessings and achieved rebirth this day.'

"Thus the demon king finished speaking, joined his palms, and withdrew.

"The Brahman woman found her way back from her dream and reflected upon this event. She then made a great vow before the image of the Flower-of-Enlightenment Tathāgata: 'I shall provide for the release from the pain of rebirth for all suffering beings for the remainder of all my eons of millennial rebirths, so that they may all be released from rebirth.'"

Then the Buddha told Mañjuśrī that the demon King Poisonless is the present Bodhisattva of Wealth. The Brahman woman is the Bodhisattva of the Earth Sanctuary.

The Two Kings

(The Buddha expressed relief that the Bodhisattva of the Earth Sanctuary has taken on the task of saving all suffering beings for the eternal future.)

As Buddha was speaking there was among those present a bodhisattva mahāsattva titled King of Everlasting Essential Existence (Dingzizai wang pusa mohesa).

The King (of Everlasting Essential Existence) addressed the Buddha, saying, "World-revered One (Shizun), the Bodhisattva of the Earth Sanctuary has made various vows through many *kalpa*s, which the World-revered One has so raptly praised. I wish that the World-revered One will give (us) an account."

Then the World-revered One told the King of Everlasting Essential Existence, "Listen attentively, listen attentively, and reflect well upon everything that I shall explain to you.

"Uncountable eons of millennia ago, there was a buddha titled the World-revered Tathāgata of All-Encompassing Wisdom (Yiqie zhichengjiu rulai, plus nine additional titles): Worthy of Offerings; of Knowing Righteousness; of Right Conduct; of Compassionate Departure; of Understanding the World; the One Who Is Unexcelled; He Who Guides Men; Master of the Heavenly Hosts; Buddha of World Reverence. The life of that buddha was sixty thousand eons of millennia. Before taking the vows as a monk, he was the ruler of a small kingdom and friend of the ruler of a neighboring kingdom. Together, they practiced the ten meritorious deeds in order to benefit all living beings. But there was another neighboring kingdom wherein all the people were evil. The two kings came together and made a plan to provide for the salvation of all. One king vowed to achieve Buddhahood as soon as possible in order to save everyone, down to the very last one. The other king vowed that he would not enter Buddhahood unless he first saved all from suffering, settled them in happiness and security, and enabled them to achieve enlightenment."

Then the Buddha told the King of Everlasting Essential Existence that the king who vowed to achieve buddhahood is the Tathāgata of All-Encompassing Wisdom. The king who vowed to save all suffering living beings and not become a buddha is the Bodhisattva of the Earth Sanctuary.

Lady Bright Eyes

Again unmeasurable eons of apocalyptic millennia ago, a buddha emerged in the world named Clear-Eyed Lotus Blossom Tathāgata (Qingjing lianhuamu rulai). The lifetime of that buddha was forty eons of millennia. In the time of his instructing by symbol, there was an arhat (saint) who went about saving the myriad living. During his teachings he met a woman named Bright Eyes (Guangmu nü) , who served him food. The arhat asked her what she desired.

Bright Eyes replied, "On the death day of my mother, I want to secure blessings to save her. But I don't know to what place of rebirth her karma has brought her."

The arhat consoled her and entered meditation to observe [where the mother was]. He saw that Bright Eyes' mother had fallen into evil karma and was suffering great pain.

The arhat asked Bright Eyes, "What did your mother do during her life? She has fallen onto an evil path and is now suffering great pain."

Bright Eyes replied, "My mother was in the habit of eating fish and turtles and the like. Of fish and turtles she was especially found of the roe. She consumed them without restraint, fried or stewed. Their numbers could amount to many times tens of thousands of lives. Revered One, have mercy, how can she be saved?"

The arhat took pity on Bright Eyes and kindly advised her, "You should recite the name of the Clear-Eyed Lotus Blossom Tathāgata with sincere devotion; have his image fashioned, painted, and carved. Then you will know of her whereabouts."

Bright Eyes listened carefully and gave up all that she loved, sought portrayals of the Tathāgata, venerated them with a respectful heart, grieving and weeping. One night later, she suddenly dreamed of a buddha with a luminous golden body, shining like Mount Sumeru.[4]

The Buddha spoke to Bright Eyes: "Your mother will soon be reborn to your family. As soon as the child becomes aware of cold and hunger, it will speak to you."

Afterward, a servant woman in her house gave birth to a child. Before it was yet three days old, it bowed its head, sobbing, and spoke thus: "The retribution of life and death is to be borne by oneself. I am your mother who has dwelled in darkness for some time. Since parting from you I fell into the Great Earth Dungeon, but am now reborn by the power of your piety into lowly birthright. But my life will be short. After thirteen years I will be condemned to punishment again. Do you have a plan that I may be liberated from this fate?"

Bright Eyes listened and knew that this was indeed her mother. Weeping, she asked, "Since you are my mother you surely know your transgressions. What evil deeds caused your fall into purgatory?"

The servant's child replied, "Slaying and slander are the causes of my retribution. Were it not for your pious merit, I could not have escaped my punishment."

Bright Eyes asked, "Can you tell me about the punishment in the Great Earth Dungeon?"

The servant's child replied, "The agony of retribution is unspeakable. A hundred thousand years is not enough for their telling."

Hearing this, Bright Eyes wept and wailed. Calling out toward space, she pleaded, "May my mother be forever freed from the earth dungeons. When she finishes these thirteen years, may she have no further heavy sins and evil ways. Buddhas of the ten directions, have compassion and listen to the great vow I make for the sake of my mother. If my mother can attain eternal liberation from the unhappy paths of hell (fire, blood, swords), lowly birthright, and woman's body, I vow before the image of the Clear-Eyed Lotus Blossom Tathāgata that, from now onward, to save and raise from rebirth the suffering beings from all of the worlds of hundreds of ten thousand millennia, from all of the earth dungeons and three evil paths. I shall enter rightful enlightenment only after all such beasts, hungry ghosts, and people who are paying for their sins have achieved buddhahood."

After she made this vow, all those present heard the Clear-Eyed Lotus Blossom Tathāgata speak thus: "Bright Eyes, you made such a great vow because of your great compassion and meritorious deeds. I foresee that your mother will have redeemed her transgressions by the age of thirteen. Then she will be reborn into a life of resolute devotion and live one hundred years. After this redemption she will be reborn into the realm of no anxiety. Then after a life of uncountable *kalpa*s, she will achieve buddhahood and deliver souls as uncountable as the sands of the Ganges River."

Then Buddha said to the King of Everlasting Essential Existence, "The arhat who enlightened Bright Eyes is the Bodhisattva of Infinite Thought (Wujinyi pusa); and the mother of Bright Eyes is the Bodhisattva of Deliverance (Jietuo pusa). Bright Eyes is the Bodhisattva of the Earth Sanctuary, who—out of compassion—vowed in the infinite far past to deliver [from suffering and rebirth] all sentient beings as numerous as the sands of the Ganges.

"In all the worlds yet to come, if there will be men or women who do no good deeds but do evil deeds instead, who do not even believe in cause and effect [with regard to morality], who are licentious and deceitful, speak with forked tongue, and who blaspheme the Great Vehicle, all beings with such karma will surely sink into end paths of retribution. But if they meet with individuals of good knowledge who encourage them with the snap of a finger to follow the Bodhisattva of the Earth Sanctuary, they will be immediately delivered from the three evil paths of retribution. Then if, with determined heart, they can venerate and piously pray, make offerings of flowers, incense, clothing, and jewels, or food and libation, they will enjoy heavenly joy for hundreds of thousands of millennia. When their heavenly blessing has ended, they will be reborn as kings and princes among men for hundreds and thousands of *kalpa*s, and will be able to remember the causal effects and details of their previous lives.

"King of Everlasting Essential Existence, such is the unimaginably great power of the Bodhisattva of the Earth Sanctuary for the benefit of all living beings. You and all bodhisattvas should remember this sutra and spread the word widely."

The King of Everlasting Essential Existence said to the Buddha, "May the Buddha have no worries. By Buddha's great divine powers, we tens of thousands of *mahābodhisattvas (pusamohesa)* will surely disseminate this sutra widely for the benefit of all living beings in the world."

After saying this to the Buddha, the King of Everlasting Essential Existence joined his palms in homage and withdrew.

—LLM

Notes

1. The six *gati* (conditions of sentient existence or modes of rebirth).
2. Honorific term of address.
3. The Buddha, Dharma (Law), and *saṃgha* (monastic community).
4. *Axis mundi* of the Buddhist universe.

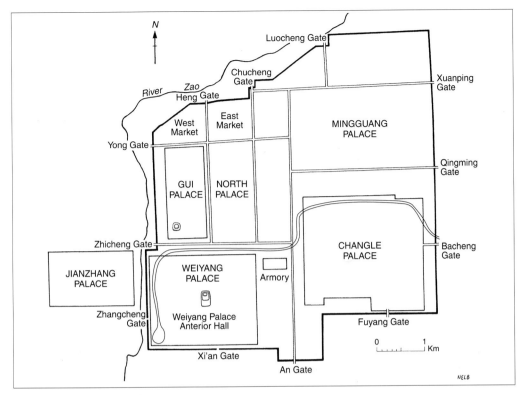

24. Plan of Western Han Chang'an in the early 1st c. B.C.E. Begun on the ruins of a palace of the Qin, the Western Han capital shown here and described in Zhang Heng's rhapsody (selection 32) was built in three main stages from the reign of the founder of the Han dynasty, Gaozu (r. 206–194 B.C.E.), through the reign of Wudi (r. 140–86 B.C.E.). Although major north-south and east-west streets of the kind described in "Kaogongji" traverse it (plate 17), Western Han Chang'an was among the least regularly shaped of China's imperial cities. Its outer wall was built to conform to the bend of the River Zao, a tributary of the River Wei roughly parallel to it just a few kilometers to the north. In addition, this ruler's city was dominated by palaces, more than would be present in any future Chinese capital.

25. Stone statue of horse trampling a "barbarian," tomb of Huo Qubing, Xingping, Shaanxi; 117 B.C.E.; Shaanxi Provincial Museum. The monumental sculpture of a horse overcoming a grotesque figure, identifiable by his eyes and heavy beard as a non-Chinese ("barbarian"), originally stood at the tomb of Huo Qubing. Although he died at the age of twenty-four, in just six years Huo had identified himself as one of Han Emperor Wu's (r. 140–87 B.C.E.) greatest generals, having already led an army of ten thousand men to victory as far West as the Altai Mountains. In recognition of his brilliant military career and valor, Han Wudi awarded him a tomb site with a high burial mound two kilometers northeast of what was to be his own grave twenty-three years later. Symbolically, the horse represents the powerful Han empire's ability to conquer the enemy. One of the largest sculptures remaining at a nonimperial tomb site from the Han period, it was found with scores of other sculptures of smaller animals in the vicinity of the mound. It is possible they originally were positioned on the mound, creating a configuration similar to isle-of-the-immortals scenes on incense burners (plate 29) and bases of money trees (plate 36).

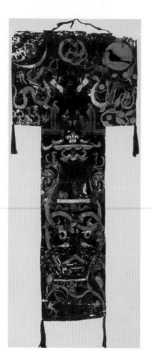

26. Silk painting excavated at Mawangdui tomb no. 1, belonging to the wife of the Marquis of Dai, near Changsha, Hunan; 1st decades of 2nd c. B.C.E. The excavation of this silk painting from the tomb of the Marchioness of Dai near Changsha, Hunan Province, in 1972, attracted the attention of every student of Han literature, religion, and art. It has been the subject of at least a dozen serious interpretative studies into the ideology of Han China as expressed in the painting. Found face down on a strikingly well-preserved corpse of a female approximately fifty years in age when she died, it is widely believed that the painting was a "guide to the soul," or graphic illustration of the dangers faced by the soul upon death when, according to certain philosophical schools of Han China, it normally separated into *hun* (celestial [yang]) and *po* (terrestrial [yin]). Some believe the deceased is represented twice, in a divination ceremony near the bottom and standing on a platform near the middle. It is also thought that some of the figures may be illustrations of descriptions in the *Chu ci* (Lyrics of Chu). A nearly identical painting was excavated in the tomb of the marquis's son and a similar one in a tomb in Linyi, Shandong. Also found in the son's tomb were detailed topographic, military, and city maps, heretofore unknown versions of classical texts, medical tracts of profound historical value, paintings of heavenly bodies including comets, and a painting of yogic exercises.

27. Burial pit no. 7 from Yangling, tomb of Han Emperor Jing, Xi'an suburbs; ca. 141–126 B.C.E. Although neither as large nor as numerous as those of the First Emperor, masses of human figurines also were found in funerary pits of later rulers of China. In the early 1990s excavation of pits at Yangling, the joint burial of Emperor Jingdi and his empress (d. 126 B.C.E.), revealed hundreds of armless naked male figures. Some wooden arms were found in the pits. It is assumed that many of the figures were clothed. Like the terra-cotta army of the First Emperor, the most sensitive feature of each sculpture is the face.

28. Interior of tomb no. 61 at Shaogou, Luoyang, Henan; Western Han. In the Han dynasty, not only royalty, but everyone who could afford to build a tomb had one. This tomb uncovered in the vicinity of Luoyang is typical of an official of the late B.C.E. or early C.E. centuries. It was standard for an official's tomb to have two main chambers or one large chamber divided by a pillar at the center. The walls and ceiling were covered with patterned brick tiles, paintings, or a combination of the two. Standard subjects of the decoration were scenes of the tomb occupant's world such as his or his and his wife's portrait, entertainment, and food or a banquet for him or them, and elements that probed Han ideas about their world and the next such as four animals associated with space and time, heavenly bodies, spirits associated with the heavenly bodies, and semihuman beings or demigods of Han myth and legend. The tomb architecture, decorations on the structure, and objects inside the tomb worked together to recreate in microcosm for the afterlife the former world of the living.

29. *Boshan* incense burner, excavated at tomb of Prince Liu Sheng, Mancheng, Hebei; ca. 113 B.C.E.; Hebei Provincial Museum. Incense burners of the type known as *boshan* are believed to be models of the isles of the immortals. Men and beasts make their way through the mountainous top of the burner, which can be detached from the watery base. The base correspondingly features water imagery. The exquisite workmanship of this burner is characteristic of objects found in the rock-carved tombs of Prince Liu Sheng, brother of the famous Han Emperor Wu, and his consort Lady Dou Wan. They may indicate the attention to detail and a taste of what will be uncovered when tombs of the emperors of the Han dynasty are excavated. The importance of the quest for immortality expressed in this bronze vessel is underscored by the fact that Liu Sheng and Dou Wan were buried in suits of jade, a material associated with longevity since ancient times in China.

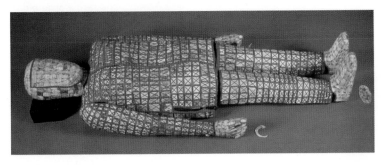

30. Jade burial garment of King Zhao Mo of Nanyue Kingdom, Guangzhou, Guangdong; 122 B.C.E.; Museum of Western Han Tomb of the Nanyue king, Guangzhou. Like those of imperial relatives in Hebei (who were buried with a replica of the isles of the immortals [plate 29]), King Zhao Mo's remains were encased in a jade shroud. His was held together with red silk rather than the gold thread used for jade suits in the north. Composed of nearly 2,300 pieces of jade, only those that covered the hands, feet, and head were sewn together; the others were pasted onto cloth with red silk decoration. Accompanying the king in his stone-walled tomb were numerous pieces of jade and a lacquer screen supported by a gilt-bronze frame. The workmanship of the objects suggests strong ties between Nanyue and the Chu state.

31. Bronze mirror with patterns resembling *T*s, *L*s, and *V*s; Eastern Han Dynasty; Freer Gallery. Highly polished bronze disks that yielded a reflection on the smooth side were common burial objects in the Eastern Han dynasty. Those with patterns on the decorated side like these are nicknamed TLV mirrors. TLV mirrors most often have a raised circular center called a boss with a dozen smaller bosses enclosed by a square. The *T*s project at the centers of the sides of the square. Surrounding the square, then, is a circle from which *L*s project at the four sides and *V*s project at the four corners. At least one more circular pattern forms the perimeter of the mirror. Decorative motifs on the TLV mirrors might include the four animals associated with the directions (vermilion bird, white tiger, black tortoise, and azure dragon), the five phases (water, fire, metal, wood, and earth), immortals, or symbols of immortality. The two perfect shapes, circle and square, represented Heaven and Earth in Han China and were the shapes that combined to form the ground plan of the ritual hall known as Mingtang.

32. Rubbing of detail from Wu Liang Shrine showing Fuxi and Nüwa, famous assassins, and other scenes, Jiaxiang, Shandong; 2nd c. C.E. It is not an exaggeration to call the motifs on the offering shrines erected by the official Wu Liang and other family members in Shandong Province a storehouse of the mind and mythology of Han China. Wu Liang Shrine is one of the first Han monuments formally identified and thoroughly studied. It possesses the recognizable style of formal silhouettes presented along straight registers; some of the scenes are labeled. Like the ones shown here, many others offer key details that make them immediately identifiable. Fuxi and Nüwa, for example, are the primogenitors of the Chinese race. Fuxi presented the Eight Trigrams to the world, as well as the institution of marriage, and music; Nüwa created humankind itself, shaping people and animals alike out of clay, and once saved humankind after creation from destruction. The two are most often shown with human heads and serpentine or fish-like tails intertwined. Below them, China's most famous hero-assassin, Jing Ke, has just thrown the blade that found its way to a pillar of the throne room rather than the heart of the First Emperor. Also famous among the scenes are tales of filial piety, a pervasive theme of Chinese popular art and literature from the Han period on (plates 45 and 46).

33. Pottery model of house; Eastern Han dynasty; University of Pennsylvania Museum of Archaeology and Anthropology. The recreation of life for the world of the tomb in Han China included models of residential architecture. The range of structures reflected the lifestyles of tomb occupants: wealthy urban nobility had grand structures with gate-towers on either side of the entry and family members or servants positioned on balconies. Those who lived in more rural China had models of country estates, sometimes, as we see here, with animals and places for them to eat and feed. Although most of the models are multistory, they are probably an exaggeration of actual residences. Birds on the roof, such as are seen here and perhaps meant to serve as guides for the soul to the heavens, were also common.

34. Pottery figurine of *liubo* players, excavated at Lingbao, Henan; Eastern Han dynasty; Henan Provincial Museum. Han lore about the activities of immortals was abundant. One of their favorite pastimes was the board game *liubo*, a contest in which men also engaged against the gods. The six sticks and board on which the game is played are all seen in this sculpture. The sculptor has captured the two players at what seems to be a decisive moment in the game. Their human expressions and animation suggest they may be men, one of them perhaps even the occupant of the tomb in which the sculpture was found. *Liubo* players and their boards also can be found on Han mirror backs (plate 31).

35. Clay entertainer, excavated in Xindu County, Sichuan; Eastern Han dynasty; Sichuan Provincial Museum. Singing and balladry, with or without musical accompaniment, are performing arts whose roots can be traced to Han and earlier times in China. Thousands of singers were employed by the First Emperor at his court. Their representations are fairly common in Eastern Han funerary art, especially in Sichuan Province. The one shown here performed to the beat of drums. Corpulent and bare-chested but with bracelets on his arms, and contorted with emotion, he seems to be losing his pants during the performance. Figurines like this, often found in nonimperial tombs, may represent members of a troupe who entertained the wealthy, nonimperial class as well as nobility. Some believe the figures are dwarfs. It has been argued that this figurine is a storyteller, but as yet, no known textual evidence supports the assertion, certainly not for storytelling of the prosimetric (*shuochang*) variety. Although entertainers including acrobats and musicians have been found in tombs in every province of Han China, so far those with such exaggerated facial expressions have been excavated only in Sichuan.

36. Money tree, excavated in Pengshan, Sichuan; Eastern Han dynasty; Sichuan Provincial Museum. Money trees were almost unknown in Chinese art history in the first half of the twentieth century, but many were found during the second half of the century. This is one of the most complete. Its clay base is a replica of a mountain populated by wild beasts, not so different from the *boshan* incense burner (plate 29). The bronze money tree lodged into it has coins of the standard Han type, *wuzhu*, made of the two perfect and symbolic shapes, circle (Heaven) and square (Earth). On the same branches are the Queen Mother of the West, who presides over the Western Paradise; the dragon and tiger throne on which she often sits; the toad, also associated with the moon and the West, who is capable of bestowing immortality; and musicians and other entertainment for her. Birds, perhaps like those on the roofs of pottery models of houses made for the same funerary world, are perched at the ends of the top branches and the summit. The money tree is both a symbol of a tomb occupant's quest for immortality and his aspirations for eternal wealth.

37. Detail of rock carving, Mount Kongwang, Lianyungang, Jiangsu; Eastern Han dynasty. The date, location(s), and route of Buddhism's entry to China are still debated. Similarly, opinions vary concerning the nature of what we today call Daoism in the Eastern Han dynasty. A unique set of carvings into a surface of approximately seventeen meters east-to-west and eight meters in height are believed to provide important clues about Chinese ideology and beliefs in the second century C.E. Among the more than one hundred images, several appear to be

seated or standing buddhas, and one a *parinirvāṇa* (death of the Buddha). Another has been identified as a Daoist in his own grotto and yet another as the Queen Mother of the West (plate 39). The name of the site, Kongwangshan, can be translated "mountain where Confucius looks into the distance." Along the mountain path up to the carving one passes a toad, sometimes associated with the moon, and an elephant, known to China because of relations with India. The complexity of the monument attests to the multiplicity of belief systems present in China in the last century of the Han dynasty, but not necessarily to a merging of those beliefs.

38. Interior of tomb no. 5, Jiayuguan, Gansu Province; 3rd–4th c. c.e. Domestic scenes and scenes of the daily life of residents of a Silk Road oasis at Jiayuguan in the Hexi corridor of Gansu Province decorated the walls of this underground tomb and others like it in the region. Measuring approximately 36 by 17 centimeters, each brick was painted with a fluid brush, and each scene was outlined in dark red-orange. The painted bricks were inserted into rows bordered by three layers of smaller bricks laid horizontally above and below. Two bricks were placed vertically between each scene in each row. In contrast to the amateurish quality of the paintings, the Jiayuguan tombs had complex structures, with two or three main chambers, numerous side niches, and ceilings formed by segmented brick vaults, comparable in size and structure to some of the most sophisticated Han burials.

39. Painting of Queen Mother of the West, western side of lower ceiling, front chamber, Dingjiazha tomb no. 5, Jiuquan, Gansu Province; ca. 386–433 c.e. Some twenty kilometers southeast of Jiayuguan and about a century later, Dingjiazha tomb no. 5 was made for a non-Chinese ruler or aristocrat of the Later Liang or Northern Liang Kingdom. In a scene that borrows heavily from Han imagery, the Queen Mother sits on her mushroom throne in her Western Paradise, wearing the headdress with two side projections called *sheng,* attended by a fox and a three-legged crow, and with a toad in a moon above her head. Her counterpart, the King Father of the East, presides with his symbolic world opposite her on the eastern wall of the front chamber of this two-room tomb. With mud-earth architecture of a desert oasis, entertainers, and scenes from the daily life of the deceased also painted on the walls, the tomb is evidence of the presence of Han ideology in China's northwest during the post-Han centuries of non-Chinese rule.

40. Ji Kang and Ruan Ji, detail of relief sculpture from south wall of tomb excavated at Xishanqiao, Jiangsu; late 4th–early 5th c.; Nanjing Museum. Poet-philosophers Ji Kang (223–262) and Ruan Ji (210–263) are two of a group of seven free-thinking individuals known as the Seven Worthies of the Bamboo Grove. Most of them knew one another, and all shared an antigovernment sentiment. Ji Kang's bare leg and Ruan Ji's exposed arm and chest, turban-like headgear, and teacup with a duck floating in it are signs of their anti-Confucian behavior. Ji Kang worked at a forge and tried to remain disengaged from politics but was nevertheless executed by the government, perhaps because of a false accusation. Ruan Ji once stayed intoxicated for sixty days to avoid marriage into a family he considered corrupt. Several other tombs with the same imagery have been found in Jiangsu, suggesting this area to have been a hotbed of Neo-Daoist sympathizers.

41. Stone sculpture from spirit path of tomb of Xiao Ji, prince of the Liang dynasty, Shishi Village, Nanjing County, Jiangsu; 529. Nanjing and Danyang counties are the locations of about thirty tombs of royalty of the Six Dynasties, the name for the period between 220 and the reunification of China in 589, during which six native Chinese dynasties ruled in succession from capitals near today's Nanjing. The greatest concentration of surviving secular monumental stone sculpture of the period is in this region. Pairs of mythological beasts and columns like these flanked the spirit path, or approach, to the burial mound along which the corpse was carried on its final journey on earth. Even in this southeastern Chinese location, hints of the Greco-Roman origins of monumental sculpture are in evidence in the fluted columns and perhaps in the lion capitals, whose origins might also be Indian or even Persian.

42. Gilt-bronze Buddha; 338 c.e.; Asian Art Museum, San Francisco. Buddhism entered China during the Eastern Han and became an important religion in China after the fall of the dynasty. As they migrated eastward from India via Central Asia, early Buddhist figures bore signs of the Western origins of the religion, including remnants of Greco-Roman sculpture introduced to today's northwest India and Pakistan in the aftermath of Alexander the Great. Before the middle of the fourth century, however, the sinicization process was well under way. The almond-shaped, pupil-less eyes, straight hairlines, and long fingers, and the sharp, parallel lines of garment folds and rounded collar in this statue are all typical of China's early Buddha images. The statue is one of the earliest Chinese Buddhist sculptures with a fixed date.

43. Multicolor silk slippers with wishes for longevity and wealth woven into the design; excavated in tomb no. 305 at the Astana graveyard, Turfan County, Xinjiang Uyghur Autonomous Region; ca. 384 B.C.E.; Xinjiang Uyghur Autonomous Region Museum. These silk slippers (23 x 8.5 x 4 cm) may have been made for use in the afterlife by a Chinese female buried in the Astana cemetery, location of hundreds of burials in the centuries after the Han through the Tang dynasty. The shoes are probably the "crimson slippers" listed in the inventory of objects buried in the tomb. The length informs us they certainly were made before the Song dynasty, when it became the practice to bind the feet of aristocratic girls as early as age five, breaking the arches and bending the toes underneath with the goal of producing enticingly tiny and delicate silk-covered appendages.

44. Relief sculpture of the "Great Departure," cave 6, Yungang, Shanxi; late 5th c. The Yungang caves site, outside the modern city of Datong in Shanxi Province, is one of the places where in the late fifth century Chinese artisans worked to transform the legends and iconography of Indian Buddhism into a Chinese system. The Buddha himself, who first appeared at Yungang as a gargantuan, inert figure with a huge, straight nose, enormous earlobes, and garment folds carefully pasted onto his robe, just thirty years later has a smooth face with Chinese features and departs on his Chinese-style horse from a palace approached by marble stairs and with a ceramic tile roof and decorative moldings on the roof ends. The scene is from the life of Prince Gautama Siddhartha before he attained enlightenment and became Śākyamuni Buddha. The umbrella over his head is still a reminder that he is an Indian prince whose head is shielded, as was that of Asian royalty since ancient times in Persia.

45. Panel of lacquer screen showing scenes of female filial piety excavated in tomb of Sima Jinlong, Datong vicinity, Shanxi; 484 C.E.; Datong City Museum. One assumes that objects buried with a person reflect his philosophical views. Thus, just as the occupant of the tomb in Jiangsu chose philosophers who opposed Confucianism to decorate his walls (plate 40), less than a century later a non-Chinese official of the Northern Wei had a screen with paragons of virtuous Confucian behavior placed in his tomb. Among several of the paragons in this scene, at the bottom we see Lady Ban, who walked behind an emperor in the first century B.C.E. rather than ride with him so as not to incite gossip, and above her the "bed scene," in which the lady is warned, "If the words that you utter are good, all men will respond. But if you depart from the principle, even your bedfellow will distrust you." These are subjects in the "Admonitions of the Court Instructress," of which a silk version in the style of the fourth-century court painter Gu Kaizhi is preserved in the British Museum.

46. Filial son Dong Yong, detail of stone-engraved panel from sarcophagus; ca. 525; Nelson-Atkins Museum of Art, Kansas City. In order to pay for his father's funeral, Dong Yong had to borrow money and subsequently indentured himself as a servant to repay the debt. On his way home from the funeral, he met a woman who asked him to marry her on the spot. Dong explained that he was not in a position to marry, since he was in debt. In a month's time, the woman returned with three hundred pieces of silk for him to use as payment. Thereupon, she revealed herself as the Spinning Maid and ascended toward the heavens. Although the ascent may shed a Daoist cast on the relief, the theme is explicitly Confucian: he who goes to any cost to honor his father with a proper funeral will reap rewards. Typical of narrative art in the early fifth century, Dong Yong is identified by name, is shown twice (as a laborer and talking to the maiden), and figures and border are carved in long, flowing lines.

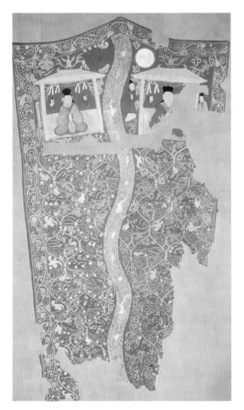

47. Lid of lacquer sarcophagus found in tomb in Guyuan, Ningxia Hui Autonomous Region; late 5th–early 6th c. In 1973, railroad workers stumbled upon the simple, single-chamber tomb, which contained this extraordinary coffin. Believed to belong to an occupant of Xianbei (Särbi) nationality, the lid exhibits symbolism of popular religion or mythology (the Queen Mother of the West and King Father of the East); on the sides are depicted Buddhist deities, paragons of Confucian filial piety, the occupant himself and presumably his wife (both in native dress), and design motifs from as far west as Sasanian Iran. In fact, a Sasanian coin dated 459–484 C.E. was also found in the tomb. The sarcophagus is evidence of the presence of Chinese ideas among the non-Chinese who populated the north at this time and of the mingling of imagery and ideology of every part of Asia in meeting points of cultures such as Guyuan at the turn of the sixth century.

48. Mahāsattva Jātaka, south side of east wall, Mogao cave 428, Dunhuang, Gansu; Northern Zhou (557–581). In this Jataka tale, or story of a former existence of the Buddha Śākyamuni, a prince (called Mahāsattva) and his two brothers come upon a hungry tigress when out on horseback (top register). The tigress is so malnourished that she does not have milk to feed her cubs. The prince offers the ultimate sacrifice, his life, to feed the baby felines. Placing himself at the feet of the tigress is not enough, however, because she is too weak to tear apart his flesh. Thus the prince ascends a mountain and throws himself to his death, making it easier for the mother tiger and her cubs to indulge (middle register). Mahāsattva's brothers are distraught when they discover him, and rush home to inform their father what has happened. In the last scene, however, it is clear that the self-sacrificing prince has attained Buddhahood. The story is told in continuous narrative, appearing in nearly ten scenes spread across the three registers of the east wall of the cave. Tiny mountains and trees no bigger than men serve as focal frames for the narration.

49. Ceiling of Mogao cave 249, Dunhuang, Gansu; Western Wei (535–554). Dunhuang is a desert town in the eastern part of Gansu Province. Beginning in the fourth century and for a thousand years afterward, monks, pilgrims, and merchants who passed through the oasis left marks of their various brands of Buddhism and artistic styles in literally thousands of caves in the area clustered in groups like Mogao, Anxi, or Yulin. Often our best knowledge of Chinese painting in the early centuries of Dunhuang's history has come from cave murals. The paintings on this ceiling include attenuated images of men, animals, and mythological beings who float across the wall along the lines with which they are painted. Those calligraphic lines, the archer turning 180 degrees to shoot from his horse in a pose known as the "Parthian shot," and the tiny mountains that frame the scene are all characteristic of sixth-century painting in China.

50. Pagoda of Songyue Monastery, Mt. Song, Henan; 523. The pagoda of Songyue Monastery is the oldest brick pagoda in China. Like all pagodas in East Asia, it traces its origins to the stupa, the Indian relic mound that began as a circular structure with an egg-shaped dome. As the pagoda made its way eastward across Central Asia to China, it became taller and more slender. In China, however, builders had no experience with circular plans. This unique twelve-sided structure may be the result of an attempt to make a circular form by craftsmen who previously had only made straight walls that joined at ninety-degree angles. Chinese brick or masonry pagodas most often have four or eight sides and, like this one, stories that replicate wooden pillars, bracket sets, and ceramic tile eaves. Also like the pagoda on Mt. Song, they tower above the low walls of a monastery as a beacon of the Buddhist faith.

51. Gilt-bronze image of Śākyamuni and Prabhūtaratna; 518; Musée Guimet. Śākyamuni is the Buddha of our age. Buddhists teach that in a future age, after a decline of the law and regeneration of the universe, Maitreya will take his place on earth and Śākyamuni will become a Buddha of the Past. This statue portrays a moment described in the *Lotus Sutra* when a Buddha of the Past named Prabhūtaratna came to earth to preach alongside Śākyamuni. This scene with two Buddhas of equal size and prominence from one of the most popular scriptures of the period of Northern and Southern dynasties is a common one in sculpture of the time. The elongated faces, torsos, and mandorlas behind the Buddhas' heads, as well as the carefully placed garment folds, are characteristic of painting and sculpture of the period between Han and Tang.

52. Procession of the empress and her entourage, Binyang cave, Longmen, Henan; 523; Metropolitan Museum of Art. Only occasionally is a secular figure found in sixth-century Buddhist art. The pair of relief sculptures from a Longmen cave outside Luoyang is one of these rare examples. Here, the Xuanwu emperor and his empress, who commissioned the excavation of the Binyang cave, are shown with their retinue in an interior that otherwise includes the Buddha himself, bodhisattvas, his first two disciples, scenes

from former lives of the Buddha known as Jatakas, and a debate between the bodhisattva Mañjuśrī and Vimalakīrti on the meaning of life and suffering. Besides a rare example of the imperial couple such as this one, mortals or sometimes just their names are found on the backs of stelae (plate 53) to commemorate donations they made of the stele itself or to the temple or monastery in which it stood.

53. Buddhist stele; mid-6th century with later repairs; Metropolitan Museum of Art. Stone slabs such as this limestone one were a standard format for Buddhist narrative in the sixth century. Always carved on the front and back and often on the two sides as well, usually the main Buddha is shown in the center front. A focal point of this stele is a story from the *Vimalakīrti-sūtra* in which the wealthy Vimalakīrti has made himself sick, knowing that Buddhist deities will come to his house to offer condolences. Bedridden, Vimalakīrti asks the bodhisattva Mañjuśrī, enthroned to the left, to instruct him on the principle of nonduality. The congregation, shaded by the undulant branches of a tree with celestial beings hovering overhead, listens to Mañjuśrī's famous answer, that it would be better to say nothing at all. When given his turn to respond, Vimalakīrti remains silent. Below Vimalakīrti and the bodhisattva sit donors, each in his own space and facing his name. The exquisite carving exhibits the heights of mid-sixth-century stonework.

54. Anji Bridge, Zhao County, Hebei; Sui period. It is believed that the Chinese may have made wooden bridges by the second millennium B.C.E., perhaps even a millennium earlier. The First Emperor of the Qin is said to have built a multispan bridge 544 meters in length. Anji Bridge, also known as the Great Stone Bridge or the Bridge of Zhao Prefecture, is the oldest stone bridge in China and the oldest open-spandrel bridge in the world. The two open arches on either side of the spandrel reduce the dead weight on the spandrel and allow flood waters to pass. The underside of the bridge is formed of twenty-eight arches, each 34 centimeters in width.

55. Xi'an from air; first half of 20th century. Chang'an, literally "everlasting peace," was the name of the capital of the Sui and Tang dynasties built southeast of the Han capital of the same name. The largest city in the world in the seventh through ninth centuries, it had a population of more than one million and an area of 84 km². Rigidly planned with straight north-south and east-west streets that divided it into 108 wall enclosed wards plus two market areas, the orthogonal arrangement was so pervasive it could still be captured in this airview of Xi'an, the city beneath which lie the ruins of the Sui-Tang capital. The widest east-west street was 220 meters; the main north-south street was about 150 meters in width. Every major street of the capital was divided into three lanes by two drainage canals.

56. Relief sculpture of imperial steed from tomb of Tang Emperor Taizong; c. 649; University of Pennsylvania Museum of Archaeology and Anthropology. Li Shimin, the Second Tang Emperor, Taizong, was a stellar military leader who solidified the empire won by his father, Tang Gaozu. Taizong loved horses. It is no wonder that six of his imperial steeds, two leaping, two prancing, and two at a stance, were sculpted in bas-relief to stand above ground in front of his funerary mound. Saluzi, a bay horse also known as Autumn Dew and as Whirlwind Victory, was one of his favorites. When the steed was wounded in battle, General Qiu Xinggong gave his

horse to Tang Taizong. Here General Qiu is shown pulling the arrow out of Autumn Dew's chest. It was reported that after the arrow was removed, the noble horse collapsed to his death.

57. Emperors Wendi and Yangdi of the Sui dynasty, detail from "Thirteen Emperors Scroll"; attributed to Yan Liben (d. 673); Museum of Fine Arts, Boston. The artist at the court of Tang Taizong to whom this handscroll is attributed is credited with presenting the design for the six imperial steeds that stood in front of the emperor's tomb (plate 56). Painters who worked for the court received official titles, but they had no freedom of choice in their subjects. They painted mainly historical subjects, current events, or specific requests such as birds or horses desired by the emperor. "Portraits" of emperors through history were typical products of a court painter. Also typical of early Chinese figure painting, every emperor is first and foremost an image of imperialism: a broad, dignified man of middle age, larger than life in comparison to his subjects, even in the cases of emperors known to have been slight or to have died as young men. Inscriptions are the only way to recognize specific emperors in the painting.

58. Fengxian cave, Longmen, Henan; 672–675. This monumental limestone grotto was carved at the request of the third Tang emperor, Gaozong. The enormous central image of the Buddha is Vairocana, the ultimate Buddha of endless light. To his immediate right and left are disciples and, flanking them, two bodhisattvas. On the sides are two pairs of guardians, who represent each of the four world quarters. The presentation is standard for the Tang dynasty, a fully developed example of the re-creation of the Buddhist world in a three-dimensional worship space. The image of the Buddha is so large that it has been speculated that Gaozong's empress, Wu Zetian (who later established herself as the emperor of her own dynasty), likened herself to the Buddha image.

59. Buddha preaching, cave 23, Kumtura, Xinjiang Uyghur Autonomous Region; Tang dynasty. Situated on the northern branch of the trade route traditionally known as the Silk Road, Kumtura is one of several sites of important Buddhist cave-temples in the Kucha region of central Xinjiang. The most famous caves in the region are at Kizil. The interiors of many of the cave-temples are covered with murals and, as seen here, green-blue and red-brown are dominant colors in many of them. This is one of six large scenes of an enthroned Buddha preaching on the north wall of the main chamber of cave 23. The iconography of specific paintings and the interrelation between paintings of single caves and sets of caves through-out the Kucha region are subjects of intense research, yet many problems remain unsolved. What is known is that, like all oases on the Silk Road, Kumtura was a meeting place for monks, merchants, and artisans from East, West, and South Asia. The stories told on the walls and the purely decorative motifs are evidence of the many cultures and religions of residents and travelers through the Kucha region.

60. Pentad of Buddhist deities, west wall niche, Mogao cave 244; ca. early 7th c. Inside or outside, in a cave-chapel or on an exterior facade such as plate 58, along the central line of a stele or painted on a wall, the arrangement of Buddhist deities and their style was standard in the Sui-Tang period. Central and largest was the main Buddha, often Śākyamuni. Flanking him and shortest in the group were *luohan* (arhats, i.e., accomplished disciples) and flanking them bodhisattvas (deities who postponed attainment of nirvana in order to help mortals attain that goal). Behind, as we see in cave 244, buddhas and other Buddhist beings filled in the Buddhist world. In the Tang dynasty, the face of

the Buddha became round with fat cheeks, and three wrinkles were sculpted onto his neck. Bodhisattvas similarly had round faces, neck wrinkles, and pursed lips, and their bodies swayed at the waist and hips, making them look feminine, a feature that was more pronounced in the eighth century than in the seventh. Monks were bald, with the most realistic faces in a Buddhist pantheon. The burst of polychrome here is typical of Buddhist painting, sculpture, and architecture of all times.

61. Main hall, Nanchan Monastery, Mt. Wutai, Shanxi; 782. The main hall of Nanchan Monastery is the earliest dated wooden hall in China and one of four wooden buildings that remain from before the year 900. All are in Shanxi Province. The structure is simple: twelve exterior pillars and bracket sets above them support the roof frame. Inside are nothing more than ceiling beams and a Buddhist altar. The hall of a humble, out-of-the way monastery, it could be entered only through the front and had windows only at the front. Also typical of its simple structure, straight posts rather than

replicas of bracket sets were placed on the lintel between the bracket sets at the tops of the columns. Some believe it survived persecutions of Buddhism in the mid-ninth century because of its simplicity and remote location.

62. Nested reliquary from Famen Monastery, Fufeng, Shaanxi. One of the most extraordinary finds of the 1980s was a two-room "underground palace" beneath the thirteen-story pagoda of Famen Monastery. Revealed were a treasury of reliquaries and containers for precious Buddhist objects, the containers themselves made of the finest materials available in Tang China. The burial of precious and exotic goods beneath the central core of a pagoda or in a statue is not rare, but the Famen Monastery contents are unique because they are known to have belonged to Tang emperors. Objects were added and removed at least seven times between 631 and 873. In fact, it is thought that this reliquary is the onè referred to in Han Yu's diatribe against the bone of the Buddha (selection 52).

63. Chinese officials and foreigners painted on east wall of ramp to tomb of Prince Zhanghuai (Li Xian), ca. 706; Qian County, Shaanxi. Upon the death of her husband in 684, Empress Wu usurped the throne of China (see plate 58). To solidify her power, she launched a ruthless campaign of executions and forced suicides of all relatives of her deceased husband who might otherwise have ruled in her place. Even her own son, Prince Zhanghuai, was forced to commit suicide at the age of thirty in the year of his father's death. In 706, after the death of Empress Wu, the bodies of the prince and his brothers, sisters, and other relatives who had suffered the same fate under Wu Zetian were exhumed and reburied with rites befitting their ranks. The foreigners on the underground approach ramp to Prince Zhanghuai's tomb, perhaps an Armenian, Korean, and Scythian, represent the many nationalities present in the capital, Chang'an, during the Tang dynasty. The specific scene may be from the funeral at which they and Chinese officials were present. Also indicating the foreign taste and exotica at the Tang court, polo, introduced to Chang'an from West Asia, is painted on a wall of this prince's tomb, the prince himself perhaps among the players.

64. Zhou Fang (ca. 730–ca. 800), "Ladies with Fans and Flowers in their Hair"; Liaoning Provincial Museum. Zhou Fang was one of the best-known painters at the Tang court in the second half of the eighth century. He is famous for his studies of court ladies. "Ladies with Flowers in Their Hair" is typical of his work. Each woman is individually spaced against a plain silk background. The subjects are mediums for the painter to show his skill at minute detail such as

hair ornaments, silk garments, paintings on fans, or the translucent cape that ladies wore over their clothing in the eighth century. Even though the painting captures the details of female attire and accoutrements, it tells us nothing about any individual subject or her emotions. Rather, each is frozen in her pose.

65. Gaochang, Xinjiang. Gaochang was the name of a Tang protectorate in the "Western Regions." With an outer wall 12 meters thick, 11.5 meters high, and 5 kilometers in circumference in the Tang period, the site was occupied almost continuously from the first century B.C.E. until the Mongolian invasions in the thirteenth century. Today its remains are about forty kilometers east of the modern city of Turfan in eastern Xinjiang. Walled in the Tang dynasty, the city was taken by a Turkic group known as the Uyghurs in the ninth century, at which point the city became known as Qoço or Kocho. Mud-earth walls and mud-earth architecture and building foundations reflecting the multiculturalism and religious syncretism at Gaochang are still very much in evidence among the enormous ruins. Much of our knowledge of Gaochang and the nearby cave-temples or towns comes from German and other European expeditions to eastern Xinjiang at the beginning of the twentieth century.

66. Panoramic map of Buddhist pilgrimage sites, Mogao cave 61; Five Dynasties period. The sweeping panoramas of Buddhist sites on the pilgrimage road is typical of one style of Chinese cartography and of paintings of architecture. Labels identify specific monasteries known to have existed and been important in the first half of the tenth century such as Foguang Monastery at the foot of Mt. Wutai. However, neither the scale of the monastery, nor distances between places, nor the relative size of figures to mountains and to architectural forms, nor buildings in a given monastery is intended to be an accurate representation of reality. Rather, the walls of cave 61 served as a kind of checklist for the pilgrim making his or her way to and from Buddhist sites of China and Dunhuang. Each temple complex is a generic composite of white-washed enclosures with red or green architectural trim that included gates, gate towers, and at least one main structure raised on a platform.

47 | Selections from the *Platform Sutra of the Sixth Patriarch*

THE CHAN (ZEN, in Japanese) Buddhist tradition developed in China during the Period of Disunion. Its First Patriarch, Bodhidharma, was an Indian monk who arrived in China about 500 C.E. Bodhidharma stressed the importance of direct experience of enlightenment through meditation. He was not concerned with the complex philosophies that marked other schools of Buddhism in China; he called Chan a school of "mind-to-mind transmission, without written texts." The *Platform Sutra of the Sixth Patriarch* encapsulates many of the key ideas of the Chan school through the life of Huineng (638–713). A native of modern Guangdong (Canton) Province and originally an illiterate firewood peddler, Huineng joined the Chan monastery run by the Fifth Patriarch, Hongren, after hearing an itinerant monk preaching. The *Platform Sutra* begins with Hongren's search for a successor to become the Sixth Patriarch. At the time, Huineng's position was quite low; he worked in the monastery's threshing room. When he became Sixth Patriarch, the Chan School split. His rival, Shenxiu, led the Northern School, while Huineng led the Southern School. Eventually, the Southern School predominated. Their differing views are encapsulated in the poems each created to express his understanding of Chan.

The *Platform Sutra* is written as though recounted by Huineng and recorded as he addressed others. Therefore, unless otherwise clear from the text, the "I" is Huineng referring to himself. The piece is divided into two sections. First is the account of how Huineng became the Sixth Patriarch; second is part of an address he delivered after revealing himself as the Sixth Patriarch to an audience at the Baolin Temple, on Nanhua Mountain in Guangdong Province. In the sermon, Huineng emphasizes the ability of everyone to achieve enlightenment by revealing the Buddha-nature each has within. The problem, as Huineng notes, is that our thoughts are entangled with the world that surrounds us, the world of *saṃsāra,* or suffering. Huineng encourages his listeners to recognize that this world is fundamentally impermanent, while our Buddha-nature is the "original mind" that brings enlightenment and is brought to light through meditation, which breaks the entanglements of *saṃsāra.*—RF

One day the [Fifth] Patriarch called the various members of the monastery together saying, "I say this to you: for common people the matter of life and death is most important. Through your devotions, all day all of you disciples only seek fields of blessings [in the next world], but not separation from the bitter seas of life and death. Yet if your inner nature is confused, of what help are blessings? You shall each go to your rooms and reflect on this yourselves. Those with wisdom, grasp the *prajñā* wisdom of the inner nature[1] and each write a verse for me. I will read your verse and, if you have understood the greater meaning, I will bestow upon you the monk's robes and Dharma,[2] and you shall become the Sixth Patriarch. Hurry! . . ."

In the middle of the night, holding a candle in his hand, the head-monk, Shenxiu, wrote his verse on the wall of the middle section of the south corridor without anyone knowing. His verse said,

The body is the tree of enlightenment;[3]
The mind is the stand for a bright mirror.
Always strive to keep it clean;
Do not let it become dusty.

. . . The Fifth Patriarch called head-monk Shenxiu into the hall, asking him, "Is the verse yours? If it is yours, you deserve to obtain my Dharma." Head-monk Shenxiu replied, "I must confess that it is indeed mine. I did not dare to seek the position of patriarch, but sought Your Holiness's kindness and compassion. Do you think your disciple has some small knowledge of the great principle?" The Fifth Patriarch answered, "If you wrote this verse, your perception is not yet complete. You have only arrived outside the gate, but not yet entered inside. If you rely upon this verse for cultivation, you will not fall into depravity. But if you use this explanation, you cannot understand ultimate enlightenment. You must enter the gate and see your own original inner nature.

"Leave now and think about this for a day or two, then write another verse for me. If by then you have entered the gate and perceived your original inner nature, I will bestow upon you the Robes and the Dharma." The head-monk Shenxiu departed. He still could not write a new verse after several days.

A young boy passed by the threshing room chanting Shenxiu's verse. I heard it and knew that this verse did not capture the inner nature or understand the greater meaning. I composed my own verse, which said,

Enlightenment truly has no tree;
The bright mirror has no stand;
Buddha nature is always pure.
Where is there any dust?

I composed another verse:

The mind is the tree of enlightenment;
The body is the stand of a bright mirror.
The mirror is fundamentally pure.
Where can it get dusty?

The disciples in the hall were all amazed at my verses. I returned to the threshing room. The Patriarch instantly saw that I understood well the greater meaning and was afraid others would know, so he said to the crowd, "He has not yet grasped it."

The Fifth Patriarch waited until midnight then called me to the hall and expounded the *Diamond Sutra*. As soon as I heard it I was suddenly enlightened, and that night I received the Dharma and no one knew. He then transmitted the Dharma of Sudden Enlightenment and the robe saying, "You are now the Sixth Patriarch. The robe is proof that has been handed down generation after generation. The Dharma is transmitted from mind to mind. You must cause people to enlighten themselves." The Fifth Patriarch said, "Huineng, since antiquity the transmission of the Dharma has dangled by a thread. If you remain here, there are those who would harm you. You must leave at once."

I took the Dharma and the robes and left in the middle of the night. The Fifth Patriarch himself saw me off at Nine Rivers courier station. I was immediately enlightened. The Fifth Patriarch instructed me, "Go and exert yourself. Take the Dharma south. Do not teach it for three years. This Dharma is difficult to propagate. Later spread moral reform and guide the deluded. If one of them gains enlightenment, it will be no different from your own." I went south after saying goodbye.

(Following are excerpts from Huineng's preaching at Baolin Temple.)

"Good friends, since its inception, our doctrine first established lack of thought as our guiding principle, lack of form as our substance, and lack of fixation as our basis. Lack of form is to exist amidst forms yet be apart from forms. Lack of thought is to be amidst thoughts yet not to think. Lack of fixation is the fundamental inner nature of people. Past, present, and future thoughts are strung together without cessation. But if you cease to think after one thought, the dharma body[4] forthwith separates from the physical body, and in the midst of thought you will not fixate upon any dharma. If you fixate upon one thought, you fixate upon thought after thought and that is called 'being fettered.' If thought after thought does not fixate on any dharma, there are no fetters. Therefore lack of fixations is the basis.

"Good friends, to be externally separate from all forms is to lack form. If you are able to separate from forms, then the substance of your nature will be pure. Therefore lack of form is the substance.

"To be unsullied in all circumstances is to lack thought. If in your own thoughts you separate from circumstances, you will not think about those dharmas. If you do not think about the multitude of things, then your thoughts will be completely eliminated. Once your thoughts cease, you will not be reborn in another place.[5] Those who study the Way must contemplate this. Do not abide in the realm of dharmas and subjectivity. Self-deception can arise, compounded by exhorting others [in this misguided view]. One's ignorance is not perceived and one even will slander the sutras and Dharma. Therefore we consider establishing lack of thought as our guiding principle.

"Because deluded people think about the circumstances surrounding them [instead of enlightenment], these thoughts give rise to perverse views. All worldly cares and careless thoughts are born from this. Therefore this school has established lack of thought as its guiding principle. When people are detached from these views, they do not give rise to thoughts. If you do not have thoughts, then even lack of thought is not established.

"Lacking is lacking what? Thinking is thinking about what? Lacking is to be detached from the worldly cares of duality. Thinking is to think about the fundamental nature of ultimate truth. If ultimate truth is the basis of thoughts, then the thoughts are the activation of ultimate truth. When one's inner nature gives rise to thought, even when seeing, hearing, perceiving and knowing, one is not contaminated in any circumstance and is always at ease. The *Vimalakīrti Sutra* says, 'Externally one is able to discern the various dharma characteristics; internally one does not move from the first principle.'

"Good friends, in this discipline sitting in meditation absolutely does not concentrate on the mind, nor does it concentrate on purity, nor does it speak of being imperturbable. If one speaks of seeing the mind, this mind is ultimately false. Because it is false like a phantasm, there is nothing to see.

"If someone speaks of seeing purity, human nature is fundamentally pure, but false thoughts obscure its ultimate truth. When one cuts off these thoughts, the original inner nature is pure. If you do not perceive the fundamental purity of your own nature, the mind creates a vision of purity that is a false purity. But falsity has no location, so those who understand this vision know it is false. Purity has no form. However, if you establish a form of purity and speak of this form of cultivation, creating this perception, you inhibit your own fundamental inner nature and are fettered by purity. If you are imperturbable, then you do not see the wrongs of others, and your inner nature is undisturbed.

"Deluded people [may] not move their own bodies, [but when] they open their mouths and speak of others being right or wrong, they violate the Way. They obstruct the Way because of their vision of the mind or of purity.

"This being so, what does this discipline mean by sitting in meditation? This discipline has no barriers. Sitting is when thoughts do not fixate upon external circumstances. Meditation is when you perceive the fundamental inner nature and are not disturbed.

"What do we mean by meditation and calmness? Meditation is to be externally separated from forms. Calmness is to be internally undisturbed. If there are external forms, but the mind is not disturbed, then the fundamental inner nature is pure and calm of its own accord. Disturbance only appears when there is contact with external things and circumstances. Meditation is to be externally separate from forms, while calmness is to be internally undisturbed. Because externally you are meditating and internally you are calm, we call it meditation and calmness. The *Vimala-kīrti Sutra* says, 'At the moment of clarity you regain the original mind.' The *Disciplines of the Bodhisattva Sutra* says, 'One's own inner nature is originally pure.' Good friends, realize that your inner nature is itself pure. Cultivate yourselves and work for yourselves. Your inner nature is the dharma body. Your practices are the Buddha's practices. Work yourself to fulfill for yourself the Buddha's Way. . . ."

On the third day of the eight month [of the second year of the Xiantian reign],[6] after they ate [in Guo'en Temple], he said to the disciples, "Each of you take your seat. I will be departing from you. . . ." Fahai said, "Your Holiness, what teaching would you leave so that people of later generations will be able to see the Buddha?" The Sixth Patriarch replied, "Listen well. If the confused people of later generations only understand all sentient beings, they will be able to see the Buddha. If they do not understand all sentient beings, even if they seek the Buddha for ten thousand *kalpa*s,[7] they will not see him. Now I teach you to understand sentient beings in order to see the Buddha, and leave you with a verse on seeing the true Buddha and being set free. The deluded do not see the Buddha, but once enlightened you will see. Fahai, please listen. Transmit the teaching for generation after generation and for ages without end."

The Sixth Patriarch said, "Listen to what I am telling you. If people in later ages want to seek the Buddha, they only need understand the Buddha's mind and all sentient beings, then they will understand the Buddha. There is Buddha mind because of sentient beings. Apart from sentient beings there is no Buddha mind.

> If deluded, then buddha is a sentient being;
> if enlightened, a sentient being is a buddha.
> If ignorant, a buddha is a sentient being;
> if wise, a sentient being is a buddha.
> If the mind is dishonest, a buddha is a sentient being;
> if impartial, a sentient being is a buddha.
> Once the mind is dishonest,
> a buddha is a sentient being.
> Once thoughts are enlightened and impartial,
> a sentient being is himself a buddha.
> My mind has Buddha within itself;
> this Buddha within is the true Buddha.
> If there were no Buddha mind within,
> where would we seek Buddha?"

—RF

Notes

1. *Prajñā* is the intuitive wisdom of Buddhism's absolute truth that all things have no permanent reality, no permanent self-identity.

2. The concept of dharma encompasses a number of different meanings. Here it points to the ultimate truth of Buddhist beliefs; hence, translated as Dharma, with a capital. At other places in the text Huineng speaks of various dharmas, meaning things that have temporary existence (people, ideas, trees, etc.), but are not ultimately true throughout time, since their existence depends upon other things and their existence is not permanent.

3. The tree under which Buddha sat in meditation until he achieved enlightenment.

4. The dharma body is not a physical body, but a term synonymous with ultimate reality. The dharma body encompasses all things, being and nonbeing.

5. There are two different interpretations of this passage. The one followed here assumes that Huineng is arguing that when one stops thinking about the physical world and its impermanent dharmas, one then breaks the cycle of rebirth and attains enlightenment. The second interpretation is that he is arguing that when one stops thinking about dharmas one is reborn into a better place, another step closer to enlightenment.

6. August 28, 713.

7. A *kalpa* is the term used for enormous lengths of time, variously defined as tens of millions of years or hundreds of millions of years.

SOME MODERN HISTORIANS have complained that the accounts of military operations found in the Chinese dynastic histories do little more than tell us that "the army of X was defeated near Y." While entries of this sort are extremely common, there are also exceptions that provide considerably more information. The text that follows is taken from the *Comprehensive Mirror for Aid in Government (Zizhi tongjian),* a comprehensive, annalistic history of China compiled by the Song scholar-statesman Sima Guang (1019–1086). It describes a battle fought in the autumn of 618 between two of the many leaders who were competing for power in the wake of the collapse of the Sui dynasty. Wang Shichong, a general nominally loyal to the Sui court, held the great city of Luoyang, where he was encircled by the forces of the rebel leader Li Mi. As food supplies ran low in the city, Wang was driven to desperate action. The following account is typical of the longer Chinese battle narratives in its reference to textual authority, its emphasis on clever stratagems and what we would now call psychological warfare, and its attention to the strategic debates at the council of war rather than the actual clash of arms. In keeping with common practice in traditional Chinese historical writing, Sima Guang based his account of the battle of Mang Mountain (Mangshan) on descriptions of the same event in earlier histories (in this case works compiled by official historians during the first half of the Tang dynasty). Since the description of Li Mi's council of war in one of these sources borrows some of its language directly from a much earlier account of a famous battle fought at the beginning of the Han dynasty, there is some question about whether the following text is a reasonably accurate account of what actually happened at Mang Mountain or a highly stylized representation of battle shaped by literary precedent and the imagination of Tang scholar-officials.—DAG

The Battle of Mang Mountain

Because the troops in the Eastern Capital (i.e., Luoyang) were weak after suffering several defeats and, moreover, the Sui generals and ministers had been massacring one another, Li Mi said that the city could be pacified within a very short time. Having monopolized political authority in Luoyang, Wang Shichong generously rewarded his officers and men, prepared weapons and equipment, and secretly planned for the defeat of Li Mi. At that time the Sui army lacked food, while Mi's army had little clothing. Shichong requested an exchange. Mi considered that this would lead to difficulties, but his aide Bing Yuanzhen and others sought private profit and persuaded Mi to consent to it. Before this, the people from the Eastern Capital who went over to Mi's side each day numbered more than a hundred. Once the defenders had obtained food, however, those who surrendered became fewer. Regretting his decision, Mi put a stop to the trade.

When Li Mi returned after smashing Yuwen Huaji,[1] many of his tough troops and fine horses were dead, and the soldiers who remained were weary and sick. Wang Shichong wished to take advantage of their weakness to attack them. Fearing that his people's hearts were not unified, he duplicitously claimed that one Zhang Yongtong, a guardsman of the Left Army, had thrice dreamt of the Duke of Zhou,[2] who had ordered him to announce his intention that Wang Shichong should keep his troops in order to assist in attacking the rebels. Shichong thereupon set up a temple for the Duke of Zhou, and whenever he sent out troops they would first stop there to pray. Shichong ordered a shaman to announce that the Duke of Zhou wished for the vice-director (i.e., Wang Shichong) to move promptly to chastise Li Mi, in which case there would be a great victory. Should he fail to follow these instructions, however, all of his troops would die of a pestilence. Shichong's soldiers were mostly men from Chu[3] who believed in superstitious talk, and they asked to be led into battle. Shichong selected his keenest troops and obtained over twenty thousand, with more than two thousand horses. On the cyclical day *renzi* (October 4, 618), he sent his army out to attack Li Mi. The banners were all inscribed with the characters of Zhang Yongtong's name, and the army's appearance was exceedingly magnificent. On the day *guichou* (October 5, 618) the army reached Yanshi and camped to the south of the Tongji Canal, over which they constructed three bridges. Leaving Wang Bodang to hold the Jinyong fortress, Li Mi personally led his elite troops out to Yanshi and took up a position on Mang Mountain[4] to await the enemy.

Li Mi summoned his generals to a conference. Pei Renji said, "Wang Shichong has arrived with all of his masses, so Luoyang must certainly be empty. We can divide our forces to hold the vital roads so that he is unable to move east, select thirty thousand elite troops, and go west along the Yellow River to threaten the Eastern Capital. When Shichong returns, we will stop our movement; should he go forth once more, we will threaten Luoyang again. If we do it this way, we will have strength to spare while they will be worn out from running for their lives; it is certain that we will defeat them." Li Mi said, "Your proposal shows great skill. At present there are three conditions under which we cannot confront the troops from the Eastern Capital: the first is that their troops are keen and their weapons sharp; the second is that they have resolved to penetrate deeply; and the third is that they are seeking battle after their food supplies have been depleted. We need only take advantage of our walls and hold fast, husbanding our strength to await their coming. If they wish for a fight they won't get it, and if they seek to flee there will be no road for them. Before ten days have passed, Shichong's head can be brought beneath my headquarters flag!" Chen Zhilue, Fan Wenchao, and Shan Xiongxin all said, "We reckon that Shichong's combat troops are

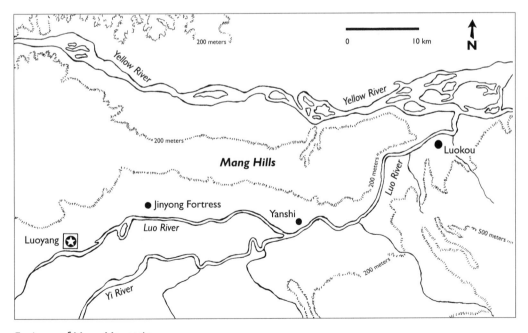

Environs of Mang Mountain

very few. They have experienced several crushing defeats, and all of them have already lost their courage. The *Methods of War*[5] says, "If double their number, then fight"—not to mention when we are more than double! Moreover, the newly adhered troops from the Yangtze and Huai rivers wish to take this opportunity to display their meritorious efforts. When we use them as our spearhead, they will be able to attain their aspiration." At that point the various generals began shouting all at once. Those who wished to give battle were seven or eight out of ten. Led astray by the opinion of the majority, Li Mi went along with them. Pei Renji contested bitterly but was unable to win the argument. He struck the ground and sighed, "Sir, you are certainly going to regret this later on."

Wei Zheng[6] spoke to the staff aide Zheng Ting, saying, "Although the Duke of Wei (i.e., Li Mi) has long been victorious, many of his brave generals and keen troops have perished, and the remaining warriors have become lax and negligent. Under these two conditions, it is difficult to counter the enemy. What is more, Shichong lacks food and has his mind set on a battle to the death, and will therefore be difficult to fight spearpoint-to-spearpoint. It would be better to resist him with deep moats and high ramparts; before ten days or at most a month have passed Shichong's grain supply will have been exhausted and he will have to retreat of his own accord. If we pursue and attack him, there is no chance that we will not be victorious." Zheng Ting replied, "That is nothing more than the usual talk of an old scholar." "This is an unorthodox strategy," Wei Zheng said; "How can you call it 'usual talk'?" With a shake of his clothing he rose and left.

Cheng Zhijie led the Inner Cavalry Army to camp with Li Mi on top of North Mang Mountain. Shan Xiongxin led the Outer Cavalry Army to camp north of Yanshi. Wang Shichong sent several hundred cavalry across the Tongji Canal to attack Shan Xiongxin's camp. Li Mi sent Pei Xingyan and Cheng Zhijie to assist Shan Xiongxin. Galloping forward in advance of the others

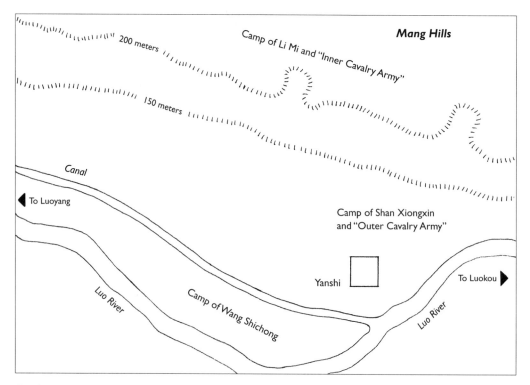

Cavalry camps

to throw himself upon the enemy, Pei Xingyan was hit by an arrow and fell to the ground. Cheng Zhijie rescued him, killing several men. Wang Shichong's army scattered before him, and he returned holding Xingyan in his arms, two riders on one horse. He was pursued by Shichong's cavalry and pierced by a lance thrust. Zhijie turned around, seized and broke the lance, cut down his pursuer at the same time, and got away together with Xingyan. When sunset came, both sides gathered their troops and returned to their respective camps. More than ten men, including Li Mi's brave general Sun Changle, had suffered serious wounds.

Having recently defeated Yuwen Huaji, Li Mi was inclined to underestimate Wang Shichong and did not prepare fortifications around his camp. During the night Shichong sent two hundred horsemen to make their way surreptitiously into the mountains to the north, where they hid themselves in ambush among the ravines. He ordered his soldiers to feed their horses and take a good meal themselves. On the morning of the day *jiayin* (October 6, 618), when he was about to join battle, Shichong harangued his troops: "This day's battle is not simply a contest that will determine victory or defeat; whether we live or die depends on this one action. If we win, it goes without saying that we will have wealth and honor; if we lose, not one of us will get away with his life. We are fighting not only on behalf of the state, but for our very lives. It is appropriate that each of you should do your utmost." At dawn, he led his soldiers to advance against Li Mi. Mi sent his troops out to meet them, but before they were able to form their ranks Shichong unleashed his assault upon them. Shichong's soldiers were all nimble braves from the Yangtze and the Huai who maneuvered as if they were flying. Before this Shichong had found a man whose facial features resembled those of Li Mi. He had him bound and concealed, and when the fighting was at its fiercest he had the man led across the front of the battle lines, raising the shout, "We've already captured Li Mi!" The soldiers all cheered. Shichong's concealed troops emerged from hiding. Descending from the heights, they rode in to take control of Li Mi's camp and set fire to the huts. Mi's forces collapsed completely, and his generals Zhang Tongren and Chen Zhilue surrendered. Mi fled toward Luokou[7] with more than ten thousand men.

—DAG

Notes

1. Yuwen Huaji, a renegade Sui general who had murdered Emperor Yang, was defeated by Li Mi in the summer of 618.

2. The Duke of Zhou was the younger brother of King Wu, who conquered the Shang people and established the Zhou dynasty in the middle of the eleventh century B.C.E. He was one of the most revered figures of Chinese antiquity, renowned for his virtue and wisdom.

3. The ancient kingdom of Chu, based in the middle reaches of the Yangtze River, lasted until the third century B.C.E. These troops came from territories that had once belonged to the Chu state, where shamanism was an important element of the local culture.

4. Mang Mountain or, perhaps more accurately, Mang Hills, is a long ridge running from east to west between the Yellow River and the Luo River. The old city of Luoyang was a few miles south of Mang Mountain.

5. This would appear to be a reference to the famous work attributed to Sun Zi, probably dating from the fifth century B.C.E. The expression that follows differs significantly from the closest parallel in the original text, however.

6. Wei Zheng (580–643) was a scholar who later became an influential minister at the court of the second Tang emperor.

7. The fortress of Luokou, east of Luoyang at the confluence of the Luo River and the Yellow River, was an important base for Li Mi's forces.

"THE TALE OF Master Yuan of Mount Lu" (Lu shan Yuan gong hua) is one of numerous manuscripts Marc Aurel Stein (1862–1943) procured from Dunhuang in 1907. Numbered S[tein] 2073, the manuscript is written in two hands on coarse, whitish paper. A colophon notes that the text was copied by Zhang Changji in the fifth year of the Kaibao era (972). The manuscript is now housed in the British Library, London, United Kingdom.

The main character of this story is the eminent monk Huiyuan (334–416), known for his contacts with contemporary gentry, exchanges with the usurper Huan Xuan (369–404), correspondence with the renowned translator Kumārajīva (344–409/413), and his teaching of *dhyāna* (meditation) practices at Mount Lu in Jiangxi Province from 373. Huiyuan emphasized the importance of worshiping Amitābha Buddha, who presides over the Western Paradise, and is famous for his essay "A Monk Does Not Bow Down before a King" (Shamen bu jing wang zhe lun). In his youth, Huiyuan diligently studied the Confucian classics and was particularly fond of Taoism. Thus he was broadly learned, not only in Buddhist precepts, but in traditional Chinese thought as well.

Another eminent monk mentioned in the text is Daoan (312–385). Daoan was one of the most influential Buddhist personalities in China during the Eastern Jin period (317–420). He stressed the need for *vinaya* (monastic rules of discipline) and immersed himself deeply in the study of *prajñā-pāramitā* (intuitive wisdom) literature. And, whereas Huiyuan encouraged the worship of Amitābha, Daoan had organized a cult to Maitreya, the Buddha of the future.

It is curious that, in real life, Huiyuan was a disciple (in fact, the favorite pupil) of Daoan, and it was his encounter with the latter in the year 354 that made him turn to Buddhism in the first place. In the present tale, however, Huiyuan is depicted as though he were the teacher of Daoan. Consequently, we can safely assume that "The Tale of Master Yuan of Mount Lu," which dates to more than half a millennium after the lifetimes of its protagonists, must have been composed for the sectarian purpose of elevating Huiyuan and his partisans over Daoan and his adherents. There are also many other aspects of the tale that are at odds with historical reality, such as the name of Huiyuan's teacher mentioned in the second paragraph, his capture by the bandit Bo Zhuang, his servitude to Prime Minister Cui, the displacement of a birthmark on Daoan's arm to Huiyuan's, his alleged authorship of an enormous commentary on the *Mahāparinirvāṇa-sūtra,* and so forth.

Without going into elaborate detail, the probable source of the massive distortions in "The Tale of Master Yuan of Mount Lu" is roughly determinable. First of all, in his *Treatise on the Three Rewards (San bao lun),* Huiyuan did write about nirvana, the central doctrine of this tale. Furthermore, he had a disciple named Daosheng who concentrated heavily on the *Nirvāṇa-sūtra* and was one of its strongest advocates. Now, when written quickly (in "grassy" style), the Chinese characters for Daoan and for Daosheng look rather similar. Thus it is quite likely that some early author had penned an attack on Daosheng (Huiyuan's student) for having appropriated Huiyuan's ideas on nirvana and that his sloppy calligraphy resulted in the transfer of his critique to Daoan (Huiyuan's teacher). To complicate matters further, there was another, later Huiyuan (523–592) who was—like Daosheng—also a staunch advocate and well-known exegete of the *Nirvāṇa-sūtra*. A contemporary of his, Tanyan (d. 588), indeed, wrote a huge commentary on this sutra in fifteen scrolls, and it was this commentary that was most influential as a guide to the text during the period when our tale was composed.

Regardless of their origin, the legends embodied in this tale were still being widely circulated as late as the fourteenth century, when Buddhist historians denounced them as false depictions of Huiyuan and Daoan. Despite all of the historical inaccuracies and legendary aspects of "The Tale of Master Yuan of Mount Lu," however, this fascinating narrative is valuable for its vivid description of medieval Buddhist lectures and debates. Finally, in terms of the development of narrative, this is the longest sustained tale to have appeared in China up to the time when it was written.

The following translation is based directly on a very close reading of the original Dunhuang manuscript. As such, it is occasionally different from all modern published versions of the text. The discrepancies result from factors such as the following: where to break sentences; where to insert punctuation; how to divide up words; how to interpret graphs that are sloppily written, erroneous, out of order, interpolated, omitted, or rubbed out; and so forth.—TS, VHM

Now, we have heard that the Dharma King[1] is magnificent and the teachings of the Buddha are imposing. The laws of the king are devoid of selfishness, and the actions of the Buddha are impartial.[2] While the king transmitted the Right Teachings, the Buddha has expounded the True Tenets. All these are now part of the twelve canonical genres.[3] They are all bridges to salvation built by Śākyamuni. After the nirvana[4] of the Tathāgata,[5] the sages have all submerged themselves in the doctrine of images.[6]

There was a monk called Zhantan[7] who had a disciple named Huiyuan. Speaking of this Huiyuan, his family lived in Yanmen.[8] There were only two brothers and no other kinsmen. The older of the two, called Huiyuan, renounced lay life and became a monk. The younger brother, called Huichi, [remained behind] to look after their mother. When Huiyuan was with monk Zhantan, he often recited the True Law and frequently read the canonical texts. He delighted in his understanding of the Third Stage of *dhyāna*[9] and realized that the [advent of the final] stage [in the development of Buddhism] was not far. Then one day, with his palms pressed together, he said to the monk, "Your disciple has humbly served you for many years already. But, in the pursuit of learning, due to my own stupidity, I am still uncultivated. Now, I would like to visit a famous mountain,[10] follow streams and cross rivers, visit priests and attend monks, and dwell as a hermit beside a precipitous gorge so that I may live out my life contentedly."

His teacher asked, "If you leave now, to which mountain do you intend to go?"

Huiyuan said, "Your disciple can't distinguish between east and west, nor do I know of north and south. I just have the desire to leave, but I don't know where I should go."

His teacher said, "If you leave now, just stay to the left of the river when you proceed on your pilgrimage. Stop when you reach Mt. Lu. That will be the place where you can cultivate yourself."

Hearing these words, Huiyuan was so pleased that he was unable to control himself. So, having received his teacher's instructions and injunctions, how dared he disobey? Then, pressing his palms together, he went forward and bowed. Twice formally bidding adieu to the monk, he embarked on his long journey.

Wending his way and taking with him a copy of the *Nirvana Sutra*,[11] Master Yuan traveled towards Mount Lu to cultivate the Way. It was the season when rays of spring shone radiantly, the beautiful flowers emitted fragrance, green willows waved supply in the breeze, and the tips of bamboos bent gracefully. He gazed upon cloudy peaks in the distance and watched winter geese hurrying homeward. Confident that his determination to learn the Way was solid, he was intent upon early attainment of the True Principles.

After walking for many days, Master Yuan arrived at Jiangzhou.[12] He walked through various byways and alleys, rested a couple of days, and then started off again. After he had gone westward for more than fifty tricents,[13] and just as he was walking along the road, he came upon a mountain. He asked someone, "What mountain is this?"

The villager answered, "This is Mount Lu."

Master Yuan said [to himself], "On the day when I first parted from my teacher, he instructed me to stop upon reaching Mount Lu. This place is where I should cultivate the Way!"

The mountain did not look like an ordinary one. What sort of unusual realm was it?

There were myriad soaring cliffs,
Thousands of interfolding plateaus;
High peaks reared upward,
Sharp crags loomed above.

Gibbons cried in dark valleys,
Tigers roared in deep ravines;
Withered pines were enwrapped by ancient wisteria,
Peach blossoms were touched by eternal freshness.

Master Yuan was eager to enjoy himself on this mountain. As the sun was about to complete its journey to the west, he entered into the depths of the mountain looking for a place to stay. Then, on the northern side of the top of Incense-Burner Peak, he built himself a temporary grass hut. From his waist he took out his fire-stone and, striking it, he lit some Priceless-Treasure incense. He sat down with his legs crossed and began reading several chapters of the *Nirvana Sutra*. The sounds of him reading the sutra were so clear and distinct that they could be heard far and near. Dharmic rhymes echoed and Sanskrit tones spread afar. Touched by [his recitation], the great rocks swayed and the hundred grasses bowed. Auspicious birds and numinous beasts all came to sing their praise.

At this time, the Mountain Spirit in his temple suddenly realized that this was an auspicious omen and was astonished like never before. The Mountain Spirit inquired, "Who's on duty today?" The stout Tree Spirit came in front of the hall and called out, "Yes, sir!" With a voice like thunder, one head with three faces, eyes like suspended mirrors, and carrying in his hands an iron staff as tall as himself, the Tree Spirit said, "I so-and-so am on duty." The Mountain Spirit responded, "So, it's you who is on duty! Just now as I was in my temple, I suddenly noticed that the rocks of the mountain were swaying and the birds and beasts were startled. Go and inspect the mountain for me. Find out what omens there are. Perhaps a sage or saint from some other place has come to my mountain. Or maybe some strange creature or spirit has taken refuge among these mountains. If it brings peace and happiness to my mountain, then admit it. If it unsettles my mountain, then you should drive it away immediately and make it leave this mountain."

The Tree Spirit called out, "Yes, sir!" He covered everywhere over hill and dale, followed along streams and crossed rivers. He even searched thoroughly under each of the trees in the mountain forest, but could not find a single person. However, when he reached the northern side of Incense-Burner Peak, he saw a monk who had built a meditation hut and, sitting cross-legged in it, was just at that moment reciting a sutra.

Seeing this, the Tree Spirit hid his spectral form and immediately changed into the body of an old man. He looked aged as a dried water willow with white hair like mulberry leaves.[14] Coming up to the hut, he greeted the monk in a loud voice. Master Yuan said, "Myriad blessings upon you!" The old man slowly came forward and started speaking: "Your disciple does not know where you come from, how you got here, and what you seek. I humbly beg you to be so kind as to grant me an explanation."

Master Yuan answered, "This poor monk has come from Yanmen to settle in this mountain for awhile and engage in cultivation of the Way."

The old man asked again, "Just now I heard your marvelous sounds. What were those sounds?"

Master Yuan answered, "The sounds you heard just now were of a poor monk reciting the sutras. When living beings hear such sounds, they invariably wish to escape sorrow and seek deliverance."[15]

When the old man heard these words, he exclaimed, "Good! Good!" Once again he inquired of the monk, "Having already come here, monk, is there anything that you need?"

Master Yuan replied, "If this poor monk can find a monastery to dwell in, then I can avoid the wind and the frost. This is the only wish that the poor monk has."

The old man said, "If you wanted something else, then there might not be any, but if it's a monastery that you desire, then this is a trivial matter. Your disciple lives in the village to the west. Wait till I reach the village and discuss the matter with various elders; then we will come and build a monastery for you." When he had finished speaking, the old man bade farewell to the monk and left.

After having taken leave of the monk, the old man was only a hundred steps away from the front of the hut when he suddenly disappeared. Instantly, he had changed back from the body of the old man into his spectral form! When he arrived in front of the hall of the Mountain Spirit, he bowed and called out, "Sir! I obeyed your order and covered everywhere over hill and dale, searching for goblins and fox-spirits, but failed to find anything. When I reached the northern side of Incense-Burner Peak, I saw a monk who had built himself a meditation hut. Sitting cross-legged, he was reciting a sutra. He said that he had come from Yanmen and had temporarily taken up residence in this mountain to engage in cultivation of the Way."

After hearing this, the Mountain Spirit could only say that he was greatly astonished. "I have guarded this mountain for countless *kalpa*s,"[16] [thought the Mountain Spirit,] "but never have I seen a monk take refuge in this mountain. All of this will bring lasting fortune to my mountain and ward off calamities." The Mountain Spirit asked again, "Does the monk who has come here need anything?"

The Tree Spirit memorialized, "I just asked him that. He doesn't really need anything, but says that he would only want a monastery to live in."

The Mountain Spirit said, "If he had wanted something else, then it may have been difficult. But, if all he needs is a monastery to dwell in, that is entirely a small matter. You don't have to go anywhere far off. Just muster out the ghosts and the spirits on this mountain on my behalf and ask them to build a monastery for this monk."

After receiving the order, the Tree Spirit, standing on the western slope, thrice knocked resoundingly [with his staff]. All of a sudden, the clouds and mists darkened. Right away, all the ghosts and spirits in the mountain arrived. That night, as they wielded their magical implements, a hundred bolts of lightning flashed and thunder pealed a thousand times. The tumultuous noise went on till dawn as the ghosts and spirits built a monastery. When dawn came, they had already completed an extraordinary monastery. Here's what it was like:[17] the multistoried towers and pavilions were no less [marvelous] than [the palaces of] the Trāyastriṃśa heaven;[18] the jeweled halls and terraces were equal to those of the Western Paradise;[19] there were dense groves of trees and thickets of bushes; flowers bloomed throughout the four seasons of the year; springs and streams flowed beside it during both spring and winter, never drying up; all the more, rare flowers and tender blossoms grew beside the cloisters of enlightenment; and magical birds of good omen flew up toward the roofs of the *vihāra*.[20]

Thereupon, when Master Yuan came out of the hut and looked, he suddenly saw a completed monastery. He gasped at how extraordinary it was. After contemplating it for a long time, Master Yuan said, "This is not something I could have done. This must be due to the mighty power of the *Mahānirvāṇa-sūtra*." Observing its rarity, Master Yuan composed the following *gāthā*:[21]

The tall, rustling bamboos turn the four seasons into spring,
The streamlets flowing in all directions clean the dust away;
Green is each branch of ivy that climbs on the walls,
Fresh is each patch of moss that covers the ground.

The distant wilderness is free from the hubbub of city markets,
The pure space has nothing vulgar as its neighbor;
The Mountain Spirit has built a *vihāra* at this place,
Monks must now be invited to turn the Dharma Wheel.

And so Master Yuan himself entered the monastery; he went to every room and walked through each courtyard. The monastery [seemed] to have everything. However, they were short of water and there was no place to fetch it. Master Yuan said, "This monastery is as perfect as the Dharma. But if there is no drinking water, how can one live here? Later, when the monks arrive, how will they get water?" As he came down in front of the Buddha Hall, he saw that there was a big rock [and thought that] there ought to be water beneath it. Master Yuan pried the rock with his staff, whereupon he found water that welled up out of the ground. To this day, it is known as the "Monk's Staff Spring." There is also a monastery called the "Monastery Built by Transformation."[22] The pool of running water beneath the monastery is called the "White Lotus Pond."

Several months after Master Yuan had moved into the monastery and settled down, an audience hurried thither from the four directions. On this day Master Yuan broadly explained the teachings of the *Mahānirvāṇa-sūtra* to his assembled followers. Within a year, the audiences were as thick as clouds, and their donations poured in like rain. All the listeners at the meeting place noted that there was an old man in the assembly who had been listening to the sutra for a year. They said that this old man never gave his name when he came and never mentioned his style when he left. He was always in his seat from the beginning of the lecture and, as soon as the lecture ended, he would go back. Master Yuan was very puzzled by this, so he asked those who sat in the same row to direct the old man to him. When the old man was called upon, he straightaway came in front of Master Yuan.

Master Yuan asked, "Where do you live, old man? You have been listening to the Dharma for a long time, yet we do not know your name or surname. We would like to know some particulars about you."

The old man answered, "Although the disciple has listened for a year, I still have not understood the doctrines in the *Nirvana Sutra*. Until I do, I cannot tell my name and surname." After he had finished speaking, the old man ran out of the monastery gate. Master Yuan tried following the old man but could not see any trace of him. Who was this person? It was the Dragon [Spirit] of the thousand-feet-deep pool of Mt. Lu. He had come to listen to Master Yuan preach the Dharma.

After he had seen the old man depart, Master Yuan would feel regretful whenever he thought of him. "This old man," thought Master Yuan, "has listened to the Dharma for almost a year, but still does not understand the meanings and the principles in the *Nirvana Sutra*. How much less can I expeditiously help all living creatures to attain enlightenment? How can I make the listeners understand? Surely, now, I must produce a commentary on the *Nirvana Sutra*." When he had finished thinking these thoughts, he informed the Buddhas of the Ten Directions, [saying,] "Now, for all sentient beings who are mired in confusion and thus have not yet been enlightened to the teachings of Mahāyāna,[23] I, your disciple, intend to make a commentary on the *Nirvana Sutra* and open the hearts of all living beings to enlightenment. They will be able to understand the Buddhist Dharma clearly and abandon falsehood to follow truth. They will be free from all trace of doubts forever." Then, in front of the Buddha Hall, he took a divine purple-cloud, fine-haired writing-brush and, informing the Buddha-Tathāgatas of the Ten Directions [of his intentions], while requesting that the Earth God and all the local spirits bear witness, [announced,] "If the saints and sages have objections, then may this brush fall down immediately." When he had finished speaking and had burnt incense, he declared his piety, then took the brush and threw it into the air. At that moment, the brush remained motionless in midair. Master Yuan knew that [his proposal] met with the approval of the Buddha-Tathāgatas. He then requested that the brush descend from midair. How do we know this? Until this day, there is still a Throw-Brush Peak at Mount Lu in Jiangzhou.

Thus did Master Yuan produce his commentary. From start to finish it took him three years to complete, but still he was afraid that there were mistakes in writing and that the purport of various passages might not be comprehensible. So he wanted to take all the more than eight hundred scrolls of the commentary outside the eastern gate of the monastery and place them on a fire. He made a big bonfire with fragrant firewood and repeatedly addressed the Buddhas of the Ten Directions, the various bodhisattvas, and the saints and sages: "For all the sentient beings who are mired in confusion and who have not yet been enlightened to Mahāyāna, I, your disciple, wanted to eliminate their doubts, so I composed this commentary. If the purport [of the commentary] is in agreement with the sutra, then I hope that the fire will not be able to burn it. If the commentary and the sutra are in conformity, then water will not be able to submerge it."

When he had finished speaking, he set the commentary ablaze. Then the crimson flames reached up to the sky and the dark smoke billowed thickly, but the sutra in the middle of all this remained completely unscathed. Master Yuan knew that the commentary had distantly met with the approval of the Buddhas. However, he was still not satisfied! So next he took the commentary to the edge of the White Lotus Pool and threw it toward the water. When the commentary was still about ten feet above the water, it remained motionless in midair. Master Yuan knew that the commentary had distantly met with the approval of the Buddhas. Later, Master Yuan took the commentary and carried it into the monastery, where he placed it in the sutra library. Afterward, there was no lack of disciples, and the people who came to listen to his lectures were exceedingly numerous. Master Yuan's propagation of the teachings of the *Mahānirvāṇa-sūtra* for the masses attracted listeners from all directions. Like pouring rain and billowing clouds they eagerly came to listen to the Dharma. From the beginning to the end, he delivered his lectures for several years.

At this time, there suddenly arose in the region of Shouzhou[24] a group of bandits led by a man surnamed Bo and called Zhuang. Speaking of this man, when young he loved doing daring things. Regardless of the danger to his life, he frequently engaged in violence and robberies. By nature he was fond of slaughter. By chance, Bo Zhuang heard someone say that at Mt. Lu in Jiangzhou there was a monastery built by magical transformation which was very wealthy. The donations the monastery received were enormous, so its riches were not inconsiderable. From far and near, he assembled a band of more than five hundred men. Traveling double-time under the starlit skies, they reached inside the borders of Jiangzhou. Quickly they encamped and settled down. Bo Zhuang then said to his band, "Do not say [anything] to anyone, lest people come to know about us. Tomorrow, when the monks have their vegetarian meal, we will go rob the monastery." Everyone voiced their agreement. Thus, there is a proverb which says, "When a person has good intentions, Heaven will support him; if he has evil aspirations, Heaven will halt him." No sooner had Bo Zhuang declared his intent at that very spot than it was already known to the local earth god. Secretly, with his magical powers, the earth god came and informed the monks at the monastery on Mt. Lu [about Bo's plans]. The word spread from room to room and was passed from courtyard to courtyard. The earth spirit, speaking from the sky, said to the monks, "Tomorrow, during the vegetarian meal, a gang of bandits will come to rob this monastery. I urge that all monks be sure to run away." The monks were frightened out of their wits when they heard this. They all ran away in different directions, fleeing as best they could.

While all the other monks were trying to escape, only monk Yunqing, the chief disciple of Master Yuan, dared not scramble off because of his devotion to and concern for his teacher. Instead, he came straight to the monk's meditation-hut and informed him, saying, "A moment ago a spirit came and reported that bandits are coming to rob this monastery. I humbly request that you kindly withdraw somewhere." Master Yuan replied, "Even though you may not have known it, I was already aware of this matter a long time ago. If [we follow] the teachings of the *Nirvana Sutra,* then there is nothing to fear. If there is fear, how can there be nirvana? You, along with the other monks, should all swiftly run away. Now that I am here in this place, I can never leave it." Yunqing, seeing that the monk would not heed his repeated request to withdraw, rained tears of sorrow. Alone, he came out of the monastery gate and followed the others in their flight.

After watching the monks leave, Master Yuan sat in the meditation-hut by himself without any fear. Soon Bo Zhuang, leading his band, approached the monastery. He arranged his army in battle formation across the ridge and had other soldiers spread out along the valley. Their war cries made the hills crumble and rocks crack. To east and west they scurried, to north and south they charged. Breaking into the monastery en masse, they shouted, "Catch them alive!" Bo Zhuang entered the monastery with his army. Hoping to find great stores of treasure, he searched each and every courtyard, but there was not a single thing in the monastery. Bo Zhuang exclaimed, "Amazing! When we were discussing our plans yesterday, no one else knew of them. Who could have informed the people in the monastery and prompted them to run away someplace?"

Bo Zhuang ordered his assistants, "Go search everywhere inside and outside of the monastery for me. If you catch any monks, bring them to me immediately!" The assistants shouted, "Yes, sir!" and searched everywhere but could not find anyone. When they reached outside the eastern gate of the monastery, they saw a monk sitting quietly in a meditation-hut. The assistants dared not disturb him, so they left stealthily and went back into the monastery, where they came straight before Bo Zhuang. They reported, "In accordance with the General's orders just now, we searched everywhere inside and outside of the monastery looking for monks, but couldn't find anyone. When we reached outside the gate of the monastery, we saw a monk and dared not let this situation go unreported." Bo Zhuang asked, "Where is the monk?" The assistants reported to the General, "We saw him sitting in the meditation-hut outside the eastern gate of the monastery." Thereupon, grasping the reins of his horse and climbing up on the saddle, Bo Zhuang rushed straight outside the eastern gate where he indeed saw a monk sitting cross-legged inside a hut. Bo Zhuang shouted at top of his voice and ordered the assistants to fetch the monk in front of his horse.

Bo Zhuang asked Master Yuan, "What riches or textiles are in this monastery of yours? Bring them out to me immediately!" Master Yuan walked towards Bo Zhuang and reported, "This monastery has always been very poor; there's nothing at all here. Although there have been a few donations, they were used entirely for daily expenses and meals. General, I dare not deceive you; there really are no riches." Bo Zhuang then closely examined Master Yuan and began to feel admiration toward him. This was because Master Yuan had the likeness of a bodhisattva and his body had a distinctive[25] silver glow, he stood seven feet[26] tall, his hair was as though daubed with lacquer, and his lips were as though dotted with vermilion. As soon as Bo Zhuang saw this, he said to his assistants, "This monk is fit to be a servant for me." He then said to Master Yuan, "I want you to be my aide. Are you willing or not?" Master Yuan stepped forward. He was willing to devote himself to become the General's slave; he consented to serve in front of Bo Zhuang's horse. Master Yuan said, "There's one other small matter that I wish you would kindly hear. Do you, General, want this poor monk's body, or do you want my karma?"[27] Bo Zhuang asked, "What do you mean by 'body,' and what do you mean by 'karma'?" Master Yuan replied, "My karma is to recite sutras. If you just want me to serve you, then here is my body. If you want this poor monk's [entire karma], then I request that you not prevent me from reciting sutras." Bo Zhuang replied, "So long as I receive your services, who would prevent you from reciting sutras?" Master Yuan agreed and followed behind the General.

When they were about a hundred paces from the monastery, Master Yuan once again addressed the General: "Please allow me to go back into the monastery and take off these monk's robes while I am there. I will return here right away to follow your banners." Bo Zhuang said, "Return quickly and do not make me angry. If you are late in coming, I will send my assistants to seize you and cut you into three parts right in front of my horse. Don't say I didn't warn you!" Master Yuan agreed, then entered the monastery and stood in front of the hall. At that time, his chief disciple Yunqing, from the top of a high peak, saw his teacher inside the monastery. He came rushing down the mountain and went straight before him. He reported to the monk, "Just now, as the wild outlaws were charging forward, I was extremely frightened. Now I am happy to see the army of bandits retreat and will share in your joy." Master Yuan said, "The *Nirvana Sutra* teaches that there is no fear; if there is fear, how can there be nirvana? From now on, you must try to improve yourself and maintain [the Dharma] well. Today, I am going to bid farewell to you forever." Yunqing asked the monk, "What could make you say such a thing?" Master Yuan replied, "Just now, outside the gate of the monastery, I gave my word to become a slave of the General. I cannot stay here for too long. You must strive to do your best later on." Hearing this, Yunqing beat himself all over until fresh blood flowed from the seven apertures [of his head].[28] After a long time, he revived and got up from the ground, then composed the following *gāthā:*

We were like birds in flight,
You, master, were like a great tree;
Now that the great tree is moving,
Where shall you send us for shelter?

Where will your transformed body dwell?
Leaving only a sentence of nirvana;
We vow to grasp the lamp of wisdom,[29]
So that we do not recklessly lose our way.

After he had finished speaking, Yunqing began to cry all the more grievously. Master Yuan said, "I am afraid that the General will blame me for being late." Master Yuan went out through the monastery gate and, catching up with the banners [of Bo Zhuang's army], followed along behind them. As the days came and the months went by, he followed them for several years.

After Yunqing saw the master leave, he once again gathered the community of monks and started giving lectures based upon the *Commentary on the Nirvana Sutra*. Invariably, the audience would shed tears like rain, just as though they were seeing the great teacher. As Yunqing had received no news of the master for several years, he gave the *Commentary on the Nirvana Sutra* to a monk named Daoan. Soon after receiving the *Commentary on the Nirvana Sutra,* Daoan took it to the Fuguang Monastery in the Eastern Capital[30] and began lecturing with it. Not knowing what sort of person Daoan really was like, the listeners were, nonetheless, touched by his lectures; they flocked to him like clouds, and donations poured in like rain.

This was the time when the Eastern Capital was under Emperor Wen[31] of the Jin dynasty. When Daoan lectured, it caused heavenly flowers to flutter down, suffusing a pleasant fragrance as they fell, and caused five-colored[32] clouds to appear. The crowds of people increased until the audiences were incalculable. They would trample the lecture mats to pieces, making it impossible to open the sessions. As a result, Daoan wrote a memorial, which he presented to Emperor Wen of the Jin: "In compliance with your orders, I have been lecturing on the *Nirvana Sutra* at the Fuguang Monastery. The audiences have increased so much that there have been scuffles on the dharma mats, making it impossible to open the sessions. I humbly beg that you issue orders bestowing special instructions." At that time, an order was issued: "Those wanting to hear Daoan's lectures must pay one bolt of silk. This will allow them to listen for one day." Since it was then a period that witnessed peace and tranquility, prices of commodities were low. Those who could pay one bolt of silk each day numbered about twenty to thirty thousand. However, as the temple courtyard was small and narrow, there was not enough space to accommodate everyone [who paid]. Once again, a memorial was sent to inform Emperor Wen: "In compliance with your orders, I inaugurated the lecture sessions at Fuguang Monastery, and as per your previous decree charged one bolt of silk. However, the audience has continued to increase, and it is difficult to control them. I humbly beg that you once again bestow special instructions." At that time an order was issued: "Those who want to listen to Daoan's lectures must pay one hundred strings of cash[33] each. This will allow them to listen for one day." Due to this interdiction, the people who came to listen to Daoan's sessions at the Eastern Capital did not exceed three to five thousand a day.

And where was Master Yuan? Master Yuan was all the while following Bo Zhuang, who attacked any prefectures and counties he came upon. In the morning he wandered through streams and fields, and in the evening he settled down in mountain forests. His hair cut level with his eyebrows[34] and a short, coarse cloth on his body, Master Yuan constantly followed behind Bo Zhuang. After several years, he began thinking about the Gates of Emptiness,[35] but there was no way he could reenter those gates. Moreover, Bo Zhuang had left a trail of crimes. He consorted with vicious rogues who loved killing and hated life. Pillage was their modus operandi.

Perchance, one day when Bo Zhuang was in the mountains, he set up camp on the eastern ridge, and Master Yuan halted for the night on the western slope. At that time, an autumn breeze suddenly stirred, the falling leaves drifted down, the hills were silent and the woods sparse, and frost nipped the grass. The wind passed into the woods and blew through the bamboos as though they were silken [strings]. The moon shone in the dark blue sky, and the scarlet mist looked like a tapestry. Beside the flowing stream, Master Yuan's heart was full of sadness. He fell into a dazed sleep and dreamed of the Buddhas of the Ten Directions,[36] all of whom appeared among the clouds with innumerable sages and wisemen. They came down to him and called out, "Bodhisattva, arise! Don't be yearning for benighted slumber. You have borne witness to the significance of nirvana; how come you are not reciting the *Nirvana Sutra* for all sentient beings?" In his dream, Master Yuan bowed reverently over and over. As he was a completely ordinary mortal,[37] it moved Akṣobhya[38] Tathāgata to grant him a prophecy. He asked Master Yuan to come closer and said, "Do not let your heart be troubled. You have a debt from the past which has not yet been repaid. Since you were once a guarantor for someone in a previous life, you have to settle the account in your present incarnation. Your creditor is not far off—he is the current Prime Minister. Bring yourself close to the Prime Minister and then sell yourself to him. Hand over the five hundred strings of cash that you get to Bo Zhuang. You can then return to Mount Lu, where I shall rendezvous with you."

Master Yuan awoke with a start from his dream and was terribly frightened. Thereupon he sat up and read a number of chapters from the *Nirvana Sutra*. This startled Bo Zhuang awake on the eastern ridge, so he asked his assistants, "What is that sound in the west?" His assistants responded, "We inform you, General, that it is the sound of the lowly slave you captured reciting sutras in the west." When Bo Zhuang heard this he got extremely angry, so he called Master Yuan to come directly before him. Rebuking him loudly, Bo Zhuang said, "If you were in a monastery, it would be all right for you to recite like this. But how could you recite a sutra when you are in attendance upon me?"[39]

Master Yuan said, "That day when you took me as a lowly slave, General, you gave me permission to recite sutras."

Bo Zhuang said, "When did I gave you permission to recite sutras?"

Master Yuan did not say anything right away, but the assistants explained, "Actually, General, you did give him permission to recite sutras."

Bo Zhuang said, "Reciting sutras is a waste of time. We've all done our share of killing, so we don't want to have to hear the sound of sutra-recitation."

Master Yuan said, "Since you won't allow me to recite sutras in a loud voice, how would it be if I recited them silently?"

Bo Zhuang said, "That will not do. The reason I captured you in the first place was because we didn't get any loot, and in the second place was because I didn't have enough slaves. So we were angry and took you prisoner. Now the amount of our money is not little and our manpower is actually quite great, so I'll let you return to your mountain and you can cultivate yourself as you wish."

Master Yuan said, "I devoted myself as your slave and agreed to serve you my entire life. If I abandon you halfway, how can this be called devotion? If the master still needs my services, then there's nothing more to talk about. However, if you do not want this lowly slave anymore, then sell me somewhere else and you'll get a bit of money to buy liquor and meat. Can't this be done?"

Hearing this Bo Zhuang laughed out loud [and said], "You are totally wrong. Only if I had bought you somewhere and possessed an old contract could I sell you. But since I took you a prisoner, how could I sell you?"

Master Yuan said, "If you do not want to sell me, then there is nothing more to talk about. But if you do want to sell me, pretend that I was born into your house as the son of a slave and then you can sell me without a contract."

Bo Zhuang said, "If I do as you say, where could I sell you?"

Master Yuan said, "If and when you want to sell your lowly slave, just take me to the Eastern Capital and you will be able to sell me off." When Bo Zhuang heard this, he became alarmed and very angry. "You low-class scoundrel!" said Bo Zhuang. "You still haven't given up your scheming tricks. You're intending to go to the Eastern Capital and make the rounds of the offices high and low, handing in accounts of my transgressions and saying that I am a bandit so that orders will be issued to capture me."

Master Yuan said, "If your lowly slave has such an intention to plot against my master, then in all future incarnations may I die and fall into hell without any hope of escaping. I only beseech you, master, not to harbor any worries. I'm definitely not [planning] such a thing." When Bo Zhuang heard this, he trusted Master Yuan. He then scattered the band under his command, keeping only three or four men. He disguised himself as a merchant and, taking three or four pack animals which he loaded with merchandise, went directly to the Eastern Capital to sell Master Yuan. He headed for the slave and horse section of the market to sell him.

Upon reaching the marketplace, Master Yuan held a sign to sell himself. Among the throngs of people, there were none who did not sigh at the sight. This was the appearance of [40] Master Yuan with his sign:

> He was seven feet tall,
> His body had a distinctive silver glow;
> His forehead was broad and eyebrows high,
> His face was like the full moon;
> His hair was as though daubed with lacquer,
> And his lips were as though dotted with vermilion;
> He marched as if a king of bulls,
> His hands hung down past his knees. [41]

As he paced back and forth, without exception the spectators gasped in admiration. The onlookers clustered together in groups of three or four, [making such comments as,] "In my lifetime, I've encountered thousands of detained lower-class people, but truly I have never seen one like this." The more they sighed the more onlookers were attracted.

At this time, Master Yuan was filled with remorse and hated himself, knowing that his debt from a previous life had not yet been paid back. He waited eagerly to sell himself in order to compensate Bo Zhuang. In a short while, his situation moved Sovereign Śakra, [42] who transformed himself and came down in the form of a messenger of Prime Minister Cui. He went directly to the slave and horse section of the market and called out to the slave and horse broker in a loud voice, "This fine chattel must not be sold to anyone else! [His services] may be enjoyed only in the residence of the current Prime Minister, Cui. [43] He may not be purchased by anyone else!" The broker, hearing this, fully believed that there were indeed such orders and so brought Master Yuan to Prime Minister Cui's residence. At this time, Bo Zhuang followed behind, but Master Yuan said to him, "There is no reason for you to come along. No matter what lies ahead, I will take the responsibility. If the Minister is pleased, then you can take all the money to the last penny."

Bo Zhuang said, "In the business that lies ahead, be sure to respond correctly and not make any mistakes."

Master Yuan exclaimed, "Yes, sir!" Then, accompanying the broker, he went directly in front of the Minister's gate. The gatekeeper asked the broker, "Who is this man that you've brought?" [The broker answered,] "I was called here by a personal messenger of the Minister because of this caitiff. I dare not sell him to anyone else, so I have especially brought him for the needs of the Minister's residence." The gatekeeper said, "Wait here while I go inside and report to the Minister." The gatekeeper then went in front of the hall and announced to the Minister, "There is a slave-broker at the gate. He has brought a lowly person to show to the Minister today. I dare not let it go unreported!" The Minister said, "Have them brought in." Thereupon, in accord with the Minister's instructions, the gatekeeper had the broker lead Master Yuan directly in front of the hall. Seeing the Minister, Master Yuan bowed and paid his respects, then stood off to one side. When the Minister took a look, he exclaimed, "Amazing! Last night I dreamed that a spirit entered my dwelling, and now I see this slave—does this not correspond with my dream?" The Minister asked the broker, "Was he born of a slave in the Bo Zhuang household, or was he bought from somewhere else?" The broker responded to the Minister, "He was born of a slave in the Bo Zhuang household." The Minister said, "Since he was born of a slave in the Bo Zhuang household, of course there won't be a contract." He asked the broker, "How much money do you want for this slave?" Before the broker could say anything, Master Yuan stepped forward and said to the Minister, "If you want to buy this lowly slave, all we ask is five hundred strings of cash." The Minister inquired, "What kind of skills do you possess to cost five hundred strings of cash?

You don't have to go into great detail. Let's just hear a general description of your talents." Master Yuan responded, "I can tell how rich a family was three hundred years ago. I also know how poor a family will be two hundred years from now. I know how to fold clothes, decoct medicine for the four seasons, and send messages. There are no questions that I cannot answer. As to various schools of calligraphy, I have a rough knowledge of a number of them. In all of these, I am ready to compete against anyone unaided. As for hoeing rice and harvesting wheat, I understand quite a bit. When it comes to business and trade, I know all the places to go. If you have some errand to send me on, I'll come like the wind and I won't be stubborn or slow. If the Minister does not believe me, I will myself write out a contract to sell myself, and then you will know that all this is true."

The Minister instructed his assistants to fetch paper and brush and give them to Master Yuan. Master Yuan took the paper and brush, then asked for an incense burner, and one was given to him immediately. After he had bowed to the Minister, he went to the front of the hall and wrote out a contract to sell himself. It was not like most contracts. Master Yuan wrote, "In such and such a year and month, I sell myself to the Minister to be his slave, to serve him with utter faithfulness till the end of his life. If I desert him halfway, in all future incarnations may I die and fall into hell. And when my punishments there are finished, may I be reborn as a beast of burden. A saddle will be placed on my back, stirrups will hang by my sides, and a bit will be inserted in my mouth as punishment for my previous transgressions. But if I serve you for the rest of your life, then in my future incarnations may I perfect the ten stages[44] of developing the Buddha-wisdom and achieve rebirth among the congregation of the buddhas." When he had finished the contract, he handed it over to the Minister. Having received it, the Minister exclaimed, "Amazing! Is this not a bodhisattva or mahāsattva who has come to my house?" And so he ordered that five hundred strings of cash be given to the broker and passed on to Bo Zhuang at once. When Bo Zhuang received the money, he dared not stay longer, so he went back and crossed the borders into Shouzhou.

Having bought the lowly slave, the Minister ordered his domestics in the western courtyard to settle Master Yuan in a room there. Aware that he had to pay off his debt, Master Yuan dared not bear a grudge against anyone else. Whether coming or going, he would invariably be at the Minister's side and run errands for him. Suddenly, one day when Master Yuan was sitting alone in his room deep into the night and had repeatedly poked the wick of the guttering lamp, he could see that the Milky Way was calm and the moon filled the sky. He sat for a long time until his eyes became blurry and he fell asleep. Once again in his dream he saw the Buddhas of the Ten Directions—all of them appeared in the void. Along with innumerable sages and wise men, they gathered like clouds and called out, "Bodhisattva, arise! Do not yearn for benighted slumber. You have borne witness to the significance of nirvana; how come you are not reciting the sutra for all sentient beings?"

Master Yuan awoke with a start. He sat up and recited the *Nirvana Sutra* until the skies brightened. The Minister was in his hall when all of a sudden he heard the sound of someone reciting a sutra. He got up and, walking slowly by himself, came in front of the gate of the western courtyard and listened to the sounds of the sutra recital. He then ordered his assistants to summon his wife. Having been summoned, the wife came in front of the western gate. Then the Minister, accompanied by his wife, listened to the reciting of the sutra until the skies brightened.

The next morning, after returning from court, the Minister ascended his hall and took a seat. Then he ordered his assistants to call the domestics of the western courtyard to him. Soon, thirty people huddled in front of the hall. The Minister inquired, "Last night in the western courtyard, which of you domestics was reciting a sutra?" At that time, the head domestic informed the Minister, "The person reciting a sutra last night was none other than the newly bought slave. The voice [you heard] reciting a sutra [was his]." Hearing that it was the new slave who was reciting the sutra, the Minister asked Master Yuan, "Were you the one who was reciting a sutra last night?" Master Yuan replied, "Yes, it was the sound of this lowly slave reciting a sutra." The Minister inquired, "What was the title of the sutra?" Master Yuan replied, "The one that I was reciting last night was the *Mahānirvāṇa-sūtra*." The Minister asked, "How many chapters of the sutra are you able to recite?" Master Yuan replied, "Your poor slave can recite the whole text in twelve scrolls, and last night I recited them all." The Minister asked, "You are not lying, are you?" Master Yuan said, "How dare I deceive you, Minister?" The Minister then ordered Master Yuan to sit down and recite the *Nirvana Sutra* again. Thereupon, Master Yuan once again opened with the sutra title, and for a second time raised the sounds of the sutra. During the entire recitation there was not a single mistake. Seeing this, the Minister frequently exclaimed, "Splendid!" Then he called the people in the residence, young and old, distinguished and lowly, all together more than three hundred persons, to come in front of the hall. The Minister ordered that from then on no one was to look down upon the new slave. At the same time he gave Master Yuan a nickname, calling him Shanqing.[45]

Every day, after retiring from the court, the Minister regularly visited the Fuguang Monastery and paid the fee of one hundred strings of cash to listen to Daoan's sutra-lectures. And on this next day, he brought Shanqing along with him to the monastery. However, as Shanqing was just beginning his service with the Minister, he was not allowed to enter the monastery to hear the sutra-lecture, but could only guard the Minister's horse outside the gate. After a short while, he saw the audience going into the monastery resembling the scudding clouds and driving rain. And then suddenly the bells stopped ringing; the title of the sutra was taken up; and the Sanskrit words that sounded at a distance gradually penetrated into his ears. When Shanqing heard this, his heart was filled with sadness. Master Yuan said to himself, "I just don't know how this Daoan is able to lecture and sing the hymns so capably. I wish one day I could once again mount the raised platform, bear witness to the fruits of the ten stages of developing Buddha-wisdom, and save all living beings from disaster. Whether with form or without, having an appearance or not, all beings are emancipated by nirvana."

After a short while, the sermon ended, and the men and women dispersed. The Minister returned to his residence. He rested for awhile in the center of the hall and, after he had composed himself, went to the upper part of the hall and took his seat there. Covering her face with her sleeve, his wife came directly in front of the Minister and said, "For several years you have been listening to the Reverend Daoan lecture on the *Nirvana Sutra* at the Fuguang Monastery. What doctrines have you heard him discuss? It is said that the *Nirvana Sutra* is infinite and illimitable. How much of the sutra do you remember? Why do you remain silent and say nothing? Why don't you explain a line or half a line of the stanzas to me?" The Minister replied, "Have you ever read the *Lotus Sutra?*" "Yes, I have read the *Lotus Sutra,*" answered the wife. The Minister said, "In that sutra, it is said, 'Speak without request and no one will listen.'"[46] The wife said, "I wish that you would say a few words [about the *Nirvana Sutra*] to the distinguished and lowly members of the residence to enlighten our minds." The Minister said, "I will explain the inner meanings of the *Nirvana Sutra* to you." The wife then ordered the domestics to sweep and clean the audience hall and erect a high wooden podium. She then called the people in the residence, the young and the old, the distinguished and the lowly, all together more than three hundred persons, to gather in front of the hall. She requested the Minister to explain the inner meaning of the *Nirvana Sutra,* and everyone was to listen in complete silence.

That night, the Minister first explained to his wife the interrelated woes of the eight kinds of suffering. The first of these is the suffering of birth. The suffering of birth: to be born, the body must depend on the shelter of the mother inside her womb. In about a month the fetus is like cheese. Then, within ninety days, it can start taking form. The males are attached on the mother's left side, the females on the right. Close to her heart and liver, the fetus is endowed with material energy and begins to take form. Thereupon, it endures various types of sufferings. It is same with the wise and the foolish, the rich and the poor. The favor of a kind mother does not vary according to her station. When the mother eats hot food, it feels no different from boiling the body in a cauldron of scalding liquid. When the mother eats cold things, it is just like being in a frigid hell. If the mother overeats, it is like being crushed between stones. And, when the mother is hungry, then one endures the suffering of being hung upside down. After a full term of ten months,[47] the time of birth approaches. The hundred bones and joints are spread out as if they were being severed by a saw. It is simply as though the four limbs were being rent from the body and the five organs were subjected to excruciating pain. There is no difference between this and being wounded by a knife or cut by a sword. One feels as though one is undergoing a thousand births and ten thousand deaths, until at last one faints and becomes insensate. One's life hangs by a thread and one has no desire to live any longer. Before long, the mother and child are separated, and there is as much blood as if a sheep had been slaughtered. The mother, in a semiconscious state, asks if it is a boy or girl. If the answer is that it's a girl, then the separation of the mother and child is considered to have been safely completed. But if the reply is that it's a boy, then the excruciating pain felt by the hundred bones and joints is forgotten, and, in her semiconscious state, she smiles faintly. This is what is called a filial son.

Now, if it is a disobedient child, how is the parturition? Inside his mother's belly, he makes her uncomfortable. He kicks the mother and does not let her rest for even a moment. Suddenly jumping onto her heart, then over to her waist, and then among the five organs, there is nowhere this child does not go. The child is born only after a full term of ten months. At that time, the child grabs hold of the mother's heart and liver, kicks her groin bones, and for days and nights cannot be contented. From here on, the mother's life is in jeopardy. The mother, believing that she is on the verge of death, shakes the earth with her cries. It is as though her heart were being carved out by a sword. Her brothers and mother have no idea what to do. Perhaps the child is someone with a grievance or to whom a debt is owed from a previous incarnation and will stop only after taking a life. Thus the mother is first forced to endure [the birth of] the child, after which she may die. This, then, is called [the suffering of] birth.

On that night, the Minister also explained to his wife the suffering of old age. The suffering of old age: the hundred years that people are granted for a lifetime are as trifling as a spark. Quickly they turn seventy or eighty and their strength begins to fade. In the beginning, one's voice is youthful and one's appearance is like a spring flower. Now, when old age comes, it is no different from the autumn grass. The skin is like that of a chicken and the hair like the feathers of a crane. The normal desires wither, vision dims, the ears become deaf, and one cannot distinguish between green and yellow. The four limbs become heavy and the hundred bones are wracked with pain. The body gradually droops farther from the sky and comes closer to the earth. At night, when sleeping on a pillowed bed, the aged person tosses and turns a thousand times. At this time, the person cannot perform any worldly affairs, just as if one were in a dream. Haven't you seen the peaches and plums alongside the roads that blossom year after year? But where are yesterday's ruddy complexions now? Once invaded by old age and sickness, the white hair can never turn black again. The youthful vigor of earlier times fades with the eight festivals;[48] the ruddy complexion of yesterday now changes with the four seasons. Everyone ages; it is the same for the rich or the poor, nor is there a distinction between the wise and the foolish. They all share in the suffering of old age. It is better, therefore, to create fields of good fortune as early as one can. Human life is over in a second, and the world passes us by right while we're watching. One must pay heed and cultivate morality. Once the human body is lost there is no way to revive it. This, then, is called the suffering of old age.

On that night the Minister also explained to his wife the suffering of illness. The wife asked, "What is the suffering of illness?" The suffering of illness: how could it be that there is solidity at the loci of the four elements?[49] Everything is due to their agglomeration: earth, water, fire, wind. An offbeat pulse is the beginning of illness. Suddenly one is so tired that one remains stuck in bed, the souls are unsettled, the spirits of the five organs are lost, the lips dry up, the tongue contracts, the brain hurts, the head aches, and the hundred bones and joints feel as if they were being severed by a saw. The pain persists throughout the night without any relief. Begging for life is of no use, begging for death is to no avail. The marvelous techniques of the world only cure people who are fated to live. How can those who are destined to die be saved? One can try curing with medicine, but [those who are destined to die] cannot be healed. For days and nights one endures all sorts of intense suffering. Some use the strong drugs of Jīvaka[50] or the needle of Bian Que,[51] but when death due to illness approaches these are of no use. The people of the world vainly accept depraved counsel and, even before they are in bed with sickness, blame the spirits and ghosts.[52] They burn money, disregard prohibitions, and vainly slaughter living creatures. This type of person falls straight into hell. The upper limit [of human life] is no more than a hundred years, and very few survive till seventy. [In general,] three people together are granted one hundred years,[53] but how much time can they [really] get? If people living in this world have access to marvelous techniques, then there ought to be those who can live a total of a thousand years. Why don't people think things through thoroughly? They vainly believe in the physicians' horrifying lies. This, then, is called the suffering of illness.

On that night, the Minister also explained to his wife the suffering of death. The suffering of death: the great desires[54] diminish, and the souls are blown away by the wind. Brothers bid long farewells, fathers and mothers are forever apart, and wives and husbands, sons and daughters can never meet again. After visitors, friends, and guests bid adieu, they can never meet again. Gold, silver, money, and other objects when spent are gone forever. Residences, shops, manors, and courtyards cannot be taken along when one goes. Due to craving and the suffering of death, when the four elements separate, the souls fly away to an unknown place. With the departure of the last mouthful of breath comes the advent of the next rebirth. But, after one dies, when can rebirth be achieved? While birth is debated as heroic, death is argued as religious merit. Rebirth is acquired according to karma, and one is assigned a new existence based on it. It is either a stay in hell, in the heavenly palace, rebirth as an animal, or as a hungry ghost—circling in the six paths of transmigration[55] without a period of rest. There's just one slight chance in ten thousand of achieving human form once again. This, then, is called the suffering of death.

On this night, the Minister also explained to his wife the suffering that comes from the five aggregates.[56] The suffering that comes from the five aggregates: the lives of the people in the world are like night and day. Pus, blood, and skin enwrap the body like fine silk. Among the five aggregates, effluvia constantly flow from the seven orifices. Within is harbored the foul smell of ordure and filth which oozes from the bones with the blood. And see how the sack of pus and dripping mucus flow day and night. It is utterly unbearable, yet completely without reality. All desires are born from a mouthful of material energy,[57] and they are the germs of the three poisons,[58] while the five viscera are the source of the five desires.[59] For this the Great Teacher[60] has the following *gāthā*:

The pus and blood inside the thin skin,
Stinking bones enwrapped by muscles;
What we see from head to toe,
Is the whole body dripping with pus.

Many sufferings of this kind assail the body. This, then, is called the suffering that comes from the five aggregates.

On that night, the Minister also explained to his wife the suffering of not getting what one seeks. Each person in the world seeks something. There are those who wish for good fortune and those who seek supreme *bodhi* (enlightenment). Within the three ages,[61] some seek the good fortune of birth in heaven. How many can enjoy the luxuries of the world or gain the wealth they seek in the realm of humans? Midway, they meet a premature demise. If one seeks gold, silver, cloth, and silk with the intention of having luxury for *kalpa* after *kalpa,* one may not even get enough food and clothing to suffice for oneself. Father, mother, and younger and older brother are each concerned with relieving their own distress. The son borne and the daughter raised, they have their own separate pursuits. If [good deeds] were not sown in the previous life, then one cannot cultivate them in a succession of *kalpas.* If one wants worldly luxury, then one must cultivate fields of blessing in the present life. Today,[62] I earnestly exhort everyone in the audience to understand that your food and clothing were determined in a previous life. Thus, the Great Master has the following *gāthā:*

What one does in the present determines what happens to one in the future;
Why not sow grains of good fortune for the future?
[The quality of] one's present life determines [the quality of one's] future life;
Why not cultivate blessings for your future life?

Many are [the sufferings of] this sort. This, then, is called the suffering of not getting what one seeks.

On that night, the Minister also explained to his wife the suffering that comes from having to meet with what is hateful. The suffering that comes from having to meet with what is hateful: the people of the world have hearts that are full of desires. When they see that someone else has a wife, they too want a wife. Within two to three years of taking a wife, they give birth to a son and plant seeds for a daughter. What may this be compared with? Like a butterfly gathering nectar from flowers, [at first] it just circles around in the air, but suddenly it sees a bunch of peonies and alights among the fragrant stamens to do its gathering. However, it does not realize that a spider has made a web on the flower and so gets tied up within it. Hundreds of twists and thousands of turns bind the butterfly in [the web], and myriad strategies to escape fail. This illustrates the suffering. Anyone who loves sexual beauty ends up like this. We see that even the young have hearts full of love and affection. Then, as the months and years pass, they have sons and daughters. When the children grow up and become adults, they are not filial to their parents. Their fivefold rebellious acts[63] fill the skies. They do not befriend wise people, but rather associate with vicious thugs. They talk without thinking and destroy the six relationships,[64] including even those with their honorable elders. If they are at home, they are a drain on one's mental vigor. If they are away from home, they are a constant source of worry. This, then, is how one often gives birth to one's enemies, and, thus, for generation after generation there is no rest. I earnestly exhort you in the audience [to accumulate] good causes,[65] thus you are aware [of what needs to be done]. If you wish to have no enemies in later generations, it would be better to cultivate the pure path in this lifetime. You will always be separated from your enemies, and your deepest emotions will not be troubled by them. How numerous are the concatenations of cause and effect[66] between men and women! Thus, the Great Master has the following *gāthā*:

> Since distant *kalpa*s, one endures drifting in the depths,
> Each and every place is visited during rebirth in the six paths;
> If [bonds] are not decisively broken off in this lifetime,
> When will there ever be an end to the mutual retribution of enemies?[67]

This, then, is called the suffering that comes from having to meet with what is hateful.

On this night the Minister also explained to his wife the suffering that comes from being apart from those whom one loves. If a family brings up a son, the parents look upon him as a pearl or jade. When he grows up and can distinguish east from west, then he leaves his native village. Night after night his parents long for him, and day after day they wait by the door till they weep with grief. They become ill from such yearning, but when can they receive care and medicine?[68] Then, all of a sudden, it is winter[69] or some festival, and the members of the family are all present. But the thoughts of the parents suddenly turn to the son far away, whereupon their breath catches in their throats and fills their breasts. This, then, is called the suffering that comes from being apart from those whom one loves.

On that night the Minister finished explaining the interrelated woes of the eight kinds of suffering. All three hundred and some members of the residence, young and old, distinguished and lowly, politely thanked the Minister. Only Shanqing was found weeping profusely and did not have anything to say. He was thinking: "I remember those days at Mt. Lu when I first lectured on the title of this sutra. It made the great rocks sway and the grasses bow. Auspicious birds and beasts came flying and filled the monastery. Clouds of good fortune lingered, all the while wreathing the sides of the Purple Hall. Auspicious breezes circled close to the edges of the Vermilion Towers. Various gods listened to the Dharma, and the ten types [of beings] heard the sutra. Those with shape and without shape, those with form and without form, all cultivated emancipation in order to achieve nirvana." Shanqing's eyes were full of tears when he finished thinking these thoughts.

The Minister felt that Shanqing's behavior was strange and asked him, "I have explained the sutra to you, so what is your reason for weeping so incessantly? Is it because you have a grievance against someone? If you have any sense, tell me the reason immediately or else look out for a flogging."

Shanqing stepped forward and addressed the Minister: "Your lowly servant doesn't really have a grievance against anyone else. It is only because Honorable Daoan's lecturing can never be impartial."

The Minister said, "Ever since the Honorable Daoan came to the capital and started lecturing, kings, nobles, generals, and ministers listen to his preaching every day. But you have never seen him preach; how could you know that his lecturing cannot be impartial?"

Shanqing stepped forward and addressed the Minister: "Last night, I followed you to the monastery. However, I was left outside the gate and could not listen to the sutra-lecture. This is how I know that Honorable Daoan's preaching cannot be impartial. Although my station in life is that of a lowly slave, I understand a bit of the Buddha's teachings. My clothes may be different from a monk's robes, but there should be no distinction in the Dharma. From this, it is clear that Daoan's preaching cannot be impartial. He doesn't know how to convey the teachings to the ears of the three classes of people, to those of four kinds of birth, nor to the ten types [of beings]."

The Minister asked, "What do you mean by 'the four kinds of birth' and 'the ten types [of beings],' and what are the 'ears of the three classes of people'? Please explain them to me in detail. Make my heart enlightened so that I clearly apprehend the Buddhist teachings."

Shanqing said, "The three classes of people: the first is the sick person on his bed; the second is the imprisoned convict; the third is people without freedom. The dharma master sitting on his raised platform does not understand how to convey his explanations everywhere to the ears of the three classes of people through skillful means.[70] When such a mistake occurs, it is an instance of not understanding how to share one's preaching impartially."

The Minister asked, "What are the four kinds of birth and the ten types [of beings]?"

Shanqing addressed the Minister: "The four kinds of birth are viviparous, oviparous, aqueous, and metamorphous.[71] These are the four kinds of birth. The ten types [of beings] are: having shape, having no shape, having form, having no form, not having form, not having no form, with four capacities, two capacities, many capacities, and no capacities. These are called the ten types [of beings]."

The Minister spoke to Shanqing: "Because I do not comprehend these things, please explain them to me in detail so that I can abandon error and seek refuge in truth."[72]

Shanqing said, "Viviparous birth: this is a person who hears the Dharma. For example, two people go to a monastery to listen to a sutra. One of them is not cupidinous and goes into the monastery to listen to the sutra. The other one is cupidinous and turns around to leave right away. The one who entered the monastery sits in meditation by himself in the Good Dharma Hall and listens to one sentence[73] of the marvelous teachings that enter into his body and soul. Thereupon his heart is filled with joy. But suddenly he remembers the one who did not enter the monastery, whereupon his heart is filled with distraction. Although there are words that he can hear, he is thoroughly depressed. Like a child in a mother's womb whose view of the sun is blocked by drifting clouds, he imperceptibly sinks into viviparous birth.

"Oviparous birth: again, this is a person who [has the opportunity to] hear the Dharma. Therefore, he goes to the monastery to listen to a sutra. Sitting in front of the Good Dharma Hall, he wants to entrust himself to the Dharma Master. However, the Dharma Master does not expound [the sutra], but instead talks about extraneous matters. Consequently, he talks of any old dharma, causing people to be confused and making it hard for them to understand. Thoroughly depressed, they soon sink into oviparous birth.

"Aqueous birth: this kind of person often receives clandestine teachings. They learn a sentence or a gāthā but do not tell it to others. They crave to enrich themselves but do not know how to disseminate [their learning] to the people. For this reason, they sink into aqueous birth.

"Metamorphous birth: for example, if someone goes to a monastery to listen to the Dharma and receives one sentence of marvelous teaching, they separately obtain an infinite and unlimited amount of meaning. The text draws out the transformative powers of the doctrine that are countless as the sands of Ganges. It is like lighting one lamp, and from that ten lamps and a hundred lamps, then a thousand lamps and from that hundreds, thousands, tens of thousands, and hundreds of thousands of lamps. From lamp to lamp, the flame is never extinguished. This is called metamorphous birth."

Then the Minister asked, "What are the ten types [of beings]?"

Shanqing said, "First, having shape: seeing the statue of a deity inside its clay niche, one worships it devoutly. Such a person even says that the Buddha is like Mount Sumeru.[74] When the mind is activated only if a shape is seen, this is called 'having shape.' Second, having no shape: where there is no nature, no nature can be seen—like the moon in the water and the wind in the air. The ten thousand dharmas are all nonexistent; there is nothing whatsoever. This is called 'having no shape.' Third, having form: supposing that one sees a handsome person on the street and says to oneself that the person is handsome because he had previously cultivated the Way. So one goes to a monastery to listen to the Dharma and sees a master who is plump and fair. Soon one takes a fancy to him and is completely captivated. Having been completely captivated, vain thoughts arise. Vain thoughts having arisen, they lead to ignorance. Having fallen prey to ignorance, there is vexation. Having been overcome with vexation, one begins to founder. Having foundered, one descends to hell. Such transgressions continue for many *kalpa*s, so that one's body and soul are both unsettled, and consequently one endures suffering. This is called 'having form.' Fourth, having no form: since the ten thousand dharmas are all empty, how could there be reality? East and west there are no traces; north and south there are no tracks. Things have nothing to do with the body and soul, which altogether far transcend the three worlds.[75] This is called 'having no form.' Fifth, not having form: when spoken of, it exists, but, when one has finished speaking, it returns to nothing. When posited, it exists, but, when no longer posited, it returns to nothing. When believed in, it exists, but, when no longer believed in, it returns to nothing. The ten thousand dharmas have nothing to do with the body and mind. This is called 'not having form.' Sixth, not having no form: without language, without speech; without going, without coming; without movement; without thought; without birth, without death—this is true reality.[76] Without going, without coming; this is the Buddha nature. This is called 'not having no form.' Seventh, two capacities:[77] people living in the world possess personhood and intelligence, which are provisionally referred to as the two capacities. There may be personhood but no intelligence, or there may be intelligence but no personhood. If personhood and intelligence do not happen to converge, then the individual will founder on an evil path. When personhood and intelligence do converge, then one can achieve birth on the path to Buddhahood. Therefore, the Great Master has the following *gāthā*:

> Personhood may be born, but intelligence not,
> Or intelligence may be born when the person is already old;
> The person loathes the late birth of intelligence,
> And intelligence loathes the premature birth of the person.
> If personhood and intelligence do not converge,
> One may repeatedly pass through old age;
> But if personhood and intelligence converge,
> One may achieve the path to Buddhahood.[78]

When one possesses both personhood and intelligence, then it is referred to as having 'two capacities.' Eighth, four capacities: the four elements of human existence belong to earth, water, fire, and wind, the four directions, and the four seas. These are called the 'four capacities.' Ninth, with many capacities: one is conversant with the ten thousand dharmas and there is nothing with which one is unfamiliar. One is knowledgeable about all the affairs of the world. When asked about sutras and books, there is nothing one cannot answer. All twelve divisions of sacred scripture have been memorized. This is referred to as having 'many capacities.' Tenth, no capacities: although one is a human, one is encumbered by everything.[79] Unable to distinguish between east and west, one is no different from an animal. This is referred to as having 'no capacities.' The above ten types [of beings] are each distinct. If you have any further doubts, please feel free to ask."

When the Minister heard these words, it was as though sweet dew[80] was entering his mind. The wife, who had also been listening to them, was filled with the perfect Buddha-truth.[81] The Minister called Shanqing to come forward [and said], "It seems from your sermon just now that you are not inferior to Daoan. Tell me some more so that my mind will be enlightened and I can have a clear understanding of the Buddhist Dharma."

Thereupon Shanqing explained to the Minister the twelve links in the chain of dependent origination,[82] which are as follows:[83] ignorance is the cause of activity, activity is the cause of consciousness, consciousness is the cause of name and form, name and form are the cause of the six senses, the six senses are the cause of contact, contact is the cause of sensation, sensation is the cause of desire, desire is the cause of grasping, grasping is the cause of existence, existence is the cause of birth, and birth is the cause of old age, sickness, death, anxiety, sorrow, suffering, and distress. Old age, sickness, death, anxiety, sorrow, suffering, and distress are the cause of ignorance. When ignorance is eliminated, then activity is eliminated. When activity is eliminated, then consciousness is eliminated. When consciousness is eliminated, then name and form are eliminated. When name and form are eliminated, then the six senses are eliminated. When the six senses are eliminated, then contact is eliminated. When contact is eliminated, then sensation is eliminated. When sensation is eliminated, then desire is eliminated. When desire is eliminated, then grasping is eliminated. When grasping is eliminated, then existence is eliminated. When existence is eliminated, then birth is eliminated. When birth is eliminated, then old age, sickness, death, anxiety, sorrow, suffering, and distress are eliminated. These are the twelve links in the chain of dependent origination.

Hearing this, the Minister exclaimed, "Excellent! Excellent!" And, at that moment, the wife sighed and obtained immeasurable fields of happiness. Shanqing then descended from the seat on the raised platform and addressed the Minister: "What Dharma Master Daoan says is like building a palace in thin air. In the end, he can never succeed! When it seems success is close, it will certainly still come crashing down. Although this slave is from a lowly class, the Buddhist Dharma is the same for all. Our clothing may be different, but our bodies are not dissimilar. Now, this lowly slave would like to go with the Minister to the monastery and have a debate with Dharma Master Daoan."

The Minister said, "If you have made up your mind, I won't stop you." And so the Minister and his wife led Shanqing into the western courtyard where he bathed with warm, scented water and changed his clothes. Then they let Shanqing return to his room to rest and wait until early next morning, when there were to be further orders.

Having returned to his room, Shanqing cleared his mind and purified his thoughts. He kept this up till dawn, not sleeping at all. Soon it was time to go to court, and Shanqing followed the Minister to the palace. After the Minister came out of court, he returned home to rest. Then he summoned Shanqing. The Minister said, "This Daoan is one of the most eminent monks in the country. You must carefully reconsider your plans."

Shanqing addressed the Minister: "There is a proverb which says, 'Entering the mountains without avoiding wolves and tigers is the bravery of the woodcutters. Entering a lake without avoiding snakes and dragons is the bravery of the fishermen.' If I can get the opportunity to debate Daoan, it will be like a thirsty person getting water or like someone who is cold having a fire. Sir, I request you to be at ease and not worry." They waited for the time of preaching to begin, and then they set off.

They soon reached [the monastery]. First, the Minister paid two hundred strings of cash and then led Shanqing into the monastery. At that time, the crowds of people who came to listen were like clouds, and donations poured in like rain. As soon as the bell rang, the lecture began. The main lecturer announced the title of the sutra, the deacon[84] recited a Sanskrit hymn, and the members of the four orders[85] looked up in reverence as if scaling Mount Gṛdhrakūṭa.[86] Daoan expected that everything would proceed happily, as though he were sitting in a meeting at the Āmravana

Garden.[87] Thereupon, with his scepter in hand and sitting on a jeweled platform, Daoan lit a large amount of priceless incense and started to proclaim the marvelous significance of the sutra. He emitted a [sacred] sound, then sang, enouncing the title of the sutra: *The Great Nirvana Sutra,* chapter "The Longevity of the Tathāgatha," section one.

Having begun the sutra lecture, Daoan praised the Buddha's majesty. First, he paid homage to the sages and the wise men, and then he extolled the virtues of the emperor. "I humbly wish that the way of the reigning emperor will be favored with the appearance of a dragon chart,[88] that his virtues may shine like a golden garden, that he may hold a golden mirror to illuminate the nine heavens,[89] and that he may follow the divine rays to visit all directions. I wish that the various kings and princes may be forever strong as golden branches, and that their jade leaves may be eternally vernal. May the princesses and the imperial consorts be forever radiant as chaste flowers. May the ministers and officials of the court be completely filial and loyal. May the provincial and county officials be pure and upright. As for the good men and good women beneath this seat in the audience, may the thousand calamities roll back with the mists and may pestilences disperse with the clouds. May disasters not invade [the realm], and may merits be copious. May sufferings end and sorrows cease on the three roads[90] of hell. May all the people in the Dharma world achieve this prosperity together." When he had finished with his invocation, Daoan intended to enter upon [a discussion of] the title of the sutra.

At that moment Shanqing stood up in the hall, and in loud voice shouted to stop the reading of the sutra title. Everyone in the four orders who saw him was shocked. Shanqing slowly came forward and, pointing at Daoan, said, "Honorable Daoan, you are very capable in preaching the Dharma. As an eminent teacher,[91] you open the sutra to lecture and sing hymns, propagating the True Tenets of the Buddha. Far and wide, you have saved those who are ignorant and those who have gone astray by propagating the sacred doctrine. Your language is brilliant and peerless within the realm. The number of living beings you have benefited is incalculable. Long have you served as a Dharma-boat[92] for those in the sea of suffering. You have borne great fruit in helping others to escape from the cycle of transmigration. But I haven't been able to determine which sutra text it is that you are lecturing on and which dharma you are propagating for all living beings. Whose commentary elaborates the True Tenets? I would like to get to the root, so I beg you to explain. Dharma Master, you are famous for your lectures throughout the land, and our ruler has proclaimed you as the best in the country. The Minister's presence here indicates his approbation, and this congenial place of worship[93] betokens dharmic joy. If Your Honor bestows a great beneficence by doing what is right and not ignoring me for being a rustic, I would be much obliged."

When Daoan heard these words, he changed color and became angry. He shouted at Shanqing, "Who are you to point in the air and scold?! The principles in the marvelous canon of our Buddha-Tathāgata are deeply profound. The Buddhist Dharma is difficult to grasp; it is not something you can comprehend. Even if I do not decline to explain [the teachings] to you, it would be like a block of rock placed in water. Although the water, by nature, is moist, it cannot penetrate into the rock. I see that your present status is that of a lowly menial. How can you just do as you please? If I commend the Buddhist Dharma to kings and high officials, only the wise among them can comprehend such teachings. Haven't you heard what the heretical books say? 'If someone is worthy of being spoken to, then speak to them. If they are not worthy of being spoken to, it would be a waste of words to do so.'[94] Even the teachings handed down by the Sage[95] recommend rejection in such cases. I will not make any explanations for an inferior, ignorant person like you. Let the deacon examine the situation and not allow anyone to cause a ruckus. The time for listening to the sutra is to be used sparingly. If you do not understand, you must lower your head, keep quiet, and pay attention to what you are hearing. The lecture mat on the dais is for proclaiming to the audience, all of whom listen to the Dharma. It's not your business to be a person who asks questions about the Dharma."[96]

Indeed, no one among the people sitting at the sermon disagreed with his opinions. Although everyone else was afraid of your Daoan, when it came to this Shanqing, his attitude was, "Who's afraid of you?" So, when Shanqing heard these words, he raised his voice all the more and, pointing at Daoan, angrily rebuked him: "Ācārya,[97] your behavior shows that you are a common monk who has lost the Way.[98] What you say and ask is not in accord with the sacred purport. The teachings bequeathed by our Tathāgata are explicit in the sutras. Dumb animals and intelligent beings are all imbued with the Buddha-nature. Have you read the *Vajracchedikā-sūtra?* Viviparous, oviparous, aqueous, metamorphous, the ten types [of beings] and the four kinds of births; having shape, having no shape, having form, having no form—everyone can achieve nirvana and this is called emancipation. Surely, I am a human. How can I be unfit to hear[99] the Dharma? I may be an inferior menial, but the Buddha-nature is unbiased. My clothes may be different from a monk's robes, but there should be no distinctions in the Dharma. Haven't you heard about Confucius who, although he was a sage, was for a long time puzzled by an argument about the sun?[100] The World-Honored One of Great Enlightenment himself had difficulty with a metal-tipped spear.[101] The layman Vimalakīrti[102] was rebuked by Prabhāvyūha. And Kṣāntivādi ṛṣi was dismembered by Kaliṅgarāja.[103] 'An honorable man doesn't cheat in a dark room'—this is a popular saying of the common literati.[104] This lowly slave is determined to ask about the text of the sutra, but it is you up there on your platform who are 'pointing in the air and scolding.' Potent medical herbs grow even on steep mountains, and lotuses bloom precisely in the mud.[105] There may be bright pearls inside of a cotton bag, while an embroidered pouch may contain useless chaff. Master of the dais, when you go into the mountains to gather timber, do not select the trees solely on the basis of their external appearance. If you do things this way, you would miss the likes of Ziyu.[106] Now, the Buddha's teachings are, in substance, equitable. They are like the sweet moisture which rains down and dampens everything all over. It cannot just keep falling and nourishing the flat fields and low grasses while withholding its benevolent moisture from hollows and hillocks. The rain is from the first impartial and natural, not giving rise to a consciousness of self and other; everything is without differentiation. Haven't you seen how the Medicine King Bodhisattva[107] demarcates the four seasons so that the five fruits, peaches, and plums follow the eight festivals[108] and are produced from the earth. In the 'Parable of Medicinal Herbs'[109] it is clearly explained that the big roots, big trees, big branches, and big leaves all depend on their original capacities and are produced from the earth. One cannot say that because some fruit is sweet the rain is sweet, or that because other fruit is sour the rain is sour. Rain, after all, has a single taste; and each of the plants that receives the rain has its own distinct nature. Only when we cultivate an impartial mind will the dharma-world[110] naturally be peaceful. The Minister is here, sir, so you should not deceive the people. Just be nice and do what is right. I hope that you will be so good as to engage in a debate with me."

Having been scolded, Daoan was deeply chagrined. He was too embarrassed to glance at the Minister, and blushed when he looked at the four orders. Then he grabbed his ruler[111] and, throwing it aside, slowly came forward. In an angry voice, he rebuked, "Shanqing, haven't you heard that it's not worth fighting an unworthy opponent even if he dies?[112] Why go to the trouble of shooting a crossbow with a draw of a thousand pounds because of the peccadilloes of a mouse? If [I start to beat] my drum at you,[113] you'd better not decline to respond. But it would be like a wren flying along with a roc. I'd be wasting my energy on you. If you have any sense, you'll lower your head, keep silent, and listen carefully. If you still fail to follow my instructions, I'll have no choice but to ask the Minister to have you caned. You will be driven out of the monastery and not be allowed to listen to the sutra. If you keep on ranting and raving, you will come to regret it!"

Hearing this, Shanqing raised his voice still higher and, pointing at Daoan across the room, said, "Such brazen, arrogant recklessness! Sir, you wear a monk's robes and often proclaim the True Sutras. Therefore, you should have an immeasurable heart, possess the conduct of the six *pāramitā*s,[114] express the *bodhi*-mind, and benefit all living beings so that they may transcend the three worlds.[115] How can your heart be without compassion or sympathy? Instead, you harm others grievously, cheat ordinary people, and request the Minister to have someone caned. This type of behavior does not accord with the True Tenets. How are the words that you utter different from those of the heretics? Ācārya, you think of yourself as the roc which presumes to raise its wings and touch the sky, and you dismiss others as wrens that spend most of their time roosting in the low grasses, unable to see the heart of the Way. Those who are rude cheat others, and those who are degenerate forget justice. Needless to say, this morning you should be cautious[116] and not speak insultingly or heedlessly. If there are any errors in my words, then I will serve as your disciple. You should hold fast to your prize and not let it slip out of your hands. But, if there is a mistake with a single word of your response, then it will be up to me to request that the Minister have you caned. You will be dragged down from your raised platform and driven out of the monastery. You will not be permitted to propagate the teachings to the public. Don't say that you weren't told!"

Having been reprimanded, Daoan kept silent without a word to utter. He was too embarrassed to glance at the Minister, and blushed when he looked at the four orders. After a long while he called Shanqing to come forward [and said], "The words that I said before were all to jest with you. You don't need to criticize me, and I won't find fault with you. When I first heard what you were saying, I was really suspicious. I thought that you actually wanted to create disorder in the lecture hall and upset the audience. Now I know that you are truly a capable person. If you ask the title of the sutra I shall respectfully answer."

Shanqing said, "Ācārya, you yourself said 'You don't need to criticize me.' The Tathāgata left behind his doctrines, and they were preserved in the sutras because of King Ajātaśatru's[117] [sponsorship. Thus the World-]Honored's discussions are known to everyone. I dare not go beyond the questions that you have allowed me to ask today. I would just like to inquire about the title of the sutra, and then I will definitely have some follow-up questions for you."

"Just now you asked this poor monk about the sutra that I lecture on," said Daoan. "It is the *Mahānirvāṇa-sūtra*. Now that you have heard the title, Shanqing, remember it clearly."[118]

Shanqing asked, "What is the meaning of *mahā*? What is the meaning of *nir*? And what is the meaning of *vāṇa*?"

Daoan answered, "*Mahā* stands for 'broad': to broadly benefit all sentient beings and help them escape from the sea of suffering. *Nir* means 'no-more-birth,' neither birth nor extinction; this is in conformity with True Thusness.[119] Neither going nor coming; this is the Buddha-nature. The word *vāṇa*: transport all sentient beings out of the three worlds and lead them to the opposite bank."[120]

Shanqing said, "The three word-segments just mentioned illustrate seven things."

"Now, Shanqing, you will hear them, so you must remember them. The first thing that they illustrate is comparable to how, when the spring sunlight becomes active, the ten thousand grasses all begin to grow. Flowers blossom everywhere no matter whether it is a shallow valley or a deep ravine. Similarly, once the name of this sutra of the marvelous Dharma was established and it was propagated and transmitted by the Tathāgata, then all sentient beings who hear the sutra, without distinguishing high or low, invariably become better. The second thing they illustrate is like tying a rope around the crooked branches of a tree [to straighten them. Similarly, hearing them] can disperse depravity and restore rectitude. The third thing they illustrate is like a bubbling spring which never dries up. Similarly, the sutra text has been in the world for a long time and has continued to spread without a respite. The fourth thing they illustrate is like the rivers and seas which enable boats with a capacity of ten thousand bushels to sail on them. Similarly, sentient beings who want to cross rivers and lakes must first rely on a long oar. The sutra text transmitted to the world can boost those aiming to escape from the mundane world.[121] Those who want to get close to and cultivate the Way must first rely on the power of the sutra. The fifth thing they illustrate is like heaven and earth which cover and support all sentient beings. If heaven and earth were completely nonexistent, upon what would the myriad images[122] stand? Since the text of the *Nirvana Sutra* exists, sentient beings can depend on it to cultivate themselves. But if the Dharma of the sutra were completely nonexistent, what could they rely on to escape from the world? The sixth thing they illustrate is like the warp and the woof which can be made into a colorful brocade or fine, white silk. Whether a long piece of thin silk or a damask, they are all because of the warp and the woof. Once the name of the marvelous sutra is established, cultivation of the Way is achieved based on this. And, totally relying on the power of the sutra, one can even attain unsurpassed wisdom.[123] The seventh thing they illustrate is like the roads and tracks which provide passage to people coming and going. People who desire to travel a thousand tricents have to start off from a road. Sentient beings who are determined to cultivate the Way must first read and recite the text of the sutra. Therefore, the ways of the later sages are taken from this.

"Although the seven meanings above are each distinct, together they explain the one word 'sutra.' Now that you have heard them, Shanqing, you must remember them."

Shanqing then asked, "The word 'sutra' by itself has so many meanings. Is there anything further regarding the name of the sutra?"

Daoan replied, "The meaning of 'nirvana' is 'immeasurable and limitless.' How could one completely finish explaining the title of the sutra? We may compare it to the thousands and tens of thousands of families and households belonging to the hundred surnames.[124] How can they be organized? It is for this reason that prefectures and counties were established, and the territories of each were divided up and boundaries were drawn. The single word 'sutra' separately proclaims tens of thousands of dharmas. Consequently, each one is different. The prefectures and counties must depend upon officials to keep records; the marvelous Dharma requires the establishment of sutra titles. If prefectures and counties do not have officials, how could the hundred surnames be ordered? The writing of commentaries on the texts of the sutras is, in a sense, to 'comb'[125] them. We may compare it to tangled hair that gets combed. When a sutra title is established for the ten thousand dharmas, the sages can thereby attain the Way. The answers that I have provided above are all based on the sutras. If you have further doubts, please feel free to ask again."

"Ācārya, I'll let you off on the seven meanings of 'sutra,'" said Shanqing. "But I have a few more questions. Would you allow me to ask them?"

Daoan replied, "This poor monk regards heavenly beings and humans as his teachers. The meanings are like bubbling springs, and the dharmas are flowing water. If you want to ask something, please do ask, and I will respond as quickly as I did when explaining your previous doubts."[126]

Shanqing said, "As for the Buddhist Dharma, all may take refuge in it. Light dust accumulates to form a mountain; falling dew adds up to flowing water. When one ladles out the latter, one cannot gauge its origin; when one journeys toward the former, one seldom can reach its limits. Yet this lowly slave [wishes] to ask the Dharma Master, like a firefly competing with the sun, or a cicada trying to hold back a chariot. Thinking himself to be a huge bird, he dares to climb onto the phoenix terrace. Under the crash of thunder, it is difficult to hear the beating of muffled drums; in front of green jade, how can a tiny dagger be presumptuous? Only the Buddha-nature is omnipresent in sentient beings.[127] Again, I ask what the essence of the Buddha-Tathāgata is."

Daoan replied, "Come closer, Shanqing. You need not be so humble. The essence of our Buddha is compassion."

Again, Shanqing asked, "Since you have said that the essence of our Buddha is compassion, why do you not save the unbelieving[128] sentient beings?"

Daoan replied, "You do not understand the real reasons. Listen while I explain. The unbelieving sentient beings are like this because they themselves have created bad karma. For example, if a family raises a boy who grows up to be a man that steals and robs in the village, when this matter is revealed he is arrested by the local authorities and is sent to jail. He is beaten, and the documents of the case are prepared. He confesses his crimes and is led to court, where it appears that his death is imminent. Although the boy's parents are kind and compassionate, how can the boy be rescued from the laws of the state? Although our Buddha is compassionate, unfortunately the power of the Buddha is not the same as the power of the boy's karma. In instances of this sort, then it will be difficult to save the person."

Shanqing asked, saying, "Although the unbelieving sentient beings have created bad karma, our Buddha is compassionate and would save even them. All that you have said just now relates to external[129] causation. What does our Buddha-Tathāgata consider to be nature?"

Daoan replied, "He takes impartiality to be nature."

Shanqing asked, "Since you have stated that nature is impartiality, why do sentient beings sink into the cycle of birth-and-death,[130] while the Buddha can testify to nirvana without residue?"[131]

Daoan replied, "Sentient beings sink into the path of evil due to ignorance and false thoughts. The Buddha can testify to nirvana without residue because everything has been extinguished."

Shanqing asked once again, "If sentient beings are ignorant and distressed[132] by delusion, what is their relationship to the Buddha nature?"

Daoan replied, "Sentient beings are characterized by ignorance and distress; the Buddha nature is characterized by everything being cut off.[133] This is why sentient beings are not separated from the Buddha and the Buddha is not separated from sentient beings. The words that I have said above are all careful answers of this sort."

Shanqing said, "Ācārya, the words that you have just spoken are greatly in error. Your lecturing, hymns, and sutra text are greatly inaccurate. It's all a bunch of thoughtless nonsense meant to please the disciples, who listen to whatever sounds good. For example, the rivers, lakes, and great seas have numerous sentient beings within them. They are either turtles and lizards, or they may be shrimp, crabs, dragons, and fish. There are many different kinds of creatures like these that belong in the water. Although fish and water have affinities, there are differences between them. If a fish does not have any water, it will die. However, if water does not have any fish, it is placid as always. Sentient beings founder when they are separated from the Buddha. The Buddha, however, remains in a quiet state when separated from sentient beings. We have heard that the Buddha is the most uniquely honored being to have appeared in the world. In his unity,[134] he far transcends the three worlds. Yet, due to his compassion, he saves the sentient beings. As for the Buddha and the common people being identical, the examples that have been given are all incorrect. In the sutra on nirvana, there are profound similes everywhere. Now, I would like to request that Your Honor briefly explain them a bit to the audience."

Daoan answered, "The similes in the *Nirvana Sutra* are quite numerous. There are three thousand major similes and eight hundred minor ones."

Shanqing interrupted and asked, "What is the meaning of 'Black Wind'?"

Daoan replied, "The Black Wind is the wind of sentient beings' ignorance. For countless *kalpa*s, sentient beings have been buffeted and shaken by this wind. This wind can be divided into eight types. To introduce their meanings individually and discuss them completely is impossible."

At this point, Shanqing knew that Daoan did not understand and could not explain the similes. Shanqing asked, saying, "Ācārya, you are acclaimed as one of the country's most virtuous[135] monks. You ought to be able to give ten answers for every question. Although you have a skull, it is without eyes. For someone to cross water, he must first know how to float. If he does not know how, it will be a waste of effort to enter the water. As for the meaning of Black Wind, who has lectured on it, and who has written the commentary on the sutra text?"

Thereupon, in his mind Daoan wanted to answer, but his mouth could not reply. And when his mouth was ready to answer, his mind could not reply. Fidgeting with his hands and feet, all he could do was exclaim, "Mea culpa! I hope that you will be compassionate and explain for me."

Shanqing said, "There's nothing whatsoever to get frightened about over the meaning of the *Nirvana Sutra*. Please relax and do not worry. I won't ask you anything else, but would simply ask your honor where you obtained the commentary on the *Nirvana Sutra*."

Daoan replied, "It was brought from the place of the Great Master Yuan at Mount Lu."

Shanqing asked, "If you were to see Master Yuan today, would you still be able to recognize him?"

Daoan replied, "If I were to see Master Yuan today, I honestly wouldn't be able to recognize him."

Shanqing asked, "Since you say you wouldn't be able to recognize him, where did you get the commentary from?"

Daoan replied, "I got it from the monk Yunqing, the chief disciple of Master Yuan."

Shanqing said, "If you are looking for someone else, then I truly am not he. But if you are looking for Master Yuan, then this lowly slave is the one."

Hearing this, Daoan became very suspicious, "I have heard," he said, "that the Great Master has a distinct mark—a fleshy protuberance around his wrist.[136] If you are indeed the Great Master, then show it to me."

Thereupon, in order to put Daoan's suspicion to rest, Master Yuan rolled up his left sleeve and, sure enough, there was a fleshy protuberance around his wrist. It emitted a bright light, which was seen by everyone in the audience. Then Daoan got up and came down from the raised platform. He beat himself all over the body until fresh blood flowed from the seven apertures.[137] Overcome with repentance, he went forward a step at a time and, out of self-hatred for not recognizing the superior person, was about to use a sharp dagger to gouge out his eyes. Tears falling like rain and wailing sorrowfully, he prostrated himself and begged the superior person to show compassion for his penitent grief.

Master Yuan said, "Do not harbor doubt or worry. There is no need for you to suffer and wail with grief. You are fully[138] a common person. How could you have recognized in me the one who expounded the meaning of nirvana?[139] I shall soon occupy my seat as teacher, but let me first apologize to the Minister. I shall then come back and preach the True Dharma to you."

And so Master Yuan went straight in front of the Minister and addressed him saying, "The days this lowly slave has served you, Minister, are few in number, and I have not performed any 'sweating-horse merits.' Abruptly entering the monastery, I disrupted the sermon. Yet I have been the recipient of Your Honor's generosity in not being blamed for this crime. Today, in front of the audience, I request that you mete out to me a painful caning."

Hearing these words, the Minister beat himself all over. On hands and knees, and with his face to the ground, he would not get up. After a long time, he revived and walked towards the superior person whom he addressed saying, "Although I am the Chief Minister, I am inept in dealing with affairs. I have benefited from the three vows[140] and been rewarded by the court. However, how could I, an ordinary mortal with carnal eyes, distinguish a sage?[141] The guilt that I bear is so great that it fills the entire universe, yet you spare me of blame. For six years you were my slave, and you often labored in my house. Sometimes I used harsh language to scold Your Honor. How should I repent for such sins?"

Master Yuan said, "This is due to my acting as a guarantor during a previous life in which debts were not settled. If one does not want to have any grievances in this life, then all accounts should be settled here. Once all debts are completely cleared, there won't be anything to be afraid of. And, from now on, when you look forward, there won't be any need for worrying."

Hearing these words, the Minister started to wail with grief all over again. He begged the honorable person for compassion, and asked him to explain the karma of his previous life.

Master Yuan said, "The Minister was a merchant in his previous life and that fellow Bo Zhuang was also a merchant. The Minister borrowed five hundred strings of cash from Bo Zhuang. In that transaction, I was the guarantor. Later, when the Minister died [before returning the money], I wanted to pay back the debt. Unfortunately, I too died [before returning the money]. After several samsaric circles, we have unexpectedly met. Because of these karmic causes, the debt that was guaranteed has been repaid."

Upon hearing this, the Minister walked forward and, wailing with grief, began to shed tears like rain. Blaming himself for his transgressions, he confessed, "Since it was I, your disciple, who contracted a debt to another person, I should have paid it back myself. How stupid I was for having given Your Honor so much trouble! I will certainly fall into hell after this lifetime."

Master Yuan said, "The debt has now been compensated, so you do not have to be apprehensive. From now on, avoid contracting further [debts]. Earnestly encourage your family members and disciples, if they have debts, to be sure to pay them back. To fulfill my duty as a guarantor, this poor monk even had to serve as a slave for six years or the matter would not have been concluded. The common person of shallow knowledge is not afraid of committing sins. But if one commits a host of sins, how can one repent?"

At this time, the audience wailed with grief and shed tears like rain. Feeling sorry for Master Yuan, they were completely filled with sadness. A thousand people gazed upon him reverently, and ten thousand sighed with admiration. On this day, everyone in the audience ceased their grudging and greed. Then, before Master Yuan had finished, he was repeatedly requested by all those present at the sermon, including the Minister, to once again mount the raised platform.

On that day, Master Yuan was like a withered tree at the edge of a cliff that had once again found spring, or like a fish that had been hooked or netted, which, when released, goes back into the rivers and seas. His heaven-endowed spirit was not like that of any ordinary person; the divine appearance of his body was rarely seen in the world. After the bells had been rung repeatedly, starting once again with the title of the sutra, he propagated [the Dharma] for the assembly. At that moment, Daoan was also sitting in the audience.

At that time, no sooner had Master Yuan begun [the lecture] with the title of the sutra than the earth responded with six types of trembling,[142] and five-colored auspicious clouds spread across the vast skies. Hundreds and thousands of heavenly beings played music together. Innumerable sages and saints made Sanskrit sounds. Crystal-clear were the sounds of the sutra, jingling were the rhymes of the Dharma. All those assembled observed these rarities, and everyone in the audience said that they were exceptional.

At that time, the Minister was once more[143] at the sermon in the Lotus Palace.[144] Once again, he unrolled the mats of Incense-Land.[145] He brought together a great assemblage of monks and nuns from the monasteries on the two main streets of the city and held a tonsure ceremony.[146] On that day, right there in the Fuguang Monastery, the Minister wrote a memorial concerning these events and presented it to Emperor Wen of the Jin dynasty.

When the emperor read the memorial, the imperial countenance was greatly delighted. "Excellent! Excellent!" he repeated. "Exceptional!" he exclaimed. He immediately issued an edict which ordered the Secretariat-Chancellery to gather representatives of the Three Doctrines—Buddhism, Daoism, and Confucianism—to go together to Fuguang Monastery and invite Master Yuan to the imperial precincts for veneration. At that time, there was another edict, which ordered the presentation of a scepter, a string of pearls,[147] a six-ringed staff,[148] and several sets of monk's robes to Master Yuan. Moreover, a royal carriage was sent to bring Master Yuan to the imperial precincts. When the edict was passed down, it was known by everyone inside and outside the imperial precincts. How stirring it was with all the officials, ministers, and Chief Ministers lined up! [The bearers of] the imperial regalia entered directly into the monastery to request the Great Master to board the carriage.

At that time, Master Yuan repeatedly declined to board the carriage. "I am an insignificant, common monk," said Master Yuan. "Although I am always grateful for My Lord's request, your subject-monk wishes to return to the mountains. This is what this poor monk wishes."

Minister Cui walked forward and addressed the monk: "I beg for compassion. Please do not turn down the invitation. The emperor is eagerly waiting in the imperial precincts especially to see you. I look up to the honorable person with reverence, first for the sentient beings of the dharma-world and, secondly, I wish that you would not turn down the emperor's request."

Only after receiving several invitations, Master Yuan began walking. All sorts of entertainers and imperial musicians were in front welcoming him. Clusters of high officials offered congratulations and wished long life to the reigning monarch.

Master Yuan, after coming out from the gate of the monastery, had walked about a hundred yards or so when he suddenly leaped up into the sky. No one knew where he was. The Minister was fearful and paid his respects. Looking toward the sky, he made the following sincere announcement: "The Great Master has limitless abilities. I wish to beg for compassion and [ask you to] accede to the king's request." He kept going as he made the announcement, winding along the way.

On that day, Master Yuan had already arrived at the gate of the council chamber before the others and respectfully received the imperial edict. Thereupon, knowing that Master Yuan had arrived, the emperor came out of the palace gate. He paid a thousand regards in reverence and expressed his devotion ten thousand times. As soon as he saw Master Yuan, the imperial countenance showed signs of great pleasure and his happiness was endless.

And so the emperor said, "It is a great joy to experience the advent of the honorable person in our small kingdom. That the people of the country are at peace and prosperous is all due to the monk."

The emperor venerated Master Yuan in the imperial precincts for a number of years. He was welcomed with admiration into the six palaces and revered with devotion in the five courtyards. From the monk, the emperor received the Threefold Refuge[149] and the Five Precepts,[150] of which there were none that he did not follow.

Ever since Master Yuan had been in the imperial precincts, he had observed that in various halls paper with characters on it was often used for unclean purposes in the privy. He scolded the people [who did so] and composed the following *gāthā:*

The Confucian child recites the Five Classics;[151]
Buddhist doctrine has established the Three Schools;[152]
Observe ritual to exercise loyalty and filial piety,
Employ flogging and banishment to carry out the nine types of agriculture.[153]
"Tall Willows"[154] and the fivefold examination essays—

The characters used to write them are the same as those in the canonical sutras.
Those who do not understand how to show respect
Use paper with writing on it for filthy purposes in the toilet.
To attain enlightenment, they will have to eliminate sins as numerous as the sands of the
    Ganges,
For which several lifetimes of repentance would not suffice;
Their bodies will be reduced to a lowly state for five hundred *kalpas*,
And they will often be born as worms in the privy.[155]

At that time, because Master Yuan had spoken the *gāthā,* everyone in the imperial precincts cultivated blessings. Suddenly one day, Master Yuan, recalling the words of Akṣobhya-tathāgata,[156] resigned from the emperor's services and said, "Your subject-monk has received His Majesty's veneration in the imperial precincts for a number of years. Now, I would like to return to Mt. Lu. I beg Your Majesty to issue a decree."[157]

Upon hearing these words, the emperor's eyes filled with tears. After a long time had passed, he said to the monk, "Our small kingdom has failed to venerate you. When you were in our imperial precincts for several years, we have unintentionally treated you with disrespect. Although we serve as the leader of the people, we are ill qualified for our role as ruler of Heaven and Earth. We appreciate very much that the honorable person has come to this small kingdom. We wish for compassion from the monk, and would request him to stay for three or four more days. Can this be done?"

Master Yuan said, "According to the teachings of nirvana, there are fundamentally no causes for us to lay hold of.[158] If one supposes that there are causes that we may lay hold of, that is all in the realm of vain thoughts. I request that Your Majesty not feel disappointed that this poor monk has made a vow to return to the mountain."

The emperor, seeing that Master Yuan's words were firm and knowing that it would be hard to make him stay since his mind was made up, issued an edict promptly to inform [the residents of] the six palaces to line up privately[159] for a farewell ceremony.[160] At that time, the emperor was filled with longing, and the Chief Minister was disconsolate. Together with the top officials of the whole kingdom, they bade farewell to Master Yuan.

Master Yuan started out on his journey, departing through the watchtowers outside the palace gate and taking leave of the imperial dwelling. Heading for Mount Lu, his way was long; gazing at the rivers and lakes, his road was distant. On that day, Master Yuan embarked on his long journey by foot, but he soon secretly manifested his supernatural powers. Once Master Yuan left Chang'an,[161] clouds formed under his feet. Like a strong man flexing his muscles,[162] he arrived at Mt. Lu in a twinkling.

Master Yuan did not return to the old monastery, but temporarily made himself a thatched hut on a steep ridge about ten tricents[163] away. In it he sat cross-legged in lotus posture and once more he sought the old scrolls. Again he raised the sounds of the sutra.

Time slipped by and several more months passed. Suddenly, Master Yuan gazed upon a high plateau and climbed to the top of it. It was a realm of steep peaks where cranes cried and deep ravines where dragons roared. Hundreds of valleys and thousands of peaks were all abloom with flowers. Over the land flowed streams that were always full; in the gardens blossomed flowers that never wither. This was a place where the Tathāgata had cultivated the Way. So Master Yuan sat upright and entered into *samādhi.*[164] Then he purified his thoughts and cleansed his heart, contemplating only the Way of the Buddha. He thought that this ephemeral life could not go on for too long and reflected that the mundane world would not endure. With his self-nature and sovereign-mind, he wanted to make a Dharma-boat in order to return to the upper world. To make the boat, Master Yuan did not use materials of the common world, nor did he need anything else. He only took passionless[165] Mahayana for the hawser, bodhi[166] and *prajñā*[167] he used for railings, the esoteric thunderbolt-handed divinities[168] for. . . .[169]

Record of copying by Zhang Changji in the fifth year (972) of the Opened Treasure reign period.[170]

—TS, VHM

Notes

1. Dharma basically means "statute" or "law." When capitalized in this story, it signifies the body of teachings expounded by the Buddha. It is the duty of a Buddhist to be knowledgeable about the Dharma and to act in accordance with it so as to achieve enlightenment. When not capitalized, dharma refers to the basic, minute elements from which all things are made, to the principle or law that orders the universe, or to the teachings of other religions than Buddhism.

2. Chinese *pingdeng* = Sanskrit *sama(tā)*. This is a key word in the story. It signifies equitableness, especially with regard to the impartiality and universality of the Buddha.

3. Sanskrit *dvādaśāṅga-dharma-pravacana*. These are: (1) *sūtra* (primarily prose discourses of the Buddha), (2) *geya* (verses which repeat the substance of the prose discourse found in the sutras), (3) *gāthā* (verses containing ideas not found in the sutras), (4) *nidāna* (historical narratives), (5) *itivṛttaka* (past lives of the disciples of the Buddha), (6) *jātaka* (past lives of the Buddha), (7) *adbhuta-dharma* (tales of miracles performed by the Buddha), (8) *avadāna* (allegories), (9) *upadeśa* (discussions of doctrine, often in question-and-answer form), (10) *udāna* (statements of the Buddha not prompted by questions from his disciples), (11) *vaipulya* (sutras that deal with broad topics), (12) *vyākarana* (prophecies of the Buddha regarding the enlightenment of his disciples). It is obvious from this list that Buddhist literature is highly elaborated and that it values narrative and parables. The richness and sophistication of the Buddhist literary tradition was one of the most attractive features of this Indian religion when it came to China.

4. Since the Sanskrit word *nirvāṇa* (literally, "blowing out; extinguishing") is found in English dictionaries, it will not be written in italics and with diacriticals below, except in the Sanskrit titles of scriptures. A particularly important term in this story, nirvana in Hinduism refers to emancipation from ignorance and the elimination of all attachment or an ideal condition of stillness, stability, and harmony. In Buddhism, it signifies the ultimate state in which one attains disinterested wisdom and compassion. When used with reference to a Buddha, it indicates the sloughing off of his mortal body.

5. Dharma King, Buddha, Śākyamuni (Sage of the Śākyas), and Tathāgata (The One Who Has Come/Gone Thus) are all different manifestations of the same person. There are serious textual problems right at the very beginning of the tale, and it is possible that the author originally intended the first, third, and fifth clauses to refer to the secular king, his laws, and his doctrines. Such an interpretation, however, would require a certain amount of emendation.

6. Sanskrit *saddharma-pratirūpaka*. The formal or imitative/image period of Buddhism, which is the second of three stages in the development of the religion: the real, the formal, and the final; or correct, semblance, and termination. These are also thought of as the three periods of a Buddha-*kalpa* (era or eon), the first lasting five hundred years, the second a thousand years, and the third also a thousand years.

7. Sanskrit *candana* (sandalwood). The author(s) of the story seem to be using a Sanskrit name for Huiyuan's teacher in order to legitimize his training in Buddhist doctrine and to distance him from his actual teacher, Daoan, who is here transformed into his antagonist.

8. In Shanxi Province.

9. This is the third *dhyāna* heaven of form, i.e., the highest paradise that is still conditioned by physical form.

10. Since famous Buddhist monasteries were often located in the mountains, saying "visit a mountain" was often tantamount to saying "visit a monastery."

11. *Nirvana Sutra*, also called the *Mahāparinirvāṇa-sūtra*. The most influential translations of this scripture are by Faxian in 418, Dharmarakṣa in 421, and Xuanzang in 652. There are, as well, other earlier and later

translations of the *Nirvana Sutra* into Chinese, several of them partial. One that may be of particular interest for the present tale is that done sometime between the years 424 and 452 by Huiyan and others. The confusing similarity of Huiyan's name to that of our hero, Huiyuan, perhaps help to account for the otherwise inexplicably close link between the latter and the *Nirvana Sutra* in this tale (see also the introduction to the tale).

As with nirvana (see n. 4), the Sanskrit word *sūtra* is now found in English dictionaries. Hence it will not be italicized and written in italics below except when it appears in the titles of Sanskrit scriptures or in philological analyses.

12. Jiang Prefecture, modern Jiujiang in Jiangxi Province.

13. A tricent *(li)* is three hundred paces or approximately one-third of a mile (< Latin *milia [passuum]*, "a thousand [paces]").

14. The images of old age in this sentence are based on literary allusions dating to works of around the years 430 and 220 respectively.

15. Sanskrit *mokṣa, mukti, vimokṣa, vimukti* (liberation, emancipation, release, escape).

16. A *kalpa* is a thousand cycles of *mahāyuga*s (periods of 12,000 years each), hence 12,000,000 years, an unimaginably long time.

17. Literally, "[all you could] see," a favorite phrase of storytellers to introduce a set piece of purple prose or verse.

18. This is the heaven of the Brahmanical god Indra.

19. Of Amitābha Buddha.

20. A sanctuary for spiritual training.

21. Stanza of Buddhist verse.

22. The original name of the monastery was "Monastery of the Illusory City."

23. The "Great Vehicle" of Buddhism, which is predominant in East Asia.

24. Shou Prefecture, approximately two hundred miles north of Mt. Lu in Anhui; modern Shou District.

25. The text refers to the silvery glow as a *xiang* (Skt. *lakṣaṇa* [distinctive mark, characteristic, or sign]). This is in keeping with the statement in the previous clause that Huiyuan had the appearance of a bodhisattva, since Buddhist iconography holds that such enlightened beings possess a certain number (often thirty-two) of *lakṣaṇa*s.

26. Equal to about 5'8" by U.S. Customary standards (1.74 meters). This would have been considerably above average for a man of the Eastern Jin period.

27. The sum total of a person's actions.

28. Eyes, ears, nostrils, and mouth.

29. This line appears to mean "May you bestow upon us the lamp of wisdom," but *chuí* (bestow) is most likely an orthographic error for *bǐng* (grasp), which has a similar appearance when handwritten.

30. Normally, "Eastern Capital" would refer to Luoyang. However, since the Jin dynasty had already abandoned the north at the time in question, that would be impossible here. Thus it is likely that the capital thought of here is that of the Eastern Jin, Jiankang, i.e., modern Nanjing (Nanking).

31. There was an Emperor Jianwen who ruled from 371 to 372 during the Eastern Jin dynasty, which would be roughly the right time for the main events and characters depicted in this story. Since the present account is largely fictional, however, it is impossible (and pointless) to determine whether he is the emperor referred to here.

32. Sanskrit *pañcarūpa-megha* or *pañcavarṇa-megha*, "five-colored" indicating auspiciousness.

33. A cash (< Portuguese *caixa* < Tamil *kācu* [copper coin] < Sanskrit *karṣa* [a weight {of precious metal}]) is a Chinese copper coin *(wen)*, one thousand of which make up a string *(chuan* or *guan)*. One hundred strings of cash would be a hundred thousand copper coins, a considerable amount.

34. Such a hairstyle was the sign of a servant.

35. Buddhism.

36. North, south, east, west, northeast, southeast, southwest, northwest, up, and down.

37. Since elsewhere throughout the text Master Yuan is described as an individual of extraordinary qualities, it does not make sense to say here that he is "completely ordinary," nor would this be likely to inspire Akṣobhya Buddha to grant him such an amazing prophecy. Hence, it is likely that the rhetorical interrogative particle *qǐ* has inadvertently been omitted by the scribe before "was." With it restored, the revised translation would be something like "As he was by no means a completely ordinary mortal . . ."

38. "Immovable"; the name of a Buddha in the east.

39. There are a number of difficult problems with these two sentences. Literally, they seem to mean, "Even if you were in a monastery and wanted to recite, it would not be permitted. All the more, now that you are in attendance upon me, how could you recite a sutra?"

40. See note 17.

41. Each line of this description consists of a conventional characteristic of heroes and handsome men in the medieval Chinese literary tradition.

42. Indra, the tutelary god of the Indo-Aryans.

43. The author seems to have dragged a mid-eighth-century Prime Minister, Cui Hao, into the story.

44. Sanskrit *daśabhūmi*.

45. Meaning literally "Good-Congratulations."

46. This sentence actually cannot be found in the *Lotus Sutra*.

47. Chinese traditionally believed that the full period of human gestation, from conception to birth, required ten months.

48. The beginnings of the four seasons, the equinoxes, and the solstices.

49. Sanskrit *mahābhūta:* earth, water, fire, and wind (or air), i.e., the four elements.

50. A famous Indian physician from the time of the Buddha. His name means "able to revive."

51. A legendary physician of the Warring States period in China. See selection 28.

52. Making several emendations to the latter part of the sentence, it may alternatively be interpreted as "when they are constantly confined to bed with sickness, beseech the spirits and ghosts."

53. In other words, most people only get to live for a little over thirty years.

54. The four passions are sexual love, sexual beauty, food, and lust.

55. The six ways (Skt. *ṣaḍ-gati*) of reincarnation or conditions of sentient existence: those of hells *(naraka-gati)*, hungry ghosts *(preta-gati)*, animals *(tiryagyoni-gati)*, malevolent nature spirits *(asura-gati)*, human beings *(manuṣya-gati)*, and heavenly beings *(deva-gati)*.

56. The five *skandhas*, which are the components of an intelligent being: form, perception, consciousness, thought, cognition. The first *skandha* is physical; the other four are mental. Attachment to the *skandhas* is a cause of suffering.

57. I.e., one's life.

58. Avarice, anger, and stupidity.

59. The desires which arise from the objects of the five senses.

60. The Buddha.

61. Past, present, and future.

62. The Minister actually says "this morning."

63. Sanskrit *pañcānantarya:* parricide, matricide, killing an arhat (saint), shedding the blood of a Buddha, and destroying the harmony of the *saṃgha* (Buddhist community).

64. Those with one's father, mother, older brother, younger brother, wife, and children.

65. So as to reap good results in the future.

66. Sanskrit *hetupratyaya*.

67. It is a common trope in Chinese literature to refer to one's lover as one's "enemy." The reasoning behind this notion is that two people are thought to be brought together in the closest possible relationship in this life to work out a grievance that one of them had against the other in a previous life. Indeed, the word translated here as "enemy" *(yuanjia)* quite literally means "person with a grievance."

68. Because the son is not there to look after them.

69. The text appears to be defective at this point. It is possible that this refers to the "winter" of the parents' life.

70. Also translated as "skill-in-means," this is the Buddhist concept of teaching known as *upāya*.

71. Sanskrit *catur-yoni,* as with (1) mammals; (2) birds, snakes; (3) worms, fishes; (4) moths (from the chrysalis), *devas* (heavenly beings), beings in hells or in newly evolved worlds.

72. The opposite qualities translated here as "error" and "truth" are often rendered as "heterodoxy" and "orthodoxy."

73. The character for "sentence" *(ju)* has been misread as the graphically somewhat similar *zi* (self).

74. The axial mountain of the universe.

75. Sanskrit *triloka* or *trailokya,* the three realms of desire, form, and pure spirit.

76. Sanskrit *bhūtatathatā* (substantial-thusness).

77. Since the "two capacities" are generally understood to be "blessedness" *(fu)* and "intelligence" or "wisdom" *(zhi),* it may be argued that everywhere in this passage "person[hood]" *(shen)* is an orthographical error for *fu* (blessedness).

78. These verses are by a Korean Zen monk named Chingak (Modern Standard Mandarin pronunciation Zhenjue [True Awareness; 870–947]) and may also be found on Dunhuang manuscript S2165.

79. The last clause is impossible to understand without emendation, but if *bù* (not) is changed to the graphically similar *yì* (also; likewise; whatever), it makes good sense.

80. Sanskrit *amṛta* (ambrosia; the nectar of immortality).

81. More literally, "[felt] as though ghee were being poured on the top of her head," i.e., as though she were being annointed with the essential truth of Buddhism.

82. Sanskrit *dvādaśāṅga pratītyasamutpāda;* the twelve *nidāna*s.

83. The following passage is severely garbled and abbreviated on the manuscript; it can only be restored by reference to its source in the chapter of the *Lotus Sutra* entitled "The Parable of the Metamorphic City."

84. Sanskrit *karmadāna* (duty-distributor), second only to the abbot of a monastery.

85. The four *varga,* namely *bhikṣu, bhikṣunī, upāsaka,* and *upāsikā* (monks, nuns, male and female devotees).

86. "Vulture Peak," the mountain in Magadha, India, near Rājagṛha, where the Buddha expounded many sutras.

87. A garden of mango trees that was supposedly donated to the Buddha by a female devotee.

88. A mythological map that was carried out of the Yellow River by dragons and horses as an auspicious omen of the legendary Yellow Emperor's reign.

89. The highest heavens (an expression frequently employed by Taoists).

90. The paths leading to the hell of fire, the hell of blood, and the hell of sharp-edged swords.

91. Sanskrit *ācārya.*

92. To ferry them to nirvana.

93. Sanskrit *bodhimaṇḍala* (circle of enlightenment).

94. Based on a passage (15.8) in the *Analects (Lunyu)* of Confucius: "The Master said, 'If you can speak to someone but fail to do so, that is to waste a person. If you cannot speak with someone but go ahead and do it anyway, that is a waste of words. The wise person wastes neither people nor words.'"

95. Confucius.

96. The syntax of this sentence is badly jumbled. What the author probably originally intended to say was roughly the following: "When the presiding elder is on his lotus mat, the audience should all listen to the Dharma. If they cause a ruckus and ask a lot of questions, they are not behaving as a person [who has come] to listen to the Dharma [should]."

97. See note 91.

98. This sentence has a couple of rare (*yōng* [commonplace, mediocre]) and miswritten (*zhi* [ambition] → *wang* [lose; lack]) graphs that require explanation and emendation to make sense.

99. *Wén* (hear) should probably be emended to *wèn* (ask about).

100. This is an allusion to a famous passage in the "Questions of Tang" chapter of the Taoist text entitled *Master Lie (Lie Zi):*

When Confucius went on an excursion to the east, he saw two boys having an argument. He asked them what it was about.

One of the boys said, "I think that the sun is closest to us when it first comes up and is farthest at noon."

The other boy thought that the sun was farthest when it first came up and closest at noon.

The first boy said, "When the sun first comes up, it is big as a chariot canopy, but at noon it is only the size of a plate or bowl. Isn't this because things that are distant seem small and things that are close seem big?"

The second boy said, "When the sun first comes up, the air is chilly, but at noon it's as hot as though one had immersed one's hand in boiling water. Isn't this because things that are close seem hot and those that are distant seem cool?"

Confucius couldn't make up his mind which of the boys was right. The two little boys laughed and said, "Who says you're so smart?"

101. In several Buddhist texts, it is mentioned that the Buddha was jabbed in the foot by a spear or sharp piece of wood because, in a previous existence, he had stabbed someone in the foot.

102. Vimalakīrti was the lay paragon of Buddhist learning who, nonetheless, was upbraided by an attendant of Mañjuśrī, the Bodhisattva who is the idealization of Wisdom.

103. The name of the ascetic literally means "Bear Insult." He was Śākyamuni Buddha in a former life and suffered mutilation in order to convert the evil King Kaliṅgarāja. His story is told, among other places, in the *Jātaka*s (tales of the Buddha's previous incarnations) and is depicted on the wall-paintings at Qizil in Eastern Central Asia.

104. This must have been a widely used expression among Confucian-minded persons in the early Tang since it is included both in "Rhapsody on a Firefly" by the poet Luo Binwang (b. 640) and in the *Family Instructions of the Grand Duke (Taigong jiajiao),* which is a collection of popular wisdom well represented among the Dunhuang manuscripts.

105. A favorite Buddhist parable found in the *Vimalakīrti-sūtra* and other texts.

106. A disciple of Confucius who had an ugly appearance but was of high moral character.

107. Bhaiṣajyarāja Bodhisattva, the healing savior.

108. See note 48.

109. A chapter of the Lotus Sutra.

110. Sanskrit *dharmadhātu,* which refers either to things in general, whether noumenal or phenomenal, or the unifying spiritual reality that serves as the basis of all things.

111. The *dianchi* (standard-ruler) of the text is an error for the graphically similar *jiechi* (boundary-ruler). The latter is a sort of paperweight kept on the table or lecture stand. Buddhist masters considered *jiechi* to be homophonous with another sinographic form meaning "precept-ruler." Aside from using the ruler as a paperweight, they would strike the table or lectern with it to draw the attention of their auditors. A totally different interpretation of the problematic phrase would read it as *sui chi diǎnlǎn* (thereupon threw aside his lecture notes).

112. It has been necessary to emend *dǐ* (bottom) to *dí* (opponent) in order to make sense of this sentence.

113. This clause may perhaps better be interpreted as "If you hear my instructions," substituting *jiào* (teaching, doctrine) for the seemingly out of place but graphically somewhat similar *qǔ* (drum).

114. The six things that ferry one across the sea of mortality to nirvana: charity, obeying the commandments, patience, zeal to progress, meditation (Zen), wisdom.

115. See note 75.

116. With appropriate emendations, the first part of this sentence more likely was intended to mean "this morning you [should] respond (*mò* [don't] → *yīng* [outstanding → respond]) to my questions (*yǔ* [speak] → *jié* [interrogate])."

117. A famous king of Magadha who was at first opposed to Buddhism but later became a generous supporter. The text is corrupt at this point and further garbled by its modern editors, but it is possible to discern the drift of Shanqing's words.

118. The text appears to be corrupt here and for the next several paragraphs. However, if one realizes that the commentary which Daoan is citing to Huiyuan (i.e., Shanqing) was actually written years earlier by Huiyuan himself, the ironies, prompts, and awkward transitions of this passage are much easier to follow.

119. See note 76.

120. The actual etymology of "nirvana" is *nir-* (out, away) + *vāṇa* (blowing), hence "blowing out; extinction."

121. I.e., those who wish to achieve nirvana.

122. Sanskrit *pratirūpa(ka),* which collectively constitute the reality of phenomena.

123. Sanskrit *anuttara bodhi,* the enlightenment of a Buddha.

124. The "hundred surnames" signifies the common people or the totality of all the Chinese surnames.

125. The Sinitic words for "comb" *(shu)* and "(sub)commentary" *(shu)* are etymologically closely linked, both deriving from a root signifying "separate; keep apart."

126. The last clause is obviously garbled. With suitable rearrangement, it may perhaps be better understood to mean "and I will now respond as I did before, [so] if you have any doubts continue speaking (i.e., asking)."

127. Sanskrit *sattva.*

128. Sanskrit *icchantika* (full of desire[s]).

129. Sanskrit *bahirdhā*, i.e., peripheral or indirect causation.

130. Sanskrit *saṃsāra* (birth and rebirth; life and death).

131. Sanskrit *aśeṣa* (without anything left over).

132. Sanskrit *kleśa*.

133. Sanskrit *sarva-nigraha-sthāna*.

134. Sanskrit *ekatva*, which may stand for *bhūtatathatā* (see n. 76).

135. Sanskrit *bhadanta* (great virtue), originally a title of the Buddha, but applied also to monks.

136. Popular legends about the historical Huiyuan recount that he was born with an inch-wide "bracelet" of flesh around his left wrist and that this was taken as a sign of his bodhisattvahood. See, for example, Imperially *Reviewed Encyclopedia of the Reign of Great Peace (Taiping yulan)* comp. 984), vol. 369. It is indicative of the strangely intertwined strands of legend and history, fantasy and reality, in this tale that, according to his biography in *Biographies of Eminent Monks (Gaoseng zhuan)*, it was Daoan who actually had a birthmark on his hand.

137. The eyes, ears, nostrils, and mouth. This sentence is a typical expression of extreme remorse that is found in many Dunhuang popular narratives.

138. To use "full[y]" in this way is awkward both in English and in Chinese, but its frequent and natural usage in Sanskrit shows to what extent Buddhist hybrid styles of "translatese" had permeated even popular narratives that were composed by individuals who almost certainly were not schooled in Indian languages. The present text is replete with such usages, but we have chosen to mention this instance only because of its obviousness and representativeness. This phenomenon of Sino-Indian linguistic and stylistic hybridity in medieval Buddhist texts is comparable to the Germanic and Slavic syntax and flavor of typical Chinese Communist writing (including that of Mao, who knew no Russian or German, but who was steeped in the translated works of Marx, Engels, and Lenin). Similarly, through the massive amounts of translation of scientific, technical, legal, administrative, and literary texts, English has had an enormous impact on the lexicon and even the grammar of Sinitic languages during the past two centuries.

139. This sentence is somewhat garbled and may also be interpreted as meaning "How could you have understood the meaning of nirvana explained by me?" But this is directly contrary to Huiyuan's own critique of Daoan in which he repeatedly stressed that it was essential for a capable teacher of Buddhist doctrine to be able to explain things in such a way that common mortals could understand them. Suffice it to say that, like most Dunhuang popular narratives, the present text is replete with such problematic constructions, a fair indication of their social status and literary nature.

140. Perhaps referring to the three vows to take refuge in the Buddha, the Dharma, and the Saṃgha (community of monks). Apart from the fact that the word translated as "vows" is written with a very strange character, there are numerous other difficulties in understanding this refractory sentence. With major restructuring and emendation, it may be rendered as ". . . I have been inept in dealing with affairs. It has already been six years (literally, 'winters') that I have used [you as my servant] morning and night."

141. This amounts to a proverb widely used in varying forms in China since at least the Tang period. Because the notion of carnal (or fleshy, physical) eyes (Skt. *māṃsacakṣus*) is clearly derived from Buddhist sources, this is another indication of the depth to which Indian concepts and linguistic usages had penetrated Chinese culture.

142. The six different types of rumblings and shakings of the earth are usually closely associated with important events in the Buddha's life. To link them with Huiyuan is to elevate him to an extremely high position.

143. Since *zài* (at) is actually a miswriting of *zuò* (do), this clause more accurately may be rendered as "the Minister sponsored the sermon in the Lotus Palace."

144. Sanskrit *Padmavimāna*, the Pure Land of the *saṃbhogakāya* (the reward-body of a Buddha).

145. This land, where the inhabitants survive on the fragrance of their superlative incense, is described in the *Vimalakīrti-sūtra*.

146. Tonsure and ordination ceremonies were sponsored by the government upon occasions of celebration.

147. For use as a rosary.

148. Sanskrit *khakkara*.

149. In the Buddha, the Dharma, and the Saṃgha.

150. Sanskrit *pañca veramaṇī* or *pañca śīla,* the five prohibitions, precepts, or commandments against killing, stealing, adultery, lying, and intoxicating drinks.

151. This line is usually considered to be corrupt and is emended to mean "Confucian doctrine emphasizes the Five Classics." In fact, it reflects a little known but very interesting body of Chinese Buddhist lore in which Confucius is referred to as "the Confucian child," his favorite disciple Yan Hui is called Guangjing (Pure Light) Bodhisattva, and Lao Zi is an avatar of Mahākāśypa, the most senior monk among the Buddha's disciples. The Five Classics are the *Book of Odes, Book of Documents, Book of Rites, Book of Changes,* and *Spring and Autumn Annals.*

152. These schools represent the ideas of emptiness or unreality (the absolute), falseness or temporary reality (the relative), and neither of the preceding.

153. This line is obviously corrupt. An alternative reading of the first part of the line might be something like "Employ irrigation and dispersal (?) . . ."

154. This is the "Changyang fu" (Rhapsody on Changyang Park) by the great Han writer Yang Xiong (53 B.C.E.–18 C.E.). It is clearly being cited here to stand for belles lettres in general.

155. These verses are also by the Korean Zen monk Chingak (see note 78).

156. This is the Buddha of the Eastern Paradise (Abirata [Delightful]).

157. The words "issue a decree" are written at the beginning of the last of the sheets of paper that are glued together to make up the scroll. The handwriting before this point, which is in columns of approximately twenty characters, has grown increasingly hurried, as though the copyist were rushing to finish the text. With "issue a decree," however, it is slower and neater, as though the copyist realized that whatever he was going to write simply had to be made to fit on this last sheet of paper. Now the handwriting becomes more deliberate and is in columns of approximately twenty-four characters. The different appearance of the handwriting before and after the break, the fact that the sheets of paper join in such a fashion as to make the columns line up poorly on either side of the seam, plus the conspicuously shorter length of the last sheet of paper in comparison with the previous sheet all led some editors in the first half of the twentieth century to mistake the last sheet as a separate text. It would appear that the copyist was simply running out of the right size paper (at thirty-four-and-a-half feet, it is already a very long scroll), grabbed a slightly longer sheet of paper as a makeshift extender in the penultimate position, then used the last sheet of paper of the proper length to complete the scroll—but not the text (see note 169).

158. Sanskrit *ārambhaṇa;* these are essentially the presumed bases of sense perceptions.

159. Presumably this was done in secret only by the top officials and without letting the populace know because they would most likely have been distraught at the prospect of Huiyuan's impending departure, and their efforts to retain him in the capital might have led to disturbances.

160. This particular ceremony features a sacrifice to the Spirit of the Roads before someone embarks on a journey.

161. The reference here to Chang'an (capital of the Tang dynasty) shows that we are purely in the realm of fiction.

162. A cliché for a swift action found in many Buddhist texts.

163. Ten tricents would be roughly three and a third miles (see n. 13).

164. The highest stage of meditation.

165. Sanskrit *anāsrava* ("undefiled," literally, "no leak / drip").

166. Intelligence.

167. Intuitive wisdom.

168. Sanskrit Vajrapāṇi, protectors of Buddhism.

169. The text breaks off in midsentence, even though the paper is not torn. The copyist merely stopped writing about one-third of the way from the end of the last sheet that makes up the scroll, allowing him room for a colophon and extra paper to wrap around the stick that serves as the end roller. As a matter of fact, the copyist had actually come very close to the end of the story, since all that remained to be told (judging from other medieval renditions) was Huiyuan's getting into the Dharma-boat and sailing up to Tuṣita Heaven.

170. The usual interpretation of the colophon is as given in the translation. Considering all of the problems with the manner in which the manuscript is brought to a close (see nn. 157 and 169), it is possible that the colophon may amount to no more than a statement of acquisition by Zhang Changji in the year 972.

THE REALM OF poetic thought explored by Tang poets had a *genius locus* all its own. There are countless lines of Tang poetry that could hardly have occurred to someone writing in English.[1] Consider this poem by Hanshan ("Cold Mountain," a place and a poet):

> Funny about the road to Cold Mountain,
> Not a trace of carts or horses.
> Hard to mark the threading streams,
> Ridge beyond ridgeline past counting.
> A profusion of herbs weeps with dew,
> Grove of pines chants in the wind.
> At a time like this where the trail is lost,
> Body asks shadow where to go?"

The last line has only five syllables in Chinese, yet a great deal of reflection went into crafting it. In the first place, it describes a concrete fact—one's shadow moves ahead of one's body. It also describes a moment of resignation—let the momentum of my journey carry me where it may! In addition, it describes one of those curious dialectical turns belonging to moments of reflection— what we project seems to have only passive movement, yet at times we follow its lead. On top of this, one could say that consciousness, which registers the body's movements with its immaterial image, resembles a shadow cast by the body's impulses. It is hard to say precisely why Tang poets strove to compress so much in a line, rather than writing discursively. Clearly the meditative concerns of Buddhism belonged to the spirit of the age, along with the suggestive aesthetic and open metaphoric spaces already established in the pre-Buddhist tradition. The form-shadow metaphor in this poem, for example, builds on similar imagery from poems by Tao Qian (365–425).

The cosmopolitan Tang culture provided an impetus toward novelty, and the compressed metrical form of *lüshi* (regulated verse) was an anvil on which poets could temper their language and work out new imagery. In terms of aesthetic achievements, Tang poetry made breakthroughs greater than the sum of any parts taken from Confucian and Buddhist philosophy. In its harmonization of means, in its transcendent flavor and time-defying crystalline visions, in its tenderness toward all phases of life, it practiced what moral ideologues could only preach. The best Tang poetry held forth a light-suffused world in which sensations paradoxically implied a spacious field of sympathy, in which particulars somehow evoked a dimension of expansive meaning. The best way to appreciate such open-ended language is to look closely at a few typical Tang poems. Here is one by Wang Wei (699?–761).

[At My] Wangchuan Retreat House, Written for Bachelor of Letters Pei Di
(Wǎng Chuān xián jū zēng Péi xiù cái Dí)

Cold mountains turning dusky green
hán shān zhuǎn cāng cùi
Autumn waters day by day purling
qiū shǔi rì chán yuán

Leaning [on my] staff outside the brushwood gate

Yĭ zhàng chái mén wài

Into the wind listen to evening cicadas

lín fēng tīng mù chán

[Over the] crossing [still] poised, the setting sun

dù tóu yú luò rì

[Above the] hamlet lane rises a lone [column of] smoke

xū lĭ shàng gū yān

Again [I] encounter Jie Yu drunk

Fù zhí Jiē Yú zùi

Crazily singing in front of five willows

kuáng gē wŭ liŭ qián

AT FIRST GLANCE this poem simply sets a scene and briefly characterizes an encounter between two persons. However, by using habits of reading encouraged by Tang poetry, the reader will find that several layers of time perception are incorporated into this simple scene. In fact, the multi-faceted manner of time's passing is a major theme of this poem. To demonstrate this, we may list twenty-one ways that time is savored in this poem: (1) in Wang Wei's presence at his retreat house—we know that Wang's life-trajectory alternated between court service and seclusion, and this poem's title indicates his current phase; (2) in the cold appearance of the mountain, which hints of approaching winter; (3) in the changing light that falls on the mountain at dusk; (4) in the seasonal waters of autumn; (5) in the purling sounds of water he is hearing at this moment; (6) in the auditory backdrop this purling has made day by day, throughout the season; (7) in the physical aging of his body, which makes him lean on his cane; (8) in the cicada sounds which mark the evening hour; (9) in the course of the sun, which is now at sunset; (10) in how the sun "remains" just a bit longer at sky's edge, moving imperceptibly; (11) in the fact that someone in the hamlet has started a cooking fire—even someone's hungry stomach is ticking off the minutes; (12) in the upward movement of the smoke column; (13) in the fact that he has been waiting while making all these observations; (14) in the fact that he encounters something that changes the mood of his day; (15) in the fact that such an encounter has happened before; (16) in how his friend Pei Di's personal qualities remind the poet of the mad recluse Jie Yu—Pei Di belongs to a character type that transcends history, so Pei Di and Jie Yu echo each other across the ages; (17) in the fact that Pei Di is drunk—when someone gets drunk, things happen faster than usual; (18) in Pei Di's song, which has a wild rhythm all its own—Wang cannot help but listen through to the end; (19) in how this quiet stream crossing has suddenly become a riotous place—just the arrival of his friend is sufficient to change the whole atmosphere; (20) in how Wang's taste for an eccentric guest reminds himself of Tao Qian, prompting him to borrow Tao's phrase and call this place "Five Willows"—Wang is joined with Tao Qian across the centuries by kindred feelings; (21) in shifts of backdrop and foreground—at the beginning we have a steady auditory background with a changing visual field (purling water with darkening hills), at the end we have a steady visual backdrop with a changing auditory foreground (Pei Di singing at the stream crossing). Reflection tells us that such multilevel shifting foci within the sensorium belong to the rich rhythm of time.

Below is a further selection of poems by Du Fu, Li Bai, and others. The poems are allowed to speak for themselves, with only a few clues to implicit meanings in the notes.

DU FU (712–770) gave poetry a new urgency by creating his own subgenre—poetic dispatches bearing witness to calamitous events of rebellion and war. Du Fu was the first Chinese poet to report the history of his own times in verse. For reasons of space, the examples given here belong to a shorter, more reflective category.

Cranes Painted by Xue Shaobao on the Exposed Wall at Tongquan Office

Eleven cranes by master Xue
Painted to look like in the Qingtian story,[2]
After so long the paint fading away
In mists of time, above the common dust.
Haughty or drooping, each with its own intent
They bear themselves with dignity like elders;
I honor the distance they aspire to
Not just these remaining flecks of pigment.
With no strain they cross ten thousand miles
Flock and wander by secret accord of souls,
Holding themselves like white phoenixes
They make no society with common songbirds.
Before this high hall collapsed
They kept company with welcome guests,
Alas that this wall should be exposed
And they end with lashing rain upon them.
High in rosy clouds is their true essence
Disdaining to drink from the muddied pool
Through unseen spaces they go where they will
Free of restraints, where none can tame them.

Overnight at White Sand Posthouse

Stopping place along the water, last rays of sun
Smoke from dwellings and then this pavilion
Beside the station, sands white as ever
Beyond the lake, grasses newly green
[In] myriad forms, the breath of spring
My lone houseboat, star in its eccentric orbit
Following waves [touched by] infinite moonlight
They grow closer in my sight—the Southern Deeps[3]

Autumn Meditations (First of Eight)

Chill of jade dewdrops wounds the maple forest
Gorge under Wu Mountain, atmosphere under a pall[4]
Between river margins, waves churning level with sky
Clouds driven through the pass, shadows brush the earth
Chrysanthemums bloom a second time to tears of other days

Lonely boat fastened to thoughts of a long-gone garden
Clothes for the cold, scissors hurry in every household
Below the fortress, laundry pounded hard at nightfall[5]

Watching Fishermen

I

At the east ferry point along the Jin River
Where bream fish jump up like liquid silver
Fishermen row out and drop big nets
To intercept the dwellers of the channel
Common fish are thrown off to the side
Red-tailed beauties stand out like a charm
The local dragon is speechless, his mermen enraged
They kick up plumes of dust in a whirlwind
Rows of chefs ply their frosty knife-blades
Heap sashimi like snow upon golden platters
Forget about the tench of Xuzhou
Carp in the Hanyin weirs are far away
Nothing can match perfect flesh of bream
But pleasure of gorging has a desolate end
Behold the shiny body gutted at morning
Its lively streak forever gone from the waters

II

Fishermen of the murky river gather at dawn
Spread nets to haul in the lunging school
Skillful boatmen race against the wind
Tridents pierce the breasted wave
Countless fry squirm from the nets
Beached in deathly heaps they twitch
Lunkers droop and fade away
Lash their tails with noses to the ground
Viewers consume a second day of treats
Push back platters and finish off the wine
This evening the river dragon goes to a new lair
Fish under these peaks will follow his stormcloud
Endless battles are raging over this land
Where have our unicorns been driven to?
Why does my kind take pleasure in this?
The sages mourn to see such desecration

Stone Niche

Bears are roaring to the left of me
Catamounts are howling on my right
Behind me run wailing ghosts
Before me the monkeys screech.

Wind blows cold under gloomy sky
Cart track obscure in deep mountains,
I pull up beneath Stone Niche
And witness a midwinter rainbow.
Who comes singing up the switchback?
A bamboo cutter's sad voice draws near.
Five years of cutting prime young stems
To keep the Hebei armory supplied.
What happens once the true shafts are gone?
How to stay on the taxman's good side then?
Helpless against the tempest from Yuyang,
Horsemen raging down upon the good folk.

Iron-Corridor Gorge

A wanderer leans into blasts of wind
Dwarfed at the edge of a precipice,
A hidden corridor runs through the chasm
Past cliffs that loom like massed iron.
A path that brushed the vault of sky
Goes into the gashed mantle of earth.
Dwarf bamboos as far as eye can see,
And ageless snow embedded in the sky.
Long trek through this brooding gorge,
Cheerless view along a glum journey,
By a stream where ice is wedged in rocks
I ride a horse that jolts me to the bone.
My fragile life is up against hidden arrows
Bandits are far from under control.
Three years of drifting place to place,
Looking back still makes my guts churn.

Overnight in a Riverside Pavilion

Darkness creeps up the mountain path
High lodge overlooks the river weir
Thin clouds settle over boulders
Lone moon tumbles in the waves
Crane follows crane in quiet flight
Pack of jackals howl over their catch
Unable to sleep I worry over warfare
No strength to set right heaven and earth

Song of My Thatched Hut Destroyed in the Wind

Winds of high autumn howl in the Eighth Month
They blow the three-ply thatch right off my roof
Rushes fly over the stream, scatter on the bank

Above they get caught in tips of tall trees
Below they skim the ground and sink in a pond
Kids from South Village seize upon my weakness
Before my eyes they turn into brazen thieves
Grab armloads of thatch and dart through the woods
I shout myself hoarse, but they will not listen
Then walk back with cane in hand, sighing.
Soon the wind grows quiet, clouds an inky shade
The autumn rain-mist darkens to gloaming
These years our thin quilts feel as cold as iron
My frail son sleeps poorly, kicks them to shreds
Leaks drip onto every bed, no corner is dry
Raindrops pelt down endlessly like rows of hemp
Since the time of troubles my sleep has been fitful
How is a wet person to get through the long night?
Somehow we need to get a thousand-roomed house
To shelter all the poor scholars, make their faces beam.
Sturdy like a mountain, impervious to storms
Ah me, if such a house could only loom before my eyes,
Let me freeze alone in a run-down hut, I would be content.

ONLY LI BAI (701–762; his name is also traditionally read as Li Bo) could have written couplets like these: "With white jade and gold to buy laughter and song, / Months of drunken haze make noblemen seem small." "New vintage in my cup, with barrels all stowed away, / Take to the waves with pretty Polly, sailing where I may." Li Bai was unique in several respects: first, for his ecstatic turn of mind, which may be related to his family's origins in Central Asia; second, for his creation of a devil-may-care persona and his self-dramatization in poetry; and third, for the ironic twist he gave to conventional imagery.

Life Is a Passing Traveler

The living are passing travelers, the dead are returnees;
Heaven and earth a roadside inn, where we grieve the dust of eons.
The rabbit in the moon pounds herbs with his pestle in vain;
Fu Sang the world-tree has been chopped up for firewood.
White bones are mute; what do green pines know of spring?
Repeated sighs at what lies ahead and behind;
What reward could there be in floating glory?[6]

Alas the Chrysanthemums at the Eastern Fence

Alas the chrysanthemums along the eastern fence[7]
Their stems are sparse, their leaves are drooping.
Though not like fine orchids, their fragrance is all their own.
Not yet having floated them in a pitcher of wine,
You leave them to glisten in vain with dewdrops.

If you fail to pick them at their time of blooming
Once the wind claims them, what can you hold dear?

Hard Road to Go

Fine pitcher of clear wine, 10,000 cash a gallon
Gourmet dishes worth a small fortune.
Push away cup and chopsticks, an end to this feasting!
I draw my sword with darting eyes, heart in a fog.
I want to cross the Yellow River, ice blocks the channel;
I want to climb Mt. Taihang, snow fills the passes.
Oh for hours of casting my hook in the azure current,
Carried off on a boat, dreaming where the sun rises.
My journey is hard, beset with false turns,
Where has it brought me now?
There will come a time to crest the waves
With wind bellying my sail, return to vast ocean.[8]

No Men among the Huns

Harsh wind driving frost chills the arid grasses
Tough as whipcord are the haughty Hun horses.
300,000 of our Chinese soldiers, and at their head
We have generals as dashing as Hu Piaoyao.
Fletching that zings like meteors stays in the quiver,
Drawn swords exhibit the gleam of lotus-etching,
Celestial soldiers go out Yumen pass in the snow.
Nomad arrows rain down on metal armor
Dragon and tiger formations lock in mortal coil.
By the moon over Taibai, we vow to smash the foe
Smash the foe, wipe his flag from the earth's face
Tread on enemy guts and wade in enemy blood.
Hang the enemy high in the sky,
Bury him by purple pass.[9]

Drinking Alone beneath the Moon

Among the blossoms, a single jar of wine;
No one else here, I ladle it out myself.
Raising my cup, I toast the bright moon,
Facing my shadow, that makes three of us.
Though the moon knows little of drinking
And shadow only trails behind me,
Let me share this moment with moon and shadow,
To find joy, take advantage of the Spring.
I sing, and the moon seems to move without moving,
I dance, and my shadow tumbles into pieces.

Sober, we're together and happy.
Drunk, we scatter in our own directions.
Intimates forever, we will wander carefree
Pledged to rendezvous in Star River distances.[10]

WANG WEI

Farm Families of Weichuan

The setting light falls on a hamlet
Oxen return through narrow lanes
An old man, concerned for his herd-boy
Leans on his staff beside a brushwood gate
A pheasant cries among rising wheat sprouts,
Silkworms sleep after eating the mulberries bare.
Fieldhands return with hoes over shoulders,
Lingering to talk and enjoy each other's company.
At this moment I long for a carefree life
And downcast I chant the song "Hard Straits"![11]

Xiang-Si [Daydreaming of Someone]

Heart-shaped seeds grow in southern climes
When spring comes, they grow new branches
May you gather many of them
These seeds are the dreamiest of all

MENG JIAO (751–814), who failed the jinshi examinations twice before passing on his third attempt and then went on to a miserable career, was a bitter man who wrote harsh poetry. Yet he could not conceal a poignant tenderness in this series of poems written to mourn the death of his infant daughter.

Nine Poems Mourning the Almond Flowers (Excerpts)

I

Chilled hands mustn't touch the water beads
Disturb the water beads, they easily fly away
Don't let startling frost sever the springtime
Springtime cut short is a gloomy time indeed.
See the fallen little flower-nipples
The hues of yesterday's infant clothes
Gathered up, they hardly fill the hand
Return at dusk, hollow and sorrowful.

V

Stepping on the ground, I fear to cause the soil pain
Or damage this tree's fragrant root
Heaven must not know of my reverence
To have snipped my descendants this way
From the hanging branch, a thousand fall
Not one fragrant life is spared
Some say it's fine to plant a tree outside
But spring beauty did not enter my door

—DM

Notes

1. Translation has done a great deal to bridge this gap. Contours of thought from one macrorealm of poetry can reappear elsewhere through translation, and from there they can enter the pool of possibilities in the new language. However, many such thought-forms are hard to catch, and whether or not they make it through the transition depends on the climate of the new era.

2. This refers to an old story about two immortal cranes which were kept in thrall by a Daoist wizard. Each year they gave birth to a baby crane which grew up and flew away.

3. According to legend, if one sails far enough into the Southern Deeps, one will curve up and around—onto the Great Sky River (the Milky Way). Du Fu feels that in his wanderings on the Yangtze, he has gotten pretty far along on the "Southern Deeps."

4. The cloud-mists of Wu Mountain were a conventional image for encountering a mountain goddess. Evidently Du Fu was not feeling romantic.

5. In the pounding sounds from the city below, Du Fu seems to hear the frustration of the laundry-women, many of whose husbands have gone off on military campaigns.

6. Li Bai turns conventional imagery on its head. The green pine, usually a symbol of endurance, is now seen as oblivious to transient joys. The world-tree becomes firewood; the journeyer recoils from oblivion that lies behind as well as ahead.

7. This line echoes the familiar image from "Drinking Wine V" by Tao Qian:

> I built a cottage right in the realm of men
> Yet there is no noise of carts and horses.
> You ask—how can that be so?
> When the mind is far, its place becomes remote
> I pick chrysanthemums by the eastern hedge
> Off in the distance gaze upon the south mountains.
> Mountain vapors glow lovely in twilight sun
> Birds returning fly together.
> There is something meaningful in this,
> I wanted to expound on it, but have gone beyond words.

8. Here Li Bai's poetic persona falls into fragments and fails to perform.

9. This is an example of Li Bai's bloody irony, in this case directed at the Tang court's jingoistic attitudes, which led to poorly conceived strategies and military disasters.

10. Again, Li Bai twists the conventional theme of celestial immortals to speak of his inner fragmentation under the influence of alcohol.

11. Referring to a poem from the *Book of Odes* which laments the decline of the Zhou kingdom.

THIS STORY IS contained in a Tang collection entitled *Dry Snacks (Ganzhuan zi),* which in its entirety is no longer extant. But about thirty-three of its entries have survived in the *Extensive Records from the Reign of Great Tranquility (Taiping guang ji),* an encyclopedic collection of stories compiled in the late tenth century. The authorship of the *Ganzhuan zi* is not well established. Some scholars attribute it to Wen Tingyun (812–872), a Tang scholar, famous for his innovative *ci* (lyric) poetry.

The *Ganzhuan zi* belongs to a special genre of prose writing, known as *biji* or note-form literature, which can be classified into three groups: historical, fictional, and philosophical. Like most other surviving pieces in the *Ganzhuan zi,* "Dou Yi" belongs in the historical group. Its content indicates that this historical narrative is apparently based on true historical figures, places, and events, with the author's dramatization.

A much truncated version of the story is found in the *Tiny Tales from Northern Dreams (Beimeng suoyan),* compiled by the Song scholar Sun Guangxian, in which the protagonist Dou Yi is referred to as Dou gong (Mr. Dou) and the descendant of Chief Minister Dou Jing.[1]

Dou Yi lived his entire life in late-eighth- and early-ninth-century Chang'an, then the largest and most prosperous metropolis in the world. Having survived the devastating An Lushan Rebellion of 755–762, the city was undergoing vigorous urban revival. Through the life and career of a successful businessman, "Dou Yi" provides us with many valuable insights into the city itself and its business practices. —VCX

Dou Yi of Fufeng was thirteen years old.[2] His various aunts on the paternal side had been royal relatives for several reign periods. His paternal uncle Dou Jiao was honorary president of the Board of Works,[3] commissioner for the palace corrals and stables, and commissioner of palace halls and parks. [Dou Jiao] owned a temple yard in Jiahui Ward (see map).[4]

Yi's relative Zhang Jingli served as aide[5] in An Prefecture.[6] After he was relieved of his duty by his replacement, he returned to the city [of Chang'an]. An Prefecture produced silk shoes. Jingli brought with him more than a dozen pairs of those to give to his nephews and nieces. All except Yi fought for them. Soon only one slightly oversized pair was left behind by the nephews and nieces. Yi bowed twice before he accepted them. Jingli asked him why. He just kept quiet. Little did they know, Yi harbored great ambitions for business success like Duanmu.[7] So he went to the market and sold them for 500 cash, which he stored away in a secret place.

Quietly he had two trowels made at a smithy, and sharpened their edges. At the beginning of the fifth month, Chang'an was covered with elm seedpods. Yi swept together more than a *hu* (bushel) of them. He then went to his uncle's (Dou Jiao) place to borrow his temple yard for study. The uncle granted his request. At night Yi would secretly rest in the Fa'an Shangren Courtyard of the Baoyi Monastery.[8] During the day, he went to the temple, where he cultivated a piece of spare land with the two trowels, digging four thousand closely aligned furrows, 5 *cun* (inches) wide and 5 *cun* deep each. Each of them was more than 20 *bu* (1 *bu* [pace] ≈ 1.5 yards [1.4 meters]) long. He fetched water to irrigate them and sowed elm seedpods into them. Summer rain soon fell, and all of the seedpods grew well. By fall, they had grown more than 1 *chi* (foot) tall and numbered in the tens of thousands.[9] The next year, the elm saplings were more than 3 *chi* tall. Yi then used an axe to chop off the shoots that were growing too closely to each other so that the saplings would be about 3 *cun* from one another. He left all those saplings that were thick and straight untouched, but cut off those that were not, and tied them up in more than a hundred bundles, each of them about 2 *chi* around. That fall happened to be gloomy and rainy, so he sold those bundles [as firewood] at more than a dozen cash each. The following year, he fetched water [to irrigate] the old elm furrows again. By fall, some of the elm trees were as thick as chicken eggs. He again chose those that were thick and straight, [but instead of saving them] chopped them off with an ax and tied them into more than two hundred bundles. This time, he increased his profit several times. Five years later, he selected more than a thousand large trees for rafters and sold them for 30,000–40,000 cash. There were no fewer than a thousand supersized timbers, large enough for making carriages, lying inside the temple yard. By then he already was running more than a hundred businesses. He accumulated silks and cloth-lined fur coats by the hundred, yet he still ate sparingly.

He then bought some black flaxen cloths from Shu (present-day Sichuan), at 100 cash per *pi* (bolt). He cut them into pieces 4 *chi* long. He then hired people to make pouches out of them. He purchased several hundred pairs of new flaxen shoes made in Neixiang.[10] Without leaving the

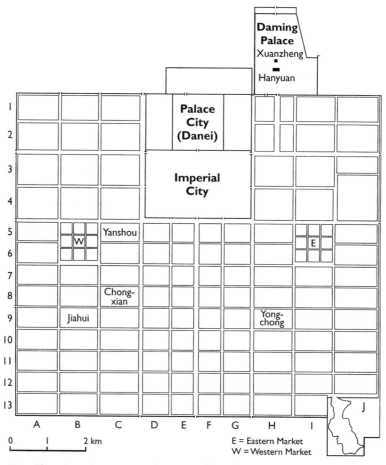

Tang Chang'an, showing its palaces, wards, and markets

temple, each day he would give out three pies and 15 cash, together with a pouch, to each one of the children from various residential wards and the Jinwu households.[11] In winter, they picked up locust seeds to fill in the pouches and turned them in. In a month's time, he amassed two cart-loads of locust seeds. He also asked children to pick up worn-out flaxen shoes, and for every three pairs of them he gave a new pair in exchange. When the news began to spread far and wide, numerous people came to turn in worn-out shoes. In a few days, he acquired more than a thousand pairs. He then sold his elm timbers large enough for carriages, raking in more than 100,000 cash. He hired day laborers to wash the worn-out shoes at the brook near the west gate of Chong-xian Ward.[12] He then had them dried in the sun and stored away in the temple yard. He bought piles of broken tiles from outside the ward gate. He then had workers wash them clean of mud at the running-water brook and transport them by cart into the temple. He set up five sets of grinding tools and three sets of filing instruments. He bought several *shi* (= *hu,* bushel) of oil-based indigo in the West Market and hired a chef to set up a kitchen stove. He recruited a large number of hired day laborers to file the worn-out shoes and grind the broken tiles. Having sieved it with a large-meshed screener, he added locust seeds and indigo into the mixture. He had his workers labor day and night to grind and beat it until it became stiff like curdled milk. The work-ers were asked to gather the mixture fresh from the mortar and were ordered to knead it with both hands into a dough of 3 *cun* across, shape it into sections of less than 3 *chi* each. He ended up hav-ing more than ten thousand sticks, which he named "dharma candles" *(fazhu).* In the sixth month of an early Jianzhong year,[13] it rained heavily in the capital city. Firewood was worth more than cassia bark.[14] Carriages were no longer seen in alleyways.[15] Yi then sold his dharma candles at 100 cash apiece. When used for cooking, they were twice as good as firewood. Yi reaped an endless amount of profit.

Previously, south of the steelyard bazaar of the Western Market there was more than 10 *mu* (1 *mu* = 240 *bu*^{2} = 6 acre [2.43 ha]) of low-lying swampland, known as the Little Sea Pond (Xiaohai chi). Located near wineshops, it became the dumping ground of the area. He asked to buy it. But the owner was unpredictable. Yi compensated him with 30,000 cash, and got the land. He set up a signpost with a pennant hanging at the top at the center of the pond. Around the pond he set up six or seven stalls for making pancakes and rice balls. He invited children to throw broken tiles at the pennant. Those who hit the target were rewarded with pancakes and rice balls. In less than a month, children of east and west Chang'an came by tens of thousands,[16] and the broken tiles which they threw [soon] filled up the pond. After measuring the area, he built a tavern of twenty bays[17] in a key location, which earned him a daily profit of several thousand cash and was excep-tionally profitable.[18] Known as the Dous' Tavern, it is still there today.[19]

Once seeing a Sogdian by the name of Mi Liang suffering from hunger and cold, Yi at once gave him some money and silk. Seven years went by, yet Yi did not ask a single question about it. When Yi met him again, out of commiseration for Mi's hunger and cold, Yi gave him another 5,000 cash. A grateful Liang told others that he would repay Dalang (Great Man, i.e., Dou Yi) eventually. One day Yi was resting at home, and before long Mi Liang appeared, telling him, "In Chongxian Ward, a small house is for sale for 200,000 cash. Dalang (Dou Yi), buy it now." Yi withdrew some extra money deposited at a treasure house *(guifang)*[20] in the Western Market and purchased the house at the market price. On the day Yi signed the title deed, Liang told Yi, "I am an expert in estimating jade. Once I saw an unusual stone in the house. Few people know about it. Used as a laundering block, it is a true piece of Yutian jade.[21] Dalang can strike it rich instantly." Yi did not believe his story. Liang said, "Please ask a jade craftsman from Yanshou Ward to examine it."[22] The craftsman was greatly amazed, and said, "This is a rare commodity indeed. I can work it into twenty sets of belt ornaments, at the price of more than a hundred strings of cash per set, which will come to a total of about three thousand strings." [Dou Yi] then asked to have the work done, which eventually brought in several hundred thousand strings of cash.[23] In addition, Yi acquired other jade pieces of various descriptions, such as containers, belt buckles, and knickknacks. The sale of these items again brought in approximately several hundred thousand strings of cash. To show his appreciation, Yi gave the house to Liang to live in, yielding to him the original title deed as well.

In front of Defender-in-Chief Li Sheng's[24] mansion, there was a small house, which was believed to be badly haunted. [Dou Yi] bought the house for its value of 210,000 cash. He enclosed the area with walls, [then] tore down the tiles and timbers and had them piled up in two separate places. Inside his property, he did farming. The Defender-in-Chief's mansion bordered on Yi's property, whose small loft-building was oftentimes an intolerable sight.[25] Li Sheng wanted to annex it to make way for a polo[26] ground. One day, he sent his men to Yi, offering to buy it. Yi firmly declined the offer, saying, "I have other use for it." During one of Li Sheng's periodic holidays, [Dou Yi] asked to see Sheng, carrying the title deed for his property with him. He said to Sheng, "Originally I bought this house for my relatives to live in. But I am afraid that my property is looking menacingly over the Defender-in-Chief's first-rate mansion. As a poor man of lowly birth, I certainly feel uneasy. Seeing that my property, spacious and idle, can be used for polo games, I now present you the original title deed, in the hope that you will graciously take care of me. Sheng was greatly pleased, saying to Yi in private, "Don't you want my humble assistance?" Yi answered, "I dare not expect that. Only, in the event of a future emergency, I might come to bother you, sir." Sheng paid increasing attention to him. Yi then cleared away the tiles and timbers and leveled the land before giving it away to Sheng for his polo games. Armed with the favors he received, Yi gathered five or six superrich merchants from the Eastern and Western Markets, and asked them, "Don't you have sons and younger brothers who aspire to secure key posts in various circuits[27] and the capital?" The merchants were overjoyed, saying to Yi, "If Dalang (Yi) soon provides shelter for our sons and younger brothers, we will pay 20,000 strings of cash for it." Yi then took the list of names of these merchants' sons and younger brothers to see Sheng, claiming that all were his relatives or friends. Sheng examined the list graciously and placed all of them in key, cushy positions in various circuits. Yi gained from it an additional tens of thousands of cash.

In Chongxian Ward, Commandant Cao Suixing found that a large tree rose [in his yard] overnight. Suixing was often concerned that its branches and leaves had grown over the years, obstructing his house and yard. He was afraid that felling the tree might result in structural damage. Then Yi paid him a visit. Pointing to the tree, he said, "Commandant, why don't you get rid of it?" Suixing answered, "It is indeed in the way. But since it is deeply rooted, to cut it may damage the roof of my house." Yi then asked to buy the tree: "I can still get rid of it for the Commandant without causing any damage. I should be able to let the tree destroy itself." The Commandant was very pleased. [Dou Yi] then paid him 5,000 cash. He discussed with the axmen how to cut down the tree. Paying them a large sum of money, he asked them to cut from top to bottom at 2 *chi* intervals. Out of the timbers he created several hundred backgammon game[29] boards and sold them at the bazaar, realizing a profit of more than a hundredfold. His astute business deals were all similar to this.

In his old age, Yi was sonless. He divided his assets among his well-acquainted relatives and friends. As to his remaining numerous businesses in various large markets[30] in west Chang'an with [daily revenues of] more than a thousand strings of cash each, he entrusted their management to the Fa'an Shangren Courtyard as its permanent property.[31] Yi constantly provided for it without even considering gain or loss.

Yi died when he was more than eighty years old. His residence remains in Jiahui Ward in the capital, where his younger brothers, nieces, and other blood relatives lived. His grandsons still live there now.[32]

—VCX

Notes

1. No Tang chief minister by the name of Dou Jing has ever been recorded in the Standard Histories.

2. Fufeng was in present-day Fufeng, Shaanxi, and west of Xi'an. There were two famous Dou lineages, the Dous of Luoyang and the Dous of Fufeng. Dou Yi apparently belonged to the Dous of Fufeng. However, it is impossible to establish connections between Dou Yi and other Dous recorded in history.

3. Dou Jiao is recorded neither in the *Old Tang History (Jiu Tangshu)* nor in the *New Tang History (Xin Tangshu)*.

4. Jiahui fang was a ward in Chang'an, located south of the Western Market.

5. *Zhangshi* was one of the top executive officers of a prefecture.

6. An Prefecture was in Hubei. Its prefectural seat was in present-day Anlu.

7. Duanmu was the surname of Duanmu Ci, commonly known as Zigong. He was one of the closest disciples of Confucius, noted for his entrepreneurship.

8. The Baoyi Monastery was located in the southwest corner of Jiahui Ward.

9. The Chinese expression *qianwan* in the text literally means "ten million." Here it is used generally to indicate the abundance of the elm saplings.

10. Neixiang was in present-day Xixia, Henan.

11. Jinwu wei (Imperial Insignia Guards) were key security forces stationed in the capitals. "*Jinwu* households" probably refers to households headed by Jinwu Guard officers.

12. Chongxian Ward was southeast of the Western Market and northeast of Jiahui Ward where the temple yard was. In the text, the ward name is given as Zongxian, which did not exist in Chang'an; it is an error for Chongxian.

13. Jianzhong (780–783) was a reign period under Emperor Dezong (r. 779–805).

14. Chinese cinnamon, used medicinally and as a spice.

15. Because there was so much mud in them that they would get stuck.

16. The expression *wanwan* or a hundred million is obviously used as a hyperbolic device.

17. A *jian* (bay) is a floor space measurement unit about 10–16 feet (3–5 meters) in length, similar to a *tsubo* in Japan.

18. The Chinese text *shuqian* (several thousand) should probably mean "several thousand *guan* (strings)," a string being composed of 1,000 cash. If such were the case, Dou would have made a daily profit of several hundred thousand cash (i.e., copper coins).

19. "Today" refers to "the middle to late ninth century."

20. A *guifang* was a primitive banking establishment.

21. Yutian, also known as Khotan, was in Xinjiang. It was famous for its jade in premodern China.

22. Yanshou Ward was to the immediate east of the Western Market.

23. In this and the preceding sentence there is confusion over the figures quoted that requires a certain amount of emendation.

24. The *taiwei* (Defender-in-Chief) was one of the Three Dukes; the title was one of the highest prestige titles in Tang China. Li Sheng (727–793) was the most powerful general under Emperor Dezong. His mansion in Chang'an was in Yongchong Ward, southwest of the Eastern Market.

25. The small loft-building *(xiaolou)* refers to Dou's house, which is made clear by the expression *fubi* (looking menacingly over) below.

26. Polo, like the Sogdians, came to China from the Western Regions (Central Asia). The importance of Central Asian and West Asian culture can scarcely be overestimated for their influence upon Tang culture.

It is not by accident that in many Tang tales Persian, Sogdians, and others from the west (like Mi Liang here) are often credited with preternatural insight or fabulous wealth.

27. A circuit *(dao)* was the highest level of local administration.

28. Cao is not recorded in the Standard Histories.

29. *Shuanglu* or *lubo (liubo),* which also appears to have come to China from Persia. Backgammon boards were often made of the finest wood and highly decorated with inlay.

30. "Various large markets" may indicate that, apart from the Western Market, other official markets might have existed in the late eighth and early ninth centuries in west Chang'an.

31. This means that Dou donated a considerable proportion of his enormous wealth to the very monastery that had given him his original opportunity to make a profit. See note 8 above.

32. The term *zhu sun* (various grandsons) does not necessarily refer to his direct descendants, since he was heirless. Here it refers to his relatives two generations below him.

KING AŚOKA (269?–232 B.C.E.) of India allegedly built numerous stupas in many lands to hold Buddhist relics known as *śarīra*. In China, the custom of building stupas was introduced together with Buddhism. During the Tang (618–907) dynasty, the best-known Buddhist relics were those contained in the stupa of the Famen Monastery (Famen si) north of the present-day county seat of Fufeng, Shaanxi Province, and sixty-five miles west of Xi'an (Tang Chang'an). A recent archaeological excavation carried out in 1987 brought to light four Buddhist relics, all finger bones, from the "underground palace" of the stupa. One of them was identified as human, and the other three were imitation relics known as "shadow bones." The former is believed to be a "true relic" of the Buddha (plate 62). In Tang times, the true relic was brought out of the monastery periodically for display and worship on seven separate occasions. In 819, it was brought out for the sixth time when the reigning emperor was Xianzong (r. 805–820). Han Yu (768–824), the most prominent stylist and prose-writer of his day, took this occasion to present this memorial to the emperor[1] in which he expressed his anti-Buddhist stand. On reading the memorial, Xianzong was so incensed that he ordered Han's execution. Later, Han's penalty was reduced to banishment to Chao Prefecture (in present-day Chaozhou, Guangdong) in the far south. Han Yu wrote another memorial as prefect of Chao Prefecture to express repentance and ask for mercy. (While in Chaozhou, Han Yu also wrote a mock memorial addressed to a crocodile that had been terrorizing the area.) He was subsequently transferred to Yuan Prefecture (in present-day Yichun, Jiangxi) before his return to the capital.—VCX

Your servant says:[2]

He humbly believes that Buddhism is a religion of the barbarians, which spread to the Middle Kingdom in Later Han (25–220 C.E.) times. It did not exist in antiquity. In the ancient past, the Yellow Emperor (Huang Di) reigned for 100 years, and lived 110 years; Shaohao reigned for 80 years, and lived 100 years; Zhuanxu reigned for 79 years, and lived 98 years; Di Ku reigned for 70 years, and lived 105 years; Di Yao reigned for 98 years, and lived 118 years; both Di Shun and Yu lived 100 years. This was a time of great tranquility under heaven. The people enjoyed peace, happiness, and longevity while there was no Buddha in the Middle Kingdom.[3]

Thereafter King Tang of Yin too lived 100 years. Tang's grandson Taiwu reigned for 75 years while Wuding reigned for 59 years. History does not record their ages, which, judging by their reign periods, should not be shorter than 100 years.[4] King Wen of Zhou lived 97 years, and King Wu 93 years, while King Mu reigned for 100 years.[5] During this period the law of the Buddha did not enter the Middle Kingdom, nor did Buddha worship bring about all this.

During the reign of Emperor Ming of Han (r. 57–75 C.E.) the law of the Buddha began to make its appearance.[6] Emperor Ming reigned for only 18 years. Thereafter chaos and destruction continued, and reign periods were short-lived. During and after the period of the Song (420–479), Qi (479–502), Liang (502–557), Chen (557–589), and the Yuan Wei (Northern Wei, 386–534) dynasties, as people became more devoted to Buddha worship, reign periods became particularly short.[7] Only Wudi of Liang (r. 502–549) reigned for 48 years. During his reign on three occasions he gave up his own body for the Buddha. At the Ancestral Temple sacrifices, he stopped making animal offerings, and limited himself to one meal of vegetables and fruits every day.[8] With Hou Jing (502–552) closing in on him, Wudi ended up dying of starvation at Taicheng.[9] His country too was destroyed soon after. Buddha worship is for the purpose of bringing good fortune, but it only results in more misfortune. In view of this, it is evident that the Buddha is not worth worshiping.

Upon taking over the imperial mantle from the Sui, [Tang] Gaozu (Li Yuan, r. 618–626) discussed the elimination [of Buddhism].[10] At that time, the ministers and courtiers were not far-sighted enough to comprehend the profundity of the Way of the ancient sages and the exigencies of the past and present so as to elucidate the sagely wisdom and correct that abuse. So the effort did not go any further, to your servant's constant regret.

I humble myself in front of the divine, holy, brilliant, and martial presence of Your Imperial Majesty, who is wise and sagely, and excels in literary accomplishment and the art of war. In the past thousands of years, no one can compare with [Your Majesty]. Not long after you ascended the throne you began to disallow ordinations of people as Buddhist monks and nuns or Daoist adepts. Nor did you permit the creation of Buddhist monasteries and Daoist abbeys.[11] Once your servant believed that the wish of Gaozu would certainly be realized under Your Majesty's hand. Nowadays, even though that has not come to pass, there is no reason to encourage it (Buddhism) to flourish again.

Now I have heard that Your Majesty instructed various monks to greet the Buddhist relic at Fengxiang, mounted a loft-building to view it, and took it in both hands into the Great Within (Danei) (see map on page 350).[12] In addition, [Your Majesty] ordered various monasteries to take turns to receive and worship the relic.

Although your servant is extremely foolish, he still knows that Your Majesty will not be deluded by the Buddha into worshiping [the relic] like this in the hope of achieving happiness and auspiciousness. This is simply a frivolous gimmick and a deceitful and exotic spectacle set up for the officials and commoners of the capital in an attempt to humor some people at a time when the harvest is good and people are happy. It cannot be true that [Your Majesty], so sagely and brilliant, believes in this sort of thing.

However, the people are inherently ignorant, susceptible to delusion, and difficult to reason with. If they should behold Your Majesty like this, they would talk about devotedly worshiping the Buddha. Everyone would say, "Even the great sage Son of Heaven is devout in his faith; who are we the ordinary people to grudge our own bodies and lives?" They would sear the tops of their heads and burn their fingers,[13] gathering in crowds of tens or hundreds. They would doff their clothes to scatter their money, from morning till night. They would emulate one another, for fear of being left behind. Old and young would all run about [doing this], abandoning their proper occupations.

If this is not henceforth banned, it (the relic) will go the rounds among various monasteries. By then, there will be people who sever their arms and cut out their flesh to make offerings [to the relic]. Corrupting our accepted mores and customs and making ourselves a laughingstock everywhere—this is no small matter.

The Buddha was originally a man of the barbarians who did not speak the language of the Middle Kingdom and was dressed in clothes of a different cut from ours. Neither did he cite the edifying discourses of the ancient sovereigns, nor did he don their proper attire. He was ignorant of the sense of duty between sovereign and subject, and the affections between father and son. If he were alive today, and were on a state mission to visit the court in the capital, and if Your

Majesty would generously receive him, [Your Majesty] would merely grant him one audience in the Hall of Manifest Government (Xuanzheng dian).[14] After one banquet was held at the Office of Foreign Relations,[15] and one set of attire was conferred on him, [Your Majesty] would have guards escort him out of the country so that he would not be able to delude the masses.

All the more, now that he has been dead for long, how can his withered and decayed bones and baleful and filthy remains be allowed into the forbidden palace? Confucius said, "Revere ghosts and spirits but keep them at a distance."[16] In antiquity, when the various princes[17] were about to hold mourning ceremonies in their states, even they would request shamans to use peach-wood charms and magic brooms to eradicate the ill-omened before they proceeded. Today for no good reason the decayed and filthy object was brought to light for Your Majesty's viewing. It was neither proceeded by shamans nor exorcised by peach-wood charms and magic brooms. No ministers have ever talked about its wrongs, and no censors have ever cited its faults. Your servant is truly mortified by this.

I pray that [Your Majesty] will have the relic delivered to the government agency concerned, which will depose of it in water or fire so as to permanently destroy its roots. If [Your Majesty] puts to rest doubts under Heaven and stops once and for all [Buddhism] from deluding posterity, all under Heaven will be aware of the achievement by you the great sage, which is hundreds of millions of times greater than that of ordinary people. Isn't that wonderful? Isn't that cause for joy?

If the Buddha should possess soul and the power to cause misfortunes, let all such calamities be visited upon your servant. Let Heaven be the witness: your servant shall never regret it.

With great gratitude and extreme sincerity, I present this memorial for Your Majesty's consideration.

Your servant in genuine fear and trepidation.[18]

—VCX

Notes

1. By genre, this is a *biao,* which is a formal, written address submitted to the throne. A *biao* is normally fairly lengthy and adheres to a particular format.

2. *Chen mou yan* (literally, "[your] vassal so-and-so says") is the formal beginning of a *biao.*

3. The rulers from Huang Di to Shun are legendary Sage Kings of the dim past. Yu was the alleged founder of the semihistorical Xia dynasty.

4. King Tang (Dayi) was the founder of the Shang dynasty. Taiwu, also known as Dawu, was the tenth sovereign of the Shang, and Wuding the twenty-third. The Shang genealogy is recorded somewhat differently in oracle-bone inscriptions than it is in the history books, which were written a thousand or more years after the kings in question lived and ruled.

5. King Wen was a predynastic leader of the Zhou people. His son, King Wu, founded the Western Zhou dynasty. King Mu was the fifth sovereign of the Western Zhou. None of the extremely long reign periods and ages of the rulers mentioned here and above can be confirmed by modern historical research.

6. Buddhism almost certainly began to trickle into China before this time albeit in an inchoate and confused fashion, but the reign of Han Mingdi is generally recognized as the period when the presence of Buddhism may be historically attested.

7. The four southern regimes of Song, Qi, Liang, and Chen were all based in Jiankang (present-day Nanjing). The Northern Wei was based first in Pingcheng (Datong), then Luoyang (east of present-day Luoyang).

8. Wudi actually gave himself up as a menial to a Buddhist monastery on several occasions, and was indeed an extraordinarily devout follower of Buddhism.

9. The Taicheng, or Terrace City, was the central palace of Jiankang under the Liang. It was sacked by Hou Jing's rebel army in 549.

10. Tang Gaozu issued, among other things, the "Edict to Purge Buddhism and Daoism" (Shatai Fo Dao zhao).

11. This is in reference to Xianzong's edict in 807. Xianzong wanted to curb ordinations for the purpose of tax benefits and the building of extravagant monasteries.

12. Fengxiang is in present-day Fengxiang, Shaanxi, west of Xi'an. Danei was an alternative name for the Palace City in Tang Chang'an.

13. Han Yu is referring to instances of self-mutilation (highly disturbing to Confucius, who set great store by the bodies bequeathed to us by our parents) that sometimes occurred out of excessive zeal on the part of Buddhist devotees.

14. The emperor held court in the Xuanzheng Hall. It was located north of the Hanyuan Hall in the Daming Palace, the second palace complex of Tang Chang'an.

15. *Libin* as a government office is not recorded in the two Tang official histories or in the *Six Canons of the Tang (Tang liu dian)*. It should be a Middle- to Late-Tang office dealing with reception of foreign guests under the Court for Dependencies (Honglu si).

16. The text is quoted from chapter 6 of the *Analects (Lunyu)*.

17. This is in reference to the Spring and Autumn period.

18. The phrase *cheng huang cheng kong* is a pro forma expression often used at the end of a memorial to show respect to the recipient.

HAN YU (768–824, styled Tuizhi) was a native of Nanyang, Dengzhou, in modern Henan Province. He was a successful examination candidate and rose through the civil bureaucracy, becoming famous as a poet and essayist. Han Yu is also traditionally credited with starting the Confucian revival known as Neo-Confucianism. In 819, he was banished to the southern reaches of the Tang empire for his criticism of the court's honoring a Buddhist relic. In the memorial he wrote to the emperor on that occasion, Han Yu criticized Buddhism not only for contravening traditional Chinese values, but also for being a foreign religion (see selection 52).

While scholars of Chinese philosophy note that Han Yu may not have contributed new concepts to the Confucian tradition, he was recognized as an inspiration by many later Neo-Confucian thinkers. In this piece he lays out his arguments against both Buddhism and Daoism, which was also prevalent during his time. The Confucian Dao (the "path" or "way" by which one is to live) is, according to Han Yu, the only true one. As opposed to the Buddhist quest for enlightenment that reaches beyond the "unreal" realm of *saṃsāra* (the cycle of repeated birth and death) in which humans live, and against Daoist notions of "nothingness," Han Yu reaffirmed Confucian belief in the ultimate reality of this world and of moral categories, writing "humaneness and righteousness are fixed terms, while the Way and Virtue (the Dao and De of Lao Zi's *Daode jing*) are by themselves substanceless positions." Furthermore, Han Yu believed that Buddhism and Daoism were inimical to the social and political order, throwing into confusion the Confucian ideals of social hierarchy and family.—RF

The Original Way

Universal love is called humaneness. When practiced appropriately it is called righteousness. What stems from these is called the Way. What is sufficient in oneself and does not depend upon externals is called virtue. Humaneness and righteousness are fixed terms, while the Way and virtue are by themselves substanceless positions. Therefore there are the ways of the gentleman and of the petty person; there are the virtues of inauspiciousness and auspiciousness. Lao Zi's belittling humaneness and righteousness was not because he did away with them, but because his perception was too small. One who sits at the bottom of a well and looks up at the sky would say the sky is small; but the sky is not small. Lao Zi considered the appearance of compassion to be humaneness and the appearance of humility to be righteousness, his belittling them is to be expected. What he called the Way was simply making a universal Way out of his own conception of the Way. It is not what I call the Way. What he called virtue was simply making a universal virtue of his own conception of virtue. It is not what I call virtue. When I speak of what I call the Way and virtue, I speak of them in terms of humaneness and righteousness, which are generally accepted terms in the world. When Lao Zi spoke of what he called the Way and virtue, he spoke of them in terms of discarding humaneness and righteousness, which was the opinionated statement of one man.

When the Zhou dynasty's Way declined and Confucius died, the books were burned in the Qin, Huang-Lao Daoism dominated the Han, and Buddhism the Jin, Wei, Liang, and Sui dynasties. Those who spoke of the Way and virtue, and humaneness and righteousness either accepted the teachings of Yang Zhu or Mo Zi, Lao Zi or Buddhism. Those who believe in one school necessarily rejected the other. What they accepted, they glorified like a ruler. What they rejected, they treated like a slave. They followed what they accepted and reviled what they rejected.

Alas! If a person in later generations wants to hear theories of humaneness and righteousness, the Way and virtue, from whom will he hear them? The Daoists say, "Confucius was our teacher's disciple." The Buddhists say, "Confucius was our teacher's disciple." Those who would be Confucians were accustomed to hearing these statements and were happy with these absurdities. They belittled themselves, saying, "Our teacher once said this, too." Not only do they say this, they also write it in their books.[1] Alas! Even if a person in later generations wants to hear theories of humaneness and righteousness, the Way and virtue, from whom will he seek them? Indeed, people delight in the strange, so they neither seek their origins nor question their consequences; they only want to hear of the strange.

In the past there were four categories of people. Now there are six.[2] In the past there was only one school of teachers. Now there are three.[3] Farmers are one type of household, but there are six types of household that eat grain. Artisans are one type of household, but there are six types that use their implements. Merchants are one type of household, but there are six that trade with them. Of course the people are impoverished and turn to thievery!

In the past there were many things that harmed people. Once the sages were established, they taught the people the Way of living together and supporting each other. They ruled the people and taught them; they drove off the insects, snakes, birds, and beasts and occupied the central plains of China. When it was cold, they clothed them; when there was hunger, they fed them. When the people lived in trees, they fell out; when they lived in the ground, they became sick, so the sages made them houses. The sages developed crafts to provide the people with implements to use. They developed trade for them to connect supply and demand. They practiced medicine to prevent the people from dying young. They created burial ceremonies for the people to extend their feelings of kindness and love. They created rituals to establish precedence of status. They created music as an emotional release. They set up government to guide the people's indolence. They created punishments to eradicate their rude obstinacy. Because the people cheated each other, they created tallies, weights, and scales to keep them honest. Because the people stole from each other, they created walls and armed soldiers to protect them. When harm came, they made preparations; when trouble arose they made defenses. Now there are those who say, "If the sages do not die, great thieves will not cease. Smash the measures and break the scales and the people will not struggle."[4] Alas! These people simply are not thinking. If there had been no sages in antiquity, people would have died out long ago. Why? Because we lack feathers, fur, scales, or shells to live in the heat and cold; because we lack claws and fangs to struggle for food.

Therefore the ruler gives commands. The minister implements the commands and extends them to the people. The people produce grain and cloth, make implements and utensils, and engage in commerce to serve their superiors. If the ruler does not give commands, then he loses that which makes him a ruler. If the minister neither implements the ruler's commands nor extends them to the people, then he loses that which makes him a minister. If the people do not produce grain and cloth, nor make implements and utensils, nor engage in commerce to serve their superiors, then they are executed.

Now the Buddhists' "Dharma" says, you must cast aside your rulers and ministers, abandon your fathers and sons, repress the way of living together and supporting each other in order to seek so-called purity and nirvana. Alas! They are fortunate to have been born after the Three Dynasties (of Xia, Shang, and Zhou) so they were not rebuked by Emperor Yu, King Tang, King Wen, King Wu, the Duke of Zhou, or Confucius. They are also unfortunate not to have been born before the Three Dynasties so they were not corrected by Emperor Yu, King Tang, King Wen, King Wu, the Duke of Zhou, or Confucius. Though their titles of emperor and king differ, these rulers were all the same in what made them sages. In the summer they made lightweight clothes; in winter they wore fur coats; they drank when thirsty and ate when hungry. Though they had different concerns, they were the same in what made them wise. Now there are those who say, "Why not have no concerns like the people of high antiquity?" This is like reprimanding someone wearing a fur coat, saying, "Why not have the simplicity of lightweight clothing?" or reprimanding someone who is starving, saying, "Why not have the simplicity of drinking?"

The tradition says, "Those in antiquity who wanted to illuminate their illustrious virtue in the world first ordered their countries. Those who wanted to order their countries first regulated their families. Those who wanted to regulate their families first cultivated themselves. Those who wanted to cultivate themselves first rectified their hearts-and-minds. Those who wanted to rectify their hearts-and-minds first made their intentions sincere."[5] However, what the ancients referred to as rectifying the mind and making the will sincere was to act with purpose. Now those who want to rectify their hearts-and-minds go beyond the world and the country, eliminating the Heavenly Constants of society: the son accordingly does not treat his father as a father; the minister does not treat his ruler as a ruler; and the people do not treat their service as service. In writing the *Spring and Autumn Annals,* Confucius considered as barbarians those feudal lords who used barbarian customs, but considered as Chinese those whose customs were similar to the Chinese. The classic says, "Barbarians with rulers are not as good as Chinese who have lost them."[6] The *Book of Odes* says, "To attack the Rong and Di, to punish Jing and Xu."[7] Now [the Buddhists] uphold the barbarians' dharma and place it above the teachings of the Former Kings. How far are they from being barbarians?

What do I call the teachings of the Former Kings? Universal love is called humaneness. When practiced appropriately it is called righteousness. What stems from these is called the Way. What is sufficient in oneself and does not depend upon externals is called virtue. Their writings are the *Book of Odes,* the *Book of Documents,* the *Book of Changes,* and the *Spring and Autumn Annals.* Their regulations are ritual, music, punishment, and government. Their people are the literati, the farmers, the artisans, and the merchants. Their roles are ruler and minister, father and son, teacher and friend, guest and host, elder and younger brothers, and husband and wife. Their clothes are hemp and silk. Their residences are houses and rooms. Their foodstuffs are millet and rice, fruit and vegetables, fish and meat.

As a Way this is easy to understand. As a teaching this is easy to practice. Therefore when practicing this for oneself, there will be satisfaction and good fortune. When practicing this for others, there will be love and openness. When practicing this for the heart-and-mind, there will be peace and contentment. When using this for the world and the country, there will be nothing you do not manage to do appropriately. Thus in life you realize your feelings, and in death you fulfill these norms. When (you are) sacrificing to Heaven, the heavenly spirits attend; when (you are) sacrificing to ancestors, the ghosts will partake.

If someone asked what sort of Way is this Way? I would respond, this is what I call the Way; it is not what was previously called the Way of Lao Zi and Buddha. Yao transmitted it to Shun. Shun transmitted it to Yu. Yu transmitted it to Tang. Tang transmitted it to Wen, Wu, and the Duke of Zhou. Wen, Wu, and the Duke of Zhou transmitted it to Confucius. Confucius transmitted it to Mencius. When Mencius died, it was not transmitted. Xun Zi and Yang Xiong grasped it but did not express its essence; they spoke of it but did not explain it fully. Prior to the Duke of Zhou [those who understood this Way] rose above and were rulers, so their concerns were acted upon. After the Duke of Zhou they fell below and were ministers, so their ideas continued.

This being so, what can be done? I say if one is not blocked, the other cannot flow; if one is not stopped, the other cannot be practiced. Turn these Buddhists and Daoists into commoners, burn their books, and turn their residences into huts. Illuminate the way of the Former Kings by teaching it. Then those without husbands or wives, those who are orphaned or childless, those who are crippled or diseased will be cared for. This, indeed, seems possible.

—RF

Notes

1. Referring to a passage in the *Book of Rites,* wherein Confucius says, "I heard it from Lao Dan." Lao Dan is a name linked to Lao Zi, so Daoists have used this as evidence that Confucius was a student of Lao Zi.

2. Confucius divided society into the literate elite, farmers, artisans, and merchants. Han Yu is arguing that Buddhist monks and Daoist priests have been added.

3. Han Yu is arguing that only Confucianism was practiced in antiquity, while in the Tang Buddhism and Daoism are also practiced.

4. From *Zhuang Zi,* chapter 10, "Rifling Trunks."

5. From the opening section of the *Great Learning.*

6. *Analects* 3.5.

7. "Bei Gong," *Book of Odes.* The Rong were non-Chinese people to the west, the Di to the north, Jing to the south, and Xu to the southeast.

THE CINDERELLA STORY is one of the world's best-loved and most widely distributed fairy tales. Occurring in many different variants, this tale of the "Ash Maiden"—who experiences glory and riches as a result of losing her slipper—is familiar to children (and adults) around the globe. Since the most widely known version of the story is European, it will undoubtedly come as a surprise to learn that the earliest exemplar of the tale is to be found in a Tang collection of exotica. Although some scholars have jumped to the conclusion that the Cinderella story itself must therefore have originated in China, this is almost certainly not the case.

A careful and close reading of the Chinese tale reveals unmistakable traces of its immediate origins in Southeast Asia, with hints that its ultimate roots lie to the west. Furthermore, this earliest "Chinese" Cinderella story (and there are many later variants within China as well) manifestly derived from fiercely independent non-Sinitic peoples. These particular non-Sinitic peoples (and we must remember that still today China has many non-Sinitic groups scattered throughout its length and breadth) lived in the far southern reaches of what is now China. At the time when the story was first written down, however, the region was only nominally and tangentially under Chinese political and military control. Culturally and socially, this part of the empire was almost completely un-Chinese.

In reading this Cinderella story, these facts should be kept clearly in mind. Indeed, the Chinese scholar who recorded the story is at pains to make explicit its non-Sinitic derivation. Duan Chengshi (ca. 800–863) was a bibliophile, word-fancier, and collector of curiosities who spent most of his life living in the Yangtze River Valley region, from the upper reaches in Sichuan to the cosmopolitan city of Yangzhou on its lower reaches. His father was the great minister Duan Wenchang (772–835), who had earned a reputation for skillfulness in governing the aboriginal peoples of the south. The elder Duan obtained a position for his son as collator of texts in the royal library. Later, as a private scholar, Duan Chengshi worked in his own well-stocked library at home. Duan had a particular penchant for all things arcane, strange, and alien. He was conversant with Buddhist literature, and especially sought out foreigners as his informants. For example, he states that he learned some of his tales from "Romans" (who may actually have been Anatolians or Syrians) and others from Indians. So devoted was Duan to the accurate description of the non-Sinitic that he even provides much valuable linguistic data in the tales that he recorded. Among the diverse topics that he wrote on were imported incenses and perfumes plus their names in the languages of the countries whence they came, medicinal herbs from abroad, falconry (introduced to China by steppe peoples), and tattooing (the history and practice of which he describes in extraordinary detail).

Duan Chengshi's aspirations in his compulsive gathering of the odd and the out-of-the-way may be gleaned from the title of the omnibus in which he gathered his records, reports, essays, and tales. That is the *Youyang zazu,* where *zazu* means something like "smorgasbord" or "miscellany" and *Youyang* is a place name referring to a mountain in Hunan (south-central China). According to legend, certain scholars who were fleeing from the "burning of the books" carried out by the First Emperor of the Qin dynasty (221–207 B.C.E.) sought refuge in this place. Upon arrival, they deposited the texts they brought with them in a cave on the mountain. These writings (which presumably survived nowhere else) were later discovered by people who had wandered into the cave. Because of this legend, the name Youyang came to signify rare and old books from from far away. Thus the entire title signifies roughly "miscellaneous morsels of lost lore." The Cinderella story recorded by Duan Chengshi fits comfortably under that rubric.

For a fuller understanding of how the Cinderella story made its way from points west to Southeast Asia, thence to the far south of the Tang imperium, and thence to central China where it was finally written down, an intensive investigation of trading patterns in the Arabian Sea, Bay of Bengal, and South China Sea is necessary. During the Tang period, there was a vibrant market economy that, judging from the products which were available and the large numbers of foreigners resident in most major cities, had distinct international dimensions. Under such conditions of flourishing long-distance trade, the transmission of the Cinderella story to the southern hinterlands of the Tang empire from India and beyond becomes much easier to comprehend.

Although an enormous amount of excellent research has been done on the various types and complicated distribution of the Cinderella story, the "Chinese" version presented here—because it is the earliest extant written version to be discovered anywhere—is important for understanding the development of this famous fairy tale. Unfortunately, the "Chinese" story is poorly known outside of a small circle of Sinologists. Those intrepid folklorists who have endeavored to make sense of it in terms of the overall evolution of the Cinderella story worldwide have been hampered by inadequate, inaccurate translations and mistaken assumptions about its cultural specificity. To facilitate future research on this intriguing topic, the present rendition provides extensive Sinological annotations, historical background, and explanations of cultural customs and beliefs. This treatment is also intended to enhance the pleasure of the general reader in encountering this charming story.—VHM

A Chinese Cinderella Story

The southern people have passed down [the story] of a tribal leader[1] in pre–Qin-Han times[2] surnamed Wu[3] whom the aborigines called "Cave Wu." He married two wives, one of whom died, leaving behind a daughter named Yexian.[4] When Yexian was young, she was intelligent and good at working[5] gold, so her father loved her. Advanced in years, the father died, whereupon Yexian was abused by her stepmother, who often ordered her to gather firewood in dangerous (steep) places and draw water from the depths. It so happened that once she caught a fish a little over two inches long with a dark red dorsal fin and golden eyes [in her bucket], whereupon she put it in a bowl of water and raised it. Day by day it grew, causing her to change the bowl several times. It grew so big that no bowl could hold it; consequently she threw it into the pond out back. Whatever extra food the girl got hold of, she right away submerged it [in the pond] to feed the fish.

When the girl went to the pond, the fish would be sure to stick its head out of the water and pillow it on the bank, but the fish would not appear when anyone else approached. The stepmother came to know about the fish, yet every time she waited for it, she never saw the fish. So she deceived Yexian, saying, "Haven't you been working too hard? I've made a new jacket for you." Whereupon she exchanged [the new jacket] for Yexian's shabby clothing. After that the stepmother ordered Yexian to fetch water from a spring that was several miles away. Then the stepmother leisurely put on Yexian's clothing, and, with a sharp knife in her sleeve, she walked toward the pond and called the fish. Right away, the fish stuck out its head, thus the stepmother killed it with the knife. The fish had already grown to more than ten feet in length. The stepmother made a meal out of its flesh, which was twice as tasty as that of an average fish. She hid its bones beneath a dung heap.[6]

The next day, when Yexian went toward the pond, she didn't see the fish anymore, whereupon she cried in the wilderness. Suddenly, there was a person[7] with hair splayed across the shoulders and wearing coarse clothing who came down from the sky and consoled Yexian, saying, "Don't cry. It was your stepmother who killed your fish. Its bones are beneath the dung. When you go back, you can take the fish bones and hide them in your room. Whatever you need you have only to pray to the bones and your wish will be granted." Yexian followed the person's instructions and was provided with gold, pearls, clothing, and food as she desired.

With the advent of the community festival, the stepmother went [to take part in it], but ordered Yexian to guard the fruit trees in the courtyard. Yexian waited until her mother had gone quite far and then went [to the festival] herself. She wore a blouse woven of kingfisher feathers and golden[8] slippers. The daughter to whom the stepmother had given birth recognized Yexian and said to her mother, "That [girl] looks very much like my older sister." The stepmother was also suspicious. As soon as Yexian was aware [that they had noticed her], she hurriedly turned back, leaving behind one of her slippers, which was picked up by a member of the tribal community. When the mother returned, all she saw was Yexian sleeping in the courtyard with her arms wrapped around one of the fruit trees, so she thought nothing more of it.

The tribal community bordered on an ocean island,[9] and on the island was a kingdom named Tuohan.[10] Tuohan was militarily powerful and ruled over scores of [other] islands.[11] Its coastal shores were more than a thousand[12] miles in length. The member of the tribal community [who had found Yexian's slipper] subsequently sold it to [the kingdom of] Tuohan. When the ruler of Tuohan obtained the slipper he ordered [the women] who were in close attendance upon him to put it on, [but even for] those with small feet, the slipper would shrink an inch [when they tried to put it on]. Then he ordered all the women in the kingdom to try it on, but in the end it did not fit any of them.

The slipper was light as a feather and made no sound [even when someone wearing it] walked on stones. The king of Tuohan suspected that the man of the tribal community had obtained it through improper[14] means, so he had the man imprisoned, shackled, and interrogated with torture. [Yet, when all was said and done,[15]] it was not known where the slipper had come from. Then [the king had the man] cast out by the side of the road with the slipper, [with instructions to search] everywhere from house to house to match[16] it. If there was a woman who could wear [the slipper], she was to be arrested and the king informed.[17] [After the man had located the matching slipper, he told the king of Tuohan, who journeyed to the tribal community to see for himself.] The king marveled at it,[18] so he searched her room and discovered Yexian [there]. He commanded her to put on the slipper, and [, when it fit, he finally] believed.

Thereafter, wearing her blouse woven of kingfisher feathers and the [golden] slippers, Yexian made a [grand] entrance. Her form[19] was like that of a heavenly being.[20] Only then did she tell everything that had happened to the king, who returned to his kingdom transporting both the fish bones and Yexian with him.

The stepmother and her daughter were soon killed when they were struck by flying stones.[21] Lamenting them, the members of the tribal community buried [the stepmother and her daughter] in a stone pit, which they called "Tomb of the Repentant Women." The members of the tribal community treated [the tomb] as a matchmaking shrine, and, when they sought a wife,[22] it would be sure to comply.

Upon reaching his kingdom, the king of Tuohan made Yexian his primary wife. [During] the first year, the king was greedy and prayed to the fish bones for unlimited treasures. [After] a year had passed, [the bones] no longer responded. Then the king buried the fish bones at the seashore, depositing them in a hundred bushels of pearls and using gold for a boundary. When the conscripted soldiers rebelled, he was planning to disburse [the pearls and gold] to provide for the troops, but one night they were washed away by the tide.

[This story] was told by Li Shiyuan, who was formerly a servant of my[23] household.[24] Shiyuan was originally the member of a tribal community in Yongzhou,[25] and he could recall many strange tales from the south.

—VHM

Notes

Material in square brackets [X] indicates additions to the Chinese text necessary for full intelligibility in English. Material in parentheses (X) indicates minimal amplification or clarification.

1. Literally, "cave host/chief," the term "cave" being used by Chinese writers during the Tang period (618–906) to designate tribal communities of non-Sinitic peoples in the area of what is now south China.

2. That is, before the Qin (221–207 B.C.E.) and Western Han (206 B.C.E.–6 C.E.) dynasties.

3. Medieval pronunciation ŋuo.

4. Medieval pronunciation jɛpɤǎn:.

5. The verb is uncertain, there being several textual variants: "panning [for]," "buckling/hooking," etc. The girl may have been proficient at spinning gold thread, a technique perfected by the Persians and other Middle Eastern peoples.

6. The author chooses an unusual word for dung heap, viz., yuqi, ancient Sinitic pronunciation *ʔiwət siər. Since the meanings of the two graphs ("lush/dense/depressed/melancholy" and "perch") make no sense as a collocation, we may assume that the word is a transcription of some non-Sinitic term. The yuqi is a filthy place that would have included garbage, excrement, and most likely ashes. Since Yexian has to scrabble through the yuqi later in the story, the dung heap here is the functional equivalent of ashes in other Cinderella stories.

7. The gender of this person is ambiguous.

8. The slippers were probably embroidered with gold thread.

9. This is a bit of an exaggeration, since Nanning (see n. 25 below) is hundreds of miles from the nearest ocean, although—to someone from central or north-central China like Duan Chengshi—in Tang times the area to the southeast of Nanning would have been thought of as intimately involved in oceanic travel.

10. Middle Sinitic d'aɣan. This is almost certainly meant to be a transcription of Dvāravati/Dvārapatī or Tavoy, Southeast Asian kingdoms that flourished during the Tang period and whose names were transcribed by Chinese in a nearly identical fashion, one which is very close to the transcription given here in our text. Both of these kingdoms were important transshipment points for long-distance trade between East and West. Dvāravati (flourished from the sixth through thirteenth centuries, with its peak in the ninth century) was especially vital in this regard and played a key role in the spread of Indian ideas and motifs to Southeast Asia (and beyond to China).

11. Perhaps a reference to the Mergui Archipelago, composed of some two hundred islands, which lies along the western edge of the Isthmus of Kra.

12. More literally, "several thousand li" (tricent = three hundred paces or approximately one-third of a mile [a thousand paces]).

13. Literally, "decrease."

14. Literally, fei Dao (not [in accord with the] Way), an expression that could signify a range of meanings from inappropriate to immoral to illegal.

15. All of the words in this set of brackets correspond to jing in the text, translated as "in the end" in the last sentence of the previous paragraph.

16. The verb in the text is *bu* (capture, arrest), but this would seem to be an error for the homophonous and graphically similar word *bu* (supplement, complement, complete).

17. The text is clearly defective at this point, there being a gap between the finding of the matching slipper and the king's being told about it.

18. It is not entirely clear precisely what the king finds so marvelous—the fact that the matching slipper was found, the fact that it was found in such a remote place, or the fact that there really was a woman who could wear such a tiny slipper.

19. The word used by Duan Chengshi for "form" is *se,* literally meaning "color," but with strong connotations of "sex." The same graph was also used to translate Sanskrit *rūpa* (form).

20. Duan Chengshi seems almost studiously to avoid comparing Yexian to a *tiannü* (heavenly woman), which would have evoked all sorts of Buddhist images (e.g., Skt. *devakanyā, devi,* or *apsaras*), referring to her instead by the more neutral *tianren* (heavenly person).

21. This would appear to be a confused allusion to death by stoning, a custom common among neither the Chinese nor their southern neighbors, but well known in the Middle East (e.g., in the Bible: "He that is without sin, let him first cast a stone"; Islam: the stoning of the devil on the Hajj). In terms of cultural ecology, this would make sense because much of the Middle East is arid, rocky land with lots of good ammunition lying around everywhere.

22. The text merely says "seek/request female," but the word "matchmaker" in the previous clause requires that "female" be understood as "wife," not "daughter" or "woman."

23. I.e., Duan Chengshi's.

24. The text reads *jiaren* (literally, "family person; member of one's family"); the author is probably referring to a family servant.

25. Modern Nanning in the province of Guangxi, a southeastern province that is the home of China's largest "minority," the Zhuang, who speak a language closely related to Thai. It is presumed that the area around Nanning was already occupied by Tai speakers during the ninth century, when Duan Chengshi wrote this story down.

ONE OF THE greatest foreign policy concerns of China's Tang dynasty (618–907 C.E.) was how to cope with the often powerful—and often belligerent—nomadic peoples to the north. Particularly troublesome had been relations with the Türks (C. Tujue), who were eventually replaced by the Uyghurs (C. Huihu); the latter dominated the northern steppe from 744 to 840. Shortly after their rise to power, the Uyghurs assisted the Tang government in the quelling of the An Lushan Rebellion (755–762), a military uprising which nearly destroyed the dynasty. After this, relations between Tang China and the Uyghurs were generally amicable, although often strained, in large part due to the horse–silk trade between them, from which the Uyghurs profited immensely, and the marriages of Tang imperial princesses to Uyghur rulers, which added to Uyghur prestige. Both of these were forced upon the Chinese by their debt to the Uyghurs.

The collapse of the Uyghur empire in 840, a result both of internal struggles and of invasion by the previously subject Kirghiz people, led to new difficulties for China, as large groups of Uyghur refugees fled to the Chinese border looking for assistance or booty. Controlling or eliminating these Uyghurs was crucial to the stability of China's vulnerable northern border.

The two documents presented below relate to this crisis. The first was written around 850–851 by a young scholar named Li Qi who was seeking to right a wrong—the indifference shown by the Tang government to a Chinese soldier named Cai Xi. As the document reveals, Cai served as a spy for the Tang, attempting to lure Uyghur refugees within striking distance; he later played a pivotal role in the Tang attack on the Uyghurs and claimed himself to have rescued the Chinese princess who was in their camp. The document gives us a look at a rare first-hand account (which Li Qi probably obtained from Cai Xi himself) of Tang military actions, Uyghur responses and suspicions, and jealousies among Chinese military leaders. It should be noted that Cai Xi's story was not incorporated into the official dynastic account of these events, which credits only the generals Liu Mian and Shi Xiong.

Li Qi's account was an effort to move the administration of the next emperor, Tang Xuanzong (r. 846–859) to recognize and reward Cai Xi's accomplishments. Cai was ultimately promoted several times, until he perished early in 863 while defending Tang positions in what is today northern Vietnam. Finally, we should note that because of Li Qi's use of archaic, "literary" terminology in this account, particularly in terms referring to the Uyghurs, this document was long unnoticed as a source for this period. It is now preserved in *juan* 803 of *Complete Tang Prose (Quan Tang wen)*.

The second document was composed by Li Deyu (787–850) and is preserved in his collected works. Li Deyu served as chief minister at the court of Tang Wuzong (r. 840–846), emperor of China during the Uyghur refugee crisis. He wrote this letter to the ruler *(qaghan)* of the Kirghiz people—who had dealt the final blow to the Uyghurs that sent the refugees fleeing to China and elsewhere—in the emperor's name. This letter thus shows the formal style of the Tang emperor's communication with another sovereign.

This letter, composed in the spring of 843 in response to a Kirghiz envoy to China (whose letter does not survive), reveals not only Tang diplomatic protocol, but also several other matters. The letter praises the Kirghiz *qaghan,* as well as the emperor's own ancestor, the great Emperor

Tang Taizong (r. 626–649), who was responsible for the expansion of the dynasty's power in its early years. In so doing, the letter seeks to gain a superior position for China vis-à-vis the Kirghiz by showing that Tang Taizong had been recognized as "Heavenly Qaghan"—a position that apparently gave him paramountcy over the steppe peoples—and had appointed the Kirghiz ruler with a Chinese title. The Kirghiz then had sent tribute to the Tang court until communications were disrupted by the rise of Uyghur power. All this would assert a superior position for China in relation to the Kirghiz.

In addition, the letter gives credence to the idea, found in several sources, of kinship between the Tang and Kirghiz ruling houses. In this relationship, China was once again in a superior position. Note that although Cai Xi's account includes a call for the Uyghurs to remember their marital ties to the Tang imperial family, the acceptance of a blood relationship between the Chinese emperor and Kirghiz *qaghan* would signify a closer (and superior) bond than the Chinese-Uyghur marital connection.

Li Deyu's letter goes on to describe the defeat of the Uyghur refugees (attributed here to Liu Mian, with no mention of Cai Xi) and then urges the Kirghiz ruler to hunt down and destroy those who had escaped. The emperor finally offers the *qaghan* a title of appointment—signifying Tang recognition of his power and position, but again placing China in a superior position.

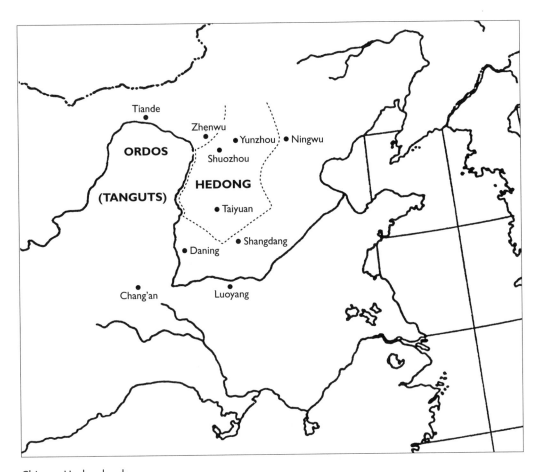

Chinese-Uyghur border

The two documents reveal both the informal ("The Account of Cai Xi") and the formal ("A Letter to the Kirghiz Qaghan") workings of the Tang administration at a time of crisis.—MRD

Li Qi, "The Account of Cai Xi"

Cai Xi is, in his own words, an assistant general. The origin of his family is unknown; from their [known] beginnings their posterity, down to Xi, have lived in the Zhenwu Army [administrative unit] in the north. [Xi] was a student of fencing; he was calm and brave, and achieved distinction through his fondness for unusual strategies. At first, before anyone knew of him, he behaved recklessly. He got into a fight with someone and [apparently] killed him. At that time, since the [later] Minister of Works Liu Mian had been made Military Governor of Zhenwu while serving as Right Vice-Director of the Department of State Affairs,[1] he heard of [the matter] and had Xi imprisoned. [Cai Xi] was about to be executed by whipping, but in the night the "dead" man revived. Thus Xi escaped death; [instead] he was banished to do garrison duty at the frontier for several years. Mian [later] was transferred to guard Hedong.[2]

At the beginning of [the reign of Emperor] Wuzong (r. 840–846), the Xiongnu[3] violated the border. [The emperor] ordered that troops be sent out from Mian's [circuit of] Hedong and from other circuits to attack them. When Xi heard that there was an incident at the border, he wished to avail himself of [the situation] to establish merit, so he escaped from the place where he was working and came to beseech Mian. He said, "In the past, Your Lordship spared Xi's[4] life. This [act] was one of Your Excellency's stretching the law to extend mercy, and it was Xi's great fortune. Now the Celestial Troops are attacking the northern savages. I humbly wish to serve at the vanguard of the army like a dog or horse. At best I would be able to repay Your Lordship's mercy; at least I beg to make amends for my own wrongdoings. Whether [the matter] concludes in life or death, [I care not]!"

After hearing this, Mian considered him resolute and upright, and ordered that he be placed among the soldiers of the government army. When they reached Daning, they heard that the Xiongnu already had entered the border at Zhenwu. At this time the Taihe Princess[5] had been abroad [among the northern nomads] for many years; [the government troops] also heard that [the military officials of] Zhenwu wanted to rescue the princess. Mian was afraid that the princess would be taken by [the military officials of] Zhenwu, and for this they would obtain great merit. He schemed and planned, but did not know what to do, nor could his generals and officers come up with a plan. Xi then requested permission to pretend to be pursuing (an) escaped criminal(s) and so reach the Xiongnu camp to sow doubt among them, causing them to enter the border at Hedong. Mian strongly approved of this plan, and so sent Xi on his way.[6]

When Xi arrived at the place where the Xiongnu [were camped], he spread the word: "Those who guard Zhenwu wish to kill you all. In Hedong, Vice-Director of the Department of State Affairs Liu is Pacification Commissioner.[7] If you do not shift [your camp] you surely will be destroyed by the forces of Zhenwu." There were those among the Xiongnu who, having heard these words, hurried to Ningwu [to submit]. [The remainder] subsequently shifted as divisions and regiments, and arrived at [the area] west of Quyue City. They were already at the border of Hedong, [but] still were more than two hundred tricents[8] from the government army.

When Xi returned and reported to Mian, [the latter] wanted to memorialize to the throne [concerning the matter], but feared an imperial edict [requiring] prisoners as evidence. Xi again [acted on Liu Mian's behalf and] captured twelve prisoners and fifteen horses. The commander (i.e., Liu

Mian) then wrote [a memorial] concerning the matter. After the emperor had learned of it, there were repeated imperial edicts ordering [Mian] to obtain the princess. Mian was distressed that the camp of the Xiongnu was [still so] far away; he wanted them to come closer, but again could not [think of a way to bring this about]. Xi then requested permission to enter their territory with goods and provisions to entice them [to approach nearer]. Mian agreed with him.

Once Xi was among the foreigners, he saw the princess, who wept while telling him of the destruction of [the state of] the northern foreigners, and of their sickness, famine, isolation, and danger, with no one to whom to appeal. Xi said to her, "The emperor is sagacious. How could the Princess not discuss entering [China for succor] along with the *chanyu*[9] and memorialize to the emperor concerning your distress?" The princess replied, "I already have discussed with the *chanyu* [the question of] letting me go. He certainly will not reconsider the matter since he already has refused!"

After she had finished speaking, Xi requested an audience with the *chanyu*. The high-[ranking] *tarqan*[10] said, "The *chanyu* [now] is separated from his native land. While he is on the path of restoring [his reign], it is not suitable for him to meet with envoys. If you have a matter [to be brought to his attention], you may only discuss it with our minister."

Xi then met with their minister. The minister said, "We are sick and hungry, having fled from ruin. The Tang [government] does not take pity on us. Today a Tang envoy has come, rejoicing that there is nothing left [of us even] to comfort." Xi replied, "Since we did not know the news of [what had happened to] the *chanyu*, we captured twelve Xiongnu; upon questioning them, only then did we learn that you have been [just] beyond the Tang border for several months. Liu Mian, Vice-Director of the Department of State Affairs in Hedong, ordered me to bring ten camel-loads of goods and provisions to deliver to the princess, the *chanyu*, and the chief ministers. He also sent an imperial edict commanding that if you are able to move southward, then it will be easy to aid those who are in need. Now your tribe is quite far [from the border]. Since [the situation] is like this, how could we have known of your thirst and hunger?" The minister said, "People are unable to comprehend legalities [when they are in such dire straits]. Recently we were starving to death and had no alternative, and so we committed offenses [against the Tang]. Certainly you have come today because of this, to mislead and kill us." He then pushed Xi out of the tent, ordered foot-soldiers with crossbows to encircle him, and said, "If you do not disclose the [actual] facts [of your coming here], they will shoot to kill!"

Xi said, "In truth, my nation ordered me to welcome you and show pity to you. If you believe me, then go [southward]; if you doubt me, then why not leave this place? For you foreigners, it will be too late for regrets! What benefit would there be in mistreating me now?" The minister said, "If we leave, what regrets can we have?" Xi said, "The *chanyu*, who is a great foreign [leader], is a relative of the Tang [imperial house].[11] There is [between them] the kindness of uncle and nephew, and the strength of mutual reliance. If you have suffered ruin, it is only fitting that you come to the Tang. But if you enter [the territories of] the various petty foreign peoples and are held in contempt by those petty foreigners, how can this not be regretted?"

The minister then said, "We would go to the Tang now, but fear that your superiors will deceive us. If you truly welcome us and encourage us to come, then swear a weighty oath with us." Xi said, "Generally those who take an oath are anxious and so there are myriad complications. Xi's oath-taking is different from this." He then stretched out his hands in front of the minister and asked him to cut off his left hand at the wrist in order to take the oath. His complexion was unchanged and his speech was quite resolute. The minister did not agree [to cut off Xi's left hand] and said, "Now, if you will cut open [the flesh above] your heart for me so that blood comes forth, and then drink it yourself, this will suffice to earn my trust." Xi then let blood flow from [the flesh] above his heart into a vessel and swore an oath, saying, "If I duplicitously mislead you into entering the Tang border, then may Heaven strike me dead—boil me alive and mince me for pickling." After he had finished speaking, he drank all the blood that was in the vessel.

The Xiongnu then trusted him, and so shifted their camp to the valleys and mountains of the frontier north of Yunzhou, sixty tricents[12] eastward from the government army. Later they were again deceitful and, saying they were going hunting, raided and plundered Zhenwu. They did not profit from being led to come [to Tang territory].

Xi had been at the savages' court for many days and feared that he would not be able to return home, so he lied to the *chanyu,* saying to him that at Yunzhou and Shuozhou he would obtain more goods and provisions for the foreigners. Therefore he was then able to return home. He told Mian everything: how he had enticed the Xiongnu to approach the border, how the Xiongnu recently had plundered Zhenwu so that their troops returning [from the raid] were wearied and worn, and also how they had made no preparations [for battle] because the Tang [imperial] family welcomed them. [He added that] if Mian would obtain the princess, he certainly should take advantage of the moment and go quickly.

Mian agreed and ordered his high-ranking military officers Shi Xiong, Wang Feng, and others all to go with Xi to the *chanyu's* camp. They surrounded it and soundly defeated [the Xiongnu].[13] Xi rushed into the camp and helped the princess onto a horse. They came out ten odd paces; [Xi] feared that the government army would not know them and would injure them by mistake, and so shouted, "This is the princess!" Shi Xiong heard him and secured them with thirty foot-soldiers. The princess was sent to Hedong, and the whole of the affair was ascribed to Liu Mian. Furthermore, [Mian] had written Xi's name in a letter, which he promised to make known to the emperor, and also said to Army Supervisor Lü Yizhong, "If not for Cai Xi, I would not have come back alive!" His [merit] thus was known [to many involved in the incident]. But when the princess was returned to the capital, Mian was elevated to [the rank of] Minister of Works and Shi Xiong was appointed Defense Commissioner of the Tiande Army. Only Xi was not made a high official. The chief commander(s) who knew of [his role] did not memorialize to the throne about it, and also the princess ultimately was unable to speak of it. [Xi's] achievements and strategies subsequently were obscured and were not made known. And yet the destruction of the Xiongnu by [the forces of] Hedong and the settling and clearing of the border dust up to now had their origins in the strength of Xi's strategies.

In the third year[14] of the Huichang period [3 February 843–23 January 844], Liu Zhen seized Shangdang in rebellion. At Taiyuan, Yang Bian took advantage of the situation and disobeyed orders, and [soon] was captured. In the fourth year [of the Huichang period, January 24, 844–February 10, 845], Shangdang was pacified. Now it is the fourth year of the [current] Emperor's Dazhong reign period [February 16, 850–February 4, 851], and the Tanguts[15] of Nanshan have rebelled. From the second year of the Huichang period[16] until the present, Xi has performed meritoriously in all punitive military expeditions. His achievements all have been noted in the records of Hedong. And when the Xiongnu were defeated, he was foremost in the attainment of merit. But this was closed off from the ears [of the emperor] by others. Up until the present there are none among the high military officers of his division and regiment who do not praise his wisdom and bravery.

I, Li Qi, say that he is great! His merit and name have been obscured; it has been altogether this way. But when the ancients said that "one's rank can be set, but one's fame cannot be taken away," it is as though they were speaking of Cai Xi. Can it be taken away from him, or can it not? At first, from the capital (i.e., Chang'an) to Luo[yang], I heard [nothing but] talk greatly praising the merit of Liu [Mian] and Shi [Xiong] in the defeat of the savages. When I reached Taiyuan and heard of Cai Xi, only then did I realize that I had been misled by [others having been] elevated instead of him. I grieve that his meritorious service and eminence still can be suppressed. Does he not have [outstanding] abilities? I consider his diligence, which has been without profit, and for this reason have investigated the matter completely and written an account to tell of it.

Li Deyu, "A Letter to the Kirghiz Qaghan"

The emperor respectfully inquires after the Kirghiz Qaghan. The summer days are lengthening; We hope that the Qaghan is resting peacefully. We soothingly approach the myriad realms and nourish the people [there] as Our own children, thinking to bring about harmony and effect the utmost probity.

General Tabuhezu and the others have arrived. We have inspected your petition. We fully understand that the Qaghan was born in a place under the Great Dipper and lives in a rustic land of frosty dew. In intelligence and strategy you are keen and effective; your abilities and determination are serenely heroic. Your majesty moves the northern regions; your fame has quickly reached the gate of the imperial palace. We admire your great achievements, which deepen Our regard for you.

The sacred virtue of Our [ancestor], Emperor Taizong, was greater than that of a hundred kings; his bravery and talent surpassed those of a thousand ancients. Within, he stabilized all the Chinese; without, he gained the submission of the hundred barbarians. In the fourth year of the Zhenguan reign period (February 18, 630–February 6, 631), the chieftains of the foreigners to the northwest came to his court and kowtowed, requesting that the emperor assume the honored title of "Heavenly Qaghan." After that, an official imperial pronouncement was issued [to the effect that] all the chieftains of the foreigners to the northwest were to call the emperor "Heavenly Qaghan." His governance of the barbarians of the four [directions] really began from this.

In the sixth year of the Zhenguan reign period (January 27, 632–February 13, 633), Taizong sent the envoy Wang Yihong to the Qaghan's own nation with an order that it be pacified. In the twenty-first year of the Zhenguan reign period (February 10, 647–January 29, 648), the chieftain of the Qaghan's own nation came to court in person, and Taizong conferred upon him the titles of General of the Left Encampment Guards and Governor-general of the Kirghiz. His tribute came to the court uninterruptedly until the end of the Tianbao reign period.[17]

Thus, the Qaghan's ancestors already received Our nation's grace and virtue. Surely in the Qaghan's nation there are persons surviving from former times who have passed down this [information] themselves. We [now respectfully] receive and carry on [Taizong's] great plan, thinking to extend our previous good [relations].

Recently We heard that after the Tianbao reign period you were cut off [from China] by the Uyghurs, who long hindered your sincere [intentions]. The Uyghurs called themselves the favorites of Heaven and did not cultivate humanity or righteousness. Their reckless actions were cruel, and they oppressed all the foreign peoples. We know that the [Kirghiz] *qaghan*s have been their enemies for generations, and [now] you have actually taken revenge, destroying their capital city and completing [your revenge] by establishing yourself as sovereign and expelling the Uyghur leaders, who have all crossed over the desert.[18] In recent times your flourishing merit and strong principles are without equal.

At the time when China was chastising rebels,[19] the Uyghurs meritoriously displayed their power. Successive emperors commended their great compliance and repeatedly favored them by forming marriage relations [with them]. Recently they lost their nation and fled, lodging at our border. At the [very] least they should have come [to Us] early in their humble sincerity, to receive Our soothing touch. Yet they acted violently, increasingly harboring wolfish intentions. Beyond the Yin Mountains, they beguiled the smaller foreign [tribes]; catching us off guard, they came to raid and plunder. They threw off restraint and afflicted our border for four years.

We levied armored troops on a large scale and long wished to eradicate them. We recently ordered the military governors of the two circuits of Youzhou and Taiyuan to serve as pacifying [commissioners] in order to display Our comforting affection. [In doing so,] We hoped that [the Uyghurs] would be penitent, and We still considered it important to be lenient and nurturing. But they treated the [Taihe] Princess with contempt and repeatedly intended to injure Us. Galloping suddenly toward Our border cities, they dared to plot robbery and thievery.

Recently Liu Mian, military governor of Taiyuan, could no longer control his anger and secretly sent out a detachment of troops [to attack the Uyghurs]. Taking advantage of their self-delusion, he made a surprise attack on their camp. The barbarian horde was greatly vanquished, and their vaulted tents were completely burned. This great evil has been maimed and has run away into hiding. We have already retrieved the Taihe Princess and brought her back to court.[20]

The surviving Uyghur troops, which do not even number a full thousand, have scattered for safety into the mountain valleys. They could certainly be seized within ten days. When I see the Princess once again, I am most deeply satisfied [by this turn of events]. Since the Qaghan is already [the Uyghurs'] enemy, it is imperative that you destroy these barbarians completely. If embers are left burning, they certainly will give rise to calamity later. We consider that when those far away have heard of this, they will be contented and at ease.

We have heard how the Qaghan originally received Our family name and became of Our own clan. The Governor of [You]beiping, [Li Guang][21] of the Han dynasty, was unequaled on earth in ability. In early adulthood he managed border affairs, and his skill in archery was such that [his arrow] could pierce a stone. After him, many of his sons and grandsons studied military strategy; for generations his was a family of commanders, down to [Cavalry] Commander [Li Ling],[22] his direct descendant through his primary wife. [Li Ling] led five thousand picked troops and penetrated deep into the great desert. The [Xiongnu] *chanyu* mobilized his entire nation to counter this, but none dared resist his awesomeness. Although he fell into [misfortune], his name terrifies the barbarians to the south and north.

Our nation has continued as descendants of the Governor of [You]beiping, and the Qaghan is a descendant of the [Cavalry] Commander.[23] Because of this, we are of the same clan, and our respectful relationship is evident. We recently heard that the Taihe Princess was rescued by some of the Qaghan's soldiers. Since our nations are of the same surname, the Qaghan sent her to be returned [to Us]. It is clear from this that the Qaghan adheres firmly to his proper and righteous heart, and stresses the goodness of loving his neighbors. We are deeply moved to sigh [in admiration], even to the point of weeping. It pains Us greatly to recall how the Princess subsequently was kidnapped by the Uyghurs and [so] for a long time could not return and how the official escorts sent by the Qaghan were all massacred. [Whenever] We think [of what happened], We are grievously pained. To this day We have not forgotten this.

We recently saw in the Qaghan's petition your inquiry after the Princess, [in which it was said that] even if the Princess had ascended to Heaven or entered the Earth, you certainly would find her. Now, out of outrage and alarm, the border general [Liu Mian] already has performed this meritorious service. The [captured] Uyghur criminals will arrive any day now, whereupon they will be executed to show Our gratitude to the Qaghan. How much more imperative it is that the [remaining] barbarian Uyghur tribes be completely annihilated! Then We will be neighboring nations with the Qaghan, and each will preserve his former border. Our good [relations] will continue, the people will be at ease, and our affairs will be conjoined as though of one body. After this, alarums along the borders will cease; bows and arrows will be sheathed. Certainly the various tribes will follow [this example], hoping for their own well-being. Knowing that our two nations will forever have a close alliance, they will believe that the Qaghan is wise and of course has calculated well.

Therefore, We have ordered President of the Court of the Imperial Stud and Vice-president of the Tribunal of Censors Zhao Fan to serve as the envoy carrying the emblems of Imperial insignia, as a response of deep sincerity. We pledge before the gods to preserve the great trust [between our two nations]. Our words are not duplicitous. Surely We need urge you no further.

Moreover, since ancient times, [leaders of] outlying peoples all have required documents of appointment from China[24] before they could control a region. Now We wish to bestow such on the Qaghan and specially add a fine title. But since We do not know the Qaghan's wishes, and moreover have been [concerned here with] expressing Our feelings, We will wait until the day Zhao Fan returns to order another envoy to carry out those formalities, thereby extending [Our wishes for] friendly relations.

We also [wish to] inquire after [the health of] the generals and ministers of your nation. [To facilitate] the dispatch of this missive, We do not address their large number here.

—MRD

Notes

1. This appointment was made ca. October 835.

2. The appointment was made in May 842.

3. That is, the Uyghurs. The Xiongnu, who rose to power at about the same time as China's Qin dynasty, were the first strong northern nomadic empire to threaten China. Therefore, Xiongnu-Chinese relations established many models for later Chinese relations with foreign peoples. It is not clear why Li Qi chose to use this archaic terminology, which is seen in many other sources as well, save for its "literary" quality (not uncommon at this time), or perhaps a desire to stigmatize the Uyghurs.

4. Here, and in a few other places where he is quoted, Cai Xi uses his given name *(ming)* to refer to himself.

5. The Taihe princess was the daughter of the Tang emperor Xianzong (r. 805–820), and the maternal aunt of Emperor Wuzong. She had been married to an Uyghur ruler in March or April 821.

6. Probably November or December 842.

7. Liu Mian was appointed Uyghur Pacification Commissioner in October 842.

8. Approximately seventy miles (113 kilometers).

9. *Chanyu* was the title of the Xiongnu ruler; the Uyghur ruler was called *qaghan*.

10. *Tarqan* was indeed an official rank of the Uyghurs, and so is the only Inner Asian term used correctly in this source.

11. That is, by marriage.

12. Approximately twenty miles (thirty kilometers).

13. In February 843.

14. The text has "second year" (February 14, 842–February 2, 843), but this is an error, as Liu Zhen's rebellion occurred in the third year of the Huichang period.

15. The Tanguts were a people who spoke a language related to Tibetan. After conflicts with other peoples, they settled in the Ordos region of North China in the ninth century, where they were under Tang rule. Later, in the early eleventh century, they established an independent state called Xia (also called Xi Xia [Western Xia]) in that same area; that state was destroyed in the thirteenth century by the Mongols.

16. See note 14 above.

17. The Tianbao reign period lasted from February 10, 742, to August 11, 756.

18. Some Uyghurs fled to China, others to Manchuria, and still others to the regions of Gansu and the Tarim Basin. Their migration into the Tarim region is particularly important, bringing significant change to that area's ethnic composition.

19. This refers to the An Lushan Rebellion.

20. The Taihe Princess arrived at the Chinese court on March 29, 843.

21. Li Guang (d. 119 B.C.E.) was a famous Han-era general whose family had been distinguished for generations for their martial abilities. He spent much of his life campaigning against the Xiongnu and held the title of Governor *(taishou)* of Youbeiping, located in the northeastern frontier region of the Han empire (in the northeast corner of modern Hebei). The name of the commandery of Youbeiping was shortened to Beiping (Northern Peace) after the Han period; hence the use of this truncated form in this document. Li Guang's life was considered of sufficient significance to be recounted in two famous Han histories, the *Shiji* of Sima Qian and the *Hanshu* of Ban Gu.

22. Li Ling (d. 74 B.C.E.) was Li Guang's grandson; although referred to in this text simply as "commander" *(duwei),* his proper title was as given. While campaigning, Li Ling was captured by the Xiongnu in 99 B.C.E. and lived among them for the rest of his days.

23. The Tang imperial house of Li claimed Li Guang as one of its ancestors. As for the connection between Li Ling and the Kirghiz, it was reported that after his capture by the Xiongnu, Li Ling was appointed by them as an officer over the Kirghiz. According to Chinese sources, some Kirghiz (apparently including this *qaghan*) considered themselves descendants of Li Ling and his troops.

24. The term used here is "Zhongguo" (Middle Kingdom).

IN 843 C.E., a war broke out between the dispersed Uyghurs, whose empire had collapsed in 840 (see selection 55), and the Tang. Subsequently, the Tang regime under Wuzong confiscated the property of the Manichaean monasteries, ostensibly because of a close connection between the Turkic Uyghurs of Inner Asia and the Manichaean religion from West Asia. This event actually initiated a general persecution of all foreign religions in China two years later. Nestorian Christianity and Zoroastrianism were wiped out, the Nestorian church returning to China only after the Mongol invasion. Manichaeanism and Zoroastrianism survived underground and only in remote areas. Buddhism, which received the brunt of the attack, not only survived in the core region of the Tang regime but also revived soon after Wuzong's reign. This account from the *Old Tang History (Jiu Tangshu), juan* 18A provides some clues as to why it was so difficult to eradicate Buddhism and explains how this Indian religion was so deeply rooted in China.—XRL, VHM

On the *gengzi* day in the seventh month of autumn (August 31, 845), the emperor (Wuzong) issued an edict to restrict the numbers of Buddhist monasteries under heaven (i.e., in the empire). The Secretariat Chancellery submitted a memorial to the throne:

According to the rules and statutes of the law *(ling, shi)*, officers of superior prefectures should perform the ceremony of burning incense in temples on anniversaries of ancestor emperors. Therefore, may Your Majesty allow one monastery in every superior prefecture wherein all the statues of sacred figures could be sheltered; monasteries in inferior prefectures should be closed. Please allow ten monasteries on the two major streets of both Chang'an (Shangdu [the Upper Capital]) and Luoyang (Dongdu [the Eastern Capital]) to stay, with ten monks allowed to remain in each monastery.

His Majesty issued an imperial order which said:

It is fitting that monasteries be allowed to remain in superior prefectures, but only those of fine workmanship may stay. Those that are dilapidated, though located in superior prefectures, should also be closed and torn down. On anniversaries when incense is to be burned, it is appropriate for officials to carry out the rituals at Taoist temples. Two monasteries are allowed to stay on each of the [two main] streets in both the Upper Capital (Chang'an) and the Lower Capital (Luoyang), and thirty monks are allowed to remain in each monastery. On the Left Street of the Upper Capital, Ci'en Monastery and Jianfu Monastery may stay. On the Right Street, Ximing Monastery and Zhuangyan Monastery may stay.

The Secretariat submitted another memorial to the throne:

As most of the monasteries under heaven are to be closed, bronze statues, bells, and gongs should be handed over to the Salt and Iron Monopoly Commissioner to be cast into coins; iron statues should be handed over to prefectures where the monasteries are located and cast into agricultural tools. Gold, silver, and brass statues and statues of other materials should be melted down for government expenditure. All the gold, silver, bronze, and iron statues in the homes of nobles *(yiguan)* and commoners *(shishu)* must be turned over to the government offices within one month after this edict is issued. Those who do not obey this order should be punished by the Ministry of the Salt and Iron Monopoly Commissioner according to the "Law of Banning Possession of Bronze." Statues made of clay, wood, and stone are allowed to remain in the monasteries as before.

The Secretariat again submitted a memorial to the throne:

Monks and nuns should not be administered by the Ministry of Sacrifices *(cibu)*. They should be administered by the Court of State Ceremonial *(honglusi)*.[1] As Buddhist monasteries are banned, other heterodox religions such as the Roman church (Nestorian church) and Zoroastrian shrines should not be allowed either. Staff of these religious institutions should be ordered to return to secular life and to their home places as taxpayers. The foreigners of those religious institutions should be returned to their proper places to be administered.

In the eighth month, a decree was issued:

I, the sovereign, have heard that, in the Three Dynasties (Xia, Shang, and Zhou) period of antiquity, there was no mention of Buddhism. Only after the Han and the Wei dynasties did the doctrine of images[2] gradually arise. Thus, the propagation of this strange custom started in that late time and, in accord with the circumstances,[3] has tainted our practices, spreading and multiplying. It has developed to the extent that, though it eats away at our national customs, we no longer notice; it seduces people and makes them confused. It has penetrated to mountains and plains all over the empire and within the city walls of the two capitals. The number of monks daily increases, and monasteries are growing in grandeur. Buddhist construction projects cost much human labor, while monastic ornaments of gold and other treasures deprive society of much benefit. Religious teachers have come to replace rulers and fathers; monastic discipline separates husband and wife. No other religion is more harmful to the law and human relations than Buddhism. Furthermore, when one farmer is not cultivating the land, there must be someone starving as a result; when one woman is not raising silkworms, there must be someone shivering in the cold.

At the present moment, there are innumerable monks and nuns under heaven who wait for farmers to feed them and women to clothe them. Temples and monasteries have been constructed extravagantly tall and ostentatiously ornamented, defying regulations and daring to imitate the style of royal palaces. During the Jin, Song, Qi, and Liang dynasties, these practices caused the depletion of material wealth and labor and the deterioration of moral standards. Moreover, my ancestors Gaozu and Taizong pacified turmoil through military force and administered China with a civil system. These two instruments are quite sufficient for running the country. How can this trivial religion from the west contend with our state structure! During the eras of Zhenguan (627–649) and Kaiyuan (713–742), there were also efforts to eliminate Buddhism. However, the eradication was not thorough, thus its influence became even greater. I, the sovereign, after broadly surveying what has been discussed in previous times and seeking out current opinion, realize that whether this corrupt practice can be eliminated depends on determination. Meanwhile, all the loyal officers inside or outside the court who assist me wholeheartedly have submitted appropriate recommendations to me, saying that the reform should be enforced. Why should I avoid this action, which will block the origin of evil that has prevailed for a thousand years, protect the integrity of the royal code enacted by a hundred kings, and benefit all the people?

When the 4,600 and more major monasteries under heaven are demolished, 260,500 monks and nuns will return to secular life to become taxpayers in the Double Tax system;[4] when more than 40,000 small monasteries and temples are demolished, several million hectares of fertile land will be confiscated, and 150,000 male and female slaves will become taxpayers in the Double Tax system. The remaining monks and nuns are to be placed under the supervision of the Bureau of Receptions (for Foreign Guests) (Zhuke), thus the fact that Buddhism is a religion for foreigners will be made obvious. The 3,000 and more followers of Christianity and Zoroastrianism are ordered to return to secular life to maintain the purity of Chinese mores.

Oh! It seems as though that which has not been carried out in the past is about to become true! How can one claim that those institutions will never be eliminated when they are completely gone? More than 100,000 idle and lazy persons have already been driven out of monasteries; thousands and thousands of those useless, colorful houses have been demolished. From now on, our motto is to be quiet and pure, and our model is to follow the principle of nonaction.[5] Our administration should be simple and efficient, following only one style. All the people of the country should be subjects of the empire. As this is the beginning of the reform, there is no known omen, so I have issued this edict clarifying matters to the court in order to make you understand my intention. . . .

On *jiachen* day in the eleventh month (December 3, 845), the emperor issued an edict:

Because monks and nuns have returned to secular life, no one is in charge of the lands for charity and houses for sick people. I am afraid the crippled and the sick will have no food supply. The two capitals should provide monasteries with a suitable amount of charity lands. Every prefecture and superior prefecture should set aside [approximately] seventeen to twenty-five acres (seven to ten hectares) and select an elder local to manage them, in order to make grain available for porridge (for the poor).

—XRL, VHM

Notes

1. It is significant that the Court of State Ceremonial was that branch of the Tang government charged with foreign relations.

2. "Doctrine of images" is a technical term referring to the second stage in the development of Buddhism, but here it is used loosely to signify Buddhism in general.

3. The emperor here uses another Buddhist technical term, *yinyuan* (Skt. *hetupratyaya*), ironically showing how the alien religion influenced even his own style.

4. The "Double Tax" was a taxation system established around 780 C.E. In this new system, taxes were calculated according to the number of laborers and the amount of property owned by the taxpaying household, not purely on the number of households as in the previous system. Taxes were collected twice a year after the harvests of the summer and autumn; thus it was called "Double Tax."

5. It is interesting that Wuzong here prescribed the Taoist notion of *wuwei* (nonpurposive action; not doing anything against nature). The Tang royal house had a fondness for Taoism because its very common surname, Li, happened to be the same as that of the supposed founder of the religion, Lao Zi. A further irony is that, although their surname can ostensibly be traced back through Li Gao (d. 417), founder of the Western Liang kingdom (400–421) in Gansu, to Li Guang (d. 125 B.C.E.), the Western Han general who also hailed from Gansu, the Tang royal family was of at least half northern, non-Sinitic blood.

THIS CELEBRATED ESSAY is the first of six sections that make up the enormously influential *Lofty Appeal of Forests and Streams (Linquan gaozhi ji)*. The text is generally accepted as reflecting the views of the great Northern Song landscape artist Guo Xi (1020?–1100?). However, the fact that Guo Xi's son, Guo Si (d. after 1123), compiled the work and that it did not begin to circulate until more than twenty years after his father's death has led some to doubt whether it was actually written entirely by Guo Xi himself. Nonetheless, Guo Si was surely the most competent spokesman for his father's ideas. His editing and the known contemporary publication of parts of the text guarantee the genuineness of the opinions expressed therein.

Guo Xi and Guo Si were both from Wenxian in Heyang (Henan Province). When he was young, the father painted in detailed fashion, particularly scenes of wintry forests. As he grew older, his brushwork became increasingly strong, and he did large-scale screens or murals. He served as an artist-in-apprenticeship in the Academy of Calligraphy under Shenzong (r. 1067–1085) and was appointed artist-in-attendance. Guo Xi considered his best work to be four scrolls of landscape with weathered rocks presented to the Confucian temple at Wenxian after his son Si had passed his middle-level examinations. Around 1085 he painted twelve large screens of landscape subjects for an important Taoist temple. A Taoist approach to nature is evident in *Linquan gaozhi*.

Guo Si, who passed the coveted *jinshi* (Advanced Scholar) degree of the civil service examinations in 1082, was said to have elevated his family through his studies. He served as an official in such posts as provincial administrator in the region of Shaanxi, and in 1117 was appointed Scholar attached to the Longtu Pavilion in the Imperial Archives. Huizong (r. 1110–1125) once ordered him to illustrate the *Classic of Mountains and Seas (Shanhai jing)*. Nonetheless, in the opinion of his contemporaries, although he had a deep understanding of painting, he could not make a name by it. On becoming an official, he began to collect his father's works, and he also edited and supplemented his father's painting manual, the first section of which is presented here. The fine literary quality of *Linquan gaozhi* is thought to result largely from the polishing and supplementing of Guo Si.—JH, VHM, SB, HYS

I. Of what does a gentleman's love of landscape consist? The cultivation of his fundamental nature in rural retreats is his frequent occupation. The carefree abandon of mountain streams is his frequent delight. The secluded freedom of fishermen and woodmen is his frequent enjoyment. The flight of cranes and the calling of apes are his frequent intimacies. The bridles and fetters of the everyday world are what human nature constantly abhors. Transcendents and sages in mist are what human nature constantly longs for and yet is unable to see. It is simply that, in a time of peace and plenty, when the intentions of ruler and parents are high-minded, purifying oneself is of little significance, and office-holding is allied to honor. Can anyone of humanitarian instinct then tread aloof or retire afar in order to practice a retreat from worldly affairs? And, if so, will he necessarily share the fundamental simplicity of (legendary recluses such as Xu You, associated with) Mount Ji and the River Ying, or participate in the lingering renown of (the Han dynasty's) Four Old Men of Mount Shang?[1] Their songs, such as the ode on "The White Pony" and the hymn to "The Purple Fungus,"[2] are all about those who had no alternative but to go into reclusion. Yet, are the longing for forests and streams, and the companionship of mists and vapors then to be experienced only in dreams and denied to the waking senses?

It is now possible for subtle hands to reproduce them in all their rich splendor. Without leaving the mat in your room, you may sit to your heart's content among streams and valleys. The voices of apes and the calls of birds will fall on your ears faintly. The glow of the mountain and the color of the waters will dazzle your eyes glitteringly. Could this fail to quicken your interest and thoroughly capture your heart? This is the ultimate meaning behind the honor which the world accords to landscape painting. If this aim is not principal and the landscape is approached with a trivial attitude, it is no different from desecrating a divine vista and polluting the clear wind.

There is a proper way to paint a landscape. When spread out on an ambitious scale it should still have nothing superfluous. Restricted to a small view it should still lack nothing. There is also a proper way to look at landscapes. Look with a heart in tune with forest and stream, then you will value them highly. Approach them with the eyes of arrogance and extravagance, then you will value them but little. Landscapes are vast things. You should look at them from a distance. Only then will you see on one screen the sweep and atmosphere of mountain and water. Figure paintings of gentlemen and ladies done on a miniature scale, if held in the hand or put on the table, may be taken in at one glance as soon as they are opened. These are the methods of looking at paintings.

It is generally accepted opinion that in landscape there are those through which you may travel, those in which you may sightsee, those through which you may wander, and those in which you may live. Any paintings attaining these effects are to be considered excellent, but those suitable for traveling and sightseeing are not as successful an achievement as those suitable for wandering and living. Why is this? If you survey present-day scenery, in a hundred miles of land to be settled, only about one out of three places will be suitable for wandering or living, yet they will certainly be selected as such. A gentleman's thirst for forests and streams is due precisely to such places of beauty. Therefore, it is with this in mind that a painter should create and a critic should examine. This is what we mean by not losing the ultimate meaning.

II. Painting also has its laws of physiognomy. The descendants of Li Cheng[3] flourished in large numbers, and all his foothills and ground areas were substantial and generous; outstanding above and abundant below, they corresponded to the indications of progeny. This is not merely in accord with physiognomy, but with general principles (of development) as well.

When you learn to paint, it is no different from learning calligraphy. If you select as models calligraphers such as Zhong You, Wang Xizhi, Yu Shinan, or Liu Gongquan,[4] after long study you should certainly achieve some similarity. As for great masters and understanding scholars, they do not restrict themselves to one school, but must select from many for comparison, and discuss widely to investigate on a broad basis in order to achieve their own style eventually. At present, artists in Qi and Lu (modern Shandong Province) work exclusively in Li Cheng's style, and artists of Guan and Shaan (modern Shaanxi) work exclusively in Fan Kuan's[5] style. Though they study all by themselves, they slavishly imitate others. Moreover, [the areas between] Shandong and Shaanxi extend for several thousand tricents, yet prefecture after prefecture, district after district, person after person they do this! Exclusive specialization has always been a fault. It is just like someone who plays but one tune and will not listen to anyone else. He cannot blame those who will not listen to him. Judging from evidence of the past, an experience common to all mankind is that human senses delight in what is new and are wearied by what is old. Hence, I consider the fact that great masters and understanding scholars do not restrict themselves to one school to be a similar phenomenon.

III. There is a good discussion on the art of writing by Liu Zihou[6] that, in my opinion, applies not only to writing. Every matter has its secret of success. Since it is the same for everything else, all the more should it not be so for painting? How can one express it? Each scene in a painting, regardless of size or complexity, must be unified through attention to its essence. If the essence is missed, the spirit will lose its integrity. The artist must complete the painting with the spirit in every part. If he does not complete it with the spirit in every part, the essence will not be clear. The artist must accord his work solemn respect. If he is not solemn, his thought will have no depth. He must be scrupulously careful throughout. If he is not scrupulous, the scene will seem unfinished.

If the creative energy that you gather is listless and you force it, the results will be insipid and indecisive. The fault is that of not attending to the essence. If your energy is dulled and you use it distractedly, the appearance will be crude and lifeless. The defect is that of not completing the painting with the spirit in every part. If you light-heartedly trifle with the subject, its forms will be summary and inadequate. The defect is that of not according solemn dignity. If you rudely disregard the subject, its construction will be careless and not cohesive. The defect is that of not being scrupulously careful.

Therefore, if indecisive, a work will offend the canon of proportion. If lifeless, it will offend the canon of refreshing purity. If it is inadequate, it will offend the canon of composition. If not cohesive, it will offend the canon of alternating rhythm. These are the gravest failings of artists, yet they can serve as a guide for the intelligent.

In the past I often saw my late father working on several paintings. Sometimes he would put one aside and ignore it. For perhaps ten or twenty days he would not give it a glance, but would repeatedly contemplate it. This was a case of having intention but lacking desire. Is not this having intention but lacking desire the listless energy he mentioned? Then again, whenever he was working at a peak of interest, he would completely forget about everything else. When his concentration was disturbed by even a single external interruption, he would put his work aside and ignore it. Is not this putting aside and ignoring the dulled energy he mentioned?

Each day he put his brush to work, he would sit by a bright window at a clean table. To left and right were lighted incense. He would lay out a fine brush and ink, wash his hands, and clean the ink-slab as though he were receiving a major guest. His spirit at ease and his intention settled, only then did he proceed. Is this not exactly what he said about not daring to trifle light-heartedly? Once the composition was laid out, he would work through it in detail. Once the painting was built up, he would add the enriching shades of ink. Though the first time seemed enough, he would work over it again. And though the second time might seem enough, he would work over it yet again. Every painting would be reworked several times from start to finish, and he would be alert as though on guard against some insidious enemy until it was done. Is this not exactly what he said about not daring to rudely disregard the subject? Whatever task you care to mention, no matter large or small, it can only thus be properly concluded. If my late father so often repeated this advice in different fashions, was it not to teach me to honor it to the end of my life, taking it as the way of progressive self-cultivation?

IV. Someone learning to paint flowers puts a plant into a deep hole to look at it from above. This shows the flowers fully in the round. Someone learning to paint bamboos selects one branch as the moonlight reflects its shadow on a plain white wall. This brings out its true form. Is there any difference in learning to paint a landscape? You must go in person to the countryside to discover it. The significant aspects of the landscape will then be apparent. To discover the overall layout of rivers and valleys in a real landscape, you look at them from a distance. To discover their individual characteristics, you look at them from nearby.

Clouds and vapors in a real landscape differ through the four seasons. They are genial in spring, profuse in summer, sparse in autumn, and somber in winter. If a painting shows the major aspect and does not create overly detailed forms, then the prevailing attitude of clouds and vapors will appear alive. Mists and haze [on mountains] in a real landscape differ through the seasons. Spring mountains are gently seductive and seem to smile. Summer mountains seem moist in their verdant hues. Autumn mountains are bright and clear, arrayed in colorful garments. Winter mountains are withdrawn in melancholy, apparently asleep. If a painting shows the major idea without distracting signs of technique, then the atmospheric conditions will seem correct.

Wind and rain in a real landscape can be grasped when seen from a distance. Near to, you may be fascinated by the motion but will be unable to examine the overall pattern in the confused flow. Shade and light in a real landscape can be comprehended if seen from a distance. From nearby your grasp will be narrowed, and you will not obtain a picture of what is hidden and what revealed by light and dark. On mountains, figures indicate paths and roads; lookout pavilions indicate scenic spots. On hills, vegetation is bright or shaded to differentiate respective distances; streams and valleys are cut short or continuous to differentiate depths of recession. On the water, fords, ferries, and various bridges hint at human activity; fishing skiffs and tackle hint at human interests.

A great mountain is dominating as chief over the assembled hills, thereby ranking in an ordered arrangement the ridges and peaks, forests and valleys as suzerains of varying degrees and distances. The general appearance is of a great lord glorious on his throne and a hundred princes hastening to pay him court, without any effect of arrogance or withdrawal [on either part]. A tall pine stands erect as the mark of all other trees, thereby ranking in an ordered arrangement the subsidiary trees and plants as numerous admiring assistants. The general effect is of a noble man dazzling in his prime with all lesser mortals in his service, without insolent or oppressed attitudes [on either part].

A tall pine standing erect is the manifestation of a host of trees. Its outward spreading indicates that it brings order to the vines, creepers, grasses, and trees, like the commander of an army bestirring those who rely on him. Its appearance resembles that of a ruler who majestically wins the approval of his age and is served by a host of lesser persons without bullying or intimidating them.

A mountain nearby has one aspect. Several tricents away it has another aspect, and ten or more tricents away yet another. Each distance has its particularity. This is called "the form of the mountain changing with each step." The front face of a mountain has one appearance. The side face has yet another appearance, and the rear face yet another. Each angle has its particularity. This is called "the form of a mountain viewed on every face." Thus can one mountain combine in itself the forms of several thousand mountains. Should you not explore this? Mountains look different in the spring and summer, the autumn and winter. This is called "the scenery of the four seasons is not the same." A mountain in the morning has a different appearance from the evening. Bright and dull days give further mutations. This is called "the changing aspects of different times are not the same." Thus can one mountain combine in itself the significant aspects of several thousand mountains. Should this not be investigated?

In spring mountains, mists and clouds stretch out unbroken, and people are full of joy. In summer mountains, fine trees offer profuse shade, and people are full of satisfaction. In autumn mountains, bright and clear leaves flutter and fall, and men are full of melancholy. In winter mountains, dark fogs dim and choke the scene, and men are full of loneliness. To look at a particular painting puts you in the corresponding mood. You seem, in fact, to be in those mountains. This is the mood of a painting beyond its mere scenery. You see a white path disappearing into the blue and think of traveling on it. You see the glow of setting sun over level waters and dream of gazing on it. You see hermits and mountain dwellers, and think of lodging with them. You see cliffside openings and streams over rocks, and long to wander there. To look at a particular painting puts you in the corresponding frame of mind, as though you were really on the point of going there. This is the wonderful power of a painting beyond its mere mood.

V. That mountains in the southeast are often strange and beautiful is not because the universe is especially partial to that area. The land there lies very low, and the floodwaters return through it, scouring out and exposing the subsurface. Thus the soil is thin and the waters are shallow. The mountains abound in strange peaks and precipitous cliffs, seeming to protrude far out beyond the stars. Waterfalls are a thousand feet high, plunging down from out of the clouds. The scarcity of cascades like that on Mount Hua[7] is not due to [mountains] not being a thousand feet high. But, even though there are solid and massive mountains, they mostly rise from the surface of the earth and not from its center.

That mountains of the northwest are often solid and massive is not because the universe particularly favors the area. The land there is very high, and full of water sources which are buried in the bulging contours of the earth. Hence the soil is thick and the waters are deep. The mountains have numerous piles of peaks, twisting through unbroken ranges of a thousand tricents or so. Great hills have summits and wind along to eminent heights in every direction of the wild terrain. The scarcity of mountains like the central Shaoshi peak of Mount Song[8] is not due to the lack of exceptional heights. But, even though there are peaks which thrust up to exceptional heights, they mostly rise from the center of the earth and not from its surface.

Mount Song has many fine streams; Mount Hua has many fine pinnacles; Mount Heng has many fine creviced peaks; Mount Chang has many fine ranges; Mount Tai has an especially fine main peak. Among the famous mountains and magnificent massifs of the empire are Tiantai, Wuyi, Lu, Huo, Yantang, Min, Emei, the Wu Gorges, Tiantan, Wangwu, Linlü, and Wudang. These are places where the treasures of heaven and earth are produced, where the caves and cottages of transcendents and sages lie hidden. Strange and towering, godlike in their beauty, their essential wonder cannot be fathomed.

If you wish to grasp their creation, there is no way more spiritual than love, no way finer than diligence, no way greater than wandering to your satiety or gazing to your fill. If all is ordered in detail in your bosom, your eye will not see the silk and your hand will be unaware of brush and ink, and through the clarity and distinctness, the depth and stillness [of your mind], everything will become your own painting. Thus did Huaisu[9] hear the nighttime waters of the Jialing River, and this sage of grass-writing achieved yet greater excellence. Thus did Lunatic Zhang[10] see the sword dance of Lady Gongsun, and the power of his brush became yet more noble.

VI. Those who wield a brush nowadays do not nourish that within to expansive fullness and do not examine that without to the point of thorough familiarity. What they experience is not comprehensive and what they discover is not quintessential. Yet, as soon as they find a piece of paper or clean off a patch of wall, they then fling down some ink quite unaware of how to pluck a scene from beyond misty reaches or to find inspiration atop stream-filled mountains. In my brash opinion, their faults can be enumerated.

What is meant by nourishing to expansive fullness? Recently a painter did a picture on the classic theme "A Benevolent Man Takes Pleasure in the Mountains," which had one old man sitting with chin in hand near a peak. In a picture on [the companion theme] "A Wise Man Takes Pleasure in the Water,"[11] he made one old man inclining in his ear before a cliff. These suffered from the fault of not reaching expansive fullness. The first theme should be depicted as in Bo Juyi's picture of his "thatched-lodge" retreat, which overflows with the mood of dwelling in the mountains. The second theme should be as in Wang Wei's picture of his estate along the Wang River, which has the pleasure of dwelling by water to the full.[12] How could the pleasure of wise or benevolent men be seen in one single figure?

What is meant by examining to the point of thorough familiarity? Artists of the present generation, when painting mountains, depict no more than four or five peaks. When painting water they depict no more than four or five waves. These suffer from the fault of not achieving thorough familiarity. In painting mountains, high and low, large and small, all should be appropriately harmonious or full to front and rear;[13] their heads should bow in due order and their limbs respond in perfect unison. The beauty of the mountains will then be satisfying. In painting water, be its surface regular or disturbed, curling in furious flight or drawn out in great stretches, its form should be natural and self-sufficient. The aspects of water will then be adequate.

What is meant by not having comprehensive experience? Painters of recent generations, if born in Wu or Yue, depict the protruding gauntness of the southeast. If they live in Xian or Qin (in Shaanxi), then they express the powerful breadth of the northwest. Those who study Fan Kuan lack the elegant charm of Li Cheng. Those who take Wang Wei as a teacher lack the structural power of Guan Tong.[14] In all these cases, their defect lies in not having comprehensive experience.

What is meant by not discovering the quintessential? A thousand-tricent stretch of mountains cannot be uniformly wondrous. A ten-thousand-tricent course of water cannot be uniformly attractive. The Taihang mountain range is pillowed against the Huaxia region, but its most eminent portion is at Linlu. Mount Tai bestrides the Qi and Lu (districts of Shandong), while its most remarkable scenery is at Longyan. If one were to paint everything in the whole sweep, how would that be different from a map? All works which do so suffer from the defect of not discovering the quintessential.

Thus, concentrating on slopes and banks leads to clumsiness. Concentrating on secluded retreats leads to insignificance. Concentrating on figures leads to vulgarity. Concentrating on lofty buildings leads to mundaneness. If you concentrate on stones, then the bones will show. If you concentrate on earth, then it will be over-fleshy. If brush-strokes are not blended together, they are called "coarse," and if coarse they lack true significance. If ink tones are not moist and rich, they are called "dried out," and if dry they lack vigor. Water that does not flow is said to be dead water; clouds that are not natural, to be frozen clouds. Mountains without light and dark areas are said to lack light effects; mountains without hidden and visible parts, to lack atmospheric haze. Since, on a mountain, where the sun shines it is light and where the sun does not shine it is dark, the constant form of a mountain is defined through light effects. Since, on a mountain, places which have atmospheric haze are hidden and places which do not are visible, the constant aspect of a mountain is defined by atmospheric haze. Hence, if hidden and visible areas are not distinguished, it is said to lack atmospheric haze.

VII. A mountain has the significance of a major object. Its form may rear up, may be arrogantly aloof. It may be lofty and broad, may sprawl. It may be vast and extensive, may be solid and bulky. It may be heroic and martial, may be sacred or awe-inspiring. It may glare down or hold court to its environment. It may be capped with further peaks or ride upon lesser slopes. It may have others which lean upon it in front or depend upon it in the rear. It may seem to gaze down from its eminence and survey the ground below. It may seem to wander down to direct its surroundings. Such are the major formations of mountains.

Water has the significance of a living object. Its form may be deep and peaceful, may be lithe and slippery. It may spread to the horizon or circle back again. It may be fat and oily, may spray out in a screen or shoot out like an arrow. It may have many sources and may flow into the distance. It may fall piercing the heavens or may splash and crash into the earth. It may bear anglers at their ease and may border happily murmuring foliage. It may embrace mists and clouds, elegant and enticing. It may shine in valleys and gorges, bright and splendrous. Such are the living formations of water.

A mountain has water as blood, foliage as hair, haze and clouds as its spirit and character. Thus, a mountain gains life through water, its adornment through vegetation, and its elegant charm through haze and clouds. Water has the mountain as its face, huts and pavilions as eyes and eyebrows, anglers as its soul. Thus, water gains its charm through the mountain, its vivacity through huts and pavilions, its ranging freedom through the anglers. Such is the interaction of mountain and water.

There are high mountains and low mountains. The arteries of the high mountain run low. Its frame opens wide; its foundation is powerful and solid. Ridge lines of rounded crests or creviced peaks crowd together and interweave in unbroken gleaming links. Such is a high mountain. Thus, this type of mountain is said to be "not isolated" and "not off-balance." The arteries of a low mountain run high. Its head comes halfway down, merging straight into its neck. The base spreads broadly, and earthen mounds bulge in profusion. It extends deep down into the earth; none can measure how far. Such is a low mountain. Thus, this type of mountain is said to be "not attenuated" and "not dispersed." If a high mountain is isolated, it is because its body is off balance. If a low mountain is attenuated, it is because its numinous energy has dispersed. Such are the configurations of mountain and water.

Rocks are nature's bones and, with bones, value is placed on their being strong and well covered, not poking through the surface. Water is nature's blood and, with blood, value is placed on its circulating and not congealing.

VIII. A mountain without haze and clouds is like spring without flowers and grass. If a mountain is without clouds, it is not refined; without water it is not charming. Without paths it is not living; without forests it is not growing. Without deep distance it seems shallow; without level distance it does not recede; and without high distance it stays low.

Mountains have three types of distance. Looking up to the mountain's peak from its foot is called the high distance. From in front of the mountain looking past it to beyond is called deep distance. Looking from a nearby mountain at those more distant is called the level distance. High distance appears clear and bright; deep distance becomes steadily more obscure; level distance combines both qualities. The effect of high distance is of lofty grandness. The idea of deep distance is of repeated layering. The idea of level distance is of spreading forth to merge into mistiness and indistinctness.

Figures in the three distances appear as follows. Those in the high distance are clear and distinct; in the deep distance they are fine and tiny; in the level distance they are remote and undisturbed. If they are clear and distinct then they cannot be short. If they are tiny then they cannot be tall. If they are remote then they cannot be large. Such are the three distances.

Mountains have three degrees of size. A mountain appears larger than a tree and a tree larger than a man. If a mountain is not dozens of times larger than a tree then it is not large at all. The tree which is not tens of times larger than a man is not large at all. In comparing the size of a tree against the size of a human figure, you begin with the leaves. In comparing the size of a human figure against a tree, you begin with the head. A number of leaves can be approximated to a human head. A human head can be made in the size of a bunch of leaves. The sizes of figures, trees, and mountains all acquire their standard in this manner. Such are the three degrees of size.

You may wish to make a mountain high, but if it is visible throughout its entirety it will not appear high. If mists enlock its waist, then it will seem high. You may wish the river to flow afar, but if it is visible throughout its entirety it will not appear long. If hidden sections interrupt its course, then it will appear long. If a mountain is visible in its entirety, not only will it no longer reach its height through soaring aloft, but you might as well paint a giant pestle. If a river is visible in its entirety, not only will it no longer go afar through twisting and bending, but you might as well paint an earthworm.

The streams and hills, woods and trees in the center twist and wind, and come forward as you set forth the scenery. If you do not suppress these details, they will satisfy the viewer's nearby scrutiny. The level plains and lofty ranges to the sides are linked together in successive layers and disappear into misty obscurity. If you do not suppress these distances, they will stretch to the utmost the beholder's far vision. "Distant mountains have no texture strokes; distant water has no waves; distant figures have no eyes."[15] They do not really lack them, but merely seem to do so.

—JH, VHM, SB, HYS

Notes

1. Xu You refused the throne when offered it by the mythical Emperor Yao. The "Four Old Men" or "Four Graybeards" retired from the world in protest against the Qin dynasty, but reemerged to support the rightful Han heir.

2. The ode on "The White Pony," poem no. 186 in the *Book of Odes (Shijing),* is about the pleasures of a leisurely visit with a treasured friend. "The Purple Fungus" is an old ballad associated with the "Four Graybeards" (see n. 1).

3. A famous painter of the Five Dynasties period (just before the Song dynasty) who was both admired and emulated by Guo Xi. Li's dates are 919–967.

4. The dates of these famous calligraphers of Han through Tang times are Zhong (151–230), Wang (322–ca. 379), Yu (558–638), and Liu (778–865).

5. A landscape master from Huayuan, Shaanxi, Fan (ca. 960–1030) himself followed Li Cheng, among others.

6. Liu Zongyuan (773–819) noted the dangers of a "trifling mind," an "indolent mind," "dulled energy," and "brash energy" in an essay on literature, "A Reply to Wei Zhongli Discussing the Way of a Teacher."

7. In Shaanxi, a northwestern province.

8. In Henan, a north-central province.

9. A poor Buddhist monk whose dates are 725–ca. 798.

10. Zhang Xu (d. 750), another master of "grass" (i.e., cursive) script.

11. These statements are attributed to Confucius in the *Analects,* 6.23.

12. Bo Juyi (772–846) and Wang Wei (701–761) are two of the most famous poets of the Tang dynasty.

13. These attributes of mountains are drawn directly from Mencius's description of the noble man (*Mencius,* 13.21).

14. A tenth-century painter who was famous for his autumn mountain scenery and paintings of forests in winter.

15. This quotation is from the "Discussion of Landscape" (Shanshui lun), attributed to the Tang poet Wang Wei (see n. 12); in slightly different versions, as "Rhapsody on Painting Landscape" (Hua shanshui fu), it is usually ascribed to the landscape painter and painting theorist Jing Hao (ca. 870–ca. 930). This protean text has at times also been attributed to Li Cheng (see n. 3).

SU SHI (STYLED Dongpo, 1037–1101) was a native of modern Sichuan. Though perhaps best known as a literary figure (he once compared his prodigious poetic output to water naturally pouring forth from a spring), he was also an important intellectual during the Song dynasty. His father, Su Xun (1009–1066), was a successful official in the Song civil service. Along with his younger brother, Su Che (1039–1112), Su Shi passed the civil service examinations in 1057. His career was marked by changing fortunes. While he was recognized by many as one of the leading minds of his day, others dismissed him as a mere litterateur; while he rose in the ranks of the bureaucracy due to his talent, he was also twice exiled for his political opinions that ran counter to the New Policies of the radical reformer Wang Anshi (1021–1086) and his followers. It is noteworthy that Su Shi here uses as his literary vehicle a genre that had long been employed in China to convey indirect criticism.

This piece was written by Su Shi for a friend who was hoping to pass the imperial examinations and gain official position. Su Shi's piece criticizes the contemporary fixation on studying poetry and the ideas of others for the sake of promotion, rather than studying to understand how the world works. Though Su held some common beliefs with other intellectuals of his day, his understanding of what constituted the Way (Dao) differed from many others. While in office he extolled Confucian values for governing, but he was personally drawn to Buddhism and Daoism. His eclectic approach to learning and his appreciation for literary creativity made him a proponent of individual paths to wisdom, rather than regimented approaches to social success and personal fulfillment.—RF

A person who was born blind did not know what the sun was. He asked the sighted about it. Someone told him, "The sun's form is like a bronze dish." [The blind man] knocked on a dish and heard its sound. Another day he heard a bell and took it to be the sun. Another person told him, "The sun's radiance is like a candle." [The blind man] grasped a candle and felt its form. Another day he felt a flute and took it to be the sun.

The difference between the sun and a dish or the sun and a flute is great, indeed, but the blind man did not know the difference. He sought from others what he had never seen. The difficulty of seeking the Way is even more extreme than [that of a blind man knowing] the sun, yet there is no difference between the blind man and others who have not understood the Way. When those who understand it inform them, even if they have a clever example and good lesson, it does not surpass the dish and candle. Is there any end to endless examples that cause us to get a bell from a pan and a flute from a candle? Therefore some of those who speak of the Way today define it based upon what they have seen, while others make abstractions based upon what they have not seen: these are both mistaken means for seeking the Way. This being so, is seeking the Way ultimately impossible?

Master Su[1] said, "The Way can be naturally developed, but cannot be sought." What do we mean by naturally developed? Sun Wu[2] said, "Those who are good at warfare develop other people and are not caused to develop by others." Zixia[3] said, "The various craftsmen live in the market in order to complete their affairs; the gentleman studies in order to realize (i.e., naturally develop) the Way." Not to seek it [from others], but to gain it oneself is precisely what we mean by realization (i.e., natural development).

There are many divers in the south who live with water every day. They are able to wade at age seven, to swim at ten, and to dive at fifteen. Now, is learning to dive something casual? There must first be those who understand the Way of water. If you live with water every day, then by the age of fifteen you will understand its Way; if you do not know water from birth, even when you are an adult you will fear boats. Therefore, when brave northerners ask the divers how they dive, if they go to a river and test what the divers have said, they always drown. Therefore not studying yet putting one's efforts into seeking the Way is always like the northerners studying diving.

The ancients used music and poetry to select literati, the literati studied various things and did not focus their will upon the Way. Now we use examinations to select literati, and the literati know about seeking the Way but do not exert effort in study. Mister Wu Yanlü of Bohai[4] has focused his will upon study. When he sought promotion in the Ministry of Rites, I wrote this "Parable of the Sun" to instruct him.

—RF

Notes

1. Probably Su Shi's father, Su Xun (1009–1066).
2. Author of the classical text on military strategy often translated under the title *The Art of War*. Believed to be a contemporary of Confucius in the sixth to fifth centuries B.C.E. See selection 17.
3. A disciple of Confucius.
4. Wu Yanlü was from Bohai, a coastal region on the border of modern Shandong and Hebei provinces. Wu served as an official in the prefectural Salt and Wine Monopoly offices in Xuzhou (in the northwest of modern Jiangsu Province) at the time that Su Shi was Xuzhou's prefect. The two often composed poetry together.

THIS IS A legend about how a silk-tapestry bag allegedly identified the missing brother, Li Yonghe (988–1050), of Emperor Renzong's (r. 1023–1063) mother, Li Chenfei (987–1032). Silk tapestry *(kesi)* became a refined art form during the Song dynasty (960–1279). However, its origin has caused much debate among textile historians. In this legend, the importance of the silk-tapestry bag's primary use as an accessory is superseded by its symbolic significance due to the famous personages associated with it. We can thus surmise the rarity of this novel weave at the time.—AS

[It is] recorded in *Notes of Eastern Pavilion (Dongxuan bi lu)* by Wei Tai (1050–1110) in the Song dynasty (960–1279) that when Empress Dowager Li (987–1032) first entered the imperial court, she was barely ten years old. She had [left behind] only one brother, who was seven years old at that time.[1] At the moment of parting, Empress Dowager Li gave [him] a handmade silk-tapestry bag with a strap. Hugging him and with tears [streaming down her face], she said, "Even if you should experience much hardship, ups and downs, you must not lose this bag. Later, if I should meet [good fortune], I will seek this bag to find you." With their sobs drowning her words, [they parted].

Thereafter, her brother [came to be] employed by a family in the business of making and cremating paper money for the dead. He strung this bag around his neck and wore it in front of his chest to keep the memory [of his sister] alive, never letting it leave his body. One day he suffered severe dysentery and was about to die. [His employer] abandoned him by the side of the road. [However,] a servant who worked in the imperial palace saw him, took pity, and adopted him. [This kind man] was puzzled by [the fact that though the sick young] man wore patched clothing, in front of his chest dangled this [splendid] bag with a strap. So [the kind man] asked about it, and the brother told him everything. When he heard the reply, the kind man was quite shocked. Apparently, he had been commissioned by the Empress Dowager to search for a bag like this to find her lost brother. The servant then again asked in detail about his surname, childhood name, and family history. Thereupon, he removed the bag and took it to the palace the next day to show the Empress Dowager and explained in full the circumstances [of how he had found it].

At that time, the Empress Dowager was awarded the title Chenfei (Imperial Consort), having just given birth to a boy, who became Emperor Renzong (b. 1008, r. 1023–1063), the sixth son of Emperor Zhenzong (r. 998–1022). [The Empress Dowager, as Imperial Consort,] was overcome with both grief and joy when she heard [about her brother]. She told Emperor Zhenzong the whole story. Emperor Zhenzong [then] awarded [her brother] the position of Palace Eunuch of the Right Duty Group.[2] This was [the story of] the one called Li Yonghe. After Renzong ascended the throne, he granted his mother posthumously the name of Zhangrui and, to glorify her family, promoted his uncle to become Commander-in-Chief of the Palace Command and

Infantry Armies in Charge of Weaponry, concurrently investing him with the symbols of Prince of the Longxi Prefecture.[3] Li Yonghe then became known as "Li, the Nation's Uncle."

—AS

Notes

1. They were natives of Hongzhou, and their father, Li Rende, served at court.
2. Because duties of this position were in the palace, it was given to individuals who had been castrated.
3. This prefecture was centered in the area of modern Lanzhou, Gansu.

THE FOLLOWING TEXT commemorates the reconstruction and expansion of the main temple of a local cult in Putian District, Fujian Province, located on China's southeast coast. The god, known by the time the inscription was composed in 1138 as the Duke of Manifest Kindness (Xian-hui hou), was the proprietary deity of a prominent local kin group, the Fang of Baidu, a small village which lay about three miles east of Putian city in the hills edging the fertile flood plain of the Mulan River. Like many prominent kin groups of the area, the Fang had abandoned their original homes, which had been in the hinterland behind Hangzhou, and settled in Putian in the late 800s, a time of widespread unrest that accompanied the fall of the Tang dynasty (618–907).

The Fang were the cult's prime benefactors at least since the eleventh century and very probably for many decades before, and they remained so at least through the twelfth century reconstruction. The text speaks to the rituals of veneration, including both the orthodox civil rituals of the scholarly elite at a time when the Confucian civil code was undergoing dramatic and long-lasting redefinition, but also the unorthodox "bloody" rituals often preferred by less exalted devotees, and it suggests the breadth of "services" which such a deity was called upon to render, including protection from drought and blight, protection from plague, and protection from marauding bandits. What is especially interesting, however, is this god's role in protecting mariners, who had become the prime movers of a major commercial revolution along the southeast coast. At least in this role, the god had been adopted by devotees outside the Fang kin group and appears to have been on the way to becoming a deity patronized by the general population. Over the next couple of centuries, however, a rival deity, the goddess popularly known as the Ancestral Mother (Mazu [or "Empress of Heaven" (Tianhou)]), who arose in a coastal village of Putian district about fifty miles to the south of Baidu, displaced the Duke of Manifest Kindness as the principal maritime deity. The cult of the Duke lingered into the fifteenth century, but completely disappears from our records thereafter while that of Mazu flourishes throughout the Chinese maritime world today.

This inscription, whose title in Chinese is "Xiangying Miao ji," was composed by Fang Lüe (*jinshi* 1106), and it was inscribed and erected by Fang Zhao (*jinshi* 1105).—HC

There is a god's temple ten tricents (ca. three miles [five kilometers]) north of Putian city that is called the Temple of the Great Official. In 1107 the Emperor Huizong (r. 1101–1126) had business in the southern suburbs (of Kaifeng, the imperial capital; i.e., the New Year's sacrifices), where he conducted sacrifices to the myriad deities. At this time, he called for reports to the local officials on the gods who were not included on the sacrificial register, be they the gods of famous mountains and great rivers or those gods that had performed meritorious service to the people. Thus the court first learned of the merit of this god from the people (i.e., the devotees). The following year (1108) the temple was granted the name "Temple of Auspicious Response" (Xiang-ying miao).

Nine years later (1116) the emperor conducted another sacrificial rite to the myriad deities at the Imperial Sacrificial Hall, and the people of our community again reported the merits of the god to the court and requested that he receive a title.[1] The Court of Imperial Sacrifices then proposed "Duke of Revealed Response" (Xianying hou). The emperor said, "I am pleased. I feel that only this god merits such prestige! It is appropriate that a place have a deity to look on so favorably." Then the emperor took up his brush and signed [the edict] naming the god "Duke of Manifest Kindness" (Xianhui hou). This was in the fourth year of Xuanhe (1122). The god [henceforth] should be treated as a noble.[2]

By the Five Dynasties era (907–960) there already was a temple where blood sacrifices were conducted by our people.[3] Among our elders there is a legend that says,

> The old temple was located north of the post station road. One evening there was terrible wind and rain and awful thunder and lightning that seemed to arise from within the temple. [The people sought out the source of the disturbance to] make offerings and burn incense, but suddenly they had no idea where they were. The following day the elders looked for where they had stopped [the night before], and they came to the base of an ancient banyan tree on Turtle Lake Mountain. They drew near and venerated [the spot], and this is the location of the present temple.[4]

The temple faces Straight Pot Mountain, and Chen Precipice embraces it from behind, while the waters of Ribbon Creek course through the grounds. Thus, although other places may have beautiful mountains and streams, nowhere can match the earthly principles [of this site]. The diviners of that time all agreed, "Gods [usually] depend on people for what they can do, but the [outstanding qualities of] this god come from the excellence of the mountains and the streams. Could this be because the local people have . . . [?? character missing[5]]?" Today there are many members of our great clan around the site of the god's temple, and there is always somebody who has attained high rank and wealth. It is all as the diviners said.[6]

As for the name "Temple of the Great Official," a tradition says that there was a local man who rose to high rank. On retirement he returned to live out his old age in the village. Every year the most talented youth among his students would join with the village elders on the day of the village festival (she) in praying to the god for abundant harvests.[7] They would carefully set out the plates and goblets, and spread the ritual vessels. Then they would bow humbly and ascend into the hall by order of age and with great filiality. It was just like the ancient village wine-drinking [ritual].[8] The village people took great pleasure [in the ritual], and so they named the temple.[9]

The god has blessed our people in many ways. Among the districts of Fujian, Putian is the most coastal. Its land is all saline, and all the arable land is unirrigated (gao; literally, "high") and without the benefit of streams. If a week passes without rain, the people may lose their crops. Whenever there is [a possibility of] drought, the people pray to the god. They never have to wait long before there is rain. Thus despite the unirrigated fields there is never drought.

[In this area] at the transition between spring and summer, conditions are cloudy and damp, and sometimes there are pestilential winds and malignant rains. Such alternations between hot and cold promote malaria, and the people suffer. At these times, the people collectively pray to the god for relief. Some even go before the god directly and use both Buddhist and Daoist rites to make offerings to him. In this way the people have suffered no disasters.

In 1117 the several prefectures were invaded by locusts . . . [missing characters]. They ate the leaves off the bamboo and trees and even the hair off the cattle and sheep. The people [of our district] were greatly afraid and prayed to the god. Thus the locusts did not dare enter an area of several miles around the temple.

In 1120 bandits from Muzhou[10] raided the granaries and killed officials. Numbering a hundred thousand, they ravaged the people throughout Jiang[nan] and [Liang]zhe and pillaged the land.[11] The court [raised? (missing character)] a million imperial guards to pacify the rebels, who then began to discuss a plan to seize boats at Dinghai (a coastal district in Zhejiang) so that they could occupy Fujian as their lair.[12] Local officials immediately reported this [to the court] and directed the people to abandon their homes to avoid [the approaching rebels]. Their claim that boats could reach the area in two days' sailing caused great fear. The masses, assisting the elderly and carrying the young, fled to find shelter in the mountains and valleys [of the interior]. As they clambered and scrambled, some even fell [to their deaths] while clusters of desperate onlookers watched from the side. Thus it was that the people abandoned their property and lost their sons and daughters, while some took their own lives in fear. But our people[13] prayed to the god, who sent them a message saying they would not be hurt. So they were at ease in their homes and none moved away. The bandits, meanwhile, were ultimately suppressed.

Three years after the imperial succession (1129),[14] the Jianzhou bandit Ye Nong, leading a force of several thousand, killed [the local] officials and rebelled.[15] They seized [a flotilla of] river boats and floated downriver [toward Fuzhou]. One evening, on reaching Nantai Creek (one of the many channels of the Min River that pass beneath the walls of Fuzhou city), they entered the outskirts of Fuzhou, where they burned the people's houses, and their strength grew rapidly. They were next planning to cross the Dayi Ford (outside Fuzhou city on the southeast side) and head south. The militia forces of the southern prefectures had not yet assembled. The communities were seized by panic, and no one was in command. But suddenly one night the bandit troops in alarm said to each other, "The government forces are arrayed, and their banners all bear the words 'Duke of Manifest Kindness.' What does this mean?" They grew afraid, and for the first time had premonitions of impending disaster. The provincial assistant fiscal intendent Zhang Mu took advantage of their indecision to cut the bridges and sink their boats in order to disrupt their plans for advancing to the south.[16]

A year later, Yang Qing led forces from the west in rebellion.[17] They entered Fujian and passed through Zhangzhou and Quanzhou, burning and pillaging and causing the people great harm. The bandits applied great pressure to our prefecture. Our local militia was outnumbered, and none had the will to resist. Suddenly the local commander Fang Di and others heard a voice in the sky: "Go quickly to the Duke of Manifest Kindness, and troops will arrive." With this the courage of our generals stiffened and the bandits fled and hid in fear and the land was at peace.[18]

In former times, when merchants ventured out to sea they had to endure wind and waves and experience difficult crossings to find profits elsewhere. Those who had not visited the temple always had bad luck. Their boats would overturn in the wind and waves, or they would meet pirates in the marshes. But then the local merchant Zhou Wei, when planning a trip to Liangzhe,[19] told the god that he was going by boat. The next thing he knew, he was assaulted with wind and waves at the Devil's Gate,[20] and in an instant everything changed. The boatmen lost their color and wailed. Zhou Wei objected, "I put my faith in the spirit of the god. It oughtn't to be like this." He then called out for help, and from the empyrean came an echo. In a moment the wind calmed and the waves settled, and the crew was spared any disaster. Similarly there was the Quanzhou captain Zhu Fang who [while preparing to] sail to Śrīvijaya[21] asked for ashes from the god's incense, which he devoutly worshiped. His boat proceeded quickly and without incident, completing the round-trip voyage within a year and earning a hundredfold profit. No one before or since has done so well, and everyone attributes his success to the god. Ever since, when merchants prepare for long voyages there is no one who does not first come and pray to the god.

I have heard that of old when sages ruled, the myriad gods performed their duties and there was no discord [in society]. The duties of gods included generating rain, protecting [the people] from calamity, reprimanding evil spirits, sweeping away the unlucky, granting wealth to good people, and punishing those who do evil. Presently the Duke receives blood sacrifices.[22] Thus the local people explained the power of his spirit in order to acquire noble title at an earlier time (i.e., 1116). He can also perform his duties [as a god] and express his loyalty [to the court] in order to merit special favor hereafter. Just as my lord, the emperor, in managing the recovery of the dynasty,[23] governed the people and served the spirits, all in their proper order. Virtue shall be praised and merit rewarded, and the Duke will be granted additional title as a result.

And so, isn't it fitting now to enlarge the god's temple in order to add to the solemn reverence of the rites, to openly acknowledge the lord's special favor, yet to privately respond to the god's gifts? The old temple was several *jian*[24] in size. Over many years, [as a result of the] rain from above and wind from beside, there was no shelter left. In 1083 Vice-Minister for Court Ceremonial Fang Jiao first expanded the landholdings [from which the temple received income]. In 1116 Fang Hui, Supervisor to the Household of the Heir Apparent, led the village people in raising funds to restore the temple.[25]

Today the god majestically faces the south, looking over his subordinates.[26] Their regalia and the rites of presenting offerings are all according to rank; it is not as it had been [before the restorations]. The worshipers pay obeisance before him, while diviners make offerings to foretell whether the future holds good fortune. In coming and going they are filled with awe. Again this is not as it was before.

[Now], at the time of the spring and autumn sacrifices, the old and young proceed [before the god] in order, offering cool wine and fragrant viands. When the god is satiated, they withdraw to the position of guests (i.e., arrayed below the god, their host), where they grasp their cups and hoist their goblets.[27] Whether they have been rewarded or punished, there are none who do not obey the god's commands. We don't know if this was the way people conducted themselves in former times.

From near and far the people come pell-mell to beg the favor of the god at his temple. They must give offerings when they have something new [to report to the god] (such as births, deaths, official appointments, and so forth), they must inform the god of their comings and goings, and they must pray [for his intercession] when they are sick. Whatever it is they come to the god for, they must divine [his response] and then follow his instructions. Again, we don't know if this was the way people conducted themselves in former times.

Since the Son of Heaven made the sacrificial offerings to Heaven and Earth (in 1116) and the Duke undertook his duties, those who come to make offerings and sacrifices [to the Duke] do so with deep sincerity. This is also unlike former times.

Since all these are unlike former times, it was inevitable that the old palace was cramped and needed to be enlarged. When the cult devotee Fang Tu first explained his plan [to restore and enlarge the temple], the followers were all happy to agree. Thus collecting the funds to underwrite costs was no trouble, and the construction was carried out without effort. There are two halls on the east and west, with space [for those who want to] rest and space for preparing vegetarian foods. Altogether the construction took eighty-two beams and cost 10,000 strings of cash. Construction began in the spring of 1134 and was finished in the summer of 1136. Since the new hall has been completed, large gatherings have assembled to make bountiful offerings to the god to induce his presence. Thus they have asked [me] to record these events.

In brief, my old house was near the temple; when I was a child I used to watch the elders as they worshiped in the hall. Subsequently I wandered the dusty roads for more than thirty years.[28] Twice I was honored with prefectural appointments in the south. Whenever I passed my home I visited [the family] graves, and I never failed to pay my respects at the temple, where I would wander about the courts and corridors and think of the ancient officials who vowed never to leave their village.[29] After I retired from office to engage in idyllic study, I returned with my household to my village, where I reflected upon my disappointments. One idle day I asked to make offerings in the temple. I hoped that when the time came I could be included among the village elders with their staffs and their slippers,[30] who with their white garments and flowing robes offer libations in the hall of the Duke. In this way I could fulfill my wish to reenact the ancient village wine-drinking ritual, but my wish has not yet been fulfilled.

I have gathered these anecdotes about the Duke to transmit to future generations. I have cleaned my inkstone and taken up my brush to record them.

Erected on the first day of the fourth month at the beginning of summer in the eighth year of Shaoxing (May 11, 1138). Inscribed by Cai Qing of Futang Village.

—HC

Notes

1. As we will learn below, this was in conjunction with an earlier restoration of the temple.

2. Note that, although the initial request for title was made in 1116, it was not until after the god had protected the region from the turmoil of the Fang La Rebellion, discussed below, that the emperor granted him title.

3. "Blood sacrifice" *(xueshi)*, the ritual offering of animal—and sometimes even human—sacrifice, has a long history in Chinese popular religion. However, since the emperors of the Song dynasty (960–1279) undertook a campaign to "civilize" the popular pantheon as part of the larger phenomenon of Confucian revival and expansion of civil ritual collectively known as Neo-Confucianism, blood sacrifice has been identified with unorthodox cults that had not received court sanction. The persistent tension between popular devotion to the Duke, manifested in the continued practice of blood sacrifice that Fang Lüe admits to later in this text, and attempts to "civilize" the deity through an overlay of orthodox civil ritual performed by the scholarly elite is an underlying theme and says much about the struggles to accommodate popular practice to the orthodox cultural trends of late imperial China.

4. This narrative refers to two spots: first, the location of an old temple "where blood sacrifices were conducted"; second, the ancient banyan tree that apparently lay somewhere apart from the old temple. The Temple of Auspicious Response is the second; we know nothing more about the first.

5. Several places in the existing stele have been marred by a gouge that cuts across several lines of text. As no transcription of the stele was taken before the gouging, the cause of which is unknown, there are spots in the text that cannot be reconstructed.

6. This discussion alludes to Chinese geomantic practice, which asserts that there is a direct correlation between topography and earthly fortune. In this case, the diviners, those who were trained in interpreting geomantic principles, maintained that the surrounding mountains provide excellent shelter from the negative forces that flow through the world, while the free flow of the water demonstrates that the temple does not interfere with the natural energy flows of the earth. It is, in short, a very auspicious site, as the success of the clan makes obvious.

7. The *she* refers to a local village organization, the community of temple devotees.

8. The village wine-drinking ritual *(xiang yin jiu)*, a celebration of academic success in which local scholars were feted by village elders, was an ancient rite first recorded in the *Rites of Zhou (Zhouli)*, one of the pre-Han Confucian classics.

9. It is not clear from the inscription when the temple was known as the Temple of the Great Official, although it was before it was renamed Temple of Auspicious Response by the imperial investiture of 1107. The name is most likely connected with Fang Jun *(jinshi* 1030) or his brother Fang Qiao *(jinshi* 1034), the two earliest members of the Baidu kin group to serve as high officials.

Fang Jun's biography (*[Guangxu] Putian xianzhi* 16:1b) says, "In the Jiayou era (1056–1064) he asked to retire on account of old age.... He lived beside his house in the Pavilion for Planting Virtue.... His followers gathered there to study." Like the unnamed "great official," Jun rose to high rank; he returned to Baidu Village following his retirement and became a teacher. It is likely, therefore, that he was the "great official," which would place the origin of the temple name sometime in the latter half of the eleventh century.

10. Muzhou is a prefecture located in southern Zhejiang (in the twelfth century known as Liangzhe), north of Fujian. Between 1120 and 1122 the coastal region south of the Yangtze River, including southern Zhejiang, was wracked by the Fang La Rebellion, one of the great mass rebellions of the Song dynasty, and the reference is clearly to this uprising. Like the major Fang kin groups of Putian, including those of Baidu Village, which was home to the compilers of the present inscription, Fang La traced his origins to the Muzhou-Xizhou border region of Liangzhe; although the Putian Fang had left Muzhou more than two centuries earlier, they no doubt shared the same ancestry. Unfortunately, but not surprisingly considering Fang La's infamy, the records of the Baidu kin make no reference to such a link.

11. Jiangnan (the area bordering the south shore of the Yangtze River that today is southern Anhui and northeastern Jiangxi provinces) and Liangzhe were two of the wealthiest and most populous provinces in all the Song empire.

12. This is an intriguing assertion that is not mentioned anywhere else in the histories of the rebellion.

13. This phrase *(wumin)* refers to the Fang kin of Baidu Village.

14. Emperor Gaozong, a collateral member of the Song imperial clan, ascended the throne in 1127, following the capture of the northern capital, Kaifeng, by the invading Jurchen forces, who seized most members of the imperial family in the process. Gaozong reestablished the Song in the south, ultimately establishing his court in Hangzhou, thereby initiating the era known as the Southern Song (1127–1279).

15. Jianzhou is located in northwestern Fujian Province, on the uppermost reaches of the Min River drainage system by which it is connected to Fuzhou and the ocean.

16. Subsequently, Ye Nong led his forces back to Jianzhou, where he was defeated by Zhang Jun (1086–1154), one of the most famous generals of the early Southern Song.

17. Like Fang La, Yang Qing was from Muzhou. He carried his rebellion into Jianzhou, in northwestern Fujian, from where Ye Nong had arisen, and later into Quanzhou.

18. More so than either of the preceding events, this narrative points directly to a private militia force of the Baidu Fang. In the 1120s and 1130s, confronted by growing social disorder that coincided with the loss of north China to the Jurchen invasions and the relocation of the court to the south, many local elite kin groups assembled such private militias.

19. Liangzhe, or "the Two Zhe," was a Song province embracing the coastal region and hinterland prefectures between northern Fujian and the Yangtze River. Hangzhou, the Southern Song capital, was in Liangzhe, and that is no doubt where Zhou Wei was headed.

20. The Devil's Gate refers to a particularly treacherous passage along the coastal route between northern Fujian and Zhejiang.

21. Śrīvijaya was a principality located on the southeast coast of the island of Sumatra in the Indonesian archipelago. It was the first of a succession of principalities that have controlled traffic through the critical Strait of Malacca between Sumatra and the Malay Peninsula and through which traffic between the Andaman Sea of the eastern Indian Ocean and the South China Sea must pass. Śrīvijaya thus was a critical linchpin in trade between China and the Indian Ocean and a frequent destination of Chinese merchants until its collapse in the fourteenth century.

22. As has been explained above (n. 3), blood sacrifice was a sign of unorthodoxy in local cults. This obviously alludes to popular practices, and so stands in contrast to orthodox practice such as Fang Lüe and the court hoped to promote.

23. This refers to the successful stabilization of the Southern Song by the Emperor Gaozong (see above, n. 14).

24. A *jian* was a measure of space, defined as the space enclosed in the distance between two columns. There was no standard size; rather the dimensions of a *jian* depended on time and place.

25. This coincides with the appeal for ennoblization recalled earlier.

26. The term rendered as "subordinates" *(zhuhou)* is a feudal expression that originally meant imperial vas-

sals. Here it refers to an array of subordinate deities, each with its own altar, all of which are subordinate to the central deity of the temple, such as one often finds in Chinese temples.

27. This all harks back to the earlier discussion of the annual village festival at which "the most talented youths . . . would carefully set out the plates and goblets, and spread the ritual vessels" in preparation for a banquet.

28. This refers to Fang Lüe's official career.

29. This line is revealing testimony to the tension so often expressed by Chinese scholars between public life as Confucian officials and the Daoist goal of idyllic retreat. Though few opted entirely for the latter, the growing Neo-Confucian critique of official life in the twelfth–thirteenth centuries and the expanding opportunities to make a living as teachers and writers gave new meaning to this tension, and this is exactly the way Fang Lüe describes his retirement in the next line.

30. The phrase *zhanglü* (literally, "staff and shoes") refers to the privilege of the elderly to carry their staff and wear their shoes inside, rather than leave them at the entrance as custom dictated.

ALL HUMAN BEINGS like things that taste sweet. We do not know if this is because mother's milk is sweet so that we acquire a craving for sweet tastes right from the moment of birth, but searching for honey was one of the major activities of humans even in the days of hunting and gathering cultures. Sugarcane, which provides most of the sugar in the world today, is a variety of grass native to New Guinea, from where it spread initially to various parts of South and Southeast Asia in Neolithic times. While sugarcane can be chewed readily, it is a difficult plant to grow and process. It requires enormous amounts of fertilizer, and constant care in the field. The rind of the cane is tough, and large amounts of cane must be crushed to make any significant quantities of juice; cane juice ferments soon after it is extracted, and the chemical changes in fermented juice prevent it from being reduced to produce sugar. Boiling vats of juice to evaporate it requires great skill and temperature control, for otherwise one ends up with a caramelized mess of molasses that, in addition to being bitter, cannot be made into sugar crystals. Finally, to make sugar, straining the thickened juice to crystallize it involves yet other technical challenges. It seems that the eastern regions of India had first developed the technique of boiling down the juice to produce a solid brown sugar sometime around 800 B.C.E. Our word "sugar" is derived from the Latin *saccharum,* which can be traced to the Sanskrit *śarkarā.*

In China, the first sweeteners were made from malted grain. The sugarcane plant was introduced in the southern regions sometime around the third century B.C.E. For many centuries, sugarcane was simply chewed and eaten like a variety of fruit; and although somewhat later sugar syrups were made from cane juice, the next step of producing a solid sugar that would keep longer and was readily transportable proved difficult. The text below gives us the history of its development. What the Indians manufactured at this time was a form of brown sugar that had evaporated most of the juice but contained all the molasses; it was called "stone honey" *(shimi)* by the Chinese probably because the hardened cakes looked like chunks of stone. Yet this was still not crystallized sugar. Then, in the eleventh century, the Chinese developed crystallized sugar, where the grains of sugar were separated from the molasses, and sugar, much as we know it now, began to be made. The text translated below records that momentous discovery and describes the process.

A Treatise on Crystallized Sugar (Tangshuang pu) is an essay in seven parts by Wang Zhuo, preface dated 1142 C.E.[1] A minor official in the 1130s from Suining Prefecture in Sichuan Province, Wang was passionately interested in the major product of his home prefecture, crystallized sugar. We do not know very much about Wang Zhou, not even the dates of his birth and death, but clearly he was one of the number of contemporary gentry-literati who were interested in introducing new crops, improving methods of cultivation, and expanding various types of manufacture. Wang obviously knew about cane cultivation and sugar processing firsthand and even inserted little asides in his text to help potential growers avoid common pitfalls. We learn also that Song-period gradations of sugar were different from today's; reddish-purple sugar, not white sugar, was considered to be the best.

Although Wang also wrote some unremarkable poems, it was his *Treatise* that secured him a place in history. It has been reprinted many times since the twelfth century and was included in the Qing-period imperially sponsored massive compendium of texts, *Siku quanshu* (Complete library in four divisions). The *Tangshuang pu* is an unusual text, for it gives both cultural history along with grounded socioeconomic data and technical information.—SM

A Treatise on Crystallized Sugar

Part 1

Crystallized sugar is also called rock sugar. Futang (Fujian), Siming (Zhejiang), Panyu (Guangdong), Guanghan, and Suining (Sichuan) have it. Of these Suining has the best. The sugar produced in the four other prefectures is insignificant, and the crystals are pulverized; the color is pale and the taste is weak. They can only be compared to the lowest grade from Suining.

That which is rare and difficult to find is precious. Because pears, oranges, tangerines, lychees, and the arbutus are not produced everywhere, they are valued in the world. But sugarcane is planted in many places, and the plants are all good; it is not at all an unusual item. However, when we come to the crystallization of cane then in all of China only the five prefectures have it, and Suining's is outstanding. Outside, among the barbarians, the Yi, the Di, the Rong, and the Man all have excellent cane. But crystallized sugar is unheard of. In the nature of things this is an inexplicable matter.

In the beginning, in the reign period of Tang Da Li (Tang Daizong, r. 763–779), there was a Buddhist monk named Zou Heshang. It is not known where he came from. Riding a white donkey, he climbed up San Mountain (Sichuan) and built a thatched hut to live in. If he needed salt, rice, firewood, or vegetables, he wrote it down on a piece of paper, tied it together with some money, and sent his donkey with the note to the market. People knew that it was from Zou. They would take the right amount of money, hang the goods on the saddle, and send the donkey home. One day, the donkey ran amok below the mountain in a field of cane shoots belonging to a man named Huang.

Huang asked Zou to pay for the damages. Zou said, "You don't know how to make sugarcane into crystallized sugar. The profit would be ten times. Would it be all right if I teach you in order to clear my debt?" When Huang tested the method the result was indeed so. From this time onward the method spread. The households making crystallized sugar near San Mountain and its vicinity all did well. No other method worked; a thousand other ways did not succeed. At the end of his life, Zou left and went north to a shrine at Lingjiu Shan in Tongquan district (Sichuan). His disciples followed him and caught up with him. All they saw was a stone statue of Mañjuśrī. Then they realized that the monk had been an incarnation of the Bodhisattva, and the white donkey was his lion. The place where Monk Zou built his thatched hut has now become the Lanka Temple. The sugar-making households paint a portrait of Zou for worship, saying that it is the likeness of Mañjuśrī. At the Fuwen Pavilion, Edict Attendant Su Zhonghu, once prefect of Suining, speaking of Sichuan, pointed to the abundant waters of Meiyan, the grace of the mountains at Langzhong, and the beauty of the rocks at Puci, not knowing that in this area the earth itself is abundant, beautiful, and graceful. The earth makes cultivation possible, sowing and reaping sweet things. The sweetest crystallized sugar in the world—isn't that because the earth is particularly good?!

Part 2

The eating of cane started with cane syrup. In Song Yu's "Summoning the Soul"[2] (Zhao hun; composed ca. 300 B.C.E.) it is said there is well-cooked turtle and roast lamb with cane syrup.

After this there was *tang* (also read *xing;* maltose, a paste-like sweetener made from grain) made from cane. Sun Liang (the prince of Wu, in the third century C.E.) sent his eunuch to the official of the imperial warehouse to get from him the sugarcane *xing* sent as tribute from Jiaozhou (the southernmost commandery during the Han, which included Guangdong, Guangxi, and northern Vietnam). Then, after this, we have stone honey. The *Guangzhi* (a Tang-period text) says sugar-cane *xing* was made into stone honey. The *Gazetteer of Eight Southern Commanderies (Nanzhong bajun zhi)* says expressed cane juice dried in the sun becomes *xing,* and this is called stone honey. The *Bencao* (the Tang pharmacopoeia) also says boil cane sugar and milk to make stone honey. The *Annals of the Tang Dynasty (Tangshi)* record that Tang Taizong sent an envoy of the country of Magadha (in India) to obtain the procedure for boiled sugar. A decree was sent to Yangzhou (in China) to present the various kinds of sugarcane, which were then pressed and drained accord-ing to the recipe obtained. The taste and color were good, better by far than that of the Western Regions (Central Asia). . . . It looks like the granulated sugar of today. . . . And that was all that was said about the technique [of making sugar] from cane. There is no word on how to make crystallized sugar. It is because crystallized sugar is not at all that old.

(Wang then gives a lengthy list of all the literary works he has surveyed since the third century that do not discuss crystallized sugar and concludes with mentions of two poets from the eleventh century, Su Shi and Huang Tingjian, who do, and notes, "The mention of the crystal-lized sugar of Suining in literature really begins with these two masters. That being the case, crys-tallized sugar is not at all ancient, and, in my opinion, its production in the four prefectures also began in recent times.")

Part 3

San Mountain is in Xiaoji district, twenty tricents east of the Fu River (in Sichuan), a remote and beautiful spot. In front of and behind the mountain, four out of every ten fields are given to cane; three out of every ten families make crystallized sugar.

There are four varieties of cane: the *du* cane, the western cane, the *fang* cane, which is referred to as the *di* cane in the materia medica (*Bencao gangmu* of 659 C.E.), and the red cane, which is referred to as the *kunlun* cane in the materia medica. The red cane is fit only for chewing raw. One can make granulated sugar from the *fang* cane and crystallized sugar from the western cane, but the color is light, and the local people do not value it. The *du* cane variety is purple and tender, and the taste is very rich. It is especially used for making crystallized sugar.

Storage and cultivation methods: Select short canes [for storage]. ([Original] note: the buds from which new cane will sprout grow between the joints; on the short ones the joints are closer together and there are more sprouts.) Dig a ditch about two feet deep; the width can be whatever is convenient. Cut off the tail-ends of the canes, stand them in the ditch upside down, and cover them with earth. If you do not invert the seed cane, rain will collect between the leaves and rot them after a while.

Cane fields are ploughed deeply after the eleventh month. Rake the dry earth energetically up and down and from side to side until like prepared noodle dough.[2] Dig a furrow which is more than a foot wide and five feet deep. Mound the earth on both sides. During the period after the fifteenth of the first lunar month and around the beginning of the second, plant the canes in rows on opposite sides. Cover them lightly with ashes, and then with earth, but no more than two inches deep. Once around the Clear Bright (Qingming) Festival (at the beginning of the fourth month) and once around the Dragon Boat (Duanwu) Festival (the beginning of the fifth month) cover them again with a thin layer of cow or pig manure mixed thoroughly with ashes. As a rule, the earth on top should not be packed in so that the shoots can appear. Around the middle of the sixth month fertilize again with night soil as above. No amount of weeding is too much, and no amount of added fresh soil can be too much, but always keep the cane sprouts exposed. Wait until they are tall enough to form clumps. And then, using a big hoe, turn over the soil from the mounds [on the sides of the furrows] and cover them completely. Harvest in the tenth month. Cane depends very heavily on the fertility of the soil. You cannot plant it with other crops mixed in. And if cane is planted in the fields this year, the five grains should be planted the following year in order to replenish the fertility of the land. Those who have extra land, alternate and plant something different for three years.

The places where crystallized sugar is plentiful: at the foot of the mountain is Lifoba, five tricents from there is Gannanba, ten tricents from there is Shijiba. West of the river, and facing the mountain, is Fengtaizhen. All together there are more than three hundred households producing sugar. The number of vats of sugar produced by each of the families varies from a maximum of several tens of vats to a minimum of one or two vats. East of the mountain are Zhang Village and Gang Kou. Behind the mountain are Nanchi and Wu villages, and to the west of the river, facing the mountain, are Fabao Yuan and Mount Ma'an. All of these have about a hundred households making sugar. However, the crystallized sugar is of medium to poor grade. On the stretch of land on the side of the mountain, there are Baishuizhen and Tuqiao. Although there are a lot of cane fields, they cannot make crystallized sugar. Every year they crush the cane and sell the cane juice to the households in front of the mountain.

Part 4

The implements used by households making sugar: There is a cane parer, used for peeling the cane, which resembles the knife used for cutting bamboo but is somewhat lighter. Then there is the cane sickle used for splitting cane, four inches thick and about a foot long, in a slightly bent shape. There is a cane bench, which looks like a small stool in one corner of which there is a hole chiseled, in which to stand a wooden fork. A bunch of cane, three to five stalks at a time, is placed in the fork, and one straddles the bench at an angle to chop them into small pieces. Then there is the cane crusher to which oxen are harnessed in order to crush the cane that has been chopped into small sections. It is made of a big piece of hard stone, is six to seven feet high, and weighs more than a thousand catties. Beneath it is a trough made of hard stone, the circumference of which is more than ten feet. Then there is an extraction basket, also called a bamboo bag, in which the cane is pressed, which is four feet high, and plaited out of this year's zi (variety of) bamboo. There is a thornwood (a particularly hard wood) pestle for tamping the cane into the extraction basin. Then there is the extraction basin into which the basket is placed, similar to the wine trough of nowadays. There is the expressing bed in which the bowl is placed. On top of this expressing bed there is a frame with a large beam. Underneath there is a revolving axle which draws down a rope to press [the bamboo basket with the prepared cane bits]. Then there is the lacquer jar, which is painted with lacquer inside and out to prevent seepage and dripping, for receiving the cane juice.

The cane is used in the tenth or eleventh month. First peel the cane. Then cut it into little bits the size of coins. The wealthy households use as many as ten to twenty people for peeling and chopping the cane. Two people peeling can supply enough for one person chopping. Next it is put into the crusher. If there is no crusher, then use a mortar and pestle. When the crushing is completed it is called "mash." Next steam the mash. After the mash has been thoroughly steamed, take it out of the earthenware cooking vat and put it in the expresser to remove all the cane juice. Pour the juice into a cauldron for boiling to steam off more water as above. The mash that results will be sugar syrup that is seven-tenths ready. Pour it temporarily into a vat. The steamed mash can also be expressed again [to yield more syrup]. In this fashion, boiling and steaming in sequence [continue] until the work is ended. Stop for three days (but if it exceeds this period then the cane [syrup] will ferment [original note]). Then boil the sugar syrup that has been accumulated again. Wait until it is nine-tenths done, and it will be thick like malt *(xing)*. ([Original] note: If you thicken it completely, the sugar becomes "sandy foot" [inferior grade sugar]). Insert bamboo [sticks] into the vats. Only then pour the syrup into the vat. [And] just cover it with a winnowing fan.

This is the method for making crystallized sugar. One may separately add fresh water to the [cane pulp that has already been expressed] and express again to make vinegar that is very sour.

Part 5

After the sugar syrup has been in the vat for two days, there will be gruel-like streaks on its surface; when you coat your fingers with it, it is like fine sand. After the fifteenth of the first lunar month, the syrup will crystallize into little lumps or clusters of grain on the tips of the bamboo sticks. Slowly the lumps will become larger like beans and then like the knuckles on a finger. Eventually they may become as large as a rock in a garden. This is commonly referred to as the bearing of the fruit. By the fifth month when the growing energy of spring and summer have already reached a peak, the crystals will no longer increase in size. Then clean out the vat. ([Original] note: if the vat is not cleaned out by the beginning of summer, it will all turn to liquid. The poorer households are eager to strain out the vats even before the fourth month.) Although the crystals have formed, there will still be some syrup. Cleaning out the vat consists of ladling out the syrup and taking out the crystals to drain and dry them. Trim off the crystals clustered and branched on the tips of the bamboo sticks without trying to cut them into any regular size and drain them. After the draining is finished, then dry them thoroughly under a hot sun and put them away in jars. The crystals that form in clumps [from the syrup still in the vat] during a four-week cycle are called "vat mirrors." They are chunks that grow out in layers like stalactites that form in the mountain caves except that they grow out sideways so they cannot be drained too abruptly. When you drain them you must sun them inside the jars for several days so that the crystals become dry and hard. Then slowly, with an iron scoop, break the crystals into several pieces and take them out. As a rule, crystals from the same jar differ in quality and color. The ones that have collected into rock-like shapes are the best, the ones that cluster on the bamboo sticks are next, the ones that cling to the sides of the jar are next, and then there are the small grains. The sandy residue is the lowest in quality, called sandy foot. The crystals that are reddish-purple in color are the highest grade, the deep amber ones the next grade, the pale yellow shade the one below, while the pale white crystals are the lowest in quality. . . .

(In the following section, part 6, Wang writes about how on the day that the vats of sugar are opened, some families strike it rich with a good crop, but they are as easily ruined if the whole lot of sugar in the jar ends up being the inferior "sandy foot." He also comments on how the great demand for sugar has led to various kinds of chicanery. In part 7 he goes on to note the various uses of sugar in the various pharmacopoeias for use as cough medicine, ointments, and for making sweetmeats. He concludes his essay with his hopes:)

Fan Weizong wrote the *Treatise on Fragrances (Xiang pu)*. Cai Junmo wrote the *Treatise on Lychees (Lizhi pu)* and the *Treatise on Tea (Cha pu)*. All are very thorough in their explications on the principles of things, and the whole world considers them accurate. Huishu (Wang Zhuo's pen name) has written the *Treatise on Crystallized Sugar (Tangshuang pu)*. I have been aware of it for a long time, and quite by chance I obtained seven chapters that I have finished studying in the Abbot's Court-yard of the Temple of the Goddess of Mercy. The future will see it compared to the works of Fan and Cai everywhere, and it will be considered brilliant.

—SM

Notes

1. This is the standard date assigned to the text, but the twentieth-century printed edition has 1155 C.E. as the date.

2. The authorship of this poem from the *Lyrics of Chu* or *Songs of the South (Chuci)* is disputed. Wang Yi (d. 158 C.E.), the editor of the *Chuci,* claims that Song Yu wrote it; Sima Qian (see selections 24, 28, and 29) states that Qu Yuan (340?–278 B.C.E.), the celebrated author of "Encountering Sorrow" (Li sao) and other famous poems in the *Chuci,* composed it.

3. The words "like noodle dough" *(ru mian)* have been omitted in the extant printed versions, but they are in the Ming manuscript version.

A DREAM OF SPLENDORS PAST IN THE EASTERN CAPITAL (Dongjing meng hua lu) is a description of life in Bianliang (modern Kaifeng, Henan Province) between the years 1117 and 1125. Its author is a shadowy figure known as Meng Yuanlao. Modern scholarship has determined that Meng Yuanlao may have been part of the extended clan headed by Meng Changling, a corrupt official who became rich by heading large construction projects. The author was literate, but not literary in the strict sense of that word. His writing alternates between several styles that are indiscriminately intermixed within the text. There are passages written in simple classical Chinese, long sections of parallel prose that provide a lyrical ambiance for each season or event, and some passages that border on the colloquial. The work seems to have been cobbled together from memory, notebooks, and invention. Unlike usual descriptions of life at the center of politics and art, *A Dream of Splendors Past* makes no mention of literati, cites no literati poetry or prose, and makes only infrequent mention of high officials. When high officials are indicated, it is only to designate certain sites or spaces within the capital that are used as points of orientation. The only people who gain mention in the book, otherwise, are shopkeepers, restaurant owners, and performers. Thus the text is very much about the netherworld of Bianliang, and centers on food, sex, entertainment, and spectacle. The preface is dated 1147, but it did not see print until 1189. Since the text is cited in other contemporary pre-1189 sources, it appears to have been widely circulated in manuscript form prior to its publication.

The work is ten chapters long, and is divided roughly in half between describing the space of the capital and detailing its annual events. In this sense, the first five chapters of the book set the stage for the events that occur in the latter five as theatrical festivals. The emperor, Huizong (r. 1100–1125), figures constantly in the text, but primarily when he appears outside the Forbidden City. Otherwise, the text details the restaurant and shop culture of the areas in the northeastern and southern parts of Bianliang. Wine shops, houses of prostitution, and commercial activities are the dominant venues, described with loving and sensuous detail. The capital that appears in the text of Meng Yuanlao recreates the memory of a particular group of capital dwellers. They were monied young gourmands, who lived a life of leisure and ease in the frenzied culture of the city, and whose contact with commercial and mercantile interests defined a social class that was not incorporated by the regular boundaries of more orthodox history.

A Dream of Splendors Past thus presented serious problems to bibliographers and historians through the ages. Its writing style was so vulgar that it was accepted only grudgingly at first. Later, as its position as progenitor of texts on capital life became solidified, it gradually was incorporated into the historical canon as a lamentation over the fall of the Northern Song. Certainly, one of the features of the text is the looming presence of Huizong, who, although not mentioned by name, stands unseen behind the text. On the one hand a vivid description of quotidian life in the capital, the book also may be seen as a subtle critique of the rampant consumerism and hedonism that marked life in the last years of Huizong's reign. Finally, we should recall that the book was indeed a "remembrance of things past," having been written after the fall of the Northern Song dynasty in 1127 and the flight of the court to the south.—SHW

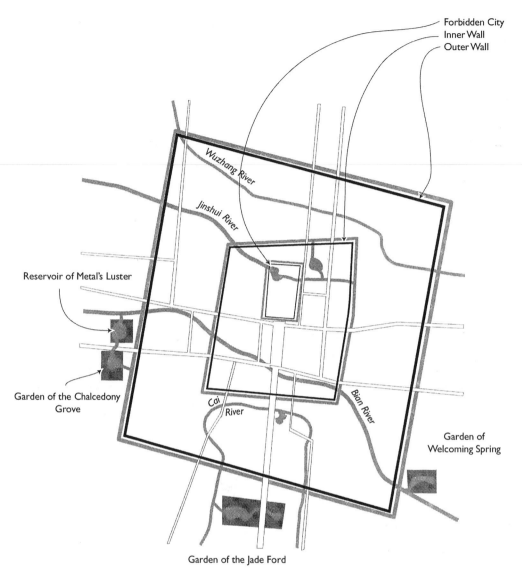

Forbidden City
Inner Wall
Outer Wall

Wuzhang River

Jinshui River

Reservoir of Metal's Luster

Garden of the Chalcedony Grove

Cai River

Bian River

Garden of Welcoming Spring

Garden of the Jade Ford

Northern Song capital

The Great Inner City

The main gateway to the Great Inner City, the Tower of Proclaiming Virtue, has five entries abreast,[1] each in vermilion and studded with golden nails. The walls are entirely of fired brick and stone, laid in alternating rows, and are carved with the figures of dragons, phoenixes, and flying clouds. The rafters are all carved, the roof beams all painted;[2] the square risers and layered purlins[3] are covered with glazed ceramic tiles. Small side pavilions bend off at ninety degrees; the balustrades are vermilion, and the door frames are of many colors. Below the tower gateyard pylons face each other; the whole is blocked with vermilion chevaux-de-frise.

Enter the main gate of the Tower of Proclaiming Virtue and one immediately encounters the Hall of Grand Felicity, in the courtyard of which are erected two towers like the bell and drum towers of a monastery.[4] On the upper floors is located the Director of Calendrical Calculations of the Astrological Service, who examines the clepsydra and who reports, holding an ivory plaque, on the double-hour and subhour segments.

Each ritual fast the emperor holds before going forth for the Great Celebration of the Suburban Sacrifice and every court assembly for the New Year are held in this hall. There are side gates on the left and right, outside the hall, called the Left and Right Gates of Enduring Celebration.[5]

On the south wall of the Inner City, there are three gateways, which are the routes to audience for the great court assemblies. On the left of the Tower of Proclaiming Virtue is the Left Ancillary Gate, and on the right it is called the Right Ancillary Gate. Just inside the Left Ancillary Gate is the Hall of Enlightenment.[6] Inside and to the west of the Right Ancillary Gate are the Tianzhang and Baowen galleries.[7] It is just about one hundred *zhang* (340 yards [314 meters]) from the palace wall to the northern corridor. Entering the Right Ancillary Gate and going east: on the northern corridor of the street are the Bureau of Military Affairs, next the Secretariat, and then the Executive Office of the Department of State Affairs—the great ministers order their affairs here when they go to and withdraw from court—next the Chancellory, and then next the secondary gates of the outer corridor of the Hall of Grand Felicity.

North another one hundred or more paces (170 yards [157 meters]) is another secondary gate, which is where the high officials dismount from their horses when they daily go to court; the other Functionaries in Retinue, Censors, and Remonstrators must dismount at the first gate and go by foot to the Hall of Patterned Virtue, where they enter the second secondary gate. Through the second secondary gate, the eastern corridor is the Eastern Side Gate of the Hall of Grand Felicity. In the western corridors are the Rear Section of the Secretariat and the Rear Section of the Chancellory, then the Institute for Drafting the Imperial History, and then a small south-facing corner gate that is exactly opposite the Hall of Patterned Virtue—which is the hall of ordinary court.

The large avenue that runs east and west in front (*sic;* back) of the Hall of Patterned Virtue goes eastward out of the Gate of Eastern Florescence and westward out of the Gate of Western Florescence. Just inside these two gates are two other opposing gates, the Left and Right Gates of Grandness and Solemnity; southward are the Left and Right Gates of the Silver Dais. From the Palace of the August Heir Apparent, just inside the Gate of Eastern Florescence, one enters the Gate of Grandness and Solemnity: on the south side of the street are the rear gate to the Hall of Grand Felicity and the Palace Audience Gates of the East and West, and the Bureaus of Ceremonies of Felicitations and Condolences, respectively; on the north side of the street is the Gate of Diffusing Heaven's Succor.

In the western corridor of the Grand North-South Avenue, facing eastward is the Hall of Distilled Radiance, which connects to the Gate of Convergent Change, through which one enters the Forbidden Center. In the gateways and towers in the eastern corridor directly across from the Hall of Distilled Radiance are the Department of Domestic Service for the Emperor, the Six Imperial Services, and the Imperial Kitchen. Usually doubled rows of the Imperial Guard are lined up at the Hall. They are on alert every segment of every hour—entering and leaving the Forbidden Center is severely monitored. Just inside the Hall are the personal attendants and the valued inner retainers, i.e., eunuchs of the imperial staff. Outside of the Hall are the offices of the Administrator of the Department of Attendance on the Interior Palace and the Imperial Pharmacy. Express runners, Functionaries of the Personal Escort, Convoy Officials, the Court of Conveyances, Elders of the Yellow Court, and the various soldiers and officers of the Inner Bureaus, official receptionists of the Bureaus of Felicitation and Condolence, and those things purchased for or sent as tribute to the Forbidden City all enter here. This is precisely why it is so bustling. The men of the various offices themselves sell rare things to eat and drink, things that would not yet be found in the urban market.

When the morning and evening meals are taken in, the Imperial Guard forms ranks between the Department of Domestic Service for the Emperor and the Hall of Distilled Radiance. They form a barrier that cannot be crossed. Above the gate to the Department is one person who calls for items, and he is called "The One Who Allocates the Food." Then someone in purple robes, capped in a cross-tailed cap and called a "Court Boy," brings a box, which he covers with a yellow dragon-embroidered box cozy. In his left hand he brings a red silk embroidered handkerchief, and enters at this point. This goes on for approximately ten boxes, and then he continues by taking twenty or more golden melon boxes in. Those things requested outside of normal hours are called "Spur-of-the-Moment Requests." Outside of the Gate of Diffusing Heaven's Succor one goes west to the Hall of the Purple Mansion (where the New Year's court is held), then next is the Hall of Patterned Virtue (where the emperor normally holds court), and next in order are the Hall of Nonactive Government, the Hall of August Ceremonies, and the Hall of Assembled Heroes (this is where the imperial feasts and the announcement of examination candidates are held).

The rear halls are called the Hall of Venerating Administration and the Hall of Protecting Harmony. The Bureau of the Personal Messengers is located in the Hall of Perceptive Thought. The rear gate is called Supporting the Northern Asterism.

The market area outside of the Gate of Eastern Florescence is especially flourishing, probably because the Forbidden Center trades here. Generally, the food and drink, the flowers and fruits fresh with each season, fish and shrimp, turtles and crabs, quail and rabbit, dried and jerked meat, gold, jade, precious baubles, and clothes sold here are the most marvelous in the world. Their quality and style are of the highest order—even if a traveler should want ten or twenty different tastes to accompany his wine, they are immediately before the eyes for the having. When the fruits, melons, and vegetables of each season first come on the market, and when such things as eggplant and calabashes first appear, each pair can cost as much as thirty or fifty strings of a thousand cash, yet the various houses of the royal offspring strive to purchase them at this expensive cost.

Avenues and Alleys at the Eastern Gate of Xiangguo (Supporting the State) Monastery

Along the Monastery East Gate Avenue are to be found shops specializing in cloth caps with pointed tails, belts and waist-wraps, books, caps, and flowers as well as the vegetarian meal of the Ding family. South of the monastery are the brothels of Managers Alley.[8] The nuns and the brocade workers live in Embroidery Alley. On the north is Small Sweetwater Alley.[9] There are a particularly large number of southern restaurants inside the alley, as well as a plethora of brothels.

Shops and Stalls along Horse Guild Avenue[10]

North, along Horse Guild Avenue and outside Old Hill-Investiture Gate,[11] on the Angled Road of the Zoroastrian Temple, lies the Prefect-north Pleasure District. In addition to the household gates and shops that line the two sides of New Fengqiu Gate Street,[12] military encampments of the various brigades and columns of the Imperial Guard are situated in facing pairs along approximately ten tricents of the approach to the gate. Other wards, alleys, and confined open spaces criss-cross the area, and are counted in the tens of thousands—no one knows their real number. In every single place, the gates are squeezed up against each other, each with its own tea wards, wineshops, stages, and food and drink.

Normally, the small-business households of the marketplace simply purchase prepared food and drink at food stores; they do not cook at home. For northern food there are the Shi Feng–style dried meat cubes[13] and the various stewed items of the House of Duan and the House of Li the Fourth, all found in front of Alum Tower. For southern food, then the Jin House located south of Xiangguo Monastery Bridge, and the House of Zhou at Ninebends are acknowledged to be the finest.

The night markets close after the third watch (11 P.M.–1 A.M.) only to reopen at the fifth (3–5 A.M.). The more boisterous places stay open until dawn. Normally, even night markets in outlying, quiet places have such items as baked sesame buns stuffed with either sour bean filling or pork tenderloin, mixed-vegetable buns, the flesh of the badger and wild fox, stews of fruit slices, blood sausages,[14] and fragrant candied fruit. Night markets are held even in the worst snowstorms and on darkest rainy days of the winter. Found there are such items as meat strips with ginger and fermented bean-paste, minced tripe with blood–paste, crystal fish–paste, fried fresh liver, clams, and crabs; walnuts, malt-sugar wheat gluten from Zezhou, cross-hatch beans, goose pears, pomegranates, Japanese quince, Chinese quince, steamed glutinous rice balls, and soup made from salted fermented bean curd (i.e., Japanese *miso*). Only after the third watch do tea-sellers appear bearing their pots, seeking to satisfy those people of the capital, both privately employed and government workers, who get off late and are able to go home only deep in the night.

Avenues and Alleys at the Southeastern Tower

Eastward from the Tower of Proclaiming Virtue is the Southeastern (literally, "South Corner") Tower, which is at the southeast corner of the Imperial City. Crossroads Avenue runs southward from here through the ginger guild; Highhead Avenue runs north, following the silk guild to the Gate of Eastern Florescence, the Gate of Morning's Radiance, to the Palace of the Precious Phylactery, and straight through to the Old Sour Jujube Gate.[15] This is where shops and vendors' displays are most bustling and boisterous. During the Xuanhe reign (1119–1125), they expanded the official roadway that lined the wall of the Forbidden City on both sides.

East from the Southeastern Tower is the Avenue of Pan's Loft. South of the avenue is an area called "Raptor Inn," which is reserved as a place where traders in eagles and hawks lodge. The rest of this area south of the street is occupied by stores and displays of true pearls, of bolts of cloth and silk, and of incense. One alleyway runs directly through to the south: it is called "Alley of the Altar for Restricting the Self." This is where gold, silver, and colored silks are traded or bartered. The buildings and their grounds are overwhelmingly impressive, and the faces of the gates are deep and broad. They appear to the eye as a dense forest. Each transaction involves thousands or even tens of thousands of strings of cash. It dazzles a person's perception.

Further to the east and north of the avenue is a site called the Wineshop of Pan's Loft. Beneath it, at the fifth watch every morning, a market forms for buying and selling clothing, books, paintings, valuable baubles,[16] rhinoceros horn, and jade.[17] At dawn appear sheeps' heads, entrails, liver, kidney and sweetbreads, udders, plain and honeycombed tripe, quail, rabbit, rock dove, pigeons, wild game, crabs, clams, and the like. Only after this session has ended do the various craftsmen come to market to buy and sell a motley of small materials. After the breakfast period, food and drink appear at the market—for instance, honey-crisp, jujube-stuffed steamed dumplings, balls of finely ground sweet bean paste, fruit cooked in scented honey, and flowered designs soaked and cooked in honey. Toward evening, hair ornaments, caps, combs, scarves and bodices, valuable baubles, tools, and the like, all of inferior quality, are put out for sale.

Further to the east and on the north is the Xu Family Calabash Stew Shop; south of the avenue is the Sang Family Pleasure Precinct.

Nearby and to the north is the Middle Pleasure Precinct and next in line the Interior Pleasure Precinct. Of the fifty or more theaters within these pleasure precincts, the Lotus Flower Theater and the Peony Theater of the Middle Pleasure Precinct and the Elephant and Yakṣa (Demon) theaters of the Central Pleasure Precinct are the largest. They can hold several thousand people. From the generation of Ding Xianxian, Wang Tuanzi, and Seventh Sage Zhang,[18] people of later times were allowed to perform here. Inside the pleasure precincts one finds many purveyors of medicinal simples, sellers of hexagram fortunes, hawkers of old clothes, those who barter and wager on food and drink, silhouette cutters, singers of ditties, and the like. One can stay here the whole day without being aware of the approach of nightfall.

Streets and Alleys Outside of the Gate of the Vermilion Bird [Excerpt]

On the western side, south of Dragonford Bridge, is the residence of Military Privy Counselor Deng;[19] further south is the Alley of the Military School; inside is the residence of Songster Zhang[20] and the Temple to the King Whose Military Might Brought Completion.[21] South of this is the Zhang Family Restaurant for Fried Dough as well as the residence of the Empress of Lustrous Integrity.[22]

Going west one comes to a large street called Large Alley Intersection and further west is the wineshop of the Loft of Cool Breezes. In the summer, people of the capital enjoy the coolness here. Further west is the Old Crow Alley Intersection, the Number One Armory, and finally the Number One Bridge.

Southward from the Large Alley Intersection is the Taoist Temple for Receiving Realized Ones. The Taoist citizens from the four quadrants are all received here. Further south and going west into Small Alley Intersection is the Monastery of Three Emulations, and going further west one comes directly to the Yinan Bridge.

South from the Small Alley Intersection is the Gate of Southern Infusion. The funeral vehicles of ordinary citizens and people of worth are not able to go through this gate to exit the city—it is said to be so because it directly faces the [major entrance] to the Great Inner [Imperial] City. It is precisely here that the pigs that citizens lead to slaughter enter the capital. Every day, until late in the evening, herds of tens of thousands of pigs, driven by no more than ten or so persons, enter the capital. There are none that run amok (all march in perfect order).

Restaurants

Generally, the largest restaurants were called "partial-tea [food shops]." They served such things as head stew, stalactite stew, pressed meat, baked sesame buns, lamb kid, large and small bones, kidneys in reduced sauce, brass-skin noodles, broad-cut noodles with ginger, twice-cooked noodles (?), cold-noodles, chess-piece pastas, and baked flour products. If one were to make it a "full-tea" meal, then one added a head stew of pickled vegetables.

There were also Sichuan restaurants that served noodles with meat, noodles with preserved meat, noodles with various forms of meat or vegetable topping, stewed meat, fried giblets of fowl, and rice served with toppings both raw and cooked.

There were also southern restaurants, which had "fish pockets," cooked minced meat with brass-skin noodles, and rice with fried fish.

In addition, calabash stew shops erected a scaffolding of heavy lintels and flowered posts that were bound together like "mountain platforms." On top of these they hung out sides of pork and mutton, twenty or thirty to the span. Just inside, the door fronts and shutters were decorated with vermilion and green; these were called "gates of pleasure."

Each of these restaurants had a courtyard with eastern and western corridors that were designated as seating compartments. When the guests sat down, a single person holding chopsticks and paper[23] then asked all of the seated guests for their orders. People of the capital were extravagant and unrestrained, and they would demand a hundred different things—some hot, some cold, some warm, some room temperature, some icy cold, as well as toppings of both lean and fat meats. Each person demanded something different. The waiter took their orders, then stood in line in front of the kitchen and, when his turn came, sang out his orders to those in the kitchen. Those who were in charge of the kitchen were called "pot masters" or were called "controllers of the preparation tables." This came to an end in a matter of moments, and the waiter—his left hand supporting three dishes and his right arm stacked from hand to shoulder with some twenty dishes, one on top of the other—distributed them in the exact order in which they had been ordered. Not the slightest error was allowed. Even the slightest mistake was reported by the guests to the head of the restaurant, who would then curse the waiter, or dock his salary, or, in extreme cases, drive him from the place.

When my kind went into a restaurant, then we used first-class ceramic bowls with shallow rims that were called "lapis bowls." Or we called it "first-class stew." Particularly fine vegetable dishes were also called "first-class pickled vegetables." Each bowl was ten *wen* (cash). If meat and noodles made up half the meal, it was called "combined stew." There was also an "individual stew," which was a half-portion. In the old days we used only spoons, but nowadays they use chopsticks.

Wine, Food, and Fruits

For the most part the cooks who sell snacks are called "Learned Ones of Fine Meals and Wine Measures." All of the young waiters in the wineshops are inclusively called "Uncle." There are also women from the neighborhood whose waists are wrapped with blue-flowered scarves and whose hair is coiled up in a precarious bun. They change the hot water for heating wine and pour out wine for the drinking party. They are commonly called "warmers of dregs." And there are common folk who come into the wineshops and who, spying young playboys drinking, attentively provide them services. They are dispatched to buy things or to go summon singsong girls, and to do things like fetch and send money and other items. They are called "idlers."

And there are others who come forward to change the hot water used to warm wine, pour wine, or sing, and sometimes even offer fruit or incense. They are called "riff-raff." And there are low-class singsong girls, who, without being summoned, come to sing in front of the tables. At the appropriate time they are given a little cash or some small item, and then they leave. This is called "petitioning the customers" or "hitting the wine seats." And there are those who sell medicinal herbs or things like fruit and radishes. They do not bother to ask if the customer is going to buy them or not, but pass them around to each of the seated guests and then collect money later. This is called "Temporarily Passing Out [the Goods]."

Such phenomena occur everywhere, except at Charcoal Zhang's and Yoghurt Zhang's near

Zhoubridge, where people of the above categories are not allowed to enter. These two places also do not sell wine snacks. They provide only fine pickled vegetables and sell only the best category of wine.

Merchants sell hair ornaments cut from silk and feathers in the shape of jade plums, moths, bees, snowy willows, and *bodhi*-tree leaves; they sell small balls of pea flour in the shape of tadpoles, and flattened fried glutinous rice balls. It is precisely these fried-glutinous-rice-ball sellers who erect green umbrellas on their bamboo racks, on top of which they fix small plum-red lamps fretted with gold. They hang lamps on the front and back of the racks and, keeping time to the beat of a drum, they twirl the racks round and round as they walk along. This is called "making it whirl."

On the Fourteenth Day of the First Month the Imperial Retinue Visits the Taoist Temple of the Five Marchmounts

On the fourteenth day of the first month, the Auriga (Charioteer, i.e., the emperor) pays a visit to the Pool for Welcoming Good Portent at the Taoist Temple of the Five Marchmounts (Sacred Peaks of the Realm), where he holds an "Imperial Presence" (this means a feast which he gives for his many officials). When it reaches eventide, he returns to the Interior.

The "Emperor's Circle" [24] and personal attendants to the emperor all wear large spherical caps, sprigs of flowers stuck in their hats, robes of red damask appliquéd with sporting lions, and waist wraps of the kings of heaven inlaid with gold, and carry various kinds of scepters. The Personal Guard all wear cross-tailed caps with the paired ends curled up and wide robes of high purple appliquéd with swans and bound with a belt.

Normally, each time the Auriga goes out, there are two hundred pairs of globed lamps of red silk appliquéd with gold leaf. These are augmented on New Year's Eve by lamps in the shape of palmate fans, made of glazed porcelain with jade staffs. The outrunners each carry a lamp globe of red silk, covered with a gem net. When the Auriga is about to arrive, outside of the several layers of the Emperor's Circle, a lone man bears a moon-shaped short-legged stool, covered in damask, on a horse. Ten or so members of the Personal Guard cluster around and prop it up, yelling out, "View the Auriga's Throne." [25]

Next in procession are some one hundred officials of the Bureau of Personnel, all in their official robes, holding staffs with globed tops covered by a net of pearls, riding on horses, anticipating any summons. The rest of the officials in close attendance are all dressed in their official clothes of violet, crimson, or green. The Grand Defenders-in-Chief of the Three Armies, military officials of the Court for Audience Reception, and the Bearers of the Imperial Arms are arrayed in front to lead the procession. "Inner Lads" are on both sides—these are strong-arms picked from the various armies, who are garbed in short damask jackets, wear small domed caps, and who keep watch with balled fists. Should anyone make a loud noise, they will be beaten until the blood flows.

Players from the Court Entertainment Bureau and the Column of Perfect Harmony lead the way, following the Auriga; cavalry formations of the various squadrons and columns play music. Beyond the Emperor's Circle that trails the Auriga, there are, on the left, the high ministers and their retinue, and on the right, the princes, the Royal House, and the Officials of the Southern Formation. [26] As the Auriga approaches, some ten men line up abreast at the gate to crack the whips. Behind the Auriga, there are small, red, embroidered parasols with crooked handles—these are also carried by palace attendants on horseback.

The Auriga enters the Lantern Mountain, and members of the Imperial Palanquin Court yell out in front of the palanquin, "Beauty comes, following the bamboo staff." The imperial palanquin makes one circuit, proceeding backward to allow a view of the Lantern Mountain. This is called "wheeling pigeons" or "treading the color spectrum." Then the Palanquin officials have a call, "It is now granted by Him to you for viewing."

The emperor ascends the Tower of Virtue Revealed. The roamers rush up to be near the Open Dais.

After the Lamps Have Been Brought In, People of the Capital Strive to Be the First to Go Out of the City to "Search Out the Spring"

South of the City: the Garden of the Jade Ford, which imitated the rectangular pond, the pavilions, and kiosks of other places,[27] and the Belvedere of the Jade Transcendent.[28] Going westward from Twisting Dragon Bend are the Ten Foot Buddha's Garden, the Garden of Grand Marshal Wang, and Meng Jingchu's Garden,[29] which is located in front of the Revered Sage (i.e., Confucius) Temple,[30] the Ridge for "Looking at the Reclining Ox,"[31] and the Shrine to the Knight Errant of the Sword.[32] Eastward from Twisting Dragon Bend there are even more gardens outside of Chen Prefecture Gate.

Outside of the Song Prefecture Gate on the east of the City are the Grove of Delight, Water Chestnut Reservoir, the Ridge of Solitary Pleasures,[33] Inkstone Terrace,[34] Spider Loft, and the Mai Family Garden. At Rainbow Bridge is the Wang Family Garden. Between Cao Prefecture Gate and the Song Gate are the Eastern Imperial Garden[35] and the Solar Brightness (Qianming) Exalting Summer/China (Xia) Nunnery.

North of the City is the Garden of Prince Consort Li.

West of the City the grand avenue of the New Zheng Prefecture Gate goes directly past the Reservoir of Metal's Luster; westward from there is a Taoist Cloister, in front of which are nothing but brothels. Further westward is the Loft for Feasting Guests. Here are pavilions and kiosks, twisting and turning ponds and dikes, swings, and painted boats. Drinkers can rent small craft on which to hold their feasts and float around to sightsee. It is just opposite the Belvedere of Auspicious Fortune and runs all the way to Plankbridge, where there are the Loft of Gathered Worthies and the Loft of Lotus Blossoms—both of which are "parting restaurants" for those going on official duties along the five highways that lead to Hedong and Shaanxi. This is where banquets are normally held to send people off. Past Plankbridge are Lower Pine Garden, Grand Minister Wang's Garden, and Apricot Blossom Ridge.

Southward, along the Alley of the Winged Tigers of the Water that runs from the corner of the Reservoir of Metal's Luster, downstream from the watermill is the Garden of Grand Preceptor Cai. South of that are the Nunnery of the Garland Sutra and Little Missy Wang's Wineshop in an alley just west of Horsewashing Bridge. Northward, along the Golden Water River is the Nunnery of the Two Zhes, the Baluo Monastery, and the Seed-Raising Garden—here the flowers and trees of all four seasons are in the thickest profusion to behold. Southward are the Liang Medicinal Herb Garden and the Garden of Grand Preceptor Tong. Further southward are the Monastery of the Iron Buddha, the Monastery of Great Fortune, and the Eastern and Western Villages of Cypress and Elm.

North of the City: Pattern-on-Heaven Slope, Cornerbridge, all the way to King Cang Jie's[36] Shrine, the Nunnery of the Eighteen Longlife Sages, and Codger Meng the Fourth's Wineshop. Northwest of the City were originally Commoner's Garden, Cang Jie's Terrace, and several "cup-floating"[37] pavilions and kiosks where people were allowed in to enjoy the spring.

Generally, the environs of the capital were replete with gardens and orchards, and there was no empty space within a hundred tricents. One after the other, fallow lands fill out with the face of spring, the pitchpipes of spring loudly proclaim clear weather, thousands and thousands of flowers strive with each other to blossom. Lithe willows lean to embrace whitewashed walls; on interlaced paths sandalwood wheels turn in the warmth, fragrant grasses are like a carpet; proud mounts neigh with head held high; apricot blossoms are like an embroidery; orioles twitter in the fragrant trees, swallows dance in the clear void. Red makeup sets tunes to music in the jeweled kiosks and storied towers, white faces sing as they walk, drawing near painted bridges and flowing waters. Raise the eyes and there are coy laughs swinging on swings; come upon any place and there is wild abandon kicking the ball. Pick the best place to search out the fragrance, and flowers and catkins drop into golden goblets; snap off kingfisher green, stick red into the hair, and bees and butterflies secretly follow homeward-bound mounts. This is then all continued by the Festival of Clear and Bright.

The Auriga Visits the Feasting Hall at the Tower of the Ford of Jewels

There is a Feast Hall south of the Tower of the Ford of Jewels. When the Auriga is on the verge of making his visit, the carts and horses of the imperial consorts are already here. Normally, people are also prohibited from entering these grounds, and there is a particular official in charge of this.

West of the Feast Hall is the Archery Hall. On the south of the Feast Hall are a crossroad, official roads, and willow-lined paths. This is where people of the capital play ball. Going west out of the Garden is the Alley of the Winged Tigers of the Water. South of the cross avenue, there is a street of old paulownia (*tung*) trees, with small orchards, pavilions, and kiosks. Going south, one crosses a painted bridge, and in the heart of the water there is a small pavilion with pinched and raised roof corners. It is surrounded by a squared pool and willow-lined walking paths; it is called Toad Pavilion. It, too, is occupied by wine houses.

Normally, just before the Auriga makes his visit, the "dry" performances are rehearsed at the main gate to the Garden. The proxy for the emperor stands on the gate. On both sides of the gate bunted boxes are raised up high, and men of worth and ordinary people are allowed to observe and enjoy the presentation of the Hundred Entertainments. When the imperial proxy reaches the Reservoir, then yellow canopies are opened up and the whips are cracked, just as in [the regular] ritual.

Each time the Grand Dragon Boat comes out and when the imperial proxy comes to the Reservoir, then the roamers increase by twofold.

On the First Day of the Third Lunar Month, the Reservoir of Metal's Luster and the Park of the Rose-Quartz Grove Are Opened

On the first day of the third lunar month, the Reservoir of Metal's Luster and the Park of the Rose-Quartz Grove are opened just outside of the Gate of Compliance to Heaven. The rituals and activities of the emperor's visit to the Reservoir are rehearsed. Although attendants of the Forbidden City, officials, and commoners are allowed to enjoy the sights, the Censorate makes a public announcement that they cannot investigate [public behavior] at this time.

The Reservoir is located north of the road that exits the Gate of Compliance to Heaven, and it is approximately nine tricents and thirty paces in circumference. The diameter is something over seven tricents.[38] After one enters the Reservoir gate, about a hundred paces west along the southern bank is the Hall Overlooking the Water, which faces north. The emperor holds a feast here when he visits to observe the races to capture the flag. In days past it was put up on the spot using multicolored tents, but during the Zhenghe reign (1111–1117) a [permanent] hall was constructed of earth and wood. Some hundred paces further to the west is the Immortals' Bridge, a triple-span arched bridge running several hundred paces north and south that has red laquered balustrades, "geese posts" in line underneath, and a pronounced hump right in the center. It is called "Camel-hump Arch," and it is shaped like an arching rainbow. Where the bridge ends there are five halls right in the center of the Reservoir on an island of rockwork. In the center of the hall that faces north an imperial awning is erected, covering a dragon couch of red laquer with gold applique, and a wind screen decorated with dragons sporting amid the clouds and waters of rivers.

Roamers are not prohibited here, and in the winding corridors of the halls, both those above and below, there is wagering for money and goods or food and drink, entertainers who perform, and stages erected on all sides. On the edges of the bridge itself are tile basins that are used for coin tossing to wager for money and goods or clothing and implements. The roamers come and go, their umbrellas and parasols everywhere you look. At the south side of the bridge a lattice gate has been erected, and just inside the gate, facing each other, are bunted lofts—every time there is a race for the flag, music is played, and singsong girls are lined up atop the lofts. Now, just across from that lattice gate, on the south side of the road, there is a very tall raised brickwork dais with a multistoried prospect tower on top. It is more than a hundred *zhang*[39] in width and is called the "Tower of the Ford of Jewels." From the front of this [dais] to the gate of the Reservoir is an [open] strip of about a hundred *zhang*. The Tower overlooks the Immortals' Bridge and the water halls below, and the Auriga comes to this place to view the mounted archers and the hundred entertainments.

On the eastern side of the Reservoir weeping willows are next to the wall and also to the water. On both sides [of the avenue delineated by these lines of willows] are bunted canopies and boxes that overlook the water; [these] can be rented to observe the race for the flag. On the eastern side of the road are wineshops and food-stands, gambling arenas, stages for entertainment, and pawnshops ([original note:] if items are not redeemed within a few days, they are released for sale right after the Reservoir closes).

Going north from here one comes straight to the rear gate of the Reservoir, which is also the West Watergate for the Bian River. The western edge of the Reservoir is devoid of any buildings; there are just weeping willows dipping into the water and wispy grasses spreading along the dike. Roamers are few here, and are mostly fishermen—droppers of the hook—who must first purchase a license at the Reservoir Office before being allowed to fish. Roamers get these fish—without quibbling about price—and draw near the water to slice them into a mince as an accompaniment to a fragrant flagon of wine. This is indeed the most wonderful taste of the whole season. When all of the water exercises are finished, the smaller dragon boats are tied up here.

On the north side of the Reservoir, directly opposite the five halls of the water palace, a huge boathouse is erected, where the large dragon boat is moored. This is called "The Cavernous Building."

The Auriga normally picks the twentieth day to make his visit. All of the companies and squadrons of the Imperial Guard put branches of flowers into their hair-wraps, and throw on dragon robes fretted with golden threads and cinches that are either golden belts or silken waist-wraps—they vie with each other to be the freshest and most original. From the imperial warehouses they issue golden spears, bows and swords sheathed in jewels, pennants embroidered with dragon and phoenix, and damask woven bridles with scarlet tassles. Their myriad horses race with each other, the sounds of their harness bells shaking the earth.

The Auriga Visits the Hall That Overlooks the Water to Give a Feast and Observe the Race for the Flag

The Auriga visits the Hall that Overlooks the Water to feast his various ministers. From the front of the hall, a covered pier on which a ceremonial guard is stationed extends into the water. Four multihued craft are arranged in a row in the water near the hall, and the hundred entertainments of the various troops are presented aboard. These include great flag twirling, lion and panther dances, the knife toss, the barbarian shield, and variety plays on ghosts and spirits. Two other boats are lined up, which are for the orchestra. There is one other small craft, with a small bunted loft lashed together on top, at the base of which are three small doors, just like the openings of a puppet stage, that open directly into the water. On the orchestra boat, the Adjutant intones the Felicitation, and music is played. The center door of the bunted loft opens up and small wooden puppets come out: a small boat is rowed by a miniature lad while a white-robed person fishes. They slowly row around in a circle, speaking to each other until music is played and a live fish is caught and brought on board. Then music is played again and the little boat goes back into the tent. This is followed by wooden puppets who play football, dance and whirl, and the like. During each of these sessions the puppets also intone a Felicitation and sing a duet of alternating lines. More music is played and [the performance] comes to an end. This is called "water puppetry."

There are also two painted boats on which swings are erected; on their sterns the acrobats climb up a pole. The Overseer of the Left and Right Troops leads the activites, and the drums and flutes match with their sounds. Then someone climbs up on the swing, and when he is nearly level with the frame of the swing, he does a tumble and somersaults into the water. This is called "water swing."

After the water skits are finished, the musicians' boats of the "hundred entertainments" line up and [the men in] each sound gongs and drums, playing music and twirling their flags [in time]. Together with the puppet boat they form two phalanxes and retire from the area. Some twenty small dragon craft, each carrying scarlet-robed soldiers, fifty or more to the boat, set up flags, drums, and gongs. On the prows of the boats military officers twirl flags and beckon the craft forward—these officers are all Commanders in the Tiger-winged Navy.

Then there are ten tiger-headed craft, with a person standing on each prow, dressed in polychrome damask and holding a small flag. Everyone else is dressed in short blue robes, with peaked headgear. They make their oars dance in unison—these are all commoners who have dropped out of their regular professions.

Two flying-fish boats, colorfully decorated with splashes of gold, are the most artful of the lot, and there are some fifty people on board, dressed in theater shirts of various hues. Scattered among them at intervals are small flags of various colors and scarlet parasols. The [people] beckon and dance to the left and right, ring small gongs, and rattle drums. There are also two loach craft which can hold only one person, who paddles by hand—these are made of a single log. They all present [rare] flowers and stones that had been presented by Zhu Mian.

The various smaller craft all race to the Cavernous Building to pull out the grand dragon boat to go to the Water Hall. The smaller dragon craft race with each other to be first to circle and glide around, to lead it on its way forward. The tiger-headed boats pull out the dragon boat with ropes. This great dragon boat is about 30 or 40 *zhang* (300–350 feet [90–100 m]) and about three or four *zhang* wide (30–35 feet [10–12 meters]). Its head and tail have gills and scales, all of which are carved and gilded with gold. The planking on the hull is a neutral color, and there are ten or more compartments on either side; these are provided for the various groups of consorts to rest in. In the center the imperial throne is set up, behind a wind screen of dragons sporting in the water. The hull itself is several feet deep, and on the very bottom are closely spaced large cast pieces of iron in a shape that mimics large silver coins, but as large as tabletops, to weigh [the boat] down and keep it from yawing and rolling. There are storied towers on top of the deck, platforms and observatories, and a railing, inside of which the imperial seat is securely placed. One person stands on the dragon's head, twirling flags, and under the awnings on the left and the right are arranged six oars that undulate as though flying through the air. [The boat] goes to one side of the Water Hall, where it is anchored.

From the front of the Water Hall to the Transcendent's Bridge, red flags are stuck in the water beforehand to mark off the distances in the water. The so-called "little dragon craft" line up in front of the Water Hall, facing each other on the east and west, and the tiger-headed, flying-fish, and other boats spread out behind them, as though making two formations. In a little while a military officer at the awning in front of the Water Hall beckons them with a red flag, and then the dragon boats all come out of formation while [the people aboard them] beat gongs and drums. The [boats] are rowed into a round formation called "Circling," and the two formations of boats race through each other's lines; this is called "Crossing Heads." Another flag and they all line up east of the five halls, where they form ranks and rows and face the Water Hall. Then a military officer on a small skiff carries out a long pole which is strung with items like damask, bunted clothing, and silver bowls. This is called "the target pole." It is stuck into the water close to the Water Hall. Once again [the boats] are summoned by flag, and two rows of boats come forward together to the sound of drumbeats. The fastest captures the flag; then [its crew] shout out "Ten Thousand Years" and make an obeisance. Together with all of the boats, like the tiger-headed craft, they line up and each race three times for the flag before it is all over. Then the smaller craft again lead the great dragon boat back into the Cavernous Building.

Inside the Reservoir and Park People Are Allowed to Wager on Goods and to Play Games

Inside the Reservoir, in addition to the areas occupied by wine-houses and entertainers, there are many small booths set up that are made out of knotted, multicolored hangings, where items are displayed that are to be won by wagering: jewels, curiosities and geegaws, bolts of cloth, tools, and vessels for tea and wine. There are those who have wagered and won 450 taels of silver from a bet of only 50 taels, even to the point that carts and horses, property and houses, singing beauties and dancing girls have all been wagered on and won. In addition to well-known games like "try the big head" and "happy at three," there are others too numerous to mention.

The fish, lotus, and fruits presented by the Office of the Reservoir and Park are rewarded at imperial pleasure according to their quality. The miniature dragon boats built by the Construction Bureau of the Rear Palace, carved from ivory and inlaid with jade, are the culmen of artistry. Of those entertainers who accompanied the Auriga to perform at the Reservoir during the Xuanhe and Zhenghe reign periods (1111–1125) were: Multi-talented Zhang, Mr. Eyes-all-over, Whiff-of-Immortality Song, and Yin Shi'an, all of whom performed on strings; and Unflappable Li, who did water puppets. The others are too numerous to count.

Food at the Reservoir: rice gruel, chilled sweet green pea soup, snails, plum wine, dried haw fruit, dried apricots, mume, crisp plums in fragrant herbs, fresh-cut fish mince, black carp, salted duck eggs, and various kinds of spicy pickled vegetables. After the water exercises are finished, noble families set up their own household music and float about the reservoir on flat black-lacquered boats pulled by two hawsers. During the Xuanhe and Zhenghe reigns there were also large and small boats for rent, and commoners were allowed use of the boats for pleasure. Their price varied.

Ceremonial Guard of the Return of the Auriga

When the Auriga returns, his head is wrapped in a small cap, and he has flowers stuck in his hair as he rides his horse. His retinue, the high officials, the hundred officers, and his ceremonial guard all are given flowers. At the beginning of the Daguan era (1107–1110), he rode a bayard. He would come to the front of the Palace of Grand Harmony and then suddenly call for Reddy,[40] and the horse would come before him. Reddy would be held back and not allowed to go forward, and the servants would say, "By this he desires to be enfeoffed." The emperor granted the title of Dragon Courser General, and then Reddy would take the bit. Now Reddy was the horse that the emperor really loved.

It was all

Damask and brocade filling the capital,
flowers' radiance flooding the eyes,
imperial scents sweeping the road,
grand music ringing in the air,
jeweled mounts racing hither and yon,
bunted boxes lining the road.
Gauzes and silks, pearls and kingfisher feathers—
door after door of spiritual transcendents;
painted galleries and red lofts—
every house a grotto precinct.
Roamers both noble and common,
horses and carts numbered in the thousands.

Singsong girls mostly rode asses in the old days, but during the Xuanhe and Zhenghe reigns they only rode horses, mantled in their "cool dusters" with their head coverings tied to the backs of their caps. Young brothel rats often followed behind them, also astride horses and dressed in light gowns and small caps. Three or four tattooed young toughs controlled the girls' horses, and they were called "flowers falling from the horse." They controlled the horses' heads with short tethers, and struck at the ground as they went along, which was called "breast tethering." They shouted and yelled as they raced and ran, competing to show off their spirited elegance. Roamers often went home with the goods they had won gambling the day long hanging from a bamboo pole. As before, there were young girls of noble families, in small palanquins studded with flowers, who let down neither their curtains nor their screens. From the first of the third month until the eighth of the fourth month, when the Reservoir was closed, there were always roamers; not a single day was ever skipped.

This month, late in spring,
the myriad flowers blaze afresh,
peony and paeonia, kerria and brier rose—

all kinds come on the market.
Flower vendors arrange them in horse-head bamboo baskets.
The sounds of singing and shouting are clear and novel, easy to heed.
[Behind] sunscreen curtains in quiet courtyards
or morning shades in high lofts,
still drowsy from last night's wine,
just waking from a pleasant dream—
hearing these [cries] one invariably is easily moved by a fresh sadness,
or feels a secret vexation tentatively rise within.
This is the most superb state of the whole season.

The various troops go out into the faubourgs and engage in joint maneuvers.

The Seventh Eve of the Seventh Month

On the eve of the seventh day of the seventh month, *mohele*[41] dolls are sold on Alum Tower Street, in the pleasure precincts outside of the Song Gate in the eastern part of town, in the pleasure precincts outside of the Liang Gate in the western part of town, outside of the northern gates, and south (on the street outside of the Gate of the Vermilion Bird), as well as inside on Horse Guild Street. [Mohele] are actually small, sculpted clay dolls. They are all placed on colored bases; some use red gauze or an azure cage; some are decorated with gold, pearls, ivory, and jade (or kingfisher feathers?). Some pairs are as expensive as several thousand strings of cash. In the Forbidden City, in the houses of the nobles, and even in those of the common citizen, seasonal items are made to be sent as festival gifts. Ducks and geese, mandarin ducks, tufted ducks, tortoises, and fish are all cast from yellow wax. These are painted bright colors and decorated with gold. They are called "water floaters."

Another practice is to smear a small board with a layer of earth, then plant prepared grains of millet and force them to sprout. Then tiny thatched huts and flowers and trees are placed on [the board], along with figures representing farmers—the whole has an air of a farming village. This is called "the grain board." Melons are also carved in intricate patterns; these are called "patterned melons."

Made-up faces of young girls are molded out of oiled flour and congealed honey and these are called "likeness foods."[42] There are hundreds of variations on this clever skill—for instance, such things as lovers' knots molded of dough kneaded with scent. If one purchases a full catty's worth, then a pair of soldiers in full armor—like the images of door guards—is included in the lot. This has always been a dandy practice, but no one knows the source of the tradition. They are called "likeness-food generals."

Sometimes green peas, soybeans, and barley are put into a ceramic dish, then soaked in water until they have produced sprouts several inches long. These are tied with colored threads of red and blue and are called "grown from seed." Rainbow-colored curtained boxes are set up in the center of the streets, where these bundles are put out for sale.

For three or four days before the evening of the seventh, carts and horses crowd the marketplaces, and the fine gauze of women fills the street as they snap off the swelling buds of lotuses, just as they are ready to bloom. This is because people of the metrocapital, skilled in fabricating double-head lotuses, take pleasure in this particular moment when they can carry them home to the admiring praise of people on the street. Even small children purchase new lotus leaves and hold them in emulation of the *mohele* dolls, which are shown holding fans. Children are specially dressed in new finery and compete with each other to vaunt their freshness and beauty.

On the evenings of the sixth and seventh days of the month, most wealthy families put together rainbow-colored lofts in their courtyards, which they call "lofts for beseeching skills." Here they lay out *mohele* dolls, flowers and fruit, wine and roast meats, pens and ink-slabs, and needles and thread. Sometimes the young lads make up poetry and the young lasses display their skills, burning incense and lining up to make obeisance to the *mohele* dolls. These activities are called "beseeching skills" *(qiqiao)*. Women thread needles while gazing at the moon. Or they put a spider into a box. The next day they inspect the box, and if the web is round and perfect, they call it "attaining skill" *(deqiao)*.[43]

In the alleyways and in the houses of singsong girls, people line up at their doors and vie with each other over who is capable of indulging most in such luxury.

—SHW

Notes

1. This records events after 1117, when the number of entries in the gate was increased from three to five.

2. The author is here using sets of ritualized literary bisyllabic terms that are interchangeable synonyms for beams and headers.

3. The two words used here originally meant square rafters and round beams or purlins; again, these are essentially words from an archaic literary vocabulary.

4. These are actually located in the courtyard of the Hall of Patterned Virtue, which is directly to the west of the Hall of Grand Felicity. This is one of several mistakes in the text that can be rectified by collation against several other descriptions of the inner city.

5. Again, the author has misplaced these gates, which are just inside the Left and Right Ancillary Gates.

6. Constructed in 1117. A hall for worshiping Heaven, the Supreme Thearch, and the royal ancestors.

7. Two of the five libraries that held the archives of various deceased emperors.

8. The term "managers" *(lushi)* derived from the old practice of feting new Advanced Scholar graduates during the Tang. One person would be appointed to oversee all of the banquet activities and supervise drinking games, including doling out wine tallies and meting out appropriate punishments.

9. So named because of the sweet water wells there. Most other wells in Kaifeng produced water laden with mineral salts.

10. From a contemporary source:

The world is troubled by mosquitoes and blackflies, and Horse Guild Avenue alone, of all places in the capital, has no mosquitoes or blackflies. Horse Guild Avenue is a place where night markets and wine houses are extremely abundant. Now mosquitoes and blackflies hate oil (i.e., smoke from oil lamps), and Horse Guild is always raucous and afloat with people and animals. Lamp fires illuminate the heavens. They are extinguished only after the fourth drum, so the place is always void of mosquitoes and black-flies. Because the road is lined for tens of tricents by herbal simples shops and since most of the owners are physicians to the state and are all extremely rich, on the five nights of the First Prime (at the beginning of the year) the lamps are a particularly overwhelming sight, and the music and acting are absolutely extraordinary. So poets often speak of the lamp fires of Horse Guild Avenue, as well.

11. The older gate of the inner wall of the city. It got its name, Old Hill-Investiture (Fengqiu), because the road which led to Fengqiu district exited through it.

12. At the newer outer wall.

13. One recipe for a similar meat cube reads: "Slice both lean and fat pork into three-inch long slices in the shape of counters and let sit overnight in a mixture of granular sugar and fagara powder. Mix thoroughly in equal portions of sugar, powder, and spices. Dry in the sun and then steam until cooked thoroughly."

14. One recipe for these blood sausages states: "Thoroughly wash out the large and small intestines of a

fat sheep. Mix cool water and fresh blood together thoroughly, half a ladle each at a time; then fill the intestines as one would for normal sausage. The fresh blood must be quickly and precisely matched. It cannot be too large a portion. If too much, it congeals and cannot be poured into the intestines."

15. Inner-wall gate through which the road to Suanzao (Sour Jujube) Prefecture ran.

16. Luxury items such as antiques, jewelry, etc.

17. This is usually understood as rhinoceros horn and jade; however, it could also mean horn that had been burnished to a jadelike luster.

18. All famous players in the Court Entertainment Bureau.

19. This was a reward for Deng Xunwu, who had been appointed in 1116 to be Military Commissioner for Protection of the Grand Army, at which time he was also appointed Co-Commissioner of Military Affairs; he was given this residence by the emperor in 1121 as a reward for being one of the prime movers behind the return of an influential minister to the capital.

20. One of the numerous entertainers and jesters favored by Huizong (r. 1100–1125), the reigning monarch.

21. Originally a site to honor Lü Shang, who helped King Wen wrest control of China in the Zhou, this was to become the major temple for honoring military heroes. By the end of the Song, some seventy-two (a Eurasian magical number) generals and military figures from the historical past were enfeoffed here as objects of sacrifice.

22. One of Huizong's concubines; originally a woman of the wineshops, her beauty captured the eye of one of Huizong's lackeys, who presented her to the emperor.

23. This could also mean paper to wipe the chopsticks with.

24. "Circle" is a metaphorical term for the personal guard.

25. Shen Gua (1030–1094) describes this paraphernalia as the "Seat of Law of the True Court," the throne the emperor sits on in his hall for normal morning court. Here, of course, it is a miniature, described as "made of aloeswood and decorated with gold. It has four legs and drooping corners, and is slightly curved in the front. It is capped by woven rattan. Each time the emperor goes out to visit a place, a veteran eunuch is employed to clasp it on a horse; it is called *jiatou*."

26. Members of the male descent line of the imperial family; they were normally given titles in the civil bureaucracy.

27. The Garden was noted for its beautiful buildings, including pavilions and kiosks; it also served as a truck garden for the Inner City, as a zoological garden, and as a wheat farm for both ritual agricultural practices and fodder for animals. The elephants used for imperial parades were housed and cared for here.

28. Located seven or eight tricents outside of the Chen Prefecture Gate, it was built during the reign of Renzong (r. 1022–1063) by a certain Taoist Chen, who turned it into a lavish garden, most noted for its three "rocks of ancient pine flowers" and two "dragon-tooth rocks." While visiting the Anguo Monastery during his exile in Huangzhou (1080–1083), the noted poet Su Shi (1036–1102; see selection 58) recalled it as one of the two sites with a lavish display of flowers:

Searching Out the Spring at Angus Temple

Abed, hearing "hundred tongues"* summon the spring winds,
Arising, seeking out flowers and willows, village after village the same;
South of the city an ancient temple enclosed with tall bamboo,
A little room, a crooked verandah that leans out over deep red.
Looking at the flowers, sighing over growing old, evokes memories of youth,
Facing wine, thinking of home, saddens an old codger.
Weakening eyes are unabashedly confused by mica windows,
Templelock strands are forced into place by mist of tea.
Far away I know that in the second month, outside of the kingly city,
At Jade Transcendent and Abundant Fortune the flowers are like the sea. . . .

*"Hundred tongues": the bush warbler (*Horornis cantans*), noted for its remarkable range of calls; also called "cowdung mynah" *(niufen bage)*. Anguo Temple was destroyed by the Jin in 1125–1126.

29. Meng Jingchu was a Director in the Court Entertainment Bureau (Jiaofang shi). Elsewhere in *Dong-jing meng hua lu,* the stoutness of his body and costume are mentioned in his role as a spirit in the "Great Court Exorcism" ceremony.

30. The temple, about a mile southwest of the city, was destroyed during the Jurchen seige of Kaifeng in 1125–1126.

31. Named for the prospect of the city wall when looked at from afar.

32. Zhu Gai, the patron saint of butchers, was a knight errant from Liang (ancient Kaifeng) during the Warring States period who hid out in the meat stalls. When the state of Qin attacked Zhao, he was sent by a third party to kill Jin Bi, who was the head of the Wei armies, and to wrest away his forces and lead them to rescue Zhao. The grave itself was located south of the city, in a park called "Butcher Boy Garden." On Clear and Bright Festival the butchers of the city would lay out wine and viands for sacrifice.

33. The place, which lay fifteen tricents east of the city wall, got its name from the following oral legend. There was a rich old man who lived here during the Song. His children were already married, and he paid no attention to the affairs of his family, but daily invited his old friends here to drink and make music. Once, when Emperor Huizong went out incognito to see him, he sighed in admiration, "Doesn't this man exemplify the pleasures of being alone?"

34. The tumulus of Zhang Yi (d. 309 B.C.E.), renowned persuader of the "horizontal" school and minister to several states. It was shaped like an inkstone, hence the name.

35. Also called "Park Perfect for Spring" (Yichun yuan) or "Welcoming Spring Park" (Yingchun yuan), it was on the site of imperial archery contests. By the year 1061 it was already in disrepair, as evinced by Wang Anshi's poem "At the Perfect-for-Spring Park" (Yichun yuan), written in that year:

> Old terraces and ponds of Yichun,
> The day draws to a close, I climb to look down on it.
> I release my belt to walk along the moss and lichens,
> Move my saddle to sit in the verdant shade.
> Trees are scattered, crying birds far away,
> Water is still, falling flowers deep down—
> No longer is there any repair or expansion,
> The ruler our king begrudges the waste of gold.

The garden was later turned into a granary complex; it also housed Huizong after he abdicated and was on his way to exile in Manchuria.

36. Cang Jie was the mythological inventor of writing.

37. Flat-topped stones or wooden tables were cut with deep grooves through which water flowed. Cups of wine were set adrift down these little channels, and guests were supposed to compose a poem (normally of four or eight lines) before the cup finished its leisurely journey down this miniature river.

38. These numbers are certainly wrong.

39. One *zhang* is equal to roughly ten feet (three meters).

40. The horse's name, Wu, is a shortened transcription of Uhulan, which is an Altaic word for "red."

41. There are many transcriptional forms of this term in Chinese characters. They represent either Sanskrit *muhūrta* (moment, instant) or *mahoraga* (serpent [in Buddhist terminology]). Although the type of doll mentioned here is often said to derive from the fat-bellied serpent called *mahoraga,* it is more like a personification of *muhūrta* signifying "diminutive, tiny."

42. The term *guoshi* (fruit/nut food) is a homophone for "exact likeness."

43. The Double Seventh festival is important because, according to an ancient legend, on the seventh night of the seventh lunar month, the Weaving Girl and the Oxherd are permitted to have their annual meeting across the Milky Way. The "beseeching skills," threading needles, and putting a spider in a box to spin its web are all related to the weaving theme of the legend.

67. Front chamber of tomb of Wang Chuzhi, Qiyanchuan Village, Quyang County, Hebei; 923. Tomb construction in China flourished uninterrupted through the first millennium C.E. and into the second. The epitaph in the center of the front chamber of the tomb, excavated in 1995, identifies this as the tomb of the military governor of three districts. The themes in murals of Han through Tang times persist here, but all are presented in styles of the tenth century. Ladies are corpulent and have especially round faces, a style that became popular in the mid-eighth century and is captured in painting of the Tang court (plate 64). An astronomical map such as was buried with the son of the woman covered by the silk painting at Mawangdui was found here too (plate 26). New, however, are replicas of screen paintings of birds and flowers and landscape painting, all of which rose to new heights in the first half of the tenth century in China.

68. Gu Hongzhong, "Night Revels of Han Xizai"; 943–960; Palace Museum, Beijing. In this opening scene from a rare example of tenth-century figure painting, the viewer is introduced to the private world of the Southern Tang (943–960) court official Han Xizai. The varying angles of the bed, tables, and screen and the use of bright red against black

and muted tones create an intensity made more emphatic by the eye contact between the female musician on the left, the bearded Han Xizai, and the red-robed official to his right. The dynamic moment so well captured here by figures, color, and props emerges only in the tenth century, separating paintings such as this one from the sometimes nearly lifeless products of the Tang court (plate 64). The intensity of this particular work is appropriate: the painter was asked by the Southern Tang ruler to visit Han's reported night revelries and present him with a painting as evidence of the unspeakable.

69. Interior of Guanyin Pavilion, Dulesi, Ji County, Hebei; 984. A year after the fall of the Tang dynasty, a man named Abaoji began forging a confederation of nomadic and seminomadic tribes in Northeast Asia. When Chinese rule reasserted itself as the Song dynasty in 960, sixteen prefectures of northern Hebei and Shanxi, including Ji County, were no longer in Chinese hands but formed the nucleus of the Liao dynasty. Yet little of the non-Chinese rulership is expressed in Guanyin Pavilion. Like many Liao wooden buildings, the pavilion is characterized by a dramatic ceiling. In addition, the interior is built around a sixteen-meter-tall image of the bodhisattva Guanyin. The pavilion uses twenty-four different types of bracket sets, more than in any contemporary Song structure but less than half the number in a Liao pagoda built seventy years later, and its two-story exterior conceals a third story visible only on the inside.

70. Remains of Liao princess of Chenguo and her husband, Xiao Shaoju, in tomb at Qinglongshan, Naiman Banner, Inner Mongolia; 1018. This excavation photograph of the tomb of the daughter of a Liao emperor and her husband, the brother of a Liao empress, reveals a burial practice of the Khitan, the people who formed the majority of the Liao ruling class. Their corpses were encased in metal wire netting, fit to each body part, and their faces were covered with golden death masks, their heads with gold crowns, and their feet with silver and gold boots. Not shown here is the preparation of the corpse beneath the metal suits. Remains of other Khitan individuals confirm textual descriptions of the draining of bodily fluids and replacement of soft tissue with vegetal matter for preservation. Although a contrast to jade suits that encased Han royalty (plate 30), the purpose of these Khitan burial garments was similar.

71. Guo Xi, "Early Spring"; 1072; National Palace Museum, Taipei. Besides the intense look at figures, the new interest in bird and flower painting, the use of ruled lines to paint architecture, and the continued painting of Buddhist subjects that reflected currently popular sects, the kind of Chinese painting known as Romantic landscape was born in the tenth century. It was a type of painting with which Chinese painters would be associated for the rest of painting history. Like Guo Xi, painters of Romantic landscape questioned the meanings of life, art, and nature in their writings and considered their art an investigation of the human spirit. "Early Spring," painted more than a century after the beginning of the tradition, includes tiny figures on a boat in the right foreground and on land in the left foreground, all about to confront the exuberance of nature as it bursts forth into spring. The placement of a monastery and hut in the midground suggests these men may reach those heights, but it is doubtful that in their journeys through life, symbolized by nature in the painting, they will reach the summit of the highest mountain peaks.

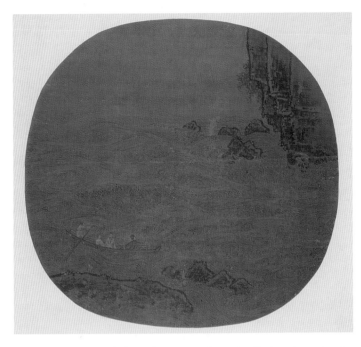

72. Li Song (fl. 1190–1230), "The Red Cliff"; Nelson-Atkins Museum of Art. Li Song was adopted by a painter in the Southern Song Academy in the capital city of Lin'an (Hangzhou) and painted at the courts of three emperors. Album leaves, the most intimate format for Chinese painting, were a common product of the Southern Song court, and many are attributed to Li Song. Among them are several paintings of peddlers that show the minutiae borne on the backs of merchants who came to the countryside to sell their wares and the locals who bought from them. In this album leaf, Li Song has chosen one of the most famous men of eleventh-century China, Su Shi (1036–1101), who expounded the theory of the *wenren,* or literatus. Wearing a red robe, Su gazes at the Red Cliff that inspired his famous ode (selection 58).

73. Detail of birds and flowers woven in silk *kesi,* (131.6 cm x 55.6 cm); Northern Song period; Liaoning Provincial Museum. Previously in the private collection of Zhu Qiqian (1872–1964), this best-known extant example of *kesi* is dated to the Northern Song dynasty. It was woven by a process called *tongjing duanwei* (literally, "woven continuously through the warp but with the weft cut"). On a simple, vertically slanted loom, the weaver first stretched the warp (purple silk) longitudinally between the warp and cloth beam and then "colored in" small areas of the weft by taking one thread of one color, wound around a small bobbin-like shuttle, back and forth latitudinally over the warp. When that area was finished, the weaver proceeded to "color" the adjacent area using another thread of a second color, section by section, until the desired motif was achieved. The result gives the impression that the silk was "carved" or "engraved," which is what the term *kesi* implies. The decorative pattern of this uncut example consists of magpies and mythical *luan* and *feng* flying amidst stylized peonies (king of flora), a Buddhist lotus, and sprigs of flowering crab apple *(haitang)* encircling a pair of confronting peacocks, each of whom holds a stalk of a vegetal scepter *(ruyi).*

74. Longxing Monastery, Zhengding, Hebei; Northern Song period and later. Song scholars are known for their advocacy of Neo-Confucianism, but the emperors continued to patronize great Buddhist monasteries. One temple complex that received attention from the Song imperial family was Longxing Monastery. Four Northern Song buildings stand there today, more than at any other religious or secular site. Towering over the monastery is the twenty-four-meter Foxiang Pavilion, constructed in 971 (and rebuilt in the twentieth century) to house a monumental bronze image of the bodhisattva Guanyin. In the same year, a side pavilion to the future Buddha Maitreya was built. Like Guanyin Pavilion at Dule Monastery (plate 69), it concealed an interior story. A pavilion that houses the monastery scriptures also dates to the Northern Song period. Its revolving sutra cabinet is a unique example of that type of structure from Song times. Finally, another unique building, a twenty-sided hall dedicated to Śākyamuni with a cruciform plan, was built in 1052. That hall and Foxiang Pavilion stood on the main building line of the monastery; the other pavilions flanked them.

75. Six types of bracket sets, from Li Jie, *Yingzao fashi*; 1st edition, 1103; 2nd edition, 1145. This page from the architectural manual presented to the court of Song Huizong in 1103 shows six types of bracket construction from the three *puzuo* (set) through the eight *puzuo*. Bracketing is just one element of the Chinese timber-frame structure which provides a symbolic visual system of a structure's rank. The more complicated the bracketing, the more eminent the structure. So far, seven *puzuo* is the highest number that survives in actual buildings, four *puzuo* the lowest. As stipulated

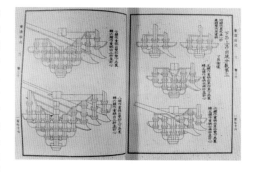

in the thirty-four-fascicle text, the Chinese wooden building skeleton is modular, and the module is generated by the section of a bracket-arm. Eight grades of timber are specified in the illustrated text, as is the number of hours expected of workers in various media of the building industry according to season. Both the frame as a whole, including ground plans, and architectural work in stone, brick, tile, and other materials for doors, windows, stairs, balustrades, etc. are described in detail.

76. "Flour Mill Powered by Waterwheel"; anonymous painting, late 10th c.; Shanghai Museum. Close observation of detail and a certain kind of realism come together in a genre of painting named *jiehua* (literally, "boundary painting"). Painting with straight edges and measured lines was ideally suited to depictions of architecture and machinery. In this handscroll painted in ink and color on silk we get a rare glimpse of Song industry. In addition, we see a unique picture of the timber frame of a building raised on high pillars, brick foundations and diagonal ramps built of patterned brick leading up to a work space, and in the background, the thatch-roofed structures where we assume the mill owners spent their day. Finally, in the foreground, goods and products necessary to the mill enterprise are transported by land and sea to the mill. In this part of the painting, the landscape elements mark the picture as a work of the Northern Song period.

77. Zhang Zeduan, detail of "Qingming Festival on the River" (Qingming shanghe tu); ca. 12th c.; Palace Museum, Beijing. No painting offers a closer look at life in the Chinese capital than this one. First painted by Northern Song court painter Zhang Zeduan, either when he was at the Huizong court of the Northern Song in Bianjing (Kaifeng) or as a reminiscence of former days after 1126 when the court moved south to escape attack by the Jurchen, this painting survives in many copies. Besides the busy lives of merchants and laborers in the capital, two famous scenes in the handscroll are a gate-tower of the city, strangely free-standing with a camel passing through it, and masses of the population crossing the bridge to the tomb area on this festival day dedicated to cleaning one's ancestors' graves at the end of the winter season.

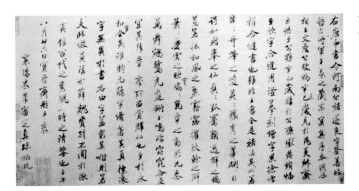

78. Mi Fu (1052–1107), colophon to "Lantingxu" (Orchid Pavilion preface), handscroll; National Palace Museum, Taipei. Mi Fu was one of the great calligraphers of the Song dynasty. Like all calligraphers, he learned from the past. In particular, he was inspired by the writing style of the fourth-century father and son masters, Wang Xizhi (307–365) and Wang Xianzhi (344–388). The "Orchid Pavilion Preface," to which Mi Fu's calligraphy is appended, is a 324-character essay on the transience of life first written by the elder Wang in the year 353. Mi Fu also is associated with a style of ink painting characterized by hazy, evocative forms. The concept of using the same brushstrokes to paint and write was fundamental to the training of Chinese poets, painters, and writers in the Song dynasty and later.

79. Ma Hezhi (act. 1130–1170), "The Seventh Month," detail of "Odes of the State of Bin"; Metropolitan Museum of Art. Ma Hezhi was a painter at the court of the first Southern Song emperor, Gaozong. Much of his oeuvre consists of paintings that illustrate poems in the *Shijing* (Book of odes). Accompanied by the text, this scene of activities of the seventh moon of the year illustrates the girls who gather mulberry leaves in their hampers while field hands work and the oriole sings. The undulating brush strokes are a trademark of this painter.

80. Chen Rong (13th century), "Nine Dragons Appearing through Clouds and Waves," handscroll; signed and dated 1244; Museum of Fine Arts, Boston. Chen Rong was a painter who specialized in dragons. In this, his most captivating work, he seizes the ferocity, energy, and spirit of China's most powerful symbol using only black ink and a few touches of shades of pink. The technique is the same one, usually without any color at all, employed by Chan (from Sanskrit *dhyāna* ["meditation"];" Zen in Japanese) Buddhist painters in southeastern China, where Chen worked during a peak century in the production of Chan painting. Like calligraphers, ink painters achieved maximum power and maximum subtlety through single brushstrokes. The paper background, on which the ink can spread, or "wash," further enhances the skill of a great ink painter.

81. Emperor Huizong, "Auspicious Cranes"; 1112; Liaoning Provincial Museum. Emperor Huizong (r. 1101–1125) was not only a patron of the arts, but also a serious painter and calligrapher. In fact, history has judged him a man devoted to the arts at the expense of his empire: it was under his watch that the northern half of Song China fell to the non-Chinese Tungusic Jurchen who formed the Jin dynasty in 1126. The omen of cranes soaring upward from the rooftops, an auspicious sign since Han times, could not save his empire. Besides gathering great artists, the Huizong court was responsible for cataloging the imperial painting col-

lection in the work *Xuanhe huapu* (Register of paintings of the Xuanhe Reign Period) and for issuing the most comprehensive building manual in Chinese history, *Yingzao fashi* (Building standards) (plate 75).

82. Great Pagoda, Great Pagoda Monastery, Ningcheng, Inner Mongolia; Liao period with later revisions. The Liao dynasty is known for extraordinary creativity in architectural design and for octagonal pagodas. Both features are exhibited in the eighty-meter-high Great Pagoda that stands at the ruins of a former Liao and Jin capital. Consisting of four parts—base, decorative band, shaft, and thirteen densely placed eave layers—the Great Pagoda was built to be seen from the outside and, as its name suggests, as a beacon from afar of the powerful non-Chinese dynasties who patronized it. The shaft features four esoteric buddhas and four esoteric bodhisattvas, and together with the center may be an ingenious replica of the nine deities in the central portion of a mandala (circular schematized representation of the cosmos) admired by Liao Buddhists. Like many Liao sites, this capital and its monasteries were revitalized during the rule of the next dynasty, Jin, who conquered them, and again by the last Chinese dynasty, Qing, whose Manchu founders and rulers were also of non-Chinese origins.

83. Back chamber, tomb of Dong Hai, Houma, Shanxi; 1196. Even by Chinese norms the interior elaboration of this tomb is extraordinary. Standard decoration in a Chinese tomb, including husband and wife occupants, their servants, their utensils, and their meal, are all present, but the latticework on the door, floral decoration on the wall beneath them, and every member of the oversized bracket sets, down to the swirls on the edges of the arms, are sculpted and painted with more attention to detail than in the past. Typical of tomb decor beginning in Song times and escalating during the Jin period, the intensity of decoration in this chamber is a marked contrast to

the tomb structure. Rarely is a Jin tomb more than a single, simple room. Even side niches are not that common. Rather than build many rooms for their afterlife, wealthy citizens such as this couple spent their money on decorating to the fullest the walls of their limited space.

84. Muqi (act. 13th c.), "Six Persimmons"; 13th c.; Daitoku-ji, Kyoto. Muqi was a Chan (Zen) Buddhist monk and a painter who worked in the vicinity of the Southern Song capital in the last half-century of Song rule. Many elements of Chan painting are represented in this work. It is, first, a painting in ink alone and, second, a study in varying levels of intensity of ink to capture the same subject, here a persimmon. Possibly painted rapidly, without indication that the painter returned to his work for touch-up, and perhaps inspired by a sudden urge to paint his subject, this exercise in drawing six pieces of fruit can be likened to the sudden attainment of enlightenment by a meditating monk. It may also be a spoof on Chinese officialdom or even the inherent foibles of man, for the painting has been nicknamed "Six Scholars," the tops of the stems recalling scholars' caps. Both the aesthetic and the technique were greatly admired in Japan, where ink paintings were collected by the ruling military leaders from the fourteenth century onward. The simplicity of paintings like this lends itself to forgery, making the authenticity of many Chan works attributed to Southern Song painters, including this one, questionable.

85. Revolving Wheel of the Six Conditions of Sentient Existence, Baodingshan, Sichuan; Southern Song. Since the second-millennium-B.C.E. culture that produced bronze men and masks at Sanxingdui (plate 10), Sichuan has been a province of art and architecture related to China, but always distinct. The rock-carved caves and relief sculpture of Baodingshan near Dazu are no exception. The six sections of the wheel, divided by ribbons that emerge from the Buddha at the center, contain illustrations of the realm of the gods, man, a battle between men and gods, the animal kingdom, hungry ghosts (unappeased spirits), and hell. Although each can be found elsewhere in Buddhist relief sculpture in China, the intensity combined with human quality of the images sets the sculpture of the Dazu cave groups apart from that of other sites.

86. Crackled celadon with azure glaze; Song; National Palace Museum, Taipei. Chinese potters have exhibited superior workmanship and instinctive ability for design since the Neolithic era. By Song times, the art of porcelain manufacture was perfected. Many wares were known for their colors; some were named for them. The word "celadon" was adopted from the color of a costume worn by a shepherd in a seventeenth-century French play. The Chinese name for the ware, *qingzi* (azure-purple), was also derived from the color. Originally the crackled effect was accidental, but it came to be highly appreciated and intentional. Celadon was one of the most appreciated of China's stonewares.

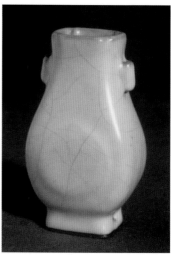

87. Dening Hall, Temple to the Northern Peak, Quyang, Hebei; 1267. The Temple to the Northern Peak was built by order of Khubilai Khaghan more than ten years before the official establishment of his government. It purpose was to pay homage to the northern of the five sacred Daoist peaks. Approached by white marble stairs, surrounded by a white marble balustrade with dragon-headed posts, and supporting two sets of roof eaves, this hall is the closest surviving example of what Khubilai Khaghan's own hall of audience in his palace-city might have looked like. Construction of such a magnificent hall for a Chinese ceremony performed by the emperor that traces its roots to pre-Han times, already before the walls of the capital were completed or South China had been taken, signaled the intentions of the Mongol conquerors of China to rule as Chinese emperors.

88. Portrait of Chabi, wife of Khubilai Khaghan; National Palace Museum, Taipei. Chabi was her husband's partner in every way. She shared his ambitions to rule a strong empire with China at the center, was watchful of his enemies, and criticized him when she believed his policy to be counter to imperial Mongolian goals. She had a reputation for practicality and frugality, recycling everything from bowstrings to animal skins. She designed broad-rimmed hats to keep the sun off people's faces and sleeveless clothing for combat. Chabi is known to have supported Buddhism in the empire and once mediated between Khubilai and his Tibetan Lamaist adviser 'Phags-pa so that the Great Khan could continue to receive his guidance but not feel threatened by the other's power. One of Khubilai's four wives but certainly the most influential, she was married to him by the year 1240. Khubilai was heartbroken when Chabi died in 1281. She is the only one of his wives whose portrait survives.

89. Zhongtong yuanbao jiaochao (primary treasure exchange note of the Zhongtong era). Paper money has been used in China since the Tang dynasty. *Zhongtong yuanbao jiaochao* was one of three paper currencies issued by the Mongols in 1260, almost twenty years before the establishment of the Yuan dynasty. The Mongols also issued coins, cast with standard or official script rather than the harder-to-read running or cursive script on Song coins, but from the beginning, the Mongol government determined that paper currency would be the dominant form of monetary exchange. This note is valued at a string of one thousand cash of copper coins, or half an ounce of silver. It was issued in denominations of 10, 20, 50, 100, 200, 300, 500, 1000, and 2000. Backed by silver and gold, paper money was the universal form of exchange under Mongolian rule: circulation of silver or gold was forbidden. When Mongolian rulers of Iran, descendants, like the Mongolian rulers of China, of the house of Chinggis Khaghan, tried to introduce paper money to their Il-Khanid empire, the population was outraged, and the ruler of Iran ended up paying for it with his life.

90. Guanxingtai (Star Observation Platform), Dengfeng, Henan; 1276. This observatory is one of nine built under the supervision of Guo Shouqing, China's most famous thirteenth-century astronomer. The platform rises 9.46 meters. Its purpose was to measure the angle of the sun in order to make a more accurate calendar. At its northern end is a niche where a stone scale was placed. At noon each day, the shadow of the sun on a crossbar fell on the scale. On the basis of that shadow, the length and number of days was calculated.

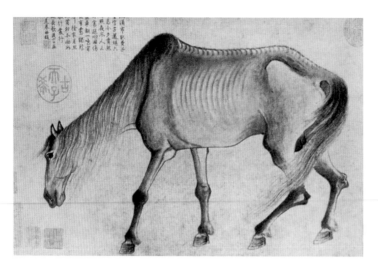

91. Gong Kai (1222–1307), "Emaciated Horse"; first half of Yuan dynasty; Osaka Municipal Museum. Gong Kai was an *yimin,* a "leftover subject," or official who had served the Song dynasty and found himself without means of support when the Mongols came to power. Like many of his compatriots, Gong fled to the Jiangnan region, southeast of the Yangtze River, and lived out his days in poverty. Tales of the heroic efforts of men like him to continue the pursuits of Chinese officialdom under adverse conditions abound. Gong, it is said, used his son's back as a painting surface since he could afford no table. Also typical of the times, Gong's paintings are on paper, a much more affordable medium than silk. Most important in this painting is its purpose—to express symbolicly his feelings about Mongolian rule. The emaciated horse with hanging head is a metaphor for the once strong China, formerly represented by a horse such as the one Tang emperor Taizong had ridden (plate 56).

92. Qian Xuan (ca. 1235–aft. 1301), "Wang Xizhi Watching Geese"; 2nd half of 13th century; Metropolitan Museum of Art. Qian Xuan was the most famous *yimin* painter. Like Gong Kai (plate 91), he had been educated in the Song bureaucratic system, attaining the highest scholarly degree awarded, but not until 1260, so he never actually served at the Song court. His paintings of figures such as this one embody several key elements of *yimin* painting: the "amateur ideal," aspects of painting of earlier periods in Chinese history, and multiple layers of overt and covert meaning and symbolism. The choice of colors is a reference to a style known as "blue and green" that had been common at the Tang court, and the use of blue for rocks together with the almost juvenile, paint-by-numbers way they are filled in are expressions of amateurism. Thus, in the same painting we have a wistful reminder of a strong China under Tang rule and a subtle assertion that an educated man should possess the ability to paint, but only as one of his many casual, or amateur, talents. The concentration of detail in one corner of the painting is a reference to a Southern Song court style, the "corner composition." The subject is a historical figure of the third century renowned not only for his calligraphy, which was inspired by the motion of geese, but for his moral integrity. The geese, themselves, may be covert symbols of warfare (especially with northern peoples). The many meanings behind the simplistic figures and bright colors were innuendoes that would have been readily understood by the literati-in-exile of Qian Xuan's day. They were the closed circle of China's former intellectual elite for whom men like Qian wrote and painted as means of venting their frustrations with politics and China's plight.

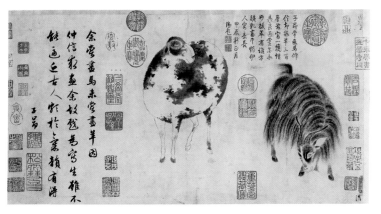

93. Zhao Mengfu (1254–1322), "Sheep and Goat"; Yuan period; Freer Gallery of Art. Zhao Mengfu is considered one of the greatest painters of the Yuan period. Yet in his own time, many viewed him as a traitor. Although a descendant of the Song royal family, he accepted an invitation to serve Khubilai Khaghan's govern-ment, which he did from 1286 to 1295. Zhao's personal battle with loyalism may be one of the meanings in this painting. On the surface it is a study in ink on paper of two animals, a standard subject for Tang painters, whom Zhao wrote he admired. However, an inscription attached to the painting suggests that the proud sheep represents a Han loyalist, Su Wu, who gave up his former status to become a sheep-herder when he was captured north of China's border, and that the humiliated goat is Su's co-officer, Li Ling, who joined with non-Chinese forces after his capture (selection 29). Whether or not this was Zhao's intent, for Yuan painters, simple subjects like this one took on meanings often far more complicated than their compositions.

94. Workshop of Ma Jun-xiang, "Jade Emperor and Terrestrial Empress," east half of north wall, Hall of the Three Pure Ones, Yongle Daoist Monastery, Ruicheng, Shanxi; 1325. Painter workshops deco-rated the walls of countless Buddhist and Daoist tem-ples in Shanxi Province in the thirteenth and four-teenth centuries. Among them, the Ma family were famous, and their paint-ings on the walls of the Hall of the Three Purities at the Yonglegong are among the finest wall paintings in China. Illustrated are more than four hundred deities of the Daoist pan-theon, making this the largest repository of Daoist imagery in China. Behind the Hall of the Three Puri-ties stands a hall dedicated to the patriarch of the Complete Perfection (Quanzhen) sect of Daoism, Lü Dongbin. Those walls, which narrate Lü's legendary life, were painted by the Zhu family workshop. Murals in the hall behind it recount the legendary life of the twelfth-century founder of Quanzhen Daoism, Wang Zhe. The four thirteenth-century buildings and fourteenth-century paintings on their walls were deemed so extraordinary that when the original site of the Daoist monastery was threatened by a modern water-works project, all existing halls, including the more than eight hundred square meters of wall paintings in them, and scores of stelae were moved upriver to Ruicheng, where they stand today.

95. Ni Zan (1301–1374), "Woods and Valley of Mount You"; 1372; Metropolitan Museum of Art. Ni Zan was born into a wealthy family from Wuxi, Jiangsu. Living in a time when the sons of wealthy men no longer expected to serve their government, families like his had nevertheless managed to own estates in southeastern China and live as members of an intellectual elite. This all changed in the 1340s, when the Mongol government made a last effort to hold onto power by raising still higher the tax base in this region, already responsible for 90 percent of their internal revenue. Like many from Jiangnan of his class, Ni Zan could not pay his taxes and was reduced to a life of poverty, living off his wealthier friends, in Buddhist monasteries, or by painting in exchange for food and shelter from local overlords who aspired to gain enough power in the south to rise against the Mongols. Ni Zan died broken and impoverished. "Woods and Valleys of Youshan" is one of about sixty paintings in similar style attributed to him: dry ink on paper, lacking all signs of humanity or enthusiasm for life.

96. Blue-and-white underglazed porcelain; Yuan period; Sackler Museum, Harvard. As in Song times, celadon was highly admired and sought after in the Yuan period. Under the aegis of Mongolian rule across Asia, Chinese celadon became available in West Asia as well as in China, so that today one of the finest collections of porcelain made in Yuan China is in the Topkapi Palace, Istanbul. The origin of blue-and-white underglazed porcelain, however, is more complicated. The technique, which included the use of blue cobalt paint and copper-red underglaze, reached its peak in the Yuan period; many scholars hold that the blue was obtained from the Muslim West, where it was particularly favored. Moreover, polychrome porcelain supposedly was considered vulgar at the Song court. Still, there may be a few examples of porcelain with colored underglaze from the late Song dynasty, leaving the role of the Western branch of the Mongol empire in the production of Yuan-period blue-and-white an unresolved issue.

63 | Zhang Jiucheng's Explanation of Zhang Zai's "Western Inscription"

ZHANG ZAI (1020–1077), a native of Chang'an, was the son of a high-ranking official. He passed the civil service examinations in 1057 and began his own successful career in the bureaucracy, until he resigned in protest of Wang Anshi's New Policies (see selection 58). As a young man, Zhang had studied Buddhism and Daoism, but found neither satisfactory. He turned his attention to Confucianism and became a friend of the brothers Cheng Hao and Cheng Yi, whose own brand of Neo-Confucianism strongly shaped Zhu Xi's thinking. Though Zhang has been linked with the early Song Neo-Confucian movement, traditionally there has been some debate about whether or not he was truly Confucian, or whether he was too influenced by Buddhism and Daoism.

The "Western Inscription" was a piece that Zhang Zai wrote on the Western Wall of his home, and one that influenced later Neo-Confucians. The original "Western Inscription" is terse and cryptic. The following is an expanded paraphrase of the original by another Song Neo-Confucian, Zhang Jiucheng (1092–1159). The latter Zhang was a native of Qiangkang, near the modern city of Hangzhou, and passed the civil service examinations in 1132. Never successful as an official, he instead became a renowned teacher. Famous for his commentaries on many classical Confucian texts, Zhu Xi later criticized him, as he did Zhang Zai, for being overly influenced by Buddhist ideas.

The "Western Inscription" is important because it laid the foundations for a Confucian cosmology that would challenge Buddhist and Daoist notions of the nature of the universe and connections between things. Here the human being is intimately connected to the world around him, but his obligations to that world are couched in examples from the Confucian tradition.—RF

Qian, the primal male energy, is my father. Kun, the primal female energy, is my mother. I am their child and live naturally between them with other people and things. My body is not limited to my own physical form. Whatever exists between Heaven and Earth—people, creatures, the land, plants, animals and insects—are all my body. My inner nature is not limited to what I see and hear, or to what I say or how I appear. Within the world, states of activity such as moving and creating, flowing and standing, or growing, flying, and swimming must have something that activates them: this is my inner nature. When Heaven and Earth give birth, those who are born into the world similar to myself are my siblings. Those that also have a place in Heaven and Earth, who live in profusion, and grow wildly are all my companions.

As I am the child of Heaven and Earth, the great ruler who governs the family affairs of Heaven and Earth is the crown prince of my father and mother. The great ministers who assist the Son of Heaven in carrying out the affairs of Heaven and Earth are the crown prince's household officials. Those of old age who were born into the world before me are like my elder brothers. I revere and treat as senior those made older by Heaven and Earth. The orphans and young children born into the world after me are like my younger brothers. I pity and so treat as juniors those made younger by Heaven and Earth. The sage harmonizes the virtues of Heaven and Earth. The worthy person is the apex of the refinements of Heaven and Earth. The decrepit and crippled, the orphaned and widowed are those of my brothers who are faltering, but have no one to whom they can tell their troubles. Protecting them in need is the way this child assists Heaven by caring for these poor people.

That I am able to delight in the commands of Heaven and Earth and not be worried even in difficulties is to be a truly filial son. One who contravenes the mind of Heaven and Earth does not love his family and opposes virtue. One who harms the humaneness of Heaven and Earth steals from his parents. One who promotes evil is a son of Heaven and Earth who is not using his natural abilities. One who acts according to the signs of Heaven and Earth, who takes appearance, speech, sight, hearing, and thought as the implementations of respect, obedience, intelligence, understanding, and perspicacity, is fulfilling the virtues of Heaven and Earth.

The affairs of Heaven and Earth are nothing more than transformation. The intentions of Heaven and Earth are nothing more than divine. If you understand transformation and plumb the depths of the divine, you will be good at emulating and implementing the affairs and intentions of Heaven and Earth. Nothing is obscured from the mind of Heaven and Earth. One who is not ashamed in the privacy of his house is not disgraced before Heaven and Earth. The mind and the inner nature are Heaven and Earth. To preserve the mind and nourish the inner nature in the middle of the night is to serve Heaven and Earth by not relaxing in the middle of the night.

Sage-emperor Yu was the son of the Lord of Chong. Because good wine can confuse the virtues, Yu hated it and so attended to the nurturing of Heaven and Earth and his parents.

The Lord of Ying Gu asked to set aside some meat for his mother in order to arouse the filial piety of Duke Zhuang of Zheng.[1] Now if I nurture the talented individuals that Heaven and Earth have given birth to, this is the same use of the filial mind.

Sage-emperor Shun, in awe and fear, did not shirk in his labors and so delighted his parents. I can match Shun's achievements if I exert myself in doing good, thereby pleasing Heaven and Earth. If the Great Shun's father was angry at him and wanted to give Shun an excessive beating, Shun would flee. If his father wanted to give him a small beating, he would bear it. On the other hand, Shen Sheng did not fully understand the Way. He considered his own death to be reverently satisfying his father's hatred.[2] This cannot be used as a model. Zhang Zai's use of this example is to show that being slandered is fate, while to accept one's death as respectfully following Heaven and Earth, like Shen Sheng's respect, is possible.[3]

Zeng Zi died a proper death.[4] If I can emulate his propriety, follow his example, and completely submit to Heaven and Earth, then this is the same as Zeng Zi's filial piety.

Bo Qi was the son of Yin Jifu. Jifu was moved by his second wife's slandering his own son to send Bo Qi out to change chariots in the frost without clothing or shoes.[5] Bo Qi obeyed his father's command. If I can be without anger, particularly towards Heaven and Earth, then this is the same as Bo Qi's filial piety.

Heaven and Earth have amply supplied our lives with wealth, high status, good fortune, and kindness; however, poverty, low status, worry, and sorrow are also expressions of Heaven and Earth's love, there to help fulfill me. If in life I serve and obey Heaven and Earth without opposition, and if in death I am at ease in their mind and will and do not cause disorder, then I will always heed the command of Heaven and Earth and be their perfectly filial son.

—RF

Notes

1. The Duke had banished his own mother, so when he was hosting the Lord of Ying Gu, the latter hoped to stir the Duke's feelings for his banished mother by acting filially toward his own mother.

2. Shen Sheng's stepmother wanted her own son to become heir, so she accused Shen Sheng of plotting his father's assassination. His father subsequently sentenced him to death. When others encouraged Shen Sheng to flee, he refused on the grounds that flight would mark him as a disobedient son.

3. Here Zhang Jiucheng seems to be disagreeing with Zhang Zai, who equally valued Shun's service to his parents and Shen Sheng's acceptance of his death sentence after being slandered. Zhang Jiucheng elaborates that Shun would serve his father when his father was reasonable, but would flee when he was not. According to Zhang Jiucheng, we should respect Shen Sheng's reverence for his parents and even be willing to die for maintaining the standards of Heaven and Earth, but not for the sake of reverencing a misguided parent.

4. Zeng Zi, one of Confucius's disciples, on the verge of death insisted that he not die on a mat given by a friend. When one of his students said he was too ill to move, Zeng Zi insisted that moving him was the proper thing to do. He was moved and died soon after.

5. This is another instance of a stepmother slandering her stepson in order to get her biological son named Heir Apparent.

64 | Zhu Xi, Introduction to the
Redacted Centrality and Commonality

ZHU XI (1130–1200), was a native of Fujian Province. His father was a civil official, and Zhu Xi himself passed the civil service examinations at the young age of nineteen. Because he had high moral standards for officials and opposed the court's policy of peaceful coexistence with the Jurchen Jin dynasty that had invaded and occupied northern China since 1127, his official career was turbulent. Of a scholarly bent, Zhu spent his career mostly filling temple sinecures, which provided him with an income, little official responsibility, and time to teach and write. He is undoubtedly one of the most influential figures in Chinese history. Though attracted to Buddhism and Daoism in the first thirty years of his life, he subsequently turned to Confucianism and became its staunch advocate. Inspired by earlier Neo-Confucian thinkers (Cheng Yi [1033–1107] in particular), Zhu Xi set about systematizing the Confucian tradition, weaving together themes as diverse as metaphysics, government, and poetry. From the classical tradition he developed a program of study with what he termed the Four Books (Confucius's *Analects,* the *Mencius,* the *Great Learning,* and *Centrality and Commonality* [i.e., the *Doctrine of the Mean*]) at the core. He used these texts and the writings of other selected Confucians to expound his belief that there is a single unitary principle that gives order to the universe. All things embody this principle and are shaped by it. Therefore, the individual's task is to understand this principle through study and apply this understanding to every facet of his life. Learning and study were necessary because, even though humans all embody this principle, everyone also has a physical body that gives rise to selfish desires. Therefore, one needs to study the works of leading Confucians to understand how to overcome one's own biased view of the world. Although during his lifetime Zhu Xi was branded a heterodox scholar, his ideas and systematized view of the Confucian tradition gained popularity. Eventually, in 1313, his commentaries upon the Classics became the foundation for the imperial civil service examinations, remaining in place until the collapse of imperial China during the early twentieth century.

This "Introduction" to one of the Four Books is a clear statement about his understanding of the Confucian tradition's origins and purpose. He uses this short piece to present his own views on the tradition's core teaching and how that core has come to be understood. Here he attempts to answer questions about the authentic transmission of core values and the moral nature of human beings.—RF

How did *Centrality and Commonality*[1] come into being? Master Zisi[2] wrote it because he worried that the transmission of the Learning of the Way would be lost. When the sages and spirits of high antiquity established the ultimate according to Heaven, the transmission of the Tradition of the Way was natural. In the Classics, the line "sincerely grasp the center" is what Sage King Yao taught Sage King Shun. The statement "the human mind is precarious; the Way's mind is subtle, it is pure and singular; sincerely grasp the center" is what Sage King Shun taught Sage King Yu. Yao's one line was perfect and complete, but Shun added three lines to it in order to clarify Yao's one line. This was necessary so posterity could aspire to it.[3]

Most would say that the mind's spirit and consciousness are unified. Yet I believe there is a difference between the human mind and the Way's mind: one is produced by the self-interest of physical form, while the other is based in the rectitude of the inner nature. This is why there are differences between those who have consciousness. Thus one mind is precarious and unstable, while the other is subtle and difficult to perceive. Yet everyone has physical form, so that even the wisest have the human mind; and everyone has inner nature, so that even the most ignorant have the Way's mind. The two are combined within the space of a square inch,[4] and if you do not know how to control them, then the precarious becomes more precarious and the subtle more subtle, and in the end the impartiality of Heavenly principle will not be able to overcome the self-interest of human desires. To be pure, examine the division between the two and do not mix them; to be singular, protect the rectitude of the fundamental mind and do not depart from it. If you act with this in mind and do not lose this focus for a moment, then the Way's mind will always be the master of the body, and the human mind will always obey its commands. Then the precarious becomes stable, the subtle becomes manifest; and whether active or still, in speech or deed, you will not make excessive mistakes.

Yao, Shun, and Yu were the world's greatest sages. Passing the rule of the world to each other was the important task in the world. When at these moments of transmission the world's greatest sages carried out the world's greatest task and their advice and warnings were nothing more than those [lines stated above], how could anything be added to this underlying principle of the world?

Various sages—such as Cheng Tang, Wen, and Wu as rulers and Gao Yao, Yi Yin, Fu Yue, the Duke of Zhou, and the Duke of Shao as ministers[5]—have borne this responsibility in turn, and all held these statements to be the transmission of the Tradition of the Way. The achievements of our Master Confucius, although he did not achieve the political position of the others, are as worthy as Yao's and Shun's because he continued the [teachings of] past sages and opened the way for future students. Yet of all his disciples, only the schools of Yan Yuan and Zeng Shen maintained these key points. Yet by the time Confucius's grandson, Zisi, became a second-generation disciple of Zeng Shen's school, the sage had been dead a long time, and heterodox doctrines had arisen.

Zisi feared that as more time went by the tradition would lose its purity. He therefore deduced the intentions of the original transmission stemming from Yao and Shun, gave it substance by using the words he had heard daily from his father and teacher as illustrations, and wrote this book, *Centrality and Commonality,* to instruct later students. He probably was deeply worried, so his words are carefully chosen; and his pondering was farsighted, so what he wrote is incisive. He said that the heavenly mandate commands the inner nature, hence the term "the Way's mind." He said the choice of good is firmly held, hence the term "pure and singular." He said the gentleman is always centered, hence the term "grasp the center." Over a thousand years later, his words are still perfectly appropriate. In selecting the works of previous sages to focus on the key points and reveal the profound, there has never been anything so clear and complete as this book.

From Zisi [the tradition] was again transmitted over two generations to Mencius, who was capable of understanding this book and maintaining the tradition of the previous sages. When he died, the tradition was lost. Therefore, our Way's survival depended upon nothing more than this text. But heterodox theories sprang up overnight and flourished, and the disciples of Lao Zi and Buddha appeared. Because their doctrines appear similar to [the sages' Heavenly] principle, they threw the truth into disorder. However, we are fortunate that this book has not been lost.

Thus when the Cheng Brothers were born,[6] they studied it and followed this thread that had not been transmitted for a thousand years. They relied upon it to critique the mistake of these two schools' apparent accuracy. Zisi's achievements were great, but were it not for Master Cheng Hao, no one would have been able to understand his thoughts based upon his text. It is a pity that Master Cheng's theories were not transmitted; yet the compilation by Shi Dun is completely derived from the writings of Cheng Hao's students, so his general ideas are clear; his more subtle words, however, have not been analyzed.[7] Though his students' own ideas are detailed and enlightening, when compared to their teacher's theories, some are tainted by Daoism and Buddhism.

When I was young, I read of Cheng Hao's ideas and humbly doubted them. However, after often being immersed in them, one morning it suddenly seemed that I had grasped his main ideas. Afterwards I dared to confront other theories and analyze their central ideas. Then I wrote the *Redacted Centrality and Commonality* in one fascicle for later gentlemen and one or two with similar minds. I also went back to Shi Dun's book, pared down his prolixity, and entitled it *The Synoptic Centrality and Commonality*. Moreover, I recorded the reasons for selecting or discarding certain interpretations and made an appendix entitled *Various Questions on Centrality and Commonality*. This completed the goals of this book: to edit and parse the text, to link the sequence of ideas, to relate the detailed and general to each other, and to present both the broad and the fine; and, in general, the similarities and differences and the advantages and disadvantages of various theories are also clarified and explained so the ideas of each are exhausted. Though I do not dare discuss lightly the transmission of the Tradition of the Way, if literati beginning their studies find it useful, then it will be some small help in practicing this old and lofty tradition.

—RF

Notes

1. *Centrality and Commonality* is a translation of the Chinese title *Zhongyong,* which has also been translated as *The Unwobbling Pivot, Application of Equilibrium,* and—more commonly—*The Doctrine of the Mean.* See selection 10.

2. A descendant of Confucius.

3. Yao, Shun, and Yu are the three legendary rulers who are credited with shaping Chinese politics and culture in the predynastic period.

4. "One square inch" is a common reference to the mind.

5. All of these men were rulers or high officials in the Shang and Zhou dynasties.

6. Cheng Hao (1032–1085) and Cheng Yi (1033–1108) were closely linked to the previous generation of scholars involved in Confucian studies: Zhou Dunyi (1017–1073) was their teacher, Shao Yong (1011–1077) their friend, and Zhang Zai (1020–1077) their uncle. However, the Chengs are credited with being the driving force behind the Confucian revival in the Song dynasty due to their ability to find coherence among diverse Confucian texts.

7. Here Zhu Xi is referring to a Song-dynasty text concerning Cheng Hao's ideas about *Centrality and Commonality* as compiled by Zhu Xi's friend, Shi Dun (1128–1182).

65 | Dragons, Tigers, and Elixirs:
Alchemy in Medieval China

CHINA'S ALCHEMICAL WRITINGS remain little-explored sources for understanding various nonofficial aspects of Chinese popular religion, natural philosophy, and medicine. Adepts who received alchemical writings from human or divine teachers saw what they had learned as a means to compound pure and powerful elixirs that could offer them and their patrons immortality and an immortal post in the divine hierarchies, as well as invincibility, power to control spirits, and higher sociopolitical standing. Adepts imagined, prepared, and used these elixirs they made for many things, but much of this variety can be seen as part of China's broad vision of self-cultivation that consolidated in Warring States and Han times.

Most of the three hundred or so earliest Chinese works that make extensive and systematic use of alchemical imagery, symbols, and terminology are included in the Ming *Daoist Canon of the Zhengtong Reign Era (Zhengtong daozang)* published in 1444–1445, but their provenance can often only be limited to a dynasty, a geographical region, or contemporary religious, technological, or philosophical developments. The earliest texts may date from the first century C.E. and the most recent to the 1440s, with the majority of titles dating to South China in Song and Yuan times. Because alchemy developed after the formative stage of China's philosophy, politics, and nature of the imperial Chinese state, its traditions employ many of these ideas and ideals, albeit in modified forms and for new and nonofficial purposes. Prominent here are activities meant to generate pure elixirs within models of cosmic process (the Way), whether they occurred in a laboratory, in the human body, through sexual union, or all three. Because of the wealth and prestige involved for the former model, alchemical activities seem to have first appealed to spiritually ambitious literati and technical masters and their potential patrons, who initially sought ad hoc patronage from the emperor or his family, but gradually wished to bolster the standing of wealthy aristocracy outside of official circles. Alchemical texts often present themselves as offering the most exalted methods of ritual and self-cultivation to foster political legitimacy and spiritual advancement.

Some of the new Daoist religious movements from the late fourth century aimed to establish themselves, in part, upon the foundations of alchemy, but made grander claims for their rituals and powers. Their attempts to supplant alchemy by selectively incorporating some alchemical ideas, gods, and methods into their religious systems and placing them at a lower level of efficacy and power than their more exalted approaches to spiritual advancement did not stop alchemists from transmitting their teachings independently to members of the imperial house and the literati. Although the Way was a unity beyond which there was nothing, efforts to embody the Way were never able to monopolize the diverse aims and ambitions of the Chinese people. Alchemy retained currency above and beyond the efforts of Daoist priests (or emperors) to limit its purview.

A single reading of a given alchemical text is often not enough to indicate whether it focuses on producing cosmic essences through laboratory work, exercises and meditation, or sexual practices. It is clear, however, that the most innovative alchemical traditions after the ninth century produced texts that regularly criticize the use of minerals and sexual practices. By the fourteenth century, these new priorities (sometimes extended to sexual practices) are regularly known as indicators of the superior Inner Elixir *(neidan)* traditions as opposed to the lesser traditions that centered on producing Outer Elixirs *(waidan)*. These priorities conformed to and advanced the priorities favored by those aspiring to become part of the emerging gentry sector of society, whose men defined themselves by their mastery of cultural refinement and philosophical speculation. Thus, while indicating the continuation of alchemical interpretations of laboratory and sexual activities, the gentry heirs to the most exalted forms of the art viewed it as a higher form of inner self-cultivation. In this way, alchemy came to be seen as a useful complement to the official state-sponsored form of Dao Learning, a superior counterpart to Chan (Zen) Buddhism, and the inner spiritual motor of some of the new forms of Daoist ritual practice.

The following three passages were written during the time of changing priorities from alchemy for the aristocracy and alchemy for gentry, but seem to focus more on laboratory-based elixirs than corporeal ones. Like most of the hundred or so extant books on laboratory alchemy, the compilation from which they came, *The Divine Grades of the Elixir Methods from the Various Lineages (Zhujia shenpin danfa),* is anonymous. It is part of the Ming Daoist Canon (its title is number 912, according to K. M. Schipper's Concordance to titles in this canon). The editor of this compendium, who most likely lived during the Southern Song (1127–1276), chose to include texts whose dates range from the ninth to twelfth centuries; most of them deal with aspects of laboratory alchemy. Like most extant alchemical texts, this one contains few clues to provenance.

The passages translated here form three consecutive (but also scarcely related) passages on the otherwise unknown *Scripture on the Golden Elixir of the Dragon and Tiger (Jindan long hu jing),* which may be the same as the *Scripture on the Great Cyclically Transformed Elixir (Da huandan jing),* both of which focus on the sources and powers of the Great Cyclically Transformed Elixir of the Dragon and Tiger (Longhu da huandan), a wondrous medicine that is often abbreviated as the Great Elixir of the Dragon and Tiger (in the first and second passages), the Great Cyclically Transformed Elixir, or just Cyclically Transformed Elixir. Despite the similarities in their names, the three passages discuss two different fundamental alchemical processes in China, and in so doing embody some of the key transitions in alchemy between the eighth and tenth centuries.

The first passage links the elixir—as transformed cinnabar—to both the roots of Chinese civilization and the foundations of the cosmos. The same character *(dan)* is used for both. The basic meaning of *dan* is cinnabar (the crystalline mineral of mercury and sulfur), and the remarkable separation of cinnabar into mercury and sulfur after heating and their recombination after cooling provided early alchemists with a basic model for one of their main alchemical processes, the product of which they called the Cyclically Transformed Elixir *(huandan).* Multiple recyclings of this cinnabar, in ritually controlled environments, produced the purest essence of the cosmic Way itself. By embodying the purest essences of the cosmic process, the refined cinnabar compounds can be understood as, in Nathan Sivin's apt phrase, "time-controlling substances."[1] Besides offering longevity and spiritual advancement, this elixir also can grant adepts or their patrons invincibility and the power to control the gods. Like its predecessor, the second passage argues for the importance of the Dragon and Tiger Elixir, which it links to a middle-grade elixir. This was appropriate for people living in the second major age of alchemy, which fell between Tang and Yuan times.

The third passage follows the major trend of later (post-Tang) Chinese alchemy in stressing that the key alchemical process centers on amalgamating refined forms of lead and mercury into an elixir. The lead-mercury amalgam discussed below becomes the alchemical process that dominated most later texts. These two refinements—which have corporeal counterparts—are given the synonyms Dragon and Tiger (for lead and mercury, respectively), thereby linking them to the most fundamental aspects of the universe, namely yang and yin and their manifold correlates. These links extended outward to the cosmos before its differentiation into the world of ordinary experience as well as backward to the endlessly generative undifferentiated state of the

Way itself, of which the elixir—whether in the laboratory or in the body—was a genuine fragment. Although embodying the very essence of the sun and moon and therefore of the cosmos, the amalgamated elixir of lead and mercury presents itself as having been very rare in earlier times and so relatively new at the time of the texts' composition, sometime between the eighth and tenth centuries.—LDS

Scripture on the Golden Elixir of the Dragon and Tiger

Marvelous Instructions on the Inner Secrets and Real Writs of the Dragon and Tiger

The [teachings of the] Great Elixir of the Dragon and Tiger (Longhu dadan) arose with the Three Sovereigns (Fuxi, Suiren, and Shennong) and were continuously passed down from High Antiquity *(shanggu),* orally transmitted and memorized by heart without ever having been written down. Since the Five Emperors (the Yellow Lord, Zhuan Xu, Yao, Shun, Yu), the methods first came to circulate in the world, and in the succeeding ages multitudes attained the Way. Since not even one or two of the Utmost Men personally transmitted the oral instructions, how much greater is it than the Five Thousand Character Text (i.e., the *Daode jing*) passed on by Lao Zi and the teachings of the Tripitaka issued by the Buddha, which merely expound the principles of non-activity *(wuwei)* and seeing Buddha-nature *(jianxing)* [respectively]? To be dead while alive—just preserving your inborn nature intact or creating gods of empty brilliance—will never make you able to become as invincible as the Cyclically Transformed Elixir. [How much better] to remain undyingly alive, protecting the Soaring Transcendents *(feixian)* without losing [your] inner constitution with these Genuine Methods in the activist mode.

Although not a few divine transcendents from antiquity to the present have attained the Way, none have mentioned anything about the Cyclically Transformed Elixir. This is because This Way is of utmost greatness, and may not be carelessly divulged. If you only teach people the methods of absorbing or emitting the radiances of the sun and moon, circuiting the seminal essence and circulating the *qi,* preserving unity by concentrating on spirits, retaining the seminal essence by [the ritualized sex of] riding women, or ingesting medicines of plants, the Five Metals or the Eight Minerals, even though you will temporarily extend your allotted number of years well beyond that of common people, you will ultimately lose the path of Everlasting Life. If you come upon waters, fires, swords, armies, poisonous creatures and wild beasts, poisonous medicines and evil calamities of the spirits, they will damage the inborn nature and natural endowments *(xing ming),* and you will be unable to leave the Grand Cycles of Cosmic Creation *(wuxing zaohua).* This being the case, none of the thousand ordinary methods will let you endure for long.

How could you not have noticed that all of the ancients whose entire families soared aloft [into the Heavens] did so through the powers of the most treasured, most revered, most valued, and most marvelous Great Cyclically Transformed Elixir? "Cyclically Transformed" means "returning back home" and "Elixir" is the name of the color crimson. This is [the process of] cinnabar exuding Realized Mercury, which, when blended *(jie)* with lead, becomes the Yellow Sprouts. The Yellow Sprouts once again become cinnabar. When fire subdues Cinnabar, it becomes the Cyclically Transformed Elixir. Whenever there are such wonders of cyclically reverting, the [product] is able to make the old become young, the dead revive, and the withered flourish. Sprinkling it on potsherds will turn them into most treasured [items]. With such efficacies of the Divine Sage, how could they not be great?

The Three Grades of Great Cyclically Transformed Elixir

The Superior Grade of the Nine Times Recycled, Golden Liquor, and Langgan Roseate Gem are the Great Cyclically Transformed Elixirs treasured in the Supreme Heavens and have not been passed down to the world. The Middle Grade of the Great Elixir of the Dragon and Tiger and the Inferior Grade of Eight Mineral [Elixirs] that transform into Quicksilver constitute the Nine Grades of the Divine Elixirs [available to human beings]. Ever since the Yellow Emperor (Huang Di) of Xuanyuan refined the elixir and soared aloft [into the Heavens], the powers of Our Great Elixir of the Dragon and Tiger have been most great! Upon entering the mouth, a single spatula [of it] will forever fix [the natural endowments] and extend the years, get rid of heteropathic and restore orthopathic [vital energies], instantly expel the [body's] Three [Deadly] Corpse-worms and Nine [Mortal] Creatures, and secure [the divinizing energies of] Essence and Spirit in the [lower] Elixir-Field without letting them escape.

The countless Divine Transcendents who attained the Way in High Antiquity completely concealed the principles of the Cyclically Transformed Elixir. Although the Elixir Scriptures (danjing) in the mundane world of dust sketch out its broad outlines, its abstruse fundamentals are totally hidden in secrecy with no oral explanations. While some in later generations have hankered after the Way, they had no starting point and blindly stumbled about on their own into decrepit old age.

I will now divulge the Heavenly Key and straightforwardly write out the method's orally transmitted explanations in order to ensure determined men who want to cultivate the Way of inborn nature and natural endowments that they need not doubt they are being deluded.

Oral Instructions on the Realized Dragon and Realized Tiger

The Realized Dragon is the Quicksilver within Cinnabar, and is the product of the descent into the ground of the Solar Light of the Grand Radiance as Realized Qi called Mercury. The Realized Tiger is the White Silver within Black Lead, and is the product of the descent into the ground of the Lunar Florescence of the Grand Darkness as Realized Qi known as Lead. Because these two treasures are endowed with the Realized Qi of the Solar Essence and Lunar Florescence, Lead contains Qi and Mercury is fundamentally Formless. None of the revered seventy-two minerals surpass Lead and Mercury in their being able to produce the Dragon and Tiger. The *Scripture on the Great Cyclically Transformed Elixir* says, "There is proof that live [unfired?] Quicksilver can secure the dead, and dead [fired?] Quicksilver can secure the living right before the eyes." How could the ranks of the walking corpses who fail to seek the Great Elixir possess spiritual powers like these? Those who come upon it have a long-held Transcendent Lot as the inherited blessings of their ancestors. Those who come upon this method should keep it secret and hidden, preserving it and being careful about divulging it lightly, since anyone who so divulges it will be punished [by Heaven]. Even though you may be as close as father and son [to someone], do not speak about it. If you come upon an Utmost Man with the same ambition who is in tune with the Way, you may transmit the Oral Instructions.

—LDS

Notes

1. "Chinese Alchemy and the Manipulation of Time," in Nathan Sivin, ed., *Science and Technology in East Asia* (New York: Science History Publications, 1977), pp. 108–122; reprinted from *Isis* 67 (1976): 513–527.

ZUQIN (1216–1287), known also as Xueyan, was a monk of the Linji (J. Rinzai) sect of Chan (Zen) Buddhism, which had by his time overwhelmed all rival denominations and established its paramount place. As one of the chief abbots of the sect, Zuqin enjoyed a prestige, both secular and ecclesiastic, seldom achieved by his Tang or Northern Song predecessors. If he was the first one in Chinese history to talk unabashedly and at length about himself, his propensity was aided by the exuberance of the vernacular finely honed during the previous two centuries by the performing arts and by the flexible format of the sermon that had adopted many theatrical devices, as well as, perhaps, by his realization that his was the representative life story of the Buddhist seeker for illumination who persevered and triumphed over all obstacles and setbacks.—PYW

When I was five years old I entered a temple. As a footboy to the abbot, listening to his conversations with visitors, I came to know that there was such a matter[1] and believed that I could achieve it. I studied sitting-in-meditation.[2] But on account of my obtuseness all my life I have suffered repeatedly and bitterly. I became a monk at sixteen and started traveling[3] at eighteen, determined to get to the bottom of this matter.

I then joined Master Tiejueyuan of Shuanglin in his assembly of sitting-in-meditation. From morning to night I stayed in the monks' hall and never went outside. Even when I was walking in the dormitory or to the washroom I held my hands in my sleeves and crossed them in front of my chest. Walking ever so slowly, I never looked left or right, nor did I see anything more than three feet in front of me. Caodong[4] masters usually taught a disciple to concentrate his mind on *gongan* (Chan paradoxes) such as "whether a dog has Buddha nature." When random thoughts and extraneous ideas occurred the disciple was supposed to visualize the character *wu* (nothingness) and balance it, ever so gingerly, on the tip of his nose. As soon as the random ideas disappeared, he would discard the character. In this fashion he silently sat, waiting for purification and maturation. After a long time perfect understanding would occur of its own accord. The Caodong method was so elaborate and perplexing that a disciple could easily spend ten or twenty years without getting anywhere. This was the reason that not too many stayed with the sect.

One day I reflected on the beginning of thoughts, and the thought of reflection immediately became an icicle, translucent and immovable. I was so frozen in my sitting meditation that the day passed in a flash. The sound of bells and drums never reached me, nor was I aware of the noon meal or any of the other scheduled activities. When the abbot heard about how well I sat he descended from the hall and came to have a look at me. He even praised me during a sermon.

At nineteen I went to Lingyin[5] as a temporary resident. I saw Miaofeng. After his death Shitian succeeded him. Yingdong was serving as the warden of the guest hall. There I met a monk-scribe who came from Chuzhou.[6] He said to me, "Brother Qin, your endeavor is like dead water; it won't do you any good. You have broken your activity and inactivity phases into two separate things." What he said about me was quite true. When I sat down, I felt I was in an unusual state, but it would disappear when I started to walk, picked up a spoon, or put down chopsticks. He said further, "To engage in Chan endeavor one must have doubts. Great doubts lead to great enlightenments; small doubts lead to small enlightenments: there is no enlightenment without doubt. To succeed one must struggle with Chan paradoxes and puzzlements." Although he did not engage himself very much in a Chan regimen, he had been to the Chan assembly led by Buan who, having been an heir of Songyuan, must have spoken cogently. I therefore decided to choose another paradox to struggle with. The one I adopted was that of "a stick of dry dung."[7] I doubted everything and stood every idea on its head. Because of the change of the paradox my earlier endeavors were all disrupted. Although I devoted myself to the new endeavor all the time—I sealed my beddings, and my back never touched the sleeping mat—I remained confused: everything seemed messy and chaotic from morning to night, whether I was walking or sitting. There was never a minute of peace or clarity. Then I heard that Abbot Tianmu had waited on Songyuan for a long time and was his heir. He must have heard Songyuan speak. Therefore I moved to Jingzi Temple.

After I enrolled as a resident I went to the abbot's office, carrying with me several sticks of incense. I fell on my knees before him and made nine obeisances, begging for instruction.

"What have you been doing?" he asked.

I gave him a full account of my endeavors, right from the very beginning.

"Have you heard," he asked, "that Linji three times asked Huangbo the meaning of Buddhism, and three times Linji was badly clubbed? Later on he jabbed Dayu three times in the ribs, saying, 'After all Huangbo doesn't know much about Buddhism.' This is the way you should look at things."[8]

The abbot further said, "When Hunyuan was the abbot of this temple I went from a temporary resident to the position of his accepted disciple. One day he said to me, 'A ready-made paradox is not acceptable. Come over and receive thirty blows.' That's the way you should see things."

Master Tianmu's words were of course meant to be uplifting, but I was not pleased. My ailment had me completely befuddled, and his medicine had only an adverse effect. I couldn't help addressing him in my mind: "You know nothing about Chan endeavors. All you have is clever verbiage." It is customary for a disciple, after having received his initial instruction from a master, to present one last round of incense and prostrate himself three times before the teacher. This is called "expressing gratitude for the good fortune." I walked out without the usual obeisances.

I stayed on in the Jingzi Temple and continued my own way of sitting-in-meditation. At that time there were seven brethren from Zhang and Quan prefectures,[9] and we formed a sitting-in-meditation group. For two years we did not open our bedding, nor did our backs ever touch the mats. There was a senior monk by the name of Xiu who also came from Zhang Prefecture, but he did not join our group. He practiced sitting-in-meditation all by himself. Every day he sat on the rush seat with his back straight as an iron pole. When he was walking he also kept his back straight, opened his eyes wide, and let his arms hang. Again he was like an iron pole. Every day he was like this. Often I tried to get close to him and talk with him, but as soon as he saw me approaching, he turned around and went in the opposite direction. For two years I got nowhere with him. As I had not made any headway in my Chan endeavor for two years, I became very tired and confused. I could no longer distinguish day from night, walking from sitting. Everything seemed to have been blended into one chaotic mess, and this utter disarray was like a lump of dank mud. One day I suddenly realized that I had not made any progress at all with my study of the Way, yet my clothes were now in shreds and my flesh wasted away. Tears began to fall unawares and I became homesick. I asked for leave to go home.

For two months I let go all the discipline. When I returned to the temple and resumed my endeavor, I felt completely reinvigorated as a result of the break, even though I had to start work from the beginning. Now I knew that to forego sleep would not help. To remain vigorous one must have deep and sound sleep in the middle of the night.

One day as I was taking a stroll in the corridor I ran into Brother Xiu. From a distance he seemed to be completely at ease, and even self-satisfied. I walked over to him and as he did not avoid me, I knew he had succeeded in some way. I asked him, "Why is it that when I tried to speak with you last year, you always avoided me?" He replied, "My respected brother, a man who genuinely works on the Tao has not even the time to clip his fingernails, much less to chat with you." He asked me about my efforts and I told him the story from the beginning. Then I said, "I am now beset by confusion and perplexity, which I cannot handle." He said, "What difficulties are there? It is only because you are not driving yourself hard enough. You must sit on a high rush seat, straighten your spine, keep every disc taut, cover up every one of your 360 bones and 84,000 pores with the word 'nothingness.' Then see what confusion and perplexity you still have." Following his advice, I found a thick rush mat and put it on my station. I sat on it and straightened my spine, making every disc taut. From top to bottom I forcibly lifted up all the 360 links of my skeleton, as if fighting alone against ten thousand enemies. When I became completely exhausted I dropped everything. Then with all my strength I made another desperate attempt. Suddenly I was no longer conscious of either my mind or my body, and I saw in front of my eyes nothing but a huge, solid substance, like a silver mountain or iron wall. This pure and clear state lasted for three days, whether I walked or sat. For three nights I did not close my eyes. In the afternoon of the third day I was walking under the gates, but I felt that I was still sitting. Suddenly I ran into Brother Xiu again. He asked me what I was doing there. I replied that I was working on the Way. "What is it that you call the 'Way'?" he asked. As I was not able to answer, I became very perplexed. Intending to go back to the hall and resume sitting-in-meditation, I first went to the back gate. Without realizing what I was doing I arrived at the back hall. The head monk there asked me, "Brother Qin, how is your work on the Way?" I replied, "I should not have asked so many people about it; now, contrary to what I expected, I am stuck." He said, "You only have to open your eyes wide and see what the principle is." I was quite struck by the last sentence and hastened back to the meditation hall. As soon as I lifted my body up to the rush seat all of a sudden everything burst open in front of me, as if the earth had collapsed. At that time I found myself unable to describe or even suggest what had happened, because I had no way to compare it with anything in this world. I didn't know what to do with my joy so I left the meditation mat and went to look for Brother Xiu. He was on the sutra table. As soon as he saw me he greeted me with folded palms and said, "Congratulations! Congratulations!" Holding each other's hand we took a stroll on the willow-shaded embankment in front of the temple. I looked up and down, viewing all the myriad things of the universe. Suddenly I realized that it was actually from my own true nature, subtle and bright, that all things flowed out, all the things that in the past had repelled my eyes and disgusted my ears, all the ignorance, troubles, perplexities, and confusion. What floated closely before my eyes now was a vast presence, absolutely silent and completely denuded of shape and form.

For more than a month I remained undisturbed. Unfortunately there was no venerable monk with great insight and skill who could get me over the top. I stayed where I was and became stagnant. This was a case of the so-called being moored in one's partial understanding, which became an obstacle to true illumination. In the middle of the night I did reach, in my deep sleep, the state of no dreams or thoughts, not hearing or seeing. But I lost the state once I woke up. There was an old saying that sleeping and waking were the same, but I was not able to comprehend it. Nor did I understand correctly the principle that "if the eyes are not asleep, dreams will vanish of their own accord; if the mind is not divided, all things will unite." As for the paradoxes of the early masters, I can understand those which contain a line of reasoning that can be ruminated upon. Those without a line of reasoning are just like silver mountains and iron walls, utterly impenetrable.

Although for many years I had been attending the lectures given by my late teacher Wu Zhun, I could almost leap through the roof every time I heard him start his lecture by asserting his primacy. It was never possible for you to open your mouth even if he had not raved about his antecedents or cited buddhas and patriarchs. Some days he could go on and on from the podium without saying anything that would have a special meaning for me.[10] When I was by myself I searched through Buddhist scriptures and the recorded sayings of old masters, yet I found not one phrase that was of any use to me. I was thus afflicted and impeded for almost ten years. Later I went with Zhong Shiliang to stay at Zhedong[11] and Tianyu Mountains.[12]

One day I was walking in front of a temple and my mind was leisurely and aimlessly wandering. I raised my eyes at random and caught sight of an ancient cypress tree. All of a sudden the sight triggered off the understanding I had reached in the past, but in the next instant it vanished. In a great burst all the obstacles also dissolved. I felt like a man who had walked into the bright sun from a dark room. From now on I no longer had doubts about life or death, the Buddha or the Patriarchs.

—PYW

Notes

1. The "matter" to which Zuqin repeatedly refers is presumably enlightenment.
2. Literal translation of *zuochan* (J. *zazen*), *Chan/zen* being derived from the transcription of Sanskrit *dhyāna* (meditation).
3. Buddhist monks, especially those belonging to the Chan/Zen school, have always been highly peripatetic. Their propensity for travel is a part of their quest for enlightenment.
4. Caodong (J. Sōtō) was another important Chan (Zen) sect.
5. The famous monastery near Lin'an, the "temporary" capital of the Southern Song dynasty in what is now Zhejiang Province.
6. Like Jingzi Temple at the end of this paragraph, also in modern Zhejiang Province.
7. The tenth-century master Yunmen Wenyan was asked by a disciple, "What is the Buddha?" He replied, "It is a stick of dry dung." This paradox was probably meant to deny all distinctions, even that between the loftiest and the vilest. The idea can be traced back to the ancient philosopher Zhuang Zi, who proclaimed that the Tao lies in urine and feces.
8. To stress the importance of self-reliance as well as the fundamental Chan belief that truth could only be conveyed through hints, gestures, and parables rather than explicit statements, the abbot here cited the experience of Linji Yixuan (?–866), the founder of the great Chan sect that bears his name (known in Japan as Rinzai). For a full account of the story see *Record of the Transmission of the Lamp (Jingde chuandeng lu)*, scroll 12. Linji went to Master Huangbo's monastery as a young monk. After several years of diligent study, he went to the master for personal instruction. Without saying a word the master struck him with his staff. Twice more he was thus rebuffed. In despair he took his leave of the master, who recommended that he go to Dayu, another Chan master of great renown. While debating with Dayu on his being ill-treated by Huangbo, Linji saw through the apparent harshness and reached illumination. To express his new understanding, he jabbed the master three times in the ribs.
9. In modern Fujian Province.
10. Eventually Zuqin was designated by Wuzhun (also known as Shifan [1178–1249]), for many years the undisputed leading abbot in the capital region (i.e., Lin'an), as his principal heir. Nevertheless the two never liked each other very much.
11. Eastern Zhejiang.
12. In Zhejiang Province.

THE MONGOLS HAD at least two writing systems of their own. The first was adapted from the Old Uyghur script, which had its origins in the Sogdian cursive script of the eighth and ninth centuries. The latter was a reduced version of the Aramaic alphabet. The second Mongol script was eponymously called 'Phags-pa after its inventor, the great Buddhist monk-adviser to Khubilai Khaghan[1] (1215–1294; r. 1260–1294). It was based upon the Tibetan script, which was, in turn, derived from a northeast Indian script by Thon mi Sambhota, a minister to the first Buddhist king, Srong btsan sgam po, during the first half of the seventh century. 'Phags-pa (1235–1280) was ordered to create a script that could be used to write all the languages of the empire, including Mongolian, Tibetan, Uyghur, and Chinese. Although 'Phags-pa successfully achieved his task around the year 1270, his efficient and accurate script did not replace the vertical Mongolian alphabet, which later evolved into the Manchu, Oirat, and other scripts. 'Phags-pa's script, however, did figure heavily in King Sejong's 1446 creation of the Korean Hangul alphabet, which lies at the heart of the writing system still used today in Korea.

Thus, while many of the Mongol rulers and their non-Chinese advisers were capable of reading and writing in their own languages, the difficult Chinese script and vast literary corpus of the Middle Kingdom—which formed a significant part of their empire—posed nearly insurmountable challenges for these overlords from the steppes. Yet they were wise (and perhaps curious) enough to realize that it was to their advantage to understand the ideology of their subjects. Hence they commanded certain court scholars, especially those who were bilingual or multilingual, to prepare vernacular exegeses of selected Chinese texts, such as the *Great Learning (Daxue), Doctrine of the Mean (Zhongyong)*, the *Four Books (Si shu), Book of Documents (Shujing)*, and so forth.

The present selection is from the *Direct Explanation of the Filial Piety Classic (Xiao jing zhijie)*, which was written by the celebrated Uyghur poet-official Guan Yunshi (Sewinch Qaya, 1286–1324). The entire first chapter is translated here, with the original Literary Sinitic (i.e., Classical Chinese) text being given in Latin (to replicate its impenetrability for the Mongol rulers, and indeed for most of the Chinese subjects) and the early Mandarin exegesis (which would have been orally more accessible, especially when accompanied by extemporaneous Mongolian amplifications) rendered in English. (It is interesting to note that the *Filial Piety Classic* was also translated into Mongolian.) For an English translation of the Literary Sinitic text upon which the Latin is based, see selection 16, section 1.

For those who know Latin, it will be obvious that there are some minor discrepancies between the Latin translation of the original Literary Sinitic text and the English translation of the same text as given in selection 16. This is because the Latin was written at a time (the early eighteenth century) when European study of Literary Sinitic was still in its infancy and hence imperfectly known. Second, Latin itself was at this time no longer of the pure, classical type, but characterized instead by late, irregular forms. The Latin translation given here was made by the Jesuit P. François Noël. It was published in Prague in the year 1711.

For clarity of reading the present selection, it is necessary to reiterate that the Latin text of

François Noël in larger size type is a translation of the original Literary Sinitic text. The smaller size English text that follows the Latin is a translation of the early Mandarin exegesis of the Literary Sinitic original. This Mandarin paraphrase-commentary was composed by the Uyghur scholar Sewinch Qaya, who was an adviser to the Mongol rulers. In other words, as you read this text, pretend that the Latin is Literary Sinitic and that the English is an early Mandarin explanation of the latter.—VHM

Filialis Observantiæ Liber, capitulum I. Totius argumenti explanatio.
The chapter which develops basic precepts and elucidates principles.

Cum domi feriaretur Zhongni (Confucius), Zhongni is the style name of Kong Fuzi (Confucius); *feriaretur* is the time when Kong Zi was dwelling at leisure, *sic* Discipulum suum *Tsem sive Tsem Tsu,* qui ad latus sedebat, Kong Zi's disciple, surnamed Zeng, named Shen, was attending him nearby, interrogavit: Kong Zi said: "Audivistíne aliquando, quænam fuerit illa priscorum Imperatorum summa virtus & potissima disciplina, The sages of the past had the best virtue and the vital way, qua totum Imperium ita suis jussis subjectum habebant, to rule over All-under-Heaven by this means, ut mutua inter omnes concordia, so that the people will be naturally complaisant, nulláque Superiores inter & Inferiores ira aut querela intercederet? that superiors and inferiors will not be resentful. Did you know that?" Mox *Tsem* assurgens: Zeng Zi got up and said: "Tuus ego rudis *Sen (nomen loquentis)* unde, quæso, potuissem illam audivisse? I am not clever; how could I know that?" Tum Confucius: Kong Zi said: "Filialis observantia, inquit, est omnium virtututum [*sic*] basis, This thing—the way of filial piety—is the root of virtuous behavior, ex qua omnis recta exurgit disciplina. the matter of teaching people first comes from within this way of filial piety. Sede, ut priùs; ego id tibi exponam. You sit down again; I will explain it for you. Filialis observantiæ initium, est non audere corpus & membra à Parentibus accepta lædere aut labefactare;[2] One's body, hair, and skin are born from one's parents, [so] we should cherish them greatly and not cause them to be injured, you see—this is the thing which ought to be the beginning of the way of filial piety; consummatio seu finis, est mores suos rìte perficere & virtutem colere, relictâ post se magni nominis famâ, qua Parentes decorentur. if one sets oneself up to do good things and leaves behind a good reputation so as to cause later people to know of it, in this manner one will succeed in manifesting the reputation of our parents—if we act in this manner, it is the completion of a life [spent following] the way of filial piety. Filialis Observantiæ This thing—the way of filial piety—initium à Parentum obsequio, at the beginning time is attentive to serving one's parents, medium à Regis servitio, in the middle is attentive to serving the government,[3] finis à morum perfectione procedit. and, if one finishes these two things of being obedient to one's parents and serving in the government, one will naturally establish one's own person. Hinc liber Carminum tom.[4] *Ta Ya* sic ait: Kong Zi again speaks words from the *Mao Odes: 'Numquid debes assidùe Majores tuos mente recolere, & eorum virtutes imitatione subsequi?* Don't fail to think of your ancestors, relying on your ancestors do good things.'"

—VHM

Notes

1. The grandson of Chinggis Khaghan (born as Temujin and also known as Genghis Khan; 1167?–1227), the creator of the Mongol empire. Khubilai (his name is also rendered variously as Qubilai Qaghan, Kubla

Khan, etc.) extended Mongol rule over the whole of China and was the first emperor of the Yuan dynasty (1279–1368).

2. The Latin text misprints *labesactare* here.

3. I.e., the emperor.

4. The word *tom.*, probably an abbreviation of *tomus,* refers to the section "Daya" (Greater Elegantiae), while *liber* refers to the *Book of Odes* as a whole.

ZHU ZHENHENG (1281–1358) was a famous "scholar-physican" of the fourteenth century, a time of innovation in medicine. Like many other literate men of his era, Zhu saw medicine as a respectable, if humble, alternative to an official career. He studied with a well known Neo-Confucian teacher from his native district of Jinhua, Zhejiang Province, but after failing the examinations he abandoned classical studies to dedicate his life to healing. Scholar physicians looked to canonical texts like *The Yellow Emperor's Inner Canon* (believed to date from the first century B.C.) as sources of medical authority, and considered prescription pharmacy—the art of devising customized herbal compounds according to cosmological patterns of yin and yang—to be the most refined clinical skill. They also sought to be recognized socially as gentlemen, but this was not always easy in a status-conscious society where their clients could outrank them and the most clinically experienced seniors might be monks or humble hereditary practitioners. In the following selections, issues of gender and class influence Zhu's account of his time in Hangzhou as a disciple of Luo Zhiti (when Zhu was forty-five years old and Luo an old man in his eighties), while status considerations also shape these stories of individual illnesses.

Zhu summed up his distinctive approach to therapy with the axiom "yang is always in surplus and yin is always deficient." Zhu was thinking of cosmological principles according to which the human organism is a microcosm of the universe at large, and the basic vitality of the body, *qi*, like the primal *qi* of Heaven and Earth, requires a balance between yang forms (heat, activity, warming and drying action) and yin forms (cold, tranquility, cooling and moistening action). But his medical essays show that Zhu thought his therapeutic axiom also applied to concrete clinical symptoms and their relief, and that it could guide the physician's understanding of human appetites and emotions. In linking the principles governing bodily health to the self-cultivation of the sage, Zhu also drew upon his earlier philosophical training in Zhu Xi's Neo-Confucianism.

Although Zhu lived and died in his native district of Jinhua as a gentleman from a respected local lineage of scholars and landowners, two of his sons followed in his footsteps as doctors. In the Ming dynasty, these family descendants and those of his many medical disciples made his medical "school of learning" famous in China and also in Japan. The following excerpts are taken from *More on the "Natural Knowledge of Phenomena" (Gezhi yulun)*—a collection of essays on medical topics he compiled in his old age at the request of his followers.—CF

Learning from a Teacher

In the summer of 1325 I first heard of Luo Taiwu [Luo Zhiti] from Chen Zhiyan [a poet]. I proceeded to pay my respects as a pupil. He rejected me with curses a half a dozen times. Only after three months of repeated visits did he finally begin to receive me. In this way I saw Master Luo treat a disorder in a monk who was suffering from emaciation, exhaustion, and jaundice. Master Luo inquired as to the origins of the disorder. The sufferer was from Sichuan, and at the time when he left to take religious vows his mother was still at home. After traveling to Zhejiang as a devotee of the Buddha for seven years, suddenly one day he thought of his mother and could not repress his longing to return home. His money belt was empty, so he simply faced west night and day, weeping. This made him sick. At the time the monk was twenty-four years old. Luo ordered that he rest peacefully at night in an adjoining chamber, and every day he gave him beef, pig belly, and sweet fat simmered and mashed into a pulp. This went on for more than two weeks. In addition, from time to time he offered soothing instructions and encouraging words. Further he said, "I will give you a money order worth ten silver pieces for travel expenses. I do not want repayment; I only wish to save your life." He watched until the young monk's physical form was somewhat revived; then he gave him a one-day treatment of three packets of *qi*-leading infusion with peach kernel" [to purge his bowels]. The patient evacuated bloody clots and phlegm accumulations. When this was finished, the next day Luo just gave him well-cooked vegetables and rice porridge and nothing more. After another two weeks the young man was his former self, and after two more weeks he was given his ten silver money order and went on his way.

This made me really understand "attack" [purging] therapies. If you prescribe to cleanse the bowels, the patient should be in a condition of sturdy repletion, and have a sound constitution. Otherwise, as pathogens leave the body, its healthy, orthodox *qi* will also be damaged; small disorders will become big ones and big ones will kill.

Every day sufferers seeking treatment came to Luo's door. He would order me to do a pulse diagnosis and report back to him. Though he lay in bed, as he listened he would explain orally which drugs treat which illness, which drugs enhance the powers of which other drugs, which drugs lead the medicine up and down which channels [within the body]. Over a year and a half he prescribed no set formulas. A single formula might "attack" and "replenish" at the same time; it might "attack" first and "replenish" later, or vice versa. In this way I came to understand that using ancient formulas to treat today's diseases makes a poor match. Isn't it as the saying goes, "To hit the mark, adapt to the times"? . . . One must cure the ill the way Han Gaozu pursued the Qin tyrant [Qin Shi Huangdi] or Zhou Wudi pursued the last ruler of the Shang dynasty. In victory they handed out money and provisions, and promulgated lenient laws, so that the damaged *qi* [of Earth] and the exhausted people were able to return to a condition of tranquility. So I determined that yin is easily enfeebled and yang is easily violent, that "attack" therapies require paying close attention to protecting healthy, orthodox *qi*. Isn't this a warning to us all?

Two Medical Cases

1. Depletion disorders and disorders of phlegm may seem like spirit possession. . . . A robust matron, Mistress Jin, attended a feast in hot summer weather. On her return her mother-in-law made inquiries and concluded that she had taken an improper seat at the banquet table. As a consequence the woman was intensely ashamed and this illness resulted. Her speech became incoherent and included the phrase "Th-This slave is at fault!" repeated over and over. Her pulses were all rapid and strung.[1] I said, "This is not a disorder from spirit pathogens. If you will only replenish her spleen, cool down her heat, and lead her phlegm out for a few days, she will be well." Her family did not believe me and called several shamans who spurted holy water and chanted incantations. In a little more than a fortnight she was dead.

Some people said, "The disorder was not due to an evil spirit, yet it was treated as if it was. What in fact so suddenly led to her death? " I said, "She went to a banquet in summer, when the weather outside was steamy hot. Spicy food went in her mouth, and her internal landscape became stagnant and hot. This was made worse by long-standing accumulations of phlegm, to which were added her shame and dejection. Suffering from phlegm and heat, what worse could be said? The shamans' method of frightening the spirits with magic rods alarmed her psyche, and her blood was disturbed; spurting holy water covered her skin and closed her pores so sweat could not flow. When sweat could not flow, steam heat within enflamed her; her blood could not be tranquilized, so that yin evaporated and yang could not survive alone. Of course she died!"

Someone said, "*Secrets of the Palace Terrace* (a sixth-century medical encyclopedia) has a section on curing with incantations. Can you reject this?" I said, "Moving spirit *qi* around is a minor art, and good for minor ailments. If it is a matter of depletion evil within and repletion evil without one must use major, orthodox methods that are well established and can be studied."

2. On Qin cassia pills: . . . Commissioner Zheng's son, aged sixteen, sought medical help, saying, "Since I was seven months old I have suffered from a urinary disorder. Every five to seven days it always appears. There is such pain that I beat the ground and cry to Heaven. Then I urinate something like lacquer or rice grains, about a cupful. In a little while its over."

I examined his pulses. With light pressure they were rough, with heavy pressure they were strung. In appearance he was thin and rather tall, and his complexion was pallid and greenish. My thought was that his father must have taken frequent potency medicines and that the residual heat in the fetus lodged in the child's Vital Gate to produce this result. So I used pills of fine tips of purple snow (*zixue* = plumbago) and yellow *nie* tree [bark], plus parasol tree (*wuzi*, probably *wutong*) dried out completely in the sun and gave him two hundred pills altogether in one dose. After a couple of hours I gave a second dose of three hundred pills taken with hot soup and solid food to settle it. After another one-half day he felt a succession of strong pains in waist and abdomen, and he then passed a discharge like lacquer and rice grains—a big bowlful. Before long his illness was eighty percent gone. Chang Zizhong later used one *liang* of orange peel plus a half *liang* each of balloon flower (*jiegeng*) and *mutong* in a single dose, and he passed a further discharge of a handful of lacquer and rice grains. Subsequently he [could] function.

A father who takes hot and dry medicines can also make his son sick, and isn't it even worse if a mother consumes these [as fertility drugs]? I record this to validate Li Gao's account of "red silk sores" (skin eruptions in infants believed caused by the sexual heat of parents' coitus).

Body, Emotions, and Moral Experience

Zhou Dunyi said that once the human psyche *(shen)* emerges into consciousness [at the beginning of life], the five human emotions *(wuxing)* are moved *(gan)* by external things, and the myriad activities of life ensue. Once there is awareness and the five emotions respond, these unstoppable motions are what we speak of as the Five Fires of the *Inner Canon*. Ministerial Fire *(xiang huo)* is easily aroused, and the adverse yang Fires of the five emotions stir each other up into random motion. Aroused Fire, in its erratic and unending transformations, burns up true yin; yin is depleted and illness results. When yin is exhausted one dies. In its form of environmental *qi*, we may speak of Princely Fire as the damp heat of summer and Ministerial Fire as [solar] fire, its fierce and violent external manifestations more intense than those of Princely Fire. So it is said, "Ministerial Fire is the thief of primordial *qi*." Master Zhou Dunyi says further, "The sage finds stability by practicing the virtues of balance, order, benevolence and justice, ruling through tranquility." Zhu Xi says, "One must make the Heart of the Way rule the self wholly, and the human heart will assent to the will [of Heaven]." This is to be good at keeping one's Fires in the proper place. When man's heart assents to the commands of the Heart of the Way and further rules [the self] in tranquility, the motions of the Five Fires will be restrained, and one's Ministerial Fire will simply support the Creative Principle *(zaohua)* enacting the succession of lives without end in its cyclical functions. How then can one's primordial *qi* be stolen?

—CF

Notes

1. The technical term in question, one of about two dozen for "pulse reading" in Chinese medicine, is *xian* and literally means "string" (as of a musical instrument). This term had also been translated as "thready." Note that the plural is used for pulse, since the doctor is conveying that he gets the same reading on all six positions—three on each wrist.

CLOUD FOREST HALL COLLECTION OF RULES FOR DRINKING AND EATING *(Yunlin tang yinshi zhidu ji)* is a Chinese cooking classic, famous in part because of the artistic genius of its author, but also because it provides a unique insight into the cuisine of central eastern China in the fourteenth century. It was written by the famous Yuan-dynasty artist Ni Zan (1301–1374), who owes his fame chiefly to his painting. He has generally been regarded as one of China's greatest masters, especially of the deceptively simple ink paintings so typical of the late-Song and Yuan dynasties (see plate 95). His work is simple, abstract, sometimes almost minimalist, and free in line and form. It is generally regarded as one of the finest examples of the tradition informed by Taoist and Chan (Zen) Buddhist ideas of art: the artist should be so perfected in skill and so intensely fused with his medium that he or she can produce exquisite pictures in a free and spontaneous manner. Skill has been overlearned to the point at which the artist need not be consciously aware of working—he can paint in a state of meditation or enlightenment. This approach to art had been a long time developing; Ni Zan stood at the culmination of an old tradition. His work is distinctive and individualist, in large part because he took this meditative-spontaneous tradition even further than his predecessors or contemporaries.

Also a poet, Ni wrote of himself:

By the eastern sea there is a sick man,
Who calls himself "mistaken" and "extreme."
When he paints walls and sketches on silk and paper,
Isn't it an overflow of his madness?[1]

Surviving among Ni Zan's writings is a book about food, the *Cloud* (or "cloudy") *Forest Hall Collection of Rules* (or "guiding principles") *for Drinking and Eating.* "Cloud Forest" was Ni's style-name or nom de plume, taken (we assume) from the Hall, his residence and studio, but bearing a deeper significance; characteristically, it connotes the hidden, secret, wild, and remote.

The book appears to be a collection of recipes for ordinary household use—directions for a kitchen staff and perhaps for his own purpose. It reflects his outlook on life and art: simplicity perfected. Ni's self-description as "mad" (a mere cliché in Yuan artistic circles) is belied by the book's down-to-earth common sense and attention to detail. Everyday foods and a few simple luxuries receive loving and careful attention. Preparation is described in minute detail. In the best Chinese and Zen tradition, amounts are left to the good judgment of the cook except when a really exact quantity must be used, and mundane details of ordinary kitchen practice are left out. Matters like cooking time are described in such terms as "when it floats to the top." The cook is assumed to have learned such things to the point at which detailed instructions are unnecessary.

Several directions for nonfood items are scattered through the book. Ni's household staff had to know how to handle incense, and, of course, the all-important matter of properly cleaning the artist's inkstones.

Most of the dishes are vegetables or seafood. Birds, wild and tame, are represented. Ni Zan was not a vegetarian, but he was aware of that Buddhist tradition; there are significantly few red meat recipes here, and there is a recipe for preparing wheat gluten to make something like the mock-meat of Buddhist monasteries.

Coming from Wuxi, Jiangsu, Ni exemplifies the cuisine that had long been typical of the region and is typical of it still. Central eastern China had been known for its aquatic foods and vegetables by the sixth century C.E. and is known for them today. Modern diners familiar with the cuisine of the region will recognize many recipes, such as the crab in wine, even though the modern recipes are not quite the same. For example, the emphasis on Chinese brown pepper is now more typical of the upper Yangtze; the barbecued pork recipe is a cognate of Cantonese *cha siu* (MSM. *cha shao*) rather than of anything currently Jiangsunese.

It is instructive to compare Ni Zan's book with the nearly contemporary *Yinshan zhengyao (YSZY)* by Hu Sihui. This work, written by a Turkic-speaker but in Chinese, was a dietary guide for the Mongol court. Writing as a Central Asian for Central Asians, in the inland dust of Dadu (Peking), Hu based almost all his recipes on meat—lamb above all. He had little truck with vegetables, and almost none with seafoods, which were rarely available in the deep interior at that time. The contrast with Ni's book is as extreme as one can find between two roughly contemporary works, at any time in the history of Chinese cookbooks. (Of course, the *YSZY* was more Turko-Mongol than Chinese, in spite of its being written in the latter language.)—ENA, TW, VHM

Cloud Forest Hall Collection of Rules for Drinking and Eating

1. How to Make Soy Sauce[2]
For each official peck[3] of crushed and yellowed soybean cake,[4] use ten catties[5] of salt and twenty catties of water. Measure accurately. Put together in large pot during the heat of summer.

2. Cooking Noodles
If one wants to eat the noodles at noon, at dawn use salted water to make up a (wheat flour) dough. Knead thirty or twenty *(sic)* times.[6] Cover and let stand. In a short while, repeat. Do this with the dough four times. Sprinkle fine starch powder on a board; roll the dough out and cut into strips. To cook: bring water to a rapid boil, stir, and put in the noodles. When the water boils rapidly again, stop the fire and then cover the pot. Turn up the fire again, let boil slowly, then take out and put in broth.

3. Sinking-Fragrance (gharuwood or lignaloes) Bundle
Sandalwood, lionstail, and betony are made into powder.[7] Add a tiny amount[8] of virgin (or early-brood) silkworm, sun-dried, and a bit of musk. Use goose-pear[9] juice to make into cakes. Burn (as incense) in a cool dry place.

4. Honeyed Stuffed Crabs[10]
Cook in salted water. When the color begins to change (to red), take out. Break up the crab and extract the meat from claws and legs. Cut this into small pieces and stuff into shell. Combine egg with a small amount of honey and mix with meat in shell. Spread some fat on the egg. Steam until the egg has just solidified. Do not overcook. For eating, it can be dipped into ground orange peel and vinegar.

5. How to Cook Crabs
Use fresh ginger, perilla,[11] cassia bark, and salt. Boil rapidly, turn the crab over, let boil rapidly again. It is then ready. It is best if eaten as soon as cooked. Thus, for one person, cook only two pieces; when those are eaten, cook more. Eat with orange peel and vinegar.

6. How to Wine-cook Crabs

Clean the crabs thoroughly, and, while they are alive, cut into two portions with the shell still intact. Then separate shell and body parts with your fingers. Cut legs and shell into small pieces. Only the upper (thicker) part of the smaller claws should be used. Open the big claws with your fingers. Cook in earthenware or tin pot, over small fire, with spring onions, Chinese brown pepper, clear wine, and some salt. In eating, do not use vinegar.

7. Cooking Wonton[12]

Chop the meat finely. Add riced bamboo shoots[13] or wild-rice shoots, chives, or *Basella rubra* tips.[14] Mix Sichuan pepper and a bit of apricot kernel paste until smooth. Wrap. The skins should start out a bit thick and small, then cut into squares. Next coat them with starch and roll them out thin. (When stuffed) put into fully boiling water that has been stirred. Do not cover. When they float up, take them out, stirring no longer. Do not use Chinese cardamom[15] in the filling because it will cause hiccups.

8. How to Cook Yellow-bird Buns[16]

Take yellow birds and chop up the brain and wings and chest meat with spring onions, brown pepper, and salt. Stuff into stomach (i.e., probably, body cavity). Use leavened dough to wrap it. Make long small rolls, flattening and rounding down the ends. Put into bamboo container and steam them. After steaming they can perhaps be treated like "lees buns": use brewing lees[17] and fragrant oil[18] and fry them, in which case they are especially delicious.

9. How to Make Cold Stirred Noodles[19]

Skin fresh ginger and press the natural juice out. Mix flower pepper powder and vinegar, and add clarified soy sauce to make a sauce. Do not add any other sauce or water. Use gelatinized meat of mandarin-fish, perch, or river fish. Immediately swish the fish in the sauce. Shrimp meat can also be used, but does not need to be gelatinized. To the sauce add finely cut coriander leaves or "fragrant herb"[20] or Chinese chive shoots. Mix the noodles that have been rinsed in fresh water into the bowl with the fish sauce. ([Original note:] When preparing the noodles, use cold meat broth with a small amount of sauce.) The gelatinized mandarin fish or the river fish should be skinned and boned, cut into thin slices, and arranged in a dish or small porcelain bowl. Simmer fish stock and fish-glue made from river-fish swim-bladder to make broth. Season the broth and pour over fish, then let cool to become gelatin.

10. A New Way to Cook Clams

Wash the clams. Open them uncooked and keep the juice in a separate container. Wash away the sand and mud, cut the clams, wash again. Do not throw the water away. Wash yet again with warm water. Then thoroughly mix a small amount of spring onion or tangerine peel shreds with the clam meat in a bowl. Filter out the dirt in the juice and wash-water, then add spring onion, Chinese pepper, and wine. Mix. Pour over the clams and eat. It is quite good.

11. "Snow Temple"[21] Vegetable

Use the hearts of green Chinese cabbage, leaving a few leaves. Cut each of the hearts into two pieces and put them in a bowl. Cut milk-cake[22] into thick pieces and cover the vegetables with it. With the hand rub out some flower pepper powder on top of the milk-cake—a small amount is enough. Add pure wine and a little salt to fill the bowl. Put in a pot and steam soft, then eat.

12. How to Cook Wheat Gluten

Use the fine wheat gluten (noodles or pieces) from Wuchong (Suzhou), newly steamed and not cooked by water. Tear into small, thin slices. Cut licorice into inch-long pieces; put these in wine and cook with water till the liquid boils off. Remove the licorice. Then use perilla leaf, tangerine peel slices, and ginger slices with the gluten and boil lightly. Take out the gluten and let cool. Then mix together thoroughly with hot oil, soy paste, flower pepper, black pepper, and apricot kernel powder. Stir the gluten with the ginger strips, tangerine, etc. repeatedly so that the flavors soak into the gluten. Dry under the sun and put in a sugar jar[23] and seal. If it is left too long and gets hard, steam it when you want to eat it.

13. Ark Shell (Cockle)

Break open four or five live cockles. Immediately arrange them in a bowl and pour their juices over them. Cook in extremely hot wine and eat without pepper or salt. When trying to break open the cockles, use a big sewing-needle to pierce them first, and opening will be easier.

14. Green Shrimp Rolls

From fresh green shrimp remove the head and shell. Leave the small tail. Use a small knife to cut them into thin pieces from the larger end to the tail. The tail should not be cut from the last piece of meat. Use spring onions, Chinese pepper, salt, wine, and enough water to submerge the shrimp. Grind up the head and shell and simmer to make a stock from which the sediment should be removed. Quick-boil[24] the shrimp meat in this stock. After having filtered the stock, serve with bamboo-shoot and preserved-ginger slices. Do not add spiced wine to the stock and do not cook too long, just enough so that it's done.

15. Mr.[25] Fragrant Snail

Break away the shell, taking the meat only, and wash. Do not use the juice in the shell. Using a small knife, cut around and around as if peeling a pear. Or one can slice it. Use chicken stock to cook quickly.

16. River Scallops

Take live ones, extract the meat, wash in wine. Cut into strips as thick as the tip of chopsticks. Cook in extremely hot wine and eat. Or just eat strips of it raw with black pepper and vinegar. When eating raw with pepper and vinegar, you can add some sugar and salt. This should be eaten cold.

17. *Zi* Fish[26]

Cut the *zi* fish into chunks as for carp. Then cook in equal measures water and wine, with ginger, Chinese pepper, and soy sauce, and eat when sauce thickens.

18. Field Snails[27]

Choose large ones. Break the shells. Take the heads. Do not let them touch water. Coat with brown sugar and let sit for as long as it takes to eat a meal. Wash. You can either cut it into thin slices and use spring onions, Chinese pepper, and wine to marinate it for a short while, then cook it quickly in clear chicken stock, or you can eat it raw after soaking it in salt, wine, and zira[28] for a few days and then eating it with clear vinegar. Do not eat this in summer.[29]

19. Quick-cooked Meat Stew

Use meat from the backbone (i.e., tenderloin), remove the tendons and membranes, and cut into pieces an inch long. Slightly score the meat, so it looks like lychees.[30] Marinate for a short while in spring onions, Chinese pepper, salt, and wine. Toss into boiling water, slightly stir, then quickly take the meat and broth and put into a container to soak. Take some clear meat broth, combine with ginger, or mountain medicine[31] pieces, or bamboo-shoot pieces and eat. Use the original broth.

20. Kidney and Stomach Crisp

"Chicken crisp"[32] is made like the previous recipe. For "chicken crisp" use white meat from the breast, cut into dice-like cubes, score like the lychee, and prepare as above.

21. How to Pickle Bamboo Shoots

Use the juice of bamboo shoots, add flowering apricot[33] (preserved by salt), sugar candy or white granulated sugar, and a small amount of raw ginger juice. Mix to taste. Put with the bamboo shoots and let soak a while. This should be eaten cold. Do not store for long.

22. How to Cook Radishes[34]

Cut into small rectangles and put these in a clean bowl. Sprinkle raw ginger strips and flower pepper grains on them. Boil a mixture of water and wine with a little salt and vinegar. While the mixture is still boiling, pour it onto the radish, cover it up immediately, and let it sit. The mixture should cover the radish.

23. How to Pickle Ginger

Use a clean cloth to wipe away the tender roots of the ginger. For every catty of ginger use one and a half catties of brewing lees and one and a half ounces of stir-fried salt.[35] Mix and put into a bottle, and sprinkle some more stir-fried salt on the surface. Seal it.

24. How to Cook Mushrooms[36]

Wash in water about four times, getting rid of all sand and mud. Then cook in chicken meat stock (or, chicken or meat stock) till they expand.

25. Duke Zheng's Method for Brewing Wine[37]

(Ingredients:) Thirty catties of white flour. A peck of mung beans, cooked soft. An ounce of *tuisha*-wood aromatic as powder. An ounce of official-quality cassia powder. Thirty lotus flower buds; use only petals and grind them—do not use the seedpods. Mash and grind sweet melon. Use a piece of coarse cloth to express through its openings about one bowl of the sweet melon meat. Mash smartweed to obtain its juice.

Mix all these together evenly till the damp and dry are combined. Wrap with a piece of cloth. Tread it out firm. Wrap it again with second-growth mulberry leaves, then tie in a hemp sack and let it air out tied to a beam. Take it out after a month, remove the mulberry leaves, and apply leaven thoroughly to the surface. Leave it out to sun and to be covered with dew at night. After about a month, put it in an earthen pot and seal it. Every thirty catties of flour can be made into seventy wine yeast cakes.

26. How to Brew[38]

Wash (glutinous rice) grain in river water till it is completely clean. Soak it for ten days and a bit more, then strain it and rinse it again with river water. The rinse water should be saved and filtered for later use. For every picul[39] of glutinous rice used, take away one peck and reserve for the second brewing. You can wait for three days to soak it. Then, for every peck of rice, use eight catties of the water strained off. Then, for a picul of flour, use four or five catties (of the rice?). To make clear wine, use only three catties. One picul of rice can be brewed per vat used. Grind up leaven (i.e., yeast) and combine with the rice. Divide into four portions, one by one. First, use a small pot to pour some water over it. Stir the mixture until it is smooth. Put each of the four portions into the vat one after another, and press them down firmly with your hands. Use a wooden ladle to sprinkle some water in the pot and cover it with a reed mat and straw. Look at the surface the next morning. If it has a big crack on the surface, put your hand inside and touch it. If it feels hard, hit with a bamboo stick. After hitting it three times, add the "reserve" rice. Use some unfiltered wine to loosen up the "reserve" rice and pour that mixture in the vat. Cover it up again. Repeat the hitting and covering if a crack appears again. It will be ready in a little over a month. Then, for every two piculs (of the mix), use eight lumps of "ash." Put one half in the unfiltered wine mix and use another bag to squeeze it. The other half is put in a bag which is in turn put into the wine. Filter to remove the dregs. Filter twice. Add the yeast cake and cook. For clear wine, do not use "reserve" rice.

How to make the ash: take mulberry ash and millet ash (the millet ash is sifted from charcoal made from unripe millet). Add hot water and roll into a ball the size of a winecup or as big as a charcoal briquette. Heat by fire till completely red. Heat it three or four times. Grind to powder before use.

27. Cooking Carp

Cut into chunks. Cook in a mix of half water and half wine. Grind peeled and sliced fresh ginger until it is a paste. Mix with flower pepper. Grind again until smooth. Gently mix with wine till liquid. First pour a little soy sauce over the fish in the pan. Bring to boil thrice. Then add the ginger-pepper mix. When it starts to boil again, take out the fish.

28. Another Way

Cut into chunks. Boil fragrant oil[40] until purified. In another pan use some of the purified oil to cook fresh ginger and Chinese pepper. Next place the fish in the pan used to heat the oil. When the fish is fried till it colors (i.e., begins to brown), add the ginger and pepper mixture and let it cook a while. Turn off the fire for a while before adding soy sauce. Then proceed as with the previous method.

29. Crabmeat Soft-shelled Turtles[41]

Take the meat out of cooked crabs. Mix thoroughly with a small amount of flower pepper. First lay some mung-bean-starch noodles on lotus leaves in the bottom of a bamboo steamer. Then put the crab meat on the noodles. Next put over this some chicken or duck egg beaten with a pinch of salt. Cover with crab spawn and steam until the egg solidifies. Remove and let it cool. Peel off the noodles. Cut the meat into medallions. Make a stock with the crab shell. Add ground ginger and flower pepper powder, and just enough starch to bind it. Put the aforementioned (medallions) in the stock or serve on a bed of spinach. This is very good.

30. Brewing-lees Buns[42]

Take buns with a delicate filling and wrap individually with yellow grass cloth or wrap the whole in one cloth. Then, first put brewing lees in a big dish, cover with a cloth, place the buns loosely on the cloth, and cover with another cloth. Then lay a thick layer of lees on the top cloth. Let it ferment overnight, then take the buns out and fry in fragrant oil. They can be kept for half a month in winter days. If (you don't eat them immediately after having fried them and) they are cold, just heat over a fire.

31. Cooking Pig's Head Meat[43]

Cut the meat into large chunks. Use half water and half wine, a pinch of salt, long slivers of the white of spring onions. Mix with flower pepper, put in a cinnabar bowl or silver pot and let cook overnight. Just before serving, put in preserved ginger slices and new[44] orange and tangerine peel shreds. If this is used in meat congee, add glutinous rice and ground fresh mountain medicine (wild Chinese yam) and eat together. One pig head can make four portions of meat congee.

32. Sichuan-style Pig's Head[45]

Use a pig's head, not cut up. Smoke over a grass and wood fire and get rid of slime. Scrape and wash till completely clean. Boil in clear water. The water should be changed a few times. Boil five times without salt. Take out of pot, let cool, and cut into willow leaf–shaped pieces. Add in long slivers of spring onion, chives, bamboo shoots, or wild-rice shoots.[46] Mix thoroughly with flower pepper, crushed apricot kernels, sesame seeds, and salt, and sprinkle with a little wine. Steam in a steamer. Roll in "hand cakes"[47] to eat.

33. Hand Cakes[48]

Use flour[49] of first quality, boiling hot water, and a little salt, stirring until smooth. Knead the dough thoroughly, then roll out pieces as big as a small bowl. Heat in a flat-based pan while sprinkling salt water on it frequently. Right after they are taken out, cover and roll them in a damp cloth.

34. Gold Carp Stomach Soup

Take a small live gold carp. Cut open the stomach. Remove the intestines. Cut away the two strips of fatty meat (of or around the stomach). Smother them with old (i.e., dry) onions, flower pepper, salt, and wine. The two pieces of fatty stomach meat should be intact and shaped like a butterfly. Make stock from the head and back-meat. Remove the meat. Put the fatty stomach meat in a colander or straining spoon and scald slightly in the stock. Wait till the fatty stomach meat is not hot, then remove bones, and mix with flower pepper or black pepper and soy sauce. Filter the earlier stock till clear like water. Add vegetables or bamboo shoots and serve.

35. Honey-brew Red Vermicelli [50]

Put real (i.e., fresh, pure) starch flour into a mold and mix thoroughly. Use thick straw-ash juice or charcoal-ash juice as cooking liquid. Pull the flour dough through the mold, which will produce thin strips. Put these strips into the cooking liquid and they will soon be done. Then serve the cooked vermicelli in clear chicken stock. Chicken shreds or meat shreds can be added on top.

36. Cooked Stuffed Lotus Rhizomes [51]

Use the best real starch flour, add a small amount of honey and musk, and pour from the bigger end into lotus rhizomes. Wrap and tie up with oil paper, then boil. When the rhizomes are cooked, slice and serve hot.

37. Tangerine Flower Tea

Jasmine tea is the same. Select average quality "small sprout" tea, and select an earthen pot for boiling. First, lay down a layer of flowers, a layer of tea, a layer of flowers, a layer of tea till the pot is full. Then tightly lay down a layer of flowers on the very top and cover it up. Put the pot under the sun and turn it over three times. Pour a shallow layer of water into a saucepan and steam the pot over a slow fire. Steam until the cover of the pot reaches its hottest, then take out. Wait till it is completely cooled down, then remove the tea from the pot. Take away the flowers, leaving only the tea. Use "lotus seed" paper to wrap up the tea and put it under the sun to dry. The paper should be opened frequently to shake the tea inside, so that it is evenly distributed, and it will be dried easily. If each pot of tea is divided into three or four paper bags the sunning will be easier. Repeat the steaming and drying processes three times, changing the flowers each time. Then the tea will be extremely good.

38. Lotus Flower Tea

In the pond, before breakfast, just as the sun rises, choose slightly opened lotus buds. Separate the petals with your fingers and put in tea leaves, filling them up. Tie with a piece of hemp string. Wait overnight, then pick the lotus the next morning, remove the tea, and wrap it up with paper and let it dry. Repeat this process three times. Put it in a tin container to store. The opening of the tin container should be tightly tied. [52]

39. How to Brew These Teas

Use a silver vessel to boil water to the crab-eye stage (i.e., just barely boiling). Now use another container to carry the tea. Pour in a small amount of water from the silver container. As soon as the tea has been submerged in the water, immediately cover the container. Wait till the tea leaves are thoroughly soaked. Put the silver vessel on the fire again until you can hear the water begin to boil. Then immediately pour in the tea leaves that have been soaked. Take the vessel away soon, return briefly to fire until it boils slightly, then drink. It is excellent.

40. Candied Citron Peel

Use mature citron. Remove everything inside including the seeds. Cut into strips. Put in boiling water and let boil once or twice. Remove from water and let it drip dry. Then, use honey, a little water—one-tenth of an ounce [53] per ounce of honey—and heat in a silver-stone pot under slow fire until the honey becomes thick and sticky. Add the citron peel, stir slightly, remove pot from fire. Wait overnight and heat again. Remove when slightly boiling. Let cool; heat once more. When it has cooled down, store it in an earthen pot and seal the opening. If less honey is used, this can be a dish to accompany wine. If it is to be used in soup, more honey should be added as necessary.

41. Fragrant Ashes

Mix thoroughly equal amounts of ash from fir twigs, autumn eggplant roots, and paper money for the dead. Pour in boiling water and make into balls. Put these ash balls in the stove and heat them with a wood fire till they turn red. Then take them out and grind them into powder. Make them into balls again with boiling water and heat till white. Add in a third part limestone chips and roll into balls again. Burn again. Put them into a bamboo colander and filter out the fine ash.

To cause the above three kinds of ash that have already been heated several times to turn white, they need to be further refined by heating ten or twenty times.

42. How to Wash Ink-slabs

Use straw ash, or burnt ash, or fragrant ash, or the ash found in temples (i.e., incense ash). (Two characters missing) and wash it. It is excellent.[54]

43. Water Dragonlets[55]

Chop finely two portions of lean pork meat to each one portion of fatty meat. Add a little spring onion, Chinese pepper, and apricot-kernel paste,[56] also a little dry, steamed cake powder (i.e., similar to breadcrumbs), and mix thoroughly. Moisten hands with vinegar and roll the dough into balls. Cover the outside with real starch flour. Boil in soup. Take them out when they float to the surface. They can be served with clear or piquant stock as desired.

44. Yellow Bird[57]

Remove skin. Take the head and wings, chop up together with spring onion and Chinese pepper. Put the chopped mixture into the body cavity and add good sweet wine. Braise in thick soup. A little salt should be added to the sweet wine.

45. White Salt Cakes[58]

Dissolve in water as much salt as is desired. Line the bottom of a colander with rough paper. Pour some of the salt water in, and put it in a clean saucepan. Wait till all the water has dripped into the saucepan. Then boil till it is dry and stir fry. Add more salt water and repeat. Mix some raw sesame with the salt, press hard, and heat with fire. Then make juice, pour into a stone bowl, and make cakes—large or small as you prefer.

46. Barbecued[59] Pig Intestines or Stomach

First boil until cooked. Then add sliced garlic, minced pork, and a pinch of salt.[60] Hang on bamboo sticks in the saucepan and cover the pan. Heat over slow fire. The saucepan should retain a cup of water in it.

47. Barbecued Pork[61]

Wash the meat clean. Rub spring onion, Chinese pepper, honey, a little salt, and wine on it. Hang the meat on bamboo sticks in the saucepan. In the pan put a cup of water and a cup of wine. Cover. Use moist paper to seal up the pan. If the paper dries out, moisten it. Heat the pan with grass bunches that should not be moved; when one is burned up, light another. Then stop the fire and leave for the time it takes to eat a meal. Touch the cover of the pan; if it is cold, remove the cover and turn the meat over. Cover it again and seal again with the moist paper. Heat again with one bunch of grass. It will be cooked when the pan cools again.

48. Barbecued Goose

Use the "barbecued pork" method. Similarly, use salt, Chinese pepper, spring onions, and wine to rub well inside the bird, and wine and honey on the outside. Put in the pan. The rest is as in the previous recipe. But the first time it is put in the pan, the stomach should be facing up; then it should be turned over with the stomach facing down.

49. A New Way with Crabs

Break open a live crab. Put aside the shell, stomach fat, and spawn. Cut the upper and lower legs into pieces the thickness of a finger and a little over an inch long. Wash them clean with water, and marinate in raw honey. After a long while, add a small amount of spring onion, Chinese pepper, and wine; mix; cook in chicken stock. Steam the stomach fat and spawn. Remove the shell and add into the stock. Serve with pickled ginger slices and clear chicken stock. Do not use the crab claws. Do not overcook.

50. Jellyfish Stew

Use prawns' heads to make a clear stock, or slices of "chicken crisp" pieces (see recipe 20 above). Add jellyfish. It is best to use only "patterned-head" jellyfish. Wash clean the prawns, cassia-peas, fresh shrimp, and chicken-crisp pieces. Mix together and serve. Fish meat can also be added.

51. How to Cook Cassia-Peas[62]

First wash clean. Put in a wine bottle, stew over a fire of husks for a while, and remove. Then change water to soak and cook for a while. Remove to serve.

52. Imitation Scallops from River Fish

Cut the meat on the back of the river fish into long sections. Cut each section into six chunks, shaped like scallops. Marinate in salt and wine, then steam. Use the remaining fish meat to make stock. Remove the bones in the head, use only the mouth and cheek. Those with the most beautiful gold color and. . .[63]

Afterword by Yao Zi (Ming Dynasty)

Manners start from drinking and eating. Drinking and eating are basic needs of humans[64]—everyday essentials for survival. However, He Yin,[65] always concerned about everything related to food, cut off only one chunk of pork from a pig, for the perfect taste; this is not a good example. Su Dongpo[66] restrained from killing during his later years and ate only vegetables; this too is not what the ancient kings had in mind for nourishing the elderly.

This book, the *Cloud Forest Hall Collection of Rules for Drinking and Eating,* is a compilation that captures the art of cooking. (According to the recipes herein,) animals are not to be ruthlessly killed or poisoned, and the vegetable dishes are exceptionally good. After a hundred generations, the author's nobility will be seen. Those who like to cook will also straighten their clothes (as a mark of respect).

Cloud Forest's given name was Zan; his style-name was Yuanzhen, his surname Ni. He was a native of Zhituo village in Wuxi County. He was born in the late-Yuan dynasty, when a host of heroes arose (against the Mongols), so he hid his talents. When the founding ancestor of the present dynasty established his capital at Jinling (Nanjing), Ni gave up his holdings and properties, left his home, and ended his life unsullied.

On the sixteenth day of the seventh month, in the autumn of the Jiayin year of the Jiajing reign period (1554), during a serious drought, suddenly there came a light breeze from the west, and sweet rain fell. The casual scholar, "Tea Dreams" Yao Zi[67] of Gouwu,[68] happily picked up his brush (to write this Afterword).

—ENA, TW, VHM

Notes

1. Translated by Susan Bush.

2. Section numbers below have been added by the translators.

3. A *dou* is a dry measure equal to approximately a dekaliter (2.64 gallons).

4. Note the specified measurements and the instruction relating thereto; compare with later recipes, where quantities are left to the chef's discretion. The same sharp contrast is seen in the *YSZY.* The time stated is *fu,* the dog days or hottest part of summer. Presumably the vat is to be left during this period and then the soy sauce drained off. Ni leaves it to the common knowledge of the kitchen staff that the beans have to be cooked first. The beans ferment into *jiang* (fermented sauce) similar to Japanese miso. Soy sauce as that term is understood in English refers to liquid drawn off from vats of fermenting *jiang. Lactobacillus,*

Aspergillus, Rhizopus, and other salt-tolerant organisms do the fermenting. The salt must be measured accurately so as to be adequate to kill unwanted organisms while not killing the desired ones.

5. A *jin* is a unit of weight equal to roughly half a kilogram (1.1 pounds).

6. The dough has to stand and undergo repeated kneadings to bring out the gluten. The amount specified is a counsel of perfection and would bring China's rather soft flour as close as possible to the ideal texture. (Lacking durum, China cannot produce Italian chewiness in noodles.) Like many Chinese works of the sort, this book directs the cook to stir the boiling noodles, to allow them to cook evenly without sticking. The word translated "broth" could imply soup, stock, or sauce.

7. The identifications of lionstail *(Leonurus macranthus)* and betony are tentative.

8. A *fen* is a unit of weight equal to about half a gram.

9. "Goose pears" are the modern Tianjin duck pears—large Chinese pears whose juice is a common cooling drink. This recipe appears to be a thrifty householder's way of using relatively ordinary ingredients to approximate the rare and valuable gharuwood incense.

10. The kind of crab *(youmou* or *qiumou)* specified is *Charybdis japonica,* a rather common species in South China. Crab is still dipped in vinegar dips, to cut the fattiness and fishy flavor and to drive away "cold." This is not cold temperature, but the cold *qi* that could injure an eater's health.

11. Perilla is an herb of the mint family, used for both seeds and leaves, the latter being intended here. These resemble purple basil in appearance and, vaguely, in their mild taste.

12. This is an early recipe for one of the Chinese foods best known to the world at large. *Huntun* ("wonton" in Cantonese pronunciation) usually refers to the soup, not the dumplings *(jiaozi),* but here the term seems to apply to the dumplings themselves (as it has come to do in English).

13. Riced shoots: literally, "bamboo shoots (cut up like) grains."

14. The basella identification is tentative.

15. *Sharen,* a type of Chinese cardamom, has a powerful and heating taste. It and other cardamoms show up in almost every recipe of this sort in the *YSZY.* Ni obviously thought such cooking was uncouth—good only for medicine! The warming properties of the seeds in question are remarked at length in the *YSZY,* and, indeed, in most Chinese books on food and health.

16. Yellow birds or yellow sparrows are, focally, Chinese yellow buntings *(Emberiza* spp.), but the name is used generally for any small yellowish or brownish bird. The word translated "buns," here as elsewhere, is *mantou,* probably a borrowing from Turkic *manty* or *mantu.* The borrowing may have gone the other way, but this is unlikely on several grounds, including the fact that today *mantou* are unstuffed, but in medieval China they had fillings, as their cognates still do in Korea and the Altaic world.

17. Brewing lees are a common pickling, marinating, coating, and flavoring agent in China, especially the central east where Ni dwelt.

18. "Fragrant oil" is probably sesame oil.

19. These are noodles that have been cooled in ice water or well water. So this is a piquant fish sauce to eat with or on them. The directions at the end are hard to follow. The fish are not easy to identify (several fish are called *lu* [sea perch], and "river fish" could be anything); any delicate, white-fleshed fish would do. The mandarin-fish *(gui)* is focally *Siniperca chuatsi,* a freshwater perch.

20. "Fragrant herb" could be basil or mint or some other herb.

21. "Temple" could possibly be a miswriting of a homonym that means "salted vegetable."

22. Milk-cake is obscure. Probably curd or a fresh cheese such as cottage cheese is meant. The dish would work best with something like the Indian *panir* or Mexican fresh cheese.

23. Sugar jar: apparently the brown ceramic maltose pot so familiar in Chinese kitchens.

24. The term implies exceedingly quick cooking—little more than a quick dip in the boiling stock.

25. "Mr."—*xiansheng*—is presumably a bit of Ni's humor.

26. Apparently a freshwater fish is meant, possibly a loach.

27. "Field snail" or "paddy snail" *(tianluo)* is a general term for small freshwater snails.

28. *Zira* or *jira* is a general Near Eastern and Indian word for apiaceous seeds. It was borrowed into China as *shiluo.* It can cover dill, fennel, aniseed, cumin, etc.

29. The prohibition against summer eating is, obviously, because the raw snails would spoil.

30. Lychee shells are rough and ridged; the direction means that one should score the meat with shallow crisscross cuts, to take the marinade.

31. "Mountain medicine" is the wild Chinese yam (*Dioscorea* spp.).

32. Obviously, a recipe has gotten dropped here, its title surviving as the (wrong) title for this recipe. Presumably one can cook kidney and stomach in the same way. "Crisp" translates *cui*, which means "succulent and juicy but offering initial resistance to bite"—like celery or, as here, like white chicken meat that has been cooked at a high temperature on the outside while staying moist and tender inside. The Chinese word does not imply crackling-crisp, as the English word generally does.

33. *Mei* is usually translated into English as "plum," but it is actually the flowering apricot *(Prunus mume)*.

34. The radish is, of course, the giant white Oriental radish.

35. Salt is, or was, typically sold in large corn-like grains in China, and these were stir-fried to break them up and provide a slight scorched taste. Impurities could be driven off or at least made safe.

36. Ni's word is one that covers any small whitish mushroom, including common market ones. The last phrase in the recipe seems to imply that we are dealing with dried ones here. This simple recipe is still widespread.

37. "Duke Zheng" may be an error for Duke Guo, a well-known brewing expert. The aromatic mentioned in the third sentence is unknown to us. Obviously this astonishing brew would be nothing like any familiar drink of today. This recipe does not actually describe the brewing itself but the preparation of wine leaven, which is essential for the process of brewing described in the next recipe.

38. This recipe, which is meant to explain what is done with the yeast in the previous recipe, is hard to follow and inadequate without specialized knowledge. Glutinous rice—the kind almost always used for brewing in China—is cooked down, mixed with yeast, and left to ferment. Then sugary, maltose-rich powder is added. The whole is mixed with enough water to prepare a mash. "Cook" at the end is confusing; cooking it would kill the yeast. Either slight heating is intended, or the yeast is to be reinoculated, or we are to understand that the wine is left to brew and then poured off and heated for drinking.

39. A *shi* (also pronounced *dan*) is a unit of weight equal to approximately 100 catties (133–143 pounds [60–64 kilograms]). "Picul" is from a Malay word signifying the maximum amount a man can carry.

40. See note 18.

41. The crabmeat is formed into little "turtles" like the familiar American candy.

42. The received name for this recipe is "sugar buns," but all sources agree that this is an obvious mistake for "brewing-lees buns."

43. The recipe may be used for a headcheese, which would be sliced and added to the separately cooked congee. The onion whites should be mixed in along with the flower pepper (though the recipe does not make this clear).

44. "New" for the citrus probably means that the peel is to be fresh, in contrast to the "old" (dried and cured) peel so often used in Chinese cooking.

45. This is for cut-up meat, not headcheese.

46. Here as elsewhere, wild-rice is not rice but *Zizania* (the "wild rice" of North America), grown in China not for its grain but for its asparagus-like shoots.

47. For the "hand cakes," see the next recipe.

48. *Shoubing* (hand cakes) is suspiciously close to the familiar *shaobing,* but the recipe is not similar, and we think this is a truly different name and recipe.

49. There is a textual problem here, but it is clear that *mian* (flour) rather than *qu* (leaven) is intended.

50. This recipe is somewhat confusing. The idea is clear: mix starch into a dough that gelatinizes. Force the dough through the sieve-like or colander-like vessel used for this in China, so that the noodles fall directly into the boiling water. Then take the noodles out. They can be mixed with soup when wanted. The main problem is the title. Perhaps the oddly named soup is in fact flavored with the honey and brew mix, producing red noodles.

51. Lotus rhizomes *(lian'ou)* are almost always translated as "roots," but they are the underwater stems of the plant. They have hollow chambers, which cooks often stuff with a wide variety of fillings.

52. This is a level of refinement worthy of the nun Adamantine, who was a tea afficionado par excellence in the novel *Dream of the Red Chamber.*

53. A *qian* is a measure of weight equal to approximately five grams.

54. The above two recipes show the extreme care that Ni took of his artist's equipment.

55. The charming name may indicate that these were originally steamed (*long* [small steamer] being a homonym of *long* [dragon]). Yet another *long* is a type of sack, whose shape may have inspired the name.

56. Use of apricot-kernel paste in meat dishes is found also in the *YSZY,* in basically Near Eastern dishes, so it may be a borrowing. (It substitutes for the very similar almond butter of the Near East.) If so, it had certainly been naturalized, since Ni Zan's recipes show no direct Near Eastern influence.

57. The "yellow bird" is almost certainly a bunting (*Emberiza* spp.). Small yellow buntings are still called by this name. However, see also comments on the recipe for yellow-bird buns (no. 8).

58. This recipe is hard to follow. The juice or stock is introduced without explanation. Most likely some water/sesame/salt mix is saved in liquid form to make the final cakes smooth and neat-appearing. Basically, this is a way to filter dirt and impurities out of salt.

59. "Barbecue" is literally "roast" or "braise," but the word "barbecue" has become the standard English term for this type of process, and indeed is the ideal word.

60. Presumably the chopped items are to be stuffed into the intestines or stomach, producing a type of sausage.

61. As noted above in the introduction, this is a version of the modern Cantonese *cha siu.*

62. Cassia-peas have nothing to do with the cassia, which is "Chinese cinnamon." They are the seeds of *Cassia tora,* a medicinal plant containing a number of drugs.

63. Here the text breaks off, and we know no more of Ni Zan's kitchen.

64. This is nearly an exact quotation from the "Operation of Ritual" (Li yun) chapter of the *Book of Rites (Li ji).*

65. Flourished mid-sixth century.

66. Su Shi (1037–1101), a famous poet, essayist, painter, and statesman of the Northern Song dynasty (see selection 58).

67. Yao Zi, who affected the pen-name Master of Tea Dreams, was a bibliophile and compiler. His self-deprecating *san ren* denotes a worthless, scatterbrained scholar; "casual" seems to get the right sense.

68. An old name for the area southeast of Wuxi (Jiangsu Province).

Tang Shi, "Lament for a Song Girl,"
Four Stanzas

TANG SHI, WHO WROTE these songs mourning the death of a young actress, lived in the end of the fourteenth and beginning of the fifteenth century. Like so many other song writers from those times, very little is known about him. He held a minor post in his home county in Zhejiang Province, but he left it for the bohemian life. He wrote prodigiously, mostly about his life and friends, the times and reminiscences of the past, and in a style that was skillful and much admired. His imagery is often imaginative and fresh and, as we see in these poems, can at times be quite moving.

The Ming Emperor Chengzu knew of Tang Shi and was pleased by him; he rewarded him often during his reign from 1402 to 1426. From this we can estimate that Tang Shi lived at least to the age of fifty and perhaps longer.

These four songs were written to a tune called "Intoxicated in the Eastern Wind" (Chen zui dong feng), which was popular during the Yuan and Ming periods. Like nearly all music of those times, this tune is lost, and we depend on the text for any insight into what the song form may have been like. The stanza structure is 6 6, 3 3 7, 7 7, which yields three "sentences." In these poems the two three-syllable lines have been augmented to five, not uncommon in this style of verse. Lines 5 and 7, both of seven syllables, have a caesura before the fourth syllable from the end, suggesting that the basic form underlying these lines is actually six syllables.—WS

I

The dark tidings wounded my whole heart,
and a thousand farewells did your dirge recall.
The butterflies work among flowers forlorn,
a phoenix weeps, the flute sings no more,
and over the poppies the long nights fall.
I despair of Death,[1] narrow and mean,
that takes the life of one so fair.

II

To the magnolia[2] a spring wind came too soon,
on a star-thistle blossom the evening rain lies.
The chamber is empty, the swallows have flown,
the roadway quiet where the cock did crow,
and whither, I ask, does your soul drift now?
How unjust is Hell's Master
that one so perfect should die so young.

III

The cadence rests and the song dies,
no frankincense burns on the plate of jade.
The song of the oriole wakes you no longer,
the cuckoo[3] it is that calls you away
and the flowers of the field await you still.
The Heralds of Hell in their dire pursuit,
heed not, I fear, the Lord of the East.[4]

IV

The mirror is flawed,[5] a lone phoenix[6] shines there;
the well-wrought harp is idle and still.
Your farewell is made to this callow youth,
and though your cruel mistress[7] is left behind too,
you, dear soul, took the Spring all away.
On Sun Terrace now no dreams of love more,
and sadly I miss the clouds and the rain.[8]

—WS

Notes

1. Yama, the Master of Hell, God of the Dead.
2. More literally, "face-powder tree," probably referring to the white cosmetic worn by the singer when she was alive.
3. The lore of the cuckoo in China is quite different from that in the West. Its call is traditionally taken to sound like the phrase *buru guiqu* (better to return home), in which "home" can refer to the resting place of the dead.
4. The Sun, the god of spring, who presides over the season of rebirth and love.
5. Because the face of the departed is no longer to be seen in it.
6. This most likely refers to the poet.
7. This may refer to a madam of a brothel or the person in charge of the entertainment troupe who had control over this singing girl.
8. Literally, "morning clouds and evening rain," a famous expression from the "Rhapsody on Gao Tang" (Gao Tang fu) in which is recounted the story of King Huai of Chu who became weary while traveling on Gao Tang Mountain and slept for a bit, whereupon he had a dream in which the Maiden of Mount Wu appeared and shared his couch with him. When he left she said to him, "I dwell upon a rise by a cliff on the southern slopes of Mount Wu; at dawn I am the morning clouds, in the evening I am the passing rain; I am there morning and evening beneath Yang Tai Mountain (here translated 'Sun Terrace')." This passage is the locus classicus for the expression "clouds and rain," which is universally used in Chinese literature as an oblique reference to sexual intimacy.

WANG YANGMING (born Wang Shouren, styled Bo'an, 1472–1529), was a native of modern Zhejiang Province. A staunch Confucian, Wang Yangming began his studies of Zhu Xi's (see selection 64) form of Neo-Confucianism at a young age. He was struck by Zhu Xi's insistence that wisdom came from "investigating things," a concept Zhu Xi developed from a phrase in the classical Confucian text the *Great Learning*. Zhu Xi argued that a unitary principle gave order to all things. However, because human beings had desires, they could not fully trust their impulses. Therefore, one needed to investigate things in the external world (books, in particular) in order to discern the universal principle that shapes and harmonizes the cosmos. At one point, frustrated by his inability to perceive this principle, Wang determined to meditate upon a piece of bamboo until he succeeded in unlocking the principle within it. His attempt was unsuccessful in terms of traditional Neo-Confucian understanding of the "investigation of things," but it led Wang to reevaluate what needed to be investigated. Ultimately, Wang developed his notion of "moral knowledge," stressing that all people have an innate ability to discern right from wrong. Once this innate moral knowledge was uncovered through study, anyone could become a sage like the legendary Yao and Shun. Wang's views contravened Zhu Xi's views, which had been adopted as the state orthodoxy promoted through the examination system. Critics said that Wang was more influenced by Chan (Zen) Buddhism than by Confucius. Wang, however, stridently defended the Confucian nature of his position by underscoring his belief in the ultimate reality of this world and by stressing that knowledge needed to be acted upon within society if an individual were to fulfill his or her potential.

In this piece, Wang Yangming relates his own explanation of a key line of the *Great Learning* that Zhu Xi had stressed to develop his program of learning in the Song: "The Way of the Great Learning depends upon illustrating illustrious virtue, loving the people, and stopping at perfect goodness." Through this explanation, Wang developed his own doctrine of moral knowledge and distinguished his project from Buddhism and Daoism.—RF

Someone asked, "The *Great Learning* is what ancient scholars considered the learning of a great person. May we dare to ask why the learning of a great person depends upon 'illuminating illustrious virtue'?" Master Yangming replied, "The great person considers Heaven and Earth and myriad things to be one body. He views the world as a single family, and China as a single person therein. The petty person differentiates the bodies and separates 'you' from 'me.' The great person's ability to consider Heaven and Earth and myriad things as one body is not merely his opinion, but it is that the humaneness in his heart-and-mind is fundamentally so. How is it that only the great person considers the universe and the myriad things as one? Even the heart-and-mind of the petty person is like this; however, he makes it petty himself. Thus if he were to see a child about to fall into a well, he would certainly feel alarm and pity, because his humaneness makes him of one body with the child.[1] Similar to the case of the child, when he perceives the mournful cries and fearful trembling of birds and animals, he would certainly feel that he cannot bear it, because his humaneness makes him of one body with the birds and animals. But birds and animals have consciousness; yet, when he sees grass being cut, he certainly feels sympathy, because his humaneness makes him of one body with the grass. But grass is alive; yet when he sees roofing tiles and rocks smashed, he certainly feels regret, because his humaneness makes him of one body with the tiles and rocks. Therefore even the mind of the petty person certainly has this humaneness that unifies everything into one body. It is rooted in the inner nature bestowed by Heaven and is numinously bright and clear. Therefore it is called illustrious virtue.

"The heart-and-mind of the petty person is alienated and blocked by the self, yet the unifying humaneness is still capable of being clear when one is not motivated by desires and not blocked by self-interest. When [one is] motivated by desires or blocked by self-interest, profit and loss strive with each other, and anger and wrath both rush forth; then one harms things and destroys the kinship one has with them. Then there is nothing one will not do, even to the point of injuring each other so the humaneness that unifies us into one body is lost. Therefore, if there are no blockages of self-interested desire, even the heart-and-mind of a petty person has the humaneness that unifies into one body just like the great person. Yet if there is even one blockage of self-interested desire, the heart-and-mind of the great person is alienated and blocked like the petty person. Thus the learning of the great person is nothing more than to dispel the blockages of self-interested desire in order to illuminate his illustrious virtue, and return to the original state of Heaven and Earth and the myriad things forming one body. You are not able to add something external to your person; [it is already within]."

Someone said, "If this is so, then why does it depend upon 'loving people'?" Wang Yangming replied, "To illuminate illustrious virtue is to establish the substance of Heaven and Earth and the myriad things being one body. To love people is to act upon Heaven and Earth and myriad things being one body. So illuminating illustrious virtue necessarily depends upon loving people; and loving people is the means by which to illuminate illustrious virtue. Therefore, if I love my father and extend this to others' fathers, and to the fathers of everyone in the world, then my humaneness really makes me of one body with my father, the fathers of others, and the fathers of everyone in the world. When I am really of one body with them, then the illustrious virtue of filial piety begins to shine forth. . . . When I am really of one body with [all elder brothers], then the illustrious virtue of fraternity begins to illuminate. As for rulers and ministers, husbands and wives, friends, even for mountains and valleys, ghosts and spirits, birds and animals, plants and trees, really there is a means by which to love them all in order to develop my humaneness that unifies into one body. After that, my illustrious virtue will begin to illuminate everything and will truly be able to unify Heaven and Earth and the myriad things into one body. This is called 'illuminating illustrious virtue in the world,' and also 'the family is settled, the state ordered, and the world pacified,' and 'inner nature is fulfilled.'"

Someone asked, "If so, then how does one come to 'stop at perfect goodness'?" [Wang] replied, "Perfect goodness is the ultimate standard of illuminating virtue and loving people. The inner nature bestowed by Heaven is purely perfect goodness. Its numinous brightness and clearness is the manifestation of highest goodness, which is the original substance of illustrious virtue. And what is called 'moral knowledge' is the manifestation of perfect goodness that allows us to know what is right is right, and what is wrong is wrong. Light or heavy, thick or thin, as the moral knowledge is stimulated, so it responds, changing and moving ceaselessly according to the situation. And so everything has heavenly balance of its own accord. This is the source of human ethics and the standards for things. It does not allow for any calculations or discussion, or any additions or deletions to it. Any calculations or discussions, or additions or deletions to it are self-interested opinions and minor wisdom, and cannot be called perfect goodness. If one is not perfectly self-controlled, pure and singular, how can one achieve this? Because later generations of people did not know that perfect goodness was in their own minds and because they used self-interested knowledge to measure and calculate the external world, they believed that each event and thing had its own set principle. Thus they were ignorant of the standards of right and wrong, and they divided and destroyed. Human desires flourished while heavenly principle failed, and the study of illuminating virtue and loving people was thrown into disorder.

"There were among the ancients those who desired to illuminate illustrious virtue; however, because they did not understand stopping at perfect goodness they pursued their self-interested mind in abstraction. They became lost in 'vacuity and emptiness' and had nothing to do with the implementation of the family, the state, and the world: these are the followers of Buddhism and Daoism. There were those who wanted to love the people; however, not understanding abiding by perfect goodness they steeped their self-interested minds in petty things. They became lost in strategies and skills and had nothing to do with the sincerity of humane love and compassion: these are the disciples of the successes of the five hegemons who valued political power. None of them understood their mistakes regarding stopping at perfect goodness.

"Therefore, the relationship between stopping at perfect goodness to illuminating virtue and loving the people is like that of the ruler and compass to squares and circles, of measurements to long and short, of the scale to heavy and light. When the square and the circle do not stop at the ruler and compass, they lose their standards. When long and short do not stop at the measurements, they deviate from their prescribed dimensions. When heavy and light do not stop at the scales, they lose their accuracy. When illuminating illustrious virtue and loving people do not stop at perfect goodness, they lose their basis. Thus it is said that stopping at perfect goodness in order to love people and illuminating illustrious virtue are the learning of the great person."

—RF

Notes

1. The parable of the child and the well is Mencius's classical argument for the innate seeds of goodness in humans. See *Mencius* II.A.6.

In Praise of Martyrs:
Widow-Suicide in Late-Imperial China

THE NOTION OF widow-fidelity is an old one in Chinese culture: widows who refused to remarry are praised in Chinese texts dating from well before the Common Era. Starting with the Han dynasty, the Chinese state honored such widows, since a wife's loyalty to her husband's family could be used to symbolize loyalty to the empire itself. Nevertheless, widow-fidelity was an ideal mostly honored in the breach before the fourteenth century. In the twelfth through the fourteenth centuries, China's intellectual elite brought Confucian teachings back to the fore after centuries of Buddhist ascendancy, and they made the ideal of wifely fidelity central to their vision of Confucian society. By the middle 1500s, local histories in every Chinese county and prefecture contained chapters praising the virtuous widows of the community. About a third of the women in these chapters were honored for suicide. No Chinese government today praises widow-suicide or discourages the remarriage of widows, and the eighteenth- and nineteenth-century emperors, even as they praised widows who did not remarry, tried to discourage them from following their husbands in death. But the essays below show us how the suicide of young widows was not only praised but romanticized in the sixteenth century, with effects that linger in popular attitudes today.

The essays below are by Wang Jiusi (1468–1551), a poet and playwright from Shaanxi Province in north-central China, whose brief official career was cut short by early-sixteenth-century court upheavals. The friendship between Wang Jiusi and Kang Hai, another Shaanxi poet and historian whose career paralleled Wang's, has been legendary for centuries. The two are known for their devotion to wine, women, and song (a hundred courtesans helped celebrate Kang Hai's sixtieth birthday), but less well known are the ties of tragedy that bound the two men. Wang's daughter was the first wife of Kang Hai's son Kang Li, and her death in childbirth was soon followed by the deaths of Kang Li; Kang Li's second wife, Yang Shengrong; her brother Yang Song; and Yang Song's wife. Wang Jiusi wrote epitaphs for them all. The two epitaphs presented here are preserved in *The Collected Works of Wang Jiusi (Mei po ji)*.

Essays praising virtuous widows were a standard subgenre of writing by educated men. Thousands of such essays are extant from the Ming and Qing dynasties, and the similarities between our two examples show us that Wang Jiusi, however profound his grief, was writing in a highly conventional style. The standard essay praising widow-suicide has a built-in tension: parents or parents-in-law must force or cajole the young widow to remarry or at least remain alive, whereas the young widow must resist them to the point of death or disfigurement. This element of resistance made a space for women to use the icon of the faithful widow as a proof of moral worth, especially after the Manchu conquest of 1644, when men and women alike called themselves "faithful widows" to the fallen Ming. But the literature in praise of faithful widows is overwhelmingly male, which raises complex questions about power, gender, and the appropriation of women's voices. Late-Qing evidence suggests that women committed suicide to punish those who damaged their reputations, a far more aggressive gesture than what we read here. But perhaps it took pathetic portraits like these to make the ideal of widow-suicide culturally acceptable.—KC

"Biography of the Martyred Wife of the Yang Family" (Yang liefu zhuan)

The martyred wife of the Yang family was the daughter of the Director of Revenue Kang Dechong, of Wugong County. She was given in marriage to Yang Song, an outstanding Lingbao County student. In the *jichou* year of the Jiajing reign period (1529), Yang Song's younger sister had married the Wugong County student Kang Li, and when Kang Li died and Yang Song's sister committed suicide, Yang rushed to her side. In his grief, he began to cough up blood. For three years he continued to cough up blood intermittently, until he finally died on the fifteenth day of the tenth month of the *xinmao* year (1531). When his illness reached its crisis, his own wife Kang promised to follow him in death.

Her parents-in-law were aware of her plans. Her father-in-law was Yang Shu'an, the Provincial Administration Commissioner, and her mother-in-law was Lady Xu, daughter of the Minister of Ritual, Xu Xiangyi. Again and again they implored her not to die, but to remain with them and make a name for herself as a filial and faithful widow. "Wouldn't that be admirable?" they said. "Why do you stubbornly insist on dying now, so as to become famous later? And aren't you even thinking about your daughter?"

But Martyr Kang replied, "I know nothing of fame; I know only that I have a husband. When I die, do not grieve for me. And if not even I am to be pitied, how much less should you pity my daughter!" Back and forth the words flew, but in the end Kang would not consent to live.

When her parents-in-law saw that she was unpersuadable, they could do nothing but weep together, and set the servants to watch over her. But the servants treated this as a matter of no great concern. Whatever crisis she might reach, where was she likely to get poison? Her parents-in-law also trusted in her safety. What they did not know was that as soon as Yang Song had become ill, Kang had purchased arsenic. On the twentieth day of this month, she seized her opportunity and secretly took it with water, and then lay down. The servants were unaware of what she had done. After some time, they noticed that her eyes were bulging and her face was red. When they called her there was no response, and only then did they realize that the crisis had arrived. They ran to inform Lady Xu, and everyone rushed in with antidotes, but they were unable to save her. She was twenty-three years old.

Ah, how heroically virtuous! She had prepared in advance her burial clothing and everything needed for her funeral, and she gave up parental love for the sake of righteousness. Her countenance was not at all perturbed or disorderly, but dignified and calm, as though the spirits attended her in death. She resembled Kang Li's wife exactly. How remarkable! How extraordinary! The Kang and Yang families had intermarried for generations, and this must have influenced both young women to sacrifice themselves. And their own natural endowments must have played a role as well. Otherwise how can we account for cases like that of Robber Zhi and his virtuous brother Hui, born of the same womb but so utterly different in conduct?[1] Then how much more must this be true of the girls from these two families? In any case, the fame of both houses will endure for generations upon generations.

The Historian observes: Alas! Who among us does not die? But if we rank the dying, there are those who esteem death lightly as a pigeon's down, while to others it is as heavy as Mount Tai. Consider, for example, Fan Zhi, one of the original courtiers of the Song dynasty.[2] The second Emperor Taizong esteemed him greatly, but remarked, "How regrettable! His only fault lay in not giving the life he owed to his sovereign Shizong. This was indeed shameful." How can a Fan Zhi be compared to our heroine, the very epitome of virtue, whose like is so rarely seen in history?

"Epitaph for Yang Shengrong, the Martyred Wife of the Kang Family" (Kang liefu Yang shi mu zhi ming)

My son-in-law was the student Kang Li (courtesy name Zikuan) of Wugong County.[3] When he died and was buried, I composed his epitaph. Now his second wife Yang has taken poison to sacrifice herself for him. Kang Li's father, the historian Kang Hai, sent a messenger rushing to tell me, saying, "The pain of her death penetrates my very heart and bones; how can I bear to speak of it? But she cannot go without an epitaph, so I dare to trouble you once again." When I heard this I could not restrain my tears. Can it really be that another young woman has died, just like my own daughter?

Kang Li would never countenance immoral behavior, saying that Heaven was certain to punish lewd or villainous deeds. Thus he never, in his twenty-two years of life, contravened the Rites.[4] Heaven must have decided to reward him by giving him this virtuous wife. But what moved her to martyrdom? Surely it was the beauty of character with which Heaven endowed her. She would not repudiate the teachings of her father and brothers.

The ancestral home of the Yang lineage was the Hongnong region (the home of the Han-dynasty founder), and the Yangs were descended from the Han-dynasty Defender-in-Chief Yang Zhen. Our heroine's great-great-grandfather served as a Censor-in-Chief, and her grandfather also had a post in the Censorate. Her father, the Provincial Administration Commissioner Yang Shu'an, was married to Lady Xu, the daughter of the Minister of Ritual Xu Xiangyi. They had four sons and four daughters, and our heroine was the youngest daughter.

She was born in the *renshen* year of the Zhengde era (1512), on the twenty-second day of the first month, just as her father, who had been serving in Zhejiang Province, received word of his promotion to the post of Vice-Commissioner in Sichuan. Thus she was named Shengrong (ascending to glory). She was born with a fondness for poetry and virtuous teachings, and when her father and brothers discussed women who had martyred themselves in the distant past, she sighed in admiration at every tale of a death for fidelity. Why, she asked, were women of the present so far below the heroines of old? In the *wuzi* year of the Jiajing era (1528), when she was seventeen,[5] she was married to Kang Li, taking the place of my deceased daughter.[6]

In the fifth month of the following *(jichou)* year Kang Li fell ill, and when his illness reached its crisis, he said to her, "If I am so unfortunate as to die, prepare an outer coffin with space for three inner coffins. Two will be for me and the daughter of Wang, and you will make the third. Can you submit to this?"[7] Weeping, she nodded and answered, "This is just what I planned. How could I do otherwise?"

Kang Li died a few days later. Yang was firmly resolved to follow him in death. Realizing this, her mother-in-law Madame Zhang and the household women kept a strict watch on her night and day.

But people in the household had been poisoning rats, and they accidentally left some of the poison in her room. Yang secretly took seven doses, but she was quickly rescued, and death was avoided.

When Madame Zhang saw that Yang could not be moved, she went to Kang Hai. He ordered that Madame Zhang and the household women encourage Yang to return home to her parents, who could try to use their ties of affection to change her mind. But Yang was consumed with regret and remorse, and she wept and cried out day and night, desiring only to die. Her parents could do nothing with her, so they had her brother Yang Song and his wife take her back to the Kang family. Anticipating her schemes, they sent an old woman to accompany her.

When she arrived at the Kang household, she threw herself on her husband's coffin and wept. She then went in to pay her respects to her mother-in-law, saying joyfully, "I thought my husband was already buried, but he is not!" Madame Zhang could tell that Yang was headed for a crisis, and she spoke to Kang Hai again. Kang answered, "Just guard her closely."

The next day, Yang got along very well with everyone who was watching her. Whenever one of them left, she would say, "Please don't go—I'll be frightened!" This led the servants to think she needed less attention, but Madame Zhang knew otherwise, and she saw to it that Yang was watched even more strictly than before.

And indeed, a few days later, at dawn on the seventh (*jihai*) day of the eleventh month, Yang arose, bathed, and deceived [her guards] by saying that last night's meal had made her thirsty and requesting a soup of pickled vegetables. She lay down in the inner chambers and drank the soup, but took two or three ounces of arsenic with it. She went to the toilet, and when she got back she knew the poison was working, and couldn't support herself. Again she deceived her guards, saying, "Just now when I went to the toilet, I saw a spirit and am feeling quite unwell."[8] Again she asked for soup of pickled vegetables, and ordered that it be extremely hot.[9] She drank three bowls in a row, saying that it made her feel a bit better.

Madame Zhang entered and was alarmed by Yang's appearance. Her suspicions were aroused, and she felt Yang's sleeve, where some arsenic remained. Madame Zhang cried out, and the rest of the household ran in to help with the rescue. But Yang calmly said to them, "My reason for returning was to die and follow my husband beneath the ground. What I said was jewelry in my bag was actually arsenic. I worried that Mother-in-law would suspect me, so I spoke falsely, but now I have taken it all. People say that there is no antidote to arsenic taken with pickled vegetables, and I felt that any antidote would deter me from my purpose. That is why I did what I did. Do not try to save me; it will put you to a lot of trouble, and you won't succeed. Just call my sister-in-law to make the final arrangements."

Of course no one obeyed her; her brother and sister-in-law were called in, and they tried to give her an antidote. She refused it, and when they attempted to force her, she bit the cup and broke it. Again they tried to give her medicine, but she clenched her teeth and refused it all. They tried to open her teeth with an iron chopstick, but she bent the chopstick. They could not force her teeth apart.

But then she said, "It's over now. I'll drink your medicine and take no more arsenic. But I did what I did because I look upon death as joy, and life as bitterness. Why do you force bitterness upon me?"

Her sister-in-law opened Yang's clothing-chest and took out her garments, all of which she had just recently sewn. Every one of her burial garments had been exquisitely prepared. The family had no choice: they dressed her in the grave clothes, and as soon as they finished, she died. Her appearance was peaceful, with no sign of turmoil. Spirits apparently were with her, and kept the poison from disturbing her countenance.

Alas! No sooner did Kang Li die than her heart was riven with grief, such that no one could prevent her death. She had been at home, with the purpose of bidding her parents farewell, for more than three months, and though everyone showered her with affection, they could not alter her resolve. With no compulsion and no anger, she died a peaceful death, unsurpassed by the enlightened and principled courtiers of old.

Right before her death, she made a pair of *lü* shoes as birthday gifts for each of her parents, and when she returned to the Kang family, she gave *lü* shoes to her parents-in-law also.[10] When we look back we can see that she was making her eternal farewell, but no one realized it at the time. How careful and precise was her planning, and how constant and long-standing her resolve!

Who would have thought an eighteen-year-old girl capable of this, especially as she had never devoted herself to study the way a man would have done? Duplicitous scholars and treacherous servants of state will hear her story and die of shame, not to mention ordinary men and women. Her case is under consideration for official recognition.[11]

Before his death, Kang Li requested that he and his wives be buried together, and his request has not been ignored. Those in the realm of darkness have no cause for regret.

Her epitaph reads:

> The verdant peaks of Guo, our ancient land,[12]
> And the northward river, brimming between its banks,
> Foster the spirit, and summon a noble band.
> Yang and Xu are families of rank:
> Brothers worth gold and jade find worthy mates
> And make an upright pattern for the age.
> Thus they bore our heroine, unsurpassed,
> Who vowed to serve the righteousness she loved.
> How easily she chose a martyr's fate.
> Her soul now free to pierce the starry realm,
> She joins the uncomplaining wives of Shun,[13]
> And looks down at our insect-driven age.
> West of the Marsh,[14] trees grace her lofty tomb,
> And spirits protect her deep, secluded realm,
> Sun, moon, and stars eclipsed by her martyr's fame.

—KC

Notes

1. The story of Robber Zhi and his virtuous brother can be found in chapter 29 of the *Zhuang Zi* (see selection 13). In the *Zhuang Zi*, the brother's name is Liuxia Ji, not Liuxia Hui as Wang Jiusi calls him here. Robber Zhi as a noted villain is referred to in the great Han-dynasty history, *Shiji*, and in various pre-Han sources.

2. Before his service to the Song dynasty, Fan Zhi had an active career in three of the so-called "Five Dynasties," which were brief and unstable hegemonies that immediately preceded the Song (960–1278). Shizong was the second emperor of the last of these "dynasties," the Posterior Zhou (951–960), and Fan Zhi did not follow Shizong or Shizong's son in death at the fall of the Zhou. (Neither, it should be noted, did the many other Posterior Zhou officials who went on to staff the new Song-dynasty bureaucracy.) Fan Zhi received the *jinshi* degree in 933/4, at the end of the Posterior Tang (923–934). He died in 963.

3. Wugong county is in Shaanxi Province.

4. The "Rites" that Kang Li never transgresses are the body of Confucian ritual (some of it codified into law) that was supposed to insure harmonious social hierarchy.

5. This is seventeen *sui*, sixteen years of age by Western reckoning.

6. This essay shows us a standard late-imperial pattern of intermarriage, in which two lineages of equal rank would each marry their daughters to the sons of the other. (Kang's original choice of Wang's daughter seems to have interrupted his own lineage pattern, and we can see this as another testimony to their friendship.)

7. Burials were often delayed, sometimes taking place years after funeral observances; this is what enables Kang Li to be buried with both his wives.

8. It was common for people (especially women) in traditional China to see evil spirits in privies, often with ill consequences.

9. The hot soup would have quickened the action of the arsenic.

10. *Lü* shoes, typically woven of straw or hemp, were the footgear of peasants. Ming encyclopedias make clear that the gentry wore them only as ritual mourning attire. Parents did *not* wear mourning for deceased children, but nevertheless *lü* shoes would have been seen as a highly symbolic gift.

11. The "official recognition" mentioned at the end of the epitaph is the process whereby a widow, the details of her case duly verified, became eligible for a government-sponsored door-marker, shrine, or arch. Such recognition was desirable not only for the edification of the community, but for the peace of mind of the family. Violent death was dangerous: if the "souls" of a martyr, however virtuous, were not ritually pacified, they could trouble the family and the community.

12. Guo, a Zhou-dynasty feudal state, covered the territory of what was Wugong County in Ming-dynasty China.

13. The wives of the legendary Sage King Shun were the daughters of his predecessor, Sage King Yao. Yao is said to have passed over his own son and selected the virtuous Shun to succeed him. Yao gave his daughters to Shun when Shun was still a lowly commoner, and their deference to their father and then to Shun made them a standard exemplar in conduct-books for women.

14. "West of the Marsh" (Hu xi) was the name of the Kang family estate. Yang was buried in the tombs of her husband's family, of which she was, after marriage, ritually a member.

ROMANCE OF THE INVESTITURE OF THE GODS *(Fengshen yanyi)* is one of a number of Ming-period (1368–1644) Chinese novels that have deep roots in popular religious beliefs. The social context of the "gods and demons novel" novels of the Ming period was that of a popular movement to combine Taoist, Buddhist, and Confucianist sectarian ideologies into a syncretistic religion. The impetus for the early composition of these novels by means of the conceit of having Buddhist and Taoist deities interact with the figures of orthodox Confucianist historiography was an intent to proselytize sectarian beliefs. Having originally served this didactic religious purpose, they became so popular that they were later absorbed into commercial channels of popular literature. Yet because the subjects of these works were the gods and immortals of popular religious belief, the interactive process linking popular religious works with popular fiction has continued to the present day. Popular religious cults continue to write, edit, and publish works of religious revelation in a style which conforms to that of popular novels.

The earliest known text of *Investiture of the Gods* dates from the Wanli period of the Ming dynasty (1573–1619). In this edition, the editor or publisher is given as Xu Zhonglin of Nanking, who is supposed to have died around the year 1566. Xu is usually cited as the original author of the text. A revised edition of *Investiture of the Gods* in one hundred chapters was published by the famous author and editor Chu Renhuo in 1695 is the one translated here.

The literary historian Liu Ts'un-yan (Liu Cunyan) firmly believes that *Investiture of the Gods* was written by Lu Xixing, who lived from 1520 until about 1601. According to Liu, Lu eventually became an ordained member of the Quanzhen sect of Taoism, a sect that fostered a syncretic approach to the "three religions."

On Taiwan today among the rural population of mountainous Puli township, authorship of *Investiture* is not ascribed to either of these men. Instead, the book is almost universally believed to have been written by Liu Bowen (Liu Ji), a capable adviser to Zhu Yuanzhang, the founder of the Ming dynasty, who is also known as the author of many seminal works in fate calculation and geomancy. The same opinion seems to have been true for many people in Peking (Beijing) in the first half of the twentieth century as well. Liu Bowen is an entity who frequently descends to take part in the seances of spirit-writing cults, so he may be regarded as a kind of "legendary archetype" or "folk spirit" responsible for composing *Investiture*. But whoever composed this fantastic novel, the text and its protagonists are reflected everywhere in the popular and performing arts surrounding popular religion in China.

The novel begins by detailing the acts of lust and cruelty which set in train the overthrow of the Shang dynasty. The gods set about systematically recruiting supernatural entities to ally with the righteous rebels of Zhou and make war on the forces of the Shang. Finally, at a grand ceremony of investiture in the final chapters of the novel, all of the souls of those killed in the wars, as well as the survivors, are given titles reflecting their famous deeds and rewarding their meritorious acts.

The following translation of excerpts from chapters 12–14 represents one of the most popular episodes from the novel, often acted out in popular theater or painted on temple walls. It is the story of Nezha (commonly called the Third Prince [San Taizi], often associated with rebellious princes such as Yongle, the third emperor of the Ming dynasty. Nezha's warlike and aggressive nature is reflected by the fact that he is often the tutelary deity of Kungfu (Gongfu) or "boxing" cults in China. Nezha is commonly considered to be a transcription of Sanskrit Naṭa, but deeper philological examination reveals that it is more likely from Sanskrit Nalakūvara or Nalakūbara, the name of the princely son of Vaiśravaṇa, one of the most important guardians of Buddhism. The name of the hero, Nezha, is only one example of the many Indic influences in this ostensibly Taoist novel. Indeed, much of the terminology of Taoist religion is derived from Buddhism. Expressions such as "primordial fire," "Divine Worthy," and "Seven Treasures" that occur in *Investiture* may be traced to Sanskrit terms. Less evident and less studied by scholars are the important Iranian motifs in the novel. However, terms such as the "Perfected" (*zhenren;* literally, "true man"), which refers to transcendent Taoist adepts who have realized the truth of the Way (Tao, Dao), are wholly indigenous coinages of Taoist religion.

Vestigial marks of the storyteller's manner are scattered throughout these chapters, yet this is merely a simulacrum of the oral traditions that fed into the novel, which is itself purely a written text. For example, the expression *kanguan* (literally, "honored viewer") is here translated as "reader," but its ultimate derivation is from the performing arts, including storytelling with pictures. Hence the emphasis on the visual aspects of the narrative. It is not by accident that many of the poems in Chinese vernacular stories and novels are preceded by the formulaic expression "all you/he could see was," followed by highly descriptive verse. Even the very last word of this selection, "session" (usually translated as "chapter" in novels such as this), is actually a reference to a unit of the storyteller's art.—GS, VHM

Chapter 12: Nezha Is Born at Chentang Pass

A poem states,

> There is a rare jewel in Golden Gleam Cave,
> It fell to earth, to give aid to the virtuous.
> The clan of Zhou develops auspicious countenance,
> The house of Shang will destroy its own spirit line.
> The fate of the empire is in capable hands,
> The ancient glories glimmer with a foxfire glow.
> When the years are in conjunction with the days:[1]
> See the vastness of the flooded fields at morning.

As the story goes, the Commander-in-Chief of Chentang Pass was named Li Jing. From his youth he had inquired into the Way and cultivated the Truth. He took as his master the Perfected Beyond Tribulation, who lived in the Western Kunlun Mountains. There he mastered the art of the Mutual Opposition of the Five Elements.[2] Because he found it difficult to lead a spiritual life, he came down from the mountains to serve the Shang ruler, King Zhow,[3] as a military commander. Thus he enjoyed the material benefits of life among men. His principal wife was of the Yin family and bore him two sons. The eldest was called Jinzha and the second Muzha. Later his wife was once more pregnant, but even after three years and six months, she still had not given birth. As a result, Li Jing was often sorely troubled in his heart. One day, he pointed at his wife's stomach. "A fetus carried more than three years and not yet born must mean it is either a goblin or a ghost," he said.

His wife was also worried. "This child is certainly no good omen," she said, "causing me thus to always be sad of heart."

Hearing this, Li Jing was very unhappy. That night at the third watch, when his wife was deep asleep, she had a dream. In it, she saw a Taoist with his hair done up into a double knot, wearing Taoist robes, who came into her bedroom. The wife scolded him. "You certainly are a Taoist without good manners! These are the women's apartments—how can you just wander in? It's really disgusting!"

"Woman, you will soon bear a good-luck child!" the Taoist replied.

The wife was not able to answer before she saw the Taoist insert something into her stomach. She awoke in a terror, her whole body covered with a cold sweat. She immediately woke up Commander Li and told him of her dream. "The dream I just now had went like thus and so. . . ."

Even before she had finished recounting it, she felt the birth pangs in her stomach. Li Jing immediately arose and went to wait in the front hall. "Pregnant for three years and six months, then a dream such as tonight's!" he thought darkly. "Certainly she will give birth, but the good or ill of the matter is not yet certain."

As he was thus sunk in worried thoughts, he saw two servants who rushed forward saying, "Master, your wife has given birth to an unnatural thing!"

Hearing this, Li Jing hurried to his wife's room, gripping his sword in his hand. In the room he saw a glowing red mass, filling the room with a strange fragrance. It was a bulging ball of flesh, round and spinning like a wheel. Li Jing was greatly startled and struck the top of the flesh-ball a blow with his sword. There was a slicing sound. The flesh-ball split in two and out jumped a small boy. His whole body had a ruddy glow, and his face was white as though powdered. On his right arm was a gold bracelet, and around his waist he wore a red band of silk brocade, glittering with gold.

This divine spirit had come down to earth and was born at Chentang Pass in order to serve as the Vanguard of Jiang Ziya. This boy was a reincarnation of the Spirit Jewel, and the ring around his wrist was called the Heaven-and-Earth Bracelet. Around his waist was the Heaven-Confusing Sash. These were treasures from the Golden Gleam Cave on Qianyuan (Celestial Prime) Mountain. Having mentioned this, I won't go into details now.

All you could see was Li Jing splitting open the flesh-ball and watching the child run about. Although Li Jing was astonished, he leaned down and picked the child up. Sure enough, it was a perfect man-child. He could not believe that it was some sort of demon and therefore he preserved its life. He gave it to this wife to see, and both of them were unable to shake off their parental affection, losing themselves in joy.

Next day, a number of the officials attached to Li Jing's retinue came to offer their congratulations. He had just dismissed them when the Commander of the Central Batallion spoke to him. "Master, there is an old Taoist outside who wishes to see you."

Since Li Jing had begun as an acolyte of the Taoists, how could he forget his origins? He replied at once, "Have him come in."

An orderly hurried to admit the old Taoist. The Taoist entered the great hall, then turned to Li Jing and greeted him. When Li Jing had completed the formalities of greeting, he offered the old Taoist the seat of honor, which was accepted without hesitation.

"Old teacher," said Li Jing, "from what famous mountain do you hail? Which illustrious cavern do you inhabit? What is your business that you have come here today?"

"I am the Perfected of Grand Unity from Golden Gleam Cave on Qianyuan Mountain. I have heard that you have had a son born to you and I have come especially to offer my congratulations. I wonder if you would consent to show him to me?"

Hearing the Taoist's words, Li Jing called the nurse to bring the child out. The Taoist took him in his arms and, looking him over, asked, "At what hour was the child born?"

"At the second watch," was Li Jing's reply.

"That is not good," said the Taoist.

"Does this mean that he will die in childhood?" asked Li Jing.

"No," answered the Taoist. "By being born at the second watch, he has offended against seventeen hundred Death Prohibitions.[4] Have you given him a name yet?"

"Not yet," replied Li Jing.

"How about letting me give him a name, and then making him my disciple?"

"I hope you will agree to be his teacher," replied Li.

"How many sons have you got altogether?" asked the Taoist.

"I have three. The oldest is called Jinzha, who is studying under the Heavenly Worthy of the Great Law, Mañjuśrī, at Cloud Mist Cave on Five Dragon Mountain. My second son is called Muzha, and his teacher is the Perfected Samantabhadra from White Crane Cave on Nine Palace Mountain. If you want this youngest boy for a disciple, just give him a name and he'll bow to you as his teacher."

"This third son," replied Taoist, "will be called Nezha."[5]

"I cannot express the depths of my gratitude, that you have given him a name, conferring on him great honor and virtue," said Li Jing. And he called his servants to provide the Taoist with a meal.

"Please don't bother," said the Taoist, "for I have a matter that requires me to return to my mountain."

In the face of such firm resolution, Li Jing could only accompany his guest to the gate, and when the proper farewells had been said, the Taoist went his way alone.

As the story goes, although there was no trouble at the pass which Li Jing was guarding, suddenly the news arrived that four hundred of the feudal lords were in rebellion. At once Li Jing gave the command to man the defenses. He gathered together his forces and drilled his soldiers, in order to defend the strategic Wild Horse Peak. As quickly as birds fly and rabbits run, time passed in the blink of an eye, so the seasons came and went. Thus before they were aware of it, seven years went by. Nezha was just seven years old but had grown to six feet in height.

In the fifth month, the weather was already hot. Since the Imperial Prince of the East, Jiang Wenhuan, had rebelled and was engaged in a great battle with Dou Rong at Wandering Soul Pass, Li Jing drilled his troops every day. But I will say no more of that.

Rather I shall tell how his third son Nezha was hot and bored, so he sought out his mother. "I would like to go and play outside the pass," he said, "but I only dare do so after asking my mother."

Since his mother loved him dearly, she replied at once, "If you want to go outside the pass to play, my son, I can send a servant to take you there. But you must not get so wrapped up in your play that you forget to come back early before your father returns from maneuvers."

"I understand," Nezha replied.

As Nezha and the servant came out of the pass, the full force of the summer sun blasted them. All you could see was

The flames of the sun scorching the dusty ground,
Turning to ashes the willow's soft green.

Wary, the traveler, as he places his foot,
And the ladies dare not venture onto the terrace.
The pleasure pavilions seem to melt in the heat;
Without a breeze, the cabanas are like ovens.
Vain to think of fragrant draughts in garden nooks,
Or of relief that distant thunder and misty rain might bring.

As I was saying, Nezha and the servant came out of the pass. After a little more than a mile, it was difficult to continue on in the hot sun. Nezha's face was brimming with sweat. "I see some shade trees ahead," Nezha told the servant. "Go and see if it is not cool underneath them."

When the servant had reached the shade of the trees, he saw that a cool breeze was stirring and that the heat was entirely dissipated. Hurriedly he returned to Nezha. "Indeed, my lord, in the shade of the willows ahead, it is very cool and a refuge from the heat," he reported.

Nezha was overjoyed to hear this, and he ran at once to the grove, where he took off his robes. He felt happy and comfortable. Suddenly he noticed the lapping of the waves against the bank and the smooth flow of the water. Truly,

On both banks, the wind is in the willows:
In the gorges, scattered rocks make the water gurgle.

Nezha ran to the water's edge. "As soon as I came out of the pass, the heat was so intense that I was covered in sweat," he cried to the servant. "Now I can wash off on this rock in the river."

"Be careful my lord," the servant replied. "I am only afraid that your father will return, so it would be better to hurry back home."

"All right," said Nezha and, taking off his clothes, he sat down on the rock. He slipped his seven-foot-long Heaven-Confusing Sash in the water and began to wash it.

Unbeknownst to him, the river was the River of the Nine Bends and formed the mouth of the Eastern Sea. When Nezha put his treasured sash into the water, it caused the water to be shot through with red flashes. Back and forth, the entire river surged; to and fro, the very earth was shaking. So Nezha took his bath, not realizing that the Crystal Palace of the Dragon King was being violently shaken.

I will say no more of Nezha bathing, but rather tell how the Dragon King of the Eastern Sea, Ao Guang, was seated in his Crystal Palace, when he heard the palace gate shaking. "There's not supposed to be an earthquake at this time," he said to his servants, "so why is the palace shaking like this? Order Ocean Patrolling Yakṣa Demon Li Gen to check the river mouth and see what manner of being is causing this ruckus!"

When the demon reached the river, he saw that the water was shot through with red flashes like fireworks and that a small boy was using a red silk cloth to dip water for bathing. The demon parted the waters and yelled. "Hey you, Kid! What kind of weird stuff are you using that causes the water to be full of red flashes and makes the Dragon King's palace shake?"

Nezha turned and saw a creature at the bottom of the river whose face was blue and hair was bright red. Protruding from his gigantic mouth were animal-like tusks, and he grasped a huge ax in his hands.

"What kind of beast are you," asked Nezha, "that you can even talk human language?"

"I am under the Dragon King's orders to keep watch on the sea," the demon replied angrily. "How dare you insult me by calling me a beast?"

Whereupon he leaped through the water and onto the bank and aimed a slash of his ax at Nezha's head. Nezha was standing there buck-naked when he saw the demon come rushing up.

He dodged and threw up his right hand with the Heaven-and-Earth Bracelet to parry the blow. Originally this Precious Weapon was a present from the Palace of Jade Vacuity of the Kunlun Mountain to the Perfected of Great Unity of Golden Gleam Cave, so how could the demon cut through it? When the bracelet came crashing down, it landed right in the middle of the demon's head, so that his brains exploded in all directions and he died right there on the riverbank.

"You've made my bracelet all dirty!" Nezha said with a laugh. So he sat back down on the rock and began to wash the bracelet. How could the Crystal Palace withstand the shaking of this second Treasure Weapon? It only lacked a little in making the whole palace collapse!

"My demon has just gone out to investigate and not yet returned," said the Dragon King. "How can there be these further disturbances?"

Even before he had got these words out of his mouth, some of his soldiers came to report. "Yakṣa Li Gen has been killed by a youth on land, so we have come especially to report!"

The Dragon King was greatly startled. "Li Gen was appointed to this post by virtue of the august command of the Jade Emperor at the Spirit Cloud Hall," he said. "Who dares thus to strike him dead?"

"Get troops ready to accompany me," he commanded. "I myself will find out who that person is."

He had not yet finished speaking when his third son, Ao Bing, stepped forward. "Why is my father angry?" he said.

When his father had told the story of the *yakṣa*'s death, his son replied, "Father, please compose yourself. I'll just go and bring the culprit back and there will be an end to the matter."

At once he ordered his troops, mounted his underwater steed, took up his engraved halberd, and left the Crystal Palace. The force of his cutting through the water caused waves to topple like mountains and billows to surge sideways, so that the tides mounted on land several feet high.

Nezha looked at the water as it moved and said, "What big waves! What big waves!"

Just then in the midst of the waves he saw a sea creature on whose back was seated a man. He was resplendently attired from head to toe. Holding a halberd in his hand, he had a brave and valiant appearance. "What person has killed our Demon General of the Sea, Li Gen?" he yelled.

"Me," said Nezha.

"Who are you?" asked the Dragon King's son.

"I am the third son of Li Jing of Chentang Pass. My father is the commander of the garrison here. That I decided to cool off here by taking a bath was no concern of this dragon general. Since he came and bothered me, what difference does it make if I killed him?"

Ao Bing cursed loudly, "You villain! Yakṣa Li Gen was an attendant of the Heavenly King's court. You had the audacity to strike him down dead, and yet still dare to make rebellious speeches!"

Thereupon Ao Bing took his halberd and thrust at Nezha. Lowering his hands, which held not an inch of iron, Nezha approached.

"Hold your hand just a second," he said. "Who are you? If you'll just tell me your name, I'll explain what happened."

"I am Third Prince Ao Bing, son of the Dragon King of the Eastern Sea."

Laughing, Nezha said, "So you are actually Ao Guang's son? If you are so rash as to think yourself grand enough to disturb me, and you and all your loaches come forth, I'll skin you all!"

The Third Prince screamed out, "You make me so mad I could die! You scoundrel, to completely lack manners!" And he again thrust at Nezha. At once Nezha reached for his seven-foot Heaven-Confusing Sash and whipped it upward, so that it seemed that a thousand balls of fire were raining from heaven. When he lashed down with the Sash, it so tightly ensnared the Third Prince that he was pulled from his underwater steed. Nezha leaped forward and placed his foot on the Third Prince's neck. He then directed a blow of the Heaven-and-Earth Bracelet at the Third Prince's temple, causing him to metamorphose into his original being, which was a serpent-like dragon. There it lay, stretched out on the ground.

"Well, I've got myself a little dragon," Nezha said. "Okay, I'll pull the nerve tendons out and make a Dragon-Tendon Belt as a gift for my father, so he can use it to bind on his armor." So Nezha pulled the Third Prince's tendons out and then took them with him as he returned inside the pass. The servant was so scared by this that his bones softened and his muscles went limp. He could hardly walk.

Arriving before the gate of the Commandant's residence, Nezha went to see his mother. "My child," she said, "what games did you play that you were gone for half the day?"

"Oh, I was just fooling around outside the pass, and before I knew it it had got late," he replied. And so saying, he went into the rear garden.

Now I shall tell how, when Li Jing returned from maneuvers, he first gave his subordinates their orders. Then he himself removed his armor and sat down in the back hall. Sadly he thought of how King Zhow was losing his grip on the government and how the four hundred vassal lords had been forced into rebellion. Daily he could see how the people were driven into ruin, and it disturbed him deeply.

Now I shall tell how Ao Guang was in his palace when he heard his dragon soldiers return. "The third son of Li Jing of Chentang Pass, Nezha, has struck the Third Prince dead!" they reported. "And he has even stripped out his tendons!"

"My son is able to rise up on the clouds and tread the rain," Ao Guang said with astonishment. "He is a true god who is merciful toward all living things. How can he have been killed? Li Jing, you went to the Kunlun Mountains in the west to study Taoism, and you and I have even exchanged bows there. Yet you let your son run wild and kill my own child. This is reason enough for a feud to last a hundred generations. How dare he pull out my son's tendons? This breaks my heart and crushes my bones!"

In great anger, Ao Guang hated not being able to revenge his son immediately. So he transformed himself into a scholar and made his way to Chentang Pass. Arriving before the commander's residence, he spoke to the gate guard. "Pass along a message for me: 'Your old acquaintance Ao Guang has come to visit.'"

The sergeant-at-arms went into the inner apartments. "Your lordship, there is an old acquaintance outside named Ao Guang who wishes to see you," he said.

"I haven't seen my elder brother for many years. What a heaven-sent pleasure to meet him today!" said Li Jing. He hurriedly arranged his robes to greet the visitor. Ao Guang came into the great hall and, after performing the rituals of greeting, he sat down. Li Jing saw the angry color in Ao Guang's face and was just about to ask why, but Ao Guang spoke first. "Li, my worthy younger brother, you have given birth to a really fine son!"

"Elder brother," Li Jing replied smiling, "we have not met for many years. Suddenly today we have this rare encounter, truly a blessing from heaven, and how can you blurt out words like these? As for me, I only have three sons. The eldest is called Jinzha, the second Muzha, and the third is Nezha. All of them are studying with famous Taoist teachers. If they are not good, at least they are not entirely worthless. I beg my elder brother not to take a mistaken view of them."

"Worthy younger brother," Ao Guang said, "it is you who have a mistaken view. How could I be wrong? Your son was bathing in the River of the Nine Bends and by using I don't know what kind of magic, he made my Crystal Palace shake as if it were about to fall down. I sent a *yakṣa* to make inquiry, but your son just killed him. My third son went to investigate, and your son also killed him. And moreover, he stripped my son's tendons from the body." When he said this, Ao Guang's heart was seized with grief. "And you still try to cover up by saying that you know nothing of the matter!" he yelled.

Li Jing smiled soothingly. "It's not my family," he answered hurriedly. "My elder brother must have made a mistake. My eldest son is on Five Dragon Mountain studying magic, the second is on the Ninth Palace Mountain doing the same, and my third son is only seven years old and does not leave the house, so how could he have done a deed of such magnitude?"

"It is exactly that third son of yours, Nezha, who did the killing," Ao Guang said.

"This is certainly most peculiar!" said Li Jing. "I hope you will not jump to premature conclusions. Let me call him out to see you."

Li Jing went back to the inner apartments. "What visitor is in the hall?" his wife, Lady Yin, asked him.

"My old friend Ao Guang," answered Li Jing. "Someone has killed his third son, and he says that it is Nezha. I am just now calling him out to be questioned about it. Where is Nezha right now?"

"It was only today that Nezha first went outside the house," the mother thought to herself, "and how does something like this happen?" Not daring to speak of the matter, she told her husband that the boy was in the back garden.

Li Jing ran to the back garden. "Nezha, where are you?" he called. He called for half an hour but there was no answer. At last he came to the door of the Crab Apple Studio, which was closed. There he again called Nezha in a loud voice. Nezha heard him and hurriedly opened the door to see his father. "My son, what are you doing here?" he asked.

"Your son was bored today and went outside the pass to the River of the Nine Bends to play," replied Nezha. "Because it was so hot, I went to wash off in the water. I didn't expect that some *yakṣa*, Li Gen, would come along, and anyway I wasn't bothering him, but he cussed at me and struck at me with his ax. So I killed him with one blow. Also I didn't know that some Third Prince called Ao Bing would strike me with his halberd, so that I had to bind him with my Heaven-Confusing Sash and draw him out on the bank. I put my foot on his neck and gave him a little blow with my bracelet, and to my surprise he turned into a dragon. I thought how dragon tendons are the most rare of things, so I stripped them out. I am just now making them into a Dragon-Tendon Belt to give to you to tie up your armor."

Li Jing just stood there with an open mouth, so frightened that he could not say a word. After a while, he yelled out, "It will be a blood feud! You have brought great misfortune on us. Go immediately to see your uncle, and hear his words."

"Don't worry, father," Nezha said, "a person isn't guilty of a crime if he acts in sincere ignorance. And besides I have not yet done anything with the tendons, so that if he wants them, they're still here in their original form. I'll go see Uncle Ao Guang immediately."

Nezha hurried to the great hall and performed the rituals of greeting. "Uncle," he said, "your nephew acted in ignorance and made this one mistake. I beg you to forgive me. Here are the tendons, still in their original form and not disturbed in the slightest."

When Ao Guang saw the tendons, he was greatly grieved. "You have such an evil son," he said to Li Jing. "And yet you can say that I am mistaken. Now he himself admits to the deed. Can you still stand aside in the matter? Moreover, my son was a True God, and Yakṣa Li Gen was appointed by the Jade Emperor. How could you and your son murder them without reason?

Tomorrow I will petition the Jade Emperor to determine whether your Taoist master yet has need for you, or whether your time has come!" Ao Guang threw up his sleeve and left. Li Jing stamped his foot and began to wail loudly, "This is a great misfortune!"

His wife heard the pitiful crying in the great hall and hurried to ask the servants what was going on. "Today your third son killed the Dragon King's son when he went outside to play," they reported. "Now the Dragon King and His Lordship have had a set-to over the matter. Tomorrow the Dragon King is going to petition the Jade Emperor about the matter, so can't you see why the master is crying?"

In panic the Lady Li ran into the front hall to see Li Jing. When he saw her arrive, he quickly ceased crying. "I tried to become a Taoist magician and failed," he said bitterly. "But how could I know that you would give birth to a son that would bring my house to extinction? The Dragon King is a true god in control of the rains, and your son has wantonly murdered one of his sons. Tomorrow if the Jade Emperor grants his petition and takes measures against us, then in two or three days you and I will both be but ghosts kneeling beneath the executioner's sword!"

When he had finished talking, he again broke out in pitiful crying. His wife also let tears fall like rain and pointed at Nezha. "I carried you for three years and six months before giving birth to you. You have no idea how much suffering I endured. Who could know that you would be the root of the extinction of our house and ancestral line?"

As Nezha saw his parents crying, he stood up uneasily, then kneeled down before them. "Father, Mother. Let me tell you something. I am not an ordinary man-child. I am the disciple of the Perfected of Great Unity who lives in Golden Gleam Cave on Qianyuan Mountain. These magic weapons of mine are all gifts from my teacher, so how can Ao Guang stand up to me? I am going straightway to Qianyuan Mountain to get my teacher to intervene in this affair. There is a saying, 'Each person is responsible for his own deeds.' How can I allow my parents to get mixed up in this matter?"

Nezha went out the door and picked up a handful of earth. He threw it up in the air and immediately became invisible. He took on his original form and rode the dust toward Qianyuan Mountain. There is a poem that serves as testimony:

> I'll bow to my master on Qianyuan Mountain,
> Tell him of the affair with Ao Guang of the Eastern Sea.
> I'll use my magic outside the Jade Emperor's gate,
> Then the Dragon King will know my magic power.

As I was saying, Nezha rode the dust cloud to Golden Gleam Cave and waited outside for his teacher's command. The Golden Mist Servant Boy reported to his master, "My elder brother awaits your command."

"Tell him to come in," said the Perfected of Great Unity.

The Golden Mist Servant Boy went to the cave entrance. "The master commands you to come in," he said to Nezha.

Nezha came up before the jade dais and threw himself down to perform the bows of greetings. "You have left Chentang Pass," said the Perfected One. "Why have you come here?"

"I would like to inform my teacher," said Nezha, "that thanks to your benevolence I was allowed to be born in Chentang Pass and live there for seven years. Yesterday I went to the River of the Nine Bends to take a bath and unexpectedly met up with the Third Prince, son of Ao Guang, who offended me with his curses. I got mad and killed him. Now Ao Guang wants to bring the case before the Jade Emperor, and my parents are terrified. I am very upset about this and can see no way out. Thus I have come up the mountain to earnestly beg my old teacher to forgive this crime which I unwittingly committed, and I hope you will see fit to save the situation."

"Although Nezha doesn't know it," the Perfected One thought to himself, "his unwittingly killing the Third Prince Ao Bing was fated by heaven. It is, of course, true that Ao Guang is king of the dragons, but his job is only to bring clouds and make rain fall. How can he act as if he does not understand the preordained signs of heaven? In bothering the courts of heaven on account of such a small matter, he truly shows that he is not aware of the proprieties!"

"Nezha, come here!" he said without hesitation. "Open up your robe." Then the Perfected One drew a Charm Character[6] over Nezha's chest with his finger. "Go to the Precious Virtue Gate of the Jade Emperor's palace and do thus and so, this and that . . . ," he ordered Nezha. "After the affair is ended, you must return to Chentang Pass and say to your parents, 'If anything more comes out of this matter, it will be taken care of by my teacher. On no account will any trouble come to my parents.' Go now."

Nezha left Qianyuan Mountain and traveled to the Gate of Precious Virtue. Truly, "The heavenly palace's extraordinary appearance finds no reflection on earth; purple mist and red clouds cover the azure heavens." All you could see was how different high heaven is:

As he rose for the first time into the upper realm,
He saw straightway the celestial city.
Ten thousand golden rays were cast forth like rainbows from the clouds.
A thousand auspicious vapors spurted from the purple aura.
He saw that the South Gate of Heaven was made of green crystal,
And was fitted out with costly cauldrons that brightly gleamed.
On both sides were four great pillars,
And coiling to the top of each
Was a cloud-raising, mist-covering red-bearded dragon.
Exactly in the middle were two jade bridges,
And standing on each bridge was a soaring Phoenix with colorful plumage.
Overall the gleam of the sunrise shimmered in the brightening mists.
The face of the sun was mottled over with a blue-green haze.
In heaven there are thirty-three palaces of the gods:
The Palace of Lingering Clouds,
The Palace of Cosmic Sands,
The Palace of Purple Atmosphere,
The Palace of Supreme Yang,
The Palace of Supreme Yin,
The Palace of Transformative Joy . . . ,
Each of them has its roof beams decorated with golden truth-hounds.
There are also the seventy-two Treasure Halls,
They are the Hall of the Morning Meeting,
The Hall of the Transcendent Empyrean,
The Hall of the Precious Light,
The Hall of the Assembled Immortals,
The Hall of the Transmitted Memorials . . . ,
Each built with pillars of jade unicorns.
The Long-life Star Terrace,

The Fortune Star Terrace,
And the Good-luck Star Terrace—
At the foot of each of them are flowers
That bloom for thousands of years without fading.
The Elixir Furnace,
The Eight Trigrams Furnace,
The Water and Fire Furnace—each of these is charged
With countless loads of fine evergreen herbs.
In the mornings the sages gather at court;
Their red silk robes are resplendent with the
Golden mist's gleaming.
On the throne of the carnelian court,
A mystic crown glitters with gold and jade.
In Spirit Cloud Treasure Hall,
A golden dragon holds a jade scepter.
In front of the Assembling Sages Pavilion
Varicolored phoenixes dance at the vermilion gate.
In the covered walks and passageways
Carved openwork is everywhere.
On all the eaves and rafters
Dragons and phoenixes wheel and soar.
Towering above all is Calabash Peak
In purple majesty, dazzling bright,
Round as a helmet, clear as a bell.
On every hand jade pendants sound:
Tightly together, thickly in layers,
Clearly ringing, roundly bulging, clear and bright
Truly, "All sorts of rare things are everywhere in heaven.
On earth each of them is a priceless treasure."
Golden watchtowers and silver phoenixes
Are paired with purple mansions.
Strange flowers and exotic trees
Reach up to the green heavens.
The moon passes by the altars paying court to the king;
Golden birds visiting the sages swoop down from on high.
If a man have the good fortune to cross into heaven,
He need never again dwell in the world of men,
Nor endure its polluting filth.

When Nezha arrived at the Precious Virtue Gate, it was still early, and he could not see Ao Guang. He noticed that none of the gates were open yet, so he stood off to one side of the Gate of the Gathering Immortals. Not long after, he saw Ao Guang arrive at the South Heaven Gate, the jades on his court dress a-tinkle. But the gate was not open yet. "I'm early," said Ao Guang. "The Yellow Turban Sergeant has not yet arrived. I'll just have to wait here."

Nezha saw Ao Guang, but Ao didn't see Nezha. Now the charm which the Perfected of the Great Ultimate had drawn over Nezha's chest was called the Invisible Body Charm, and that's why Ao Guang couldn't see Nezha. Watching Ao Guang waiting there, Nezha's temper flared up and he strode toward the Dragon King. Lifting up the Heaven-and-Earth Bracelet, he struck Ao Guang in the back behind his heart. He struck him a blow like a hungry tiger pouncing on his supper and flattened him out on the ground. Then Nezha hurried up and aimed a kick in the same place.

If you don't know whether Ao Guang lived or died, you'll have to hear about it in the next chapter.

Chapter 13: The Immortal Taiyi Subdues the Rock Demon [Summary]

Nezha beat Ao Guang and pulled some scales from his body, causing the Dragon King to cry for mercy. Nezha made him transform into a small snake and took him back to see his father, Li Jing. The Dragon King was released by Li Jing and threatened terrible revenge. Meantime Nezha went to the garden and climbed to the drum tower, where he found a bow and three arrows. The bow was one used by the Yellow Emperor to defeat Chi You in the archetypic struggle for hegemony of the Chinese empire. Nezha shot an arrow into the air; it struck and killed a disciple of the goddess Shijia. She captured Li Jing. Li Jing got Nezha to confess and brought him before the goddess to be punished. Nezha killed another of her disciples and then used his magic weapons to attack the goddess herself. The goddess captured the magic weapons, so Nezha fled to seek the help of his master, the Perfected of Great Unity. The Perfected One fought and defeated the goddess, but when Nezha returned home, he found the Dragon King Ao Guang besieging his parents. Feeling guilty for causing his parents such troubles, Nezha determined to commit suicide by disembowelment. "Now I am going to split open my belly, scoop out my guts, and slice off my flesh from the bones and return them to my parents."

Nezha's mother gathered up his corpse and buried it in a wooden coffin according to the rites. In life Nezha had depended on his mortal spirits and eternal souls. He originally was a valuable shell that had metamorphosed by using the essence of blood to create a soul and spirits.

Chapter 14: Nezha Is Transformed into a Lotus Blossom

A poem states:

> The magical power of the gods is hard to measure;
> They have mysterious methods of returning the dead to life.
> A small red pill suffices to restore the treasure of life,
> A few stray lotus leaves reanimate the soul.
> In traversing the world it will not do to use a polluting frame;
> To become a god, one must have incense offerings to restore life's vigor.
> He returns across the bounds of this world, seeking his divine master:
> The dynasty of Zhou depends on his aid and assistance.

As I was saying, the Golden Cloud Boy entered the cave and reported to the Perfected of Great Unity: "My elder brother Nezha is acting dumb and blind; wafting to and fro, his movements are checked by the wind—why, I don't know."

When the Perfected One heard this, he knew immediately what had happened and hurried out of the cave. "Nezha!" he ordered, "this is not your place of rest. Return to Chentang Pass and appear to your mother in a dream. Tell her that forty tricents from the pass is a place called Emerald Screen Mountain. On top of the mountain is an open space where you should tell your mother to build a temple for you. If you receive incense smoke there for three years, you can again be returned to the world of men and aid the true prince. Hurry, and do not tarry on your way."

Hearing this, Nezha left the Perfected One's mountain and came to Chentang Pass, arriving exactly at the third watch. He went into the bedroom of his mother. "Mother, it's Nezha," he said. "At present my mortal energies and eternal souls have nothing upon which they can rely. I hope that you will take to heart the agony of my death. Forty tricents from here is a mountain called Emerald Screen Mountain. I am asking you to build a temple for me there, so that I can receive some incense smoke, and after a while be reborn into heaven. I appreciate my mother's kind virtue, which is as deep as heaven is vast."

His mother awoke and, realizing it was just a dream, began to weep bitterly.

"Wife," Li Jing asked, "why are you crying?" She told him of what had happened in her dream. "You are still crying about that boy," he said angrily, "even though he caused us a great deal of harm. There's a common saying: 'dreams follow what the heart inspires.' It is only because you think of him so much that you dream so often of his soul appearing to you. You should not be so superstitious." His wife did not answer.

The next night Nezha again appeared to her in a dream. On the third night he came again. She would scarcely fall asleep before he appeared before her eyes, and before she knew it, six or seven days had passed. Since Nezha had an aggressive temperament in life, in death his spirit was also capable and ambitious. Therefore he appealed to his mother: "I have begged you for several days, but you refuse to recall the agony of my death. You refuse to build a temple for me. I therefore intend to haunt you till you can find no repose anywhere in your house."

His mother woke up but did not dare to say anything to her husband. Instead she secretly gave several ounces of silver to one of her trusted servants. She sent him to Emerald Screen Mountain to undertake the construction of a temple and to set up an image of Nezha in it. In less than a month, the work was complete. Nezha manifested his divinity on Emerald Screen Mountain, touching the hearts of all people. If a thousand favors were asked, Nezha granted a thousand favors. When ten thousand favors were asked, Nezha responded to the ten thousand requests. Because of this the people sought to give the temple dignity, and kept everything in the best order. All you could see was

> Eight horoscopic characters cut into the temple wall,
> Copper rings arranged as handles, right and left on the vermilion doors,
> The carved porches of blue tiles with three-foot overhangs,
> Scattered cypress trees around two-story terraces.
> The altar and their furniture are all covered with gold,
> The dragon flags and phoenix banners are magnificently embroidered.
> The hooks that hold up the curtains are like half-moons in heaven,
> While on the dusty floor stand the gruesome judges of the dead.
> Sandalwood incense smoke gracefully curls into clouds of color;
> Every day, the people come in droves to the rites and rituals.

Nezha occupied Emerald Screen Mountain manifesting his divinity, and from all the four quarters, from near and far, the people all came to offer incense, as numerous as ants, more with every passing day. Among those who sought good fortune, or those who sought to change bad luck to good, there was not one whose prayers were not answered. As quickly as the birds fly or rabbits run, or like an arrow reflecting light and shadow in its flight, more than half a year passed unnoticed.

Now I shall tell how the Imperial Prince of the East, Jiang Wenhuan, had mobilized four hundred thousand men and horses in order to avenge his father, and he was engaging Dou Rong at Wandering Soul Pass in severe fighting. Dou Rong was not able to gain the victory against him, so Li Jing had deployed his troops at Wild Horse Pass in order to protect the lines. One day as he was bringing his men back, he passed by Emerald Screen Mountain. From horseback Li Jing saw the coming and going of the people, supporting the aged and carrying the young. In making their oferings of incense, the men and women were as numerous as ants, people and smoke piled one upon the other. "This is Emerald Screen Mountain," Li Jing said. "Why should people be coming here in such a steady stream?"

"About half a year ago," an orderly replied, "a god began to manifest his divinity here. For a thousand prayers there were a thousand answers; for ten thousand favors asked, ten thousand favors are granted. If good fortune is asked, good fortune comes; if misfortune must be averted, then the misfortune is dissipated. Because of this, the people are overawed and come to offer incense."

Li Jing heard out his orderly; then he thought to question his Central Batallion Commander. "What is the name of this god?"

"It is the temple of Nezha," the officer replied.

Li Jing was very angry. "Bivouac the men here," he commanded, "while I ride up the mountain to take a look."

As Li Jing rode his horse up to take a look, men and women had to dodge away to allow him and his horse to reach the temple gate. There he saw hanging high over the gate a wooden tablet, and written on it was "Temple of Nezha." Going inside the temple, he saw the image of Nezha, verily as though alive, and the Judges of Hell standing to the right and left. Li Jing pointed at the image. "You filthy beast! When you were alive you harassed and harmed your parents; now that you are dead you mislead the common people." So saying he took his Six-Strand Whip and with a single blow broke the gilded image of Nezha into pieces. His anger rose even higher, and he kicked over the judges of the dead. Then he gave the order to set fire to the temple buildings and burn them down. To the myriads of worshipers, he gave a command: "This is not a god. You may not offer incense to him." And he scared the crowds of people so badly that they quickly left the mountain. Li Jing got back up on his horse to leave, but his anger would not die down. There is a poem as proof:

When the brave warrior came upon Emerald Screen Mountain,
It surprised him to see the people offering incense there.
With a blow of his whip the gilded image is turned to smithereens,
With a kick from his foot, the judges of hell meet with calamity.
The temple precincts are consumed with raging fire,
The smoke penetrates to the sky in fierce billows.
Just because a stroke of anger rebounded to the heavens,
Father and son must meet in battle many times.

As the story goes, Li Jing and his soldiers returned to the fortress at Chentang Pass, where they dismounted and scattered after receiving their orders.

Li Jing went in to the inner apartments where his wife, Lady Yin, greeted him. "You gave birth to a really fine son," he scolded her, "and even now he leaves me a legacy of injury. You have built a temple for him, and incited the common people with lies. If you are trying to make me lose this official position of mine, you have just about done it. Powerful ministers are at the helm of state, men like Fei Zhong and You Hun, with whom I have no dealings. If someone were to send this information to the capital and a traitor were to accuse me for having a connection with unorthodox gods, then my years of meritorious service would be lost. And all because of what you have done, woman! Today I burned down the temple you built for Nezha. If you once again have a temple built for him, I won't just let the matter drop!"

Now I shall speak no more of Li Jing, but will tell how Nezha was not at the temple that day, having gone on an outing. When he returned, he saw that the buildings had been destroyed and the mountain was still red with the flames, the smoke and fire not yet extinguished. The two Judges of Hell came to meet him, trying to swallow their sobs. "What happened?" Nezha asked.

"It was the military commander of Chentang Pass, Li Jing," the judges replied. "He suddenly appeared on the mountain with his soldiers and smashed your image to pieces. Then he burned the temple. Why this happened, we don't know."

"I have nothing more to do with you, Li Jing," Nezha said, "since I have returned blood and bone to my father and mother. Why should you then smash my image and burn my temple? You leave me with no place to repose."

Nezha was very unhappy in his heart, and he was sunk in thought for a long time. Then he set out to return to Qianyuan Mountain. Since Nezha had been receiving incense for half a year, he had some form and substance. In a short while he had reached his teacher's cave on the high mountain. The Golden Cloud Boy took Nezha in to see the Perfected of Great Unity. "Why aren't you in your temple receiving incense?" asked the Perfected One. "Why have you come here?"

Kneeling down before him, Nezha replied, "My image was smashed to bits by my father, and he also burned down my temple. I have nothing to depend on; thus I came to see my teacher. I beg of you to save me."

"It is Li Jing's fault," said the Perfected One. "You have already returned your flesh and bones to your father and mother, so he has nothing to say about your living on Emerald Screen Mountain. If he does not now allow you to receive incense, how are you supposed to take on a corporeal form? Moreover, it is not long till Jiang Ziya is to come down from the mountain. Enough of this—I intend to do you a favor."

And he gave orders to Golden Cloud Boy: "Bring me two lotus blossoms and three lily pads from the Pond of the Five Lotuses." The servant boy hurried to get the lotus leaves and blossoms and placed them on the ground. The Perfected One took the blossoms and tore off the petals, making them into the three faculties. He then took the stems from the leaves and cut them up to make the three hundred bones. The three lotus leaves he laid out on top, middle, and bottom, corresponding to the realms of Heaven, Earth, and man. Taking an alchemical pill of *jindan* he placed it in the middle of the figure he had made. Using magic formulae of the Taoists of Former Heaven, he made the forces of fate rotate nine times and made the directions distinct, orienting to the dragon and the tiger. Thus the Perfected One lightly impelled the mortal spirits and eternal souls of Nezha to enter the lotus-leaf form.[7]

"Nezha," he shouted, "what are you waiting for? Take up human form!"

With an echoing yell, a man came springing up. His face was as if powdered white, and his lips as if painted red. His eyes gleamed, and he was sixteen feet tall. This was none other than Nezha transformed into the lotus blossom, and seeing his teacher, he fell down and bowed on the ground before him. "Li Jing's destroying your image is truly a thing that is hard to bear," the Perfected One said.

"Even though my master will give help," replied Nezha, "it will still be a difficult matter to get revenge."

"Come with me into my peach garden," said the Perfected One. There he gave to Nezha the

Fire-Tip Lance and, after a short practice session, Nezha was completely the master of it. Nezha at once wished to descend the mountain and seek revenge.

"Now that you have mastered the technique of the lance, I want to give you these Fire-Wind Wheels. In addition I am going to give you a Spirit Charm and a Secret Incantation."

The Perfected One handed Nezha a leopard-skin bag with the Heaven-and-Earth Bracelet and the Heaven-Confusing Sash inside it. It also contained a golden roof tile. "Go to Chentang Pass," the Perfected One told him. Nezha kowtowed in thanks to his teacher, mounted the Fire-Wind Wheels, and holding the Fire-Tip Lance in his hands, he journeyed to Chentang Pass. There is a poem as proof:

> Two lotus blossoms became his body,
> Spirit Jewel appears on earth for the second time.
> In his hand he holds the Purple Flame Snake Lance,
> Underfoot he treads the Golden Cloud Fire-Wind Wheels.
> The magic in his leopard-skin bag will pacify the empire,
> The power within his embroidered sash will bring good fortune to the people.
> The sages of successive eras are in the vanguard of power,
> The deeds written in the official histories will shine for ten thousand years.

As the story goes, Nezha entered Chentang Pass and arrived at the headquarters. "Li Jing, come out double-quick to see me!" he yelled loudly.

An orderly reported this: "The Third Master is outside. He is standing on the Fire-Wind Wheels and holding the Fire-Tip Lance. He is calling out the general's name for some reason. What are your orders?"

"What a lot of crap!" Li Jing yelled. "How can someone die and then come back to life again?"

He had no sooner spoken than another messenger arrived to report: "General, he says if you are too slow in coming out, then he will just come in hunting for you."

Li Jing was terribly angry. "How can such a thing be?" he said, and taking up his inlaid halberd, he mounted up on a black horse and came out of the headquarters. He saw Nezha riding upon the Fire-Wind Wheels and holding the Fire-Tip Lance in his hands, looking hardly anything like he previously did.

"You filthy animal!" Li Jing shouted with alarm. "You were a monster before you were ever born, and now you come to life after death—again you come around here to make trouble for me!"

"Li Jing," Nezha replied, "I have returned my flesh and blood to you. I have not interfered with you in any way. Wherefore then did you come to Emerald Screen Mountain and break my image to pieces, and set my temple on fire? Today I aim to avenge that blow of your whip!" And taking up his lance, he thrust it right toward Li Jing's face.

Li Jing parried with his halberd, reined his horse in a whirling turn, and halberd struck on lance. Nezha's strength was without bounds, and after three or four passes, Li Jing was under such a furious attack that his horse reared up and threw off the rider. Li Jing was taxed to the utmost; his muscles ached and the sweat ran in rivulets down his back. All he could do was flee off to the southeast.

"Li Jing," Nezha called out, "don't think that I will spare you this time. Even if I don't kill you, I won't give up without doing something worse!" And he charged forward in pursuit. In a very short time, Nezha was about to catch up since his Fire-Wind Wheels were fast, and Li Jing's horse was slow. Li Jing panicked and had to dismount. He threw up a cloud of dust and took off on it. "The magical arts of the five elements are but ordinary things of the Taoist initiate," said

Nezha with a laugh. "Do you think to escape me on a cloud of dust?" And giving a stamp of his foot, he mounted up on his Fire-Wind Wheels. Just hear the raging sound of a fire storm, how the flying clouds are split open with lightning, as Nezha hurtles forward in pursuit!

"If he catches me this time," Li Jing thought to himself, "he will surely kill me with his lance. What is to be done?" Li Jing saw how Nezha was gradually overtaking him, and just as the jaws of no escape were about to close on him, he heard the sound of a man singing:

At the edge of the pool's clear water, the moon is shining bright;
The verdant willows top the banks, and peach blossoms bloom.
Parting is but the fragrance of the breeze:
Wisps of flying clouds high in the sky.

Looking at him, Li Jing saw the form of a Taoist novice, wearing a kerchief in his hair and Taoist robes with large sleeves. On his feet were hempen sandals with silken straps. Actually, it was Muzha, disciple of the Sage of Saving Righteousness of White Crane Cave on Ninth Palace Mountain. "Father," said Muzha, "here I am."

Seeing that it was his second son, Muzha, Li Jing felt relieved. Nezha, seeing that Li Jing was talking to a Taoist novice, pressed his wheeled pursuit even faster. Having caught up, he got down from his wheels. Muzha stepped forward. "Hold on!" he bellowed. "You vile spawn! You have a lot of nerve! For a son to kill his father, that's patricide and against all morality! Turn around and leave right away, or I won't even let you die a decent death!"

"Who are you?" asked Nezha. "Whose tiny gob emits such big words?"

"You don't even recognize me, do you? I am none other than Muzha."

When Nezha knew that it was his second brother, Muzha, he spoke up at once: "Brother, you don't know the facts of the matter." And he told him the details of what had happened at Emerald Screen Mountain. "Was Li Jing at fault, or am I at fault?" he asked.

"Nonsense!" bellowed Muzha. "There is no such thing in the world as parents being at fault!"

"But I cut open my belly and split my guts, and returned my flesh and blood to him. Now I have no relationship with him; how can there be anything of parent and son between us?"

"What a rebellious child!" Muzha said angrily, and taking up his sword in hand he slashed at Nezha.

Nezha parried with his lance. "Muzha," he said, "I have no quarrel with you. Why don't you just stand aside and let me take vengeance on Li Jing?"

"You vile spawn!" bellowed Muzha. "How dare you commit such a monstrous sin?" And once more he attacked with his sword.

"This is brought about by universal fate—one of us must die if the other is to live." So saying, with the lance in his hand Nezha thrust at Muzha's face. Thrusting and parrying with their weapons, the two matched each other step for step, in a battle of brothers. Seeing Li Jing standing off to one side, Nezha was afraid that he would escape. Thinking quickly, Nezha knocked up the sword with his lance, and used his free hand to take the Golden Rooftile and throw it up in the air. Muzha could not defend against this, and the roof tile hit him directly behind the heart. He fell down on the ground. Nezha immediately mounted his wheels to capture Li Jing, who turned and ran.

"Even if you flee to the islands of the sea," Nezha called out, "only chopping off your head will serve to quench my hatred."

Li Jing fled in desperation, like a bird flying in search of a forest or fish darting within a net, without regard to the points of the compass. After the chase had continued for a little while, it appeared to Li Jing as though matters were once more at a desperate pass. "Enough! Enough!

Enough!" he sighed to himself. "I don't know what terrible sin I, Li Jing, must have committed against my parents in a former existence: not only was I unsuccessful on the Way of transcendence, but I also gave birth to a monster such as this Nezha! If it must be thus, would it not be better to take my halberd and kill myself, rather than endure such an insult from this evil son of mine!" Just as he was about to raise his hand and put an end to it all, he heard a voice calling out, "General Li! Don't make a move! Wait for me!" Then he heard a song:

> On the borders of the fields the fresh breeze brushes the willows,
> Flowers wave upon the water's face out in the pond.
> If you ask where is the place of my repose:
> My home is deep among the white clouds.

The singer was none other than the Divine Worthy of Mañjuśrī's Great Law from Celestial Cloud Cave on Five Dragon Mountain, and he approached with a hair-duster in his hand.

"Old teacher," Li Jing said as he saw him approach, "will you save my life?"

"You go into my cave," said the Divine Worthy, "and I will wait here a little while for him."

Nezha, heroic and dauntless, came riding up on his Fire-Wind Wheels, pursuing with his lance in hand. When he saw the Taoist there, how did he look?

> His two-horned topknot cleaves the clouds.
> His Taoist robes are girdled with a silken belt.
> He wanders hither and thither, his form trained in the Tao.
> Inside him are hidden the many secrets of the black arts.
> He was a student of the sage Primal Beginning in the Palace of Jade Vacuity,
> And he has gathered with the immortals at the dwelling of the Jade Mother of the West;
> His extraordinary endowments were achieved by manipulating the five elements,
> And he had practiced transcendence and nourished the Way under the Emperor of Heaven.

As the story goes, Nezha saw the Taoist standing on the mountainside, but he could not see Li Jing. "Reverend Sir," said Nezha, "did you see a general pass by here?"

"If you are referring to General Li Jing," replied the Divine Worthy, he has gone into my Celestial Cloud Cave. What do you wish of him?"

"Reverend Sir," Nezha replied, "he is my enemy. If you would be so good as to have him come out of your cave, then the affair has nothing to do with you. But if Li Jing should escape me, then you will have to suffer thrusts of my lance in his stead."

"Who are you," the Taoist asked, "that you hate enough to want to kill even me with your lance?"

Nezha didn't know who the Taoist was, so he freely replied, "I am Nezha, disciple of the Perfected of Great Unity from Golden Gleam Cave on Qianyuan Mountain. You must not underestimate me."

"I have never heard that the Perfected of Great Unity had a disciple by the name of Nezha," said the Taoist. "Why don't you go somewhere else to play your boorish games. At my place here I don't allow such rudeness. If you pull that sort of stunt around here, I'll hang you up in my peach garden for three years and give you three hundred blows of my staff."

How could Nezha know good from evil? He took his lance and made a pass, trying to skewer the Divine Worthy. The Taoist turned and ran away into his cave, whereupon Nezha mounted his wheels and chased after him. The Divine Worthy turned and saw that Nezha was drawing close, so he took an object out of his sleeves. This was called the Concealed Dragon Club, or also the

Golden Lotus of Seven Treasures. He threw this up in the air, and at once a wind sprang up in every quarter, clouds and fog obscured the sky, dust and dirt went flying, and as the club came down it did so with a screaming sound. Nezha was confused so deeply that he did not know north from south; his senses were almost obliterated, so how could he distinguish east from west? Over his neck dropped a ring of gold, and two other rings encased his thighs: he was encased by yellow gold, immobilized like a pillar standing there.

When Nezha's eyes cleared so that he could see, he could not move a muscle.

"Well, my good little sinner," said the Divine Worthy, "you have certainly made a nuisance of yourself." To Jinzha he said, "Bring the staff!"

Jinzha hurried off to get the staff and then presented it to the Divine Worthy. "Here it is," he said.

"Beat him for me," commanded the Divine Worthy.

Harkening to the command of his teacher, Jinzha took the staff and gave Nezha a stroke with it. The primordial fire came exploding out of Nezha's seven orifices. "That's enough now," the Divine Worthy said. So Jinzha went back into the cave.

"I pursued Li Jing and wasn't able to overtake him," Nezha thought to himself. "Instead I have got a beating from this guy's staff, and what's more I can't even run away!" Nezha gnashed his teeth in deep hate, yet there wasn't anything for him to do but stand right there and let his anger rise up to the very heavens. Reader! The Perfected of Great Unity clearly sent Nezha to this place in order to blunt his bloodlust. The Perfected One knew in advance what would happen. Nezha was at the peak of vexation when he saw through the window a man wearing a loose robe with wide sleeves. On his feet were hempen sandals with silken straps—it was none other than the Perfected of Great Unity. When Nezha saw him, he cried out, "Master! I beseech you to save your disciple this once!" He called to his master several times, but the Perfected One just walked right past him without paying any attention and went on to the cave.

"The Perfected of Great Unity is here," announced White Cloud Boy.

The Divine Worthy came out of the cave to greet him. Taking the Perfected One by the hand, he said with a smile, "Your disciple asked me to teach him some things."

The two immortals sat down together. "Because Nezha has broken the prohibition against killing so many times," said the Perfected of Great Unity, "I sent him here for you to blunt his bloodlust. Who could have known that he would commit a crime against even you, Divine Worthy?"

The Divine Worthy commanded Jinzha to release Nezha and let him come in. Jinzha went up to Nezha. "Your teacher is calling you," he said.

"You clearly can't do anything with me," said Nezha. "How have you pulled the wool over my eyes, making it so I can't move a muscle? And still you come to make fun of me!"

"Close your eyes," said Jinzha with a laugh. So Nezha closed his eyes. Jinzha wrote a charm character, then picked up the Concealed Dragon Club. Quickly Nezha opened his eyes, but the encircling rings were not to be seen. Nezha bowed his head. "Good, good, good. Today I've had to eat a great deal of crow, but now I'll just go in the cave and see my master; surely he'll have a plan for me."

He and his brother went inside the cave, where he saw the Taoist who had had him beaten sitting on the left and his master sitting on the right. "Come over and kowtow before your honorable elder uncle," said the Perfected of Great Unity.

Nezha did not dare to disobey his teacher, so he had to kneel down and kowtow. "Thank you for beating me," Nezha said. Then he turned and bowed before his teacher. The Perfected of

Great Unity called to Li Jing to come in. Li Jing threw himself down and bowed before them. "This affair of Emerald Screen Mountain," said the Perfected One to him, "must not be underestimated. You and your son must not be at odds over this matter."

Standing to one side, Nezha's anger rose to his face like a raging fire, and he was full of so much hatred for Li Jing that he wished he could swallow him alive. The two transcendents already knew what he was thinking. "From now on, you two must not hold any grudges," said the Perfected One. Then he commanded Li Jing: "You may go home first." Li Jing thanked the Perfected One and went on out. This made Nezha so mad that, although he did not dare to say anything, he stood off to one side and pulled at his ears and rubbed his cheeks. He made long sighs and took short breaths. The Perfected One laughed to himself and then said, "Nezha! You can also go. Return and guard my cave carefully. I am going to play a game of chess with your uncle here and I will come in a little while."

When Nezha heard these words, a flower bloomed in his heart. "I understand you perfectly," he answered. He hurried out of the cave and mounted up on his Fire-Wind Wheels. Then he once more began the pursuit of Li Jing. After a good while, Nezha saw in front of him Li Jing riding along on his cloud of dust. "Li Jing," he yelled. "Stop trying to get away! Here I come!"

When Li Jing saw him, he cried out in anguish, "How could the Taoist have broken his promise? When he let me leave first, he should not have let Nezha leave the mountain if he meant to help me. Yet now he has let Nezha come chasing after me soon after I left. This is really not following through with one's promise. What am I going to do?" He had no choice but to run away as fast as he could.

So Nezha chased Li Jing: he chased him so close that Li Jing could not find the road to heaven nor a gate into the earth. Just when things were at their most dangerous point, Li Jing saw a Taoist sitting on a rock and leaning against a pine tree on a hilltop. "Can that be Li Jing down at the foot of the hill?" the Taoist said.

Li Jing raised his head up and saw the Taoist. "Master!" Li Jing said. "This old general is indeed Li Jing!"

"What's the trouble?" asked the Taoist.

"Nezha is coming right behind me," said Li Jing. "I hope you will condescend to save me."

"Hurry up the hill," said the Taoist. "Stand here behind me and I will save you."

Li Jing climbed up the hill and hid himself behind the Taoist. He had not yet caught his breath when he saw Nezha come riding up to the foot of the hill on his Fire-Wind Wheels with a whoosh. Nezha saw the two men standing there and gave a grim laugh: "Can it be that I must again suffer defeat?" Mounted on his wheels he came up the hill.

"Are you Nezha?" the Taoist asked.

"That's just who I am," answered Nezha. "Why have you told Li Jing to stand there behind you?"

"Why are you chasing him?" asked the Taoist. Once again Nezha told the story of Emerald Screen Mountain.

"But on Five Dragon Mountain you came to an agreement about the matter," said the Taoist. "Since you are chasing him again, you have broken your promise."

"You have nothing to do with us," said Nezha. "It's my business if I just want to grab him in order to satisfy my hatred."

"Since you're unwilling—," said the Taoist, and then he turned to Li Jing. "Fight a bout or two with him and let me see how it comes out."

"Master," Li Jing replied, "this bastard is possessed of limitless strength. This old general has no chance of beating him."

The Taoist stood up and spit at Li Jing, then gave him a clap on the back with his open palm: "You must try a round with him for me; I'm here and it won't matter."

Li Jing could only take up his halberd and attack. Nezha parried with his Fire-Tip Lance. And father and son fought one another there on the hill, making fifty or sixty passes. This time Nezha was pressed by Li Jing till the sweat filled his face and ran over his whole body like a river. As Nezha found himself unable to ward off the blows of the halberd, he thought to himself, "At first Li Jing couldn't stand up to me, but now this Taoist spits on him and gives him a clap on the back—that must be the reason why he is winning. I've got a plan to counter that. I'll just give a feint, and use it to kill the Taoist first. Afterwards Li Jing will be no trouble."

Giving a twist of his body, Nezha jumped outside the circle of combat. With his lance he thrust at the Taoist. The Taoist opened his mouth, and from it emitted a single White Lotus Blossom which blocked the lance. "Li Jing!" commanded the Taoist. "Grab it!" At once Li Jing took hold of the lance.

"You miserable criminal!" the Taoist said to Nezha; "your quarrel is with your father. I have no enmity with you. Why should you try to kill me? It is lucky that my White Lotus Blossom blocked your thrust, or I would have fallen victim to your nasty plot. How can you explain yourself?"

"Well," said Nezha, "before Li Jing could not stand up to me. But when you told him to fight me, why did you spit on him and give him a clap on the back? This is clearly because you have set demons to keep me from winning. Because of this I wanted to take my anger out on you by killing you."

"What a miserable criminal," said the Taoist, "to dare to try to kill me!"

Nezha was furious. He flourished his lance and thrust it right at the Taoist's head. The Taoist jumped off to one side, then threw his sleeve up in the air. At once an auspicious cloud was emitted and a purple mist rolled forth. An object fell down onto Nezha, and he was entrapped in an exquisite pagoda. The Taoist clapped both his hands on the top of the pagoda, and at once flames erupted inside it. Nezha was burnt so badly that he screamed for mercy.

"Nezha," said the Taoist from the outside, "do you acknowledge Li Jing as your father?"

Nezha could only scream, "Old Master, I recognize him as my father!"

"Since you have acknowledged Li Jing as your father," said the Taoist, "I will let you loose." At once he picked up the pagoda. Nezha opened his eyes wide and looked all over his body, but was not burned in the slightest. "How can such strange things happen?" thought Nezha to himself. "This Taoist is truly a sorcerer."

"Nezha," said the Taoist, "since you acknowledge Li Jing as your father, you may kowtow before him."

Nezha was very much set against doing this, but the Taoist threatened to conjure up the pagoda again, so Nezha had no other choice but to suppress his anger and swallow his grumbling. He fell down on his knees and bowed down before Li Jing, but his expression betrayed his unwillingness.

"Call him father," said the Taoist. Nezha would not say anything. "Nezha," said the Taoist, "if you don't call him father, then you haven't really given in, so I'll just use this Golden Pagoda to burn you up again."

"Father!" Nezha said in terror, "I concede that I was wrong!"

Even though Nezha said these words, in his heart he had not given up, and he secretly gnashed his teeth. "Li Jing," he thought to himself, "are you always going to have this Taoist at your side?"

Then the Taoist called to Li Jing. "Kneel down," he said, "so that I can give you the secret formula for this Gold Pagoda. If Nezha is not obedient, you can conjure this pagoda to burn him up."

This made Nezha cry out in anguish inside.

"Nezha," said the Taoist, "from now on you and your father must get along together. There will come a time when both of you will be ministers in the same hall, serving the shining prince. Both of you will earn true merit. You must not again even mention the things that have henceforth come between you. Nezha, you may leave."

Seeing how matters stood, Nezha had no choice but to return to Qianyuan Mountain. Li Jing knelt down before the Taoist.

"Master," he said, "you have made known to me the virtue of the Tao and saved me from a dangerous extremity. May I ask your name and origin? What is the cave where you reside?"

"This poor Taoist is the Burning Lamp Sage of Original Awareness Cave on Spirit Hawk Mountain. You were not able to cultivate the Tao to perfection and had to seek fame and fortune among men. Now King Zhow of the Shang dynasty has lost virtue, and there will be great upheaval in the empire. You need not serve any longer as an official, but should hide yourself instead among the mountains and valleys. Forget fame and fortune in the meantime and wait until King Wu of the Zhou arises. Then you may again come forth to earn merit and take up your profession."

Li Jing knocked his head on the ground, then returned without a word to Chentang Pass.

The Taoist had really been asked by the Perfected of Great Unity to come to this place and refine Nezha's nature and to make the relationship between father and son a whole and perfect one. Afterwards Li Jing and his three sons would be elevated to gods while still living men. Li Jing is none other than the Pagoda-Holding Heavenly King.

A person of later times wrote a poem about this which says,

From the exquisite pagoda of yellow gold
Stream ten thousand rays of light toward heaven.
If Burning Lamp[8] had not used his powerful magic,
Father and son could not have been brought together.

This was the second time that Nezha had entered the world at Chentang Pass. Afterwards Jiang Ziya came down from the mountain in order to respond to the seven-year imprisonment of King Wen (of the Zhou) at Youli. If you don't know what happened in that matter, listen to me explain it in the next session.

—GS, VHM

Notes

1. The implication is that dominion over the vastness of empire is dependent on events determined by the intersection of different temporal cycles.

2. The reference is to a set of five cyclically interacting components (sometimes called phases) which, related to categories of time and space, determines the character or outcome of events.

3. The last king of the Shang dynasty was named Zhòu. To distinguish him from the Zhōu dynasty, which succeeded the Shang, his name is spelled Zhow.

4. Once again the reference is to a set of cyclically interacting components relating to time and space. Such calculations are important in selecting names and may result in children being affiliated to foster parents if the time of their birth is in conflict with that of their parents.

5. The names of Nezha's two older siblings are taken from components of the "five elements" system mentioned in note 2. Since the Xia dynasty is connected with "wood" *(mu)*, the Shang dynasy with "metal"

(jin), and the Zhou dynasty with "fire" *(huo)*, Nezha's emblematic association with fire and his burning temperament is symbolically appropriate in the historical context. The name Nezha is derived from an Indian original (see introduction), but the components may imply exorcism and furious activity. Nezha's father Li Jing is identified with the Buddhist guardian deity Vaiśravaṇa.

6. A talismanic symbol, often containing Chinese-character-like emblematic elements that "command" the realization of the intent of the written charm or spell.

7. This whole passage is redolent of the anciently attested Chinese rituals of "summoning the soul" *(zhao-hun)*, in which an image or object (usually made of rice or rice straw, but here it is the lotus, more evocative of Buddhist iconography) is made to be the seat of being during death rituals. The *jindan* or "vermilion pill" is the alchemically transformed elixir or essence of gold and cinnabar, confering immortality on those who ingest it.

8. Sanskrit Dīpaṃkara, the name of the twenty-fourth Buddha before Śākyamuni.

THE IMPERIAL GOVERNMENT of China functioned largely on paper. Reports and proposals were submitted as memorials to the emperor, and the emperor promulgated decisions and policies in edicts and rescripts. The documents accumulated until they were too numerous to be conveniently consulted, and from time to time they were collected, organized, and published as the *Collected Statutes (Huidian)*. The first Ming work of this type was the *Official Duties of All the Offices (Zhusi zhizhang)*, compiled in 1393. This was followed by the *Collected Statutes of the Great Ming Dynasty (Da Ming huidian)*, compiled and revised over a period of several decades, finally promulgated in 1510 and printed the next year. A supplement was compiled, but not printed, in 1549. An updated edition of the entire work was completed in 1587 and subsequently printed. The documents in the *Collected Statutes* were sorted and grouped under the headings of the Six Ministries and several other top-tier government agencies, and arranged chronologically within those headings.

When modern scholars of late-imperial China mine the riches of the *Collected Statutes* of Ming and Qing, they may translate the term *Huidian* or romanize it. Some translate the *dian* of the title as "administrative law" or "statutes." Others, especially certain legal scholars, banish the *huidian* from the domain of law altogether, while focusing on the Ming and Qing penal codes *Da Ming lü* and *Da Qing lüli*. They translate *dian* as "institutes" and describe the *Huidian* not as a law code but as an encyclopedic description of government offices.

The front matter of the 1587 edition includes a preface to the 1503 edition by the Hongzhi emperor. This document, unremarkable though it may be when it is read in its traditional Chinese context, takes the modern reader into an unfamiliar world, a world in which a fallible but well-disposed humankind is properly ordered and governed by the principles *(li)* that were discovered by the ancient sages in the patterns of an eternally unfolding cosmic order. The laws and institutions of the Chinese empire derived their ultimate authority not from the will of the emperor, but from their putative conformity with these eternal principles. It was the task of government constantly to maintain that conformity under ever-changing circumstances.

In the extravagant language of his preface, the emperor commends his dynasty's *Collected Statutes* to all his subjects as a faithful expression of the Principle of Heaven (Tianli) and as a comprehensive design for ordering the world in harmony with the cosmos.—RT

Imperial Preface to the *Revised Edition of the Collected Statutes of the Ming*

WE perceive that, when the ancient emperors and kings turned their attention to the world, each of them had the statutes *(dian)* proper to his own time. And they used [those statutes] to perfect the government of all within the four seas. Even though there were additions and deletions, and continuities and changes over the course of time, and even though discrepancies could not be avoided, the important thing is that they never departed from a single "lodging place" *(yu)* of the Principle of Heaven.[1]

Perfect indeed is the Principle of Heaven! And therefore it is the work of humankind to bequeath [the statutes] to posterity without man-made corruption or confusion. Although they may be relaxed in their application to particular cases, there is that in them that cannot be changed.

Yao and Shun attained sagehood in the time of the states of Tang and Yu.[2] For the first time ever they fixed the laws *(fa)*[3] as circumstances required. In the domains of liturgy, learning, number, and measure, the Principle of Heaven now found spontaneous expression, and nothing was left out. As the rules accumulated, they were broad and ample; as they issued forth, they were lofty and clear. Exalted and resplendent, they could not be improved upon.

The sages of the three royal [houses], Yu, Tang,[4] and Wen and Wu (founders of Xia, Shang, and Zhou dynasties) could only look back upon Yao and Shun from afar, and yet they gradually amplified their statutes *(dianzhi)*. Perfectly indeed did [their laws] conform to the principle *li!* In this way they brought about the felicity and prosperity of the Great Harmony (Taihe),[5] and everywhere a return to [true] government.

Later generations were unable to rise to their level. Following the Qin dynasty, the Han, Tang and Song [dynasties] were praised for their good government, and many worthy rulers[6] arose among them. This may be called the [age of] "Lesser Tranquility" (Xiaokang).[7] However, the statutes were applied in a corrupt and careless manner. Because they were mixed up with human behavior, they did not wholly express the Principle of Heaven.[8] It was for this reason that the Song Confucian Mr. Ouyang said that their government proceeded from duality *(chu yu er)*.[9] How then can one say that there was no explanation for their failure to emulate the government of antiquity?

Our Exalted Emperor Taizu (r. 1368–1398), having attained the virtue of a sage, expelled the barbarian Yuan dynasty and came into possession of All under Heaven. In all events [desiring] to practice unified government and exercise unified authority, he would invariably summon the multitude of Confucian scholars and consult with them. While respecting the laws of antiquity, he gave careful consideration to what was appropriate in the immediate circumstances, leaving something out here or adding something there. Gloriously the Principle of Heaven was applied [in his laws]. His divine plans and sage-like decisions excelled those of the ages, and he wholly purged the vulgar accretions of later times. Our Emperors Taizong Wenhuangdi (r. 1399/1403–1424), Renzong Zhaohuangdi (r. 1425), Xuanzong Zhanghuangdi (r. 1426–1435), Yingzong Ruihuangdi (r. 1436–1449/1457–1464), and Xianzong Chunhuangdi (r. 1465–1487) followed one another as sage has succeeded sage.[10] From first to last they were of one mind. Even when they deleted or added as required by the circumstances, they all were guided by this Way. And that is precisely how this Great Peace (Taiping)[11] of more than a hundred years has come to pass![12]

WE have simply accepted the appointment of Heaven (Tianxu).[13] From the time of OUR enthronement until the present, [WE] have toiled early and late in the hope of being able to perpetuate the brilliance of OUR forebears. But their fundamental laws that had issued forth intermittently during their successive reigns had yet to be brought together and unified. WE therefore commanded the Confucian officials *(ruchen)* to bring forth all the hitherto hidden documents in the possession of the various government offices and consult the official records.[14]

All those who serve in government or are concerned with ritual have compiled the [documents] for their respective offices. Every office and agency has classified its documents and put them in order. Each office [now] has charge of its proper business and each matter comes before the appropriate office. [This compilation] shall be called the *Collected Statutes of the Great Ming Dynasty (Da Ming huidian)*.

When the compilation was finished and presented to US, it contained 180 chapters. WE have read it section by section. The main points have been emphasized, the sections of the code separated, and the particular items distributed among them. It is even as the sun and the moon lend their beauty to the heavens, and the myriad stars obediently show themselves forth.

The laws and institutions of our sage progenitor and our divine ancestors, which have lasted more than a hundred years, have been carefully considered [in light of] the old and the new, and serve as a model for a myriad of generations. In this collection, nothing has been lost!

[WE] have commanded that the printing blocks be cut so that [the *Huidian*] may be published here and in the provinces. Then the world will have it and none will depart from it in favor of heterodox doctrines, and none will hasten after present advantage. In every undertaking, from the imperial court to All under Heaven, nothing [will be done that is] too large or too small, too subtle or too coarse. Everything will conform to the Principle of Heaven and have its appropriate application. Accumulate it and it becomes deep; grasp it and it will long endure. Then will the dynastic patrimony *(guojia)*[15] be prosperous and enlightened and enjoy the reign of peace and harmony. It may be compared to Tang and Yu (i.e., Yao and Shun), and surpass the Three Dynasties. And this [felicity] may be handed down undiminished. Consequently, we have written this to serve as its preface.

Hongzhi 15, 12th month, 11th day (January 8, 1503)

—RT

Notes

1. The "Principle of Heaven" may be understood as the cosmic master principle in which all of the particular principles of the phenomenal world were subsumed. The great Song Neo-Confucian thinker Zhu Xi (see selection 64) resolved the paradox of the unity and multiplicity of the Principle of Heaven by using the metaphor of the moon and its reflections. Here "lodging-place" is understood to be the particularization of Tianli as the immanent principle of discrete phenomena.

2. The sage rulers Yao and Shun ruled in Tang and Yu, respectively.

3. *Fa* is normally translated as "law"; especially in Legalist contexts it implies a penal code. Taking the next sentence into consideration, *fa* should be understood in a more general sense to include all the rules and orders issued with the authority of the emperor.

4. Yu and Tang here are different characters from those used to write the names of the states of Yao and Shun mentioned in the first sentence of the previous paragraph.

5. The *locus classicus* of Taihe as "universal harmony" may be found in the *Yijing* commentary on the first hexagram, where it is associated with the cyclical culmination of yang.

6. *Xianjun.* A category ranked just behind the sages.

7. *Xiaokang.* The *locus classicus* of the expression may be found in the "Liyun" chapter in the *Liji,* where the text refers to the rule of (Xia) Yu, (Shang) Tang, and (Zhou) Kings Wen, Wu, and Cheng, and the Duke of Zhou.

8. This confrontation between "human behavior" or "human artifice" *(renwei)* and the "Principle of Heaven" succinctly expresses the contradiction between wayward humankind and the encompassing cosmos, and this in spite of the belief that humankind was especially endowed by Heaven with the faculty of moral choice.

9. The "duality" was presumably that of Heaven and humankind. "Mr. Ouyang" is presumably Ouyang Xiu (1007–1072), the great Song stylist, historian, statesman, and political thinker.

10. Note that the reign of the Jianwen emperor (1399–1402) has been absorbed into that of Taizong, and that of Daizong (1450–1456) has been absorbed into that of Yingzong.

11. A sociopolitical ideal that goes back to the late-third century B.C.E.

12. In the foregoing outline of Chinese history, the text presents us with a tripartite scheme. First came a golden age of the sages, Yao and Shun and the founders of the Xia, Shang, and Zhou, who initiated and perfected human civilization. The second was the Lesser Tranquility of the Han through Song dynasties, when the Principle of Heaven was only partially honored despite the efforts of some good rulers. The third period was the Ming dynasty, a new golden age initiated by the founding sage, Zhu Yuanzhang, and continued by his sagely heirs. This self-serving "history" invokes the authority of the classical version of the Three Ages in the *Gongyang Commentary* on the *Spring and Autumn Annals*.

13. This is the title of a Jin dynasty (265–316) drum song. According to the words of the song, "The sage ruler (i.e., the first emperor of Jin) obediently succeeded his father (who was king of Jin), and then accepted the abdication (of the last Wei emperor in 1265). He liberally assisted the Great Transformation (Hongji dahua) and caused other men to use their talents to the full."

14. This would have been the decree of 1497.

15. Often translated as "nation" or "state" (in its modern legal sense), but these renderings are anachronistic in this context. The ancient classical sense denotes the fief and the families of its great officials.

ONE OF THE GREAT Chinese inventions was the civil service system based on merit, with recruitment to the bureaucracy through government schools and an examination system. National Universities and civil service examinations existed during most dynasties, sometimes as two separate routes, but more often as two interrelated routes within one recruitment system for the bureaucracy.

The idea that government officials should be chosen on basis of moral integrity and merit rather than heredity can be dated back to Confucius (551–479 B.C.E.) and to the Warring States period (403–256 B.C.E.), during which the concept of *shi*, "warrior-official," gradually changed meaning to become "scholar-official." The *shi* began to emerge as a social class of officials who gained their status from achievement rather than heredity. The Qin (221–206 B.C.E.) and Han (206 B.C.E.–220 C.E.) dynasties built on these ideas and organized bureaucracies of nonfeudal, non-hereditary administrators. Emperor Wu (141–87 B.C.E.) of the Former Han dynasty (206 B.C.E.–9 C.E.), under the influence of Dong Zhongshu, adopted Confucianism as the state ideology, established a National University (Taixue) in 124 B.C.E., and began systematic recruitment of civil servants through recommendations and written examinations. This marked an important turning point in Chinese history, since Confucianism was for the first time made the state ideology and the basis for the school curriculum and the examination system, a role it was to maintain into the twentieth century.

After the fall of the Han, control of the recruitment system largely reverted to the powerful local families until the Sui dynasty (589–618), when a system of examinations based on the Han model was reestablished, made more elaborate, and had a Confucian curriculum as the basis for the examinations. Therefore, the civil service merit system is usually considered to have begun in the Sui and Tang (618–906) dynasties. During the Tang, schools and examinations were further expanded, and a substantial number of the government officials came through the examination system. Recruitment through regular examinations now became an effective means to strengthen and protect the central government against the powers of regionalism and the hereditary aristocracy, and by the middle of the Tang the examination system had produced a large bureaucracy of merit. There were different universities and specialized colleges in the capital, and degrees were awarded in different fields such as classics, letters, law, calligraphy, and mathematics. Of these, the *jinshi* (Presented Scholar) degree in letters became the most prestigious and chief recruitment route to the bureaucracy.

The examination system further grew in importance during the Song dynasty (960–1279). The *jinshi* examination, which put more emphasis on reasoning ability than on mere memorization, continued to be the most important. After 1065, until the examination system was finally abolished in 1905, examinations were held every three years, except for the first fifty years of the Yuan dynasty (1260–1368), when examinations were temporarily discontinued in favor of the school system and because of the Mongol rulers' reluctance to employ Chinese as officials. The subject matter for the examinations was the Four Books and Five Classics as interpreted by Zhu Xi (1130–1200) and Song philosophers of his school. In the Song, Ming, and Qing (1644–1912), the examination system made possible a high degree of upward social mobility into the official class. In the early Ming, the National University was the main recruitment source for the civil service. Over two hundred men per year entered civil service through the *jinshi* examination during Northern Song (960–1125) and an average of ninety per year under the Ming (1368–1644). However, provincial examination *juren* (Recommendee) degree holders as well as graduates from the National University were also recruited into the civil service during the Ming.

During many of the major dynasties, such as the Han, Tang, Song, and especially during the Ming, the National University played an important role in the recruitment system for the civil service. After the establishment of the National University in 124 B.C.E., the enrollment grew from originally fifty students to a thousand in 41 B.C.E. By 132 C.E. the University had 240 buildings and 1,850 rooms, and the enrollment was said to have exceeded thirty thousand by the middle of the second century. The enrollment in early Ming was some fifteen thousand students in 1424. During the Tang dynasty there were three universities and several colleges for special subjects in the capital. The three universities were the Guozixue for sons of officials of the third rank and above, the Taixue for sons of officials of the fifth rank and above and members of the upper aristocracy, and the Simenxue for sons of officials of the seventh rank, members of the lower aristocracy, and commoners. The Song dynasty took over this system, but with more commoners and sons of lower-ranking officials admitted. The Yuan established three Guozixue, one each for the study of Mongolian, Muslim languages, and Chinese. All three were open to sons of officials and commoners equally.

In the Ming dynasty there was one National University (Guozijian) in each of the two capitals, Beijing and Nanjing. Although some students were also now admitted because of their fathers' official rank, they never constituted more than a few percent of the whole student body. The large majority of students were recruited from among the examination first-degree holders *(shengyuan)* in the local schools through recommendation and examinations, with quotas set for the number of "tribute students" *(gongsheng)* each school could recommend. In the Ming, the National University played an unprecedented role as a major recruitment source for the civil service, and university students had to serve on internships in some government office before they could graduate. During the early Ming the overall majority of officials came from the university rather than the examination system, and the university continued to have an important role as recruitment source for the lower bureaucracy throughout the dynasty.

By the middle of the fifteenth century, the examination system and the *jinshi* degree began to replace the university as the chief recruitment channel for the higher offices in the central government. The ranking system for officials during the Ming and Qing consisted of nine grades, with each grade subdivided into two degrees, a and b. All officials were thus classified into eighteen ranks with 1a being the highest and 9b the lowest. The National University continued throughout the Ming to supply lower-ranking officials for the local governments and teachers for the local government schools, as well as candidates for the examinations. Under the Qing, however, the National University had a rather low enrollment and played an insignificant role as a recruitment source for the civil service.

With the renewed emphasis on the *jinshi* degree, the private academies *(shuyuan)* became more important as places to prepare for the examinations. The private academies first began to flourish during the eleventh century as centers for higher learning, scholarly debate, and preparation grounds for the candidates in the examination system. By the middle of the sixteenth century, *shuyuan* had begun gradually to take over the government schools' role as centers for preparing for the examinations for the higher degrees, *juren* and *jinshi,* and maintained this role through the late Ming and the Qing.

Under the Ming, *juren* degree holders had a special advantage as potential official appointees. Candidates who ranked low in the metropolitan examination for the *jinshi* degree were recorded on special additional lists known as *fubang* (supplementary list). These so-called *fubang juren* were allowed to enter the National University to continue their studies while waiting for the next metropolitan examination three years later. Both *juren* and regular university graduates *(jiansheng)* could, as mentioned earlier, be directly appointed to official posts, although, after the fifteenth century, most often as lower local government officials or as teachers in the local schools. Since it was possible at times to purchase one's entry into the university, the Ming system of civil service recruitment offered a number of access routes into civil service which was unprecedented and also unsurpassed by the following Qing dynasty.—JLH

The Chapter on Schools in the *History of the Ming Dynasty (Ming shi), juan* 69, "Treatise on Recruitment for the Civil Service," Chap. 1.

The Recruitment *(xuanju)* System for the Civil Service can be roughly divided into four different methods: (1) recruitment through the school system *(xuexiao)*, (2) through the examination system *(kemu)*, (3) through special recommendation *(jianju)*, and (4) through selection based on qualifications *(quanxuan)*. In schools men are educated, through examinations they are promoted, through special recommendations they are summoned from the various corners of the empire, and through selection based on qualifications they are distributed evenly [throughout the bureaucracy]. In this way all talented men in the empire will be recruited.

Under the Ming system it was the civil service examinations in particular that flourished, and the ministers and grand secretaries *(qingxiang)* all came through this route. The schools served to produce talented men to participate in the examinations. [However], those who received official appointment directly through the school route were considered secondary to those who had come through the examination route. [Those who advanced through any] other than these routes were [called] miscellaneous functionaries *(zaliu)*. However, the recruitment paths of *jinshi*,[1] *ju-gong* (i.e., *juren* and *gongsheng*),[2] and *zaliu* were all three employed side by side. Although sometimes one route received more emphasis than the other two, the others were not abandoned. The recommendation route flourished at the beginning of the dynasty but was later discontinued because of the emphasis on the examination system. Selection based on qualifications is at the very core of official service, and without it there would be no route through which to advance. Through a systematic description of the details of these four routes, the causes underlying the merits and faults of the recruitment system during 270 years of its existence can be readily seen.

To participate in the civil service examinations *(keju)*,[3] candidates had to advance through the school system. Those, however, who began their official careers directly from the school system need not to have gone through the examination system. There were two types of schools: (1) the National University *(guoxue)*, and (2) prefectural *(fuxue)*, subprefectural *(zhouxue)*, and district schools *(xianxue)*. Students from the prefectural, subprefectural, and district schools who entered the National University could then become eligible for official appointment. Those who did not enter the university could not get official appointments. Students who entered the National University were all known as *jiansheng* (university students). Students who entered by virtue of their *juren* degree were referred to as *jujian*; those who were *shengyuan* were called *gongjian* (tribute students); sons and younger brothers of ranking officials were called *yinjian* (students through protection); and those who gained admission through financial contributions were referred to as *lijian* (students by precedent [of financial contribution]). Moreover, within the *gongjian* category there were *suigong* (annual tribute student), *xuangong* (tribute student by special selection), *en'gong* (tribute student by imperial grace), and *nagong* (tribute student by financial contribution).[4] Within the *yinjian* category there were *guansheng* (students recommended by officials) and *ensheng* (students by imperial grace).[5]

The National University was founded at the beginning of the Ming, in the year 1365. In 1368, the first year of the Hongwu reign (1368–1398), Emperor Taizu (Zhu Yuanzhang, 1328–1398)[6] ordered that sons and younger brothers of ranking officials *(pinguan zidi)* and [sons of] the common people who were outstanding and mastered the Chinese script should become students at the university.

From among the university students, Guo Qi, Wang Pu, and others, altogether more than ten students, were selected to study with the Heir Apparent in the inner palace. Upon oral examination by the emperor in the Jinshen Pavilion, they all were found to have good appearance and to be both intelligent and refined, and they gave detailed and elegant answers to the questions. Emperor Taizu was pleased and bestowed lavish gifts upon them.

When the empire had been brought to peace, the emperor ordered in a proclamation that students be selected from prefectural, subprefectural, and district schools to enter the national university. Moreover, younger *juren* degree holders, such as Zhao Weiyi, and tribute students, such as Dong Chang and others, were also selected to study at the university and were given clothing and cloth. These students were then ordered to practice clerical work in the various government offices [as preparation for their official careers]. They were then referred to as *lishi jiansheng* (intern students). The most outstanding students in this group, such as Li Kuo and others, were selected to enter the Wenhua Hall and the Wuying Hall[7] to discuss classical texts. They were called junior fellows *(xiao xiucai)*. Those scholars who were of outstanding talent and learning and who were both bright and refined in their appearance were assigned to study extensively and thoroughly the encyclopedic literature and the disciplines of ethics and statecraft so as to prepare themselves for service in high positions. They were called senior fellows *(lao xiucai)*.[8]

At the beginning of the dynasty the Yingtian Prefectural School was changed into the National University. Later the university was moved to the foot of the Jiming (Cock's Crow) Mountain.[9] At that time the name was changed from Guozixue to Guozijian[10] and the offices of chancellor *(jijiu)* and director of studies *(siye)*, as well as those of proctor *(jiancheng)*, erudites *(boshi)*, lecturers *(zhujiao)*, preceptors *(xuezheng)*, teaching assistants *(xuelu)*, archivist *(dianji)*, quartermaster *(zhangzhuan)*, and registrar *(dianbu)* were established. The students were enrolled into six different departments *(tang)*: the Shuaixing (Following One's True Nature) Department, the Xiudao (Cultivating the Way) Department, the Chengxin (Making the Mind Sincere) Department, the Zhengyi (Defining the Sense of Right) Department, the Chongzhi (Ennobling One's Ambition) Department, and the Guangye (Broadening One's Learning) Department.[11] Next to the school were dormitories to lodge the students. These were known as *haofang* (registered lodgings).

Students received generous stipends in food, and each season they were given cotton and silk cloth and embroidered silk cloth, as well as sets of clothing, headgear, and boots. On all official holidays, such as New Year's Day and the Lantern Festival, students were given holiday money. Empress Xiaozi (Empress Ma, 1332–1382)[12] ordered that grain be stored inside the university and established more than twenty "Red Granaries" *(hongcang)* to support the wives and children of the students. Students who were not yet married and served on internships were given money to pay for their wedding, and in addition two sets of women's clothing and a monthly stipend of two bushels *(shi)* of rice.[13] Students who had stayed long in the capital and whose parents were still alive, or if their parents were dead, whose grandparents or great-uncles or -aunts were alive, were all sent home to visit their families. Each student was given one set of clothing and five *ding* in paper money toward travel expenses. Such was the generous and kind treatment of the students.

The method of teaching them [was as follows]. Each morning the chancellor and the director of studies would take their seats in the [Yilun] Hall, while the chief officers from the registrar down, and the subordinate officials from the proctor down, would stand at their assigned places. After the students completed the greeting ceremony, they would be asked questions on the Classics and the Histories and receive instruction standing with their hands folded.

Only the first and the fifteenth of the month were holidays. All other days the students attended the [lecture] hall and took their meals together in the dining hall. Lectures *(huijiang)*, student lectures *(fujiang)*,[14] and recitation classes *(beishu)* held on a rotating basis were the standard schedule.

The subjects of study were, in addition to the Four Books and one's Classic of concentration *(benjing)*, the *Florilegium of Explanations (Shuoyuan)* by Liu Xiang, the *Penal and Administrative Codes of the Ming Dynasty (Da Ming lü* and *Da Ming ling)*, calligraphy, mathematics, and the *Imperial Grand Pronouncement (Yuzhi da gao)*. Each month students were examined on their interpretation of the Classic [of concentration] and on their interpretation of the [Four] Books,[15] one essay question in each subject, and on their ability to write the following types of documents: proclamation *(zhao)*, announcement *(gao)*, memorial *(biao)*, essay *(ce)*, free discussion *(lun)*, and judgment *(panyu)*, two essays in any two formats.[16] Each day they were required to practice more than two hundred characters of calligraphy in the style of one of the following masters: Wang Xizhi, Wang Xianzhi, Zhi Yong, Ouyang Xun, Yu Shinan, Yan Zhenqing, or Liu Gongquan.

In each class one student was selected to serve as student prefect *(zhaizhang)* and oversee the work of the other students. In their dress, pace, and table manners students were required to maintain a serious and appropriate appearance. At night they had to sleep within the university. If a student had legitimate reasons to leave the premises, he had to report this to the teaching officials in charge of his class. The student prefect would then be ordered to accompany the student to file a petition with the chancellor.

The proctor was responsible for keeping a Register of Accumulated Misdemeanors *(jiqian bu)*. Students who did not obey the rules were recorded in the register. Second- and third-time offenders were convicted and punished. Fourth-time offenders were punished even with banishment to some distant region *(faqian anzhi)*. The articles of the University Regulations were revised many times and maintained a good balance between leniency and strictness. For the various halls and the dormitories, the taking of meals and bathing, in all cases there were prohibitory regulations *(jinli)*. As for home leaves for the purpose of visiting one's parents or getting married, there were fixed time limits according to the distance of the journey. Those students who transgressed the time limits were punished to serve as jail wardens *(dianshi)* in some distant region; some were demoted to become clerks *(li)*.

The officials in charge of teaching were invariably selected from among senior scholars. Song Na (chancellor 1383–1390), Wu Yong (chancellor 1382–1383), and others were recruited from among the Confucian scholars to become chancellors. Song Na in particular became known as a famous teacher.[17]

Of all candidates who passed the *jinshi* examination over the years, many came from the National University. In 1388, Ren Hengtai passed as number one in the Palace Examination. Emperor Taizu summoned Song Na, praised and rewarded him, and ordered that the names of the successful candidates be inscribed on a stele to be erected at the university gate. In 1391, when Xu Guan passed as number one, it was also like this. From that time on, steles with the names of the successful *jinshi* examination candidates were erected for each examination.[18]

Each year the provincial surveillance offices throughout the empire would select *shengyuan* over twenty who were honest and prudent, and dignified and cultivated in their behavior, to be sent to the university for an entrance examination. *Juren* who had failed in the metropolitan examination *(huishi xiadi)* entered the university to complete their studies.

Later, in response to a memorial by Remonstrator Guan Xian, it was stipulated that prefectural, subprefectural, and district schools each should annually send one tribute *shengyuan (suigong sheng-yuan)*, and this became established practice. The Hanlin Academy would examine them in their interpretation of the Classics and the Four Books, one essay question each, and on their ability to write a judgment essay *(panyu)*, one question. Those who passed the examination with the highest grade were enrolled in the National University [at Nanjing], while those who received the second grade were admitted to the National University at Zhongdu (the "Central Capital," at Fengyang, Anhui).[19] Those who failed were sent back [to their schools], and [the students and] the responsible officials were punished through the withholding of food stipends and salaries.

As a result young scholars from all provinces gathered like clouds in the capital. From Yunnan and Sichuan came aboriginal official students *(tuguan sheng)*. Countries such as Japan, Liuqiu, and Siam also all had official students *(guansheng)* who studied at the National University. These students were often bestowed generous gifts, and those who accompanied them were also presented with gifts. Throughout the Yongle (1403–1425) and Xuande (1426–1436) reigns this practice was continued. By the time of the Chenghua (1465–1487) and Zhengde (1506–1521) reigns, students were still arriving from Liuqiu (the Ryukyus, modern Okinawa).

The establishment of a National University in Zhongdu took place in Hongwu 8 (1375). In the twenty-sixth year (1393) it was abolished, and the teachers and students were all included into the National University in the capital (Nanjing). In Yongle 1 (1403) the Beijing National University was first established. In the eighteenth year (1420), when the capital was moved [from Nanjing to Beijing], what had been the Capital National University changed its name and became Nanjing National University, and for the university students a distinction came to be made between those of the northern national university and those of the southern.[20]

Emperor Taizu was concerned that the sons and younger brothers of the military officials received training only in the military arts and rarely had any experience in the study of letters. He ordered the Chief Military Commission to select students from these young men to enter the National University. Those who resided at Fengyang studied at the Zhongdu National University. The Duke of Han, Li Shanchang (1314–1390), and others were ordered to evaluate the standing of the teachers and the students and rank them into different classes. The Duke of Cao, Li Wenzhong (1339–1384), was put in charge of university affairs to maintain discipline and watch over [the students].

Later many sons and younger brothers of the dignitaries *(xunchen)* also entered the university to study. In Jiajing 1 (1522) it was ordered that those dukes, marquises, and earls who had not yet been appointed to office and were under thirty years of age should study at the university. When shortly thereafter it was ordered that also those who had already been employed should enter, the younger family members of the dignitaries and the imperial inlaws vied to be admitted to the university for its prestige.

The students in the Six Departments were promoted according to a system of credit point accumulation *(jifen zhi fa)*. Two directors of studies, one of the left and one of the right, each supervised three departments. Students who had mastered the Four Books but not yet their Classic were registered in the Zhengyi, Chongzhi, and Guangye departments. Those who had spent more than a year and a half in one of these departments and had shown excellence both in their literary style and reasoning ability were advanced to the Xiudao and Chengxin departments. After another year and a half [in one of these departments], those students who had a good command of both classics and history and had shown excellence in both style and reasoning were admitted to the Shuaixing Department.

Only students in the Shuaixing Department could accumulate credit points. The credit-point system was as follows. In the first month of each quarter students were examined on their interpretation of their Classic of concentration by one essay question. In the second month they were required to write one free discussion *(lun)* and one court document[21] in the style of either a proclamation *(zhao)*, announcement *(gao)*, or memorial *(biao)*. In the third month they would write one essay *(ce)* on subjects from the classics and the histories, and two judgments on given cases *(panyu)*.

In each examination, if both the style and reasoning were good, the student would receive one point. If the reasoning was good but the style inferior, he would be given half a point. If [both reasoning and style] were inferior and there were mistakes, no point was given. Those who accumulated eight points in one year were considered to have graduated and were granted status qualifying them for official appointment *(chushen)*. Those who did not obtain the required number of credit points had to remain at the university and continue their training. If there were students who displayed particularly outstanding talent and learning, a memorial would be submitted so that the emperor could personally appoint them.

In the year Hongwu 26 (1393), Liu Zheng, Long Tan, and others, altogether some sixty-four university students, were appointed as Administration Commisioners *(buzheng shi,* rank 2b), Surveillance Commissioners *(ancha shi,* 3a), Administration Vice-Commissioners *(canzheng,* 3b), Assistant Administration Commisioners *(canyi,* 4b), Surveillance Vice-Commissioners *(fushi,* 4a), Assistant Surveillance Commissioners *(qianshi,* 5a), and other officials. Such was the manner in which students were all of a sudden employed in important positions. Those who were appointed as high-ranking officials in various parts of the empire were innumerable.

Li Kuo and others were promoted from the Wenhua and Wuying halls to become censors. Kuo was shortly afterwards transferred to the position of Supervising Secretary *(jishi zhong)* and concurrently Recorder *(lushi)* in the princely establishment of Qi. It would seem then that recruitment for the censorial government positions *(taijian)* was also done from the National University. However, the positions that students were most often appointed to were those of rank six and below in the prefectural, subprefectural, and district administrations.

At first, due to the warfare and destruction that had taken place in the north, people there rarely knew the importance of learning. Therefore, Lin Boyun and others, altogether 366 university students, were dispatched to teach in these various northern localities. Later [teachers] were also sent to the other provinces. Students in the prime of their life who were good at literary composition were selected and appointed as instructors *(jiaoyu)* in district schools or similar officials.

Although Taizu occasionally put into practice the civil service examination system, the majority of officials were recruited from among the university students *(jiansheng)* and from men of outstanding talent promoted through special recommendation *(jianju rencai)*. Consequently, at that time, of the men appointed to official posts in the capital and throughout the empire, National University students were the majority.

After two reign changes, the *jinshi* degree gradually became more important, and the system of special recommendation was abolished. The *juren* and *gongsheng* routes also gradually became less important.[22] Although the original system of credit accumulation and intern service was not formally changed, the chancellors of both the Southern and Northern University, Chen Jingzong, Li Shimian, and others paid much attention to the restoration of the original order. Thus, these institutions had already become different from the time of their first implementation.

The tendency of the public sentiment was to emphasize only the *jinshi* degree. The promotions and demotions of an official's career were already decided the day he presented himself as a candidate for office. Unless a *jiansheng* could pass the civil service examinations with distinction, he would not succeed [in reaching high office], even though he had come from the school for training government officials. Such were the circumstances of one thing adding on to another.

When the precedent of purchase of studentships (*nasu*, "contributing grain") had been set, the system of official ranks gradually became mixed. When common people were allowed also to enter the university [simply] by virtue of being holders of the first degree (*shengyuan*)—they were then referred to as *minsheng* (student from the people), or *junxiu* (refined and elegant man)—the status of the university students declined even further.

Thus, although they all came from the National University, *jujian* and *gongsheng* were appointed as assistant prefects *(fu zuoer)* in prefectures and head officials *(zhengguan)* in the subprefectures and districts, while *guansheng* and *ensheng* were selected to serve in lower capital offices: the six ministries *(bu)*, the departments *(yuan)*, commissions *(fu)*, guards *(wei)*, bureaus *(si)*, and courts *(si)*. These were still known as the "regular route" *(zhengtu)*.

Students by purchase (*yuanli jiansheng*, "students by set precedent of [financial] contribution"), on the other hand, were only selected to become Vice-Magistrates *(zuoer)* in the subprefectures and districts or subordinate officials *(shouling guan)* in the prefectures. Those who were given posts in the central government were appointed as subordinate officials in such offices as the Court of Imperial Entertainments (Guanglu si) and the Directorate of Imperial Parks (Shanglinyuan jian). Those who wished to serve in distant places were employed in Yunnan, Guizhou, Guangxi, and where vacancies occurred as principal subordinate officials in the Administrative Office of the Guards (Junwei yousi shouling) in the border provinces, and to fill vacancies as instructors *(jiaoshou)* in the guard schools *(weixue)* and in the princely establishments *(wangfu)*. For the rest of their careers these men would belong to the "irregular route" *(yitu)*.

The practice of admitting *juren* to the National University began during the Yongle reign (1403–1425). Of the candidates who ranked low (and did not pass as *jinshi*) in the metropolitan examination *(huishi xiadi)*, those who were outstanding were immediately listed by the Hanlin Academy so that they could enter the university and wait for a later examination. They were given a stipend equivalent to the salary of an instructor in a district school *(jiaoyu)*. In the metropolitan examinations at this time there were supplementary lists *(fubang)* of successful candidates (who did not pass as *jinshi*). These *juren* were generally appointed as local teaching officials. Therefore, those who were admitted to the university were also given this salary.

In the year Xuande 8 (1433), Minister of Rites Hu Ying and Grand Secretaries Yang Shiqi and Yang Rong were ordered to select Long Wen and others, altogether twenty-four *fubang juren*, to be sent to the National University to study. Every three months the Hanlin Academy would examine these students on their literary ability. Like the Hanlin bachelors *(shujishi)* they were treated with exceptional favor. Later, no special second examination was given. *Fubang [juren]* over twenty-five years of age were appointed to teaching positions, while those under twenty-five could either return home to study (*yiqin*, "to stay close to their parents") or enter the university to study. Finally, no distinction was made on the basis of seniority, and both those who wished to return home and those who wished to enter the university were allowed to do so.

The term *yiqin* means that the candidate returned to his home town to study, i.e., he studied while being close to his family *(yiqin yiye)*. There were also the categories of leave called *dingyou* (mourning for one's parents), *chenghun* (getting married), *xingqin* (visiting one's parents), and *song youzi* (accompanying one's child home), all of which, following the precedent set by the *yiqin* leave, had fixed time limits set for the return to the university.

During the Zhengtong reign (1436–1449), there were many vacant teaching positions in the empire, but *juren* were contemptuous of the low status of these positions and for the most part did not wish to be appointed. In Zhengtong 13 (1448), Censor Wan Jie requested that the Ministry of Rites be ordered to recruit more *fubang* to fill the teaching positions. Officials from the ministry replied that seven out of ten *juren* preferred to study at home or enter the university, while only three wished to take up teaching positions, and that it was merely appropriate to let each follow his own inclination. As a result the proposal was not implemented.

By the time of Chenghua 13 (1477), Censor Hu Lin submitted a proposal saying, "Of the teaching officials in the empire, very many are *suigong*. Neither in their speech nor conduct, nor in their literary ability are they qualified to serve as the teachers of others. We ask that more *juren* be recruited for employment in these positions and that the appointment of *gongsheng* be discontinued." After deliberation by the ministry it was decided that *suigong* should be recruited as before (originally stipulated), and teaching officials who held the *juren* degree should still be permitted to participate in the metropolitan examinations. From this time on, the number [of *juren*] who took up teaching positions gradually increased.

During the Jiajing reign (1522–1566), because both National Universities at Nanjing and Beijing had become almost empty of students, it was recommended that *juren* who had failed in the metropolitan examination should all be sent to the universities, and deadlines were set to make them hurry. Yet, in the end, *juren* who did not wish to enroll in the university could not be persuaded by force to do so. Subsequently, in addition to the annual tribute students, from time to time it also became necessary to recommend, "tribute students by special selection" *(xuan gong)* to fill the vacancies in the university.

Gongsheng who entered the university were originally *shengyuan* selected from the local schools, and since each school was ordered to annually send up one tribute student, they became known as annual tribute students *(suigong)*. The regulations governing this system were changed many times. . . .

(Here follows a long section describing the *gongsheng* system, changes in the annual *suigong* quotas, recommendation standards, other student categories and their status and prospects for official appointment. These regulations were changed many times due to the government's concern about maintaining a steady flow of students in and out of the university so as to recruit the best talents for the bureaucracy. The system was also, as seen above, influenced by the steadily growing importance of the examination system, especially the *jinshi* degree, from the midfifteenth century on.)

The institution of *lijian,* or university students by purchase, began in Jingtai 1 (1450). Because of the critical situation on the frontier, people throughout the empire who gave contributions of grain *(na su)* or horses *(na ma)* were allowed to enter the university to study. The number of students [admitted in this manner] was limited to one thousand. The system was practiced for four years and then discontinued.

In Chenghua 2 (1466), because of the great famine in Nanjing, the commanding officer [of Nanjing] submitted a proposal asking to let those sons and grandsons of officials, the military, and the common people who gave contributions of grain enter the university. The Minister of Rites, Yao Kui (1414–1473) responded, saying, "The National University is the place for nurturing talent. In recent years the provinces have sent up forty-year-old *shengyuan,* and those who contribute grass or horses begin to count in the tens of thousands. The oversupply of candidates is beyond control. Now, if wealth is taken as a substitute for virtue, the scholarly spirit *(shifeng)* will surely become more vulgar each day." The emperor agreed and rejected the commanding officer's proposal.

Nevertheless, later sometimes, in years of famine, or when there were disturbances on the frontier, or when some major construction project was undertaken, the practice was reintroduced following earlier precedent. In the end it could never be prevented.

Such were the main developments of the different categories of university students: the *jujian,* the *gongjian,* the *yinjian,* and the *lijian.*

—JLH

Notes

1. During the Ming and Qing dynasties the examination system consisted of three degrees: *shengyuan, juren,* and *jinshi.* The *shengyuan* degree was awarded after a student had passed a series of examinations in the local (prefectural, subprefectural, or district) school, *juren* after examination at the provincial level, and *jinshi* at the metropolitan examination given at the capital.

2. *Gongsheng* (tribute students) were *shengyuan* in the local schools who were recommended for study at the National University (Guozijian) in Beijing or Nanjing.

3. *Keju* is the usual term referring to the examination system.

4. *Suigong* (annual tribute students) were recommended, usually each year, according to a special quota set for the different local administrative units. During the first half, at least, of the Ming dynasty the vast majority of university students belonged to this group. *Xuangong* (tribute students by special selection) were from time to time after 1504 selected in addition to the annual quota to increase the number of students in the university. *En'gong* (tribute students by imperial grace) were selected on special occasions, such as the emperor's birthday or other celebrations. *Nagong* (tribute students by financial contribution) was introduced as a new category in 1450, when the government was in need of funds after the military defeat against the Oirats at Tumu and the peasant rebellion of Deng Maoqi. It was later resorted to from time to time when the government was in financial straits, although officials often spoke out against the practice.

5. *Guansheng* were sons of officials of the seventh rank or higher allowed to study at the university because of their father's rank. After 1457 this privilege was restricted to officials of the third rank and up. This category also included sons or relatives of non-Chinese tribal chiefs in the frontier areas *(tuguan zidi)* and foreign students *(waiyi zidi)* from countries like Korea, Japan, Liuqiu (the Ryukyus, modern Okinawa), Vietnam, and Siam. *Ensheng* (students by imperial grace) are to be distinguished from *en'gong,* who were tribute students added to the regular quota on special occasions. *Ensheng* were students admitted individually by special imperial orders. They were often sons of officials who had served meritoriously in government or who had died for their country or for remonstrating loyally with the emperor and were honored posthumously this way.

6. For his biography and biographical data on many other persons mentioned in this chapter, see Luther Carrington Goodrich and Chaoying Fang, eds., *Dictionary of Ming Biography (1368–1644)* (New York: Columbia University Press, 1976).

7. These two offices were under the direction of the Hanlin Academy, the highest academic institution in the government, which provided literary and scholarly assistance to the emperor and the court. The Hanlin Academy drafted proclamations and other state documents, compiled imperially sponsored books, and read and explained the Classics and histories to the emperor and to his family.

8. A few decades later, during the Yongle reign (1403–1425), the Grand Secretariat took form, evolving from the Hanlin Academy, and its members came also almost exclusively from within the Hanlin Academy. From the 1420s on, the grand secretaries continued to be the highest officials in the bureaucracy.

9. The university was moved in 1382 to a newly built large campus on the southern slope of Jiming Mountain in the northern part of Nanjing, just south of Xuanwu Lake. It is now roughly the site of Nanjing Institute of Technology.

10. Universities (also referred to as Taixue, Guoxue, or Guozixue) existed during most dynasties, although sometimes only nominally. It was during the Ming that this institution reached its highest point of development and importance as recruitment source for the civil service.

11. The departments or "Halls" are listed here in declining order of difficulty in the Confucian curriculum. The names are taken from various passages in the Classics.

12. See her biography in Goodrich and Fang, *Dictionary of Ming Biography,* 1023–1026.

13. This was a very generous stipend, being in the range of the average salary for an elementary teacher in the seventeenth and early-eighteenth century. Also in the early Ming, the monthly salary of a teacher in a local school was around this level: 2.5 bushels for an instructor in a subprefecture *(xuezheng)* and 2 bushels for an instructor in a district school *(jiaoyu)*. Assistant instructors *(xundao)* also received 2 bushels. It seems that teachers also received a monthly stipend in rice of 0.6 bushel, the same amount given to students who received a stipend *(lingsheng)*. During the Ming, one bushel of rice equaled approximately one tael *(liang)* of silver. It seems unlikely that university students also received this stipend in later reigns.

14. On days for student lectures, students were asked to give lectures on the topic covered in the teacher's lecture the previous day.

15. The four major Confucian canonical texts: the *Great Learning (Daxue)*, the *Doctrine of the Mean (Zhongyong)*, *Analects of Confucius (Lunyu)*, and *Mencius (Meng Zi)*.

16. There were many similarities between the examinations given in the university and the provincial *(juren)* and metropolitan *(jinshi)* examinations. In the provincial and metropolitan examinations, which lasted fifteen days, in the first part (nine days) candidates were examined on the interpretation of the Four Books (three questions) and the Classics (four questions). Each essay had to be at least three hundred characters long. In the second part (three days) they were examined on a free discussion *(lun);* one question, judgment *(pan);* five questions; and answer to one question written in the form of either a proclamation *(zhao)*, announcement *(gao)*, or memorial *(biao)*. In the third part (three days) the examination consisted of five essays on questions from the Classics and histories and contemporary affairs. The emphasis on the highly sylistic form of presenting the answers, the so-called "eight-legged essay" *(baguwen)*, began, according to Gu Yanwu (1613–1682; see selection 83) during the Chenghua reign (1465–1488).

17. Song Na also became famous as one of the most stern disciplinarians in the history of the university.

18. Many of these steles are still standing and can be seen at the site of the National University in Beijing, now the Beijing Municipal Library (Shoudu tushuguan).

19. For a brief period (1375–1393) during the Hongwu reign, a second National University existed at Taizu's home town, Fengyang, which Taizu had designated as the Middle Capital. The National University at Beijing was established 1403 by the Yongle emperor, Taizong.

20. From the time Emperor Taizong made his old seat as prince of Yan, Beijing, an auxiliary capital in 1403, two universities coexisted throughout the rest of the Ming dynasty. After the capital was formally changed to Beijing (1421), the Ming continued to have two capitals, with Nanjing being the auxiliary. Central government agencies were duplicated in the two cities, although in the auxiliary capital these were primarily concerned with administration of the surrounding areas.

21. The term used here is *neike* (literally, "inner subject/branch/department"); now used only in the sense of "internal medicine" (as opposed to *waike* [surgery]), but it is unlikely to have had that meaning in the present context.

22. The *juren* degree holders and the *jiansheng,* however, continued throughout the Ming to serve as the recruitment pool for lower government offices and for many higher and midlevel posts in the local administration. Many became teachers in the local schools. From the late fifteenth century on, higher officials in the central government and at the provincial level, as well as head officials at the local level, almost without exception came from among the *jinshi* degree holders. The changing emphasis in the recruitment system towards the *jinshi* degree holders took place gradually over the fifteenth century, until in late Ming and during the Qing it was almost a prerequisite for official appointment.

EXTENSIVE RECORDS ON FOUR FOREIGN LANDS (Siyi guang ji) was compiled by Shen Mou-shang, a native of Jiangsu Province on China's eastern coast. Written at the end of the sixteenth or the beginning of the seventeenth century, Shen's notice on Bengal is partly based on earlier accounts of Bengal and India in *New Dynastic History of the Tang (Xin Tang shu)*, compiled by Ouyang Xiu (1007–1072) and Song Qi (998–1061); *Records of Foreign Countries along the West Ocean (Xiyang fanguo zhi)*, written by Gong Zhen in 1434; *An Overall Survey of the Star Raft (Xingcha shenglan)*, written by Fei Xin in 1436; *An Overall Survey of the Shores of the Oceans (Yingyai shenglan)*, written by Ma Huan in 1457 (?); and *Records on Tribute from the Countries in the Western Ocean (Xiyang chaogong dianlu)*, written by Huang Shencong in 1520. Shen's work, however, has the most comprehensive account of medieval Bengal. Not only is there a general description of the geography, customs, and products of Bengal, there is also a detailed discussion on the language and script of this important region of India. In addition, there is a listing of 303 Bengali words transcribed into Chinese.

Between 1409 and 1423 at least seven Ming (1368–1644) embassies visited the kingdom of Bengal. Among these, the embassies lead by Hu Xian in 1415 and 1420 are most famous and noteworthy. One of the main aims of these Ming missions seems to have been the establishment of a military alliance between China and Bengal. This interest in military collaboration between the two countries may have stemmed from Bengal's request for Chinese help in its war against the neighboring state of Jaunpur. Although the extant sources are silent about the result of the military diplomacy between Bengal and China, the Chinese embassies seem to have collected an enormous amount of information about the East Indian kingdom. In fact, much of Shen Moushang's knowledge about Bengal may have come from the information originally gathered by Hou Xian and his entourage. Shen Moushang's notice is important evidence of the Ming court's political interest in and diplomatic contacts with South Asia. At the same time, Shen's record of various commodities and Bengali vocabulary indicates the commercial interest and the participation of Chinese merchants in Sino-Indian trade.—NCS

The Frontiers of Bengal

The Kingdom of Bengal is [in] Tianzhu[1] (India). It was [called] Shendu[2] during the Han dynasty (206 B.C.E.–220 C.E.). It is also known as Magadha or Brahmana. In the east, it reaches the sea and [borders] Zhancheng.[3] In the west, it extends to Jibin[4] and the kingdom of Bosi,[5] while some say it reaches to the kingdom of Jingangbaozuo,[6] [which is] also called Zhaonamuer.[7] In the south it reaches the sea, and to the north it extends to Congling.[8] The region is thirty thousand tricents wide and divided into five Indias: East, West, South, North, and Middle.

The Route from the Kingdom of Sūmatra to Bengal

Sailing by boat from the Kingdom of Sumendara,[9] and taking [the way through] the Mao mountain[10] and the Cuilan islands,[11] it takes twenty days of travel under favorable northwestern winds. The first place reached is the port of Chati.[12] This is where the river branches out and where all the ocean-going junks moor. Again, rowing on a small boat one can enter the bay [after traveling] a distance of more than five hundred tricents. The name of [this] place is Suonaergang.[13] After landing on the shore and walking southwest for more than thirty stations,[14] one reaches [the capital of the] kingdom. There are outer and inner city walls; and all the big and small government offices are all located within the city.[15]

The Land Route to Bengal

The land route, starting from Chittagong, is sixteen stations to Sonarjiang (Sonargaon). Then from the city moat it is another twenty stations to Banduwa,[16] the capital of the kingdom.

The Hills and Rivers of Bengal

The Wuling (Five Peaks) Mountains are very high and covered with luxurious forest.[17] The people [of the kingdom] dwell together [on the banks of] Jiapili river.[18]

The Kingdom of Bengal

Bengal is [also known as] East India. India has five kingdoms: East India borders the sea and adjoins Champā; West India connects to the Kingdom of Daqin;[19] South India borders the sea; and North India borders the Snowy Mountains.[20] The Kingdom of East India, or [as] some say the Kingdom of West India, is the place where Śākyamuni attained Buddhahood. During the time of Emperor Ming (r. 58–76) of the Han dynasty, the Buddhist doctrines of India entered China. Their custom is to give up the body and cremate the corpse. This is called *chapi*.[21] From this [custom] originated the cremation system prevalent among the poor people in China.

The kings of Middle India are surnamed Qilizhi, also called Shali.[22] The kingdom has existed for generations without rebellions or [attempts] to murder the ruler. The capital, called Chabuheluo,[23] is situated on the banks of the Kauryala River. There are several hundred other cities with established chiefs. There are several dozen other countries having established kings. During the times of Emperor Yang (r. 605–617) of the Sui dynasty (581–618), Pei Ju was sent to establish contacts with the countries in the Western Regions. The places he could not reach were India and Fulin.[24] The emperor expressed regret over this.

During the Wude reign period (618–627) [of the Tang dynasty], there was great chaos in the kingdom [of Middle India]. Its King Śīlāditya, in order to check the advance [of enemy] troops, mounted an attack on the four [other kingdoms of] India. The elephants were not unharnessed, nor were soldiers unarmored, and [eventually] the four other Indias became vassals of the northern kingdom.

In the fifteenth year of the Zhenguan era (641), Śīlāditya declared himself the king of Magadha and sent tribute missions [to the Tang court]. Emperor Taizong, then, ordered the Commandant of Fleet-as-Clouds Cavalry, Liang Huai[jing], [to go to Magadha] as a Pacifier Commissioned with Special Powers. Śīlāditya was very surprised [with the arrival of the embassy] and asked the people of his kingdom, "Have envoys of Mahācīnasthāna (i.e., the Great China Country) come to my country since the ancient times?" Everyone replied, "No." Some said that the Middle Kingdom was [in fact] Mahācīnasthāna. Then [the king], directing all his ministers, faced east and prostrating he received the [imperial] edict.

In the twenty-second year [of the Zhenguan era (648)], the Emperor [Taizong] sent the lead envoy Wang Xuance, holding the title of Right Defense Guard Commandant, and others to Śīlāditya's country. [However, by this time] his vassal Aluonashun[25] [of] the Tīrabukti [kingdom] had murdered Śīlāditya and established himself [as the king]. He dispached soldiers to attack Xuance. Xuance was the only [person] who was able to escape to Tibet. There he gathered troops from Nepal and other countries and routed Aluonashun. The captive Aluonashun was presented before the [Tang] emperor.[26]

In the third year of the Yongle reign period (1405) of the present dynasty,[27] an envoy from the king of the Kingdom [of Bengal], Aiyasiding,[28] came to the [Ming] court. The emperor [in return] presented the king [gifts consisting of] four bolts each of hemp, silk, and gauze silk, and eight bolts of thin silk. Three bolts of hemp, silk, and gauze silk, and six bolts of thin silk were presented to the queen. The emperor ordered an envoy to go to India to invite a foreign monk. After arriving in the [Chinese] capital, [the foreign monk] was housed in the Linggu Monastery, where he taught people to chant Oṁ-maṇi-padme-hūṁ. Li Jiding, a Reader-in-Waiting of the Hanlin Academy, remarked, "If he has supernatural powers, then he should be well versed in Chinese! Why does he wait for a translator and [only] then comprehends [Chinese]? In fact, the Oṁ-maṇi-padme-hūṁ that he utters actually means, 'I have cheated you.' The people do not understand this."[29]

In the sixth year [of the Yongle reign period (1408)], the king of the country sent his envoy who entered through Taicang[30] to pay tribute [to the Ming court]. In the twelfth year [of the Yongle reign period (1414)], King Jianfuding[31] sent his minister Bajiyi with a memorial written on gold leaf. [The envoy] presented tribute consisting of a giraffe and other local products. The emperor in return presented four bolts of brocade and sixty bolts of thin silk to the king. Other rewards were also given to the headmen.

In the thirteenth year [of the Yongle era (1415)], the emperor ordered Vice-Director Hou Xian and others to lead a fleet of ships, and as per an imperial edict present rewards to the king, queen, and the headmen of the kingdom. [When the mission arrived in Bengal], the king of that kingdom sent the local chieftain with presents including clothes and other offerings, and more than a thousand men and horses went out to welcome [them].

From Chittagong port, it is a distance of sixteen stations to Sonargaon. [This place] has a city moat, streets, and markets where merchandise is stockpiled and business is brisk. Once again, attendants, on elephants and horses, were sent out to welcome [the Chinese envoys] with presents and offerings.

After twenty stations one arrives in Panduā. This is the king's capital. The city walls are majestic, the streets and markets full of adjoining shops that stockpile merchandise in large quantities. The king's palaces are all built with bricks and mortar; the brick-laid steps are high and broad. The roofs of halls are flat and coated with white lime. There are three inner gates and nine long halls whose pillars are all covered and ornamented with brass and engraved with designs of flowers and animals.

[On the day the court received the Chinese envoys], over a thousand mounted troops with shining armor were placed on the left and right sides of the long corridor. Stout warriors wearing shining armor and helmets, and holding sharp swords, bows, and arrows lined up outside. The sight was grand and full of pomp. More than a hundred umbrellas made of peacock feathers were arranged on the left and right sides of the court. In addition, over a hundred elephant[-mounted] troops were placed in front of the palace. In the main hall, the king sat cross-legged on the high throne inlaid with eight [types of] jewels. The king's sword lay across his knees. He then ordered two people holding silver staffs and wearing turbans to lead the way [for the Chinese envoys]. After each five steps, they shouted once and then stopped when they reached the center [of the court]. Next, two people holding golden staffs led [the envoys] further forward according to the previous ritual. Bowing, the king received the imperial edict and kowtowed,[32] and after touching it to his forehead started reading. After the gift-receiving ceremony ended, a carpet was spread on the floor of the hall to receive our imperial envoys. A reception was arranged for our [accompanying] officers and soldiers. Roasted beef and mutton were served, and, as wine was prohibited due to fear of its corrupting nature and the resulting loss of decorum, rose water and scented honey were served as drinks.

After the reception ended, the king again presented a golden helmet, golden waist belts, golden vases, and golden bowls to the imperial envoy. Each of the vice-envoys under him received a silver helmet, silver waist belts, silver vases, and silver bowls. And [to] the officials under them golden waist belts and hemp thread were presented. The Head Wardrobe [Officer] and the soldiers received silver coins. It is evident that the country is prosperous and has a sense of etiquette. Later, [the king] personally arranged a golden container and [wrote] a memorial on a golden leaf, and sent envoys and ministers with local products to present to the [Chinese] court. Since this time tributary envoys [from Bengal] have occasionally come [to China].

The Administrative System of Bengal

The kingdom has a written language and is skillful in calendar-making. It has a yamen with bureaucrats of various ranks and is [in charge of] certifying credentials of [businessmen], geomancers, and physicians. The headman is called Basi-sālar. The color and style of dress used by the king and the headman conform to the system of the Muslims. Punishments include breaking off hands and feet, severing nose or ears, flogging, imprisonment, etc. For smaller offenses a fine is imposed. Days and months are fixed according to a twelve-month year. There is no intercalary month. The gates of houses all face east.

The Customs of Bengal

The weather [of the kingdom], throughout the four seasons, is always hot like summer. The land is vast; the arable land is fertile and [therefore] produces four crops a year. It is not necessary to weed and sow [because] crops grow naturally in all seasons. The people believe in oath taking and propagandize against cursing. They can inform the dragons to stir up clouds and start the rains. Men and women [of the kingdom] work hard at tilling and weaving. Their customs are pure and honest.

The wealthy people build boats, and many of them go to foreign countries to trade. The appearance of most of the people is dark. There are very few people of white [complexion]. The men all shave their heads. The males wrap their heads with white cloth. They wear long white upper garments. On the lower [part of the body] they wrap a kerchief of various colors. On their feet they wear goatskin shoes stitched with golden threads. The full dress is very orderly.

The women wear short blouses and wrap colored cotton cloth or silk satin around [their bodies]. They do not use rouge, [yet] they are naturally graceful. From their ears hang precious ornaments, [and] around their necks hang necklaces. Their hair is heaped up on the back portion of the head. They wear four bracelets plated with gold and have rings on fingers and toes. They show respect by licking the feet and touching the heels of people.

The language of the kingdom is mostly Bengali, which constitutes a group of its own. There are also people who speak Parsi.

Funeral rites and marriage ceremonies are performed according to Muslim customs. Although commercial transactions may amount to thousands of gold [pieces], prices are fixed with the use of hands and there are never any regrets and accusations. They have all sorts of shops, bathing houses, wine-sellers, and food merchants. All types of skilled workers and artisans are also available. The people do not have tea, [and so] they offer betel nuts to the guests.

The kingdom has a type of people called Hindus. They do not eat beef, and when eating and drinking men and women [sit in] separate places. When the husband dies, [the wife] does not take a husband again. And, when the wife dies, [the husband] does not remarry. If the orphans and widows do not have anyone to support them, then the whole village takes turn to sustain them. They are not allowed to go to another village to beg for food. Their integrity is worthy of acclaim.

In the marketplace there is a type of women of the streets who wear black, green, or white flowery blouses, and wrap a green towel around the lower [part of the body]. In addition, [they] string together garlands of coral and amber beads in pearlized niter matrices, and wear them festooned on their shoulders and head. On the upper arms they wear pink armlets made from melted saltpeter. When people hold feasts, they invite these women for entertainment. They sing foreign songs and also are very well versed at dancing.[33]

There is also a class of people called Genxiaosulunai.[34] They are households of musicians. Every day during the fifth watch they go to the main gates of the headman or wealthy families. One person blows a *śanāi,* another beats a small drum, and one beats a big drum. In the beginning [the beating of drums] is slow, but following the beat it gradually gets faster and faster. Afterwards, they proceed to the next family blowing the *śanāi* and beating the drums. During feast times, they beg for money and goods at various places by performing jugglery.

In addition, there is a class of people who, together with their wives, move about dragging ropes tied to a big tiger. When they reach a household they begin their performance. Unfastening [the rope], they make the tiger sit on the ground. The man, with a bare body, leaps toward the tiger by himself and kicks and beats it. The tiger, letting out its anger, roars. The man then engages the tiger in several rounds of duels. He also inserts his fist into the tiger's mouth, reaching all the way into its throat. After the act is over, the rope is once again tied around the head of the tiger. The tiger lies down on the ground soliciting food. The people then feed it meat and reward [the husband and wife] with money and goods on the ground.

There are several varieties of liquor: coconut, rice, palm, zizania,[35] and heated wines. The king uses money minted from silver called *tākā.* The official weight of each equals three [of our copper] coins. Their official [size] is 1.2 inches [in diameter]. There is writing on the face [of the *tākā*]. Trade is conducted based on prices fixed according to this currency. In the markets on the streets, [people] also use cowries. The foreign word for it is *kaoli,*[36] and [prices] may also be quoted in numbers [of cowries]. The products of the country include gold, silver, satin, silk, blue-and-white-patterned porcelain, copper, iron, musk, vermilion, mercury, and straw-matting.

The Products of Bengal

Paddy is harvested four times a year. The stalks are so tall that a camel could get swallowed up in them. The grains of rice are fine, long, and mostly red in color. Millet, barley, sesame, and beans are available. Jackfruits are as big as a basket and taste sweet. Amalas have aromatic flavor and taste sour. [There are] plantains, sugarcane, jujubes, betel nuts, and granulated sugar. Mulberry trees are used to raise silkworms, [from whose cocoons] silk can be made.

[The people] chew the leaves of the *lailuo* (?) tree, which is like a pear tree. [The *lailuo* tree] grows in the depths of mountain valleys. It is guarded by a gigantic poisonous snake. In order to pick the leaves, one must shoot the branches with arrows. When birds [pick the leaves up from the ground] with their beaks and fly away from the tree, the leaves are gathered by shooting the birds.

[There are] melons, vegetables, and ginger. Buffaloes that are slaughtered are black and have long sharp horns that measure four feet and more. Once in every ten days [the horns] are cut. If not, then [the buffalo] dies of exhaustion. People drinking the blood of [these buffaloes] can live for five hundred years.

[There are also] camels, ivory, rhinoceros, cows, horses, goats, ghee, lions, leopards, gibbons, chickens, ducks, kingfishers, rock sugar, and fish.

There are various categories of cloths: one type is ragged cloth, which foreigners call *beibo*.[37] It is over three feet in width and fifty-six to [fifty-]seven feet in length. This cloth is white and fine like notepaper made of floss silk. One type is ginger-yellow cloth, which the foreigners call *man-zheti*.[38] It is more than four feet in width and fifty feet in length. It is like netting or gauze. One type is *zhanboletali*.[39] It is more than three feet in width and sixty feet in length. The thread of the cloth is fine, and [it] is like gauze. All [such cloths] are used to wrap the head. One type is *shataer*.[40] It is two feet in width and forty feet in length. It looks like *sansuo* (?) cloth. One type is *maheimale*.[41] It is about four feet in width and more than twenty feet in length. On the reverse [side] it has flannel tufts about one and a half to two inches thick. This is the [so-called] *tūla* [cotton] cloth.

Cotton flannels, patterned silk towels, silk, and quilt covers [are also produced]. White paper is made from tree bark. It is bright, fine, and smooth like deerskin. Crystals, agate, coral, pearls, gems, wrought-iron swords, spears, red beads, jade stones, raw salt, lacquerware, dishes, and bowls [are also produced].

Tribute Items from Bengal

Horses, saddles, vessels and utensils made of gold and glass, blue-and-white-patterned porcelain, *sahaci* (?), *jhamaratali* (?) cloth, *xibaibi* (?) cloth, *tūla* cloth, crowns of cranes, rhinoceros horns, kingfisher and oriole feathers, crystallized sugar, frankincense, ripe gharuwood, sandalwood incense, vine incense, black clay, purple glue, fine rattan work, black wood, sapan wood, pepper, [and] coarse jute.

Kingdom of Zhaonapuer

[This] kingdom is in India, and it is the ancient Buddhist kingdom. In the eighteenth year of the Yongle reign period (1420), its king, Yibulajin,[42] invaded the kingdom of Bengal a number of times. [The Chinese emperor] has sent envoys with imperial decrees instructing the kingdom [to desist].

Gifts to Bengal

In the third year of the Yongle reign period (1404), [the emperor] presented four bolts each of hemp and gauze silk, and eight bolts of fine silk to the king [of Bengal]. To the queen [he presented] three bolts each of hemp and gauze silk, and six bolts of fine silk. In the twelfth year [of the Yongle reign period] (1413), [the emperor] presented four bolts of brocade and sixty bolts of damask silk fabrics to the king. [He also] had different amounts of gifts for the headmen and other officials.

The [Tian]zhu (Indian) Script

[According to] Indian canons, writing was created by three people. They are known as Brahma, Kharoṣṭha (or Kharoṣṭhī), and [Ji] Cangjie. Brahma, of the Ābhāsvara Heaven, transmitted the writing system of the *brahmaloka* to India. It is written from right [to left]. Kharoṣṭha created the writing system in the Western Regions. It is written from left [to right]. Both combine sounds and rhymes (i.e., consonants and vowels) to form words. The writing systems of various foreigners all evolve from these [two systems]. Ji Cangjie lived in China. [He] created simple characters from the appearance of various objects. Compound characters were formed by the complementarity of shape and sound. This [kind of phonological] discussion is merely the farfetched interpretation of clever monks and cannot be deeply trusted. However, the so-called consonants are fifty in all. Sixteen of these are patterned on inflections, and thirty-four consonants are categorized according to the Siddham plosive letters. Today [I am] recording them:

e (a)	long *a* (ā)	*yi* (i)	long *yi* (ī)	*wen?* (u)	long *huo* (ū)	*li* (r̥)	short? *li* (l̥)
yi	long *lu*	*yi* (e?)	long *ai* (ai)	*wu* (o)	long *ou* (au)	*er*	short? *wu*

Below are the sixteen inflections according the *Dictionary of Indian Grammar and Philology* and other instructional [manuals]. Of those [sixteen inflections] that [I have] transmitted today, if the seventh, eighth, ninth, and tenth sounds are removed, then there are only twelve inflections. This is because these four inflections are already covered by the third and fourth inflections. The thirty-four consonants are categorized according to five phonological qualities:

Velars

ge (ka)	*ke* (kha)	????	*jie*	*ne* (ṅa)

Dentals

????	????	????	????	*ni* (na)

Lingual

????	????	????	cha	nu

Gutturals

tan	????	chi	da	na

Labials

bo	deng	mo	po	ma (ma)

ye (ya)	????	luo (la)	bo	she (śa)

sha (sha)	sa (sa)	he (ha)	cha

The above [nine inflections] are blended from gutturals and lingual plosives and are based on sounds and rhymes. Thus, they may be combined to create innumerable [words].

The script of Western Heaven:

ming	wang	shen	de	si	yi	xian	bin

"Barbarians from four [directions] have all submitted to the kind virtues of the Ming emperor."[43]

an	ma	ni	compounded ba	mi	hong

"Oṁ-maṇi-padme-hūṁ."

—NCS

Notes

1. Literally, "heavenly bamboo."
2. From Sanskrit Sindhu, the name for the river Indus.
3. Champā, in Southeast Asia.
4. Kāpiśī region, in present-day Afghanistan.

5. Persia.

6. Literally, "the kingdom of the Jeweled Diamond Throne."

7. Jaunpur.

8. Pamir Mountains.

9. Sūmatra, in Southeast Asia.

10. Poulo Weh, an island on the northern coast of Sūmatra.

11. Nicobar and Andaman Islands.

12. Chittagong, in present-day Bangladesh.

13. Sonargaon, about fifteen milies from Dhaka, the modern capital of Bangladesh.

14. A station or stage was a stop on highways used for courier service in ancient China. The distance between two stations was approximately ten miles. Thus, to travel thirty stations would mean a total distance of roughly three hundred miles.

15. This entire passage, with few minor differences, seems to have been borrowed from Ma Huan's *Yingyai shenglan*.

16. Panduā.

17. It is not clear which mountains Shen is referring to here. Wuling usually refers to the five ranges in the southern borders of the Chinese empire, especially during the Qin dynasty (221–206 B.C.E.).

18. Kauryala?

19. Daqin normally refers to the Roman Empire, especially the eastern part, but here it probably refers loosely to Persia and other lands to the west of India.

20. Hindu Kush.

21. Pāli *jhāpeti;* Sanskrit *dhyāpayati.*

22. Kṣatriya, i.e., the warrior class.

23. Champāran?

24. Farang.

25. Aruṇāśa?

26. The Tang court's diplomatic relations with King Śīlāditya (better known as Harṣa) of Kanauj, and the Chinese envoy Wang Xuance's battle with Aluonashun, the usurper of Harṣa's throne, is the most popular episode in Chinese accounts of India. This battle is reported to have taken place at Champāran, which Shen, perhaps erroneously, designates as the capital of Middle India.

27. I.e., the Ming.

28. Ghiyas-ud-din Azam Shah?

29. Li Jiding's assertion is both hilarious and specious. The Sanskrit *dhāraṇī* (mantra, incantation) actually means "Oṁ (a sacred sound), jewel in the lotus." Li misheard the Sanskrit as very colloquial Mandarin, *"An ba ni hong"* (I have cheated you).

30. In present-day Zhejiang Province.

31. Saif-ud-din?

32. It is highly unlikely that the Indian king actually did this, although the Chinese who reported the visit may have well wished (and perhaps even imagined) that he had done so.

33. These are the famous Indian nautch girls.

34. The Bengali term for this group of people is not clear. However, it seems to be a combination of two (or more?) musical instruments. *Gengxiao,* for example, may stand for *kaṇgsa* and *sulunai* for *śanāi.*

35. A type of edible aquatic grass.

36. I.e., *korī.*

37. *Bafta?*

38. *Pachad?*

39. *Chambaratāli/jhamaratāli?*

40. *Chautāli?*

41. Shanbeft?

42. Ibrahim Shargi?

43. The Bengali letters here are apparently transcriptions of Chinese words.

THE SHAOLIN MONASTERY is famous the world over for its martial techniques. The monastery, which was founded during the late fifth century, is situated at the foot of Mount Song, in today's Henan Province. The earliest recorded instances of its monks' participation in warfare date from the seventh century. On one occasion, the monks warded off bandits who attacked their monastery. On another (in 621), they assisted in the campaign of the future Tang emperor, Li Shimin (r. 627–649), against another contender to the throne, Wang Shichong. Following his victory, the Tang emperor handsomely rewarded the Shaolin monks, appointing one of them general.

Although Tang sources record two instances of Shaolin participation in warfare, they allude neither to regular military training at the monastery nor to a specific martial technique in which its monks specialized. Indeed, the earliest evidence that the martial arts were practiced at the monastery postdate the Tang period by no less than seven centuries. Late-Ming authors are the first to describe regular martial practice at the Shaolin Monastery. At that period (the sixteenth and seventeenth centuries), Shaolin monks specialized in staff-fighting. The staffs they employed, approximately 8.5 feet (2.6 meters) long, were made either of wood or of iron.

Following is a brief passage from the earliest extant manual of Shaolin fighting, *Exposition of the Original Shaolin Staff Method*, which was authored around 1610 by a martial-arts expert named Cheng Zongyou (style: Chongdou). Cheng spent more than ten years at the Shaolin Monastery, studying its staff-method. In the following passage, he sketches the monastery's history, as well as his own experiences there. He also outlines a Shaolin legend, which attributes the monastery's staff-method to a divine being named Jinnaluo (Skt. Kiṃnara). According to this etiological legend, Jinnaluo was incarnated as a lowly menial at the Shaolin Monastery. When the monastery was attacked by bandits, he emerged from its kitchen (where he tended the stove) and, wielding a "divine staff" *(shengun),* warded off the aggressors.—MS

The Shaolin Monastery is named after the Shaoshi Mountain. This mountain is adjacent to the Central Sacred Peak [Mount Song], for which reason the latter is known as Taishi (Big *shi*), whereas the Shaolin [Mountain] is known as Shaoshi (Small *shi*).[1]

During the Taihe reign period (477–499), the Northern Wei emperor, Xiaowendi, founded the monastery for monk Batuo. In the third year of Emperor Xiaomingdi's Xiaochang reign period (527), Bodhidharma (Damo) crossed [the river] eastward.[2] He sat nine years in meditation, facing the Shaoshi cliffs. He left his image, [cast by his shadow,] on the wall. Eminent monks gathered in response, and one after the other translated Bodhidharma's doctrine.

During the Sui dynasty's Kaihuang reign period (581–600), 100 *qing* (approximately 250 acres [100 hectares]) of the Cypress Valley Village's (Baigu tun) lands were bestowed upon the monastery.

During the early Tang period, the [Shaolin] monk Tanzong and his fellows raised troops to fight the usurper [Wang Shichong]. They captured his nephew, Renze, and expressed their loyalty to the Tang dynasty. Emperor Taizong (Li Shimin; r. 627–649) praised their heroic spirit and appointed

Tanzong general. He rewarded all the other [fighting monks] with land. Taizong repeatedly issued imperial letters proclaiming his sympathy to the Shaolin monks and expressing his concern for their well-being. In addition, he bestowed upon the monastery forty *qing* (approximately 100 acres [40 hectares]) of land and a water mill. These constitute to this day the [Cypress] Valley estate.

During the Yuan dynasty's Zhizheng reign period (1341–1367) the Red Troops (Hongjun) revolted. The monastery was badly ravaged by this sect. Luckily, just then somebody came out of the monastery's kitchen and reassured the monks, saying, "You should all be calm. I will ward them off myself." Wielding a divine staff *(shengun)*, he threw himself into the stove. Then, breaking out, he emerged from [the stove], and stood astride Song Mountain and the Imperial Fort (Yuzhai). The Red Troops disintegrated and withdrew.[3]

The monastery's residents marveled at this event. A monk addressed the crowd, saying, "Do you know who drove away the Red Troops? He is the Mahasattva Guanyin (Guanyin dashi), incarnated as King Jin'naluo (Skt. Kiṃnara)." Therefore they wove a wickerwork statue of him, and to this day they continue to practice his [fighting] technique.

Among King Jin'naluo's successors there was a Master Hama, who apparently was similar to him. He transmitted the Buddhist doctrine to Jingtang, and the techniques of hand-combat *(quan)* and staff-fighting *(gun)* to Biandun. The latter once saved someone among the Miao people [in southwest China]. Therefore, the Miao venerated him, and deified him.

I have come to the conclusion that there are no fighting monks *(wuseng)* in the land. Only the Shaolin clerics are worthy of the title ["fighting monks"], for they attend to the protection of the [Buddhist] faith. The Shaolin Monastery is nestled between two mountains: that of culture *(wen)* and that of fighting *(wu)*. Indeed this monastery has transmitted the method of staff-fighting and the doctrines of the Chan sect alike, for which reason scholars throughout the land have always admired it.

Since my youth I was determined to learn the martial arts. Whenever I heard of a famous teacher I wouldn't hesitate to travel far to gain his instruction. Therefore I gathered the necessary travel expenses, and journeyed to the Shaolin Monastery, where I spent, all in all, more than ten years. At first I served Master Hongji, who was tolerant enough to admit me into his class. Even though I gained a sketchy understanding of the [staff]-method's broad outlines, I didn't master it.

At the time Master Hongzhuan was already an old man in his eighties.[4] Nevertheless his staff method was superb, and the monks venerated him the most. Therefore I turned to him as my next teacher, and each day I learned new things I had never heard of before. In addition, I befriended the two Masters Zongxiang and Zongdai, and I gained enormously from practicing with them. Later I met Master Guang'an, one of the best experts in the Buddhist technique. He had inherited Hongzhuan's technique in its entirety, and had even improved upon it. Guang'an tutored me personally, and revealed to me wonderful subtleties. Later I followed him out of the monastery, and we traveled together for several years. The marvelous intricacy of the staff's transformations, the wonderful swiftness of its manipulations—at first I didn't grasp them, but gradually I became familiar and was enlightened. I chose this field as my specialty, and I believe I did have some achievements.

As for archery, riding, and the arts of sword and spear, I paid quite some attention to their investigation as well; however by that time my energy of half a lifetime had already been spent. My great uncle, the military student *(wuxuesheng)* Yunshui, and my nephews Junxin and the National University student *(taixuesheng)* Hanchu had studied with me once at Shaolin. They pointed out that so far the Shaolin staff method had been transmitted orally only, from one Buddhist master to the next. Since I was the first to draw illustrations and compile written formulas for it, they suggested I publish these for the benefit of like-minded friends. At first I declined, saying I wasn't equal to the task. But then illustrious gentlemen from all over the land started commending the supposed merits of my work. They even blamed me for keeping it secret, thereby depriving them. So finally I found some free time, gathered the doctrines handed to me by teachers and friends, and combined these with what I had learned from my own experience. I commissioned an artisan to execute the drawings, and, even though my writing is somewhat vulgar, I added to the left of each drawing a rhyming formula *(gejue)*.

Put together these drawings and formulas constitute a volume, which I titled *Exposition of the Original Shaolin Staff Method.* Just casting a glance at one of the drawings would probably suffice to figure the position depicted therein. Thus the reader will be able to study this method without the aid of a teacher. Despite an apparent simplicity, each sentence captures the secret of victory and defeat, each drawing harbors the essence of movement. Even though staff-fighting is called a trivial art, its explication in this book is the result of strenuous effort.

If this book assists like-minded friends in reaching the other shore, if they rely upon it to strengthen the state and pacify its borders, thereby enhancing the glory of my teachers' methods, then yet another of my goals would be accomplished.

—MS

Notes

1. The word *shi* literally means "chamber" (probably referring to caves in the mountains).

2. That is to say, he came from India to China. Bodhidharma was the first patriarch of Chan (Zen) Buddhism in China.

3. A distance of several miles separates Mount Song from the Imperial Fort. Only a giant of supernormal dimensions could have stood astride both, indicating that inside the blazing stove Jinnaluo underwent a process of transformation. That this is what Cheng Zongyou had in mind is confirmed by other late-Ming sources, which specify that Jinnaluo grew several hundred feet tall. The saint's supernormal dimensions explain why the Red Troops dispersed upon seeing him.

It is possible that Jinnaluo grew into supernormal dimensions following the example of Sun Wukong, the simian protagonist of the Journey to the West cycle (which predates the Jinnaluo legend). Like Jinnaluo, Sun Wukong, who is armed with a magic staff, masters the art of transformation. Here then we have an example of the impact of popular literature (in this instance, the Journey to the West cycle) on monastic lore.

4. A spear-manual attributed to Hongzhuan is available in the seventeenth-century anthology *Record of Hands and Arms (Shou bi lu).*

PROBABLY WRITTEN IN the very last years of the Ming dynasty, "A Handful of Snow" (Yi peng xue) is a dramatic interpretation of events at the Ming court about a century earlier. Yan Shifan, the son of the corrupt minister of state Yan Song, hears of a priceless heirloom jade cup, the eponymous "handful of snow," owned by the aristocrat Mo Huaigu. Mo Huaigu refuses to hand over the cup, and instead has a forgery made to give to Yan. When the forgery is uncovered, Mo Huaigu is arrested. At the last minute, his loyal steward Mo Cheng substitutes himself for his master and is beheaded in his stead. When the head is sent back to the capital to be examined, it arouses suspicion, and the general who oversaw the execution, Qi Jiguang, is interrogated.

In this act (Act 18: "Investigating the Head"), the skull of the beheaded is examined. Tang Qin—a former friend of Mo Huaigu who betrayed him and now works for Yan Shifan—has his suspicions, but after making a deal with Mo's concubine Xueniang, he goes along with the original ruling.

The playwright, Li Yu (ca. 1615–1671), is widely recognized as the most outstanding of the famous Suzhou dramatists who wrote during the Ming-Qing transition period. He was an authority on tunes and musical techniques and was known for his broad learning. Unsuccessful as an official, he channeled his energy toward writing. His early plays (of which "A Handful of Snow" is one) emphasized social status and didacticism, while his later plays (after the collapse of the Ming in 1644) are more given to heroism and realism.—TL

(LU BING *in cap and belt*, SERVANT *following, enters.*)
LU BING (*To the tune of "Striding to the Moon"*):

> In my unicorn robes billowing colored silk, gold seal hanging from my elbow,
> I don't admire even a giant of letters.
> Coldly holding to the rigor of the law, I accept no bribes.
> Mercy like spring rain and justice like fall frost all come from my hands.

The anthill thinks Mount Tai lowly; things are topsy-turvy just like this. I might as well heartily drink of fine wine, and know nothing of the situation at court or in the country.

I am Lu Bing, the Commander of the Imperial Bodyguard.[1] I administer punishments and am in charge of the military outfits of the Six Ministries. Wielding the law, the Five Chief Military Commissions are under my jurisdiction.

Steely-faced, inspiring fear, who cares if the people involved are from princely and powerful families? Armed with awe-inspiring Imperial proclamations, all I do is uphold the power like lightning that strikes and thunder that destroys. Single-mindedly I obey Xiao He's law,[2] so that all the nations might know the emperor's power.

Today I have received an imperial command that there was a mistake with Chamberlain Mo's head. We have seized and interrogated Regional Commander Qi. I think it's a terrible outrage that Mo Wuhuai—over something as small as a jade cup—butted heads with the Yan family, to the point of getting executed.

Moreover, it ended up implicating innocents, and got increasingly vicious. Alas! Could I Lu Bing agree to a false verdict—a "Perhaps it was so"[3]—and bear a terrible reputation for ten thousand generations to come?

It is only that the command orders it, so I will question them, and get this affair settled. Tell the standardbearers, and have them bring in Commander Qi and others together.

(*All assent.* SERVANT *carries a bucket and leads forth* QI JIGUANG *and* XUEYAN *in chains.*)

QI JIGUANG (*To the tune of "Facing the River Plum"*):

My total sincerity Heaven knows;
Slandered, what shame is there in bearing lotus seeds?[4]

XUEYAN:

That loyal soul in the Nine Plains[5] I have sworn to follow;
To repay him in my heart with one death,
My name will be preserved for eternity.

SERVANT (*Calls out*): Accused gentleman, enter; accused lady, face the judge.

(QI JIGUANG *looks at* LU BING *and bows politely but does not kneel.* LU BING *stands.*)

LU BING: Please bring the sagely proclamation forward.

(SERVANT *supports proclamation with both hands.* QI JIGUANG *weeps and kneels.*)

QI JIGUANG: Oh! His Sageliness!

All the blood in my chest
And the steel at my waist
Will protect forever the gold cup of a homeland, to keep it whole.
This lonely loyalty honors the emperor's palace.
With the virtue of Su Wu,[6]
With the tongue of Changshan,[7]
Once my work for this fertile soil is done, I will have filled a box with accusations,
I beseech the perspicuity of the emperor for punishing thunder and cleansing snow.

(*He kneels.*)

LU BING: Bring the Imperial Pronouncement. (*They all assent.* SERVANT *dressed in a plain black robe enters, along with* TANG QIN *in an official cap and belt and* YAN'S LIEUTENANT *in military garb.*) Will it be rain and dew from the highest level of heaven, warmth of three springs; or a road of wind and frost, and a summer cold spell?

SERVANT: According to the command we got from Your Lordship, we have brought Registrar Tang and the general who originally captured Mo Huaigu to investigate and examine the head.

(TANG QIN *goes through the procedure for participating in court proceedings.* YAN'S LIEUTENANT *kowtows.*)

SERVANT: To answer your lordship, we will quickly perform the examination, and report back with a decision on the punishment.

LU BING: Understood. You two can stay for the interrogation. The steward can go for now.

SERVANT: Yes.

To uncover a criminal needs some art.
To bring a secret to life one must be like a god.

(*Exits.* LU BING *sits.*)

LU BING: Qi Jiguang, do you admit your crime?

QI JIGUANG: I received a commission for an important feudatory, a carved bamboo tally for a vital border area.

I let loose arrows that shocked like lightning.
That chaotic brutal wind gave rise to white feathered darts.

Wielding a spear, I turned back the sun,

My valiant accomplishments gave glory to my home.

I claim the achievement of opening up lands on the frontier; I have not had the disaster of killing generals or losing troops. I dare not crow over my achievements, but I have no reason to admit any guilt.

LU BING: How could you release the criminal Mo Huaigu, kill under false pretenses someone innocent, substitute this false head, and trick the court?

QI JIGUANG: Whether Mo Huaigu was guilty I do not dare to argue on his behalf. It will all come out by itself eventually. But how could I with only passing knowledge of Mo Huaigu entrap myself to death? Sir, please keep in mind Qi Jiguang!

(To the tune of "New Lad from Liangzhou.")

Swearing loyalty like the one at Juyang,[8]

Reporting my achievements like that Huaiyin,[9]

How could I deceive like that Chen Ping who tricked Chu?

LU BING: On that day was there anyone else who was overseeing the beheading?

*(*TANG QIN *faces* YAN'S LIEUTENANT.)*

TANG QIN: Tell us why he wasn't executed immediately after his capture, and why a night elapsed.

YAN'S LIEUTENANT: I oversaw the beheading. When we got him that night, Qi Jiguang refused to behead him immediately, so we postponed it one night. On the next day he was taken out, bound. In fact one couldn't distinguish him clearly.

QI JIGUANG: Alas! On that day, all the troops saw him. And moreover you

Oversaw it with your eyes wide open.

With that official order, you personally took charge of the bagged-up head.

TANG QIN: The top of Chamberlain Mo's head used to have three tiers, and at the back of his head there was a bump like a fist, and all of this was known well by the Registrar. *(Points at the head.)* Now the top of the head is pointed, and the back of the head smooth—is it not that the head is false?

QI JIGUANG: Woe! According to what you say, Chamberlain Mo must have had three heads and six arms; how could we prove anything to you? It's all

Capturing the wind, and grabbing at shadows.

It's slandering, and spraying people with poison.

Wrongly accusing the innocent, you have rejected all government structure.

TANG QIN: Chamberlain Mo originally wanted to flee to you, and then he just happened to fall into your hands. That would precisely be according to a treacherous plot.

QI JIGUANG: Could it be that on the road there was no one familiar with him?

You would have it so that a shadow of a snake in a cup would have to be pursued.

Mistaking the couple in the cart for ghosts, would you pull your bow and wrongly incriminate people?

LU BING: Bring Xueyan over here. Whether the head is real, and whether it's truly your master, you certainly can tell. Tell us now, and if you should lie, I shall use torture.

Examining these dead bones,

Testing out that live mouth.

Tell us the truth and do not delay.

Can the law

Be so lightly spared?

XUEYAN: My lord! Oh me! *(To the above tune.)*

In life together imprisoned,

Torture follows the cangue and handcuffs I wear.

Painfully I gaze at the hungry blade, but there is no one to save me.

(Pointing at YAN'S LIEUTENANT.*)* It's just this general here. If he has some

Slight suspicions,

Before the torture starts, may he raise up the spears and lances.

TANG QIN: It's hardly even a few scraps of bone now.

XUEYAN: For other people it's all guesswork. But I shared a bed with him; could it be that I would not know him? My lord, my master never had a three-tiered head. *(Clutching the head and weeping.)* Just these

Bones I shared a blanket with,

Skull I shared a pillow with,

I will cleave to you through nine deaths.

TANG QIN: My Lord, this is a case of

Slick talk which disputed is still treacherous plots.

But I didn't know that the law could be softened like melted iron.

LU BING: It seems that we must still carefully examine it, and not hold to a single person's perspective and implicate innocents.

Although the law is set up,

We must accommodate circumstance.

How can we bear to use harsh tortures and not shine some light into the overturned bowl of injustice?

Real and fake,

We must investigate carefully.

SERVANT *(As* COMMANDANT *enters):* The imperial proclamation has arrived. *(*LU BING *kneels.)* Charioteer Shang's crime is not pardoned. Lu Bing, the Commander of the Imperial Body-guard, is ordered to report after his immediate execution.

*(*LU BING *expresses thanks for the emperor's grace and stands.)*

LU BING: Take each of the criminals back to the wings for now; when I return from overseeing this beheading, I will return to interrogate them.

*(*SERVANT *responds.)*

LU BING *(To* YAN'S LIEUTENANT*):* Before in Jizhou you watched the beheading; now come with me to see someone tied up and killed.

YAN'S LIEUTENANT: Yes.

LU BING:

Before it is asked for, the Duke of Huaiyin's head has been presented,

At the banks of the marsh. Qu Yuan's soul responds to its summons.

*(*YAN'S LIEUTENANT *and* SERVANT *exit.)*

SERVANT: Lord Qi and Lord Tang are ordered to return to the wings.

TANG QIN: I'm not disappearing anywhere; I'm just going to wait here.

QI JIGUANG: Supreme loyalty for days and days attracts the notice of both foreign and native; with *qi* regulating ice and frost, heaven and earth know.

(Exits with SERVANT. XUEYAN *weeps.* TANG QIN *looks at* XUEYAN *and imitates her gestures.)*

TANG QIN *(To the above tune):*

I spy on her pretty looks, exceptionally tender and shy;

Moreover her loneliness is to be endured with me.

Old Mo is dead, and we never need mention him again. And even if he isn't dead,

He's fled for his life with no time to spare.

Will you be able to embrace his blanket and bedclothes again?

(Looks around and then says to her) Miss Xue, Miss Xue, the head is dead. Why do you weep over it?

(She does not respond.)

TANG QIN: Do you want to live?

XUEYAN: A perfectly good life—why shouldn't I want to live?

TANG QIN: But your life depends entirely on

My lightly flapping tongue

With its deceiving, keen lips.

The road to life or death can fork sharply.

XUEYAN: Even forgetting your friendship of yore with my master, you would still want to pre-serve the law of heaven. One person has already died, and now you want to harm us!

TANG QIN: People nowadays care nothing for old friendships—much less for the law of heaven. It's just that if I say the head is real, you live. If I say it's fake, even a plain old death sentence isn't a certainty. If I even hint at this, you won't be allowed to live.

XUEYAN: If you just go along for a word, that would be your own hidden virtue.

To be pardoned to life and excused from death I rely on your virtuous lordship,

By engraving it in bone and inscripting it in my heart I would repay your virtue.

TANG QIN: To speak about gratitude is just empty, useless words. If you just do what I say on one matter, then I'll save your two lives.

XUEYAN: What matter?

TANG QIN *(Singing quietly):*

Wenjun was widowed,

Xiangru played the lute.[10]

It truly is that

The god of marriage has long decided who will be paired.

If you should agree,

I'll open up a way for you to live.

XUEYAN *(Sings in an aside to the above tune):*

The pity that a young beauty should have sworn to die and been left to the mercy of fate!

If I put off this beast, disaster will touch my living friend.

TANG QIN: Don't be suspicious. Whether you are willing or unwilling will decide for me.

XUEYAN: I fear

Receiving the mockery of others

Carrying my lute into another's boat.

TANG QIN: Mockery is empty. Death is real. Don't get the wrong idea.

XUEYAN: All right! All right! I just want you to use

A word to break the shackles of prison,

A phrase to answer heaven.

And what need is there for me to feel sorrow for the green, green willow?[11]

TANG QIN: I'll say it; just don't you regret anything.

XUEYAN: What kind of talk is that?

My golden word is worth a mountain.

If I should go back on it, then let the sword fall down!

TANG QIN *(Jumps around):* That's as it should be! Great! Great!

XUEYAN: You swear an oath. It would be good if you could vindicate me in one shot.

TANG QIN: Don't get suspicious, miss. *(Kneeling to heaven.)* I, Tang Qin,

> Do deeply bow,
>
> Do earnestly swear:
>
> If I go back on my word, I will truly be a beast.
>
> Let the sword fall,
>
> And my head part from my body.

> *(LU BING enters; YAN'S LIEUTENANT and SERVANT follow.)*

> Right after leaving the prison where breath is cut out of the body,
>
> We've returned to where souls are summoned.

(SERVANT enters with QI JIGUANG in tow.)

LU BING: General, come here. On that earlier occasion, you oversaw the beheading; how does it compare with what you just saw?

YAN'S LIEUTENANT: Yes, that was just the way I saw him tied up and executed.

LU BING: I would say only the binding was set. You saw it from afar, but when you originally saw him bound you were facing him. Could it be that the person you saw the next night you did not recognize?

QI JIGUANG: With respect to your honor, though I was a friend of Mo Huaigu, could it be that the general's word could be bought? If I die what regret will I have, when I'll surely return as an avenging ghost?

LU BING: Don't be rash. I still need to review this matter carefully. Registrar Tang, come here. This is no small matter—three lives hang on this moment. You should identify him again.

TANG QIN: I've been pondering over this also. He was tied up and beheaded right before the general—that's the case, no question. But the contours of the skull are slightly different. It's probably the case that the living man's tendons and bones were stretched out, and after death they all contracted. *(To the tune of "Each Section Tall.")*

> Carefully exploring the real situation.
>
> Expend some hesitation.
>
> Perhaps it's that the bones and tendons have shrunk and do not look as they used to.

QI JIGUANG:

> The point of suspicion is past;
>
> The cause of uncertainty is resolved.
>
> A longstanding grievance is broken open.

XUEYAN:

> In life and after death, there was no error.
>
> I expect the net of the law to open and expand, and waves of mercy to descend.

> *(Together.)*

> A bright mirror hung on high, shining into the darkness.
>
> Spring returns and the rains wet the dried dead trees.

LU BING: The overseer of the beheading was not mistaken; he corroborates what the general saw. The skull was not mistaken—it has passed through the Registrar's careful examination. And now there is nothing more to say on the matter. *(He writes.) (To the above tune.)*

> This humble official examined the beheaded criminal,
>
> Went to the root of the matter.
>
> I detained the people, acted according to the law, and personally oversaw everything.

The head was again impounded;
Its frame had shrunk.
It's not false—
Not one differed from this opinion by a word.
(Together.)
From now on this enmity will be crossed through with a pen.
We hear the golden rooster holding in its beak announcement of an amnesty, and passing
along the drip of the lotus waterclock.

LU BING: Let us hold it for now, and wait for the imperial reply to decide its outcome.

QI JIGUANG: Yes.

LU BING:
I have held fairly to the law of the land, and my conscience is clear.

QI JIGUANG:
I have relied on heaven's sun to shine on dirt and impurity.
(Together.)
Standing on our tiptoes we've seen
The power of thunder and lightning turned into the flow of the rain.

(LU BING exits.)

TANG QIN *(To* SERVANT): Take Miss Xue to stay elsewhere. Don't let her stay with Commander
Qi.

(SERVANT assents.)

Envoi

QI JIGUANG:
The gentleman just relies on righteousness.

XUEYAN:
Life and death are to be awaited without any shame.

TANG QIN:
In all matters preserve good will,
It makes it easier to meet up again later.

—TL

Notes

1. Lu Bing was a historical figure who was a son of Emperor Shizong's wet-nurse.

2. Xiao He was a minister of the Western Han who codified its laws. Later, "Xiao He's law" came to stand for the law in general.

3. The Song official Qin Gui (*jinshi* 1115) condemned the patriot Yue Fei (1103–1141) with the words *"Moxu you"* (Perhaps it was [so]). Although he lacked documentary evidence of Yue Fei's treachery, Qin Gui used these words to suggest Yue Fei's crimes. Few can now understand the grammatical and lexical properties of these three syllables, but they are still used today as a single unit (often with an adjectival ending, hence *moxuyou de*) that conveys the meaning "baseless, groundless, trumped-up, fabricated."

4. Reference to a Han-dynasty general who transported a cartful of lotus seeds but was accused of having stolen a whole cartful of pearls.

5. The Nine Plains were the traditional burial site of the nobles of the Warring State of Jin; the reference here is to Mo Cheng, the dead and buried steward.

6. A Han-dynasty emissary to the Huns, Su Wu spent nineteen years in captivity without faltering in loyalty.

7. During the An Lushan Rebellion (755–763), Yan Gaoqing, the Prefect of Taishan (or Changshan), was defeated, but refused to submit, instead unceasingly shouting insults at the rebel. Before he was executed, he had his tongue sliced off.

8. In the Tang dynasty, the rebel An Lushan besieged the city of Juyang; the loyal general there held on until death.

9. Han Xin, the right-hand man of Liu Bang (247–195 B.C.E.), the founder of the Han dynasty, was enfeoffed Duke of Huaiyin.

10. A reference to the most famous remarried widow in Chinese literature, Zhuo Wenjun, who fell in love with the poet Sima Xiangru (179–117 B.C.E.).

11. An allusion to the Tang short story "The Tale of Miss Liu" (Liushi zhuan), the green willow refers to remarriage.

THE REQUIEM *(JIWEN)* began in ancient China as a performative text accompanying the rites of sacrifice and libation to the dead. The importance of the genre may be seen from the fact that, in the Tang period, writers from minor clans depended on fees for such writings to meet their living expenses. The present piece, written by an obscure member of the literati, contains a moving portrait of a three-year-old girl. The grieving father (Shen Cheng; 1588?–1624), recalling all the details of her innocent wiles and revelries, her little games and amusing mimicries, has succeeded in making her the most fully realized child in traditional Chinese literature.—PYW

On the twenty-third day of the Eleventh Month of the *jiwei* year in the Wanli reign (1619) the eldest daughter Azhen of Shen Cheng died of complications from smallpox. She was temporarily interred in North Cemetery. Her mother, Madame Bo, chanted Buddhist scriptures daily in the hope of gaining blessings in the afterlife for her. In addition, she urged me to write a plea for her, but I could not for some time bear to touch the pen. On the third seventh day[1] of my daughter's death, having prepared food for offering to her, I wrote the following as a way of mourning for her. The text would be burned on the playground where she used to romp.

Alas, what a sad occasion! You were named Azhen because you were born in the year *bingchen* (1616). The character *zhen* was a combination of *bing* and *chen*. When you were born I was not pleased. A man over thirty wanted a son, not a daughter. But you won me over before you had completed your first year. Even then you would respond with giggles each time I made a face at you. You were then cared for by nurse Zhou. Whenever you became hungry, you were brought to your mother to be suckled. After you were fed, your nurse would carry you back to her room. As she had to get up many times during the night, she stayed in her day clothes all night. Because of you, she went through a great deal of hardship. Your mother would be angered if you were brought to her too often, but you would cry if your wish was not immediately gratified.

Last year, *wuwu* (1618), was a bad year for me. As I had to leave for the examinations, I parted from you reluctantly several times. Nurse Zhou died, and I failed my examinations. When I came home you greeted me by holding on to my sleeves and demanding gifts of toys. With you by my side my unhappiness was relieved. As you grew more teeth, you became more intelligent. Addressing your parents, you pronounced the words "dad" and "mom" perfectly. You often knocked on the door and then quickly went inside and asked, "Who is there?" When my nephew came you called him "brother." He teased you by pretending to snatch your toys; you darted and dashed away. When your mother's younger brother came, you seized him by his jacket while gleefully shouting, "Mom! mom!" When your uncle [my older brother] came you acted the part of host. Holding up a wine cup, you invited your honored guest to drink. Everybody burst out laughing. After you were born your grandfather went to the country and then you went to Suzhou. As a result you had not seen each other for more than a year. When you two met again you were asked if you knew who he was. Without hesitation you responded, "By his white hat and white beard I know he is my granddad." Your maternal grandfather you had never seen before. As soon as you saw him for the first time you pronounced that he came from Peking. Your maternal grandmother loved you as if you had been her own child. Several times she took you back with her to Suzhou. There in the middle of the night you would ask her for toys, and at dawn you would demand fruit. When your parents wanted to keep you home you refused, turning to me and saying, "Granny will miss me." In the Sixth Month of this year you developed a skin rash. I went to Suzhou to bring you home. You kept on rubbing the troubled spots and looked sad. But you dared not cry, thinking that crying would displease us. Every time you reached for fruit or candy you always watched the reaction of your parents. You would not put the food into your mouth unless there was a sign of approval. During your play sometimes you injured your hand. Your little eyes would glower at the wound, but you would hide your hand when you saw adults approaching. Your mother was too strict. From time to time she would discipline you for fear that your habits would be carried into adulthood. Although I agreed with her, I said to her when you were not around, "A little child cannot be expected to know right and wrong. Let her be until she is a little older."

When you were still in Suzhou your parents were about to return home to Loudong. You were asked whether you would go back with them. You couldn't make up your mind. When you did come back I was overwhelmed with joy. We played together—I taunted you and surprised you, and you would play along by feinting dumb. You carried jujubes in a small basket and sipped porridge in a low chair. Sometimes you recited the *Great Learning* while bowing to Amituofo.[2] Sometimes you would play a guessing game with me, and the winner would chase the loser around the house. When you finally caught me you laughed jubilantly and clapped your hands. Who would have believed that not quite half a month later you would breathe your last? Was it decreed by Heaven, or was it simply fate? Who could fathom the mystery? When you were stricken I sent for the doctors. Some said you had measles; others believed it was the flu. It did not seem to be the flu, and it may have been measles. Looking back, I still cannot understand what happened. You had always been an articulate child, but then you could not talk. Your voice was gone and you could hardly breathe. You could do nothing but open and shut your eyes. The family surrounded you and wept, and tears also flowed from your eyes. Alas, it is too painful to say any more!

It is the way of the world that one does not weep over the death of a daughter. But a man like me, who is still poor and friendless in his prime, should be content to have only daughters. He should have been happy to have a daughter as intelligent as you. Who would have expected the gods to treat me so cruelly! Ten days before you were stricken your sister Axun, younger than you by two years, came down with the same illness. Three days after she died you were also gone.

Now that you no longer have playmates, you should at least have the company of your sister, whom you knew well. You can walk now, but she is still unsteady on her feet. Hold her by the hand wherever you go. Be nice to her and compete not! If you meet again your nurse, ask her to guide you to your father's first wife, Madame Gu, and his mother, Madame Min. They will take you girls in. That was why I had you temporarily interred next to Gu. She will look after you, while you must take good care of your baby sister. In the future I shall choose a plot and make a permanent resting place for all of you.

I have been thinking of you all the time. If you know how much I miss you you will come back, again and again, in my dreams. If fate permits, be reborn as my next child. For such hopes I am sending you a copy of the *Diamond Sutra* as well as other books of spells and incantations. There are also offerings of meat and paper money for your use. When you see the King of the Underworld kneel down with raised hands and plead for mercy. Say the following to him: "Although I die young, I am truly guiltless. I was born into a poor family, and I never complained about the hardships. Fearing the God of Thunder, I never wasted even a grain of rice. I have always worn my simple clothes with care. I am too young to bring suitable gifts for Your Majesty. Please have pity on me and shield me from the exactions of ghosts."[3] Just say the words to him and don't cry or make noises. You must not forget that the Underworld is different from home.

I am writing this but you cannot read. I shall call your name and let you know that your father is here. Azhen, Azhen, your sad father is mourning you.

—PYW

Notes

1. Chinese funeral ceremonies customarily extended for seven seven-day periods.
2. In her innocent ignorance she mixed a Confucian text with a Buddhist divinity.
3. It was, and still is, believed by the Chinese that the Underworld is ruled by a bureaucracy ever ready to exact gifts and bribes from the new entrants.

IN THE FIRST DECADES of what we call the seventeenth century, the Ming, founded in 1368, was an old dynasty beset by many problems: ineffectual emperors, bureaucratic corruption and factionalism, an outmoded revenue system, a disgruntled military sector, and, consequently, lack of success in dealing with ever more serious challenges from rebel movements in the heartland and bellicose Manchus on the northeastern frontier. In 1644 a rebel army seized the main capital, Beijing, where the current emperor committed suicide. Taking advantage of the chaotic situation in North China, the Manchus penetrated a key pass in the Great Wall, defeated the rebels, and claimed the right to rule China under their own Qing dynasty.

There ensued almost twenty years of conflict between advancing Manchu-Qing forces (composed increasingly of surrendered native Chinese armies) and forces led by officials and imperial clansmen who remained loyal to the Ming dynasty. A series of Ming resistance courts were set up in the southern provinces (and even in Burma), to be eliminated one by one under relentless Qing campaigns until the last fugitive Ming court was destroyed and the last Ming claimant was executed in 1661–1662.

Zhang Kentang was one among many Ming officials who adhered staunchly to a Confucian creed of loyalty to the state under which one had lived as an adult, and especially under which one had been privileged to serve in office. This creed had grown more absolute among the political elite since the Song resistance to the Jurchen and Mongol "barbarians" in the twelfth through thirteenth centuries. In 1625 Zhang had passed the highest civil service examination and thereafter had risen in the bureaucratic ranks from district magistrate, to censor in the capital, to regional inspector for Fujian Province, to governor of that province. In 1645, when the Ming resistance court in the auxiliary capital, Nanjing, collapsed under Qing attack, Zhang helped to establish a successor court under the Ming prince of Tang in Fujian, while at the same time loyalists in Zhejiang Province, to the north, also rallied around another scion of the Ming imperial line, the prince of Lu. Zhang labored mightily in a number of concurrent, high positions to extend the sway of the Fujian court into the central provinces. But he was hampered by the obstructionism of a regional warlord—of the ilk that inexorably gained control of all the loyalist regimes. Specifically, Zhang led a naval contingent which was to spearhead a concerted campaign to recover Jiangnan, but the warlord blocked any follow-through, and Zhang's flotilla was left waiting on islands off the Zhejiang coast while the situation in Fujian went from bad to worse.

In 1646 both the Zhejiang and Fujian courts were wiped out by the Manchus, and many supporters who refused to surrender or collaborate resorted to living in remote coastal enclaves or on coastal islands, such as those on which Zhang Kentang already was stationed in the Zhoushan Archipelago (see maps). Taking up residence in the walled city of Wengzhou on Dai Island, Zhang tried to persuade another naval warlord who dominated that maritime region to coordinate with the remnant loyalists forces of the prince of Lu from Zhejiang—to no avail. The coastal loyalist element remained fragmented while the Qing built up its naval capability on Hangzhou Bay and at the mouth of the Yangtze River. That buildup eventually led to Qing campaigns on the offshore islands to clear up sites, such as Wengzhou, of collusion between loyalists and renegade militarists, beginning in the autumn of 1651.

Zhang, having foreseen this inevitability, attained especially glowing martyrdom by committing suicide with his whole household—except his young grandson, Zhang Maozi—as the invading soldiers approached. The *Record of Life beyond My Due (Yusheng lu)* is Maozi's written recollection of how, and statement of belief on why, he survived the massacre of Wengzhou and the dreadful hardships that befell him afterward.

Zhang Maozi was not alone in recording his experiences during the Qing conquest. The seventeenth century is remarkable for the number and variety of diaries, memoirs, and other autobiographical writings that were generated by a combination of several factors: rising literacy, the popularization of a philosophy that stressed individual thoughts and feelings, unprecedented political struggles, and both natural and man-made calamities, such as widespread epidemics and protracted warfare. But Maozi's account is unusual in its vividness and in the intensity of emotion expressed with mastery by such a young writer—the *Yusheng lu* having been written when the author was only eighteen years old.

It also is notable for exhibiting several characteristics of autobiographical memory, particularly memory of traumatic events. We see that the rememberer is very concerned—one might say obsessed—with reconciling senseless experiences with his perceived role in life, with fitting otherwise inexplicably unjust occurrences into both a self-schema and a cosmic schema. Only then can he be psychologically reconciled with what has happened. For a fatherless only grandson in a prominent upper-class family of Maozi's culture and era, self and cosmos were united especially strongly in filiality, that is, the sacred duty to fulfill the life-giving impulses of Heaven and Earth by reverencing and perpetuating one's male family line (the patriline). Also, in an overwhelmingly

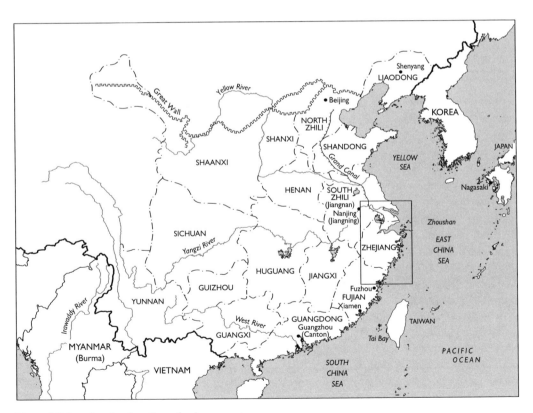

Map of China showing location of enlargement

Detail showing the Zhoushan Archipelago

agricultural civilization such as that of premodern China, identification of one's patriline with a certain place—with the family fields and especially the ancestral graveyard—had been emblematic of the landholding class since ancient times.

Whatever purely physical illness Maozi suffered after his release from prison, it is clear from the standpoint of present-day psychotherapy that he also was fraught with "survivor guilt" and other symptoms of what we now call posttraumatic syndrome. In his mind, horrifying caricatures of things that have shocked his psychosomatic system are as though on perpetual automatic replay, until something occurs that helps him give positive meaning to it all. Having "realized" why he has been put through such trials, Maozi recalls each instance of wishing he had died with his family as a virtual incantation which activated the cosmic powers that sustained him.

We enter Maozi's memoir near the beginning, having learned that his father died in the fateful year of 1644. We also have learned that in the next year, as the security of Jiangnan became imperiled, Maozi, then eleven, and his mother had been escorted by a member of this official family's personal guard, Adjutant Ru Yingyuan, from the ancestral home in Huating (to the east of Tai Lake in the rich Yangtze Delta) to Fujian Province to join the family patriarch, Zhang Kentang. But after less than another year, the resistance regime of the prince of Tang was destroyed. Maozi, his mother, and the rest of his grandfather's household had to flee the mainland and join Zhang Kentang, along with many loyalists from Zhejiang and Fujian, on the Zhoushan Archipelago— which became for many of them a last refuge.—LS

A Record of Life beyond My Due

In 1646, Grandfather was summoned to Wengzhou to plot strategy with former commanders and others who were supporting the prince of Lu. Not long after that, [the diehard resistance in] Fujian collapsed, and Grandfather bared his sword intending to cut his own throat. I was in a state of panic, when Master Ru came to Grandfather's study and spoke with him. For a long time I heard nothing, but finally Grandfather said, in noble resignation, "I am a high official, so I should not die merely as would a [private] individual." He further said, "The Zhang family has only one grandson." Then it seemed that Master Ru replied, "Leave the matter to me." The following day I suddenly heard that Master Ru had left for Luojia[1] to live as a Buddhist monk.

After that, Grandfather was at Wengzhou for six years, during which he constructed a pavilion with "Snowy Union" written on its entrance plaque.[2] Sometimes when he returned there from his outer office, he would lift his head and gaze upward. Before his left thumb could loosen his belt, he would stamp his foot and sigh deeply. Or he would stay there alone talking to himself, standing up and pacing around. Or he would write long letters and seal them firmly before giving them to a messenger. When a report would arrive from somewhere, he again would gnash his teeth in anger and then sigh as he burned it.

When I would come back from our family school to wish Grandfather well, I would see this and think it odd. So I brought it up with my teacher, Master Song, who said, "My son, what you've noted is your grandfather discussing certain plans that are not carried out, conferring on the appointment of certain men who then are not made use of, recommending cooperation or noncooperation with, punishments or rewards for, certain figures and then having his advice come to naught." At that time, I didn't know what "certain plans" or "certain men" my teacher was referring to, but I do now.

Regularly, when Grandfather was in the company of my grandmothers [his four concubines], he would say softly to them, "If the day comes when there's an incident, I alone will die. You should look out for yourselves." But they would respond in unison, "If our lord were determined to die, we would be capable of going first." Wengzhou, of course, was like a feeble mantis praying before the maw of a powerful whale, and the second day of the ninth month of 1651 eventually came.

Oh, do I still dare tell of when that day actually arrived?—when thunderous explosions rent the earth, and clouds of black smoke engulfed the city wall, when so many submitted their documents in surrender or hid themselves after opening the gates? While others were in pandemonium looking for ways to save their own lives, Grandfather sat in the Pavilion of Snowy Union, adjusted his cap and robe, and lifted his pen to compose a final poem. He called me before him and, pointing to the name-plaque of the pavilion, said, "This is where my waters are stilled. Only because it would not have been right for me, a high official, to end my life merely as a private individual [have I delayed suicide until now]. But you must not die; you must remain and continue the Zhang family line."

He then pulled out a length of silk and looped it over the center beam. Just as the dust on that beam stirred, a shout arrived that Grandfather's disciple Su Zhaoren . . . had hanged himself in the outer corridor. Probably they had long planned for that day. Grandfather again righted his cap and dashed back to the main building, calling out, "Wait a bit for me!" There, my concubine-grandmothers, Mesdames Fang, Zhou, Qiang, and Bi,[3] as well as my mother, Dame Shen, and my little sister, Maoqi, had already vied to go ahead of one another in hanging themselves, one by one, with lengths of silk they had torn. Grandfather faced south, kowtowed, and returned to the silk noose on the pavilion's center beam. Oh, can I still bear to tell of it? His male and female servants all cut off their breath by casting themselves into the well. Altogether, twenty-seven people followed my grandfather in death.

At the time I could only pace back and forth, tugging at my grandfather's robe and pulling on my mother's sleeve in complete loss of my whole world. Though Grandfather had orderd me not to die, I certainly did not wish to live. My own length of silk was already knotted when Adjutant Lin Zhican and his younger brother Lin Guiqu bundled me away. A troop of renegade soldiers turned to look at us, and in that moment I lost track of Zhican and his group. I only saw blood from people's heads and arms spurting all over my body.[4] Falling amidst the grasses in a weedy slough, I said, "This is the death of me!" But then I thought to myself, "It would have been better to die beside Grandfather and Mother than die here."

My hair afloat, I looked up and found that I'd been seized by a soldier, and again I thought to myself, "It would have been better to die beside Grandfather and Mother." But the soldier left after taking my armlet—one that my mother, with an intention I hadn't understood—previously had instructed me to always wear and never set aside. The soldiers who arrived after that had no such prize to take, so they stripped me bare. Bound straight up by my clothes being taken off, top and bottom, I couldn't readily get away. But then somehow I was released, completely naked. As another soldier approached, I said to myself that I surely would die. But, on the contrary, that soldier, as though pitying me, said, "Can you help me heft this sack?"

He tossed me a tattered bag to cover my body and had me follow him, saying, "We can't go by way of the gate; if we do, I'll lose my sack and you your life. Now we have to leap the city wall"— which was thirty feet (nine meters) high. Again, I thought to myself how much better it would have been to die beside Grandfather and Mother. But then—don't ask me how—I made it down without injury and, moreover, managed to carry that sack and wade across the moat to the southern outskirts of town, amidst a great din of killing and flight.

The soldier, again, led me into the grass around the edge of the moat, and at sunset we reached the Daolong Shrine. The soldier pointed to a place in the back of the shrine and told me to lie low there, that he was letting me go. At the time I didn't understand why he was treating me so generously. Now I realize that the soldier was a southerner—one in what's called the Green Standard Army—and thus was always humiliated by Eight-Banner soldiers [who would take his booty].[5] In order to protect his sack of loot, he protected me.

The other soldiers camping in the shrine, who spied out and pursued refugees as though they were rabbits, did not bed down until well after dark. Two other people who were hiding with me in the same place planned a joint escape. Altogether, in one valiant, swift move, we scaled the wall. But halfway over, I knocked loose a tile, which sounded an alarm as it fell. The soldiers all got up and conducted a big search. Suddenly a huge cat came down from the eave, bringing with it another loose tile that made the same sound. The soldiers said, "It's just the cat," and discontinued their search.

So up I went again over the wall and scurried a distance of one or two miles. From afar I saw what seemed to be a river and headed toward it. The others who had been hiding with me [in the back of the shrine] had halted by a sandbank. They said, "This is the shore of East River. If we wade across fast, perhaps we'll survive." At that hour the night tide was at full flow, the waves were high, and the riverbanks were far apart. So I thought to myself, "This is no mere moat. If I wade into this I'll die; if I don't, I'll die anyway. It would have been better to die beside Grandfather and Mother than to die like this." Suddenly a large bamboo log came floating downstream, so I used it to get across.

But then the wild grass became so tall that I didn't know where I was. Thorny brambles came in on me like ten thousand knives and a thousand arrowheads, and flowing blood covered my feet. So I took off the crude sack that had been hiding my nakedness and used it to step on, picking the sack up and laying it down over and over. As I drew near the foot of a hill, the east was turning light. It was the third day of the month.

I entered a small hermitage where the monk comforted me with some gruel. But, while the bowl felt real in my hands, the gruel seemed unreal to me. The monk said that Xie Beach was not far away, so I followed him there on the double and reached the home of an old acquaintance, Zhang Linbo. As we shook hands, I felt disoriented as though in a dream. I thought about having no way to inquire about the souls of my grandfather and mother, and I wondered, as a grandson and son with some modicum of conscience, having fled far from them to save my own life, how I could bear up for even twenty-four hours.

After several days, word came that when soldiers entered the Pavilion of Snowy Union, seeing a radiance issuing from my grandfather's clothing and a lifelike color in his face, they all fell prostrate in astonishment and did not dare to go near. On a subsequent day I learned that the Qing Grand Marshal, pursuing fugitives, had reached Putuo, where a monk named Wufan came out and, bowing deeply, entreated the commander, saying, "I formerly was a commander myself under Grand Secretary Zhang, but I resigned and became a monk six years ago. At the time, knowing that the Grand Secretary surely would die [rather than surrender or flee], I promised him that I would take care of his remains." The Qing Grand Marshal said angrily, "If he had deserved to die, then why should you now want to bury him?" and he ordered that the monk be bound, naked, and threatened with a knife. But the monk, unmoved, said, "A good man does not lamely try to prolong his life. Would you still be angry if I stuck out my neck [for beheading] after the burial is done?" The whole array of advisers to the Grand Marshal sighed in amazement at how exceptional the monk was. So the commander told him, "You knew that your leader was determined to die, and indeed, he hanged himself with his whole family. I have already explicitly ordered the troops not to abuse his remains. I hereupon permit you to go and bury him." And so it was done.[6]

[Upon hearing this,] I said in anguish, "That must have been Master Ru Yingyuan. How distressing! What I as a grandson was unable to do, Master Ru risked his life to accomplish. How can I go on living?" Moreover, after a while I heard sounds of refugees being rounded up in the vicinity, so I took leave of Zhang Linbo, saying, "It would have been better to follow Grandfather and Mother in death. If I keep hiding here I'll implicate you." I went out and turned myself in to an administrator named Qiao, who took pity on me. But on the twenty-eighth, an order arrived from the supreme commander that I be remanded for interrogation. I was placed in a watertight compartment of a troop ship, tied with other prisoners—two on either end of a several-foot length of rope—so that four men all had to sit or lie down together. When we cried out ceaselessly in hunger, they would lower down pieces of broiled beef which, when they reached our lips, proved to be dripping with fresh blood. By the next day we'd found it was best for all to lie back as a unit. If I tried to sit up individually, the others' necks would get twisted; if one of the others tried to get up, our necks would get yanked up with his motion. After three days like that, we reached the checkpoint at Dinghai,[7] and when I looked back toward the Pavilion of Snowy Union, it was removed from me by a vast sea of billowing waves.

It had been raining constantly for a long time, and on the road I sank to my shins in pasty mud and horse manure. With two or three other prisoners I was questioned by tribunals at five or six places. Everyone agreed that the young boy was guiltless, but they were unwilling to release me right away. After seven days of being spattered with mire, my face didn't even look human. I thought to myself that I surely could die of weariness and miserable humiliation—and how much better it would have been to die beside Grandfather and Mother.

Within the first ten days of the tenth month, I was confined as a criminal in the Ningbo jail. According to the jailer's regulations, ten thousand coins bought exemption from the earthen pit, another ten thousand released one from the night-pen, another two hundred got one a few sheaves of straw [to lie on], and if the money continued, an inmate could massage his chest while sunning his back under the eaves. One [escort to] a tribunal hearing required money; one visit with relatives required money; one service of food and drink required money. Otherwise, inmates were roughed up going out and coming back, were not allowed to see their kin, or had their food and drink spilled or rudely snatched away. There was no question that I'd be put down in the earthen pit.

The pit was over twenty feet deep and about thirty feet wide—pitch black without a ray of sun. The floor felt extremely damp to the touch, so I had to use things that seemed to be reeds, pieces of firewood, or a rotten wood ladle to make a seat. When I'd sat for quite a while, I felt as though clammy worm- or snake-like creatures were wriggling around my lower legs. During the night, I lay in a cage which resembled a bed but was more narrow.[8] I was forced to lie with my two arms spread out on planks and held in restraints about half the size of tea trays—those for my upper arms and shoulders were about half the size of wash basins. For my neck and feet, also, there were restraints. Wherever there were restraints, my skin became discolored by the blood and sweat of I-don't-know-who. My five extremities were rendered as useless as those of a corpse, and only my torso was left to breathe. Below my neck there was a round wooden peg, which could be moved in and out [of a choke-harness] like a door bolt. This was removed only when one died. Worse, the [guards] would attach rocks to a prisoner's topknot, which would cause his neck to hang down [onto the peg] and, sure enough, cut his breath off within a couple hours. [It was so dank that] paper would get wet in no time. Packs of rats, fully a foot long, would contend to snap at my cheeks, so I didn't dare open my eyes. [But then] lice from my cup would trail into my eyelashes.

I passed out for a long time, but then I heard the bell and rattle used by the guards, and shortly one of them came and unblocked the cage enough so that I could see some daylight. Then, what was left of some juice was lowered down in a mottled red-and-white box made of woven bamboo. I didn't know where it had come from. In a few days, more people—who said their surname was Luo—joined me in the pit. They padded one another by lying back to back, and their tears flowed together in a single stream. By chance some rays of light came down from between chinks in the tiles and made egglike [shapes on the floor]. Thereupon I was able to see that what, the day before, I'd thought might be reeds, kindling, or a rotten wood ladle actually were parts of dried human skeletons! Again, I thought that I surely would die in that place and how much better it would have been to die beside Grandfather and Mother.

Suddenly, the guards were passing the call for "Master Zhang," and I thought it quite odd that, out of the blue, they were using "master" as a term of address for me. Emerging from the pit by means of a rope, I saw one man with a sallow face and a few missing teeth and another with a long, narrow, pock-marked face and a slight beard. The latter said, "I am Lu Zhouming, and this is my younger brother, Chunming." I didn't have the vaguest idea [who they were]. Zhouming continued, "Ever since the troops went to Wengzhou, we've been inquiring everywhere about gentlemen who may have died in the calamity, and we heard first of all about [your grandfather]. Then yesterday on the road, we encountered a lame man begging for food to take to the jail. Out of curiosity, we inquired of him and learned that he is your [family's] man Sun who lives hereabouts. We then bribed the jail guard to make another inquiry." I said tearfully, "That's [our] servant Sun Ji!" and it occurred to me that the bamboo box lowered into the pit had been from him.

Chunming then said, "From now on I will provide your morning and evening meals," as he presented a container of food. Before I could even straighten my chopsticks, some emaciated men [who'd been standing] around us ran up and seized [the food] with filthy claws like contending hawks or wolves. In no time, it was all gone, the few morsels that fell to the ground having been scuffled over by the weak. Chunming said, "It looks like I'll have to get you out of this jail."

Then a secretary to the prefect, a Master Gao, came to review cases of incarceration. Seeing me and inquiring into why I was there, he was appalled. He spoke of the past when he had been the first literatus to be elevated [to civil service eligibility] by my grandfather during his magistracy of Jun County.[9] Then, sighing tearfully, he began to do what he could to help, sternly ordering the jail guards to keep the perverse and overbearing prisoners away from me. From that point, I no longer was confined in the pit or the night-pen, I was able to eat and drink, and I was allowed to see not only the servant Sun Ji but also my teacher, Master Song, who came along.

In the first part of the eleventh month, word came that a monk was begging to be allowed in. I said to myself, "It surely is Wufan." When the door opened, at first he didn't recognize me [by my appearance]. But then he recognized my voice and embraced me tightly in greatest anguish, saying, "At first they said you'd been sent to the provincial capital [Hangzhou]. I've gone back and forth four times now." I asked him where he was staying, and he replied, "After I requested custody of [your grandfather's] remains, the supreme commander was suspicious of my living across the sea, so he had me transferred to [the monastery] on Tiantong [Mountain].[10] You're not looking very well. How can you go on living here for long?"

I responded by telling him of Chunming's intention [to get me released], but I also told him that I should have died with my grandfather and mother, so I really couldn't burden anyone with [saving me from death in jail]. On another day, I heard that Chunming had requested of the authorities [that I be released]—unsuccessfully, and on the following day that Wufan had requested my release—unsuccessfully, and then that his whole monastic community had done so—unsuccessfully, and then that Wufan had asked to take my place in confinement—unsuccessfully. Chunming also made a joint appeal with [five other gentlemen]—all to no avail.

Then Wufan came in with some pigs' trotters and a flagon of wine [ostensibly] to make an offering to the Jail God. The only plan [he could conceive] to resolve my long incarceration was to get the guards drunk. Chunming came to see me and said resolutely, "For some time now these feet of mine have given up on treading the public tribunal. If this doesn't work, what in the world will!" The next day Wufan came in with his hand at his brow and said, "Good fortune. A Mister Liu the Honest and Filial[11] from Fujian has come to visit the head official. When Chunming told him about you, he declared gallantly that, since your grandfather had beneficially governed his home province, and besides, had died out of loyalty to his state, he [Liu] felt obligated [to get you released]. He pulled back his sleeves in determination as he rose and headed into the government compound."

Chunming straightway got more than forty people to corroborate [what was being said about my case]. Only then did the official in charge begin to change his attitude. He ordered an inquiry into Chunming's background, [in the course of which] Chunming's neighbors confirmed that he is the son of the former (i.e., Ming-dynasty) chief minister of the Court of Judicial Review, that he lives in a corner of the city to the west of Moon Lake, that his family has always engaged in agriculture, and that they are solidly conscientious and scholarly, the younger men all ranking among the civil-service licentiates. Thereupon, the official ordered Chunming to come and assume the public duty of, first, bringing me before him in audience. He gruffly addressed Chunming, saying, "I know you have a home. Today I'm giving Maozi over to you. Don't test [the security of] that home [by using the boy's presence in any untoward way]." Thus, I got out of jail and went to live with Chunming.

At the house west of the lake there was cold rain and falling snow. People told me it was the eleventh of the twelfth month. Alas, from the beginning of the ninth month to that time, it had been altogether a hundred days. My body had become inured to a tragic existence, the painful disruption to my mind had become a fixed state, and whenever I thought or spoke of my [deceased] elders I felt as though I would break apart. One night my grief was so injurious that I became ill.

My delirium was filled with sounds of cannon balls smashing the city walls; of foot soldiers and cavalry cutting and killing; of dwellings collapsing in fire; of my grandfather, mother, four concubine-grandmothers, and little sister grasping lengths of silk, ready to use them, and shouting at me to get away; of [the Lin brothers'] and other victims' blood being spattered and flesh being ripped. Suddenly I was in a viney, muddy slough; then falling down a wall that seemed ten thousand feet high; then going under as I tried to wade across a moat; then the tile from the [shrine] wall had aroused the soldiers to make a search, and I had gone into the rising tide on the East River shore, but neither the cat nor the bamboo had come. Then I was down in the pit where ten-foot, venomous serpents with shiny spots reared their heads, bared their tongues, and spit fire; where the rats turned into fierce-looking tigers which flared their tails as they pounced toward the restraining rack; and where the jail guards had red hair, blue jowls, and two protruding fangs. When—brandishing gigantic clubs—[the guards] came to dun me for money they'd suddenly announce receipt of an order to march me to the marketplace, where I'd see an executioner—silk pennon fluttering from his topknot—raising high a white sword as though practicing [to behead me]. And I still would think to myself, how much better it would have been to die beside Grandfather and Mother.

It went on like that for two months, during which Chunming rushed in both doctors and soothsayers, and no one in the household had any leisure time. He personally tended the stove to decoct my medicine, not even noticing when the flames had consumed half of his sleeves. At the beginning of the second month of 1652, I was able to stand with the aid of a staff. How grievous! If it hadn't been for the strenuous efforts of Chunming and others in getting me out of jail, this illness probably would have rendered me the same as those in the pit whose remains I mistook for reeds, kindling, and a rotten wood ladle.

Eating and sleeping day after day in an upper-story [room]—what more could one ask for in such a vastly fortunate life beyond one's due? Anyway, [the old family] courtyard [surely having] become a thicket of brush and [my family] having lost its official registration, [no matter how] high I might climb or how far I might look, [I could see] no home to return to. But that my grandfather's bones were still at Wengzhou, sending up will-o'-the-wisps from the shallow soil, was a matter so urgent that [I felt] it could not wait half a day. On the fifteenth of the eleventh month, Wufan made a request of the Vice-General, Sir Zhang, who replied, "[Since] the grandfather killed himself [i.e., did not resist the Qing assault], what blame does the youngster bear? Why not enable him, at last, to return home?" And he forthwith took it upon himself, like Chunming before, to obtain permission from the official in charge.

Oh! Creeping on the ground in supplication for [travel] funds, I am about to carry my grandfather's bones back to our ancestral graveyard.[12] A ritual cup of wine and a scoop of grain, one mourner's wail, and [my mission] will be over. Perhaps then I can be pardoned for tolerating [so much] grief, fecklessly muddling through to the present. As the new year approaches, I especially reflect back on that second day of the ninth month, 1651, when I should have died by hanging myself but didn't because of Adjutant Lin; when I should have died in the massacre of the city but didn't because of the soldier lugging the sack; when I should have died at Daolong Shrine but didn't because of the cat that knocked down the tile; when I should have died at the shore of East River but didn't because of the floating bamboo log. Ultimately, I should have died either of incarceration or [the resulting] illness but didn't because of the heroic stratagems of Chunming and other gentlemen.

Now, it might have been predicted that I would die as a guest in another's home, but Sir Zhang has been so cooperative and, moreover, has unexpectedly enabled me to return [to Huating]. Could it be that the Emperor of Heaven and the Empress of Earth have been moved by the bitter resolve of my forebears and have specially preserved this unfilial, weak body of mine to fulfill their plan to return Grandfather home? Or that, in this decadent age when upright ways have withered away, they have made use of this refugee's hardships to make glowingly manifest [the example left to us by] humane and noble persons? Although such persons seek only to amass virtue, not to make their voices heard afar, how could I not but broadcast [the virtue of my grandfather], as well as that of the five wives,[13] to the four quarters! For this reason, in grief and distress I cry out laments as I kowtow [in respect to the deceased] and present this narrative.

Grandfather's governance of Jun County can be told of by the people of Jun, so that aspect of his excellence has been made known by the prefect's secretary, Mr. Gao. His service as regional inspector and then as governor of Fujian Province can be told by the people of Fujian, so that aspect of his excellence has been made known by the Filial and Honest Mr. Liu. I am not capable of recounting those affairs, nor do I need to do so. I [now just] reverently set forth his suicide poem, as follows:

> For twenty years, among the people, my empty name was well known,
> But for dignity late in life, my labors lost, there was only the gardener's role.[14]
> Randomly rhapsodizing on [the theme of] "return," in shame I stilled my resolve
> To somewhat carry forth the "righteous spirit" of Wen Shan.[15]
> My monarch's kindness yet unrepaid, I consumed myself with useless cares,
> Not lacking the Way of the minister when it came to bearing hardship.
> Consigning these words to the pens of historians of all time,
> I enjoin them not to lightly strike the phrase "[died in his official] cap and gown."

ABOUT THREE-QUARTERS of a century later, Zhang Maozi's original manuscript of the *Record of Life beyond My Due* came into the possession of a well-known historian of Zhejiang local history, Quan Zuwang (1705–1755), having been passed down by Quan's great-grandfather. Quan's postscript reads, in part,

> Maozi, having gotten out [of jail], was housed in Mr. Lu's Studio for Watching the Sun, so sick that he almost died. In his illness he wrote out the *Record,* articulating at length the difficulties he suffered in captivity, such that one can hardly bear to finish reading it. But the content is firmly true and the style is sufficient to convey that truth. At the time, Maozi was not yet twenty years of age, so one can sense that he was a genuine prodigy. When he had recuperated, the stalwart Fan Zhaozhi from Jiaochuan[16] escorted him back to Huating, and [Ru] Yingyuan got the family home back in order. But before long Maozi died. The orchid was severed; the jade was broken. The sacrifices in the lineage of a great family of state were discontinued.[17] How lamentable.

—LS

Notes

1. A very small island southeast of Putuo Island in the Zhoushan Archipelago. Often such small islands near Putuo are included when "Putuo" is spoken of. The Putuo island cluster was famous for its many monasteries and Buddhist culture. See map on page 530.

2. In the surrounding garden were a plum tree and and pear tree, the branches of which interpenetrated,

creating an impression of heavy snow in the spring when the trees blossomed. In this context, the traditional associations of snow with purity and cold with adversity come into play, suggesting a place where men of pure resolve maintained contact with one another under adverse conditions.

3. That Zhang Kentang apparently was a widower, that his only son had died, and that only Maozi remained to perpetuate the patriline may account for Zhang's having taken so many concubines in his advanced years.

4. The Lin brothers both were hacked to death.

5. The Green Standard armies were made up of surrendered Chinese soldiers, in contrast to the Eight-Banner forces, which had fought for the Qing from the beginning of the Manchu rise to power. The latter were considered more reliable by the Qing leadership, both in loyalty and in fighting ability, and thus held higher status and prestige.

6. In fact, because there was no means, in the aftermath of the massacre, to obtain suitable coffins in Wengzhou, Ru was unable to dress the remains of Zhang Kentang and his household members in the way favored in Confucianism, preserving the bodies whole. He had to resort to the way preferred in Buddhism, cremation. The residue of the bones of Zhang, the womenfolk, and the others such as the disciple Su Zhaoren were collected in three respective urns, which Ru buried near his hermitage on Luojia Island.

7. Located at the mouth of the Yong River, Dinghai was an important defense point for Ningbo, on the river to the southwest. At this time, the checkpoint was called Dinghai, and a corresponding garrison town on the main island of the Zhoushan group was called Zhenhai. Later the names of these two places were reversed.

8. Traditional-style Chinese beds were enclosed on three sides, often with a curtain on the fourth side.

9. In northwestern Henan Province.

10. A scenic high point to the east-southeast of Ningbo.

11. A conventional title given by the authorities to certain paragons of the local elite. Later in the Qing period, a system was formalized whereby bestowal of the title "Filial, Honest, and Four-Square" gave recipients certain advantages in taking the civil service examinations.

12. Actually, Ru Yingyuan was unable to convey the remains to Maozi because travel between the islands and the mainland again had become prohibitive, resistance forces having reoccupied the Zhoushan bases. So he persuaded Maozi to make the trip home, carry out the ritual to settle his grandfather's soul with just the spirit tablet (a wooden plaque, regarded as the seat of the soul of the deceased person whose name was written on it), and wait for a more peaceful time to retrieve the actual remains. However, both Maozi and Yingyuan died before that more peaceful time came, and the island burial place became lost in the underbrush until it was sought out by Zhang Kentang's principal biographer, Quan Zuwang, in 1726.

13. The grandfather's four concubines and one daughter-in-law, Maozi's mother.

14. An allusion to the *Analects (Lunyu)* 13.4, in which Confucius (seeing his role as that of an adviser on morality and policy) declines to give advice on farming or gardening, deferring on those subjects to old, experienced farmers and gardeners. The sense in Zhang Kentang's poem is that Zhang had not been able to sustain his proper role as a statesman.

15. The famous minister of the Southern Song dynasty, Wen Tianxiang (1236–1283), who maintained his loyalty to the fugitive Song court as it was pursued by the Mongols to the seaboard of far southern China and finally eliminated in 1279. Wen was captured by the Mongols and later executed, but not before writing some patriotic poems and an account of his upright deportment in captivity, which greatly inspired later generations of Han-Chinese loyalists. The most famous of such poems by Wen was called "Song of the Righteous Spirit" (Zhengqi ge), which is alluded to in this line of Zhang's poem.

16. The archaic name of a river in northwestern Hunan Province.

17. An allusion to a passage in the *Zuo Commentary (Zuozhuan)* to the *Spring and Autumn Annals (Chunqiu)* chronicle of Duke Wen, fifth year (622 B.C.E.), concerning the extinction of two ancient states, Lu and Liao, by the superpower Chu. An observer remarked, "So suddenly have the sacrifices ceased to the [founding family line] of Gaotao Tingjian! Their virtue no longer will be put into effect, and the people will be without aid. How lamentable."

FENG MENGLONG (1574–1646) makes a strident statement of the value of popular song in his Preface to the *Mountain Songs (Xu Shan'ge)*.[1] He argues that the genuine affect of popular song could remedy the false ethical teachings that plagued the late Ming (late sixteenth–early seventeenth century). The claim is riddled with contradictions. The strategy of his argument hinges on understanding of the "Airs of the States" (Guofeng)[2] and the way they "sway" *(feng)* their listeners, investing that term with several different meanings. He places Ming popular song in the lineage of the Airs, noting that even these bawdy songs should be valued as unmediated expression of the common folk. He also draws a parallel between the popular song texts and the writings of the Grand Historian,[3] supposedly compiled from popular sources. Both aspects of the preface balance notions of the social utility of popular literature and an interest in simplicity and unselfconsciousness. Feng's comments in the first pages of the *Mountain Songs* anthology set out to show the broad significance of the literature in dialect (specifically the Wu dialect of the lower Yangtze Valley). Such comments and the loose classification of the songs based on themes such as passion, jealousy, songs on objects *(yongwu),* and so on treat the love songs with high seriousness. However, the songs and their subject matter are closely tied to the world of courtesans and the entertainment quarters. The claim that the "Mountain Song" is the contemporary equivalent of the ancient Airs is a defensive posture commonly taken by preface writers to works of questionable content, but it is meant to be at least partially humorous.—KL

Preface to the *Mountain Songs*

Since the first written records, each age has had its songs and rhymes. The Grand Historian set forth [songs] called the *feng* and *ya,* which are revered. Since the Laments of Chu and Tang regulated verse [departed from the standard of the *Book of Odes*], people strive for formal elegance and grace, and the expression of a common human nature was consequently not considered in the realm of poetic endeavor. Consequently, such verse is distinguished as "Mountain Song." This refers to [songs by] farmers and rural people which are straightforward expressions of intent, and with which high officials and literati do not concern themselves. So long as these songs are not included in the realm of *shi* poetry and are not the concern of respectable officials and scholars, they are increasingly despised, and the minds of the singers, in turn, become increasingly shallow. What is popular now are all tunes on amorous themes.[4] Although these are bawdy songs of the kind that were censured in the "Airs of the States," Confucius recorded them.[5] He felt that as they expressed genuine feeling they should not be excluded [from the *Book of Odes*]. Although the "Mountain Songs" are extremely vulgar, are they not the direct descendants of the Airs of Zheng and Wei? In our degenerate times, there may be false poetry and prose, but there is no false "Mountain Song." Because "Mountain Songs" do not vie for social preeminence with *shi* poetry, they are not trifling or false. Since they are not trifling and false, then should I not collect them to preserve what is genuine?

Ah! People these days want to see things like what the Grand Historian set forth in ancient times. If what is found among the common people in recent times is like this, perhaps [current popular song] can also be said to be representative of all forms of discourse on affairs.[6] Songs like [those to the tune] "Hanging Branch" (Guazhi'er) achieve the aim of using genuine feeling such as is shared by men and women to rid us of the false medicine of Confucian ethical teachings. It is for this reason that I compiled, first, [the anthology] *Hanging Branch* and then the *Mountain Songs.*

"Laughter" (Xiao)

A southeast wind sweeps through
A fresh new blossom opens among the leaves.
Young wife, don't giggle.
Passion is most often born of laughter.

Feng Menglong's marginal comment on this song clarifies the relationship between the vulgar pronunciation of the words *sheng* 生 (to give rise to), *sheng* 聲 (pitch/tone), and *zheng* 爭 (to strive/contest). These are all pronounced in accordance with common spoken usage and fall in the rhyme categories *jiang* and *yang* (in the *Zhong-yuan Yinyun* [Rhyming patterns of the Central Plains]). Feng Menglong likens the dialect and its phonetic characteristics and related lore to local games in the following note:

> There are a great number of examples like this. One couldn't possibly record them all. The people of Wu sing about Wu, and [their songs] can be likened to local games such as striking tiles or tossing coins. They don't need to circulate the realm like the laws issued by the imperial court.

He compares the second song in the *Mountain Songs* to the Odes of the Zhou royal household and the Domestic Regulation [in the *Book of Rites*]. The third entry abruptly shifts from high seriousness to humor, with a ribald song text entitled "The Sixteen Steps of Lovemaking" (Shiliu buxie) that Feng recalls hearing when he was young. The opening sequence demonstrates the humor of the Mountain Songs as well as the strategy he uses to publish material about love and sex that is clearly associated with the courtesans' milieu.

"Going" (Zou)

"My lover has gone by the front gate seven or eight times.
Standing at the gate, I can only wave a hand."
She is just like a newborn chick, her mother watches her that closely.
At the front and rear of the storage room, both sides simmer.

Another way to sing this is:

I have conceived a passion for someone over on that side of the bridge.
Across the street from me, the wine shop hangs a sign at both entrances.
Wine brewed from cork tree bark sells, sold so my gut feels such burning it hurts.[7]
One million storage chambers face me, and both sides simmer. (*juan* 1:7)

The *Mountain Songs* use conventionalized phraseology such as "My girl has . . ." (*Jie'er sheng-lai . . .*). This kind of conventionalized phrasing resembles what Milman Parry and Albert Lord designated formulaic language in oral epic verse, with a limited vocabulary keyed to specific topics and themes. However, Feng Menglong notes many texts that he reworded to improve or add a twist to a common theme. In this way, there is a peculiar counterpoint between highly conventionalized language and subject matter and the editorial emphasis on invention in the dialect songs. Two examples from a series of nine such songs in the second chapter of "Love Songs in Four Lines" (Siqing siju) are selected here.

My girl has . . . (First of nine)

My girl has a good figure.
She's like a rice transport with its cabin brimming full with husks never opened.
While he wants to buy into rice, she wants to sell it off.
He makes inquiries into how to get inside through some hole. (*juan* 2:13)

My girl has . . . (Fourth of nine)

My girl has sophistication.
But when we share a pillow she is not fair and square.
The girl is like those long-legged, speckled mosquitoes in the middle of summer,
Who get their mouths into me and sing in satisfaction. (*juan* 2:13b)

Single-minded (Zhuanxin)

The girl cannot stitch; she cannot thread a needle.
All she can do is entwine herself in love affairs.
She says, "Oh my love,
It's not that your gal can't do her sewing.[8]
I'm only afraid you, my love, would get distracted." *One could say this.*[9] (*juan* 2:20b)

An Exchange (Jiaoyi)

The lad has loved me, and I too have loved him,
But dare not make our stolen pleasures public knowledge.
The maid has her dear husband and the lad has dependents too.
Could we not make an exchange and both form a pair? (*juan* 3:24)

Feng Menglong comments: "In such an exchange, who would be the middleman?"

THE FOLLOWING SONG describes the preparation of a cold salad of cucumber to wittily suggest a scene of passionate lovemaking. Such use of double entendre, or play on the discrepancy between the written meaning and the way the words can be heard, is characteristic of the Wu-dialect Mountain Songs. Countless songs describe ordinary objects using such play on homophones, with an especially large number in chapter six, "Songs on Objects in Four Lines" (Yongwu siju) and chapter seven, "Love Songs in Varied Forms" (Siqing zati). Incidentally, this example playfully upends the wording of songs describing women, "My girl has . . ." and puts the cucumber first.

Cucumber (Huanggua)

The cucumber always reminds me of my girl,
Making out to be clever, tender, gentle, and fragrant. Push down on her:
One plate, a second plate—cutting in countless fine strands and dressing her in garlic.[10]
I imagine you have a tendency to get jealous.
The girl says, "My love, Oh! You push me to the limit, pushing straight into my 'palace.'[11]
Now I am soaked in water and limp, collapsed in a heap." (*juan* 7:57)

—KL

Notes

1. The *Mountain Songs (Shan'ge)* and *Hanging Branches (Guazhi'er)* were published before 1618 under the collective title *Childish Obsessions in Two Fascicles (Tongchi er nong)*.

2. One of the three main sections of the *Book of Odes (Shijing)*.

3. Sima Qian (145?–86? B.C.E.), author of the *Records of the Grand Historian (Shiji)*; see selections 28 and 29.

4. *Pu*, translated "tunes," seems to refer to a type of verse. Particular tunes were supposed to have been used consistently to convey similar emotions.

5. "Bawdy songs" are literally *sangjian Pu shang zhi yin* (songs [sung] amidst the mulberry on the banks of the River Pu) in the kingdom of Wei (present-day Henan), referring to the place where licentious songs were said to be current in the *Book of Rites (Liji)*, "Record of Music" (Yueji).

6. The phrase *lunshi zhi lin*, translated as "all forms of discourse on affairs," alludes to *Mencius* 5B:8.

7. The bark of the cork tree (*Phellodendron amuense*) is used in Chinese medicine as a tonic, diuretic, alterative, aphrodisiac, and antirheumatic. Li Shizhen (1518–1593), author of the famous pharmacopoeia entitled *Bencao gangmu* (see selection 36, introduction), wryly notes "To see the complete list of difficulties for which it is prescribed, one would be led to think it is a universal panacea." See *Chinese Medicinal Herbs*, translated and researched by F. Porter Smith and G. A. Stuart (San Francisco: Georgetown Press, 1973), pp. 316–317.

8. The phrase translated "do sewing" (*zuo shenghuo* [literally, "make a living; do work"]) is common usage for *zuo zhenxian huo* (to do thread-and-needle work), but also has the sense of "making love."

9. The comment rendered in italics is an interlinear note in small script.

10. Line two reads like a description of feminine grace, but sounds like a recipe for adding scallion to the crisp cucumber to enhance its fresh aroma. The bisyllabic compound *kuobao* in line two, meaning "to embrace," is a homophone in the Wu-dialect for "peel" and "hit." In line three, "countless fine strands" (of silk) is a homophone for endless longing. "Dressing her in garlic" sounds like "I plan to accompany you," perhaps for the night.

11. The translation "have a tendency to get jealous" is idiomatic. Line four could more literally be taken "This I imagine is [perfect for someone] fond of eating vinegar." Line five shifts to first person feminine voice, writing out a graphic description of penetration, with "palace" signifying the uterus or womb. The written form of *kuo* ("push" or "contract") is a homophone for the Wu-dialect *kuo* (to peel) and describes cutting the fruit's skin away to the flesh within.

FANG YIZHI (1611–1671) was a native of Tongcheng (in Anhui Province). The scion of a distinguished family, he was a member of the literary group that called itself the Restoration Society (Fushe). His association with this politically oriented society caused him to flee to the southeast when a wholesale arrest of its antiquarian, anticorruption members was initiated. Disguised as a medicine seller, he managed to stay out of harm's way and eventually became an itinerant monk after the Manchus consolidated their new empire.

The breadth of Fang's interests was enormous, including the classics, literature, calligraphy, painting, history, geography, astronomy, music, mathematics, medicine, phonology, and philology. Fang Yizhi was a skeptic, yet open to compelling, new ideas. He was extraordinarily well-versed in the past, but also emphasized present-day utility. Above all, he possessed a scientific spirit that stressed the importance of evidence.

Perhaps Fang Yizhi's greatest contributions were in the realm of philology. Fang was familiar with the *Aid for the Eyes and Ears of Western Literati (Xiru ermu zi)*, the first romanized glossary of Chinese words. This pathbreaking work, published in 1626, was compiled by Nicolas Trigault (Jin Nige; 1577–1628), a fellow Jesuit of the great Matteo Ricci (Li Madou; 1552–1610), who was responsible for the creation of a systematic scheme for transcribing Mandarin in roman letters. Fang Yizhi's writings include some vague statements that indicate he was aware of the advantage of transcribing Sinitic sounds with an alphabet, which would make him the first Chinese to recognize the profound and far-reaching significance of romanization.

Fang Yizhi lived during the fall of the Ming and the beginning of the Qing dynasties. Another tragic figure who endured the tumultuous transition from native-dominated dynasty to foreign-controlled empire (compare selection 80), Fang can be seen as part of an intellectual movement away from the abstract moral philosophy that dominated the Ming period, and upon which some Qing scholars blamed the collapse of the dynasty. In this short piece, Fang discusses his view of intellectual pursuits. In it, he clearly differs from earlier Neo-Confucian thinkers, yet maintains certain fundamental Neo-Confucian ideas. One of the key terms is "activating point" *(shenji)*, a concept that is difficult to grasp and may only have been fully understood by Fang himself. Furthermore, given the tremendous instability of the age, one wonders how Fang would have answered his own final question.—VHM

Everything in the universe is a thing. People are born into the middle of them. At birth we live in a body and our body lives in the world. What we perceive and use are all affairs, and an affair is a thing. The sages instituted the beneficial use of implements in order to make life easier and brought order to their hearts-and-minds according to the apparent and innate patterns of things. Implements certainly are things, and the heart-and-mind is a thing. If we go deeper and speak of the inner nature, the inner nature is also a thing. When we thoroughly examine the universe, the universe is a thing. When you follow reasoning to a point you cannot understand, turn to something you can understand to grasp it—use the concrete to understand the hidden. The most abstruse thing is a concrete fact: it is the ultimate activating point for all things and mysterious transformations. If we examine the source of inactivity and activity, we understand the activating point.

Things have their own reasons for being. If we truly examine them on the grand scale of cosmic time or the small scale of plants and insects, and if we categorize their characteristics, assess their good and bad points, infer their permanent and temporary features—that is to engage in material investigation. Material investigation consists of understanding the activating point. There are those who go so far as to sweep aside material investigation and rashly begin discussing the activating point in order to illuminate the most abstruse mysteries, and they ignore material things. Who will be able to bring together the manifest and innate characteristics of things, and tie together the study of the singular activating point and the numerous material things and so understand the mysteries?

In the Wanli reign period (1573–1620) learning from the distant West came to China. It is skilled in material investigation, but weak in discussions of understanding the activating point. Thus, when wise literati have used it, their material investigation is still incomplete. It is only because Confucian scholars control the study of human activities like government and society. The sages penetrated the mysteries, categorized the myriad things, and put their knowledge in the *Book of Changes*. Calendrics, government regulations, medicine, and divination can all be derived through frequent study of the River Diagram and the Hexagram Judgments in the *Book of Changes*—wherein the discussion of the ultimate activating point is most thorough. But how are scholars to plumb its depths?

—RF

GU YANWU'S (1613–1682) name was celebrated by twentieth-century Chinese nationalists for his loyalty to the fallen Ming dynasty and for his refusal to lend his distinguished name to service of the new Manchu Qing dynasty. Gu has also been revered by intellectual modernizers for his innovative emphasis on empirically based research methods, which became the dominant trend of scholarship during the eighteenth and early nineteenth centuries. Gu came from a leading family of Suzhou Prefecture whose members had served and been honored by the Ming dynasty over several generations. Gu was strongly influenced by his family's tradition of learning, which was guided by practical and realistic historical studies rather than the fashionable Neo-Confucian moral philosophy.

In his youth Gu was known as an eccentric personality, and he was particularly contemptuous of the artificial style of learning required in preparation for the civil service examinations during the Ming dynasty. From his early manhood Gu was actively involved in privately sponsored scholarly efforts directed at redefining China's cultural legacy, in response to the social and political crisis of his time. Gu is reputed to have held civil office briefly in the Southern Ming regime based in Nanjing and to have participated in guerrilla activities against Qing forces in the Jiangnan (south of the lower reaches of the Yangtze River) region. After escaping a predatory neighbor's malicious intrigues against his reputation and his life, Gu fled his home region and passed his last twenty-five years as a sojourner in North China, carrying the remains of his family's library with him. Through much of that time, two of Gu's nephews served in high office under the new Qing dynasty, so Gu was not entirely alienated from official patronage during this era of violence and disorder.

Gu's mature thought is best known through his two writings published during his lifetime: *Record of Daily Learning (Ri zhi lu)*, and *Five Treatises on Phonology (Yin xue wu shu)*. The former contains the essence of his thought on Confucian statecraft. It was a carefully distilled digest of Gu's wide readings, intended to serve as a resource for reviving moral standards, social order, and normative government, and reflects his strong bias against the Manchu Qing dynasty. His second major work, on phonology, was directed at recovering accurate knowledge of lost ancient poetic rhymes by inductive inference from abundant evidence found in core Confucian classical texts. It has been hailed as a path-breaking example of empirical research *(kaozheng)*, and it was very influential as a model for later Qing dynasty scholarship. The possibility of indirect Western influence on Gu's scholarly method, from Jesuit missionaries who transmitted Western science to China in the late-Ming period, has been raised by some modern scholars.

Gu's concern to recover ancient pronunciations is significant in the context of contemporary issues during his lifetime. Gu maintained that the Ming dynasty's decline was primarily due to the corruption of normative personal relationships among the governing elite. He believed that growth of the central and provincial bureaucracies in recent centuries had led to dominance of impersonal and artificial associations between civil officials, with negative effects on the quality of administration and on the morale and behavior of local elites. District magistrates serving at the lowest level of administration were required not to be natives of the region where they served, which often made them unable to speak the language of the local people, so they became unduly reliant on their clerks for knowledge of local affairs. And, among the officials themselves, Gu explicitly linked the outbreak of disruptive bureaucratic factions to officials' inability to speak with each other in any language other than the artificial "official speech" (*guanhua*, i.e., Mandarin). Indeed, the Manchus' primary strategy for consolidating their regime took advantage of this psychological alienation between the elite of different dialect regions.

Gu sought above all to promote harmony among the educated elite in their understanding of normative Confucian values. Gu's classical idealism led him to suppose that this goal could be approached if scholars in all regions would learn to recite the classical texts in a culturally authoritative and uniform pronunciation, rather than in their own mutually divergent and discordant modern topolects. Gu recognized some of the problems faced by twentieth-century proponents of a standard national language, but his approach differed from theirs in its aims, scope, and means. He employed empirical methods in the service of strengthened commitment to Confucian values, not in the service of science or democracy. So Gu had no interest in finding a socially universal or merely functional solution to the problem of oral communication between ordinary people of different regions. Rather, he sought to revive awareness, among the educated governing elite, of their appropriate aspirations for society and the state.—TB

The *Book [of Rites] (Liji)* says, "When sounds (*sheng*) form patterns (*wen*), these are called 'harmonic tones' (*yin*)." When there is a patterned text (*wen*), then rhymes (*yin*) exist. When rhymes are arranged together, it is poetry. After poetry is formed, then it is set to music. These all come from Heaven and are not man-made.

In the Three Dynasties of high antiquity (Xia, Shang, and Zhou), texts were all based on the Six Classics, and people were all educated in their local community schools. Their natures were trained and transformed to be moderate and harmonious, and when they expressed themselves in [rhyming] sounds (*yin*), these never failed to accord with righteousness. Thus the *Rites of Zhou (Zhouli)* says that the royal court's chief ceremonial officer "in the ninth year convenes the musicians and scribes [from the various feudal states], instructs them in [correct] written and spoken forms [of words], and determines [normative] sounds and tones." This is a means by which to integrate moral standards and reconcile social customs, and one dare not neglect it.

For this reason, although the 305 poems of the *Book of Odes (Shijing)*—from the sacrificial songs of the Shang dynasty down to Marquis Ling of Chen (r. 612–598 B.C.E.)—[had originated in] a broad area of fifteen feudal states and over more than a millennium's time, still their rhymes were undifferentiated. [In the *Book of Documents (Shangshu; Shujing)* there are] the *Song* by the sage-ruler Shun and its *Continuation* by his minister Gaoyao, as well as the Viscount of Ji's *Statement* [of royal perfection]; [in the *Book of Changes (Yijing)* there are] the appended *Judgments* by King Wen and the Duke of Zhou. [The rhymes in all these] are entirely like [the rhymes in the *Book of Odes*]. Thus, the 305 poems of *Odes* are a guide to the rhymes of classical antiquity."

By the Wei (220–265) and Jin (265–420) dynasties and thereafter, antiquity was ever more remote, and [examples of] nonclassical verse (*ci*) and rhymed prose (*fu*) were ever more abundant. Later, rhymes [originally called *yin*, referring to the integral sound of a full monosyllabic word] became called by the name *yun* [referring only to the final segment of a fragmented sound]. By the time of Zhou Yong in the Six Dynasties Song (420–479) period and Shen Yue in the Liang period (502–557), charts systematically distinguishing the four tones had been constructed.

But from the Qin (221–210 B.C.E.) and Han (206 B.C.E.–220 C.E.) dynasties, writing had gradually turned away from ancient models, and in the Eastern Jin (318–420) dynasty [this trend] became increasingly extreme. So, when Shen Yue made his charts, he was not able to base them on the *Odes* [from high antiquity], or to make supplementary references to [*Li*] *Sao* (Encountering Sorrow) and the Masters [of the Warring States period], in order to compile an imperishable classic. Rather, Shen Yue based his tone charts only on the rhymes used in the rhymed prose of various writers since the time of Ban [Gu] and Zhang [Heng, both of the Eastern Han dynasty], and in the [pentasyllabic] poetry of varous writers since Cao [Zhi] and Liu [Cheng, both of the Jian'an era (196–219) in the late Eastern Han]. Shen Yue wrote a definitive work on this subject, with the result that modern rhymes circulated while ancient rhymes fell into disuse; this was the first major transformation in the history of rhymes.

Coming down into the Tang (618–906) period, composition of poetry and rhymed prose was used to select civil officials, and the uniform standard for their rhymes was the [set of 206 rhyme groups in] Lu Fayan's *Countertomic Rhymes* (*Qieyun;* completed 601, in the Sui dynasty). Although there were [various] commentaries concerned with use of single or multiple [rhyme groups to classify certain characters], still the division of rhyme groups remained unchanged. At the time of the [Northern] Song reign period Jingyou (1034–37) there were some slight changes. Then, during the late years of [Southern Song] Emperor Li Zong (r. 1225–1264), Liu Yuan, a native of Pingshui district, for the first time merged the 206 rhyme groups into 107 groups. In the Yuan dynasty (1279–1368) Huang Gongshao's work *Assembled Rhymes* (*Yun hui*) followed this [example], which has been continued to the present. Thus, the Song rhymes were circulated and the Tang rhymes fell into disuse; this was the second major transformation in the history of rhymes.

As each age became more distant [from antiquity], the transmission [of ancient models] became ever more corrupted. The demise of this Way occurred more than two thousand years ago now. I have immersed my mind [in this subject] for [many] years, but only after obtaining a copy of [the 1101 C.E. redaction of *Qie yun,* known as] *Expanded Rhymes* (*Guang yun*) did I comprehend its essential principles and understand its applications. On this basis, I used the Tang-dynasty writers [represented in *Guang yun*] to correct the errors of the Song-dynasty writers, and used the ancient classics to correct the errors of Shen Yue and the Tang writers.

As for the rhymes of high antiquity, their division in groups is now put in order; this is a matter of the most profound significance and cannot be left unclarified. So I set forth the changes of ancient and modern rhymes, probed the reasons for their differences, and composed *Treatise on Rhymes* (*Yin lun*) in three chapters, to examine and rectify the most ancient rhymes. I annotated the 305 poems [of the *Odes*] and wrote *The Original Rhymes of "Odes"* (*Shi ben yin*) in ten chapters. I annotated [the *Book of*] *Changes* (*Yijing*) and wrote *The Rhymes of "Changes"* (*Yi yin*) in three chapters. I clarified Shen Yue's errors of classification, and one by one used the ancient rhymes to correct them, so I wrote *Corrections to "Tang Rhymes"* (*Tang yun zheng*) in twenty chapters. I comprised ancient rhymes in ten groups, and wrote *Table of Ancient Rhymes* (*Gu yin biao*) in two chapters. From this time, the text of the Six Classics can be read [accurately aloud]. As for the other writings of the various [Eastern Zhou dynasty] Masters, they may vary more or less, but not by very much.

[As Confucius said,] "That Heaven has not allowed this culture to be entirely lost" [indicates that] a new sage will surely arise who can cause modern speech to be restored to the pure ancient model. Confucius said, "Not until I returned to Lu from Wei was the music in Lu corrected, nor did the courtly modes and hymns there each fully [re]gain its proper role." Truly, there is hope that someone may accomplish this in future.

—TB

IN 1697, MERELY FOURTEEN years after the Qing (Manchu) conquest of Taiwan, an adventurous traveler, Yu Yonghe (literary name, Canglang, fl. 1697), volunteered for a sulfur expedition to the island. A private secretary serving in Fujian, Yu was among the first Chinese literati to travel to Taiwan. Although Taiwan is located less than a hundred miles off the southeastern coast of China, prior to the troubles surrounding the end of the Ming dynasty it was considered a "remote island far beyond the seas," and few besides fishermen and pirates had ever traveled there. Originally inhabited by various indigenous peoples of hypothetical "Austronesian" descent, Taiwan was a colony of the Dutch between 1624 and 1661. In 1661, the Ming loyalist Zheng Chenggong (Koxinga) ousted the Dutch and established Taiwan as a base for a war of resistance against the Manchu Qing dynasty. Sending the Admiral Shi Lang against these rebel troops, the Qing conquered the island in 1683. The Qing court officially annexed the island in the following year, making Taiwan a part of Fujian Province.

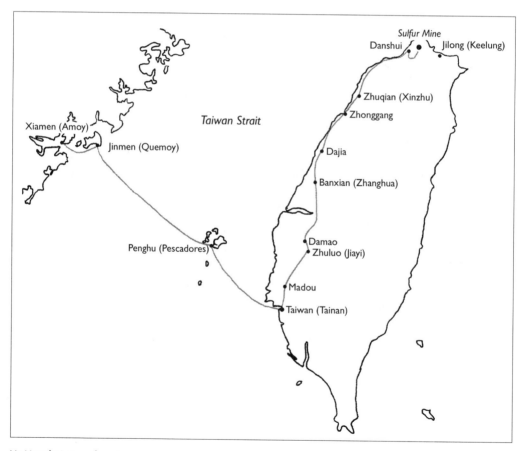

Yu Yonghe's travel route

Taiwan was thus still a wild frontier—inhabited by "savages" *(fan)*[1] and remnants of the rebel troops in mountain hideaways—at the time when Yu made his arduous journey. It was also a place known for malarial "miasmas" and other environmental dangers. Yet, as Yu tells us in his diary, his lust for adventure had sparked a desire to see this new frontier ever since it had been annexed to the Chinese empire. His opportunity came in 1697, when he joined an expedition to Taiwan to obtain sulfur, a vital strategic item. Yu traveled to Taiwan from Xiamen (Amoy) via Penghu (the Pescadores), taking four days to cross the treacherous Taiwan Strait. Arriving in a southern port near Taiwan prefectural city (now Tainan), Yu spent ten months on the island, trekking north over land to the sulfur mines in the area of Danshui and Jilong (Keelung). He composed a diary recording his experiences, which is now known as the *Small Sea Travelogue (Pihai jiyou).*

As one of the earliest first-hand accounts of frontier Taiwan, this work was highly regarded by both Qing frontier officials and Japanese colonial officials who took the island in 1895. Qing readers valued Yu's account not only for the information he recorded, but also for his vivid description and prose style, which is unusually lively for a travel diary. *Small Sea Travelogue* is thus one of the most important texts for the study of Qing Taiwan. Unfortunately, the details of the author's life are obscure, and we know little about him other than his composition of this celebrated text. It appears that he was a rather ordinary private secretary, who produced a vivid and fascinating account of an extraordinary journey. In this selection, some of the highlights of Yu's travelogue, which is divided into three volumes, are introduced, translated, and annotated.—ET

Small Sea Travelogue, vol. 1

(In the first section, Yu describes the circumstances surrounding his journey and the details of his voyage outward from Fujian towards the Pescadores and Taiwan. He describes at length the perils and the wonders of being at sea. Once he reaches Taiwan, he establishes himself at Taiwan prefectural city, the seat of the local Chinese frontier administration.)

I entered Min [Fujian] in the spring of 1691, passing through Jianning and Yanjin to reach the City of Banyans (Rongcheng), Fuzhou. In the beginning of autumn I left Fuzhou and traveled through Xinghua and Quanzhou to Shima in Zhangzhou. Before long, I also went to Zhangpu, Haideng, Longyan, Ningyang, all subordinate towns, as well as various villages along the shore, and then returned to Shima. Also I crossed to Xiamen (Amoy) by skiff, returning after five days. In 1692, I returned again to Fuzhou and stayed at the *yamen*[2] of Wang Zhongqian. So I had traveled through six of the eight prefectures of Fujian. In the autumn of 1693, I went on duty to Taining. I moored my boat beneath the city walls of Shaowu, spent two nights there, and returned. The next year I went to Wuping in Dingzhou, going upstream from Yanjin. I climbed the heights of Tieyan and crossed the dangers of Jiulong. In the space of half a year, I went back and forth four times. Of all the mountains and streams and hidden depths, there was not a single one that I didn't walk through and see with my own eyes. Thus, I completed my travels of the eight prefectures of Fujian.

The prestige of our dynasty is spread far and wide. The rebel Zheng (Koxinga)[3] has rendered his allegiance. Taiwan lies far beyond the Eastern Ocean; since antiquity until the present day, there has never been a tribute mission sent to China. Now we have divided the land into districts and counties, established governmental offices, levied taxes and tribute, opened sea routes for continuous traffic back and forth, and added a ninth to the eight prefectures of Fujian;[4] it is truly a feat. By nature I am addicted to travel, and don't avoid obstacles or danger. I had often said that since Taiwan has already been put on the map, if I couldn't survey the place, I wouldn't be satisfied. In the winter of 1696, there was a fire at the gunpowder storehouse at Fuzhou; more than 500,000 [*jin*]⁵ of niter gunpowder were destroyed with not a shred left. The person in charge was reprimanded and ordered to compensate for the loss. Jilong and Danshui in Taiwan produce sulfur rocks, and we were to go in search of it. I laughed joyfully and said, "It's my dream come true!" In the first month of 1697, I packed my luggage and observed the abstinences in preparation for travel. My colleagues, Master Yan Shengping (Youtao), Master Qiu Shaoyi, Master Hu Shenfu, Master He Xiangchen, Master Chen Ziwei, my cousin Zhao Lüzun, and my nephew Zhou Zailu, all bid me fond farewell. The servants Xu Wen, Yu Xing, and Long Dexi were asked to accompany me. Master Cao Lüyang sent me off, and Master Wang Yunsen traveled with me.

[First month] 24th—Noon, I went out of South Gate. I arrived at the Great Bridge [of Nantai], and met with rain. I stayed at Lüyang's lodging place.

25th—The weather cleared slightly; I traveled thirty tricents and crossed the Wulong River. After the night, the fog began to clear, and the river glistened like silk. Looking out at the reflection of the Net of Stars Pagoda in the harbor, it was like a needle hanging upside down in the water. Therefore, I composed a quatrain:

> The billowing waves of the river flow day and night,
> From a distance I look at the summit of Mount Five Tigers.
> From Haimen gazing three thousand tricents,
> All you can see is the floating Net of Stars Pagoda.

By night I arrived at Fangkou, and saw a certain Master Shi and Master Dong Zanhou. Master Dong was the eldest son of the magistrate of Zhuluo, and Shi was his uncle. So I agreed to travel together with them.

26th—We passed Longing Peak and I recalled that I had passed this peak six times since I had come to Min. In recent years my teeth have become soft and my hair gray. I was suddenly inspired and wrote this poem:

> For seven years I've been a servant in Min,
> Six times I've been dyed by the dust of Longing Peak.
> All I have is the gray color of my temples,
> Going past once and returning anew again.

That night I stayed on Fisherman's Creek.

27th—We set out at dawn. We traveled by sedan chair in the morning light of a lightly cloudy sky. The villagers carried ploughs and led oxen, going back and forth over the mounds. The time when I would withdraw from service was drawing near, and I could not contain my excitement. I composed this poem:

> The color of the mountains is clearer in the dawn,
> The sound of the creek is quiet as it flows naturally.
> People speaking on the other side of the bank,
> The barking of dogs emerges from the secluded [a corner of] village.
> A light rain wets my clothes,
> A slight chill makes the traveler melancholy.
> White clouds are really to be envied,
> Rolling over the mountain peaks.

By noon we got to Puwei; the sedan-chair bearers placed the sedan chair in the boat. Although I was taking a boat, I was actually sitting in the sedan chair. The boatman held a bamboo pole and pulled the boat while walking on the shore; the boat moved very quickly. Poling a boat from shore and sitting in a sedan chair on a boat, two strange things at once. This could only be seen at this place. Along the bank were many old banyan trees; the roots and trunks were all twisted in knots, in all sorts of strange configurations. There were more than ten trees lined in a row for half a tricent which actually belonged to a single trunk. I once moored the boat beneath these trees, and remember it to this day. I still cherish its dense flourishing as I did in the past. . . . [6]

[Second month] 23rd— . . . After a while, black clouds spread in all directions, and the stars were totally covered. I remembered that my friend Master Yan Youtao had said, "At sea, in the pitch of night, you can't see a thing, but when you strike the water, you are able to see." I struck it and water splashed up, sending rays of light flying like dozens of bushels of bright pearls, spreading out over the surface of the water, like crystals shimmering. After a long time it began to fade. What a wondrous sight! In the middle of the night a slight breeze began to stir. The captain set the rudder in order preparing to set out. Then I went to bed.

24th—Rising in the morning I saw that the color of the sea had turned from dark emerald to light black. Looking back, I could still faintly see the islands of the Pescadores. After a while, they slowly faded beyond the clouds. In front of us we could hazily see the various mountains of Taiwan. As we went on, the water turned pale blue, then became white, and then we saw the mountain peaks of Taiwan's prefectural city laid out in front of us. On the shore it was all shallow sand. On the beach there were numerous fishermen's huts. Small skiffs were continually going back and forth. Looking at Lu'er Gateway, we could see it was the place where the sand spits of both shores came together. The "gateway" was more than a tricent wide. Looking at it there didn't seem to be anything terribly strange or dangerous. . . .

25th— . . . After two days, I began to pay calls. I saw Prefect Master Jin, Vice-Prefect Master Qi, Registrar Master Yin, Prefect of Zhuluo Master Dong, and Prefect of Fengshan Master Zhu. Also through Vice-Prefect Master Qi I met my friend Mister Lü Hongtu. We grasped each other's hands eagerly. He had not expected me to suddenly make an overseas journey and thought that I had fallen from the sky. I was really excited to meet an old friend in a strange land. We spent many a full day together and were even closer than we had been when we served together in Fuzhou. We wrote, did archery, composed songs, played pitching pots; there was nothing we did not do. In our leisure we discussed the ancient and the modern. We appreciated the strange and resolved doubts. Also we obtained a copy of the Taiwan prefectural gazetteer and investigated Taiwan's conditions, poring over it together.

Taiwan is to the southeast of the eight Min, separated by more than a thousand tricents [7] of sea. In past dynasties there were no links to China (Zhongguo [the Middle Kingdom]); the Chinese did not know that this piece of land existed. Even geographic maps, comprehensive gazetteers, and other such books, which contain very detailed records of all the barbarians, do not include the name Taiwan. Only "Admiral Zheng He's [8] Ocean Travels" in the Ming compilation of state documents mentions "drawing well water at Chikan," and it doesn't specify where this "Chikan" is. Only the Pescadores, in the Ming, belonged to Tong'an County of Quan district in Fujian. Fishermen from Zhangzhou and Quanzhou all gathered there to pay the annual fishing taxes. During the Jialong period (1522–1573), Liuqiu (the Ryukyus) [9] occupied it. In the Ming, people held this territory in contempt and simply abandoned it. We have no means of verifying whether or not Liuqiu ever had sovereignty over Taiwan.

As for the people of Taiwan, the locals are savages. Their language cannot be understood in

China. Moreover, they have no written language and no way to record events of earlier times. During the Wanli reign (1573–1620), the island was occupied by the Dutch ([original note:] the Dutch are what we now call the "Red Hairs"). They built the two cities of Taiwan and Chikan ([original note:] Taiwan is today called Anping, and Chikan is now Tower of the Red Hairs).[10] From research we know the year was 1621. The two cities appear much like those in the pictures of buildings drawn by the Europeans. They are not more than ten sixth-acres in area.[11] Their purpose is primarily for stationing canons and defending the port. There are no parapets or watchtowers as there are on the city walls of China to secure the inhabitants. When our dynasty was established, those in the four directions submitted [to the dynasty]. Only Koxinga held out at Jinmen (Quemoy) and Xiamen (Amoy), making numerous raids. . . .

. . . Fengshan County is located to the south [of the Taiwan prefectural capital—present-day Tainan]. Southward from the border of Taiwan County, it extends to the ocean by Shama jetty, a total of 495 tricents. From the shore eastward to Dagou'a harbor at the base of the mountains, it is 50 tricents wide. There are eleven villages of pacified savages, called Upper Danshui, Lower Danshui, Lili, Qieteng, Fangsuo, Dazeji, Yahou, and Dalou. The preceding are eight plains villages, which remit taxes and perform corvée. There are those called Qieluotang, Langqiao, and Beimanan. These three are in the mountains. They only remit taxes and do not perform corvée. In addition, there are the Kuilei savages and the wild savages in the mountains, whose villages have no names. Zhuluo district is located to the north. The pacified savage villages are Xin'gang, Jialiuwan (pronounced Gelawan), Ouwang (pronounced Xiaolang), Madou, etc., 208 villages, aside from which there are Ge'anan (pronounced Geyalan), etc., 36 villages. Although these are not wild savages, they do not remit taxes. It is hard to record everything [about them]. North from the border with Taiwan County, to the northwest corner, then turning to the great ocean by Big Jilong village at the northeast corner, it extends 2,315 tricents. The [territory] under the administration of the three counties is only the plains between the mountain range and the shore. The wild savages in the deep mountains do not communicate with the outside world. Outsiders cannot enter; it is impossible to know the conditions there.

Small Sea Travelogue, vol. 2

(After having settled in the prefectural city, Yu begins to make preparations for the sulfur expedition. In order to obtain this precious product, Yu is compelled to travel north to Danshui and Jilong, where the sulfur mines are located. To get to these remote regions, Yu must travel through indigenous territory and dense mountain jungle. What he encounters there is so strange to him that he calls it "No-Man's-Land."[12] He is led on this trek by local Chinese and indigene guides.)

Due to my sulfur mission, I've spent over two months living in Taiwan prefectural city, buying cloth, oil, sugar; smelting large kettles; getting knives, axes, hoes, and ladles made; ordering large and small wooden pails; making scales, rulers, peck and bushel measures; and making all sorts of other preparations. The cloth is to trade with the savages for sulfur ore. The oil and large kettles are for refining sulfur. The sugar is necessary because the workers must frequently drink and bathe with sugar water in order to counter the poisonous sulfur fumes. The hoes are to level the earth and build platforms. The knives and axes are to chop firewood and clear weeds. The ladles are for removing the sulfur from the pots. The small buckets are for solidifying the sulfur. The large buckets are for storing water. The scale, ruler, peck, and bushel measures are for weighing and measuring various items. I also bought millet, salt, baskets, cauldrons, bowls and chopsticks, etc. for one hundred people. I estimated that I spent about 980 gold. I bought a large boat to transport it all. Having put about 70 percent of the supplies on board, I felt that the boat was overloaded and privately began to worry. So I halted the loading and bought another boat in order to transport the remainder; the cost was half that of the first boat. Someone said, "There are large and small boats, which can transport various amounts. Now you haven't filled this one nearly to capacity; why have you spent more for no reason?" I said, "I suddenly became worried. I'm about to divide the cargo in two and have each boat transport half. It's not just for transporting the remainder." The speaker laughed to himself and left. Master Wang felt that the plans were already set and didn't want to rearrange things. I thus dropped my plan to split the cargo in two.

My affairs having been settled, I planned to board the boat at dawn. The Prefect Master Jin (name Zhiyang, sobriquet Dounan) and the Vice-Prefect Master Ji (name Tiwu, sobriquet Cheng'an) said to me, "Haven't you heard how horrible the environment at Danshui is? Whenever people go there, they fall ill. Whenever they fall ill, they always die. Whenever the workers hear that they are being sent to Jilong or Danshui, they all sigh in despair as though being sent to the "end of the world." The custom is for navy men to change duty in the spring and fall, and they consider it great luck to return alive. If these tough workers are like this, how will you be able to bear it? Why don't you order a servant to go along while you yourself stay at the prefectural city to oversee operations from afar?" I said, "For this journey we have hundreds of savages and craftsmen. Moreover, we will be going close to the wild savages. If we have no means by which to quell them, I'm afraid that there will be difficulties, causing trouble in the territories [which we control]. Moreover, I have accepted this mission; how can I refuse to go?" The next day, Lieutenant-Colonel Master Yin (name Fu), and Captain Qi of Fengshan (name Jiacan), both from my native place, came to stop my journey. They said, "Last fall Zhu Youlong tried to plot sedition. Brigade-General Master Wang ordered a captain low-ranking military officer to lead a hundred men to guard Danshui. After only two months, not a single person returned. If it's like this going to Danshui, it will be even worse going to Jilong, which is beyond Danshui." Again they said, "A certain county functionary went with four companions but returned alone. These are all recent events; why don't you look out for yourself, Master?" I laughed, "My life is governed by fate. Heaven controls it. What is the environment to me? I have thought it over carefully; I must go." Master Yin and prefectural military officer Master Shen (name Changlu) made herbal medicines and various other remedies such as poison antidotes and prescriptions to ward off pestilence for me and bid me over and over to take care of myself.

Then there was my fellow-provincial, Master Gu (name Fugong) from Huangyan, who had followed his father, Mr. [Gu] Nanjin, to take up a post as regional commissioner in Jiangnan and live in Jingkou. In 1659, he was abducted and taken to Taiwan. He lived in Taiwan for a long time, becoming very familiar with the terrain. He and I had been like old friends since the first time we met. He too came to me and said, "The environment harms people, and the demon creatures cause trouble beyond what the expert can prepare for. If you wish to avoid difficult terrain and seek level ground, stay safe and avoid danger, you must consider everything. Do you know the sea routes? All seafaring boats do not fear the open ocean, but fear close mountains; they are not troubled by deep waters, but are troubled by shallow waters. Boats are floating objects by nature, with masts to ride the wind and rudders to navigate the waters. Even though it is not easy for strong winds and waves to sink them, if you run into reefs they will sink, and if you get stuck on sand bars they will break up. Disaster will be immediate. Now, going from the prefectural city to Jilong, the boat must pass through sand and rapids, and if you meet with winds there are no ports in which to harbor. It is twice as dangerous as the open seas. How can it be better than going by land? Now you want to take me along, but if we must go by boat, then I wish to decline."

I said, "I'll follow your instructions."

Master Wang's plans were set, and in the end he boarded the boat. We couldn't convince him otherwise. I went with Master Gu and led a bunch of slaves; we took to the road in heavy carts. Fifty-five workers followed. It was the seventh day of the fourth month. We passed a savage village and changed carts. The carts were pulled by brown calves. We ordered local savages to drive. That day we passed Dazhou Creek, Xin'gang village, Jialiuwan (pronounced Gelawan) village, and Madou village. Although these were all the dwellings of savages, there were fine trees and shady woods. The houses were tidy and clean, not inferior to our own villages in China.

I said, "Who says that the savages are vile? How can you trust what others say?"

Master Gu said, "Xin'gang, Gelawan, Ouwang, and Madou were all major villages during the time of the rebel Zheng. He issued an order exempting all youths who could go to the town and study from forced labor, in order to gradually civilize them. The savages of the four villages thus know the value of agriculture, and of saving and storing goods; every household is industrious and prosperous. Moreover, they are close to the prefectural city, and are used to seeing the manners of the market town. Therefore, among all the savage villages their customs are superior. Ouwang is close to the ocean. It's not on the thoroughfare, but is especially prosperous and thriving; it's a pity you can't see it. After this I'm afraid that the farther we go the more vile it will become."

Indeed I could see that the men and women of the four villages had uncoiffed hair and went without pants, still following their old customs. It was really vile. At Madou we changed carts and headed for Daoluoguo. The savages could not understand the language of the servants. I saw that the officers had set out a meal for me while we were on the road and thought that I should go over to them. We drove to Jialixing, and by the time that we arrived it was already the second watch. I asked where the sleeping quarters were to be, and they were in the camp. Before long, I went to Commandant Master Zhao's place. Master Zhao's personal name was Zhen. He was a native of Tianxiong. He was filial and honest, and was on good terms with my friend Master Hou Jingzhi. We talked about various old friends in Tianxiong, Pinggan, Yexia, and Pingtai. He [remembered] everything. These were all the affairs of the past thirty years. I heard the water clock drip for half an hour, and then I went to bed.

[Fourth month] 8th—We still rode the same cart, and returned to Madou village. We changed carts and crossed Maogangwei Creek and Tiexianqiao Creek, and arrived at Daoluoguo village. It was almost dusk. I thought of Master Wang sailing on the large junk, riding the southern wind and covering a thousand tricents in a flash. I estimated that I would arrive behind him. So I traveled by night, crossing creeks such as Jishui (Swift Water) and Bazhang (Eight Palms). It was already dawn when we reached Mount Zhuluo. I was so tired I fell asleep sitting up. Just when the day was getting hot, we crossed Niutiao (Cow Jump) Creek. We passed Damao (Hit Cat) village and crossed Shandie (Piled Mountains) Creek.[13] Then we passed Taliwu village and arrived at Chaili village, where we spent the night. I estimate that we traveled two days and nights by cart. On the cart I was tired and wanted to sleep, but every time we got to a sheer cliff or a deep ravine, I would be startled awake again. The savage cart drivers I saw were all covered with blue tattoos. On their backs were outstretched wings of birds. From their shoulders to their navels they had net patterns cut in slanting strokes. On each shoulder there was the likeness of a human head, revolting and terrifying. From their wrists to their elbows, they piled tens of iron bracelets. Also there were some who used them to make their ears large.

10th—We crossed Huwei (Tiger Tail) Creek, and Xiluo (Western Conch) Creek. The creeks were two or three tricents wide. One could walk on the sand flats, and when the carriages passed they left no tracks; it was like a kind of "sheet-iron" sand. The sand and water were all black, due to the fact that the Taiwanese mountains are all colored by black earth. Another thirty tricents and we came to Dongluo (Eastern Conch) Creek. It was exactly as wide as Xiluo (Western Conch) Creek, but the water was deeper and more rapid. The buffaloes hitched to the shafts were afraid of drowning. They simply lay down and floated. Ten or so savage boys supported the wheels in order to get them across. Thus most of them did not sink below the surface. Once across, we met with rain. We galloped for thirty tricents and arrived at Dawu township, where we stayed the night. As for the savages that we saw that day, many more had tattooed their bodies. Their earrings became as large as plates. But they tied back their hair. Some had braids, some had little buns. Also they used three feathers from the chicken's tail as tassels, which they stuck in their buns. The feathers swayed in the breeze. They thought it looked beautiful. There were also three young girls working with mortar and pestle. One of them was rather attractive. They appeared in front of outsiders naked, but their composure was dignified.

11th—We went thirty tricents and arrived at Banxian village. The host of the inn greeted the guests respectfully, setting out food and drink. He said, "Past this point it is mostly stone roads. Traveling by cart is not easy. Rest for a while to get rid of your fatigue." So we stayed overnight there. From Mount Zhuluo to this place, many of the savage women that we saw were white and pleasing.

12th—We passed Yasu village and reached Dadu village. All along the route were large and small clusters of rocks. The carts drove on top [of them]. Crouching all day we were extremely fatigued. On top of that there was the overgrown jungle. The grass buried you up to the shoulders. . . . The appearance of the savages turned increasingly vile.

13th—We crossed Da Creek, passed Shalu village, and arrived at Niuma village. The village huts were very cramped. When it rained, they got totally wet. I borrowed a sleeping platform that the savages had set up outside the windows of the huts. I climbed a ladder and went up. Even though there was no door or railing, I was pleased that it was high and clean.

14th—It was cloudy and foggy, and rained hard. We couldn't travel. After noon the rain stopped. I heard the sound of the ocean roaring; it was like the sound of the raging tidal bore at Hangzhou. It did not stop all day. A villager said, "The roar of the ocean is the evidence of the rain."

The fifteenth and sixteenth it rained all day. The creek in front was agitated with new water. We did not dare proceed.

17th—A slight clearing of the skies. My bed faced the mountains, but they were blocked by fog for five days. I was disappointed at not being able to see the foothills. Suddenly I saw it clearing, and was ecstatic. I thought of wild savages jumping from ridge to ridge. This mountain really is like a hedgerow; you can't tell what the mountains which lie beyond are like. I was going to climb the foothills to see the view. A villager said, "Wild savages often hide in the jungle hunting deer. When they see people they shoot arrows immediately. Be prudent and don't go!" I nodded to him, but took my walking stick, and pushing aside weeds and thorns, made my way up. When I ascended the peak the weeds were thick and tangled, and there was nowhere to place my feet. The trees in the forest were like hedgehog bristles—branches connected and leaves overlapped. The shade was so dense it was like night during the day. When I looked up to the heavens it was like peering at the sky from the bottom of a well; from time to time you could just get a glimpse. Although there was a mountain directly in front of my eyes, the dense foliage blocked it, so that I couldn't get a view. There were only wild apes jumping and squatting above and below, making noises at the people, like old people coughing. Also there was an old ape, like a five-foot-tall child, squatting and glaring angrily. When the wind swept across the tops of the tress, it made a soughing sound which chilled one to the bone. The water from the waterfall flowed by. I looked for [the waterfall] but couldn't find it. A long snake slithered out beneath my ankles, giving me a fright. So I went back.

18th—It rained heavily again. It was the weather of a strong typhoon. My clothes were soaked through. In front of the steps it was all mud. One couldn't step through it. I paced up and down depressed, then composed a poem:

> The savage huts are like ant hills,
> The thorny underbrush hangs down on the road.
> The typhoon wind invades the low window,
> The sea mist attacks the stairs.
> Avoiding the rain, I wear clogs everywhere,
> To the bed supported on tortoise shells is added a ladder.
> The stream in front has newly risen,
> I hesitate and wish to find a roosting place.

After a while, a savage woman arrived. Hair tangled and bone-thin, her appearance was inhuman. She raised her hands and made hand signals, as if she wanted something. I looked for some food and gave it to her. When the villagers saw, they quickly waved her away, saying "This woman knows magic; she is skilled at putting curses on people; don't let her get close."

25th—I took a cart together with Master Wang. We proceeded in double stages.[14] We crossed three high peaks and arrived at Zhonggang village, where we ate lunch. We saw a very fat ox, locked in a wooden cage, outside of the gate. Its head was lowered and feet were cramped; it was unable to stand up. The villagers said, "This ox is just beginning to be put to the harness. We train it by this means." They also said, "at Zhuqian and Nankan on the route ahead there are many wild oxen in the mountains. . . ."

[Beginning of the fifth month]—After several days, all the heads of various villages arrived, namely from twenty-three villages including Balifen, Mashaoweng, Inner Beitou, Outer Beitou, Mount Jizhou, Mount Dadong, Little Jilong, Big Jilong, Jinbaoli, Nan'gang, Walie, Baizhe, Limo, Wuliuwan, Leili, Laoli, Xiulang, Balangpan, Qiwuzu, Dadayou, Lizu, Fang'ayu, Mailizhekou. They were all led by the head village of Danshui. The local leaders were divided into head [chief] and vice-chief. We gave them cheap wine, fed them sugar cubes, and gave them one *zhang*[15] or so of cloth, and they all left happily. Moreover, we traded cloth with the savages for ore; for each seven feet of cloth we obtained one basket of ore.[16] Weighing it, altogether we got about 270 or 280 catties.[17] The next day, savages, both men and women, arrived in a continuous stream carrying ore in *mangge* [canoes].

The ore was variously brown and black. The color was rich and the quality heavy, and there were sparks. When you rubbed it between the fingers, there was a wonderful soughing noise. If it is not like this, then it is inferior. The refining method: pound it into a powder and let it dry in the sun. First put ten or so catties of oil into the kettle; slowly add the dry ore. Make a frame in the shape of a cross with large bamboo, and have two people hold each end and stir. The sulfur in the ore comes out upon contact with oil. As the oil and ore melt together, frequently add ore and oil until the kettle is full. You use approximately eight hundred or nine hundred catties of ore, and as for oil, the amount depends on the quality of ore. The workers from time to time scoop out some of the liquid with a metal spade and let it run down the side in order to examine it. If it's too much, they add ore; not enough, they add oil. If there is either too little or too much oil, then you will ruin the sulfur. If the ore is good and you use the appropriate amount of oil, then from one kettle you can get four hundred or five hundred catties of pure sulfur. If not, you can get anything from about two hundred or so to a few dozen catties. Even though the key to the process lies in the oil, the workers attend to the strength of the fire; it seems as though this makes a slight difference. I asked the savages where the sulfur ore was produced, and they pointed to the foothills behind the thatched hut. The next day I dragged Master Gu to go there.

We took a *mangge* and ordered two savage boys to row. We entered by the stream; at the end of the stream was Inner Bai village. We called for some locals to guide us. We turned east and went half a tricent, then entered jungle. The stalks of the weeds were over one *zhang* high. We parted them with both hands and entered sideways. The hot sun touched the tips of the weeds, and the hot summer air was steaming; it was oppressively humid. The path under the grass twisted and turned and was only wide enough for a snake to crawl on. Gu was well equipped for hiking and walked with the guide. They suddenly advanced; I followed behind with the attendants. I was only five paces behind him, yet we could no longer see one another. I was afraid we would lose each other. We would call to one another to gauge the distance of our separation.

We walked about two or three tricents, crossed two small streams (which we waded across), then again entered the deep jungle. The trees were dense and shady. Large or small we could not distinguish their names. Old vines wound around them like coiling dragons or serpents. When the wind passed leaves would drop, some as big as one's palm. Also there were giant trees which grew up splitting the earth. With two leaves sprouting, they were already ten spans big. The guide called these "cedar." When cedars begin to grow, they already have an entire trunk. Over many years they grow solid, but never increase in size. So they are the same in principle as bamboo. From the tops of the trees came the sounds of myriad types of birds. Though the ear could hear them, the eye could not see them. A cool wind struck the flesh, almost making you forget the sweltering heat. Again we crossed five or six hills, and reached a large stream. The stream was four or five *zhang* wide. The water flowed over bare rocks, giving it an indigo color. The guide said that this water originally came from the sulfur caves, where there was a bubbling spring. I tested it with one finger and it was still quite hot. I leaned on my walking stick and crossed over by stepping on bare rocks. We went two or three more tricents and the forest suddenly ended; for the first time the mountains in front could be seen. Then we crossed a small peak, and I felt that the ground beneath my shoes was gradually getting hot. I saw that the color of the vegetation was a withered lifeless brown. As I gazed at the lower foothills of the mountain in front, I saw strands of white vapor rising, like mountain clouds being suddenly spit out, shaking and waving amid the blue peaks. The guide pointed and said, "That is the sulfur cave." When the wind passed, the sulfurous odor was horrible. We went another half tricent. No plants grew here, and the ground was broiling hot. The mountains on both sides had giant rocks which had been eroded by sulfur fumes, eaten away into powder. There were fifty or so streams of white vapor, all rushing out from under the ground. Pearl-like bubbles were spit up, flying up over a foot in the air. I hitched up my clothes and went over to the side of the cave and looked in. I heard an angry thunderous noise rocking the earth, and the sound of crashing waves and boiling cauldrons. The ground was precarious, as though it were about to shake. It struck fear in my heart. Within an area of a hundred sixth-acres, it was really like a giant boiling cauldron, and I was walking on the lid. The only thing that was keeping me from falling in was the fact that the hot air was causing it to swell up. Among the giant rocks on the right was one particularly large cave. Thinking that giant rocks would not fall, I climbed atop a rock and looked down. Poisonous flames assaulted one from the cave, making it impossible to look at it directly. When they hit my head it felt as if my brain would split. I quickly retreated a hundred paces. On the left was a stream which made a sound like a toppling mountain. It was the source from which the bubbling spring came. I went back to the deep forest for a short rest. Then I followed the old path and returned. My clothes were infused with sulfur fumes, which would not disperse for days. For the first time I realized that the ceaseless mountain-toppling, cliff-crumbling, ear-splitting noise was the sound of the bubbling in the sulfur caves. I wrote two poems to commemorate [my visit]:

> The Creator gathered these strange structures,
> A surging, bubbling spring in the high peaks.
> Angry thunder will flip the earth over on its axis,
> A poisonous fog shakes the cliff tops.
> In the emerald torrent the pine grows withered,
> In cinnabar mountains plants are about to go up in flames.
> Fairy mountains Peng and Ying are far off in my gaze,
> The boiling rocks welcome the gods.

> In May there are few travelers,
> On the western slope there is a volcano.
> Who knows where the bubbling spring lies?
> So I set out on a difficult journey.
> Falling powder melts the precarious rocks,
> The sulfur stains in script-like blotches.
> A rumbling noise spreads for ten tricents,
> It's not the echoing of the current.

People had said that the environment of this place was harmful, with contagious diseases and numerous perils. That was the judgment of the various gentlemen of Taiwan prefectural city. At first I did not believe them, but having been here only a short while, the slaves became sick, and nine out of ten of the workers fell sick! Even the cook got sick. There was no one to take charge of the cooking. Master Wang had barely escaped from drowning, and now had come down with dysentery and couldn't keep any fluids down. Day and night there were about seventy or eighty rows [of sick men] until gradually they overflowed the beds. By the side of my bed, there were sick men all around. All I could hear was their moaning and trembling, as though singing an endless chorus. I resented not having superhuman strength. How could I nurse all of them? So I sent them all back on a boat. Moreover, Master Gu had to return to the provincial capital on other business. I alone could not leave. . . .

Looking out over the plain, [you see] nothing but luxuriant grasses. The vigorous vegetation covers your head; the feeble vegetation comes up to your shoulders. When the carriage passes through this growth, it is like being in the Underworld. The tips of the grasses graze your face and cut your neck. The mosquitoes and flies suck your flesh like starving vultures and hungry tigers; you can't beat them off. The blazing sun beats down on you, and your neck and back are about to split open. You've already exhausted the suffering and toil of the human world. Then, when you get there, instead of four walls and a tiled roof, there is only thatch; from all sides the wind enters like arrows. In bed you constantly see the sky. The green weeds grow up into the bed; as soon as you pull them up they sprout again. When it rains, it is like a flood in the hut. After the rains have passed, you still have to wear clogs to bed for ten days. The strumming of the cicadas and the piping of the worms rise up from beneath the bed, and the tide reaches the steps from time to time. [When you] go out of the hut, the weeds bury your shoulders, and the old trees are gnarled; it is indescribable. Horrid clumps of bamboo grow up in their midst. Within a foot of you not a thing can be seen. At night, cobras with their swollen necks make noises next to the pillows in every room. From time to time they snort like cows. They have the strength to swallow deer. Small snakes chase people and are as fast as flying arrows. At night, I don't dare go beyond the threshold of the house. The sea wind howls angrily; everything resounds. The forests and valleys shake and rock. The hut and bed are on the verge of collapsing. In the middle of the night the apes howl, sounding like ghosts crying. A single lamp flickers, and I sleep next to those who are on the verge of dying from malaria. What are Ziqing's remote frontier and Xinguo's marshes next to this?[18]

Liu Zihou[19] said, "Bozhou is not a place fit for humans to live." Let Zihou know of this place, and he would regard Bozhou as a paradise. The night that I arrived, there was a fisherman who had built his hut south of the harbor, separated from my dwelling by the water. He had folded some cloth as a mat and pillow and had gone to sleep. In the middle of the night, arrows came in from the outside, piercing the top layer of the pillow twenty-eight times. Luckily, his brain was not injured. He remained in dreamland when another arrow entered, penetrating his arm. His companions pursued the bandits, but failed to capture them. When they examined the arrow, it turned out to be the type that the savages use to shoot deer. Also there was a villager killed on the road. This all happened within the space of a few days. My thatched hut is in No-Man's-Land. From time to time I see savages coming and going in the jungle; no one can make out where they come from. When there are arrows being shot in the depths of night, how can I not be on guard? In this place, there are threats all around, and every minute I am on the verge of death! My body is not made of metal or stone; my strength is no greater than that of a mouse or rat. Moreover, I'm in my hoary years, and have an aged mother at home. How can I then forget the warning I received when I was getting ready to set forth, about remaining too long in a land of danger and death? It's just because I am resolute and brave by nature. I always advance and never retreat; in planning for others and planning for myself, I earnestly hope to accomplish something. Moreover, all my life I have been through dangers and encountered difficulties; why should I stop with just this one undertaking? Now I am old! If I were willing to stop in the middle of this endeavor, because of one thought of shame, wouldn't I lose my former self? Now, those who have fallen ill have left, and those who haven't fallen ill have also left out of fear of disease and danger. Who was left to complete this task? Wouldn't it have been better not to have come then, rather than to leave early now? Who could force me? Now, since I've come, isn't it useless to regret anything else? My will is habitually resolute. My spirit is so true that the mountain ghosts yield and the demon of disease also keeps far away from my sojourner's dwelling. Moreover, it was indeed due to my passion for travel that I came. I once said, "In searching for the exotic and visiting scenic spots, one must not fear risky inclinations: if the voyage is not dangerous it will not be exotic; if the inclination is not risky, it will not be exhilarating." Taibo [Li Bo] climbed Mount Hua,[20] and regretted not taking along one of Xie Tiao's[21] startling couplets; he scratched his head and complained to Heaven. Changli [Han Yu][22] climbed to the summit of Mount Hua and, crying bitterly, composed a letter taking leave of his family. The Magistrate of Huayin used a hundred stratagems to get him down, and only then was he able to descend.[23] They were all obsessed with a passion for travel. Although I would not dare to compare myself with the worthies of the past, what I have passed through on this journey would make Changli and Taibo envious. Moreover, Penglai Island is in sight, and the waters of the Ruoshui can be cupped in the hand.[24] If Qin Shihuang and Han Wudi were to hear of this, would they not roll over in their graves?[25]

Small Sea Travelogue, vol. 3

(In the last section, Yu describes the completion of his expedition and his return to China. This section is filled with his observations about the relation between China and Taiwan, an island that had long been considered "beyond the seas" and remote from "China proper." He finally makes a plea both for the humanity of the native "savages" and for the benefits of colonizing Taiwan. Yu bases his arguments on the need to civilize the "savages," and the need to strengthen China's position in the international arena. Upon arriving back in China, Yu gives his final judgment on the exotica he has seen and expresses his pleasure at returning to his home and old friends.)

Since I have come overseas, and moreover have traveled to the farthest and most remote areas, personally traveling through No-Man's-Land, walking over hill and dale, through the mountains and rivers, seeing the conditions, savage customs, and popular sentiment of all of Taiwan (not just being there myself but actually exploring), how can I not write something in order to leave a record by which to let people know of this world and these people? At the time, I would often go out at dawn with my walking stick, then take a boat at dusk, in order to survey the surroundings and explore the terrain.

. . . People argue that Taiwan is simply "a ball of mud beyond the sea, that is unworthy of development by China. It is full of naked and tattooed savages who are not worth defending. It is a daily waste of Imperial money for no benefit. It would be better to evacuate the people and vacate the land." Don't they know that if we abandon it, someone else will take it? If we vacate it, they will not have difficulty bringing in immigrants to populate it. Ai!

. . . The wild savages rely on their ferociousness and from time to time emerge and plunder, burning houses and killing people. Then they return to their lairs, and no one can approach them. Every time they kill someone, they remove the head and go back and cook it. They scrape the flesh from the skull and apply red and white paint to it. They place it in the doorway, and their fellows regard those with the most skulls as heroes. They live as if in a dream, as if drunk. They don't know to civilize [themselves]. They are really mere beasts! But they are just like tigers and leopards; if you come across them, they will bite. Like snakes and vipers, if you run up against them, they will bite. If you don't approach their caves, they have no intent of poisoning you.

. . . If we could civilize them with rites and righteousness; refine them with the *Book of Odes* and the *Book of Documents;* cultivate them in the way of storing what they have and preparing for shortages; regulate them with clothing, food and drink, marriage and funeral customs; make them all understand love for relatives, respect for elders, obedience to their lords, and affection for superiors; enlighten their minds to the enjoyment of life and repress their obstinate and hostile natures; then, at the longest, it would take one hundred years, and at the fastest, thirty years, to see their customs change and see them comply with the rites and teachings. How would they be any different from the Chinese?

. . . Because they are of a different kind, people discriminate against them. They see them without clothing and say, "They don't know cold." They see them walking in the rain and sleeping under the dew and say, "They don't get sick." They see them running for long distances with heavy loads and say, "They really have endurance." Ai! Aren't they also human?! Look at their limbs, their bodies, their skin and bones; in what way are they not human, so that you say these things? You can't gallop a horse all night; you can't harness an ox crookedly, or else they will get sick. If oxen and horses are this way, how much the more so for people? . . . Enjoying fullness and warmth, suffering from hunger and cold, hating labor and delighting in idleness and pleasure, this is human nature. You may consider these people different, but what need is there to consider their nature different? The humanitarian gentleman will know not to reject my words. . . .

[Tenth month] 12th—Riding the slight breeze, I helped the boat along with a paddle. I could see the great Nantai Bridge. Young Zhou Xuanyu led several servants in a small skiff to welcome me. When I saw them I was overjoyed. Xuanyu and I took the small skiff together and went to the great bridge, where we went ashore. Entering the city, we went to meet those good friends who had seen me off so long ago. Only Qiu Shaoyi, He Xiangchen, and my nephew Zhou Zailu were in. The others had either returned home or gone to other places, and we couldn't see them. Only Lü Hongtu crossed the ocean and returned before me. I was quite happy. Seeing once again the sights of the city, I remembered that for half a year I had been living in No-Man's-Land. It was a world apart. I wonder how it compares with changing into a crane and going back [to Heaven as an immortal]. In the past I desired to travel overseas. I said that the waters of the Ruoshui could be held in the hand, and that the three mountains of the immortals could be reached.[26] Now that my eyes have seen all of the vast wilderness, and my feet have exhausted the solitary precipices, I know that these so-called immortals are no more than a naked, tattooed race! Even if this is the elysium of the immortal islands Peng and Ying, it can't compare to my hometown with its misty hazes over boundless waters, and the fife and drum of painted pleasure boats. These are extraordinary and wonderful rain or shine—quite enough to keep my thoughts attached [to them no matter where I go].

—ET

Notes

1. The word "savage" is used here as a translation of the Chinese *fan*. Qing writers employed this pejorative term to refer to the indigenous peoples of Taiwan.

2. Government office.

3. Zheng Chenggong, or Koxinga, took Taiwan as a base for his Ming loyalist rebel army in 1661, ousting the Dutch, who had colonized the island in 1624. Zheng's descendants held the island until 1683, when they were defeated by Qing forces.

4. Fujian was divided into eight prefectures. When China first took possession of Taiwan, the island was made part of Fujian Province, thus adding a ninth prefecture.

5. Approximately 660,000 pounds (300,000 kilograms).

6. In the portion of the text that has been omitted, the author explains that he transfers to an ocean-going sampan.

7. Taipei is actually only about 150 miles (241 kilometers) from Fuzhou. The figure of 1,000 tricents (approximately 330 miles [531 kilometers]) thus exaggerates by more than doubling the distance. As a matter of fact, although Yu Yonghe cites many distances, some of which seem to be of a precise nature (e.g., 2,315 tricents from the south to the north of Taiwan, which is nearly four times the actual length of the island), they are highly unreliable and inaccurate throughout.

8. Admiral Zheng He, the great eunuch Muslim commander of the Ming fleet, led seven major naval expeditions between 1405 and 1433, exploring the seas as far as Africa.

9. Now Okinawa, a part of Japan.

10. Tower of the Red Hairs is located in Tainan, Taiwan.

11. One sixth-acre *(mu)* is equivalent to approximately 733.5 square yards (677 square meters).

12. What is translated as "No-Man's-Land" here is literally "Non-human land." The author uses the phrase to describe Taiwan as a place unfit for habitation by civilized men.

13. All of the place names have meanings. A few of them are translated here to give an idea of what they are like.

14. This means that they skipped every other rest stop that would normally have been scheduled.

15. One *zhang* is equivalent to approximately 141 inches (3.6 meters).

16. A Chinese foot is equivalent to approximately 14.1 inches.

17. A catty is equivalent to approximately 1.33 pounds (0.6 kilograms).

18. Ziqing is the sobriquet of Su Wu, a famous statesman of the second century B.C.E. who was sent by the Han emperor Wudi on a mission to the Xiongnu (Hun) Khan. He was imprisoned by the Khan and later sent into the wilds, where he lived for nineteen years as a shepherd. Xinguo refers to Wen Tianxiang

(1236–1282), who was famous for his loyalty to the Song dynasty (960–1279) and his resistance to the invading Mongols who overthrew the Song. In 1276 he was sent on a mission to a Mongol camp, where he was imprisoned. Later he escaped and fought with the imperial forces in Zhangzhou, Fujian. He was known for leading troops into the barbarian wilderness. He was honored with the title Lord of Xinguo (True to the State).

19. Liu Zihou is the style name of Liu Zongyuan (773–819), a famous Tang-dynasty (618–907) literatus who is often credited with establishing the travelogue genre. Bozhou is in present-day Guizhou.

20. Li Bo (701–762) was a famous Tang-dynasty poet and inebriate. Mount Hua is one of the five sacred mountains of China. It is located in today's Shaansi Province, in the south of Huayin County. It was traditionally renowned as a Taoist holy place and as a scenic spot.

21. Xie Tiao (464–499) was famous for the originality of the couplets in his landscape poems.

22. Han Yu (768–824) was one of the most eminent poets and essayists of the Tang dynasty.

23. In 803, Han Yu climbed Mount Hua with some companions. It is said in Li Zhao's *Supplement to the State History of the Tang* that when Han reached the summit, he became afraid that he would be unable to descend. He then wept and made out a last will to his family. The magistrate of Huayin eventually reached him and helped him to descend.

24. Penglai is one of three mythical islands of immortals fabled to be located in the middle of the Eastern Sea. See note 25. The Ruoshui is the name of a river said to run near the dwelling place of the goddess, the Queen Mother of the West.

25. According to legend, the ancient Emperor Qin Shihuang, founder of the Qin dynasty, had sent a mission overseas in search of the three islands of the immortals and the magical herbs of immortality. Another legend has it that Han Wudi, Emperor Wudi of the Han, once met with the Queen Mother of the West and attempted to obtain the secrets of immortality from her.

26. The three mountains of the immortals are the mythical mountains Fangzhang, Penglai, and Yingzhou, said to be located in the middle of the Eastern Sea.

"MIAO ALBUMS" OF GUIZHOU Province are handpainted ethnographic manuscripts of non-Han peoples that were first made during the eighteenth century. Under the Yongzheng emperor (r. 1723–1735) the administration of much of Guizhou shifted from the hereditary control of local headmen to the regular imperial bureaucracy. Confucian officials newly assigned to posts in the region found these documents a useful tool for acquainting themselves with the customs and beliefs of the non-Han peoples whom they would be governing. Each album leaf names and depicts a distinct group, enumerates where its members lived and how they dressed, and describes customs and practices by which they could be identified. The colorful illustrations focus primarily on themes relating to livelihood, religious festivals, courtship rituals, proclivity to violent behavior, and other practices of individual groups found to be of interest. The illustrations that follow depict a range of courtship and marriage practices.—LH

Caijia Miao are located in Guizhu, Xiuwen, Weining, Dading, and Pingyuan.[1] The men wear felt upper garments. The women put their hair up using felt, and adorn it with blue cloth. The style

Figure 85.1. Songjia (untitled album, Ethnologisches Museum, Abteilung Ostasien, Staatliche Museen Preussischer Kulturbesitz, Berlin, #46973). The woman's parents are shown wielding sticks against the "bride snatchers." Belying the kidnapping, the bride appears to be dressed up for the event, her trousseau well-prepared and packed into the basket strapped to one man's back.

resembles a cow's horn; it is more than a foot tall. They must use long hairpins to fasten it up. They wear short upper garments and long skirts. Father-in-law and daughter-in-law do not speak with each other. When a woman's husband dies they bury her with him. The woman's family will send a group of people to snatch her away to avoid this fate. (See plate 110.)

Songjia Miao are under the jurisdiction of Guiyang. The men wear caps and have long robes. The women pin their hair up and wear short skirts. When it is time for a marriage to take place, the man's family sends people for the bride. The woman's family in turn leads a group of relatives to try to prevent her departure. This is called snatching a bride from her parents. (See fig. 85.1.)

Kayou Zhongjia are located in Guiyang, Anshun, Nanlong, Pingyue, and Duyun prefectures. They are fond of blue clothing. Women cover their heads with patterned kerchiefs. Their upper garments are short, and rounded at the bottom. They cut the fabric to fit the body, neither increasing nor decreasing the amount even in the cold of winter or the heat of summer. Their skirts are long and finely pleated, with panels of alternating colors. Their big festival is on the sixth day of the sixth month. Every year during the first month of spring the unmarried men and women gather together and dance under the moon. They sing and dance in the wilderness. They use colorful cloth, tying it up into a small ball like a melon. It is called a flower ball *(hua qiu)*. Those whose sentiments of deep affection are in harmony toss the ball back and forth, and then become intimate. Whenever they come together, whether for weddings or funerals, the pair is

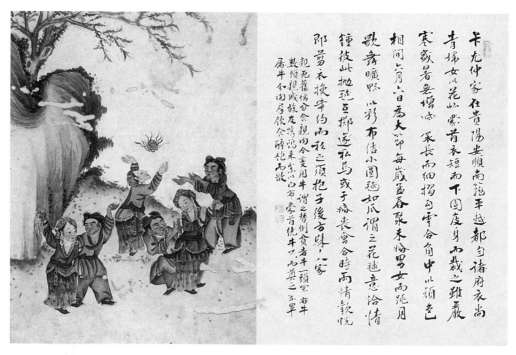

Figure 85.2. Kayou Zhongjia ("Miaoman tu," Fu Ssu-nien Library, Academia Sinica). The Kayou Zhongjia are pictured in a natural setting in which their "moon dance" was held. Three men and three women cavort in pairs. Note the colorful balls of cloth that are tossed back and forth between amorous couples. In this illustration each person depicted appears to have found a mate with whom their "sentiments of deep affection are in harmony."

always joyful and contented. They cut pieces from their clothing and exchange belts. Thus engaged, they elope. Only after the woman bears a child does she become part of her husband's family.

When a parent dies the old custom was to divide up the flesh and eat it. Now this has changed; they use water buffalo instead. This is called changing the custom *(ti li)*. The poor use one head of cattle, the wealthy use several head. Relatives, clansmen, and friends bring chicken to sacrifice. They cover their heads with white cloth, circle the buffalo, cry, and offer libations to it. When the sacrifice is over, they kill and dress the buffalo and divide up the meat. The guests eat and drink until sated and inebriated and then disperse. (See fig. 85.2.)

Tooth-breaking Gelao are located in Qianxi, Qingzhen, and Pingyue departments and counties. When a woman marries, she must first have her two front teeth knocked out for fear of harming her husband's family. These are the so-called chiseling-teeth people. They cut their hair in front and wrap it up behind. This has the meaning of getting married *(qu qimei)*.[2]

Figure 85.3. Daya Gelao ("Miaoman tu," Fu Ssu-nien Library, Academia Sinica). The "tooth-breaking" ritual, which characterizes this group of Gelao, is shown taking place within the privacy of a fenced area outside the house. A group of six women, including the bride, participates. The bride is seated and leans her head back; another woman supports it, holding it by the jaw. A third woman grasps the bride's right arm. The oldest woman present—judging by her wrinkles and darker skin—is responsible for breaking the bride's front teeth. Seated next to the bride, she holds a mallet in her right hand and a chisel in her left in preparation for the task at hand. A fifth woman, located off to the right of the group, holds a tray or basket in which the chisel and mallet are sometimes depicted in other Miao albums. The sixth woman looks on from inside the house. The only male present is separated from these activities by the fence and gate in the foreground of the illustration.

The Gelao are also called Geliao. There are five different groups who do not intermarry. They have dishevelled hair and go barefoot. They value life lightly; they will die for their companions. They weave strips of gingham into "barrel skirts," which they wear around their waists horizontally without pleats. Men and women alike make clothes. This is so with all five varieties. (See fig. 85.3.)

—LH

Notes

1. These are all place-names in Guizhou Province. The Caijia Miao are shown in color plate 110, where the man on the right carries a hoe and a basket for moving earth as if he is ready to dig the woman's grave. The other two men appear to be holding on to the woman as if to make sure she does not get away. Sometimes illustrations of the Caijia show a more hopeful scene; a man with a bedroll on his back coming over a bridge to reclaim the woman for her natal family.

2. *Qimei* literally means "even with the eyebrows," but it is also an expression that refers to a married couple.

97. Stage, Dongyang, Linfen County, Shanxi, Yuan. Chinese drama has its roots in performing arts dating back to Han and earlier times (plate 35). Even in the Tang dynasty, however, opera is believed to have been performed in temporary structures. The first known stationary stages are from the Song dynasty. In Jin times, Shanxi Province became a center for authorship and performance of popular drama, especially those parts of southern Shanxi where workshops painted the walls of Daoist and Buddhist monasteries beginning in the thirteenth century (plate 94). In the early fourteenth century, a troupe of actors who performed at the Guangsheng Monastery was painted on the walls of one of its halls, about two hundred kilometers north of Yonglegong. The stage in Dongyang is halfway between Yongle Daoist Monastery and Guangsheng Buddhist Monastery.

98. Shen Zhou (1427–1509), "Thousand Buddha Hall and Pagoda of the 'Cloudy Cliff' Monastery," album leaf from "Twelve Views of Tiger Hill, Suzhou"; Cleveland Museum of Art. Shen Zhou was a country gentleman with plenty of wealth and an uncomplicated and unpretentious lifestyle who spent his entire life in the immediate vicinity of Suzhou, a city that prided itself in its beauty and its cultivated gentility. He was also the greatest painter of his day and is one of the best known and most recognizable in the history of China. "Twelve Views of Tiger Hill," probably painted after about 1490 and thus one of his later works, is typical of his subjects and his style. The subject is what he knew best, his own city (named Wu in the third century and earlier) and the places in it where he passed his many leisure hours. Marks of Shen Zhou's brush are the architectural drawings made with parallel lines but without the use of a guiding straight edge, faceless figures, foliage dominated by a wet brush, and lavish use of orange-pink and blue tones.

99. Zhou Chen (ca. 1450–aft. 1535), detail from "Beggars and Street Characters"; 1516; Cleveland Museum of Art. Zhou Chen was a professional painter, not a scholar, about whose life we know little. His portraits of twenty-four men he observed out of his window one day is unique, even among the work of men who sold their paintings to support themselves. This has led

to speculation about the painter's purpose. Were these twelve pairs of figures on paper inspired by Buddhist paintings of monks? Was this a social or moral commentary about the reality of life in Suzhou, so different from the city portrayed by the elder painter Shen Zhou (plate 98)? Or was it just a study, sketches in ink and color for some greater work he thought would interest his clientele?

100. Qiu Ying (1494/5–1552), "Saying Farewell at Xunyang," hand-scroll; Nelson-Atkins Museum of Art, Kansas City. Qiu Ying was a professional artist who painted in the city of Suzhou. His lifestyle was a contrast to those of many contemporary artists in the beautiful southeastern city where literate men painted and built gardens purely as pastimes. The subjects and styles of Qiu Ying's paintings appealed to a wealthy mercantile population that also resided in Suzhou. "Saying Farewell at Xunyang" is typical. It illustrates "The Lute Song," a poem by Bo Juyi, written in 816, that would have been known to anyone who bought the painting. In the poem, Bo comes to the riverbank to bid farewell to a friend whose boat is docked there. Across the water he hears some of the most beautiful lute music he has ever experienced. He rightly supposes that the musician was trained in the capital, Chang'an. Indeed, she had been a famous courtesan in her youth and, now past her prime, was married to a local tea merchant. The painter not only chooses a famous subject of the Tang dynasty, he paints in the archaistic "blue and green" manner of Tang painters, which had previously experienced a renaissance in both Song and Yuan painting (plate 92). Qiu Ying's Suzhou clientele also would have been aware of these stylistic predecessors. Finally, the outlines of the mountains, the other natural elements, and the figures also harken back to Tang styles as they had been interpreted by Song and Yuan painters.

101. Dong Qichang (1555–1636), "The Qingbian Mountains"; 1617; Cleveland Museum of Art. Dong Qichang was the most influential painter of his era and one of the most influential in the history of Chinese painting. His fame is derived not from his paintings so much as his writings. Dong was an art historian, a critic of Chinese painting and Chinese painters. He conceived of a framework, a clearly artificial one, for grouping all painters of the past into two schools, the Northern and the Southern. The categories were chosen in emulation of the two main schools of Chan (Zen) Buddhism. Dong determined that the Southern school should be the superior, and into this group he placed literati painters and others he considered great such as Jing Hao, Dong Yuan, and Juran of the tenth century, Mi Fu (plate 78) of the Song, and Ni Zan of the Yuan (plate 95). Northern school painters were court artists and those who used more color in their paintings, including Ma Yuan and Zhao Boju of the Song. Dong's treatises on painting had such a great influence that the success of painters for the next several centuries often depended on their adherence to old masters whose work had been sanctioned by Dong Qichang.

102. Five marble bridges and Gate of Great Harmony, Forbidden City; Ming period with later additions. Beijing is the epitome of Chinese urban planning, the direction toward which imperial designs in China had been heading for two millennia prior to the fifteenth century. Borrowing the location of its main axial line from Khubilai Khaghan's capital, which lies underneath it, its water sources from the Jin (1115–1234) city that lies beneath the ruins of Khubilai's capital, and its layout from the earliest prescriptions for Chinese urban planning (plate 17), Beijing is linked to every period of China's past. Beijing also provides the world with its most powerful images of China: enclosure by walls, access through gates rather than directly into a building or building group, construction along long lines, and courtyards. Finally, it is an ultimate image of imperial privacy, for only the golden roof tiles are visible from the outside.

103. Altar of Heaven complex, Beijing; 15th c. and after. Whereas the Forbidden City is the supreme image of imperial China, the Altar of Heaven complex is the ultimate symbol of the unique role of the emperor in China. Here, not only is every detail of the building complex perfectly and rigidly planned, but every structure is also symbolic. The three main structures combine the two perfect shapes of Chinese construction, the circle symbolizing Heaven and the square symbolizing Earth, seen on the mirror back from the Han dynasty (plate 31). At the winter solstice the emperor ascended the three platforms of the Circular Mound to report to Heaven the events of the year. In the first moon of the year, he returned, this time to the Hall for Prayer for a Prosperous Year, the only circular, three-roof structure in China, to obtain the confidence of Heaven and make supplications for a year of prosperity. Besides this altar complex, imperial Beijing had an Altar of Agriculture, an Altar of Earth, Altars of the Sun and Moon, twin Altars of Soil and Grain, and an Ancestral Temple, each within its own walled complex of buildings.

104. Forest of Pagodas, Shaolin Monastery, Dengfeng County, Henan. The forest of more than 220 pagodas, some of which date from the Tang dynasty, represents just one facet of the Shaolin Monastery. It was founded in 496, in the shadow of the sacred peak, Mount Song, just three years after the Northern Wei dynasty had moved its capital to Luoyang, about sixty kilometers northwest of the monastery. The Indian Buddhist monk Bodhidharma, first patriarch of Chan (Zen) Buddhism in China, is purported to have spent nine years meditating toward a cave wall at the Shaolinsi in the 520s and 530s. Less than a kilometer away stands the oldest wooden building in Henan, the main hall of Chuzu Hermitage, dated to 1125. Five kilometers in another direction is the oldest pagoda in the province (plate 50). Finally, Shaolin Monastery's monks have been famous for centuries for their dexterity in the martial arts (selection 77).

105. Merchant residence, Hong Village, Yi County, Anhui; Ming period. Some of the earliest extant Chinese residences are in Anhui Province. Many of them belonged to merchant families. Anhui houses most often are two stories, rare examples of multistory, residential construction in premodern China. The reason for the high buildings was limited space: they are rarely more than three bays in width. Supported by timber frames, covered with whitewashed brick, with flat, gable sides known as "firm mountain roofs," and built around sky

wells rather than courtyards, the simple, rigid exteriors often concealed elaborately carved wooden decoration, embellished building parts, and roof supports. In other words, a family's monetary wealth was visible only within. Like most traditional Chinese residences, a main central room in the back area was formal, reserved for the display of precious possessions or ancestral portraits. However, whereas in one-story courtyard-style houses the sleeping rooms would flank the main chamber, here they were upstairs. Hong Village has been designated a UNESCO World Heritage Site.

106. Garden of the Humble Administrator, Suzhou; 16th c. Gardens are the one setting in which Chinese construction principles break down. The Garden of the Humble Administrator was built by the Ming court censor Wang Xianchen. Its name comes from a line in a poem by fourth-century scholar-official Pan Yue, who achieved fame but was nevertheless disappointed with officialdom and retired to plant trees and cultivate a vegetable garden. He wrote that working the land was his way of ruling. In 1551, Wang's friend, the painter Wen

Zhengming, painted eight album leaves depicting scenes from the garden. Descended from a family of successful officials, Wen failed the national exams for an official position at least ten times between 1495 and 1522. Wen Zhengming, whom some have likened to the humble, or unsuccessful, administrator, painted in a studio in Wang Xianchen's garden.

107. Chen Hongshou (1599–1652), the poet Tao Yuanming, detail of "Episodes from the Life of Tao Qian"; 1650; Honolulu Academy of Fine Arts. The first half of the sixteenth century was a period of political upheaval in China, culminating with the overthrow of the Ming dynasty and establishment of the Manchu dynasty named Qing in 1644. The coincident period of late Ming to early Qing is always described as one of the most innovative in Chinese painting history, comparable in new developments to the tenth century and the period of Mongolian rule. The intro-

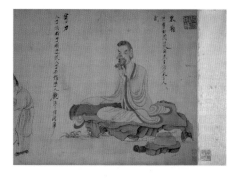

spection on the personality of the fourth-century poet Tao Yuanming (Qian), author of the famous poem "Returning Home," had also been a subject for the Yuan painter Qian Xuan, whose oeuvre was marked by political undertones (plate 92). This work is typical of Chen's probing in a disconcerted manner beneath the skin of his subject. The politically and emotionally frustrated painter has added an aspect of the absurd to his work, penetrating beyond the work of his predecessors, who had used figure painting merely to express political and social injustice.

108. Manchu ceremonial armor made for the Xianfeng emperor (r. 1851–1861), Palace Museum, Beijing. Although the Qing dynasty quickly adapted to a facade of Chinese imperialism following native models of the Ming dynasty, the predynastic Qing were seminomadic Manchus who originated in the territory of China's three northeastern provinces (former Manchuria). In the early seventeenth century, the Manchus organized themselves militarily according to Eight Banners, each symbolizing one of the main tribes that had come together to forge a united empire. In their imperial capital in Shenyang, Liaoning Province, occupied by the man who became the founder of the Manchu dynasty, Nurhaci, beginning in 1625, each Banner had its own hall. Today those small buildings house ceremonial and military regalia of the seventeenth-century Bannermen. The eight banners also were blazed in front of the Manchu summer palaces in Chengde, Hebei Province.

109. Main temple *(vihaan)* of Tai Buddhist temple complex, Wat Gang, Meng Zhe, Xishuangbanna (Sipsongpanna), Yunnan. The nationality of the ruling family of Qing China was Manchu, but ethnic groups from every part of China comprised and sometimes tormented the empire. Today they are called "minorities," and the ethnicity of the region of Yunnan Province known as Xishuangbanna, which shares a border with Myanmar (Burma), is Tai (pronounced Dai). In the Qing period, almost every Tai village had a temple complex like this one, consisting of a main temple that contains a statue of the Buddha at one end, one or two pagodas, monks' quarters, a wall around the complex, and a causeway connecting a gate of that wall to the entrance of the main temple. Just as the buildings of Xishuangbanna resemble those of contemporary Burma, architecture at other Chinese borders followed forms of Tibet, Mongolia, regional styles of Fujian or Guangxi, and so forth. Today, all are considered Qing architecture, whose main feature might be called multiculturalism. Although Wat Gang is a living monastery, the building in the photograph has the startlingly early date of 748.

110. Scene from "Miaoman tu" (illustrated albums describing the customs of the southern "ethnic minority" Miao); 18th–19th c. Ethnologisches Museum, Staatliche Museen Preussischer Kulturbesitz, Berlin. The Miao were one of the scores of so-called "ethnic minorities" that populated every edge of the Qing Chinese border. The Miao lived in Guizhou and Yunnan. Albums such as these emphasized the deep-seated differences—in physical features, ritual, and the dress, foods, and manners of daily life—between their subjects and the people of the Yellow River Valley and Central Plain. Miao is the Modern Standard Mandarin transcription of Hmong. The Hmong are found in many parts of Southeast Asia today and, since the Vietnam War, in large numbers as refugees in North America and elsewhere. When they were painted, the albums were of interest to non-Miao perhaps more than to the Miao themselves (selection 85).

111. Yonghegong, Beijing; 1694 and later. Lamaist Buddhism, which traced its origins to the region of Nepal-Tibet, had first become popular in China under Mongolian rule. Under the Qing court, it flourished all the more. The Yonghegong is the most famous and important lamasery in Beijing. The buildings on the site of the Yonghegong were constructed in 1694 by the Kangxi emperor (r. 1662–1722) as a residence for his fourth son, whom he probably did not antici-

pate would succeed him. Upon his father's death after the extraordinarily long reign of sixty years, this son became the Yongzheng emperor (r. 1723–1736), whereupon he moved into the Forbidden City and his residence automatically attained the status of a place where an emperor has resided. Thus it could never be used for a secular purpose. Yongzheng's successor, the Qianlong emperor (r. 1736–1796), converted the former residence, first replacing its green roof-tiles with imperial golden ones and then in 1644 officially turning it into a lamasery, which it remained through the rest of imperial times. Since antiquity, religious architecture in China had borrowed its forms from secular architecture. Sometimes, as was the case here, a residence became a religious institution.

112. Ruins of Yuanming-yuan, Beijing; late 18th c. and later. The Qing emperors had five gardens, usually referred to as summer palaces, northwest of Beijing. The most famous was Yiheyuan, best known by the name Summer Palace, reconstructed between 1751 and 1764 by the Qianlong emperor in honor of his mother's sixtieth birthday. Nearby Yuanmingyuan, actually three gardens that shared boundaries, was

constructed over a period of 150 years. In the mid-eighteenth century, Castiglione (plate 114) was one of the Europeans at the Qianlong court asked to make designs for some of its buildings. To aid them, they sent to Europe for books on architecture. The destruction evident in this photograph was the result of burning in 1860 during the Anglo-French attack on Beijing.

113. Shitao (Daoji) (1641–c. 1710), detail of "Peach Blossom Spring"; Freer Gallery of Art. Shitao is one of the seventeenth-century painters of the Ming-Qing transition who is labeled an "individualist." A descendant of the Ming imperial family whose father was killed in political unrest of 1644, he sought refuge in a monastery for a time, then became a professional painter, and in 1684 acknowledged the Qing government. Shitao's style is hard to characterize, thereby leading to the association with individuality. He wrote that he was opposed to copying old masters without allowing for the inspiration of one's own eyes and that the power of painting was in the primordial line. It would be impossible to say a painting is typical of his work, but "Peach Blossom Spring" is characteristic. Here the artist has taken as his theme Tao Yuanming's (365–427; see plate 107) essay about a wanderer who stumbles upon an arcadian community that has endured for centuries with no knowledge of the outside world and its political turmoil. Although many painters before Shitao had dealt with the essay, none of the paintings approached the expressive strokes of Shitao.

114. Guiseppe Castiglione (1688–1766), "Chinese Ladies-in-Waiting in the Yuanmingyuan"; Völkerkunde Museum, Hamburg. Guiseppe Castiglione was one of the Jesuits who worked in a studio with Chinese court painters inside the Forbidden City. Although books printed in Europe and knowledge of Western painting techniques were available in China during the Ming dynasty, they flourished at the courts of Kangxi, Yongzheng, and Qianlong. Castiglione was more responsible for the interest in European techniques in China than any other Jesuit painter, in large part because of the seriousness of his study of Chinese painting. Through exploration of light, shading, and perspective he created a unique and truly Sino-Western style. The hanging scroll "Chinese Ladies-in-Waiting in the Yuanmingyuan" is typical of Castiglione's unique success as a Sino-European painter. The theme of the painting, court ladies, even court ladies playing a board game, is an old one. The hanging scroll format is equally old and a trademark of Chinese painting. Although using Chinese colors, the techniques employed by the painter are Western. This painting has two levels of Westernization beyond the typical ones in Castiglione's oeuvre: ladies of eighteenth-century courts in Beijing sometimes wore the clothing of European women, especially when they had themselves painted. In addition, the setting for the painting is a room of the summer palace complex Yuanmingyuan (plate 112), parts of which were designed by Castiglione and other Europeans in imitation of baroque architecture. Guiseppe Castiglione went by the Chinese name Lang Shining. When he died in Beijing, he was buried there. It is said that the Qianlong emperor erected a stele in his memory.

115. Chang Dai-chien (Zhang Daqian) (1899–1983), "Through Ancient Eyes"; ca. 1920–1922; Metropolitan Museum of Art. Some would call Chang Dai-chien the master synthesizer of the thousand-plus-year history of Chinese painting that preceded him, and others would call him a rogue and forger whose oeuvre befuddled even the greatest twentieth-century connoisseurs of Chinese painting. An eccentric who modeled aspects of his life after those of a Chinese scholar-official, Chang sought public attention through his four simultaneous marriages, meeting with Picasso in 1956, and claims after he left China in 1949 that he had painted certain masterpieces in major museums of the West assigned to some of China's most famous artists. Whether or not all the works he painted or claimed to have painted are correctly attributed, Chang Dai-chien's unique twentieth-century career epitomizes the fine line between the age-old and uniquely Chinese practice of admiring and copying the old masters as a sign of greatness and respect, on the one hand, and the Western disdain for forgery, on the other.

116. Xu Bing (1955–), "Tianshu" (Book from the sky); ca. 1989. Contemporary Chinese artists are reaching out in many directions to find new modes of expression in an ever-changing world. There could be perhaps no greater sacrilege than to tamper with the script *(wenzi)* that lies at the heart of Chinese culture *(wenhua)*. Yet that is exactly what Xu Bing has done in the most profound way. Probing the characters from every angle imaginable, he has deconstructed the matrix that—more than anything else—has defined Chinese tradition for the past three thousand years. At the same time, Xu Bing's work points to an exciting future in which the barriers between Chinese culture and global culture will be obliterated. Here we see meticulously carved and printed woodblock graphs that look like characters but are not. In later projects, the artist has written English words in the square shape of Chinese characters and has created Chinese characters that morph into alphabetic form.

117. Fuyou Road, Shanghai; 2002. The challenges of the late twentieth and early twenty-first centuries are far greater than modernization. China, its cities, its buildings, and all its art forms, the tangible and intangible features that have defined Chinese civilization for several millennia, face powerful outside images more rapidly than at any time in the past. The main shopping thoroughfare of China's most contemporary city is a contrast of the neon signs of foreign venture capitalists and profiles of Chinese-style buildings.

YUAN MEI (1718–1796) was a poet and an iconoclast whose hedonistic life mirrored the independent spirit which he championed in his writings. His ideas were forward-looking yet deeply rooted in his era. He lived by his wits, writing funeral essays for patrons and publishing his own works, yet he could never have succeeded without ties to men of influence, made during his early years in the Hanlin Academy and his short career as magistrate. The Qing was a time when scholars like Gu Yanwu (see selection 83) were repudiating the Neo-Confucian orthodoxy of Song thought, in favor of an evidential, pragmatic approach to the classics. Yuan Mei did not buy into the idealistic tendencies of Song thought either, but what he most objected to was the idea of an imposed Dao-lineage. Yuan Mei was interested in forming a rewarding personal synthesis, and his sole criterion for any philosophy was whether it could contribute to one's emotional wholeness. He did not care for Buddhism, yet karma was a key part of his worldview, and much of his favorite poetry incorporates a Chan (Zen) aesthetic. He even named his garden "Suiyuan" (Garden of Mr. Sui), which is a pun on "go along with karma."

To the extent that was possible in his times, Yuan Mei was an advocate of independent womanhood. He stood against the practice of footbinding, but judiciously confined his opinion to his personal letters. He praised educated women, accepted women students, some of them unmarried, and even published a book titled *Poems by the Female Disciples of Sui Garden (Suiyuan nüdizi shixuan)*. Although some later moralists (Liang Qichao [1873–1929; see selection 90] among them) found his loose behavior disgusting, he was fairly scrupulous in his relations with women students from good families. He met with them in groups or with chaperones, during social visits at his garden. His relations with them helped created a carefree, romantic aura around Sui Garden which probably helped him sell *Suiyuan Poetry Talks (Suiyuan shihua)* and other books. Because the Sui Garden was a famous literary gathering spot, perhaps Yuan Mei was partly justified in claiming that his Sui Garden was a prototype for the Daguan Garden in Cao Xueqin's *Dream of the Red Chamber.*

As for Yuan Mei's behavior with singing girls and handsome male actors, of which he made no secret, that was wholly a different story. One can understand the viewpoint of moralists when reading, in his collection of letters, that he "found oblivion while lying atop a woman, rather than on a meditation mat."

As an arbiter of taste, Yuan Mei was a tireless promoter of other people's poetry. He wrote prefaces and arranged for publication of much work. He had little interest in rules, conventions, and cumbersome metrical technique. This can be seen in the selections from his *Suiyuan Poetry Talks* below. Yuan Mei looked for a fresh, individual outlook; he believed each true poet says certain things that no one else can say better. The other two selections below, which reflect his opposition to overarching philosophies, are taken from his letters and his essays.

Yuan Mei's literary career points to a revolution in personal taste that was already changing Chinese classical literature from within, even as powerful external forces were bearing down upon it.—DM

Yuan Mei's Letter to Xiang Jinmen

I appreciate the concern shown in your recent letter, in which you clarified some points on the *Laṅkāvatāra-sūtra* for me. In view of certain serious fallacies, I must pen a few more lines to explain myself to you. I once remarked that people differ in their natures just as much as in their faces. Some have a taste for jujubes, and roast meat does not appeal to them; some have a taste for lychee fruit, and wild greens do not appeal to them. Liu Yong was said to be fond of nibbling scabs. [The *Annals of Master Lü* tells us that] a man with bad body odor was once banished to the seaside, only to be chased by someone who found that appealing. Even if the gourmet Yi Ya came to life, he could not tell us why this is so.

Buddhism has been in China for two thousand years, so it would be impractical to suppress it and foolish to elevate it. Emperor Jing of the Han said, "A meat eater who abstains from horse liver cannot be accused of narrow tastes."[1] Gao Qianzhi of the Northern Qi said, "Buddhism is one of the nine subsidiary teachings." These two statements were right on the mark. By my inborn nature I am not fond of Buddhism or Daoism, or even Neo-Confucianism. Down through the years I have not let a day go by without opening a book. I still have not delved far enough into the classics and dynastic histories, so how would I find time to pursue heterodox studies? This would only drain my energy and take up precious time. Since I don't have time to read about it, I also don't have time to refute it. It's enough to "keep myself empty and go along with it," as Zhuang Zi says. When I was forty, my old friend Cheng Mianzhang suddenly urged me to read the *Laṅkāvatāra-sūtra*. He thought that a person of my intelligence would feel at home with this book. Who would have thought that partway through I would be dozing over its pages! The places he thought marvelous seemed humdrum to me; what he thought profound I found to be turgid. Why was this? Our natures are different, and I have no incense-burning karma from my past life. As for the word karma, though it comes from Buddhism, after a lifetime of experience I am convinced of it, and it is the one thing from Buddhism which I believe fills a gap in our sagely classics. Obviously I am empty of preconceptions in this; in all things I only seek what makes sense. I don't have an us-and-them mentality about Confucianism versus Buddhism. When you heard me using the word "turgid," you rose to the defense of the Buddhist religion. You quoted the phrase *fei-hu-xi*[2] from an old Music Bureau poem, and you mentioned Yang Xiong's *Scripture of Great Mystery* to prove that ancient Chinese books also have unclear passages. Of course there is no lack of obscure phrases in old Chinese books. Many of these are scraps of old dialect or proverbs that lost meaning over time. They are not turgid for the sake of turgidity, but the mantras and *dhāraṇi*s in Buddhist scriptures are turgid for the sake of turgidity. You tell me that all these mantras have meanings that can be written down in plain language. What about obscure lines in the old Music Bureau songs? They are scraps of Qi or Lu dialect, and I challenge you to tell me what they mean now. As for Yang Xiong's *Classic of Great Mystery,* it is like the *Classic of Wondrous Archery* by Liao Xi of Northern Wei: both of these books exploit obscurities and parade oddities, so they have been ignored by later generations. Chen Qufei of the Song said, "Yang Xiong was fond of marvels, which is why his work is not marvelous." Su Dongpo judged it even more harshly: "He tries to decorate shallowness with profundity." Opinion on this is already settled.

Moreover, you caution me that my arguments have certain weak spots; you are concerned that believers will spy them out and attack me, to the point that I won't have any ground to stand on. On this point you are wrong. If I thought of Buddhist doctrine as ground to stand on, then I would worry about being attacked, and your concern would be justified. However, I do not draw on Buddhism for my grounds of argument: I fear I would be tempted by it to set off on a wayward path. When it comes to grounds of argument, I have my own place to stand. Why should I worry about coming under attack? If I am attacked as an ignoramus, I will be pleased to hear it. If I am attacked as a "deluded man with no concept of Buddhist truth," I will be even more pleased. Why? Followers of different paths do not make plans together. Yan Yuan was laughed at for not understanding birdcalls as well as Gongyechang; Zigong was laughed at for lacking Jiegelu's ability to understand the mooing of cows.[3] Neither of these worthies was bothered in the slightest.

What is more, given your admiration for the subtleties of Buddhist scriptures, you yourself are a believer. If you want to attack me, then attack me. Why must you put words in the mouths of others who will direct hypothetical attacks against me? A phoenix soars a thousand fathoms above the earth, while an oriole frets over being driven from his crack between roof-tiles. I humbly suggest that this line of argument is not worthy of you.

At the close of your letter you say, "All the gentry and court officials nowadays pay honor to the Buddha. You alone, Sir, come forth to preside over the teaching of names, trying your utmost to reverse its decline."[4] Again, I take issue with what you say. All my life I have acted according to my Heaven-given nature, and I don't like making statements to put myself on a pedestal. I stand on the worth of my own opinions. I dislike Buddhism in the same way that I push aside a piece of meat that, to me, seems tainted. I avoid listening to mantras and chanting, simply because they do not appeal to my sensory preferences. I make no claim to perfect discrimination in sound and taste, and I don't set myself up as a high-minded arbiter. It has always struck me that King Wen sought the Way all his life and never thought he found it, but Mencius and Han Fei Zi both assumed the mantle of the Way-lineage. Self-important people have set out to refute Yang Zhu and Mo Zi in one era,[5] and similar people have tried to refute Buddhism and Daoism in the next. They have grieved over the Yellow River's murkiness and tried to clear it with their tears. This shows the temperament of a bookish dreamer and contributes little to society. I am not like them. I don't play up to the Buddha, and I don't refute the Buddha. I do not believe the nine subsidiary teachings, and I don't suppress them. Why? Variation is in the nature of things. Zixia said, "Even a minor path has something worth looking into, but if I take it too far, I fear getting bogged down. A superior man does not do this."[6] Buddhism and Daoism are examples of minor paths. To allow them to preach Dharma and attract followers, giving a livelihood to many unoccupied people—this is part of the greatness of Heaven and Earth. If Confucius and the Duke of Zhou came back to life, they would not disagree with this statement. (*Chidu* [Letters] chap. 7, no. 178)

From "Approaches to Writing for Exam Candidates"

. . . What we call the Dao is something empty and formless. People say that so-and-so transmitted the Dao and so-and-so received it. Has anyone ever seen it resting on someone's shoulders or carried on someone's back? Yao, Shun, Yu, and Gao lived in the same era. Does this mean that there were four lineage-bearers in one era? Wouldn't that be a bit crowded? From the time of Confucius and Mencius to the time of Cheng Yi and Zhu Xi, a thousand years passed without a lineage-bearer. Wasn't that spaced a bit too widely? There are people who draw diagrams of transmission to show the trunk and branches of the Dao-lineage. But how do they handle those who seclude themselves for a higher aim? How do they handle the ones who withdraw from society without regret? Some may say, "We base the lineage on those who leave written works." But how would they handle worthy men who do great deeds yet don't repose their ideals in empty words? Won't we need to get rid of the notion of Dao-lineage before the teaching of sages can truly expand? (*Wen ji* [Collected prose] chap. 24, p. 2)

Remarks from *Suiyuan Poetry Talks*

From the *Book of Odes* right up to today, any poem which gets passed down has to possess *xing-ling*.[7] It has nothing to do with cobbling things together. (*Shihua,* chap. 5)

Mr. Xi'ai said, "As the genre of 'poetry comments' flourishes, poetry dies." Formerly I did not know what he meant, but later I read *Poetry Talks from Yuyang,* and I sighed to find that although Song poetry is worth keeping, we might as well dispense with poetry comments from the Song. Pi Guanye has these lines: "The stroller breaks a willow wand to stir the floss / A swallow flies with fallen petals daubed in mud." This is a fine couplet, but Pei Guangyue says, "When willow floss is in the air, the ground should not be muddy." A Tang poet has these lines: "Outside of Suzhou City at Cold Mountain Temple / Bells in the night reach the traveler's boat." This is a fine couplet, but Ou Gong ridicules it because temple bells don't ring at night. Other writers of "poetry comments" mention temple bells rung at night to support these lines. This kind of discussion causes inspiration to die on the vine. If people indulge in such poetry comments, they might as well give up on poetry! (*Shihua,* chap. 8)

Once I visited a monastery and saw this poem written in small characters on the wall: "A man returns through flowers to a girl's pealing voice / His wife buys wine, wants a poem for the occasion / She tells of early blooms, more lush than years gone by / Fragrant glimmer even lovelier at night / In storm at dawn wondering can they last? / 'Had you returned in triumph three days sooner / Your eyes could have feasted on splitting buds.'" At the end was written "Viewing peonies with my wife" without signature. Some laughed at the simplicity, but I said, "It has *xing-ling* through and through: it must be by an accomplished poet." (*Shihua,* chap. 12)

Li Xiaocun was adept at writing quatrains, but he was criticized for reaching after unusual imagery. This does not allow for what Wen Zisheng said: "A line of text is easy to write; a craggy ridge is hard to trace." A poet like Xiaocun lives up to the word "craggy." Here is his "Taizhou Boat Lodgings": "Misty sandbar haloed moon, a hard-to-make-out shape / Is that someone's night-dress skimming past the reeds? / Long-haired maid with ready hand at oar / This dewy night agrees to take a person home." Here is his "Night Passing Red Bridge": "Sky vaults and moon rises, trailing its jade rope / Wine like agate lantern ruddy along both banks / Singing voices down the line, wind stirs water / Light boats in clusters, west of painted bridge." Also, here is his "Waste Garden": "Whose courtyard consummates its own spring? / Moss on windowsill, dust on desk / At least the dog next door still cares / Over the fence barks at a flower thief." Also, here is his "Clear Stream": "Whitewashed wall brushed by fallen petals / Pavilions through the gloomy shade of trees / Wind-driven drizzle on unraised blind / No one there, but haunting just the same." Also, here is his "Refusal to Sit for a Portrait": "Having a shape, I only care to hide it / Lacking talent, I know this body's an encumbrance." These are Xiaocun's best pieces, but *Cullings of a Fool's Retirement* only chooses "Remembering Whitegate," which has this couplet: "Willows in late wind, wine in deep alley / Peach blossoms near spring stream, woman behind curtain." This is nothing but a lineup of pretty-sounding words, at the lowest level. People who give up *xingling* for style let the best things go by the wayside. (*Shihua,* chap. 13)

As for the two poets of Tongcheng, Fang Funan and Fang Nantang are equally well known. Yumen likes Funan and I am partial to Nantang. Why? Because the bones of his poetry are pure. Funan studied Li Shangyin and Du Fu,[8] but in the end he was encumbered and his *xingling* was closed off prematurely. (*Shihua,* chap. 13)

Inspector Liu Tingji of the Han army was a poet during the Kangxi emperor's reign. Some thought his poems too frivolous, but the *xingling* running through them cannot be denied. Look at his "Fisherfolk": "To each family its own fishing boat / A marriage made to float upon the water / Girl of thirteen boy of fifteen / Lower their eyes whenever they meet." Look at this couplet from "Random Lines": "Idle flowers are best viewed idly / Snapped off to take home they are no longer fresh." (*Shihua,* chap. 14)

Huang Yunxiu says, "Having no poems, you busy yourself over books." Fang Ziyun says, "Studies neglected, you get *xingling* poems." Liu Xiashang says, "Reading too long, poetic thoughts get bogged." These statements could only have been uttered by persons who knew reading and poetry well. (*Shihua,* chap. 3)

Chan Master Whitecloud wrote this *gāthā:* "A fly drawn by the light bumps the window paper / Unable to pass it tastes much suffering / Suddenly it chances on the route it came by / And knows its eyes have fooled it all through life." Chan Master Xuedou wrote this verse: "A rabbit exposed on a road / Is borne away by a passing hawk / Then the hawk for lack of awareness / Vainly sniffs the log where it stood. . . . " Though these are Chan discourses, they are compatible with poetry. (*Shihua,* chap. 4)

In the past when reading Sun Yuanru's poems, I felt he was a rare talent. Later on seeing his recent works, I found his brilliance much diminished. Looking into the reason, I found that he had retreated into textual studies. Sun knew of my feelings and wrote the following for me: "Pile books body-high to learn the writer's craft / From a cul-de-sac reach heaven then make *xingling* poems / Judgment of ages can hardly fall on me / Deep into the classics I flee from your genius pen." (*Shihua,* chap. 16)

In the final years of the Kangxi reign, among commoners good at poetry, there were Qu Siqi of Nanjing and Li Keshan of Suzhou. Unlike the style of Strawcoat Zhu, both were forlorn and high-minded. I have seen few poems by Li Keshan. Qu was good at five-word lines in the old-style, with technique superior to Strawcoat's. In terms of *xingling,* he could not equal Ma Qiutian, Shen Fangzhou, Qiu Huajing, and the poet I mentioned who wrote on a monastery wall. Here is Qu Siqi's "Viewing Fall Colors": "On Mount Censer's layered peaks / Hard-won view at rim in setting light / Bells resound to the world below / Voices close to *deva*-realms[9] / Red leaves vie in color-riot / Autumn blooms quietly lovely / Wind-swept slope above wooded valley / Bird bound home through chill mist." Here is a couplet from "Mochou Lake": "Ever since the lovely one departed / Here have grown the most fragrant herbs." From this chill, detached atmosphere, we can imagine what sort of person he was. (*Shihua buyi* [Poetry talks supplement], chap. 1)

Xu Shuixiang of Baoshan, who concentrated on poetry and did not prepare for civil exams, died at the age of twenty-two. Ten days before his death, while lying sick in bed, he told his father, "I have been taken to see the Underworld lord of Dongting Lake. My life's blood has gone into poetry. Please have copies made for my friend Pu Xiangchun's collection." Before he heard of the young man's death, Pu dreamed he and Xu were happily conversing and the young man said he had died four days earlier. Since then Xu apprenticed himself to Master Zhao Qinqiu and was making great strides in learning about poetry. With a laugh he faded from Pu's sight. Pu then printed Xu's poems with the title *One Hundred Omissions.* Here is Xu's "Autumn Seaside Mood": "A thousand finned families make an aquatic county seat / High-piled jetty looms in a curve before my sight / Heaven submerges a poor city under azure waves / Lord in strife with his creatures for a foot of ground / Masts from Fusang[10] sailing to many destinations / Disk of sun peeking makes islands radiant / Water stretching vast to eyes' limit / Surprise that gusts of autumn stir few waves." Here is a couplet from "Mourning Han Qi": "West Lake has been here for this family of Song times / Good for viewing in old age from a donkey's back." Here is a couplet from "Comes the Night": "Though jade is best cherished when left uncut / Can't help picking the flowers I view." This truly comes from *xingling.* (*Shihua buyi,* chap. 1)

In the year 1736 I entered the capital, and in 1741 I tested into the Hanlin Academy. I spent my youthful years under the tutelage of Li Wenzhen from Anxi, and my studies were based on his standards. In poetry he did not strive for perfect technique, but he let *xingling* flow out here and there. Look at this from his "Poem for He Yimen": "Though learned you do not hanker for a post / Writing for the occasion, you can feed a family / Your table is ringed by wine-loving guests / Your door is thronged by booksellers' carts." This is a true picture of Yimen's life. Here are two lines from Li's "Limpid Shade": "Urging a drinking companion, I get drunk first / Letting itself be taken, the pawn cares only to win." Here are two lines from "Peaceful Dwelling": "Half of those who visit fancy your calligraphy / All of those who knock have flowers for your vase." These are memorable lines from his collection *Utter Beauty.* (*Shihua buyi,* chap. 2)

Someone brought me a certain powerbroker's poems and asked if I would put them in my *Poetry Talks.* When reading them I could hardly keep my eyes open, so I told him, "The poems have clarity of diction and good technique, but if I want to find fault, there's nothing to find fault with; if I want to make fun of them there's nothing to make fun of; if I want to select some, there are none that stand out. Confucius said, 'Firm of will and woodenly silent—this is close to humaneness.' As for your eminent friend's poems, without venturing to say they are wooden, I'll admit they're close to humaneness, but not to poetry." The friend said, "His language fits his solemn subjects." I said, "I don't think so. When the pen has magic, it brings loyalty and justice alive. When the pen is dull, even songs about lads and lasses will lack fascination." (*Shihua buyi,* chap. 2)

To make the realm of one's poems expansive and their feeling lively, it takes diligent study and thoughtfulness. You should have something to say and content yourself with the aims of poetry expressed by Confucius and Mencius. If you insist on multiplying strictures, narrowing possibilities, and putting your *xingling* in manacles, to the point that your poems lose the joy of being alive, aren't you making yourself a mannequin? (*Shihua buyi,* chap. 3)

Going through my old papers, I found a quatrain by Yin Sicun: "On a moonlit night the lamp burns on and on / After heavy meals I rise late now and then / Pressing cares add frost around my temples / I fear to recall the days of my youth." This was probably a favorite piece I kept from work Yin had sent me for a critique. I also kept his verse on redeeming winter jackets from a pawnshop: "The sight of this familiar clothes box / Brightens my old wife's features / Our maid appears with iron in hand / To press each hem and sleeve / Alas the wrinkles are too deep / No iron can unrumple them." These express *xingling* in his own inimitable way. (*Shihua buyi,* chap. 4)

Xiangyan and I made an excursion to Tiantai, so we left our lakeside tower for a month. Coming back we found the desk covered with letters that had caught up to us in our travels, all connected with bygone infatuations. Xiangyan wrote this couplet: "New letters to greet us covering the desktop / Flowers of our absence are withered near the wall." And this couplet is from "Farewell to West Lake": "Prospects of unforgettable friendship / Memories of uncompleted poems." These lines are full of *xingling,* expressed by the telling vagaries of Xiangyan's pen. (*Shihua buyi,* chap. 5)

Lady Kong Jingting of Juqu was . . . of willowy build and had the manners of one from a good family. In the Spring of 1791 she came to view flowers in my garden with her mother-in-law. Her household members raved about her. She was fond of quietude and accomplished at poetry. I remember poems she sent to her husband: "Watching phases of the moon since you have left / Alone by a lone lamp, tears thread down my cheek / Moon at edge of sky stirs my strongest feelings / Each side knows the others parting sorrow." "Wishing to confide my sorrow to a notebook / Pace in silence, lean against a window / O dear, let us not undo our sweet vow / What a waste of scented sheets to sleep alone." Both poems have their own way of showing *xingling.* (*Shihua buyi,* chap. 7)

Master Tanzun has a poem called "Excursion to Incense-Realm Monastery": "Drizzle pauses at the wane of day / Pine cones drop down from steep bluff / Crowd of peaks loom on steep massif / Precarious bridge enwrapped in final rays / Autumn sounds disturb a traveler's dream / Chill air against a poetry-chanting shirt / From empty edge emerges subtle scent / Heaven's flowers for sure beyond this world." Here is his "Black Butterfly": "You fly beyond any list, tracing curve of an old vine / Carried on membrane wings under a horse being groomed / You fly real as life into my Lacquer Garden dream / Sure enough I've reached the land of sweet darkness." Here is a couplet from "Autumn Willow": "Village house in westering sun—a thousand detached lines / Asleep upstairs in east wind—memories come and go." This is from his "Written as a Gift": "Chill pure frost on November Yantai bluff / Fine river rain all through the course of Spring." These are rare expressions of *xingling,* utterly unlike the common tone. (*Shihua buyi,* chap. 9)

Miss Yan Ruizhu of Wujiang showed unique intelligence by age eighteen. She pawned her hair ornaments to pay tuition and study under me. I asked, "Have you read *Cangshan Poems?*" She said, "If I hadn't, I wouldn't come to study under you. Other people's poems have good lines, but don't hang together, or they hang together but don't have good lines. But you, Sir, combine the two. I especially like your parallel prose, so I memorized your thousand-word plaque at the Zhongsu Shrine." I asked, "That piece has many allusions; do you know where they come from?" She said, "I know almost half of them. People say your metrical prose has allusions, but don't they know your poetry has them too? Your poems emphasize *xingling,* so the language is transformed: it carries ideas from the philosophers, but people find it familiar and do not notice. It is like salt in water: one can only know the presence of salt by taste, but no grains of salt are seen. One would have to read ten thousand volumes with great care to point out your sources." (*Shihua buyi,* chap. 10)

"In Stillness" by Yuan Mei: "Mastery in stillness is when you see *xingling* / Deserted well becomes a night-bubbling spring / Thread of spider silk hangs plainly before you / Unless you take time it can easily be missed." (*Shi ji* [Collected verse] chap. 28)

—DM

Notes

1. Emperor Jing presided over the first appearance of Buddhism in China.

2. Three meaningless syllables, like "tra-la-la," used to fill out the melody of a line of verse. However, seduced by the surface signification of the characters used to write these three syllables, Chinese scholars came up with all sorts of fantastic nonsense about what they presumably *meant,* such as "concubine breathes faintly" or "concubine shouts 'hog'!"

3. Zigong was one of Confucius's disciples.

4. Confucianism is sometimes called "the teaching of names" because Confucius advocated the rectification of names to make government ethical.

5. During the Warring States period, Yang Zhu advocated hedonism and Mo Di (i.e., Mo Zi) advocated universal love. Both were treated as heterodox teachers by Mencius.

6. Zixia was a disciple of Confucius who actively propagated the master's teachings after his death. This statement is quoted from the last section of the *Analects.*

7. *Xingling* is a key term in Yuan Mei's poetics. Though sometimes translated as "spirit and mind" or "sensibility," it refers to the *inspiration* that wells up from one's individual nature.

8. Two of the most celebrated poets of the Tang dynasty.

9. I.e., the realms of heavenly beings.

10. Fusang is the world-tree, which grows beyond the eastern horizon.

IN THE THIRD CENTURY B.C.E. the first imperial dynasty of China, the Qin, erected the Great Wall as a barrier between their agrarian civilization and groups of pastoralist nomads who occupied the steppes and highlands of Inner Asia. Although the nomads lived off their herds, they had also perfected the art of horseback warfare and were a constant threat to China's peace. At times the sedentary agrarian Chinese would invade the pasture lands of these nomads and convert them to agricultural use. The reverse would happen as well, the nomads turning bandit and crossing the boundary into China. The Great Wall was built to block such nomads' entry, but it also marked a natural ecological frontier between the arid steppes where herding was natural and the more fertile, better-watered plains where farming was the preferred way of life.

Sometimes the nomads would form a tribal confederation, develop a charismatic leader, create a state with a mighty army of horsebacked bowmen, and conquer China itself. The Tibetans did this in the eighth century, occupying Chinese-speaking territory up to the outskirts of the capital and briefly taking Chang'an itself in the year 763. The Mongol nomadic state actually conquered China in the thirteenth century, creating the Yuan dynasty. The Manchus did this again in the seventeenth century, founding the Qing dynasty.

Between these two poles of sedentary conquest of nomads and nomadic conquest of the sedentary, China and its surrounding traveling, tented nomads carried on an active and complex foreign policy. The Chinese would send tribute, gifts, or assistance to the nomads, dispatch diplomats and regional administrators, incorporate their leadership by granting them office, and chronicle their political and cultural life.

Nomadic policy toward the Chinese is more difficult to know, because the nomads were slower to develop literacy and keep written chronicles. But here is an oral epic of the Tibetans which presents their side of the Tibetan-Chinese interaction and gives us an unusually intimate glimpse at some of the attitudes of the surrounding nomad pastoralist milieu.

It is interesting to think about the contrasting positions of Chinese histories and diplomatic records, which view the pastoralist warriors at their frontiers as "barbarians," and the nomadic sense of respect tinged with greed reflected here in the Tibetans and by other ethnic leaders visiting the Chinese court. In the background is an unwritten understanding that the frontier kingdoms and confederations at times raid the Chinese and at times conduct policy with them, at times are their adversaries, but as often send religious leaders to the Chinese court to teach the emperor and his retinue. Recent histories in the West give a more nuanced view of the relationship between China and its so-called "frontiers."[1] The pastoralists beyond the Great Wall are no longer barbarians harrying the edge of Chinese civilization, but a complex and rich cultural sphere of their own based on a different ecology.

The Tibetan *Gesar of Ling* is a gigantic oral epic sung by Tibetan bards and written down over the last few centuries in many different forms. Versions of it can be found in China, Mongolia, Tibet, and among tribal peoples of Inner Asia. It tells the story of an enlightened hero, Gesar of Ling, who protects the land of Tibet from anti-Buddhist invaders. Like an Achilles or an Aeneas, he uses his military prowess and leadership abilities. But, more importantly, he uses the unique, ironic, humorous, outrageous, and vast perspective of a buddha. Seeing things from the cosmic point of view gives him a unique sense of skillful means to overcome enemies while creating a civilization based on the Buddhist principles of compassion and wisdom. Possessing the power of a buddha to see beyond mere appearance to the ultimate level of reality gives Gesar magical powers that make him a sorcerer knight, as if King Arthur and Merlin were joined in one man.

The lore that combines alchemical magic with skill in weaponry and political inscrutability is shared to a degree by his future subjects, the people of the land of Ling.

Ling is a land of Tantric steppe warriors. Their religion is a peculiar kind of Buddhism which does not turn away from the world to a purer sphere, but achieves enlightenment by seeing the phenomenal world as sacred in every detail. This means that the buddhas in the epic teach not ascetic denial of worldly things, but alchemical transmutation of the ordinary into magical reality. Magical reality is enlightened reality. The unenlightened world is made up of merely physical things, of objects, people, plants, and animals. The enlightened world is made up of the kind of things found in expositions of alchemical Taoism: power places, gods, heroes, animistic spirits, and vital energies.

A word should be said about the expression "White Ling," which occurs constantly in the epic. It means, in effect, Ling the Good. It distinguishes Ling from the enemy kingdoms which surround it. These enemies are usually demons or reincarnations of demons. And so the opposite of "White" in this case would be something like "demonic."

In the same way, society itself is represented in what the authors of the epic would consider to be an enlightened society. This means that the state and national identity are constituted not by laws with executive arms to enforce them, but by kinship relations and tribal compacts to create political entities. Customs of mediation and blood money are used instead of courts to settle disputes between them. Crimes are not punished, but likewise settled by mediation and what we call today "restorative justice." When mediation does not work there is tribal warfare to rectify imbalances that occur where trust is betrayed or there has been a failure to adjudicate the wrong.

The genealogy that begins the passage lays out therefore not simply the names and descent of the important families in the epic, but the basic structure of the ideal Tibetan state—a land where every relationship is not merely legal or contractual, but real in the sense of being a blood connection or a tribal compact. Sense of place, sense of family, sense of country become one experience in the shamanistically holistic world of the epic.

This excerpt is from volume 2 of a nine-volume version of the *Gesar* sung and read in northeastern Tibet, principally in Qinghai and Gansu provinces. It records the life and religious beliefs of the warlike high-altitude nomadic herders. Their wealth is found in their herds of yak and *dri* (female yaks), cows, horses, and sheep. They live most of the year in yak-hair tents, moving to fortress castles in the winter. They have farms as well, but their agriculture does not typically use irrigation or the more-efficient techniques of the Chinese farmers. Their population, therefore, is sparse compared to China's, and many of their goods are gained through trade with their neighbors. When trade will not do, raiding and banditry are considered an equally honorable alternative. If they are caught by their victims, then mediation and restorative justice are the usual resort.

They are followers of Tibetan Buddhism, but their daily ritual life combines elements of Indian Buddhism with shamanistic practices found across Inner Asia, including some elements of ancient Chinese alchemical Taoism. All nomads ride armed to the teeth, for there are no police or governmental authorities. Legal disputes are handled by mediators who rely on a vast invisible corpus of proverbs to decide cases. Instances of murder, kidnaping, and theft are settled before negotiation by vendetta and after negotiation by exchanges of blood money. Often opposing parties will settle disputes through exchanges of blood-price simply to avoid the military conflict of vendetta.

Ling is a Tibetan-speaking country and stands in the reader's eyes for Tibet itself. The Ling view of nationality is based on tribal notions, with all legal structures created by kinship relations and blood oaths of loyalty. This passage begins by introducing us to the Mukpo clan, the tribe of Tibetans who rule the Kingdom of Ling. We meet some of Ling's greatest warriors—in particular, the king of Ling, Chipön, the epic's Agamemnon, and the fiery Buddhist warrior, Gyatsa Zhalkar, the epic's Achilles.

The shamanistic version of Buddhism practiced in the epic includes a complex machinery of gods and special powers that surround the warrior. Every warrior has developed a sort of "battle aura" called *wang thang,* literally, a "field of power." This invisible shield of light glows about the hero or heroine's shoulders and head, creating an impression of invincibility. In addition to this charisma, there is a group of "patron deities" that perch on the warrior's armor and bodily centers. One of them is called a *garuda,* a magical bird spirit that usually perches on the head. There are also father and mother gods on the shoulders and heart center, and body gods to protect both the body and the family name. There is also the all-important life-force *(srog)* dwelling as a sort of treasury of energy in the heart. Also in the heart is the life-essence *(la),* a kind of second soul that departs just before the body dies, and the *tshe* or life-duration energy—a force that determines longevity. To support the *srog,* keep the *la* from wandering, and increase the *tshe,* the warrior must lead a stainless life and do rituals of gathering and reversal of negative forces. Chief among the forces that must be gathered, collected, and nourished is the ancient notion of "windhorse," which is found both in China and Tibet. This is a power of upliftedness and élan—a personal energy of dignity and innate success. When the power of a hero's windhorse is raised, not only is life-force increased, but the field of power opens like a radiant flower, and the warrior seems to glow. Then local spirits and matrices of energy associated with dignity, confidence, and upliftedness are drawn to the body and land on it. These complexes of energy are called "war-gods." They come in many varieties and occupy their special positions on the body, the armor, the horse, and the weapons. This translation mentions many deities of the class of wargods. Some are like household spirits. Others, like the *nyen,* are independent gods of mountains and natural phenomena.

The ability to invoke, control, and increase these energies and gods is an essential art taught by the Tibetan epic and practiced by its Buddhist heroes—a sort of warrior's magic. The ceremony of invocation that ends this translation is an example of such a ritual practice. In this ceremony a column of smoke is created and a host of deities is asked to descend down via the smoke to bless the assembly. The highest gods who descend are actually Buddhist deities. The lower ones are native Tibetan war-gods.

The events in this reading show Zhalkar and two other young knights from other tribal kingdoms meeting with the Chinese emperor. He is their maternal uncle, for their fathers have (all through policy) married Chinese wives. This is actually indicated in Zhalkar's family name, Gyatsa, which means "Chinese nephew." In the epic the names of heroes indicate both their patriarchal and matriarchal descent. The name "Gyatsa" indicates that his mother was Chinese. Thus, in the Tibetan epic, even the Chinese emperor is a tribal leader, addressing the Tibetan and Inner Asian princes as if he were more a patriarchal chief of chiefs, head of all clans, rather than the ruler of a politically and legally constituted state. He gives amazing weapons that fire the imagination of Tibetan bards, who dream of the technological superiority of the Chinese, and remind us that these nomadic pastoralists get most of their manufactured goods from surrounding agrarian civilizations.

Then, when Zhalkar returns from China, he discovers that his cousin has been killed in battle. There is a debate about whether or not Zhalkar will lead the Ling army on a mission of revenge. Numerous proverbs are bandied as exercises in nomadic judicial rhetoric. To the Tibetan this scene is very funny, because Gyatsa's youthful anger drives him out of control, and he harshly criticizes the most virtuous person in the epic, Chipön, the chief of Ling.

The scene then moves to the conquered land, Gog. There the family of the future mother of Gesar of Ling is preparing to flee, along with her adopted father, Ralo, from the returning Lingite hordes. In the confusion, Gogmo, Gesar's future mother, is separated from her family and wanders, along with her dowry of magical possessions, into the camp of the Ling invaders.

This is a fateful moment, for Ling gains not only Gogmo's treasure, but also the magical woman who will give birth to a warrior buddha, the future savior of Ling, Gesar. This sudden windfall is accepted as a sign of future good fortune, and a smoke offering is performed to maximize the blessings of the event. The stage is thereby set for the coming miraculous birth of the great Tibetan enlightened hero, Gesar of Ling.

Identification of proper names and Tibetan or Sanskrit for translations of technical terms may be found in the glossary at the end of this reading.—RK

Now, in the Clan of Mukpo Dong, the royal line of Chöphen Nagpo (Black Dhama Benefit) originated from his three wives: Serza (Wife from the Ser Tribe), Omza (Wife from Om), and Changza.[2] They each had three sons. The son of Ser was Lhayag Darkar (Good Divine White Silk). The son of Ombu was Trichang Pagyal (Wolf Throne Royal Warrior). The son of Chang was Dragyal Bum-me (Victorious over Enemies, Ten Thousand Flames). From these three came the Greater, Lesser, and Middle lineages of Mukpo Dong.[3]

In the Lesser or Cadet Lineage, the princely son of King Dragyal Bum-me was Thogmey Bum (Beginningless Ten Thousand).[4] And Thogmey's son was Chöla Bum (Ten Thousand for the Dharma). Chöla Bum had three wives, and they were Rongza (Wife from Rong), Gaza (Ga Wife), and Muza (Mu Wife), these three.[5]

Rongza's son was an incarnation of the Pandita Suvarna born as the chief Chipön Rongtsha Tragen (Rong Maternal Nephew Old Falcon). He was smart. His intelligence and knowledge were as bright as the morning sky. His skill and compassion were like the moisture and warmth of the earth in spring. His commands were straightforward like lines drawn with a ruler. He could distinguish the right or wrong of his subjects' actions like splitting bamboo. Unruly strong men he would yoke and supress. But he would protect the weak and humble like his own parents. He was the chief man among the brothers and cousins, the Brethren of Ling. At meetings his was the final word.[6] He was the general of all the bandits who tamed enemies. Although he was born in the clan of the Lesser Lineage, he was respected as the principal chief of all Ling.

To Gaza was born a son named Yugyal (Turquoise Victory), who while warring with Hor was lost in battle to the Hor.[7] To Muza was born an emanation of the Brahmin Sudatta named Senglön (Lion Minister).[8] At birth he was

> Outwardly gentle like a white silk scarf from China,
> Inwardly gentle like white butter candy
> With a warm, gentle feeling like the sun in Spring.
> His gentle mind was loose and relaxed like a knot in a scarf.
> His body was a heap of splendor
> And his speech a flute of brilliant and melodious sound.
> He gained control over the mechanism of his luminous mind.
> He was a sky fortress of many war-gods
> And a castle surrounded by *werma*s.
> He was the life stone that attracts the oath-bound protectors.[9]

Chipön, the chief, married Bödza Metog Tashi Tso (Tibetan Wife Flower Auspicious Lake). Their eldest son was Yuphen Tag-gyal (Turquoise Benefit Tiger King). The middle son was Lenpa Chögyal (Moron Dharma King). The younger son was Nanchung Yutag (Neglectful Turquoise

Tiger). And there was a daughter named Lhamo Yudrön (Goddess Turquoise Lamp), making four altogether.

Senglön wed Gyaza Lhakar Drönma (Chinese Wife Divine White Lamp). In the year of the female Water Ox in the twelfth month their son was born, whose face was like the moon.

> His mind was as vast as the sky.
> All of his actions were dharma activity.
> To his enemies he was a bitter thorn bush.
> To his friends, he was a white silken scarf.
> To the warriors he was a ferocious tiger.
> He had the Six Abilities of a Warrior, like a fierce Horpa bird of prey.[10]

Everyone in his family called him Zhalu Nyima Rangshar (Dear Little Face of the Self-arising Sun). Outsiders called him Gyatsa Zhalkar of Clan Bumpa. For thirteen days the gurus did Long-Life Prosperity ceremonies for him. The paternal elders (fathers and uncles) did aspiration prayers, and the maternal elders danced and sang to celebrate his birth. The name of the Greater Lineage's leader was Divine Son Namkhai Senzhal. The leader of the Middle Lineage was Lingchen Tharpa Sönam (Great Ling Merit of Liberation). The leader of the Younger Lineage was Chipön, and these three offered a scarf inscribed with these verses of auspicious prayer to the neck of dear little Zhalkar:

> All is well by day and well by night;
> All is well even before the dawn,
> Bringing continuous well-being both day and night,
> May the auspiciousness of the Rare and Precious Three Jewels[11] pervade everywhere.

And Chipön answered:

> "Oh, the great district of the white class of the gods possesses
> This first sign of the spread of its field of power.[12]
> Of dreams that come true it is the head
> And will be the first to tame the Enemies of the Four Directions.
> Listen to the silk scarf of this song undistractedly."

And then the three leaders sang this song:

> Ala thala thala the song is sung.[13]
> We offer this song—offer it to the great god Brahma.
> Offer it to the Country God Magyal Pomra,
> To the strict and mighty *zodor* Gedzo
> And the god of males Nyentag Marpo (Red Nyen Tiger).
> May the expanse of their great sovereignty cover the sky.
> Great continent of the earth, may it contain all this.
>
> In case you don't recognize this place, it is Chisö Yagi Khado.
> It is the great gathering place Tagthang Tramo (Colorful Tiger Plain).
> It is the site of joyful and happy reunions
> In the great four-cornered yak-hair tent.
>
> If you don't know the likes of me—
> I am King Chipön of Rongza.

Those who accompany me in this song are the leaders of the Greater and Middle lineages.
We three brother leaders offer this song.

Today the stars in the sky are excellent.
On earth the time is right and the signs are excellent.
Now when the three excellences unite,
On the birth celebration of the future chieftain of Mupa
White Ling is engaged in song and dance.
May the divine gurus perform longevity, prosperity, and smoke-purification rituals.
May the mothers and aunts make excellent prayers.
May the fathers and brothers have open minds in their methods.
According to the sayings passed on by ancient Tibet:[14]

"The gods, Three Jewels, and dear leaders, these three—
If you supplicate, make offerings, and show respect to them,
All desirable necessities will arise.

Trade, husbandry, and taming enemies, these three—
If accomplished with diligence are the source of prosperity.

Horses, wives, and houses, these three—
To decorate them and keep them clean is for your own good."

Earlier on it was a custom in the land of Ling
Since the time of Ling's founder Chöphen Nagpo,
That when the enemy came, we raised our spears as one.
When goods came, we portioned them with the blade of a knife and shared.[15]

As for the Gold or Ser Family in the Elder Lineage, at the birthday celebration they
have given

Ten paṭas of yellow gold,
Golden armor replete with silken ruffles,
A golden helmet with a yellow silken victory banner crest,
A sword with a golden guard,
A golden horse named Soaring Golden Bird Gait,
A golden saddle with golden bridle and gold crupper—
All adorned with a silken golden scarf of auspiciousness,
These were the nine offerings of yellow gold.

For the birth celebration of the child of Ombu, from Middle Ling they have given
In a stupa[16] of white conch
A melodious conch with clockwise turning.
Conch armor and a golden martial robe,
Conch helmet with white silk crest flags,
The sword named "Wishing, Cuts at a Touch,"
With a guard of refined white silver.
The horse with Mongolian gait[17] White Moon Color.
Silver saddle, silver bridle, and silver crupper—
The nine white conch articles were offered.

I, Chipön of the Mu family of the Lesser Lineage, give
A piece of White Sixth turquoise[18] called Essence Milk Drop,
Turquoise armor called Crag Mountain Meteorite-Proof,
A turquoise helmet called Vast as the Sky
Adorned with silk flags called Rich Like Massing Clouds,
The ancestral wealth of Chur lha (Coral God), Chief of Jiang,
A blonde horse[19] with a turquoise-beaded mane and a saddle adorned with turquoise,
With matching turquoise bridle and crupper.
I give the sword "Cuts the Enemy to Pieces in Vendetta,"
And along with it a blue silken hand-guard tie,
A fish-gut scarf from Nyatra Bakha—
These are the nine blue turquoise offering articles
Offered by the family of the Lesser Lineage at the birthday celebration.

The Three Lineages of the Six Districts of Ling
Are called Great, Middle, and Lesser
Not because of any difference in the greatness of their achievements or fame,
But because they were earlier or later
In the ancestral lineage of Chöphen Nagpo.
They all came from the same paternal tribe.
The lineage leaders were three golden flowers.
They were the initiatory vase placed on the crown of the head.
Whatever words they spoke were like *amṛta*[20] on the tip of the tongue.
Whatever actions they performed were for the general weal of the Six Districts.

According to the ancient sayings of the Tibetans:

> When he keeps the Dharma school in the square monastery, the lama,
> Master of the precious vase of sutras and tantras,
> Is learned in the path, the three trainings, and practice.

> When he holds the tribunal of the dear imperial chieftain,
> The master of the golden throne of exalted status
> Is great in the extent of his action, field of power, and knowledge.[21]

Just so, in the Lineage of the White Snow Lionness,
Turquoise Mane[22] only inhabits the regions of snow,
Never thinking to go down to the bustling town,

Just so, in the Lineage of the Children of Turquoise Dragons,
The dragon thunders his roar only in the clouds.
Never thinking to wander aimlessly through foreign lands,

In just that way the lineage of the children of Mukpo Clan
Suppresses from above the other districts,
Never thinking to accomplish other than our clan's affairs.

Furthermore, even though the royal parasol of the sun
Gives warmth to the four continents,
If the conch moon did not rise in the sky
Who could find their way in the pitch darkness of night?
The stars may sparkle, but without the sun they are useless.

In this world of Jambudvīpa, the Twelve Countries of Tibet
Are bordered on four sides by Four Demon Kingdoms.
The gods have ordained their subjugators to be the kingdom of White Ling.
In combat, before the warriors with form
And the hardy picked troops girded for battle,
The three heads of Ling will dawn like the sun.
He who presses down the necks of the formless obstructing spirits,[23]
Devil harrier[24] of gods, cannibal demons, and ghosts,
Who is not human, but pretends to be a man and a boy,
Who is first the one to whom the imperial gods all bow down,
Second, the one *nyen*s and body gods circumambulate,
Third, the one to whom the king of the *nāga*s[25] Tsugna Rinchen makes offerings,
And fourth, the one whose body has obtained miraculous powers,
May he be born to ornament White Ling.

Where in the lineage of the three brothers of the Mukpo Dong
He will be born has already been ordained.
All of this is the fervent wish of Ling.
This fervent wish has burst forth from my mouth.
It is both an outburst and a prophecy.
By the excellent auspicious connections of these words of truth,
May this golden sun of the lineage of leaders,
That great covering, fill the sky with its vast protecting sovereignty.
May the great vessel of the earth be able to contain it.
May all that has been sung in this song turn to the Dharma.
May this whole song be as meaningful as it is melodious.
If the song has caused confusion, I confess the fault.
If the words have caused harm, I beg your forgiveness.
May the Six Districts of Ling hold this in their hearts.

Then Upper, Middle, and Lower Ling celebrated the birth with vast and extensive song and dance. As for Zhalkar, in one month's time he grew as much as other children would grow in a year. When Zhalkar came of age, the Chinese emperor invited his three nephews: the son of Sadam of Jang named Nyitri Karchen (Twenty Thousand Great Stars); Lhabu Legpa (Auspicious Godling), a son of the Achen tribe of Hor; and Zhalu Karpo, the son of Senglön Dong Bumpa. He gave each of them wealth from the natural resources of his own country and from nowhere else: each one got a horse, a sword, and armor as the main articles. Beyond that, gold, silver, tea, silk, and so forth, about a hundred gifts were bestowed.

Then he said, "Oh, dear little nephews, you three who know how to succeed in your aims, listen to the white scarf of this song without distraction. Do not forget the fruit of this meaning—hold it in your mind. Here are three words of completely flawless advice." Saying that he broke into song:[26]

"Ala the song begins this way.
And thala is the sound of the melody.
Undeceiving Refuge, the Rare and Precious Three Gems,
Inseparably abide as my crown ornament.

In case you don't know what place this is,
This is the Magic Palace of the Chinese Lord.

In case you don't know the likes of me—
Spanning the great, vast, azure firmament,
Extending across the face of the dense earth,
I am the ruler of China.

Now, listen to me and you will hear
These well-known sayings of days gone by:

> Mount Meru, the ocean, and a great leader, these three
> Are best liked when firm and unmoving.
> Conversation, counsel, and arrows, these three
> Are best when straight, not crooked or bent.
> Lawsuits, bows, and lassos, these three—
> Are best if they bend wherever they go.

Even if there are turmoil and battle between the divisons of the Great Districts,
The great leader should still be a single unmoving fortress.
The paternal lineage[27] of the Chinese is whiter than a conch.
One may not harm it, it is like gold.
The three horses—Pheasant, Peacock, and Duck—
Are the horse wealth of the country of China in the east.
These will be the horses beneath you, my three nephews.

First, the conch armor called White Excellent God,
Second, the turquoise armor called Defeat Ten Thousand, Master a Thousand,
Third, meteoric iron armor called Slate Mountain Lightning-Proof.
This armor was magically forged by the Eight Classes of Non-Men.[28]
With armor like this the castle of life[29] cannot be pierced by steel-blue weapons.
Oh my three dear ones, Zhal, Nyitri, and little Lha,
I give you this armor as your companion for life.
May it make your bodies indestructible.

In the Imperial Eastern Land of China
Three cranes were fed with iron dust.
After they vomited the dust back up,
At the very first rays of dawn,
It was forged by a Rākṣasa blacksmith
Into the sword Guzi Skydawn,
With male iron, like the wrath of a *heruka,*
Female iron smiling like a *heruki,*
And son iron like a shooting star.
Patterns on the blade like banking southern clouds.
Just holding it suppresses the eight classes of gods with splendor.
Striking with it reduces iron mountains to dust.
Nyitri Karchen of Jang, I offer this to you.

The iron dust that the cranes shat out
Was taken by the blacksmith of the king of the Tsen gods, Yamshud (Death Overlord).
In the obscure darkness of night he forged the sword
Azi Blazing Poison Slasher.

The nape of the sword is bright like the predawn glow;
The belly of the blade is dark like the epitome of darkness;
Patterns on the blade are like swirling waves in the ocean;
Hard tempered iron is like an angry Rākṣasa;
Iron so flexible, it can be knotted like a cord.
Striking, it eats the enemy's flesh.
Lha'u Legpo of Hor, I offer this to you.

The iron left in the birds' stomachs
When the Morning Star shone was magically forged
By the blacksmith of the The'u rang gods.
It was forged with brass and metallic salts
And forged from iron salts and molten metal.
The cold water in which it was tempered is the blood of Rākṣasas.
War-gods throng the good nape of this sword,
The teeming war-gods boost you with constant boasting.
Gandharvas throng the black-bellied edge of the blade.
The *gandharvas* gather there groaning [for blood].[30]
Patterns swirl on the blade like the ocean—
The pounded imprint like swelling waves.
If you strike a river's course with it
This wind sword is called "Reverses the River's Flow."
When it is in the country of China,
It bears the name "Splendidly Suppressing a Thousand Sword Points."
This is your patriarchal sword, Chieftain Zhalu.

And here is some gold, silver, and silk,
Varieties of tea and so forth that I offer.
Offerings by the hundreds to each of you in celebration—
All this in honor of the joyful meeting of uncle and nephews.

To keep the seat of an imperial leader of the Great Districts,
One must hold down the necks of the mighty and
Protect the humble as your own parents,
And be straight in secular affairs like a bamboo shaft.
One must be open-minded like the expanse of sky at break of day,
With means and wisdom like the rising sun.
Then the administration of the countries will be gentle, like the earth and water in Spring.
Do not be obsessive in the activities you perform.
If you can't handle the enemy and he overcomes you,
No protector will come to save you in your weakness.
If you put black thoughts in your mind
You will never be taken for a righteous lawgiver.

According to ancient Tibetan proverbs:

> 'On nine round-trips to China with a White *garuda dzo,*[31]
> You may not mean to wound its back with a heavy burden,
> But if the business be profitable it just might happen.

Riding your noble steed nine round-trip journeys to raid,
You may not mean to whip its buttocks,
But if you are after rich booty, it just might happen.

Swearing oaths of friendship nine times,
You may not intend to hurt each other's feelings with black words,
But if the mind gets stirred to anger, it just might happen.'

Heart essence of China, my three nephews,
Close relatives that you are, do not think to bicker with each other.
Still if there is a conflict between the Great Districts, it will probably occur.
Think about it and don't let your attitude change.
It is pointless for three young brothers to show each other black faces.
If one brother's sword is thrust in its sheath, let all be sheathed together.
And bind the three brothers' horses in one corral together.

The welfare of the white mother lineage is prime.[32]
Although the honorable *garuda* is great in power,
Garuda would never bear his talons and fight in space.
To the king of birds, the welfare of his own kind is prime.

Although the three potencies of the white snow lions are complete,
They would never quarrel with fellow animals on the earth.
To the king of beasts the welfare of wild beasts is prime.

If you understand this, it is molasses to the ear.
If you don't, I will not explain it.
Three princes, keep this in mind."

After he spoke, everyone was filled with delight. Then the three princes with their ministers, retinue, horses, mules, and so forth each happily returned to his own place.

While Bumpa Gyatsa was traveling from Gorgeous Upper White Ling to China, war broke out between Gog and Ling. The Eighteen Clans of Gog were destroyed by Ling. In the end the son of Chipön, Lenpa Chögyal, was lost to Gog. For some time they kept this secret from Gyatsa.

One day Gyatsa went hunting close to the spring called White Lady Myriad Swirls. He had just killed a deer when two wandering villagers from Ling, a mother and son, came there. She recognized that he was Gyatsa and said, "Hey, you must be Gyatsa. Wow, this is great!

With you White Ling is the best.
Without you, we're nothing.

It's really true. Last year while Gyatsa was away, Gog and Ling fought and even though Ling destroyed the Eighteen Clans of Gog, what was the point, since Lenpa Chögyal, Chipön's cherished heart son, was killed? Even now, in the districts of White Ling they are saying that Gyatsa will take revenge. And by the way, since I'm already standing here before the greatly kind leader, won't you please give me a piece of this meat you've caught?"

He gave her whatever meat she wanted and carefully asked her questions. She spoke without concealing anything. Regret that he had not been there in Gog pierced Zhalkar's heart like an arrow. Instantly he departed for Chipön's Falcon Fortress: "Oh Uncle King Chipön, aren't you like the saying:

'First a miserable failure in one's own affairs;
Second, a useless pimp when it comes to others.
Third and finally, just being full of shit.'

You have kept this a secret from your own people, but blabbed it to the other hundred provinces," he said, and broke into this short warrior's song.

"The song is ala thala thala.
Thala is the melody.
I bow at the feet of the Refuge, the Ocean of Victorious Ones.
In case you don't recognize this place,
It is the rich Falcon Castle Sky Fortress.
In case you don't recognize the likes of me,
I am Gyatsa Zhalkar of Bumpa.
I'm the nephew of the Emperor of China.
Now, then, Your Highness King Chipön,
Everyone says your great intelligence is bright as the dawning sky.
But plunged in obscurity, your sky never dawned.
The ancient sayings talk of what we should tell:

'If the minister embezzles food, tell the chief;
If someone is lost to the enemy, inform the warriors.
If there's been a robbery, dispatch someone clever in pursuit.'

With these three tellings all is well.
But you, man, just to hide your faults to yourself,
So that the chiding words of a beggar woman loaded me with ridicule and shame.

My older brother Lenpa Chögyal—
When I think of him now, my heart winds are depressed.
Two things brought the death of my older brother:
First, meaningless battle with Gog.
Second, allowing intermarriage with Hor.[33]
It all started with the black shadow of Yellow Hor,
Kunga's ill-omened daughter.
These two brought the downfall of my elder brother.
Kunga's daughter, Zima Lake—
Send her tear-marked face back to Hor.
She must not be allowed to remain in White Ling.
For I have lost my older brother to Gog.

Yes, and his avenger shall be Gyatsa.
For I am Zhalkar, like a white snow lion.
The six skills of a warrior are my flourishing turquoise mane.
Since I eat the red meat of my enemy like a hunter eats game,
I don't need the help of carnivore foxes.

I Gyatsa am the best red tiger of all,
Armor and weapons shine on my body like the six smiles of a tiger.[34]

Since I can drink the heart's blood of the enemy ponies,
I don't need any spotted leopards butting in.

Now I'll stay no longer. I go to the land of Upper Gog—
First to take revenge ninefold.
Second, to avenge myself further, to drink the enemy's heart blood.
And third, to see to it that the land of Gog is no more.
If I do not succeed, Gyatsa is like a corpse.
If you understand this speech, it is molasses to the ear.
If you don't, I'm not going to explain this song.
Chipön keep this in your mind."

Just as he had spoken, Gyatsa decided to depart alone without any more discussion. Chipön thought to himself:

"It's best not to go to war at this time.
But I won't manage to convince Zhalkar not to go.
And how could he possibly go alone?
I must tell him how everything happened."

With this thought, he began to sing a song which told the whole story and described the discussion about plans for sending a reinforcement army:

"I can't help but sing this song.
If I don't sing it, there's nothing left to do.
When happy, this is a marvelous song for tea and liquor.
When sad, it's a song to restore one's mind.

Undeceiving Three Jewels of Refuge
And worldly *zodor*s of White Ling,
Come here today to befriend Chipön.
Precious gem of the divine lineage of Bumpa,
With a relaxed mind, please listen to what I have to say.

Last year, we argued with Gog about land and people.
And since we couldn't settle on a treaty or accord,
War finally broke out between Gog and Ling.
The chieftain of Tagrong, Zigphen,
Plus Chipön, Lenpa Chögyal, and
Maternal nephew-uncle Denma Changtra, these three
Could remain no longer and left for the Upper Land of Gog.
They annihilated the Eighteen Clans of Gog.[35]
But it didn't help, for still in the final outcome
Lenpa Chögyal was slain.

Then, so that Ling could have its ninefold revenge,
The entire male gender was killed
And Gog became a land full of mourning widows.

But in the neighborhood of Ralo Tönpa[36]
Everyone was concealed by the *lha, lu,* and *nyen.*[37]

Thus the Ling soldiers could not see them and they were left behind.
I can't conceive how you could possibly conquer them now.
Their protector and refuge is known as Urgyen Padmasambhava.
Their guardian is the *nāga* King Tsugna Rinchen for
The *nāga* Tsugna's daughter is in Gog.

What I, Chipön, think is
In the ancient Mother Tablets[38] of the Mupko clan there is this prophecy:

> 'That jewel within the ocean[39]
> Will be taken by the mouse from the pinnacle of the victory banner.
> Whatever of the White is desired will be accomplished.'

If you think about it, doesn't this apply here?
Last year during the turmoil of battle it was a case of the proverb:

> 'Raising a really long club
> To strike the snout of a really short old dog.
> The undesired harvest of famine
> Brings down weakness, suffering, and exhaustion of merit.'

After the battle the brethren put their heads together in Ling,
But I, Chipön was without my son.
According to the ancient proverbs:

> 'Just because the King of Birds moults feather and wing,
> That doesn't make the white crag move or shake.
> Just because the golden-eyed fish is caught on a hook,
> Don't think that the ocean will grow or shrink.
> If you lose one eye in battle,
> Don't think that you can take revenge your whole life.'

Knowing I'm sonless does not torment me,
Because you, nephew Gyatsa, are alive and well.
I have no thought to seek revenge.
I swear this is true on the ancestral Hundred Thousand Verse Scripture.[40]
Let me tell you these most dark mystery words:

First the daughter of the *nāga* King Tsugna,
Second, the *dri*[41] cow with prosperity horns,
Third, the Fine Blue Nine-winged Tent,
Fourth, the Twelve Scriptures of the Nāgas in a Hundred Thousand Verses—
These most precious inner treasures of the cold-blooded *nāga*s[42]
Are now the inner wealth of Ralo Tönpa.
I wonder if these four could come to belong to Ling?
If that happened, whatever we wish would be fulfilled.
When the year of the mouse begins
I think the prophecy will come to pass.

Keep these words as the jewel within your collar.
If you go, there's no reason for you to go alone.

Go shoulder to shoulder with Zigphen of Tagrong.
Let Denma bring up the rear guard.
Go with an army seventy thousand strong.
You must go arm in arm with all of the kinsmen.
To the *zodor* country gods
Make offerings and praise them with smoke and windhorse.[43]
Dear chieftain Zhalkar, for your first raid
Perhaps you can win the booty without a fight.
If you understand these words, they're molasses to your ear.
If not, I'm not going to explain it.
Chieftain Zhalkar, keep this in your heart."

Then the kinsmen had a productive discussion. The very next morning messages and messengers were sent to the upper, lower, and middle regions of Ling like falling snow. The cousins and nephews decided among themselves that they would dispatch seven armies of ten thousand to Gog. Three days later at the crack of dawn, in the Assembly Hall Tagthang Tramo (Colorful Tiger Plain) they gathered in a state of perfect readiness.

Then Trothung[44] thought, "Even though Zhalu of the Bumpa clan is a white snow lion, still he can be caught by the hand. Although he's a red tiger, you can still hold him down by the ears. If his cousins and brothers and his relief army follow him to Gog, then the land of Gog will be no more, they will utterly annihilate it. This daughter of Nāga Tsugna along with the *nāga* wealth will be our booty. Zhalu will become legendary throughout Tibet. Even though all the treasures we capture will become the general property of Ling, yet it's certain that the daughter will belong to the Younger Lineage[45] and not to my clan. I'm going to have to do something about this.

Therefore I'll be a stool pigeon and do Kyalo a great favor. Afterwards I will ask him to give the *nāga* princess to Tagrong as my personal portion of the booty. Along with her I will certainly acquire some of the wealth of the *nāga*s. Even if that doesn't work out, she holds the name of her father, the *nāga* Tsugna Rinchen. What could be better than that anyway?"

He placed a charm of swift flight on a golden arrow and attached this letter to its neck:

> "Respectfully presented to Ralo Tönpa Gyaltsen of Gog:
> From Trothung the Chieftain of Tagrong.
>
> The blood price for killing Chipön's son last year is that Bumpa Zhalkar, leading seven armies of ten thousand mighty warriors, is determined to attack you tomorrow. Fighting won't get you out of this. Therefore by nightfall it is important for you to escape to a safe and remote place. Now I have done you a great favor. Henceforth, if there's a good turn you can do me, don't forget what I've done for you."

Then he conjured and enjoined the arrow to land on the top of Ralo's tent. He shot it from the peak of Gedzo Rimar Wangzhu. With a sound of sparks, the arrow struck the top of the tent. Ralo quickly noticed that there was a letter tied to its neck. He read and understood the meaning and instantly sent messengers and messages throughout the land of Gog. But the mules and horses were unable to carry the turquoise tent and the Hundred Thousand Verse Nāga treasure. They were barely able to carry the *dri* horn *nāga* treasure.

That very night they began their journey, traveling to the border of the province of Hor in the region of Ma (Mashöd). During their nightime escape, the *dri* carrying the *nāga* treasure turned around and went back up the path. The *nāga* daughter saw this, but no one else did. Because the moment of destiny had come, although the *nāgini* was riding a horse, she dismounted. Feeling more inclined to walk, she set out after it, but was unable to catch the running *dri*. Her horse got loose and went back following the clan. Although she called back to them, by the power of karma, no one could hear her. She followed after the *dri* along the banks of the Ma River valley. When she stopped, the *dri* would stop as well. Whether she went quickly or slowly, the *dri* would do the same, and so she couldn't quite catch up with it. Several times she almost caught it, but it would continue down the path, the *nāginī* still chasing the *dri*. The path they took wandered about aimlessly. During that time it never even occurred to her that she might be suffering from hunger, thirst, pain, or exhaustion.

Just then the Ling army, its armor and weapons flashing, arrived in the country of Gog. The land of Gog had become empty. There was nothing left except cushions and beds.

The Ling soldiers gathered for a meeting and Zhalkar, Sengtag Adom, and so on, all the young warriors, were sent on reconnaisance to find out where the people of Gog had gone. Some soldiers said, "We don't know where they've gone. All these soldiers are just going to tire ourselves out to no end. Why don't we just go back?"

Then Chipön said, "Although we may be following them for just a little silver, wherever the soldiers of the White Ling go, they have never returned empty-handed, with no booty. How could we possibly leave without a victory? So let's have Senglön perform a divination and base our decision on that." Then Senglön did an arrow divination and respectfully gave them as the outcome:

"If we go as far as the time it takes to drink tea, then
Beauty is nectar to the eyes;
The refined essence of the nectar is inexhaustible,
And the treasure trove that fulfills all needs and desires will be ours.
Without fighting it will fall into our hands.
We will not need to slide our weapons in their sheaths.
The arrow will not be notched in the bow.
Victory will be decided by our field of power alone."

Then Trotung of Tagrong thought, "That divination was amazing. It must be a sign that all of this will eventually come round to Tagrong. However, it is certain that today there will be no booty." Trothung thought he might have to seek advantage by accusing Senglön of making an inaccurate divination. So he derisively said, "Hah! If your victory in this empty land occurs without even notching the arrow in the bow or sliding the swords from their sheaths, then the fee for your divination today should be the booty itself."

Chipön, who knew how great the booty would be, said, "Well then, if that is the chief of Tagrong's decision today, then let it be that way. Now let's boil some tea and make a smoke offering to the gods. Then we'll go."

Then they went out to gather juniper for the smoke offering.

Now, it turns out that before this all happened, Ralo Tönpa had asked his guru, Dorje Gyaltsen (Vajra Banner), for counsel. The lama predicted that in this year Ralo's wealth would be taken away and he would be attacked by enemies. He had better make many smoke offerings and accumulate appeasement and expiation offerings to the war-gods. Ralo, therefore, had prepared offerings enough to fill a hundred yak saddlebags—varieties of woods, rhododenrons, juniper, tamarisk, and wormwood. These prepared offerings the men of Ling discovered and gathered up to make their own smoke offering—a great smoke offering that would fill all of space.

Chipön said, "Today the auspicious connection is excellent, because this is the first raid of the warrior Gyatsa. Mikyong Karpo (Sengtag Adom), he whose castle Pala is a support around which the war-gods of White Ling flock, do you now invoke the gods and raise a song that will cause the war-gods to alight on the body of the warrior![46] You other mighty warriors, raise aloft your threefold panoplies, arrows, and spears, and stand at attention."

Then there came the warrior Sengtag Adom, a white man with a white horse bearing a white flag and a white helmet with white pennants, his white cape covering his back. He bore spear pennants, banners, and a divine white lasso. Adorned with these nine whites—white as though they had emerged from the white gods themselves—he raised this song like a haughty snow lion in his prime:

"The song begins with ala ala ala
Thala gives the melody.
The refuge, the Rare and Supreme Three Jewels,
Please remain inseparable as my crown ornament.
If you don't know this place,
It has degraded into an empty desert of the black enemy,
A place White Ling has conquered,
The fatherland of Gog Ralo Tönpa.
In case you don't know the likes of me,
I am Seng Adom, a wolf among men
From the Maroon Palace of Kyutri.
This horse is Thousand Mountains Treasury of Wealth.
I am the emanation son of Mount Machen Pomra in the East and
The heart son of the god, White Brahma.
Today, the day of auspiciousness,
We make a smoke offering to please the gods of the Rare and Supreme Three Jewels.
First from the morning side of the valley, we gather the juniper.
Then from the shady side rhododendrons,
And third from between them the white tamarisk:
These three are known to be the deathless *amṛta* trees.
Buddha Locana is the oven for burning.[47]
Māmakī is the water we sprinkle.
We melt with the power of Pāṇḍaravāsinī
We summon with the wind of Samaya Tārā.
It blazes in the expanse of the space of Dhātvīśvari.
Clouds of smoke are the self-manifestation of emptiness,
The spontaneous, natural, continuous treasure of all that is desired.
By making this smoke offering of the *amṛta* of appearance-emptiness[48]
To the Dharmakāya-Vajradhara,
The Sambhogakāya—the victorious five buddha families,[49]
And the Nirmāṇakāya—three protectors bodhisattvas[50]—
The three tutelary deities of White Ling, may all be purified.

First Guru Padmasambhava,
Second Great Ling Glorious Lion,
And third, the teacher of the Ling clan, Guide of Enlightenment.
By the three lamas of Ling may all be cleansed.

Ḍākinī Yeshe Tsogyal,
The only mother, the Queen of Accomplishments,
And Manene Exalted Lady Queen.[51]
By these three ladies of Ling may all be cleansed.

The great god, White Brahma
Lord of the Nyen, Five Topknots,
And the *nāga* King Tsugna Rinchen:
By these three deities that protect White Ling may we be purified.

Red Nyentag (Red Nyen Tiger),
Oath-bound Vajrasadhu,
Life Lord of the Three Worlds, Pehar:
By these three, the protectors who uphold the ancestral heritage of Mugpo Dong, may all
    be purified.

The war-god who abides on the top of the white helmet,
The *garuda*s who encircle the vulture-feathered silk headdress,
And the war-gods who rest on the black armor,
Those war-gods who surround the warrior like a cape of eight auspicious symbols,
The war-gods who alight on the shield,
Who surround the whip and guard the perimeter,
The war-gods who alight on the dawn-colored spear pennants,
On the sight of the single notched straight arrow
And on the supreme white bowstring and the blade of the sword,
And on the magic slingshot propelled by the winds—
By all the war-gods who surround these may all be purified.

One war-god delivers into our hands
The vow-corrupting unruly enemies.
One conquers all comers at all costs.
One war-god kills just by a touch of his weapons:
May these three kindred war-god victors of the land cleanse all.

Some war-gods make one unseen by the enemy, some make us proof against weapons,
And the life force free from threats. All these protectors surround like a tent:
May these three brotherhoods of protecting war-gods cleanse all.

Pleasing speech, prosperity, and
Raising windhorse to give universal victory,
By the three brethren war-gods who increase these, may all be cleansed.
The noble stallion's fancy baubles and trappings,
The four hooves like wheels of wind,
And the downy vulture feathers protruding from his ears,
May the war-gods that surround the horse cleanse all.
May the *werma* who fill the heavens cleanse all.
May the great gong whose sound fills intermediate space cleanse all.

Above we offer silk banners filling the sky,
Like white clouds of the war-gods *tha ra ra.*[52]

People fill the space between
With the dragon sound of Ki So *u ru ru.*
The face of the earth is covered with horses.
The rain of *siddhis*[53] is falling *si li li*—
Inconceivable reward of the six grains.

Thus do these war-gods mark the white day
Of the first raid of Chieftain Gyatsa.
The enemy aggression could not bear the splendor of his presence.
Look how they fled in the depths of the black earth.
After the black enemy is suppressed under ground
Then the many sparkling rewards will fall in our own hands.
First, the dharmic wealth of the gods above—
May we today gain that as our reward.
Second, the increasing wealth of the humans in the middle—
May we today be apportioned that as our reward.
Third, the inexhaustible wealth and riches of the *nāgas* below—
May we have our portion of that booty today.

White Ling and the gods are integral to each other.
The aims of the white gods will be fulfilled.
May White Ling be ornamented with myriad colorful rewards.
May this account prevail throughout the world.
May whatever we wish for be spontaneously achieved.
May the myriad rewards arrive in our hands.
Although it may be necessary for this army to be deployed for a year,
We are prepared even to encircle the southern continent of Jambudvīpa.
May whatever prayers we make come to pass.

If you understand this song, it will be molasses to your ears.
If not, I am not going to try to explain it.
Cousins and brothers of Ling keep this in your mind."

As they rode off, they shouted in unison the warrior cry of Ki So and Lha Gyal Lo (Divine Victory).[54]

—RK

Glossary

We have decided in this translation to give English approximations of the important Tibetan names that are familiar to people who know this epic, the "household names." In italics next to the glossary entries we give the actual complex Tibetan spelling and sometimes the Sanskrit as well, if this is important. Where both Tibetan and Sanskrit are given, Tibetan is indicated by "Tib." and Sanskrit by "Skt." The bolded entries are given in the form in which they are commonly found in English texts.

Achen—name of a tribe and a region in the Kingdom of Hor, in the area of the upper Yellow River.
amrita—Tib. *bdud rtsi;* Skt. *amṛta*—literally, "anti-death [potion]"—refers to a milky drink that

confers eternal life and is the sole possession of the gods. Used metonymically for any delicious drink.

Anu Zigphen—*A nu gZig 'phen*—Youthful Leopard Leap—one of the Thirty Mighty Warriors, a chieftain of the Tagrong tribe. In some traditions he is Trothung's oldest son, in others his brother.

appeasement and fulfillment offerings—*rngan gsol*—ceremonies of sacrifice to correct the opposition of gods caused by violation of taboo or other transgressions.

body god—*sku lha*—a deity who protects the body of a specific warrior, much like the patron gods that perch on the head, shoulders, and chest of warriors.

Bodza Metog Tashi Tsho—*bod bza' Me tog bkra shis mtsho*—Wife of Tibet Flower Auspicious Lake—Chipön's wife.

buddha families, five—In Tantric symbolism each of the five points of the mandala (north, south, east, west, and center) is inhabited by a buddha and his consort, representing five styles of energy in which enlightenment and confusion both are manifest. The five buddhas are Akṣobhya in the East, Amitābha in the West, Amoghasiddhi in the North, and Ratnasambhava in the South, plus the famous Vairocana Buddha in the center. These five primordial buddhas and their consorts participate in most empowerments in the epic.

Buddha Locana—*sangs rgyas sPyan ma*—the female buddha representing the element of earth.

cannibal demons—Tib. *srin po;* Skt. *rākṣasa*—fearful demons with long tongues, claws, and fangs; enemies to humankind and sometimes eat humans. They are much in evidence in the Indian epic tradition.

Chöphen Nagpo—*Chos phan Nag po*—Black Dharma Benefit—a founder of the royal lineage of Mukpo Dong. Chöphen Nagpo had three famous wives: Serza, Amza, and Changza. Ser (gSer), Am ('Am), and Chang (sPyangs) are three tribes with an important relationship with the Mukpos, probably through the politics of the tribal state of Ling. *Za* here means wife *(gza')*. By marrying into these leading families, Chöphen Nagpo increased the power of the Mukpo. These three wives gave birth respectively to the three lineages of Ling, the so-called Elder, Cadet, and Middle lineages.

Chur lha—*byur lha*—name of a chief of Jang. It may mean "Mishap God" or "Coral God" (if *bhur lha* is really *bhyi ru lha*).

country god—*yul lha*—literally, "god of the place." A term for a native Tibetan deity, usually attached to a specific place. Sometimes this refers to a god of the hunt.

Ḍākinī—*mkha' 'gro ma*—a wrathful or semiwrathful female deity who signifies the absolute as a messenger principle. The *ḍākinī*s are tricky and playful women who can be seductive, motherly, or punishing as they serve the Tantric practitioner, bringing messages of enlightenment and guidance. They represent the basic space out of which the play of samsara and nirvana arises. There are also lower goddesses who are essentially fairies or demonesses deputized by Buddhism. These two are sometimes called *ḍākinī*s in Tibetan texts. There is a group of *ḍākinī*s who are female extensions of the basic principle of Buddhahood. They manifest as female *yidam*s (meditional deities) in the style of the five families of buddhas and are named by those families, as Buddhaḍākinī, Vajraḍākinī, and so forth.

Denma—*'Dan ma*—the famous chief minister of Gesar, his tactical planner and first disciple. If it were not that Gesar himself is a supreme trickster, one would say that Denma is the Odysseus figure in the epic. His full name is Denma Changtra *('Dan ma Byang khra* or *sPyang khra).* He is also called *tsha zhang* Denma, meaning literally "maternal nephew-uncle Denma" and *tsha rgyal,* maternal nephew-king. All of these titles refer to the fact that he is related through female descent to Ling, an important ally from the Den clan.

Dorje Gyaltsen—*rDo rje rGyal mtshan*—Ralo Tönpa's guru.

dzo—*mdzo*—the result of crossing a yak bull with a cow; the male offspring serve as beasts of burden and the females are good milk producers.

enemies in the four directions, four—*phyogs bzhi'i dgra bzhi*—also known as the *māra*s (or devils) of the Four Directions *(phyogs bzhi' bdud bzhi).* These are the four principal anti-Buddhist kingdoms that Gesar must oppose. They are listed in the first chapter of the first book of the epic. These include Lutsen in the north, King Gurkar from Hor, and Sadam, king of Jang. The fourth enemy is different in various lists.

field of power—*dbang thang*—literally, "field of power" or "charisma"—an important part of the cosmology of Tibetan village and nomadic culture, the *wang thang,* as it is pronounced, is an aura that surrounds the body and makes a person's actions penetrating and effective. It can be gathered, collected, and built up into a powerful force. Sometimes this expression is translated as "authentic presence" because it is regarded in a subtle way as a kind of field of wealth and fortunate power. People who are naturally successful and natural leaders are all born with an impressive *wang thang.* Modern martial arts culture sometimes calls this a "battle aura."

Five Topknots—Tib. *zur phud lnga pa;* Skt. *Pañcaśika*—the king of the *nyen* (mountain gods). A figure associated with the great *nyen* Nyenchen Thangla. In China, Pañcaśika was identified with Five Terraces Mountain (Wutai shan) in northern Shanxi, a sacred Buddhist site that attracted pilgrims from East Asia, Central Asia, and South Asia.

fortress—*rdzong*—often refers to an administrative district dominated in theory by a single fort. The epic speaks of the Twelve Great Fortresses of Ling *(gLing rDzong chen bcu gnyis),* actually meaning twelve countries in Tibet.

gandharva—*'dri za*—the Tibetan word for this deity literally means "smell eater"; refined beings alleged to live on fragrances. They are celestial musicians. Sometimes in the epic, *gandharva*s are wrathful martial deities. This is unusual.

garuda—*'khyung*—a gigantic divine bird first prominently mentioned in the first book of the great Indian epic, the *Mahābhārata.* In Hinduism he is the mount of Viṣṇu. In Tibetan religion he is the king of the birds and a divine principle of vast mind.

Gedzo—*ge 'dzo*—name of a local deity, a *nyen* (mountain god); one of the most important native Tibetan deities in the epic. He is the *nyen* of the mountain Gedzo Rimar Wangzhu *(ge 'dzo ri dMar dBang zhu)* in Eastern Tibet.

Gedzo Rimar Wangzhu—*ge 'dzo ri dMar dBang zhu*—another name for Gedzo and the name of a mountain where he resides.

ghosts—Tib. *'byung po;* Skt. *bhūta*—a class of pathetic invisible spirits of the same order as *preta*s (hungry ghosts). Sometimes called "elementals," following the literal meaning of *bhūta* and the fact that this class of deities may include spirits of fire, earth, water, etc.

god of males—*skyes lha*—short for *skyes po lha;* a type of war-god, akin to the "five patron gods" who perch on a warrior's body and protect him in battle. They have the appearance of strong men and are decorated with jewels.

gods, eight classes of—*lha sde brgyad*—a traditional list of kinds of native Tibetan deities. The list varies, but it usually includes *lha, nyen, naga*s, war-gods, and other non-Buddhist deities.

Gog—*'Gog*—the country of Kyalo Tönpa Gyaltsen, neighboring Ling. Because Gesar's mother lived in Gog, the possession of Tönpa Gyaltsen, she is known as Gogmo, the woman from Gog.

Gog, eighteen clans of—*'gog pha tsho bco brgyad*—literally, "the eighteen father districts of Gog." These, apparently, are areas of Gog organized according to clans patriarchally derived.

Guide of Enlightenment—*Byang chub 'Dren pa*—a guru in Ling.

Gyatsa Zhalkar—*rGya tsha zhal dkar*—Chinese Nephew White Face; half-brother of Gesar, grandson of the Chinese emperor. His father is Senglön and his mother is Gyaza (rGya bza' Lha dkar sGron ma). In many ways Gyatsa is the model of a perfect Tibetan warrior. Indeed, he is one of the Seven Super Warriors. He is of the Bumpa clan, which is in the Lesser or Cadet order of Ling; hence he is also known as Gyatsa Zhalkhar of Bumpa ('Bumpa'i rGya tsha Zhal dkar).

Gyatsa Nyima Rangshar—*rGya tsha Nyima Rangshar*—Chinese Maternal Nephew Sun Self-Arising; the clan's name for Gyatsa Zhalkar.

Gyaza Lhakar Drönma—*lha-dkar sGronma*—Chinese Wife Divine White Lady of the Lamp—Senglön's first wife.

heruka—*khrag 'thung*—a wrathful male *yidam* (meditional or tutelary deity) at the level of enlightenment of complete Buddhahood. The Tibetan *khrag 'thung* means "blood drinker," for the wrathful form of *heruka*s is borrowed from depictions in the iconography of monstrous vampires. In Tantric symbolism the *heruka* "drinks the blood of ego-clinging and dualistic thinking."

heruki—female *heruka*.

Jambudvīpa—*Dzam bu gLing*—the southern continent or island of the Buddhist world-system. It is named after the *jambu* (rose-apple) tree. Jambudvīpa is roughly equivalent to planet Earth in the Western cosmological system—the world populated by human beings, so "Jambudvīpa" is often simply translated as "the world" or "the whole world."

life stone—*bla rdo*—a magical stone that holds the life essence or magical essence and power of an individual or a whole group.

lu—Tib. *glu;* Skt. *nāga*—a dragon or water spirit. See *nāga*.

Magyal Pomra—*rMa rgyal sPom ra*—a *nyen* (q.v.), a mountain god of very high standing in the Tibetan native pantheon. Magyal Pomra is the deity of the Machen Pomra mountain range, also called Amnye Machen. It is a series of peaks in the heart of the Golok district in Qinghai Province. Magyal Pomra is a highly enlightened *nyen* and servant of the cause of Buddhism, a co-worker in the plots of Padmasambhava, the deathless founder of Tibetan Tantra.

Manene—a goddess who is a sort of divine mother and guide to Gesar of Ling. *Ma* means "mother," and *ne-ne* or *a-ne* is an affectionate or diminutive for the paternal aunt. Or it can refer more generally to a woman of the older generation. Manene has many names, one of the most popular being Nam-men Karpo Manene (*gNam sman dKarpo Ma ne ne* [White Sky Goddess]).

meditational deity—*yi dam;* the Tantric *(vajrayāna)* practitioner's personal deity, who embodies the practitioner's awakened nature. *Yidam* is explained as a contraction of *yid kyi dam tshig,* the *samaya* or commitment of one's mind. *Yidam*s are *sambhogakāya* buddhas, who are visualized in accordance with the psychological makeup of the practitioner. They are male or female, wrathful or peaceful, and carry symbolic ornaments which are an esoteric commentary on the nature and manifestation of the practitioner's mind.

Mikyong Karpo—*Mi skyong dKar po*—another name for Sengtag Adom.

Mother Tablets—*ma yig*—an ancient collection of proverbs and prophecies for the kingdom of Ling.

Mu—*dMu*—a tribe in the Younger Lineage of Ling. Gesar's human father is Senglön, whose mother was known as Muza (Wife from the Mu Tribe). Thus Gesar is closely related to the Mu of the Cadet Lineage, as is Chipön, the chieftain of the Cadet Lineage.

Muza—*rMu-rdza;* Wife from the Mu Tribe—wife of Chöla Bum of the Cadet Lineage.

nāga—Tib. *klu,* pronounced *lu*—dragons, serpents, a class of deities associated with water in all its forms. Iconographically they are usually represented with human torsos and blue-skinned serpent-like lower bodies. The women have turquoise hair. As an Indic deity the *nāga*s figure prominently in the Indian epic tradition, particularly the *Mahābhārata,* which begins with a description of the war between the *nāga*s and Garuda. But the word *lu* also refers to a native Tibetan deity associated with water and representing one of the three levels of the cosmos in native Tibetan religion: *lha, nyen,* and *lu. Nāgī* is a female *lu.* The most famous of the *lu* or *nāga*s is Tsugna Rinchen, the king of the *nāga*s, who rules a realm at the bottom of the ocean.

non-men—*mi ma yi*—term for any sort of worldly deities.

Nyatra Bakha—*Nya spra Bakha*—name of a legendary fish in Hor.

nyen—*gnyen*—gods of mountain ranges. In the threefold hierarchy of native deities (*lha, nyen,* and *lu*), which matches the Confucian divisions of Heaven, Earth, and Man, they occupy the middle realm between Heaven and the Underworld, equivalent to the sides of mountains. Famous *nyen* are Machen Pomra and Nyenchen Thanglha, and Gesar's patron Gedzo. *Nyen* are usually powerful gods who exercise a certrain proprietorship over the lands where their mountain ranges lie and are thus often called *sa-bdag,* Earth lords.

Nyentag—*sNyan stag*—Nyen Tiger; the name of a tutelary deity of Gesar who has the form of a war-god. Also known as Red Nyen Tiger (gNyan stag dMar po).

Nyentag Marpo—*gNyan stag dMar po*—Red Nyen Tiger—a mountain god who occurs in the Gesar epic. *See* Nyentag.

Nyitri Karchen—*Nyi khri sKar chen*—Twenty Thousand Great Stars—the son of Sadam of Jang, a nephew of the emperor of China. Sadam in later volumes will be a great enemy of Ling, and Gesar will kill him during a war with the Jang.

Omza—*Om bza'*—Wife from the Om Tribe. *See* Chöphen Nagpo.

Padmasambhava—*pad ma 'byung*—the Tantric magician who brought Tantra to Tibet. His name means "born from a lotus," an indication of his magical origins. Padmasambhava is regarded as a completely enlightened buddha who still dwells on a demon island on another continent and still works to protect the Dharma in Tibet. He is one of the principal objects of devotion in Tibetan religion.

Pehar—a Central Asian deity that was brought to Tibet at the time of the founding of the Tibetan empire and became a guardian of the first monastic center, Samye. He is easily identifiable by his peculiar circular hat.

Ralo Tönpa—*See* Tönpa Gyaltsen of Kyalo.

Rongza—*Rong bza';* Wife from Rong—wife of Chöla Bum of the Lesser Lineage.

rākṣasa—*srin-po*—cannibal demons; horrific, man-harming monsters. They figure prominently in Indian poetry and in epics. They assume many forms and are called "cannibal demons" because they have the habit of eating their victims.

sambhogakāya—*longs spyod rdzogs sku*—the form of a buddha who appears to spiritually advanced people in visions and wears magnificent, colorful, symbolic ornaments. In the threefold division of buddhas into body, speech, and mind, the *sambhogakāya* buddhas represent the speech principle.

select portion—*phud*—the first bit of food or drink, which is offered to the Three Jewels before any other offerings are made or a meal of enlightened communication is consumed.

Sengtag Adom—*seng stag A dom;* Lion Tiger Primal Bear—a leader in the Middle Lineage of Ling, one among the group called "the Thirty Fathers and Uncles of Ling," and one of the Seven Super Warriors; one of the most famous warriors of his clan.

Serza—*gSer bza'*—Wife from the Ser Tribe. *See* Chöphen Nagpo.

smoke offering—*lha sangs;* pronounced *lha sang;* literally, "divine purification"; a ceremony in which clouds of juniper smoke are offered along with tea, liquor, and various rites from native Tibetan religions. The *lha* or gods are invited to descend the column of smoke and purify the place.

Soaring Golden Bird Gait—*gser bya ldin 'gros*—a horse given to Zhalkar by the Ser tribe at his birthday celebration.

Tantra—an esoteric form of Buddhism based on the notion of transmuting negativity into enlightenment through ritual practices, complex yogas, and sophisticated meditation techniques.

the'u rang—*the'u rang*—one of the eight classes of gods, a class of local deities generally harmful to humankind. According to one description, the *the'u rang* are invisible one-legged demons who ride mounted on tornados. They are harmful to children and are also the deities to whom gamblers pray when they are playing dice. One who receives the blessings of the *the'u rang* will win in gambling but must become a servant of the *the'u rang* after death.

Three Protectors—*rigs gsum mgon po*—literally, "protectors of the three families"; the three bodhisattvas who represent respectively wisdom *(prajñā)*, compassion *(karuṇā)*, and power *(bala)*: Mañjuśrī, Avalokiteśvara, and Vajrapāṇi.

Three Trainings—Tib. *bslab gsum*; Skt. *trīśikṣa*—training in discipline *(śila)*, meditation *(samādhi)*, and wisdom *(prajñā)*.

Tönpa Gyaltsen of Kyalo—*skya lo ston pa rgyal mtshan*—literally, "Teacher Victory Banner of Kyalo"; the leader of the wealthy class of Ling. He is the father of Drugmo, Gesar's future bride, and a leader in the province of Gog.

Trichang Pagyal—*Khri spyang dPa' rgyal*—Wolf Throne Victorious Warrior, son of Chöphen Nagpo and Omza; founder of the Middle Lineage of Ling.

tsen—*btsan*—Deities associated with rocks and the sides of mountains. In the threefold order of gods *(lha, nyen,* and *lu)*, they stand in the middle or intermediate space between heaven and earth with the *nyen*. Often represented as red in color, and everything associated with them (e.g., armor, horse, lance, banner, snare, dog) is also depicted as red.

Tsugna Rinchen—*gtsug na rin chen*—literally, "Jewel in the Crest"; the king of the *nāga*s and maternal grandfather of Gesar. "Jewel in the Head" refers to a classical Asian belief that every serpent has a jewel in its head just above and between the eyes.

Urgyen Padma—one of the many names of the Tantric yogi who founded Tibet, Padmasambhava, the Lotus Born from the Country of Uḍḍiyāna (Urgyen), a Central Asian kingdom taken by Tibetans to be almost a magical land.

Vajradhara—*rDo rje Chang*—the primordial buddha, the divine source of the Tantric teachings of the New Translation School, the second great school of Tantric Buddhism, which arose in eleventh-century Tibet. Vajradhara means "Holder of the Vajra," the *vajra* being an adamantine scepter that symbolizes transcendent skillful means. He is a *dharmakāya* buddha, that is, a deity who represents the mind and ultimate nature of the Buddha.

Vajrasadhu—*rDo rje Legs pa*—one of the most important protector deities in Tibet; a wrathful protector riding a brown ram, holding the implements of a blacksmith. He is often classed with the *nyen* or mountain deities, equal in power to Nyenchen Thangla. In the *Gesar* epic he works closely with Padmasambhava to serve the cause of Gesar.

windhorse—*(rlung rta)*—1. an ancient Sino-Tibetan diagram that shows four beasts, sometimes the eight trigrams of the Chinese *Book of Changes (Yijing)*, and a flying horse with a flaming jewel on its saddle. It is often presented on a flag or pennant that flaps in the wind and thereby propagates blessings and uplifted windhorse (see next meaning) to the place. These "windhorse" flags can be found by the hundreds before a Tibetan residence or temple, decorating flagpoles and cords stretched between two high places. 2. Windhorse is also a kind of energy of dignity, confidence, and personal power that must be awakened by a warrior in order to have success in battle. A person with perpetually fully opened windhorse has a field of power about him that gives him an air of success and invincibility. This field is called *wang thang (dbang thang;* "field of power" or "authentic presence"). *See* "field of power." One of the aims of the *Gesar* epic as a didactic piece within its own culture is to teach the art and consequences of controlling one's windhorse.

Yeshe Tsogyal—*ye shes mtsho rgyal*—a famous female *tantrika,* consort of Padmasambhava, one of the founders of Tantrism in Tibet.

yidam—*See* meditational deity.

zodor—a class of worldly deities from the Bönpo pantheon and native Tibetan religion. In the epic the *zodor* is usually the god of Mount Magyal Pomra or Gedzo, a special epic mountain god who protects and advises Gesar. Often the *zodor* is the country god *(yul lha),* the local naturally existing deity who is the "proprietor" *(bdag po)* of the land.

Notes

1. A good summary of this scholarship is given in *The Perilous Frontier: Nomadic Empires and China, 221 B.C. to A.D. 1757,* by Thomas Barfield (Oxford: Blackwell, 1996). Barfield is an anthropologist whose work on nomads in Afghanistan led him to a vast comparative study of nomads worldwide. In this book he advances the work of historians who have been developing a more complicated picture of Chinese-nomadic political relationships by looking at ecological and cultural issues as well as the political chronologies.

2. In Tibetan chronicles black is often the color of ancestral gods. The name "Mukpo" means "swarthy" and is the name of Gesar's family. Since this is a living epic still sung, there is in fact a large Mukpo clan in existence that claims this genealogy as the history of the founding of their clan.

3. The genealogy of the family of the hero is important in any epic, from the "begats" sections of the Judeo-Christian Bible to the catalog of the ships in the *Iliad.* There is one peculiarity in this Tibetan pastoralist genealogy: it describes both the patriarchal and matriarchal descent lines of the heroes. Here is one understanding of the meaning of this genealogy. At the point of its founding the Mukpo clan divided into three sublineages that took up residence respectively in the highlands, the middle lands, and the lowlands of the area around a sacred mountain named Machen Pomra. The Elder Lineage took up the highlands and descended from the daughter-in-law who was the eldest. She was sent by her father-in-law into the highlands to find a magical object that would provide a name for the family of her sublineage. She found a golden yoke and the name of her family became Ser, which means "gold." She was called Serza, the wife of the Ser family, thus naming her branch of the Mukpo clan according to its feminine origins.

4. The Bum family is a subset of the Cadet Lineage. They probably gained their name from their possession of a valuable copy of the *Hundred Thousand Line Perfection of Wisdom Sutra,* which is often a sacred object in a Tibetan family.

5. Chöla Bum's three wives are denominated by the names of their original families. So, for example, Rongza is "the wife from the Rong Clan." This means that she is partly still under the protection of that clan, which must keep good relations with the Mukpos. Her male sons are named not according to their paternal descent from Mukpo Dong, but according to their mother's line. So they are called Rongtsha, "nephew of Rong."

6. *Blo phug* (the last word)—literally, "mind cave." The innermost mind, that upon which one must depend in a counsel.

7. The Hor were a neighboring tribal kingdom that also had at times a tributary relationship with China. The battle between Ling and Hor is a historical event and also the basis for the longest chapter of the *Gesar* epic, "The War against the Hor."

8. Senglön is the father of Gesar. He and Chipön, the chief of Ling, are two of the most important characters in the epic. Both of them, therefore, are seen as descendants of Indian tantric saints. Thus the Tibetan text expresses a typical Tibetan position: that they are politically connected with China, but culturally descended from India.

9. War-gods, *werma*s, and oath-bound protectors—*dgra lha, werma, dam can chags pa'i.* These are three kinds

of local deities important in Tibetan cosmology. The war-gods are deities and complexes of energy that invest the body of the warrior, sitting on his or her head, two shoulders, and heart center. Iconographically they are represented as small armored warriors. A Tibetan knight who has all the war-gods perched upon his or her body has a "battle aura" of immense power and is difficult to defeat. *Werma*s are like *dralha*s. They gather around warriors whose contemplative powers are strong and invest the weapons with power. The oath-bound protectors are local deities that have been bound magically by Buddhist masters and now must serve the Buddhist cause. The shrines where these deities are worshiped as spirits of the land and environment are called "castles" and "fortresses" because they are usually found in nature as piles of rocks that look like Tibetan fortifications. A life stone *(bla rdo)* is a magical stone which holds the life essence, the magical essence, and power of an individual or a group.

10. This passage includes an untranslatable honorific punning on Gyatsa Zhalkar's name. He is a *rgya dar* (Chinese silken scarf), a *rgya stag* (Bengal tiger), and a *rgya khra* (bird of prey). The word *rgya* means a different thing in each context. It is parallel to the use of the word *'jam*, which means "soft" in Chipön's praises. Chipön is *phyi 'jam* (outwardly soft), *nang 'jam* (inwardly soft), *dro 'jam* (warm and soft), and *lhod 'jam* (loose and soft). But the word *'jam* is not a pun on any of Chipön's many names. There are, however, two famous Tibetan lama/scholars whose names begin with the word 'Jam: Jamgön Kongtrül and Jamyang Khyentse Özer—two gurus of the nineteenth-century editor of the epic. This would explain the oddness of the line translated "He gained control over the mechanism of his luminous mind" (see the seventh line of the first verse passage), which has within it syllables from the names of these two gurus. This passage praising Chipön could be a tribute in code to these two great *yogin*s who were, according to the colophons, active in encouraging this edition of the epic.

11. The objects of refuge for all Buddhists: the Buddha, the Dharma (the teachings), and saṃgha (the monastic community).

12. The "field of power" *(wang thang)* is the charisma an individual or country possesses when it is going to be successful in its endeavors. It plays about the shoulders of warriors like the "battle aura" in modern Asian cartoons. It is an aspect of the merit developed by Ling through previous good deeds and moments of courage of its inhabitants. Here the birth of a noble warrior such as Zhalkar is a first sign of the merit that the entire country of Ling possesses—the merit to develop a great aura of power and be successful in the future. It is a first sign of the coming of their greatest warrior, Zhalkar's as yet unborn half-brother, Gesar of Ling.

13. "Ala" and "thala" are the Tibetan equivalent of "tra-la-la." With these sounds the bard singing this song gives the melody for the rest of the song.

14. Aphorisms are an important part of Tibetan literature, in part because the legal system depends on the services of mediators who employ proverbs and gnomic expressions to decide cases and disputes. There are at least three kinds of aphorisms: the ancient tradition of Tibetan sayings *(gna' mi bod kyi gtam rgyun)*, proverbs *(gtam dpe)*, and elegant sayings *(legs bshad)*. The ancient Tibetan sayings are considered a distinct oral corpus in themselves, different from the thousands of proverbs in current usage.

15. If goods came, it was the custom to portion them with the blade of a knife *(grogs byung na gri rtses kham bkos dar; grogs* means "possessions" or "goods"—valuable things such as clothes and food that come your way). The expression *gri rtses* literally means "with the trip of a knife" and *gam* means "a bite" or "a morsel." The idea is that in the old days somebody who gained something would share it with everybody else, holding the meat, for example, in their teeth and cutting off a piece with their knife to share with the others.

16. Originally a burial mound covering relics of a saint. Some stupas are domed and pinnacled architectural monuments dedicated to a buddha; others are small ornamental reliquaries of the same shape.

17. Mongolian gait—*rTa 'gros ldan*. This is the special way of running Tibetans teach their horses to make them give a smooth ride, so that the rider need not post. It looks like the high-stepping gait used by horses in a steeplechase.

18. White Sixth turquoise—*gyu drug*—a kind of turquoise, the highest-quality turquoise. If you put a drop of milk on it, it turns the milk pink, indicating the gem's high quality. We do not know what the other five orders of turquoise are, but think that perhaps in medicine there are five other turquoises.

19. *Rta rag pa*—black mane and tail, yellow body, black feet, and sometimes a black muzzle.

20. A divine nectar drunk by the gods and symbolically given to humans in initiation ceremonies. *Amṛta* means "anti-death potion."

21. An interesting list of three qualities a political leader must have, which seem to be compared to the three disciplines of the path: morals, meditation, and wisdom. Field of power is the aura of power that grows and develops around the shoulders of an individual—the person's charisma. The sense of knowledge in this case is not metaphysical knowledge, but practical knowledge, knowledge of the people.

22. The mythical creature called a Snow Lion is supposed to have a turquoise mane. There is actually a magnificent creature in Tibet called a "Snow Leopard" (also called an "ounce"; *Leo uncia*), but it does not have a wondrous green mane.

23. These are invisible demonic forces posed against Ling and its Buddhist society. Some of them are great forces such as the *tanma*, who appeared as Giant Oxen to oppose Padmasambhava's coming to Tibet. Others cause sickness and disease. All must be defeated by Gesar's magic.

24. The term "devil harrier" is the equivalent of the Tibetan *lha sring 'byung bo'i ltag bdud la / mi min 'phrul gyi mi bu zhig*. This passage refers to Gesar who, as an enemy of the world of invisible monster spirits, is a *māra* (devil) to them. He is a devil who "devils the back of the neck" *(ltag bdud)* of gods, *rākṣasa*s (demons), and ghosts or elementals.

25. *Nāga* is a Sanskrit word meaning "serpent." It refers to mythical beings that usually were thought of as inhabiting watery lands. When ideas about *nāga*s were transmitted to China, the Sanskrit word was translated as *long* (dragon), resulting in considerable confusion. The name *nāga* is also applied to a brachycephalic Negrito people of eastern Assam and to their land (Nāgaland). For more information, see the glossary preceding these notes.

26. This Tibetan epic view of the Chinese emperor makes him speak like a tribal chieftain, even down to the singing of epic songs of advice and the deployment of numerous village proverbs.

27. The term "paternal lineage" is the equivalent of the Tibetan *pha rus dung,* which literally means "the tribal lineage of the fathers," a distinction of special importance in the epic, where maternal as well as paternal descent is noticed.

28. The Tibetan *mi min sde brgyad* is a mysterious category, reminiscent of the Eight Classes of gods.

29. This probably means the life-force and life-essence at one's heart-center.

30. Usually *gandharva*s are described as elegant, invisible, cosmic musicians playing softly on divine instruments. Here, however, they have become just another wrathful deity in the armies of the Buddhist warriors.

31. A *dzo* is the offspring of a yak bull and various types of cows from India.

32. In this case the mother lineage is probably a reference to the fact that the three "nephews" are related to the Chinese emperor and each other through marriages. The maternal descent of each of these warriors is a point of prime political importance, a sort of alliance that should prevent war between them.

33. Lenpa Chögyal was married to a daughter of Kunga from one of the three divisions of the Kingdom of Hor, the Yellow Hor. The fourth and longest volume of the epic describes the war between Ling and Hor. This is a war actually attested by history. At this point in the epic war with Hor has not yet broken out, but apparently Gyatsa Zhalkar already harbors animosity against the Hor, for he regards Lenpa Gyögyal's marriage to a foreign woman from Hor as ill-starred. All this, of course, was predicted by the Chinese emperor, who fruitlessly, as it turned out, warned the three nephews against internecine struggle.

34. The tiger's stripes are described poetically as being shaped like six smiles, so poetically the tiger is called Six Smiles, just as the snow lion is called Turquoise Mane.

35. The word for clan here is *pha rus,* which means "paternal clan." The sense is that they killed all the men in the province.

36. Ralo Tönpa is a wealthy man in Gog. The future mother of Gesar has become his possession, a servant to him. She is actually a *nāgī,* a dragonness, in disguise. Her father, Tsugna Rinchen, is the king of the *nāga*s. At the insistence of the all-powerful, godlike Tantric yogi Padmasambhava, Tsugna has allowed his daughter to wander across the earth as a human so that her fate can lead her to Ling. Now the moment has come. This war will set her free from Gog, and she will be captured by Ling. There she will be known as Gogmo (the woman from Gog). She will marry Senglön and father Gesar.

37. A threefold division of local deities that matches the Confucian notion of Heaven, Earth, and Man. *Lha* are sky gods matching heaven. *Lu* are dragons and stand for Earth and water. *Nyen* are mountain gods and stand between the two realms of Heaven and Earth, the way Man mediates between Heaven and Earth. In this case the three levels of reality are part of a conspiracy to make sure that the mother of Gesar and her family are not harmed.

38. Tibetan *ma yig,* perhaps short for *gdod-ma,* meaning "primordial texts." But in the epic they are taken to be paired with the *pha 'bum,* "father hundred thousand verses," as if there is a male and female ancient collection of prophecies and proverbs for Ling.

39. The jewel is the *nāga* princess. "Victory banner" is a takeoff on Ralo Tönpa Gyaltsen's full name, "Gyaltsen" meaning "victory banner." The "pinnacle" refers to the fact that the *nāga* princess took with her the best of the *nāga* kingdom's treasures. "Mouse" refers to the year that Gyatsa will actually go and fight Gog and win the princess—that is, this very year, the year of the mouse or rat. "White" here refers to White Ling, whose wishes will be fulfilled by the raiding expedition because the *nāga* princess will give birth to the new king of Ling, Gesar.

40. One of the most precious possessions of the Ling tribe is a richly ornamented copy of the Buddhist *Hundred Thousand Line Perfection of Wisdom Sutra.* In fact, one of the major families in Ling is named after this book, Bum *('Bum),* meaning "a hundred thousand."

41. A female yak.

42. These precious things—a lovely blue tent, a precious ornamented scripture, and a *dri* with magic horns—are all considered as a sort of dowry that goes with Gogmo, a gift from the fabulous wealth of the *nāga*s.

43. To "praise the war-gods" means to perform the tribal ceremonies of making a purificatory smoke offering and flying windhorse flags. This ceremony involves the creation of an altar with banners of the four directions, the elements, and other essentially Taoist symbols. The power of a warrior's charisma and good fortune, known as "windhorse," is summoned, and mythical animals that represent the elements and the four directions are invoked: red fire tiger, blue thunder dragon, white snow lion, and red *garuda.* An offering of purificatory smoke is made in the midst of this arrangement. These practices are central to the Gesar epic and much discussed in the epic, where warriors perform these ceremonies in order to increase their personal power and to have victory in battle and politics.

The practices are shared by the Chinese tradition, where they are thought of as ancient Taoist rituals. See, for example, chapter 49 of the Chinese martial epic, *Romance of the Three Kingdoms (Sanguo yanyi),* where a strategic general, Zhuge Liang, performs this ceremony to control the winds. His version of the ritual involves one uniquely Chinese element, invocation of the seven stars of the Big Dipper. Luo Guanzhong, *Three Kingdoms: A Historical Novel,* trans. Moss Roberts (Berkeley: University of California Press, 1991), p. 372.

44. Trothung is Gesar's uncle, but an evil man who invariably causes harm because of his selfishness and self-serving political policy. He always fails, however, perhaps because he is an emanation of the Buddhist deity Hayagrīva, the horse-headed slayer of demons. In any case, in this scene he typically gives bad advice designed to help himself and betray his friends, but it all backfires to the good of Ling, and he becomes a laughingstock.

45. Younger Lineage—*chung rgyud*—that is, to the clan of Zhalkar, which is known as the Younger or Lesser Lineage because it descends from the founder of Ling's (Chöphen Nagpo's) youngest son. This lineage is also often referred to as the Cadet Lineage.

46. One of the principal aims of a smoke offering is to raise a column of smoke down which the war-gods may descend. These energy principles alight on the warrior's head, shoulders, and breast and, dwelling there, uplift the warrior and protect him or her in battle.

47. Now the elements are represented in Indic Tantric Buddhist style as the five consorts of the five primordial buddhas. Locanā (Spyan ma) is the female Buddha consort who represents the element of Earth. Therefore she becomes the hearth or stove, which is the basis or ground for the offering. The other female buddhas are represented in the rest of the stanza. Māmakī, the buddha of water (bDag gi ma); Pāṇḍaravāsinī, the buddha of fire (Gos dkar mo); Samaya Tārā, the buddha of air (Dam Tshig sGrol ma), and Dhātvīśvarī, the buddha of space (dByings kyi dBang phyug ma).

48. Appearance-emptiness is Tibetan *snang stong,* a metaphysical term from Tantric philosophy. The Tantric philosophy evolved to explain smoke offerings is interesting and involved.

The nature of the phenomenal world (appearance) is emptiness. Therefore, some schools of Buddhist philosophy declare that there is no truly existent appearance, but only emptiness. In Tantra, however, one realizes the emptiness of appearance without losing the experience of appearance or the phenomenal world. Thus Tantric enlightenment involves a simultaneous realization of the vividness of appearance and of its emptiness. Because appearance is vivid, though empty, the gods who represent the phenomenal world of hearth, home, the elements, the war-gods, and so forth may be invoked. For although the gods are empty by nature, appearance teems with them as the vivid self-expression of the ground of being.

49. The lords of the five female buddhas, the five consorts. See the glossary preceding these notes.

50. The *dharmakāya, sambhogakāya,* and *nirmāṇakāya* are the three levels or aspects of the Buddha: the mind, speech, and body. In this chant the mind of the Buddha, the ultimate nature of the Buddha, is represented by the primordial buddha Vajradhara. The form Buddha takes when he manifests himself in visionary appearances is represented by the colorful, symbolically coded *sambhogakāya* buddhas, the buddhas of the five families. The *nirmāṇakāya* is represented by the three protectors: the bodhisattvas of Wisdom, Compassion, and Energy.

51. Three patron goddesses of Ling. The first, Yeshe Tsogyal, is a famous *yogini.* The second is a protective deity. The third is the divine aunt, a goddess, of Gesar of Ling.

52. Tibetan is filled with onomatopoeic sounds in three syllables. Usually these sounds represent natural sounds, but sometimes they represent situations. *Tha ra ra* is the sound of clouds of war-gods or in some cases the sound of poisonous clouds spreading. It may not be a sound at all, but just a feeling. More ordinary ones are, for example, *khyi li li,* the sound of a tempest, or *ur ru ru,* thunder, or *zi ri ri,* the buzzing of bees.

53. *Siddhi* is a Sanskrit word meaning "successful achievement" or "fulfillment." These are supranormal faculties attained by spiritually perfected *yogins.* Aside from advanced yogic techniques, such powers may also be attained by alchemy, herbs, medicines, Tantric rites, and specific mantras (magic verbal formulas).

54. This refers to a victory yell that is given when Tibetans reach the top of a mountain or accomplish some feat: *Ki Ki So So Lha Gyal-lo. Ki Ki* and *So So* are simply victorious sounds. *Lha Gyal-lo* means "Divine Victory" or "The gods are victorious."

A Nineteenth-century Fable

LIKE MANY OTHERS in this book, the following selection combines popular and literary influences in both form and content. The author, Shao Binru, was a native of Sihui County in Guangdong Province who made his living storytelling but also wrote stories in literary style.[1] This tale mixes colloquial and literary Chinese and has a long commentary in Cantonese topolect. The content reflects folk beliefs of Buddhist origin; the successive confrontations of a scholar with a spirit medium and with judges in Hell, as well as the dramatic lightning and thunderclaps, would fit perfectly in one of the folk operas so popular in South China. Yet a Neo-Confucian authorial voice controls the unorthodox subject matter and especially the final outcome. Shao consciously tried to be both entertaining and morally elevating.[2]

The tale divides into three parts, playing on familiar themes or tropes of Chinese fictional and historical writing, but in each case with an original twist. The first part is in a long tradition of victorious elite confrontations with spirit mediums, except that this spirit medium gets her posthumous revenge; the second is based on the idea, derived from popular Buddhism, that the dead person has to be reviewed by the Courts of Hell and, if appropriate, punished for lifetime transgressions before being permitted to rest in peace;[3] here the scholar Zhang Jixing is returned to his original identity on earth and given the chance to redeem himself. The last part presents a Neo-Confucian view of the good life, but the idea of redemptive good deeds is Buddhist in inspiration.[4]

The tale is particularly illuminating on the tension between the attitudes of the educated and uneducated (elite and folk) in the late Qing, a tension often hard to comprehend from the outside. Not unlike the Jesuits who went to China in the late Ming, those few Republican-period Chinese writers who tried to rehabilitate Confucianism represented it as agnostic and rationalistic, and fundamentally different from the "superstitious" beliefs and practices common among the people. It followed, in their view, that the elite of Qing scholars and officials must have disliked popular religion for much the same reason, but both premise and deduction were incorrect. The elite view of what might loosely be called magical practice was, in fact, more complex. Divination, for example, was widely practiced by scholars and officials, though with the aid of written texts. And stories of filial deeds in the Confucian spirit not uncommonly included magical intervention, which was held to be produced by the sincere emotion of the mourner. Zhang's public humiliation of the ghost wife is inspired by the rectitude of the Confucian scholar, yet it is effected through the magical power of cursing, a notion appropriated from folk practices.

If Qing elites themselves indulged in magic, why did they find shamanism so objectionable? This tale suggests answers. Notice that what Zhang Jixing dislikes about the spirit medium is not what she believes, but how she conducts herself and what effect she has on local folk. Notice how Zhang himself achieves contact with the supernatural world: certainly not in the medium's disorderly manner of possession by a god. Neo-Confucians were not rationalists, but participated in the same moral cosmic order as ordinary folk, though in a different spirit.

The tale mentions only one Court of Hell, but in the standard folk understanding of late-imperial times, there were ten. The notion was integral to the funeral ritual sequence widely practiced by many rich and poor families alike. Each court dealt with specific crimes and misdeeds, and in principle, the investigation and judgments covered the same period of time as the period of mourning. In many parts of South China, seven of the Ten Courts (a concept deriving from Buddhism) were navigated in the main mourning period of forty-nine days (with rites conducted every seven days after death seven times), and the last three courts after a hundred days, one year, and three years. Three years had been the standard mourning period prescribed by the early Confucians.

Ideas of retribution and reward, though Buddhist in origin, were not seen as contradictory to orthodox Confucian expectations that the gentleman do good selflessly. (A similar perspective to this tale is taken by ledgers of merit and demerit, some of them precisely quantified, in which Ming and Qing writers spelled out the effects of good and bad deeds.) The Neo-Confucian virtues of self-examination and practical morality dominate Shao's rendering of the story. This is evident if we ask why Zhang's treatment of the spirit medium is considered unjust, how he decides on his own conversion, and how he rehabilitates himself as a good person.—DSS

Zhang the King of Hell [5]

During the Qianlong reign (1736–1795) in Hangzhou, Zhejiang Province, there was a junior licentiate *(xiucai)* named Zhang Jixing whose conduct was fundamentally immoral. He had mistreated his neighbors and done many appalling things, and was the butt of everyone's jokes and curses.

One day he paid a visit to a friend. They heard that there was a woman in one of the villages who "did the ghost wife" *(zuo guipo)* [6] and who could call forth gods and summon ghosts. The women who believed and consulted her were many beyond counting. Zhang Jixing and his friend also went to watch her in action. At that moment the ghost wife was burning incense and performing her rites, with ghostly voice and breathing, ghost-like behavior and talk, in pursuit of the dark way of the ghosts. The crowd believed a true ghost had arrived, and everyone was standing quietly listening, with their palms pressed together, fearful of not displaying sincerity. When Zhang Jixing saw this, he flew into a rage, walked to the front, and slapped her across the mouth, saying, "Your weird nonsense deceives the masses and cheats everyone of their money. If I were Yama the King of Hell I would have to twist off your head!"

The sight of this dispelled the mood; losing interest, people vacantly dispersed. Several days later, around the woman's neck a large welt appeared, changing into a decapitating wound, and she died. People were shocked by this strange occurrence, and thereafter called Zhang Jixing "Zhang the King of Hell" (Zhang Yanwang).

Several years later Zhang Jixing fell ill. In a dream two strangers resembling official lictors asked him to accompany them. They arrived at a Court of Hell,[7] which was spacious and magnificent, with two gods seated to the left and right behind rolled-up screens. The god in the middle was sitting behind a hanging bamboo screen that concealed his face. Zhang Jixing asked the gods, "What are your orders in bringing me here?"

The gods told him, "There is a ghost wife who has accused you, that is why we brought you. To curse the ghost wife was quite fair in principle and you did no wrong, but you yourself are not a proper and upright person. You must count, one by one, the many bad things you have done in your life and take cognizance of them."

They told assistants to give him a powder board *(fenpai)* [8] and ordered him to write them down on it. Zhang Jixing took up a brush, straightaway filling two boards with writing, but still felt he was not done. The gods said, "These crimes are more than enough. In your opinion what punishment do you deserve?"

Zhang Jixing thought for a long time, and answered, "I should be struck by thunder."[9]

The gods replied, "That punishment is insufficient. You shall be struck three times."

Rolling up the central screen, they told Jixing to look up. He saw that the image of the god in the central seat had a face just like his own. On waking, he realized that in a former existence he had been a god of Hell who had erred and been sent to Earth as a human by way of punishment. Shortly the two lictors came again to escort him home to his quarter [in Hangzhou]. At once he was terrified, as if waking up from a nightmare, his body bathed in sweat.

All day he thought about it, and realized that the roots went back a long way. Just because he had had no inhibitions, [the lack of which had] led [him] to extremes of criminality and disgrace, he was to suffer punishment by thunder, throwing away half a lifetime of study. It was clear to him that he had violated all the principles of the sages. And to a greater extent than people of [merely] low character he had aroused the hatred of others in his lifetime and would be punished by the ghosts in death. He wondered to himself how an ambitious, strapping, seven-foot-tall[10] man could willingly turn bad and pursue a futile life in the world. Even though he had done wrong and repentance would not be easy, by being a good man for one day [at a time] he could yet say he was not willing to give up on himself. At once he resolved to do this; having taken this step, his resolve remained unshaken. From then on, he washed clean his former wrongs and turned bad into good.

Suddenly one day thunder and lightning came together, knocking Jixing dead to the ground; but at once he revived. Several months later, while he was watching the theater in front of the stage, the sound of thunder came again. Jixing knew he would be hit and called on the crowd quickly to make their escape. Before he had finished speaking, sure enough he was struck dead; but he soon returned to life. He hurried home, and taught conscientiously in country schools, showing his resolution and earnestness. Again he heard the rumble of thunder like a great drum shaking the earth. Jixing was afraid that the third time he would be killed and could hardly return to life again. So he hid under a table of black lacquer.[11] A crash of thunder completely burned up the coverlet and mosquito net, but Jixing escaped death.

Zhang Jixing knew the number of his *kalpa*s[12] had expired, but he continued to be assiduous in cultivating goodness, toiling on his essays. In three years he passed the second-level *(juren)* civil examination, and he enjoyed the fruits of success for another ten years before his death. Zhang Jixing often used his own experience as a lesson for others to be ready to acknowledge having spoken wrongly. Those who manage to live long do so through the power of acting contritely.

—DSS

Notes

1. The eighteen tales of Shao's *Colloquial Tales Exhaustively Discussed (Suhua qingtan),* published in 1870, are set mostly in Guangdong, Zhejiang, Shaanxi, and Sichuan during the Ming or Qing periods.

2. Shao's own colloquial commentary drives home the moral message. See note 11 for an example.

3. In formal Buddhism, people were said to be reborn into a new existence, moving up in the social scale or down to the animal world depending on the level of transgression, but in late-imperial times, popular belief was more focused on the experience of Hell.

4. The same is true of the moralistic textbooks produced in the seventeenth and eighteenth centuries by local scholars.

5. Zhang Yanwang, after the god in charge of Hell, Yanluo wang (Skt. Yamarāja, i.e., King Yama).

6. In Guangdong, the term "ghost wife" *(guipo)* was used for any widow, reflecting the belief that the dead husband would inflict misfortune on any other man who took her as a wife. Here it is a local term for a spirit medium.

7. As the commentary explains, each of the Ten Courts of Hell had its own king. Zhang Jixing is not one of the conventional names for these kings.

8. This was a wooden board painted white (i.e., a "whiteboard") that was used for writing down notes in black ink.

9. The understanding was that death by lightning was inflicted by the thunder ax of the God of Thunder, as the commentary mentions.

10. During the Qing period, the Chinese foot length *(chi)* was actually longer than the English foot, about thirteen inches. Moving backward in history, the *chi* becomes progressively smaller (in the Warring States period it is only equal to about nine inches). The reference here to a "seven-foot-tall man" is probably just a conventional epithet based on earlier standards. For the late-Han period, for example, it would work out to just over six feet by modern English standards. This would have to be considered tall for a Chinese man at any point in Chinese history, including the present.

11. Believing perhaps that because black lacquer could not be penetrated by light, it could protect against the lightning aspect of thunder. How, one might ask, could the mighty God of Thunder be so easily foiled? Shao explains to his listeners in a commentary: "It was not that the God of Thunder feared black lacquer. If parents hit a child who really understands his [or her] error and sincerely repents, hiding at the bottom of the bed, the parents sometimes will refrain from hitting [the child again]." Similarly the God of Thunder stayed his hand because Jixing had sincerely repented.

12. Unimaginably long and recurring periods of time, here referring to countless rebirths.

BIOGRAPHIES OF WOMEN, published in anthologies or collections, have a long history in China that begins with a work titled *Lienü zhuan,* or *Biographies of Women,* attributed to the Han statesman Liu Xiang (79–8 B.C.E.). Compiled in the first century before the Common Era, *Lienü zhuan* was reprinted hundreds of times. (One of the short biographies below mentions a woman lecturing to her female relatives on stories about "chaste women of old," some of which would surely have come from Liu Xiang's original book, perhaps from one of the Qing facsimile reprints of a Song classic edition dating from the twelfth or early thirteenth century. These reprints, fully illustrated, enjoyed great popularity in genteel households during the eighteenth and nineteenth centuries.) Although Liu Xiang's original work displayed all kinds of "womanly" qualities, from cleverness and resourcefulness to depravity, his anthology became the prototype for the biographies of "exemplary women" *(lienü)* that, by late-imperial times, focused almost exclusively on Confucian virtues, especially wifely fidelity. Biographies of exemplary women were considered necessary parts of every official dynastic history, later making their way into provincial and county histories (gazetteers). By the Qing period their production had become a minor historical industry, and in the hands of unimaginative editors, most *lienü* biographies were reduced to formulaic cant.

The stories that follow are modeled after Liu Xiang's original work, in that each is intended to illustrate for the reader a particular female virtue and all are lively tales. They are selected from a collection printed in 1831, *Precious Records of the Maidens' Chambers (Langui baolu),* one of the first anthologies of female biographies edited and published by a woman. The compiler, Wanyan Yun Zhu, was born into an elite Han Chinese family (surnamed Yun) in 1771. She married a Manchu of the Wanyan clan, a relatively rare crossing of ethnic boundaries in her day. She died in 1833, barely two years after completing this work and another mammoth compendium of women's poetry. Yun Zhu was widely admired as a literary patron, avidly collecting poems from female writers throughout the empire and printing books at her own Studio of Rosy Fragrance, where she commandeered editorial assistance from her granddaughters.

In many ways the stories Yun Zhu selected for her anthology are "representative" of the *lienü* genre. In fact, most of them are slightly condensed versions of "official" biographies printed a century before in the *Comprehensive Gazetteer of the Empire (Da Qing yitong zhi),* first published in 1744. What is significant about these particular stories, however, is what they tell us about Yun Zhu's own tastes and about her assessment of the tastes of the female reading audience for whom the stories are intended. As contemporary readers will see, the appeal of these tales was perhaps supposed to lie in Confucian moral lessons: showing especially how filial daughters, faithful wives, chaste women, and dutiful daughters-in-law should behave. Yun Zhu's preface to her collection asserts that these moral lessons are what attracted her to the stories. In fact, though, as Yun Zhu surely recognized, the plots of these tales also make them fun to read. Murder and revenge, suicide and self-sacrifice, miracles and mysteries, exotic places, tribal peoples are what give these *lienü* biographies their bite and make their heroines memorable.

In the larger context of Chinese history, Yun Zhu's *lienü* stories yield other insights. The Manchus who ruled the Qing empire (1644–1911) organized political campaigns promoting womanly virtue, which the Qing emperors personally honored with special commendations composed in calligraphy by the emperor's own hand. (Readers will note that these commendations are mentioned frequently in the stories below.) So, on one level these Qing *lienü* stories trumpet the success of Manchu rule by celebrating imperial power spreading Confucian values throughout the realm, even into the borderlands where non-Han peoples lived. On the other hand, as the plot lines tell us, in China's villages and towns, gossip and myth infused women's virtuous deeds with magical efficacy that was experienced and preserved in miracles, shrines, and sacred spaces. It is this tension between official, top-down political and moral indoctrination and local, grassroots cultural invention, that makes these stories so rich—not to mention their bold narrative style, sparked by lively dialog and impassioned outbursts, faint but unmistakable echoes of Liu Xiang's magnificent work.—SLM

The Story of Li Sanjie (Third Elder Sister)

Third Elder Sister Li came from Luyi (eastern Henan Province, near the Shandong border). Her father, Qisheng (The Unicorn Rises), had no sons and four daughters. Once while on the road, her father had a quarrel with a kinsman named Chu and was injured. All the witnesses were fearful and intimidated, and no one dared to demand restitution. Third Elder Sister, greatly distressed, took the case to court. After three years, the perpetrator had still not been punished. So she changed into a man's clothes and stationed herself outside the walls of the imperial court, cut her flesh, and wrote in blood. As her cries rose, the sound of the drum responded from within. Orders concerning the case were issued to the provincial governor, with the result that Chu and his son both died in prison. Third Elder Daughter still resented the fact that their heads were not exposed in the marketplace. She put on plain clothes and with the demeanor of a mourner, she wept day and night. Everyone in the area recognized her righteousness. Each day she was approached by persons offering betrothal gifts in exchange for her hand. To this she responded, "As long as my mother is alive, I will never marry." In time she buried her father, adopted an heir for her paternal grandparents, and arranged her younger sisters' marriages. When at length her mother, née Zhang, died, she arranged for the burial, then took a sash and strangled herself. That was in the thirty-seventh year of Kangxi (1698). Early in the Qianlong reign, an imperial commendation was ordered for her grave, and the county magistrate Xu Tan composed an epitaph. Local people gave her the posthumous title "Filial Martyr" *(xiao lie)*. Hu Tianyou of Shanyin (in Zhejiang Province) composed a poem recording these events.

    Editor's note: The grave mound is located three tricents east of the wall of Luyi County seat, in Henan Province.

The Story of Wang Wenlan's Wife, née Yun

Wang Wenlan's wife, née Yun, came from Wujin [a wealthy area in Jiangsu Province]. When her father, Zongxun, was ill, she cut a piece of her flesh to offer him.[1] After her father died, she served her birth mother, née Liu, and even following her marriage to Wang, she continued to look after her. One day a fire broke out in the home where her mother lived. Her mother was very old and did not know what to do. Yun braved the fire, entered the home, and carried her mother out in her arms. All of the hair on her body was burned, but otherwise she suffered no ill effects. People were amazed at the depth of her filial devotion. She was honored with an imperial commendation early in the Qianlong reign.

The Story of the Three Wang Girls

The three Wang girls were from Jintan (Jiangsu Province). Two were the daughters of Wang Chanjin. One was the daughter of Wang Yi. They lived by the shores of Changtang Lake. At the end of the Ming during an army mutiny they fled into the marshes near the lake to hide. When the rebels found out where the girls were hiding, they made a raft and poled out, pulling the three up onto the raft. The three girls joined hands back-to-back, with their arms tightly intertwined. When the raft reached a place where the current was running swiftly, they suddenly began rocking their bodies and pounding their feet, and the raft capsized, throwing everyone into the water. All drowned. The next day the rebel corpses floated to the surface, but there was no sign of the three girls' bodies. More than a month later, when the rebels had dispersed, the two families came to the spot looking for the girls' corpses. Only then did the bodies appear, with the hands and arms still linked as they had been in life. Fathers and mothers wept, and grasping the girls' hands, freed them at last. They were buried in a grave mound by the lake. The tree that grew there later had three branches, all intertwined.

The Story of the Martyred Wife of Shanqi

The martyred wife of Shanqi was from Huizhou (the home of wealthy merchants in Anhui Province). No one knows her surname. She had only been married a few months when her husband died. She had neither children nor parents-in-law nor brothers-in-law to depend on. She vowed to die to preserve her chastity. Her parents wanted to betroth her to another family, but as they prepared to do this, she heard of it and said, "My life is done." She sacrificed at her husband's grave, changed into new clothes, and walked to the mouth of the stream that runs through the town. At the time, the water from the mountains was rushing in great torrents. She threw herself into the waves and died. Her body floated for several miles before a tree on the bank stopped it. A stonemason saw the corpse and tried to loosen her clothes, but they were all tied in such tight knots[2] that he was unable to undo them. Suddenly, the corpse rose up and cried in a loud voice, "My parents wanted to steal my chastity so I died! How dare you, a lowly man, act this way? I will snatch your soul!" Having spoken, the corpse fell to the ground. Everyone who saw this gasped in amazement.

The Story of "Powdered Elder Sister"

The woman known as "Powdered Elder Sister" was from Gaoyou (Jiangsu). Her father, whose surname was Ze, was known as "Old Man." She was betrothed to a certain person, but he went off to beg one year during a famine and after more than a decade passed, he still had not returned. One day the woman's father happened to meet him in the market town. He said to the father, "I want you to return my brideprice to me, so you can betroth your daughter to somebody else." The girl's father, delighted, got out the money and gave it to the man, who was equally pleased, so they signed a contract. But when the father went home and reported this to his daughter, she cried aloud for a long time and when night fell, hanged herself.

The Story of Sun Xiugu

Sun Xiugu was from Qiantang (i.e., Hangzhou, Zhejiang). When she was fifteen she was betrothed to Yang Wenlong, but before they were married, Wenlong went off to Quzhou [by river, to the southwest of the province] in company with his father, a petty trader. Xiugu remained at home with her future mother-in-law, née Hou. There was a man named Yan Tuji who was a troublemaker in the neighborhood. He waited until her mother-in-law was ill and bedridden, then sneaked into the house to try to assault Xiugu. Xiugu bit off her finger and bore the pain, driving him away. Later, however, he returned, and she was frightened that she would not be able to escape, so she drank poison and died. At the time it was high summer, but her body looked as if it were still alive for many days afterward. When these events became known, she received an imperial commendation, and Tuji was arrested and punished. The local people buried her, and the governor Zhang Min erected a stele at her grave.

Editor's note: The grave is located outside the present-day city of Hangzhou in Zhejiang, to the east of Rosy Dawn Hill on the north shore of West Lake.

The Story of the Woman Named Kang

Kang was from Xing County (Shanxi), the daughter of the *juren* degree-holder Kang Tiyuan. While still a young girl she was betrothed to Liu Shiqi. Just when they were to marry, he developed epilepsy. His condition steadily worsened, and so it was proposed that she break off the engagement. She vowed to die and steadfastly refused. Tiyuan was pleased by her determination and went ahead with the marriage. She was nineteen at the time. She cared for her ill husband for forty years until Shiqi died. She remained a virgin all her days.

The Story of the Concubine, née Hu, of a Man Named Deng

The woman née Hu was from Beiping (a town outside the capital?).[3] She was the concubine of one Deng of Tongan (Fujian Province). His legal wife, née Cai, was jealous of her and kept her locked up in a secluded room. When Deng passed away, the wife let her out. Hu bowed before Deng's coffin, strangled herself, and died. Tucked into her sash was a poem with the following stanza: "I'll follow the wild butterfly over the green grass; we'll hold hands together 'til we reach the ghostly door."

The Story of Lu Xiang's Wife, née Zhang

Lu Xiang's wife, née Zhang, was from Lou County (in prosperous Songjiang Prefecture, Jiangsu). Her mother-in-law was a former prostitute. Together with her son, the mother-in-law tried to force Zhang into prostitution, but she resisted. When they began to beat her to force her to submit, she secretly went to the Wan'an Bridge, threw herself into the water, and died. Eight days later when they retrieved her corpse, her face looked as if she were still alive. Her clothing was tied tightly in knots from top to bottom.[4] Neighbors erected a shrine beside her grave.

The Story of Zhang Guixi[5]

Yin Chun's wife Zhang Guixi was from She County (a commercial center in Anhui, renowned as the home of wealthy merchants and strictly moral women). Chun was a servant of the Huang family. His mistress, née Cheng, was an educated woman. When she lectured to her daughters-in-law about chaste women of old,[6] Zhang would stand nearby listening carefully to every word. When Chun died, she closed the door and hanged herself. Members of the family saved her from death. Then she stopped eating. The mistress wept and pleaded with her, but she said, "Your servant's wife's decision cannot be changed. From the time I heard you talking about *lienü,* my mind was made up." And so she starved to death.

The Story of the Wife, née Liu, of a Man Named Wang

The woman née Liu, from Huairen (in far northern Shanxi, near the border of Inner Mongolia), was the wife of a man named Wang. His family was poor. Her mother-in-law was old, and her husband could not support her. Liu worked at gathering firewood and grinding flour to eke out a living. One day during a great famine, a powerful merchant was offering to buy the children and women of starving people. Liu said to her husband, "We shall all be dead at any moment. If the merchant buys me for a lot of money, it will surely be enough to preserve the lives of your aging mother and our frail children. Send me to [meet him in] the outskirts of the city. Once you have the money, I will look after myself." He did as she instructed him. When they reached the outskirts of the city, the merchant ordered her husband to escort them beyond the border to prevent any unexpected turn of events. Four days later, they took lodging in Tiancheng [in Inner Mongolia]. After handing over the money, the merchant sent her husband away and went to an outer room. When he returned, wearing his finest clothes, Liu tricked him into getting drunk. Then taking her hatpin, she punctured her throat and died. The merchant fled in terror. On the roadways everyone talked about the "starving wife with extraordinary purity."

The Story of Xuan Gong's Wife, née Song

Xuan Gong's wife, née Song, was a native of Zhuji (part of Shaoxing Prefecture, a conservative center of literary culture in Zhejiang Province). Her husband died before she had borne a son. At the time she was in her seventeenth year, and she was very beautiful. A Huai'an merchant (i.e., a merchant from an area known for its commercial wealth and political connections) bribed her late husband's elder brother and made a plot to abduct her, but a neighbor's wife found out about it and told her. Upon hearing of this, one night she stitched up all of her upper and lower garments, stole out of the house, walked to a canal dike, and threw herself into the water. The weather was cold at the time, and the water had frozen into ice. She died beneath the layers of ice. Her brother-in-law mistakenly believed that she had run away to hide. Soon afterward, a fierce wind blew up, causing waves many feet high, and her corpse washed up on one of the embankments. The water there had always been muddy and turbid, but after her death it became clear and pure. The official in charge of the area built a shrine for martyred wives to honor her. He gave the spot on the embankment the name "Chaste Suicide."

The Story of Yisonga's Wife Xiguang

Xiguang, a member of the Niohuru clan, was a Manchu. She was married to the son of the minister Yonggui, an assistant vice-minister named Yisonga. When her husband became ill, she cut a piece of her own flesh to prepare medicine to cure him,[7] but to no avail. She vowed to follow him in death, but as her husband's illness worsened, he said to her, "My father is old, my younger brothers and sisters are still young, and our two daughters have not yet married. My life is over, but these matters still need attention." Xiguang wept and assured him that she understood. After he died, she remained faithful for ten years, seeing to each of these matters one by one. The day after her second daughter's wedding, she composed a heptasyllabic poem to testify to her steadfast vows, then hanged herself. Yonggui copied the poem and sent it with a memorial to the throne. The emperor responded by granting her an imperial commendation.

The Story of a Zhuang Wife, née Luo

A wife from the Zhuang people from Lipu (Guangxi Province), née Luo, was widowed young and vowed to remain faithful to her dead husband. Zhuang tribal custom pays little attention to rules of propriety for young women, and singing is very important in their culture. But when people sang songs to entice her, she remained steadfast and unmoved. She served her mother-in-law with utmost filiality and reared her son to adulthood, suffering alone for more than fifty years.

The Story of the Chieftain's Daughter, Zhen'e

The [Miao?] chieftain's daughter Zhen'e was from Dading (in western Guizhou). When she was young, she was betrothed to a man named Jia, but before they could be married her parents, concerned about Jia's poverty, wanted to betroth her to another man. She hardened her resolve and refused. When they began to coerce her, she killed herself. In Kangxi 29 (1690) the governor Tian Wen personally wrote an inscription for her imperial commendation.[8]

—SLM

Notes

1. This practice, known as *gegu* (cutting the thigh), required boiling a piece of one's own flesh and feeding the broth as a medicine to an ailing elder, usually a parent. It was considered by many to be the utmost sign of filial reverence, though periodically the practice was condemned by the Chinese government, echoing the views of officials and scholars who regarded it as a perversion of Confucian values.

2. Tying clothing in knots was a sign of moral determination to keep the body inviolate, even in death. See a similar motif in the story of Liu Xiang's wife, below.

3. Although the place-names in this story are not precisely identified, it is possible that this concubine was acquired by her patron during travels north to the capital. This would help to explain the wife's extreme animosity and also the romantic innuendo in the poem, which suggests a love affair between a female entertainer and a traveling merchant or official.

4. See note 2 above.

5. This story is a pointed example of the ways in which the model *lienü* had been transformed by Qing times. In fact, Liu Xiang's *Biographies* contains few stories of widows who killed themselves. The story dramatizes the narrowing focus of Confucian ideals for women in the Qing period, when widow suicides and chaste martyrs, along with faithful widows who refused to remarry in order to serve their parents-in-law, were the main recipients of imperial commendation.

6. Quite possibly drawing on Liu Xiang's *Biographies of Women* (see introduction).

7. See note 1 above.

8. Tian Wen (1635–1704), appointed governor of Guizhou Province in 1688, was recognized for his leadership in developing policies to promote education and to minimize the costs of military action in that province, which was then being colonized by Han settlers who were under attack by Miao [Hmong] tribes resisting their encroachments. For the Miao people, see selection 85.

90 | Kang Youwei, "An Investigation into the Reforms of Confucius"

KANG YOUWEI (1858–1927; *jinshi* 1895), born in Nanhai (Guangdong Province), lived at the end of the Qing dynasty. Already by his early twenties, Kang had visited Hong Kong and Shanghai. He was deeply impressed by what he saw in both places and realized that the "men from across the seas" who had built up both of the vibrant enclaves from sleepy fishing villages could not be dismissed as ignorant barbarians. Consequently, he began to acquire books about the West and read them assiduously. Kang's first attempt at social reform occurred in 1883, when he tried to have footbinding of women abolished in his own village.

While in Peking to take examinations in 1888, and in the aftermath of the disastrous Sino-French War, Kang submitted to the throne his celebrated "Ten Thousand Character Memorial." Although this and other proposals from Kang around that time were never called to the emperor's attention, they set the tone for the reform movements of a decade and more later. Upon returning to Canton, Kang established a progressive academy and accepted as his students such future intellectual luminaries as Liang Qichao (1873–1929).

In 1898, Kang Youwei was a leading adviser to the Guangxu emperor, when the latter attempted to reform the imperial system. This "Hundred Days' Reform" resulted in an internal coup against the emperor by his aunt, Empress Dowager Cixi, and the execution or exile of reform-minded men like Kang. The piece below may be read as Kang's attempt to revitalize the Confucian tradition that had grown moribund and conservative as a political philosophy. It may also be interpreted as an attempt to answer the challenges posed by the introduction of Western thought to China. In doing so, Kang Youwei stresses the flexibility of the sages' responses to their times and places the blame for China's not having achieved the goals of Great Peace and Grand Unity upon those who corrupted the textual and institutional norms of Confucianism.—VHM, RF

[Some] 2,376 years after Confucius's death I read his words. I pondered deeply and was disconsolate, crying out, "Alas! Why have I not witnessed the order of an age of Great Peace and been delighted by the Grand Unity?" Why has our China of two thousand years, a place of thousands of square miles, the progeny of innumerable gods, not witnessed the order of an age of Great Peace and been delighted by the Grand Unity? Why has this great land early on not witnessed the order of the Great Peace and been delighted by the Grand Unity?

Heaven grieved over the numerous difficulties of people in the world, so the Black Emperor sent down his essence and relieved the people's cares.[1] [Confucius] was divine, a Sage King, teacher of myriad generations, guardian of myriad peoples, and instructor of the world. He was born into a world of chaos and according to this world of chaos established the model of the three ages and devoted himself to the Great Peace.[2] He established the idea of the three ages in the country of his birth, but focused on the grand unification of everything in the world—far and near, great and small—as one. He thereupon used the primal energy of *qi* to unify with Heaven, was humane based upon Heaven, taught of the various creatures based on the shifting forms of divine energy, and created humane government based upon the compassionate heart-and-mind. By his teachings he unified spirits and the land, aristocracy and commoners, insects and plants; but he loved his fellow humans above all, and so established the *Spring and Autumn Annals'* institutions as those of a new king practicing humaneness to supplant the standards of bravado and warfare of the Period of Chaos. His Way is based in the divine, accords with the universe, nurtures the myriad things, and benefits innumerable generations. He understood what is fundamental, and comprehended minor policies. Great and small, refined and coarse, the natural elements and all directions are all included in his Way! These institutions are nothing more than establishing Heaven in primal energy, establishing Earth in this one Heaven, establishing human affairs in this single Earth, in these affairs establishing regulations according to the times, exerting himself in practicing humaneness, and worrying about the people's worries to dispel the people's troubles.

The *Book of Changes* says, "Books do not exhaust words, and words do not exhaust ideas." The *Book of Odes, Book of Documents, Book of Rites, Book of Music, Book of Changes,* and the *Spring and Autumn Annals* were Confucius's books, and his oral transmissions to seventy disciples were his words. These institutions are nothing more than his words to save the people according to the times, like changing clothes according to the season.

In the Former and Later Han dynasties, rulers, ministers, and scholars reverently used this government Confucius had used to restrain the chaos found in the *Spring and Autumn Annals,* but they mixed it with the methods of hegemons, and so did not fully implement Confucius's institutions. These beginnings of the sage's institutions were uprooted in the Xin dynasty by Liu Xin.[3] The forged *Zuo Commentary* to the *Spring and Autumn Annals* was widely used, and the ancient text was corrupted. During the Xin dynasty, they edited Confucius's Classics and said they were the Duke of Zhou's. They demoted Confucius's status from that of a Sage King to an early teacher. Study of the *Gongyang Commentary* was abandoned; the idea of reforming institutions was buried; the theory of the Three Ages was diminished; the order of Great Peace and the delight of the Grand Unity were tarnished and not illuminated, repressed and not promulgated.[4] Our culture and heritage were mixed with literary studies, with Buddhism and Daoism during the Wei, Jin, Sui, and Tang dynasties, and were corrupted by the customs of the Di and Qiang peoples, of the Turks, Khitans, and Mongols. Not only did these people not understand the Great Peace, but they lost the proper means of seeking the Han people's goal of bringing order to chaos, and so were unsuccessful. Consequently, the people of China suffered the harsh government of cruel rulers and barbarians for two thousand years. The loss is grievous!

Master Zhu Xi was born after people stopped studying the Great Peace. He actively advocated and promulgated it. He often spoke of righteousness, but rarely spoke of humaneness. He understood self-reflection for correcting one's faults, but did little to relieve the people's troubles. His views were obstructed by the doctrines of the Period of Chaos, and so he did not understand the rectitude of the Great Peace and Grand Unity, but instead was confused by Buddhism and Daoism. The Way of Confucius withered, so that those who considered it a means of governing could only achieve incomplete peace of the Eastern Zhou, the Liu Shu, and the Later Liang dynasties (who could not reunify China).

Heaven pitied the people and led them with light. The rays of the sun were like shining crystal. When I was a small child I dreamt I grasped a ritual vessel and carried it west. Then I perceived the divine music of Heaven and again saw the beauty and richness of the official musicians of the imperial ancestral temples. When I reached the gate I cut away the thorny overgrowth and cleared the path. I dispelled the clouds and mist and looked upon the sun and moon. There was another world, and it was not human.

I do not dare to hide the Great Way, and so have made a careful examination of this with many of my students for the past eight years, deleting the confusing, and completely clarifying the important points in making this examination of reform systems.

—RF

Notes

1. Kang is using a legend that the divine Black Emperor fathered Confucius, thus giving Confucius divine status himself.

2. Kang is building upon the tradition that Confucius said the world would go through three stages: the worlds of Chaos, Rising Peace, and Great Peace.

3. Liu Xin (ca. 50 B.C.E.–23 C.E.) and his father, Liu Xiang (79–78 B.C.E.), were prominent scholars working in the Imperial Library in the Former Han dynasty (206 B.C.E.–9 C.E.). In this capacity, they cataloged a number of previously lost texts. Wang Mang usurped the throne from the Han dynasty and proclaimed the beginning of the Xin dynasty (literally the "New" dynasty), over which he ruled from 9 to 24 C.E. Wang Mang and Liu Xin were friends with similar textual interests. Wang Mang is credited with recovering the classical text known as the *Rites of Zhou,* upon which he based much of his governmental policies. Liu Xin is particularly famous for rediscovering the *Zuo Commentary* to the *Spring and Autumn Annals,* though some have argued that he forged it to give classical sanction to the political views he shared with Wang Mang.

4. The idea of the Three Ages is first found in the *Gongyang Commentary;* the *Zuo Commentary* does not mention them.

LU XUN[1] (1881–1936) is generally regarded as the greatest Chinese writer of the twentieth century. He never produced a novel, but he wrote numerous memorable short stories and countless essays and letters that had an enormous impact on modern China. Among his most celebrated works are "The True Story of Ah-Q" (A-Q zhengzhuan), "Diary of a Madman" (Kuangren riji), and "My Old Hometown" (Guxiang). Lu Xun was also a deeply learned chronicler and critic of Chinese literature; his *Brief History of Chinese Fiction (Zhongguo xiaoshuo shilüe)* remains authoritative to this day.

But Lu Xun was much more than an outstanding littérateur. He was also a trenchant social commentator whose impassioned pleas for reform were instrumental in guiding China's path toward progress—even for many decades after his death. He made bitterly honest comments on virtually all aspects of Chinese institutions, culture, and customs. Among the subjects that attracted Lu Xun's attention was the Chinese script. So deep were his feelings about the Chinese writing system that he was reported to have proclaimed shortly before his death, *"Hanzi bu mie, Zhongguo bi wang"* (If Chinese characters do not fade away, China will perish!). While this is admittedly a radical formulation of the problem posed by China's archaic script in the context of efforts to modernize the nation, Lu Xun was by no means the first Chinese scholar to blame the writing system for his nation's backwardness. Indeed, Lu Xun had been preceded by dozens of individuals from the late-Qing period onward who had devised simple and more efficient writing systems, including alphabets, for the various Chinese languages. And, as early as the Song dynasty, the renowned and erudite polymath Zheng Qiao (1104–1162) had noted some of the deficiencies of the Chinese script.

Lu Xun returned to the subject of the Chinese writing system on numerous occasions throughout his career, but his most sustained and probing examination of the characters is to be found in the remarkable text translated here. Because *An Outsider's Chats about Written Language (Menwai wentan)* is both enormously informative and richly entertaining, we have chosen to present the text in its entirety. It should be noted that the first word of the title, *Menwai,* is multivalent. Among its applicable meanings here are "outdoors" and—with *han* (man, fellow) understood at the end—"novice, layman, greenhorn." Since Lu Xun was deeply familiar with the script, its nature, and history, he was obviously being polite in styling himself a *menwai(han).*

Menwai wentan first appeared in the pages of the "Free Discussions" (Ziyou tan) supplement of the influential Shanghai newspaper *Shen bao,* from August 24 through September, 1934 under the pseudonym Hua Yu. This name may literally be rendered as "China's Prison," but it is also a perfect homophone for "China's Language," a pun that was almost surely in the back of Lu Xun's mind when he chose it for this particular work.—VHM

1. Introduction

I'm told that the heat in Shanghai this year hasn't been equaled in the past sixty years. During the day, we'd go out to grub for a living, and, in the evening, we'd return with our heads hanging. In our rooms it would still be hot, and, on top of that, there were mosquitoes. At such times, paradise could only be found outdoors *(menwai)*. Probably because [Shanghai is] next to the sea, there's always a breeze so you don't need to fan yourself. The neighbors who lived in the flats and garrets in the vicinity would also sit outside. Although we knew each other somewhat, we didn't often have a chance to meet. Some of them were shop clerks, others were proofreaders in publishing houses, and still others were accomplished draftsmen. Everybody would be totally exhausted and sighing over how hard life was. But at least this was a time when we were free, and so we would talk freely.

The limits of our conversations were actually quite broad. We talked about the drought, praying for rain,[2] picking up girls,[3] a three-inch shrunken mummy,[4] foreign rice,[5] naked gams,[6] and we also talked about classical writing, vernacular language, and colloquial speech.[7] Because I'd written several pieces in the vernacular language, when it came to such subjects as classical writing, they were particularly interested in hearing what I had to say, and, to oblige them, I did speak a great deal. In this way, we passed two or three nights before we were diverted by other topics and, at any rate, had exhausted the subject. Little did I expect that, a few days later, several of my neighbors would ask me to write out what I had said.

Among them, there were those who believed me because I had read some old books, others who believed me because I had read a few foreign books, and still others who believed me because I had read both old books and foreign books. But several of them, on the contrary, for these very reasons did not believe me and said that I was a "bat."[8] When I touched upon classical writing, they would say with a smile, "You're not one of the eight great prose stylists[9] of the Tang and Song periods. Can we believe you?" When I talked about colloquial speech, they again said with a smile, "You're not one of the toiling masses. What sort of big talk are you feeding us?"

Yet there is some truth to this. When we were discussing the drought, mention was made of an official who went to the countryside to inspect the drought conditions. He claimed that there were some places that really wouldn't have had to experience the drought but were now experiencing it because the peasants were lazy and had not manned the irrigation pails. But one newspaper carried a report about a sixty-year-old man who, because his son had died of exhaustion while manning the irrigation pails and, seeing that the drought continued as before, committed suicide since he had no other way out. The views of the official and the country-folk are so far apart as this! Such being the case, I'm afraid that ultimately my evening chats are no more than the idle words of an outsider in his leisure.

After the tropical storm passed, the weather became a bit cooler; but *(sic)* I finally fulfilled the wishes of those who had hoped that I would write out my opinions. What I have written is much simpler than the words I had spoken, but the overall import differs little and may be considered a copy for my peers to read. At the time, I simply relied on my memory to cite old books here and there. The spoken word, like the wind, rushes past the ear, and so it is not important if you make some mistakes. Committing it to paper made me hesitate, and, furthermore, I was stymied by not having the original texts to check. All I can do is ask my reader to correct my errors as he encounters them.

Written and inscribed on the night of August 16, 1934

2. Who Invented the Written Word?

Who invented the written word?

We are accustomed to hearing stories about how a certain thing was always invented by a sage of ancient times. Naturally, we would ask the same question about the written word. At once, there is an answer from some forgotten source: writing was invented by Cang Jie.[10]

This is what is advocated by most scholars, and naturally they have their sources for it. I have even seen a portrait of this Cang Jie. He was a monkish[11] old man with four eyes. It would seem that, if one is going to create writing, he'd first off better have an unusual visage. Those of us who have just two eyes are not only insufficiently talented; even our features are unsuited for the task.

However, the author of the *Book of Changes* ([original note:] I don't know who he was) was rather more intelligent. He said, "In high antiquity, government was carried out with knotted cords[12] [to make records]. The sages of subsequent ages substituted [written] documents and contracts for these." He does not mention Cang Jie but only says "the sages of subsequent ages." And he does not mention "invented" but only speaks of an exchange. He was really being very cautious. Perhaps, without thinking about it, he did not believe that in antiquity there could have been a person who created a large number of graphs all by himself so he just gives us this one vague sentence.

But what sort of figure was responsible for replacing knotted cords with documents and contracts? Was he a writer? That's not a bad answer, judged from the current reality of the so-called "writers" who are most fond of flaunting their writing skills but utterly inept when their pens are snatched away from them. Indeed, one must first think of them, and, indeed, they ought to expend a bit of effort on behalf of their own bread-winning tool. Yet this is not true. Although people in prehistoric times sang songs when they worked and sang songs when they were wooing, by no means did they make drafts of their songs or keep manuscripts of them. This is because, even in their dreams, they wouldn't have been able to conceive of selling manuscripts of their poems or of compiling their collected works. Furthermore, in the society of that time, there were no newspaper publishers and bookstores, so writing was of no utility whatsoever. According to what some scholars tell us, it would appear that those who devoted their labors to script must have been the historians.

In primitive society, at first there were probably only mages[13] [who were in charge of spiritual and ritual matters]. It was not until after a period of gradual evolution when things became complicated that there was a need to record such matters as sacrifice, hunting, war, and so forth. The mages were then forced to think of a way to make records in addition to carrying out their basic duty of "inviting the spirits to descend."[14] This is the beginning of "the [professional] historian."[15] Moreover, as we can tell from the phrase "[cause the exploits of the feudal lords to] rise up to Heaven,"[16] another of their basic duties was to burn the booklets in which they had recorded the major events concerning their tribal chieftain and his administration so that god above could read them. Consequently, they likewise had to write compositions, although this was probably something that occurred subsequently. Still later, duties were divided up even more clearly, whereupon there came into being the historian, who specialized in keeping records of things. Script is an indispensable instrument for the historian. Some ancient has said, "Cang Jie was the Yellow Emperor's historian."[17] We cannot trust the first part of the sentence, but the fact that it does point out the relationship between history and script is very interesting. As for the later "men of letters" who used script to write such fine lines as "Oh, my love! Ah, I am dying!" they were merely enjoying the fruits of others' labors and "do not merit consideration here."

3. How Did the Characters Come into Existence?

According to the *Book of Changes,* before there were documents and contracts, there clearly were knotted cords. Whenever the country-folk where I'm from have something important they want to do the next day and are afraid of forgetting it, they often say, "Tie a knot in your belt!" Then did our ancient sages also use a long cord in which they tied a knot for everything? I'm afraid this wouldn't work. If there were only a few knots you could still remember [what they signified], but once there were many it would be hopeless. Or perhaps that was precisely something like the eight trigrams[18] of Emperor Fuxi,[19] with three cords in each unit. If all were unknotted that would be *qian* (male, Heaven), but if all three had a knot in the center that would be *kun* (female, Earth). I'm afraid this isn't right either. If there were only eight units, you still might be able [to get by], but if there were sixty-four units, it would be difficult to remember [what they all stood for], much less if there were 512 units![20] There still survives in Peru the *quipu.*[21] It uses a horizontal cord and a number of vertical strings hanging from it which, pulled back and forth, are knotted [and unknotted]. Although it looks like a net without really being one, it seems as though it could actually be used to represent a relatively large amount of ideas. I suspect that the knotted cords of our prehistoric ancestors were like this. However, since they were replaced by documents and contracts and were not the direct ancestors of the latter, there's no harm setting them aside for the moment.

The "Goulan Stele Inscription"[22] of Emperor Yu[23] of the Xia dynasty was forged by Taoists. The oldest characters that we can see on genuine artifacts are the oracle-bone inscriptions and bronze inscriptions of the Shang dynasty.[24] But these are already quite advanced, so it is virtually impossible to find a single primitive form. Occasionally, however, one can glimpse a small amount of realistic pictography, for example a deer or an elephant. From these pictographic shapes, one can discover clues related to script: the Chinese script is founded on pictography.

The buffalo painted in the Altamira Caves[25] of Spain are famous remains of primitive man, and many art historians say that this is truly "art for art's sake," that primitive man painted them for amusement. But this explanation cannot escape from being overly "modern,"[26] because primitive man did not have as much leisure as nineteenth-century[27] artists. He had a reason for painting each buffalo, something that had to do with buffalo, whether it was hunting the buffalo or casting a spell on them. Even now people gawk at the advertisements for cigarettes and movies [posted] on walls in Shanghai. One can imagine what a commotion such an extraordinary sight must have caused in unsophisticated, primitive society! As they looked at [the paintings], they would come to know that this thing [called] a buffalo could, after all, be drawn on a flat surface with lines. At the same time, it seems as though they came to recognize [the drawing as a graph representing the word] "buffalo." While admiring the artists' ability, nobody invited them to earn some money by writing their autobiography, so their names have passed into obscurity. However, there was more than one Cang Jie in [ancient] society. Some of them carved designs on sword hilts; others drew pictures on doors. [Such pictographic representations] made an impression and were passed on from mind to mind, from mouth to mouth. [In this fashion,] the number of characters increased [to the point that], once the scribes collected them, they could make do to record events. I suspect that the origins of Chinese writing are to be found within this sort of process.

Naturally, later on there must have been a continual increase in the number of characters, but this is something that the scribes could have managed by themselves. By inserting the new characters—which, moreover, were pictographic—among the familiar characters, others would have easily guessed what they signified.[28] Even up to the present time, China is still producing new characters. However, if anyone is intent on being a new Cang Jie, they will surely fail. Zhu Yu[29] of [the southern kingdom of] Wu and Wu Zetian[30] of the Tang [dynasty] both created bizarre characters, but all their efforts were wasted.

Nowadays, it is Chinese chemists who are the best at creating characters. [The characters they come up with for] the names of many elements and compounds are very hard to recognize, and it is even difficult to read out their sounds. To tell the truth, whenever I see [such characters] I get a headache. I feel that it would be far better and more straightforward to use the Latin names current in all other nations. If you are incapable of recognizing the twenty-some letters [of the Roman alphabet]—please pardon me for speaking bluntly—then you probably won't be able to learn chemistry very well either.

4. Writing Characters Is Like Drawing Pictures

In both the *Rites of Zhou (Zhouli)*[31] and the *Explanation of Simple and Compound Graphs (Shuo wen jie zi)*,[32] it is said that there are six different methods for forming characters.[33] Here I won't discuss [all six], but will only say a few things related to the pictographs.

Pictographs may be "based upon the body which is close at hand or on objects that are far away."[34] That is, by drawing an eye you have *mu* 目 (eye) and by drawing a circle and adding a few rays you get *ri* 日 (sun). Of course, that is very clear and convenient. But sometimes you hit a brick wall. For example, if you want to draw the edge of a knife blade, how do you go about it? If you don't draw the back of the knife blade, you can't depict the edge of the blade. At this stage, you have to come up with a novel idea, [such as] adding a short line along the blade edge to indicate "here; this place," thus creating the graph *ren* 刃 (knife edge). This is already getting to seem a bit troublesome to handle, and it is all the more so when you have something that has no form to represent. In such cases, all you can do is come up with an "ideational" graph, which may also be called a "conjunct" graph. A hand placed on a tree is *cai* 采 (pluck), and a heart placed between a roof and a bowl yields *ning* 寜 (peaceful, serene, tranquil) because one is at peace when one has food and shelter. However, if you want to write the *ning* of *ningke* 寧可 (would rather), then you've got to add a line beneath the bowl to show that this is [a different character, which] merely borrows the sound of *ning* [meaning "peaceful, serene, tranquil"].

Conjunct graphs are more troublesome than pictographs, since you have to draw at least two components. [For a more complicated conjunct] character like *bao* 寶 (treasure), you have to draw a roof (top), a string of jade (middle left), a jar (middle right), and a cowry shell (bottom) for a total of four components. It looks to me as though the character for "jar" is actually a combination of the two forms for mortar and pestle, so all together there are five components.[35] Just for this one character *bao* you have expended a lot of effort.

But [even this method] won't [always] work, because there are some things that cannot be depicted and other things that one does not know how to depict. For example, the leaves of the pine and the cypress are of different types, and it is possible to distinguish them. But writing, after all, is writing; it cannot be as refined as painting. When you come right down to it, you just have to stick it out. To get us out of this sticky situation, along comes [the principle of character formation called] *xiesheng* (symphonetic)[36] in which meaning and shape part company.[37] [With *xiesheng* characters,] this is already [to adopt the principle of] recording the sounds [of words for things instead of trying to draw their shapes]. Therefore, some people say that this was [further] progress for Chinese writing. They're right. We may indeed call this progress, yet the foundation is still that of drawing pictures. For example, *cai* 菜 (vegetable) is classified under the *cao* (grass) radical and has the sound of *cai*[38] (pluck). [To write this character, you must] draw a clump of grass [at the top], a claw [in the middle], and a tree [at the bottom]: three components. [Another example,] *hai* 海 (sea) is classified under the *shui* (water) radical and has the sound *mei*[39] ("each, every"). [To write this character, you must] draw a river [on the left side] and a lady[40] wearing a cap (?)[41] [on the right side]: also three components. To sum up, if you want to write [Chinese] characters, you are forever compelled to draw pictures.

But the ancients were by no means stupid. They had long since simplified the pictographs so that they became distanced from realistic representations. Seal[42] characters with their curved lines still bear the traces of picture-drawing. But with the development of the clerical script[43] up to the standard script[44] of today, [the characters have grown] poles apart from [the archaic] pictographs. However, the foundation has by no means changed. Even after [the characters had grown] poles apart [from their archaic ancestral forms], they became pictographs that no longer bore a resemblance to the objects they represented. Although [the characters were now] simpler to write, they were exceedingly difficult to recognize. [You simply] had to memorize them arbitrarily one by one. Furthermore, there are still some characters that even today are by no means simple. For example, if you ask a child to write *luan* 鸞 (a mythical bird like the phoenix) or *zao* 鑿 (chisel), it's very hard to fit inside a half-inch square unless he practices for five or six months.

Another complication is that, due to sound changes that have occurred between antiquity and the present, there are many symphonetic *(xiesheng)* graphs whose phonophores have gotten quite out of tune. Nowadays, who still pronounces *hua* 滑 (slippery) as *gu* 骨 (bone)[45] or *hai* (sea) as *mei* (each, every)?[46]

The ancients handed down writing to us. Admittedly, this is a tremendous heritage for which we should be thankful. However, at the present time, when pictographs no longer resemble the objects they are supposed to represent, and when symphonetic graphs have gotten out of tune, our thanks cannot but be a bit hesitant.

5. Did Language and Script Coincide in Ancient Times?

Having reached this point, I would like to speculate a bit on the question of whether or not language and script coincided in ancient times.

With regard to this question, although modern scholars have by no means come to a clear conclusion, it seems from listening to their manner of speaking that they probably consider them to have coincided, and the further back we go the more closely they coincided. Nonetheless, I'm rather doubtful of that, because the easier a script is to write, the easier it is to make what one writes coincide with speech. But the Chinese pictographs are so hard to draw that I suspect that our forefathers all along stripped away unimportant words.

The *Book of Documents (Shujing)*[47] is so hard to read that it would seem it might well serve as evidence that it was based on spoken language. But research has not yet precisely revealed the spoken language of the Shang and Zhou people [whom it purports to be about]. Perhaps it was more prolix [than the terse written language of the *Book of Documents*]. As for the ancient books of the Zhou and Qin, although their authors used a small amount of their local topolects, the writing was roughly the same [regardless of what part of China and which speech community they hailed from]. And, even if it was fairly close to the spoken language, what they were using was a standardized Zhou-Qin vernacular, not at all a Zhou-Qin colloquial. All the more it goes without saying for the Han dynasty that, although Sima Qian[48] (d. ca. 86 B.C.E.) was willing to render [a few of] the hard-to-understand expressions of the *Book of Documents* into contemporary terminology.

Yet it was only in special instances that he adopted a bit of popular phraseology, such as when Chen Shě's[49] old friend sees that he has become king, he exclaims with surprise, "Wow! Shě, you're a splendacious guy as *de facto* king!"[50] I suspect that the four words "as *de facto* king" in this sentence have undergone refinement by His Lordship the Grand Scribe.

Well, then, shouldn't the children's rhymes, the proverbs, and the folk songs quoted in ancient books be authentic popular language of the time? In my estimation that's hard to say too. Chinese men of letters, by temperament, were quite fond of rewriting the compositions of others. The most obvious example of this is that "The Song of the Prince of Huainan,"[51] though it was the same Han-period folk song from the same place, is recorded in two different versions in the *History of the Han (Hanshu)* and in the *Annals of the Former Han (Qian Han ji).*[52]

One goes:

A foot of cloth can yet be sewn,
A peck of grain can yet be husked,
But these two brothers cannot countenance each other.

The other goes:

A foot of cloth will make you snuggly warm,
A peck of rice will stuff your tummy,
But these two brothers do not countenance each other.

If we compare [these two versions], it seems as though the latter is [closer to] the original, yet it's possible that even [in this version] some things have been omitted and that it is merely a summary. Later, the recorded sayings[53] and the storyteller's scripts[54] of the Song period, [as well as] the spoken portions of Yuan drama[55] and southern plays,[56] are also summaries. It's just that the language they used was relatively common and that the words they omitted were relatively few, so that people felt they were "clear as speech."

My surmise is that Chinese language and script all along have not at all coincided. The main reason for this is that the characters are difficult to write, so that the only recourse is to abbreviate somewhat. The writing of the ancients was [thus] a digest of the spoken language of the time. Therefore, when we write Classical Chinese,[57] we are using pictographs that no longer bear a resemblance to the objects they are supposed to represent and symphonetic graphs that are not necessarily in tune to limn on paper a digest of the spoken language of the ancients that no modern person would say and that few can understand. Just think! Wouldn't it be difficult?

6. Consequently Literature Became a Rare Commodity

Writing had its inception among the people, but later it became the exclusive possession of the privileged. According to the surmise of the author of the *Book of Changes,* "In high antiquity, government was carried out with knotted cords [to make records]." Thus, even knotted cords already belonged to the rulers. By the time [writing] fell into the hands of the mages and scribes, it was even more so, inasmuch as they served under the chieftains and over the populace. As society evolved, the scope of those individuals who learned to write expanded, but [writing] was largely still restricted to the privileged. As for the common people, they were illiterate not because they lacked the tuition fees, but simply because they were considered unfit since [writing] was restricted only to those who qualified. Furthermore, they were not even permitted to look at books. Before woodblock printing developed in China, a good book would invariably be hidden away in the imperial libraries and depositories, so that not even scholars knew its contents.

Since writing belonged to the privileged, it was something dignified and mysterious. Still today, Chinese characters are very dignified. We often see hanging on the wall baskets with the maxim "Cherish paper that has characters on it." When it comes to written charms that can dispel evil and cure sickness, that is due to their mysteriousness. Since writing possesses dignity, then whoever knows how to write will be dignified by his association with it. If new dignitaries keep appearing day after day, this would not be beneficial to the old dignitaries. What is more, once those who can write become numerous, the mysteriousness of writing would diminish. The power of Taoist talismans, which seem to be made up of characters, is due to the fact that, aside from Taoist priests, nobody can read them. Therefore, those who can write are certain to keep a tight grip on [this skill].

In Europe, during the Middle Ages, all literature and learning were in the monasteries. Literacy in Croatia was restricted to monks until the nineteenth century. The spoken language of the people had deteriorated to the point that it was barely adequate for the old way of living. When they wanted to carry out reform, all they could do was import a lot of new words from abroad.

In addition to the limitations of social status and economic means, our Chinese characters present another high threshold to the masses: their difficulty. If you don't spend ten or so years on them, it's not easy to cross this threshold alone. Those who cross over it are the scholar-officials, and these same scholar-officials do their utmost to make writing as difficult as possible because it makes them especially dignified, surpassing all other ordinary scholar-officials. Yang Xiong[58] of the Han dynasty, who had a fondness for strange characters, had this failing. When Liu Xin[59] wished to borrow the manuscript of his *Regional Speech (Fang yan)*,[60] Yang threatened to commit suicide.[61] In the Tang dynasty, Fan Zongshi's[62] essays were written in such a fashion that others could not punctuate them, and Li He[63] wrote poems that were incomprehensible. They all did this for the same reason. Another method is to write characters that no one else knows. A crude way of doing that us to look up a few old characters from the *Kangxi Dictionary*[64] and insert them in your writing. Another, more sophisticated, way is—like Qian Dian[65]—to write out the whole of Liu Xi's *Explanation of Terms (Shiming)*[66] in small-seal script.[67] Recently, Mr. Qian Xuantong[68] copied out Taiyan's[69] "Catechism of Minor Learning" (Xiaoxue wenda)[70] in the [small-seal] graphs of [Xu Shen's] *Shuo wen*.

Chinese characters and the Chinese literary language are already difficult enough by their own nature. On top of that, the scholar-officials have purposely devised all of these additional difficulties that get added on. Such being the case, how could anyone hope that the masses would have any affinity for the Chinese writing system? But the scholar-officials precisely want it to be this way. If the characters were easy to recognize and everybody could master them, then they would not be dignified, and the scholar-officials would lose their dignity along with them. Those who say that the written vernacular is not as good as Classical Chinese take this as their starting point. Nowadays, when those who talk about "the language of the masses" *(dazhong yu)* say that it is only necessary to teach the masses a "thousand-character curriculum,"[71] the roots of such thinking also lie in this.

7. Illiterate Authors

Our predecessors called the digest of ancient spoken language written out in such a difficult script *wen*,[72] while those today who are slightly more progressive call it *wenxue*.[73] But this word *wenxue* was not adopted from [the pronouncement of Confucius in the *Analects*]:[74] "In *wen xue*, there are Zi You and Zi Lu." Rather, it was imported from Japan, where it was their translation of the English word "literature."[75] People who can compose this kind of *wen* (refined writing)—and nowadays it is permissible to write in the vernacular—are called "men of letters" or they are called "authors."

The primary requirement for the existence of literature is the ability to write. Therefore, of course, there cannot be any "men of letters" among the illiterate multitudes. But there are authors among them. Don't laugh until you hear the rest of what I have to say. I believe that, before humankind had writing, there were already creative works. Unfortunately, there was no one to record them, nor was there any way to record them. Our earliest ancestors originally couldn't even speak. In order to work cooperatively, they had to express their ideas; thus they gradually learned to produce complex sounds. Suppose they were carrying wood and found it very difficult but didn't know how to express this. If one among them called out, "Heave-ho! Heave-ho!" this is [a kind of] creation, and if everybody else—out of admiration—adopted this expression, then that was tantamount to publication. And if it were preserved in some form of notation, that would be literature. Whoever did so would be an author, a man of letters, and he would belong to the "Heave-ho School."[76] We need not laugh, for although such a work may indeed be quite childish, there are many respects in which the ancients were not up to moderns, this being one of them. Take, for example, these Zhou-dynasty lines:

> *Guan! guan!* cry the ospreys
> On an island in the river;
> Graceful is the fair maiden,
> A fit mate for the gentleman.

Since this is the first stanza [of the first poem] in the *Poetry Classic (Shijing)*,[77] we are so overawed by it that all we can do is kowtow submissively. However, if such a poem had not been written in the past and a modern poet were to write a vernacular poem utilizing these ideas, I suspect that—no matter which newspaper supplement he submitted it to—chances are nine out of ten that it would be stuffed into the waste basket.

> Ah, a pretty girl!
> She's a good match for the young lord.

What kind of talk is this?

Even among the pieces in the "Airs of the States" (Guofeng),[78] there are quite a few that were the creations of anonymous illiterates. Because they were relatively outstanding, these were handed down by word of mouth. The officials [who were sent out to the various states] selected and recorded these poems as reference materials for the government.[79] No one knows how many other poems must have disappeared. The two great epics of the Greek poet Homer[80]—let us assume for the moment that there actually was such a person—may also be considered as originally being oral recitations, while the extant texts were recorded by others. Poems such as the "Midnight Songs"[81] and the "Songs without Accompaniment"[82] of the Eastern Jin through the Qi and Chen dynasties,[83] and the "Bamboo Branch Lyrics" and the "Willow Branch Lyrics"[84] of the Tang dynasty were all originally anonymous creations. They were transmitted by literary men who selected and polished them. While these polished verses have admittedly been preserved, it's a pity that they surely must have lost a great deal of their original character. Still today, there are ballads, rustic songs, fishermen's songs, and so forth everywhere, and these are all the works of illiterate poets. There are children's tales and folk narratives which are the works of illiterate creators of fiction. These are all illiterate authors.

However, because [we are dealing with] works that have not been recorded and that, moreover, are easily lost, the extent of their circulation can not be very wide, and the number of people who know about them will also be small. Occasionally, when men of letters encounter a bit [of this sort of oral literature], they are invariably surprised, and absorb it into their own works as new nourishment. When an old literature deteriorates, a new transformation may be initiated by the adoption of folk literature or foreign literature. Such examples are frequently to be seen in the history of literature. Although illiterate authors may not be as refined as men of letters, they are solid and refreshing.

If we want their works to be enjoyed by everyone, we must enable such authors to write, and, at the same time, we must enable readers to be literate and even to be able to write themselves. In a word, we must make writing accessible to everyone.

8. How to Make Writing Accessible to the Masses

There were already [attempts] to make writing accessible to the masses at the end of the Qing dynasty.

> Don't beat a drum, don't strike a gong!
> Listen to me sing a Grand Peace Song. . . .

This was an imperially issued ditty[85] for instructing the masses. Aside from this, the scholar-officials also published some vernacular newspapers, but their intention was only that the people should be able to understand them when they were read aloud, not that they should be able to write things out themselves.[86] The *Thousand Character Textbook for Commoners* presumes the possibility of [teaching people] to be able to write out a few things, but it's only enough for writing accounts and letters. If one wishes to write out whatever thoughts are in one's mind, its limited number of characters is insufficient. [Such curricula] are like a prison in which the prisoners are given a plot of land which, however, is restricted, so that all they can do is walk, stand, sit, and lie down in their closed quarters, but can definitely not run outside of the iron bars that have been erected.

Lao Naixuan[87] and Wang Zhao[88] both devised simplified characters which were quite progressive and whereby one could write words according to their sounds. In the early years of the Republic, when the Ministry of Education wanted to devise an alphabet, these two men were members of the committee [charged with that task].[89] Mr. Lao sent a representative, but Mr. Wang attended personally. They had a great fight with Mr. Wu Zhihui[90] over whether or not to keep the entering tones.[91] The fight was so frantic that Mr. Wu's padded trousers fell down when he sucked in his belly. Nonetheless, after repeated deliberations they did come up with something that they called Letters for Annotating Sounds (*zhuyin zimu*). At the time, there were quite a few people who thought that *zhuyin zimu* could replace the characters. In fact, however, this didn't work out because *zhuyin zimu*, after all, are nothing more than simplified tetragraphs,[92] just like Japanese *kana*.[93] It's all right if a few [of these symbols] are sandwiched [between the characters] or if they are [attached as phonetic] annotations to the sides of the characters, but if you want them to stand alone, they're not up to it. It's easy to get them mixed up when writing, and they are readily confused in reading. When the committee members called them Letters for Annotating Sounds, they were well aware of their limited capabilities. If we look at [the situation in] Japan, there are those who advocate reducing [the number of] characters, there are those who advocate Romanization, but nobody advocates using only kana.

Somewhat better is to use [National] Romanization ([Guoyu] Luomazi).[94] I suppose that the person who did the most advanced research on this subject was Mr. Zhao Yuanren,[95] but I'm not very clear about it. [National Romanization] uses the internationally current roman letters for spelling—now even Turkey[96] has adopted them—a string of letters [are joined to form] a word; it's exceptionally clear and good. But, for an outsider like me, it seems as though that method of spelling is still too complicated. Of course, if one wants to be precise, then one must be fastidious, but when something is excessively complicated, then it becomes difficult and constitutes an obstacle to popularization. It would be better to have something else that is simple yet not crude.

Now let us examine the New Latinization for a moment. The *Daily International Digest*[97] has published a pamphlet titled "Latinization of Written Chinese," and a supplement to the combined issues for June and July, 1934 of *La Mondo* (The World)[98] [entitled] "Lingva Scienco" [Language Science] also introduced this [system of spelling]. These publications are so cheap that anyone interested may buy a copy to read. The New Latinization uses only twenty-eight letters, and the spelling is easy to learn. "Man" is *rhen,* "home" is *fangz.* "I eat fruit" is *Wo ch goz.* "He is a worker" is *Ta sh gungrhen.* It is now being tried out among overseas Chinese and it has seen some success, but so far it's only for the northern topolects.[99] But I suppose, after all, that most people in China speak one of the northern topolects—not Pekingese—so that if, in the future, there really is a kind of popular written language that can be used everywhere, it will likely be based mainly on the northern topolects. For present purposes, so long as minor modifications are made after due consideration, enabling it to be compatible with various particular, local pronunciations, this spelling system can be used even in remote parts of the country.

Thus, provided that one recognizes twenty-eight letters and learns a few rules for spelling and writing, then anyone but a lazybones or an imbecile can read and write. Moreover, Latinization has another advantage: one can write fast. The Americans say, "Time is money." But I think that time is life. To squander other people's time for no reason is, in fact, no different than robbing and murdering them. However, those like us who sit idly chatting in the cool [evening] breeze are exceptions!

9. Specialization or Popularization?

Having come thus far, we run into a big problem: spoken Chinese languages are quite different in various parts of the country. If we merely divide them up roughly, there are the five groups of the northern topolects, Jiangsu and Zhejiang topolects, the topolects of Hunan, Hubei, Sichuan, and Guizhou, the topolects of Fujian, and Cantonese. Furthermore, there are also minor differences within these five groups. Now, if we use Latinization to write, should we write in Standard Mandarin, or should we write in colloquial? If we write in Standard Mandarin, many people do not know it. If we write colloquial, people from other places won't be able to read it, and this will cut them further off from each other, which would not be as good as the characters that circulate throughout the country. This is a great defect.

In my opinion, let each locality write its own colloquial during the initial stage. At the beginning, it is not necessary to be concerned whether people in other places understand the meaning. Before the introduction of Latinization, our illiterates never used characters to exchange information anyway; hence there are no new disadvantages. On the contrary, there is at least the new advantage that people in the same district will be able to exchange ideas and absorb knowledge. Of course, by the same token, we also need people to write some beneficial books. Yet the question remains whether the language of the masses in various places should, after all, in the future turn toward the direction of specialization or popularization.

In the topolects and in colloquial speech, there are quite a few profound expressions. Where

I'm from we call them "pithy expressions."[100] They are very interesting to use, much like allusions in Classical Chinese, and there is a distinct pleasure in hearing them. Specialization would entail allowing the topolects from various places to develop more fully by refining their grammar and vocabulary. This would be beneficial to literature, for it would be far more interesting than just using vague generalities in one's writing. But specialization has its own dangers. I don't know linguistics, but when we observe animals, we note that they are bound to perish whenever they become [overly] specialized. Already before there were human beings, there were many animals and plants that died out because they became too specialized. Thus, they lost their ability to evolve and were unable to adapt to changes in the environment.

Fortunately, we human beings cannot yet be said to be overly specialized animals, so please don't worry. The masses have [their] literature, but they should not sacrifice themselves for it. Otherwise, that would be as ridiculous as the living sages who want to make martyrs of eighty percent of the Chinese people by keeping them illiterate in order to preserve the characters. Therefore, I think that, during the initial period, we should use the topolects. However, at the same time, common grammar and vocabulary should be brought in. First use that which is innate; this is [the means to] popularize writing in a given locality. [After that,] add that which is new; this is [the means to] popularize writing throughout the entire country.

Of course, a system devised by a few scholars in their study usually won't work, but just letting things take their own course is not a good approach either. Today on the wharves, in public offices, and in universities there is already something like common speech *(putonghua)*. When people speak, it is neither the National Language (Guoyu),[101] nor is it the language of the capital (Pekingese), with each person having their own local accent and intonation. Yet neither is it a topolect, and even if they pronounce it with difficulty and must make an effort when listening, still—when all is said and done—they can speak and understand it. If we regularize [this language of the wharves, offices, and universities] and help it to develop, it can become a part of the language of the masses,[102] or perhaps even the main force. When I said that we should "add that which is new" to the topolects, the source of "the new" lies in this. Once this language which stems from nature but has that which is man-made added to it becomes widespread, our common spoken and written language will have been largely unified.

After this, naturally there will still be more to do. After many months and years, when the spoken and written language becomes even more unified, something that is as good as pithy [local] expressions and more lively than classical allusions will gradually take shape, making literature all the more brilliant. This is not something that will happen immediately. Just think of the characters which advocates of the "National Essence"[103] hold to be so precious. Didn't it take three to four thousand years to end up with such a pile of bizarre achievements?

As for who should take the initiative in this, that goes without saying: enlightened scholars. Some may say, "The work of the masses must be done by the masses themselves."[104] Of course, that does make sense, but we must look at the role of the speaker. If the speaker is one of the masses, then it is partially right, the right part being that [the masses] should take care of their own affairs, but the wrong part is refusing the help of others. If, however, the speaker is a scholar, then it is completely different: he is using pretty phrases to monopolize writing and to protect his own dignity and honor.

10. There's No Need to Panic

However, without necessarily even taking any real action, the mere mention of this is enough to cause some people to panic.

First they say that those who advocate language and writing for the masses *(dazhong yuwen)* are "political propagandists in the literary realm like Song Yang,"[105] meaning that they are rebels. Putting a red[106] cap on them is the easiest way to oppose them. Yet, at the same time, this means that, for their own peace of mind, they would rather that eighty percent of Chinese remain illiterate. And, as for verbal propaganda, there ought to be eighty percent who are deaf and dumb. But this is outside the framework of "chatting about written language," so here I needn't say too much about it.

Of those who are particularly concerned about literature, I now see that there are two types. One type is afraid that if the masses can all read and write, then everybody will become men of letters. This is like the good man [in the fable] who was afraid that the sky would fall down. I mentioned earlier that, among the illiterate masses, there have all along been authors. I haven't been to the countryside for a long time, but in the past if the peasants had a bit of leisure—for example, if they were relaxing in a cool place—then somebody would tell stories. But the storyteller was usually a special person who was relatively more experienced and a clever talker who could keep people listening, was easy to understand, and moreover was interesting. This was an author and, if you copied down what he said, it would be literature. If there were someone whose language was insipid, yet was excessively loquacious, nobody would want to listen to him and would even unleash many sarcastic remarks in his direction—satire. We've already been playing around with Classical Chinese for several thousand years and with written vernacular for ten-odd years; but are all who can write men of letters? Even if we all become men of letters, this is not like being warlords or bandits since it would not be harmful to the people. All we'd do is read each other's works.

Another type is afraid that [the quality of] literature would be lowered. The masses are not cultivated in the old literature. Compared to the refined literature of the literati, perhaps they may appear to be "low," but they have not been tainted by the chronic maladies of the old literature. Therefore, what they compose is vigorous and fresh. I've already mentioned how anonymous literature such as the "Midnight Songs" (Ziye ge) can give new strength to the old literature. Now there are also many folk songs and [folk] stories that have been introduced. In addition, there are popular dramas, such as the autobiographical [speech] by the Ghost of Impermanence[107] in "Mulian[108] Rescues His Mother," which I quoted in *Dawn Flowers Plucked at Dusk (Zhao hua xi shi).*[109] He says that, because he sympathized with another ghost and let him temporarily go back to earth for half a day, he was unexpectedly punished by Yama.[110] From then on, [he decided] never to be lenient again,

> Even if you are [protected by] a wall of bronze or iron!
> Even if you are a relative of the emperor!

How human, how conscience-stricken, how law-abiding, and how resolute! Is this something that our men of letters could produce?

This is the authentic work of peasants and craftsmen who perform such plays in their free time, borrowing the theme of Mulian's travels to string together many tales. Except for "The Young Nun Goes down the Mountain,"[111] they are completely different from the woodblock printed text of the "Record of Mulian Rescuing His Mother."[112] Among the scenes there is one called "Wu Song Kills the Tiger"[113] in which two men—one strong and one weak—do the acting. First the strong man takes the part of Wu Song and the weak man the part of the tiger. The weak man complains when he is beaten roundly by the strong man who says, "You're a tiger. If I don't beat you, won't you bite me to death?" All that the weak man can do is ask to exchange [roles], but when he is bitten mercilessly by the strong man and grumbles, the strong man says,

"You're Wu Song. If I don't bite you, won't I be beaten to death by you?" I think that, compared to the fables of the Greek, Aesop,[114] or of the Russian, Sologub,[115] this is in no way inferior.

If we were to go out into every part of the country to collect them, I suspect that there would be many more works of this sort. However, they naturally have their defects. They have all along been cut off from modern thought by the shackles of our difficult script and difficult literary style. Therefore, if we want Chinese culture to advance as one, we must promote the language of the masses and the literature of the masses. All the more, our writing must be Latinized.

11. The Masses Are by No Means as Stupid as the Scholars Imagine

But this time, no sooner were the language and writing of the masses mentioned than various valiant generals have taken advantage of the opportunity to join the fray. Their backgrounds are not all of a kind, but they all attack the vernacular, translations, Europeanized grammar, and new terms. They all fly the flag of the masses, saying that none of these things is understood by the masses, so they are unacceptable. Among them are some who were originally classicists. They avail themselves of this to assail the vernacular and translations that are right before them. This is the old tactic of "making alliances with those who are distant while attacking those who are near."[116] Others among them are slothful persons who have never studied hard. Before the language of the masses succeeds, they want the vernacular to fail, so that they will be left with an empty arena where they can boast wildly. As a matter of fact, they are good friends of Classical Chinese, so I don't want to say anything more about them. What I want to talk about now are those well-intentioned but mistaken individuals who, either because they belittle the masses or because they belittle themselves, are prey to the same failing as the scholars of old.[117]

Scholars often belittle others, thinking that sentences which are relatively new or relatively difficult must be thoroughly swept away for the sake of the masses, even though they themselves can understand such sentences, since the masses cannot understand them. In speaking and writing, the more ordinary the better. If these views develop further, they will imperceptibly become a new school of the national essence.[118] Sometimes, wanting the language and writing of the masses to spread quickly, they propose that everything should suit the taste of the masses, and they even go so far as to say that an effort should be made to "cater to the masses." They intentionally use a lot of swear words to ingratiate themselves with the masses. Naturally, this shows that they are making extraordinary efforts, but if they keep on this way, they will end up becoming new buffoons for the masses.

Speaking of the term "masses," it has a broad range of meaning, including various sorts and types of people. But even if it's an illiterate who can't recognize the simplest character, to my mind they really aren't so stupid as the scholars think. They want knowledge, new knowledge. They want to learn, and they can pick things up. Of course, if [they're confronted with] a mouthful of new grammar and new vocabulary, they won't understand anything. But if one picks out what is essential and gradually infuses them with it, they will be able to accept it. Their ability to absorb [new things] may well exceed that of scholars with more preconceived ideas. Newborn babies are all illiterate, but by the time they are two years old they understand many words and can say many words. To them, these are all completely new terms and new grammar. They don't have to look them up in *Mr. Ma's Grammar (Ma shi wentong)*[119] or *Fountain of Words (Ciyuan)*,[120] nor do they need a teacher to explain them. After listening to them a few times, they understand the meaning through comparison. This is also the way that the masses can pick up new vocabulary and new grammar; this is how they make progress. Therefore, although the proposals of the new national essence school seem as though they were put forward for the masses, in actuality they have served to hold them back. Nonetheless, we cannot adopt a laissez-faire attitude toward the masses either, since their understanding of things in some respects, after all, is still beneath that of those enlightened scholars [who have their interests at heart]. If discrimination is not regularly exercised for them, they may mistakenly choose what is useless, or even what is harmful. Therefore, the new buffoonery of "catering to the masses" is unacceptable.

[Judging] from the instruction of history, in the beginning all reforms are the duty of the enlightened intellectuals. These intellectuals, however, must study, think hard, be decisive, and have perseverance. They may also employ various expedients, yet without deceiving others. They use inducements, but by no means do they cater [to others]. They do not belittle themselves by acting as clowns for everybody, nor do they belittle others by treating them as their own underlings. They are simply individuals among the masses. I think that only in this way can the cause of the masses be carried out.

12. Coda

I've already said quite a lot. In short, words alone will not suffice; what's important is action. We need lots of people to act: the masses and the vanguard. All sorts of people are needed to act: educators, men of letters, linguists. . . . This is an urgent necessity right now, even if it is like sailing against the current, when all you can do is tow the boat from the bank. To be sure, sailing with the current is pleasant, but even then it is necessary to have a steersman.

Although we can discuss the best methods for towing and steering, in general the greatest benefit derives from practice. No matter how we look at the wind or the water, our goal is always the same: Forward!

Everyone probably has his own opinion, so now let me hear what brilliant ideas each of you [has to offer on this subject].

—VHM

Notes

1. This is but one of the more than a hundred pen names and pseudonyms employed by Zhou Shuren. Lu Xun was born into a prominent gentry family of Shaoxing, Zhejiang, which had been a center of learning for centuries.

2. The year 1934 was one of serious drought in the south and terrible floods in the north. The Guomindang / Kuomintang (KMT; Nationalist) government invited the Ninth Panchen Lama and the Living Buddha of Anqin to perform public prayers for rain.

3. A reference to the semiscandalous news at the beginning of August, 1934 concerning a Secretary of State named Chu Minyi, who was photographed in slightly compromising situations with a young beauty.

4. Probably as a diversion from the unbearable heat, the newspapers reported the finding of the desiccated corpse of the Drought God named Hanba. The tiny mummy, which apparently had but one eye in the top of its head, was actually exhibited in the house of wonders called "The World" (Shijie).

5. Due to the crop failure resulting from the prolonged drought, China had to spend a tremendous amount of silver to purchase American rice during this period.

6. During the New Life campaign of Generalissimo Chiang Kai-shek and his wife, Soong Mei-ling, regulations governing the dress of women were promulgated on June 7, 1934. Among these were very precise

rules concerning how many inches of skin below the knee could be exposed and a prohibition against exposure of female toes and elbows. Offenders were subject to arrest.

7. Whether to write in the dead, classical language or in a style more nearly approximating the spoken language had been a topic of much debate already from before the time of the May Fourth Movement of 1919. Lu Xun is credited with writing the first modern vernacular *(baihua)* short story, "The Diary of a Madman" (1918). Even though the Republican authorities had replaced Classical Chinese as the medium of government and education, there was a constant struggle to keep from backsliding into the old habit of teaching elementary students Classical Chinese and requiring middle-school students to master the Four Books *(Analects, Mencius,* the *Great Learning,* and the *Doctrine of the Mean;* see selections 7, 9, 10, 64). As a matter of fact, intense discussions on the appropriateness of such a policy had erupted in May, 1934, when an archconservative scholar named Wang Maozu launched an attack against restricting the medium of instruction to written vernacular materials. In the following months, well over a hundred articles on the subject appeared in Shanghai newspapers and journals alone. Lu Xun himself participated in these debates, publishing several essays of his own in which he argued against the reintroduction of Classical Chinese. His completion of *Menwai wentan* at the end of the summer of 1934 was undoubtedly stimulated by this vigorous pedagogical confrontation. It is not surprising that, still at the beginning of the twenty-first century, conservative activists in mainland China (with support from abroad) are pushing for the partial restitution of Classical Chinese and the gradual deemphasis of reading and writing vernacular.

8. An allusion to Aesop's fable on "The Bat and the Weasels," in which a bat successively escapes being eaten by two weasels by telling the one that it is a mouse and the other that it is a bird. Since Lu Xun was competent in both classical and vernacular writing styles, a few of his interlocutors must have been skeptical that he was a master of either.

9. Han Yu and Liu Zongyuan of the Tang dynasty; Ouyang Xiu, Su Xun, Su Shi (Dongpo), Su Zhe, Wang Anshi, and Zeng Gong of the Song dynasty were considered by later critics to be the best prose writers of their day.

10. The supposed mythical inventor of the Chinese script.

11. Lu Xun uses the Sanskrit word *dhūta.*

12. This immediately calls to mind the *quipu* of early Incan civilization. Lu Xun discusses the *quipu* in more detail in the next section.

13. The word Lu Xun uses here, *wū* (archaic pronunciation **mʸag*), is almost invariably translated as "shaman." However, judging from their duties described in the oracle-shell and bone inscriptions, they were not at all like typical Tungusic shamans. Rather, they clearly resembled ancient Iranian mages. Indeed, there is persuasive archaeological, paleographic, and linguistic evidence that the *wu* were actually magi (<Greek *mágos* < Old Persian *maguš;* cf. Avestan *moγu*). Later, however, roughly from the Warring States period on, *wū* loses its original Iranian signification and comes to be applied to individuals who were engaged in essentially shamanistic practices. See the following note.

14. By late Warring States times, the *wu* did evolve into religious practitioners much more akin to Tungusic shamans, of which communication with the gods and spirit travel were characteristic activities.

15. The word used here is *shi* (archaic pronunciation **srʸɔʔ* [indefinite final consonant or consonant cluster]), more accurately rendered as "scribe" in the earliest stages of the Chinese script. The sinograph used to write this word depicts a hand holding a drill for making marks in hard surfaces such as bone. It is more than a mere curiosity to note that the Indo-European etymological root of the English words "scribe" and "script" is **skrībh,* which means "cut / scratch / mark [a surface]."

16. From the *Book of Rites (Liji),* chapter "Ritual Implements" (Li qi).

17. From the *History of the Han (Hanshu),* "Table of Past and Contemporary Persons" (Gu jin ren biao).

18. Eight symbols which are each composed of various combinations of three solid lines or lines that are broken in the middle (☰, ☷, ☵, ☲, ☳, ☶, ☱, ☴) and represent the basic elements of natural philosophy. Two trigrams joined together make up a hexagram. There are sixty-four hexagrams, and their manipulation constitutes the fundamental system of divination in the *Book of Changes.*

19. By one common account, Fuxi was the mythical founder of Chinese civilization, having taught the Chinese people how to make nets, hunt and fish, and raise animals. He supposedly also established the institutions of marriage and created the eight trigrams.

20. The number 512 is eight times 64, so Lu Xun appears to be hypothesizing an even more complicated system of enneagrams (nine-line symbols).

21. Spelled "Quippus" by Lu Xun, this word is derived from Quechua *khipu,* which designates a device consisting of a cord with knotted strings of various colors attached to it that is used for recording events, keeping accounts, and so forth.

22. Located on Goulou Peak of Hengshan (one of the five sacred mountains of China) in Hunan Province, it was allegedly carved by Yu in commemoration of his controlling the flood. The inscription is composed of seventy-seven strange characters that are hard to decipher. The Tang poet Han Yu (768–824), in a poem entitled "Mt. Goulou," has the line "On the top of Mt. Goulou is [reported to be] the stele of divine Yu." Yet, in the same poem, the following line also occurs: "[Even though you] search in a thousand and ten thousand places, it's nowhere to be found." From this it is evident that the legend of the Goulou stele had already been concocted over a millennium before the time of Lu Xun. By the early part of the sixteenth century, scholars of rather dubious reputation had begun to write treatises "explaining" the inscription. Since there had been no previous mention of the existence of an inscription on Mt. Goulou consisting of seventy-seven characters, critical modern scholarship regards it as a notorious Ming forgery by Taoists.

23. The legendary first emperor of the semihistorical Xia dynasty, he was said to have quelled the flood that covered China.

24. In other words, around 1200 B.C.E.

25. Discovered in 1879, these caves hold some of the finest paleolithic art in the world.

26. Lu Xun uses the Chinese transcription *(modeng)* of the English word.

27. The call for "art for art's sake" began with the French author Théophile Gautier (1811–1872) and was taken up by other late-nineteenth-century European writers and critics.

28. Lu Xun is simplifying matters in many respects. First of all, pure pictography was already insufficient for expressing the limited range of topics covered in the oracle-bone and bronze inscriptions. Even in these earliest known stages of Chinese writing, scribes had to use ideographic, phonophoric, and other principles to be able to express themselves. Furthermore, beyond a very limited number of fairly obvious pictographs, it is difficult for those who are untutored in a given script to figure out the precise meanings of symbols that were originally designed as pictographs. For example, oracle-bone characters like those for "turtle" and "horse," which are among the most highly pictographic characters, are almost never correctly identified when shown to individuals who have not already studied the script intensively.

29. A scholar-official who was active around 253–258, he was said to have made up more than a thousand strange characters.

30. The only woman in Chinese history who set herself up as emperor and established her own dynasty, the Zhou, Wu Zetian (623/625–705) promulgated twelve (some accounts say nineteen) new characters (including one for her personal name [Zhao], one for the name of her dynasty [Zhou], and one for Heaven [Tian] in the year 690, when she assumed the throne. Her brief empire collapsed with her death in 705 and reverted to the Tang.

31. This work purports to be a detailed description of the administrative structure and governmental organization of the Zhou dynasty. It is traditionally dated to the Warring States period (475–221 B.C.E.), but it is not even mentioned by title before the year 90 B.C.E. and does not surface as a text until the Han interregnum of Wang Mang (45 B.C.E.–23 C.E.; r. 9–23 C.E.), who relied on it heavily in a vain attempt to shore up the dubious legitimacy of his Xin (New) dynasty.

32. Completed by Xu Shen (ca. 55–ca. 149 C.E.) in the year 100, this is the first systematic and comprehensive dictionary of Chinese characters. Although it was hugely influential from the time it was presented to the emperor in the year 121 C.E. until the twentieth century, modern scholarship has increasingly called into question its lexicographical principles and findings, which are based on late and severely limited data.

33. These are the so-called *liu shu* (six writings): *zhishi* (indicative [ideographs]), *xiangxing* (representational [pictographs]), *xingsheng* (semanto-syllabic [pictophonetic graphs]), *huiyi* (conjunct [etymonic graphs]), *zhuanzhu* (transferred [graphic-etymonic pairs]), and *jiajie* (borrowed [phonetic loans]).

34. This sentence is quoted from the *Book of Changes,* "Great Treatise" (Xi ci [da zhuan]), part II, section 2, where it occurs in a passage describing how Baoxi (i.e., Fuxi; see n. 19 above) devised the trigrams after contemplating the natural phenomena of Heaven and Earth.

35. Lu Xun is correct in stating that *fou* 缶 was originally composed of two components, but they were not a mortar and a pestle. Instead, the earliest forms of the graph show an earthen jar with the upper part as its lid and the lower part as its body. Characters with *fou* as their radical usually have something to do with earthenware. The character for *bao* potentially could be looked up by any of its four main components, which are all radicals, but is conventionally classified under the "roof" radical at the top.

36. The term *xiesheng* literally means "harmonious sound(s)," hence the English coinage "symphophonetic." Functionally, however, it is identical to the term already mentioned in note 33 for the most common means of character formation, namely *xingsheng* (pictophonetic). Whether called *xiesheng* or *xingsheng*, such graphs amount to approximately 85 percent of the total. This type of graph consists of a radical (the "picto-" part) which gives a hint at the meaning ("tree," "grass," "metal," "water," "hill," etc.) and a phonophore (the sound-bearing element) which provides an indication of the sound.

37. By this, Lu Xun means that *xiesheng/xingsheng* graphs do not attempt to portray the likeness of the thing specified. Rather, they convey an idea of the sound of the word indicated by the graph, together with a general suggestion of its meaning.

38. Except that *cài* meaning "vegetable" is pronounced in the fourth tone, with a following pitch, while *cǎi* meaning "pluck" is pronounced in the third tone, with a low, dipping pitch. The phonophoric portion of a graph may be even less precise than that in *cài* (vegetable). For example, depending upon the characters in which it occurs, the phonophore *jian* 兼 may be variously read as *jiǎn, jiàn, qiān, qiǎn, qiàn, xián, xiǎn, lián, liǎn, liàn, zhuàn, zuàn, qiè*, etc. This is obviously not a precisely rigorous system of phonetic notation.

39. This is another excellent example of how the phonophoric portion of pictophonetic characters often gives grossly inadequate information about how they should be pronounced. Depending upon the character in which it occurs, the phonophore *mei* 每 may be variously read as *méi, mèi, huǐ, huì, hǎi, mǐn, yù, fán*, etc. It should be pointed out that the last two items cited (*yù* and *fán*) may incorporate the *mei* phonophore for purely visual purposes and thus not be phonologically related to it. Furthermore, while the plethora of Mandarin pronunciations for characters having the *mei* and *jian* (see n. 38) phonophores is bewildering, there are historical reasons for the production of such disparate sounds. Two thousand years ago, all of the graphs existing at that time that incorporated the *mei* or *jian* phonophores would surely have sounded much more like each other than they do today. Unfortunately, a satisfactory reconstruction of the sounds of early Sinitic has still not been achieved, although scholars have been working assiduously for the last century to determine the sounds of the characters in ancient times.

40. Lu Xun is referring to the bottom right element of the graph, *mu* 母, which means "mother" when it stands alone. The earliest pictographic forms of the character depicted a woman kneeling down with her breasts exposed (the two dots of the modern graph are the vestigial nipples), the symbol of a mother who nurses her children. By extension, *mu* also indicates the older female generation or simply female.

41. The question mark is Lu Xun's. The earliest forms of the graph for *mei* (each, every) actually depict a kneeling woman with an elaborate ornament stuck in her hair.

42. Large- and small-seal characters (*dazhuan, xiaozhuan*) were the next main stages in the development of the Chinese script after oracle-bone and bronze inscriptional forms. They were current in the Spring and Autumn (770–476 B.C.E.) and Warring States (475–221 B.C.E.) periods respectively.

43. This stage in the development of the Chinese script, called *lishu* (also referred to as "official script" in English), took place roughly during the Han dynasty (206 B.C.E.–220 C.E.).

44. The last main stage in the development of the Chinese script, called *kaishu* (also referred to in English as "regular script" or "model script"), became popular from the latter part of the Han dynasty.

45. It is interesting to observe that, moving roughly from north to south China, the graph for *hua* (slippery) has the following pronunciations (the small circles indicate tones; the romanization here is that of the International Phonetic Alphabet [IPA], with *k* being pronounced as we normally pronounce "g" and the question mark without a dot signifying a glottal stop): ₒ*xua, xuaʔₒ, xuʋʔₒ, xuæʔₒ, ɦuaʔₒ, ɦoₒ, faₒ, uaₒ, uaˀ, uatₒ, vatₒ, watₒ, huatₒ, kutₒ, kukₒ, kouʔₒ, xuaₒ, koₒ*. From this data, it is evident that many of the southern topolects (which are more conservative than northern topolects) not only still pronounce *hua* (slippery) with an initial "g" sound, but that some of them still retain the final consonant that the etymological root for this word must originally have possessed.

46. The relationship between *hai* and *mei* is discussed in note 39 above.

47. The *Shujing* is a disparate collection of texts concerning the Shang and Zhou dynasties whose dates of composition vary widely, with the bulk probably coming from the late Warring States and Han periods.

48. Author of the *Records of the Grand Historian (Shiji;* see selections 28 and 29).

49. Also called Chen Sheng (d. 209 B.C.E.), Chen Shě was the leader of a peasant rebellion toward the end of the Qin dynasty.

50. In this sentence, the words for "Wow" and "splendacious" are highly colloquial terms that probably reflect the local language of the rebels. Only in extremely rare instances have such unpolished expressions survived the redactional processes of Chinese historiography and literature. Indeed, as Lu Xun points out, the rest of the sentence is in standard Literary Sinitic or Classical Chinese, revealing that the historian could not resist improving the language of his original sources after all.

51. The prince, Liu Zhang, was the younger brother of Emperor Wen (r. 180–157 B.C.E.). Accusing the prince of insurrection, the emperor banished him to the far southwest (Sichuan). The prince died of starvation en route to his place of banishment, causing the people to commemorate him with this song.

52. The *Hanshu,* by Ban Gu of the Eastern Han dynasty, is the official Chinese history of the Former or Western Han dynasty. It was begun by Ban Gu's father, Ban Biao, and finished up by his sister Ban Zhao and the scholar Ma Xu. The *Qian Hanji* was compiled by Xun Yue (148–209), also of the Eastern Han. The second version of the poem, however, does not actually occur in Xun Yue's work, but rather in the "Exegesis of the 'Great Exploits' of Huainan" (Huainan "Honglie" jiexi) by Gao You, yet another Eastern Han scholar. Perhaps because he was working from memory, Lu Xun makes a few other minor errors in quoting the two versions. As quoted in scroll 44 of the *History of the Han,* the first version lacks the word *neng* (can) in the last line. As quoted in scroll 118 of the *Records of the Grand Historian,* however, it appears exactly as quoted by Lu Xun. As recorded by Gao You, the first line of the second version originally had *zeng* (pongee [rough silk from wild silkworms]) instead of *bu* (cloth) and *haotongtong* (really nice) instead of *nuantongtong* (snuggly warm). And in the third line of this version, the word *neng* (can) occurs, just as in the third line of the poem in the *Records of the Grand Historian.*

53. The term used here, *yulu,* refers especially to the records of the words and deeds of Chan (Zen) masters. After the genre was well established by the Buddhists, it was taken up by certain Neo-Confucian scholars. The spoken portions of *yulu* can be highly vernacular. However, since they seem to reflect a koine, we cannot be sure that any of the *yulu* are accurate transcriptions of the topolectal speech patterns of individuals who, after all, hailed from various parts of China.

54. Lu Xun uses the word *huaben* (literally, "tale-root"), which is one of the most misunderstood terms in the study of Chinese literature. Although it is usually loosely interpreted as signifying "prompt-books" of the Song and Yuan periods, recent research has shown that the vast majority of *huaben* are literary creations of the Ming and Qing periods. While they are manifestly vernacular in nature, still less so than *yulu* do *huaben* faithfully preserve the spoken language of the Song and Yuan periods.

55. Translated literally as "miscellaneous drama," *zaju* constitutes the first formal theatrical tradition of China and was the most glorious and rich literary manifestation of the Yuan period (1279–1308).

56. The term *chuanqi* (literally, "transmission of the strange") normally signifies either Tang-period classical fiction or southern-style drama of the Ming and Qing periods. Since neither of these terms is appropriate in this case, Lu Xun must have been thinking of *nanxi* (southern plays), which do have their roots in the late-Song and Yuan periods and are considered to be the direct forerunners of Ming *chuanqi.*

57. Lu Xun writes *guwen* (old writing). This may also be referred to as Literary Sinitic.

58. Yang Xiong (53 B.C.E.–18 C.E.) was one of China's greatest early rhapsodists. However, in his moralistic old age, he rejected his entire output in the *fu* (rhyme-prose, rhapsody)—an important early literary genre—as being frivolous and trivial.

59. The son of the famous scholar, writer, and bibliophile of the Western Han Liu Xiang (79–8 B.C.E.), Liu Xin (ca. 50 B.C.E.–23 C.E.) was himself a distinguished scholar, statesman, astrologist, and bibliographer.

60. The complete title of the work is *Youxuanshi zhe juedai yu shi bie guo fang yan* (Obsolete Words Collected by Light Chariot Envoys with Glosses on the Regional Speech from Individual States [David Knechtges]; or Local Words of Different "Countries," Explained by the Language of Bygone Generations [as Collected] by the Imperial Messenger[s] [Who Traveled] in the Light Cart [Paul L-M. Serruys]). Scholars have been debating the authorship of this book for centuries, with some saying that it is impossible for Yang

Xiong to have written it and others saying that it was definitely compiled by him. Regardless of who the author was (most modern scholars believe that it actually was Yang Xiong's work), *Fang yan* is the first extant work dealing with the local languages of the Chinese empire, although there is good evidence that investigations of regional speech and writing habits were carried out before the Han dynasty in Zhou and Qin times. Indeed, the first words in the complete title of the book attributed to Yang Xiong refer to an old Zhou-dynasty office, the Royal Commissioner (Youxianshi), whose chief was periodically sent out from the capital to gather information about regional dialects and languages, local folk songs, and other aspects of culture in which the government was interested. It should also be noted that the term *fangyan,* as a bisyllabic word, has long (for at least a century) been misleadingly translated as "dialect." Since many Sinitic (i.e., "Chinese") *fangyan* are mutually unintelligible, linguistically it would be more precise to refer to them as separate languages. Some *fangyan,* however, are mutually intelligible variants of the same language. Therefore, to avoid confusion, scholars have recently begun to use the word "topolect" as a more neutral and accurate rendering of *fangyan,* which, in the most literal sense, means "speech [pattern characteristic of a] place." This is identical with the meaning of "topolect." The irony of all this is that the modern bisyllabic Mandarin term *fangyan* was probably created as an inaccurate calque for the English word "dialect." There is no indication that Chinese referred to local speech patterns as *fangyan* before the modern period. (Judging from the title and contents of *Fang yan,* which deals strictly with individual words [actually characters], this was certainly not what Yang Xiong meant by the collocation of *fang* and *yan,* although whoever calqued *fangyan* from "dialect" was obviously inspired by the title of the Han-period book.) Instead, if premodern Chinese referred to local speech patterns at all, it was as *xiang tan* (village chatting [the *tan* being the same graph as in the title of Lu Xun's work translated here]), with no idea whatsoever of their being related or linguistically classifiable in a hierarchical or cladistic scheme.

The *Fang yan* attributed to Yang Xiong contains over eleven thousand local terms culled from the length and breadth of the Han empire. Although it is a valuable collection of basic data for historical linguists, the compilers were seriously hampered by the lack of a convenient and reliable method for making phonetic transcriptions.

61. Yang Xiong attempted to commit suicide by leaping out of the upper story of a building when he was falsely implicated in a plot against the usurper, Wang Mang. This occurred in 10 C.E., three years after Yang Xiong is said to have finished his compilation of *Fang yan* (Liu Xin [see n. 59] actually did commit suicide for his anti–Wang Mang actions, which he felt compelled to engage in after the usurper had killed three of his sons.) Lu Xun uses the Shanghai expression "jump into the Whangpoo [River]" to indicate suicide. In a letter written in response to Liu Xin's request to see the manuscript of *Fang yan,* Yang Xiong replies that, for twenty-seven years, he had traveled widely with brush in hand taking notes on the local languages of the realm. Since, however, the manuscript was incomplete at the time Liu Xin requested it, Yang Xiong was not willing to let others see it. If someone forced him to turn it over, he would commit suicide instead. This, of course, seems like an extreme reaction to scholarly interest in one's work. However, aside from the fact that Yang Xiong was by nature high-strung, the reputation of Liu Xin and his father, Liu Xiang, who were notorious for "editing" the works of others and, in so doing, somehow making them their own, must have been a factor in Yang Xiong's response.

62. Fan, who died around the year 821, wrote refractory prose that many readers could make no sense of at all.

63. Li He (790–816) was a well-known Tang poet whose verse was so recherché and strange that it thoroughly bewildered even the most learned scholars.

64. Named after the Manchu Kangxi emperor (r. 1662–1722) of the Qing dynasty who sponsored its compilation, this dictionary contains 47,315 characters. A goodly portion of these characters is so obscure that either the sound or the meaning (or both the sound and the meaning) is unknown. Still another large group of characters in this dictionary are odd, little-used variants of more common graphs. The *Kangxi Dictionary* was the standard unabridged reference for Chinese characters up to the early part of the twentieth century, when lexicons with even greater numbers of bizarre and outmoded sinographs were compiled. It was not long before the barrier of 50,000 characters was broken, then 80,000, and after that 100,000 different forms were dredged up. Now there are online computer dictionaries with 120,000 different Chinese characters. It is, of course, a monumental problem to order such a multiplicity of discrete items made up of from one to sixty-four brush strokes that are of eight basic types. Xu Shen's *Shuo wen jie zi* (see n. 32), which had 9,353

graphs, divided them up into 540 "radicals" (classifying components). The *Kangxi Dictionary,* with a vastly larger number of graphs, reduced that figure to 214 (already employed by a lexicographer named Mei Yingzuo in the late Ming). Until recently, serious Sinologists were obliged to memorize the 214 radicals of the *Kangxi Dictionary.* Now, however, a mind-numbing plethora of other numbers of radicals and completely different ordering methods has been devised. None of these has won acceptance as a widely recognized standard means for looking up the characters, leaving Chinese lexicography and information processing in a chaotic state.

65. A philologist of the Qing period whose dates are 1744–1806.

66. The *Shiming* adopted the novel approach of employing homophones or near-homophones to explain words. The compiler's paronomastic (punning) glosses are fanciful, at times bordering on the absurd, but his dictionary is nonetheless valuable to modern researchers for the phonological information it contains. Liu Xi's dates are unknown, but *Shiming* was completed around the year 200 C.E.

67. By the time of Qian Dian, this obsolete form of the sinographs would have been readable only to a small handful of antiquarians, learned seal engravers, and specialists in the history of the Chinese script.

68. Around the time of the May Fourth Movement, the tumultuous period of cultural renaissance that erupted in 1919, Qian Xuantong (1887–1939) was among the more progressive thinkers who advocated thorough reform of the Chinese script and languages. Later, however, like many erstwhile enthusiasts for modernization and change, he adopted a far more conservative stance. It is undoubtedly for this reason that Lu Xun mentions him in this sentence, which is fairly saturated with multiple layers of irony.

69. Zhang Taiyan (1868–1936) was one of the most ardent intellectuals of the late-Qing period who were not only opposed to the ineffective Manchu government, but who rejected the entire Confucian ideology that served as the foundation of the imperial system. Like Qian Xuantong (see n. 68) and so many other youthful reformers, he became more backward-looking as he grew older.

70. "Xiaoxue wenda" literally means "Questions and Answers on Minor Learning." "Minor Learning" here signifies traditional (pre-Buddhist, pre-Western) script and language studies, in contrast to *daxue* (major learning), i.e., moral inculcation. (In modern times, under Japanese influence, *xiaoxue* has come to mean "primary school" and *daxue* now means "university.") Zhang Taiyan's "A Catechism of Minor Learning" explains words on the basis of *Shuo wen jie zi* (see nn. 32 and 64), China's first dictionary. Qian Xuantong was so impressed by Zhang Taiyan's work that he copied it out in the ancient small-seal script in which *Shuo wen jie zi* had originally been written.

71. This was also a hot topic right around the time Lu Xun wrote these chapters, with the major book publishers variously issuing *A Thousand Character Textbook for Commoners, A Thousand Character Textbook for the Masses, A Thousand Character Textbook for Citizens, A Thousand Character Textbook for Young and Old,* and so forth. Although a thousand characters cover approximately 90 percent of all occurrences in typical writing, this amount is grossly inadequate for full literacy. The result of reading at this level would be such that one would fail to recognize one out of every ten morphemes in a text, an unacceptably high degree of incomprehension. Lu Xun viewed Chinese educators who promoted such policies of instruction for the masses as elitist and condescending. In his opinion, they failed to confront fundamental flaws in the character writing system.

72. The earliest form of the graph used to write this word depicted a man with a tatoo on his chest. The basic idea that it conveyed was that of "ornament, pattern." Gradually, the word evolved to mean "refined," "culture," and "writing," its primitive signification being preserved only in such old expressions as *wen shen* (tattoo the body). It is supremely ironic that the most rarefied manifestation of Chinese civilization has its origins in the cultural practices belonging to the "barbarian" nomads of the north and northwest.

73. The Mandarin bisyllabic word *wenxue* means "literature," but the two graphs used to write this word signify "culture, refinement, writing, etc." and "learning." The enormous leap from *wen* plus *xue* to *wenxue* is explained in the following sentences and notes.

74. See selection 7. In this particular passage of the *Analects* (11.3), Confucius is praising two of his favorite disciples. The two syllables *wen* and *xue* are not joined because they have not yet fused into a single word. The exact meaning of *wen xue* in this passage of the *Analects* is contested, with translations running from "culture" (surely an imprecise rendering) to "literary acquirements" (a mystifying formulation in its own right) to "familiarity with old documents" (probably fairly close to what Confucius actually meant). Regardless of the bewildering range of interpretations for *wen xue* in this *Analects* passage, all scholars agree

that it does not mean "literature." In the centuries following Confucius, *wen xue* acquired the following different connotations: literati learning, scholarship, literary talent, formal documents, the name of a section in the educational system, instructor, and clerk (the last two terms being official titles). As late as *A New Account of Tales of the World (Shishuo xinyu)* by Liu Yiqing (403–444), where *wen xue* is used as a chapter heading ("Letters and Scholarship"), the two morphemes had not fused into a single concept. Their fusion and adoption to convey the notion of "literature" was still far in the future.

75. *Wenxue*, the characters for which are pronounced *bungaku* in Japanese, is one of many important new words that were coined in Japan to cope with Western ideas and things. Around the end of the nineteenth century and the beginning of the twentieth century, a flood of such loans and calques were borrowed into Chinese languages. Having himself been an overseas student in Japan, Lu Xun was well aware of China's indebtedness to Japan for such basic modern terms as those for "biology," "train," and "democracy." A special category of such borrowings were "round-trip words" that started out in China with one meaning, had a new meaning attached to them in Japan, and were then brought back to China with that new meaning displacing the earlier one. *Wenxue* was one of these words; others are those for "culture," "civilization," "grammar," "physics," "analysis," and "religion."

76. This is a reference to the well-known author and humorist Lin Yutang (1895–1976), who in late April and early May of 1934 had written a series of articles criticizing the primitiveness of the "literature of the masses" *(dazhong wenyi)*. He had specifically sneered at the shallowness of ancient work songs and chants such as "Heave-ho! Heave-ho!" In the following sentences, Lu Xun deliberately invokes what is perhaps the earliest icon of Chinese men of letters.

77. One of the Confucian classics (see selection 6).

78. One of the three main sections of the *Book of Odes*. The "Airs of the States" are generally considered to be based on folk songs that were collected in various regions of the Zhou empire. The other two main sections of the *Book of Odes* are the courtly "Elegantiae" (Ya) and the stately "Hymns" (Song [pronounced *soong*]).

79. The theory being that this would enable the rulers to gauge the sentiments of the people through their verse.

80. Homer (9th c. B.C.E.), author of the *Iliad* and the *Odyssey*, was an illiterate, blind bard.

81. "Ziye" was the eponymous creator of this genre of poetry. Her name means something like "Girl of the Night." The poems she created, and those of later poets modeled after them, were full of suggestive double entendres.

82. These songs were said to be spontaneous lamentations of the people for a dead prince. Like the "Midnight Songs," they were characteristic of the south.

83. I.e., the Six Dynasties period (317–589).

84. The "Zhuzhi ci" and the "Liuzhi ci" were mostly heptasyllabic poems by well-known Tang poets, such as Bo Juyi (772–846) and Liu Yuxi (772–842), who modeled their works on particular folk-song genres. These poems were used for both entertainment and education.

85. Realizing that the traditional educational system was unsuited to the twentieth century, the Qing government in 1901 abolished the rigidly formulaic "eight-legged essay" of the civil service examination system, established schools, and promoted popular education. In 1906, the authorities went further and compiled stories and songs written in the vernacular for use in teaching. The lines quoted here are from one of these songs.

86. Already in the early-Qing dynasty, with roots stretching back still further to the Yuan, there was an informal practice of writing out vernacular paraphrases of classical texts that could be read aloud to those who were illiterate in characters (see selection 67). Perhaps the best examples of this are the vernacular renderings of the "Sacred Edict" of the Kangxi emperor (r. 1662–1722) prepared by individual local magistrates to be read out to the citizens of their districts. The authorities were eager to communicate the wishes of the government to the people, but realized that Classical Chinese, even when read aloud, was completely unintelligible to them. Because these vernacular paraphrases were not considered proper literature, very few of them have survived. It was only at the beginning of the twentieth century that the Qing government began a small-scale, programmatic effort to make vernacular materials available from a central source.

87. An official, statesman, and educator of the late-Qing and early-Republican periods, Lao Naixuan (1843–1921) based his simplified writing system on that of Wang Zhao (see n. 88). Unlike Wang, however,

who emphasized Mandarin and whose efforts were restricted to the north, Lao (who was from Zhejiang) believed that it would be most efficient if learners first became literate in their own topolects, so he added some symbols that were especially meant for sounds in southern languages.

88. A late-Qing reformer from Hebei, Wang Zhao (1859–1933) had spent time in Japan and was inspired by the *kana* syllabaries to modify a small group of Chinese characters so that they could stand for initials (of which there were fifty) and finals (of which there were fifteen).

89. This meeting was convened in February and went on for more than a month because of differences of opinion between northerners and southerners about which sounds needed to be represented by the alphabet they were supposed to design. Lu Xun was himself a member of the committee, so he would have been intimately familiar with its workings. Eventually, the committee did come up with thirty-nine Letters for Annotating Sounds *(zhuyin zimu),* which they used to specify the standard pronunciation of more than 6,500 characters. The "alphabet" (based on radically simplified characters) and the standard pronunciations were promulgated in 1918. *Zhuyin zimu* were renamed *zhuyin fuhao* (Symbols for Annotating Sounds) in 1930, because it was realized that they were not really letters of an alphabet, but were actually more like a syllabary that could also be used to indicate initials, medials, and finals. *Zhuyin fuhao* are now known informally as *Bo po mo fo* after the first four symbols of the set.

90. The Chairman of the Committee to Unify Reading Pronunciations (Duyin tongyi hui) was Wu Zhihui (1866–1953); and the Vice-Chairman was Wang Zhao (see n. 88). Wu Zhihui was born in Jiangsu, spent significant amounts of time in Shanghai, and was a close associate of Cai Yuanpei (1868–1940), the great scholar and educator who hailed from Zhejiang. Thus Wu Zhihui was unmistakably southern in his orientation.

91. The entering tones are final consonants *(-p, -t, -k)* that were present in Middle Sinitic. Although the entering tones have been lost in most modern northern Sinitic languages, they are still preserved in most Sinitic languages south of the Yangtze.

92. See note 89. "Tetragraphs" is a translation of *fangkuaizi,* which literally means "square[-shaped] graphs," a designation that derives from the fact that all characters, no matter how many strokes they have, must fit into the same size square space. Another common term for the characters is *hanzi,* which may be literally rendered as "sinograph."

93. The *kana* constitute a true syllabary that comes in three forms: angular *katakana* for onomatopoeia and transcription of foreign words, rounded *hiragana* for grammatical components and for spelling words, and *furigana* (both angular and rounded) when attached to Chinese characters to indicate their sounds.

94. Following the rules of the system itself, this was called *Gwoyeu Romatzyh,* or GR for short. GR was adopted by the Nationalist government in 1928 as its second official system for indicating the sounds of characters. The most obvious distinguishing feature of GR is that, instead of using numbers or diacritical marks to indicate the four tones, it employs various combinations of letters.

95. Known as Y. R. Chao in the West, Zhao (1892–1982) was the principal designer of this system. Although GR is considered by many linguists to be elegant and sophisticated, Lu Xun criticized it several times as being excessively complicated and difficult to learn.

96. Kemal Ataturk, the great Turkish leader, promoted the switch from the Arabic script (poorly suited for Turkic languages) to the Roman alphabet. The new policy went into effect on January 1, 1929.

97. The *Meiri guoji wenxuan* was a series inaugurated in Shanghai on August 1, 1933. The pamphlet in question was number 12 in the series. It appeared on August 12, 1933.

98. This was a journal put out by advocates of Esperanto in Shanghai.

99. This refers to the two hundred thousand Chinese workers living in the Soviet Union at the time Lu Xun was writing.

100. Lu Xun uses the term *lianhua* (literally, "refined talk") from his own district of Shaoxing. This is a good example of the many topolecticisms that have enriched the national, standard language of Mandarin.

101. At present, "Putonghua" refers to Standard Mandarin as spoken in mainland China, "Guoyu" to Standard Mandarin as spoken on Taiwan, and "Huayu" to Standard Mandarin as spoken in Hong Kong and Singapore. While there are slight differences of pronunciation, tone, and vocabulary among them, they are all basically the same language. (The differences in writing—simplified/reformed versus complicated/traditional characters—are much greater than are the differences in the standard language.) At the time Lu Xun was writing, *putonghua* simply meant "common speech" and had not yet become fixed as the official designation of the standard national language of the People's Republic of China (which didn't exist then).

In Lu Xun's day, "Guoyu" was the official designation of the standard national language of the Republic of China. When Chiang Kai-shek and the Nationalist Party government were defeated by the Communists under Mao Zedong and went to Taiwan, they took the name "Guoyu," together with the Standard Mandarin language it signified, and imposed them on the Southern Min speakers and aborigines on the island whose languages were very different. During the 1950s through 1970s, the National Language Movement (Guoyu yundong) on Taiwan was strict, thorough, and successful, but with democratization under Chiang Ching-kuo (Chiang Kai-shek's son and successor as President of the Republic of China on Taiwan), Taiwanese, Hakka, and the other non-Mandarin languages of Taiwan have increasingly been reasserting their place in government, business, literature, and education.

102. The term used here is *dazhongyu,* which is often translated as "common language," a rendering that leaves it open to confusion with *putonghua* (see n. 101).

103. The proponents of the quintessence of Chinese culture *(guocui)* were archconservative diehards opposed to reform and modernization.

104. Such sentiments concerning the "language of the masses" (*dazhongyu;* see n. 102) were frequently uttered during the mid-1930s. For example, in the July 7, 1934, issue (no. 21) of Human Words *(Ren yan)* weekly, Zhang Kebiao wrote, "Literature in the language of the masses will only be true literature of the language of the masses when it is created by the masses themselves."

105. Song Yang is a pseudonym of the Communist writer Qu Qiubai (1899–1935), who succeeded Chen Duxiu (1879–1946) as General Secretary of the Chinese Communist Party. This sentence is quoted from an article by the anti-Communist, pro-Confucian Li Yansheng entitled "From Literature in the Language of the Masses to Literature in the National Language," which appeared in the August 1, 1934, issue of *Shenbao.* In this article, Li—who was an ardent supporter of the Chinese characters and Classical Chinese—alleged that the movement for literature written in the language of the masses was Communist inspired.

106. I.e., Communist.

107. Wuchang (Skt. Anitya).

108. Sanskrit Maudgalyāyana, the name of a most filial son who goes down to hell to rescue his mother, a theme about which there have been enormously popular stories and dramas from the Tang period to the present. Lu Xun wrote about Mulian dramas in a couple of his essays.

109. A collection of Lu Xun's essays first published in 1928.

110. King of Hell.

111. To "go down the mountain" means to leave a monastery or cloisters and return to secular life. The episode about the young nun leaving behind her religious life was a favorite that was often performed separately.

112. A Ming-period drama written by Zheng Zhizhen of Xin'an in Anhui Province, who explains that he drew on folk plays to compose it.

113. This is a famous episode from the Ming novel *Water Margin (Shuihu zhuan),* in which the drunken hero beats a formidable tiger to death with his bare hands after smashing his club to smithereens on a rock. The fact that it is totally unrelated to the Mulian story did not deter the peasants who put on folk plays about the latter from inserting it into their performances.

114. Although Aesop was said to have lived in the sixth century B.C.E., the celebrated collection of over three hundred fables that was edited by later persons and survives to this day contains many elements from Indian and Arabian sources.

115. F. Sologub (1863–1927) was a poet and author of fiction who also wrote fables, ten of which Lu Xun translated and published.

116. This is the advice given to a king in the "Biography of Fan Ju," *Records of the Grand Historian,* by Sima Qian (see n. 48 and selections 28 and 29), the strategy being to ally oneself with distant kingdoms but to attack one's neighbors. The analogy employed here is to praise the language of the masses, which was still far off, but to attack the written vernacular, which had already been current since the time of the May Fourth Movement (1919). This was the position of individuals such as Wang Maozu (see n. 7), who, in the mid-1930s, espoused Classical Chinese, while claiming that they were not opposed to the language of the masses.

117. All of the views reflected in this and the following paragraph were expressed in articles and books published in Shanghai during the period from June through August of 1934.

118. See note 103.

119. Awkwardly based on Greek and Latin paradigms, this is the first grammar of Classical Chinese and the first systematic grammar of any Sinitic language written by a Chinese. (European scholars had been writing grammars of vernacular and classical Sintic languages for a couple of centuries by the time *Mr. Ma's Grammar* appeared in 1898.) Its author, Ma Jianzhong (1844–1900), was educated in Catholic schools in China and in Paris. He became a member of the diplomatic corps with particular expertise as a translator.

120. A classically oriented dictionary of approximately seventy thousand entries compiled by the Commercial Press of Shanghai (who also published *Mr. Ma's Grammar* and many other important linguistic and literary works at the very end of the nineteenth century and during the first half of the twentieth century). First published in 1915, *Ciyuan* has since been reissued in numerous different editions.

XU BING WAS BORN in Chongqing (Sichuan) in 1955, although his ancestral roots lie in Wenling (Zhejiang). After graduating from upper middle school in 1973, Xu Bing was sent down to the countryside for reeducation the following year. He shared a house with four other students in Huapen Commune, a village consisting of thirty-nine peasant families who worked their poor land in Yanqing District northwest of Beijing (Peking). Aside from carrying out his mandatory farming duties, Xu Bing found time to help edit and produce a newsletter entitled (after a line of Chairman Mao's verse) "Brightly Colored Mountain Flowers in Full Bloom" (Lanman shanhua). Already in his graphics for this newsletter, as well as in his exquisitely written and illustrated chalkboard announcements, Xu Bing's exceptional talent was evident. With the end of the Cultural Revolution in 1976, it became possible for him to return to Beijing. In 1977, Xu Bing was admitted to the Central Academy of Fine Arts. After graduating in 1981, he stayed on to teach and continue his studies at the academy; he received his Master of Arts in 1987.

Following a lengthy period of preparation, Xu Bing's monumentally iconoclastic installation exhibition, *Book from the Sky (Tianshu),* opened at the China Art Gallery (Beijing) in 1988. The combination of the severe criticism to which Xu Bing was subjected for this work and the generally repressive climate that ensued upon the massacres in and around Tiananmen Square on June 4, 1989, compelled him to emigrate to the United States in 1990. Since moving to New York, his artistic creativity has flourished.

Xu Bing is one of the foremost Chinese artists working today. His formidable international reputation, however, is based not on painting or sculpture, but rather on graphic arts. Xu Bing is particularly noted for the bold and daring transformations that he works upon the Chinese characters. He has now gone far beyond the utterly impenetrable *Book from the Sky* that is so perfectly familiar and thoroughly redolent of tradition for Chinese viewers. Among his recent experiments have been the exhibition of copulating pigs whose skin is covered with inscrutable alphabetic and character writing, English words written in the shape of Chinese characters, and Chinese characters morphing into alphabetic form and even taking flight as winged fowl.

Xu Bing continues to probe the relationship between language and writing. Living in the cosmopolis of New York City, he has ample subject matter to stimulate his interest and broaden his vision. While it is impossible to predict what his next experiments will be, it is likely that his preoccupation with the cultural conditioning of script will remain a vital concern. In the essay below, the artist expresses verbally what his art demonstrates graphically.—ALH, VHM

Many strange dialogues are recorded in the annals of Chan (Zen) Buddhism. In the *Collected Works of Buddhism* is the question, "What is Buddha?" The master responds, "The neigh of a wooden horse." How could the Buddha be the neigh of a wooden horse? A student might ponder this all day without arriving at a conclusion, yet perhaps the day will come when he "suddenly bumps upon the proper road and realizes what has been clouding his vision." Such "sudden realization" in Chan Buddhism is called Enlightenment. This Chan method of revelation can lead you to understand the errors in your thinking and everyday logic. The real origins of truth cannot be found in a literal, logical answer but instead must be "searched for in the living word."

Buddhists believe that "if you look for harmony in the living word, then you will be able to reach Buddha; if you look for harmony in lifeless sentences, you will be unable to save yourself." The complicated lives and cultural experiences of my generation of mainland Chinese have verged on the absurd. Society has constantly presented us with extraordinary difficulties. We have to face them and find effective responses. My work and my method of thinking have been my "search for the living word," my response to the realities of the past and my own cultural experiences.

Our lives and cultural background are a jumbled knot of socialism, the Cultural Revolution, the Reform Period, Westernization, modernization—all these complexities are reflected quite naturally in my work. For example, when I began using so-called modern language in my work, people noted a strong element of traditional culture and "bookishness." Even when I had completed some extremely experimental works with living animals, the same classic sensibility pervaded.

From where does this bookishness come? In reality, members of my generation were never truly educated in orthodox Chinese culture. Much of what we learned was remolded by Mao Zedong (1893–1976). Mao hoped to create a new culture that dispensed with the old but at the same time was not Western. This sort of change formed an extremely important part of our cultural background. It influenced our modes of thinking and even speaking. The mainland China of the past was closed, but it was not traditional. This is a particularly interesting reality, and we must decide how to confront it.

Mao's transformation of culture was meant to "touch people to their very souls." Most deeply rooted was his transformation of language, because the Chinese language directly influences the methods of thinking and understanding of all Chinese people. To strike at the written word is to strike at the very essence of the culture. Any doctoring of the written word becomes in itself a transformation of the most inherent portion of a person's thinking. My experience with the written word has allowed me to understand this.

When each member of the Chinese cultural community first begins his or her education, he or she must spend years memorizing thousands of characters. This process is a sort of ceremony in homage to the culture, and it leaves all Chinese with an extreme sense of respect for the "written word." My generation, however, was irreparably affected by the campaign to simplify characters. This remolding of my earliest memories—the promulgation of new character after new character, the abandonment of old characters that I had already mastered, the transformation of new characters and their eventual demise, the revival of old characters—shadowed my earliest education and left me confused about the fundamental conceptions of culture.

In my own personal experience, this feeling of a culture being turned upside down was particularly pronounced. My parents worked on a university campus—my father was in the department of history and my mother worked in the department of library sciences—and I became familiar with all sorts of books at a very early age. But books seemed strange to me then because I could not read them—I was too young. And when I finally *could* read them, I was not *allowed* to read them. These were the years when we could no longer read whatever we chose. We read Mao's "Little Red Book." After the Cultural Revolution, I returned to the libraries to read or skim book after book. Before long, China began to experience a "cultural warming." I read so much and participated in so many conversations on culture that my mind was in a constant state of chaos. My psyche had been clogged with all sorts of random things. I felt as if I had lost something. I felt the discomfort of a person suffering from starvation who had just gorged himself. It was at that point that I considered creating a book of my own that might mirror my feelings (the *Book from the Sky*). And then, already past thirty-five, I moved to the United States and began learning yet another way of speaking and writing. Traces of the conflict that arose between my actual level of knowledge and my ability to express that knowledge can be found in my later works.

Throughout my life, I have always felt that I am incapable of entering culture, and at the same time I am unable to escape it. I have been around lots of books, but I never once read one closely. I am not a cultured person, but I know my fair share of words. When I was young, my father required that I write a page of characters each day. In the beginning, I would trace red characters in books like the *Square Word Calligraphy Red Line Tracing Book* that I use in *Classroom Calligraphy*. Later I would practice copying calligraphy with rubbings from famous classical stelae as my models. A calligrapher must sit up straight and show great concentration. Eventually this became both a habit and an interest of mine. Even when I was sent to work on a production team in the countryside, I continued to practice calligraphy from time to time. This was an unusual practice during that period. In the Asian world of letters there is a thing called *tongzi gong,* or precocious skill. It might be said that I had such a skill, yet in my mind I have never truly created calligraphy, because my earliest experience with the brush—the tracing of red characters and the copying of classical stelae—was not calligraphy: it was simply writing characters. To be precise, it was a method of cultural conditioning and a rite of cultural passage. I never thought of it as art.

This skill of mine came of use during the Cultural Revolution. I found that an element of traditional culture could be used to revolutionize one's fate, somewhat like my later works. At the time there was a saying: "Use your pen as your weapon and shoot down revolutionary gangs." My father was a reactionary. No one spoke of "tradition" during the Cultural Revolution; instead we spoke of "blood relationships." I was labeled "the bastard son of a reactionary father." My family background was polluted, but I could write well, so I was grudgingly allowed to become a useful person, a "writing tool." To be honest, I am very resourceful, but at that time all I could manage to do was what I do well in order to rid myself of my blemished family history. I sat in the Propaganda Office for hour upon hour, writing and painting. Big-character posters and leaflets made of tightly written small characters, they were all as carefully and neatly done as professionally printed words. Even the largest slogan posters were perfect on my first try. Each character was standard and forceful. I could write them quickly and extremely well. I have written so much, and now as I think back, it seems as if I was then like the Buddhist copiers of old. They did not need to understand the meaning of each sutra that they copied. They had only to copy and recopy a lifetime's worth of sutras to gain entrance into the next world.

I say that preparing all those posters was like copying sutras because, although it was very difficult work, I was very willing to do it. Dedication to a particular action is part of my personality. I research new fonts that appear in newspapers, and I pay attention to new forms of writing. For example, one can turn the character *qi* in the name of one of China's famed leaders, Liu Shaoqi (1898–1969), on its side to become *gou,* or "dog," but the character is still read as *qi.* In writing the compound character *zhong,* meaning loyal, you can combine in one character the ancient and modern forms of the Chinese language. The lower half of *zhong* is the heart radical, which can be written in pictographic form so that it resembles an actual heart. The *zhong* radical, written in its modern form, acts as the phoneme. Ancient and modern aspects of the Chinese language can thus be fused to create signs of interesting and provocative form and meaning. Pasting such creatively written characters all over a room's four walls results in the equivalent of a modern installation. Chinese people did this type of creative linguistic manipulation—writing *dog* in Liu Shaoqi's name to declare hatred of him or emphasizing the heart shape in the character *zhong* to express dedication to Chairman Mao—to show their extreme emotions during turbulent times.

Later I was sent to the countryside as part of Mao's rustication program. In an impoverished, remote village, I became a "scholar." Besides writing posters and printing newspapers, I became expert at making decorative banners for weddings, funerals, and holidays. At the New Year, the villagers requested that I combine the four characters in the phrase *huang jin wan liang* (ten thousand catties of gold) to form a single character. They also asked me to write *zhao cai jin bao* (bringing in wealth and riches) as a single character. When someone died, I was asked to string together a series of strange characters to form what looked like a stream in the nether world. The uniqueness of Chinese characters has encouraged a tradition of "playing upon words" since time immemorial. That village was quite remote, so it still maintained many of the old customs.

Rarely in the turbulent, ever-changing reality of modern Chinese society can a person read with dedication. Those who truly understand the meaning of reading will know how to "read" into the rich text that is Chinese society. This tremendous "volume" is as difficult to interpret as the famous Chan texts. You must be able to find your way through the emptiness and locate meaning in the midst of chaos. You must use Chan methods to gain understanding.

Years ago when I carved the *Book from the Sky,* friends said that there was something wrong with me. They had become accustomed to a deviant society, but they were not used to employing atypical methods to respond to that society. Now that I have written these words that both are and are not English words (Square Word Calligraphy), friends say that the feeling is right. I think my friends understand me. Their response tells me that not only does this method suit me from a technical perspective, but also, more important, these characters hint at something that is very much like me and my state of mind.

I love using the written word to create works of art. My creations are words and yet simultaneously are not words. They look familiar, but you cannot name them. They have been disguised to look different internally and externally.

These masked "words," like computer viruses, have a purpose in the human mind. In the space between understanding and misunderstanding, as concepts are flipped, customary modes of thought are thrown into confusion, creating obstacles to connections and expression. It is by opening up these unopened spaces that we may revisit the origins of thought and comprehension.

Art has value because it is genuine, not false. If you create art, the material "you" will mercilessly reveal you in all your complexity. Perhaps in life you can hide, but in art it is impossible. Regardless of whether you hope to hide or to flaunt an idea, it will all be recorded. That which belongs to you is yours. You may wish to get rid of it, but you cannot. Then there are those things that do not belong to you and, regardless of your effort, will never belong to you. All of this is decided by fate. This might sound fatalistic, but it is what I have experienced. In reality, this "fate" is what you experience: it is your cultural background and your life. It determines the inclination and style of your art. Your background is not of your own choosing; this is especially true for mainland Chinese artists. As far as I am concerned, artistic style and taste are not man-made; they are heaven-sent.

—ALH, VHM

The bibliography on China is enormous and growing exponentially. It would obviously be impossible to provide complete coverage of even one aspect of Chinese studies. Rather, the works included here are meant to be representative of the vast amount of published information that is available on China. It is also hoped that the books and articles mentioned here may prove useful for those who wish to follow up on the selections or who have been asked to write a paper on a related topic. In keeping with the aims of the *Hawai'i Reader on Traditional Chinese Culture* (see Introduction), this list of suggested readings is divided into a number of subject areas. The categories of this list are arranged as follows:

General	Ethnography and Folklore	Neighboring Peoples
Archaeology	Gender and Sex	Science and Technology
Art and Architecture	History and Statecraft	(including Medicine)
Biography	Languages and Scripts	Society and Customs
Commerce	Law	Taiwan
Culinary Arts	Literature	Thought (including Military Arts
Daily Life	Music and Opera	and Strategy) and Classics
Education and Literacy	Myth and Religion	

GENERAL

Blunden, Caroline, and Mark Elvin. *Cultural Atlas of China*. New York: Facts on File, 1983; rev. 1998.

Dillon, Michael, ed. *China: A Cultural and Historical Dictionary*. Durham East Asia Series. Richmond, Surrey: Curzon, 1998.

Herrmann, Albert. *An Historical Atlas of China*. Chicago: Aldine, 1966.

Loewe, Michael, ed. *Early Chinese Texts: A Bibliographical Guide*. Early China Special Monograph Series, 2. Berkeley: Society for the Study of Early China and Institute of East Asian Studies, University of California, 1993.

O'Neill, Hugh B. *Companion to Chinese History*. New York: Facts on File, 1987.

Perkins, Dorothy. *Encyclopedia of China: The Essential Reference to China, Its History and Culture*. Chicago: Fitzroy Dearborn, 1999.

Tregear, T. R. *China: A Geographic Survey*. London: Hodder and Stoughton, 1980.

Wilkinson, Endymion. *Chinese History: A Manual*. Harvard-Yenching Institute Monograph Series, 46, 52. Cambridge, Mass.: Harvard University Asia Center, 1998; rev. and enlgd., 2000.

Zurndorfer, Harriet T. *China Bibliography: A Research Guide to Reference Works about China Past and Present*. Leiden: E. J. Brill, 1995; Honolulu: University of Hawai'i Press, 1999.

ARCHAEOLOGY

Barnes, Gina L. *China, Korea, and Japan: The Rise of Civilization in East Asia*. London: Thames and Hudson, 1993.

Chang, Kwang-chih. *The Archaeology of Ancient China*. New Haven, Conn.: Yale University Press, 1986, 4th ed., rev. and enlgd.

———. *Shang Civilization*. New Haven, Conn.: Yale University Press, 1980.

Keightley, David N., ed. *The Origins of Chinese Civilization*. Berkeley and Los Angeles: University of California Press, 1983.

Li, Chi. *The Beginnings of Chinese Civilization*. Seattle: University of Washington Press, 1957.

————. *The Formation of the Chinese People: An Anthropological Study.* Cambridge, Mass.: Harvard University Press, 1928.

Shaughnessy, Edward, L., ed. *New Sources of Early Chinese History: An Introduction to the Reading of Inscriptions and Manuscripts.* Early China Special Monograph Series, 3. Berkeley: Society for the Study of Early China and Institute of East Asian Studies, University of California, 1997.

————. *Sources of Western Zhou History: Inscribed Bronze Vessels.* Berkeley and Los Angeles: University of California Press, 1991.

ART AND ARCHITECTURE

Akiyama Terukazu and Matsubara Saburo. *The Arts of China.* Vol. 2: *Buddhist Cave Temples.* Tokyo and Palo Alto, Calif.: Kodansha International, 1969.

Barnhart, Richard, et al. *Three Thousand Years of Chinese Painting.* New Haven, Conn.: Yale University Press, 1997.

Bush, Susan. *The Chinese Literati Painters.* Cambridge, Mass.: Harvard University Press, 1971.

————, and Hsio-yen Shih, eds. *Early Chinese Texts on Painting.* Cambridge, Mass., and London: Harvard University Press, 1985.

Chen, Shih-hsiang. *Biography of Ku K'ai-chih.* Berkeley and Los Angeles: University of California Press, 1953.

Davidson, J. LeRoy. *The Lotus Sutra in Chinese Art.* New Haven, Conn.: Yale University Press, 1954.

Dunhuang Institute of Cultural Relics. *The Art Treasures of Dunhuang.* Hong Kong: Joint Publishing, 1981.

Hsu, Cho-yun, and Katheryn M. Linduff. *Western Chou Civilization.* Early Chinese Civilization Series. New Haven, Conn., and London: Yale University Press, 1988.

Li, Xueqin. *Eastern Zhou and Qin Civilizations.* Tr. K. C. Chang. Early Chinese Civilization Series. New Haven, Conn., and London: Yale University Press, 1985.

Li, Zehou. *The Path of Beauty: A Study of Chinese Aesthetics.* Tr. Gong Lizeng. Oxford: Oxford University Press, 1994.

Liang, Ssu-ch'eng, and Wilma Fairbank, eds. *A Pictorial History of Chinese Architecture.* Cambridge, Mass.: MIT Press, 1984.

Rawson, Jessica, ed. *Mysteries of Ancient China: New Discoveries from the Early Dynasties.* London: British Museum Press; New York: George Braziller, 1996.

Shaughnessy, Edward L. *Sources of Western Zhou History: Inscribed Bronze Vessels.* Berkeley and Los Angeles: University of California Press, 1991.

Sickman, Laurence, and Alexander Soper. *The Art and Architecture of China.* Baltimore, Md.: Penguin, 1956.

Steinhardt, Nancy S. *Chinese Imperial City Planning.* Honolulu: University of Hawai'i Press, 1990.

————. *Chinese Traditional Architecture.* New York: China Institute in America, 1984.

————, et al. *Four Thousand Years of Chinese Architecture.* New Haven, Conn.: Yale University Press, 2002.

Sullivan, Michael. *The Arts of China.* Berkeley and Los Angeles: University of California Press, 1999.

Sze, Mai-mai. *The Way of Chinese Painting.* New York: Vintage, 1959.

Thorp, Robert L., and Richard E. Vinograd. *Chinese Art and Culture.* New York: Harry N. Abrams, 2001.

Wheatley, Paul. *The Pivot of the Four Quarters: A Preliminary Enquiry into the Origin and Character of the Ancient Chinese City.* Chicago: Aldine, 1971.

Wu, Hung. *Monumentality in Early Chinese Art and Architecture.* Stanford, Calif.: Stanford University Press, 1995.

Yang, Xiaoneng, ed. *The Golden Age of Chinese Archaeology.* Washington, D.C.: National Gallery, 1999.

Yee, Chiang. *Chinese Calligraphy.* London: Methuen, 1955.

BIOGRAPHY

Boorman, Howard L., ed. *Biographical Dictionary of Republican China.* New York: Columbia University Press, 1967–1971.

Franke, Herbert, ed. *Sung Biographies.* 4 vols. Wiesbaden: F. Steiner, 1976.

Giles, Herbert A., comp. *A Chinese Biographical Dictionary.* Shanghai (?): Kelly and Walsh, 1898, various rpts.

Goodrich, L. C., and Chaoying Fang, eds. 2 vols. *Dictionary of Ming Biography: 1368–1644.* New York: Columbia University Press, 1976.

Hummel, Arthur W., ed. *Eminent Chinese of the Ch'ing Period*. Washington, D.C.: Government Printing Office, 1943.

Loewe, Michael. *A Biographical Dictionary of the Qin, Former Han, and Xin Dynasties Periods, 221 B.C.–A.D. 24*. Leiden: Brill, 2000.

de Rachewiltz, Igor; Hok-lam Chan; Hsiao Ch'i-ch'ing; and Peter W. Grier, eds. *In the Service of the Khan: Eminent Personalities of the Early Mongol Yuan Period (1200–1300)*. Wiesbaden: Harrassowitz, 1993.

Wu, Pei-yi. *The Confucian's Progress: Autobiographical Writings in Traditional China*. Princeton, N.J.: Princeton University Press, 1990.

COMMERCE

Clark, Hugh R. *Community, Trade, and Networks: Southern Fujian Province from the Third to the Thirteenth Century*. Cambridge: Cambridge University Press, 1993.

von Glahn, Richard. *Fountain of Fortune: Money and Monetary Policy in China, Tenth to Seventeenth Centuries*. Berkeley and Los Angeles: University of California Press, 1996.

Peng, Xinwei. *A Monetary History of China*. Tr. Edward H. Kaplan. 2 vols. Bellingham: Western Washington University Press, 1994.

Yang, Lien-sheng. *Money and Credit in China: A Short History*. Cambridge, Mass.: Harvard University Press, 1952.

Yü, Ying-shih. *Trade and Expansion in Han China: A Study in the Structure of Sino-Barbarian Economic Relations*. Berkeley and Los Angeles: University of California Press, 1967.

CULINARY ARTS

Anderson, E[ugene] N. *The Food of China*. New Haven, Conn.: Yale University Press, 1988.

Buell, Paul D., and Eugene N. Anderson. *A Soup for the Qan: Chinese Dietary Medicine of the Mongol Era as Seen in Hu Szu-hui's* Yin-shan cheng-yao. Appendix by Charles Perry. London and New York: Kegan Paul International, 2000.

Chang, K. C., ed. *Food in Chinese Culture: Anthropological and Historical Perspectives*. New Haven, Conn.: Yale University Press, 1977.

Chung, Henry. *Hunan Style Chinese Cookbook*. New York: Harmony, 1978.

Gwinner, Thomas. 1988. *Essen und Trinken: Die Klassische Kochbuchliteratur Chinas*. Frankfurt am Main: Haag unter Herchen. Heidelberger Schriften zur Ostasienkunde, Band 11.

Ho, Kenneth. *The World of Food: China*. New York: Crowell, 1973.

Lee, Calvin B. T., and Audrey Evans Lee. *The Gourmet Chinese Regional Cookbook*. New York: G. P. Putnam's Sons, 1976.

Lo, Kenneth H. C. *Peking Cooking*. London: Faber and Faber, 1971.

McCawley, James D. *The Eater's Guide to Chinese Characters*. Chicago: University of Chicago Press, 1984.

Sabban, Françoise. "Cuisine à la coeur de l'Empereur de Chine au XIVe siècle." *Médiévales* 5 (1983): 32–56.

Simoons, Frederick. *Food in China*. Boca Raton, Fla.: CRC, 1991.

DAILY LIFE

Benn, Charles. *Daily Life in Traditional China: The Tang Dynasty*. Westport, Conn.: Greenwood, 2002.

Gernet, Jacques. *Daily Life in China on the Eve of the Mongol Invasion, 1250–1267*. Tr. H. M. Wright. Stanford, Calif.: Stanford University Press, 1970; French original, 1959.

Loewe, Michael. *Everyday Life in Early Imperial China*. New York: Putnam, 1968.

EDUCATION AND LITERACY

Chaffee, John W. *The Thorny Gates of Learning in Sung China: A Social History of Examinations*. Cambridge: Cambridge University Press, 1985.

———, and Wm. T. deBary, eds. *Neo-Confucian Education: The Formative Stage*. Berkeley and Los Angeles: University of California Press, 1989.

Connery, Christopher Leigh. *The Empire of the Text: Writing and Authority in Early Imperial China*. Lanham, Md.; Boulder, Colo.; New York; Oxford: Rowman and Littlefield, 1998.

Elman, Benjamin, and Alexander Woodside, eds. *Education and Society in Late Imperial China, 1600–1900*. Berkeley and Los Angeles: University of California Press, 1994.

Kracke, E. A., Jr. *Civil Service in Early Sung China, 960–1067*. Cambridge, Mass.: Harvard University Press, 1953.

Lee, Thomas H. C. *Education in Traditional China: A History*. Leiden, The Netherlands; and Boston, Mass.: Brill, 2000.

Lewis, Mark Edward. *Writing and Authority in Early China*. Albany: State University of New York Press, 1999.

Meskill, John Thomas. *Academies in Ming China: A Historical Essay*. Tucson: University of Arizona Press, 1982.

Rawski, Evelyn Sakakida. *Education and Popular Literacy in Ch'ing China*. Ann Arbor: University of Michigan Press, 1979.

ETHNOGRAPHY AND FOLKLORE

Bodde, Derk. *Festivals in Classical China: New Year and Other Annual Observances during the Han Dynasty, 206 B.C.–A.D. 220*. Princeton, N.J.: Princeton University Press, 1975.

Eberhard, Wolfram. *China's Minorities: Yesterday and Today*. Belmont, Calif.: Wadsworth, 1982.

———. *Chinese Festivals*. New York: Henry Schuman, 1952.

———, ed. *Studies in Chinese Folklore and Related Essays*. Bloomington: Indiana University Press, 1970.

Hostetler, Laura. *Qing Colonial Enterprise: Ethnography and Cartography in Early Modern China*. Chicago: University of Chicago Press, 2001.

Moser, Leo J. *The Chinese Mosaic: The Peoples and Provinces of China*. Boulder, Colo.: Westview, 1985.

Olson, James S. *An Ethnohistorical Dictionary of China*. Westport, Conn.: Greenwood, 1998.

Schafer, Edward H. *Shore of Pearls*. Berkeley and Los Angeles: University of California Press, 1970.

GENDER AND SEX

Ayscough, Florence. *Chinese Women: Yesterday and To-Day*. Cambridge, Mass.: Riverside, 1937.

Bernhardt, Kathryn. *Women and Property in China, 960–1949*. Stanford, Calif.: Stanford University Press, 1999.

Beurdeley, Michel, ed. *Chinese Erotic Art*. Tr. Diana Imber. Secaucus, N.J.: Chartwell, 1969.

Birge, Bettina. *Women, Property, and Confucian Reaction in Sung and Yüan China*. Cambridge Studies in Chinese History, Literature and Institutions. Cambridge: Cambridge University Press, 2002.

Bray, Francesca. *Technology and Gender: Fabrics of Power in Late Imperial China*. Berkeley and Los Angeles: University of California Press, 1997.

Brownell, Susan, and Jeffrey N. Wasserstrom, eds. *Chinese Femininities, Chinese Masculinities: A Reader*. Berkeley and Los Angeles: University of California Press, 2002.

Cahill, Suzanne. *Transcendence and Divine Passion: The Queen Mother of the West in Medieval China*. Stanford, Calif.: Stanford University Press, 1993.

Cass, Victoria. *Dangerous Women: Warriors, Grannies, and Geishas of the Ming*. Lanham, Md.: Rowman and Littlefield, 1999.

Chang, Kang-i Sun, and Haun Saussy, eds. *Women Writers of Traditional China: An Anthology of Poetry and Criticism*. Stanford, Calif.: Stanford University Press, 1999.

Cutter, Robert Joe, and William Gordon Crowell, trs. *Empresses and Consorts: Selections from Chen Shou's* Records of the Three States *with Pei Songzhi's Commentary*. Honolulu: University of Hawai'i Press, 1999.

Ebrey, Patricia. *The Inner Quarters: Marriage and the Lives of Chinese Women in the Sung Period*. Berkeley and Los Angeles: University of California Press, 1993.

Edwards, Louise P. *Men and Women in Qing China: Gender in* The Red Chamber Dream. Sinica Leidensia. Leiden: Brill, 1994.

Furth, Charlotte. *A Flourishing Yin: Gender in Chinese Medicine, 960–1665*. Berkeley and Los Angeles: University of California Press, 1999.

Gilmartin, Christina K.; Gail Hershatter; Lisa Rofel; and Tyrene White, eds. *Engendering China: Women, Culture, and the State*. Cambridge, Mass.: Harvard University Press, 1994.

Goldin, Paul. *The Culture of Sex in Ancient China*. Honolulu: University of Hawai'i Press, 2002.

Guisso, Richard W., and Stanley Johannesen, eds. *Women in China: Current Directions in Historical Scholarship.* Youngstown, N.Y.: Philo, 1981.

van Gulik, R. H. *Sexual Life in Ancient China.* Ed. Paul R. Goldin. Leiden: Brill, 1961; rev. ed., 2003.

Hinsch, Bret. *Passions of the Cut Sleeve: The Male Homosexual Tradition in China.* Berkeley and Los Angeles: University of California Press, 1990.

———. *Women in Early Imperial China: Asian Voices.* Lanham, Md.: Rowman and Littlefield, 2002.

Ko, Dorothy. *Teachers of the Inner Chambers: Women and Culture in Seventeenth-Century China.* Stanford, Calif.: Stanford University Press, 1994.

———. *Every Step a Lotus: Shoes for Bound Feet.* Berkeley and Los Angeles: University of California Press, 2001.

———; Joan Piggott; and JaHyun Kim Haboush, eds. *Gender and Text in Confucian China, Korea, and Japan.* Berkeley and Los Angeles: University of California Press, 2002.

Lai, Karyn, ed. "Feminism and Chinese Philosophy." *Journal of Chinese Philosophy* 27.2 (2000).

Levy, Howard S. *Chinese Footbinding: The History of a Curious Erotic Custom.* New York: W. Rawls, 1966.

Li, Chenyang, ed. *The Sage and the Second Sex: Confucianism, Ethics, and Gender.* Chicago and La Salle, Ill.: Open Court, 2000.

Li, Yu-ning, ed. *Chinese Women through Chinese Eyes.* Armonk, N.Y., and London: M. E. Sharpe, 1992.

Mann, Susan. *Precious Records: Women in China's Long Eighteenth Century.* Stanford, Calif.: Stanford University Press, 1997.

McMahon, Keith. *Misers, Shrews, and Polygamists: Sexuality and Male-Female Relations in Eighteenth-Century Chinese Fiction.* Durham, N.C.: Duke University Press, 1995.

O'Hara, Albert Richard. *The Position of Women in Early China According to the* Lieh Nü Chuan *(Biographies of Eminent Chinese Women).* Washington, D.C.: Catholic University of America Press, 1945; rpt. Taipei: Mei Ya, 1971.

Raphals, Lisa. *Sharing the Light: Representations of Women and Virtue in Early China.* SUNY Series in Chinese Philosophy and Culture. Albany: State University of New York Press, 1998.

Rouzer, Paul F. *Articulated Ladies: Gender and Male Community in Early Chinese Texts.* Harvard-Yenching Institute Monograph Series 53. Cambridge, Mass.: Harvard-Yenching Institute, 2001.

Schafer, Edward H. *The Divine Woman: Dragon Ladies and Rain Maidens in T'ang Literature.* Berkeley and Los Angeles: University of California Press, 1973.

Sommer, Matthew H. *Sex, Law, and Society in Late Imperial China.* Law, Society, and Culture in China. Stanford, Calif.: Stanford University Press, 2000.

Swann, Nancy Lee. *Pan Chao: Foremost Woman Scholar of China.* New York and London: Century, 1932; rpt. Ann Arbor: Center for Chinese Studies, University of Michigan, 2001.

T'ien, J-K. *Male Anxiety and Female Chastity: A Comparative Study of Ethical Values in Ming-Ch'ing Times.* Leiden: Brill, 1988.

Tsai, Kathryn Ann, tr. *Lives of the Nuns: Biographies of Chinese Buddhist Nuns from the Fourth to Sixth Centuries.* Honolulu: University of Hawai'i Press, 1994.

Tseng, Chi-feng. *Testimony of a Confucian Woman.* Athens: University of Georgia Press, 1993.

Tung, Jowen R. *Fables for the Patriarchs: Gender Politics in Tang Discourse.* Lanham, Md.: Rowman and Littlefield, 2000.

Wang, Ping. *Aching for Beauty: Footbinding in China.* Minneapolis: University of Minnesota Press, 2000.

Watson, Rubie S., and Patricia Buckley Ebrey, eds. *Marriage and Inequality in Chinese Society.* Berkeley and Los Angeles: University of California Press, 1991.

Widmer, Ellen, and Kang-i Sun Chang, eds. *Writing Women in Late Imperial China.* Stanford, Calif.: Stanford University Press, 1997.

Wile, Douglas. *Art of the Bedchamber: The Chinese Sexual Yoga Classics including Women's Solo Meditation Texts.* Albany: State University of New York Press, 1992.

Wolf, Margery, and Roxane Witke, eds. *Women in Chinese Society.* Studies in Chinese Society. Stanford, Calif.: Stanford University Press, 1975.

Wu, Yenna. *The Chinese Virago: A Literary Theme.* Cambridge, Mass.: Council on East Asian Studies, Harvard University, 1995.

Yang, Lien-sheng. "Women Rulers in Imperial China." *Harvard Journal of Asiatic Studies* 23 (1960–1961), 47–61.

Zurndorfer, Harriet T., ed. *Chinese Women in the Imperial Past: New Perspectives.* Sinica Leidensia, 44. Leiden: Brill, 1999.

HISTORY AND STATECRAFT

Beeching, Jack. *The Chinese Opium Wars.* New York: Harcourt Brace Jovanovich, 1976.

Bielenstein, Hans. *The Bureaucracy of Han Times.* Cambridge Studies in Chinese History, Literature, and Institutions. Cambridge: Cambridge University Press, 1980.

Bloodworth, Dennis, and Ching Ping Bloodworth. *The Chinese Machiavelli.* New York: Farrar, Straus, and Giroux, 1976.

Bodde, Derk. *China's First Unifier: A Study of the Ch'in Dynasty as Seen in the Life of Li Ssu.* Sinica Leidensia, 3. Leiden: E. J. Brill, 1938; rpt., Hong Kong: Hong Kong University Press, 1967.

Chang, K. C. *Art, Myth, and Ritual: The Path to Political Authority in Ancient China.* Cambridge, Mass.: Harvard University Press, 1983.

Ch'ien Mu. *Traditional Government in Imperial China: A Critical Analysis.* Tr. Chün-tu Hsüeh and George O. Totten. Hong Kong: Chinese University Press, 1982.

Creel, Herrlee G. *The Origins of Statecraft in China.* Chicago and London: University of Chicago Press, 1970.

Crump, J. I., Jr., tr. *Chan-kuo ts'e.* Rev. ed. Michigan Monographs in Chinese Studies 77. Ann Arbor: Center for Chinese Studies, University of Michigan, 1996.

———. *Intrigues: Studies of the* Chan-kuo ts'e. Ann Arbor: University of Michigan Press, 1964.

Dreyer, Edward L. *Early Ming China.* Stanford, Calif.: Stanford University Press, 1982.

Dubs, Homer H. *The History of the Former Han Dynasty by Pan Ku.* 3 vols. Baltimore, Md.: Waverly, 1938–1955.

Durrant, Stephen W. *The Cloudy Mirror: Tension and Conflict in the Writings of Sima Qian.* SUNY Series in Chinese Philosophy and Culture. Albany: State University of New York Press, 1995.

Eberhard, Wolfram. *A History of China.* 4th ed. Berkeley and Los Angeles: University of California Press, 1977.

Ebrey, Patricia Buckley. *The Cambridge Illustrated History of China.* Cambridge: Cambridge University Press, 1996.

Fairbank, John K., and Denis Twitchett, eds. *The Cambridge History of China.* 15 vols. Cambridge: Cambridge University Press, 1978–.

Fitzgerald, C. P. *The Empress Wu.* Vancouver: University of British Columbia Press, 1970.

Frodsham, J. D., comp. *The First Chinese Embassy to the West.* Oxford: Clarendon, 1974.

Gardner, Charles S. *Chinese Traditional Historiography.* Cambridge, Mass.: Harvard University Press, 1938, 1961.

Gernet, Jacques. *Ancient China: From the Beginnings to the Empire.* Tr. Raymond Rudorff. Berkeley and Los Angeles: University of California Press, 1968.

———. *A History of Chinese Civilization.* Tr. J. R. Foster and Charles Hartman. 2nd ed. New York: Cambridge University Press, 1996.

Granet, Marcel. *Chinese Civilization.* Tr. Kathleen E. Innes and Mabel Brailsford. New York: Knopf, 1930.

Hartman, Charles. *Han Yü and the T'ang Search for Unity.* Princeton, N.J.: Princeton University Press, 1986.

Hucker, Charles O. *The Traditional Chinese State in Ming Times.* Tucson: University of Arizona Press, 1961.

Jenner, W. J. F. *The Tyranny of History: The Roots of China's Crisis.* London: Allen Lane, Penguin, 1992.

Karlgren, Bernhard. *The Book of Documents.* Stockholm: Museum of Far Eastern Antiquities, 1950.

Leslie, Donald Daniel; Colin Mackerras; and Wang Gungwu, eds. *Essays on the Sources for Chinese History.* Canberra: Australian National University, 1973.

Levy, Howard S., tr. *Biography of An Lu-shan.* Berkeley and Los Angeles: University of California Press, 1960.

Liu, James T. C. *Reform in Sung China: Wang An-shih (1021–1086) and His New Policies.* Cambridge, Mass.: Harvard University Press, 1959.

Loewe, Michael. *Crisis and Conflict in Han China: 104 B.C. to A.D. 9.* London: George Allen and Unwin, 1974.

———, and Edward L. Shaughnessy, eds. *The Cambridge History of Ancient China: From the Origins of Civilization to 221 B.C.* Cambridge: Cambridge University Press, 1999.

Martin, H. Desmond. *The Rise of Chingis Khan and His Conquest of North China.* New York: Octagon, 1977.

Maspero, Henry. *China in Antiquity.* Tr. Frank A. Kierman, Jr. Amherst: University of Massachusetts Press, 1978.

Pulleyblank, E. G. *The Background of the Rebellion of An Lu-shan.* London: Oxford University Press, 1955.

Schaberg, David. *A Patterned Past: Form and Thought in Early Chinese Historiography.* Harvard East Asian Monographs 205. Cambridge, Mass., and London: Harvard University Asia Center, 2001.

Sima Qian. *Records of the Grand Historian.* Han Dynasty, 2 vols. Qin Dynasty, 1 vol. Tr. Burton Watson. Hong Kong and New York: *Renditions*-Columbia University Press, 1993.

Spence, Jonathan. *Emperor of China.* New York: Alfred A. Knopf, 1974.

———, and John W. Wills, Jr., ed. *From Ming to Ch'ing.* New Haven, Conn.: Yale University Press, 1979.

Ssu-ma Ch'ien. *The Grand Scribe's Records.* 9 vols. projected. Ed. William H. Nienhauser, Jr. Bloomington: Indiana University Press, 1994–.

———. *Records of the Historian: Chapters from the* Shih Chi *of Ssu-ma Chi'en.* Tr. Burton Watson. New York: Columbia University Press, 1969.

Struve, Lynn A. *The Southern Ming, 1644–1662.* New Haven, Conn.: Yale University Press, 1984.

———. *Voices from the Ming-Qing Cataclysm: China in Tigers' Jaws.* New Haven, Conn.: Yale University Press, 1993.

Teng, Ssu-yü, and John K. Fairbank. *China's Response to the West.* Cambridge, Mass.: Harvard University Press, 1954.

Twitchett, Denis. *The Writing of Official History under the T'ang.* Cambridge: Cambridge University Press, 1992.

Wakeman, Frederic, Jr. *The Great Enterprise: The Manchu Reconstruction of Imperial Order in Seventeenth-Century China.* 2 vols. Berkeley and Los Angeles: University of California Press, 1985.

Watson, Burton. *Ssu-ma Ch'ien, Grand Historian of China.* New York: Columbia University Press, 1958.

———. *The Tso chuan: Selections from China's Oldest Narrative History.* Translations from the Oriental Classics. New York: Columbia University Press, 1989.

Wittfogel, Karl. *Oriental Despotism: A Comparative Study of Total Power.* New Haven, Conn.: Yale University Press, 1957.

———, and Feng Chia-sheng, eds. *History of Chinese Society: Liao (907–1125).* Philadelphia: American Philosophical Society, 1949.

Wright, Arthur F. *The Sui Dynasty.* New York: Alfred A. Knopf, 1978.

LANGUAGES AND SCRIPTS

Baxter, William H. *A Handbook of Old Chinese Phonology.* Berlin: Mouton de Gruyter, 1992.

Boltz, William G. *The Origin and Early Development of the Chinese Writing System.* American Oriental Series, 78. New Haven, Conn.: American Oriental Society, 1994.

Branner, David Prager. "A Neutral Transcription System for Teaching Medieval Chinese." *T'ang Studies* 17 (1999): 1–169.

DeFrancis, John. *The Chinese Language: Fact and Fantasy.* Honolulu: University of Hawai'i Press, 1984.

Forrest, R. A. D. *The Chinese Language.* London: Faber and Faber, 1948.

Karlgren, Bernhard. *The Chinese Language: An Essay on Its Nature and History.* New York: Ronald Press, 1949.

———. *Sound and Symbol in Chinese.* London: Oxford University Press, 1929; rev. ed., Hong Kong: Hong Kong University Press, 1962.

Keightley, David N. *Sources of Shang History: The Oracle Bone Inscriptions of Bronze Age China.* Berkeley and Los Angeles: University of California Press, 1978.

Norman, Jerry. *Chinese.* Cambridge Language Surveys. Cambridge: Cambridge University Press, 1988.

Ramsey, S. Robert. *The Languages of China.* Princeton, N.J.: Princeton University Press, 1987.

Yang, Paul Fu-mien. *Chinese Linguistics: A Selected and Classified Bibliography.* Hong Kong: Chinese University of Hong Kong, 1974.

LAW

Bodde, Derk, and Clarence Morris. *Law in Imperial China.* Cambridge, Mass.: Harvard University Press, 1967.

Ch'ü, T'ung-tsu. *Law and Society in Traditional China.* Paris: Mouton, 1961.

Duyvendak, J. J. L., tr. *The Book of Lord Shang: A Classic of the Chinese School of Law.* Probsthain's Oriental Series 17. London: A. Probsthain, 1928.

van Gulik, R. H., tr. and annot. *T'ang-yin pi-shih, Parallel Cases from under the Peartree: A Thirteenth-Century Manual of Jurisprudence and Detection.* Leiden: Brill, 1956.

Hulsewé, A. F. P. *Remnants of Ch'in Law: An Annotated Translation of the Ch'in Legal and Administrative Rules of the 3rd Century B.C. Discovered in Yün-meng Prefecture, Hu-pei Province, in 1975.* Sinica Leidensia, 17. Leiden: Brill, 1985.

————. *Remnants of Han Law.* Vol. 1: *Introductory Studies and an Annotated Translation of Chapters 22 and 23 of the History of the Former Han Dynasty.* Sinica Leidensia, 9. Leiden: Brill, 1955.

McKnight, Brian E., and James T. C. Liu, trs. *The Enlightened Judgments: Ch'ing-ming chi: The Sung Dynasty Collection.* Albany: State University of New York Press, 1999.

Meijer, M. J. *Murder and Adultery in Late Imperial China: A Study of Law and Morality.* Sinica Leidensia, 25. Leiden: Brill, 1991.

Johnson, Wallace, tr. and annot. *The T'ang Code.* 2 vols. Princeton, N.J.: Princeton University Press, 1979, 1997.

Peerenboom, R. P. *Law and Morality in Ancient China: The Silk Manuscripts of Huang-Lao.* SUNY Series in Chinese Philosophy and Culture. Albany: State University of New York Press, 1993.

LITERATURE

Birrell, Anne. *Popular Songs and Ballads of Han China.* 2d ed. Honolulu: University of Hawai'i Press, 1993.

Campany, Robert Ford. *Strange Writing: Anomaly Accounts in Early Medieval China.* Albany: State University of New York Press, 1996.

Chang, Kang-i Sun. *The Evolution of Chinese Tz'u Poetry: From Late T'ang to Northern Sung.* Princeton, N.J.: Princeton University Press, 1980.

Chaves, Jonathan. *The Columbia Book of Later Chinese Poetry.* New York: Columbia University Press, 1986.

Crump, James I. *Chinese Theater in the Days of Kublai Khan.* Tucson: University of Arizona Press, 1981.

————. *Song-Poems from Xanadu: Studies in Mongol-Dynasty Song-Poetry (San-ch'ü).* Ann Arbor: Center for Chinese Studies, University of Michigan, 1993.

————. *Songs from Xanadu.* Ann Arbor: Center for Chinese Studies, University of Michigan, 1983.

Dolby, William. *A History of Chinese Drama.* London: Paul Elek, 1976.

Edgerton, Clement, tr. *The Golden Lotus.* New York: Paragon, 1962, rpt.

Frodsham, J. D. *The Murmuring Stream: The Life and Works of the Chinese Nature Poet Hsieh Ling-yun (385–433), Duke of K'ang-lo.* 2 vols. Kuala Lumpur: University of Malaya Press, 1967.

Goodrich, L. Carrington. *The Literary Inquisition of Ch'ien Lung.* Baltimore, Md.: Waverly, 1935.

Hawkes, David, tr. and annot. *Ch'u-tz'u: The Songs of the South; An Ancient Chinese Anthology.* Oxford: Clarendon, 1959; Boston: Beacon, 1962; rev. ed. as *The Songs of the South: An Anthology of Ancient Chinese Poems by Qu Yuan and Other Poets.* Harmondsworth: Penguin, 1985.

————, tr. *The Story of the Stone: A Chinese Novel in Five Volumes by Cao Xueqin.* Vol. 5, John Minford, tr. Harmondsworth: Penguin, 1973–1986.

Hightower, James Robert, tr. and annot. *The Poetry of T'ao Ch'ien.* Oxford: Clarendon, 1970.

Hsia, C. T. *The Classic Chinese Novel: A Critical Introduction.* New York: Columbia University Press, 1968; Ithaca, N.Y.: Cornell University Press, 1996.

Idema, Wilt L. *Chinese Vernacular Fiction: The Formative Period.* Leiden: Brill, 1974.

————, and Stephen H. West. *Chinese Theater 1100–1450: A Source Book.* Wiesbaden: Franz Steiner, 1982.

Karlgren, Bernard, tr. *The Book of Odes.* Stockholm: Museum of Far Eastern Antiquities, 1950.

Knechtges, David R. *The Han Rhapsody: A Study of the Fu of Yang Hsiung (53 B.C.–A.D. 18).* Cambridge: Cambridge University Press, 1976.

————, tr. and annot. *Wen xuan, or Selections of Refined Literature.* 8 vols. projected. Princeton, N.J.: Princeton University Press, 1982–.

Liu, James J. Y. *The Art of Chinese Poetry.* Chicago: University of Chicago Press, 1962.

————. *Chinese Theories of Literature.* Chicago: University of Chicago Press, 1975.

Lu Hsün (Lu Xun). *A Brief History of Chinese Fiction.* Tr. Yang Hsien-yi and Gladys Yang. Peking: Foreign Languages Press, 1959.

Ma, Y. W., and Joseph S. M. Lau, eds. *Traditional Chinese Stories: Themes and Variations*. New York: Columbia University Press, 1978.

Mackerras, Colin. *Chinese Drama: From Its Origins to the Present Day*. Honolulu: University of Hawai'i Press, 1983.

Mair, Victor H. *Painting and Performance: Chinese Picture Recitation and Its Indian Genesis*. Honolulu: University of Hawai'i Press, 1988.

————. *T'ang Transformation Texts: A Study of the Buddhist Contribution to the Rise of Vernacular Fiction and Drama in China*. Cambridge, Mass.: Council on East Asian Studies, Harvard University, 1989.

————, ed. *The Columbia Anthology of Traditional Chinese Literature*. New York: Columbia University Press, 1994.

————, ed. *The Columbia History of Chinese Literature*. New York: Columbia University Press, 2001.

————, ed. *The Shorter Columbia Anthology of Traditional Chinese Literature*. New York: Columbia University Press, 2000.

————, tr. and annot. *Tun-huang Popular Narratives*. Cambridge: Cambridge University Press, 1983.

————, and Tsu-Lin Mei. "The Sanskrit Origins of Recent Style Prosody." *Harvard Journal of Asiatic Studies* 51.2 (1991): 375–470.

Nienhauser, William H., Jr., ed. and comp. *The Indiana Companion to Traditional Chinese Literature*. Bloomington: Indiana University Press, 1986; rev. rpt. Taipei: Southern Materials Center, 1988; Vol. 2, 1998.

Owen, Stephen. *The End of the Chinese "Middle Ages": Essays in Mid-T'ang Literary Culture*. Stanford, Calif.: Stanford University Press, 1996.

————. *The Great Age of Chinese Poetry: The High T'ang*. New Haven, Conn.: Yale University Press, 1981.

————. *Poetry of the Early T'ang*. New Haven, Conn.: Yale University Press, 1977.

————, comp. and tr. *Readings in Chinese Literary Thought*. Harvard-Yenching Institute Monograph Series. Cambridge, Mass.; and London: Harvard University Press, 1992.

————, ed. *An Anthology of Chinese Literature*. New York: W. W. Norton, 1996.

Plaks, Andrew. *The Four Masterworks of the Ming Novel*. Princeton, N.J.: Princeton University Press, 1987.

Pound, Ezra, tr. *The Confucian Odes*. New York: New Directions, 1959.

Rickett, Adele Austin, ed. *Chinese Approaches to Literature from Confucius to Liang Ch'i-ch'ao*. Princeton, N.J.: Princeton University Press, 1978.

Roberts, Moss, tr. *The Three Kingdoms: A Historical Novel, Attributed to Luo Guanzhong*. Berkeley and Los Angeles: University of California Press, 1991.

Roy, David T., tr. *The Plum in the Golden Vase, or Chin P'ing Mei*. Princeton, N.J.: Princeton University Press, 1993– (2 vols. published to date).

Saussy, Haun. *The Problem of a Chinese Aesthetic*. Stanford, Calif.: Stanford University Press, 1993.

Schlepp, Wayne. *San-ch'ü: Its Technique and Imagery*. Madison: University of Wisconsin Press, 1970.

Shapiro, Sidney, tr. *Outlaws of the Marsh*. 3 vols. Peking: Foreign Languages Press, 1980.

Shih, Chung-wen. *The Golden Age of Chinese Drama: Yüan Tsa-chü*. Princeton, N.J.: Princeton University Press, 1976.

Van Zoeren, Stephen. *Poetry and Personality: Reading, Exegesis, and Hermeneutics in Traditional China*. Stanford, Calif.: Stanford University Press, 1991.

Wagner, Marsha. *The Lotus Boat: The Origins of Chinese Tz'u Poetry in T'ang Popular Culture*. New York: Columbia University Press, 1984.

Waley, Arthur. *The Life and Times of Po Chü-i, 772–846 A.D.* London: George Allen and Unwin, 1949.

————. *The Poetry and Career of Li Po, 701–762 A.D.* London: George Allen and Unwin, 1950.

————, tr. *The Book of Songs: The Ancient Chinese Classic of Poetry*. Ed. with addtl. trans., Joseph R. Allen. New York: Grove, 1960, 1996.

————, tr. *Monkey*. London: John Day, 1942; rpt. New York: Grove, 1958.

Watson, Burton. *Early Chinese Literature*. New York: Columbia University Press, 1962.

————. *Chinese Rhyme-Prose: Poems in the Fu Form from the Han and Six Dynasties Periods*. New York: Columbia University Press, 1971.

————. *The Columbia Book of Chinese Poetry: From Early Times to the Thirteenth Century*. New York: Columbia University Press, 1984.

West, Stephen H. *Vaudeville and Narrative: Aspects of Chin Theater*. Wiesbaden: Franz Steiner, 1977.

Yu, Anthony C., tr. *The Journey to the West*. 4 vols. Chicago: University of Chicago Press, 1977–1983.

MUSIC AND OPERA

Chan, Sau Y. *Improvisation in a Ritual Context: The Music of Cantonese Opera.* Hong Kong: Chinese University Press, 1991.

DeWoskin, Kenneth J. *A Song for One or Two: Music and the Concept of Art in Early China.* Michigan Papers in Chinese Studies 42. Ann Arbor: Center for Chinese Studies, University of Michigan, 1982.

Johnson, David, ed. *Ritual Opera and Operatic Ritual: "Mu-lien Rescues His Mother."* Chinese Popular Culture Project. Berkeley: Chinese Popular Culture Project, University of California, 1991.

Lieberman, Frederic. *Chinese Music: An Annotated Bibliography.* 2nd ed. New York: Garland, 1979.

Malm, William P. *Music Cultures of the Pacific, the Near East, and Asia.* Englewood Cliffs, N.J.: Prentice Hall, 1967.

Wiant, Bliss. *The Music of China.* Hong Kong: Chung Chi, 1965.

Yung, Bell. *Cantonese Opera: Performance as Creative Process.* Cambridge: Cambridge University Press, 1989.

————; Evelyn S. Rawski; and Ruby S. Watson, eds. *Harmony and Counterpoint: Ritual Music in a Chinese Context.* Stanford, Calif.: Stanford University Press, 1996.

MYTH AND RELIGION

Birrell, Anne. *Chinese Mythology: An Introduction.* Baltimore and London: Johns Hopkins University Press, 1993.

————, tr. *The Classic of Mountains and Seas.* London: Penguin, 1998.

Bodde, Derk. "Myths of Ancient China." In *Mythologies of the Ancient World,* ed. Samuel Noah Kramer, pp. 367–408. Garden City, N.J.: Anchor Books, Doubleday, 1961.

Bokenkamp, Stephen R., with Peter Nickerson. *Early Daoist Scriptures.* Berkeley and Los Angeles: University of California Press, 1997.

Boltz, Judith M. *A Survey of Taoist Literature, Tenth to Seventeenth Centuries.* China Research Monograph 32. Berkeley: Institute of East Asian Studies, University of California, 1987; rpt. (with Corrigenda), 1995.

Buswell, Robert E., Jr., ed. *Chinese Buddhist Apocrypha.* Honolulu: University of Hawai'i Press, 1990.

Chen, Kenneth K. S. "Anti-Buddhist Propaganda during the Nan-ch'ao." *Harvard Journal of Asiatic Studies* 15 (1952), 166–192.

————. *Buddhism in China: A Historical Survey.* Princeton, N.J.: Princeton University Press, 1964.

———— *The Chinese Transformation of Buddhism.* Princeton, N.J.: Princeton University Press, 1973.

Creel, Herrlee G. *"What Is Taoism?" and Other Studies in Chinese Cultural History.* Chicago: University of Chicago Press, 1970, 1977.

Cronin, Vincent. *The Wise Man from the West.* New York: Dutton, 1955.

Dean, Kenneth. *Taoist Ritual and Popular Cults in Southeast China.* Princeton, N.J.: Princeton University Press, 1993.

Dunne, George H. *Generation of Giants.* Notre Dame, Ind.: University of Notre Dame Press, 1962.

Gernet, Jacques. *China and the Christian Impact: A Conflict of Cultures.* Tr. Janet Lloyd. Cambridge: Cambridge University Press, 1986.

Giles, H. A. *The Travels of Fa-hsien.* London: Routledge and Kegan Paul, 1959.

Goodrich, Anne Swann. *Chinese Hells: The Peking Temple of Eighteen Hells and Chinese Conceptions of Hell.* St. Augustin: Monumenta Serica, 1981.

Granet, Marcel. *The Religion of the Chinese People.* Tr. Maurice Freedman. New York: Harper and Row, 1975.

de Groot, J. J. M. *The Religious System of China.* 6 vols. Leiden: Brill, 1892–1910; rpt., Taipei: Southern Materials Center, 1989.

Hansen, Valerie. *The Changing Gods of Medieval China, 1127–1276.* Princeton, N.J.: Princeton University Press, 1990.

Israeli, Raphael. *Muslims in China: A Study in Cultural Confrontation.* Copenhagen: Scandinavian Institute of Asian Studies, 1980.

Kohn, Livia, ed. *Daoism Handbook.* Handbook of Oriental Studies (Handbuch der Orientalistik), Sect. 4, Vol. 14. Leiden: Brill, 2000.

Kublin, Hyman, ed. *Jews in Old China: Some Western Views.* New York: Paragon, 1971, rpt.

Lach, Donald F. *The Preface to Leibniz' Novissima Sinica.* Honolulu: University of Hawai'i Press, 1957.

Leslie, Donald D. *The Survival of the Chinese Jews.* Leiden: Brill, 1972.

Lopez, Donald S., Jr., ed. *Religions of China in Practice.* Princeton, N.J.: Princeton University Press, 1996.

Mair, Victor H. "Old Sinitic *myag,* Old Persian *maguš,* and English 'Magician.'" *Early China* 15 (1990): 27–47.

Maspero, Henry. *Taoism and Chinese Religion.* Tr. Frank A. Kierman, Jr. Amherst: University of Massachusetts Press, 1981.

Mather, Richard. "The Landscape Buddhism of the Fifth-Century Poet Hsieh Ling-yün." *Journal of Asian Studies* 18 (1958): 67–79.

Pollak, Michael. *Mandarins, Jews, and Missionaries.* Philadelphia: The Jewish Publication Society of America, 1980.

Poo, Mu-chou. *In Search of Personal Welfare: A View of Ancient Chinese Religion.* SUNY Series in Chinese Philosophy and Culture. Albany: State University of New York Press, 1998.

Robinet, Isabelle. *Taoism: Growth of a Religion.* Tr. Phyllis Brooks. Stanford, Calif.: Stanford University Press, 1997.

Schipper, Kristofer M. *The Taoist Body.* Tr. Karen C. Duval. Berkeley and Los Angeles: University of California Press, 1993.

Shapiro, Sidney. *Jews in Old China.* New York: Hippocrene, 1984.

Thompson, Laurence G., comp. *Chinese Religion in Western Languages: A Comprehensive and Classified Bibliography of Publications in English, French, and German through 1980.* Association for Asian Studies Monograph, 41. Tucson: University of Arizona Press, 1985.

———. *Chinese Religion: Publications in Western Languages 1981 through 1990.* Ed. Gary Seaman. Association for Asian Studies Monograph, 47. Los Angeles: Ethnographics Press, Center for Visual Anthropology, University of Southern California, 1993.

———. *Chinese Religion: Publications in Western Languages.* Volume 3: *1991–1995.* Ed. Gary Seaman. Association for Asian Studies Monograph and Occasional Paper Series, 58. Los Angeles: Ethnographics Press, Center for Visual Anthropology, University of Southern California, 1998.

Varg, Paul. *Missionaries, Chinese and Diplomats.* Princeton, N.J.: Princeton University Press, 1958.

Wagner, Rudolf G. *A Chinese Reading of the Daodejing: Wang Bi's Commentary on the Laozi with Critical Text and Translation.* Albany: State University of New York Press, 2002.

Waley, Arthur, tr. *Chiu Ko—The Nine Songs: A Study of Shamanism in Ancient China.* London: George Allen and Unwin, 1955.

———. *The Real Tripitaka.* London: George Allen and Unwin, 1952.

———. *The Way and Its Power.* London: Allen and Unwin, 1934.

Welch, Holmes. *Taoism: The Parting of the Way.* Boston: Beacon, 1957.

———, and Anna Seidel, eds. *Facets of Taoism: Essays in Chinese Religion.* New Haven, Conn.: Yale University Press, 1979.

Weinstein, Stanley. *Buddhism under the T'ang.* Cambridge: Cambridge University Press, 1987.

Werner, E. T. C. *A Dictionary of Chinese Mythology.* Shanghai: Kelly and Walsh, 1932; numerous reprints.

Wright, Arthur F. *Buddhism in Chinese History.* Stanford, Calif.: Stanford University Press, 1959 and later rpts.

Zürcher, E[rik]. *The Buddhist Conquest of China: The Spread and Adaptation of Buddhism in Early Medieval China.* 2 vols. Leiden: Brill, 1959.

NEIGHBORING PEOPLES

Bagchi, P. C. *India and China: A Thousand Years of Cultural Relations.* Rev. ed. Bombay: Hind Kitabs, 1950.

Barfield, Thomas J. *The Perilous Frontier: Nomadic Empires and China, 221 BC to AD 1757.* Oxford: Basil Blackwell, 1989; rev. 1996.

Bawden, C. R. *The Modern History of Mongolia.* New York: Frederick A. Praeger, 1968.

Beckwith, Christopher I. *The Tibetan Empire in Central Asia: A History of the Struggle for Great Power among Tibetans, Turks, Arabs, and Chinese during the Early Middle Ages.* Princeton, N.J.: Princeton University Press, 1987; rev. 1993.

Buttinger, Joseph. *The Smaller Dragon: A Political History of Vietnam.* New York: Frederick A. Praeger, 1959.

Cleaves, Francis W., ed. and tr. *The Secret History of the Mongols.* Cambridge, Mass.: Harvard University Press, 1982.

Crossley, Pamela. *The Manchus*. Cambridge, Mass.: Blackwell's, 1997.

Di Cosmo, Nicola. *Ancient China and Its Enemies: The Rise of Nomadic Power in East Asian History*. Cambridge: Cambridge University Press, 2002.

———, ed. *Warfare in Inner Asian History (500–1800)*. Leiden: Brill, 2002.

Fairbank, John K., ed. *The Chinese World Order: Traditional China's Foreign Relations*. Cambridge, Mass.: Harvard University Press, 1968.

Franck, Irene M., and David M. Brownstone. *The Silk Road*. New York: Facts on File, 1986.

Hall, D. G. E. *A History of South-East Asia*. 4th ed. New York: St. Martin's, 1981.

Hall, John W. *Japan from Prehistory to Modern Times*. New York: Delacorte, 1970.

Hammer, Ellen. *Vietnam: Yesterday and Today*. New York: Holt Rinehart and Winston, 1966.

Hulsewé, A. F. P. *China in Central Asia: The Early Stage, 125 B.C.–A.D. 23*. Leiden: E. J. Brill, 1979.

Janhunen, Juha. *Manchuria: An Ethnic History*. Mémoires de la Société Finno-Ougrienne, 222. Helsinki: The Finno-Ugrian Society, 1996.

Jagchid, Sechin, and Van Jay Symons. *Peace, War, and Trade along the Great Wall: Nomadic-Chinese Interaction through Two Millennia*. Bloomington: Indiana University Press, 1989.

Kahn, Paul. *Secret History of the Mongols*. San Francisco: North Star, 1984. An adaptation of Cleaves, 1982.

Knapp, Ronald G. *China's Island Frontier: Studies in the Historical Geography of Taiwan*. Honolulu: University of Hawai'i Press, 1980.

Lamb, Alistair. *Asian Frontiers: Studies in a Continuing Problem*. New York: Praeger, 1968.

Lattimore, Owen. *Inner Asian Frontiers of China*. New York: American Geographical Society, 1940.

Lee, Ki-baik. *A New History of Korea*. Tr. Edward W. Wagner. Cambridge, Mass.: Harvard University Press, 1984.

Lee, Robert H. G. *The Manchurian Frontier in Ch'ing History*. Cambridge, Mass.: Harvard University Press, 1970.

Liu, Xinru. *Ancient India and Ancient China: Trade and Religious Exchanges, AD 1–600*. New Delhi: Oxford University Press, 1988.

Mackerras, Colin, ed. and tr. *The Uighur Empire according to the T'ang Dynastic Histories: A Study in Sino-Uighur Relations, 744–840*. Columbia: University of South Carolina Press, 1973.

Maenchen-Helfen, Otto J. *The World of the Huns: Studies in Their History and Culture*. Ed. Max Knight. Berkeley and Los Angeles: University of California Press, 1973.

Mallory, J. P., and Victor H. Mair. *The Tarim Mummies: Ancient China and the Mystery of the Earliest Peoples from the West*. London: Thames and Hudson, 2000.

Mills, J. V. G., tr. and annot. *Ma Huan Ying-yai sheng-lan: "The Overall Survey of the Ocean's Shores" (1433)*. Bangkok: White Lotus, 1997, rpt.

———, tr. and annot. *Hsing-ch'a sheng-lan: "The Overall Survey of the Star of the Raft by Fei Hsin."* Wiesbaden: Harrassowitz, 1996.

Morse, H. B. *The International Relations of the Chinese Empire*. 3 vols. London: Longmans, 1910–1918.

Pan, Yihong. *Son of Heaven and Heavenly Qaghan: Sui-Tang China and Its Neighbors*. Bellingham: Western Washington University Press, 1997.

Phillips, E. D. *The Mongols*. New York: Praeger, 1969.

Ray, Haraprasad. *Trade and Diplomacy in India-China Relations: A Study of Bengal during the Fifteenth Century*. New Delhi: Radiant, 1993.

Reischauer, Edwin O. *Ennin's Diary*. New York: Ronald, 1955.

———. *Ennin's Travels to T'ang China*. New York: Ronald, 1955.

Sansom, George. *A History of Japan*. Vol. 1: *To 1334*. Vol. 2: *1334–1615*. Vol. 3: *1615–1837*. Stanford, Calif.: Stanford University Press: 1958, 1961, 1963.

Schafer, Edward H. *The Golden Peaches of Samarkand: A Study of T'ang Exotics*. Berkeley and Los Angeles: University of California Press, 1963.

Shakabpa, Tsepon W. D. *Tibet: A Political History*. New Haven, Conn.: Yale University Press, 1967.

Sinor, Denis, ed. *The Cambridge History of Early Inner Asia*. Cambridge: Cambridge University Press, 1990.

Smith, Richard J. *Chinese Maps: Images of All Under Heaven*. Hong Kong: Oxford University Press, 1996.

Snellgrove, David, and Hugh Richardson. *A Cultural History of Tibet*. Boulder, Colo.: Prajna, 1980.

Stein, R. A. *Tibetan Civilization*. Tr. J. E. Stapleton Driver. London: Faber and Faber, 1972.

Waldron, Arthur. *The Great Wall of China: From History to Myth.* Cambridge: Cambridge University Press, 1990.

Watson, Francis. *The Frontiers of China.* New York: Praeger, 1966.

Wiens, Herold J. *China's March toward the Tropics.* Hamden: Shoestring, 1954.

SCIENCE AND TECHNOLOGY (INCLUDING MEDICINE)

Bodde, Derk. *Chinese Thought, Society, and Science: The Intellectual and Social Background of Science and Technology in Pre-Modern China.* Honolulu: University of Hawai'i Press, 1991.

Carter, Thomas F. *The Invention of Printing in China and Its Spread Westward.* Rev. L. Carrington Goodrich. New York: Ronald, 1955.

Cullen, Christopher. *Astronomy and Mathematics in Ancient China: The* Zhoubi suanjing. Cambridge: Cambridge University Press, 1996.

Harper, Donald. *Early Chinese Medical Literature: The Mawangdui Medical Manuscripts.* The Sir Henry Wellcome Asian Series. London and New York: Kegan Paul International, 1998.

Ho Peng Yoke. *Li, Qi and Shu: An Introduction to Science and Civilization in China.* Hong Kong: Hong Kong University Press, 1985; rpt., Mineola, N.Y.: Dover, 2000.

Laufer, Berthold. *Paper and Printing in Ancient China.* New York: B. Franklin, 1973, rpt.

Libbrecht, Ulrich. *Chinese Mathematics in the Thirteenth Century: The* Shu-shu Chiu-chang *of Ch'in Chiu-shao.* Cambridge, Mass.: MIT Press, 1973.

Liu, Yanchi. *The Essential Book of Traditional Chinese Medicine.* Vol. 1: *Theory.* Vol. 2: *Clinical Practice.* Tr. Fang Tingyu and Chen Laidi. Ed. Kathleen Vian and Peter Eckman (vol. 1); Ed. Barbara Gastel (vol. 2). New York: Columbia University Press, 1988, 1995.

Mazumdar, Sucheta. *Sugar and Society in China.* Cambridge, Mass.: Harvard University, Asia Center Publications, 1998.

Needham, Joseph, et al., eds. *Science and Civilisation in China.* 7 vols. projected. Cambridge: Cambridge University Press, 1954–.

Perkins, Dwight. *Agricultural Development in China.* Aldine, 1969.

Porkert, Manfred. *The Theoretical Foundations of Chinese Medicine: Systems of Correspondence.* MIT East Asian Science Series, 3. Cambridge, Mass.: MIT Press, 1974.

Qian, Wen-yuan. *The Great Inertia: Scientific Stagnation in Traditional China.* London; Sydney; and Dover, New Hampshire: Croom Helm, 1985.

Sivin, Nathan. *Medicine, Philosophy, and Religion in Ancient China: Researches and Reflections.* Aldershot, U.K.; and Brookfield, Vt.: Variorum, 1995.

———. *Science in Ancient China: Researches and Reflections.* Aldershot, U.K.; and Brookfield, Vt.: Variorum, 1995.

———. *Traditional Medicine in Contemporary China.* Science, Medicine, and Technology in East Asia, 2. Ann Arbor: Center for Chinese Studies, University of Michigan, 1987.

Unschuld, Paul U. *Medicine in China: A History of Ideas.* Berkeley and Los Angeles: University of California Press, 1985.

———. *Medicine in China: A History of Pharmaceutics.* Berkeley and Los Angeles: University of California Press, 1986.

Twitchett, Denis. *Printing and Publishing in Medieval China.* New York: Frederic C. Beil, 1983.

Ware, James. *Alchemy, Medicine, Religion in the China of* A.D. *320: The* Nei P'ien *of Ko Hung* (Pao-p'u tzu). Cambridge, Mass.: MIT Press, 1966.

SOCIETY AND CUSTOMS

Berkowitz, Alan. *Patterns of Disengagement: The Practice and Portrayal of Reclusion in Early Medieval China.* Stanford, Calif.: Stanford University Press, 2000.

Brokaw, Cynthia K. *The Ledgers of Merit and Demerit: Social Change and Moral Order in Late Imperial China.* Princeton, N.J.: Princeton University Press, 1991.

Ch'ü, T'ung-tsu. *Han Social Structure.* Ed. Jack L. Dull. Han Dynasty China, 1. Seattle and London: University of Washington Press, 1972.

Ebrey, Patricia. *Chu Hsi's Family Rituals*. Princeton, N.J.: Princeton University Press, 1991.

————. *Confucianism and Family Rituals in Imperial China: A Social History of Writing about Rites*. Princeton, N.J.: Princeton University Press, 1991.

————. *Family and Property in Sung China: Yuan Ts'ai's Precepts for Social Life*. Princeton, N.J.: Princeton University Press, 1984.

Ho, Ping-ti. *The Ladder of Success in Imperial China: Aspects of Social Mobility, 1368–1911*. New York: Columbia University Press, 1980.

Holzman, Donald. "The Place of Filial Piety in Ancient China." *Journal of the American Oriental Society* 118.2 (April–June 1998): 185–200.

Hsu, Cho-yun. *Ancient China in Transition: An Analysis of Social Mobility, 722–222 B.C.* Stanford Studies in the Civilizations of Eastern Asia. Stanford, Calif.: Stanford University Press, 1965.

Hymes, Robert P., and Conrad Schirokauer, eds. *Ordering the World: Approaches to State and Society in Sung Dynasty China*. Berkeley and Los Angeles: University of California Press, 1993.

Johnson, David; Andrew J. Nathan; and Evelyn S. Rawski, eds. *Popular Culture in Late Imperial China*. Berkeley and Los Angeles: University of California Press, 1985.

Keightley, David N. *The Ancestral Landscape: Time, Space, and Community in Late Shang China (ca. 1200–1045 B.C.)*. Berkeley: Institute of East Asian Studies, University of California, 2000.

Mather, Richard B., tr. *Shih-shuo Hsin-yü: A New Account of Tales of the World*. Minneapolis: University of Minnesota Press, 1976.

Shahar, Meir, and Robert Weller, eds. *Unruly Gods: Divinity and Society in China*. Honolulu: University of Hawai'i Press, 1996.

Teng, Ssu-yü, tr. *Family Traditions of the Yen Clan*. Leiden: E. J. Brill, 1988.

Vervoorn, Aat. *Men of the Cliffs and Caves: The Development of the Chinese Eremitic Tradition to the End of the Han Dynasty*. Hong Kong: The Chinese University Press, 1990.

TAIWAN

Davidson, James. *The Island of Formosa: Historical View from 1430 to 1900*. New York: Macmillan, 1903.

Keliher, Macabe. *Out of China, or Yu Yonghe's Tale of Formosa: A History of Seventeenth-Century Taiwan*. Taipei: SMC Publishing, 2003.

Knapp, Ronald G. *China's Island Frontier: Studies in the Historical Geography of Taiwan*. Honolulu: University of Hawai'i Press, 1980.

Meskill, Johanna Menzel. *A Chinese Pioneer Family: The Lins of Wu-feng, Taiwan, 1729–1895*. Princeton, N.J.: Princeton University Press, 1979.

Pickering, W. A. *Pioneering in Formosa: Recollections of Adventures among Mandarins, Wreckers, and Head-hunting Savages*. London: Hurst and Blackett, 1898.

Rubinstein, Murray A. *Taiwan: A New History*. Armonk, N.Y.: M. E. Sharpe, 1999.

Shepherd, John. *Statecraft and Political Economy on the Taiwan Frontier, 1600–1800*. Stanford, Calif.: Stanford University Press, 1993.

THOUGHT (INCLUDING MILITARY ARTS AND STRATEGY) AND CLASSICS

Ames, Roger T. *The Art of Rulership: A Study of Ancient Chinese Political Thought*. Honolulu: University of Hawai'i Press, 1983; rpt., Albany: State University of Albany Press, 1994.

de Bary, William Theodore. *Neo-Confucianism Orthodoxy and the Learning of the Mind-and-Heart*. New York: Columbia University Press, 1981.

————, and the American Council of Learned Societies, Subcommittee on Studies of Chinese Civilization, ed. *The Unfolding of Neo-Confucianism*. Studies in Oriental Culture, 10. New York: Columbia University Press, 1975.

Bol, Peter K. *This Culture of Ours: Intellectual Transitions in T'ang and Sung China*. Stanford, Calif.: Stanford University Press, 1992.

Brooks, E. Bruce, and A. Taeko Brooks. *The Original Analects: Sayings of Confucius and His Successors*. New York: Columbia University Press, 1998.

Chan, Wing-tsit, comp. and tr. *A Source Book in Chinese Philosophy*. Princeton: Princeton University Press, 1963.

Elman, Benjamin. *Classicism, Politics, and Kinship: The Ch'ang-chou School of New Text Confucianism in Late Imperial China*. Berkeley and Los Angeles: University of California Press, 1990.

———. *From Philosophy to Philology: Social and Intellectual Aspects of Change in Late Imperial China*. Cambridge, Mass.: Harvard University Council on East Asian Studies, 1984, 1990.

Goldin, Paul R. *After Confucius: Studies in Early Chinese Philosophy*. Honolulu: University of Hawai'i Press, 2004.

———. *Rituals of the Way: The Philosophy of Xunzi*. Chicago and La Salle: Open Court, 1999.

Goldman, Merle, and Leo Ou-fan Lee. *An Intellectual History of Modern China*. Cambridge and New York: Cambridge University Press, 2002.

Graff, David A. *Medieval Chinese Warfare, 300–900*. London and New York: Routledge, 2002.

Graham, A. C. *Disputers of the Tao: Philosophical Argument in Ancient China*. La Salle, Ill.: Open Court, 1989.

Hall, David L., and Roger T. Ames. *Thinking through Confucius*. SUNY Series in Systematic Philosophy. Albany: State University of New York Press, 1987.

Henderson, John. *The Construction of Orthodoxy and Heresy: Neo-Confucianism, Islamic, Jewish, and Early Christian Patterns*. Albany: State University of New York Press, 1999.

———. *Scripture, Canon, and Commentary: A Comparison of Confucian and Western Exegesis*. Princeton, N.J.: Princeton University Press, 1991.

Holcombe, Charles. *In the Shadow of the Han: Literati Thought and Society at the Beginning of the Southern Dynasties*. Honolulu: University of Hawai'i Press, 1994.

Ivanhoe, Philip J., and Bryan W. Van Norden, eds. *Readings in Classical Chinese Philosophy*. New York and London: Seven Bridges, 2001; rpt., Indianapolis and Cambridge, Mass.: Hackett, 2003.

K'ang, Yu-wei. *Ta T'ung Shu: The One World Philosophy of K'ang Yu-wei*. Tr. Lawrence G. Thompsen. London: Allen and Unwin, 1958.

Kierman, Frank A., Jr., ed. *Chinese Ways in Warfare*. Cambridge, Mass.: Harvard University Press, 1974.

Liang Ch'i-chao. *Intellectual Trends in the Ch'ing Period*. Tr. Immanuel C. Y. Hsu. Cambridge, Mass.: Harvard University Press, 1959.

Nivison, David S. *The Ways of Confucianism: Investigations in Chinese Philosophy*. Ed. Bryan W. Van Norden. Chicago and La Salle, Ill.: Open Court, 1996.

Sun Tzu. *The Art of War*. Tr. Samuel B. Griffith. New York: Oxford, 1963.

———. *The Art of War*. Tr. and comm. Denma Translation Group. Boston: Shambhala, 2001.

Wagner, Rudolf G. *The Craft of a Chinese Commentator: Wang Bi on the* Laozi. SUNY Series in Chinese Philosophy and Culture. Albany: State University of New York Press, 2000.

———. *Language, Ontology, and Political Philosophy in China: Wang Bi's Scholarly Exploration of the Dark* (Xuanxue). SUNY Series in Chinese Philosophy and Culture. Albany: State University of New York Press, 2003.

———., tr. *A Chinese Reading of the* Daodejing: *Wang Bi's Commentary on the* Laozi *with Critical Text and Translation*. SUNY Series in Chinese Philosophy and Culture. Albany: State University of New York Press, 2003.

Wang, Aihe. *Cosmology and Political Culture in Early China*. Cambridge Studies in Chinese History, Literature and Institutions. Cambridge: Cambridge University Press, 2000.

Wile, Douglas. *Lost T'ai-chi Classics from the Late Ch'ing Dynasty*. Albany: State University of New York Press, 1996.

———. *T'ai Chi's Ancestors: The Making of an Internal Art*. New York: Sweet Ch'i Press, 1999.

Zhu Xi. *Learning to Be a Sage: Selections from the Conversations of Master Chu Topically Arranged*. Tr. Daniel K. Gardner. Berkeley and Los Angeles: University of California Press, 1990.

Plate numbers are in **boldface.**

Adler Planetarium & Astronomy Museum, Chicago, Illinois: **13** (Celestial chart, attributed to Qian Yong [1826] [P-69])

Ancient Chinese Architecture, Beijing, 1982: **50** (p. 53); **61** (p. 65); **69** (p. 82); **90** (p. 125); **103** (p. 161)

Ancient City of Xi'an (pamphlet), n.d.: **25** (p. 16)

The Arthur M. Sackler Museum, Harvard University Art Museums: **96** (Large plate with foliate rim and peacock decoration. Yuan dynasty [1279–1368] mid-14th c. Jiangxi Province, Jingdezhen. Blue-and-white ware: porcelain with decoration painted in underglaze cobalt blue and with molded decoration on the rim and cavetto. D. 48.8 cm. Gift of Richard B. Hobart. Photo by Photographic Services © 2003 President and Fellows of Harvard College)

Art Treasures of Dunhuang, Hong Kong, 1981: **48**

The Asian Art Museum of San Francisco: **8** (Rhinoceros *zun.* The Avery Brundage Collection, B60 B1+. Reproduced by permission); **42** (Seated Buddha, dated 338. Later Zhao dynasty [319–350]. Gilt bronze. The Avery Brundage Collection, B60B1034. Reproduced by permission)

Ba Shu qingtongji, Chengdu, 1990: **18** (pl. 21).

The British Museum: **19** (Chinese bronze figure of two wrestlers, dated ca. 5th–4th c. B.C.E., formerly in the collection of Capt. G. Spencer Churchill)

China Building Industry Press: **102**

Chinese Imperial City Planning: **24** (fig. 52)

The Cleveland Museum of Art: **98** (Shen Zhou [1427–1509]. *Twelve Views of Tiger Hill* [detail]. Ming dynasty. Album leaf, ink and slight color on paper, 31.1 × 40.2 cm. Leonard C. Hanna, Jr., Fund, 1964.371); **99** (Zhou Chen [c. 1450–after 1536]. *Beggars and Street Characters* [detail]. Ming dynasty. Handscroll, ink and color on paper; 31.9 × 244.5 cm overall. John L. Severance Fund, 1964–94); **101** (Dong Qichang [1555–1636]. *The Qingbian Mountains.* Ming dynasty. Hanging scroll, ink on paper, 224.5 × 67.2 cm. Leonard C. Hanna, Jr., Bequest, 1980.10)

Cui, *Pingyang Jinmu zhuandiao,* Taiyuan 1999: **83** (pl. 22)

Daitoku-ji: **84**

Sara Davis: **109**

Dazu grottoes, Beijing, 1984: **85** (p. 75)

Dunhuang Mogao ku, Beijing: **49** (vol. 1, 1982, pl. 107); **60** (vol. 2, 1984, pl. 172); **66** (vol. 5, 1987, pl. 56)

Ethnologisches Museum, Berlin: **110, Fig. 85.1** (Photographs by Margaret Framken, 1999)

The Freer Gallery of Art, Smithsonian Institution, Washington, D.C.: **31** (Mirror, Han dynasty, 1st–2nd century. Bronze: 14.3 cm. Purchase, F1937.30); **93** (Zhao Mengfu [1254–1322]. *Sheep and Goat,* ca. 1300. Handscroll, ink on paper; 27.5 × 406.1 cm. Purchase F1931.4); **113** (Shitao [1642–1707]. *Peach Blossom Spring.* Qing dynasty [1690s–early 1700s]. Handscroll, ink and color on paper; 25.0 × 157.8 cm. Purchase, F1957.4)

Fu Ssu-nien Library, Academia Sinica, Taipei: Fig. 85.2, Fig. 85.3

Guyuan Bei Wei mu qiguanhua, Yinchuan, 1988: **47** (1st color pl.)

Han-Tang bihua, Beijing, 1974: **63** (pl. 75)

Historical Relics Unearthed in New China, Beijing: **29** (1998, pl. 98); **45** (1972, pl. 135)

Honolulu Academy of Arts: **107** (Chen Hongshou [1598–1652]. *Episodes from the Life of Tao Qian (Yuanming)* [detail]. Qing dynasty [1644–1911]. Ink and slight color on silk; 30.5 cm × 3.08 m. Purchase, 1954 [1912.1])

Huang, *Han-Wei Luoyang bihua mu,* Beijing, 1996: **28** (p. 90)

Jiayuguan bihua fajue baogao, Beijing, 1985: **38** (pl. I)

Jiuquan Shiliuguomu bihua, Beijing, 1989: **39** (western ceiling [pl. 1])

Kaogu: **2** (1990, no. 7, pl. 1); **4** (1983, no. 1, pl. 4)

Courtesy of Ronald Knapp: **54, 105**

Kumutula shiku, Beijing, 1992: **59** (pl. 56)

Liao Architecture: **70** (fig. 266); **75** (fig. 36)

Liaoning Provincial Museum: **73** (Gao Hanyu, *Zhongguo lidai zhi ran xiu tulu,* Hong Kong, 1986, p. 74, cat. no. 74)

Liaoningsheng Bowuguan canghua, Shanghai, 1983: **81** (pl. 9)

Liaoning Zhongda wenhua shiyi, Liaoning, 1990: **3** (p. 26)

Li Xueqin, *The Wonder of Chinese Bronzes,* Beijing, 1980: **16** (pl. 22)

Li Yuming et al., *Shanxi gujianzhu tonglan,* Taiyuan, 1986: **97** (p. 261)

Courtesy of Liu Heping: **76**

Longmen, 1986: **58**

Victor Mair: **11**

The Metropolitan Museum of Art: **52** (*The Emperor and His Court as Donors.* Northern Wei dynasty [386–534], ca. 522. Longmen, Binyang cave. Limestone with traces of polychromy; 208 × 394 cm. The Metropolitan Museum of Art, Fletcher Fund, 1935. [35.146] Photograph © 2000 The Metropolitan Museum of Art); **53** (Buddhist stele, with scene of the disputation of Mañjuśrī and Vimalakīrti. Style of Northern Qi dynasty, 550–577; inscription dated 533–545. Limestone; h. 308 cm, w. 112.4 cm, d. 30.5 cm. Rogers Fund, 1929. [19.72]. Photograph © 1991 The Metropolitan Museum of Art); **79** (Ma Hezhi [active ca. 1130–ca. 1170] and assistants. *Odes of the State of Bin.* Detail no. 2: scene 1, *The Seventh Month,* left half. Southern Song dynasty [1127–1279]. Handscroll, ink, color, gold and silver on silk; 27.6 × 711.6 cm overall. Purchase, Gift of J. Pierpont Morgan, by exchange, 1973. [1973.121.3]. Photograph © 1981 The Metropolitan Museum of Art); **92** (Qian Xuan [ca. 1235–before 1307]. *Wang Xizhi Watching Geese.* Yuan dynasty [1260–1368], ca. 1295. Handscroll, ink and color on paper; 23.2 × 92.7 cm. Purchase, Gift of The Dillon Fund, 1973 [1973.120.6]. Photograph © 1981 The Metropolitan Museum of Art); **95** (Ni Zan [1306–1374]. *Woods and Valley of Mount Yu,* Yuan dynasty [1260–1368], ca 1372. Hanging scroll, ink on paper; 95.3 × 35.9 cm. Purchase, Ex coll.: C. C. Wang Family, Gift of The Dillon Fund, 1973 [1973.120.8]. Photograph by Malcolm Varon. Photograph ©1991 The Metropolitan Museum of Art); **115** (Zhang Daqian [1899–1983]. *Through Ancient Eyes.* 1920–1922. Album leaf mounted as a hanging scroll. Ink and color on paper; 33.3 × 33.3 cm. Bequest of John M. Crawford, Jr., 1988. [1939.363.189]. Photograph © 1995 The Metropolitan Museum of Art)

Musée des arts asiatiques–Guimet, Paris: **51** (Buddha Śākyamuni and Prabhūtaratna. © Photo RMN)

Museum of Fine Arts, Boston: **57** (Attributed to Yan Liben [d. 673]. *The Thirteen Emperors.* Tang dynasty, 2nd half of 7th century [with later replacement]. Handscroll; ink and color on silk; 5.3 × 531 cm. Denman Waldo Ross Collection; 31.643; **80** (Chen Rong, Chinese, 1st half of 13th century. *Nine Dragons.* Chinese, Southern Song dynasty, dated 1244. Ink and touches of red on paper; 46.3 × 1096.4 cm. Francis Gardner Curtis Fund, 17.1697)

Museum für Völkerkunde Hamburg: **114** (Guiseppe Castiglione [1688–1766]. *Chinese Ladies-in-waiting in the Yuanmingyuan.* © Museum für Völkerkunde Hamburg)

Nanchao lingmu shike, Beijing, 1981: **41** (pl. 3)

National Palace Museum, Taipei, Taiwan, Republic of China: **71, 78, 86, 88**

Nelson-Atkins Museum of Art, Kansas City, Missouri: **46** (*Episode from Stories of Filial Piety* [side of a stone sarcophagus], dated 525. Northern Wei dynasty [386–534]. Engraved gray limestone; 62.2 × 223.5 cm overall. [Purchase: Nelson Trust] 33-1543/2. Photograph by Jamison Miller); **72** (Li Song [act. 1190–1230]. *The Red Cliff.* Southern Song dynasty [1127–1279]. Album leaf mounted as a hanging scroll, ink and color on silk, ivory roller; 26.0 × 24.8 cm. [Purchase: Nelson Trust] 49-79. Photograph by Robert Newcombe); **100** (Qiu Ying [1494–1552]. *Saying Farewell at Hsun-yang.* Ming dynasty [1368–1644]. Handscroll, ink and full color on paper in blue-green style; 33.6 × 399.7 cm. [Purchase: Nelson Trust] 46-50)

Osaka Municipal Museum of Art: **91** (Gong Kai [1222–1307], *Emaciated Horse*)

Palace Museum, Beijing: **77**

A Panoramic View of the Temples in China, vol. 1, Beijing, 1990: **74** (p. 61)

Michele Pirazzoli-T'Serstevens, *Han Civilization of China,* Oxford (Phaidon), 1982: **34**

Qin Shi Huangdi Mausoleum Museum, Xiyang village, Lingtong County, Shaanxi: **23**

Victor H. Mair is professor of Asian and Middle Eastern Studies at the University of Pennsylvania. He holds a Ph.D. from Harvard University and a M. Phil. from the School of Oriental and African Studies (University of London). Mair is the author of numerous works on Chinese language and literature and is the general editor of the ABC Chinese Dictionary series. He has also organized several archeological investigations in Central Asia.

Nancy S. Steinhardt is professor of East Asian art at the University of Pennsylvania and curator of Chinese art at the University Museum of Archaeology and Anthropology. She received her Ph.D. in fine arts from Harvard University in 1981. Steinhardt is author of *Chinese Traditional Architecture* (China Institute, 1984), *Chinese Imperial City Planning* (University of Hawai'i Press, 1990), and *Liao Architecture* (University of Hawai'i Press, 1997); editor of *Chinese Architecture* (Yale University Press, 2002); and has written more than fifty scholarly articles on topics in the areas of East Asian art, architecture, and city planning.

Paul R. Goldin, who received his Ph.D. from Harvard University, is currently associate professor of Chinese thought at the University of Pennsylvania. He is the author of *After Confucius: Studies in Early Chinese Philosophy* (University of Hawai'i Press, 2005), *The Culture of Sex in Ancient China* (University of Hawai'i Press, 2002), and *Rituals of the Way: The Philosophy of Xunzi* (Open Court, 1999). In addition, he has edited the new edition of R. H. van Gulik's classic study, *Sexual Life in Ancient China* (Brill, 2003).

Production Notes for
Mair / Hawai'i Reader in Traditional Chinese Culture

Cover and interior designed by April Leidig-Higgins
with text and display in Garamond MT, captions in Scala Sans

Composition by Josie Herr

Printing and binding by The Maple-Vail Book Manufacturing Group

Printed on 60# Text White Opaque, 426 ppi